COLLECTING CHILDREN'S BOOKS

FRONT COVER ILLUSTRATION:
A plate from the 1929 Charles Folkard
edition of *Alice's Adventures in Wonderland*

Published in the United Kingdom 2007
by Diamond Publishing, Room 101
140 Wales Farm Road, London W3 6UG

Printed in India by Replika Press Pvt Ltd

ISBN No. 978-0-9532601-7-1

COLLECTING
CHILDREN'S
BOOKS

COMPILED BY

EDITOR
Jonathan Scott

CONSULTANTS
David Adland
John Cowen
Clarissa Cridland
Richard Dalby
Jason Draper
June Hopper
Barbara Richardson
David Schutte
Ann F. Smith
Stuart Webb
David Whitehead
Norman Wright

DESIGN
Elizabeth Moore

PRODUCTION
Val Cutts

PUBLISHER
Andy McDuff

Contents

Foreword

Welcome to the new edition of *Collecting Children's Books*, the definitive price guide to collectable books and annuals. The new edition has been fully updated and greatly expanded to include more than 60 new subjects and 3,000 new entries, making a total of over 15,000 separate items. Of course, this book could never have got off the ground without the expertise and hard work of *BMC*'s expert contributors, and our thanks go out to all those who helped with this and previous editions.

The last edition was produced in the wake of some fantastic prices achieved by J.K. Rowling's firsts. Since then a host of new faces have burst onto the scene as the media searched for the next 'Harry Potter'. The hype has faded, and many have fallen by the wayside, but the best of this fresh crop of collectable authors and illustrators are listed. That is not to say we have abandoned older authors. Indeed relatively new faces such as Philip Pullman and G.P. Taylor rub shoulders with long overdue entries for Ogden Nash and Victorian adventure writer George Manville Fenn, to name but a few. We have also added new general subjects, such as a round-up of fictional airmen under the heading 'Biggles Rivals'. Comic collectors will also find 'Issue 1' values now listed alongside famous annuals like *Beano* and *Dandy*, plus a seperate entry of the 'Top 50 British Comics'.

While new authors come and go, it remains the case that the old established names represent the safest investment, with price increases in many cases exceeding inflation. The rarest books of Beatrix Potter, Lewis Carroll, Edward Lear, Kenneth Grahame, Charles Dickens, J.R.R. Tolkien, Rudyard Kipling and A.A. Milne are the 'blue chip' items, while many of what might be termed the 'second division' names have continued to hold their own – Enid Blyton, Arthur Ransome, W.E. Johns, C.S. Lewis, Rupert the Bear and Elsie J. Oxenham. Others, such as G.A. Henty, have stalled or even decreased in value.

We have greatly expanded the introductory section to be a complete guide to collecting children's books, with terms, hints and trends, which we hope will be useful to those new to collecting, and an aide-memoire to old hands. We've also improved the index by including major character/series names. So now if you remember reading the 'Teddy Lester' books but can't recall the author, just look under 'T'.

Children's books are endlessly fascinating, not least from a financial viewpoint. The frailest item can be worth hundreds of pounds, and it is often an author's last — as well as earliest — works which command the highest prices. Sometimes you'll pick up a bargain, at other times you will have to pay the full going rate for a long sought-after title. The biggest change of all in book collecting has been the internet. When the first edition of this book was issued in 1995, the internet was still very young. By the second, in 2001, it had been begrudgingly accepted. Today it has become a favoured (if dangerous) hunting ground for many collectors, and the post-'Harry Potter', web-savvy bibliophile, is a wily old bird, wary of hype and false profits. Whether you hunt online, on the shopfloor, or at book fairs and auctions, *Collecting Children's Books* is here to help you. Good luck and happy hunting!

Introduction

In this expanded introductory section you will find all you need to know about book collecting, and how to get the most out of this book. There are technical terms, tips on how to identify a first edition, grading the value of a book, the relative value of reprints, a useful survey of variant jackets and bindings, an expanded glossary of terms, plus advice on condition, storage, illustrated gift-books and many other aspects of children's books.

i) How to use the guide

This book provides a complete list of children's works by collectable authors and illustrators, with a guide to the value of every first edition. All the entries have been checked by a team of expert consultants, which includes dealers, writers and bibliographers.

It's designed to be an easy-to-use reference work for the collector and dealer. Its basic layout is simple: the entries are arranged alphabetically by the author or illustrator's surname or by the first word of the book/series title. The books themselves are listed chronologically, beginning with the major series and ending with a section on miscellaneous titles ('Others'). With illustrators, works both written and illustrated by the artist are listed separately before those for which they simply provided the artwork.

Certain books have, of course, been reprinted many times, often in very desirable illustrated or 'collector's' editions. These are all grouped together immediately after the first edition, in chronological order. Where a single edition is available in both trade and 'De Luxe' formats, then the trade edition is always listed first. Ordinary reprints are not listed.

Each entry has four components:

1) the title (in bold);

2) an opening bracket, which contains details of: i) the book's contents, including any important contributions from other authors and/or illustrators; and, ii) its format, including bindings, dustjackets and — with limited editions — the number of copies printed and whether or not they were signed and/or numbered;

3) a second bracket, which gives the name of the publisher and the date of publication. With undated books, the year of publication is given in square brackets, like this: "(Blackie, [1934])". Where a book has been published before or after the date printed on the title-page, the actual year of publication is given in square brackets: "(Blackie, 1933 [1934])";

4) the current value of the first edition of the book (in bold).

Because of their very nature, most children's books are normally subject to quite a lot of wear and tear, so there are very few around in Fine condition. For this reason, most prices given in this volume are either for books in Good (up to 1900) or Very Good condition (after 1900). Only books by contemporary authors are graded as being in Fine condition.

Illustrated editions of classic works are listed under both the author's and the artist's name. However, the precise number of illustrations in each edition is given only in the section devoted to the artist — in the first of the two brackets.

ii) Quick glossary

To help you understand the information in this book, it is worth knowing the precise meaning of the following words:

BINDINGS: Unless otherwise stated, the first editions of all the books we've listed were issued in cloth bindings with dustjackets.

WRAPPERS: a paper cover, either gummed or sewn onto the pages of the book.

PAPERBACK: a modern, small-octavo softcover book, usually with glossy 'wrappers'.

BOARDS: covers of unbound, stiff card, often with a cloth spine. 'Laminated' boards are those with a glossy, hard-wearing covering, and are usually found on books and annuals from the mid-1960s onwards. In modern trade volumes, the boards are typically covered in paper or cloth. In special editions, they may also be covered in leather or other materials. Many are also published with a picture laminated onto the boards (permabound, illustrated boards, or pictorial boards).

LEATHER: There are several types of leather commonly used in book-binding. 'Morocco' is a hard-wearing leather of Islamic origin made from goat-skin, which first came into use in Britain in the late 17th century. Leather has a natural grain and sub-categories of Morocco, which can be identified by the grain, include Levant, Niger and Hard-Grain. Crushed morocco has been ironed and pressed and has no noticeable grain. Other types of leather include the cheapest – sheep, roan – and the most commonly used, calf. 'Quarter bound' refers to a book with a leather spine, the sides covered with cloth or paper. Half Bound books normally have leather spine and corners, while the rest of the cover is boards or paper.

VELLUM: fine, cream or white leather-like material made from the skin of a young animal — usually calf, but sometimes lamb or kid. Note that this 'weathers' very easily and is rarely found in better than Good condition. Some ultra-expensive limited edition giftbooks are actually printed on vellum.

JAPANESE VELLUM: a stiff, glossy handmade paper, often used for the pages of De Luxe editions, and sometimes as a substitute for real vellum in bookbinding.

DUSTJACKETS: Most dustjackets are printed on matt or glossy paper. 'Glassine' jackets are made from a highly-transparent, almost cellophane-like paper, and are usually entirely plain.

MULTI-VOLUME EDITIONS: Where an edition comprises more than one volume, the exact number is given in the first bracket. In all cases, the value quoted refers to the complete set, as is clearly marked before the price.

ILLUSTRATION: any pictorial decoration that is larger than vignette-size.

VIGNETTE: a small decorative device normally inserted at the end of a chapter.

PLATE: any full-page illustration, in colour or black-and-white. It is often printed on glossier paper than the text itself.

TIPPED-IN PLATE: one that is gummed along one edge only. It is often mounted on thicker paper than is used for the pages themselves.

iii) What decides the price?

A book's age does not necessarily guarantee its value or collectability. The major factors are scarcity, demand, fashion and condition. Pricing rare books is always a challenge. Top specialist dealers, especially those based in London, will invariably charge more than general booksellers, while, at the other extreme, we all know someone who has paid a couple of pounds for a first of Arthur Ransome's *Swallows and Amazons* or Richmal Crompton's *William the Lawless*! Our values reflect those charged by non-specialist dealers – i.e. dealers who may specialise in say children's books, but don't specialise further on *just* 'Biggles', for example.

Many books which appeared in extremely small limited editions seem to turn up more frequently on the rare book market than less collected titles which had editions of a few thousand copies, but which were issued in more perishable and ephemeral bindings. With desirable modern children's editions, a mint jacket is often worth more to collectors than the book it protects.

As has been said, the majority of values relate to books in Very Good condition in Very Good dustjackets. But if you have a 'Good' copy of a book that we have given a 'Very Good' value for in one of our bibliographies, you can calculate the approximate value of your copy by using the 'Ready Reckoner' at the back of this book.

All the values quoted in this book are *selling* prices. If you walk into your local children's bookshop and offer a VG copy of *William the Lawless*, then he or she would be most unlikely to offer you more than half of the price we quote. On the other hand, if you were advertising the book in the 'For Sale' section of this book's parent magazine, then we would recommend that you ask for the full amount.

iv) Indentifying a first edition

The term first edition has come to mean 'first edition, first printing' – in other words the *first print run* of a book's first edition. A first edition may actually go through many printings before its text is significantly changed.

When a book goes back to press after a textual change, it becomes the second edition. Identifying a first edition can be relatively straightforward: many publishers use a statement such as 'First published in Great Britain 1965', which denotes the first printing assuming of course that it is not followed by any other publishing dates. A third printing, for example, would give the same statement but it would be followed by the words 'third printing' or 'third impression' or 'reprinted 1966, 1967'.

The term 'True First Edition' is often used by dealers to indicate which of two first editions from different countries actually came first. Books are often printed in the US and UK at the same time, but just as often they appear sometimes weeks, months and even years before the other. Roald Dahl's *Charlie and the Chocolate Factory*, for example, was issued in the UK by Allen & Unwin in 1967, *three years after* it first appeared in the US.

The 'first trade edition' refers to the first regularly published edition for release to the book trade and the general public and as a term is used to differentiate it from a Deluxe binding of the first edition, which may have been issued simultaneously, or from a limited edition which preceded it. Similarly 'first published edition' is a term usually employed to differentiate the book in question from a privately printed, restricted circulation edition. 'First English edition' would be used where the true first edition was issued in a different country, or occasionally used where the book was first published in a different language. 'First separate edition' is applied to a story, poem or chapter which may have previously appeared as part of another book, but appeared here for the first time in a stand-alone volume. Another phrase which crops up is 'first edition thus', which refers to a book that has appeared previously, but first appeared with some major revision, or with new illustrations.

Attributes that can help prove that the book in your hands is a particular edition (such as the first printing of the first edition), may include such things as the printed price, special coloured pages, codes or statements printed inside, or typographical errors. It is also possible to prove firsts by something's absence – a missing ISBN number, for example, where subsequent printings have one. The term 'identification points' is pointless jargon for these clues.

In the 1990s many book publishers on both sides of the Atlantic started using a numbering system, sometimes coupled with a 'First Edition' statement. If you see a set of numbers on the copyright page (it can be descending: '987654321' or split: '13579108642'), the smallest number printed establishes the print run. A number that stated: '98765' would be a 5th printing of that edition. When the publisher runs out of numbers and still wants to print more, they start again with a larger set of numbers (from 20 down to 11 perhaps). Of course publishing companies have the uncanny knack of not always conforming to any given convention – even their own.

v) Other collectable editions

ADVANCE or PROOF COPY: When a publishing company has accepted material for publication they embark on a series of steps that culminates in the 'First Edition'. Many (but not all) of the larger companies produce what could loosely be termed a 'mock edition' of the book. It is usually in soft cover and is sent to a select group of readers and critics. These may result in corrections to spelling, grammar, punctuation, coherency, etc. This mock edition, not intended for sale, is referred to as an 'advance reading copy' or 'publisher's proof copy', and examples do find their way onto the secondhand market. Although optimistic internet sales often post these items at higher prices than the true first edition, the majority are in fact less valuable partly because of the quality of the bindings, the numbers produced, and because it is the *true* first edition – the item closest to the author's original vision – which most interests collectors. In this book we have not listed advance/proof copies apart from when they have achieved impressive prices.

ASSOCIATION/PRESENTATION COPIES: Prices in this book relate to ordinary unsigned first editions (unless otherwise stated). However, collectors should note that the highest prices are achieved by books that have a personal inscription by the author/illustrator to a friend, relative or collaborator. These are called 'association copies', and are particularly sought-after by collectors. Association copies usually sell for *at least* twice as much as unsigned ones, and where the dedicatee has a particularly close link with the work concerned – maybe they were the original inspiration for one of the characters, or designed or illustrated the book – then the price achieved may be many times our quoted value.

SIGNED COPIES: Where ordinary signed copies are concerned, the general rule is that an author or illustrator's signature will always increase a book's value, whether it's a first edition or a reprint. Two factors affect the size of the increase: 1) the rarity of an author's signature; and, 2) the nature of the inscription. In these days of promotional tours, it's quite common for an author to sign literally hundreds of copies of a new book, so these won't increase the book's value by more than five or ten pounds. On the whole, signatures are much rarer in volumes from before the war, and in these cases a plain inscription would raise the value by 100% and, with the most collectable authors, as much as 500%. Generally speaking, editions in which the author, or illustrator, or occasionally some other famous person has signed the book increases its value, but simple flat signed copies are better than personal messages to the fan – indeed these can even *detract* value in the eyes of some collectors.

DELUXE EDITION: Also known as *edition de luxe*, this term is applied to a special printing of a particular book, produced to higher specifications on higher quality paper and often encased in better quality bindings, or perhaps in a protective slipcase.

LIMITED EDITION: An edition limited to a stated number of copies, usually specially bound and numbered or lettered and signed by the author and, perhaps, others who contributed to the book – an illustrator or photographer. Not all limited editions are collectable – some publishers produce limiteds that are little more than the sheets of the trade edition bound in different boards and maybe in a slipcase; while others publish editions they term 'limited', but for which they will not state the number of copies produced. Many issue books under the 'Collector's Edition' tag, which may have some difference in binding or design to the standard edition, but are frequently produced in huge quantities. A true 'limited edition' should have a 'limitation' page that will state how many copies were printed and the number assigned to any given copy.

PRIVATELY PRINTED: This can either refer to a volume that was produced by the author, or friend of the author's, own private press, or an edition for which the author paid for both the printing and distribution. Beatrix Potter's debut is a famous example.

PIRATED EDITION: An edition produced and sold without the permission of (or payment to) the author.

vi) Reprints – how much are they worth?

As we noted above, for a book to qualify as a 'new edition', the text must have been reset and/or new text or illustrations added. With most modern first editons, any later edition is not as desirable as the first. With children's books, on the other hand, new editions might feature a new set of previously unpublished illustrations, or occasionally have had the text revised or enlarged by the author. Needless to say, both variations are of considerable interest to collectors, especially if the new illustrations are by a collectable artist like Arthur Rackham or Edmund Dulac. To take *Alice in Wonderland* as an example – although the first edition is the most valuable, there have been countless later illustrated editions, some of which are very desirable and costly.

What about a later *impression* of the first edition? Basically, five factors affect the value of a later impression of a collectable book: 1) the rarity of the first impression; 2) the number of the later impression; 3) its condition; 4) its similarity to the original; and, 5) whether or not it's still in print.

It goes without saying that the rarer the first impression, the more valuable will be the second. Any 'Biggles' fan will know that the most sought-after titles are the five published by John Hamilton in the 1930s, and many collectors are happy to accept a reprint instead of the first impression. A second or third impression of a book like *'Biggles' of the Camel Squadron* (1934) can sell for as much as £100 even *without* the jacket, while a second impression *with* the jacket might be worth half as much as the first.

The second factor to consider is the lateness of the impression. For obvious reasons, collectors who either can't find or afford a first print of a favourite book would rather have a second impression than, say, an eighth – providing, of course, that they were identical in condition and format – and this, quite naturally, is reflected in the values.

Of all the factors that decide the value of a later impression, the most important is format. Put quite simply, if collectors can't have a first edition, then they want their substitute to look as much like the original as possible – the same publisher, binding, illustrations, paper, dustjacket, everything. Even if a reprint dates from ten or twenty years after the first printing, it will still be collectable if in all essentials it is the *same book* as the first. Even the smallest change in format can lower the value of a reprint – in 1919 Beatrix Potter's publishers Frederick Warne became a limited company, with the result that all her books subsequently had the words 'F. Warne & Co. Ltd.' printed on their front boards rather than simply 'F. Warne & Co.'. As a result the reprints are much cheaper than earlier examples. Of course, not all changes in format are for the worse. For the second impression of *The Hobbit*, Tolkien provided four new colour plates to go with the black-and-white illustrations in the original printing, and these account for its relatively high price on the collector's market.

The other crucial component is the dustjacket. It's a more or less universal rule that reprints with dustjackets hold their value a lot better than those without them. A collector may be willing to pay good money for a first impression of *Just William* (1922) *without* a dustjacket, but if he's got to settle for a later one, then he'll definitely want the jacket.

The following guidelines are worth bearing in mind when valuing later impressions: 1) Reprints that are identical in format to the first impression are usually the most valuable, except where there are later editions illustrated by collectable artists; 2) where the format is the same, condition is more important than the date of a reprint; 3) reprints with dustjackets are much more desirable than those without (again, providing that the format is identical); 4) the rarer the book, the greater the parity between the price of the first impression and those of early reprints. This is particularly the case with illustrated books.

Most of the gift books by Arthur Rackham, Edmund Dulac and the other 'Golden Age' illustrators went through several printings, and these have almost invariably been accompanied by a gradual decline in production standards – for instance, the number of illustrations has been reduced, or these have been reproduced directly onto the page rather than being 'tipped-in'. The quality of reproduction can also drop, meaning colours in later printings are less vibrant. If you are particularly interested in illustrated books it's always worth inspecting the plates before buying (if only to check they're all present).

vii) The value of dustjackets

Also known as dust wrapper, dust cover Dustjackets were originally designed to protect the cloth covers of hardback books during their journey from printers to reader. According to Carter (*ABC For Book Collectors*, 1952) the earliest recorded dustjacket dates from 1832, but examples earlier than the 1880s very rarely survive. These earliest jackets were purely functional – plain paper, later examples printed with simple generic designs or the publisher's in-house adverts. Pictorial dustjackets began to appear (occasionally) from the early 1900s onwards, especially in the US.

There are many examples of books from the late-Victorian/Edwardian period that may well have been issued in jackets, but as neither the jackets nor the records proving the jackets' existence survive, it is impossible to tell – which is why we rarely ascribe a with-jacket value to books from this era. However, although pre-1914 jackets are sometimes staggeringly rare, as a general rule of thumb it is fair to assume that the majority of post-1900 hardback titles *were* originally issued in jackets. A famously rare example from this era would be Kenneth Grahame's *The Wind in the Willows* (Methuen, 1908) which was issued in a simple buff jacket whose one-colour illustration and titles mirrored the decorations of the cloth bindings it protected.

The jacket, when it survives, can hold important information about the book's age and whether it's a first printing. The most obvious clue is often the price, which may change for a second impression or edition. Although some jackets have the price on the rear spine, it is more common to find the pricing on what is called the 'front flap'. It is common for jackets to be price-clipped, which *greatly* reduces their value.

Prior to the 1980s the only numbers that appeared on a dustjacket were the ones that some publishers used for their own identification purposes. During the 1980s most children's books started carrying an ISBN number on the back or the inside rear flap. In the last 15 years most of the ISBN numbers are printed together with a computer bar code. These numbers, or sometimes the lack of a number, can be important points of identification.

Because of the huge value a dustjacket can add to a first edition, it is not uncommon to come across a jacket off a newer printing that has been used to replace the original dustjacket (if damaged or missing). This is known as marrying. Sometimes this may be done in the hope that it goes unnoticed by the buyer. It may be easy to spot by anyone with knowledge of the correct first edition jacket, while at other times it may be impossible to tell – in which case it becomes more or less irrelevant.

viii) Condition, investment & preservation

Many collectors insist on only Fine or Mint condition, while others are perfectly happy to build up a set of titles by their favourite author or on a particular subject in any condition, so long as they are clean and complete. Dealers generally use a scale that begins with the term 'as New' or 'Mint'. 'Fine' is used for one close to this standard, 'Very Good' when minor flaws first appear, 'Good' for a book that shows normal wear and defects, 'Fair' is a worn book with defects and perhaps missing endpapers, while 'Poor' or 'Reading Copy' are used for those books that have significant wear and defects. Defects should always be described to a buyer and the more rare and valuable the book, the more reason to be exact in a description. A slash is frequently used to differentiate the description of the book and the jacket – so Very Good/Very Good or VG/VG means a Very Good book in a Very Good dustjacket.

The famous term 'foxing' refers to paper that has become discoloured with brownish spots. According to Carter (*ABC For Book Collectors*, 1952) the term was first noted in 1848 and may be derived from the colour of the spots. It is usually caused by damp or poor ventilation, combined with metallic or chemical impurities in the paper. The term 'Rubbed' is used when describing condition to indicate wear – usually to the extremities of the book i.e. the spine, joints, etc.

Some book collectors see themselves as investors. A careful study of the market enables one to buy books that appreciate in value, sometimes at a rate far higher than most stocks and shares – or so they claim. In reality it's always best to collect what interests you rather than what you think may be valuable. Nevertheless, the 'Harry Potter' phenomenon has increased interest in this area. Perhaps the best example is the first issue of children's comic *Dandy*, which was published by D.C. Thomson in 1937 with the 'Express Whistler' free gift. In June 1985 we at *Book & Magazine Collector* valued it at £25-£50. In 2004 a 'superb' copy, with the original gift and an announcement of the new comic cut from the previous week's *Hotspur*, sold for £20,350.

Not everyone will see their children's books as an 'investment', but most will want to ensure that the value of their library doesn't depreciate. The enemies of your collection are legion and include heat, moisture, insects, rodents, dust, sunlight, greases, oils, solvents, migrating acids, pollution (especially sulphur dioxide), reading and children. There are lots of specialist storage solutions on the market which work very well and are certainly worth considering. However, for those with a limited budget, there are various steps that can ensure the preservation of your collection. Before installing bookshelves, you must choose a suitable room. Rooms in which the temperature and humidity stay relatively constant and where it never becomes too hot or too cold, are preferable in the long run. The room should not be exposed to direct sunlight (or at least not the wall you intend to use for storing books) as the rays of the sun can have a disastrous effect on any book – bleaching jacket spines, yellowing pages, and even warping the entire book. It's also best if shelves are not directly above a radiator, or, if you have children, within reach of toddlers' inquisitive hands!

Shelves should not fit too closely over the books – books that only just squeeze in are likely to warp due to pressure on the top of the spine and cover. The spine is also likely to be knocked out if the book is used a lot. The other consideration is the depth of shelf – a book which is being balanced on three quarters of its width over the edge of a shelf that is too shallow may develop a weak spine over time.

Most will prefer to use wood shelves, metal boxes and filing cabinets. Be aware however that some woods are acidic and release fumes that can damage your volumes, while some paints are also harmful to paper. Ordinary cardboard boxes are naturally acidic and are the major cause of premature deterioration of paper collections. In general plastics are a good choice for storage but make sure that the products – sleeves, wrappers, boxes, etc – have been specifically designed for long-term storage. There are also plenty of acid-free paper and card products on the market.

As a general rule, it's best not to attempt any restoration or repairs yourself – the damage adhesive tape can do to a book's value is hard to overstate. There are plenty of professional restoration firms out there who can work miracles – transforming torn, seemingly hopeless dustjackets, into pristine items. But their services don't come cheap, so you need to take into consideration the cost effectiveness of undertaking restoration.

Most dealers will have cleaned and checked books before sale, but with books purchased from charity shops, stalls, and jumble sales it's worth giving them a once over. In the case of a hardback book, the first thing to do is to give the cover and spine a brushing with a reasonably firm, fine brush. Paperbacks deteriorate far more quickly, but grubby glossy card covers can also be cleaned up by hot water mixed with washing up liquid, carefully applied. If the book has a peeling or split spine, it is possible to effect some repairs rather than having it rebound (which can detract from its value). However, experiment on a damaged book of little importance before progressing to the more prized items. A little super-glue to the spine will often work wonders if the spine is then held firmly in position while it dries. Other minor repairs include removing unwanted inscriptions or pencil and ink stains – there are several good ink and pencil erasers on the market, but use light pressure to avoid making a hole in the page.

Dustjackets cause lots of problems. Brand new jackets can be preserved, if only by removing them while the book is read (thereby turning tables on the origins of dustjackets which were originally designed to protect the book). Older dustjackets are far more problematic as they tend to be flimsy and prone to tears, stains and creasing. Minor marks can be rubbed out by an eraser, creases can be folded out, and the jacket kept separately in clear wrappers (which are available from most bookdealers). Ex-library copy jackets are often protected by a tight plastic wrapping – although this does keep the jacket in good condition, it is almost impossible to remove without damaging it.

ix) The internet

The internet has fuelled interest in collecting in general, not least through online auction sites such as eBay, and has also seen a shift in the whole emphasis of the book trade. While doom-laden stories about the slow death rattle of the secondhand bookshop are common, in reality, a great many are doing very well indeed by trading both traditionally, on the shop floor, and through the internet, while others have chosen to concentrate solely on the latter. The internet has also revolutionized the search for books, enabling you to browse the stock of dealers from around the world. There are vast sites listing millions of books plus resources for checking book details. However, there are disadvantages: some of the prices charged for books online are frankly laughable; there have been many documented cases of forged signed editions; the descriptions of condition can be unreliable; and information is frequently wrong. The internet is all very well, but you can't beat the atmosphere of an old independent bookshop, a regional fair, or a bustling auction house.

Antiquarian Booksellers' Association: *www.aba.org.uk*

Provincial Booksellers Fairs Association: *www.pbfa.org*

Dominic Winter Book Auctions: *www.dominic-winter.co.uk*

Bloomsbury Auctions: *www.bloomsbury-book-auct.com*

British Library: *www.bl.uk*

Sotheby's: *www.sothebys.com*

Christie's: *www.christies.com*

Bonhams: *www.bonhams.com*

Abebooks: *www.abebooks.co.uk*

Alibris: *www.alibris.com*

eBay: *www.ebay.co.uk*

Amazon: *www.amazon.co.uk*

x) More useful terms

BACKSTRIP: The part of a book where the sections are united by sewing or stapling. While 'backstrip' is also used to describe the portion of outer cover which encloses this, the term 'SPINE' is preferable.

COPYRIGHT PAGE: In modern trade editions this is the page – usually the verso of the title page – that contains the publication and copyright information.

ENDPAPERS: In a hardcover book the first and last blank page is glued to the inside of the board on the front and back to fasten the boards to the bound pages. These glued pages are referred to as the front endpaper (or paste-down endpaper) or the rear endpaper. The next blank pages at front and back are referred to as the front free endpaper and rear free endpaper.

EX-LIBRARY COPY: A book that has at one time been in a lending library, and so it is likely that condition will have been compromised. The majority of the 500 first editions of *Harry Potter and the Philosopher's Stone* found their way into the library system, which adds to the rarity of really fine examples. The term is sometimes confised with 'Ex-Libris' which refers to a bookplate/ownership label, usually pasted into the front free endpaper of a book. 'Ex-Libris' means from the collection or library of.

FLAPS: The parts of the dustjacket that are folded inside the cover of the book – between the PASTE-DOWNS and the front and rear free-ENDPAPERS.

FORE-EDGE: Opposite the spine, where the pages open.

FRONTISPIECE: Illustration facing the title-page.

HALF-TITLE PAGE: The page that precedes the title page, containing only the title of the book.

HEAD: When the book is closed the top edge of the pages forms the 'head'. Some publishers will colour the 'head' of a book, and this can sometimes help identify a particular edition of a book. A gilt head is always called 'top edge gilt'.

HEADBAND: A (usually) silk band at the head and foot of the SPINE.

HEAD-PIECE: A decorative element or vignette at the head of a chapter.

SPINE: The bound side of the pages.

VERSO / RECTO: The left-hand page of an open book – the 'back' of a page. / The right-hand page of an open book – the 'front' of a page.

TAIL: The bottom of the pages.

TAILPIECE: A small, sometimes decorative device for a blank space in the lower part of a page – often used at the end of a chapter

TITLE PAGE: The page preceding the text that carries on its recto the book's title, the author's name and the publisher (plus sometimes their location and logo). On the reverse side of this page is usually found publishing and copyright information – sometimes known as the 'copyright' or 'acknowledgments' page.

TITLES: The titles on the boards of a hardcover book, or the wrappers of a paperback. Gold letters are called 'gilt', while a picture or title engraved with no colour is called 'blind stamped'.

ADAMS, Richard

British author. Born: Richard George Adams in Berkshire, 1920. Studied at Bradfield College and Worcester College, Oxford. Worked for the Civil Service between 1948 and 1974. Won Guardian Award and Carnegie Medal for *Watership Down*. Past President of the RSPCA.
Prices are for books in Very Good condition with dustjackets where applicable.

WATERSHIP DOWN (Rex Collings, 1972) £1,000
WATERSHIP DOWN (first illustrated edition; in slipcase) (Penguin/Kestrel, 1976) £50
SHARDIK (Lane/Rex Collings, 1974) £20
NATURE THROUGH THE SEASONS (non-fiction; science texts by Max Hooper) (Kestrel, 1975)..............£20
THE TYGER VOYAGE (verse; illustrated by Nicola Bayley) (Cape, 1976)...£30
THE SHIP'S CAT (verse; illustrated by Alan Aldridge) (Cape, 1977)...£25
THE PLAGUE DOGS (illustrated by A. Wainwright) (Lane, 1977)..£20
NATURE DAY AND NIGHT (non-fiction; illustrated by David Goddard; science texts by Max Hooper) (Kestrel, 1978)...............£12
THE WATERSHIP DOWN FILM PICTURE BOOK (Lane, 1978)..£20
THE IRON WOLF and Other Stories (illustrated by Yvonne Gilbert and Jennifer Campbell) (Lane, 1980)........£12
THE BUREAUCATS (illustrated by Robin Jacques) (Viking, 1985) £25
TALES FROM WATERSHIP DOWN (short stories) (Hutchinson, 1996)..£12

AESOP'S 'FABLES'

Collection of moral tales reputedly written by the Greek storyteller, Aesop, who lived on the island of Samos in the middle years of the Sixth Century BC. First printed in England by Caxton in 1484, and reissued many times since.
Prices are for books in Very Good condition.

AESOP'S FABLES Retold by Rev Thomas James (illustrated by John Tenniel) (Murray, 1852)....................£100
AESOP'S FABLES Revised and rewritten by J.B. Rundell (illustrated by Ernest Griset) (Cassell, Peter & Galpin, [1869])........£100
SOME OF AESOP'S FABLES (illustrated by Randolph Caldecott; translated by Alfred Caldecott) (Macmillan, 1883)...............£35
THE BABY'S OWN AESOP Being the Fables condensed in rhyme by W.J. Linton
(illustrated by Walter Crane) (Routledge, 1887 [1886])..£125
AESOP'S FABLES (illustrated by Charles Robinson) (Dent: 'Banbury Cross' series, 1895) £125
THE FABLES OF AESOP (illustrated by E.J. Detmold) (Hodder & Stoughton, 1909) £125
THE FABLES OF AESOP (illustrated by E.J. Detmold; limited to 750 copies, signed by the artist)
(Hodder & Stoughton, 1909) £500
AESOP'S FABLES Preface by Gordon Home (illustrated by Charles Folkard) (A. & C. Black, 1912)...........£35
AESOP'S FABLES A new translation by V.S. Vernon Jones, with an introduction by G.K. Chesterton.
(illustrated by Arthur Rackham) (Heinemann, 1912)..£200
AESOP'S FABLES A new translation by V.S. Vernon Jones, with an introduction by G.K. Chesterton.
(illustrated by Arthur Rackham; limited to 1,450 copies, signed by the artist) (Heinemann, 1912).................£1,000
AESOP'S FABLES Retold by Blanche Winder (illustrated by Harry Rountree) (Ward Lock, [1924])...........£40
AESOP'S FABLES (illustrated by Louis Rhead) (Harper, US, [1927])..£45
THE FABLES OF ESOPE Translated out of Frensshe into Englysshe by William Caxton
(illustrated by Agnes Miller Parker; limited to 250 copies) (Gregynog Press, 1931).................................£1,450
AESOP'S FABLES Edited by Michael Hague (Holt, US, 1985)...£35

AHLBERG, Allan and Janet

British husband-and-wife author/illustrator team. Born in 1938 and 1944 respectively, Allan and Janet Ahlberg met at Sunderland Teacher Training College, and were married in 1969. They collaborated on many books for young readers, although not all Allan's 100-plus titles were illustrated by Janet. Janet died in November 1994.
Prices are for books in Very Good condition with dustjackets where applicable.

HERE ARE THE BRICK STREET BOYS by Allan Ahlberg (illustrated by Janet Ahlberg) (Collins, 1975) £20
A PLACE TO PLAY by Allan Ahlberg (illustrated by Janet Ahlberg) (Collins, 1975)................................£20
SAM THE REFEREE by Allan Ahlberg (illustrated by Janet Ahlberg) (Collins, 1975)..............................£20
THE OLD JOKE BOOK by Allan and Janet Ahlberg (Kestrel, 1976)..£30
FRED'S DREAM by Allan Ahlberg (illustrated by Janet Ahlberg) (Collins, 1976).................................£20
THE GREAT MARATHON FOOTBALL MATCH by Allan Ahlberg (illustrated by Janet Ahlberg) (Collins, 1976).........£20
BURGLAR BILL by Allan and Janet Ahlberg (Heinemann, 1977)...£25
THE VANISHMENT OF THOMAS TULL by Allan and Janet Ahlberg (A. & C. Black, 1977) £25
JEREMIAH IN THE DARK WOODS by Allan and Janet Ahlberg (Kestrel, 1977) £20
EACH, PEACH, PEAR, PLUM by Allan and Janet Ahlberg (Kestrel, 1978) £35
COPS AND ROBBERS by Allan and Janet Ahlberg (Heinemann, 1978) £25
THE LITTLE WORM BOOK by Allan and Janet Ahlberg (Granada, 1979 [1981]) £15
THE ONE AND ONLY TWO HEADS by Allan and Janet Ahlberg (Collins, 1979) £15

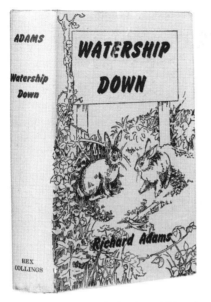

*The first edition of Richard Adams' most celebrated and collectable novel, **Watership Down** (1972).*

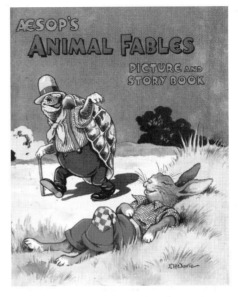

*Over the years **Aesop's Fables** have been endlessly reimagined and reissued by children's publishers.*

TWO WHEELS, TWO HEADS by Allan and Janet Ahlberg (Collins, 1979)..£25
SON OF A GUN by Allan and Janet Ahlberg (Heinemann, 1979)..£25
FUNNYBONES by Allan and Janet Ahlberg (Heinemann, 1980)..£25
A PAIR OF SINNERS by Allan Ahlberg and John Lawrence (Granada, 1980)...£20
MR BIFF THE BOXER by Allan Ahlberg (illustrated by Janet Ahlberg) (Viking, 1980).................................£12
MR COSMO THE CONJURER by Allan Ahlberg (illustrated by Joe Wright) (Viking, 1980)............................£12
MRS PLUG THE PLUMBER by Allan Ahlberg (illustrated by Joe Wright) (Viking, 1980)...............................£12
MRS WOBBLE THE WAITRESS by Allan Ahlberg (illustrated by Janet Ahlberg) (Viking, 1980).....................£12
MASTER SALT THE SAILOR'S SON by Allan Ahlberg (illustrated by André Amstutz) (Kestrel, 1980)............£12
MISS JUMP THE JOCKEY by Allan Ahlberg (illustrated by André Amstutz) (Viking, 1980)...........................£12
PEEPO! by Allan and Janet Ahlberg (Kestrel, 1981)...£35
MASTER MONEY THE MILLIONAIRE by Allan Ahlberg (illustrated by André Amstutz) (Viking, 1981)............£12
MISS BRICK THE BUILDER'S BABY by Allan Ahlberg (illustrated by Colin McNaughton) (Viking, 1981).........£12
MR AND MRS HAY THE HORSE by Allan Ahlberg (illustrated by Colin McNaughton) (Viking, 1981)...............£12
MR BUZZ THE BEEMAN by Allan Ahlberg (illustrated by Faith Jaques) (Viking, 1981).................................£12
MR TICK THE TEACHER by Allan Ahlberg (illustrated by Faith Jaques) (Viking, 1981).................................£12
MRS LATHER'S LAUNDRY by Allan Ahlberg (illustrated by André Amstutz) (Viking, 1981)...........................£12
THE BABY'S CATALOGUE by Allan and Janet Ahlberg (Kestrel, 1982)...£35
THE BABY'S CATALOGUE FRIEZE by Allan and Janet Ahlberg (Kestrel, 1982)..£20
DOUBLE DUCK by Allan Ahlberg and Eric Hill (Granada: 'Help Your Child To Read' series, 1982)................£10
SILLY SHEEP by Allan Ahlberg and Eric Hill (Granada: 'Help Your Child To Read' series, 1982)...................£10
POORLY PIG by Allan Ahlberg and Eric Hill (Granada: 'Help Your Child To Read' series, 1982)....................£10
RUBBER RABBIT by Allan Ahlberg and Eric Hill (Granada: 'Help Your Child To Read' series, 1982)..............£10
FAST FROG by Allan Ahlberg and Eric Hill (Granada: 'Help Your Child To Read' series, 1982)......................£10
BAD BEAR by Allan Ahlberg and Eric Hill (Granada: 'Help Your Child To Read' series, 1982).......................£10
THE HA-HA BONK BOOK by Allan and Janet Ahlberg (Kestrel, 1982)...£10
HIP-HIPPO-RAY by Allan Ahlberg and André Amstutz (Granada: 'Help Your Child To Read' series, 1983)......£10
MISTER WOLF by Allan Ahlberg and André Amstutz (Granada: 'Help Your Child To Read' series, 1983).........£10
KING KANGAROO by Allan Ahlberg and André Amstutz (Granada: 'Help Your Child To Read' series, 1983).....£10
SPIDER SPY by Allan Ahlberg and André Amstutz (Granada: 'Help Your Child To Read' series, 1983)...........£10
TELL-TALE TIGER by Allan Ahlberg and André Amstutz (Granada: 'Help Your Child To Read' series, 1983).....£10
TRAVELLING MOOSE by Allan Ahlberg and André Amstutz (Granada: 'Help Your Child To Read' series, 1983)......£10
TEN IN A BED by Allan Ahlberg and André Amstutz (Granada, 1983)...£12
WHICH WITCH? by Allan and Janet Ahlberg (Heinemann: 'Daisychain' series, 1983).................................£25
THAT'S MY BABY by Allan and Janet Ahlberg (Heinemann: 'Daisychain' series, 1983)...............................£12
SUMMER SNOWMAN by Allan and Janet Ahlberg (Heinemann: 'Daisychain' series, 1983)...........................£12
READY, TEDDY, GO by Allan and Janet Ahlberg (Heinemann: 'Daisychain' series, 1983)............................£25
PLEASE MRS BUTLER by Allan Ahlberg (verse; illustrated by Fritz Wegner) (Kestrel, 1983).......................£20

CLOWNING ABOUT by Allan and Janet Ahlberg and André Amstutz (Heinemann, 1984) £25
MONSTER MUNCH by Allan and Janet Ahlberg and André Amstutz (Heinemann, 1984) £25
THE GOOD OLD DOLLS by Allan and Janet Ahlberg and André Amstutz (Heinemann, 1984)................................. £25
RENT-A-ROBOT by Allan and Janet Ahlberg and André Amstutz (Heinemann, 1984) £25
YUM YUM by Allan and Janet Ahlberg (Viking Kestrel, 1984)... £6
PLAYMATES by Allan and Janet Ahlberg (Viking Kestrel, 1984) £6
BEAR'S BIRTHDAY by Allan Ahlberg (Walker: 'Red Nose Readers' series, 1985).. £10
JUMPING by Allan Ahlberg (illustrated by Colin McNaughton) (Walker: 'Red Nose Readers' series, 1985).............. £6
SO CAN I by Allan Ahlberg (illustrated by Colin McNaughton) (Walker: 'Red Nose Readers' series, 1985).............. £6
BIG BAD PIG by Allan Ahlberg (Walker: 'Red Nose Readers' series, 1985).. £6
FEE FI FO FUM by Allan Ahlberg (illustrated by Colin McNaughton) (Walker: 'Red Nose Readers' series, 1985)......................... £6
HAPPY WORM by Allan Ahlberg (illustrated by Colin McNaughton) (Walker: 'Red Nose Readers' series, 1985)....................... £6
HELP! by Allan Ahlberg (illustrated by Colin McNaughton) (Walker: 'Red Nose Readers' series, 1985) £6
MAKE A FACE by Allan Ahlberg (illustrated by Colin McNaughton) (Walker: 'Red Nose Readers' series, 1985) £6
PUSH THE DOG by Allan Ahlberg (illustrated by Colin McNaughton) (Walker: 'Red Nose Readers' series, 1986) £6
CRASH! BANG! WALLOP! by Allan Ahlberg (illustrated by Colin McNaughton) (Walker: 'Red Nose Readers' series, 1986) £6
SHIRLEY'S SHOPS by Allan Ahlberg (illustrated by Colin McNaughton) (Walker: 'Red Nose Readers' series, 1986) £6
ME AND MY FRIEND by Allan Ahlberg (illustrated by Colin McNaughton) (Walker: 'Red Nose Readers' series, 1986).............. £6
THE CINDERELLA SHOW by Allan and Janet Ahlberg (Viking, 1986) £12
THE JOLLY POSTMAN by Allan and Janet Ahlberg (Heinemann, 1986)... £30
THE JOLLY POSTMAN'S LETTERS (Heinemann, 1986)... £25
THE CLOTHES HORSE and Other Stories by Allan and Janet Ahlberg (Viking Kestrel, 1987)............................ £15
WOOF! by Allan Ahlberg (Viking, 1987).. £20
TELL US A STORY by Allan Ahlberg (illustrated by Colin McNaughton) (Walker, 1987).. £20
ONE, TOW, FLEA! by Allan Ahlberg (illustrated by Colin McNaughton) (Walker, 1987).. £20
MASTER BUN THE BAKER'S SON by Allan Ahlberg (illustrated by Fritz Wegner) (Viking, 1988)........................ £10
MISS DOSE THE DOCTOR'S DAUGHTER by Allan Ahlberg (illustrated by Faith Jaques) (Viking, 1988)............ £10
MR CREEP THE CROOK by Allan Ahlberg (illustrated by André Amstutz) (Viking, 1988) £10
MRS JOLLY'S JOKE SHOP by Allan Ahlberg (illustrated by Colin McNaughton) (Viking, 1988)........................... £10
THE MIGHTY SLIDE by Allan Ahlberg (Viking, 1988)... £12
STARTING SCHOOL by Allan Ahlberg (Viking, 1988) £15
BYE BYE BABY by Allan and Janet Ahlberg (Heinemann, 1989) £25
HEARD IT IN THE PLAYGROUND by Allan Ahlberg (Viking, 1989)... £12
BLACK CAT by Allan Ahlberg (Heinemann, 1990).. £12
MYSTERY TOUR by Allan Ahlberg (Heinemann, 1990) £12
BLOW ME DOWN by Allan Ahlberg (illustrated by Colin McNaughton) (Walker, 1990) £12
LOOK OUT FOR THE SEALS! by Allan Ahlberg (illustrated by Colin McNaughton) (Walker, 1990)..................... £12
THE JOLLY CHRISTMAS POSTMAN by Allan Ahlberg (illustrated by Janet Ahlberg) (Heinemann, 1991) £35
MRS BUTLER SONGBOOK by Allan Ahlberg and Colin Matthews (illustrated by Fritz Wegner) (Viking, 1992) £15
THE BEAR NOBODY WANTED by Allan and Janet Ahlberg (Viking, 1992) £40
PET SHOP by Allan Ahlberg (illustrated by André Amstutz) (Little Mammoth, 1992)... £15
SKELETON CREW by Allan Ahlberg (illustrated by André Amstutz) (Heinemann, 1992)....................................... £15
BUMPS IN THE NIGHT by Allan Ahlberg (illustrated by André Amstutz) (Heinemann, 1993)............................... £7
GIVE THE DOG A BONE by Allan Ahlberg (illustrated by André Amstutz) (Heinemann, 1993) £12
IT WAS A DARK AND STORMY NIGHT by Allan Ahlberg (illustrated by Janet Ahlberg) (Viking, 1993) £20
THE GIANT BABY by Allan Ahlberg (illustrated by Fritz Wegner) (Viking, 1994)... £10
THE JOLLY POCKET POSTMAN by Allan Ahlberg (illustrated by Janet Ahlberg) (Heinemann, 1995).................. £12

AIKEN, Joan

British author. Born: Sussex, 1924, the daughter of the American poet, Conrad Aiken. Joined *Argosy* magazine as features editor in 1955. As well as her children's books, she wrote a large number of adult works, notably several volumes of horror and fantasy stories. Died: 2004.

Prices are for books in Very Good condition with dustjackets where applicable.

'Wolves of Willoughby Chase' series

THE WOLVES OF WILLOUGHBY CHASE (illustrated by Pat Marriott) (Cape, 1962).. £75
BLACK HEARTS IN BATTERSEA (illustrated by Robin Jacques) (Cape, 1965).. £60
NIGHTBIRDS ON NANTUCKET (illustrated by Pat Marriott) (Cape, 1966) £80
THE WHISPERING MOUNTAIN (illustrated by Pat Marriott) (Cape, 1968) £80
THE CUCKOO TREE (illustrated by Pat Marriott) (Cape, 1971).. £45
MIDNIGHT IS A PLACE (illustrated by Pat Marriott) (Cape, 1974).. £25
THE STOLEN LAKE (illustrated by Pat Marriott) (Cape, 1981).. £35
DIDO AND PA (illustrated by Pat Marriott) (Cape, 1986) £30
IS (illustrated by Pat Marriott) (Red Fox, 1993) £12
COLD SHOULDER ROAD (Cape, 1995) £12
DANGEROUS GAMES (Cape, 1999).. £8
MIDWINTER NIGHTINGALE (Cape, 2004) £8
THE WITCH OF CLATTERINGSHAWS (Cape, 2005) £8

Others

ALL YOU'VE EVER WANTED and Other Stories (illustrated by Pat Marriott) (Cape, 1953) £80
MORE THAN YOU BARGAINED FOR and Other Stories (illustrated by Pat Marriott) (Cape, 1955).....................£80
THE KINGDOM AND THE CAVE (novel; illustrated by Dick Hart) (Abelard Schuman, 1960) £45
A NECKLACE OF RAINDROPS and Other Stories (illustrated by Jan Pienkowski) (Cape, 1968).......................£35
A SMALL PINCH OF WEATHER and Other Stories (illustrated by Pat Marriott) (Cape, 1969).........................£25
ALL AND MORE (contains 'All You've Ever Wanted' and 'More Than You Bargained For'; illustrated by Pat Marriott)
  (Cape, 1971)..£25
THE KINGDOM UNDER THE SEA and Other Stories (illustrated by Jan Pienkowski) (Cape, 1971)..................£30
A HARP OF FISHBONES and Other Stories (illustrated by Pat Marriott) (Cape 1972) £25
ARABEL'S RAVEN (illustrated by Quentin Blake) (BBC, 1972) £20
THE ESCAPED BLACK MAMBA (illustrated by Quentin Blake; paperback) (BBC, 1973)..............................£20
ALL BUT A FEW (paperback) (Puffin, 1974)..£8
THE BREAD BIN (illustrated by Quentin Blake; paperback) (BBC, 1974)...£8
MORTIMER'S TIE (illustrated by Quentin Blake; paperback) (BBC, 1976) £8
ANGEL INN (Cape, 1976)..£12
A BUNDLE OF NERVES: Stories of Horror, Suspense and Fantasy (Gollancz, 1976)...............................£12
THE FAITHLESS LOLLYBIRD and Other Stories (illustrated by Pat Marriott) (Cape, 1977)..........................£25
TALE OF A ONE-WAY STREET and Other Stories (illustrated by Jan Pienkowski) (Cape, 1978)...................£30
MICE AND MENDELSON (illustrated by Babette Cole; music by John Sebastian Brown) (Cape, 1978).............£20
GO SADDLE THE SEA (novel; illustrated by Pat Marriott) (Cape, 1978)..£30
MORTIMER AND THE SWORD EXCALIBUR (illustrated by Quentin Blake; paperback) (BBC, 1979) £8
THE SPIRAL STAIR (illustrated by Quentin Blake; paperback) (BBC, 1979)..£8
A TOUCH OF CHILL: Stories of Horror, Suspense and Fantasy (Gollancz, 1979) £12
ARABEL AND MORTIMER (contains 'Mortimer's Tie', 'Mortimer and the Sword Excalibur' and
  'The Spiral Stair'; illustrated by Quentin Blake) (Cape, 1980)..£20
MORTIMER'S PORTRAIT ON GLASS (illustrated by Quentin Blake) (BBC, 1980) £8
MR JONES'S DISAPPEARING TAXI (illustrated by Quentin Blake; paperback) (BBC, 1980).........................£8
THE SHADOW GUESTS (novel) (Cape, 1980)...£20
A WHISPER IN THE NIGHT: Stories of Horror, Suspense and Fantasy (Gollancz, 1982) £20
MORTIMER'S CROSS (illustrated by Quentin Blake) (Cape, 1983)..£20
THE KITCHEN WARRIORS (BBC, 1983) £20
BRIDLE THE WIND (novel; illustrated by Pat Marriott) (Cape, 1983)...£25
ARABEL AND THE ESCAPED BLACK MAMBA (illustrated by Pat Marriott) (Cape, 1984)............................£20
UP THE CHIMNEY DOWN and Other Stories (illustrated by Pat Marriott) (Cape, 1984).............................£20
MORTIMER SAYS NOTHING (illustrated by Quentin Blake) (Cape, 1985)...£20
THE LAST SLICE OF RAINBOW (Cape, 1985) £20
PAST EIGHT O'CLOCK (illustrated by Jan Pienkowski) (Cape, 1986) £20
THE MOON'S REVENGE (illustrated by Alan Lee) (Cape, 1987)...£20
THE TEETH OF THE GALE (novel) (Cape, 1988)...£25
THE MYSTERY OF MR JONES'S DISAPPEARING TAXI (illustrated by Quentin Blake) (Cape, 1988) £20
A FOOT IN THE GRAVE (illustrated by Jan Pienkowski) (Cape, 1989) £20
MORTIMER'S PORTRAIT ON GLASS (illustrated by Quentin Blake) (Cape, 1990) £10
A FIT OF SHIVERS (short stories) (Gollancz, 1990)...£12
MORTIMER AND ARABEL (with Lizza Aiken) (illustrated by Quentin Blake) (BBC, 1992) £10
A CREEPY COMPANY (short stories) (Gollancz, 1993) £10
THE WINTER SLEEPWALKER (illustrated by Quentin Blake) (Cape, 1994)..£10
A HANDFUL OF GOLD (illustrated by Wayne Anderson; paperback) (Hodder, 1998)....................................£10
MOON CAKE (illustrated by Wayne Anderson; paperback) (Hodder, 1998)...£3

AINSLIE, Kathleen

British author-illustrator. Her work covers a period from 1900 to 1910. Her stocking-sized children's books
with hand-written texts and Dutch doll characters were influenced by Florence K. Upton's slightly earlier
'Golliwog' series.
Prices are for books in Good condition.

OH! POOR AMELIA JANE! (Castell, [1900]) £50
CATHERINE SUSAN'S LITTLE HOLIDAY (Castell, [1900]) £60
ME AND CATHERINE SUSAN (Castell, [1903]) £60
AT GREAT-AUNT MARTHA'S (Castell, [1904]) £50
ME AND CATHERINE SUSAN EARNS AN HONEST PENNY (Castell, [1905])...£50
LADY TABITHA AND US (Castell, [1905]) £50
CATHERINE AND ME'S COMING OUT (Castell, [1905]) £50
CATHERINE AND ME'S GOES ABROAD (Castell, [1905]) £50
SAMMY GOES A `HUNTING (Castell, [1905]) £40
CATHERINE SUSAN'S CALENDAR 1906 (Castell, [1905]) £60
"WHAT I DID" (Castell, [1906]) £40
MOPS VERSUS TAILS (Castell, [1907]) £45
DEAR DIRTY DOLLY (Castell, [1908]) £60

CATHERINE SUSAN'S CALENDAR 1910 (Castell, [1909])..£60
CATHERINE SUSAN IN HOT WATER (Castell, [1910]) £40
VOTES FOR CATHERINE SUSAN AND ME (Castell, [1910]) £40

ALCOTT, Louisa M.

American author. Born: Louisa May Alcott in Pennsylvania in 1832, but lived most of her life in Boston. Published her first novel, *Moods*, in 1866, and achieved immediate and lasting fame with the follow-up, *Little Women* (1868). Died: 1888.

Prices are for books in Very Good condition.

FLOWER FABLES (Briggs, US, 1855)...£200
MOODS (Routledge, [1866])...£150
LITTLE WOMEN, or Meg, Jo, Beth and Amy (Roberts Bros, US, 1868)..£3,000
LITTLE WOMEN, or Meg, Jo, Beth and Amy (Sampson Low, 1868)..£600
LITTLE WOMEN (illustrated by H.M. Brock) (Seeley, 1908)...£40
LITTLE WOMEN (illustrated by M.V. Wheelhouse) (Bell, 1909) £40
LITTLE WOMEN Introduction by Flora Klickmann (illustrated by Harold Copping) (R.T.S., 1912)........£40
LITTLE WOMEN (illustrated by Jessie Willcox Smith) (Little Brown, US, 1915)...................................£60
LITTLE WOMEN (illustrated by Millicent E. Gray) (Hodder & Stoughton, 1922) £40
LITTLE WOMEN (illustrated by Percy Tarrant) (Harrap, 1922) £40
LITTLE WOMEN (illustrated by S. Van Abbe) (Dent, 1948)...£30
LITTLE WOMEN (illustrated by Rene Cloke) (Gawthorn [1949])...£35
LITTLE WOMEN Part 2 (Roberts Bros, US, 1869)..£2,000
GOOD WIVES (Sampson Low, 1869)...£300
GOOD WIVES (illustrated by H.M. Brock) (Seeley, 1905)..£40
GOOD WIVES (illustrated by M.V. Wheelhouse) (G. Bell, 1911)..£40
GOOD WIVES (illustrated by Harold Copping) (R.T.S., 1913) £40
GOOD WIVES (illustrated by S. Van Abbe) (Dent, 1953)...£30
ON PICKET DUTY (James Redpath, US, [1864])..£200
HOSPITAL SKETCHES AND CAMP AND FIRESIDE STORIES (Sampson Low, 1870)........................£125
AN OLD FASHIONED GIRL (Sampson Low, 1870)..£90
AN OLD FASHIONED GIRL (illustrated by Jessie Willcox Smith) (Little Brown, US, 1902) £50
LITTLE MEN: Life at Plumfield with Jo's Boys (Sampson Low, 1871) £200
MY BOYS (Volume One of 'Aunt Jo's Scrapbag'; precedes first US edition) (Sampson Low, 1871) £100
SHAWL STRAPS (Volume Two of 'Aunt Jo's Scrapbag') (Sampson Low, 1873 [1872])......................£100
CUPID AND CHOW CHOW (Volume Three of 'Aunt Jo's Scrapbag') (Sampson Low, 1873) £90
SOMETHING TO DO (Ward Lock, [1873])..£70
FIRESIDE AND CAMP STORIES (Ward Lock, 1873)..£70
WORK: A Story of Experience (precedes first US 'Experience'; two volumes) (Sampson Low, 1873)....£145
EIGHT COUSINS, or The Aunt Hill (Sampson Low, 1875)..£100
BEGINNING AGAIN: Being a Continuation of 'Work' (Sampson Low, 1875) £100
SILVER PITCHERS and Other Stories (Sampson Low, 1876)...£90
A MODERN MEPHISTOPHELES (Sampson Low, 1877) £50
ROSE IN BLOOM: A Sequel to 'Eight Cousins' (Sampson Low, 1877 [1876]).....................................£75
ROSE IN BLOOM (illustrated by Rodney Shackell; issued with dustjacket) (Hart-Davis, 1967) £20
UNDER THE LILACS (precedes first US appearance; issued in eleven monthly parts; illustrated) (Sampson Low, 1877-78) £100
UNDER THE LILACS (first one-volume edition) (Sampson Low, 1878)..£60
JIMMY'S CRUISE IN THE 'PINAFORE' (Volume Five of 'Aunt Jo's Scrapbag') (Sampson Low, 1879)....£50
JACK AND JILL (Sampson Low, 1880)..£55
AN OLD FASHIONED THANKSGIVING and Other Stories (Volume Six of 'Aunt Jo's Scrapbag') (Sampson Low, 1882) £45
PROVERB STORIES (Sampson Low, 1882)..£40
SPINNING WHEEL STORIES (Sampson Low, 1884)..£40
LULU'S LIBRARY (Sampson Low, 1886 [1885])...£40
JO'S BOYS: And How They Turned Out (Sampson Low, 1886)...£120
JO'S BOYS (illustrated by Harry Toothill) (Dent, 1960)...£20
A GARLAND FOR GIRLS (Blackie, 1888)..£35
RECOLLECTIONS OF MY CHILDHOOD DAYS (Sampson Low, 1890) £30
COMIC TRAGEDIES: Written by 'Jo' and 'Meg' (Sampson Low, 1893) £44

ALDIN, Cecil

British illustrator. Born: Slough, 1870. Studied at South Kensington School of Art. Worked as a comic illustrator in the 1890s before achieving great success as a sporting artist. Contributed to the *Boy's Own Paper* and *Oxford Annual*. Retired to Majorca in 1930. Died: 1935.

Prices are for books in Very Good condition.

SPOT, AN AUTOBIOGRAPHY (fourteen mono illustrations by Cecil Aldin) (Houlston, 1894) £200
WONDERLAND WONDERS by Rev John Isabell (mono frontispiece and nineteen illustrations by Cecil Aldin;
    also includes contributions by Louis Wain) (Home Words, 1895)...£100

This Edition, numbered and signed by the Artist, is limited to three hundred and eighty copies, of which three hundred and fifty are for sale, and thirty are for presentation.

This is No. 244

Aldin has long been a favourite with collectors. Pictured is a unique pencil sketch illustration added to a signed limitation page.

THE HOUSE ANNUAL (Gale & Polden, 1902) £75
THE YOUNG FOLKS' BIRTHDAY BOOK (Hills, 1902) £50
THE SNOB: Some Episodes in a Mis-spent Youth by Walter Emanuel (nineteen colour plates by Cecil Aldin)
(Lawrence & Bullen, 1904).. £100
A GAY DOG: The Story of a Foolish Year by Walter Emanuel (24 colour plates by Cecil Aldin) (Heinemann, 1905)............. £150
THE DOGS OF WAR by Walter Emanuel (Bradbury Agnew, [1906])... £100
THE HAPPY ANNUAL (with John Hassall) (Heinemann, 1907)... £80
OLD CHRISTMAS by Washington Irving (27 colour plates, six mono plates and decorations by Cecil Aldin)
(Hodder & Stoughton, 1908) £145
FARM FRIENDS FOR LITTLE FOLK (with other illustrators, including Arthur Rackham) (Blackie, 1908) £100
THE PLAYTIME PICTURE BOOKS. With verses by Richard Waylett (series; includes 'The Doggie Book')
(Lawrence & Jellicoe, 1909)... each £150
PUSSY AND HER WAYS (Henry Frowde/Hodder & Stoughton, [1909]).. £250
DOGGIE AND HIS WAYS (Henry Frowde/Hodder & Stoughton, [1909]).. £250
THE BLACK PUPPY BOOK (Henry Frowde/Hodder & Stoughton, [1909]) £250
THE WHITE PUPPY BOOK (Henry Frowde/Hodder & Stoughton, [1909]) £250
THE WHITE KITTEN BOOK (eleven colour plates by Cecil Aldin) (Henry Frowde/Hodder & Stoughton, [1909])........ £250
PICKLES, A PUPPY DOG'S TALE (24 colour illustrations by Cecil Aldin) (Henry Frowde/Hodder & Stoughton, [1909])......... £350
ROUGH AND TUMBLE (Henry Frowde/Hodder & Stoughton, [1909]) £350
FIELD BABIES (24 colour plates by Cecil Aldin) (Henry Frowde/Hodder & Stoughton, [1910]) £200
THE TWINS (24 full-page colour plates by Cecil Aldin) (Henry Frowde/Hodder & Stoughton, [1910])............ £325
THE RED PUPPY BOOK (twelve colour plates) (Henry Frowde/Hodder & Stoughton, [1910]) £175
MY PETS (Henry Frowde/Hodder & Stoughton, [1910]).. £75
AN OLD-FASHIONED CHRISTMAS EVE by Washington Irving (Hodder & Stoughton, 1910) £35
AN OLD-FASHIONED CHRISTMAS DAY by Washington Irving (Hodder & Stoughton, 1910) £35
THE POSTHUMOUS PAPERS OF THE PICKWICK CLUB by Charles Dickens (two volumes; Vol. 1 has thirteen
colour plates, Vol. II has eleven colour plates) (Chapman & Hall/Lawrence & Jellicoe, 1910) £200
MY BOOK OF DOGGIES: Stories and Pictures for Little Folk (with other artists, including Arthur Rackham)
(Blackie, [1910]).. £125
PUPPY TAILS by Richard Waylett (Lawrence & Jellicoe, [1910]) £125
HANDLEY CROSS or Mr Jorrocks' Hunt by Robert Smith Surtees (two volumes) (Edward Arnold, [1911])............ £100
FARM BABIES by May Byron (24 full-page colour illustrations by Cecil Aldin) (Henry Frowde/Hodder & Stoughton, [1911]) £300
FARMYARD PUPPIES (twelve colour illustrations by Cecil Aldin) (Henry Frowde/Hodder & Stoughton, [1911]) £175
MERRY AND BRIGHT (24 full-page colour illustrations by Cecil Aldin) (Henry Frowde/Hodder & Stoughton, [1911])........ £300
MAC: A Story of a Dog (Henry Frowde/Hodder & Stoughton, [1912])... £300
THE MONGREL PUPPY BOOK (twelve colour plates by Cecil Aldin) (Henry Frowde/Hodder & Stoughton, [1912]) £200
BLACK BEAUTY by Anna Sewell
(eighteen plates in colour and endpapers especially drawn for this edition by Cecil Aldin) (Jarrold, [1912])............. £150
WHITE-EAR AND PETER: The Story of a Fox and a Fox-Terrier by Neils Heiberg (sixteen colour plates by Cecil Aldin)
(Macmillan, 1912).. £175
CECIL ALDIN'S HAPPY FAMILY by May Byron (six parts; illustrated in colour by Cecil Aldin;
also issued in a single volume edition) (Henry Frowde/Hodder & Stoughton, [1912]) .... each £75
CECIL ALDIN'S MERRY PARTY by May Byron (six parts; illustrated with many full-page pictures in colour by Cecil Aldin;
also issued as a single-volume edition) (Henry Frowde/Hodder & Stoughton, 1913) .... each £75
MY DOG by Maurice Maeterlinck. Translated by A. Teixeira de Mattos (six colour plates by Cecil Aldin) (Allen, 1913)............. £75
ZOO BABIES by G.E. Farrow (Frowde/Hodder & Stoughton, 1913) £135
THE MERRY PUPPY BOOK (36 colour plates by Cecil Aldin) (Milford, 1913)................................. £300
THE UNDERDOG by Sidney Trist (four illustrations by Cecil Aldin) (Animals' Guardian, 1913)............ £75
CECIL ALDIN'S RAG BOOK, THE ANIMALS' SCHOOL TREAT by Clifton Bingham (24 colour illustrations by Cecil Aldin)
(Dean: 'Rag Book' series No. 70, [1913]).. £150
THE BOBTAIL PUPPY BOOK (verse) (Henry Frowde/Hodder & Stoughton, [1914]).......................... £200
JACK AND JILL by May Byron (illustrated by Cecil Aldin) (Henry Frowde/Hodder & Stoughton, [1914]) £300
THE DOG WHO WASN'T WHAT HE THOUGHT HE WAS by Walter Emanuel (24 colour plates by Cecil Aldin)
(Raphael Tuck, [1914])... £300
ANIMAL REVELS by May Byron (Henry Frowde/Hodder & Stoughton, [1914])............................... £75
ANIMAL FROLICS by May Byron (Henry Frowde/Hodder & Stoughton, [1914]) £75
MOUFLOU by Ouida (T.C. & E.C. Jack, 1915).. £100
THE CECIL ALDIN PAINTING BOOKS (contains 'The Puppy Book', 'The Normandy', 'The Cat and Dog Book' and
'The Pied Piper of Hamelin') (Lawrence & Jellicoe, [1915])... each £100
JOCK AND SOME OTHERS by Richard Waylett (sixteen full-page colour illustrations and
fifteen black-and-white illustrations by Cecil Aldin) (Gale & Polden, [1916]) £250
THE MERRY PARTY (Humphrey Milford, [1918]) £150
BUNNYBOROUGH (Humphrey Milford, [1919]) £275
GYP'S HOUR OF BLISS by Gladys Davidson (Collins, 1919) £200
THE GREAT ADVENTURE (seventeen colour plates by Cecil Aldin) (Humphrey Milford, [1920])............ £200
CECIL ALDIN LETTER BOOKS (Humphrey Milford, [1920]) £100
US (Humphrey Milford, [1922]) £150
DOGS OF CHARACTER (Eyre & Spottiswoode, 1927)... £75
A DOZEN DOGS OR SO by P.R. Chalmers (thirteen colour plates by Cecil Aldin) (Eyre & Spottiswoode, 1927)............. £120
SLEEPING PARTNERS: A Series of Episodes (twenty colour plates by Cecil Aldin) (Eyre & Spottiswoode, [1929])............. £250

JERRY: The Story of an Exmoor Pony by Eleanor E. Helme and Nance Paul
(eleven full-page black-and-white illustrations by Cecil Aldin) (Eyre & Spottiswoode, [1930]) **£45**
AN ARTIST'S MODELS (twenty colour plates by Cecil Aldin) (Witherby, 1930)................................**£200**
MRS TICKLER'S CARAVAN (with Pat Wood) (Eyre & Spottiswoode, 1931)................................**£50**
LOST, STOLEN OR STRAYED by Marion Ashmore (thirty black-and-white illustrations and colour frontispiece by Cecil Aldin)
(Eyre & Spottiswoode, 1931)..**£45**
FLAX, POLICE DOG by Svend Fleuron. Translated from Danish by E. Gee Nash
(ten black-and-white illustrations by Cecil Aldin) (Eyre & Spottiswoode, [1931])................................**£35**
THE BUNCH BOOK by James Douglas (51 black-and-white illustrations and coloured frontispiece by Cecil Aldin)
(Eyre & Spottiswoode, 1932)..**£35**
THE JOKER, AND JERRY AGAIN by Eleanor E. Helme and Nance Paul (Eyre & Spottiswoode, 1932) **£45**
THE CECIL ALDIN BOOK (eight colour plates and 95 black-and-white illustrations by Cecil Aldin)
(Eyre & Spottiswoode, 1932)..**£45**
SCARLET, BLUE AND GREEN by Duncan Fife (four colour plates, seven half-tone and 25 mono illustrations by Cecil Aldin)
(Macmillan, 1932)..**£75**
HIS APOLOGIES by Rudyard Kipling (Doubleday Doran, US, 1932)................................**£45**
DOGS OF EVERY DAY by Patrick Chalmers (twelve full-page mono plates by Cecil Aldin) (Eyre & Spottiswoode, 1933) **£75**
WHO'S WHO IN THE ZOO (four colour plates and 35 full-page black-and-white illustrations by Cecil Aldin)
(Eyre & Spottiswoode, 1933)..**£50**
HOTSPUR THE BEAGLE by John Vickerman (Constable, 1934)................................**£50**
JUST AMONG FRIENDS (Eyre & Spottiswoode, 1935) **£175**
HOW TO DRAW DOGS (47 pages of sketches by Cecil Aldin; foreword by Gwen Aldin) (John Lane: The Bodley Head, 1935) ...**£150**
SMUGGLERS' GALLOWS by Stanton Hope (Eyre & Spottiswoode, 1936)................................**£30**
BUNNYBOROUGH (reissue of 1919 edition; fifteen colour plates by Cecil Aldin; issued in dustjacket)
(Eyre & Spottiswoode, 1946)..**£45**

'ALICE' BOOKS

Lewis Carroll's *Alice's Adventures in Wonderland* (1865) and *Through the Looking-Glass* (1872 [1871]) have been illustrated by countless artists. What follows is a list of the most collectable editions. See also CARROLL, Lewis.
Prices are for books in Very Good condition (with dustjackets after 1940).

'Alice's Adventures Under Ground'

ALICE'S ADVENTURES UNDER GROUND (red cloth binding) (Macmillan, 1886)................................**£200**
Ditto (variant binding) (Macmillan, 1886)..**£2,000**
JUSTIN TOOD EDITION (Gollancz, 1988)..**£30**
ANTONY BROWNE EDITION (Julian MacRae, 1988)..**£30**
HELEN OXENBURY EDITION (Walker, 1999) **£20**

'Alice's Adventures in Wonderland'

FIRST [WITHDRAWN] EDITION (illustrated by John Tenniel; red cloth binding) (Macmillan, 1865)................................**£200,000+**
FIRST US EDITION (illustrated by John Tenniel; red cloth binding) (Appleton, US, 1866 [1865]) ....**£5,000+**
FIRST UK EDITION (illustrated by John Tenniel; red cloth binding) (Macmillan, 1866 [1865]) ....**£3,000+**
FIRST GERMAN EDITION (as 'Alice's Abenteuer Im Wunderland'; translated by Antonie Zimmermann)
(Macmillan und Comp, 1869)..**£300**
FIRST FRENCH EDITION (as 'Aventures d'Alice au Pays des Merveilles'; translated by Henry Bué)
(Macmillan and Co, Londres, 1869)..**£300**
FIRST ITALIAN EDITION (as 'Avventure d'Alice nel Paese delle Meraviglie'; translated by T. Pietrocòla-Rossetti)
(Macmillan and Co, Londra, 1872)..**£300**
'PEOPLE'S EDITION' (illustrated by John Tenniel; green cloth binding) (Macmillan, 1887) **£50**
'THE NURSERY ALICE' (illustrated by John Tenniel; boards) (Macmillan, 1890)................................**£150**
PETER NEWELL EDITION (Harper, US, 1901) **£150**
BLANCHE McMANUS EDITION (Mansfield, US, 1896)..**£80**
BLANCHE McMANUS EDITION (Ward Lock, 1907)..**£80**
CHARLES ROBINSON EDITION (Cassell, 1907) **£150**
ARTHUR RACKHAM EDITION (with a poem by Austin Dobson; green cloth binding) (Heinemann, [1907])................................**£300**
ARTHUR RACKHAM EDITION (De Luxe Edition, with poem by Austin Dobson; limited to 1,130 copies; white vellum binding)
(Heinemann, [1907])..**£1,750**
THOMAS MAYBANK EDITION (Routledge, 1907)..**£100**
MILLICENT SOWERBY EDITION (Chatto & Windus, 1907)..**£150**
HARRY ROUNTREE EDITION (Nelson, 1908)..**£100**
THOMAS HEATH ROBINSON EDITION (illustrated by Thomas Heath Robinson and Charles Pears)
(William Collins, 1908)..**£30**
MABEL LUCIE ATTWELL EDITION (boards or cloth binding) (Raphael Tuck, [1910])................................**£200**
FRANK ADAMS EDITION (Blackie, 1912)..**£40**
ALICE B. WOODWARD EDITION (Bell, 1913) **£100**
A.E. JACKSON EDITION (Frowde, 1915) **£150**
MARGARET TARRANT EDITION (Ward Lock, 1916) **£150**
A.L. BOWLEY EDITION (Raphael Tuck, 1921)..**£50**
GWYNNED HUDSON EDITION (Hodder & Stoughton, 1922) **£150**
WILLY POGANY EDITION (Dutton, US, 1929)..**£50**
WILLY POGANY EDITION (De Luxe Edition, signed by the artist) (Dutton, US, 1929) **£250**

'ALICE' BOOKS

The King and Queen of Hearts inspecting tarts in the coutroom. A famous John Tenniel illustrations from the first edition of **Alice's Adventures in Wonderland** *(1865).*

ANTHONY RADO EDITION (Newman Wolsey, [c 1944]) £40
EILEEN SOPER EDITION (Harrap, 1947)..£40
MARAJA EDITION (W.H. Allen, 1958) £40
RALPH STEADMAN EDITION (Dobson, 1967) £70
SALVADOR DALI EDITION (Random House, US, 1969)...£3,000
BARRY MOSER EDITION (University of California Press, US, 1982)...£50
BARRY MOSER EDITION (De Luxe Edition) (Pennyroyal Press, US, 1982) £3,000
MICHAEL HAGUE EDITION (Holt, US, 1985) £25
MICHAEL HAGUE EDITION (Methuen, 1985)..£20
JUSTIN TODD EDITION (Gollancz, 1988) £30
ANTONY BROWNE EDITION (Julia MacRae Books, 1988)...£30
HELEN OXENBURY EDITION (Walker, 1999)..£20
DIDIER MUTEL EDITION (limited to 50 signed copies; in slipcase) (Mutel, Paris, 2002) £2,500

'Through the Looking-Glass'

FIRST EDITION (illustrated by John Tenniel) (Macmillan, 1872 [1871]) £400
'PEOPLE'S EDITION' (illustrated by John Tenniel; green cloth binding) (Macmillan, 1887) £50
BLANCHE McMANUS EDITION (Mansfield, US, 1899)..£50
PETER NEWELL EDITION (Harper, US, 1902) £100
HELEN MUNRO EDITION (Nelson, 1937) £30
RALPH STEADMAN EDITION (MacGibbon & Kee, 1972) £60
QUENTIN BLAKE EDITION (in slipcase) (Folio Society, 1976)...£30
QUENTIN BLAKE EDITION (facsimile edition; issued with dustjacket)
    (Windward, 1980) £10
WASP IN A WIG (the first appearance in print, exclusive to *The Sunday Telegraph*, of the lost chapter from
    Through The Looking Glass, with illustrations by Ralph Steadman, Sir Hugh Casson, Peter Blake & P. Procktor)
    (Telegraph Sunday Magazine No.51, 1977)..£5
WASP IN A WIG a 'suppressed' episode of **Through the Loking-Glass** (Macmillan, 1977) £10

Combined Editions

JOHN TENNIEL EDITION (92 illustrations by John Tenniel, including sixteen in colour) (Macmillan, 1911) £80
MERVYN PEAKE EDITION (Continental, Sweden, 1946)..£200
MERVYN PEAKE EDITION (Wingate, 1954) £120
THE COMPLETE ALICE AND HUNTING OF THE SNARK (illustrated by Ralph Steadman) (Jonathan Cape, 1986).............£40

'ALLY SLOPER' ANNUALS

The best-known of the early British comics, featuring the world's first regular strip cartoon character, Ally Sloper, an accident-prone, gin-drinking misfit originally created by Charles Henry Ross. He first appeared on 14th August 1867 in the pages of the weekly magazine, *Judy*, achieving his own comic, *Ally Sloper's Half Holiday*, on 3rd May 1884. The title continued in various incarnations until 1923, but it is the early 'special numbers' that are most collected today.

Prices are for numbers in Very Good condition.

ALLY SLOPER'S HALF HOLIDAY (W.J. Sinkin, 3rd May 1884)..£40
ALLY SLOPER'S CHRISTMAS HOLIDAYS (W.J. Sinkin, December 1884)..£40
ALLY SLOPER'S CHRISTMAS HOLIDAYS (W.J. Sinkin, 1885-1914)...each £35
ALLY SLOPER'S SUMMER NUMBER (W.J. Sinkin, 1880)..£35
ALLY SLOPER'S SUMMER NUMBER (W.J. Sinkin, 1881-1887)...each £30

ANDERSEN, Hans

Danish author. Born: Hans Christian Andersen in Odense, Denmark, 1805. Had little formal education. Began his literary career with a novel, *The Improvisatore* (1835), but achieved his greatest success with his *Eventyr fortalte for Børn* (*Tales Told for Children*) of the same year. His stories were first published in English in 1846, and their popularity in Britain brought him the friendship of Charles Dickens, amongst others. Died: 1875.

Prices are for books in Good condition (pre-1900) and Very Good condition (post-1900) in original binding.

Tales: Early Editions

WONDERFUL STORIES FOR CHILDREN (translated by Mary Howitt) (Chapman & Hall, 1846).....................£800
A DANISH STORY BOOK (illustrated by Count Pocci; translated by Charles Boner) (Joseph Cundall, 1846) £600
DANISH FAIRY LEGENDS AND TALES (translated by Caroline Peachey) (W. Pickering, 1846)....................£400
THE SHOES OF FORTUNE and Other Tales (illustrated by Otto Speckter; translated by Charles Boner)
    (Chapman & Hall, 1847)...£150
A PICTURE BOOK WITHOUT PICTURES (translated by Meta Taylor) (Bogue, 1847) £150
TALES FOR THE YOUNG (illustrated by the Dalziel Bros) (Burns, 1847) £150
A CHRISTMAS GREETING TO MY ENGLISH FRIENDS (translated by Lockmeyer; dedicated to Charles Dickens)
    (R. Bentley, 1847)..£150
THE DREAM OF LITTLE TUK and Other Tales (illustrated by Count Pocci; translated by Charles Boner)
    (Grant & Griffiths, 1848) £400

TALES AND FAIRY STORIES (illustrated by H. Warren; translated by Madame de Chatelain) (Routledge 1853) **£150**
DIAMOND SPARKS (illustrated by Henry Warren, George Routledge, 1853).. **£150**
THE SAND-HILLS OF JUTLAND (translated by Anne Bushby) (Richard Bentley, 1860)... **£150**
THE ICE MAIDEN (illustrated by Pearson after Zwecker; translated by Bushby) (R. Bentley, 1853)................................ **£100**
THE WILD SWANS (J. Haddock, 1863) **£100**
STORIES AND TALES (illustrated by the Dalziel Bros after A.W. Bayes; translated by H.W. Dulken) (Routledge, 1864) **£100**
WHAT THE MOON SAW and Other Tales (illustrated by the Dalziel Bros after A.W. Bayes; translated by H.W. Dulken)
(Routledge, 1866 [1865]).. **£100**
OUT OF THE HEART: Spoken to the Little Ones (illustrated by the Dalziel Bros; translated by H.W. Dulken)
(Routledge, 1867).. **£100**
THE WILL O' THE WISPS ARE IN TOWN and Other Tales (illustrated by Swain; translated by A. Plesner and
S. Rugeley-Powers) (Strahan, 1867) **£200**
LATER TALES (illustrated by Otto Speckler, Alfred Cooper, and others, translated by Caroline Peachey,
A. Plesner, H. Ward, and others) (Bell & Daldy, 1869) **£150**
THE WOOD NYMPH (translated by A.M. and A. Plesner) (Sampson Low, 1870) **£80**
THE WHITE SWAN and Other Tales (illustrated by Alice Havers; translated by Mrs H.B. Paull)
(Hildesheimer & Faulkner, 1873).. **£100**
STORIES AND FAIRY TALES (illustrated by Gaskin; translated by Oskar Sommer; two volumes)
(George Allen, 1893) .... the set **£175**

Important Illustrated Editions (with dustjackets where applicable)
'E.V.B.' [ELEANOR VERE BOYLE)
FAIRY TALES (quarto) (Sampson Low, 1872 [1871]) **£600**
FAIRY TALES (with two extra colour plates by E.V.B.; small folio) (Sampson Low, 1872 [1871])............................ **£800**
ARTHUR GASKIN
STORIES AND FAIRY TALES (In two volumes, limited to 300 sets) (George Allen, 1893) .... the set **£300**
WILLIAM HEATH ROBINSON
DANISH FAIRY TALES AND LEGENDS (Sands, 1897) **£100**
FAIRY TALES (Constable, 1913).. **£600**
FAIRY TALES (Edition De Luxe, in vellum binding; limited to 100 copies, signed by the artist) (Constable, 1913)............... **£3,000+**
HELEN STRATTON
FAIRY TALES (George Newnes, 1899)... **£80**
CHARLES ROBINSON, THOMAS HEATH ROBINSON & WILLIAM HEATH ROBINSON
FAIRY TALES (translated by Mrs E. Lucas) (Dent, 1899) **£100**
FAIRY TALES New Edition (Hodder & Stoughton, [1923]) **£100**
FAIRY TALES Boots edition (reissue of 1923 edition) (Hodder & Stoughton [1927]) **£60**
MAXWELL ARMFIELD
FAIRY TALES (J.M. Dent, 1910) **£60**
EDMUND DULAC
STORIES (Hodder & Stoughton [1911]).. **£300**
STORIES (Hodder & Stoughton [1911]; Edition De Luxe; limited to 750 copies, signed by the artist) **£1,500**
A. DUNCAN CARSE
FAIRY TALES (A. & C. Black, 1912) **£40**
FAIRY TALES (A. & C. Black, 1912; Edition De Luxe; limited to 500 copies, signed by the artist & publishers)........................ **£200**
MABEL LUCIE ATTWELL
FAIRY TALES (Raphael Tuck, [1914]).. **£150**
HARRY CLARKE
FAIRY TALES (George G. Harrap, 1916) **£350**
FAIRY TALES (Edition De Luxe; limited to 125 copies, signed by the artist) (George G. Harrap, 1916) **£1,750**
MARGARET TARRANT
FAIRY STORIES (Ward Lock, 1917).. **£60**
HONOR C. APPLETON
FAIRY TALES (Nelson, [1920]).. **£200**
ANNE ANDERSON
FAIRY TALES (Collins, 1924) **£120**
KAY NIELSEN
FAIRY TALES (in dustjacket and publisher's box) (Hodder & Stoughton [1924]) .... **£1,500+**
FAIRY TALES (Edition De Luxe; limited to 500 copies, signed by the artist, approx.
250 copies in blue cloth [and dustjacket], and 250 in white vellum binding) (Hodder & Stoughton, [1924])...................... **£3,000**
WILLI HARWERTH
THE RED SHOES (limited edition, signed by the artist) (D. Cleverdon, 1928).. **£80**
CHRISTINE JACKSON
HANS ANDERSEN: FORTY STORIES [i.e. FORTY-TWO STORIES] (translated by M.R. James, with d/j)
(Faber & Faber, 1930).. **£40**
ARTHUR RACKHAM
FAIRY TALES (with d/j) (George G. Harrap, 1932) **£400**
FAIRY TALES (publisher's special binding in full morocco) (George G. Harrap, 1932)... **£300**
FAIRY TALES (Edition De Luxe; limited to 525 copies, signed by the artist) (George G. Harrap, 1932) **£1,500**
REX WHISTLER
FAIRY TALES AND LEGENDS (with d/j) (Cobden-Sanderson, 1935)... **£50**
FAIRY TALES AND LEGENDS (limited to 200 copies, signed by the artist) (Cobden-Sanderson, 1935) **£350**

Hans Andersen's Fairy Tales have been illustrated by a host of celebrated artists, including Mabel Lucie Attwell.

'There sat the dog with the eyes as big as teacups'. The Harry Clarke edition (1916) included this plate for 'The Tinderbox'.

FRITZ KREDEL
ANDERSEN'S LIFE AND STORIES (in two volumes, translated by Jean Hersholt, limited to 1,500 sets,
 signed by the artist and translator, in slipcase) (Limited Editions Club, US, undated) ....the set **£100**
THE COMPLETE ANDERSEN (in six volumes, translated by Jean Hersholt, limited to 1,500 sets,
 signed by the artist and translator) (Limited Editions Club, US, undated)..the set **£300**
ROBIN JACQUES
HANS ANDERSEN: FORTY-TWO STORIES (translated by M.R. James, with d/j) (Faber & Faber, 1953) **£30**
E.H. SHEPARD
FAIRY TALES (translated by L.W. Kingland, with d/j) (OUP, 1961) **£30**
SHIRLEY HUGHES
FAIRY TALES (with d/j) (Blackie, 1961) **£30**
MICHAEL FOREMAN
HANS ANDERSEN: HIS CLASSIC FAIRY TALES (with d/j) (Victor Gollancz, 1976) **£20**
EDWARD ARDIZZONE
ARDIZZONE'S HANS ANDERSEN (with d/j) (Andre Deutsch, 1978) **£30**
MICHAEL HAGUE
MICHAEL HAGUE'S FAVOURITE HANS ANDERSEN FAIRY TALES (with d/j) (Holt, US, 1981)........................**£30**
Ditto (Edition De Luxe, limited to 300 signed copies, with original drawing, in slipcase) (Holt, US, 1981) **£200**

ANDERSON, Anne

Scottish illustrator. Born: Scotland, 1874, but lived in Argentina, then Berkshire. Married the illustrator
Alan Wright, with whom she collaborated on several children's books. Died: 1930.

Prices are for books in Very Good condition with dustjackets where applicable.

AUCASSIN AND NICOLETE. Translated and edited with introduction by Harold Child (A. & C. Black, 1911)...........**£100**
THE DANDY ANDY BOOK (twelve colour plates by Anne Anderson) (Nelson, [1911]) **£125**
THE FUNNY BUNNY ABC: A Book of Bunnies and Bairnies with Pictures for Painting (Nelson, [1912]) **£100**
THE GATEWAY TO CHAUCER (sixteen colour plates by Anne Anderson) (Nelson, 1912) **£85**
THE DARING-DUCKIE BOOK (with Alan Wright) (twelve colour plates by Anne Anderson) (Nelson, 1914) **£100**
OLD FRENCH NURSERY SONGS by Horace Mansion (Harrap, [1915]) **£125**
OLD ENGLISH NURSERY SONGS (eight plates by Anne Anderson) (Harrap, [1915])......................................**£135**
THE BUSY BUNNY BOOK (illustrated by Anne Anderson and Alan Wright) (Nelson, [1916]).............................**£100**
THE NAUGHTY NEDDY BOOK (with Alan Wright) (Nelson, [1916])..**£100**
THE GILLY FLOWER GARDEN BOOK (Nelson, [c.1916]) **£120**
THE ROSIE POSY BOOK (Nelson, [c.1917])..**£120**
TWO BOLD SPORTSMEN (with Alan Wright) (Nelson, 1918)...**£80**
RIP by E.W. Garrett (Humphrey Milford, 1919)...**£70**
THE PATSY BOOK: Being the Adventures of Patsy, Patty and Pat (Nelson, [1919])....................................**£80**
HOP O'MY THUMB (Nelson, [c.1920])..**£80**
TUB TIME TALES by Madeline Barnes (Blackie, 1920)..**£110**
THE JACKIE JACKDAW BOOK (Nelson, 1920)..**£100**
THE JACKY HORNER ABC (Dean, [c.1920])...**£80**
THE HOUSE ABOVE THE TREES by Ethel Eliot (Thornton Butterworth, 1921) **£150**
FIRESIDE STORIES by Madeline Barnes (Blackie, 1922)...**£90**
GRIMM'S FAIRY TALES (Collins, [1922])..**£100**
SING-SONG STORIES by Agnes Grozier Herbertson (illustrated by Anne Anderson and Alan Wright) (Milford, [1922])............**£90**
COSY-TIME TALES by Natalie Joan (Nelson, [1922]) **£100**
THE ANNE ANDERSON FAIRY-TALE BOOK (Nelson, [1923]) **£90**
HANS ANDERSEN'S FAIRY TALES (Collins, [1924])..**£120**
COSY CHAIR STORIES by Peggy Morrison (Collins, [1924]) **£90**
THE ISLE OF WIRRAWOO by A.L. Purse (illustrated by Anne Anderson and Alan Wright)
 (Humphrey Milford/OUP, 1924)...**£80**
HEIDI by Johanna Spyri (translated by Helene S. White) (Harrap, 1924)..**£100**
WANDA AND THE GARDEN OF THE RED HOUSE (Humphrey Milford, 1924) **£80**
THE WATER BABIES by Charles Kingsley (T.C. & E.C. Jack, [1924])..**£150**
LITTLE RHYMES FOR LITTLE FOLKS by Mrs H. Strang (Humphrey Milford, 1925) **£60**
THE OLD MOTHER GOOSE NURSERY RHYME BOOK (Nelson, [1926]) **£100**
MR PICKLES AND THE PARTY by Constance Heward (Warne, [1926]) **£60**
THE CUDDLY KITTY AND THE BUSY BUNNY (illustrated by Anne Anderson and Alan Wright) (Nelson, 1926) **£100**
THE PODGY-PUPPY (illustrated by Anne Anderson and Alan Wright) (Nelson, [1927]).................................**£120**
A SERIES OF FAIRY TALES (six parts; written by Anne Anderson) (Nelson, [1928])...........................each **£35**
A SERIES OF FAIRY TALES (three parts; written by Anne Anderson) (Collins, [1929])......................each **£35**
PLAYTIME ABC (written by Anne Anderson) (Collins, 1930)..**£50**
MERRY FOLK (written by Anne Anderson) (Collins, 1930)...**£75**
THE ANNE ANDERSON PICTURE BOOK (fairy tales by Hans Andersen and the
 Grimm brothers accompanied by numerous coloured and black-and-white illustrations by Anne Anderson)
 (Collins, [1943])...**£120**
THE COSY CORNER BOOK (Collins, [1943]) **£100**
PRETENDER PEGGY by Violet Methley (T.C. & E.C. Jack, no date)...**£50**
THE SLEEPY-SONG BOOK by Horace Mansion (Harrap, no date)..**£120**

ANDERSON, Gerry

British TV producer. Born: 1929. Creator of some of the most popular children's TV shows of the 1960s and '70s, including *Stingray* and *Thunderbirds*. These series inspired a number of collectable spin-off novels and annuals.

Prices are for books in Very Good condition.

Annuals and Large Hardbacks

TWIZZLE ADVENTURE STORIES (Birn Brothers, 1959) £20
MORE TWIZZLE ADVENTURE STORIES (Birn Brothers, 1960) £20
TWIZZLE STORY BOOK (Birn Brothers, 1960) £20
TV PLAYLAND 1965 (with three 'Twizzle' stories) (TV Publications, 1965)...£15
TORCHY AND HIS TWO BEST FRIENDS STORY BOOK (Daily Mirror, 1962) £20
TORCHY GIFTBOOK (Daily Mirror, 1960) £20
TORCHY GIFTBOOK (Daily Mirror, 1961) £20
TORCHY GIFTBOOK (Daily Mirror, 1962) £20
TORCHY GIFTBOOK (Daily Mirror, 1963) £20
TORCHY GIFTBOOK (Daily Mirror, 1964) £20
FOUR FEATHER FALLS ANNUAL (Collins, 1960) £50
TEX TUCKERS FOUR FEATHER FALLS (Collins, 1961) £20
FOUR FEATHER FALLS (Collins, 1961)..£50
MIKE MERCURY IN SUPERCAR (Collins, 1961)..£40
SUPERCAR — A LITTLE GOLDEN BOOK (Golden Press, 1962)...£25
SUPERCAR ANNUAL (Collins, 1962)..£35
SUPERCAR ANNUAL (Collins, 1963)..£35
GIRL TELEVISION AND FILM ANNUAL 1963 (with 'Supercar' feature) (Odhams, 1963) £12
FIREBALL XL5 — A LITTLE GOLDEN BOOK (Golden Press, 1963)...£20
ATV TELEVISION SHOWBOOK (with 'Fireball XL5' feature) (Purnell, 1963)...£10
FIREBALL XL5 ANNUAL (Collins, 1963)..£50
FIREBALL XL5 ANNUAL (Collins, 1964)..£35
FIREBALL XL5 ANNUAL (Collins, 1965)..£25
FIREBALL XL5 ANNUAL (Collins, 1966)..£25
ITV ANNUAL 1964 (with 'Fireball XL5' feature) (TV Publications, 1964)..£12

*The **Stingray Annual** was one of many spin-off publications inspired by Gerry Anderson's hit TV shows of the Sixties.*

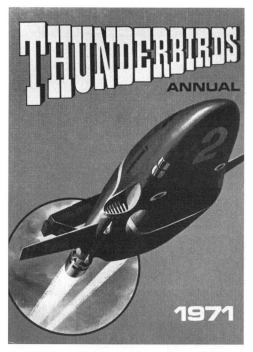

*The 1971 **Thunderbirds Annual** features 'Thunderbird 2' on the cover and now sells for £8 in Very Good Condition.*

STINGRAY TELEVISION STORY BOOK (PBS, 1965)...£15
STINGRAY ANNUAL (City Magazines, 1965)..£30
STINGRAY ANNUAL (City Magazines, 1966)..£20
STINGRAY — THE DEADLY ALLIANCE (World Distributors, 1965)..£12
STINGRAY IN 'DANGER IN THE DEEP' (World Distributors, 1966)......................................£12
THUNDERBIRDS — THE TARGET (large storybook) (World Distributors, 1966).....................£12
THUNDERBIRDS TELEVISION STORY BOOK (PBS, 1966)...£12
THUNDERBIRDS ANNUAL (City Magazines, 1966)...£35
THUNDERBIRDS ANNUAL (Century 21, 1967)..£25
THUNDERBIRDS ANNUAL (Century 21, 1968)..£15
CAPTAIN SCARLET AND THUNDERBIRDS ANNUAL (Century 21, 1969).............................£30
THUNDERBIRDS ANNUAL 1971 (Century 21, 1970)...£12
THUNDERBIRDS ANNUAL (Purnell, 1972)...£15
LADY PENELOPE IN 'THE CITY OF DARKNESS' (World Distributors, 1966).......................£25
LADY PENELOPE ANNUAL (City Magazines, 1966)..£30
LADY PENELOPE ANNUAL (Century 21, 1967)...£25
LADY PENELOPE ANNUAL (Century 21, 1968)...£20
LADY PENELOPE ANNUAL (Century 21, 1969)...£12
PENELOPE 1971 (IPC Magazines)..£6
PENELOPE 1972 (IPC Magazines)..£6
TV21 ANNUAL (City Magazines, 1965)..£12
TV21 ANNUAL (City Magazines, 1966)..£12
TV21 ANNUAL (Century 21, 1967)...£12
TV21 ANNUAL (Century 21, 1968)...£12
TV21 ANNUAL (Century 21, 1969)...£12
CANDY AND ANDY (features Thunderbirds) (Century 21, 1967)...£10
CANDY AND ANDY STORYBOOK: The Duck Who Could Not Swim (Century 21, 1968).........£10
CANDY AND ANDY (Century 21, 1968)..£10
CANDY AND ANDY (Century 21, 1969)..£10
CAPTAIN SCARLET ANNUAL (Century 21, 1967)...£30
CAPTAIN SCARLET ANNUAL (Century 21, 1968)...£20
THE ANGELS ANNUAL (Century 21, 1967)...£25
THE ANGELS STORYBOOK 1 (Century 21, 1967)...£10

Joe 90 never quite enjoyed the success of Thunderbirds and Stingray, but the tie-in annuals still sell for up to £8.

The third of the six Lady Penelope annuals published between 1966 and 1972. She also featured in three spin-off novels.

THE ANGELS STORYBOOK 2 (Century 21, 1968)..£10
JOE 90 ANNUAL (Century 21, 1968)...£25
JOE 90 ANNUAL (Century 21, 1969)...£25
JOE 90 TOP SECRET (Century 21, 1969)..£20
JOE 90 DOSSIER (large paperback) (Century 21, 1969) £10
JOE 90 STORYBOOK — JOSEPH NINESKI (Century 21, 1968)...£15
JOE 90 STORYBOOK — APPOINTMENT WITH DEATH (Century 21, 1968) £15
JOE 90 STORYBOOK — DOUBLE AGENT (Century 21, 1968) £15
JOE 90 STORYBOOK — THE CRACKSMAN (Century 21, 1969) £15
UFO ANNUAL (Century 21, 1971) £12
COUNTDOWN (features 'UFO', 'Captain Scarlet' and 'Thunderbirds') (Purnell, 1972) £20
COUNTDOWN 1973 (features 'UFO', 'Captain Scarlet' and 'Thunderbirds') (Purnell, 1973) £12
TV ACTION 1974 (features 'UFO' and 'Protectors') (Purnell, 1974) £12
PROTECTORS 1974 (Polystyle, 1974)...£12
SPACE 1999 ANNUAL (World Distributors, 1975)..£12
SPACE 1999 ANNUAL (World Distributors, 1976)..£10
SPACE 1999 ANNUAL (World Distributors, 1977)..£10
SPACE 1999 ANNUAL (World Distributors, 1978)..£10
SPACE 1999 ANNUAL (World Distributors, 1979)..£15
TERRAHAWKS ANNUAL (World Distributors, 1983) £7
TERRAHAWKS ANNUAL (World Distributors, 1984) £7
TERRAHAWKS ANNUAL (World Distributors, 1985) £7

Novels (all paperback unless otherwise indicated)
SUPERCAR — BLACK DIAMOND TRAIL (hardback) (World Distributors, 1961) £25
STINGRAY by John Theydon (illustrated by Peter Archer) (Armada, 1965) £10
STINGRAY AND THE MONSTER by John Theydon (Armada, 1966) £10
THUNDERBIRDS by John Theydon (illustrated by Peter Archer) (Armada, 1966)............................£10
THUNDERBIRDS by John Theydon (reissue) (Titan, 1989) £6
THUNDERBIRDS ARE GO by Angus P. Allan (Armada, 1966) £10
CALLING THUNDERBIRDS by John Theydon (Armada, 1966)..£10
CALLING THUNDERBIRDS (reissue) (Titan, 1990)..£5
THUNDERBIRDS — RING OF FIRE by John Theydon (Armada, 1966)..£8
THUNDERBIRDS — OPERATION ASTEROIDS by Angus P. Allan (hardback) (World Distributors, 1966) £20
THUNDERBIRDS — LOST WORLDS by John W. Jennison (hardback) (World Distributors, 1966) ..£22
LADY PENELOPE IN 'A GALLERY OF THIEVES' by Kevin McGarry (hardback)
    (World Distributors, 1966)...£30
LADY PENELOPE IN 'COOL FOR DANGER' by Kevin McGarry (hardback) (World Distributors, 1966) £30
LADY PENELOPE AND THE ALBANIAN AFFAIR by John Theydon
    (illustrated by Chris Highton) (Armada, 1966)...£10
CAPTAIN SCARLET AND THE MYSTERONS by John Theydon (Armada, 1967)............................£8
CAPTAIN SCARLET AND THE MYSTERONS (reissue) (Titan, 1989) £5
CAPTAIN SCARLET AND THE SILENT SABOTEUR by John Theydon (Armada, 1967) £8
CAPTAIN SCARLET AND THE SILENT SABOTEUR by John Theydon (reissue) (Titan, 1990)........£5
THE ANGELS AND THE CREEPING ENEMY by John Theydon (Armada, 1968) £10
JOE 90 AND THE RAIDERS by Tod Sullivan (Armada, 1968) £4
JOE 90 IN REVENGE by Howard Elson (Armada, 1969)..£4
THE SECRET SERVICE — THE DESTROYER by John Theydon (Armada, 1969) £4
THE SECRET SERVICE — THE V.I.P. by John Theydon (Armada, 1969)...£4
UFO by Robert Miall (Pan, 1970)...£6
UFO by Robert Miall (Piccolo, 1971) £6
UFO 2 by Robert Miall (Pan, 1971)...£6
THE PROTECTORS by Robert Miall (Pan, 1973)..£4
SPACE 1999: Breakaway by E.C. Tubb (Orbit, 1975)...£6
SPACE 1999: Breakaway by E.C. Tubb (hardback) (Dobson, 1975)..£10
SPACE 1999: Moon Odyssey by John Rankine (Orbit, 1975)...£6
SPACE 1999: Moon Odyssey by John Rankine (hardback) (Dobson, 1975)....................................£10
SPACE 1999: The Space Guardians by Brian Ball (Orbit, 1975) £6
SPACE 1999: The Space Guardians by Brian Ball (hardback) (Dobson, 1975) £10
SPACE 1999: The Collision Course by E.C. Tubb (Orbit, 1975) £6
SPACE 1999: The Collision Course by E.C. Tubb (hardback) (Dobson, 1975) £10
SPACE 1999: Lunar Attack by John Rankine (Orbit, 1975)...£6
SPACE 1999: Lunar Attack (hardback) (Dobson, 1975)..£10
SPACE 1999: Astral Quest by John Rankine (Orbit, 1975) £6
SPACE 1999: Astral Quest by John Rankine (hardback) (Dobson, 1975) £10
SPACE 1999: Alien Seed by E.C. Tubb (Orbit, 1976)...£6
SPACE 1999: Alien Seed (hardback) (Arthur Barker, 1976) £10
SPACE 1999: Android Planet by John Rankine (Orbit, 1976) £6
SPACE 1999: Android Planet by John Rankine (hardback) (Arthur Barker, 1976).............................£10

SPACE 1999: **Rogue Planet** by E.C. Tubb (Orbit, 1977) **£6**
SPACE 1999: **Rogue Planet** by E.C. Tubb (hardback) (Arthur Barker, 1977)...**£10**
SPACE 1999: **Earthfall** by E.C. Tubb (Orbit, 1977) **£6**
SPACE 1999: **Planets of Peril** by Michael Butterworth (Star, 1977)..**£6**
SPACE 1999: **Planets of Peril** by Michael Butterworth (hardback) (Wingate, 1977)...**£10**
SPACE 1999: **Mind-Breaks of Space** by Michael Butterworth and J. Jeff Jones (Star, 1977)............................**£6**
SPACE 1999: **Mind-Breaks of Space** by Michael Butterworth and J. Jeff Jones
    (hardback) (Wingate, 1978) **£10**
SPACE 1999: **The Space-Jackers** by Michael Butterworth (Star, 1977)..**£6**
SPACE 1999: **The Psychomorph** by Michael Butterworth (Star, 1977)..**£6**
SPACE 1999: **The Time Fighters** by Michael Butterworth (Star, 1977) **£6**
TERRAHAWKS by Jack Curtis (Sparrow, 1984)...**£4**
TERRAHAWKS STORYBOOK (Purnell, 1984)...**£3**
TERRAHAWKS (8 novels) (Purnell, 1984/5).. each **£3**

APPLETON, Honor C.

British illustrator. Born: 1879. Best known for her illustrations to Mrs H.C. Cradock's 'Josephine' books.
Also contributed to *Blackie's Annuals*. Died: 1951.

Prices are for books in Very Good condition.

Books Written and Illustrated by Honor C. Appleton

THE BAD MRS GINGER (Grant Richards: 'Dumpy Books for Children' series No. 16, 1902)....................................**£105**
DUMPY PROVERBS (Grant Richards: 'Dumpy Books for Children' series No. 24, 1903) **£110**
BABIES THREE (Nelson, [1921])...**£110**
ME AND MY PUSSIES (Nelson, 1924) **£100**

Books by Mrs H.C. Cradock Illustrated by Honor C. Appleton

JOSEPHINE AND HER DOLLS (Blackie, 1916 [1915])..**£140**
JOSEPHINE'S HAPPY FAMILY (Blackie, 1917 [1916])...**£90**
JOSEPHINE IS BUSY (Blackie, 1918) **£100**
THE BIG BOOK OF JOSEPHINE (contains 'Josephine and her Dolls', 'Josephine's Happy Family' and 'Josephine is Busy')
    (Blackie, [1919])..**£200**
WHERE THE DOLLS LIVED (ten illustrations by Honor C. Appleton) (SPCK, [1919]) **£100**
JOSEPHINE'S BIRTHDAY (Blackie, 1920 [1919])...**£100**
JOSEPHINE, JOHN AND THE PUPPY (Blackie, [1920]) **£90**
PEGGY'S TWINS (SPCK, [1920]) **£65**
THE HOUSE OF FANCY (O'Connor, 1922) **£65**
PEGGY AND JOAN (Blackie, [1922])..**£65**
JOSEPHINE KEEPS SCHOOL (Blackie, [1925])..**£80**
THE BONNY BOOK OF JOSEPHINE (contains 'Josephine,'John and the Puppy', 'Josephine's Birthday' and
    'Josephine Keeps School') (Blackie, [1926])..**£160**
JOSEPHINE GOES SHOPPING (Blackie, [1926])..**£75**
THE BEST TEDDY BEAR IN THE WORLD (Nelson, [1926])...**£50**
PAMELA'S TEDDY BEARS (Jack, [1927]) **£55**
JOSEPHINE'S CHRISTMAS PARTY (Blackie, [1927])..**£75**
THE WORLD'S BEST STORIES FOR CHILDREN (Blackie, 1930) **£45**
JOSEPHINE KEEPS HOUSE (Blackie, 1931)...**£70**
THE JOSEPHINE DOLLY BOOK (contains 'Josephine's Happy Family', 'Josephine, John and the Puppy' and
    'Josephine is Busy') (Blackie, [1934]) **£160**
JOSEPHINE'S PANTOMIME (Blackie, 1939)..**£65**
JOSEPHINE GOES TRAVELLING (Blackie, 1940) **£65**
JOSEPHINE KEEPS HOUSE (Blackie: 'Josephine Miniatures' series, [1953])...**£40**
JOSEPHINE'S PANTOMIME (Blackie: 'Josephine Miniatures' series, [1953]) **£40**
JOSEPHINE GOES TRAVELLING (Blackie: 'Josephine Miniatures' series, [1953]) **£40**
JOSEPHINE'S CHRISTMAS PARTY (Blackie: 'Josephine Miniatures' series, [1953]) **£40**
JOSEPHINE KEEPS SCHOOL (Blackie: 'Josephine Miniatures' series, [1953])..**£40**
JOSEPHINE, JOHN AND THE PUPPY (Blackie: 'Josephine Miniatures' series, [1953])......................................**£40**

Other Books Illustrated by Honor C. Appleton

TOWLOCKS AND HIS WOODEN HORSE by Alice Appleton
    (Grant Richards: 'Dumpy Books for Children' series No. 20, 1903)..**£75**
PERRAULT'S FAIRY TALES (twelve colour illustrations by Honor C. Appleton; translated by S.R. Littlewood)
    (Herbert Daniel, [1911])..**£65**
SONG OF INNOCENCE by William Blake (twelve colour illustrations by Honor C. Appleton; preface by Thomas Secombe)
    (Herbert Daniel, [1911]) **£55**
OUR NURSERY RHYME BOOK. Edited by L. and F. Littlewood
    (Herbert & Daniel, [1912]) **£40**
CHILDREN IN VERSE. Edited by Thomas Burke (Duckworth, 1913)...**£80**
BETTY'S DIARY by Dorothy Russell (Blackie, 1914) **£45**
HOW I TAMED THE WILD SQUIRRELS by Eleanor Tyrrell (Nelson, 1914) **£55**

THOSE MYSTERIOUS CHILDREN by Dorothy Russell (Blackie, [1915])...£55
THE CHILD OF THE SEA. Retold by S.R. Littlewood
(Simpkin, Marshall, Hamilton & Kent, 1915) £35
BETTY AND THE BOYS by Dorothy Russell (T.C. & E.C. Jack, [1917])..£50
THE SECRET PASSAGE by Dorothy Russell (T.C. & E.C. Jack, [1917])..£40
ST GEORGE FOR ENGLAND by Basil Hood (Harrap, 1919) £20
A CHRISTMAS CAROL by Charles Dickens (eight colour illustrations by Honor C. Appleton)
(Simpkin, Marshall, Hamilton, Kent, 1920)...£45
FAIRY TALES by Hans Christian Andersen (Nelson, [1920])...£200
THE THIRTEENTH ORPHAN by Christine Chaundler (Nisbet, 1920) £30
SNUFFLES FOR SHORT by Christine Chaundler (Nisbet, [1921]) £25
BROTHER RABBIT and Other Stories by Sara Cone Bryant
(with others) (Harrap, 1926) £30
MARJORY'S WHITE RAT by Penelope Leslie (Blackie, 1926) £25
WEE WILLIE WINKIE by Ada M. Marzials (Harrap, 1932)..£25
THE BOOK OF FAIRY STORIES (with Nora Fry) (Harrap, 1935) £25
THE BOOK OF ANIMAL TALES by Stephen Southwold (Harrap, 1936)...£35
HEATHER THE SECOND by May Wynne (Nelson, 1938)...£20
THE CHILDREN'S SWISS FAMILY ROBINSON. Adapted by F.H. Lee (Harrap, 1938)..£25
THE CHILDREN'S KING OF THE GOLDEN RIVER. Adapted by F.H. Lee from John Ruskin (Harrap, 1940) £25

'THE ARABIAN NIGHTS'

Collection of popular tales from the Middle East dating from the Eighth Century and afterwards. Amongst the best known are 'Aladdin', 'Ali Baba' and 'Sinbad the Sailor'. First published in France between 1704 and 1717, and in England from 1706 onwards, originally in chapbooks.

Prices are for books in Very Good condition.

THE ARABIAN NIGHTS (four volumes; illustrated with engravings from designs by R. Westall) (Booker, 1819) £500
DALZIELS' ILLUSTRATED ARABIAN NIGHTS' ENTERTAINMENTS. Text revised by H.W. Ducken (published in parts; illustrated by various eminent artists, engraved by the Brothers Dalziel) (Ward, Lock & Tyler, [1864 & 1865]).................£750
ALADDIN, or The Wonderful Lamp; Sinbad The Sailor; Ali Baba. Revised by M.E. Braddon (illustrated by Gustave Doré)
(Maxwell, [1880]) £350
FAIRY TALES FROM THE ARABIAN NIGHTS. Edited and arranged by E. Dixon
(illustrated by J.D. Batten) (Dent, 1893)...£50
THE ARABIAN NIGHTS' ENTERTAINMENTS (illustrated by W. Heath Robinson, Helen Stratton, A.D. McCormick,
A.L. Davis and A.E. Norbury) (Newnes/Constable, 1899) £175
THE CHILD'S ARABIAN NIGHTS (illustrated by W. Heath Robinson) (Grant Richards, 1903).......................................£400
THE ARABIAN NIGHTS' ENTERTAINMENTS. Selected and retold for children by Gladys Davidson
(illustrated by Helen Stratton) (Blackie, [1906])..£40
THE ARABIAN NIGHTS Edited with an introduction by W.H.D. Rouse (illustrated by Walter Paget) (Nister, [1907]) £40
FAIRY TALES FROM THE ARABIAN NIGHTS Edited and arranged by E. Dixon (illustrated by John D. Batten;
reprint of 1893 edition) (Dent, 1907) £30
STORIES FROM THE ARABIAN NIGHTS Retold by Laurence Housman (illustrated by Edmund Dulac)
(Hodder & Stoughton, 1907) £350
STORIES FROM THE ARABIAN NIGHTS Retold by Laurence Housman (illustrated by Edmund Dulac)
(limited to 350 copies, signed by the artist) (Hodder & Stoughton, 1907) £1,750
THE ARABIAN NIGHTS Their best-known tales retold by Kate Douglas Wiggin and Nora Smith
(illustrated by Maxfield Parrish) (Werner Laurie, [1909])...£50
THE ARABIAN NIGHTS (illustrated by René Bull) (Constable, 1912)..£170
THE ARABIAN NIGHTS (illustrated by Charles Folkard; preface by Gordon Home) (A. & C. Black, 1913)...............................£50
MORE TALES FROM THE ARABIAN NIGHTS (illustrated by Willy Pogány) (Holt, US, 1915)...£50
TALES FROM THE ARABIAN NIGHTS (illustrated by A.E. Jackson) (Ward Lock, 1920) £40
THE ARABIAN NIGHTS' ENTERTAINMENTS (illustrated by Louis Rhead) (Harper, US, [1923]).......................................£45
THE ARABIAN NIGHTS: Tales from the Thousand and One Nights (illustrated by E.J. Detmold)
(Hodder & Stoughton, [1924]) £350
THE ARABIAN NIGHTS: Tales from the Thousand and One Nights (illustrated by E.J. Detmold;
limited to 100 copies, signed by the artist) (Hodder & Stoughton, [1924]) £1,000
STORIES FROM THE ARABIAN NIGHTS Edited by Frances J. Olcott (illustrated by Monro S. Orr) (Harrap, 1934) £40
TALES FROM THE ARABIAN NIGHTS (illustrated by Frank C. Papé) (Hutchinson, [1934]).......................................£30

ARDIZZONE, Edward

British illustrator. Born: Haiphong, China, in 1900, although brought up in England. Studied at Claysmore School and Westminster School of Art. Married in 1929. Served as an official war artist during the Second World War. As well as his many children's books, he illustrated a large number of classics, including the works of Dickens, Trollope and Thackeray. Contributed to *Radio Times*, *Punch*, the *Strand* and the *London Magazine*. Died: 1979.

Prices are for books in Very Good condition with dustjackets where applicable.

Books Written and Illustrated by Edward Ardizzone
LITTLE TIM AND THE BRAVE SEA CAPTAIN (OUP, [1936]) £500

LITTLE TIM AND THE BRAVE SEA CAPTAIN (revised edition) (OUP, 1955)..£30
LUCY BROWN AND MR GRIMES (OUP, [1937])...£300
LUCY BROWN AND MR GRIMES (revised edition) (The Bodley Head, 1970)..£40
TIM AND LUCY GO TO SEA (OUP, [1938])...£300
TIM AND LUCY GO TO SEA (revised edition) (OUP, 1958)..£25
NICHOLAS THE FAST-MOVING DIESEL (Eyre & Spottiswoode, [1947]) £300
PAUL, THE HERO OF THE FIRE (paperback) (Puffin, 1948) £40
PAUL, THE HERO OF THE FIRE (revised edition) (Constable, 1962)..£20
TIM TO THE RESCUE (OUP, 1949)...£250
TIM AND CHARLOTTE (OUP, 1951) £170
TIM IN DANGER (OUP, 1953)...£125
TIM ALL ALONE (OUP, 1956)...£75
JOHNNY THE CLOCKMAKER (OUP, 1960) £60
TIM'S FRIEND TOWSER (OUP, 1962)...£60
PETER THE WANDERER (OUP, 1963) £60
DIANA AND HER RHINOCEROS (The Bodley Head, 1964)..£50
SARAH AND SIMON AND NO RED PAINT (Constable, 1965)...£55
TIM AND GINGER (OUP, 1965) £55
THE LITTLE GIRL AND THE TINY DOLL by Aingelda and Edward Ardizzone (Constable, 1966) £45
TIM TO THE LIGHTHOUSE (OUP, 1968) £45
JOHNNY'S BAD DAY (The Bodley Head, 1970)...£30
TIM'S LAST VOYAGE (The Bodley Head, 1972)..£35
SHIP'S COOK GINGER: Another Tim Story (The Bodley Head, 1977) £30
THE ADVENTURES OF TIM (The Bodley Head, 1985)..£25

Books Illustrated by Edward Ardizzone

TOM, DICK AND HARRIET by Albert N. Lyons (Cresset Press, 1937) £250
GREAT EXPECTATIONS by Charles Dickens (Limited Editions Club, US, 1939)...................................£350
MIMFF by H.J. Kaeser (OUP, 1939) £50
PEACOCK PIE by Walter de la Mare (Faber, 1946) £75
THE PILGRIM'S PROGRESS by John Bunyan (Faber, 1947) £60
THREE BROTHERS AND A LADY by Margaret Black (Acorn Press, 1947) £45
A TRUE AND PATHETIC HISTORY OF DESBAROLLDA, THE WALTZING MOUSE by Noel Langley
   (Lindsay Drummond, 1947)...£55
HEY NONNY YES: Passions and Conceits from Shakespeare. Edited by Hallam Fordham (John Lehmann, 1947).............£35
CHARLES DICKENS' BIRTHDAY BOOK. Edited by Enid Dickens Hawksley (Faber, 1948) £50

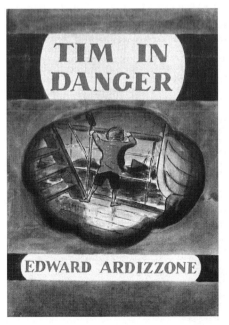

Amongst the most collectable of Edward Ardizzone's many works are those featuring the redoubtable boy hero, Tim.

Tim in Danger, published in 1953 and now worth £125, sees Tim having to find his runaway friend Ginger.

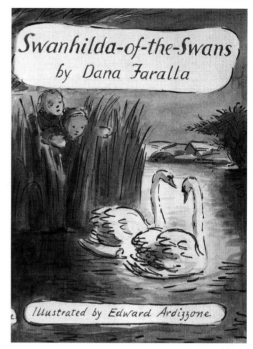

*Ardizzone provided the illustrations for Cecil Day Lewis's classic children's novel, **The Otterbury Incident** (1948).*

*Even a less familiar title like **Swanhilda-of-the-Swans** (1964) is worth £35 thanks to its Edward Ardizzone illustrations.*

THE OTTERBURY INCIDENT by Cecil Day Lewis (Putnam, 1948) £50

THE ROSE AND THE RING by W.M. Thackeray (Guilford Press/Wilfrid David, 1948) £30

MIMFF IN CHARGE by H.J. Kaeser (translated by David Ascoli) (OUP, 1949) £35

THE TALE OF ALI BABA. Translated by J.C. Mardrus and E. Powys Mathers
(Limited Editions Club, US, 1949) £250

SOMEBODY'S ROCKING MY DREAMBOAT by Noel Langley and Hazel Pynegar (Arthur Barker, 1949) £30

THE HUMOUR OF DICKENS (News Chronicle, 1952) £15

THE BLACKBIRD IN THE LILAC by James Reeves (OUP, 1952) £45

MIMFF TAKES OVER by H.J. Kaeser (OUP, 1954) £30

THE FANTASTIC TALE OF THE PLUCKY SAILOR AND THE POSTAGE STAMP by Stephen Corrin
(Faber, 1954) £25

THE LITTLE BOOKROOM by Eleanor Farjeon (OUP, 1955) £45

THE SUBURBAN CHILD by James Kenward (CUP, 1955) £35

MINNOW ON THE SAY by Philippa Pearce (OUP, 1955) £60

DAVID COPPERFIELD by Charles Dickens (abridged by S. Wood) (OUP, 1955) £30

BLEAK HOUSE by Charles Dickens (abridged by S. Wood) (OUP, 1955) £30

SUN SLOWER, SUN FASTER by Meriol Trevor (Collins, 1955) £30

PIGEONS AND PRINCESSES by James Reeves (Heinemann, 1956) £40

ST LUKE'S LIFE OF CHRIST (translated by J.B. Phillips) (Collins, 1956) £25

WANDERING MOON by James Reeves (Heinemann, 1957) £35

A STICKFUL OF NONPAREIL by George Scurfield (limited to 500 copies; issued without dustjacket) (CUP, 1956) £70

HUNTING WITH MR JORROCKS by Robert Surtees. Edited by Lionel Gough (OUP, 1956) £45

PREFABULOUS ANIMILES by James Reeves (Heinemann, 1957) £35

THE SCHOOL IN OUR VILLAGE by Joan M. Goldman (Batsford, 1957) £30

THE BOY DOWN KITCHINER STREET by Leslie Paul (Faber, 1957) £30

LOTTIE by John Symonds (The Bodley Head, 1957) £30

MIMFF-ROBINSON by H.J. Kaeser
(translated by Ruth Michaelis and Jena & Arthur Ratcliff) (OUP, 1958) £30

THE STORY OF JOSEPH by Walter de la Mare (Faber, 1958) £30

JIM AT THE CORNER by Eleanor Farjeon (OUP, 1958) £40

PINKY PYE by Eleanor Estes (Constable, 1959) £30

THE NINE LIVES OF ISLAND MACKENZIE by Ursula Moray Williams (Chatto & Windus, 1959) £25

TITUS IN TROUBLE by James Reeves (The Bodley Head, 1959) £40

EXPLOITS OF DON QUIXOTE (abridged by James Reeves) (Blackie, [1959]) £30

STORY OF MOSES by Walter de la Mare (Faber, 1959)..£30
ELFRIDA AND THE PIG by John Symonds (Harrap, 1959) £35
HOLIDAY TRENCH by Joan Ballantyne (Nelson, 1959) £20
THE GODSTONE AND THE BLACKYMOR by T.H. White (Cape, 1959) £40
THE STORY OF SAMUEL AND SAUL by Walter de la Mare (Faber, 1960)...................£30
KIDKNAPPERS AT COOMBE by Joan Ballantyne (Nelson, 1960) £25
THE RIB OF THE GREEN UMBRELLA by Naomi Mitchison (Collins, 1960) £30
ELEANOR FARJEON'S BOOK. Edited by Eleanor Graham (paperback) (Puffin, 1960)......£15
MERRY ENGLAND by Cyril Ray (Vista Books, 1960)..£35
ITALIAN PEEPSHOW by Eleanor Farjeon (OUP, 1960) £30
THE PENNY FIDDLE: Poems for Children by Robert Graves (Cassell, 1960) £80
BOYHOODS OF THE GREAT COMPOSERS (two volumes) (OUP, 1960 & 1963).........the set £50
HURDY GURDY by James Reeves (Heinemann, 1961)..£40
NO MYSTERY FOR THE MAITLANDS by Joan Ballantyne (Nelson, 1961)...................£35
DOWN IN THE CELLAR Nicholas Gray (Dobson, 1961)..£30
THE ADVENTURES OF HUCKLEBERRY FINN by Mark Twain (Heinemann, 1961).......£35
THE ADVENTURES OF TOM SAWYER by Mark Twain (Heinemann, 1961)..................£40
STORIES FROM THE BIBLE by Walter de la Mare (Faber, 1961)..................................£35
THE WITCH FAMILY by Eleanor Estes (Constable, 1962)..£35
NAUGHTY CHILDREN by Christianna Brand (Gollancz, 1962).....................................£45
SAILOR RUMBELOW AND BRITANNIA by James Reeves (Heinemann, 1962)............£40
PETER PAN by J.M. Barrie (Brockhampton Press, 1962)..£50
A RING OF BELLS by John Betjeman (John Murray, 1962)...£50
THE STORY OF LET'S MAKE AN OPERA by Eric Crosier (OUP, 1962) £25
THE SINGING CUPBOARD by Dana Farralla (Blackie, 1962).....................................£40
MRS MALONE by Eleanor Farjeon (OUP, 1962) £45
STIG OF THE DUMP by Clive King (paperback) (Puffin Original, 1963).....................£35
KALEIDOSCOPE by Eleanor Farjeon (OUP, 1963)..£45
SWANHILDA-OF-THE-SWANS by Dana Faralla (Blackie, [1964])...............................£35
ANN AT HIGHWOOD HALL by Robert Graves (Cassell, 1964).....................................£85
THREE TALL TALES by James Reeves (Abelard-Schumann, 1964) £35
THE ALLEY by Eleanor Estes (Harcourt Brace, US, 1964)..£30
NURSE MATILDA by Christianna Brand (Brockhampton Press, 1964).......................£50
ISLAND OF FISH IN THE TREES by Eva-Lis Wuorio (Dobson, 1964) £35
THE LAND OF RIGHT UP AND DOWN by Eva-Lis Wuorio (Dobson, 1965).................£35
OPEN THE DOOR Edited by Margery Fisher (Brockhampton Press, 1965) £30
THE STORY OF JACKIE THIMBLE by James Reeves (Chatto & Windus, 1965)..........£30
OLD PERISHER by Diana Ross (Faber, 1965)..£30
THE OLD NURSE'S STOCKING BASKET by Eleanor Farjeon (OUP, 1965)................£30
THE TRUANTS and Other Poems for Children by John Walsh (Heinemann, 1965)......£30
THE GROWING SUMMER by Noel Streatfeild (Collins, 1966)......................................£35
LONG AGO WHEN I WAS YOUNG by E. Nesbit (Whiting & Wheaton, 1966)................£35
DADDY LONGLEGS by Jean Webster (Brockhampton Press, 1966) £40
THE LAND OF GREEN GINGER by Noel Langley (paperback) (Puffin, 1966).............£15
THE DRAGON by Archibald Marshall (Hamish Hamilton, 1966)..................................£25
THE SECRET SHOEMAKER and Other Stories by James Reeves
    (Abelard-Schumann, 1966)...£40
TIMOTHY'S SONG by W.J. Lederer (Lutterworth Press, 1966)....................................£25
THE YEAR ROUND by Leonard Clark (Hart-Davis, 1966)...£25
RHYMING WILL by James Reeves (Heinemann, 1967)...£25
MIRANDA THE GREAT by Eleanor Estes (Harcourt Brace, US, 1967)......................£20
A LIKELY PLACE by Paula Fox (Macmillan, [1967])..£20
KALI AND THE GOLDEN MIRROR by Eva-Lis Wuorio (World Publishing, 1967).......£30
THE STUFFED DOG by John Symonds (Arthur Barker, 1967).....................................£25
NURSE MATILDA GOES TO TOWN by Christianna Brand (Brockhampton Press, 1967)......£25
ROBINSON CRUSOE by Daniel Defoe (Nonesuch Press, 1968)................................£45
UPSIDE-DOWN WILLIE by Dorothy Clewes (Hamish Hamilton, 1968)........................£20
SPECIAL BRANCH WILLIE by Dorothy Clewes (Hamish Hamilton, 1969)..................£20
THE ANGEL AND THE DONKEY by James Reeves (Hamish Hamilton, 1969).............£20
DICK WHITTINGTON Retold by Kathleen Lines (The Bodley Head, 1970).................£15
FIRE BRIGADE WILLIE by Dorothy Clewes (Hamish Hamilton, 1970)........................£25
HOW THE MOON BEGAN by James Reeves (Abelard-Schumann, 1971)...................£20
THE OLD BALLAD OF THE BABES IN THE WOOD (The Bodley Head, 1972) £15
THE SECOND BEST CHILDREN IN THE WORLD by Mary Lavin (Longmans, 1972)......£15
THE TUNNEL OF HUGSY GOODE by Eleanor Estes (Harcourt Brace, US, 1972).......£15
THE LITTLE FIRE ENGINE by Graham Greene (The Bodley Head, 1973)..................£100
THE LITTLE TRAIN by Graham Greene (The Bodley Head, 1973)..............................£100
COMPLETE POEMS FOR CHILDREN by James Reeves (Heinemann, 1973).............£25
THE NIGHT RIDE by Aingelda Ardizzone (The Bodley Head, 1973)...........................£15

The first British editions of Mark Twain's **A Yankee in King Arthur's Court** *(1889) and the first book in T.H. White's* **The Once and Future King** *tetralogy.*

THE LITTLE HORSE BUS by Graham Greene (The Bodley Head, 1974)..**£100**
THE LITTLE STEAM ROLLER by Graham Greene (The Bodley Head, 1974)...**£100**
THE LION THAT FLEW by James Reeves (issued without dustjacket) (Chatto & Windus, 1974)..........................**£25**
NURSE MATILDA GOES TO HOSPITAL by Christianna Brand (Brockhampton Press, 1974) **£25**
MORE PREFABULOUS ANIMILES by James Reeves (Heinemann, 1975) **£25**
ARDIZZONE'S KILVERT (Cape, 1976)..**£25**
ARCADIAN BALLADS by James Reeves (Heinemann, 1977) **£20**
ARDIZZONE'S HANS ANDERSEN (Deutsch, 1978)..**£30**
A CHILD'S CHRISTMAS IN WALES by Dylan Thomas (Dent, 1978)..**£35**
THE JAMES REEVES STORY BOOK (Heinemann, 1978) **£25**
ARDIZZONE'S ENGLISH FAIRY TALES (Deutsch, 1980)..**£25**

ARTHURIAN LEGENDS

The legend of King Arthur has been retold in countless stories and poems, many of them presented in beautiful illustrated editions. Caxton's edition of Sir Thomas Malory's *Le Morte D'Arthur* (1469-70) was particularly influential, attracting the attention of Spenser and Milton and later, Tennyson.

Prices are for books in: (i) Good condition in a contemporary leather binding (pre-1850); (ii) Good condition in the original binding (1851-1900); (iii) Very Good condition in the original binding without dustjackets (1901-20) or with dustjackets (1921 to present).

Original Romances, Translations and Renditions

LE MORTE D'ARTHUR (reprint of 1498 De Worde edition on vellum; two volumes; boxed)
  (Shakespeare Head Press, 1933)..the set **£10,000**
LE MORTE D'ARTHUR (William Stansby, 1634)...**£8,000**
LE MORTE D'ARTHUR (edited by Robert Southey) (Longman, 1817)..**£800**
LE MORTE D'ARTHUR (illustrated by Aubrey Beardsley; two volumes; publisher's binding)
  (Dent, 1893 & 1894)...the set **£800**
LE MORTE D'ARTHUR (illustrated by W. Russell Flint; four volumes)
  (Riccardi Press, 1910-1911)..the set **£700**
LE MORTE D'ARTHUR (illustrated by Charles Gere) (Ashendene Press, 1913) **£2,500**
HISTORIA REGUM BRITANNIAE by Geoffrey of Monmouth (Paris, 1508) ....n/a
HISTORIA REGUM BRITANNIAE (as 'The British History'; translated by Aaron Thompson)
  (Bohn, 1842)..**£75**
THE MABINOGION. Edited by Lady Charlotte Guest (three volumes) (London, 1849).......................the set **£125**
THE MABINOGION. Edited by Gwyn and Thomas Jones
  (Golden Cockerel Press, 1948)...**£350**

THE LEGENDS OF KING ARTHUR AND HIS KNIGHTS by James Knowles (Griffith and Farran, 1862) £80
THE LEGENDS OF KING ARTHUR AND HIS KNIGHTS (illustrated by Lancelot Speed)
(Frederick Warne, 1912)..£20
IDYLLS OF THE KING by Alfred Lord Tennyson (Moxon, 1859)..£600
IDYLLS OF THE KING (illustrated by Gustave Doré) (Moxon, 1868)...£300
THE BOY'S KING ARTHUR by Sidney Lanier (Scribner's, US, 1880)...£60
THE BOY'S KING ARTHUR (illustrated by N.C. Wyeth) (Scribner's, US, 1917)...£50
THE BOOK OF ROMANCE by Andrew Lang (Longman, 1902)..£30
TALES OF KING ARTHUR AND THE ROUND TABLE by Andrew Lang (Longman, 1905).....................................£20
THE STORY OF KING ARTHUR AND HIS KNIGHTS by Howard Pyle (Scribner's, US, 1903) £200
THE STORY OF THE CHAMPIONS OF THE ROUND TABLE by Howard Pyle (Scribner's, US, 1905)...................£200
THE STORY OF SIR LAUNCELOT AND HIS COMPANIONS by Howard Pyle (Scribner's, US, 1907).....................£200
THE STORY OF THE GRAIL AND THE PASSING OF ARTHUR by Howard Pyle (Scribner's, US, 1911).................£200
STORIES OF KING ARTHUR by A.L. Haydon (illustrated by Arthur Rackham) (Cassell, 1910)............................£150
KING ARTHUR'S KNIGHTS by Henry Gilbert (illustrated by Walter Crane) (T.C. & E.C. Jack, 1911) £125
ERIC AND ENID by Chretien de Troyes. Edited by W.W. Comfort (Dent: 'Everyman's Library', 1914)....................£8
THE ROMANCE OF KING ARTHUR AND HIS KNIGHTS OF THE ROUND TABLE
(illustrated by Arthur Rackham; trade edition) (Macmillan, 1917) £300
THE ROMANCE OF KING ARTHUR AND HIS KNIGHTS OF THE ROUND TABLE by Alfred W. Pollard (illustrated by
Arthur Rackham; De Luxe Edition : limited to 500 copies on vellum, signed by the author) (Macmillan, 1917)......£1,000
SIR GAWAIN AND THE GREEN KNIGHT Edited by J.R.R. Tolkien and E.V. Gordon (with errata slip) (OUP, 1925)...£700
KING ARTHUR AND THE KNIGHTS OF THE ROUND TABLE by Roger Lancelyn Green
(paperback) (Penguin, 1953)..£10
KING ARTHUR AND THE ROUND TABLE by Alice M. Hadfield (Dent, 1953)...£15
THE ACTS OF KING ARTHUR AND HIS NOBLE KNIGHTS by John Steinbeck (Farrar, Straus & Giroux, US, 1976)....£20

Modern Arthurian Fiction

A YANKEE AT THE COURT OF KING ARTHUR by Mark Twain
(illustrated by Dan Beard) (Chatto & Windus, 1889)..£175
CIAN OF THE CHARIOTS by William H. Babcock (Lothrop, US, 1898) £35
SIR MARROK by Allan French (Century, US, 1902)...£35
UTHER AND IGRAINE by Warwick Deeping (Outlook, 1903) £30
THE LIFE OF SIR AGLOVALE DE GALIS by Clemence Housman (Methuen, 1905)...£40
THE CLUTCH OF CIRCUMSTANCE by Dorothy Senior (Black, 1908)..£30
THE BOY APPRENTICED TO AN ENCHANTER by Padriac Colum (Macmillan, 1920) £35
THE FAMOUS TRAGEDY OF THE QUEEN OF CORNWALL AT TINTAGEL IN LYONESSE by Thomas Hardy (play)
(Macmillan, 1923)..£60
PERRONIK THE FOOL by George Moore (Boni & Liveright, US, 1924)...£35
GALAHAD: Enough of His Life to Explain His Reputation by John Erskine (Bobbs-Merrill, US, 1926) £20
LAUNCELOT: A ROMANCE AT THE COURT OF KING ARTHUR by Ernest Hamilton (Methuen, 1926)..................£25
LAUNCELOT AND THE LADIES by Will Bradley (Harper, UK/US,1927)..£25
THE GRAVE OF ARTHUR by G.K. Chesterton (poem; wrappers) (Faber: 'Ariel Poems' series, 1930) £15
THE GRAVE OF ARTHUR by G.K. Chesterton (De Luxe Edition; poem; limited to 350 copies, signed by the author;
illustrated by Celia Fiennes) (Faber: 'Ariel Poems' series, 1930)..£275
PENDRAGON by W. Barnard Faraday (Methuen, 1930)...£40
TRISTON AND ISOLDE : RESTORING PALAMEDE by John Erskine (Bobbs-Merrill, US, 1932)..........................£20
THE LITTLE WENCH by Philip Lindsay (Nicholson & Watson, 1935)..£25
THE SWORD IN THE STONE by T.H. White (Collins, 1938)..£600
THE WITCH IN THE WOOD by T.H. White (Collins, 1940)..£600
THE ILL-MADE KNIGHT by T.H. White (Collins, 1941)...£400
THE BEAR OF BRITAIN by Edward Frankland (Macdonald, 1944)..£40
PORIUS by John Cowper Powys (Macdonald, 1951)..£40
THE ENCHANTED CUP by Dorothy James Roberts (Appleton-Century-Crofts, US, 1953)..................................£40
LAUNCELOT MY BROTHER by Dorothy James Roberts (Appleton-Century-Crofts, US, 1954)...........................£30
THE ENCHANTED CUP by Dorothy James Roberts (Hutchinson, 1954) £30
THE QUEEN'S KNIGHT by Marvin Borowsky (Random House, US, 1955)..£30
TO THE CHAPEL PERILOUS by Naomi Mitchison (Allen & Unwin, 1955)..£40
GARETH OF ORKNEY by E.M.R. Ditmas (Faber, 1956)..£35
BIRTH OF A LEGEND by Mary Mitchell (Methuen, 1956)..£40
THE GREAT CAPTAINS by Henry Treece (The Bodley Head, 1956) £35
THE ONCE AND FUTURE by T.H. White (omnibus edition; contains 'The Sword in the Stone',
' The Witch in the Wood', 'The Ill-Made Knight' and 'The Candle in the Wind') (Collins, 1958)...........................£150
THE PAGAN KING by Edison Marshall (Doubleday, US, 1959)...£25
THE LANTERN BEARERS by Rosemary Sutcliff (illustrated by Charles Keeping) (OUP, 1959) £35
SWORD AT SUNSET by Rosemary Sutcliff (Hodder & Stoughton, 1963)...£30
KINSMEN OF THE GRAIL by Dorothy James Roberts (Little Brown, US, 1963)...£30
KING OF THE WORLD'S EDGE by H. Warner Munn (paperback) (Ace Books, US, 1967)...................................£20
THE DUKE OF WAR by Walter O'Meara (Harcourt, Brace & World, US, 1966) £25
THE GREEN MAN by Henry Treece (The Bodley Head, 1966)..£30
THE SHIP FROM ATLANTIS by H. Warner Munn (paperback) (Ace Books, US, 1967).......................................£20

THE EMPEROR ARTHUR by Godfrey E Turton (Doubleday, US, 1968) £15
THE CRYSTAL CAVE by Mary Stewart (Hodder & Stoughton, 1970) £15
TRISTAN AND ISEULT by Rosemary Sutcliff (The Bodley Head, 1971) £15
DRUSTAN THE WANDERER by Anna Taylor (Longman, 1971) £12
KING OF THE LORDLESS COUNTRY by Roy Turner (Dobson, 1971) £15
THE HOLLOW HILLS by Mary Stewart (Hodder & Stoughton, 1973) £15
MERLIN'S RING by H. Warner Munn (paperback) (Ballantine Books, US, 1974) £10
THE GREEN KNIGHT by Vera Chapman (Rex Collings, 1975) £20
THE BRIGHT-HELMED ONE by Jayne Viney (Robert Hale, 1975) £20
THE CRIMSON CHALICE by Victor Canning (Heinemann, 1976) £20
KING ARTHUR'S DAUGHTER by Vera Chapman (Rex Collings, 1976) £20
THE KING'S DAMOSEL by Vera Chapman (Rex Collings, 1976) £20
THE CIRCLE OF THE GODS by Victor Canning (Heinemann, 1977) £20
PENDRAGON by Douglas Carmichael (Blackwater Press, US, 1977) £100
ARTORIUS REX by John Gloag (Cassell, 1977) £20
PARSIVAL, or A KNIGHT'S TALE by Richard Monaco (Macmillan, 1977) £20
THE BOOK OF MERLYN by T.H. White (University of Texas Press, US, 1977) £30
ARTHUR REX by Thomas Berger (Delacorte Press, US, 1978) £25
THE IMMORTAL WOUND by Victor Canning (Heinemann, 1978) £20
THE SWORD AND THE FLAME by Catherine Christian (Macmillan, 1978) £15
THE SWORD AND THE FLAME (as 'The Pendragon') (Knopf, US, 1979) £12
PERCIVAL AND THE PRESENCE OF GOD by Jim Hunter (Faber, 1978) £35
MERLIN by Robert Nye (Hamish Hamilton, 1978) £35
LANCELOT by Peter Vansittart (Peter Owen, 1978) £25
THE MAGIC CUP by Andrew M. Greeley (McGraw-Hill, US, 1979) £25
THE GRAIL WAR by Richard Monaco (paperback) (Pocket Books, US, 1979) £10
THE LAST ENCHANTMENT by Mary Stewart (Hodder & Stoughton, 1979) £15
THE LIGHT BEYOND THE FOREST by Rosemary Sutcliff (The Bodley Head, 1979) £15
HAWK OF MAY by Gillian Bradshaw (Simon & Schuster, US, 1980) £20

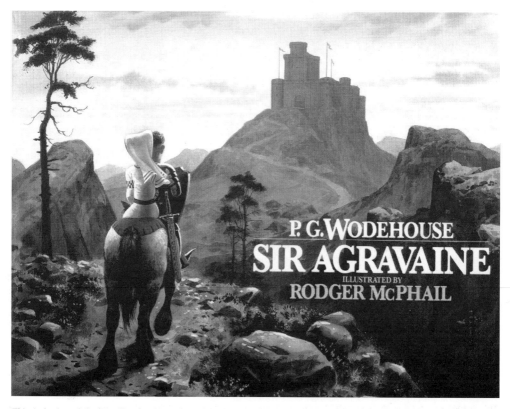

This Arthurian tale by 'Blandings' author, P.G. Wodehouse, was published in 1984 and now sells for £20 in Very Good condition.

THE CRIMSON CHALICE by Victor Canning (omnibus edition: 'The Crimson Chalice',
'The Circle of the Gods' and 'The Immortal Wound') (Heinemann, 1980) **£15**
FIRELORD by Parke Godwin (Doubleday, US, 1980) **£25**
THE FINAL QUEST by Richard Monaco (Putnam, US, 1980) **£15**
KINGDOM OF SUMMER by Gillian Bradshaw (Simon & Schuster, US, 1981) **£20**
GUINEVERE by Sharan Newman (St Martin's Press, US, 1981) **£20**
THE ROAD TO CAMLANN by Rosemary Sutcliff (The Bodley Head, 1981) **£15**
THE SWORD AND THE CIRCLE by Rosemary Sutcliff (The Bodley Head, 1981) **£15**
THE MISTS OF AVALON by Marion Zimmer Bradley (Knopf, US, 1982) **£150**
IN WINTER'S SHADOW by Gillian Bradshaw (Simon & Schuster, US, 1982) **£20**
THE IDYLLS OF THE QUEEN by Phyllis Ann Karr (paperback) (Ace Books, US, 1982) **£10**
THE CHESSBOARD QUEEN by Sharan Newman (St Martin's Press, US, 1983) **£20**
THE WICKED DAY by Mary Stewart (Hodder & Stoughton, 1983) **£15**
BELOVED EXILE by Parke Godwin (paperback) (Bantam Books, US, 1984) **£10**
SIR AGRAVAINE by P.G. Wodehouse (Blandford Press, 1984) **£20**
THE LAST RAINBOW by Parke Godwin (paperback) (Bantam Books, US, 1985) **£10**
BLOOD AND DREAMS by Richard Monaco (paperback) (Ace Books, US, 1985) **£10**
GUINEVERE EVERMORE by Sharan Newman (St Martin's Press, US, 1985) **£20**
MERLIN'S BOOKE by Jane Yolen (Ace Books, US, 1986) **£25**
TALIESIN by Stephen Lawhead (Crossway, US, 1987) **£20**
CHILD OF THE NORTHERN SPRING by Persia Woolley (Poseidon, US, 1987) **£20**
DOWN THE LONG WIND by Gillian Bradshaw (omnibus edition: contains 'Hawk of May',
'Kingdom of Summer' and 'In Winter's Shadow'; paperback) (Methuen, 1988) **£10**
MERLIN DREAMS by Peter Dickinson (Gollancz, 1988) **£20**
MERLIN by Stephen Lawhead (Crossway, US, 1988) **£20**
THE WHITE RAVEN by Diana L Paxson (Morrow, US, 1988) **£25**
THE COMING OF THE KING by Nikolai Tolstoy (Bantam, 1988) **£20**
PARSIFAL by Peter Vansittart (Peter Owen, 1988) **£20**
THE ROAD TO AVALON by Joan Wolf (New American Library, US, 1988) **£20**
ARTHUR by Stephen Lawhead (Crossway, US, 1989) **£20**
WHITE NUN'S TELLING by Fay Sampson (paperback) (Headline, 1989) **£5**
WISE WOMAN'S TELLING by Fay Sampson (paperback) (Headline, 1989) **£5**
BLACK SMITH'S TELLING by Fay Sampson (paperback) (Headline, 1990) **£5**
QUEEN OF THE SUMMER STARS by Persia Woolley (Poseidon, 1990) **£20**
GUINEVERE: THE LEGEND IN AUTUMN by Persia Woolley (Poseidon, 1991) **£20**
TALIESIN'S TELLING by Fay Sampson (paperback) (Headline, 1991) **£5**
DAUGHTER OF TINTAGEL by Fay Sampson (omnibus edition: contains 'Morgan' series; paperback)
(Headline, 1992) **£8**
HERSELF by Fay Sampson (paperback) (Headline, 1992) **£5**
THE SKY STONE by Jack Whyte (trade paperback) (Viking, Canada, 1992) **£20**
THE FOREST HOUSE by Marion Zimmer Bradley (Michael Joseph, 1993) **£20**
DRUID SACRIFICE by Nigel Tranter (Hodder & Stoughton, 1993) **£20**
THE SINGING SWORD by Jack Whyte (trade paperback) (Viking, Canada, 1993) **£20**
THE KINGMAKING by Helen Hollick (Heinemann, 1994) **£12**
PENDRAGON by Stephen Lawhead (Morrow, US, 1994) **£15**
THE EAGLES' BROOD by Jack Whyte (trade paperback) (Viking, Canada, 1994) **£15**
THE WINTER KING by Bernard Cornwell (Michael Joseph, 1995) **£12**
PENDRAGON'S BANNER by Helen Hollick (Heinemann, 1995) **£12**
THE KING'S EVIL by Haydn Middleton (Little Brown, US, 1995) **£12**
THE PRINCE AND THE PILGRIM by Mary Stewart (Hodder & Stoughton, 1995) **£12**
THE SAXON SHORE by Jack Whyte (trade paperback)
(Viking, Canada, 1995) **£15**
ENEMY OF GOD by Bernard Cornwell (Michael Joseph, 1996) **£12**
BLACK HORSES FOR THE KING by Anne McCaffrey (Harcourt Brace, US, 1996) **£20**
THE KNIGHT'S VENGEANCE by Haydn Middleton (Little Brown, US, 1996) **£10**
THE QUEEN'S CAPTIVE by Haydn Middleton (Little Brown, US, 1996) **£12**
LADY OF AVALON by Marion Zimmer Bradley (Viking, 1997) **£12**
THE ENCHANTRESSES by Vera Chapman (Gollancz, 1997) **£12**
EXCALIBUR by Bernard Cornwell (Michael Joseph, 1997) **£12**
SHADOW OF THE KING by Helen Hollick (Heinemann, 1997) **£12**
GRAIL by Stephen Lawhead (Avon, US, 1997) **£12**
THE SORCEROR by Jack Whyte (trade paperback; two volumes) (Viking, Canada, 1997) .... the set **£15**

ASHFORD, Daisy

**British author. Born: 1890. Best known for her story, *The Young Visiters* (1919), written when she was nine.
Died: 1972.**

Price is for books in Very Good condition with dustjackets.

THE YOUNG VISITERS, or Mr Salteena's Plan Preface by J.M. Barrie (Chatto & Windus, 1919) **£125**
THE YOUNG VISITERS (illustrated by Heather Corlass) (Zodiac Press, 1949) **£15**

A selection of famous rarities by avidly-collected illustrator Mabel Lucie Attwell. All her first editions, when they survive in good condition, are valuable items. She produced more than forty annuals between 1922 and 1976, worth between £50 and £200 today.

THE YOUNG VISITERS (illustrated by Posy Simmonds) (Chatto & Windus, 1984)...£15
DAISY ASHFORD: HER BOOK (contains 'A Short Story of Love and Marriage', 'The True History of Leslie Woodcock',
'Where Love Lies Deepest' and 'The Hangman's Daughter; with Angie Ashford's 'The Jealous Governes')
(Chatto & Windus, 1920) £60
LOVE AND MARRIAGE (illustrated by Ralph Steadman) (Rupert Hart-Davis, 1965)..£20
WHERE LOVE LIES DEEPEST (illustrated by Ralph Steadman) (Rupert Hart-Davis, 1966) £20
THE HANGMAN'S DAUGHTER and Other Stories (OUP, 1983) £10

ASIMOV, Isaac

American science fiction author. Born: 1920. Best known for *I, Robot* and the 'Foundation' series and countless works of non-fiction, the famously prolific writer also penned SF books and stories children. Please
note that in the US, the six 'Starr' novels were written as 'Paul French'. Died: 1992.

Prices are for books in Very Good condition with dustjackets where applicable.

DAVID STARR: SPACE RANGER (Doubleday, US, 1953) ....£100+
DAVID STARR: SPACE RANGER (World's Work, 1953) £90
LUCKY STARR AND THE PIRATES OF THE ASTEROIDS (Doubleday, US, 1954) £80
LUCKY STARR AND THE PIRATES OF THE ASTEROIDS (World's Work, 1954) £80
LUCKY STARR AND THE OCEANS OF VENUS (Doubleday, US, 1954) £70
LUCKY STARR AND THE OCEANS OF VENUS (as 'OCEANS OF VENUS'; paperback)
(New English Library, 1974) £5
LUCKY STARR AND THE BIG SUN OF MERCURY (Doubleday, US, 1956) £70
LUCKY STARR AND THE BIG SUN OF MERCURY (as 'BIG SUN OF MERCURY'; paperback) (N.E.L., 1974)......£5
LUCKY STARR AND THE MOONS OF JUPITER (Doubleday, US, 1957) £60
LUCKY STARR AND THE MOONS OF JUPITER (as 'MOONS OF JUPITER'; paperback) (N.E.L., 1974) £5
LUCKY STARR AND THE KINGS OF SATURN (Doubleday, US, 1958) £60
LUCKY STARR AND THE KINGS OF SATURN (as 'RINGS OF SATURN'; paperback) (N.E.L., 1974) £5
NORBY THE MIXED-UP ROBOT (Walker, US, 1983) (with Janet Asimov)..£50
NORBY THE MIXED-UP ROBOT (Methuen, 1984)..£30
NORBY'S OTHER SECRET (Walker, US, 1984) (with Janet Asimov)..£50
NORBY'S OTHER SECRET (Methuen, 1985) £30
NORBY AND THE LOST PRINCESS (Walker, US, 1985) (with Janet Asimov) £40
NORBY AND THE LOST PRINCESS (Methuen, 1986)..£30

ATKINSON, Mary Evelyn

British author. Born: Mary Evelyn Atkinson in 1899. Wrote several Arthur Ransome-style children's stories
featuring the Lockett family. Died: 1974.

Prices are for books in Very Good condition with dustjackets.

AUGUST ADVENTURE (illustrated by Harold Jones) (Cape, 1936)...£50
MYSTERY MANOR (illustrated by Harold Jones) (John Lane: The Bodley Head, 1937)....................................£40
THE COMPASS POINTS NORTH (illustrated by Harold Jones) (John Lane: The Bodley Head, 1938) £40
SMUGGLERS' GAP (illustrated by Harold Jones) (John Lane: The Bodley Head, 1939)...................................£30
GOING GANGSTER (illustrated by Harold Jones) (John Lane: The Bodley Head, 1940) £30
CRUSOE ISLAND (illustrated by Harold Jones) (John Lane: The Bodley Head, 1941)....................................£30
CHALLENGE TO ADVENTURE (illustrated by Stuart Tresilian) (John Lane: The Bodley Head, 1942) £25
THE MONSTER OF WIDGEON WEIR (illustrated by Stuart Tresilian) (John Lane: The Bodley Head, 1943) £25
THE NEST OF THE SCARECROW (illustrated by Stuart Tresilian) (John Lane: The Bodley Head, 1944)................£25
PROBLEM PARTY (illustrated by Stuart Tresilian) (John Lane: The Bodley Head, 1945) £25
CHIMNEY COTTAGE (illustrated by Dorothy Craigie) (The Bodley Head, 1947)..£20
THE HOUSE ON THE MOOR (illustrated by Charlotte Hough) (The Bodley Head, 1948)...................................£20
THE 13TH ADVENTURE (illustrated by Charlotte Hough) (The Bodley Head, 1949) £20
STEEPLE FOLLY (illustrated by Charlotte Hough) (The Bodley Head, 1950)..£20
CASTAWAY CAMP (illustrated by Charlotte Hough) (The Bodley Head, 1951) £20
HUNTER'S MOON (illustrated by Charlotte Hough) (The Bodley Head, 1952) £20
THE BARNSTORMERS (illustrated by Charlotte Hough) (The Bodley Head, 1953)...£20
RIDERS AND RAIDS (illustrated by Sheila Rose) (The Bodley Head, 1955)...£15
UNEXPECTED ADVENTURE (illustrated by Sheila Rose) (The Bodley Head, 1955)..£15
HORSESHOES AND HANDLE BARS (illustrated by Sheila Rose) (The Bodley Head, 1958) £15
WHERE THERE'S A WILL (illustrated by Wendy Marchant) (Nelson, 1961) £15

ATTWELL, Mabel Lucie

British illustrator. Born: East London, 4th June 1879. Married the illustrator, Harold Cecil Earnshaw, in 1908.
As well as illustrating such children's classics as *Peter Pan* and *Alice in Wonderland*, Attwell produced
her own series of postcards, annuals and 'midget books'. She also drew a comic-strip for the magazine, *The
Passing Show*, and contributed to *Pearsons*, *The Strand* and other magazines. Died: 1964.

Prices are for books in Very Good condition.

'Bunty and the Boo Boos' Books
BUNTY AND THE BOO BOOS (Valentine, [1921-22])...£150

THE BOO BOOS AND BUNTY'S BABY (Valentine, [1921-22])..£150
THE BOO BOOS AT SCHOOL (Valentine, [1921-22])..£140
THE BOO BOOS AT THE SEASIDE (Valentine, [1921-22])..£140
THE BOO BOOS AT HONEYSWEET FARM (Valentine, [1921-22])..£140
THE BOO BOOS AND SANTA CLAUS (Valentine, [1921-22]) £140

Annuals

THE LUCIE ATTWELL ANNUAL NO. 1 (Partridge, 1922)...£200
THE LUCIE ATTWELL ANNUAL NO. 2 (Partridge, 1923)...£175
THE LUCIE ATTWELL ANNUAL NO. 3 (Partridge, 1924)...£150
LUCIE ATTWELL'S CHILDREN'S BOOK (Partridge, 1925-32) ....each £150
LUCIE ATTWELL'S ANNUAL (Dean, 1934-35, 1937-1941)...each £125
LUCIE ATTWELL'S ANNUAL (Dean, 1942) ....each £50
LUCIE ATTWELL'S ANNUAL (Dean, 1945-1968) ....each £50
LUCIE ATTWELL'S ANNUAL (Dean, 1969-1974)...each £50

Other Books Written and Illustrated by Mabel Lucie Attwell

PEGGY: The Lucie Attwell Cut-Out Dressing Doll (Valentine, [1921])......................................£175
STITCH STITCH (Valentine, [1922])..£125
COMFORTING THOUGHTS (Valentine, [1922]) £50
BABY'S BOOK (Raphael Tuck, [1922])..£75
ALL ABOUT BAD BABIES (John Swain, [c.1925])...£50
ALL ABOUT THE SEASIDE (John Swain, [c.1925])..£45
ALL ABOUT FAIRIES (John Swain, [c.1925])..£55
ALL ABOUT THE COUNTRY (John Swain, [c.1925])...£50
ALL ABOUT SCHOOL (John Swain, [c.1925]) £50
ALL ABOUT FIDO (John Swain, [c.1925])...£75
LUCIE ATTWELL'S RAINY-DAY TALES (with other authors) (Partridge, [1931])............................£125
LUCIE ATTWELL'S ROCK-AWAY TALES (with other authors) (London, 1931)...............................£80
LUCIE ATTWELL'S FAIRY BOOK (Partridge, 1932)..£150
LUCIE ATTWELL'S HAPPY-DAY TALES (Partridge, [1932])..£80
LUCIE ATTWELL'S QUIET TIME TALES (Partridge, [1932])...£80
LUCIE ATTWELL'S PAINTING BOOK (Dean, [1934])...£55
LUCIE ATTWELL'S GREAT BIG MIDGET BOOK (Dean, [1934])...£80
LUCIE ATTWELL'S GREAT BIG MIDGET BOOK (different from above) (Dean, [1935])......................£80
LUCIE ATTWELL'S PLAYTIME PICTURES (Carlton Publishing Co, 1935).....................................£65
LUCIE ATTWELL'S STORY BOOK (Dean, [1943]) £55
LUCIE ATTWELL'S STORY BOOK (different from above) (Dean, [1945]).....................................£55
LUCIE ATTWELL'S JOLLY BOOK (Dean, [1953]) £45
LUCIE ATTWELL'S NURSERY RHYMES POP-UP BOOK (Dean, 1958)...£40
LUCIE ATTWELL'S STORYTIME TALES (Dean, [1959])...£40
LUCIE ATTWELL'S BOOK OF VERSE (Dean, 1960) £35
LUCIE ATTWELL'S BOOK OF RHYMES (Dean, 1962)..£35
STORIES FOR EVERYDAY (Dean, 1964) £20
A LITTLE BIRD TOLD ME (Dean, 1964) £20
A LITTLE BIRD TOLD ME ANOTHER STORY (Dean, 1966) £20
TINIES' BOOK OF PRAYERS (Dean, 1967)..£25
LUCIE ATTWELL'S TINY RHYMES POP-UP BOOK (Dean, 1967)..£30
LUCIE ATTWELL'S TELL ME A STORY POP-UP BOOK (Dean, 1968)..£30
LUCIE ATTWELL'S BOOK OF RHYMES (Dean, 1969)..£15

Books Illustrated by Mabel Lucie Attwell

THAT LITTLE LIMB by May Baldwin (Chambers, 1905) £55
THE AMATEUR COOK by K. Burrill (Chambers, 1905)...£90
TROUBLESOME URSULA by Mabel Quiller-Couch (Chambers, 1905) £70
DORA: A High School Girl by May Baldwin (Chambers, 1906)..£70
TURQUIOSE AND RUBY by L.T. Meade (Chambers, 1906)...£70
A BOY AND A SECRET by Raymond Jacberns (Chambers, 1908)..£50
THE LITTLE TIN SOLDIER by Graham Mar (Chambers, 1909)..£50
THE FEBRUARY BOYS by Mrs Molesworth (Chambers, 1909)..£70
OLD RHYMES (Raphael Tuck, 1909)...£40
THE OLD PINCUSHION by Mrs Molesworth (Chambers, 1910) £80
MOTHER GOOSE (Raphael Tuck, 1910)..£170
ALICE IN WONDERLAND by Lewis Carroll (twelve colour plates by Mabel Lucie Attwell) (Raphael Tuck, [1910])...................£200
MY DOLLY'S HOUSE ABC ('untearable' pages) (Raphael Tuck, [c.1910])..................................£150
GRIMM'S FAIRY TALES (four full-page illustrations by Mabel Lucie Attwell) (Cassell, [1910])......£120
TABITHA SMALLWAYS by Raymond Jacberns (Chambers, 1911)..£60
GRIMM'S FAIRY STORIES (twelve colour plates by Mabel Lucie Attwell) (Raphael Tuck, 1912) £150
TROUBLESOME TOPSY AND HER FRIENDS by May Baldwin (Chambers, 1913) £50
HANS ANDERSEN'S FAIRY TALES (twelve colour plates by Mabel Lucie Attwell) (Raphael Tuck, [1914])...................£150

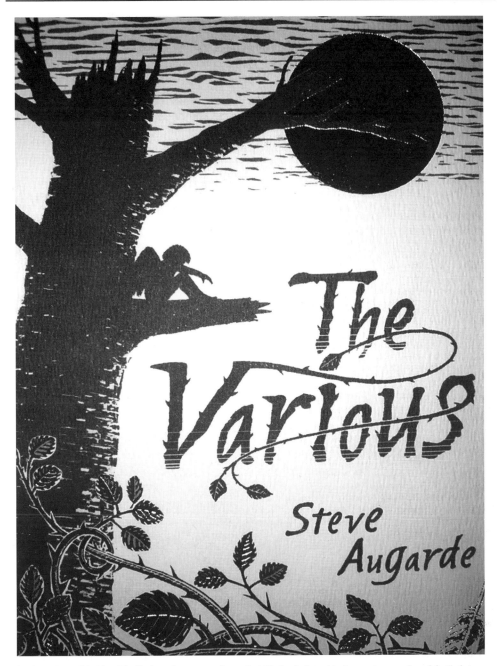

Steve Augarde's debut, **The Various,** *became a modern collectable thanks in part to its sumptuous embossed dustjacket.*

PETER PAN AND WENDY by J.M. Barrie (Hodder & Stoughton, [1921])...£300
THE LOST PRINCESS: A Fairy Tale by Marie, Queen of Roumania (Partridge, 1924)..£100
CHILDREN'S STORIES (Whitman Publishing Co., [c.1930])..£200

AUGARDE, Steve

British author/illustrator. Born in Birmingham, this award-winning children's writer had already written over 70 picture books for younger children, before his first novel attracted the attention of book collectors. He also provided the artwork and music for two animated BBC television series.

Prices are for books in Fine condition with dustjackets where applicable.

THE VARIOUS (David Fickling, 2003) £45
THE VARIOUS (signed) (David Fickling, 2003)..£75
THE VARIOUS (signed, dated, inscribed, with unique b&w illustration) (David Fickling, 2003) £150
THE VARIOUS (signed, dated, inscribed, with unique colour illustration) (David Fickling, 2003)....................£300
THE VARIOUS (paperback) (Corgi Children's, 2004)...£5
CELANDINE (David Fickling, 2005) £10
CELANDINE (paperback) (Corgi Children's, 2006)..£5

'AUNT JUDY'S' CHRISTMAS VOLUMES

Spin-offs from *Aunt Judy's Magazine*, one of the most popular children's periodicals of the Nineteenth Century. Launched in 1866, it was originally edited by Mrs Margaret Gatty and featured serials, poems, articles and readers' letters. Among the illustrators who contributed to the title were George Cruikshank and Randolph Caldecott.

Prices are for volumes in Very Good condition.

AUNT JUDY'S CHRISTMAS VOLUME (annual; contributors include Lewis Carroll, Hans Andersen;
    artists include George Cruikshank, Randolph Caldecott, etc.; collated from 'Aunt Judy's Magazine')
    (Bell & Daldy, 1866-1885) £50
AUNT JUDY'S MAGAZINE (monthly) (Bell & Daldy, 1866)..each £10

'AUNT LOUISA' BOOKS

Pseudonym of Laura B.J. Valentine. Born: 1814. Died: 1899. Best known as a compiler of toy books for children.

Prices are for books in Very Good condition.

AUNT LOUISA'S LONDON GIFT BOOK (Warne, 1867)...£175
AUNT LOUISA'S NURSERY FAVOURITES (illustrated by K. Greenaway) (Warne, 1870) £350
AUNT LOUISA'S LONDON TOY BOOKS (series of titles) (Warne, c.1870-1880)......................................each £50
AUNT LOUISA'S BIRTHDAY GIFT (Warne, 1875)..£175
AUNT LOUISA'S SUNDAY BOOK (Warne, c.1878)..£175
AUNT LOUISA'S BOOK OF NURSERY RHYMES (Warne, 1880)..£75
AUNT LOUISA'S BOOK OF ANIMAL STORIES (Warne, [1899])...£70
AUNT LOUISA'S FIRST BOOK FOR CHILDREN (Warne, 1902)...£50
AUNT LOUISA'S BOOK OF COMMON THINGS (Warne, c.1910)..£40

AVERY, Gillian

British author. Born: Gillian Elise Avery in Reigate, Surrey, 1929. Worked as a reporter and as an illustration editor before publishing her first story, *The Warden's Niece*, in 1957. Many of her books are set in the Victorian era.

Prices are for books in Very Good condition with dustjackets.

THE WARDEN'S NIECE (illustrated by Dick Hart) (Collins, 1957)..£75
TRESPASSERS AT CHARLCOTE (illustrated by Dick Hart) (Collins, 1958)...£50
JAMES WITHOUT THOMAS (illustrated by John Verney) (Collins, 1959) £50
THE ELEPHANT WAR (illustrated by John Verney) (Collins, 1960)...£50
TO TAME A SISTER (illustrated by John Verney) (Collins, 1961)...£50
THE GREATEST GRESHAM (illustrated by John Verney) (Collins, 1962)..£35
THE PEACOCK HOUSE (illustrated by John Verney) (Collins, 1963)..£35
THE ITALIAN SPRING (illustrated by John Verney) (Collins, 1964)..£30
CALL OF THE VALLEY (illustrated by Laszlo Acs) (Collins, 1966)...£25
A LIKELY LAD (illustrated by Faith Jaques) (Collins, 1971)..£25
ELLEN'S BIRTHDAY (illustrated by Krystyna Turska) (Hamish Hamilton, 1971)..£15
ELLEN AND THE QUEEN (illustrated by Krystyna Turska) (Hamish Hamilton, 1971).......................................£15
JEMIMA AND THE WELSH RABBIT (illustrated by J. Lawrence) (Hamish Hamilton, 1972) £15
FREDDIE'S FEET (illustrated by Krystyna Turska) (Hamish Hamilton, 1976) £15
HUCK AND HER TIME MACHINE (Collins, 1977)..£15
MOULDY'S ORPHAN (illustrated by Faith Jaques) (Collins, 1978)...£15
SIXPENCE! (illustrated by Antony Maitland) (Collins, 1979) £15
THE LOST RAILWAY (Collins, 1980)..£15
ONLOOKERS (Collins, 1983)..£15

AWDRY, The Rev W.

British author/illustrator, creator of 'Thomas the Tank Engine'. Born Wilbert Vere Awdry in Ampfield, Hampshire, in 1911. Studied at Dauntsey's School, St. Peter's Hall, Oxford, and Wycliffe Hall, Oxford. Served as Rector of Elsworth and Vicar of Elmneth in Norfolk. As well as the 'Thomas the Tank Engine' books, he wrote several books for adults on steam railways. Died: 1997. His son Christopher (b1940) began writing more stories for the series in 1983. *Really Useful Engines* was the first of 14 penned by Christopher.

*Prices are for books in Very Good condition with dustjackets where applicable. * Indicates books written by Christopher Awdry.*

'Railway' series
1. THE THREE RAILWAY ENGINES (illustrated by William Middleton) (Edmund Ward, 1945) £125
2. THOMAS THE TANK ENGINE (illustrated by Reginald Payne) (Edmund Ward, 1946) £175
3. JAMES THE RED ENGINE (illustrated by C. Reginald Dalby) (Edmund Ward 1948) £125
4. TANK ENGINE THOMAS AGAIN (illustrated by C. Reginald Dalby) (Edmund Ward, 1949) £125
5. TROUBLESOME ENGINES (illustrated by C. Reginald Dalby) (Edmund Ward, 1950) £90
6. HENRY THE GREEN ENGINE (illustrated by C. Reginald Dalby) (Edmund Ward, 1951) £90
7. TOBY THE TRAM ENGINE (illustrated by C. Reginald Dalby) (Edmund Ward, 1952) £90
8. GORDON THE BIG ENGINE (illustrated by C. Reginald Dalby) (Edmund Ward, 1953) £90
9. EDWARD THE BLUE ENGINE (illustrated by C. Reginald Dalby) (Edmund Ward, 1954) £90
10. FOUR LITTLE ENGINES (illustrated by C. Reginald Dalby) (Edmund Ward, 1955) £90
11. PERCY THE SMALL ENGINE (illustrated by C. Reginald Dalby) (Edmund Ward, 1956) £70
12. THE EIGHT FAMOUS ENGINES (illustrated by John T. Kenney) (Edmund Ward, 1957) £70
13. DUCK AND THE DIESEL ENGINE (illustrated by John T. Kenney) (Edmund Ward, 1958) £50
14. THE LITTLE OLD ENGINE (illustrated by John T. Kenney) (Edmund Ward, 1959) £50
15. THE TWIN ENGINES (illustrated by John T. Kenney) (Edmund Ward, 1960) £50
16. BRANCH LINE ENGINES (illustrated by John T. Kenney) (Edmund Ward, 1961) £50
17. GALLANT OLD ENGINE (illustrated by John T. Kenney) (Edmund Ward. 1962) £50
18. STEPNEY THE 'BLUEBELL' ENGINE (illustrated by Gunvor and Peter Edwards) (Edmund Ward, 1963) £35
19. MOUNTAIN ENGINES (illustrated by Gunvor and Peter Edwards) (Edmund Ward, 1964) £35
20. VERY OLD ENGINES (illustrated by Gunvor and Peter Edwards) (Edmund Ward, 1965) £35
21. MAIN LINE ENGINES (illustrated by Peter and Gunvor Edwards) (Edmund Ward, 1966) £35
22. SMALL RAILWAY ENGINES (illustrated by Peter and Gunvor Edwards) (Kaye & Ward, 1967) £25
23. ENTERPRISING ENGINES (illustrated by Gunvor and Peter Edwards) (Kaye & Ward, 1968) £25
24. OLIVER THE WESTERN ENGINE (illustrated by Gunvor and Peter Edwards) (Kaye & Ward, 1969) £25
25. DUKE THE LOST ENGINE (illustrated by Gunvor and Peter Edwards) (Kaye & Ward, 1970) £25
26. TRAMWAY ENGINES (illustrated by Gunvor and Peter Edwards) (Kaye & Ward, 1972) £25
*27. REALLY USEFUL ENGINES (illustrated by Clive Spong) (Kaye & Ward, 1983) £8
*28. JAMES AND THE DIESEL ENGINES (illustrated by Clive Spong) (Kaye & Ward 1984) £8
*29. GREAT LITTLE ENGINES (illustrated by Clive Spong) (Kaye & Ward, 1985) £8
*30. MORE ABOUT THOMAS THE TANK ENGINE (illustrated by Clive Spong) (Kaye & Ward, 1986) £8
*31. GORDON THE HIGH-SPEED ENGINE (illustrated by Clive Spong) (Kaye & Ward, 1987) £8
*32. TOBY, TRUCKS AND TROUBLE (illustrated by Clive Spong) (Kaye & Ward 1988) £5
*33. THOMAS AND THE TWINS (illustrated by Clive Spong) (Heinemann, 1989) £5
*34. JOCK THE NEW ENGINE (illustrated by Clive Spong) (Heinemann, 1990) £5
*35. THOMAS AND THE GREAT RAILWAY SHOW (illustrated by Clive Spong) (Heinemann, 1991) £5
*36. THOMAS COMES HOME (illustrated by Clive Spong) (Heinemann, 1992) £5
*37. HENRY AND THE EXPRESS (illustrated by Clive Spong) (Heinemann, 1993) £5
*38. WILBERT THE FOREST ENGINE (illustrated by Clive Spong) (Heinemann. 1994) £5
*39. THOMAS AND THE FAT CONTROLLER'S ENGINES (illustrated by Clive Spong) (Heinemann, 1995) £5
*40. NEW LITTLE ENGINE (illustrated by Clive Spong) (Heinemann, 1996) £5
THE CLASSIC LIBRARY STATION BOX (boxed set containing all 26 original books by Rev. W. Awdry) (Heinemann, 2002) £130

Other 'Thomas' titles
'RAILWAY' SERIES: WELSH EDITIONS
1. Y TRI INDIAN TREN ('Three Railway Engines'; illustrated by C. Reginald Dalby) (Edmund Ward, [1950]) £35
2. THOMAS YR INJIAN DANC ('Thomas the Tank Engine'; [illustrated by Reginald Payne]) (Edmund Ward, [1950]) £35
3. JAMES YR INJIAN COCH ('James the Red Engine'; illustrated by C. Reginald Dalby) (Edmund Ward, [1950]) £35
4. THOMAS INJIAN-DANC ETO ('Tank Engine Thomas Again'; illustrated by C. Reginald Dalby) (Edmund Ward, [1950]) £35

PAINTING BOOKS (all paperback)
1. SCENES FROM 'THOMAS THE TANK ENGINE' FOR YOU TO PAINT (Edmund Ward, [1950]) £25
2. SCENES FROM 'JAMES THE RED ENGINE' FOR YOU TO PAINT (Edmund Ward, [1950]) £25
3. SCENES FROM 'THE THREE RAILWAY ENGINES' FOR YOU TO PAINT (Edmund Ward, [1952]) £25
4. SCENES FROM 'TROUBLESOME ENGINES' FOR YOU TO PAINT (Edmund Ward, [1952]) £25

'MODEL ENGINE' BOOKS (all paperback)
1. THOMAS THE TANK ENGINE AND ANNIE (Edmund Ward, [1957]) £35
2. PERCY WITH CLARABEL THE COACH (Edmund Ward, [1957]) £35
3. GORDON THE ENGINE AND HIS TENDER (Edmund Ward, [1957]) £35
4. JAMES THE RED ENGINE AND HIS TENDER (Edmund Ward, [1957]) £35

POP-UP BOOKS
BERTIE THE BUS AND THOMAS THE TANK ENGINE (from No. 4) (Kaye & Ward, 1983) £18
THE FLYING KIPPER AND HENRY THE GREEN ENGINE (from No. 6) (Kaye & Ward, 1983) £18
HENRY THE GREEN ENGINE AND THE ELEPHANT (from No. 6) (Kaye & Ward, 1984) £18
HENRY THE GREEN ENGINE GETS OUT (from No. 6) (Kaye & Ward, 1983) £18
JAMES THE RED ENGINE AND THE TROUBLESOME TRUCKS (from No. 3) (Kaye & Ward, 1984) £12
PERCY THE SMALL ENGINE TAKES THE PLUNGE (from No.12) (Kaye & Ward, 1984) £12
THOMAS THE TANK ENGINE AND THE TRACTOR (from No. 2) (Kaye & Ward, 1984) £12
THOMAS THE TANK ENGINE GOES FISHING (from No. 2) (Kaye & Ward, 1983) £18

OMNIBUS EDITIONS
RAILWAY STORIES (illustrated by C. Reginald Dalby and John T. Kenney) (Kaye & Ward, [1982]) £12
MORE RAILWAY STORIES (illustrated by C. Reginald Dalby and John T. Kenney) (Kaye & Ward, 1983) £12

OTHERS
THE REVEREND W. AWDRY'S RAILWAY SERIES SURPRISE PACKET (produced In the railwayman's satchel;
    illustrated by Peter Edwards) (Kaye & Ward, 1972) £25
THOMAS'S CHRISTMAS PARTY (illustrated by Cllve Spong) (Kaye & Ward, 1984) £12
THOMAS'S ABC (illustrated by T. Wells) (Heinemann, 1987) £5
THOMAS'S COUNTING BOOK (illustrated by T. Weils) (Heinemann, 1987) £5
THOMAS THE TANK ENGINE PRESS-OUT MODEL BOOK (illustrated by K. Stott) (Kaye & Ward, 1987) £8
HELLO THOMAS (LIFT-THE-FLAP BOOK) (Heinemann, 1988) £6

Other books by Rev W. Awdry

'BELINDA' SERIES
BELINDA THE BEETLE (illustrated by Ionicus) (Brockhampton Press, 1958) £35
BELINDA BEATS THE BAND (illustrated by John T. Kenney) (Brockhampton Press, 1961) £35

'SODOR' TITLES
RAILWAY MAP OF THE ISLAND OF SODOR (illustrated by C. Reginald Dalby) (Edmund Ward, 1958) £50
Ditto Revised Edition (illustrated by C. Reginald Dalby) (Kaye & Ward, 1971) £25
ISLAND OF SODOR: ITS PEOPLE, HISTORY, AND RAILWAYS (with George Awdry) (Heinemann, 1987) £12

This montage of classic 'Thomas the Tank Engine' titles gives some idea of the range of covers to be found in the series.

B

'BB'

British author-illustrator. Born: Denys James Watkins-Pitchford in Northamptonshire in 1905. Studied at Royal College of Art, subsequently working for many years as art master at Rugby School. Also wrote many works for adults, notably on wildlife and field sports, and illustrated most of his own titles. Awarded an MBE in 1989. Died: 1990.

Prices are for books in Very Good condition with dustjackets.

Books Written and Illustrated by 'BB'

WILD LONE: The Story of a Pytchley Fox (Eyre & Spottiswoode, 1938) £150
MANKA, THE SKY GIPSY: The Story of a Wild Goose (Eyre & Spottiswoode, 1939) £150
THE LITTLE GREY MEN: A Story for the Young in Heart (No colour plates) (Eyre & Spottiswoode, 1942) £225
THE LITTLE GREY MEN: A Story for the Young in Heart (eight colour plates) (Eyre & Spottiswoode, 1946) £225
BRENDON CHASE (Hollis & Carter, 1944) £150
THE LITTLE GREY MEN: A Story for the Young in Heart (eight colour plates by 'BB') (Eyre & Spottiswoode, 1946) £150
DOWN THE BRIGHT STREAM (Eyre & Spottiswoode, 1948) £175
BB's FAIRY BOOK: MEETING HILL (Hollis & Carter, 1948) £175
THE WIND IN THE WOOD (Hollis & Carter, 1952) £175
FAIRY TALES OF LONG AGO (Dent, 1952) £25
THE FOREST OF BOLAND LIGHT RAILWAY (Eyre & Spottiswoode, 1955) £120
MONTY WOODPIG'S CARAVAN (Ward, 1957) £500
BEN THE BULLFINCH (Hamish Hamilton, 1957) £500
WANDERING WIND (Hamish Hamilton, 1957) £450
ALEXANDER (Blackwell, 1957 [1958]) £100
MONTY WOODPIG AND HIS BUBBLEBUZZ CAR (Ward, 1958) £100
MR BUMSTEAD (Eyre & Spottiswoode, 1958) £80
THE WIZARD OF BOLAND (Ward, 1959) £80
BILL BADGER'S WINTER CRUISE (Hamish Hamilton, 1959) £350

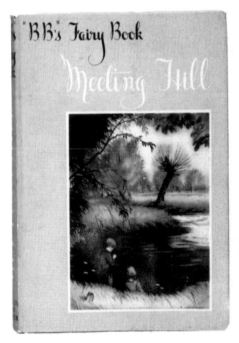

The splendid 'scraperboard' dustjacket of the first edition of 'BB's' classic adventure story, Brendon Chase (1944). Like all of the illustrations in the book, it is signed with his real name.

'BB' also wrote a number of children's stories featuring fairies and other fantastic creatures. Meeting Hill was published by Hollis & Carter in 1948 and is now worth £175.

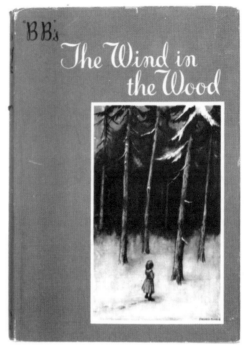

'BB's **The Little Grey Men** *was issued in 1942, with no colour plates, and again in 1946 with eight colour plates.*

The Wind in the Wood *(1952) was the third children's book by 'BB' to be published by Hollis and Carter.*

BILL BADGER AND THE PIRATES (Hamish Hamilton, 1960) **£350**
BILL BADGER'S FINEST HOUR (Hamish Hamilton, 1961)..**£175**
THE BADGERS OF BEARSHANKS (Ernest Benn, 1961) **£125**
BILL BADGER'S WHISPERING REEDS ADVENTURE (Hamish Hamilton, 1962) **£350**
LEPUS THE BROWN HARE (Benn, 1962)..**£125**
BILL BADGER'S BIG MISTAKE (Hamish Hamilton, 1963)..**£275**
BILL BADGER AND THE BIG STORE ROBBERY (Hamish Hamilton, 1967)......................................**£350**
THE WHOPPER (Benn, 1967)..**£500**
AT THE BACK O'BEN DEE (Benn, 1968) **£250**
BILL BADGER'S VOYAGE TO THE WORLD'S END (Kaye & Ward, 1969) **£125**
THE TYGER TRAY (Methuen, 1971)..**£250**
THE POOL OF THE BLACK WITCH (Methuen, 1974)..**£125**
LORD OF THE FOREST (Methuen, 1975)..**£100**
STORIES OF THE WILD (with A.L.E. Fenton and A. Windsor Richards) (Benn, 1975) **£50**
MORE STORIES OF THE WILD (with A. Windsor Richards) (Benn, 1977) **£50**
A CHILD ALONE (Joseph, 1978) **£35**

Books Illustrated by 'BB'
THE LONG NIGHT by William Mayne (No d/j) (Blackwell, 1957 [1958]) **£125**
THIRTEEN O'CLOCK by William Mayne (Blackwell, 1959)..**£50**
THE BIRDS OF THE LONELY LAKE by A. Windsor Richards (Benn, 1961)..**£30**
PRINCE PRIGIO AND PRINCE RICARDO by Andrew Lang (Dent, 1961)..**£30**
THE ROGUE ELEPHANT by A.R. Channel (Dobson, 1962) **£40**
GRANNY'S WONDERFUL CHAIR by Frances Browne (Dent, 1963) **£30**
THE LOST PRINCESS by George MacDonald (Dent, 1967)..**£50**

BAGNOLD, Enid
British author. Born: Rochester, Kent, in 1889. Studied art in London before serving as a nurse in the Great War. Had her greatest success with *National Velvet* (1935), but also wrote several adult novels and plays, notably the drama, *The Chalk Garden* (1956). Died: 1981.
Prices are for books in Very Good condition with dustjackets.

ALICE AND THOMAS AND JANE (Heinemann, 1930)..**£50**
NATIONAL VELVET (Heinemann, 1935) **£200**

BALLANTYNE, R.M.

Scottish author. Born: Robert Michael Ballantyne, 1825. Apprenticed to the Hudson Bay Company at the age of sixteen and sent off to Canada, where he worked as a fur trader. Returned to Scotland where, in 1848, he published an account of his life in Canada, followed, in 1856, by his first adventure novel, *Snowflakes and Sunbeams, or The Young Fur-Traders*. Amongst his many other works are *The Coral Island* (1858) and *The Gorilla Hunters* (1861). Also an accomplished painter and lecturer, and an Elder of the Free Kirk of Scotland. Described by Stevenson in the dedicatory poem to *Treasure Island* as "Ballantyne the brave". Died: 1894.

Prices are for books in Good condition.

SNOWFLAKES AND SUNBEAMS, or The Young Fur-Traders (illustrated by the author) (Nelson, 1856) £1,500
THREE LITTLE KITTENS by 'Comus' (verses and music) (Nelson, [1856]) £60
MY MOTHER by 'Comus' (Nelson, 1857)..£60
THE BUTTERFLY'S BALL by 'Comus' (Nelson, 1857) £75
MISTER FOX by 'Comus' (Nelson, 1857)...£60
UNGAVA: A Tale of Esquimaux Land (Nelson, 1858 [1857]) £60
THE CORAL ISLAND: A Tale of the Pacific Ocean (illustrated by the author) (Nelson, 1858 [1857]) £6,000
THE ROBBER KITTEN by 'Comus' (Nelson, 1858)..£75
MARTIN RATTLER, or A Boy's Adventures in the Forests of Brazil (Nelson, 1858)......................................£75
MEE-A-OW! or Good Advice to Cats and Kittens (Nelson, 1859) £75
THE WORLD OF ICE, or Adventures in the Polar Regions (Nelson, 1860 [1859])...£75
THE DOG CRUSOE: A Tale of the Western Prairies (Nelson, 1861 [1860])...£100
THE GOLDEN DREAM, or Adventures in the Far West (Shaw, 1861 [1860]) £100
THE GORILLA HUNTERS: A Tale of the Wilds of Africa (Nelson, 1861) £1,500
THE RED ERIC, or The Whaler's Last Cruise: A Tale (illustrated by William Coleman) (Routledge, 1861) £75
MAN ON THE OCEAN: A Book for Boys (Nelson, 1863 [1862])..£75
THE WILD MAN OF THE WEST: A Tale of the Rocky Mountains (illustrated by Johann Zwecker)
    (Routledge, 1863 [1862])...£100
BALLANTYNE'S MISCELLANY (fifteen volumes) (Nisbet, 1863-1886)...each £50
GASCOYNE, THE SANDAL-WOOD TRADER: A Tale of the Pacific (Nisbet, 1864 [1863]) £75
THE LIFEBOAT: A Tale of Our Coast Heroes (Nisbet, 1864)...£60
FREAKS ON THE FELLS, or Three Months' Rustication: And Why I did not Become a Sailor
    (Routledge, 1865 [1864])...£75
THE LIGHTOUSE: Being the Story of a Great Fight Between Man and the Sea (Nisbet, 1865)............................£60
SHIFTING WINDS: A Tough Yarn (Nisbet, 1866)..£60
SILVER LAKE, or Lost in the Snow (Jackson, 1867) £60
FIGHTING THE FLAMES: A Tale of the London Fire Brigade (Nisbet, 1868) £75
AWAY IN THE WILDERNESS, or Life Among the Red-Indians and Fur-Traders of North America
    (Porter & Coates, U.S., 1869)..£100
DEEP DOWN: A Tale of the Cornish Mines (Nisbet, 1869)...£60
ERLING THE BOLD: A Tale of the Norse Sea-Kings (illustrated by the author) (Nisbet, 1869).........................£60
THE FLOATING LIGHTS OF THE GOODWIN SANDS: A Tale (illustrated by the author) (Nisbet, 1870)...................£60
THE IRON HORSE, or Life on the Line: A Tale of the Grand National Trunk Railway (Nisbet, 1871)...................£100
THE NORSEMEN IN THE WEST, or America Before Columbus (Nisbet, 1872) £75
THE PIONEERS: A Tale of the Western Wilderness (Nisbet, 1872)..£75
BLACK IVORY: A Tale of Adventure among the Slavers of East Africa (Nisbet, 1873)..................................£75
LIFE IN THE RED BRIGADE: A Story for Boys (Routledge [1873])...£50
THE OCEAN AND ITS WONDERS (Nelson, 1874)...£30
THE PIRATE CITY: An Algerine Tale (Nisbet, 1875) £75
RIVERS OF ICE: A Tale Illustrative of Alpine Adventure and Glacier Action (Nisbet, 1875) £50
UNDER THE WAVES, or Diving In Deep Waters: A Tale (Nisbet, 1876)...£50
THE SETTLER AND THE SAVAGE: A Tale of Peace and War in South Africa (Nisbet, 1877)...............................£75
IN THE TRACK OF THE TROOPS: A Tale of Modern War (Nisbet, 1878)..£50
JARWIN AND CUFFY: A Tale (Warne, [1878])..£50
SIX MONTHS AT THE CAPE, or Letters to Periwinkle from South Africa (Nisbet, 1879 [1878]) £75
POST HASTE: A Tale of Her Majesty's Mails (Nisbet, 1880 [1879]) £75
PHILOSOPHER JACK: A Tale of the Southern Seas (Nisbet, 1880)..£60
THE LONELY ISLAND, or the Refuge of the Mutineers (Nisbet, 1880) £60
THE REDMAN'S REVENGE: A Tale of the Red River Flood (Nisbet, 1880)..£75
THE COLLECTED WORKS OF ENSIGN SOPHT, LATE OF THE VOLUNTEERS (Nisbet, 1881) £150
MY DOGGY AND I (Nisbet, [1881])...£60
THE GIANT OF THE NORTH, or Pokings Round the Pole (Nisbet, 1882 [1881]) £75
THE KITTEN PILGRIMS, or Great Battles and Grand Victories (illustrated by the author) (Nisbet, [1882])...........£75
THE BATTERY AND THE BOILER, or Adventures in the Laying of Submarine Cable (Nisbet, 1883 [1882])..............£75
THE MADMAN AND THE PIRATE (Nisbet, 1883)..£60
BATTLES WITH THE SEA, or Heroes of the Lifeboat and Rocket (Nisbet, 1883)...£60
THE YOUNG TRAWLERS: A Story of Life and Death and Rescue on the North Sea (Nisbet, 1884)......................£60
DUSTY DIAMONDS CUT AND POLISHED: A Tale of City-Arab Life and Adventure (Nisbet, 1884 [1883])...............£60
TWICE BOUGHT: A Tale of the Oregon Gold Fields (Nisbet, 1885 [1884]) £60

BALLANTYNE, R.M.

THE ROVER OF THE ANDES: A Tale of Adventure in South America (Nisbet, 1885)..................£60
THE ISLAND QUEEN: A Tale of the Southern Hemisphere (Nisbet, 1885).............................£60
RED ROONEY, or Last of the Crew (Nisbet, 1886)...£60
THE BIG OTTER: A Tale of the Great Nor'West (Routledge, 1887 [1886])..............................£60
BLUE LIGHTS, or Hot Work in the Soudan: A Tale of Soldier Life (Nisbet, 1888)....................£60
THE MIDDY AND THE MOORS: An Algerine Story (Nisbet, 1888).....................................£60
THE CREW OF THE WATER WAGTAIL: A Story of Newfoundland (Nisbet, [1889])...................£60
THE GARRETT AND THE GARDEN, or Low Life High Up; and JEFF BENSON, or The Young Coastguardsmen
(Nisbet, [1890])..£60
CHARLIE TO THE RESCUE: A Tale of the Sea and the Rockies (illustrated by the author) (Nisbet, 1890)............£60
THE COXSWAIN'S BRIDE, or The Rising Tide and Other Tales (illustrated by the author) (Nisbet, 1891)............£60
THE HOT SWAMP: A Romance of Old Albion (Nisbet, 1892) £60
HUNTED AND HARRIED: A Tale of the Scottish Covenanters (Nisbet, [1892])........................£50
THE WALRUS HUNTERS: A Romance of the Realms of Ice (Nisbet, 1893)............................£50
FIGHTING THE WHALES (Blackie, [1915])...£20
THE JOLLY KITTEN BOOK (Blackie, [1925])..£30
BALLANTYNE OMNIBUS FOR BOYS (Collins, [1932])..£10

BANNERMAN, Helen

Scottish author. Born: Helen Brodie Cowan Watson in Edinburgh in 1863. Married an army doctor and settled in India, where she wrote *Little Black Sambo* (1899) to amuse her children. The success of this little picture book — the copyright of which she sold for £5 — prompted her to produce several more in the same style and format. She died in her native Scotland in 1946.

Prices are for books in Very Good condition.

THE STORY OF LITTLE BLACK SAMBO (anonymous)
(Grant Richards: 'Dumpy Books for Children' series No. 4, 1899)..£6,000
THE STORY OF LITTLE BLACK MINGO (anonymous) (Nisbet, 1901)....................................£250
THE STORY OF LITTLE BLACK QUIBBA (anonymous) (Nisbet, 1902)..................................£250
LITTLE DEGCHIE-HEAD: An Awful Warning to Bad Babas (anonymous) (Nisbet, 1903) £200
PAT AND THE SPIDER: The Biter Bit (anonymous) (Nisbet, 1904).....................................£175
THE STORY OF THE TEASING MONKEY (anonymous) (Nisbet, 1906)..................................£100
THE STORY OF LITTLE BLACK QUASHA (anonymous) (Nisbet, 1908) £120
THE STORY OF LITTLE BLACK BOBTAIL (anonymous) (Nisbet, 1909) £100
THE STORY OF SAMBO AND THE TWINS (Nisbet, [1937])..£60
THE STORY OF LITTLE WHITE SQUIBBA (Chatto & Windus, 1966)....................................£30

BARKER, Cicely Mary

British author-illustrator. Born: 1895. Best known for her 'Flower Fairies' books, in which fairy children are shown dressed as different types of flowers. Died: 1973.

Prices are for books in Very Good condition.

THE CHILDREN'S BOOK OF HYMNS (Blackie & Son, [c.1920]) £50
FLOWER FAIRIES OF THE SPRING (poems and pictures by C.M. Barker) (Blackie, [1923]).........£80
FLOWER FAIRIES OF THE SUMMER (poems and pictures by C.M. Barker) (Blackie, [1925]).......£70
FLOWER FAIRIES OF THE AUTUMN: With the Nuts and Berries they Bring (poems and pictures by C.M. Barker)
(Blackie, [1926])..£60
THE BOOK OF FLOWER FAIRIES (contains the above three books) (Blackie, [1927]) £250
FLOWER FAIRIES OF THE WINTER (Warne, [1925]) £125
AUTUMN SONGS WITH MUSIC (from 'Flower Fairies of the Autumn'; music by Olive Linnell; twelve coloured plates)
(Blackie, [1926])..£125
SPRING SONGS WITH MUSIC (from 'Flower Fairies of the Spring'; music by Olive Linnell; twelve coloured plates)
(Blackie, [1926])..£125
SUMMER SONGS WITH MUSIC (from 'Flower Fairies of the Summer'; music by Olive Linnell; twelve coloured plates)
(Blackie, no date) £125
OLD RHYMES FOR ALL TIMES (collected, edited and illustrated by C.M. Barker) (Blackie, [1928])............£100
FLOWER SONGS OF THE SEASONS (music by Olive Linnell; twelve coloured plates) (Blackie, [c.1930]) £125
BEAUTIFUL BIBLE PICTURES (six cards painted by C.M. Barker) (Blackie, [1932])..................£30
A LITTLE BOOK OF RHYMES NEW AND OLD (collected, edited and illustrated by C.M. Barker) (Blackie, [1933])............£45
THE LITTLE PICTURE HYMN BOOK (illustrated and decorated by C.M. Barker) (Blackie, [1933])............£50
A FLOWER FAIRY ALPHABET (poems and pictures by C.M. Barker) (Blackie, [1934]).................£90
A LITTLE BOOK OF OLD RHYMES (collected, edited and illustrated by C.M. Barker) (Blackie, [1936])............£40
HE LEADETH ME: A Book of Bible Stories by Dorothy O. Barker (illustrated by C.M. Barker) (Blackie, [1936])............£40
THE LORD OF THE RUSHIE RIVER (story and pictures by C.M. Barker) (Blackie, [1938]) £45
FAIRIES OF THE TREES (poems and pictures by C.M. Barker) (Blackie, 1940) £50
WHEN SPRING CAME IN AT THE WINDOW: A One-Act Play (with songs from 'Flower Fairies of the Spring';
music by Olive Linnell) (Blackie, 1942)..£65
FLOWER FAIRIES OF THE GARDEN (poems and pictures by C.M. Barker) (Blackie, [1944]) £60
GROUNDSEL AND NECKLACES (story and pictures by C.M. Barker) (Blackie, [1946]).................£40
FLOWER FAIRIES OF THE WAYSIDE (poems and pictures by C.M. Barker) (Blackie, [1948]) £60

FAIRIES OF THE FLOWERS AND TREES (contains 'Flower Fairies of the Wayside',
'Flower Fairies of the Garden' and 'Fairies of the Trees') (Blackie, [1950])...**£200**
LIVELY STORIES (five books: 'The Little House', 'Do You Know?', 'The Click-Clock Man',
'The Why Girl' and 'Hutch the Peg Doll') (Macmillan, 1954-1955)..each **£40**
CICELY BARKER'S FLOWER FAIRY PICTURE BOOK (Blackie, [1955])..**£75**
LIVELY NUMBERS (three books: 'The Little Man', 'The Little Boats' and 'The Lazy Giant') (Macmillan, 1960-1962).........each **£40**
THE RHYMING RAINBOW (Blackie, 1977)...**£20**
THE FAIRIES' GIFT (Blackie, 1977)...**£20**
FLOWER FAIRIES MINIATURE LIBRARY (poems and illustrations from the 1920s Flower Fairies series;
four miniature books: 'Spring Flower Fairies', 'Summer Flower Fairies', Blossom Flower Fairies' and
'Berry Flower Fairies'; in slipcase) (Blackie & Son Intervisual, 1981)...the set **£35**
SIMON THE SWAN (Blackie, 1988) **£40**

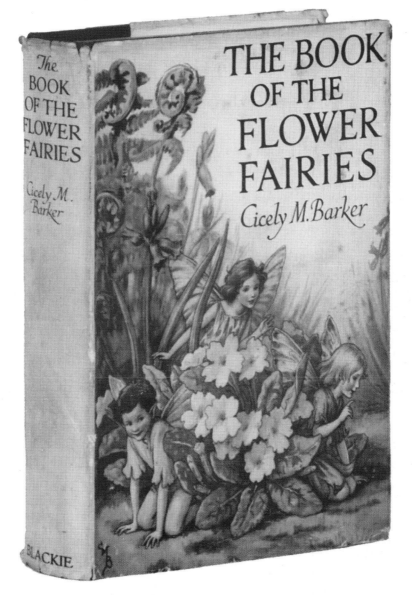

*The Book of the Flower Fairies (Blackie, 1927) contained three previous collections of poems and
pictures by British author-illustrator Cicely M. Barker and very rarely survives with its dustjacket intact.*

BARKLEM, Jill

British author-illustrator. Born: Epping, 1951. She studied illustration with Fritz Wegner at St Martin's College of Art in London. Her 'Brambly Hedge' series began in 1980.

Prices are for books in Very Good condition with dustjackets where applicable.

Books Written and Illustrated by Jill Barklem

SPRING STORY (Collins, 1980)..£25
SUMMER STORY (Collins, 1980)...£20
AUTUMN STORY (Collins, 1980)...£20
WINTER STORY (Collins, 1980)...£20
BRAMBLY HEDGE: The Seasons — Summer, Winter, Autumn, Spring (in decorative slipcase) (Collins, 1981)....................£70
THE SECRET STAIRCASE (Collins, 1983)..£20
THE HIGH HILLS A Brambly Hedge story (Collins, 1986) £20
SEA STORY (Collins, 1990)..£20
THE BRAMBLY HEDGE TREASURY (Harper Collins, 1991) £10
POPPY'S BABIES A Brambly Hedge story (Collins, 1994)...£25
BRAMBLY HEDGE Sliding Picture Books (four little volumes: 'Wilfred's Birthday', 'Poppy & Dusty's Wedding',
   'Primrose's Adventure' and 'The Snow Ball') (Collins, 1995)..£25
WINTER STORY Colouring Book (from the 'Brambly Hedge' stories) (Collins, 1996)......................................£5
SPRING STORY Sticker Book (from the 'Brambly Hedge' stories) (Collins, 1997)...£5
BABY MICE IN BRAMBLY HEDGE (illustrated boards; contains 'Summer Story' and 'Poppy's Babies') (Collins, 1999)............£10

BARRIE, J.M.

Scottish author. Born: James Matthew Barrie in Kirriemuir ('Thrums'), Scotland, in 1860. Barrie's favourite reading as a child were 'penny dreadfuls' and the works of R.M. Ballantyne, James Fenimore Cooper and Robert Louis Stevenson. After studying in Edinburgh, he became a journalist on the *Nottingham Journal* before moving to London in 1885, where he worked as a freelance. Enjoyed success with the plays *Quality Street* and *The Admirable Crichton*, before achieving lasting fame with *Peter Pan*, first produced in 1904. Became a baronet in 1913. Died: 1937.

An Arthur Rackham plate from **Peter Pan in Kensington Gardens**, *a particularly popular edition of Barrie's story.*

Prices are for books in Very Good condition with dustjackets where applicable.

THE LITTLE WHITE BIRD (novel including first mention of Peter Pan) (Hodder & Stoughton, 1902) £80
PETER PAN IN KENSINGTON GARDENS (Extracts from THE LITTLE WHITE BIRD.
  With 50 colour plates by Arthur Rackham) (Hodder & Stoughton, [1906]) £1,500
PETER PAN IN KENSINGTON GARDENS (Edition De Luxe, limited to 500 copies, signed by Arthur Rackham)
  (Hodder & Stoughton, [1906]) £4,000
PETER PAN IN KENSINGTON GARDENS (New edition, with 50 colour plates and 12 drawings by Arthur Rackham)
  (Hodder & Stoughton, 1912) £1,000
PETER PAN IN KENSINGTON GARDENS (Edition De Luxe, not signed) (Hodder & Stoughton, [1912]) £1,500
PETER PAN IN KENSINGTON GARDENS (facsimile of the 1912 Rackham De Luxe edition;
  limited to 500 numbered copies) (Hodder & Stoughton, 1983) £200
THE PETER PAN PICTURE BOOK Edited by D. O'Connor (illustrated by Alice B. Woodward)
  (Hodder & Stoughton, 1907) £90
PETER AND WENDY (First edition in novel form. Illustrated by F.D. Bedford) (Hodder & Stoughton, [1911]) £150
THE PETER PAN PORTFOLIO (Illustrated by Arthur Rackham; Limited to 500 copies, numbered 101 to 600,
  signed by publisher, engravers and printers) (Hodder & Stoughton, 1912) £3,000
THE PETER PAN PORTFOLIO (illustrated by Arthur Rackham; edition limited to twenty copies,
  each plate signed by the artist) (Hodder & Stoughton, 1912) £10,000
THE STORY OF PETER PAN (illustrated by Alice B. Woodward) (Hodder & Stoughton, 1914) £50
THE PETER PAN PAINTING BOOK (illustrated by John Hassall) (Hodder & Stoughton, [1915]) £40
PETER AND WENDY (illustrated by Mabel Lucie Attwell; with dustjacket) (Hodder & Stoughton [1921]) £300
PETER PAN, or The Boy Who Would Not Grow Up (play) (Hodder & Stoughton, 1928) £60
PETER PAN AND WENDY (illustrated by Gwynedd Hudson; with dustjacket) (Hodder & Stoughton, 1931) £200
THE BLAMPIED EDITION OF PETER PAN (with dustjacket) (Hodder & Stoughton, 1939) £150
PETER PAN (illustrated by Nora S. Unwin; with dustjacket) (Hodder & Stoughton, 1951) £35
PETER PAN CHILDREN'S ALBUM (Walt Disney, 1952) £40
PETER PAN (Walt Disney, 1953) £40
WHEN WENDY GREW UP: An Afterthought (play; issued with dustjacket) (Nelson, 1957) £20
PETER PAN (illustrated by Edward Ardizzone) (Brockhampton Press, 1962) £50
PETER PAN (illustrated by Trina Schart Hyman) (Hodder & Stoughton, 1980) £20
PETER PAN (illustrated by Michael Hague) (Holt, U.S., 1987) £40

BATES, H.E.

British author. Born: Herbert Ernest Bates in Higham Ferrers, Northants, in 1905. Best known for his adult novels, including *The Purple Plain*, *Love for Lydia* and the 'Larkins Family' series, but also wrote a handful of children's titles. Died: 1974.

Prices are for books in Very Good condition with dustjackets.

ACHILLES AND THE DONKEY (illustrated by Carol Barker) (Dennis Dobson, 1962) £40
ACHILLES AND DIANA (illustrated by Carol Barker) (Dennis Dobson, 1963) £40
ACHILLES AND THE TWINS (illustrated by Carol Barker) (Dennis Dobson, 1964) £40
THE WHITE ADMIRAL (illustrated by P. Chapman) (Dennis Dobson, 1968) £40

BAUM, L. Frank

American author. Born: Lyman Frank Baum in Chittenago, New York, in 1856. Launched his career as a children's writer with *Mother Goose in Prose* (1897), following this three years later with *The Wonderful Wizard of Oz* (1900). Many more 'Oz' books followed, along with several other children's fantasies. After his death in 1919, the series was continued by Ruth Plumly Thompson and John R. Neill.

Prices are for books in Very Good condition.

'Oz' books

THE WONDERFUL WIZARD OF OZ (illustrated by W.W. Denslow) (George M. Hill, US, 1900) £15,000
SECOND US EDITION (as THE NEW WIZARD OF OZ; illustrated by W.W. Denslow) (Bobbs-Merrill, US, 1903) £700
FIRST UK EDITION (as THE NEW WIZARD OF OZ; illustrated by W.W. Denslow) (Hodder & Stoughton, 1906) £900
FILM TIE-IN EDITION (as THE WIZARD OF OZ: the original story on which the film is based;
  illustrated by W.W. Denslow, with 4 colour stills from the MGM film) (Hutchinson, UK, [1939]) £325
BAUM EDITION (Dent, 1965) (illustrated by L. Frank Baum) £30
ANNOTATED EDITION (as THE ANNOTATED WIZARD OF OZ; edited by Michael Patrick Hearn)
  (Clarkson N. Potter, US, 1973) £70
HAGUE EDTION (illustrated by Michael Hague) (Holt, US, 1982) £40
POP-UP WIZARD OF OZ (Pop-up version, with illustrations by Robert Sabuda, in the style of W.W. Denslow)
  (Simon & Schuster, 2000) £15
THE MARVELOUS LAND OF OZ (illustrated by John R. Neill; red or light green binding) (Reilly & Britton, US, 1904) £4,000
THE MARVELOUS LAND OF OZ (illustrated by John R. Neill) (Fleming H. Recell, 1904) £900
THE MARVELOUS LAND OF OZ (as THE MARVELLOUS LAND OF OZ; illustrated by John R. Neill)
  (Hodder & Stoughton, 1906) £500
OZMA OF OZ (illustrated by John R. Neill) (Reilly& Britton, US, 1907) £3,000
OZMA OF OZ (illustrated by John R. Neill) (Hutchinson, 1942) £75
DOROTHY AND THE WIZARD IN OZ (illustrated by John R. Neill) (Reilly & Britton, US, 1908) £3,000
THE ROAD TO OZ (illustrated by John R. Neill) (Reilly & Britton, US, 1909) £3,000

BAUM, L. Frank

THE EMERALD CITY OF OZ (illustrated by John R. Neill) (Reilly & Britton, US, 1910) **£3,000**
THE PATCHWORK GIRL OF OZ (illustrated by John R. Neill) (Reilly & Britton, US, 1913) **£3,000**
TIK-TOK OF OZ (illustrated by John R. Neill) (Reilly & Britton, US, 1914)... **£1,750**
THE SCARECROW OF OZ (illustrated by John R. Neill) (Reilly & Britton, US, 1915) **£1,000**
RINKITINK IN OZ (illustrated by John R. Neill) (Reilly & Britton, US, 1916) **£800**
THE LOST PRINCESS OF OZ (illustrated by John R. Neill) (Reilly & Britton, US, 1917) **£1,750**
THE TIN WOODMAN OF OZ (illustrated by John R. Neill) (Reilly & Britton, US, 1918) **£1,750**
THE MAGIC OF OZ (illustrated by John R. Neill) (Reilly & Lee, US, 1919) **£700**
GLINDA OF OZ (illustrated by John R. Neill) (Reilly & Lee, US, 1920) **£700**

'Little wizard' books

THE COWARDLY LION AND THE HUNGRY TIGER (illustrated by John R. Neill) (Reilly & Britton, US, 1913) **£100**
LITTLE DOROTHY AND TOTO (illustrated by John R. Neill) (Reilly & Britton, US, 1913) **£100**
TIK-TOK AND THE NOME KING (illustrated by John R. Neill) (Reilly & Britton, US, 1913) **£100**

All THIS TIME DOROTHY and her companions had been walking through the thick woods. The road was still paved with yellow brick, but these were much covered by dried branches and dead leaves from the trees, and the walking was not at all good.

There were few birds in this part of the forest, for birds love the open country where there is plenty of sunshine; but now and then there came a deep growl from some wild animal hidden among the trees. These sounds made the little girl's heart beat fast, for she did not know

One of W.W. Denslow's chapter heading illustrations from the first edition of
***The Wonderful Wizard of Oz** (1901), showing Dorothy, Toto and the Cowardly Lion.*

OZMA AND THE LITTLE WIZARD (illustrated by John R. Neill) (Reilly & Britton, US, 1913) **£100**
OZMA AND THE LITTLE WIZARD (as PRINCESS OZMA OF OZ) (Hutchinson, 1942) **£50**
JACK PUMPKINHEAD AND THE SAWHORSE (illustrated by John R. Neill) (Reilly & Britton, US, 1913) **£100**
THE SCARECROW AND THE TIN WOODMAN (illustrated by John R. Neill) (Reilly & Britton, US, 1913) **£100**
THE SCARECROW AND THE TIN WOODMAN (as SCARECROW AND THE TIN WOODMAN OF OZ) (Hutchinson, 1942) ..**£50**
LITTLE WIZARD STORIES OF OZ (comprises all the above titles; illustrated by John R. Neill) (Reilly & Britton, US, 1914) **£500**

Other 'Oz' books
PICTURES FROM THE WONDERFUL WIZARD OF OZ (booklet) (George W. Ogilvie, US, [1903]) **£250**
DENSLOW'S SCARECROW AND TIN MAN (booklet) (G.W. Dillingham, US, 1904) **£250**
THE WOGGLE-BUG BOOK (illustrated by Ike Morgan) (Reilly & Britton, US, 1905) **£1,750**
THE OZ TOY BOOK: Cut-Outs for the Kiddies (illustrated by John R. Neill) (Reilly & Britton, US, 1915) **£500**
THE LAND OF OZ STORY BOOK (Hutchinson, 1941) **£100**

'Oz' books by other authors
RUTH PLOMLY THOMPSON (All illustrated by John R. Neill and published by Reilly & Lee)
THE ROYAL BOOK OF OZ (1921); KABUMPO IN OZ (1922); THE COWARDLY LION OF OZ (1923); GRAMPA IN OZ (1924); THE LOST KING OF OZ (1925); THE HUNGRY TIGER OF OZ (1926); THE GNOME KING OF OZ (1927); THE GIANT HORSE OF OZ (1928); JACK PUMPKINHEAD OF OZ (1929); THE YELLOW KNIGHT OF OZ (1930); PIRATES IN OZ (1931); THE PURPLE PRINCE OF OZ (1932); OJO IN OZ (1933); SPEEDY IN OZ (1934); THE WISHING HORSE OF OZ (1935); CAPTAIN SALT IN OZ (1936); HANDY MANDY IN OZ (1937); THE SILVER PRINCESS IN OZ (1938); OZOPLANING WITH THE WIZARD OF OZ (1939)
JOHN R. NEILL (All illustrated by the author and published by Reilly & Lee)
THE WONDER CITY OF OZ (1940); THE SCALAWAGONS OF OZ (1941); LUCKY BUCKY IN OZ (1942);
JACK SNOW (Both illustrated by Frank Kramer and published by Reilly & Lee)
THE MAGICAL MIMICS IN OZ (1946); THE SHAGGY MAN OF OZ (1949)
OTHERS
Cosgrove, Rachel: THE HIDDEN VALLEY OF OZ (illustrated by 'Dirk' Gringhuis) (Reilly & Lee, 1951); McGraw, Eloise Jarvis & Wagner, Lauren McGraw: MERRY GO ROUND IN OZ (Reilly & Lee, 1963); McGraw, Eloise Jarvis & Wagner, Lauren McGraw: THE FORBIDDEN FOUNTAIN OF OZ (Int. Wizard of Oz Club, 1980); Martin, Dick: THE OZMAPOLITAN OF OZ (Int. Wizard of Oz Club, 1986); Maguire, Gregory:WICKED: The Life & Times of The Wicked Witch of the West (HarperCollins, US, 1995)

Other books by Frank L. Baum
MOTHER GOOSE IN PROSE (illustrated by Maxfield Parrish) (Way & Williams, US, 1897) **£3,000**
MOTHER GOOSE IN PROSE (illustrated by Maxfield Parrish) (Duckworth, 1899).................**£700**
FATHER GOOSE: HIS BOOK (illustrated by R.F. Seymour) (George M. Hill, US, 1899) **£3,000**
FATHER GOOSE: HIS BOOK (illustrated by R.F. Seymour) (George M. Hill, US, 1900) **£1,000**
SONGS OF FATHER GOOSE: a selection of verses set to music by Alberta N. Hall (George M. Hill, US, 1900) **£500**
A NEW WONDERLAND (illustrated by Frank Berbeck) (Russell, US, 1900) **£1,750**
THE ARMY ALPHABET (illustrated by Harry Kennedy) (George M. Hill, US, 1900) **£900**
THE NAVY ALPHABET (illustrated by Harry Kennedy) (George M. Hill, US, 1900) **£900**
AMERICAN FAIRY TALES (illustrated by Ike Morgan, Harry Kennedy and N.P. Hall) (George M. Hill, US, 1901) **£1,000**
DOT AND TOT OF MERRYLAND (illustrated by W.W. Denslow) (Hill, US, 1901) **£1,000**
THE MASTER KEY: An Electrical Fairy Tale (Bowen-Merrill, US, 1901) **£500**
THE MASTER KEY: An Electrical Fairy Tale (Stevens & Brown, [1902]) **£500**
THE LIFE AND ADVENTURES OF SANTA CLAUS (illustrated by Mary Cowles Clark) (Bobbs-Merrill, US, 1902) **£700**
THE LIFE AND ADVENTURES OF SANTA CLAUS (illustrated by Mary Cowles Clark) (Stevens & Brown, 1902)...........**£600**
THE SURPRISING ADVENTURES OF THE MAGICAL MONARCH OF MO AND HIS PEOPLE
(illustrated by F. Berbeck) (Bobbs-Merrill, US, 1903) **£600**
THE ENCHANTED ISLAND OF YEW (illustrated by Fanny Cory) (Bobbs-Merrill, US, [1903]) **£500**
QUEEN ZIXI OF IX, or The Story of the Magic Cloak (illustrated by Frederick Richardson) (Century, US, 1905) **£600**
QUEEN ZIXI OF IX (same as above, but with different title page) (Hodder & Stoughton, 1905) **£350**
JOHN DOUGH AND THE CHERUB (illustrated by John R. Neill) (Reilly & Britton, US, 1906) **£600**
JOHN DOUGH AND THE CHERUB (with John Dough Mystery form intact) (Reilly & Britton, US, 1906)...........**£800**
JOHN DOUGH AND THE CHERUB (illustrated by John R. Neill) (Constable, 1906) **£500**
THE LAST EGYPTIAN: A Romance of the Nile (illustrated by Francis P. Wightman) (Reilly & Britton, US, 1908) **£300**
THE SEA FAIRIES (illustrated by John R. Neill) (Reilly & Britton, US, 1911) **£500**
SKY ISLAND (illustrated by John R. Neill) (Reilly & Britton, US, 1912) **£500**

BAWDEN, Nina
British author. Born: London, 1925. A high reputation in books for adults and children, and notable for and *Carrie's War* (1973) and *The Peppermint Pig* (1975).
Prices are for books in Very Good condition with dustjackets where applicable.

DEVIL BY THE SEA (Collins, 1957)..................**£50**
THE SECRET PASSAGE (Gollancz, 1963)..................**£40**
ON THE RUN (Gollancz, 1964) **£30**
THE WHITE HORSE GANG (Gollancz, 1966) **£30**
THE WITCH'S DAUGHTER (illustrated by Shirley Hughes) (Gollancz, 1966)..................**£30**
A HANDFUL OF THIEVES (Gollancz, 1967) **£20**
THE RUNAWAY SUMMER (Gollancz, 1969)..................**£20**

As this photograph clearly shows, S.G. Hulme Beaman's famous 'Toytown' books were issued in a wide variety of formats.

SQUIB (illustrated by Shirley Hughes) (Gollancz, 1971) £20
CARRIE'S WAR (Gollancz, 1973) £30
THE PEPPERMINT PIG (illustrated by Alexy Pendle) (Gollancz, 1975) £30
REBEL ON A ROCK (sequel to 'Carrie's War') (Gollancz, 1978) £20
THE ROBBERS (illustrated by Charles Keeping) (Gollancz, 1979) £20
WILLIAM TELL (illustrated by Pascale Allamand) (Cape, 1981) £15
KEPT IN THE DARK (Gollancz, 1982) £15
THE FINDING (Gollancz, 1985) £15
PRINCESS ALICE (illustrated by Phillida Gili) (Deutsch, 1985) £15

BAYLEY, Nicola

British illustrator. Born: 1949. Produced *Nicola Bayley's Book of Nursery Rhymes* in 1975 and illustrations for books by Richard Adams, Russell Hoban and William Mayne.

Prices are for books in Very Good condition with dustjackets where applicable.

Books Written and Illustrated by Nicola Bayley

BOOK OF NURSERY RHYMES (Cape, 1973) £50
NICOLA BAYLEY'S BOOK OF NURSERY RHYMES (eight volumes; pictorial boards) (Cape, 1975) ....the set £65
PUSS IN BOOTS (pop-up book) (Cape, 1976) £30
ONE OLD OXFORD OX (pictorial boards) (Cape, 1977) £15

PUSS IN BOOTS (pop-up) (Greenwillow, 1977) £15
ELEPHANT CAT (Walker, 1984) £15
CRAB CAT (Walker, 1984) £15
SPIDER CAT (Walker, 1984) £15
POLAR BEAR CAT (Walker, 1984) £15
BEDTIME & MOONSHINE (Walker, 1987) £20
HUSH-A-BYE-BABY (eight volumes; pictorial boards) (Sainsbury's, 1985) .... the set £25
AS I WAS GOING UP AND DOWN (eight volumes; pictorial boards) (Sainsbury's/Walker Books, 1985) ...... the set £25
THE NECESSARY CAT (Walker, 1998) £10

Books Illustrated by Nicola Bayley
THE TYGER VOYAGE by Richard Adams (Cape, 1976) £30
LA CORONA AND THE TIN FROG by Russell Hoban (Cape, 1979) £25
THE PATCHWORK CAT by William Mayne (Cape, 1981) £30
THE MOULDY by William Mayne (Cape, 1983) £25
BOY by Paul Manning (Macmillan, 1987) £15
TAIL FEATHERS FROM MOTHER GOOSE by Iona Opie (illustrated by Maurice Sendak, Janet Ahlberg,
    Nicola Bayley, Quentin Blake, John Burningham and Anthony Browne) (Walker, 1988) £25
THE MOUSEHOLE CAT by Antonia Barber (Walker, 1990) £20
FUN WITH MRS THUMB by Jan Mark (Walker, 1993) £10

BEAMAN, S.G. Hulme
British author-illustrator. Born: Sydney George Hulme Beaman in London in 1886. Began as a toymaker, but then turned to drawing strips in which the characters were all represented as toys. His popular 'Toytown' stories, featuring Larry the Lamb, were later adapted for BBC Radio's *Children's Hour*, remaining firm favourites until the programme's demise in 1964. Beaman died in 1932.

Prices are for books in Very Good condition with dustjackets where applicable.

ALADDIN (retold and illustrated by S.G. Hulme Beaman) (John Lane The Bodley Head, 1924) £70
THE ROAD TO TOYTOWN (1925) £100
THE SEVEN VOYAGES OF SINBAD THE SAILOR (retold and illustrated by S.G. Hulme Beaman)
    (John Lane The Bodley Head, 1926) £80
'OUT OF THE ARK' BOOKS (six books) (Warne, [1927]) .... each £30
TALES OF TOYTOWN (written and illustrated by S.G. Hulme Beaman) (Humphrey Milford, 1928) £150
JOHN TRUSTY (written and illustrated by S.G. Hulme Beaman) (Collins, [1929]) £50
WIRELESS IN TOYTOWN (written and illustrated by S.G. Hulme Beaman) (Collins, 1930) £80
THE SMITH FAMILY by H.C. Craddock (illustrated by S.G. Hulme Beaman) (Nelson, [1931]) £40
THE TOYTOWN MYSTERY (written and illustrated by S.G. Hulme Beaman) (Collins, [1932]) £80
STORIES FROM TOYTOWN (written and illustrated by S.G. Hulme Beaman) (OUP, 1938) £65
TOYTOWN SERIES (also known as 'The Adventures of Larry the Lamb'; illustrated by Ernest Noble)
    (Lapworth, [1942-1947]) .... each £30
LARRY THE LAMB (illustrated by S.G. Hulme Beaman) (Collins, 1946) £60
TOYTOWN TALES (illustrated by George Moreno) (News of the World, [1952]) £40
THE CRUISE OF THE TOYTOWN BELLE (play; adapted by Hendrik Baker; paperback) (Samuel French, [1953]) £30
TOYTOWN SERIES (Oldbourne, 1957-1961) .... each £20

'BEANO'
Probably the best-known of all British comics, published by D.C. Thomson of Dundee. The comic itself first appeared on 30th July 1938. Among the title's most popular characters are Dennis the Menace, Biffo the Bear, Beryl the Peril and the Bash Street Kids.

Prices are for comics/annuals in Very Good condition (with cover description in brackets).

BEANO ISSUE 1 (D.C. Thomson, 30th July 1938) £10,000
THE BEANO BOOK 1940 (Pansy Potter holding see-saw for Big Eggo and other 'Beano' characters) £3,000
THE BEANO BOOK 1941 (Big Eggo and other 'Beano' characters appearing from large eggs) £1,000
THE BEANO BOOK 1942 (Lord Snooty playing bagpipes) £900
THE MAGIC BEANO BOOK 1943 (Big Eggo and others in three-legged race) £700
THE MAGIC BEANO BOOK 1944 ('Beano' characters in pillow fight) £550
THE MAGIC BEANO BOOK 1945 (Big Eggo and others playing leap-frog) £450
THE MAGIC BEANO BOOK 1946 (Big Eggo pulling others along in a cart) £400
THE MAGIC BEANO BOOK 1947 ('Beano' characters gathered around Big Eggo; quarto) £300
THE MAGIC BEANO BOOK 1948 (Big Eggo and others playing musical instruments; quarto) £250
THE MAGIC BEANO BOOK 1949 (Biffo, Big Eggo and others around a taxi; quarto) £200
THE MAGIC BEANO BOOK 1950 (Biffo, painting portrait of Big Eggo; quarto) £150
THE BEANO BOOK 1951 (Biffo riding on mechanical horse) £100
THE BEANO BOOK 1952 (Biffo nailing pictures of 'Beano' characters to cover) £75
THE BEANO BOOK 1953 (Jack Flash carrying 'Beano' characters on trips to the moon) £70
THE BEANO BOOK 1954 (Biffo hangs from a tree; Dennis holding lobster) £65
THE BEANO BOOK 1955 (Policeman stopping Dennis and Biffo from fishing) £55
THE BEANO BOOK 1956 (Biffo looking at Bash Street Kids) £55

'BEANO'

THE BEANO BOOK 1957 (Dennis kicking ball which rebounds off various characters).................................£55
THE BEANO BOOK 1958 (Biffo juggling; Dennis freeing bees from hive)..£55
THE BEANO BOOK 1959 (Dennis playing leapfrog with a goat) £55
THE BEANO BOOK 1960 (Biffo completing Bash Street Kids jigsaw) £45
THE BEANO BOOK 1961 ('Beano' in large letters; with characters at top and bottom of cover) £45
THE BEANO BOOK 1962 (Jonah dancing on mast of sinking ship)..£45
THE BEANO BOOK 1963 (Bash Street Kids on large swing) £45
THE BEANO BOOK 1964 (Buster tickling Biffo with feather)...£45
THE BEANO BOOK 1965 (two children blowing up a Biffo balloon)...£40
THE BEANO BOOK 1966 (dated '1966' on cover) £30
THE BEANO BOOK 1967-69 ....each £25
THE BEANO BOOK 1970 ....£15
THE BEANO BOOK 1971-72 ....each £12
THE BEANO BOOK 1973-74 ....each £10
THE BEANO BOOK 1975-77 ....each £8
THE BEANO BOOK 1978-80 ....each £5
THE BEANO BOOK 1981-Present ....each £5

'BEEZER'

Another popular British comic published by D.C. Thomson. The comic itself was launched on 21st January 1956, the first *Beezer Book* appearing the following year. Among the title's best-known characters were Ginger, Baby Crocket and 'Pop, Dick and Harry'.

Prices are for comics/annuals in Very Good condition (with cover description in brackets).

BEEZER ISSUE 1 (D.C. Thomson, 21st January 1956) £125
THE BEEZER BOOK 1958 ....£65
THE BEEZER BOOK 1959 ....£20
THE BEEZER BOOK 1960-65 ....each £15
THE BEEZER BOOK 1966-69 ....each £12
THE BEEZER BOOK 1970-74 ....each £6
THE BEEZER BOOK 1975-77 ....each £4
THE BEEZER BOOK 1978-91 ....each £4

Two early issues from the great British comic publishers D.C. Thomson. **Beano** *was launched in July 1938,* **Beezer** *in January 1956.*

BELLOC, Hilaire

British author. Born: Joseph Hilaire Pierre René Belloc in 1870. Educated at the Oratory School in Birmingham and Balliol College, Oxford. Belloc wrote a large number of adult works, many of them reflecting his Catholic faith, as well as some very popular collections of humorous verses for children. Died: 1953.

Prices are for books in Very Good condition.

VERSES AND SONNETS (Ward & Downey, 1896) £200
THE BAD CHILD'S BOOK OF BEASTS (illustrated by Basil Blackwood) (Alden Press, 1896)............£120
MORE BEASTS (FOR WORSE CHILDREN) (illustrated by Basil Blackwood) (Arnold, 1897) £100
A MORAL ALPHABET (illustrated by Basil Blackwood) (Arnold, 1899)..£100
CAUTIONARY TALES FOR CHILDREN (illustrated by Basil Blackwood) (Eveleigh Nash, 1908).........£70
MORE PEERS (illustrated by Basil Blackwood) (Stephen Swift, 1911)..£60
NEW CAUTIONARY TALES (illustrated by Nicolas Bentley) (Duckworth, 1930) £70
NEW CAUTIONARY TALES (illustrated by Nicolas Bentley; De Luxe edition: limited to 110 copies, signed by the author)
    (Duckworth, 1930) £150
CAUTIONARY VERSES: The Collected Humorous Verses of Hilaire Belloc (Duckworth, 1939)............£50

BEMELMANS, Ludwig

Austrian author. Born in 1898 and emigrated to America in 1914. Notable for his 'Madeline' picture books, with verse texts. *Madeline's Rescue* (1953) won the Caldecott Medal. Died: 1962.

Prices are for books in Very Good condition with dustjackets where applicable.

'Madeline' Books

MADELINE (Simon & Schuster, U.S., 1939) £150
MADELINE (Derek Verschoyle, 1952)...£80
MADELINE'S RESCUE (Viking Press, U.S., 1953)..£125
MADELINE'S RESCUE (Derek Verschoyle, 1953) £80
MADELINE AND THE BAD HAT (limited to 985 copies, signed by the author) (Viking Press, U.S., 1956) £175
MADELINE AND THE BAD HAT (trade edition) (Viking Press, U.S., 1957) £125
MADELINE AND THE BAD HAT (Deutsch, 1958)..£60
MADELINE AND THE GYPSIES (Viking Press, U.S., 1959)..£100
MADELINE AND THE GYPSIES (Deutsch, 1961)..£60
MADELINE IN LONDON (Viking Press, U.S., 1961)..£100
MADELINE IN LONDON (Deutsch, 1962)...£60
MADELINE'S CHRISTMAS (completed by Madeline and Barbara Bemelmans) (Viking Kestrel, U.S., 1985) £15
MADELINE'S CHRISTMAS (completed by Madeline and Barbara Bemelmans) (Deutsch, 1985) £15

Others

HANSI (Viking Press, U.S., 1934)...£100
HANSI (Lovat Dickson, 1935)...£60
THE GOLDEN BASKET (Viking Press, U.S., 1936) £60
THE CASTLE NUMBER 9 (Viking Press, U.S., 1937) £60
QUITO EXPRESS (Viking Press, U.S., 1938) £60
ROSEBUD (Random House, U.S., 1942)...£50
A TALE OF TWO GLIMPS (CBS, U.S., 1947) £20
THE HAPPY PLACE (Little Brown, U.S., 1952) £20
THE HIGH WORLD (Harper, U.S., 1954) £20
THE HIGH WORLD (Hamish Hamilton, 1958) £15
PARSLEY (Harper, U.S., 1955) £20

BERESFORD, Elisabeth

British author and creator of the Wombles. Born: Paris in 1926, the daughter of the popular novelist, J.D. Beresford. Educated at Brighton and Hove High School, and served in the WRNS during the war. Married the TV presenter, Max Robertson, in 1949, and subsequently wrote extensively for television, which provided the subject for her first book. Best known for *The Wombles* (1968) and its many sequels, but has also written children's fantasies and adult romances.

Prices are for books in Very Good condition with dustjackets where applicable.

'Wombles' Books

THE WOMBLES (illustrated by Margaret Gordon) (Benn, 1968)..£75
THE WANDERING WOMBLES (illustrated by Oliver Chadwick) (Benn, 1970)....................................£50
THE INVISIBLE WOMBLE and Other Stories (illustrated by Ivor Wood) (Benn, 1973) £50
THE WOMBLES IN DANGER (Benn, 1973)...£25
THE WOMBLES AT WORK (illustrated by Barry Leith) (Benn, 1973)...£20
THE WOMBLES GO THE SEASIDE (World Distributors, 1974) £22
THE WOMBLES GIFT BOOK (illustrated by Margaret Gordon and Derek Collard) (Benn, 1975)...........£15
THE SNOW WOMBLE (illustrated by Margaret Gordon) (Benn, 1975) £15
TOMSK AND THE TIRED TREE (illustrated by Margaret Gordon) (Benn, 1975)..................................£22

WELLINGTON AND THE BLUE BALLOON (illustrated by Margaret Gordon) (Benn, 1975) **£20**
ORINOCO RUNS AWAY (illustrated by Margaret Gordon) (Benn, 1975) **£12**
THE WOMBLES MAKE A CLEAN SWEEP (illustrated by Ivor Wood) (Benn, 1975) **£20**
THE WOMBLES TO THE RESCUE (illustrated by Margaret Gordon) (Benn, 1975)... **£12**
THE WOMBLES OF WIMBLEDON (contains 'The Wombles at Work' [illustrated by Barry Leith] and
'The Wombles to the Rescue' [illustrated by Margaret Gordon]) (Benn, 1976) **£12**
THE MACWOMBLE'S PIPE BAND (illustrated by Margaret Gordon) (Benn, 1976) **£12**
MADAME CHOLET'S PICNIC PARTY (illustrated by Margaret Gordon) (Benn, 1976) **£12**
BUNGO KNOWS BEST (illustrated by Margaret Gordon) (Benn, 1976) **£20**
TOBERMORY'S BIG SURPRISE (illustrated by Margaret Gordon) (Benn, 1976)... **£12**
THE WOMBLES GO ROUND THE WORLD (illustrated by Margaret Gordon) (Benn, 1976) **£12**
THE WORLD OF THE WOMBLES (illustrated by Edgar Hodges) (World Distributors, 1976) **£12**
WOMBLING FREE (illustrated by Edgar Hodges) (Benn, 1978) **£12**

Others

THE TELEVISION MYSTERY (Parrish, 1957) **£30**
THE FLYING DOCTOR MYSTERY (Parrish, 1958) **£22**
TROUBLE AT TULLINGTON CASTLE (Parrish, 1958).. **£22**
COCKY AND THE MISSING CASTLE (illustrated by Jennifer Miles) (Constable, 1959).................................... **£22**
GAPPY GOES WEST (Parrish, 1959)... **£22**
THE TULLINGTON FILM-MAKERS (Parrish, 1960) **£12**
TWO GOLD DOLPHINS (illustrated by Peggy Fortnum) (Constable, 1961)... **£12**
DANGER ON THE OLD PULL'N PUSH (Parrish, 1962) **£10**
STRANGE HIDING PLACE (Parrish, 1962)... **£10**
DIANA IN TELEVISION (Collins, 1963)... **£10**
THE MISSING FORMULA MYSTERY (Parrish, 1963)... **£10**
THE MULBERRY STREET TEAM (illustrated by Juliet Pannett) (Friday Press, 1963).. **£12**
AWKWARD MAGIC (illustrated by Judith Valpy) (Hart-Davis, 1964) **£10**
THE FLYING DOCTOR TO THE RESCUE (Parrish, 1964) **£10**
HOLIDAY FOR SLIPPY (illustrated by Pat Williams) (Friday Press, 1964) **£12**
GAME, SET AND MATCH (Parrish, 1965).. **£20**
KNIGHTS OF THE CARDBOARD CASTLE (illustrated by C.R. Evans) (Methuen, 1965)..................................... **£10**
TRAVELLING MAGIC (illustrated by Judith Valpy) (Hart-Davis, 1965).. **£10**
THE HIDDEN MILL (illustrated by Margery Gill) (Benn, 1965)... **£10**
PETER CLIMBS A TREE (illustrated by Margery Gill) (Benn, 1966) **£10**
FASHION GIRL (Collins, 1967) **£10**
THE BLACK MOUNTAIN MYSTERY (Parrish, 1967).. **£10**
LOOKING FOR A FRIEND (illustrated by Margery Gill) (Benn, 1967).. **£10**

The Wombles

Elisabeth Beresford

Illustrated by MARGARET GORDON

The book that introduced the world to the 'Wombles' in 1968. Jacketed copies in Very Good condition are now worth £50.

Cecil Aldin's works remain very popular with collectors of children's books.

*Both these plates come from important illustrated editions of Hans Andersen's **Fairy Tales**.*
Above is an example by Harry Clark, the plate opposite is by the great Victorian illustrator 'E.V.B.'.

Several rare first editions from L. Frank Baum's very collectable and influential 'Oz' series.

The WONDER-FUL WIZARD of OZ
BY L. FRANK BAUM
PICTURES BY W.W. DENSLOW

THE MAGIC of OZ
By L. Frank Baum
Illustrated by John R Neill

DOROTHY and the WIZARD in OZ
By L. Frank Baum

OZMA OF OZ
L. FRANK BAUM

Glinda of Oz
by L. Frank Baum
Illustrated by Jno R Neill

THE EMERALD CITY OF OZ
L. Frank Baum

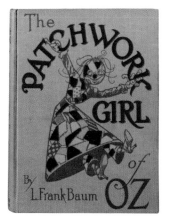

The PATCHWORK GIRL of OZ
By L. Frank Baum

Tik-Tok of OZ
By L. Frank Baum

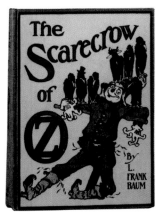

The Scarecrow of OZ
BY L. FRANK BAUM

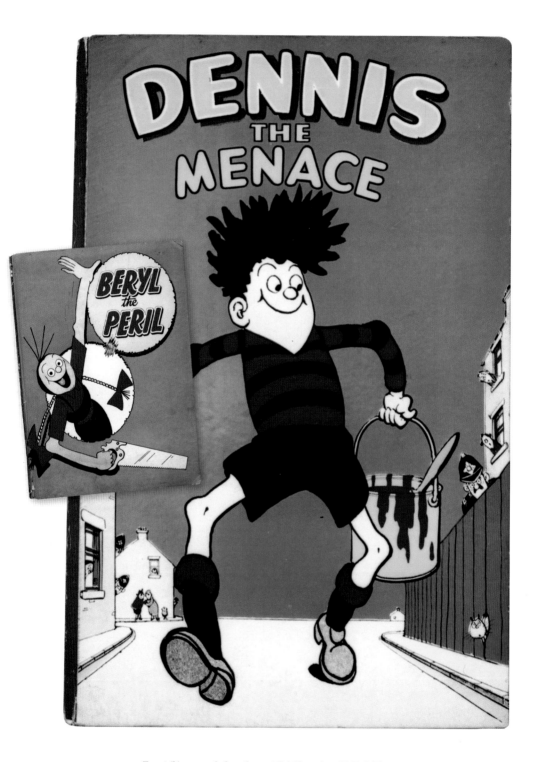

Two striking annuals from the great British comic stable D.C. Thomson.

The much-loved 'Faraway Tree' series from the prolific Enid Blyton.

*Three perveyers of the 'schoolgirl' story, including the ever-popular
Elinor Brint-Dyer, plus the less well-known Angela Brazil and Elsie J. Oxenham.*

The adventures of William Brown remain very collectable and are hard to find with their dustjackets intact.

*Several 'Alice' rarities including the first edition of **Alice's Adventures in Wonderland** (above left), its sequel **Through the Looking Glass**, and the later facimile edition of **Alice's Adventures Under Ground** – the book's original title. Pictured opposite are a number of collectable illustrated editions. The famous withdrawn edition of **Alice's Adventures in Wonderland** is currently worth £200,000.*

Roald Dahl remains one of Britain's most popular children's writers. MAny of his early books were published first in America, long before they appeared in the UK.

*Despite a dip in the popularity of Disney books and
annuals with collectors, they remain highly desirable items.*

*Randolph Caldecott (above) and Kate Greenaway (opposite)
dominated children's book illustration during the Victorian era.*

TRUE TO THE
OLD FLAG...
A TALE OF THE AMERICAN WAR
OF INDEPENDENCE...
BY G. A. HENTY

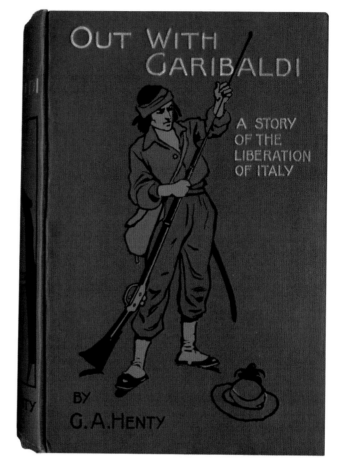

OUT WITH
GARIBALDI

A STORY
OF THE
LIBERATION
OF ITALY

BY
G·A·HENTY

G.A.HENTY

WITH CLIVE
IN INDIA

YOUNG·BUGLERS
G·A·HENTY
THE·BOYS
POCKET·LIBRARY

IN·TIMES of PERIL
G·A·HENTY
THE·BOYS
NEW·LIBRARY

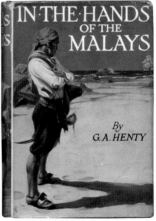

IN·THE·HANDS
OF THE
MALAYS

By
G·A·HENTY

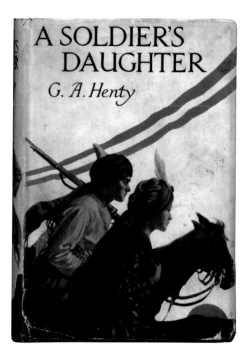

Some examples of the boys' adventure novels of G.A. Henty. It is very rare to find them in such good condition, and with the dustjackets intact.

W.E. Johns remains as popular as ever with collectors. Starting with the first 'Biggles' book **The Camels Are Coming**, these are some of his most valuable hardbacks. Also pictured is the very rare first paperback edition of **Mossyface**, which he wrote under the name 'William Earle', and the first in his little-known SF series, which began in 1954 with **Kings of Space**.

Five books in the 'Narnia' series by C.S. Lewis, including the first **The Lion, The Witch and The Wardrobe**.

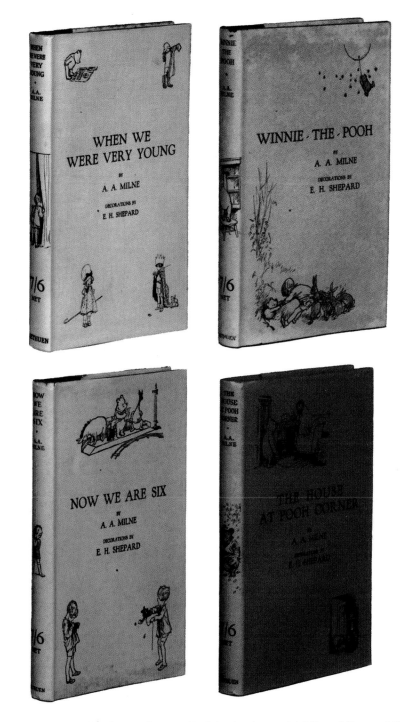

Dustjacketed first editions of the four phenomenally successful collaborations between A.A. Milne and illustrator E.H. Shepard.

Various Beatrix Potters including the second private printing (top left) and first trade edition (top right) of her debut **Peter Rabbit**; *the first privately printed (above left) and trade editions (above right) of* **The Tailor of Gloucester**; *and a host of other collectables including ordinary trade editions, and deluxe copies of her most famous works.*

THE TALE OF
MRS. TITTLEMOUSE

BY
BEATRIX POTTER

F. WARNE & Cᵒ

THE TALE OF
TIMMY TIPTOES

BY
BEATRIX POTTER

F. WARNE & Cᵒ

THE TALE OF
JOHNNY TOWN-MOUSE

BY
BEATRIX POTTER

F. WARNE & Cᵒ

THE · TALE · OF
LITTLE
PIG ROBINSON

By
BEATRIX · POTTER

The Tale of
Benjamin Bunny

Beatrix Potter

The Tale of
Tom Kitten

Beatrix Potter

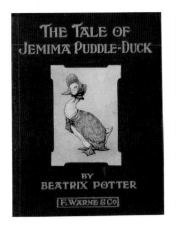

THE TALE OF
JEMIMA PUDDLE-DUCK

BY
BEATRIX POTTER

F. WARNE & Cᵒ

JEANNOT LAPIN

PAR
BEATRIX POTTER

F. WARNE & Cᵒ Lᴰ

The Story of
Tabbykin Town

In School and at Play

The collectable incarnations of 'Rupert', from early books by Mary Tourtel, to the very expensive Rupert Annuals.

The beautifully bound Christmas gift-books all illustrated by Arthur Rackham. The plate on the right comes from **Gulliver's Travels**.

The books of these modern authors have all become regulars at auction. The UK first editions
in Philip Pullman's 'His Dark Materials' trilogy, the first self-published edition of G.P. Taylor's
Shadowmancer, and Steve Augarde's second children's novel **Celandine**.

*The first editions, rare paperback proof copies and signed deluxe
editions of the first three books in the 'Harry Potter' series.*

*The striking wrapparound dustjacket for the first edition of **The Hobbit** was designed by the author himself.*

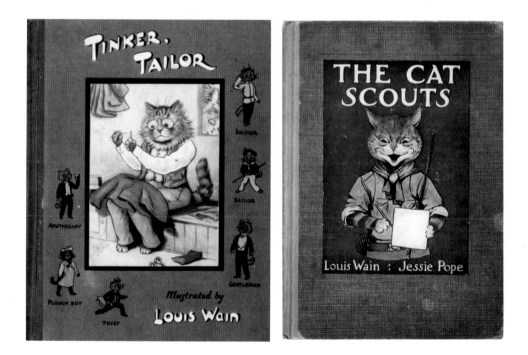

A selection of books and annuals by the very collectable cat artist Louis Wain.

*The very rare **Gran'pop's Annual** by illustrator Lawson Wood.*

THE ISLAND BUS (illustrated by Robert Hodgson) (Methuen, 1968) £10
SEA-GREEN MAGIC (illustrated by Ann Tout) (Hart-Davis, 1968)...£10
DAVID GOES FISHING (illustrated by Imre Hofbauer) (Benn, 1969) £10
GORDON'S GO-KART (illustrated by Margery Gill) (Benn, 1970)..£10
STEPHEN AND THE SHAGGY DOG (illustrated by Robert Hales) (Methuen, 1970)...............................£8
VANISHING MAGIC (illustrated by Ann Tout) (Hart-Davis, 1970) £8
DANGEROUS MAGIC (illustrated by Oliver Chadwick) (Hart-Davis, 1972) £8
THE SECRET RAILWAY (illustrated by James Hunt) (Methuen, 1973)..£8
INVISIBLE MAGIC (illustrated by Reg Gray) (Hart-Davis, 1974) £8
SNUFFLE TO THE RESCUE (illustrated by Gunvor Edwards) (Kestrel, 1975)...£8
TOBY'S LUCK (illustrated by Doreen Caldwell) (Methuen, 1978) £8
SECRET MAGIC (illustrated by Caroline Sharpe) (Hart-Davis, 1978) £8
THE HAPPY GHOST (illustrated by Joanna Carey) (Methuen, 1979) £8
THE TREASURE HUNTERS (illustrated by Joanna Carey) (Methuen, 1980)...£6
CURIOUS MAGIC (illustrated by Jayel Jordan) (Granada, 1980)..£6
THE FOUR OF US (illustrated by Trevor Stubley) (Hutchinson, 1981)..£6
THE ANIMALS NOBODY WANTED (illustrated by Joanna Carey) (Methuen, 1982) £6
THE TOVERS (illustrated by Geoffrey Beitz) (Methuen, 1982)...£6
JACK AND THE MAGIC STOVE Retold by Elisabeth Beresford (illustrated by Rita van Bilsen) (Hutchinson, 1982).................£6
THE ADVENTURES OF POON (illustrated by Dinah Shedden) (Hutchinson, 1984) £6
THE MYSTERIOUS ISLAND (illustrated by Joanna Carey) (Methuen, 1984)...£6
ONE OF THE FAMILY (illustrated by Barry Thorpe) (Hutchinson, 1985)...£6
THE GHOSTS OF LUPUS STREET SCHOOL (illustrated by Oliver Chadwick) (Methuen, 1986)..................£5
STRANGE MAGIC (illustrated by Judith Valpy) (Methuen, 1986)..£5
ONCE UPON A TIME STORIES (illustrated by Alice Englander) (Methuen, 1987)..£5
EMILY AND THE HAUNTED CASTLE (illustrated by Kate Rogers) (Hutchinson, 1987) £5
THE SECRET ROOM (Methuen, 1987)...£5
THE ARMADA ADVENTURE (Methuen, 1988)..£5
THE ISLAND RAILWAY (Hamish Hamilton, 1988)...£5
ROSE (Hutchinson, 1989)...£5
THE WOODEN GUN (Hutchinson, 1989)...£5
CHARLIE'S ARK (Methuen, 1989)...£5
TIM THE TRUMPET (Blackie, 1992)..£5
JAMIE AND THE ROLLA POLA BEAR (Blackie, 1993)..£5
LIZZY'S WAR (Simon & Schuster, 1993) £5

'BERYL THE PERIL' ANNUALS

Popular spin-off annual from the *Beano* comic. Published biennially by D.C. Thomson, but irregularly in later years (post-1981).

Prices are for annuals in Very Good condition.

BERYL THE PERIL 1959 ....£85
BERYL THE PERIL 1961 ....£35
BERYL THE PERIL 1963 ....£30
BERYL THE PERIL 1965 ....£25
BERYL THE PERIL 1967 ....£20
BERYL THE PERIL 1969 ....£20
BERYL THE PERIL 1971 ....£15
BERYL THE PERIL 1973 ....£15
BERYL THE PERIL 1975 ....£12
BERYL THE PERIL 1977 ....£10
BERYL THE PERIL 1979 ....£5
BERYL THE PERIL 1981-Present ....each £3

BESTALL, Alfred

British author-illustrator. Born: Alfred Edmeads Bestall in Mandalay, Burma, on 14th December 1892. Studied at Rydal School and Central School of Art, London, subsequently contributing work to *Blighty*, *Punch* and the *Tatler*, as well as illustrating works by Blyton, Dumas and other children's authors. Took over the *Daily Express*'s 'Rupert' strip from Mary Tourtel in 1935, and continued with the character until 1973. Awarded an MBE in 1985. Died: 1986.

Prices are for books in Very Good condition with dustjackets where applicable.

THE PLAY'S THE THING! by Enid Blyton (Home Library Book Co., [1927]) £100
MYTHS AND LEGENDS OF MANY LANDS. Retold by Evelyn Smith (Nelson, 1930) £85
THE SPANISH GOLD-FISH by Dudley Glass (Warne, [1934]) £85
MOTHER GOOSE (Warne, 1937)..£85
SCHOOLGIRL'S OWN ANNUALS (illustrated by Alfred Bestall and others) (1923 onwards) ....each £25
SCHOOLGIRL'S ALBUM (illustrated by Alfred Bestall and others) (1925-27) ....each £20
PLAYS FOR OLDER CHILDREN by Enid Blyton (Newnes, 1940)...£30
PLAYS FOR YOUNGER CHILDREN by Enid Blyton (Newnes, [1940]) £30
THE BOY NEXT DOOR by Enid Blyton (Newnes, 1944)..£40
THE LAND OF THE CHRISTMAS STOCKING by Mabel Buchanan (Latimer House, 1948) £30

BETJEMAN, John

British poet and architectural historian. Born: North London, 1906. Educated at Marlborough and Oxford University. Wrote many volumes of poetry and prose, but produced only two children's titles. Knighted in 1969, and appointed Poet Laureate in 1972. Died: 1984.

Prices are for books in Very Good condition with dustjackets.

A RING OF BELLS Introduced and selected by Irene Slade (new version of 'SUMMONED BY BELLS',
    revised for children; illustrated by Edward Ardizzone) (John Murray, 1962)...£50
ARCHIE AND THE STRICT BAPTISTS (illustrated by Phillida Gili) (John Murray, 1977) £30

'BIGGLES' Rivals

Below are a selection of collectable books featuring airmen adventurers in the style of 'Biggles'. For the complete 'Biggles' entry see 'JOHNS, W.E.'.

Prices are for books in Very Good condition with dustjackets where applicable.

'Ted Scott' by Franklin W. Dixon

OVER THE OCEAN TO PARIS or, TED SCOTT'S DARING LONG-DISTANCE FLIGHT (Grosset & Dunlap, US, 1927) £50
RESCUED IN THE CLOUDS or, TED SCOTT, HERO OF THE AIR (Grosset & Dunlap, US, 1927) £50
OVER THE ROCKIES WITH THE AIR MAIL or, TED SCOTT, LOST IN THE WILDERNESS (Grosset & Dunlap, US, 1927) ...£50
FIRST STOP HONOLULU or, TED SCOTT OVER THE PACIFIC (Grosset & Dunlap, US, 1928) £45
SEARCH FOR THE LOST FLYERS or, TED SCOTT OVER THE WEST INDIES (Grosset & Dunlap, US, 1928) £35
SOUTH OF THE RIO GRANDE or, TED SCOTT ON A SECRET MISSION (Grosset & Dunlap, US, 1928) £35
ACROSS THE PACIFIC or, TED SCOTT'S HOP TO AUSTRALIA (Grosset & Dunlap, US, 1928) £35
LONE EAGLE OF THE BORDER or, TED SCOTT AND THE DIAMOND SMUGGLERS (Grosset & Dunlap, US, 1929) £25
FLYING AGAINST TIME or, TED SCOTT BREAKING THE OCEAN TO OCEAN RECORD (Grosset & Dunlap, US, 1929) £25
OVER THE JUNGLE TRAILS or, TED SCOTT AND THE MISSING EXPLORERS (Grosset & Dunlap, US, 1929) £20
LOST AT THE SOUTH POLE or, TED SCOTT IN BLIZZARD LAND (Grosset & Dunlap, US, 1930) £30
THROUGH THE AIR TO ALASKA or, TED SCOTT'S SEARCH IN NUGGET VALLEY (Grosset & Dunlap, US, 1930) £20
FLYING TO THE RESCUE or, TED SCOTT AND THE BIG DIRIGIBLE (Grosset & Dunlap, US, 1930) £20
DANGER TRAILS OF THE SKY or, TED SCOTT'S GREAT MOUNTAIN CLIMB (Grosset & Dunlap, US, 1931) £20
FOLLOWING THE SUN SHADOW or, TED SCOTT AND THE GREAT ECLIPSE (Grosset & Dunlap, US, 1932) £30
BATTLING THE WIND or, TED SCOTT FLYING AROUND CAPE HORN (Grosset & Dunlap, US, 1933) £45
BRUSHING THE MOUNTAIN TOP or, TED SCOTT AIDING THE LOST TRAVELLER (Grosset & Dunlap, US, 1934) £45
CASTAWAYS OF THE STRATOSPHERE or, TED SCOTT HUNTING THE VANISHED BALLOONISTS (Grosset & Dunlap, US, 1935) £25
HUNTING THE SKY SPIES or, TESTING THE INVISIBLE PLANE (Grosset & Dunlap, US, 1941) £100
THE PURSUIT PATROL or, CHASING THE PLATINUM PIRATES (Grosset & Dunlap, US, 1943) £100

'Andy Lane' by Eustace L. Adams

FIFTEEN DAYS IN THE AIR (Grosset & Dunlap, US, 1928) £25
OVER THE POLAR ICE (Grosset & Dunlap, US, 1928) £25
RACING AROUND THE WORLD (Grosset & Dunlap, US, 1928) £30
THE RUNAWAY AIRSHIP (Grosset & Dunlap, US, 1929) £30
PIRATES OF THE AIR (Grosset & Dunlap, US, 1929) £30
ON WINGS OF FLAME (Grosset & Dunlap, US, 1929) £25
THE MYSTERIOUS MONOPLANE (Grosset & Dunlap, US, 1930) £25
THE FLYING WINDMILL (Grosset & Dunlap, US, 1930) £25
THE PLANE WITHOUT A PILOT (Grosset & Dunlap, US, 1930) £30
WINGS OF ADVENTURE (Grosset & Dunlap, US, 1931) £30
ACROSS THE TOP OF THE WORLD (Grosset & Dunlap, US, 1931) £35
PRISONERS OF THE CLOUDS (Grosset & Dunlap, US, 1932) £35

'Bill Bruce' by Major Henry Arnold

BILL BRUCE AND THE PIONEER AVIATORS (A.L. Burt, US, 1928) £25
BILL BRUCE, THE FLYING CADET (A.L. Burt, US, 1928) £20
BILL BRUCE BECOMES AN ACE (A.L. Burt, US, 1928) £20
BILL BRUCE ON BORDER PATROL (A.L. Burt, US, 1928) £20
BILL BRUCE AND THE TRANS-CONTINENTAL RACE (A.L. Burt, US, 1928) £20
BILL BRUCE ON FOREST PATROL (A.L. Burt, US, 1928) £20

'Rex Lee' by Thomson Burtis

REX LEE, GYPSY FLYER (Grosset & Dunlap, US, 1928) £35
REX LEE ON THE BORDER PATROL (Grosset & Dunlap, US, 1928) £25
REX LEE, RANGER OF THE SKY (Grosset & Dunlap, US, 1928) £25
REX LEE, SKY TRAILER (Grosset & Dunlap, US, 1929) £25
REX LEE, ACE OF THE AIR MAIL (Grosset & Dunlap, US, 1929) £20
REX LEE, NIGHT FLYER (Grosset & Dunlap, US, 1929) £20
REX LEE'S MYSTERIOUS FLIGHT (Grosset & Dunlap, US, 1930) £25
REX LEE, ROUGH RIDER OF THE AIR (Grosset & Dunlap, US, 1930) £25
REX LEE, AERIAL ACROBAT (Grosset & Dunlap, US, 1930) £25
REX LEE TRAILING AIR BANDITS (Grosset & Dunlap, US, 1931) £25
REX LEE, FLYING DETECTIVE (Grosset & Dunlap, US, 1931) £25

*The last of the six 'Bill Bruce'
yarns. An American hero who
is largely forgotten today, all six
were first published in 1928.*

'Rud Riley' by Thomson Burtis
DAREDEVILS OF THE AIR (Grosset & Dunlap, US, 1932) **£15**
FOUR ACES (Grosset & Dunlap, US, 1932) **£15**
WING FOR WING (Grosset & Dunlap, US, 1932) **£15**

'Jack Ralston' by Ambrose Newcomb
THE SKY DETECTIVE or, HOW JACK RALSTON GOT HIS MAN (Goldsmith, US, 1930) **£25**
EAGLES OF THE SKY or, WITH JACK RALSTON ALONG THE AIR LANES (Goldsmith, US, 1930) **£25**
WINGS OVER THE ROCKIES or, JACK RALSTON'S NEW CLOUD CHASER (Goldsmith, US, 1930) **£25**
THE SKY PILOT'S GREAT CHASE or, JACK RALSTON'S DEAD STICK LANDING (Goldsmith, US, 1930) **£25**
TRACKERS OF THE FOG PACK or, JACK RALSTON FLYING BLIND (Goldsmith, US, 1931) **£25**
FLYING THE COAST SKYWAYS or, JACK RALSTON'S SWIFT PATROL (Goldsmith, US, 1931) **£25**

'Tim Murphy' by Graham M. Dean
DARING WINGS (Goldsmith, US, 1931) **£35**
SKY TRAILS (Goldsmith, US, 1932) **£25**
CIRCLE 4 PATROL (Goldsmith, US, 1933) **£20**
TREASURE HUNT OF THE S-18 (Goldsmith, US, 1934) **£20**

'Baldy's Angels' by Captain Robert Hawke
BALDY'S ANGELS (paperback) (Boys' Friend Library 369; Amalgamated Press, 1933) **£10**
THE DEATH SQUADRON (paperback) (Boys' Friend Library 377; Amalgamated Press, 1933) **£10**
THE AIR MUSKETEERS (paperback) (Boys' Friend Library 385; Amalgamated Press, 1933) **£10**
BEHIND THE ENEMY LINES (paperback) (Boys' Friend Library 400; Amalgamated Press, 1933) **£10**
WAR BIRDS (paperback) (Boys' Friend Library 433; Amalgamated Press, 1934) **£10**
SKULL OF THE SKIES (paperback) (Boys' Friend Library 462; Amalgamated Press, 1935) **£10**
FLAMING WINGS (paperback) (Boys' Friend Library 486; Amalgamated Press, 1935) **£10**
BALDY OF THE 'CAMEL' CORPS (paperback) (Boys' Friend Library 509; Amalgamated Press, 1936) **£10**
FIGHTING FURIES (paperback) (Boys' Friend Library 548; Amalgamated Press, 1936) **£10**
SPARKY DRIVES ON! (paperback) (Boys' Friend Library 600; Amalgamated Press, 1937) **£10**
THE HUMAN SHADOW (paperback) (Boys' Friend Library 700; Amalgamated Press, 1939) **£10**

'Bill Bolton' by Lt Noel Sainsbury Jr
BILL BOLTON, FLYING MIDSHIPMAN (Goldsmith, US, 1933) **£20**
BILL BOLTON AND THE FLYING FISH (Goldsmith, US, 1933) **£20**
BILL BOLTON AND THE HIDDEN DANGER (Goldsmith, US, 1933) **£20**
BILL AND THE WINGED CARTWHEELS (Goldsmith, US, 1933) **£20**

DAVE DAWSON,
FLIGHT
LIEUTENANT

by

R. SIDNEY BOWEN

THE WAR ADVENTURE SERIES

HUTCHINSON & CO. (Publishers) LTD.
LONDON : NEW YORK : MELBOURNE

The fifth in R. Sidney Bowen's 'Dave Dawson' adventures, issued by Hutchinson .

'Colin Standish' by Percy F. Westerman
THE AMIR'S RUBY (Blackie & Son, 1932) £25
THE WESTOW TALISMAN (Blackie & Son, 1934) £25
STANDISH OF THE AIR POLICE (Blackie & Son, 1935) £20
STANDISH GETS HIS MAN (Blackie & Son, 1938) £25
STANDISH LOSES HIS MAN (Blackie & Son, 1939) £25
STANDISH PULLS IT OFF (Blackie & Son, 1940) £25
STANDISH HOLDS ON (Blackie & Son, 1941) £25

'Jaggers' by John Templer
JAGGERS, AIR DETECTIVE (OUP, 1936) £20
JAGGERS SWOOPS AGAIN (OUP, 1937) £20
JAGGERS AT BAY (OUP, 1938) £20

'John Wentley' by J.F.C. Westerman
JOHN WENTLEY TAKES CHARGE (Collins, 1938) £25
JOHN WENTLEY INVESTIGATES (Collins, 1939) £25
JOHN WENTLEY WINS THROUGH (Collins, 1940)..£25

'Dave Dawson' by R. Sidney Bowen
DAVE DAWSON AT DUNKIRK (Hutchinson, 1941) £30
DAVE DAWSON WITH THE R.A.F. (Hutchinson, 1941) £30
DAVE DAWSON IN LIBYA (Hutchinson, 1941) £30
DAVE DAWSON ON CONVOY PATROL (Hutchinson, 1941) £35
DAVE DAWSON - FLIGHT LIEUTENANT (Hutchinson, 1941)..£35
DAVE DAWSON AT SINGAPORE (Hutchinson, 1942) £35
DAVE DAWSON WITH THE PACIFIC FLEET (Hutchinson, 1942) £30
DAVE DAWSON WITH THE AIR CORPS (Hutchinson, 1942) £30
DAVE DAWSON WITH THE COMMANDOS (Hutchinson, 1942) £30

DAVE DAWSON ON THE RUSSIAN FRONT (Hutchinson, 1943) £20
DAVE DAWSON WITH THE FLYING TIGERS (Hutchinson, 1943) £20
DAVE DAWSON ON GUADACANAL (Hutchinson, 1943) £20
DAVE DAWSON AT CASABLANCA (Hutchinson, 1944) £35
DAVE DAWSON WITH THE EIGHTH AIR FORCE (Hutchinson, 1944).. £150
DAVE DAWSON AT TRUK (Hutchinson, 1946) £200

'Steve Knight' by Tedd Copp
THE MYSTERY OF THE DEVIL'S HAND (Grosset & Dunlap, US, 1941) £20
THE BRIDGE OF BOMBERS (Grosset & Dunlap, US, 1941) £20
THE PHANTOM FLEET (Grosset & Dunlap, US, 1941) £20

'A Yankee Flier' by A.L. Avery
A YANKEE FLIER WITH THE R.A.F. (Grosset & Dunlap, US, 1941) £30
A YANKEE FLIER IN THE FAR EAST (Grosset & Dunlap, US, 1942) £30
A YANKEE FLIER IN THE SOUTH PACIFIC (Grosset & Dunlap, US, 1943)................................... £30
A YANKEE FLIER IN NORTH AFRICA (Grosset & Dunlap, US, 1944) £30
A YANKEE FLIER IN ITALY (Grosset & Dunlap, US, 1944) £30
A YANKEE FLIER OVER BERLIN (Grosset & Dunlap, US, 1944) £20
A YANKEE FLIER IN NORMANDY (Grosset & Dunlap, US, 1945) £20
A YANKEE FLIER ON A RESCUE MISSION (Grosset & Dunlap, US, 1945) £20
A YANKEE FLIER UNDER SECRET ORDERS (Grosset & Dunlap, US, 1946) £20

'Lucky Terell' by Canfield Cook
SPITFIRE PILOT (Grosset & Dunlap, US, 1942) £25
SKY ATTACK (Grosset & Dunlap, US, 1942) £25
SECRET MISSION (Grosset & Dunlap, US, 1943) £25
LOST SQUADRON (Grosset & Dunlap, US, 1943) £25
SPRINGBOARD TO TOKYO (Grosset & Dunlap, US, 1943) £25
WINGS OVER JAPAN (Grosset & Dunlap, US, 1944) £25
THE FLYING JET (Grosset & Dunlap, US, 1945) £25
THE FLYING WING (Grosset & Dunlap, US, 1946) £25

'Rockfist Rogan' by Frank S. Pepper *(writing as Hal Wilton)*
ROCKFIST ROGAN (Stewart Pepper & Son, 1950)... £30
ROCKFIST AT THE NORTH POLE (Stewart Pepper & Son, 1951)... £30
ROCKFIST IN THE KINGDOM OF THE KHAN (Stewart Pepper & Son, 1952)............................. £30

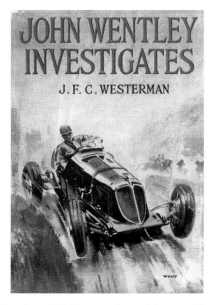

Percy's son J.F.C. Westerman also created a memorable airman hero, who went by the name of John Wentley.

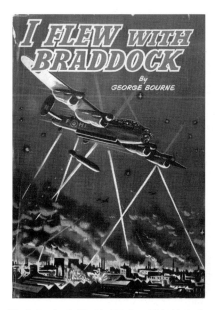

The first and only 'Braddock' to be published in book form was encased in this marvelous dustjacket.

There were nine 'Yankee Flyer' books published between 1941 and 1946 and all are very hard to find today.

Another morale-boosting 'Lucky Terrell Flying Story' by Canfield Cook, published in America in 1943.

The Amir's Ruby, the first of seven 'Standish' stories, is very rarely found in its original jacket.

The first adventure in the 'Battler Britton' series, first issued in these paperback wrappers by Fleetway in 1958.

'Red Randall' by R. Sidney Bowen
RED RANDALL AT PEARL HARBOR (Grosset & Dunlap, US, 1944) £25
RED RANDALL ON ACTIVE DUTY (Grosset & Dunlap, US, 1944) £25
RED RANDALL OVER TOKYO (Grosset & Dunlap, US, 1944) £25
RED RANDALL AT MIDWAY (Grosset & Dunlap, US, 1944) £25
RED RANDALL ON NEW GUINEA (Grosset & Dunlap, US, 1944) £25
RED RANDALL IN THE ALEUTIANS (Grosset & Dunlap, US, 1945) £25
RED RANDALL IN BURMA (Grosset & Dunlap, US, 1945) £25
RED RANDALL'S ONE MAN WAR (Grosset & Dunlap, US, 1946) £40

'David Wilshaw' by Captain A.O. Pollard
DAVID WILSHAW (AIR DETECTIVE) INVESTIGATES (Hutchinson, 1955) £30
THE POISONED PILOT (Hutchinson, 1956) £30
THE GOLDEN BUDDHA (Hutchinson, 1956) £30

'Braddock' by George Bourne
I FLEW WITH BRADDOCK (D.C. Thomson & John Leng, 1957) £20

'Hunter Hawk' by Eric Leyland & T.E. Scott-Chard
OUTLAWS OF THE AIR (Edmund Ward, 1957) £15
THE ATOM PLANE MYSTERY (Edmund Ward, 1958) £15
SMUGGLERS OF THE SKY (Edmund Ward, 1959) £15
COMMANDOS OF THE CLOUDS (Edmund Ward, 1959) £15
COMET ROUND THE WORLD (Edmund Ward, 1959) £15
THE SECRET WEAPON (Edmund Ward, 1960) £15
BANDIT GOLD (Edmund Ward, 1962) £15

'Battler Britton'
BATTLER BRITTON, WAR ACE (paperback) (Thriller Comics Library No 160; Fleetway, 1958) £8
BOOK I & II (Fleetway, 1960 & 1961) ....each £15

'Steve Canyon' by Milton Caniff
OPERATION CONVOY (Grosset & Dunlap, US, 1959) £20
OPERATION SNOWFLOWER (Grosset & Dunlap, US, 1959) £20
OPERATION FOO LING (Grosset & Dunlap, US, 1959) £20
OPERATION EEL ISLAND (Grosset & Dunlap, US, 1959) £20

'Dogfight Dixon'
DOGFIGHT DIXON, R.F.C. (paperback) (Thriller Picture Library No 307; Fleetway, 1960) £5
TRAITOR PILOT (paperback) (Air Ace Picture Library 297; Fleetway, 1966) £3
COURAGE-SKY HIGH (paperback) (Air Ace Picture Library 300; Fleetway, 1966) £3
THE MARK OF DOOM (paperback) (Air Ace Picture Library 305; Fleetway, 1966) £3
CLASH OF ARMS (paperback) (Air Ace Picture Library 307; Fleetway, 1966) £3
CHAIN OF COMMAND (paperback) (Air Ace Picture Library 312; Fleetway, 1966) £3
FLYING JOKER (paperback) (Air Ace Picture Library 316; Fleetway, 1966) £3
THE TROJAN WAR HORSE (paperback) (Air Ace Picture Library 320; Fleetway, 1966) £3
BALKAN BATTLE (paperback) (Air Ace Picture Library 325; Fleetway, 1967) £3
THE PHANTOM CAMEL (paperback) (Air Ace Picture Library 328; Fleetway, 1967) £3
HAWKS OF THE DESERT (paperback) (Air Ace Picture Library 332; Fleetway, 1967) £3

BIRO, Val
British author-illustrator. Born: Balint Stephen Biro in Budapest, Hungary, on 6th October 1921. Came to Britain in July 1939 to study art, subsequently working as a freelance illustrator and producing his first solo work, *Bumpy's Holiday*, in 1943. He is best known for the 'Gumdrop' series featuring an old Austin motor-car.
Prices are for books in Very Good condition with dustjackets where applicable.

BUMPY'S HOLIDAY (Sylvan Press, [1943]) £60
THE WONDERFUL WIZARD OF OZ by L. Frank Baum (Dent, 1965) £30
GUMDROP: The Adventures of a Vintage Car (Brockhampton Press, 1966) £60
GUMDROP AND THE FARMER'S FRIEND (Brockhampton Press, 1967) £30
GUMDROP ON THE RALLY (Brockhampton Press, 1968) £30
GUMDROP ON THE MOVE (Brockhampton Press, 1969) £30
GUMDROP GOES TO LONDON (Brockhampton Press, 1971) £25
THE HONEST THIEF: A Hungarian Folk Tale (Brockhampton Press, 1972) £10
GUMDROP FINDS A FRIEND (Brockhampton Press, 1973) £25
BUSTER IS LOST (Macmillan, 1974) £10
GUMDROP IN DOUBLE TROUBLE (Brockhampton Press, 1975) £20
A DOG AND HIS BONE (Macmillan, 1975) £10
BRER RABBIT AND THE TAR BABY by Enid Blyton (Hodder & Stoughton, 1975) £10
GUMDROP AND THE STEAMROLLER (Hodder & Stoughton, 1976) £18
GUMDROP POSTS A LETTER (Knight Books, 1976) £18
GUMDROP ON THE BRIGHTON RUN (Hodder & Stoughton, 1976) £15

GUMDROP HAS A BIRTHDAY (Hodder & Stoughton, 1977)..£10
THE DEVIL'S CUT by Clive King (Hodder & Stoughton, 1978)..£20
GUMDROP GETS HIS WINGS (Hodder & Stoughton, 1979)..£10
HUNGARIAN FOLK-TALES (OUP, 1980)..£10
GUMDROP FINDS A GHOST (Hodder & Stoughton, 1980)..£10
JUNGLE SILVER by H.E. Todd (Hodder & Stoughton, 1981)..£8
GUMDROP AND THE SECRET SWITCHES (Hodder & Stoughton, 1981)...£10
GUMDROP AT SEA (Hodder & Stoughton, 1982)...£10
THE MAGIC DOCTOR (OUP, 1982)..£10
GUMDROP MAKES A START (Hodder & Stoughton, 1982)..£8
GUMDROP AND HORACE (Hodder & Stoughton, 1982)...£8
GUMDROP RACES A TRAIN (Hodder & Stoughton, 1982)..£8
GUMDROP GOES TO SCHOOL (Hodder & Stoughton, 1983)..£8
THE WIND IN THE WILLOWS (Purnell, 1983)..£20
GUMDROP GETS A LIFT (Hodder & Stoughton, 1983)..£8
GUMDROP AT THE ZOO (Hodder & Stoughton, 1983)..£8
GUMDROP IN A HURRY (Hodder & Stoughton, 1983)...£8
FABLES FROM AESOP (eighteen volumes) (Ginn & Wright, 1983-1988)...........................the set £125
GUMDROP'S MAGIC JOURNEY (Hodder & Stoughton, 1984)...£8
GUMDROP FISHING (Hodder & Stoughton, 1984)..£8
GUMDROP HAS A TUMMY-ACHE (Hodder & Stoughton, 1984)...£8
GUMDROP IS THE BEST CAR (Hodder & Stoughton, 1984)...£8
GUMDROP ON THE FARM (Hodder & Stoughton, 1984)...£8
GUMDROP AND THE MONSTER (Hodder & Stoughton, 1985)...£8
THE HOBYAHS (OUP, 1985)..£10
THE PIED PIPER OF HAMELIN (OUP, 1985)..£10
TALES FROM HANS ANDERSEN (eighteen volumes) (Ginn & Wright, 1985-1989)................the set £75
THE DONKEY THAT SNEEZED (OUP, 1986)..£10
GUMDROP TO THE RESCUE (Hodder & Stoughton, 1986)...£5
GUMDROP AT SEA (Hodder & Stoughton, 1987)...£5
GUMDROP AND THE DINOSAUR (Hodder & Stoughton, 1988)..£5
DRANGO DRAGON (Ladybird, 1989)...£4
PETER CHEATER (Ginn, 1989)...£5
JACK AND THE BEANSTALK (OUP, 1989)...£10

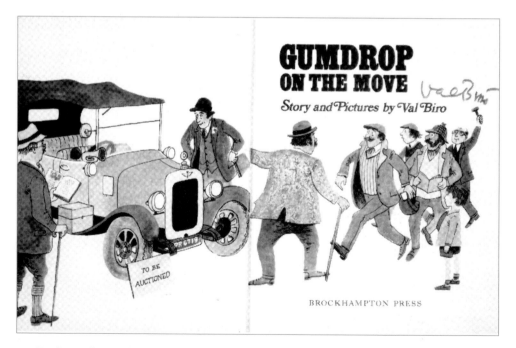

Gumdrop on the Move (1969) *was the fourth book to feature the little car. It is now worth £30 in Very Good condition.*

TOBIAS AND THE DRAGON: A Folk Tale from Hungary (Blackie, 1989)..£10
GUMDROP AND THE PIRATES (Hodder & Stoughton, 1989)..£5
THE THREE LITTLE PIGS (OUP, 1990) £10
LOOK AND FIND A.B.C. (Hippo Books, 1990) £5
MIRANDA'S UMBRELLA (Blackie, 1990)...£5
GUMDROP AND THE ELEPHANT (Hodder & Stoughton, 1990)..£5
GUMDROP AND THE BULLDOZERS (Hodder & Stoughton, 1991)..£5
GUMDROP FOR EVER! (paperback) (Puffin, 1991)...£5
GUMDROP'S MERRY CHRISTMAS (Hodder & Stoughton, 1992)...£8
THREE BILLY GOATS GRUFF (OUP, 1992) £5
BOASTING MONSTERS (Longman, 1994) £5
MONSTER FEAST (Longman, 1994)...£5
MONSTER PACK (Longman, 1994)...£5

Books by Anthony Buckeridge

TYPICALLY JENNINGS! (dustjacket and black-and-white frontispiece by Val Biro) (Collins, 1971)............£45
JENNINGS SOUNDS THE ALARM: Seven Plays for Radio (illustrated by Val Biro; paperback) (David Schutte, 1999)...........£12
JENNINGS SOUNDS THE ALARM (100 copies signed by author and artist; paperback) (David Schutte, 1999) £30
JENNINGS BREAKS THE RECORD: Seven More Plays for Radio
(illustrated by Val Biro; paperback) (David Schutte, 2000) £12
JENNINGS BREAKS THE RECORD (100 copies signed by author and artist; paperback) (David Schutte, 2000).....................£30
JENNINGS JOINS THE SEARCH PARTY: Plays for Radio Volume 3
(illustrated by Val Biro; paperback) (David Schutte, 2001) £12
JENNINGS JOINS THE SEARCH PARTY
(100 copies signed by author and artist; otherwise as above; paperback) (David Schutte, 2001)......................£30
JENNINGS TO THE RESCUE: Plays for Radio Volume 4 (illustrated by Val Biro; paperback) (David Schutte, 2002)..............£12
JENNINGS TO THE RESCUE
(100 copies signed by author and artist; otherwise as above; paperback) (David Schutte, 2002)......................£20
JENNINGS AND THE ROMAN REMAINS: Plays for Radio Volume 5
(illustrated by Val Biro; paperback) (David Schutte, 2002) £12
JENNINGS AND THE ROMAN REMAINS
(100 copies signed by author and artist; otherwise as above; paperback) (David Schutte, 2002)......................£20
INTRODUCING REX MILLIGAN (illustrated by Val Biro; paperback) (David Schutte, 2002)..............................£15
INTRODUCING REX MILLIGAN (100 copies signed by author and artist; paperback) (David Schutte, 2002) £25

'BLACK BOB' ANNUALS

Popular series of spin-off annuals, published by D.C. Thomson, featuring the Dandy's 'wonder dog', Black Bob. Note that the books were published biennially between 1951 and 1965, and that there was no edition for 1963.

Prices are for annuals in Very Good condition.

BLACK BOB 1950 ....£75
BLACK BOB 1951 ....£40
BLACK BOB 1953 ....£30
BLACK BOB 1955 ....£30
BLACK BOB 1957 ....£25
BLACK BOB 1959 ....£20
BLACK BOB 1961 ....£20
BLACK BOB 1965 ....£20

BLACKWOOD, Algernon

English writer. Born: 1869. Highly collectable author, best known for his tales of the supernatural and macabre. His most famous story was *The Willows*, which H.P. Lovecraft considered the finest supernatural tale in English literature. He also penned several stories for children, all issued by Basil Blackwell and mostly also published in the 'Joy Street' annuals. Died: 1951.

Prices are for books in Very Good condition.

SAMBO AND SNITCH (Basil Blackwell, 1927) £60
SAMBO AND SNITCH (Appleton, US, 1927)...£60
MR CUPBOARD (Basil Blackwell, 1928)...£50
BY UNDERGROUND (Basil Blackwell, 1928)..£50
THE PARROT AND THE CAT (Basil Blackwell, 1931)..£50
THE ITALIAN CONJUROR (Basil Blackwell, 1932)..£50
MARIA (OF ENGLAND) IN THE RAIN (Basil Blackwell, 1933) £50
SERGEANT POPPETT AND POLICEMAN JAMES (Basil Blackwell, 1934) £50
THE FRUIT STONERS (Basil Blackwell, 1935)..£50
HOW THE CIRCUS CAME TO TEA (Basil Blackwell, 1936) £50
THE ADVENTURES OF DUDLEY AND GILDEROY Adapted by Marion B. Cothren (Dutton, US, 1941)...................£20
THE ADVENTURES OF DUDLEY AND GILDEROY Adapted by Marion B. Cothren (Faber, 1941) £20

Quentin Blake provided the illustrations for several Roald Dahl books, including **Matilda** *(1988), today worth £50.*

Algernon Blackwood is best known for his tales of the supernatural, but also wrote several works for children.

BLAKE, Quentin

British author-illustrator. Born: Sidcup, Kent, in 1932. Illustrated his own work and that of many others, notably Roald Dahl. He was a tutor at the Royal College of Art from 1965 to 1988. He won the Kate Greenaway Medal for *Mr Magnolia*, the Kurt Maschler Award for *All Join In* and the international Bologna Ragazzi Prize for *Clown*. He was awarded the OBE in 1988. He was appointed the first Children's Laureate in May 1999.

Prices are for books in Very Good condition with dustjackets where applicable.

Books Written and Illustrated by Quentin Blake

PATRICK (Cape, 1968) £40
JACK AND NANCY (Cape, 1969) £40
BAND OF ANGELS (Gordon Fraser, 1969) £15
ANGELO (Cape, 1970) £30
THE ADVENTURES OF LESTER (BBC, 1971) £30
SNUFF (Jonathan Cape, 1973) £25
THE PUFFIN BOOK OF IMPROBABLE RECORDS (with John Yeoman; paperback) (Puffin, 1975) £15
HORSESHOE HARRY AND THE WHALE (Dobson, 1976) £25
THE BED BOOK (Faber, 1976) £45
THE ADVENTURES OF LESTER ('Jackanory Stories') (BBC, 1977) £50
MISTER MAGNOLIA (Cape, 1980) £25
ACE DRAGON LTD (Cape, 1980) £15
QUENTIN BLAKE'S NURSERY RHYME BOOK (Cape, 1983) £20
THE STORY OF THE DANCING FROG (Cape, 1984) £20
A LAMP FOR THE LAMB CHOPS (Methuen, 1985) £20
DON'T PUT MUSTARD ON THE CUSTARD (Deutsch, 1985) £20
MRS ARMITAGE ON WHEELS (Cape, 1987) £20
ABC (Cape, 1989) £15
QUENTIN BLAKE BOOK OF NONSENSE VERSE (Viking, 1994) £30
CLOWN (Cape, 1995) £15
THE GREEN SHIP (Cape, 1998) £15
FANTASTIC DAISY ARTICHOKE (Cape, 1999) £10

Books Illustrated by Quentin Blake

PUNKY, MOUSE FOR A DAY by John Moreton (Faber, 1962) £15
UNCLE by J.P. Martin (Cape, 1964) £50

UNCLE CLEANS UP by J.P. Martin (Cape, 1965)..£50
UNCLE AND HIS DETECTIVE by J.P. Martin (Cape, 1966)..£45
UNCLE AND HIS TREACLE TROUBLE by J.P. Martin (Cape, 1967)......................................£45
ALBERT THE DRAGON AND THE CENTAUR by Rosemary Weir (Abelard-Schuman, 1968)......£20
UNCLE AND CLAUDIUS THE CAMEL by J.P. Martin (Cape, 1969)...£45
MR HORROX AND THE GRATCH by James Reeves (Abelard-Schuman, 1969)......................£25
CARLSON by Natalie Savage (Blackie, 1972)...£15
ARABEL'S RAVEN by Joan Aiken (BBC, 1972)...£15
MOUSE TROUBLE by John Yeoman (Macmillan, 1972)..£15
MCBROOM'S ONE-ACRE FARM by S. Fleischman (Chatto & Windus, 1972)........................£15
THE ESCAPED BLACK MAMBA by Joan Aiken (BBC, 1973)...£15
UNCLE AND THE BATTLE FOR BADGERTOWN by J.P. Martin (Cape, 1973)........................£45
HOW TOM BEAT CAPTAIN NAJORK AND HIS HIRED SPORTSMEN by Russell Hoban (Cape, 1974)......£25
THE BREAD BIN by Joan Aiken (paperback) (BBC, 1974)..£5
MIND YOUR OWN BUSINESS by Michael Rosen (Deutsch, 1974)...£15
A NEAR THING FOR CAPTAIN NAJORK by Russell Hoban (Cape, 1975)..............................£25
A GREAT DAY FOR UP! by Dr Seuss (Collins, 1975)..£15
MORTIMER'S TIE by Joan Aiken (paperback) (BBC, 1976)..£5
THE HUNTING OF THE SNARK by Lewis Carroll (in slipcase) (Folio Society, 1976)..............£30
THE HUNTING OF THE SNARK by Lewis Carroll (facsimile edition; issued with dustjacket)
(Windward, 1980)...£10
COLD COMFORT FARM by Stella Gibbons (in slipcase) (Folio Society, 1977)......................£20
THE ENORMOUS CROCODILE by Roald Dahl (Cape, 1978)...£35
MORTIMER AND THE SWORD EXCALIBUR by Joan Aiken (BBC, 1979)...............................£15
THE SPIRAL STAIR by Joan Aiken (paperback) (BBC, 1979)...£5
ARABEL AND MORTIMER by Joan Aiken (contains 'Mortimer's Tie', 'Mortimer and the sword Excalibur'
and 'The Spiral Stair') (Cape, 1980)...£15
MORTIMER'S PORTRAIT ON GLASS by Joan Aiken (paperback) (BBC, 1980)......................£5
MR JONES'S DISAPPEARING TAXI by Joan Aiken (paperback) (BBC, 1980).........................£5
THE TWITS by Roald Dahl (Cape, 1980)..£50
ACE DRAGON LTD by Russell Hoban (Cape, 1980)..£15
GEORGE'S MARVELLOUS MEDICINE by Roald Dahl (Cape, 1981).....................................£45
THE BFG by Roald Dahl (Cape, 1982)...£50
ROALD DAHL'S REVOLTING RHYMES by Roald Dahl (Cape, 1982).....................................£50
MORTIMER'S CROSS by Joan Aiken (BBC/Cape, 1983)...£15
THE WITCHES by Roald Dahl (Cape, 1983)...£50
HOW THE CAMEL GOT HIS HUMP by Rudyard Kipling (Macmillan, 1984)..........................£15
DIRTY BEASTS by Roald Dahl (Cape, 1984)...£30
MORTIMER SAYS NOTHING by Joan Aiken (Cape, 1985)...£15
THE GIRAFFE, THE PELLY AND ME by Roald Dahl (Cape, 1985)...£45
SMELL JELLY SMELL FISH by Michael Rosen (Walker, 1986)..£15
ASK DR PETE by Doctor Peter Rowan (Cape, 1986)...£15
THE RAIN DOOR by Russell Hoban (Gollancz, 1986)...£20
THE MARZIPAN PIG by Russell Hoban (Cape, 1986)...£20
SPOLLJOLLY-DIDDLY-TIDDLYITIS by Michael Rosen (Walker, 1987)..................................£15
MATILDA by Roald Dahl (Cape, 1988)..£50
TAIL FEATHERS FROM MOTHER GOOSE by Iona Opie
(illustrated by Quentin Blake and others) (Walker, 1988)..£30
RHYME STEW by Roald Dahl (Cape, 1989)..£25
ALPHABEASTS by Dick King-Smith (Gollancz, 1990)...£15
ESIO TROT by Roald Dahl (Cape, 1990)..£20
VICAR OF NIBBLESWICKE by Roald Dahl (Century,1991)...£20
ROALD DAHL'S GUIDE TO RAILWAY SAFETY by Roald Dahl (pamphlet) (British Rail, 1991)......£15
A HANDFUL OF GOLD by Joan Aiken (Cape, 1995)...£10
CHARLIE AND THE CHOCOLATE FACTORY by Roald Dahl (Viking, 1995)..........................£10
FANTASTIC MR FOX by Roald Dahl (Viking, 1996)...£15
BREAKFAST WITH DOLLY by John Hedgecoe (Collins, 1996)..£15
CHARLIE AND THE CHOCOLATE FACTORY by Roald Dahl (Puffin hardback, 1997)...........£20
UP WITH THE BIRDS by John Yeoman (Hamilton, 1998)..£10

'BLUE PETER' ANNUALS

The BBC's hugely popular twice-weekly magazine programme for children was launched in 1958 and has inspired a number of spin-off books and annuals.

Prices are for annuals in Very Good condition.

BLUE PETER NO. 1 (BBC, 1964)..£100
BLUE PETER NO. 2 (BBC, 1965)..£35
BLUE PETER NO. 3 (BBC, 1966)..£20
BLUE PETER NO. 4 to No. 9 (BBC, 1967-72) ....each £10
BLUE PETER NOS. 5 to Present (BBC, 1973 to present)..each £6

BLYTON, Enid

The most successful British children's author of the twentieth century. Born: Enid Mary Blyton in London on 11th August 1897, and spent her childhood in the suburb of Beckenham. After school, studied to be a kindergarten teacher, at the same time submitting verses and stories to various magazines, including *Teachers' World*. Her first book, a volume of poems entitled *Child Whispers*, was published in 1922, and was followed by *The Enid Blyton Book of Fairies* (1924), *Sunny Stories for Little Folk* (1926) and countless other works. Best known for the 'Famous Five' (1942 onwards) and 'Secret Seven' (1949 onwards) series, and the phenomenally popular 'Noddy' books (1949 onwards). Died: 1968.

Prices are for books in Very Good condition with dustjackets where applicable.

'Famous Five' Books

FIVE ON A TREASURE ISLAND: An Adventure Story (illustrated by Eileen Soper) (Hodder & Stoughton, 1942) £1,200
FIVE GO ADVENTURING AGAIN (illustrated by Eileen Soper) (Hodder & Stoughton, 1943)......................................£500
FIVE RUN AWAY TOGETHER (illustrated by Eileen Soper) (Hodder & Stoughton, 1944) £500
FIVE GO TO SMUGGLERS' TOP (illustrated by Eileen Soper) (Hodder & Stoughton, 1945) £500
FIVE GO OFF IN A CARAVAN (illustrated by Eileen Soper) (Hodder & Stoughton, 1946)......................................£500
FIVE ON KIRRIN ISLAND AGAIN (illustrated by Eileen Soper) (Hodder & Stoughton, 1947)................................£500
FIVE GO OFF TO CAMP (illustrated by Eileen Soper) (Hodder & Stoughton, 1948)...£120
FIVE GET INTO TROUBLE (illustrated by Eileen Soper) (Hodder & Stoughton, 1949)..£100
FIVE FALL INTO ADVENTURE (illustrated by Eileen Soper) (Hodder & Stoughton, 1950) £75
FIVE ON A HIKE TOGETHER (illustrated by Eileen Soper) (Hodder & Stoughton, 1951)...£55
FIVE HAVE A WONDERFUL TIME (illustrated by Eileen Soper) (Hodder & Stoughton, [1952])..................................£55
FIVE GO DOWN TO THE SEA (illustrated by Eileen Soper) (Hodder & Stoughton, 1953)..£45
FIVE GO TO MYSTERY MOOR (illustrated by Eileen Soper) (Hodder & Stoughton, 1954) £45
FIVE HAVE PLENTY OF FUN (illustrated by Eileen Soper) (Hodder & Stoughton, 1955) £40
FIVE ON A SECRET TRAIL (illustrated by Eileen Soper) (Hodder & Stoughton, 1956) £40
FIVE GO TO BILLYCOCK HILL (illustrated by Eileen Soper) (Hodder & Stoughton, 1957)..£40
FIVE GET INTO A FIX (illustrated by Eileen Soper) (Hodder & Stoughton, [1958]) £35
THE FAMOUS FIVE SPECIAL (contains 'Five Go Off to Camp', 'Five Go Off in a Caravan' and
    'Five Have a Wonderful Time'; illustrated by Eileen Soper) (Hodder & Stoughton, 1959)......................................£35
FIVE ON FINNISTON FARM (illustrated by Eileen Soper) (Hodder & Stoughton, [1960]) £35
FIVE GO TO DEMON'S ROCKS (illustrated by Eileen Soper) (Hodder & Stoughton, 1961)..£35
FIVE HAVE A MYSTERY TO SOLVE (illustrated by Eileen Soper) (Hodder & Stoughton, 1962)....................................£35
FIVE ARE TOGETHER AGAIN (illustrated by Eileen Soper) (Hodder & Stoughton, 1963) £35
THE FAMOUS FIVE BIG BOOK (contains 'Five on a Treasure Island', 'Five Go Adventuring Again' and
    'Five Run Away Together'; illustrated by Eileen Soper) (Hodder & Stoughton, 1964)..£35
FIVE HAVE A PUZZLING TIME & OTHER STORIES (paperback) (Red Fox, 1995)...£5
THE FAMOUS FIVE ADVENTURE (Script of the Famous Five stage play; limited to 350 numbered copies)
    (Wright, 2000)..£30

'Adventure' Books

THE ISLAND OF ADVENTURE (illustrated by Stuart Tresilian) (Macmillan, 1944)...£550
THE CASTLE OF ADVENTURE (illustrated by Stuart Tresilian) (Macmillan, 1946)...£250
THE VALLEY OF ADVENTURE (illustrated by Stuart Tresilian) (Macmillan, 1947) £200
THE SEA OF ADVENTURE (illustrated by Stuart Tresilian) (Macmillan, 1948)...£150
THE MOUNTAIN OF ADVENTURE (illustrated by Stuart Tresilian) (Macmillan, 1949)..£120
THE SHIP OF ADVENTURE (illustrated by Stuart Tresilian) (Macmillan, 1950)..£120
THE CIRCUS OF ADVENTURE (illustrated by Stuart Tresilian) (Macmillan, 1952) £80
THE RIVER OF ADVENTURE (illustrated by Stuart Tresilian) (Macmillan, 1955) £75

'Secret Seven' Books

AT SEASIDE COTTAGE (illustrated by Eileen A. Soper; boards, no dustjacket) (Brockhampton Press, [1947]).........£35
SECRET OF THE OLD MILL (illustrated by Eileen A. Soper; boards, no dustjacket) (Brockhampton Press, [1948])...................£45
THE SECRET SEVEN (illustrated by George Brook) (Brockhampton Press, 1949)..£65
SECRET SEVEN ADVENTURE (illustrated by George Brook) (Brockhampton Press, 1950)......................................£45
WELL DONE, SECRET SEVEN (illustrated by George Brook) (Brockhampton Press, 1951).................................£45
SECRET SEVEN ON THE TRAIL (illustrated by George Brook) (Brockhampton Press, 1952)..............................£45
GO AHEAD SECRET SEVEN (illustrated by Bruno Kay) (Brockhampton Press, 1953) £35
GOOD WORK, SECRET SEVEN! (illustrated by Bruno Kay) (Brockhampton Press, 1954)...................................£35
SECRET SEVEN WIN THROUGH (illustrated by Bruno Kay) (Brockhampton Press, 1955) £35
THREE CHEERS SECRET SEVEN (illustrated by Burgess Sharrocks) (Brockhampton Press, 1956)....................£30
WHERE ARE THE SECRET SEVEN (Australian booklet) (Weeties breakfast cereal, 1956)..................................£55
SECRET SEVEN MYSTERY (illustrated by Burgess Sharrocks) (Brockhampton Press, 1957)............................£25
PUZZLE FOR THE SECRET SEVEN (illustrated by Burgess Sharrocks) (Brockhampton Press, 1958) £25
SECRET SEVEN FIREWORKS (illustrated by Burgess Sharrocks) (Brockhampton Press, 1959)........................£25
GOOD OLD SECRET SEVEN (illustrated by Burgess Sharrocks) (Brockhampton Press, 1960) £25
SHOCK FOR THE SECRET SEVEN (illustrated by Burgess Sharrocks) (Brockhampton Press, 1961)..................£25
LOOK OUT SECRET SEVEN (illustrated by Burgess Sharrocks) (Brockhampton Press, 1962)..........................£25
FUN FOR THE SECRET SEVEN (illustrated by Burgess Sharrocks) (Brockhampton Press, 1963)......................£25

Four examples of Enid Blyton's most avidly collected series of books, starring the Famous Five and all illustrated by Eileen Soper.

'Mystery' Books

THE MYSTERY OF THE BURNT COTTAGE (illustrated by J. Abbey) (Methuen, 1943) £750
THE MYSTERY OF THE DISAPPEARING CAT (illustrated by J. Abbey) (Methuen, 1944)...................................£200
THE MYSTERY OF THE SECRET ROOM (illustrated by J. Abbey) (Methuen, 1945) £150
THE MYSTERY OF THE SPITEFUL LETTERS (illustrated by J. Abbey) (Methuen, 1946) £90
THE MYSTERY OF THE MISSING NECKLACE (illustrated by J. Abbey) (Methuen, 1947)................................£90
THE MYSTERY OF THE HIDDEN HOUSE (illustrated by J. Abbey) (Methuen, 1948) £90
THE MYSTERY OF THE PANTOMIME CAT (Methuen, 1949) £70
THE MYSTERY OF THE INVISIBLE THIEF (Methuen, 1950) £70
THE MYSTERY OF THE VANISHED PRINCE: Being the Ninth Adventure of the Five Find-Outers and Dog
(illustrated by Treyer Evans) (Methuen, 1951)..£70
THE MYSTERY OF THE STRANGE BUNDLE (illustrated by Treyer Evans) (Methuen, 1952) £60
THE MYSTERY OF HOLLY LANE (illustrated by Treyer Evans) (Methuen, 1953) £60
THE MYSTERY OF TALLY-HO COTTAGE (illustrated by Treyer Evans) (Methuen, 1954) £60
THE MYSTERY OF THE MISSING MAN (illustrated by Lilian Buchanan) (Methuen, 1956).............................£60
THE MYSTERY OF THE STRANGE MESSAGES (illustrated by Lilian Buchanan) (Methuen, 1957).....................£60
THE MYSTERY OF BANSHEE TOWERS (illustrated by Lilian Buchanan) (Methuen, 1961) £50

'Barney Junior Mystery' Books

THE ROCKINGDOWN MYSTERY (illustrated by Gilbert Dunlop) (Collins, [1949])..£35
THE RILLOBY FAIR MYSTERY (illustrated by Gilbert Dunlop) (Collins, [1950]) £30
THE RING O'BELLS MYSTERY (illustrated by Gilbert Dunlop) (Collins, 1951)..£25
THE RUBADUB MYSTERY (illustrated by Gilbert Dunlop) (Collins, 1952) £25
THE RAT-A-TAT MYSTERY (illustrated by Gilbert Dunlop) (Collins, 1956) £25
THE RAGAMUFFIN MYSTERY (illustrated by Gilbert Dunlop) (Collins, 1959) £25

'St. Clare's School' Books

THE TWINS AT ST. CLARE'S (Methuen, 1941) £300
THE O'SULLIVAN TWINS: Another School Story about St. Clare's (Methuen, 1942) £45
SUMMER TERM AT ST. CLARE'S (Methuen, 1943)..£40
CLAUDINE AT ST. CLARE'S (Methuen, 1944)..£35
THE SECOND FORM AT ST. CLARE'S (illustrated by W. Lindsay Cable) (Methuen, 1944)..............................£35
FIFTH FORMERS AT ST. CLARE'S (illustrated by W. Lindsay Cable) (Methuen, 1945)..................................£35

'Malory Towers' Books

FIRST TERM AT MALORY TOWERS (illustrated by Stanley Lloyd) (Methuen, 1946)......................................£40
THE SECOND FORM AT MALORY TOWERS (illustrated by Stanley Lloyd) (Methuen, 1947) £35

*The complete dustjacket by Stuart Tesilian which encased the second book in the 'Adventure' series, **The Castle of Adventure** (1946).*

THIRD YEAR AT MALORY TOWERS (illustrated by Stanley Lloyd) (Methuen, 1948)...£35
THE UPPER FOURTH AT MALORY TOWERS (illustrated by Stanley Lloyd) (Methuen, 1949).............................£35
IN THE FIFTH AT MALORY TOWERS (illustrated by Stanley Lloyd) (Methuen, 1950) £35
LAST TERM AT MALORY TOWERS (illustrated by Stanley Lloyd) (Methuen, 1951)...£35

Numbered 'Noddy' Books

NO. 1: NODDY GOES TO TOYLAND (Sampson Low, 1949)..£80
NO. 2: HURRAH FOR LITTLE NODDY (Sampson Low, 1950)...£60
NO. 3: NODDY AND HIS CAR (Sampson Low, 1951)..£50
NO. 4: HERE COMES NODDY AGAIN! (Sampson Low, 1951) £45
NO. 5: WELL DONE, NODDY! (Sampson Low, 1952)..£45
NO. 6: NODDY GOES TO SCHOOL (Sampson Low, 1952) £45
NO. 7: NODDY AT THE SEASIDE (Sampson Low, 1953)...£45
NO. 8: NODDY GETS INTO TROUBLE (Sampson Low, 1954) £45
NO. 9: NODDY AND THE MAGIC RUBBER (Sampson Low, 1954)...£45
NO. 10: YOU FUNNY LITTLE NODDY (Sampson Low, 1955)..£45
NO. 11: NODDY MEETS FATHER CHRISTMAS (Sampson Low, 1955) £45
NO. 12: NODDY AND TESSIE BEAR (Sampson Low, 1956)..£40
NO. 13: BE BRAVE, LITTLE NODDY! (Sampson Low, 1956)..£40
NO. 14: NODDY AND THE BUMPY-DOG (Sampson Low, 1957) £40
NO. 15: DO LOOK OUT, NODDY! (Sampson Low, 1957)..£40
NO. 16: YOU'RE A GOOD FRIEND, NODDY! (Sampson Low, 1958) £40
NO. 17: NODDY HAS AN ADVENTURE (Sampson Low, 1958) £40
NO. 18: NODDY GOES TO SEA (Sampson Low, 1959) £40
NO. 19: NODDY AND THE BUNKEY (Sampson Low, 1959) £40
NO. 20: CHEER UP, LITTLE NODDY! (Sampson Low, 1960)...£40
NO. 21: NODDY GOES TO THE FAIR (Sampson Low, 1960) £40
NO. 22: MR PLOD AND LITTLE NODDY (Sampson Low, 1961)..£40
NO. 23: NODDY AND THE TOOTLES (Sampson Low, 1962) £40
NO. 24: NODDY AND THE AEROPLANE (Sampson Low, 1964)...£40

Other 'Noddy' Books

NODDY'S HOUSE OF BOOKS ('The Tiny Noddy Book Nos. 1-6'; pictorial wraps; in cardboard case;
issued without dustjackets) (Sampson Low, [1951])..the set **£125** (each **£12**)
THE BIG NODDY BOOK (illustrated by Beek; issued without dustjacket) (Sampson Low, 1952) £40
ENID BLYTON'S NODDY PAINTING BOOKS (Robinson, [1952])...£20
ENID BLYTON'S NODDY COLOUR STRIP BOOK (illustrated by Beek) (Sampson Low, [1952]) £20

The third in the 'Adventure' series sees the children marooned in a valley after a plane trip goes horribly wrong.

BLYTON, Enid

ENID BLYTON'S NODDY'S ARK OF BOOKS (five books; in ornamental cardboard case; issued without dustjackets) (Sampson Low, [1952]) .... the set **£125** (each **£12**)
THE NEW BIG NODDY BOOK (Sampson Low, 1953) **£30**
NODDY CUT-OUT MODEL BOOK (Sampson Low, 1953) **£75**
NODDY'S GARAGE OF BOOKS (five books; illustrated by Beek; pictorial wraps; in cardboard case; issued without dustjackets) (Sampson Low, [1953]) .... the set **£125** (each **£12**)
ENID BLYTON'S NODDY GIANT PAINTING BOOK (issued without dustjacket) (Sampson Low, [1954]) **£20**
ENID BLYTON'S NODDY POP-UP BOOK (issued without dustjacket) (Sampson Low, [1954]) **£35**
NODDY STRIP BOOKS (pictorial wraps; issued without dustjackets) (Sampson Low, [1954]) .... each **£20**
NODDY'S CASTLE OF BOOKS (five books; illustrated by Beek; pictorial wraps; in ornamental cardboard case; issued without dustjackets) (Sampson Low, [1954]) .... the set **£125** (each **£12**)
A DAY WITH NODDY (Sampson Low, [1956]) **£25**
ENID BLYTON'S BOOK OF HER FAMOUS PLAY 'NODDY IN TOYLAND' (Sampson Low, [1956]) **£60**
ENID BLYTON'S NODDY PLAY DAY PAINTING BOOK (issued without dustjacket) (Sampson Low, [1956]) **£20**
NODDY AND HIS FRIENDS (pop-up picture book; issued without dustjacket) (Sampson Low, [1956]) **£30**
THE NODDY TOY STATION BOOK NOS. 1-5 (in cardboard case) (Sampson Low, [1956]) .... the set **£125** (each **£12**)
NODDY'S NEW BIG BOOK (Sampson Low, 1957) **£25**
MY BIG EARS PICTURE BOOK (Sampson Low, [1958]) **£25**
MY NODDY PICTURE BOOK (Sampson Low, [1958]) **£25**
NODDY'S SHOP OF BOOK NOS. 1-5 (in cardboard case) (Sampson Low, [1958]) .... the set **£125** (each **£12**)
NODDY'S OWN NURSERY RHYMES (Sampson Low, [1958]) **£25**
A.B.C. WITH NODDY (Sampson Low, [1959]) **£20**
NODDY'S CAR PICTURE BOOK (Sampson Low, 1959) **£15**
NODDY'S TALL BLUE (GREEN-ORANGE-PINK-RED-YELLOW) BOOK (set of six books) (Sampson Low, [1960]) .... each **£45**
NODDY AND THE TUBBY BEARS (rag book) (Dean, 1960) **£20**
NODDY'S ONE, TWO, THREE BOOK (Sampson Low, [1961]) **£15**
NODDY'S TOYLAND TRAIN PICTURE BOOK (Sampson Low, [1961]) **£15**
A DAY AT SCHOOL WITH NODDY (Sampson Low [1962]) **£15**
ENID BLYTON'S NODDY (board book) (Purnell, [c.1963]) **£15**
NODDY TREASURE BOX (Sampson Low, [1965]) **£20**
LEARN TO COUNT WITH NODDY (Sampson Low, [1965]) **£15**
LEARN TO GO SHOPPING WITH NODDY (Sampson Low, [1965]) **£15**
LEARN TO READ ABOUT ANIMALS WITH NODDY (Sampson Low, [1965]) **£15**
LEARN TO TELL THE TIME WITH NODDY (Sampson Low, [1965]) **£15**
NODDY AND HIS FRIENDS: A Nursery Picture Book (Sampson Low, 1965) **£15**
NODDY AND BIG-EARS (Sampson Low, [1967]) **£15**
NODDY AND HIS PASSENGERS (Sampson Low, [1967]) **£15**
NODDY AND THE MAGIC BOOTS: With 'Noddy's Funny Kite' (the cover bears the title 'Noddy's Funny Kite') (Sampson Low, [1967]) **£15**
NODDY AND THE NOAH'S ARK ADVENTURE PICTURE BOOK (Sampson Low, [1967]) **£15**
ENID BLYTON'S NODDY (board book) (Purnell, 1967) **£15**
NODDY IN TOYLAND PICTURE BOOK (Sampson Low, 1967) **£15**
NODDY'S TOYLAND ABC PICTURE BOOK (Sampson Low, [1967]) **£15**
NODDY'S AEROPLANE PICTURE BOOK (Sampson Low, [1967]) **£15**

Strip Books (all in pictorial wraps, and issued without dustjackets)

MARY MOUSE AND THE DOLLS HOUSE (Brockhampton Press, [1942]) **£15**
MORE ADVENTURES OF MARY MOUSE (Brockhampton Press, [1943]) **£15**
LITTLE MARY MOUSE AGAIN (Brockhampton Press, [1944]) **£15**
HALLO, LITTLE MARY MOUSE (illustrated by Olive F. Openshaw) (Brockhampton Press, [1945]) **£15**
MARY MOUSE AND HER FAMILY (illustrated by Olive F. Openshaw) (Brockhampton Press, [1946]) **£15**
HERE COMES MARY MOUSE AGAIN (Brockhampton Press, 1947) **£15**
HOW DO YOU DO, MARY MOUSE (Brockhampton Press, 1948) **£15**
WELCOME MARY MOUSE (illustrated by Olive F. Openshaw) (Brockhampton Press, [1950]) **£15**
WE DO LOVE MARY MOUSE (Brockhampton Press, 1950) **£15**
A PRIZE FOR MARY MOUSE (Brockhampton Press, [1951]) **£15**
HURRAH FOR MARY MOUSE (Brockhampton Press, 1951) **£15**
MARY MOUSE AND HER BICYCLE (illustrated by Olive F. Openshaw) (Brockhampton Press, [1952]) **£15**
MANDY, MOPS AND CUBBY AGAIN (Sampson Low, 1952) **£15**
MANDY, MOPS AND CUBBY FIND A HOUSE (Sampson Low, 1952) **£15**
MR TUMPY PLAYS A TRICK ON SAUCEPAN (Sampson Low, 1952) **£15**
MARY MOUSE AND THE NOAH'S ARK (illustrated by Olive F. Openshaw) (Brockhampton Press, [1953]) **£15**
CLICKY THE CLOCKWORK CLOWN (Brockhampton Press, 1953) **£15**
MANDY MAKES CUBBY A HAT (Sampson Low, 1953) **£15**
MR TUMPY IN THE LAND OF WISHES (Sampson Low, 1953) **£15**
MARY MOUSE TO THE RESCUE (Brockhampton Press, [1954]) **£15**
MANDY, MOPS AND CUBBY AND THE WHITEWASH (Sampson Low, [1955]) **£15**
GOBO IN THE LAND OF DREAMS (Sampson Low, [1955]) **£15**
MARY MOUSE IN NURSERY RHYME LAND (Brockhampton Press, [1955]) **£15**
MR TUMPY IN THE LAND OF BOYS AND GIRLS (Sampson Low, [1955]) **£15**

BOM BOOK (Brockhampton Press, 1956) £15
A DAY WITH MARY MOUSE (illustrated by Frederick White) (Brockhampton Press, [1956]) £15
BOM THE LITTLE TOY DRUMMER (Brockhampton Press, 1956) £15
MARY MOUSE AND THE GARDEN PARTY (illustrated by Frederick White) (Brockhampton Press, [1957])..............£15
BOM AND HIS MAGIC DRUMSTICK (Brockhampton Press, 1957) £15
BOM GOES ADVENTURING (illustrated by R. Paul Höye) (Brockhampton Press, 1958)..........................£15
CLICKY GETS INTO TROUBLE (illustrated by Molly Brett) (Brockhampton Press, [1958])........................£15
MARY MOUSE GOES TO THE FAIR (illustrated by Frederick White) (Brockhampton Press, [1958]) £15
BOM AND THE RAINBOW (illustrated by R. Paul Höye) (Brockhampton Press, 1959).............................£15
HELLO BOM AND WUFFY DOG (illustrated by R. Paul Höye) (Brockhampton Press, [1959])...................£15
MARY MOUSE HAS A WONDERFUL IDEA (illustrated by Fred White) (Brockhampton Press, [1959])........£15
BOM AND THE CLOWN (Brockhampton Press, 1959) £15
CLICKY AND TIPTOE (illustrated by Molly Brett) (Brockhampton Press, 1960) £15
HERE COMES BOM (illustrated by R. Paul Höye) (Brockhampton Press, [1960]) £15
MARY MOUSE GOES TO SEA (illustrated by Fred White) (Brockhampton Press, [1960]) £15
BOM GOES TO MAGIC TOWN (Brockhampton Press, 1960) £15
BOM AT THE SEASIDE (illustrated by R. Paul Höye) (Brockhampton Press, 1961) £15
BOM GOES TO THE CIRCUS (illustrated by R. Paul Höye) (Brockhampton Press, [1961]) £15
HAPPY BIRTHDAY CLICKY (illustrated by Molly Brett) (Brockhampton Press, [1961]) £15
MARY MOUSE GOES OUT FOR THE DAY (illustrated by Fred White) (Brockhampton Press, [1961])......£15
HAPPY HOLIDAY, CLICKY (illustrated by Molly Brett) (Brockhampton Press, 1961) £15
FUN WITH MARY MOUSE (illustrated by R. Paul Höye) (Brockhampton Press, 1962).............................£15
MARY MOUSE AND THE LITTLE DONKEY (illustrated by R. Paul Höye) (Brockhampton Press, [1964])......£15

Miscellaneous and Related Titles

NASH & PALL MALL MAGAZINE (March 1917, August 1917 and September 1918 issues; in original covers)................ each £35
TEACHER'S WORLD MAGAZINE (issues including Blyton contributions, from 1922 onwards)...................... each £8
CHILD WHISPERS (poems; pictorial card covers) (J. Saville, [1922])...£250
CHILD WHISPERS(issued with dustjacket) (J. Saville, 1923)..£225
CHILD WHISPERS(perfect bound card covers) (J. Saville, 1923)..£225
RESPONSIVE SINGING GAMES (large format, card covers; issued without dustjacket) (J. Saville, 1923)............£100
REAL FAIRIES (poems; issued with dustjacket) (J. Saville, 1923)...£225
REAL FAIRIES (perfect bound pictorial card covers) (J. Saville, 1923)...£225
SONGS OF GLADNESS (words by Enid Blyton, music by Alec Rowley; card wraps; issued without dustjacket)
   (J. Saville, 1924)..£100
TEN SONGS FROM 'CHILD WHISPERS' (music by Sydney Twinn; card wraps; issued without dustjacket) (J. Saville, 1924)............£100
THE ZOO BOOK (Newnes, [1924])..£30
THE ENID BLYTON BOOK OF FAIRIES (Newnes, [1924]) £60
SPORTS AND GAMES (illustrated by Richard Ogle; boards) (Birn, 1924)...£150
Ditto (as 'Playtime'; pictorial boards) (Birn, 1932) £160
SILVER AND GOLD (poems; illustrated by Lewis Baumer) (Nelson, [1925]) £100
THE ENID BLYTON BOOK OF BUNNIES (Newnes, [1925]) £60
READING PRACTICE NOS. 1-5, 8, 9 & 11 (others not published; issued without dustjackets) (Nelson, [1925-1926]) .... each £15
THE ENID BLYTON BOOK OF BROWNIES (illustrated by Ernest Aris) (Newnes, [1926]) £60
TALES HALF TOLD (Nelson, 1926)...£75
THE BIRD BOOK (illustrated by Ronald Green; plates) (Newnes, [1926])...£25
THE TEACHER'S TREASURY. Edited by Enid Blyton (three volumes) (Newnes, [1926])..................... each £15
SUNNY STORIES FOR LITTLE FOLKS MAGAZINES (Edited by Enid Blyton, 240 issues) (Newnes, [1926-1936])........... each £8
THE WONDERFUL ADVENTURE (pictorial baords, no d/j. Only known copy was discovered by a BMC reader) (Birn Brothers, 1927)....£350
THE ANIMAL BOOK (illustrated by K. Nixon) (Newnes, [1927]) £20
A BOOK OF LITTLE PLAYS (Nelson, 1927) £25
THE PLAY'S THE THING: Musical Plays for Children (music by Alec Rowley; illustrated by Alfred E. Bestall)
   (Home Library Book Co., [1927]) £250
LET'S PRETEND (illustrated by I. Bennington Angrave) (Nelson, [1928])...£45
AESOP'S FABLES RETOLD (Nelson, 1928)...£25
OLD ENGLISH TALES RETOLD (Nelson, 1928)..£25
PINKITY'S PRANKS and Other Nature Fairy Stories: Retold (Nelson, 1928)...£25
TALES OF BRER RABBIT RETOLD (Nelson, 1928) £25
ENID BLYTON'S NATURE LESSONS (Evans, 1929) £15
TARRYDIDDLE TOWN (Nelson, 1929) £25
THE BOOK AROUND EUROPE (pictorial boards) (Birn, 1929) £125
THE KNIGHTS OF THE ROUND TABLE (Newnes, [1930])..£30
TALES FROM THE ARABIAN NIGHTS. Retold By Enid Blyton (Newnes, [1930])......................................£30
TALES OF ANCIENT GREECE (Newnes, [1930])...£30
TALES OF ROBIN HOOD (Newnes, [1930])..£30
PICTORIAL KNOWLEDGE (Enid Blyton was assistant editor and contributed the verse section; ten volumes)
   (Newnes, 1930) .... the set £40
MY FIRST READING BOOK (Birn, [1933]) £30
CHEERIO! A Book for Boys and Girls (Birn, [1933])...£60
LETTERS FROM BOBS (paper wrappers) (Privately printed by Enid Blyton, 1933).....................................£80

FIVE MINUTE TALES: Sixty Short Stories for Children (Methuen, 1933) £30
LET'S READ (Birn, [1933]) £25
READ TO US (Birn, 1933) £25
THE ADVENTURES OF ODYSSEUS: Stories from World History Retold (Evans, 1934) £20
THE STORY OF THE SIEGE OF TROY: Stories from World History Retold (Evans, 1934) £20
TALES OF THE ANCIENT GREEKS AND PERSIANS: Stories from World History Retold (Evans, 1934)......£20
TALES OF THE ROMANS: Stories from World History Retold (Evans, 1934) £20
THE ENID BLYTON POETRY BOOK (Methuen, 1934) £35
THE RED PIXIE BOOK (issued with dustjacket) (Newnes, [1934]) £75
ROUND THE YEAR WITH ENID BLYTON: A Year's Nature Study for Children (four books: 'Spring', 'Summer',
'Autumn' and 'Winter'; issued without dustjackets) (Evans, [1934]) ....the set £20
TEN-MINUTE TALES: Twenty-Nine Varied Stories for Children (Methuen, 1934) £25
THE OLD THATCH SERIES (eight volumes; issued without dustjackets) (W. & A.K. Johnston, 1934-1935) ....each £12
TREASURE TROVE READERS ('Junior' series only compiled by Enid Blyton ['Senior' series complied by Cyril Midgley];
issued without dustjackets) (A. Wheaton, 1934-1935) ....each £12
THE STRANGE TALE OF MR WUMBLE (pictorial wraps; issued without dustjacket) (Coker, [1935]) £20
HOP, SKIP AND JUMP (pictorial wraps; issued without dustjacket) (Coker, [1935]) £20
THE TALKING TEAPOT and Other Tales (Coker, [1935]) £20
BRER RABBIT. Retold by Enid Blyton ([1935]) £20
THE CHILDREN'S GARDEN (Newnes, [1935]) £25
THE GREEN GOBLIN BOOK (Newnes, [1935]) £80
HEDGEROW TALES (illustrated by Vere Temple) (Methuen, 1935) £20
NATURE OBSERVATION PICTURES (32 pictures from 'The Birds of the British Isles' by T.A. Coward;
selected by and with footnotes by Enid Blyton; in four folders) (Warne, 1935) £40
BIRDS OF THE WAYSIDE AND WOODLAND by Thomas A. Coward.
Edited and with introductory chapters by Enid Blyton (Warne, 1936) £20
FIFTEEN-MINUTE TALES: Nineteen Stories for Children (Methuen, 1936) £25
THE FAMOUS JIMMY (illustrated by Benjamin Rabier) (Muller, 1936) £25
SIX ENID BLYTON PLAYS (Methuen, 1936) £20
THE YELLOW FAIRY BOOK (Newnes, [1936]) £45
ADVENTURES OF THE WISHING-CHAIR (illustrated by Hilda McGavin) (Newnes, [1937]) £950
MORE LETTERS FROM BOBS (paper wrappers) (Privately printed by Enid Blyton, 1933) £80
ENID BLYTON'S SUNNY STORIES (new series) (Newnes, 1937-1953) ....each £4
THE ADVENTURES OF BINKLE AND FLIP (illustrated by Kathleen Nixon) (Newnes, [1938]) £30
BILLY-BOB TALES (illustrated by May Smith) (Methuen, 1938) £30
HEYO, BRER RABBIT! Tales of Brer Rabbit and His Friends. Retold by Enid Blyton (Newnes, 1938) £40
MR GALLIANO'S CIRCUS (Newnes, [1938]) £400
THE SECRET ISLAND (No first edition in original dustjacket currently known) (Blackwell, 1938) £1,000
THE OLD THATCH (second series; eight volumes) (W. & A.K. Johnston, 1938-1939) ....each £10
HURRAH FOR THE CIRCUS! Being the Further Adventures of Mr Galliano and his Famous Circus
(illustrated by E.H. Davie) (Newnes, 1939) £100
NAUGHTY AMELIA JANE! (Newnes, 1939) £150
THE WISHING BEAN and Other Plays (Blackwell, 1939) £20
THE ENCHANTED WOOD (Newnes, 1939) £1,000
THE BLYTON-SHARMAN MUSICAL PLAYS FOR JUNIORS (words by Enid Blyton; six books) (Wheaton, 1939)......each £12
CAMEO PLAYS BOOK NO. 4. Edited by George H. Holroyd (only Book No. 4 is by Enid Blyton) (Arnold, 1939)......£12
HOW THE FLOWERS GROW and Other Musical Plays (Wheaton, 1939) £12
SCHOOL PLAYS: Six Plays for School (Blackwell, 1939) £15
BOBS AGAIN (paper wrappers) (Privately printed by Enid Blyton, 1940) £80
NEWS CHRONICLE BOYS' AND GIRLS' CIRCUS BOOK (News Chronicle, 1940) £40
BOYS' AND GIRLS' CIRCUS BOOK (illustrated by Hilda McGavin) (Newnes, [1940]) £35
BOYS' AND GIRLS' STORY BOOK (Newnes, 1940) £35
NEWS CHRONICLE BOYS' AND GIRLS' BOOK (News Chronicle, 1940) £25
THE SECRET OF SPIGGY HOLES (Blackwell, [1940]) £200
BIRDS OF OUR GARDENS (illustrated by Roland Green and Ernest Aris) (Newnes, 1940) £20
THE CHILDREN OF CHERRY-TREE FARM (illustrated by Harry Rountree) (Country Life, 1940) £40
THE LITTLE TREE-HOUSE: Being the Adventures of Josie, Bun and Click (illustrated by Dorothy M. Wheeler) (Newnes, [1940]) £45
MISTER MEDDLE'S MISCHIEF (illustrated by Joyce Mercer and Rosalind M. Turvey) (Newnes, 1940) £40
THE NAUGHTIEST GIRL IN THE SCHOOL (Newnes, 1940) £60
PLAYS FOR OLDER CHILDREN (from 'The Play's the Thing'; illustrated by Alfred Bestall) (Newnes, [1940]) £30
PLAYS FOR YOUNGER CHILDREN (from 'The Play's the Thing'; illustrated by Alfred Bestall) (Newnes, [1940]) £30
TWENTY-MINUTE TALES (Methuen, 1940) £20
TALES OF BETSY-MAY (illustrated by J. Gale Thomas) (Methuen, 1940) £25
THE TREASURE HUNTERS (illustrated by E. Wilson and Joyce Davies) (Newnes, 1940) £75
CHILDREN OF KIDILLIN (first published under the pseudonym 'Mary Pollock') (Newnes, 1940) £25
THREE BOYS AND A CIRCUS (first published under the pseudonym 'Mary Pollock') (Newnes, 1940) £25
THE ADVENTURES OF MR PINK-WHISTLE (Newnes, 1941) £75
FIVE O'CLOCK TALES: Sixty Five-Minute Stories for Children (Methuen, 1941) £15
THE FURTHER ADVENTURES OF JOSIE, CLICK AND BUN (illustrated by Dorothy M. Wheeler) (Newnes, [1941])......£35

*Individual issues of the fortnightly **Enid Blyton's Magazine** from the 1950s (above) are now worth £4 in Very Good condition.*

THE SECRET MOUNTAIN: Being the Third Story of the Strange Adventures of the Secret Island Children
   (Blackwell, 1941) £75
THE ADVENTUROUS FOUR (Newnes, 1941)..£50
THE BABAR STORY BOOK. Told by Enid Blyton (Methuen, 1941)...£60
A CALENDAR FOR CHILDREN (Newnes, 1941)..£100
ENID BLYTON'S BOOK OF THE YEAR (Evans, 1941) £15
THE CHILDREN OF WILLOW FARM: A Tale of Life on a Farm (illustrated by Harry Rountree) (Country Life, 1942) £35
THE NAUGHTIEST GIRL AGAIN (Newnes, 1942)..£50
MORE ADVENTURES ON WILLOW FARM (Country Life, 1942)..£30
SIX O'CLOCK TALES: Thirty-Three Short Stories for Children (illustrated by Dorothy M. Wheeler) (Methuen, 1942)...........£20
SHADOW, THE SHEEP-DOG (Newnes, 1942)...£120
THE LAND OF FAR-BEYOND (Methuen, 1942)..£150
I'LL TELL YOU A STORY (illustrated by Eileen A. Soper) (Macmillan, 1942)................................£30
I'LL TELL YOU ANOTHER STORY (Macmillan, 1942) £25
ENID BLYTON'S HAPPY STORY (Hodder & Stoughton, 1942)..£25
HELLO, MR TWIDDLE! (illustrated by Hilda McGavin) (Newnes, 1942)..£30
THE FURTHER ADVENTURES OF BRER RABBIT. Retold By Enid Blyton (Newnes, 1942)............£30
ENID BLYTON'S LITTLE BOOKS (pictorial wraps; issued without dustjacket) (Evans, [1942])....... each £15
CIRCUS DAYS AGAIN (Newnes, 1942)...£100
ENID BLYTON'S READERS (Books 1-3; issued without dustjackets) (Macmillan, 1942)............... each £10
JOHN JOLLY AT CHRISTMAS TIME (paper wrappers) (Evans, 1942) £100
THE CHILDREN'S LIFE OF CHRIST (Methuen, 1943)...£15
THE SECRET OF KILLIMOOIN (Blackwell, 1943)...£100
SEVEN O'CLOCK TALES: Thirty Short Stories for Children (Methuen, 1943)...............................£20
DAME SLAP AND HER SCHOOL (illustrated by Dorothy M. Wheeler) (Newnes, [1943])...............£30
THE MAGIC FARAWAY TREE (illustrated by Dorothy M. Wheeler) (Newnes, 1943) £950
ENID BLYTON'S MERRY STORY BOOK (illustrated by Eileen A. Soper) (Hodder & Stoughton, 1943)............£30
BIMBO AND TOPSY (illustrated by Lucy Gee) (Newnes, 1943)..£25
THE JOLLY FAMILY PICTURE STORY BOOKS (Evans, [1943])...£25
THE ADVENTURES OF SCAMP (published under the pseudonym 'Mary Pollock') (Newnes, 1943) £25
JOHN JOLLY BY THE SEA (paper wrappers) (Evans, 1943) £90
JOHN JOLLY ON THE FARM (paper wrappers) (Evans, 1943)..£90
SMUGGLER BEN (published under the pseudonym 'Mary Pollock') (Laurie, 1943) £40
THE TOYS COME TO LIFE (illustrated by Eileen A. Soper) (Brockhampton Press, [1944]).............£30
BILLY AND BETTY AT THE SEASIDE (Valentine, [1944])..£60
THE BOY NEXT DOOR (illustrated by A.E. Bestall) (Newnes, 1944)..£150
ENID BLYTON'S NATURE LOVER'S BOOK (illustrated by Donin Nachshen and Noel Hopkin) (Evans, 1944) £15
THE CHRISTMAS BOOK (illustrated by Treyer Evans) (Macmillan, 1944)....................................£20

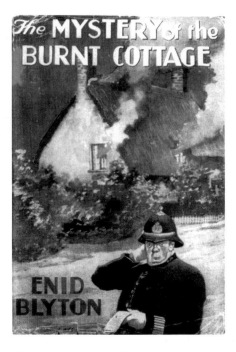

The 1939 first edition of **The Enchanted Wood** *is very rare in its dustjacket and is currently valued at £1,000.*

The first in the very collectable 'Mystery' series of books, first issued in 1943 and illustrated by J. Abbey.

COME TO THE CIRCUS (illustrated by Eileen A. Soper) (Brockhampton Press, [1944])..£30
EIGHT O'CLOCK TALES (illustrated by Dorothy M. Wheeler) (Methuen, 1944)..£20
ENID BLYTON'S JOLLY STORY BOOK (illustrated by Eileen Soper) (Hodder & Stoughton, 1944)...........................£25
POLLY PIGLET (illustrated by Eileen A. Soper) (Brockhampton, [1944]) £35
RAINY DAY STORIES (illustrated by Nora S. Unwin) (Evans, [1944]) £30
TALES FROM THE BIBLE (illustrated by Eileen A. Soper) (Methuen, 1944)..£25
TALES OF TOYLAND (illustrated by Hilda McGavin) (Newnes, 1944) £30
AT APPLETREE FARM (Brockhampton Press, 1944) £30
A BOOK OF NAUGHTY CHILDREN (Methuen, 1944) £30
THE DOG THAT WENT TO FAIRYLAND (Brockhampton Press, 1944) £25
JOLLY LITTLE JUMBO (Brockhampton Press, 1944)...£30
ENID BLYTON READERS BOOKS 4-6 (Macmillan, 1944) ....each £8
THE THREE GOLLIWOGS (Newnes, 1944)..£200
THE BLUE STORY BOOK (illustrated by Eileen A. Soper) (Methuen, 1945)...£25
ROUND THE CLOCK STORIES (illustrated by Nora S. Unwin) (National Magazine Co., 1945)...........................£20
THE CARAVAN FAMILY (illustrated by William Fyffe) (Lutterworth Press, 1945) £20
THE BROWN FAMILY (illustrated by E. and R. Buhler) (News Chronicle, [1945])...£20
THE CONJURING WIZARD and Other Stories (illustrated by Eileen A. Soper) (Macmillan, 1945).......................£30
THE ENID BLYTON NATURE READERS NOS. 1-20 (Macmillan, [1945])...each £8
THE FAMILY AT RED ROOFS (illustrated by W. Spence) (Lutterworth Press, 1945) £30
THE FIRST CHRISTMAS (photographs by Paul Henning) (Methuen, 1945)..£15
HOLLOW TREE HOUSE (illustrated by Elizabeth Wall) (Lutterworth Press, 1945) £20
THE NAUGHTIEST GIRL IS A MONITOR (Newnes, 1945)...£30
THE RUNAWAY KITTEN (illustrated by Eileen A. Soper) (Brockhampton Press, [1945])..£30
THE TWINS GO TO NURSERY-RHYME LAND (illustrated by Eileen A. Soper) (Brockhampton Press, [1945]) £30
ENID BLYTON'S SUNNY STORY BOOK (Hodder & Stoughton, 1945)...£20
THE TEDDY BEAR'S PARTY (illustrated by Eileen A. Soper) (Brockhampton Press, [1945]) £30
JOHN JOLLY AT THE CIRCUS (paper wrappers) (Evans, 1945) £50
AMELIA JANE AGAIN (Newnes, 1946)...£35
THE BAD LITTLE MONKEY (illustrated by Eileen A. Soper) (Brockhampton Press, [1946]) £30
THE CHILDREN AT HAPPY HOUSE (illustrated by Kathleen Gell) (Blackwell, 1946)...£25
CHIMNEY CORNER STORIES (illustrated by Pat Harrison) (National Magazine Co., 1946) £25
THE ENID BLYTON HOLIDAY BOOK (Sampson Low, [1946])...£25

Noddy Goes to Toyland was the first of 24 books featuring the popular characters, Noddy and Big Ears, worth £80 today.

The hugely-prolific Enid Blyton wrote this rare collection of poems, which was issued in J. Saville in 1923.

ENID BLYTON'S GAY STORY BOOK (illustrated by Eileen Soper) (Hodder & Stoughton, 1946) £30
JOSIE, CLICK AND BUN AGAIN (illustrated by Dorothy M. Wheeler) (Newnes, [1946]) £35
THE LITTLE WHITE DUCK and Other Stories (illustrated by Eileen A. Soper) (Macmillan, 1946)....................£25
THE PUT-EM-RIGHTS (illustrated by Elizabeth Wall) (Lutterworth Press, 1946) £15
THE RED STORY BOOK (Methuen, 1946)...£25
TALES OF GREEN HEDGES (illustrated by Gwen White) (National Magazine Co., 1946)...............................£20
THE SURPRISING CARAVAN (illustrated by Eileen A. Soper) (Brockhampton Press, 1946) £30
THE TRAIN THAT LOST ITS WAY (illustrated by Eileen A. Soper) (Brockhampton Press, [1946]) £30
ENID BLYTON NATURE READERS NOS. 21-30 (Macmillan, 1946).. each £8
THE FOLK OF THE FARAWAY TREE (illustrated by Dorothy M. Wheeler) (Newnes, 1946) £75
THE ADVENTUROUS FOUR AGAIN (Newnes, 1947) £40
THE GREEN STORY BOOK (illustrated by Eileen A. Soper) (Methuen, 1947)..£20
THE HAPPY HOUSE CHILDREN AGAIN (illustrated by Kathleen Gell) (Blackwell, 1947)................................£30
HOUSE-AT-THE-CORNER (illustrated by Elsie Walker) (Lutterworth Press, 1947) £25
JINKY NATURE BOOKS (four books) (Arnold, [1947]) .... each £8
MORE ABOUT JOSIE, CLICK AND BUN (illustrated by Dorothy M. Wheeler) (Newnes, 1947).......................£30
ENID BLYTON'S LUCKY STORY BOOK (illustrated by Eileen Soper) (Hodder & Stoughton, 1947) £25
RAMBLES WITH UNCLE NAT (illustrated by Nora S. Unwin) (National Magazine Co., [1947]) £20
THE SAUCY JANE FAMILY (illustrated by Ruth Gervis) (Lutterworth Press, 1947) £25
A SECOND BOOK OF NAUGHTY CHILDREN: Twenty-Four Short Stories (illustrated by Kathleen Gell)
(Methuen, 1947) £25
THE SMITH FAMILY (Books 1-3 by Enid Blyton [Books 4-6 by Rose Fyleman]) (Arnold, [1947]) .... each £10
ENID BLYTON'S TREASURY (published for Boots) (Evans, 1947) £25
BEFORE I GO TO SLEEP: A Book of Bible Stories and Prayers for Children at Night
(illustrated by Grace Lodge) (Latimer House, 1947)..£30
THE VERY CLEVER RABBIT (Brockhampton Press, 1947) £25
LITTLE GREEN DUCK and Other Stories (Brockhampton Press, 1947) £25
MISCHIEF AT ST. ROLLO'S (published under the pseudonym 'Mary Pollock') (Newnes: 'Tower House' series, 1947)..............£25
THE SECRET OF CLIFF CASTLE (published under the pseudonym 'Mary Pollock')
(Newnes: 'Tower House' series, 1947)..£25
MISTER ICEY-COLD (Blackwell, 1948)..£25
THE ADVENTURES OF PIP (Sampson Low, [1948]) £25
THE BOY WITH THE LOAVES AND FISHES (illustrated by Elsie Walker) (Lutterworth Press, 1948)..............£12

BLYTON, Enid

ENID BLYTON'S BRER RABBIT BOOK (first of a series, followed by 2nd-8th 'Brer Rabbit Books')
(Latimer House, 1948)..each **£15**
JUST TIME FOR A STORY (illustrated by Grace Lodge) (Macmillan, 1948)..**£20**
LET'S GARDEN (illustrated by William McLaren) (Latimer House, 1948)..**£25**
LET'S HAVE A STORY (illustrated by George Bowe) (Pitkin, [1948]) **£20**
THE LITTLE BUTTON-ELVES (Coker, [1948])..**£20**
THE LITTLE GIRL AT CAPERNAUM (illustrated by Elsie Walker) (Lutterworth Press, 1948).................**£10**
BRER RABBIT AND HIS FRIENDS. Retold by Enid Blyton (Coker, 1948)...**£16**
ENID BLYTON'S BEDTIME SERIES (two parts) (Brockhampton Press, 1948) ....each **£12**
CHILDREN OF OTHER LANDS (Coker, [1948])..**£16**
COME TO THE CIRCUS! (a different work from the 1944 Brockhampton book; illustrated by Joyce M. Johnson)
(Newnes, 1948)..**£20**
MORE ADVENTURES OF PIP (Marston, [1948]) **£20**
NOW FOR A STORY (illustrated by Frank Varty) (Harold Hill, 1948)..**£15**
THE RED-SPOTTED HANDKERCHIEF and Other Stories (illustrated by Kathleen Gell) (Brockhampton Press, [1948]) **£25**
SIX COUSINS AT MISTLETOE FARM (illustrated by Peter Beigel) (Evans, 1948)....................................**£20**
TALES OF OLD THATCH (Coker, 1948)..**£20**
TALES OF THE TWINS (illustrated by Eileen A. Soper) (Brockhampton Press, [1948])............................**£15**
THEY RAN AWAY TOGETHER (illustrated by Jeanne Farrar) (Brockhampton Press, [1948])..................**£15**
WE WANT A STORY (illustrated by George Bowe) (Pitkin, [1948])..**£25**
ENID BLYTON READERS BOOK NO. 7 (Macmillan, 1948) **£7**
ENID BLYTON'S MERRY CHRISTMAS CARDS (card covers) (H.A. & W.L. Pitkin, 1948) **£40**
ENID BLYTON'S BIRTHDAY CARDS (card covers) (H.A. & W'L. Pitkin, 1948) **£70**
NATURE TALES (Johnston, 1948)...**£10**
TALES AFTER TEA (Werner Laurie, 1948) **£20**
ENID BLYTON'S BLUEBELL STORY BOOK (Gifford, [1949])..**£30**
HUMPTY DUMPTY AND BELINDA (Collins, [1949])..**£30**
A BOOK OF MAGIC (Macmillan, 1949)...**£16**
BUMPY AND HIS BUS (illustrated by Dorothy K. Wheeler) (Newnes, 1949)..**£25**
ENID BLYTON'S DAFFODIL STORY BOOK (Gifford, [1949]) **£30**
THE DEAR OLD SNOWMAN (Brockhampton Press, [1949])..**£25**
THE ENID BLYTON BIBLE STORIES: OLD TESTAMENT (Macmillan, 1949)...**£20**
THE ENID BLYTON PICTURES: OLD TESTAMENT by John Turner (Macmillan, 1949).............................**£20**
JINKY'S JOKE and Other Stories (illustrated by Kathleen Gell) (Brockhampton Press, [1949]) **£20**
MR TUMPY AND HIS CARAVAN (illustrated by Dorothy M. Wheeler) (Sidgwick & Jackson, 1949)..........**£40**
MY ENID BLYTON BEDSIDE BOOK (first of a series, followed by Enid Blyton's 2nd-12th 'Bedside Books')
(Arthur Barker, 1949)...each **£20**
A STORY PARTY AT GREEN HEDGES (illustrated by Grace Lodge) (Hodder & Stoughton, 1949)..........**£20**
TALES AFTER SUPPER (Werner Laurie, 1949)..**£10**
A CAT IN FAIRYLAND (Pitkin, 1949)...**£25**
CHUFF THE CHIMNEY SWEEP (Pitkin, 1949)...**£25**
THE CIRCUS BOOK (Latimer House, 1949) **£20**
DON'T BE SILLY, MR TWIDDLE (Newnes, 1949)..**£25**
THOSE DREADFUL CHILDREN (illustrated by Grace Lodge) (Lutterworth Press, 1949).........................**£25**
ENID BLYTON'S GOOD MORNING BOOK (illustrated by Don & Ann Goring) (National Magazine Co., 1949)........................**£20**
OH, WHAT A LOVELY TIME (Brockhampton Press, 1949)..**£20**
ROBIN HOOD BOOK (Latimer House, 1949) **£20**
TINY TALES (Littlebury, 1949)..**£20**
THE STRANGE UMBRELLA and Other Stories (Pitkin, [1949])...**£25**
THE ENCHANTED SEA and Other Stories (Pitkin, [1949]) **£25**
A RUBBALONG TALE SHOWBOOK ('Show Book' series No A1, devised by Jack Chambers;
complete with all cut-outs; boards) (Werner Laurie, 1950) **£250**
MARY MOUSE SHOWBOOK (devised by Jack Chambers; complete with all cut-outs; boards) (Werner Laurie, 1950) **£250**
THE ASTONISHING LADDER and Other Stories (illustrated by Eileen A. Soper) (Macmillan, 1950)......**£25**
THE MAGIC KNITTING NEEDLES and Other Stories (Macmillan, 1950)..**£25**
THE MAGIC SNOW-BIRD and Other Stories (Pitkin, [1950])..**£25**
THE THREE NAUGHTY CHILDREN and Other Stories (illustrated by Eileen A. Soper) (Macmillan, 1950)............**£20**
THE WISHING CHAIR AGAIN (Newnes, 1950)..**£25**
SIX COUSINS AGAIN (illustrated by Maurice Tulloch) (Evans, 1950)...**£20**
SMUGGLER BEN (Werner Laurie, 1950)...**£15**
TRICKY THE GOBLIN and Other Stories (illustrated by Eileen A. Soper) (Macmillan, 1950)..................**£25**
RUBBALONG TALES (illustrated by Norman Meredith) (Macmillan, 1950)...**£30**
THE POLE STAR FAMILY (illustrated by Ruth Gervis) (Lutterworth Press, 1950)......................................**£20**
ENID BLYTON'S POPPY STORY BOOK (Gifford, [1950])..**£20**
THE SEASIDE FAMILY (illustrated by Ruth Gervis) (Lutterworth Press, 1950)..**£20**
MR PINK-WHISTLE INTERFERES (illustrated by Dorothy M. Wheeler) (Newnes, 1950)..........................**£25**
ENID BLYTON'S BOOK OF THE YEAR (illustrated by Eileen Soper; music by Alec Rowley) (Evans, 1950) **£20**
MISTER MEDDLE'S MUDDLES (illustrated by Rosalind M. Turvey and Joyce Mercer) (Newnes, 1950)...**£25**
ENID BLYTON LITTLE BOOK NO. 1 (first of a series, followed by Nos. 2-6) (Brockhampton, [1950])...............each **£10**
THE ENID BLYTON PENNANT SERIES (thirty books) (Macmillan, 1950)..each **£7**

ENID BLYTON READERS BOOKS NOS. 10-12 (Macmillan, 1950) .... each **£7**
ROUND THE YEAR WITH ENID BLYTON (Evans, 1950) **£10**
ROUND THE YEAR STORIES (Coker, 1950) **£15**
TALES ABOUT TOYS (Brockhampton Press, 1950) **£20**
WHAT AN ADVENTURE (Brockhampton Press, 1950) **£20**
THE YELLOW STORY BOOK (illustrated by Kathleen Gell) (Newnes, 1950) **£20**
PIPPY AND THE GNOME and Other Stories (Pitkin, 1951) **£15**
THE PROUD GOLLIWOG (Brockhampton Press, 1951) **£15**
THE QUEEN ELIZABETH FAMILY (illustrated by Ruth Gervis) (Lutterworth Press, 1951) **£15**
BENJY AND THE PRINCESS and Other Stories (Pitkin, [1951]) **£15**
THE BOOK OF BROWNIES (illustrated by Ernest Aris) (Newnes, [1951]) **£25**
THE BUTTERCUP FARM FAMILY (illustrated by Ruth Gervis) (Lutterworth Press, 1951) **£20**
ENID BLYTON'S BUTTERCUP STORY BOOK (Gifford, [1951]) **£20**
THE FLYING GOAT and Other Stories (Pitkin, [1951]) **£25**
ENID BLYTON'S GAY STREET BOOK (illustrated by Grace Lodge) (Latimer House, [1951]) **£25**
JOSIE, CLICK AND BUN, AND THE LITTLE TREE HOUSE (reprint of 'The Little Tree House' [1940];
    illustrated by Dorothy M. Wheeler) (Newnes, [1951]) **£25**
A PICNIC PARTY WITH ENID BLYTON (illustrated by Grace Lodge) (Hodder & Stoughton, 1951) **£20**
THE RUNAWAY TEDDY BEAR and Other Stories (Pitkin, [1951]) **£25**
THE SIX BAD BOYS (illustrated by Mary Gernat) (Lutterworth Press, 1951) **£25**
'TOO-WISE' THE WONDERFUL WIZARD and Other Stories (Pitkin, [1951]) **£25**
UP THE FARAWAY TREE (illustrated by Dorothy M. Wheeler) (Newnes, 1951) **£40**
TALES OF ANCIENT GREECE (reissue; illustrated by Anne and Janet Johnstone) (Latimer House, [1951]).......... **£12**
DOWN AT THE FARM (Sampson Low, 1951) **£20**
FATHER CHRISTMAS AND BELINDA (Collins, 1951) **£20**
FEEFO, TUPPENY AND JINKS (abridged edition of the 'Green Goblin Book' [1935]) (Staples Press, 1951) **£20**
THE LITTLE SPINNING MOUSE and Other Stories (Pitkin, 1951) **£25**
ENID BLYTON'S ANIMAL LOVER'S BOOK (Evans, 1952) **£15**
ENID BLYTON'S BRIGHT STORY BOOK (illustrated by Eileen Soper) (Brockhampton Press, 1952) **£20**
THE ENID BLYTON BIBLE PICTURES: NEW TESTAMENT (Macmillan, [1952]) **£20**
THE QUEER ADVENTURE (illustrated by Norman Meredith) (Staples Press, 1952) **£20**
THE STORY OF MY LIFE (Pitkin, [1952]) **£30**
WELCOME, JOSIE, CLICK AND BUN! (illustrated by Dorothy M. Wheeler) (Newnes, 1952) **£25**
THE VERY BIG SECRET (illustrated by Ruth Gervis) (Lutterworth Press, 1952) **£20**
ENID BLYTON'S SNOWDROP STORY BOOK (Gifford, [1952]) **£25**
ENID BLYTON'S OMNIBUS! (illustrated by Jessie Land) (Newnes, 1952) **£20**
ENID BLYTON TINY STRIP BOOKS (first of a series) (Sampson Low, [1952]) .... each **£12**
MY FIRST ENID BLYTON BOOK (first of a series, followed by the 2nd and 3rd 'Enid Blyton Books')
    (Latimer House, 1952) .... each **£20**
MY FIRST NATURE BOOK (first of a series, followed by the 2nd and 3rd 'Nature Books'; illustrated by Eileen A. Soper)
    (Macmillan, 1952) .... each **£7**
THE CHILDREN'S JOLLY BOOK (with W.E. Johns and others) (Odhams, 1952) **£15**
COME ALONG TWINS (Brockhampton Press, 1952) **£12**
THE MAD TEAPOT (Brockhampton Press, 1952) **£12**
THE TWO SILLIES and Other Stories. Retold By Enid Blyton (Coker, 1952) **£20**
THE SECRET OF MOON CASTLE (Blackwell, 1953) **£40**
SNOWBALL THE PONY (illustrated by Iris Gillespie) (Lutterworth Press, 1953) **£15**
THE STORY OF OUR QUEEN (illustrated by F. Stocks May) (Muller, 1953) **£15**
WELL REALLY, MR. TWIDDLE! (illustrated by Hilda McGavin) (Newnes, 1953) **£25**
THE CHILDREN'S BOOK OF PRAYERS. Chosen by Enid Blyton (Muller, [1953]) **£15**
ENID BLYTON'S CHRISTMAS STORY (advent calendar; illustrated by Fritz Wegner) (Hamilton, [1953]) **£30**
THE ENID BLYTON BIBLE STORIES: NEW TESTAMENT (fourteen books) (Macmillan, 1953 [1954])............ each **£6**
ENID BLYTON'S MAGAZINE (March 1953-September 1959) .... each **£4**
GOBO AND MR FIERCE (Sampson Low, 1953) **£12**
HERE COME THE TWINS (Brockhampton Press, 1953) **£12**
LITTLE GIFT BOOKS. Translated by Enid Blyton (first of a series; illustrated by Pierre Probst) (Hackett, 1953)............... each **£20**
PLAYWAYS ANNUAL by Enid Blyton and others (Lutterworth Press, 1953) **£10**
VISITORS IN THE NIGHT (Brockhampton Press, 1953) **£12**
THE ADVENTURE OF THE SECRET NECKLACE (illustrated by Isabel Veevers) (Lutterworth Press, 1954) **£15**
THE CASTLE WITHOUT A DOOR and Other Stories (Pitkin, [1954]) **£15**
THE CHILDREN AT GREEN MEADOWS (illustrated by Grace Lodge) (Lutterworth Press, 1954) **£20**
ENID BLYTON'S FRIENDLY STORY BOOK (illustrated by Eileen Soper) (Brockhampton Press, 1954) **£20**
ENID BLYTON'S GOOD MORNING BOOK (illustrated by Willy Schermelé) (Juvenile Productions, [1954])........... **£20**
THE GREATEST BOOK IN THE WORLD (illustrated by Mabel Peacock) (British & Foreign Bible Society, [1954])............ **£15**
THE LITTLE TOY FARM and Other Stories (Pitkin, 1954) **£15**
BIRTHDAY TIME BOOKS (Brent Press, 1954):
    A SURPRISE FOR MARY (paper wrappers) **£25**
    A HAPPY BIRTHDAY (paper wrappers) **£25**
    THE TWO BIRTHDAYS (paper wrappers) **£25**

THE WONDERFUL BIRTHDAY (paper wrappers)..£25
ALL ABOUT BABIES (paper wrappers)..£25
TALES ABOUT TOYS (paper wrappers)..£25
ENID BLYTON'S MARIGOLD STORY BOOK (Gifford, [1954])..£25
MERRY MISTER MEDDLE! (illustrated by Rosalind M. Turvey and Joyce Mercer) (Newnes, 1954) £25
MORE ABOUT AMELIA JANE! (illustrated by Sylvia I. Venus) (Newnes, 1954) £30
ENID BLYTON'S MAGAZINE ANNUAL (first of a series of four) (Evans, [1954]) .... each £15
LITTLE STRIP PICTURE BOOKS (Sampson Low, 1954) .... each £10
ENID BLYTON'S AWAY GOES SOOTY (illustrated by Pierre Probst) (Collins [printed in the Netherlands], [1955])...................£20
BENJY AND THE OTHERS (illustrated by Kathleen Gell) (Latimer House, 1955)................................£20
BIBLE STORIES FROM THE OLD TESTAMENT (illustrated by Grace Lodge) (Muller, [1955])..........£10
ENID BLYTON'S BOBS (illustrated by Pierre Probst) (Collins [printed in the Netherlands], [1955])........£20
FINDING THE TICKETS (play) (Evans, 1955) £15
ENID BLYTON'S FOXGLOVE STORY BOOK (Gifford, [1955])...£25
HOLIDAY HOUSE (illustrated by Grace Lodge) (Evans, [1955]) £15
ENID BLYTON'S LITTLE BEDTIME BOOKS (series of eight books) (Sampson Low, [1955]).......... each £12
MISCHIEF AGAIN! (photographs by Paul Kaye) (Collins, 1955) £15
MORE CHIMNEY CORNER STORIES (illustrated by Pat Harrison) (Macdonald, 1955) £20
THE MOTHERS' MEETING (play) (Evans, 1955) £12
MR PINK-WHISTLE'S PARTY (illustrated by Dorothy M. Wheeler) (Newnes, 1955) £22
MR SLY-ONE AND THE CATS (play) (Evans, 1955)..£15
ENID BLYTON'S NEDDY THE LITTLE DONKEY (illustrated by Romain Simson) (Collins [printed in the Netherlands], [1955]) £20
PLAYING AT HOME: A Novelty Book (story by Enid Blyton; devised and illustrated by Sabine Schweitzer) (Methuen, 1955)........£160
RUN-ABOUT'S HOLIDAY (illustrated by Lilian Chivers) (Lutterworth Press, 1955)..........................£20
THE CHILD WHO WAS CHOSEN (Waterloo & Sons, 1955)..£50
LET'S HAVE A CLUB OF OUR OWN! (Waterloo & Sons, 1955)..£50
ENID BLYTON'S CHRISTMAS WITH SCAMP AND BIMBO (Collins, [1955])....................................£20
ENID BLYTON'S SOOTY (illustrated by Pierre Probst) (Collins [printed in the Netherlands], [1955]) £20
THE TROUBLESOME THREE (illustrated by Leo) (Sampson Low, [1955])......................................£15
ENID BLYTON'S 'WHAT SHALL I BE?' (illustrated by Pierre Probst) (Collins [printed in the Netherlands], [1955]) £15
WHO WILL HOLD THE GIANT? (play) (Evans, 1955)..£15
BIBLE STORIES FROM THE NEW TESTAMENT (illustrated by Grace Lodge) (Muller, 1955)..........£10
BIMBO AND BLACKIE GO CAMPING (illustrated by Pierre Probst) (Collins, 1955) £20
ENID BLYTON'S FAVOURITE BOOK OF FABLES, from the Tales of La Fontaine (Collins, 1955) £25
GOLLIWOG GRUMBLED (Brockhampton Press, 1955)..£20
LAUGHING KITTEN (photographs by Paul Kave) (Harvill, 1955)..£15
ENID BLYTON'S ANIMAL TALES (illustrated by Romain Simon) (Collins [printed in the Netherlands], [1956])......................£20
THE CLEVER LITTLE DONKEY (illustrated by Romain Simon) (Collins [printed in the Netherlands], [1956]) ..£20
COLIN THE COW-BOY (illustrated by R. Caillé) (Collins [printed in the Netherlands], [1956])............£20
FOUR IN A FAMILY (illustrated by Tom Kerr) (Lutterworth Press, 1956)..£15
LET'S HAVE A PARTY (photographs by Paul Kaye) (Harvill, 1956)..£15
SCAMP AT SCHOOL (illustrated by Pierre Probst) (Collins [printed in the Netherlands], [1956])........£20
A STORY BOOK OF JESUS (illustrated by Elsie Walker) (Macmillan, 1956) £10
ENID BLYTON'S BOM PAINTING BOOK (Dean, [1957]) £15
CHILDREN'S OWN WONDER BOOK (containing contributions by Enid Blyton and others) (Odhams, 1957) £10
NEW TESTAMENT PICTURE BOOKS NOS 1-2 (Macmillan, 1957).. each £5
THE BIRTHDAY KITTEN (illustrated by Grace Lodge) (Lutterworth Press, 1958) £35
ENID BLYTON'S LITTLE BEDTIME BOOK (four books; all different work from the earlier book of the same title)
(Sampson Low, [1958]) .... each £12
MR PINK WHISTLE'S BIG BOOK (Evans, 1958)..£20
RUMBLE AND CHUFF (illustrated by David Walsh) (Juvenile Productions, [1958])..........................£20
TALES AFTER TEA (Collins, 1958) £10
ENID BLYTON'S MYSTERY STORIES (contains 'The Secret of Cliff Castle' and 'Smuggler Ben') (Collins, 1959)...................£10
ENID BLYTON'S DOG STORIES (contains 'Three Boys and a Circus' [1940] and 'The Adventures of Scamp' [1943])
(Collins, 1959) £10
ADVENTURE STORIES (Collins, 1960)..£10
ADVENTURE OF THE STRANGE RUBY (illustrated by Roger Payne) (Brockhampton Press, 1960)................£15
HAPPY DAY STORIES (illustrated by Marcia Lane) (Evans, 1960)..£15
WILL THE FIDDLER (illustrated by Grace Lodge) (Instructive Arts, [1960])....................................£20
OLD TESTAMENT PICTURE BOOKS (Macmillan, 1960) .... each £5
TALES AT BEDTIME (illustrated by Hilda McGavin) (Collins, 1960) £15
THE BIG ENID BLYTON BOOK (Hamlyn, 1961)..£15
THE MYSTERY THAT NEVER WAS (illustrated by Gilbert Dunlop) (Collins, 1961) £20
CIRCUS DAYS AGAIN (May Fair Books, 1962)..£10
THE FOUR COUSINS (illustrated by Joan Thompson) (Lutterworth Press, 1962) £15
STORIES FOR MONDAY (issued without dustjacket) (Oliphants, 1962)..£20
STORIES FOR TUESDAY (Oliphants, 1962) £20
THE BOY WHO WANTED A DOG (illustrated by Sally Michel) (Lutterworth Press, 1963)................£10
TALES OF BRAVE ADVENTURE. Retold by Enid Blyton (stories about Robin Hood and King Arthur) (Dean, [1963])..............£12

Two key Blyton rarities including her first collection of poems **Child Whispers** *(£250), issued in pictorial card covers in 1922.*

BRER RABBIT AGAIN (Dean, 1963)...£8
THE ENID BLYTON STORYBOOK FOR FIVES TO SEVENS (illustrated by Dorothy Hall and Grace Shelton)
(Parrish, [1964])..£25
HAPPY HOURS STORY BOOK (Dean, [1964])..£15
ENID BLYTON'S SUNSHINE PICTURE STORY BOOK (first of a series)
(World Distributors [printed in the Netherlands], [1964])...£15
STORYTIME BOOK (Dean, 1964)..£15
TELL-A-STORY BOOKS (World Distributors, 1964)..each £6
TROUBLE FOR THE TWINS (Brockhampton Press, 1964) £12
ENID BLYTON'S SUNSHINE BOOK (Dean, [1965])..£12
THE BOY WHO CAME BACK (illustrated by Elsie Walker) (Lutterworth Press, 1965)...............................£10
THE MAN WHO STOPPED TO HELP (illustrated by Elsie Walker) (Lutterworth Press, 1965) £10
EASY READER (first of a series; issued without dustjacket) (Collins, 1965)..£8
ENID BLYTON'S BRER RABBIT'S A RASCAL (Dean, 1965)..£12
TALES OF LONG AGO Retold by Enid Blyton (Dean, 1965) £12
ENID BLYTON'S PIXIE TALES (Collins, 1966)..£12
ENID BLYTON'S PIXIELAND STORY BOOK (Collins, 1966) £12
ENID BLYTON'S PLAYBOOK (first of a series) (Collins, [1966])..£12
ENID BLYTON'S FIRESIDE TALES (Collins, 1966) £12
THE HAPPY HOUSE CHILDREN (Collins, 1966)..£15
ENID BLYTON'S BEDTIME ANNUAL (Manchester, 1966) £15
THE FAIRY FOLK STORY BOOK (Collins, 1966) £15
ENID BLYTON'S GIFT BOOK (Purnell, 1966) £15
STORIES FOR BEDTIME (Dean, 1966)..£12
STORIES FOR YOU (Dean, 1966) £12
JOHN AND MARY (series of nine books; illustrated by Fromont) (Brockhampton Press, 1966-68) ....each £8
HOLIDAY ANNUAL STORIES (Low Marston, 1967)...£12
HOLIDAY MAGIC STORIES (Low Marston, 1967)..£12
HOLIDAY PIXIE STORIES (Low Marston, 1967) £12
HOLIDAY TOY STORIES (Low Marston, 1967) £12
THE PLAYTIME STORY BOOK NOS 1-14 (World Distributors, 1967)...each £6
ADVENTURES ON WILLOW FARM (Collins, 1968) £10
BROWNIE TALES (Collins, 1968) £10
ONCE UPON A TIME (Collins, 1968) £10
THE BEAR WITH BOOT-BUTTON EYES and Other Stories (Purnell, 1975) £5
DAME ROUNDY'S STOCKINGS and Other Stories (Purnell, 1975) £5
THE DOG WITH THE LONG TAIL and Other Stories (Purnell, 1975)...£5
THE GOBLIN AND THE DRAGON and Other Stories (Purnell, 1975)...£5
THE GOOD OLD ROCKING HORSE and Other Stories (Purnell, 1975) £5
THE LITTLE SUGAR MOUSE and Other Stories (Purnell, 1975) £5
BRER RABBIT AND THE TAR BABY (illustrated by Val Biro) (Hodder & Stoughton, 1975) £10

BOND, Michael

British author. Born: 1926. Worked as a cameraman for the BBC during the 1950s, before turning to writing following the success of *A Bear Called Paddington* (1958). As well as Paddington, Bond has created several other popular children's characters, including Thursday, Parsley the Lion and Olga da Polga.

Prices are for books in Very Good condition with dustjackets where applicable.

'Paddington' Story Books

A BEAR CALLED PADDINGTON (illustrated by Peggy Fortnum) (Collins, 1958) £150
MORE ABOUT PADDINGTON (illustrated by Peggy Fortnum) (Collins, 1959)...£75
PADDINGTON HELPS OUT (illustrated by Peggy Fortnum) (Collins, 1960)..£65
PADDINGTON ABROAD (illustrated by Peggy Fortnum) (Collins, 1961)..£65
PADDINGTON AT LARGE (illustrated by Peggy Fortnum) (Collins, 1962) £65
PADDINGTON MARCHES ON (illustrated by Peggy Fortnum) (Collins, 1964)..£65
THE ADVENTURES OF PADDINGTON (contains 'A Bear Called Paddington' and 'More About Paddington') (Collins, 1965).....£30
PADDINGTON AT WORK (illustrated by Peggy Fortnum) (Collins, 1966)..£40
PADDINGTON GOES TO TOWN (illustrated by Peggy Fortnum) (Collins, 1968)..£40
PADDINGTON TAKES THE AIR (illustrated by Peggy Fortnum) (Collins, 1970)..£35
PADDINGTON 'BLUE PETER' STORYBOOK (Collins, 1973) £25
PADDINGTON TAKES A BATH (illustrated by Barry Wilkinson) (Collins, 1976)...£15
PADDINGTON GOES TO THE SALES (illustrated by Barry Wilkinson) (Collins, 1976) £15
PADDINGTON'S NEW ROOM (illustrated by Barry Wilkinson) (Collins, 1976)...£15
PADDINGTON TAKES THE TEST (illustrated by Peggy Fortnum) (Collins, 1979).......................................£35
PADDINGTON AT HOME (Collins, 1980)...£15
PADDINGTON GOES OUT (Collins, 1980)..£15
PADDINGTON ON SCREEN: A Second Blue Peter Storybook (illustrated by Barry Macey) (BBC, 1981) £15
PADDINGTON'S STORYBOOK (anthology; illustrated by Peggy Fortnum) (Collins, 1983) £12

Paddington 'Young Set' Books

PADDINGTON BEAR (illustrated by Fred Banbery) (Collins, 1972) £20
PADDINGTON'S GARDEN (illustrated by Fred Banbery) (Collins, 1972) £15
PADDINGTON AT THE CIRCUS (illustrated by Fred Banbery) (Collins, 1973) £12
PADDINGTON GOES SHOPPING (illustrated by Fred Banbery) (Collins, 1973)..£12
PADDINGTON AT THE SEASIDE (illustrated by Fred Banbery) (Collins, 1975).......................................£12
PADDINGTON AT THE TOWER (illustrated by Fred Banbery) (Collins, 1975) £12

*The very first 'Paddington' book, **A Bear Called Paddington** (1958), and the third in the series, **Paddington Helps Out** (1960).*

PADDINGTON'S PICTURE BOOK (anthology; contains 'Paddington Bear', 'Paddington's Garden', 'Paddington at the Circus', 'Paddington Goes Shopping', 'Paddington at the Tower' and 'Paddington at the Seaside') (Collins, [1978]) £12

Paddington 'First' Picture Books
PADDINGTON AND THE KNICKERBOCKER RAINBOW (illustrated by David McKee) (Collins, 1984) £12
PADDINGTON AT THE ZOO (illustrated by David McKee) (Collins, 1984) £12
PADDINGTON AT THE FAIR (illustrated by David McKee) (Collins, 1985) £12
PADDINGTON'S PAINTING EXHIBITION (illustrated by David McKee) (Collins, 1985) £12
PADDINGTON AT THE PALACE (illustrated by David McKee) (Collins, 1986) £12
PADDINGTON MINDS THE HOUSE (illustrated by David McKee) (Collins, 1986) £12
PADDINGTON AND THE MARMALADE MAZE (illustrated by David McKee) (Collins, 1987) £12
PADDINGTON'S BUSY DAY (illustrated by David McKee) (Collins, 1987) £12
PADDINGTON'S MAGICAL CHRISTMAS (illustrated by David McKee) (Collins, 1988) £12

Picture Books Written with Karen Bond
PADDINGTON'S LONDON (David Booth/Hutchinson, 1986) £10
PADDINGTON AT THE AIRPORT (illustrated by Toni Goffe) (David Booth/Hutchinson, 1986) £10
PADDINGTON POSTS A LETTER (Crocodile, 1987) £10
PADDINGTON'S COLOURS (Crocodile, 1986) £10
PADDINGTON'S BUS RIDES (Hutchinson, 1986) £10
PADDINGTON'S CLOCK BOOK (Hutchinson, 1986) £10

Paddington 'Pop-Up' Books
PADDINGTON'S POP-UP BOOK (Collins, 1977) £30
PADDINGTON'S SHOPPING ADVENTURE (Collins, 1981) £18
PADDINGTON'S BIRTHDAY TREAT (Collins, 1981) £18
PADDINGTON AND THE SNOWBEAR (Collins, 1981) £18
PADDINGTON AT THE LAUNDERETTE (Collins, 1981) £18

Other 'Paddington' Titles
PADDINGTON'S BIRTHDAY BOOK Compiled by Brenda Bond (illustrated by Peggy Fortnum) (Collins, 1969) £20
THE GREAT BIG PADDINGTON BOOK (illustrated by Ivor Wood) (Collins, 1976) £12
PADDINGTON'S LOOSE-END BOOK: An ABC of Things to Do (illustrated by Ivor Wood) (Collins, 1976) £10
PADDINGTON'S PARTY BOOK (illustrated by Ivor Wood) (Collins, 1976) £10
FUN AND GAMES WITH PADDINGTON (with Lesley Young) (Collins, 1977) £10
PADDINGTON'S CARTOON BOOK (illustrated by Ivor Wood) (Collins, 1979) £10
PADDINGTON BEAR RAG BOOK: DRESSING (Dean's Rag Book Co., 1982) £12
PADDINGTON'S DAY OF ACTION (illustrated by Barry Macey) (Paddington & Co., 1983) £10
PADDINGTON'S FIRST PUZZLE BOOK (Crocodile, 1987) £10
PADDINGTON'S SECOND PUZZLE BOOK (Crocodile, 1987) £10

'Thursday' Books
HERE COMES THURSDAY (illustrated by Daphne Rowles) (Harrap, 1966) £20
THURSDAY RIDES AGAIN (illustrated by Beryl Sanders) (Harrap, 1968) £20
THURSDAY AHOY! (illustrated by Leslie Wood) (Harrap, 1969) £20
THURSDAY IN PARIS (illustrated by Leslie Wood) (Harrap, 1971) £20

'Parsley' Books
PARSLEY'S GOOD DEED (illustrated by Esor) (BBC, 1969) £12
THE STORY OF PARSLEY'S TAIL (illustrated by Esor) (BBC, 1969) £12
PARSLEY'S LAST STAND (BBC, 1970) £12
PARSLEY'S PROBLEM PRESENT (BBC, 1970) £12
PARSLEY THE LION (illustrated by Ivor Wood) (Collins, 1972) £12
PARSLEY PARADE (illustrated by Ivor Wood) (Collins, 1972) £12

'Olga Da Polga' Books
THE TALES OF OLGA DA POLGA (illustrated by Hans Helweg; paperback) (Puffin, 1971) £12
OLGA MEETS HER MATCH (illustrated by Hans Helweg) (Longman, 1973) £15
THE FIRST BIG OLGA DA POLGA BOOK (illustrated by Hans Helweg) (Longman, 1975) £12
THE SECOND BIG OLGA DA POLGA BOOK (illustrated by Hans Helweg) (Longman, 1975) £12
OLGA CARRIES ON (illustrated by Hans Helweg) (Kestrel, 1976) £6

'J.D. Polson' Books
J.D. POLSON AND THE LIBERTY HEAD DIME (illustrated by Roger Wade-Walker) (Octopus, 1980) £20
J.D. POLSON AND THE DILLOGATE AFFAIR (illustrated by Roger Wade-Walker) (Hodder & Stoughton, 1981) £20
J.D. POLSON AND THE GREAT UNVEILING (illustrated by Roger Wade-Walker) (Hodder & Stoughton, 1982) £20

Others
THE DAY THE ANIMALS WENT ON STRIKE (illustrated by Jim Hodgson) (Studio Vista, 1972) £20
MICHAEL BOND'S BOOK OF MICE (Purnell [printed in Holland], [1972]) £12
MR CRAM'S MAGIC BUBBLES (illustrated by Gioia Fiammenghi; paperback) (Puffin, 1975) £6
WINDMILL (illustrated by Tony Cattaneo) (Studio Vista, 1975) £20
THE CARAVAN PUPPETS (illustrated by Vanessa Julian-Ottie) (Collins, 1983) £15

George E. Studdy's 'Bonzo the Dog' featured in a number of annuals between 1936 and 1952. This one dates from 1949.

'BONZO' BOOKS AND ANNUALS

A popular series of books and annuals featuring Bonzo the Dog, the creation of the British artist George E. Studdy (1878-1948). Bonzo first appeared in 1912 and, as well as books, inspired postcards, toys and a series of silent animated films.

Prices are for annuals in Very Good condition (with cover description in brackets).

'Bonzo' Annuals
BONZO LAUGHTER ANNUAL [1935] £140
BONZO'S ANNUAL (Bonzo sitting on throne) [1936] £125
BONZO'S ANNUAL (Bonzo dressed as clown with balloon) [1937] £120
BONZO'S ANNUAL (Bonzo skipping) [1938] £120
BONZO'S ANNUAL (Bonzo and jack-in-the-box) [1947] £50
BONZO'S ANNUAL (Bonzo with a donkey and cart) [1948] £50
BONZO'S ANNUAL (Bonzo wearing a fez and firing a peashooter) [1949] £50
BONZO'S ANNUAL (Bonzo with parrot) [1950] £50
BONZO'S ANNUAL (Bonzo as a cowboy) [1951] £45
BONZO'S ANNUAL (Bonzo on a moon rocket) [1952] £40
THE BONZO PORTFOLIO (1-10) ....the set £250

'Bonzo' Books
BONZO'S HAPPY DAY (Dunlop Press, no date) £150
BONZO'S LEAP YEAR (Dunlop Press, no date) £150
BONZO'S HAPPY FAMILY (Dunlop Press, no date) £150
BONZO'S LITTLE HOLIDAY (Dunlop Press, no date) £150
BACHELOR BONZO (Dunlop Press, no date) £150
BONZO'S BRAN PIE (Dunlop Press, no date) £150
BONZO PAINTING BOOK (J. Swain, [1924]) £150
MR BONZO COMES TO TOWN (J. Swain, [1925]) £150
BAD BOY BONZO (J. Swain, [1925]) £150
BONZO'S SEASIDE HOLIDAY (J. Swain, [1925]) £150
BONZO'S COUNTRY HOLIDAY (J. Swain, [1925]) £150
THE GOOD DEEDS OF BONZO (J. Swain, [1925]) £150
THE ADVENTURES OF BONZO (J. Swain, [1925]) £150
THE BONZO BOOK (Partridge, [1925]) £200
THE NEW BONZO BOOK (Partridge, [1927]) £200
THE BONZOOLOO BOOK (Partridge, [1929]) £200
BONZO AND US (Partridge, 1931) £160
BONZO: The Great Big Holiday Book (cover shows Bonzo on rocking horse) (Dean, 1934) £75
BONZO: The Great Big Holiday Book (cover shows Bonzo's head) (Dean, 1934) £75
BONZO COLOURING BOOK (Dean, [1934]) £70

'BOOKANO' BOOKS

Popular series of pop-up books designed and published by S.L. Giraud under the Strand Publications imprint between 1934 and 1951. Note that during the war years (Nos. 7-13) the books were compiled from previously used material. In the mid-Thirties (probably 1936), the title was changed from *Bookano Annual* to *Bookano Stories*.

Prices are for books in Very Good condition.

BOOKANO STORIES: With Pictures that Spring Up in Model Form (edited by S.L. Giraud)
 (Strand Publications: 'Bookano Living Pictures' series, [1936]) £70
BOOKANO ZOO: Animals in Fact, Fancy and Fun (edited and produced by S.L. Giraud)
 (Strand Publications, [1939]) £65
BOOKANO NO 1: Goblins in a Carpenter's Shop, with Sound Effects of Sawing Wood! (Strand Publications, 1934) £90
BOOKANO NO 2: Cottage, with Semi-Transparent Fairy (Strand Publications, 1935) £80
BOOKANO NO 3 (Strand Publications, 1936) £70
BOOKANO NO 4 (Strand Publications, 1937) £70
BOOKANO NO 5 (Strand Publications, 1938) £60
BOOKANO NO 6 (Strand Publications, 1939) £60
BOOKANO NO 7 (Strand Publications, 1940) £60
BOOKANO NO 8 (Strand Publications, 1941) £60
BOOKANO NO 9 (Strand Publications, 1942) £60
BOOKANO NO 10 (Strand Publications, 1943) £55
BOOKANO NO 11 (Strand Publications, 1944) £55
BOOKANO NO 12 (Strand Publications, 1945) £55
BOOKANO NO 13 (Strand Publications, 1946) £55
BOOKANO NO 14 (Strand Publications, 1947) £55
BOOKANO NO 15 (Strand Publications, 1948) £55
BOOKANO NO 16: Tower Bridge (Strand Publications, 1949) £80
BOOKANO STORIES NO. 17 (Strand Publications, 1950) £90

BOSTON, Lucy M.

British author. Born Lucy Maria Wood in Southport, Lancashire, in 1892. Studied at Somerville College, Oxford, before training as a nurse and serving in France during the Great War. In 1935, she bought the 800-year-old Hemingford Grey Manor in Cambridgeshire, which inspired *The Children of Green Knowe* (1954) and five sequels, all illustrated by her son, Peter. Died: 1990.

Prices are for books in Very Good condition with dustjackets.

'Green Knowe' Books

THE CHILDREN OF GREEN KNOWE (illustrated by Peter Boston) (Faber, 1954) £50
THE CHIMNEYS OF GREEN KNOWE (illustrated by Peter Boston) (Faber, 1958).. £30
THE RIVER AT GREEN KNOWE (illustrated by Peter Boston) (Faber, 1959) £30
A STRANGER AT GREEN KNOWE (illustrated by Peter Boston) (Faber, 1961)... £35
AN ENEMY AT GREEN KNOWE (illustrated by Peter Boston) (Faber, 1964).. £30
THE STONES OF GREEN KNOWE (illustrated by Peter Boston) (The Bodley Head, 1976) £25

Others

YEW HALL (Faber, 1954).. £35
THE CASTLE OF YEW (illustrated by Margery Gill) (The Bodley Head, 1965).. £18
THE SEA-EGG (illustrated by Peter Boston) (Faber, 1967)... £18
THE HOUSE THAT GREW (illustrated by Caroline Hemming) (Faber, 1969).. £18
PERSEPHONE (Collins, 1969).. £15
THE HORNED MAN (play) (Faber, 1970) £15
NOTHING SAID (illustrated by Peter Boston) (Faber, 1971)... £15
THE GUARDIANS OF THE HOUSE (illustrated by Peter Boston) (The Bodley Head, 1974)................................. £15
THE FOSSIL SNAKE (illustrated by Peter Boston) (The Bodley Head, 1975) £15
TIME IS UNDONE (limited to 750 copies; wraps) (Privately printed, 1977).. £15

'E.V.B.'

British illustrator. Born Eleanor Vere Boyle in 1825. Inspired by Richard Doyle and the Pre-Raphaelites, Eleanor Vere Boyle became the first important woman illustrator of the early Victorian era, in the generation preceding Kate Greenaway. Disguising her gender under the alias 'E.V.B.', she would most famously illustrate a ground-breaking English edition of Andersen's *Fairy Tales*, and go on to become one of the most popular writer-gardeners of the nineteenth century. Died: 1916.

Selected bibliography. Prices are for books in Good condition in their original bindings.

CHILD'S PLAY (Addey, 1852) £200
A CHILDREN'S SUMMER (Addey, 1853) £200
A NEW CHILD'S PLAY (Sampson Low, 1877) £150
CHILD'S PLAY (omnibus) (Sampson Low, 1881 [December 1880]) £150
THE MAY QUEEN by Alfred Tennyson (Sampson Low, 1861 [December 1860])... £200
FAIRY TALES by Hans Christian Andersen (Sampson Low, 1872 [December 1871]) £600
FAIRY TALES (with two extra plates by EVB; small folio) £800

'BOYS' FRIEND LIBRARY'

Some collectable issues of the 'Boys' Friend Library', the British story journal.

Prices are for issues in Very Good condition.

Original series

No 1 'Jack, Sam and Pete's Adventure in Africa' by S. Clarke Hook (Sept 1906) £20
No 4 'Birds of Prey' by Maxwell Scott (Oct 1906)... £12
No 10 'Sexton Blake's Honour' Anon (Jan 1907).. £15
No 30 'Tom Merry & Co' by Martin Clifford (Nov 1907) £20
No 37 'Tom Merry's Conquest' by Martin Clifford (Jan 1908) £20
No 47 'Gilbert Nameless' by Morton Pike (April 1908).. £10
No 115 'Guy of the Greenwood' by Morton Pike (April 1910).. £12
No 200 'Canvas And Caravan' by R.W. Comrade (Aug 1912).. £15
No 259 'The Longbows of England' by Morton Pike (April 1914) £12
No 288 'The Boy Without a Name' by Frank Richards (Jan 1915)... £25
No 328 'Rivals and Chums' by Frank Richards (Mar 1916) £25
No 458 'Robin Hood and His Merry Men' by Morton Pike (May 1919) £10
No 504 'In Trackless Space' by R.W. Comrade (April 1920).. £25
No 514 'Nipper at St. Franks' by R.W. Comrade (Jul 1920).. £15
No 681 'A Trip To Mars' by Fenton Ash (Sept 1923) £25
No 688 'The Devil Tree of Eldorado' by Frank Aubrey (Oct 1923) £125
No 704 'Pots of Money' (anonymous [E.S. Brooks]) (Feb 1924).. £15

New series

No 44 'Wings of Adventure' by Paul Quinton (April 1926)...
No 167 'The Flying Beetle' by George E. Rochester (Nov 1928)...

*Eleanor Vere Boyle ('E.V.B') was the most important female illustrator from the generation preceding Kate Greenaway. This plate comes from the 1872 edition of **Fairy Tales** by Hans Christian Andersen.*

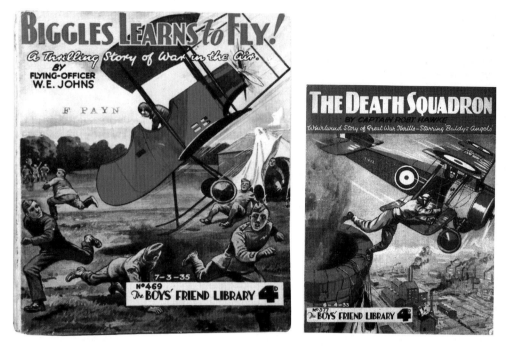

*Two issues from the popular Boys' Friend Library including the very scarce **Biggles Learns to Fly!** by W.E. Johns.*

No 171 'The Scarlet Squadron' by George E. Rochester (Dec 1928) £15
No 204 'Crooked Gold' (anonymous [Leslie Charteris]) (Aug 1929)...£250
No 266 'The Rio Kid' by Ralph Redway (Dec 1930) £12
No 331 'King of the Islands' by Charles Hamilton (April 1932)..£12
No 369 'Baldy's Angels' by Captain Robert Hawke (Feb 1933) £15
No 405 'Captain Justice' by Murray Roberts (Nov 1933) £15
No 469 'Biggles Learns to Fly' by W.E. Johns (Mar 1935)..£1,000
No 482 'The Mystery Man of Mayfair' by Warder Lynk (Jun 1935) £12
No 491 'Sir Anthony – Crook' by Warder Lynk (Aug 1935)..£12
No 501 'Biggles in France' by W.E. Johns (Nov 1935) £1,100
No 610 'Biggles Goes To War' by W.E Johns (Feb 1938) £250
No 614 'The Camels Are Coming' by W.E. Johns (Mar 1938)..£250
No 617 'The Cruise of the Condor' by W.E. Johns (April 1938)..£250
No 621 'Biggles Flies East' by W.E. Johns (May 1938) £250
No 625 'The Spyflyers' by W.E. Johns (1938) £250
No 630 'Biggles Flies Again' by W.E. Johns (1938) £250
No 634 'The Mark of the Buccaneer' by R. Gordon (Aug 1938) £60
No 654 'The Laughing Buccaneer' by R. Gordon (Jan 1939) £60
No 701 'The Trail of the Flying Bomb' by George E. Holmes (Jan 1940)..£15
No 702 'The Hooded Stranger' by Gerald Verner (Jan 1940) £15
No 721 'The Grim Joker' by Gerald Verner (June 1940) £15
No 722 'The Phantom of Scotland Yard' by 'Barry Weston' [Gwyn Evans] (June 1940) £15

'BOY'S OWN' ANNUALS

Bestselling British story annual, described by its publisher, the Religious Tract Society, as "an illustrated volume of pure and entertaining reading". The paper itself was launched on 18th January 1879, the first annual appearing later that year. Although the paper survived until February 1967, the last annual was published in 1940.

Prices are for annuals (bound volumes) in Very Good condition.

VOLUMES 1 (with colour plates) (January-September 1879)..£75
VOLUMES 2-36 (with double-page sporting prints and special supplements where issued)
(October 1879-September 1914)..each £40
VOLUMES 37-58 (with colour plates) (October 1914-September 1935)..each £45
VOLUMES 59-63 (with colour plates) (October 1935-September 1940)..each £30

BRADBURY, Ray

American science fiction author. Born: 1920. The author of the classic *Fahrenheit 451*, *Dark Carnival* and *Something Wicked This Way Comes* also penned these very collectable children's SF books.

Prices are for books in Very Good condition with dustjackets.

SWITCH ON THE NIGHT (Pantheon, US, 1955) (1st state, 'Pantheon Books' on title page).........................£450
SWITCH ON THE NIGHT (Pantheon, US, 1955) (later states, 'Pantheon Books/Random House')...................£325
SWITCH ON THE NIGHT (Hart-Davis, 1955)...£170
R IS FOR ROCKET (Doubleday, US, 1962)...£170
R IS FOR ROCKET (Hart-Davis, 1968)...£115
S IS FOR SPACE (Doubleday, US, 1966)..£115
S IS FOR SPACE (Hart-Davis, 1968)...£100
THE HALLOWEEN TREE (Knopf, US, 1972) (black cloth stamped in orange and white)..............................£80
THE HALLOWEEN TREE (Knopf, US, 1972) (white cloth stamped in orange and brown, no d/j)...................£30
THE HALLOWEEN TREE (Hart-Davis MacGibbon, 1975) £35
WHEN ELEPHANTS LAST IN THE DOORYARD BLOOMED: Celebrations for Almost Any Day in the Year
(Knopf, US, 1973)...£15
WHEN ELEPHANTS LAST IN THE DOORYARD BLOOMED (Hart Davis MacGibbon, 1975) £15
WHERE ROBOT MICE AND ROBOT MEN RUN ROUND IN ROBOT TOWNS: New Poems Both Light and Dark
(Knopf, US, 1977)...£15
WHERE ROBOT MICE AND ROBOT MEN RUN ROUND IN ROBOT TOWNS
(Granada, UK, 1979)...£15
THE HAUNTED COMPUTER & THE ANDROID POPE (Knopf, US, 1981)..£15
THE HAUNTED COMPUTER & THE ANDROID POPE (Granada, 1981)...£15
DOGS THINK THAT EVERY DAY IS CHRISTMAS (Gibbs-Smith, US, 1997)..£10
AHMED AND THE OBLIVION MACHINES (paperback) (Avon, US, 1998) £10

BRADLEY, Helen

British author-illustrator. Born: Lancashire, 1900. Began painting in her sixties, producing a series of distinctive Lowryesque scenes reminiscent of her Edwardian childhood that were collected in four books.

Prices are for books in Very Good condition with dustjackets.

AND MISS CARTER WORE PINK: Scenes from an Edwardian Childhood
(Cape, 1971)..£25
MISS CARTER CAME WITH US (Cape, 1973) £25
'IN THE BEGINNING' SAID GREAT-AUNT JANE (Cape, 1975) £20
THE QUEEN WHO CAME TO TEA (Cape, 1978) £20

BRAZIL, Angela

British author. Born: Preston, 1868. Attended Manchester High School, Ellerslie College and finally Heatherly's, where she studied art. Her first school story, *The Fortunes of Philippa* (1907), was followed by many others, including *The Jolliest Term on Record* (1915) and *A Patriotic Schoolgirl* (1918). Died: 1947.

Prices are for books in Very Good condition with dustjackets where applicable.

A TERRIBLE TOMBOY (illustrated by Angela and Amy Brazil) (Gay & Bird, 1904)....................................£250
THE FORTUNES OF PHILIPPA (Blackie, 1907 [1906])..£125
THE THIRD CLASS AT MISS KAYE'S (Blackie, 1909 [1908])..£125
THE NICEST GIRL IN THE SCHOOL (Blackie, 1910)...£90
BOSOM FRIENDS: A Seaside Story (Nelson, [1910])..£70
THE MANOR HOUSE SCHOOL (illustrated by F. Moorsom) (Blackie, 1911)...£65
A FOURTH FORM FRIENDSHIP (Blackie, 1912)..£65
THE NEW GIRL AT ST. CHAD'S (Blackie, 1912)..£65
A PAIR OF SCHOOLGIRLS (Blackie, [1912])...£65
THE MISCHIEVOUS BROWNIE (play) (Paterson: 'Children's Plays' series No. 1, [1913])............................£65
THE FAIRY GIFTS (play) (Paterson: 'Children's Plays' series No. 2, [1913])..£65
THE ENCHANTED FIDDLE (play) (Paterson: 'Children's Plays' series No. 3, [1913])..................................£65
THE WISHING PRINCESS (play) (Paterson: 'Children's Plays' series No. 4, [1913])....................................£60
THE LEADER OF THE LOWER SCHOOL (Blackie, [1914])...£65
THE YOUNGEST GIRL IN THE FIFTH (Blackie, [1914])...£65
THE GIRLS OF ST. CYPRIAN'S (Blackie, [1914])...£65
THE SCHOOL BY THE SEA (Blackie, [1914])...£65
THE JOLLIEST TERM ON RECORD (illustrated by Balliol Salmon) (Blackie, [1915]).................................£60
FOR THE SAKE OF THE SCHOOL (Blackie, [1915]) £60
THE LUCKIEST GIRL IN THE SCHOOL (illustrated by Balliol Salmon) (Blackie, [1916])............................£60
THE SLAP-BANG BOYS (T.C. & E.C. Jack, [1917])..£60
THE MADCAP OF THE SCHOOL (illustrated by Balliol Salmon) (Blackie, [1918]).....................................£60
A PATRIOTIC SCHOOLGIRL (illustrated by Balliol Salmon) (Blackie, [1918])...£60
FOR THE SCHOOL COLOURS (illustrated by Balliol Salmon) (Blackie, [1918])...£60
A HARUM-SCARUM SCHOOLGIRL (illustrated by John Campbell) (Blackie, [1919]) £60

Even without their colourful dustjackets, many of Angela Brazil's books are still very handsome and desirable volumes.

Although not as avidly sought as Elinor Brent-Dyer, Angela Brazil remains very popular with collectors of schoolgirl stories.

THE HEAD GIRL AT THE GABLES (illustrated by Balliol Salmon) (Blackie, [1919])................£60
TWO LITTLE SCAMPS AND A PUPPY (illustrated by E. Blampied) (Nelson, [1919])................£65
A GIFT FROM THE SEA (illustrated by A.E. Jackson) (Nelson, [1920])................£100
A POPULAR SCHOOLGIRL (illustrated by Balliol Salmon) (Blackie, [1920])................£100
THE PRINCESS OF THE SCHOOL (illustrated by Frank Wiles) (Blackie, [1920])................£100
A FORTUNATE TERM (illustrated by Treyer Evans) (Blackie, [1921])................£100
LOYAL TO THE SCHOOL (illustrated by Treyer Evans) (Blackie, [1921])................£100
MONITRESS MERLE (illustrated by Treyer Evans) (Blackie, [1922])................£100
THE SCHOOL IN THE SOUTH (illustrated by W. Smithson-Broadhead)
    (Blackie, [1922])................£100
THE KHAKI BOYS and Other Stories (Nelson, [1923])................£100
SCHOOLGIRL KITTY (illustrated by W.E. Wightman) (Blackie, [1923])................£100
CAPTAIN PEGGIE (illustrated by W.E. Wightman) (Blackie, [1924])................£70
MY OWN SCHOOLDAYS (autobiography) (Blackie, [1925])................£115
JOAN'S BEST CHUM (illustrated by W.E. Wightman) (Blackie, [1926])................£70
QUEEN OF THE DORMITORY and Other Stories (illustrated by P.B. Hickling)
    (Cassell, 1926)................£70
RUTH OF ST. RONAN'S (illustrated by F. Oldham) (Blackie, [1927])................£65
AT SCHOOL WITH RACHEL (illustrated by W.E. Wightman) (Blackie, [1928])................£65
ST CATHERINE'S COLLEGE (illustrated by Frank Wiles) (Blackie, [1929])................£60
THE LITTLE GREEN SCHOOL (illustrated by Frank Wiles) (Blackie, [1931])................£60
NESTA'S NEW SCHOOL (illustrated by J. Dewar Mills) (Blackie, [1932])................£60
JEAN'S GOLDEN TERM (Blackie, [1934])................£60
THE SCHOOL AT THE TURRETS (Blackie, [1935])................£60
AN EXCITING TERM (Blackie, [1936])................£50
JILL'S JOLLIEST SCHOOL (Blackie, 1937)................£50
THE SCHOOL ON THE CLIFF (illustrated by F.E. Hiley) (Blackie, [1938])................£50
THE SCHOOL ON THE MOOR (illustrated by Henry Coller) (Blackie, [1939])................£50
THE NEW SCHOOL AT SCAWDALE (illustrated by M. Mackinlay)
    (Blackie, [1940])................£50
FIVE JOLLY SCHOOLGIRLS (Blackie, [1941])................£35
THE MYSTERY OF THE MOATED GRANGE (Blackie, [1942])................£35
THE SECRET OF THE BORDER CASTLE (illustrated by Charles Willis) (Blackie, [1943])................£35
THE SCHOOL IN THE FOREST (illustrated by J. Dewar Mills) (Blackie, [1944])................£35
THREE TERMS AT UPLANDS (illustrated by D.L. Mays) (Blackie, [1945])................£35
THE SCHOOL ON THE LOCH (illustrated by W. Lindsay Cable) (Blackie, [1946])................£35

BREARY, Nancy

British author who started to write her school stories for girls in the 1940s, concentrating on separate stories rather than series, with a strong focus on mystery.

Prices are for books in Very Good condition with dustjacket.

GIVE A FORM A BAD NAME (Newnes, 1943)................£40
TWO THRILLING TERMS (Blackie, 1943)................£40
NO PEACE FOR THE PREFECTS (Newnes, 1944)................£35
THE LOWER FOURTH EXCELS ITSELF (Newnes, 1945)................£35
A SCHOOL DIVIDED (Newnes, 1945)................£35
THIS TIME NEXT TERM (Blackie, 1945)................£35
JUNIOR CAPTAIN (illustrated by D.L. Mays) (Blackie, 1946)................£35
THE SNACK BOAT SAILS AT NOON ! (illustrated by Alfred Sindall) (Newnes, 1946)................£35
THE IMPOSSIBLE PREFECT (illustrated by Leo Bates) (Blackie, 1947)................£35
JUNIORS WILL BE JUNIORS (Newnes, 1947)................£35
THE FORM THAT LIKED TO BE FIRST (illustrated by W. Spence) (Blackie, 1948)................£35
IT WAS FUN IN THE FOURTH (illustrated by Joan Martin May) (Newnes, 1948)................£35
RACHEL CHANGES SCHOOLS (illustrated by D.L. Mays) (Blackie, 1948)................£30
MAINLY ABOUT THE FOURTH (Newnes, 1949)................£30
FIVE SISTERS AT SEDGEWICK (illustrated by W. Spence) (Blackie, 1950)................£30
DIMITY DREW'S FIRST TERM (Newnes, 1951)................£25
THE RELUCTANT SCHOOLGIRL (illustrated by Louis Ward) (Blackie, 1951)................£25
HAZEL HEAD GIRL (illustrated by W. Spence) (Blackie, 1952)................£25
AT SCHOOL WITH PETRA (illustrated by Newton Whittaker) (Blackie, 1953)................£25
FOURTH FORM DETECTIVES (illustrated by Newton Whittaker) (Blackie, 1954)................£25
THE RIVAL FOURTHS (illustrated by Frank Haseler) (Blackie, 1955)................£25
STUDY NUMBER SIX (illustrated by Betty Ladler) (Blackie, 1957)................£25
THE MYSTERY OF THE MOTELS (illustrated by Victor Bertoglio) (Blackie, 1958)................£25
SO THIS IS SCHOOL! (illustrated by Drake Brookshaw) (Blackie, 1959)................£25
THE AMAZING FRIENDSHIP (illustrated by Drake Brookshaw) (Blackie, 1960)................£25
THE FOURTH WAS FUN FOR PHILIPPA (illustrated by Drake Brookshaw)
    (Blackie, 1961)................£25

BRENT-DYER, Elinor M.

British author. Born: Gladys Eleanor May Dyer in South Shields in 1894. Studied at the City of Leeds Training College during the Great War, working as a teacher for the next thirty years. Submitted stories to various magazines and anthologies before publishing her first book, *Gerry Goes to School*, in 1922. This was followed three years later by *The School at the Chalet* (1925), the first of her long-running series of novels set at a chalet school in the Tyrol. Died: 1969.

Prices are for books in Very Good condition with dustjackets.

'Chalet School' Books

THE SCHOOL AT THE CHALET (Chambers, [1925])	£500
JO OF THE CHALET SCHOOL (Chambers, [1926])	£500
THE PRINCESS OF THE CHALET SCHOOL (Chambers, [1927])	£400
THE HEAD-GIRL OF THE CHALET SCHOOL (Chambers, 1928)	£400
THE RIVALS OF THE CHALET SCHOOL (Chambers, 1929)	£400
EUSTACIA GOES TO THE CHALET SCHOOL (Chambers, 1930)	£400
THE CHALET SCHOOL AND JO (Chambers, 1931)	£400
THE CHALET GIRLS IN CAMP (Chambers, 1932)	£400
THE EXPLOITS OF THE CHALET GIRLS (Chambers, 1933)	£400
THE CHALET SCHOOL AND THE LINTONS (Chambers, 1934)	£400
THE NEW HOUSE AT THE CHALET SCHOOL (Chambers, 1935)	£400
JO RETURNS TO THE CHALET SCHOOL (Chambers, 1936)	£400
THE NEW CHALET SCHOOL (Chambers, 1938)	£300
THE CHALET SCHOOL IN EXILE (with Brisley dustjacket) (Chambers, 1940)	£500
THE CHALET SCHOOL IN EXILE (with non-Brisley dustjacket) (Chambers, 1940)	£200
THE CHALET SCHOOL GOES TO IT (Chambers, 1941)	£200
THE HIGHLAND TWINS AT THE CHALET SCHOOL (Chambers, 1942)	£200
LAVENDER LAUGHS IN THE CHALET SCHOOL (Chambers, 1943)	£200
GAY FROM CHINA AT THE CHALET SCHOOL (Chambers, 1944)	£150
JO TO THE RESCUE (Chambers, 1945)	£200
THREE GO TO THE CHALET SCHOOL (Chambers, 1949)	£100
THE CHALET SCHOOL AND THE ISLAND (Chambers, 1950)	£100
PEGGY OF THE CHALET SCHOOL (Chambers, 1950)	£100
CAROLA STORMS THE CHALET SCHOOL (Chambers, 1951)	£100
THE CHALET SCHOOL AND ROSALIE (paperback) (Chambers, 1951)	£300
THE WRONG CHALET SCHOOL (Chambers, 1952)	£100
SHOCKS FOR THE CHALET SCHOOL (Chambers, 1952)	£100
THE CHALET SCHOOL IN THE OBERLAND (Chambers, 1952)	£100
BRIDE LEADS THE CHALET SCHOOL (Chambers, 1953)	£150
CHANGES FOR THE CHALET SCHOOL (Chambers, 1953)	£150
JOEY GOES TO THE OBERLAND (Chambers, 1954)	£150
THE CHALET SCHOOL AND BARBARA (Chambers, 1954)	£100
TOM TACKLES THE CHALET SCHOOL (Chambers, 1955)	£100
THE CHALET SCHOOL DOES IT AGAIN (Chambers, 1955)	£150
A CHALET GIRL FROM KENYA (Chambers, 1955)	£100
MARY-LOU OF THE CHALET SCHOOL (Chambers, 1956)	£100
A GENIUS AT THE CHALET SCHOOL (Chambers, 1956)	£100
A PROBLEM FOR THE CHALET SCHOOL (Chambers, 1956)	£100
THE NEW MISTRESS AT THE CHALET SCHOOL (Chambers, 1957)	£100
EXCITEMENTS AT THE CHALET SCHOOL (Chambers, 1957)	£100
THE COMING OF AGE OF THE CHALET SCHOOL (Chambers, 1958)	£100
THE CHALET SCHOOL AND RICHENDA (Chambers, 1958)	£100
TRIALS FOR THE CHALET SCHOOL (Chambers, 1959)	£100
THEODORA AND THE CHALET SCHOOL (Chambers, 1959)	£100
JOEY AND CO IN TIROL (Chambers, 1960)	£100
RUEY RICHARDSON – CHALETIAN (Chambers, 1960)	£100
A LEADER IN THE CHALET SCHOOL (Chambers, 1961)	£100
THE CHALET SCHOOL WINS THE TRICK (Chambers, 1961)	£100
A FUTURE CHALET SCHOOL GIRL (Chambers, 1962)	£150
THE FEUD IN THE CHALET SCHOOL (Chambers, 1962)	£100
THE CHALET SCHOOL TRIPLETS (Chambers, 1963)	£100
THE CHALET SCHOOL REUNION (with identification key) (Chambers, 1963)......£150 (with original yellow band: £200)	
JANE AND THE CHALET SCHOOL (Chambers, 1964)	£150
REDHEADS AT THE CHALET SCHOOL (Chambers, 1964)	£150
ADRIENNE AND THE CHALET SCHOOL (Chambers, 1965)	£150
SUMMER TERM AT THE CHALET SCHOOL (Chambers, 1965)	£150
CHALLENGE FOR THE CHALET SCHOOL (Chambers, 1966)	£150
TWO SAMS AT THE CHALET SCHOOL (Chambers, 1967)	£150
ALTHEA JOINS THE CHALET SCHOOL (Chambers, 1969)	£150
PREFECTS OF THE CHALET SCHOOL (Chambers, 1970)	£150

The 'Chalet School' series by Elinor Brent-Dyer remain her most collectable books, with values ranging from £150 to £500.

Related Titles

THE CHALET BOOK FOR GIRLS (issued without dustjacket) (Chambers, [1947]) £80
THE SECOND CHALET BOOK FOR GIRLS (issued without dustjacket) (Chambers, 1948) £80
THE THIRD CHALET BOOK FOR GIRLS (Chambers, 1949) £200
THE CHALET GIRLS' COOKBOOK (Chambers, 1953) £200

'La Rochelle' Books

GERRY GOES TO SCHOOL (illustrated by Gordon Browne) (Chambers, [1922]) £200
GERRY GOES TO SCHOOL (Lippincott, U.S., 1923) £200
A HEAD GIRL'S DIFFICULTIES (Chambers, [1923]) £200
THE MAIDS OF LA ROCHELLE (Chambers, [1924]) £200
SEVEN SCAMPS (Chambers, [1927]) £200
HEATHER LEAVES SCHOOL (Chambers, 1929) £200
JANIE OF LA ROCHELLE (Chambers, 1932) £200
JANIE STEPS IN (Chambers, 1953) £60

'Chudleigh Hold' Books

CHUDLEIGH HOLD (Chambers, 1954) £60
THE CONDOR CRAGS ADVENTURE (Chambers, 1954) £60
TOP SECRET (Chambers, 1955) £60

Others

A THRILLING TERM AT JANEWAY'S (Nelson, [1927]) £150
THE NEW HOUSE MISTRESS (Nelson, [1928]) £60
JUDY THE GUIDE (Nelson, [1928]) £150
THE SCHOOL BY THE RIVER (Burns, Oates & Washbourne, [1930]) £600
THE FEUD IN THE FIFTH REMOVE (Girl's Own Paper, [1932]) £100
THE LITTLE MARIE-JOSÉ (Burns, Oates & Washbourne, 1932) £600
CARNATION OF THE UPPER FOURTH (Girl's Own Paper, [1934]) £100
ELIZABETH THE GALLANT (Thornton Butterworth, 1935) £400
MONICA TURNS UP TRUMPS (Girl's Own Paper, [1936]) £100
CAROLINE THE SECOND (Girl's Own Paper, [1937]) £400
THEY BOTH LIKED DOGS (Girl's Own Paper, [1938]) £400
THE LITTLE MISSUS (Chambers, 1942) £150
THE LOST STAIRCASE (Chambers, 1946) £80

A complete set of Elinor Brent-Dyer's four 'travel' paperbacks issued by Chambers in the early 1950s. Together they're worth around £2,400.

LORNA AT WYNYARDS (Lutterworth Press, 1947)..£150
STEPSISTERS FOR LORNA (illustrated by John Bruce) (Temple, 1948)..£150
FARDINGALES (Latimer House, 1950)..£150
VERENA VISITS NEW ZEALAND (paperback) (Chambers, 1951)..£600
BESS ON HER OWN IN CANADA (paperback) (Chambers, 1951)..£600
A QUINTETTE IN QUEENSLAND (paperback) (Chambers, 1951)..£600
SHARLIE'S KENYA DIARY (paperback) (Chambers, 1951)..£600
THE 'SUSANNAH' ADVENTURE (Chambers, 1953) £80
NESTA STEPS OUT (Oliphants, 1954) £150
KENNELMAID NAN (Lutterworth Press, 1954)..£150
BEECHY OF THE HARBOUR SCHOOL (Oliphants, 1955) £100
LEADER IN SPITE OF HERSELF (Oliphants, 1956)..£100
THE SCHOOL AT SKELTON HALL (Parrish, 1962)..£150
TROUBLE AT SKELTON HALL (Parrish, 1963)..£150

Books Containing Stories by E.M. Brent-Dyer (All but 'My Favourite Story' issued without dustjackets)

SUNDAY AND EVERYDAY READING FOR THE YOUNG (contains Elinor M. Brent-Dyer's 'Jack's Revenge')
(Wells Gardner Darton, 1914) £60
THE BIG BOOK FOR GIRLS (contains Elinor M. Brent-Dyer's 'The Lady in the Yellow Gown') (Humphrey Milford/OUP, 1925)............£40
THE GOLDEN STORY BOOK FOR GIRLS (contains Elinor M. Brent-Dyer's 'The Lady in the Yellow Gown')
(Humphrey Milford/OUP, 1931) £40
STORIES OF THE CIRCUS, BOOK 4 (magazine; contains Elinor M. Brent-Dyer's 'Carlotta to the Rescue') ([c.1931]) £60
THE CHILDREN'S CIRCUS BOOK (contains Elinor M. Brent-Dyer's 'Carlotta to the Rescue') (Associated Newspapers, [c.1934]) £40
COME TO THE CIRCUS (contains Elinor M. Brent-Dyer's 'Carlotta to the Rescue') (P.R. Gawthorn, [c.1938])............£40
THE SECOND CORONET BOOK FOR GIRLS (contains Elinor M. Brent-Dyer's 'Cavalier Maid') (Sampson Low, no date) £30
MY FAVOURITE STORY (contains Elinor M. Brent-Dyer's 'Rescue in the Snows') (Thames, no date) £30
SCEPTRE GIRLS' STORY ANNUAL (contains Elinor M. Brent-Dyer's 'House of Secrets') (Purnell, no date) £30
GIRL'S OWN ANNUAL VOL. 57 (contains Elinor M. Brent-Dyer's 'The Robins Makes Good') (Girl's Own, no date).................£60
MY TREASURE HOUR BUMPER ANNUAL (contains Elinor M. Brent-Dyer's 'The Chalet School Mystery')
(Murrays Sales & Service Co., 1970)..£40

BRIGGS, Raymond

British author-illustrator. Born: Raymond Redvers Briggs in Wimbledon in 1934. Studied at the Wimbledon School of Art and the Slade School of Fine Art, subsequently working on advertisements and book covers before producing his first solo work, *Midnight Adventure*, in 1961. His distinctive 'comic strip' style was first seen in *Father Christmas* (1973), and has been used to great effect in *Fungus the Bogeyman* (1977), *The Snowman* (1978) and other books.

Prices are for books in Very Good condition with dustjackets where applicable.

'Father Christmas' Books

FATHER CHRISTMAS (Hamish Hamilton, 1973)..£70
FATHER CHRISTMAS GOES ON HOLIDAY (Hamish Hamilton, 1975)..£50
THE COMPLETE FATHER CHRISTMAS (contains 'Father Christmas' and 'Father Christmas Goes on Holiday')
    (Hamish Hamilton, 1978)..£40
THE FATHER CHRISTMAS MINI BOOK (Hamish Hamilton, 1989)..£10
THE FATHER CHRISTMAS BOOK OF THE FILM (paperback) (Puffin, 1992)..................................£5
THE FATHER CHRISTMAS BLOOMING DIARY 1994 (paperback) (Puffin, 1992) £5
FATHER CHRISTMAS HAVING A WONDERFUL TIME: A Story Book with Postcards (Hamish Hamilton, 1993)..................£10

'Fungus the Bogeyman' Books

FUNGUS THE BOGEYMAN (Hamish Hamilton, 1977)...£50
FUNGUS THE BOGEYMAN PLOP-UP BOOK (Hamish Hamilton, 1982)...£30

'Snowman' Books

THE SNOWMAN (Hamish Hamilton, 1978)..£50
THE SNOWMAN: The Party (board book) (Hamish Hamilton, 1985) £7
THE SNOWMAN: Dressing-Up (board book) (Hamish Hamilton, 1985) £7
THE SNOWMAN: Walking in the Air (board book) (Hamish Hamilton, 1985) £7
THE SNOWMAN: Building the Snowman (board book) (Hamish Hamilton, 1985)...........................£7
THE SNOWMAN: A Pop-up Book with Music (with Ron Van Der Meer) (Hamish Hamilton, 1986).......£35
THE SNOWMAN: Address Book (Hamish Hamilton, 1987)..£10
THE SNOWMAN BOOK OF THE FILM (paperback) (Puffin, 1988)..£5
THE SNOWMAN MINI BOOK (Hamish Hamilton, 1989) £5
THE SNOWMAN STORY BOOK (Random House, 1990)...£5
THE SNOWMAN CHRISTMAS BOOK (Ladybird, 1990)...£4
THE SNOWMAN FLAP BOOK (Random House, 1991)..£5
THE SNOWMAN CLOCK BOOK (Random House, 1991) £5
THE SNOWMAN TELL THE TIME BOOK (Hamish Hamilton, 1991)..£5
THE SNOWMAN SOFT AND SMALL BABY BOOK (Hamish Hamilton, 1993)....................................£5

Other Books Written and Illustrated by Raymond Briggs

MIDNIGHT ADVENTURE (Hamish Hamilton, 1961) £50
THE STRANGE HOUSE (Hamish Hamilton, 1961)...£40
RING-A-RING O'ROSES (Hamish Hamilton, 1962)..£45
SLEDGES TO THE RESCUE (Hamish Hamilton, 1963)...£40
THE WHITE LAND: A Picture Book of Traditional Rhymes and Verses (Hamish Hamilton, 1963)........£40
FEE FI FO FUM: A Picture Book of Nursery Rhymes (Hamish Hamilton, 1964)...............................£35
THE MOTHER GOOSE TREASURY (Hamish Hamilton, 1966)..£60
JIM AND THE BEANSTALK (Hamish Hamilton, 1970) £20
GENTLEMAN JIM (Hamish Hamilton, 1980)..£25
WHEN THE WIND BLOWS (Hamish Hamilton, 1982)...£20
THE TIN-POT GENERAL AND THE OLD IRON WOMAN (Hamish Hamilton, 1984)..........................£20
UNLUCKY WALLY (Hamish Hamilton, 1987)..£20
UNLUCKY WALLY TWENTY YEARS ON (Hamish Hamilton 1989) £15
THE MAN (Random Century/Julia MacRae Books, 1992)..£15
THE BEAR (Hamish Hamilton, 1994)..£12
ETHEL AND ERNEST: A True Story (Cape, 1998)...£10

Books Illustrated by Raymond Briggs

PETER AND THE PISKIES: Cornish Folk and Fairy Tales by Ruth Manning-Sanders (OUP, 1958)........£25
THE ONION MAN by Alan Ross (Hamish Hamilton: 'Antelope' series, 1959) £20
DANGER ON GLASS ISLAND by Alan Ross (Hamish Hamilton: 'Antelope' series, 1963)....................£20
THE WRECK OF MONI by Alan Ross (Hamish Hamilton: 'Antelope' series, 1963) £20
MYTHS AND LEGENDS. Edited by Jacynth Hope-Simpson (Hamish Hamilton, 1964)......................£25
WHISTLING RUFUS by William Mayne (Hamish Hamilton, 1964) £25
THE DAY THE TOWN WENT SILENT by Friedrich Feld (Blackie, 1965)..£25
THE FLYING 19 by James Aldridge (Hamish Hamilton, 1966)..£20
JIMMY MURPHY AND THE WHITE DUESENBERG by Bruce Carter (Hamish Hamilton, 1968)...........£25
LINDBERGH THE LONE FLIER by Nicholas Fisk (Hamish Hamilton, 1968).....................................£25
RICHTOVEN THE RED BARON by Nicholas Fisk (Hamish Hamilton, 1968).....................................£25
THE CHRISTMAS BOOKS. Edited by James Reeves (Heinemann, 1968) £30

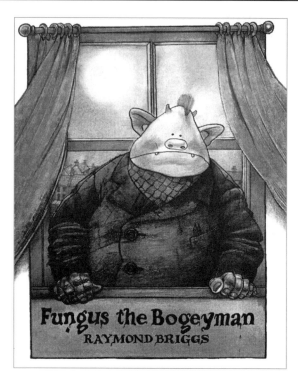

The first edition of Raymond Briggs' Fungus the Bogeyman is now worth £50 in Very Good condition.

FIRST UP EVEREST by Showell Styles (Hamish Hamilton, 1969)..£25
SHACKLETON'S EPIC VOYAGE by Michael Brown (Hamish Hamilton, 1969)..£25
THE ELEPHANT AND THE BAD BABY by Elfrida Vipont (Hamish Hamilton, 1969)..............................£20
FESTIVALS by Ruth Manning-Sanders (Heinemann, 1970)..£25
THE TALE OF THREE LANDLUBBERS by Ian Serraillier (Hamish Hamilton, 1970).........................£20
THE FAIRY TALE TREASURY Selected by Virginia Haviland (Hamish Hamilton, 1972)....................£40
THE FORBIDDEN FOREST by James Reeves (Heinemann, 1973) £25
THIS LITTLE PUFFIN – FINGER PLAYS AND NURSERY GAMES Edited by Elizabeth Matterson (Viking, 1975) £10
ALL IN A DAY by Mitsumasa Anno (Hamish Hamilton, 1986) £8

BRISLEY, Joyce Lankester

British author-illustrator. Born: Joyce Lankester Brisley in 1896. Creator of 'Milly-Molly-Mandy' (Millicent Margaret Amanda), who featured in a long-running series of books, beginning in 1928 with *Milly-Molly-Mandy Stories* and continuing until 1967. Brisley died in 1978.

Prices are books in Very Good condition with dustjackets.

MILLY-MOLLY-MANDY STORIES (Harrap, 1928) £150
MORE OF MILLY-MOLLY-MANDY (Harrap, 1929)..£100
LAMBS'-TAILS AND SUCHLIKE: Verses and Sketches (Harrap, 1930) £60
FURTHER DOINGS OF MILLY-MOLLY-MANDY (Harrap, 1932) £70
THE DAWN SHOPS and Other Stories (Harrap, 1933) £50
MARIGOLD IN GODMOTHER'S HOUSE (Harrap, 1934) £70
BUNCHY (Harrap, 1937)..£55
THREE LITTLE MILLY-MOLLY-MANDY PLAYS FOR CHILDREN (Harrap, 1938) £60
MY BIBLE-BOOK (Harrap, 1940)...£45
THE ADVENTURES OF PURL AND PLAIN (Harrap, 1941) £55
MILLY-MOLLY-MANDY AGAIN (Harrap, 1948)..£60
ANOTHER BUNCHY BOOK (Harrap, 1951)...£35
MILLY-MOLLY-MANDY & CO (Harrap, 1955)...£55
MILLY-MOLLY-MANDY AND BILLY BLUNT (Harrap, 1967)..£35
CHILDREN OF BIBLE DAYS (Harrap, 1970)...£12
THE JOYCE LANKESTER BRISLEY BOOK Edited by Frank Walters (anthology) (Harrap, 1981)....£12

BROOKE, L. Leslie

British author-illustrator. Born: Leonard Leslie Brooke in Liverpool in 1862. Began work as an artist in 1889, illustrating books by Mrs Molesworth, Andrew Lang and Edward Lear. Also wrote/illustrated his own series of 'picture books', beginning with *Johnny Crow's Garden* (1903). Father of Henry Brooke, who became British Home Secretary. Died: 1940.

Prices are for books in Very Good condition.

THE LIGHT PRINCESS and Other Stories by George MacDonald (Blackie, [1890]) £125
NURSE HEATHERDALE'S STORY by Mrs Molesworth (Macmillan, 1891) £40
THE GIRLS AND I: A Veracious History by Mrs Molesworth (Macmillan, 1892) £40
MARY: A Nursery Story for Very Little Children by Mrs Molesworth (Macmillan, 1893) £40
MY NEW HOME by Mrs Molesworth (Macmillan, 1894) £40
THE CARVED LIONS by Mrs Molesworth (Macmillan, 1895) £30
SHEILA'S MYSTERY by Mrs Molesworth (Macmillan, 1895) £30
THE ORIEL WINDOW by Mrs Molesworth (Macmillan, 1896) £30
MISS MOUSE AND HER BOYS by Mrs Molesworth (Macmillan, 1897) £30
THE NURSERY RHYME BOOK Edited by Andrew Lang (Warne, 1897) £100
A SPRING SONG by Thomas Nash (Dent, 1898) £40
THE JUMBLIES and Other Nonsense Verses (Warne, [1900]) £100
THE PELICAN CHORUS and Other Nonsense Verses (Warne, 1900) £100
NONSENSE SONGS AND STORIES (Warne, 1900) £100
JOHNNY CROW'S GARDEN: A Picture Book (Warne, 1903) £150
THE STORY OF THE THREE LITTLE PIGS (Warne, [1904]) £80
TOM THUMB (Warne, [1904]) £50
THE GOLDEN GOOSE BOOK (Warne, [1905]) £120
JOHNNY CROW'S PARTY: Another Picture Book (Warne, 1907) £100
LESLIE BROOKE'S CHILDREN'S BOOKS (seven books) (Warne, [1907-1922]) .... each £30
THE HOUSE IN THE WOOD and Other Old Fairy Stories (Warne, [1909]) £35
THE TAILOR AND THE CROW: An Old Rhyme with New Drawings (Warne, [1911]) £50
THE MAN IN THE MOON: A Nursery Rhyme Picture Book (Warne, [1913]) £40
ORANGES AND LEMONS: A Nursery Rhyme Picture Book (Warne, [1913]) £30
A NURSERY RHYME PICTURE BOOK (two books) (Warne, [1913 & 1922]) .... the pair £50
NURSERY RHYMES (Warne, [1916]) £60
RING O'ROSES: A Nursery Rhyme Picture Book (Warne, [1922]) £60
JOHNNY CROW'S NEW GARDEN (Warne, 1935) £45

'THE BROONS' ANNUALS

Long-running cartoon strip drawn by Dudley Watkins and featuring a 'typical' Scottish family. Launched in the 'Fun' section of the *Sunday Post* on 8th March 1936, the first annual – published by D.C. Thomson – appearing at Christmas 1939. They were subsequently issued biennially, although there were no editions for 1944 and 1946 because of paper shortages. Note that the annuals were undated before 1968.

Prices are for annuals in Very Good condition (with cover description in brackets for undated annuals).

THE BROONS 1940 (portraits of the Broon family with names below) £1,800
THE BROONS 1942 (head and shoulders profile of Maw and Paw in oval frame) £900

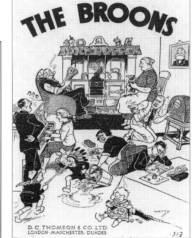

*The first annual featuring 'Scotland's happy family', **The Broons**. This is now valued at £1,800 for a Very Good copy. The title-page from this book, featuring artwork from the regular 'Broons' and 'Oo Wullie' artist, Dudley Watkins.*

THE BROONS 1948 (Paw in a chair with newspaper and Maw with tea tray; this cover was also used on the 1974 annual) ... **£650**
THE BROONS 1950 (Broons family standing smiling at reader) **£500**
THE BROONS 1952 (Broons family sitting around a table smiling at the reader) **£400**
THE BROONS 1954 (Maw and Paw dancing the highland fling).. **£150**
THE BROONS 1956 (Broons family sitting in front of a window).. **£150**
THE BROONS 1958 (Broons family playing board games on a table and the floor)... **£80**
THE BROONS 1960 (Broons family at the dinner table; calendar in background reads 'Jan 25') **£60**
THE BROONS 1962 (Broons family at home; two boys playing board games, Maw standing) **£50**
THE BROONS 1964 (Broons family on a mountain top)... **£35**
THE BROONS 1966 (Broons family crossing a road)... **£30**
THE BROONS 1968 .... **£20**
THE BROONS 1970 .... **£15**
THE BROONS 1972-74 .... each **£15**
THE BROONS 1976-80 .... each **£15**
THE BROONS 1982-Present .... each **£5**

BROWN, Pamela

British author. Born: Colchester, Essex, in 1924. Having trained for the stage herself, she frequently brought this interest to her novels whether historical or contemporary, notably *The Swish of the Curtain*. Died: 1989.

Prices are for books in Very Good condition with dustjackets where applicable.

THE SWISH OF THE CURTAIN (illustrated by Newton Whittaker) (Nelson, 1941)... **£50**
THE SWISH OF THE CURTAIN (revised edition, Brockhampton Press, 1971).. **£35**
THE SWISH OF THE CURTAIN (revised edition, Goodchild, 1984)... **£25**
MADDY ALONE (illustrated by Newton Whittaker) (Nelson, 1945).. **£30**
GOLDEN PAVEMENTS (illustrated by Newton Whittaker) (Nelson, 1947)... **£25**
BLUE DOOR ADVENTURE (illustrated by Newton Whittaker) (Nelson, 1949).. **£25**
TO BE A BALLERINA AND OTHER STORIES (illustrated by Marcia Lane Foster) (Nelson, 1950) **£25**
FAMILY PLAYBILL (illustrated by Marcia Lane Foster) (Nelson, 1951) **£25**
THE TELEVISION TWINS (illustrated by Marcia Lane Foster) (Nelson, 1952) **£25**
HARLEQUIN CORNER (illustrated by Marcia Lane Foster) (Nelson, 1953)... **£25**
THE WINDMILL FAMILY (illustrated by Marcia Lane Foster) (Nelson, 1954) **£25**
LOUISA (illustrated by Sax) (Nelson, 1955)... **£25**
MADDY AGAIN (illustrated by Drake Brookshaw) (Nelson, 1956)... **£25**
THE BRIDESMAIDS (illustrated by Peggy Beetles) (Brockhampton Press, 1956).. **£25**
SHOWBOAT SUMMER (illustrated by Charles Paine) (Brockhampton Press, 1957).. **£25**
BACK-STAGE PORTRAIT (illustrated by Drake Brookshaw) (Nelson, 1957)... **£25**
UNDERSTUDY (illustrated by Drake Brookshaw) (Nelson, 1958) **£25**
FIRST HOUSE (illustrated by Drake Brookshaw) (Nelson, 1959) **£25**
AS FAR AS SINGAPORE (illustrated by Peggy Beetles) (Brockhampton Press, 1959) **£25**
THE OTHER SIDE OF THE STREET (illustrated by Nathan Mayer) (Brockhampton Press, 1965)................................... **£20**
THE GIRL WHO RAN AWAY (illustrated by Nathan Mayer) (Brockhampton Press, 1968)... **£20**
A LITTLE UNIVERSE (illustrated by Faith Jaques) (Brockhampton Press, 1970)... **£20**
SUMMER IS A FESTIVAL (Brockhampton Press, 1972) **£20**
LOOKING AFTER LIBBY (Brockhampton Press, 1974)... **£20**
EVERY DAY IS MARKET DAY (Hodder & Stoughton, 1977) **£20**
THE MGM GIRLS Behind the Velvet Curtain by Peter Harry Brown and Pamela Ann Brown (Harrap, 1984)........................ **£20**
THE FINISHING SCHOOL (Goodchild, 1984)... **£20**

BRUCE, Dorita Fairlie

British author. Born Dorita Morris Fairlie Bruce in Spain on 20th May 1885. Her happy years at a boarding school in Roehampton inspired a whole series of girls' stories, the best-known featuring the character 'Dimsie', who appeared in her first book, *The Senior Prefect* (1921). She also wrote four historical novels. Died: 1970.

Prices are for books in Very Good condition with dustjackets.

'Dimsie' Books

THE SENIOR PREFECT (OUP, 1921).. **£350**
DIMSIE MOVES UP (OUP, 1921)... **£175**
DIMSIE MOVES UP AGAIN (OUP, 1922)... **£125**
DIMSIE AMONG THE PREFECTS (OUP, 1923)... **£115**
DIMSIE GROWS UP (OUP, 1924)... **£100**
DIMSIE, HEAD-GIRL (OUP, 1925) **£100**
DIMSIE GOES TO SCHOOL (reissue of 'The Senior Prefect') (OUP, 1925) **£60**
DIMSIE GOES BACK (OUP, 1927).. **£100**
THE DIMSIE OMNIBUS (contains 'Dimsie Goes to School', 'Dimsie Moves Up' and 'Dimsie Moves Up Again';
'Dimsie Goes to School' was originally published under the title 'The Senior Prefect') (OUP, 1932)..................... **£65**
THE NEW DIMSIE OMNIBUS (contains 'The New House-Captain', 'The Best House in the School' and
'Captain of Springdale') (OUP, 1935) **£60**

DIMSIE INTERVENES (OUP, 1937) £75
DIMSIE CARRIES ON (OUP, 1942) £75

'Nancy' Books
THE GIRLS OF ST. BRIDE'S (OUP, 1923) £240
THAT BOARDING SCHOOL GIRL (OUP, 1925) £100
THE NEW GIRL AND NANCY (OUP, 1926)..£100
NANCY TO THE RESCUE (OUP, 1927) £80
THE BEST BAT IN THE SCHOOL (OUP, 1931)...£90
NANCY AT ST. BRIDE'S (OUP, 1933) £70
NANCY IN THE SIXTH (OUP, 1935) £100
THE DORITA BRUCE OMNIBUS (contains 'Nancy at St. Bride's', 'That Boarding School Girl' and
'The New Girl and Nancy') (OUP, 1937) £60
NANCY RETURNS TO ST. BRIDE'S (OUP, 1938) £70
NANCY CALLS THE TUNE (illustrated by Margaret Horder) (OUP, 1944) £55

'Springdale' Books
THE NEW HOUSE-CAPTAIN (OUP, 1928) £125
THE BEST HOUSE IN THE SCHOOL (OUP, 1930) £125
CAPTAIN OF SPRINGDALE (OUP, 1932) £125
THE NEW HOUSE AT SPRINGDALE (OUP, 1934)..£125
PREFECTS AT SPRINGDALE (OUP, 1936) £125
CAPTAIN ANNE (OUP, 1939)..£125

'School on the Moor' Books
THE SCHOOL ON THE MOOR (OUP, 1931)..£110
THE SCHOOL IN THE WOODS (OUP, 1940) £400
TOBY AT TIBBS CROSS (illustrated by Margaret Horder) (OUP, 1942)...£100

'Sally' Books
SALLY SCATTERBRAIN (illustrated by Margaret Horder) (Blackie, 1956) £85
SALLY AGAIN (illustrated by Betty Ladler) (Blackie, 1959) £85
SALLY'S SUMMER TERM (illustrated by Joan Thompson) (Blackie, 1961) £85

Historical Novels
THE KING'S CURATE (John Murray, 1930)...£450
MISTRESS-MARINER (John Murray, 1932)...£450
A LAVEROCK LILTING (OUP, 1945) £50
THE BEES ON DRUMWHINNIE (illustrated by Margaret Horder) (OUP, 1952) £50

Others
WILD GOOSE QUEST (Lutterworth Press, 1945)...£80
THE SERENDIPITY SHOP (illustrated by Margaret Horder) (OUP, 1947)..£85
TRIFFENY (illustrated by Margaret Horder) (OUP, 1950)...£100
THE DEBATABLE MOUND (illustrated by Patricia M. Lambe) (OUP, 1953)..£80
THE BARTLE BEQUEST (illustrated by Sylvia Green) (OUP, 1955)..£100

BRUNA, Dick
Dutch author-illustrator. Born: Holland, 1927. Creator of an outstandingly successful series of small picture books for very young children. The now-familiar square format appeared from 1959 onwards, and include the 'Miffy' and 'Snuffy' books.
Prices are for books in Very Good condition with dustjackets where applicable.

Books Written and Illustrated by Dick Bruna
THE LITTLE BIRD (Methuen, 1962)..£15
TILLY AND TESSA (Methuen, 1962) £15
THE FISH (Methuen, 1962) £5
CIRCUS (Methuen, 1963)..£5
LITTLE BIRD TWEET (Methuen, 1963) £5
THE EGG (Methuen, 1964)...£5
THE KING (Methuen, 1964) £5
MIFFY (Methuen, 1964) £10
MIFFY AT THE SEASIDE (Methuen, 1964)...£10
THE CHRISTMAS BOOK (Methuen, 1964) £10
MIFFY IN THE SNOW (Methuen, 1965)..£10
MIFFY AT THE ZOO (Methuen, 1965)...£10
THE SAILOR (Methuen, 1966) £5
THE SCHOOL (Methuen, 1966) £5
THE APPLE (Methuen, 1966) £5
PUSSY NELL (Methuen, 1966) £5
LITTLE RED RIDING HOOD (Methuen, 1967) £5
TOM THUMB (Methuen, 1967)...£5

BRUNA, Dick

CINDERELLA (Methuen, 1968)...£5
SNOW WHITE AND THE SEVEN DWARFS (Methuen, 1968)...............................£5
B IS FOR BEAR (Methuen, 1967)..£5
A STORY TO TELL (Methuen, 1968)..£5
I CAN COUNT (Methuen, 1968)...£5
I CAN READ (Methuen, 1969)..£5
I CAN READ MORE (Methuen, 1969)...£5
SNUFFY (Methuen, 1970)..£5
SNUFFY AND THE FIRE (Methuen, 1970)...£5
MIFFY'S BIRTHDAY (Methuen, 1971)...£5
MIFFY GOES FLYING (Methuen, 1971)...£5
ABC (frieze) (Methuen, 1971)..£5
MY VEST IS WHITE (Methuen, 1973)..£5
I CAN COUNT MORE (Methuen, 1973)..£5
123 (frieze) (Methuen, 1974)...£5
ANIMAL (frieze) (Methuen, 1975...£5
ANOTHER STORY TO TELL (Methuen, 1976)...£5
LISA AND LYNN (Two Continents, U.S., 1975)...£5
MIFFY AT THE PLAYGROUND (Methuen, 1976)...£5
DICK BRUNA'S ANIMAL BOOK (Methuen, 1976)...£5
I AM A CLOWN (Methuen, 1976)...£5
MIFFY IN HOSPITAL (Methuen, 1976)..£5
I CAN READ DIFFICULT WORDS (Methuen, 1977)..£5
I CAN DRESS MYSELF (Methuen, 1977)..£5
POPPY PIG (Methuen, 1978)..£5
POPPY PIG'S GARDEN (Methuen, 1978)..£5
MIFFY'S DREAM (Methuen, 1979)..£5
MY TOYS (Methuen, 1980)..£5
READ WITH MIFFY (frieze) (Methuen, 1980)..£5
POPPY PIG GOES TO MARKET (Methuen, 1981)...£5
WHEN I'M BIG (Methuen, 1981)..£5
I KNOW ABOUT NUMBERS (Methuen, 1981)...£5
DICK BRUNA'S WORD BOOK (Methuen, 1982)...£5
MIFFY'S BICYCLE (Methuen, 1984)..£5
MIFFY AT SCHOOL (Methuen, 1984)..£5
I KNOW ABOUT SHAPES (Methuen, 1984)...£5
I CAN MAKE MUSIC (Methuen, 1984)...£5
FARMER JOHN (Methuen, 1984)...£5
THE LIFEBOAT (Methuen, 1984)...£5
FIND MY HAT (Methuen, 1984)..£5
BACK TO FRONT (Methuen, 1984)..£5
MY SPORT BOOK (Methuen, 1984)...£5
BLUE BOAT (with Peter Jones) (Methuen, 1984)..£5
MY HOUSE (Methuen, 1984)...£5
PLAYING IN WINTER (Methuen, 1984)..£5
MY PLAYTIME (Methuen, 1985)...£5
MY STREET (Methuen, 1985)...£5
MY GARDEN (Methuen, 1985)...£5
MY ANIMALS (Methuen, 1985)..£5
MIFFY'S BOOK OF COLOUR (Methuen, 1986)..£5
POPPY PIG'S BOOK (Methuen, 1987)...£5
SNUFFY'S PUPPY (Methuen, 1987)..£5
BEAR'S SPRINGTIME (Methuen, 1987)..£5

de BRUNHOFF, Jean

French author-illustrator, best known as the creator of Babar the Elephant. Born in Paris in 1899, de Brunhoff studied at the École Alsacienne. His first 'Babar' book, *L'Histoire de Babar, le petit eléphant*, was published in 1931, appearing in Britain three years later under the title *The Story of Babar, the Little Elephant*. Following de Brunhoff's death in 1937, the series was continued by his son, Laurent.

Prices are for UK editions in Very Good condition.

THE STORY OF BABAR, THE LITTLE ELEPHANT (Methuen, 1934).................£300
BABAR'S TRAVELS (Methuen, 1935)..£200
BABAR THE KING (Methuen, 1936)..£180
BABAR'S ABC (Methuen, 1937)...£200
BABAR'S FRIEND ZEPHIR (Methuen, 1937)...£150
BABAR AT HOME (Methuen, 1938)..£175
BABAR AND FATHER CHRISTMAS (Methuen, 1940)......................................£140

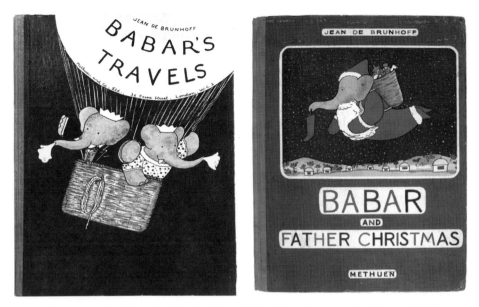

The second and last 'Babar' books by Jean de Brunhoff before his son Laurent continued the series in 1948.

'Babar' Books by Laurent de Brunhoff
BABAR AND THAT RASCAL ARTHUR (Methuen, 1948)...£80
PICNIC AT BABAR'S (Methuen, 1950)..£80
BABAR'S VISIT TO BIRD ISLAND (Methuen, 1952)...£60
BABAR'S CASTLE (Methuen, 1962)...£45
SERAFINA THE GIRAFFE (illustrated by Laurent de Brunhoff) (Methuen, 1964 [1965])................£40
BABAR'S FRENCH LESSONS (Cape, 1965)..£40
SERAFINA'S LUCKY FIND (illustrated by Laurent de Brunhoff) (Methuen, 1967)...........................£35
BABAR AND THE PROFESSOR (Methuen, 1972)...£30
BABAR'S BOOK OF COLOUR (Methuen, 1985)..£25

BUCKERIDGE, Anthony
British author. Born: London, 1912. Taught in a prep school, having his first success as a writer with a handful of adult plays broadcast on BBC Radio. These were followed by a series of radio scripts featuring the schoolboy, Jennings, who subsequently featured in two dozen books, beginning with *Jennings Goes to School* (1950). Buckeridge has also written four novels featuring the grammar schoolboy, Rex Milligan. Died: 2004.

Prices are for books in Very Good condition with dustjackets.

'Jennings' Books
JENNINGS GOES TO SCHOOL (dustjacket and colour frontispiece by S. van Abbé) (Collins, 1950)..............£80
JENNINGS FOLLOWS A CLUE (dustjacket and colour frontispiece by S. van Abbé) (Collins, 1951) £60
JENNINGS' LITTLE HUT (dustjacket and colour frontispiece by S. van Abbé) (Collins, 1951) £60
JENNINGS AND DARBISHIRE (dustjacket and colour frontispiece by S. van Abbé) (Collins, 1952)............£50
JENNINGS' DIARY (dustjacket and colour frontispiece by S. van Abbé) (Collins, 1953).........................£50
ACCORDING TO JENNINGS (illustrated by S. van Abbé) (Collins, 1954)...£45
OUR FRIEND JENNINGS (illustrated by Mays) (Collins, 1955) £45
THANKS TO JENNINGS (illustrated by Mays) (Collins, 1957) £40
TAKE JENNINGS, FOR INSTANCE (illustrated by Mays) (Collins, 1958)..£40
JENNINGS, AS USUAL (illustrated by Mays) (Collins, 1959)...£40
THE TROUBLE WITH JENNINGS (illustrated by Mays) (Collins, 1960) £35
JUST LIKE JENNINGS (illustrated by Mays) (Collins, 1961)...£40
LEAVE IT TO JENNINGS (illustrated by Mays) (Collins, 1963)...£40
JENNINGS, OF COURSE! (illustrated by Mays) (Collins, 1964)...£40
ESPECIALLY JENNINGS! (illustrated by Mays) (Collins, 1965) £40
A BOOKFUL OF JENNINGS (anthology) (Collins, 1966) £40
JENNINGS ABOUNDING (illustrated by Mays) (Collins, 1967) £45
JENNINGS IN PARTICULAR (illustrated by Mays) (Collins, 1968) £45

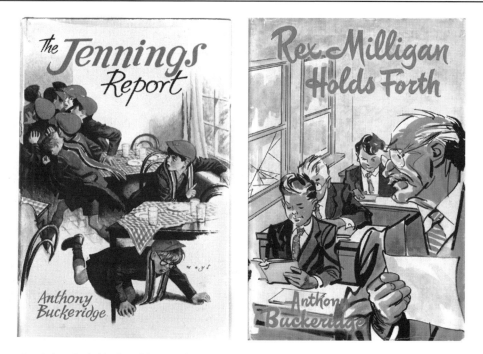

Two Anthony Buckeridge first editions including a later 'Jennings' book and the third installment in the little known 'Rex Milligan' series.

TRUST JENNINGS! (illustrated by Mays) (Collins, 1969)..£45
THE JENNINGS REPORT (illustrated by Mays) (Collins, 1970)..£80
TYPICALLY JENNINGS! (dustjacket and black-and-white frontispiece by Val Biro) (Collins, 1971)............£45
THE BEST OF JENNINGS (anthology; revised reissue of 'A Bookful of Jennings' [1966]) (Collins, 1972) £40
SPEAKING OF JENNINGS (Collins, 1973)..£40
JENNINGS AT LARGE (paperback original) (Armada, 1977)..£20
JENNINGS AT LARGE (first hardback edition) (Severn House, 1980)...£45
JENNINGS ABOUNDING!: A Comedy with Music (play; paperback) (Samuel French, 1980) £5
JENNINGS AGAIN! (illustrated by Rodney Sutton) (Macmillan, 1991)..£20
THAT'S JENNINGS (illustrated by Rodney Sutton) (Macmillan, 1994)..£20
JENNINGS SOUNDS THE ALARM: Seven Plays for Radio (illustrated by Val Biro; paperback) (David Schutte, 1999)..........£12
JENNINGS SOUNDS THE ALARM (100 copies signed by author and artist; paperback) (David Schutte, 1999) £30
JENNINGS BREAKS THE RECORD: Seven More Plays for Radio
    (illustrated by Val Biro; paperback) (David Schutte, 2000) £12
JENNINGS BREAKS THE RECORD (100 copies signed by author and artist; paperback) (David Schutte, 2000).......£30
JENNINGS JOINS THE SEARCH PARTY: Plays for Radio Vol 3
    (illustrated by Val Biro; paperback) (David Schutte, 2001) £12
JENNINGS JOINS THE SEARCH PARTY
    (100 copies signed by author and artist; otherwise as above; paperback) (David Schutte, 2001)..............£30
JENNINGS TO THE RESCUE: Plays for Radio Vol 4 (illustrated by Val Biro; paperback) (David Schutte, 2002) £12
JENNINGS TO THE RESCUE
    (100 copies signed by author and artist; otherwise as above; paperback) (David Schutte, 2002)..............£20
JENNINGS AND THE ROMAN REMAINS: Plays for Radio Vol 5
    (illustrated by Val Biro; paperback) (David Schutte, 2002) £12
JENNINGS AND THE ROMAN REMAINS
    (100 copies signed by author and artist; otherwise as above; paperback) (David Schutte, 2002)..............£20

'Bligh Family' Books
A FUNNY THING HAPPENED! (Lutterworth Press, 1953) £40

'Rex Milligan' Books
REX MILLIGAN'S BUSY TERM (illustrated by Mazure) (Lutterworth Press, 1953) £40
REX MILLIGAN RAISES THE ROOF (illustrated by Mazure) (Lutterworth Press, 1955)...........................£40
REX MILLIGAN HOLDS FORTH (illustrated by Mazure) (Lutterworth Press, 1957)................................£40
REX MILLIGAN REPORTING (illustrated by Mazure) (Lutterworth Press, 1961) £40

The very first issue of Bunty is worth £50 today, and came with a free Ladybird Ring!

This is the first of the Diana For Girls annual, published by D.C. Thomson between 1965 and 1969.

INTRODUCING REX MILLIGAN (illustrated by Val Biro; paperbackl) (David Schutte, 2002) **£15**
INTRODUCING REX MILLIGAN (100 copies signed by author and artist; paperback) (David Schutte, 2002) **£25**

Others
STORIES FOR BOYS Edited by Anthony Buckeridge (Faber, 1957) **£15**
IN AND OUT OF SCHOOL Edited by Anthony Buckeridge (Faber, 1958) **£15**
STORIES FOR BOYS 2 Edited by Anthony Buckeridge (Faber, 1965) **£15**

'BUNTY'
British comic first published by D.C. Thomson in 1958. Other girls' annuals issued by D.C. Thomson are also listed.

Prices are for comics/annuals in Very Good condition.

BUNTY (No. 1, 1958) **£50**
BUNTY (1958-2001) .... each **£3**
BUNTY FOR GIRLS (annual) 1959-1963 .... each **£12**
BUNTY FOR GIRLS (annual) 1964-1969 .... each **£10**
JUDY FOR GIRLS (annual) 1964-1969 .... each **£10**
DIANA FOR GIRLS (annual) 1965-1969 .... each **£10**

BURNETT, Frances Hodgson
Anglo-American author. Born: Frances Eliza Hodgson in Manchester in November 1849. Following the death of her father, the family emigrated to America in 1865, where Frances remained until 1898, supporting her family through her writing. She produced a number of adult novels before enjoying huge success with her children's stories, *Little Lord Fauntleroy* (1886) and *The Secret Garden* (1911), the latter inspired by her nine-year residence at Maytham Hall in Rolvenden, Kent. She moved back to the United States in 1908, where she died in 1924.

Prices are for books in Very Good condition.

SURLY TIM and Other Stories (Armstrong, U.S., 1877) **£250**
SURLY TIM and Other Stories (Ward Lock, [1877]) **£150**
OUR NEIGHBOUR OPPOSITE (stories) (Routledge, [1878]) **£80**
NATALIE and Other Stories (Warne, [1879]) **£80**
LINDSAY'S LUCK (stories) (Scribner, U.S., [1878]) **£80**
LINDSAY'S LUCK (stories) (Routledge, 1879) **£70**
THE TIDE ON THE MOANING BAR and A QUIET LIFE (stories) (Routledge, [1879]) **£65**

BURNETT, Frances Hodgson

LITTLE LORD FAUNTLEROY (Warne, 1886)..£250
SARA CREWE, or What Happened at Miss Minchin's (Unwin, 1887) £85
SARA CREWE, or What Happened at Miss Minchin's and Editha's Burglar
(Warne, 1888)..£80
LITTLE SAINT ELIZABETH and Other Child Stories (Warne, 1890) £30
CHILDREN I HAVE KNOWN: And Giovanni and the Other
(Osgood McIlvaine, 1892 [1891])...£50
THE ONE I KNEW THE BEST OF ALL (illustrated by Reginald Birch) (Warne, 1893)...............£30
THE CAPTAIN'S YOUNGEST, PICCINO and Other Child Stories (illustrated by R.B. Birch) (Warne, 1894) £25
TWO LITTLE PILGRIMS' PROGRESS: A Story of the City Beautiful (Warne, 1895)...............£45
IN THE CLOSED ROOM (illustrated by Jessie Willcox Smith) (McClure Philips, U.S., 1904)......£100
A LITTLE PRINCESS: Being the Whole Story of Sara Crewe Now Told for the First Time
(illustrated by Harold Pifford) (Warne, 1905)...£200
RACKETTY-PACKETTY HOUSE by Queen Crosspatch. Spelled by F.H. Burnett (Warne, 1907)............£100
THE TROUBLES OF QUEEN SILVER-BELL (Warne, 1907)...£100
THE COZY LION told by Queen Crosspatch (illustrated by Harison Cady) (Century, U.S., 1907)..........£60
THE COZY LION (issued with dustjacket) (Tom Stacey, 1972)..£15
THE SPRING CLEANING told by Queen Crosspatch (illustrated by Harrison Cady) (Century, U.S., 1908) £65
THE SPRING CLEANING (issued with dustjacket) (Tom Stacey, 1973).................................£15
THE SECRET GARDEN (illustrated by Charles Robinson) (Heinemann, 1911)........................£350
THE SECRET GARDEN (illustrated by E.H. Shepard) (1956)..£50
THE SECRET GARDEN (illustrated by Michael Hague) (Holt, U.S., 1987)...............................£30
THE LAND OF THE BLUE FLOWER (Putnam, 1912)...£20
MY ROBIN (illustrated by Alfred Brennan) (Stokes, U.S., 1912)..£45
MY ROBIN (Putnam, 1913)..£20
THE LOST PRINCE (Hodder & Stoughton, 1915)..£70
THE LITTLE HUNCHBACK ZIA (illustrated by Charles Robinson) (Heinemann, 1916)..............£60

BURNINGHAM, John

British author-illustrator. Born: Farnham, Surrey, in 1936. Studied at the Central School of Art, London, 1956-59. Married the illustrator Helen Oxenbury in 1964. Won the Kate Greenway Medal in 1964 and 1971 and the Kurt Maschler Award in 1984. Illustrated the three volumes of Ian Fleming's *Chitty-Chitty-Bang-Bang* (1964-65).

Prices are for books in Very Good condition with dustjackets where applicable.

Books Written and Illustrated by John Burningham

BORKA: THE ADVENTURES OF A GOOSE WITH NO FEATHERS (Cape, 1963).......................£40
THE MOUSE WHO WANTED TO PLAY THE BALALAIKA (Cape, 1964).................................£35
ABC (illustrated by John Burningham and Leigh Taylor) (Cape, 1964).....................................£35
HUMBERT, MISTER FIRKIN AND THE LORD MAYOR OF LONDON (Cape, 1965).................£25
CANONBALL SIMP (Cape, 1966)..£25
HARQUIN, THE FOX WHO WENT DOWN TO THE VALLEY (Cape, 1967)..............................£30
SEASONS (Cape, 1969)...£40
MR GUMPY'S OUTING (Cape, 1970)..£35
MR GUMPY'S MOTOR CAR (Cape, 1973)...£30
COME AWAY FROM THE WATER, SHIRLEY (Cape, 1977)...£25
TIME TO GET OUT OF THE BATH, SHIRLEY (Cape, 1978)...£25
WOULD YOU RATHER (Cape, 1978)..£30
THE SHOPPING BASKET (Cape, 1980)..£25
AVOCADO BABY (Cape, 1982)...£20
GRANPA (Cape, 1984)...£20
WHERE'S JULIUS? (Cape, 1986)...£20
JOHN PATRICK NORMAN McHENNESSY: The Boy Who Was Always Late (Cape, 1987) £20

Books Illustrated by John Burningham

CHITTY-CHITTY-BANG-BANG, THE MAGICAL CAR: ADVENTURE NUMBER 1 by Ian Fleming (Cape, 1964) £200
CHITTY-CHITTY-BANG-BANG, THE MAGICAL CAR: ADVENTURE NUMBER 2 by Ian Fleming (Cape, 1964) £200
CHITTY-CHITTY-BANG-BANG, THE MAGICAL CAR: ADVENTURE NUMBER 3 by Ian Fleming (Cape, 1965) £200
THE COMPLETE ADVENTURES OF THE MAGICAL CAR (omnibus edition) (Cape, 1971) £80
THE WIND IN THE WILLOWS by Kenneth Grahame (pictorial slipcase) (Viking, 1983) £100

Others

BIRDLAND (wall frieze) (Cape, 1966)...£12
LIONLAND (wall frieze) (Cape, 1966)...£12
STORYLAND (wall frieze) (Cape, 1966)..£12
JUNGLELAND (wall frieze) (Cape, 1968)..£12
WONDERLAND (wall frieze) (Cape, 1968)...£12
AROUND THE WORLD (two wall friezes) (Cape, 1972) £12
AROUND THE WORLD IN EIGHTY DAYS (Cape, 1972)...£25

LITTLE BOOKS (readers, eight books: 'The Baby' 'The Rabbit', 'The School', 'The Snow', 'The Blanket', 'The Cupboard', 'The Dog' and 'The Friend' (Cape, 1974) .... the set **£12**
NUMBER PLAY (six books: 'Count Up', 'Read One', 'Ride off', 'Pigs Plus', 'Just Cats' and 'Five Down') (Walker, 1983) .... the set **£12**
FIRST WORDS (six books: 'Cluck Baa', 'Skip Trip', 'Slam Bang', 'Sniff Shout', 'Wobble Pop' and 'Jangle Twang') (Walker, 1984) .... the set **£12**
PLAY AND LEARN (three books: '123', 'Opposites' and 'Colours') (Sainsbury-Walker, 1985) .... the set **£12**
TAIL FEATHERS FROM MOTHER GOOSE by Iona Opie (illustrated by Maurice Sendak, Janet Ahlberg, Nicola Bayley, Quentin Blake, John Burningham and Anthony Browne) (Walker, 1988) **£30**

BUTTERWORTH, Nick

British author-illustrator. Born: Kingsbury, London, in 1946. Worked as a freelance graphics artist and as a TV-AM children's programme presenter. He produced a regular illustrated story, 'Upney Junction', for the *Sunday Express.*

Prices are for books in Fine condition with dustjackets where applicable.

Books Written and Illustrated by Nick Butterworth

B.B.BLACKSHEEP AND FAMILY: A Collection of Nursery Rhymes (Macdonald, 1981) **£15**
TREASURE TROVE AT UPNEY JUNCTION (Macdonald, 1983) **£10**
INVASION AT UPNEY JUNCTION (Macdonald, 1983) **£10**
A MONSTER AT UPNEY JUNCTION (Macdonald, 1983) **£10**
A WINDY DAY AT UPNEY JUNCTION (Macdonald, 1983) **£10**
JACK THE CARPENTER AND HIS FRIENDS (Sainsbury's/Walker, 1986) **£10**
TOM THE GREENGROCER AND HIS FRIENDS (Sainsbury's, 1986) **£10**
JULIE THE PAPER GIRL AND HER FRIENDS (Sainsbury's, 1986) **£10**
ONE SNOWY NIGHT (HarperCollins, 1989) **£7**
THE SECRET PATH (HarperCollins, 1990) **£7**
AFTER THE STORM (HarperCollins, 1993) **£7**
THE RESCUE PARTY (HarperCollins, 1983) **£7**
THE CROSS RABBIT (HarperCollins, 1995) **£5**
THE FOX'S HICCUPS (HarperCollins, 1996) **£5**
A YEAR IN PERCY'S PARK (HarperCollins, 1995) **£8**
THE HEDGEHOG'S BALLOON (HarperCollins, 1996) **£7**
THE BADGER'S BATH (HarperCollins, 1996) **£7**
TALES FROM PERCY'S PARK (omnibus) (HarperCollins, 1996) **£7**
THE OWL'S LESSON (HarperCollins, 1997) **£5**

Others

TALES FOR A PRINCE (illustrated by Mick Inkpen, M. Ursell and Krystyna Turska) (Hodder & Stoughton, 1988) **£10**
JAKE AGAIN by Annette Butterworth (Hodder & Stoughton, 1996) **£6**

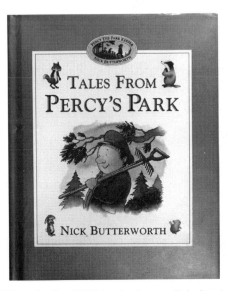

Nick Butterworth is a comparatively recent arrival on the collecting scene. This title first appeared in 1995.

This omnibus from 1996 brings together several tales featuring Butterworth's best-known creation, 'Percy the Park Keeper'.

C

CALDECOTT, Randolph

British illustrator. Born: Chester, 1846. Worked as a bank clerk before moving to London at the age of 26, where he studied at the Slade School of Art. His work for *London Society* magazine led to a fruitful partnership with the printer, Edmund Evans, with whom he produced a series of popular picture books, notably *The Diverting History of John Gilpin* (1878) and *Ride a Cock Horse* (1884). Also contributed to the *Graphic* and other magazines. Caldecott was an important influence on Beatrix Potter. Died: 1886.

Prices are for Books in Very Good condition.

Randolph Caldecott's 'Picture Books' (all printed by Edmund Evans and issued in sewn stiff card covers)

THE DIVERTING HISTORY OF JOHN GILPIN (Routledge, [1878])..£30
THE HOUSE THAT JACK BUILT (Routledge, [1878])..£30
ELEGY ON THE DEATH OF A MAD DOG by Oliver Goldsmith (Routledge, [1879])..................................£70
THE BABES IN THE WOOD (Routledge, [1879])...£30
THE THREE JOVIAL HUNTSMEN (Routledge, [1880])...£30
SING A SONG FOR SIXPENCE (Routledge, [1880])..£30
THE QUEEN OF HEARTS (Routledge, [1881]) £30
THE FARMER'S BOY (Routledge, [1881])..£30
THE MILKMAID (Routledge, [1882])..£30
HEY DIDDLE DIDDLE and BYE BABY BUNTING (Routledge, [1882]) £30
THE FOX JUMPS OVER THE PARSON'S GATE (Routledge, [1883]) £30
A FROG HE WOULD A-WOOING GO (Routledge, [1883])...£30
COME LASSES AND LADS (Routledge, [1884])...£30
RIDE A-COCK HORSE TO BANBURY CROSS and A FARMER WENT TROTTING UPON HIS GREY MARE
　(Routledge, [1884])...£30
AN ELEGY ON THE GLORY OF HER SEX, MRS MARY BLAIZE by Oliver Goldsmith
　(Routledge, [1885])...£30
THE GREAT PANJANDRUM HIMSELF (Routledge, [1885])...£30

Two examples of Randolph Caldecott's very popular picture books, still in fine condition for their age.

R. CALDECOTT'S PICTURE BOOK (Volume One, containing the first four 'Picture Books')
(Routledge, [1879])..**£55**
R. CALDECOTT'S PICTURE BOOK (Volume Two, containing the second four 'Picture Books')
(Routledge, [1881])..**£55**
R. CALDECOTT'S COLLECTION OF PICTURES & SONGS (single-volume reissue of
'R. Caldecott's Picture Book' Volumes One and Two) (Routledge, [1881])..**£50**
THE HEY DIDDLE DIDDLE PICTURE BOOK (contains four 'Picture Books') (Routledge, [1883])................**£50**
THE PANJANDRUM PICTURE BOOK (contains four 'Picture Books') (Routledge, [1885])........................**£50**
THE COMPLETE COLLECTION OF RANDOLPH CALDECOTT'S PICTURES AND SONGS
(contains all sixteen 'Picture Books', with a preface by Austin Dobson; limited to 800 copies; engraved,
printed and signed by Edmund Evans) (Routledge, U.K./U.S., 1887)...**£250**
R. CALDECOTT'S PICTURE BOOKS (contains the first four 'Picture Books') (Routledge, [1889 & 1892]) **£50**
R. CALDECOTT'S SECOND COLLECTION OF PICTURES AND SONGS (a one-volume reissue of
'The Hey Diddle Diddle Picture Book' and 'The Panjandrum Picture Book') (Warne, [1895])....................**£50**
R. CALDECOTT'S COLLECTION OF PICTURES AND SONGS (reissue of 1881 edition) (Warne, [1896]) **£50**
R. CALDECOTT'S PICTURE BOOK NO. 1 (four volumes; together contain fourteen 'Picture Books')
(Warne: U.K./U.S., [1906-1907])..each **£50**
MINIATURE PICTURE BOOKS (miniature editions of each 'Picture Book;
four volumes containing four 'Picture Books' each were also published)
(Warne, U.K./U.S., [1906-1907]) ....each **£25**

Other Books Illustrated by Randolph Caldecott

FRANK MILDMAY, or The Naval Officer by Captain Marryat (six full-page black-and-white
illustrations by Randolph Caldecott; engraved by Edmund Evans; with a memoir by F. Marryat)
(Routledge, U.K./U.S., [1873])...**£45**
BARON BRUNO, or The Unbelieving Philosopher and Other Fairy Stories by Louisa Morgan
(eight black-and-white illustrations by Randolph Caldecott) (Macmillan, 1875)......................................**£45**
OLD CHRISTMAS. From the Sketch Book of Washington Irving
(second edition; 120 black-and-white illustrations by Randolph Caldecott; arranged and engraved by J.D. Cooper)
(Macmillan, 1876)..**£35**
BRACEBRIDGE HALL, or The Humorists by Washington Irving (116 black-and-white illustrations by Randolph Caldecott;
arranged and engraved by J.D. Cooper) (Macmillan, 1877 [1876])..**£35**
WHAT THE BLACKBIRD SAID: A Story in Four Chirps by Mrs Frederick Locker
(four full-page black-and-white illustrations of birds by Randolph Caldecott) (Routledge, 1881)..................**£45**
JACKANAPES by Juliana Horatia Ewing (SPCK, 1884 [1883]) **£20**
SOME OF AESOP'S FABLES WITH MODERN INSTANCES (Macmillan 1883)...**£30**
DADDY DARWIN'S DOVECOTE: A Country Tale by Juliana Horatia Ewing (SPCK, [1884]) **£20**
LOB LIE-BY-THE-FIRE by Juliana Horatia Ewing (SPCK, [1885])..**£20**
FABLES DE LA FONTAINE (selected and introduced by Louis M. Moriarty) (Macmillan, 1885)...................**£30**
JACK AND THE BEANSTALK by Hallam Tennyson (Macmillan, 1886)...**£30**
THE OWLS OF OLYNN BELFRY by A.Y.D. (Field & Tuer, [1886])..**£30**
JACKANAPES by Juliana Horatia Ewing (contains 'Daddy Darwin's Dovecote' and 'Lob Lie-By-The-Fire')
(SPCK, [1892])..**£25**
RANDOLPH CALDECOTT'S PAINTING BOOK (SPCK, [1895])..**£45**
RANDOLPH CALDECOTT'S PAINTING BOOK (first series) (Warne, U.K/U.S., [1902]) **£35**

CAMERON, Katharine

Scottish illustrator. Born: Glasgow, 1874. Studied at the Glasgow School of Art and in Paris. Illustrated many children's books, and was a contributor to *The Yellow Book*. Married the artist, Arthur Kay, in 1928. Died: 1965.

Prices are for books in Very Good condition.

IN FAIRYLAND: Tales Told Again by Louey Chisholm (T.C. & E.C. Jack, 1904)......................................**£85**
THE WATER BABIES by Charles Kingsley (T.C. & E.C. Jack, [1905])..**£60**
STORIES OF KING ARTHUR'S KNIGHTS by Mary MacGregor (T.C. & E.C. Jack, [1905])..........................**£40**
THE ENCHANTED LAND by Louey Chisholm (T.C. & E.C. Jack, 1906)...**£100**
LEGENDS AND STORIES OF ITALY FOR CHILDREN by Amy Steedman (T.C. & E.C. Jack, [1909])...............**£30**
'IN FAIRYLAND' SERIES by Louey Chisholm (T.C. & E.C. Jack, [1910]) **£35**
CELTIC TALES by Louey Chisholm (T.C. & E.C. Jack, [1910]) **£45**
IN A CITY GARDEN by James R. Aitken (Foulis, 1913) **£35**
WHERE THE BEE SUCKS: A Book of Flowers. Poems chosen by Iola A. Williams (Medici Society, [1929]) **£35**
IAIN THE HAPPY PUPPY: Being the Autobiography of a West Highland White Terrier
(written and illustrated by Katherine Cameron) (Moray Press, 1934)...**£35**

CAMPBELL, Roy

Poet. Born: Durban, Natal 1901. Campbell's celebrated legacy include several books of poetry, two autobiographical works, two travel books, a percipient little study of the Spanish poet, Garcia Lorca, and a children's novel. Died: 1957.

Prices are for books in Very Good condition with dustjackets.

THE MAMBA'S PRECIPICE (illustrated by Dolf Reiser) (Frederick Muller, 1953).....................................**£25**

THE 'CAPTAIN' MAGAZINE

British boys' magazine, published by Newnes between 1899 and 1924. Its best-known contributor was P.G. Wodehouse, who submitted many of his early school stories to the title.

Prices are for volumes in Very Good condition.

THE CAPTAIN MAGAZINE: A Magazine for Boys and Old Boys. Vol. 1 (April-September 1899)..£45
THE CAPTAIN MAGAZINE Vols. 2-25 (October 1899-September 1911) .... each £35
THE CAPTAIN MAGAZINE Vols. 26-46 (October 1911-March 1922) .... each £30
THE CAPTAIN MAGAZINE Vols. 47-50 (April 1922-March 1924) .... each £25

CARR, J.L.

English author. Born: Yorkshire, 1912. Loved by collectors and the literary establishment alike, the author of *A Month in the Country* and *The Battle of Pollock's Crossing* also penned several children's works. Died: 1994.

Prices are for books in Very Good condition.

THE RED WINDCHEATER (paperback) (Macmillan, 1970)..£5
THE DUSTMAN (paperback) (Macmillan, 1972) £5
THE GARAGE MECHANIC (paperback) (Macmillan, 1972)..£5
THE OLD FARM COAT (paperback) (Macmillan, 1974) £5
RED FOAL'S COAT (paperback) (Macmillan, 1974)...£5
THE GREEN CHILDREN OF THE WOODS (paperback) (Longman, 1976) £5
AN EAR-RING FOR ANNA BEER (as 'Jim Carr', paperback) (Macmillan, 1976)...£5
GONE WITH THE WHIRLWIND (as 'Jim Carr', paperback) (Macmillan, 1980)...£5

CARROLL, Lewis

British author. Born: Charles Lutwidge Dodgson in Daresbury, Cheshire, in 1832. Educated at Rugby School and Christ Church College, Oxford. Received Studentship of the college in 1852 and appointed Sub-Librarian in 1855. His first humorous pieces appeared in the *Comic Times* in that year. Inspired by his friendship with the young Alice Liddell, he wrote *Alice Adventures Under Ground* in 1864, the book appearing under the title *Alice's Adventures in Wonderland* the following year. The sequel, *Through the Looking-Glass, and What Alice Found There*, was published in 1871. As well as his various books of nonsense, he also wrote several pamphlets and was an accomplished photographer. Died: 1898.

Prices are for books in Very Good condition in the original cloth (with dustjackets after 1930).

'ALICE' BOOKS

'Alice's Adventures Under Ground'

ALICE'S ADVENTURES UNDER GROUND (red cloth binding) (Macmillan, 1886)..£200
ALICE'S ADVENTURES UNDER GROUND (variant binding) (Macmillan, 1886)...£2,000
JUSTIN TOOD EDITION (Gollanz, 1988)...£30
ANTONY BROWNE EDITION (Julian MacRae, 1988)..£30
HELEN OXENBURY EDITION (Walker, 1999) £20

'Alice's Adventures in Wonderland'

FIRST [WITHDRAWN] EDITION (illustrated by John Tenniel; red cloth binding) (Macmillan, 1865)..................£200,000+
FIRST US EDITION (illustrated by John Tenniel; red cloth binding) (Appleton, US, 1866 [1865]) ....£5,000+
FIRST U.K. EDITION (illustrated by John Tenniel; red cloth binding) (Macmillan, 1866 [1865]) ....£3,000+
FIRST GERMAN EDITION (as 'Alice's Abenteuer Im Wunderland'; translated by Antonie Zimmermann)
    (Macmillan und Comp, 1869)..£300
FIRST FRENCH EDITION (as 'Aventures d'Alice au Pays des Merveilles'; translated by Henry Bué)
    (Macmillan and Co, Londres, 1869)..£300
FIRST ITALIAN EDITION (as 'Avventure d'Alice nel Paese delle Meraviglie'; translated by T. Pietrocòla-Rossetti)
    (Macmillan and Co, Londra, 1872)..£300
'PEOPLE'S EDITION' (illustrated by John Tenniel; green cloth binding) (Macmillan, 1887) £50
'THE NURSERY ALICE' (Illustrated by John Tenniel; boards) (Macmillan, 1890)......................................£150
PETER NEWELL EDITION (Harper, US, 1901) £150
BLANCHE McMANUS EDITION (Mansfield, US, 1896)..£80
BLANCHE McMANUS EDITION (Ward Lock, 1907)...£80
CHARLES ROBINSON EDITION (Cassell, 1907) £150
ARTHUR RACKHAM EDITION (with a poem by Austin Dobson; green cloth binding) (Helnemann, [1907])...........£300
ARTHUR RACKHAM EDITION (De Luxe Edition, with poem by Austin Dobson; limited to 1,130 copies; white vellum binding)
    (Heinemann, [1907])..£1,750
THOMAS MAYBANK EDITION (Routledge, 1907) £100
MILLICENT SOWERBY EDITION (Chatto & Windus, 1907) £150
HARRY ROUNTREE EDITION (Nelson, 1908)..£100
THOMAS HEATH ROBINSON EDITION (illustrated by Thomas Heath Robinson and Charles Pears)
    (William Collins, 1908)..£30
MABEL LUCIE ATTWELL EDITION (boards or cloth binding) (Raphael Tuck, [1910]) £200

*The original simple bindings for the first edition of **Through the Looking-Glass**, illustrated by John Tenniel (Macmillan, 1872).*

CARROLL, Lewis

*A plate from Arthur Rackham's 1907 edition of **Alice in Wonderland**. Unusually, most of the De Luxe copies of this book were not signed.*

WILLY POGANY EDITION(De Luxe Edition, signed by the artist) (Dutton, US, 1929) **£250**
CHARLES FOLKARD EDITION (A. & C. Black, 1929)... **£40**
MARIE LAURENCIN EDITION (Black Sun Press, Paris, 1930) **£2,000**
MARIE LAURENCIN EDITION (with extra plates) (Black Sun Press, Paris, 1930)....................... **£5,000**
FIRST RENE CLOKE EDITION ('The Radiant Step', 1934) **£30**
SECOND RENE CLOKE EDITION (P.R. Gawthorn, [c 1943]) **£30**
ANTHONY RADO EDITION (Newman Wolsey, [c 1944]) **£40**
EILEEN SOPER EDITION (Harrap, 1947)... **£40**
MARAJA EDITION (W.H. Alien, 1958) **£40**
RALPH STEADMAN EDITION (Dobson, 1967) **£70**
SALVADOR DALI EDITION (Random House, US, 1969)... **£3,000**
BARRY MOSER EDITION (University of California Press, US, 1982)..................................... **£50**
BARRY MOSER EDITION (De Luxe Edition) (Pennyroyal Press, US, 1982) **£3,000**
MICHAEL HAGUE EDITION (Holt, US, 1985) **£25**
MICHAEL HAGUE EDITION (Methuen, 1985)... **£20**
JUSTIN TODD EDITION (Gollancz, 1988)... **£30**
ANTONY BROWNE EDITION (Julia MacRae Books, 1988)... **£30**
HELEN OXENBURY EDITION (Walker, 1999)... **£20**
DIDIER MUTEL EDITION (limited to 50 signed copies; in slipcase) (Mutel, Paris, 2002) **£2,500**

'Through the Looking-Glass'

FIRST EDITION (illustrated by John Tenniel) (Macmillan, 1872 [1871]) **£400**
'PEOPLE'S EDITION' (illustrated by John Teniel; green cloth binding) (Macmillan, 1887) **£50**
BLANCHE McMANUS EDITION (Mansfield, US, 1899)... **£50**
PETER NEWELL EDITION (Harper, US, 1902).. **£100**
HELEN MUNRO EDITION (Nelson, 1937) **£30**
RALPH STEADMAN EDITION (MacGibbon & Kee, 1972)... **£60**
WASP IN A WIG (the first appearance in print, exclusive to *The Sunday Telegraph*, of the lost chapter from *Through The Looking-Glass*, with illustrations by Ralph Steadman, Sir Hugh Casson, Peter Blake & P. Procktor) (Telegraph Sunday Magazine No.51, 1977).. **£5**
WASP IN A WIG a 'suppressed' episode of **Through the Loking-Glass** (Macmillan, 1977) **£10**

Combined Editions

JOHN TENNIEL EDITION (92 illustrations by John Tenniel, including sixteen in colour) (Macmillan, 1911) **£80**
MERVYN PEAKE EDITION (Continental, Sweden, 1946) **£200**
Ditto (Wingate, 1954).. **£120**
THE COMPLETE ALICE AND HUNTING OF THE SNARK (illustrated by Ralph Steadman) (Jonathan Cape, 1986)............. **£40**

Other Children's Books

PHANTASMAGORIA and Other Poems (Macmillan, 1869) **£300**
Ditto (Miniature edition with illustrations by Arthur B. Frost) (Macmillan, 1911)........................ **£30**
THE HUNTING OF THE SNARK, An Agony In Eight Fits (Macmillan, 1876)........................ **£400**
Ditto (with illustrations by Peter Newell) (NY: Harper , 1903) **£60**
Ditto (with illustrations by Mervyn Peake) (Chatto & Windus, 1941) **£60**
Ditto (with illustrations by Harold Jones; limited edition of 900 copies; morocco, slipcase) (Whittington Press, 1975) **£150**
Ditto (with illustrations by Ralph Steadman) (Dempsey, 1975).. **£30**
Ditto (with illustrations by Quentin Blake, slipcase) (Folio Society, 1976)........................... **£20**
Ditto (Facsimile edition) (Windward, 1980) **£20**
RHYME? AND REASON? (with illustrations by Arthur B. Frost and Henry Holiday) (Macmillan, 1883)................ **£150**
A TANGLED TALE (with illustrations by A.B. Frost) (Macmillan, 1885).............................. **£150**
SYLVIE AND BRUNO (with illustrations by Harry Furniss) (Macmillan, 1889) **£100**
SYLVIE AND BRUNO CONCLUDED (with illustrations by Harry Furniss) (Macmillan, 1893) **£60**
THREE SUNSETS & OTHER POEMS (with illustrations by Gertrude B. Thomson) (Macmillan, 1898) **£80**
THE LEWIS CARROLL PICTURE BOOK (with illustrations by Lewis Carroll) (T. Fisher Unwin, 1899)............... **£150**
FEEDING THE MIND (Preface by William H. Draper) (Chatto & Windus, 1907)................... **£40**
BRUNO'S REVENGE (Collins, [1924])... **£60**
FURTHER NONSENSE, VERSE AND PROSE (with photos by Carroll and illustration by H.M. Bateman) (T. Fisher Unwin, 1926)........ **£80**
THE COLLECTED VERSE OF LEWIS CARROLL (illustrations by Tenniel, Frost, Holiday, Furniss and Carroll) (Macmillan, 1932)...... **£100**
FOR THE TRAIN (Edited by Hugh J. Schonfield, illustrations by C.H. Bennett & W. McConnell) (Denis Archer, 1932)............... **£60**
Ditto (limited edition) (Denis Archer, 1932).. **£100**
THE RECTORY UMBRELLA AND MISCHMASCH (Edited by Florence Milner) (Cassell, 1932)................... **£60**

CAVE, Patrick

British children's author. Born in Bath. Author of several widely acclaimed 'Young Adult' novels.

Prices are for books in Fine condition with dustjackets where applicable.

NUMBER 99 (paperback) (Oxford University Press, 2001) **£8**
LAST CHANCE (paperback) (Oxford University Press, 2002) **£8**
SHARP NORTH (Simon & Schuster, 2004) **£10**
BLOWN AWAY (Simon & Schuster, 2005) **£10**

This edition of Pinocchio was published by Collins and is now valued at £25 in Very Good condition with the jacket.

This American paperback was published in 1939 to coincide with the Disney film. Very Good copies are valued at £800.

'CHATTERBOX' ANNUALS

Long-running British children's annual. The magazine itself was founded in 1866 as a rival to the 'penny dreadfuls' of the time, and contained both serials and factual/religious articles. It ceased publication in 1948.

Prices are for annuals in Very Good condition.

CHATTERBOX 1866 (William Mackintosh, [1866]) £45
CHATTERBOX 1867-1929 (William Mackintosh/Wells Gardner & Darton).. each £35
CHATTERBOX 1930-1956 (Wells Gardner & Darton/Dean) .... each £10

CHRISTOPHER, John

British author. Born: Christopher Samuel Youd in 1922. An accomplished science fiction writer for adults, he is one of the few authors to write successfully in the field for children. Many of his works are grouped together in trilogies.

Prices are for books in Very Good condition with dustjackets.

THE WHITE MOUNTAINS (Hamish Hamilton, 1967)..£35
THE CITY OF LEAD AND GOLD (Hamish Hamilton, 1967)..£35
THE POOL OF FIRE (Hamish Hamilton, 1968)...£35
THE LOTUS CAVES (Hamish Hamilton, 1969)...£20
THE GUARDIANS (Hamish Hamilton, 1970) £20
THE PRINCE IN WAITING (Hamish Hamilton, 1970) £20
BEYOND THE BURNING LANDS (Hamish Hamilton, 1971) £20
THE SWORD OF THE SPIRITS (Hamilton Hamilton, 1972)..£20
DOM AND VA (Hamish Hamilton, 1973) £20
A FIGURE IN GREY (written under the pseudonym 'Hilary Ford') (World's Work, 1973) £15
WILD JACK (Hamish Hamilton, 1974) £15
IN THE BEGINNING (Longman, 1975)..£15
EMPTY WORLD (Hamish Hamilton, 1977) £15
FIREBALL (Gollancz, 1981) £15
NEW FOUND LAND (Gollancz, 1983)...£15
DRAGONDANCE (Viking Kestrel, 1986)..£15

'CHUMS' ANNUALS

British boys' annual, published between 1892 and 1941. It was a less popular rival to the *Boy's Own Paper*. Vols. 1-34 published by Cassell, Vol. 35 onwards published by Amalgamated Press.

Prices are for annuals (bound volumes) in Very Good condition.

VOLUME 1 (1892-1893) £35
VOLUMES 2-22 (1893-1914)..each £25
VOLUMES 23-26 (1914-1918)..each £25
VOLUMES 27-42 (1918-1935)..each £25
VOLUMES 43-48 (1935-1941)..each £20

CLARKE, Harry

Illustrator. Born: Dublin, 1889. Stained glass artist and book illustrator Harry Clarke was a major figure in the Irish Arts and Crafts Movement. He was picked up by London publisher Harrap, and his first book illustrations appeared in the 1916 edition of Hans Christian Andersen's *Fairy Tales*. Died: 1931.

Prices are for books in Very Good condition.

FAIRY TALES by Hans Andersen (cloth) (Harrap, 1916) £350
FAIRY TALES by Hans Andersen (full leather) (Harrap, 1916) £500
FAIRY TALES by Hans Andersen (limited to 125 signed copies; vellum) (Harrap, 1916) £1,750
FAIRY TALES by Carles Perrault (cloth) (Harrap, 1923)..£250
FAIRY TALES by Carles Perrault (bound in Persian levant leather)(Harrap, 1923) £500

COLFER, Eoin

Irish author. Born: 1967. His first novel, *Benny and Omar*, was published by the O'Brien Press in October 1998. He wrote many children's books before his very collectable 'Artemis Fowl' novels, about a 12-year-old criminal mastermind, made his name.

Prices are for books in Fine condition with dustjackets where applicable.

ARTEMIS FOWL (with variant non-holographic dustjacket) (Viking, 2001) £100
ARTEMIS FOWL (with holographic dustjacket) (Viking, 2001) £50
ARTEMIS FOWL (uncorrected proof; pictorial soft covers) (Viking, 2001) £75
ARTEMIS FOWL (paperback) (Hyperion, US, 2001) £20
THE ARCTIC INCIDENT (Viking, 2002) £20
THE ETERNITY CODE (Viking, 2003)..£20
THE SEVENTH DWARF (paperback original; new short Artemis adventure) (Puffin, 2004) £12
THE OPAL DECEPTION (Viking, 2005)..£15
THE LOST COLONY (Viking, 2006)..£10

COLLINS, Norman

British publisher, television executive and author. Born: Buckinghamshire, 1907. The creator of *London Belongs to Me* and other noted bestsellers also wrote two collectable children's books. Died: 1982.

Prices are for books in Very Good condition with dustjackets.

BLACK IVORY (Collins, 1948) £15
BLACK IVORY (Duell, Sloan & Pearce, US, 1948)..£12
LITTLE NELSON (Collins, 1981) £12

COLLODI, Carlo

Italian author. Born: Carlo Lorenzini in Florence in 1826. Took his pseudonym from the name of his mother's home town. Worked as a journalist and founded his own satirical magazine, before turning to children's writing. Best known for *Pinocchio*, which was first serialised in 1881. Also translated Perrault's tales. Died: 1890.

Prices are for books in Very Good condition.

LE AVVENTURE DI PINOCCHIO (first edition in book form; illustrated by E. Mazzanti) (Florence, 1883)............................£25,000
THE STORY OF A PUPPET, or The Adventures of Pinocchio (translated by M.A. Murray) (Unwin, 1892) £5,000
ADVENTURES EVERY CHILD SHOULD KNOW: The Marvellous Adventures of Pinocchio
  Edited by Mary E. Burt, from an original translation by A.G. Capriani (illustrated by Emily Hall Chamberlin)
  (Doubleday, U.S., 1909)..£250
PINOCCHIO: The Tale of a Puppet (illustrated by Charles Folkard; translated by M.A. Murray) (Dent, 1911)..............£100
PINOCCHIO (illustrated by Maria L. Kirk) (Lippincott, U.S., 1920)...£85
PINOCCHIO (illustrated by Jack Tinker) (Lippincott, U.S., [1930]) £70
PINOCCHIO (illustrated by K. Wiese; translated by M.A. Murray) (Nelson, 1938) £35
THE ADVENTURES OF PINOCCHIO (illustrated by A.H. Watson) (Collins, 1939)........................£30
WALT DISNEY'S PINOCCHIO (limited to 100 numbered copies; comb-bound) (Collins, [1939])........................£200
WALT DISNEY TELLS THE STORY OF PINOCCHIO (paperback) (Whitman No 556, U.S., 1939)........................£900
WALT DISNEY'S VERSION OF PINOCCHIO (pictorial boards) (Collins, 1940)................................£60
PINOCCHIO (illustrated by Charles Folkard; translated by M.A. Murray, revised by G. Tassinari) (Dent, 1951) £35

THE ADVENTURES OF PINOCCHIO AND PIP, or The Little Rose-Coloured Monkey
(illustrated by Will Nickless; introduction by David Davis) (Collins, 1954) £25
PINOCCHIO. Adapted by Allen Chafee (illustrated by Lois Lenski) (Publicity Products, [1954]) £20
THE ADVENTURES OF PINOCCHIO (illustrated by Roberto Innocenti) (Cape, 1988) £15

COMICS, Great British

This selected price guide appeared with '50 Great British Comics' chosen by comics experts Norman Wright and David Ashford in the December 2006 issue of *Book & Magazine Collector*.

Prices are for comics in Very Good condition without any free gifts.

BATTLE PICTURE WEEKLY (Amalgamated Press/Fleetway/IPC, 8th March 1975).............................£12
BEANO (DC Thomson, 30th July 1938)...£10,000
BEEZER (DC Thomson, 21st January 1956) £135
BOYS WORLD (Longacre, 26th January 1963)...£35
BUFFALO BILL (Boardman, October 1948) £20
BUNTY (DC Thomson, 18th January 1958) £55
BUSTER (Amalgamated Press/Fleetway/IPC, 28th May 1960) £90
CLASSIC IN PICTURES (Amex, 1949)..£12
COLOURED SLICK FUN (Swan, 1945)...£12
COMET (Allen/Amalgamated Press, 20th September 1946)...£12
COMIC CUTS (Amalgamated Press/Fleetway/IPC, 17th May 1890) £125
COMMANDO (DC Thomson, July 1961) £275
COWBOY COMICS LIBRARY (Amalgamated Press/Fleetway/IPC, May 1950) £100
DANDY (DC Thomson, 4th December 1937)..£7,000
DYNAMIC THRILLS (Swan, January 1951)..£12
EAGLE (Hulton/LongacreOdhams/IPC, 14th April 1950) £170
(JUNIOR) EXPRESS (SUPER COLOUR) WEEKLY (Beaverbrook/TV, 18th June 1950) £12
FILM FUN (Amalgamated Press/Fleetway/IPC, 17th January 1920) £90
GIRL (Hulton/LongacreOdhams/IPC, 2nd November 1951) £55
HAPPY DAYS (Amalgamated Press/Fleetway/IPC, 8th October 1938)..£80
ILLUSTRATED CHIPS (Amalgamated Press/Fleetway/IPC, 6th September 1890) £125
KNOCKOUT (Amalgamated Press/Fleetway/IPC, 4th March 1939)..£190
LION (Amalgamated Press/Fleetway/IPC, 23rd February 1952)...£90
LONE STAR (DCMT/Atlas, November 1952)..£12
MAGIC (DC Thomson, 22nd July 1939) £1,300
MARVELMAN/YOUNG MARVELMAN (Miller, 3rd February 1954)...£35
MICKEY MOUSE WEEKLY (Odhams, 8th February 1936) £130
PRINCESS (Amalgamated Press/Fleetway/IPC, 30th January 1960)..£12
PUCK (Amalgamated Press/Fleetway/IPC, 30th July 1904) £40
RADIO FUN (Amalgamated Press/Fleetway/IPC, 15th October 1938).......................................£225
RAINBOW (Amalgamated Press/Fleetway/IPC, 14th February 1914) £90
RANGER (Amalgamated Press/Fleetway/IPC, 18th September 1965)...£35
ROY CARSON (Boardman, 1948)...£20
SCHOOL FRIEND (Amalgamated Press/Fleetway/IPC, 20th May 1950) £35
SPACEMAN (Gould-Light, 1953) £25
SPARKLER (Amalgamated Press/Fleetway/IPC, 20th October 1934)..£55
SUN (Allen/Amalgamated Press, 11th November 1947) £12
SUPER DETECTIVE LIBRARY (Amalgamated Press/Fleetway/IPC, March 1954) £90
SWIFT (Hulton/LongacreOdhams/IPC, 20th March 1954)...£35
SWIFT MORGAN (Boardman, 1948)..£20
THRILLER COMICS LIBRARY (Amalgamated Press/Fleetway/IPC, November 1951).........................£110
TIGER (Amalgamated Press/Fleetway/IPC, 11th September 1954) £80
TIT-BITS SCIENCE-FICTION COMICS (Pearson, 1953)..£40
TOPPER (DC Thomson, 7th February 1953)...£135
TV CENTURY 21 (City, 23rd January 1965)...£175
2000AD (Amalgamated Press/Fleetway/IPC, 26th February 1977) £80
VALIANT (Amalgamated Press/Fleetway/IPC, 6th October 1962)..£40
VICTOR (DC Thomson, 26th February 1961)...£40
WAR PICTURE LIBRARY (Amalgamated Press/Fleetway/IPC, September 1958) £20
WHAM! (Odhams, 20th June 1964)..£55

COOKSON, Catherine

British novelist. Born County Durham, 1906. The prolific and popular romantic novelist (although she always preferred to call her works 'historical novels'), whose works went on to sell more than 100,000,000 copies, also penned a handful of children's stories. Died: 1998.

Prices are for books in Very Good condition in dustjackets.

MATTY DOOLIN (Macdonald, 1965) £20
JOE AND THE GLADIATOR (Macdonald, 1968) £15
THE NIPPER (Macdonald, 1970) £15

*Six Great British comics chosen by **BMC's** comic experts Norman Wright and David Ashford.*

BLUE BACCY (Macdonald, 1972) £15
OUR JOHN WILLIE (Macdonald, 1974) £12
MRS FLANAGAN'S TRUMPET (Macdonald, 1976) £12
GO TELL IT TO MRS GOLIGHTLY (Macdonald, 1977) £12
LANKY JONES (Macdonald, 1980) £12
NANCY NUTALL AND THE MONGREL (Macdonald, 1982) £12

COOLIDGE, Susan

American author. Born: Sarah Chauncy Woolsey in Cleveland, Ohio, in 1845. Spent most of her childhood in New Haven, Connecticut, and worked as a nurse during the Civil War. Her first children's book, *The New-Year's Bargain* (1872), was quickly followed by *What Katy Did*. She also wrote several volumes of verse and edited the letters of Fanny Burney and Jane Austen. Died: 1905.

Prices are for books in Very Good condition.

THE NEW YEAR'S BARGAIN (illustrated by Addie Ledyard) (Roberts Brothers, U.S.,1872)....................................£85
THE NEW YEAR'S BARGAIN (illustrated by Addie Ledyard) (Warne, [1872]) £40
WHAT KATY DID (illustrated by Addie Ledyard) (Roberts Brothers, U.S., 1873)..£200
WHAT KATY DID (illustrated by Addie Ledyard) (Ward & Lock, [1873])..£150
WHAT KATY DID AT SCHOOL (Roberts Brothers, U.S., 1874)...£175
WHAT KATY DID AT SCHOOL (Ward & Lock, 1874)..£100
LITTLE MISS MISCHIEF and Other Stories (illustrated by Addie Ledyard) (Roberts Brothers, U.S., 1874)............£80
LITTLE MISS MISCHIEF and Other Stories (illustrated by Addie Ledyard) (Ward & Lock, [1874]) £35
MISCHIEF'S THANKSGIVING and Other Stories (illustrated by Addie Ledyard) (Roberts Brothers, U.S., 1874)....£70

MISCHIEF'S THANKSGIVING and Other Stories (illustrated by Addie Ledyard) (Routledge, [1875])...£35
NINE LITTLE GOSLINGS (Roberts Bros, U.S., 1875)..£40
FOR SUMMER AFTERNOONS (Roberts Brothers, U.S., 1876)..£20
EYEBRIGHT (Roberts Brothers, U.S., 1879)...£50
EYEBRIGHT (Routledge, [1879])...£30
CROSS PATCH and Other Stories (illustrated by Ellen Oakford) (Roberts Brothers, U.S., 1881) £35
CROSS PATCH and Other Stories (illustrated by Ellen Oakford; same as above, but with different title-page) (Bogue, 1881)..£35
A GUERNSEY LILY (Roberts Brothers, U.S., 1881 [1880])...£55
A GUERNSEY LILY (Bogue, 1881)..£55
A ROUND DOZEN (Roberts Brothers, U.S., 1883)..£30
A LITTLE COUNTRY GIRL (Roberts Brothers, U.S., 1885) £20
WHAT KATY DID NEXT (illustrated by Jessie McDermot) (Roberts Brothers, U.S., 1886)................................£175
WHAT KATY DID NEXT (illustrated by Jessie McDermot) (Ward & Lock, [1887]) £175
WHAT KATY DID NEXT (illustrated by Jessie McDermot) (Blackie, 1903 [1902])..£100
CLOVER (Roberts Brothers, U.S., 1888)..£60
JUST SIXTEEN (Roberts Brothers, U.S., 1889)..£30
IN THE HIGH VALLEY (Roberts Brothers, U.S., 1890)..£70
IN THE HIGH VALLEY (Blackie, 1959) £25
THE BARBERRY BUSH (Roberts Brothers, U.S., 1893)...£25
NOT QUITE EIGHTEEN (Roberts Brothers, U.S., 1894)..£25
AN OLD CONVENT SCHOOL IN PARIS (Roberts Brothers, U.S., 1895)...£25
CURLY LOCKS (Little Brown, U.S., 1899) £25
A LITTLE KNIGHT OF LABOR (Little Brown, U.S., 1899) £25
LITTLE TOMMY TUCKER (Little Brown, U.S., 1900) £25
TWO GIRLS (Little Brown, U.S., 1900) £25
UNCLE AND AUNT (Little Brown, U.S., 1901)...£25
LITTLE BO-PEEP (Little Brown, U.S., 1901)...£25
THE RULE OF THREE (Henry Altemus, U.S., 1904)..£20
A SHEAF OF STORIES (Little Brown, U.S., 1906) £20

CORKRAN, Alice

British author. Wrote several children's works, but is best known for *Down the Snow Stairs* (1887), a fantasy partly inspired by the works of Lewis Carroll. Died: 1916.

Prices are for books in Very Good condition.

THE ADVENTURES OF MRS WISHING-TO-BE and Other Stories (Blackie, 1883 [1882]) £25
DOWN THE SNOW STAIRS or From Good-Night to Good-Morning (illustrated by Gordon Browne) (Blackie, 1887 [1886])...£50
MARGERY MERTON'S GIRLHOOD (illustrated by Gordon Browne) (Blackie, 1888 [1887]) £40
MEG'S FRIEND (illustrated by Robert Fowler) (Blackie, 1889 [1888]) £25
JOAN'S ADVENTURES AT THE NORTH POLE AND ELSEWHERE (Blackie, 1889 [1888]).................................£35

CORMIER, Shawn

American author. Born: 1967. New children's author whose debut *Nomadin* attracted a lot of interest among collectors of 'ultra modern' firsts.

Prices are for books in Very Good condition.

NOMADIN (paperback; signed/dated/inscribed) (Pine View Press, 2003)...£50
NOMADIN (paperback) (Pine View Press, 2003) £7
NIDEMON: sequel to Nomadin (paperback) (Pine View Press, 2005)..£7

CRADOCK, Mrs H.C.

British author of the 'Josephine' series and other children's books, many of them illustrated by Honor C. Appleton. Also wrote the 'Teddy Bear' series.

Prices are for books in Very Good condition.

THE CARE OF BABIES: A Reading Book for Girls (Bell, 1908) £70
JOSEPHINE AND HER DOLLS (illustrated by Honor C. Appleton) (Blackie, 1916 [1915]) £140
JOSEPHINE'S HAPPY FAMILY (illustrated by Honor C. Appleton) (Blackie, 1917 [1916])................................£90
JOSEPHINE IS BUSY (illustrated by Honor C. Appleton) (Blackie, 1918)...£100
EVERYDAY STORIES TO TELL TO CHILDREN (Harrap, 1919)..£50
THE BIG BOOK OF JOSEPHINE (contains 'Josephine and her Dolls', 'Josephine's Happy Family' and
   'Josephine is Busy'; illustrated by Honor C. Appleton) (Blackie, [1919])..£200
WHERE THE DOLLS LIVED (illustrated by Honor C. Appleton) (SPCK, [1919])...£100
JOSEPHINE'S BIRTHDAY (illustrated by Honor C. Appleton) (Blackie, 1920 [1919]) £100
JOSEPHINE, JOHN AND THE PUPPY (illustrated by Honor C. Appleton) (Blackie, [1920])...............................£90
PEGGY'S TWINS (illustrated by Honor C. Appleton) (SPCK, [1920])...£65
THE HOUSE OF FANCY (illustrated by Honor C. Appleton) (O'Connor, 1922)...£65
PEGGY AND JOAN (illustrated by Honor C. Appleton) (Blackie, [1922]) £65

Two Walter Crane rarities: a version of American author Nathaniel Hawthorne's **Wonder Book** *and the classic* **Baby's Own Aesop**.

THE STORY OF PAT (SPCK, [1923])...£30
JOSEPHINE KEEPS SCHOOL (illustrated by Honor C. Appleton) (Blackie, [1925]) £80
THE BONNY BOOK OF JOSEPHINE (contains 'Josephine, John and the Puppy',
   'Josephine's Birthday' and 'Josephine Keeps School'; illustrated by Honor C. Appleton) (Blackie, [1926])...............£160
JOSEPHINE GOES SHOPPING (illustrated by Honor C. Appleton) (Blackie, [1926]).....................................£75
THE BEST TEDDY BEAR IN THE WORLD (illustrated by Honor C. Appleton) (Nelson, [1926]) £50
PAMELA'S TEDDY BEARS (illustrated by Honor C. Appleton) (Jack, [1927])...£55
JOSEPHINE'S CHRISTMAS PARTY (illustrated by Honor C. Appleton) (Blackie, [1927]) £75
ELIZABETH (illustrated by Doris Burton) (Nelson, [1930])...£30
JOSEPHINE KEEPS HOUSE (illustrated by Honor C. Appleton) (Blackie, 1931)..£70
THE SMITH FAMILY (illustrated by S.G. Hulme Beaman) (Nelson, [1931]) £35
BARBARA AND PETER (illustrated by Doris Burton) (Nelson, [1931])...£30
THE JOSEPHINE DOLLY BOOK (contains 'Josephine's Happy Family', 'Josephine, John and the Puppy' and
   'Josephine is Busy'; illustrated by Honor C. Appleton) (Blackie, [1934])......................................£160
ADVENTURES OF A TEDDY BEAR (illustrated by Joyce L. Brisley) (Harrap, 1934)..£60
MORE ADVENTURES OF A TEDDY BEAR (illustrated by Joyce L. Brisley) (Harrap, 1935)...............................£50
IN TEDDY BEAR'S HOUSE (illustrated by Joyce L. Brisley) (Harrap, 1936) £50
JOSEPHINE'S PANTOMIME (illustrated by Honor C. Appleton) (Blackie, 1939) £65
TEDDY BEAR'S SHOP (illustrated by Joyce L. Brisley) (Harrap, 1939)...£40
JOSEPHINE GOES TRAVELLING (illustrated by Honor C. Appleton) (Blackie, 1940).....................................£65
TEDDY BEAR'S FARM (illustrated by Joyce L. Brisley) (Harrap, 1941)..£40
THE JOSEPHINE MINIATURES (six books: 'Josephine Keeps House', 'Josephine's Pantomime',
   'Josephine Goes Travelling', 'Josephine's Christmas Party', 'Josephine Keeps School' and 'Josephine,
   John and the Puppy'; illustrated by Honor C. Appleton) (Blackie, [1953]) .... each £40

CRANE, Walter

British illustrator. Born: Liverpool, 1845. Formed a successful partnership with the printer, Edmund Evans, for whom he illustrated many 'yellowback' novels and a long-running series of children's 'picture books', published by Warne and Routledge. Died: 1915.

Prices are for books in Very Good condition.

Warne's 'Sixpenny Toybooks' Illustrated by Walter Crane

THE HOUSE THAT JACK BUILT (Warne, 1865)...£150
THE COMICAL CAT (Warne, 1865) £100
THE AFFECTING STORY OF JENNY WREN (Warne, 1865) £100
THE RAILROAD ALPHABET (Warne, 1865)...£100
THE FARMYARD ALPHABET (Warne, 1865)..£100
COCK ROBIN (Warne, 1866) £100
A GAPING-WIDE-MOUTH WADDLING FROG (Warne, [1866])...£100

CRANE, Walter

Routledge's 'Sixpenny' and 'Shilling Toybooks' Illustrated by Walter Crane

THE OLD COURTIER (Routledge, 1867)...£75
MULTIPLICATION TABLE IN VERSE (Routledge, [1867])..£75
CHATTERING JACK'S PICTURE BOOK (Routledge, [1867])..£75
HOW JESSIE WAS LOST (Routledge, [1868])...£75
GRAMMAR IN RHYME (Routledge, [1868])..£75
ANNIE AND JACK IN LONDON (Routledge, [1869])...£75
ONE, TWO, BUCKLE MY SHOE (Routledge, [1869])...£75
THE FAIRY SHIP (Routledge, 1870)..£75
THE ADVENTURES OF PUFFY (Routledge, 1870)...£75
THIS LITTLE PIG WENT TO MARKET (Routledge, [1871])..£75
KING LUCKIEBOY'S PARTY (Routledge, [1871])..£75
KING LUCKIEBOY'S PICTURE BOOK (contains 'King Luckieboy's Party', 'This Little Pig Went to Market'
   and 'The Old Courtier') (Routledge, 1871) £150
ROUTLEDGE'S BOOK OF ALPHABETS (contains 'The Railroad Alphabet' and 'The Farmyard Alphabet')
   (Routledge, 1871) £125
NOAH'S ARK ALPHABET (Routledge, 1872) £100
MY MOTHER (Routledge, 1873)...£100
ALI BABA AND THE FORTY THIEVES (Routledge, 1873) £75
CINDERELLA (Routledge, 1873) £75
WALTER CRANE'S NEW TOY BOOK (contains eight previously published titles) (Routledge, 1873) £250
WALTER CRANE'S PICTURE BOOK (contains eight previously published titles) (Routledge, 1874) £250
VALENTINE AND ORSON (Routledge, 1874) £90
PUSS IN BOOTS (Routledge, 1874) £90
OLD MOTHER HUBBARD (Routledge, 1874)..£90
THE MARQUIS OF CARABAS' PICTURE BOOK (Routledge, [1874]) £90
THE ABSURD ABC (Routledge, 1874) £80
THE FROG PRINCE (Routledge: 'Walter Crane Shilling' series, 1874) £70
GOODY TWO SHOES (Routledge: 'Walter Crane Shilling' series, 1874)...............................£80
BEAUTY AND THE BEAST (Routledge: 'Walter Crane Shilling' series, 1874) £80
THE ALPHABET OF OLD FRIENDS (Routledge: 'Walter Crane Shilling' series, 1874) £75
LITTLE RED RIDING HOOD (Routledge, 1875)...£75
JACK AND THE BEANSTALK (Routledge, 1875)...£75
THE BLUEBEARD PICTURE BOOK (Routledge, [1875])...£75
BABY'S OWN ALPHABET (Routledge, 1875) £75
THE YELLOW DWARF (Routledge: 'Walter Crane Shilling' series, 1875) £75
THE HIND IN THE WOOD (Routledge: 'Walter Crane Shilling' series, 1875).....................£75
PRINCESS BELLE ETOILE (Routledge: 'Walter Crane Shilling' series, 1875) £75
ALADDIN'S PICTURE BOOK (Routledge: 'Walter Crane Shilling' series, 1875 [1876])..........£75
SONG OF SIXPENCE TOY BOOK (Warne, [1876])..£75
THE THREE BEARS PICTURE BOOK (Routledge, [1876])...£75
THE SLEEPING BEAUTY IN THE WOOD (Routledge, 1876)...£75
WALTER CRANE'S PICTURE BOOKS VOL. 1: The Little Pig: His Picture Book (John Lane, 1895)............£55
WALTER CRANE'S PICTURE BOOKS VOL. 2: Mother Hubbard: Her Picture Book (John Lane, 1897)..........£55
WALTER CRANE'S PICTURE BOOKS VOL. 3: Cinderella's Picture Book (John Lane, 1897)...............£55
WALTER CRANE'S PICTURE BOOKS VOL. 4: Red Riding Hood's Picture Book (John Lane, 1898).........£55
BEAUTY AND THE BEAST PICTURE BOOK (John Lane: 'Large' series Vol. 1, 1901)..................£45
GOODY TWO SHOES PICTURE BOOK (John Lane: 'Large' series Vol. 2, 1901)......................£45
THE SONG OF SIXPENCE PICTURE BOOK (John Lane: 'Large' series Vol. 3, 1909) £45
THE BUCKLE MY SHOE PICTURE BOOKS (John Lane: 'Large' series Vol. 4, 1910) £45
PUSS IN BOOTS and THE FORTY THIEVES (John Lane, 1914)..£45
THE SLEEPING BEAUTY and BLUEBEARD (John Lane, 1914)..£45
THE THREE BEARS and MOTHER HUBBARD (John Lane, 1914) £45

Other Books Illustrated by Walter Crane

ROUTLEDGE'S COLOURED PICTURE BOOK (contains 'King Grisly Beard', 'The Fairy Ship' and
   'The Adventures of Puffy'; illustrated by Walter Crane and others) (Routledge, [1871]) £200
OUR OLD UNCLE'S HOME by Mother Carey (1872)..£100
MRS MUNDI AT HOME by Walter Crane (Marcus Ward, 1875) £100
TELL ME A STORY by Mrs Molesworth (Macmillan 1875)..£80
CARROTS by Mrs Molesworth (Macmillan, 1876) £80
THE QUIVER OF LOVE: A Collection of Valentines (illustrated by Walter Crane and Kate Greenaway)
   (Marcus Ward, 1876)..£90
THE BABY'S OPERA: Old Rhymes With New Dresses by Walter Crane (Routledge, 1877)............£150
THE CUCKOO CLOCK by Mrs Molesworth (Macmillan, 1877) £80
MOTHER GOOSE'S JINGLES (illustrated by Walter Crane, H. Weir and others) (London, 1878 [1877])......£80
GRANDMOTHER DEAR by Mrs Molesworth (Macmillan, 1878) £60
THE BABY'S BOUQUET by Walter Crane (Routledge, 1878) £150
THE TAPESTRY ROOM by Mrs Molesworth (Macmillan, 1879) £60
A CHRISTMAS CHILD by Mrs Molesworth (Macmillan, 1880) £60

THE NECKLACE OF PRINCESS FIORIMONDE by Mary de Morgan (Macmillan, 1880) £60
THE FIRST OF MAY: A Fairy Masque by John R. Wise (limited to 300 copies, signed by the artist)
(Sotheran, 1881)... £500
THE FIRST OF MAY: A Fairy Masque (folio; limited to 200 copies, signed by the artist) (Sotheran, 1881) £500
THE ADVENTURES OF HERR BABY by Mrs Molesworth (Macmillan, 1881)... £40
ROSY by Mrs Molesworth (Macmillan, 1882) £40
HOUSEHOLD STORIES by the Brothers Grimm (Macmillan, 1882) £90
PAN PIPES: A Book of Old Songs by Theodore Marzials (Routledge, 1883) £150
TWO LITTLE WAIFS by Mrs Molesworth (Macmillan, 1883)... £40
CHRISTMAS-TREE LAND by Mrs Molesworth (Macmillan, 1884) £40
THE GOLDEN PRIMER Parts 1 and 2 by Professor J.M.D. Meiklejohn (two volumes) (Blackwood, [1884]) .... the set £60
FOLK AND FAIRY TALES by Constance C. Harrison (Ward & Downey, 1885) £70
SLATEANDPENCILVANIA: Being the Adventures of Dick on a Desert Island by Walter Crane
(Marcus Ward, 1885)... £150
US by Mrs Molesworth (Macmillan, 1885) £40
LITTLE QUEEN ANNE by Walter Crane (Marcus Ward, 1886) £160
POTHOOKS AND PERSEVERANCE, or The ABC Serpent by Walter Crane (Marcus Ward, 1886)..................... £180
A ROMANCE OF THE THREE Rs by Walter Crane (Marcus Ward, 1886) £160
LEGENDS FOR LIONEL IN PEN AND PENCIL by Walter Crane (Cassell, 1887) £60
THE BABY'S OWN AESOP by Walter Crane (Routledge, 1887 [1886]) £125
FOUR WINDS FARM by Mrs Molesworth (Macmillan, 1887) £40
LITTLE MISS PEGGY by Mrs Molesworth (Macmillan, 1887) £40
A CHRISTMAS POSY by Mrs Molesworth (Macmillan, 1888) £40
THE HAPPY PRINCE and Other Tales by Oscar Wilde (illustrated by Walter Crane and G. Jacomb-Hood)
(David Nutt, 1888) £750
FLORA'S FEAST: A Masque Of Flowers by Walter Crane (Cassell, 1889) £125
THE RECTORY CHILDREN by Mrs Molesworth (Macmillan, 1889)... £40
THE CHILDREN OF THE CASTLE by Mrs Molesworth (Macmillan, 1890) £40
QUEEN SUMMER, or The Tourney of the Lilly and the Rose by Walter Crane (Cassell, 1891)........................ £125
A WONDER BOOK FOR BOYS AND GIRLS by Nathaniel Hawthorne (sixty designs by Walter Crane)
(Osgood, McIlvaine, 1892) £175
STUDIES AND STORIES by Mrs Molesworth (A.D. Innes, 1893) £40
THE HISTORY OF REYNARD THE FOX by F.S. Ellis (David Nutt, 1894) £75
THE STORY OF THE GLITTERING PLAIN by William Morris (limited to 250 copies) (Kelmscott Press, 1894)................... £2,000
THE MERRY WIVES OF WINDSOR by William Shakespeare (George Allen, 1894)... £60
TWO GENTLEMEN OF VERONA by William Shakespeare (Dent, 1894)... £60
THE FAERIE QUEEN by Edmund Spenser (issued in nineteen parts) (George Allen, 1894-97)................................... the set £600
THE FAERIE QUEEN by Edmund Spenser (issued in six volumes; limited to 1,000 sets) (George Allen, 1897).......... the set £800
CARTOONS FOR THE CAUSE (Twentieth Century Press, 1896) £500
A FLORAL FANTASY IN AN OLD ENGLISH GARDEN by Walter Crane (Harper, 1898) £125
THE SHEPHERD'S CALENDAR by Edmund Spenser (Harper, 1898) £80
TRIPLETS by Walter Crane (limited to 750 numbered copies) (Routledge, 1899) £250
THE BOOK OF WEDDING DAYS (Longmans Green, 1889)... £175
DON QUIXOTE. Translated by Judge Parry (Blackie, 1900)... £60
WALTER CRANE'S PICTURE BOOK (contains 'The Baby's Opera', 'The Baby's Bouquet' and
'The Baby's Own Aesop'; limited to 750 copies; vellum binding) (Warne, 1900)... £350
A MASQUE OF DAYS by Charles Lamb (Cassell, 1901) £250
FLOWERS FROM SHAKESPEARE'S GARDEN by Walter Crane (Cassell, 1906) £150
THE CHILD'S SOCIALIST READER by A.A. Watts (Methuen, 1907) £70
THE ROSEBUD and Other Tales by Arthur Kelly (Fisher & Unwin, 1909) £100
KING ARTHUR'S KNIGHTS by H. Gilbert (T.C. & E.C. Jack, 1911).. £75
RUMBO RHYMES by Alfred C. Calmour (Harper, 1911) £175
ROBIN HOOD by H. Gilbert (T.C. & E.C. Jack, 1912).. £75
THE STORY OF GREECE by M. MacGregor (T.C. & E.C. Jack, [1913])... £60
THE KNIGHTS OF THE ROUND TABLE by H. Gilbert (T.C. & E.C. Jack, [1915]) £60

CROMPTON, Richmal

British author. Born: Richmal Crompton Lamburn in Lancashire in 1890. Studied at London University,
subsequently becoming Classics mistress at Bromley High School before being compelled to retire because
of illness. Best known for the enormously popular 'William' books, although she also wrote several novels for
adults. Died: 1969.

Prices are for books in Very Good condition with dustjackets.

'William' Books

JUST WILLIAM (illustrated by Thomas Henry; this book's first edition is smaller than the usual Crown 8vo size,
measuring 7"x 4.25"; the first edition is also identified by the unnumbered pages of adverts at the rear of the
volume; red boards) (Newnes, [1922])... £1,500
MORE WILLIAM (illustrated by Thomas Henry; red boards) (Newnes, 1922)... £1,500
WILLIAM AGAIN (illustrated by Thomas Henry; red boards) (Newnes, 1923).. £1,000
WILLIAM THE FOURTH (illustrated by Thomas Henry; red boards) (Newnes, 1924) £900

WILLIAM AND WHITE SATIN   177

"SHE'S A SOPPY OLD LUNY!" DORITA REMARKED
SWEETLY.

One of the Thomas Henry illustrations from Richmal Crompton's 'William' stories.

STILL WILLIAM (illustrated by Thomas Henry; red boards) (Newnes, [1925])...£900
WILLIAM THE CONQUEROR (illustrated by Thomas Henry; red boards) (Newnes, [1926]) £900
WILLIAM THE OUTLAW (illustrated by Thomas Henry; red boards) (Newnes, [1927])...................................£800
WILLIAM IN TROUBLE (illustrated by Thomas Henry; red boards) (Newnes, [1927]) £800
WILLIAM THE GOOD (illustrated by Thomas Henry; red boards) (Newnes, [1928]) £800
WILLIAM (illustrated by Thomas Henry; blue boards) (Newnes, [1929])..£1,000
WILLIAM THE BAD (illustrated by Thomas Henry; blue boards) (Newnes, 1930)..£1,000
WILLIAM'S HAPPY DAYS (illustrated by Thomas Henry; blue boards) (Newnes, [1930]) £1,000
WILLIAM'S CROWDED HOURS (illustrated by Thomas Henry; blue boards) (Newnes, [1931]) £1,000
WILLIAM THE PIRATE (illustrated by Thomas Henry; blue boards) (Newnes, 1932)...................................£1,000
WILLIAM THE REBEL (illustrated by Thomas Henry; buff boards) (Newnes, [1933]) £1,000
WILLIAM THE GANGSTER (illustrated by Thomas Henry; blue boards) (Newnes, [1934]) £1,000
WILLIAM THE DETECTIVE (illustrated by Thomas Henry; brown boards) (Newnes, 1935) £1,000
SWEET WILLIAM (illustrated by Thomas Henry; green boards) (Newnes, [1936]).......................................£1,000
WILLIAM THE SHOWMAN (illustrated by Thomas Henry; green boards) (Newnes, [1937])..........................£1,000
WILLIAM THE DICTATOR (illustrated by Thomas Henry; green boards) (Newnes, [1938]) £1,000
WILLIAM AND A.R.P. (illustrated by Thomas Henry; green boards) (Newnes, 1939) £1,000
JUST WILLIAM: The Story of the Film (stories selected from six of the 'William' books,
   together with the script of the film) (Newnes, 1939) £100
WILLIAM AND THE EVACUEES (illustrated by Thomas Henry; green boards) (Newnes, 1940).................£900
WILLIAM DOES HIS BIT (illustrated by Thomas Henry; green boards) (Newnes, 1941) £650

WILLIAM CARRIES ON (illustrated by Thomas Henry; green boards) (Newnes, 1942)...................................**£650**
WILLIAM AND THE BRAINS TRUST (illustrated by Thomas Henry; green boards) (Newnes, 1945)...................................**£200**
JUST WILLIAM'S LUCK (illustrated by Thomas Henry; green boards) (Newnes, 1948)...................................**£85**
WILLIAM THE BOLD (illustrated by Thomas Henry; green boards) (Newnes, 1950)...................................**£115**
WILLIAM AND THE TRAMP (illustrated by Thomas Henry; green boards) (Newnes, 1952)...................................**£90**
WILLIAM AND THE MOON ROCKET (illustrated by Thomas Henry; green boards) (Newnes, 1954)...................................**£55**
WILLIAM AND THE SPACE ANIMAL (illustrated by Thomas Henry; green boards) (Newnes, 1956)...................................**£55**
WILLIAM'S BAD RESOLUTION (reissue of 'William and A.R.P.') (Newnes, 1956)...................................**£20**
WILLIAM THE FILM STAR (reissue of 'William and the Evacuees') (Newnes, 1956)...................................**£20**
WILLIAM AND THE ARTIST'S MODEL: A Play in One Act (pamphlet) (J. Garnet Miller, 1956)...................................**£15**
WILLIAM'S TELEVISION SHOW (illustrated by Thomas Henry; green boards) (Newnes, 1958)...................................**£60**
WILLIAM THE EXPLORER (illustrated by Thomas Henry; green boards) (Newnes, 1960)...................................**£60**
WILLIAM'S TREASURE TROVE (illustrated by Thomas Henry; green boards) (Newnes, 1962)...................................**£60**
WILLIAM AND THE WITCH (illustrated by Thomas Henry and Henry Ford; green boards) (Newnes, 1964)...................................**£90**
WILLIAM AND THE MONSTER (illustrated by Peter Archer and Thomas Henry; paperback) (Armada, 1965)...................................**£10**
WILLIAM THE ANCIENT BRITON (illustrated by Peter Archer and Thomas Henry; paperback) (Armada, 1965)...................................**£10**
WILLIAM THE CANNIBAL (illustrated by Peter Archer and Thomas Henry; paperback) (Armada, 1965)...................................**£10**
WILLIAM THE GLOBETROTTER (illustrated by Peter Archer and Thomas Henry; paperback) (Armada, 1965)...................................**£10**
WILLIAM AND THE POP SINGERS (illustrated by Henry Ford; green boards) (Newnes, 1965)...................................**£90**
WILLIAM AND THE MASKED RANGER (illustrated by Henry Ford; green boards) (Newnes, 1966)...................................**£90**
WILLIAM THE SUPERMAN (illustrated by Henry Ford; green boards) (Newnes, 1968)...................................**£150**
WILLIAM THE LAWLESS (illustrated by Henry Ford; red boards) (Newnes, 1970)...................................**£850**

'Jimmy' Books
JIMMY (Newnes, 1949)...................................**£70**
JIMMY AGAIN (illustrated by Lunt Roberts) (Newnes, 1951)...................................**£50**
JIMMY THE THIRD (illustrated by Lunt Roberts; paperback) (Armada, 1965)...................................**£20**

CUNLIFFE, John
British author Born: Lancashire, 1933. Creator of 'Postman Pat' in 1981, and also notable for his 'Giant' and 'Farmer Barnes' stories.
Prices are for books in Very Good condition with dustjackets where applicable.

'Farmer Barnes' Books
FARMER BARNES BUYS A PIG (illustrated by Carol Barker) (Deutsch, 1964)...................................**£25**
FARMER BARNES AND BLUEBELL (illustrated by Carol Barker) (Deutsch, 1965)...................................**£15**
FARMER BARNES AT THE COUNTY SHOW (illustrated by Jill McDonald) (Deutsch, 1969)...................................**£15**
FARMER BARNES AND THE GOATS (illustrated by Jill McDonald) (Deutsch, 1971)...................................**£10**
FARMER BARNES GOES FISHING (illustrated by Jill McDonald) (Deutsch, 1972)...................................**£10**
FARMER BARNES AND THE SNOW PICNIC (illustrated by Joan Hickson) (Deutsch, 1974)...................................**£10**
FARMER BARNES FELLS A TREE (illustrated by Joan Hickson) (Deutsch, 1977)...................................**£8**
FARMER BARNES AND THE HARVEST DOLL (illustrated by Joan Hickson) (Deutsch, 1977)...................................**£8**
FARMER BARNES' GUY FAWKES DAY (illustrated by Joan Hickson) (Deutsch, 1978)...................................**£8**

'Giant' Books
THE GIANT WHO STOLE THE WORLD (illustrated by Faith Jaques) (Deutsch, 1971)...................................**£5**
THE GIANT WHO SWALLOWED THE WIND (illustrated by Faith Jaques) (Deutsch, 1972)...................................**£5**
GIANT KIPPERNOSE AND OTHER STORIES (illustrated by Fritz Wegner) (Deutsch, 1972)...................................**£5**
GIANT BROG AND THE MOTORWAY (illustrated by Alexy Pendle) (Deutsch 1976)...................................**£5**

'Postman Pat' Books
POSTMAN PAT AND THE MYSTERY THIEF (illustrated by Celia Berridge) (Deutsch, 1981)...................................**£8**
POSTMAN PAT'S TREASURE HUNT (illustrated by Celia Berridge) (Deutsch, 1981)...................................**£8**
POSTMAN PAT'S SECRET (illustrated by Celia Berridge) (Deutsch, 1981)...................................**£8**
POSTMAN PAT'S RAINY DAY (illustrated by Celia Berridge) (Deutsch, 1982)...................................**£8**
POSTMAN PAT'S DIFFICULT DAY (illustrated by Celia Berridge) (Deutsch, 1982)...................................**£8**
POSTMAN PAT'S FOGGY DAY (illustrated by Celia Berridge) (Deutsch, 1982)...................................**£8**
POSTMAN PAT'S TRACTOR EXPRESS (illustrated by Celia Berridge) (Deutsch, 1983)...................................**£8**
POSTMAN PAT TAKES A MESSAGE (illustrated by Celia Berridge) (Deutsch, 1983)...................................**£8**
POSTMAN PAT'S THIRSTY DAY (illustrated by Celia Berridge) (Deutsch, 1984)...................................**£8**
POSTMAN PAT GOES SLEDGING (illustrated by Celia Berridge) (Deutsch, 1984)...................................**£8**
POSTMAN PAT'S LETTERS ON ICE (illustrated by Celia Berridge) (Deutsch, 1985)...................................**£5**
POSTMAN PAT'S BREEZY DAY (illustrated by Celia Berridge) (Deutsch, 1985)...................................**£5**
POSTMAN PAT TO THE RESCUE (illustrated by Celia Berridge) (Deutsch, 1986)...................................**£5**
POSTMAN PAT'S SUMMER STORYBOOK (illustrated by Celia Berridge) (Deutsch, 1987)...................................**£5**
POSTMAN PAT'S PARCEL OF FUN (illustrated by Stuart Trotter) (Deutsch, 1987)...................................**£5**
POSTMAN PAT'S WINTER STORYBOOK (illustrated by Celia Berridge) (Deutsch, 1987)...................................**£5**
POSTMAN PAT MAKES A SPLASH (illustrated by Joan Hickson) (Deutsch, 1987)...................................**£5**
POSTMAN PAT'S ZODIAC STORYBOOK (illustrated by Celia Berridge) (Deutsch, 1989)...................................**£5**
POSTMAN PAT'S THREE WISHES (Deutsch, 1990)...................................**£5**

CUNLIFFE, John

'Beginners' Books
POSTMAN PAT'S ABC STORY (illustrated by Joan Hickson) (Deutsch, 1986)...£4
POSTMAN PAT'S 123 STORY (illustrated by Joan Hickson) (Deutsch, 1986)...£4

'Easy Reader' Books
POSTMAN PAT'S WET DAY (illustrated by Joan Hickson) (Deutsch, 1986)...£4
POSTMAN PAT'S MESSY DAY (illustrated by Joan Hickson) (Deutsch, 1986)..£4
POSTMAN PAT ON SAFARI (illustrated by Joan Hickson) (Deutsch, 1986)..£4
POSTMAN PAT AND THE GREENDALE GHOST (illustrated by Joan Hickson) (Deutsch, 1987)..........................£4
POSTMAN PAT AND THE CHRISTMAS PUDDING (illustrated by Joan Hickson) (Deutsch, 1987).........................£4
POSTMAN PAT PLAYS FOR GREENDALE (illustrated by Joan Hickson) (Deutsch, 1988)......................................£4

'Baby' Books
A DAY WITH POSTMAN PAT (illustrated by Celia Berridge) (Deutsch, 1985)...£3
POSTMAN PAT AND THE SUMMER SHOW (illustrated by Celia Berridge) (Deutsch, 1985).................................£3

Others
THE ADVENTURES OF LORD PIP (illustrated by Robert Hales) (Deutsch, 1970) £10
RIDDLES AND RHYMES AND RIGMAROLES (illustrated by Alexy Pendle) (Deutsch, 1971)...........................£10
THE KING'S BIRTHDAY CAKE (illustrated by Faith Jaques) (Deutsch, 1973)..£10
THE GREAT DRAGON COMPETITION AND OTHER STORIES (illustrated by Alexy Pendle) (Deutsch, 1973).......................£10
THE FARMER, THE ROOKS AND THE CHERRY TREE (illustrated by Prudence Seward) (Deutsch, 1974) £10
SMALL MONKEY TALES (illustrated by Gerry Downes) (Deutsch, 1974)..£10
MR GOSLING AND THE RUNAWAY CHAIR (illustrated by William Stobbs) (Deutsch, 1978).........................£10
MR GOSLING AND THE GREAT ART ROBBERY (illustrated by William Stobbs) (Deutsch, 1979)..................£10
SARA'S GIANT AND THE UPSIDE-DOWN HOUSE (illustrated by Hilary Abrahams) (Deutsch, 1980)..........................£8
OUR SAM: THE DAFTEST DOG IN THE WORLD (illustrated by Maurice Wilson) (Deutsch, 1980)......................£8
THE MINISTER'S CAT (illustrated by David Parkins) (Deutsch, 1989) £8
ROSIE AND JIM AND THE GLASS BLOWERS (illustrated by Celia Berridge) (Deutsch, 1993)...........................£5

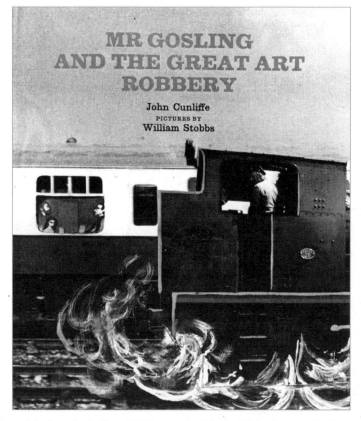

Mr Gosling and the Great Art Robbery (1979) is the work of John Cunliffe, best known for his 'Postman Pat' titles.

D

DAHL, Roald

British author. Born: Llandaff, Wales, in 1916, of Norwegian parents. Educated at Repton School, and worked for the Shell Oil Company before serving with the RAF in North Africa during the Second World War. His first children's book, *The Gremlins* (1943), came out of his wartime experiences, and was followed by several other classic works, including *James and the Giant Peach* (1961) and *Charlie and the Chocolate Factory* (1964), most of which were first published in America. Died: 1990.

Prices are for books in Very Good condition with dustjackets where applicable.

THE GREMLINS From the Walt Disney Production 'A Royal Air Force Story' (Random House, US, [1943]) £1,250
THE GREMLINS (boards; issued without dustjacket) (Collins, [1944]) £700
THE GREMLINS (Ayres & James, Australia, [1944]) £750
JAMES AND THE GIANT PEACH (illustrated by Nancy Ekholm Burket) (Knopf, US, 1962) £350
JAMES AND THE GIANT PEACH (illustrated by Michael Simeon; boards; issued without dustjacket) (Allen & Unwin, 1967) £100
JAMES AND THE GIANT PEACH (illustrated by Emma Chichester Clark) (Unwin Hyman, 1990) £8
JAMES AND THE GIANT PEACH (illustrated by Quentin Blake) (Viking International, 1995) £8
JAMES AND THE GIANT PEACH (illustrated by Lane Smith) (Knopf, US, 1996) £6
CHARLIE AND THE CHOCOLATE FACTORY (illustrated by Joseph Schindelman) (Knopf, US, 1964) £850
CHARLIE AND THE CHOCOLATE FACTORY (illustrated by Faith Jaques; boards; issued without dustjacket) (Allen & Unwin, 1967) ... £175
CHARLIE AND THE CHOCOLATE FACTORY (illustrated by Michael Foreman) (Unwin Hyman, 1985) £15
CHARLIE AND THE CHOCOLATE FACTORY (illustrated by Quentin Blake; hardback) (Viking International, 1995) £10
THE MAGIC FINGER (illustrated by William Pene du Bois) (Harper & Row, US, 1966) £100
THE MAGIC FINGER (boards; issued without dustjacket) (Allen & Unwin, 1968) £60
THE MAGIC FINGER (illustrated by Tony Ross) (Viking International, 1993) *(first issued as a paperback by Puffin in 1989)* £10
THE MAGIC FINGER (illustrated by Quentin Blake) (Viking International, 1995) £10
FANTASTIC MR FOX (illustrated by Donald Chaffin) (Knopf, US, 1970) £35
FANTASTIC MR FOX (boards) (Allen & Unwin, 1970) £50
FANTASTIC MR FOX (illustrated by Tony Ross) (Unwin Hyman, 1988) £8
FANTASTIC MR FOX (illustrated by Quentin Blake) (Viking International, 1996) £8
CHARLIE AND THE GREAT GLASS ELEVATOR (illustrated by Joseph Schindelman) (Knopf, US, 1972) £150

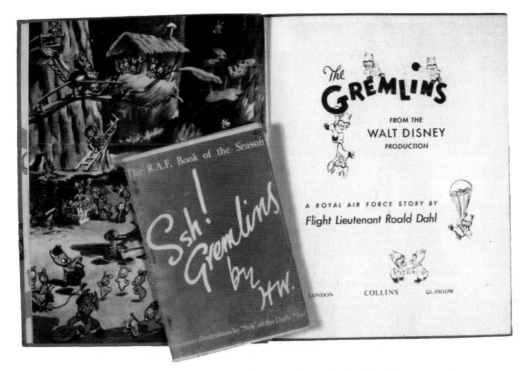

Roald Dahl's first and rarest book, written for the Walt Disney production **The Gremlins** *which was never made.*

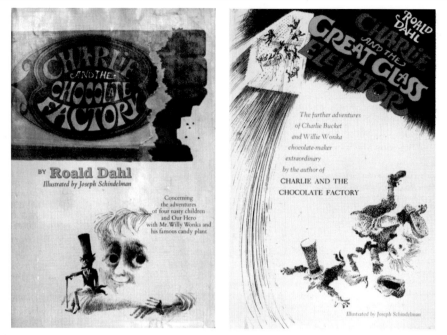

*The first US editions of Roald Dahl's bestselling **Charlie and the Chocolate Factory** and its sequel **Charlie and the Great Glass Elevator**.*

CHARLIE AND THE GREAT GLASS ELEVATOR (illustrated by Faith Jaques; boards) (Allen & Unwin, 1973)..........................£60
CHARLIE AND THE GREAT GLASS ELEVATOR (illustrated by Michael Foreman) (Unwin Hyman, 1986).................£8
CHARLIE AND THE GREAT GLASS ELEVATOR (illustrated by Quentin Blake) (Viking International, 1995)..........................£8
THE COMPLETE ADVENTURES OF CHARLIE & MR WILLY WONKA (illustrated by Faith Jaques) (Allen & Unwin, 1978).....£30
THE COMPLETE ADVENTURES OF CHARLIE & MR WILLY WONKA (illustrated by Michael Foreman) (Unwin Hyman, 1978).....£15
DANNY, THE CHAMPION OF THE WORLD (illustrated by Jill Bennett) (Knopf, US, 1975) £20
DANNY, THE CHAMPION OF THE WORLD (Jonathan Cape, 1975)..........................£50
DANNY, THE CHAMPION OF THE WORLD (illustrated by Quentin Blake) (Jonathan Cape, 1994) £10
THE WONDERFUL STORY OF HENRY SUGAR and Six More (Knopf, US, 1977) £20
THE WONDERFUL STORY OF HENRY SUGAR and Six More (Jonathan Cape, 1977)..........................£40
THE ENORMOUS CROCODILE (illustrated by Quentin Blake) (Knopf, US, 1978)..........................£20
THE ENORMOUS CROCODILE (Jonathan Cape, 1978) £35
THE TWITS (illustrated by Quentin Blake) (Jonathan Cape, 1980) £50
THE TWITS (Knopf, US, 1981)..........................£15
GEORGE'S MARVELLOUS MEDICINE (illustrated by Quentin Blake) (Jonathan Cape, 1981)..........................£40
GEORGE'S MARVELLOUS MEDICINE (Knopf, US, 1982) £20
THE BFG (illustrated by Quentin Blake) (Jonathan Cape, 1982)..........................£50
THE BFG (Farrar, Straus & Giroux, US, 1982)..........................£15
ROALD DAHL'S REVOLTING RHYMES (illustrated by Quentin Blake; issued without dustjacket) (Jonathan Cape, 1982)...............£50
ROALD DAHL'S REVOLTING RHYMES (Knopf, US, 1983)..........................£30
THE WITCHES (illustrated by Quentin Blake) (Jonathan Cape, 1983)..........................£50
THE WITCHES (Farrar, Straus & Giroux, US, 1983)..........................£20
DIRTY BEASTS (illustrated by Rosemary Fawcett; issued without dustjacket) (Jonathan Cape, 1983)..........................£40
DIRTY BEASTS (Farrar, Straus & Giroux, US, 1983) £20
DIRTY BEASTS (illustrated by Quentin Blake) (Jonathan Cape, 1984) £25
BOY: Tales of Childhood (memoir) (Jonathan Cape, 1984)..........................£20
THE GIRAFFE AND THE PELLY AND ME (illustrated by Quentin Blake) (Jonathan Cape, 1985)..........................£40
THE GIRAFFE AND THE PELLY AND ME (Farrar, Straus & Giroux, US, 1985)..........................£15
GOING SOLO (memoir; illustrated by Quentin Blake) (Jonathan Cape, 1986) £15
MATILDA (illustrated by Quentin Blake) (Jonathan Cape, 1988)..........................£50
MATILDA (Viking, US, 1988)..........................£30
RHYME STEW (illustrated by Quentin Blake) (Jonathan Cape, 1989) £25
RHYME STEW (Viking, US, 1990)..........................£20
ESIO TROT (illustrated by Quentin Blake) (Jonathan Cape, 1990) £20
ESIO TROT (Viking, US, 1990)..........................£10
ROALD DAHL'S GUIDE TO RAILWAY SAFETY (illustrated by Quentin Blake; pamphlet) (British Rail, 1991) £15
THE VICAR OF NIBBLESWICKE (illustrated by Quentin Blake) (Random Century, 1991)..........................£20

THE VICAR OF NIBBLESWICKE (Viking, US, 1992)......£12
THE MINPINS (illustrated by Patrick Benson) (Jonathan Cape, 1991)......£20
THE MINPINS (Viking, US, 1991)......£12
MY YEAR (illustrated by Quentin Blake) (Jonathan Cape, 1993)......£12
MY YEAR (Viking, US, 1993)......£8
THE ROALD DAHL TREASURY (various illustrators) (Jonathan Cape, 1997)......£12
THE ROALD DAHL TREASURY (Viking, US, 1997)......£12
THE MILDENHALL TREASURE (illustrated by Ralph Steadman) (Jonathan Cape, 1999)......£12
THE MILDENHALL TREASURE (illustrated by Ralph Steadman) (Knopf, US, 2000)......£10

'DAN DARE' BOOKS AND ANNUALS

Popular British comic character, originally featured in the *Eagle* (1950-69) and later in *Lion*. Inspired many spin-off publications and items of ephemera.

Prices are for books and annuals in Very Good condition.

DAN DARE SPACE BOOK (1953)......£75
DAN DARE: PILOT OF THE FUTURE With Realistic Pop-Up Pictures (1953)......£65
DAN DARE (pop-up) (1954)......£65
DAN DARE PICTURE CARD ALBUM (with cards) (1954)......£60
DAN DARE PICTURE CARD ALBUM (without cards) (1954)......£50
DAN DARE'S ANASTASIA JET PLANE ('Presso Book')......£45
DAN DARE'S SPACESHIP ('Presso Book')......£50
THE HORLICKS SPACEMAN'S HANDBOOK......£60
DAN DARE ON MARS ('Eagle Novel', 1956)......£45
DAN DARE INTERPLANETARY STAMP FOLDER (1950s)......£40
DAN DARE'S SPACE ANNUAL (1963)......£20
DAN DARE ANNUAL 1974......£12
DAN DARE: PILOT OF THE FUTURE (novelisation of the first 'Dan Dare' serial; paperback)
  (New English Library, 1977)......£5
THE MAN FROM NOWHERE (Dragons Dream, 1979)......£10
DAN DARE ANNUAL 1979......£4
DAN DARE ANNUAL 1980......£4
ROGUE PLANET (Dragons Dream, 1980)......£10
REIGN OF THE ROBOTS (Dragons Dream, 1981)......£10
DAN DARE: PILOT OF THE FUTURE (illustrated by Frank Hampson and others; softcover)
  (Hamlyn, 1981)......£12
DAN DARE: PILOT OF THE FUTURE (Hawk, 1987)......£20
DAN DARE ANNUAL 1987......£3
RED MOON MYSTERY/MAROONED ON MERCURY (Hawk, 1988)......£20
OPERATION SATURN (Hawk, 1989)......£12
PRISONERS OF SPACE (Hawk, 1990)......£12
DAN DARE DOSSIER (1990)......£20
DAN DARE HOLIDAY SPECIAL 1990......£3
DAN DARE HOLIDAY SPECIAL 1991......£3
MAN FROM NOWHERE (Hawk, 1991)......£12
DAN DARE ANNUAL 1991......£3
DARE by Grant Morrison and Rian Hughes (softcover; 1991)......£6
ROGUE PLANET (Hawk, 1992)......£12
REIGN OF THE ROBOTS/THE SHIP THAT LIVED (Hawk, 1993)......£12
THE PHANTOM FLEET (Hawk, 1993)......£12
TERRA NOVA TRILOGY (Hawk, 1993)......£12
PROJECT NIMBUS AND OTHER STORIES (Hawk, 1994)......£12
SOLID SPACE MYSTERY AND OTHER STORIES (Hawk, 1995)......£12
DARE: THE FINAL VOLUME (Hawk, 1995)......£12
DAN DARE 3D BOOK OF JET PLANES (given free with 'Eagle'; in original envelope)......£35
DAN DARE STAMP ALBUM......£40

'DANDY'

Popular British comic, published by D.C. Thomson of Dundee. The comic itself was launched on 4th December 1937, the first annual, entitled *The Dandy Monster Comic*, appearing in 1939. Among the title's many well-known characters are Desperate Dan and Korky the Cat. Note that the annuals were undated before 1966, after which they were dated on the cover.

Prices are for comics/annuals in Very Good condition (with cover description in brackets).

'The Dandy'

DANDY ISSUE 1 (price is for comic without the original 'Express Whistler' free gift) (DC Thomson, 4th December 1937)......£7,000

'The Dandy Monster Comic'

1939 (Korky, Desperate Dan, monkeys and other characters holding the 'y' of 'Dandy')......£3,000
1940 (Korky the Cat hanging from a trapeze)......£1,250

1941 (Korky leading others in band)..£750
1942 (Desperate Dan towing others in boat)..£1,000
1943 (Korky leading others in boat)...£550
1944 (Korky on football kicked by Desperate Dan)..£550
1945 (Korky on skis and Desperate Dan on logs)..£400
1946 (Korky and others in stars)...£300
1947 (Korky being tossed in blanket)..£300
1948 (Korky and others as puppets)..£250
1949 (Korky in top hat with cigar, and Desperate Dan; quarto)..£200
1950 (Korky with kettle on beach, pouring hot water into the sea; quarto)..£150
1951 (Korky as ringmaster in circus, and Desperate Dan holding an elephant; quarto).......................................£100
1952 (Korky's toyshop, with toy Desperate Dan pushing tin of red paint onto Korky; quarto)..............................£75

'The Dandy Book'

1953 (six sets of Korky with mice and dinner table)...£75
1954 (four sets of Korky hiding a fish under top hat)...£60
1955 (four sets of Korky fishing by 'no fishing' sign)...£60
1956 (four sets of Korky in front of 'Korky's Joke Shop')...£60
1957 (three sets of Korky stealing fish from train)...£50
1958 (three sets of Korky catching fish with magnet in rowing boat)..£45
1959 (three sets of Korky sitting in an umbrella, in a canoe)...£40
1960 (three sets of Korky eating meal, with chained letter box)...£40
1961 (three sets of Korky balancing an egg on his nose)..£40
1962 (three sets of Korky leaning on a lamp-post)..£40
1963 (four sets of Korky wearing sailor suit and looking through porthole)...£40
1964 (Korky in a deckchair eating a pie)..£40
1965 (two sets of Korky with pantomime horse)..£40
1966 (dated '1966' on cover)...£30
1967-69 ....each £25
1970 ....£15
1971-72 ....each £10
1973-74 ....each £10
1975-77 ....each £8
1978-80 ....each £8
1981-Present ....each £5

*The first two editions of **The Dandy Monster Comic** issued in 1939 (left) and 1940, and worth £3,000 and £1,250 respectively.*

DARCH, Winifred

British author. Born: Brighton, 1884. Worked as a High School Mistress before writing popular school stories for girls.

Prices are for books in Very Good condition.

CHRIS AND SOME OTHERS (illustrated by Savile Lumley) (OUP, 1920) £25
JEAN OF THE FIFTH (OUP, 1923) £25
POPPIES AND PREFECTS (illustrated by Charles E. Brock) (OUP, 1923).. £25
CECIL OF THE CARNATIONS (illustrated by Mary Strange Reeve) (OUP, 1924)................................ £25
HEATHER AT THE HIGH SCHOOL (illustrated by C.E. Brock) (OUP, 1924).. £20
KATHERINE GOES TO SCHOOL (illustrated by M.D. Johnston) (OUP, 1925)...................................... £20
GILLIAN OF THE GUIDES (illustrated by M.D. Johnston) (OUP, 1925)... £20
THE NEW SCHOOL AND HILARY (illustrated by Mary Strange Reeve) (OUP, 1926) £20
VARVARA COMES TO ENGLAND (illustrated by M.D. Johnston) (OUP, 1927)................................... £20
CICELY BASSETT, PATROL LEADER (illustrated by M.D. Johnston) (OUP, 1927) £20
THE UPPER FIFTH IN COMMAND (illustrated by M.D. Johnston) (OUP, 1928) £20
FOR THE HONOUR OF THE HOUSE (illustrated by M.D. Johnston) (OUP, 1929)............................. £20
THE FIFTH FORM RIVALS (OUP, 1930) £20
THE LOWER FOUTH AND JOAN (illustrated by M.D. Johnston) (OUP, 1930) £20
MARGARET PLAYS THE GAME (illustrated by E. Brier) (OUP, 1931) £20
THE GIRLS OF QUEEN ELIZABETH'S (OUP, 1932)... £20
THE SCHOOL ON THE CLIFF (illustrated by M.D. Johnston) (OUP, 1933).. £20
THE NEW SCHOOLGIRL OMNIBUS (contains 'Chris & Some Others', 'Heather at the High School' and 'Jean of the Fifth') (OUP, 1934) .. £25
THE HEAD GIRL AT WYNFORD (illustrated by Reginald Mills) (OUP, 1935).. £15
SUSAN'S LAST TERM (illustrated by Margaret Horder) (OUP, 1936) £15
THE WINIFRED DARCH OMNIBUS (contains 'For the Honour of the School', 'Cicely Bassett,
     Patrol Leader' and 'Margaret Plays the Game') (OUP, 1936)... £25
ELINOR IN THE FIFTH (illustrated by Margaret Horder) (OUP, 1937).. £15
ALISON TEMPLE – PREFECT (illustrated by Gilbert Dunlop) (OUP, 1938) £15
THE SCHOLARSHIP AND MARGERY (OUP, 1938)... £15
THE NEW GIRL AT GRAYCHURCH (illustrated by Gilbert Dunlop) (OUP, 1939)................................ £15

DAVIDSON, Lionel

British crime author. Born: Hull, in 1922. One of only a handful of writers to have won the Crime Writers' Association Gold Dagger on more than two occasions. Davidson also penned a handful of children's books, which are avidly sought by his fans.

Prices are for books in Very Good condition with dustjackets.

As 'Lionel Davidson'

UNDER PLUM LAKE (Cape, 1980) £25

As 'David Line'

SOLDIER AND ME (Harper, US, 1965)... £20
RUN FOR YOUR LIFE (Cape, 1966).. £20
MIKE AND ME (Cape, 1974) £20
SCREAMING HIGH (Cape, 1985) £20

DE LA MARE, Walter

British author. Born: Walter John de la Mare in London in 1873, of Huguenot descent. Studied at St. Paul's School, leaving at the age of sixteen to work for the Anglo-American Oil Company. His first book was a volume of poems entitled *Songs of Childhood* (1902), and this was followed by several more verse collections — notably *Peacock Pie* (1913) — as well as novels, of which the best-known is *Memoirs of a Midget* (1921). Received a Civil List pension in 1908. Died: 1956.

Prices are for books in Very Good condition (with dustjackets after 1940).

SONGS OF CHILDHOOD by Walter Ramal (verse) (Longmans Green, 1902).................................... £300
SONGS OF CHILDHOOD (verse; enlarged, revised edition; illustrated by Estella Canziani) (Longmans, 1923)......................... £40
SONGS OF CHILDHOOD (verse; illustrated by Marion Rivers-Moore) (Faber, 1942) £25
THE THREE MULLA-MULGARS (Duckworth, 1910) £40
THE THREE MULLA-MULGARS (illustrated by Dorothy Lathrop) (Duckworth, 1921)........................ £25
THE THREE MULLA-MULGARS (illustrated by J.A. Shepherd) (Selwyn & Blount, 1924) £25
A CHILD'S DAY: A Book of Rhymes (verse; illustrated by Carine and Will Cadby) (Constable, 1912) £100
PEACOCK PIE: A Book of Rhymes (verse) (Constable, 1913) £40
PEACOCK PIE (verse; illustrated by W. Heath Robinson) (Constable, [1916]).................................... £80
PEACOCK PIE (verse; illustrated by C. Lovat Fraser) (Constable, [1924])... £35
PEACOCK PIE (verse; illustrated by Jocelyn Crowe) (Faber, 1936) £25
PEACOCK PIE (verse; illustrated by Rowland Emett) (Faber, 1941)... £30
PEACOCK PIE (verse; illustrated by Edward Ardizzone) (Faber, 1946) £80
CROSSINGS: A Fairy Play (illustrated by Randolph Schwabe; music by C. Armstrong Gibbs) (Beaumont Press, 1921) £40

DE LA MARE, Walter

DOWN-ADOWN-DERRY: A Book of Fairy Poems (verse; illustrated by Dorothy P. Lathrop) (Constable, 1922) £100
BROOMSTICKS and Other Tales (illustrated by Bold) (Constable, 1925) £30
MISS JEMIMA (illustrated by Alec Buckels) (Blackwell, [1925])..£30
LUCY (illustrated by Hilda T. Miller) (Blackwell, [1927])..£30
OLD JOE (illustrated by C.T. Nightingale) (Blackwell, [1927])...£30
TOLD AGAIN: Traditional Tales (illustrated by A.H. Watson) (Blackwell, 1927) £30
STORIES FROM THE BIBLE (illustrated by Theodore Nadajen) (Faber, 1929) £20
STORIES FROM THE BIBLE (illustrated by John Farleigh) (Faber, 1933) £30
STORIES FROM THE BIBLE (illustrated by Edward Ardizzone) (Faber, 1961) £40
DESERT ISLANDS AND ROBINSON CRUSOE (illustrated by Rex Whistler; issued with dustjacket) (Faber, 1930)..................£50
DESERT ISLANDS AND ROBINSON CRUSOE (illustrated by Rex Whistler; De Luxe edition:
 limited to 650 copies, signed by the author) (Faber/Fountain Press, 1930)...£250
POEMS FOR CHILDREN (verse; contains 'Songs of Childhood', 'Peacock Pie' and other poems) (Constable, [1930]) £35
TOM TIDDLER'S GROUND: A Book of Poetry for the Junior and Middle Schools
 Edited by Walter de la Mare (verse) (Collins, [1932]) £15
THE LORD FISH and Other Tales (illustrated by Rex Whistler; issued with dustjacket) (Faber, 1933).....................£60
THE LORD FISH and Other Tales (illustrated by Rex Whistler; limited to signed sixty copies) (Faber, 1933) £250
THE THREE ROYAL MONKEYS, or The Three Mulla-Mulgars (illustrated by J.A. Shepherd) (Faber, 1935) £20
THIS YEAR: NEXT YEAR (verse; illustrated by Harold Jones) (Faber, 1937) £150
ANIMAL STORIES: Chosen, Arranged and in Some Part Rewritten (verse) (Faber, 1939).....................................£25
BELLS AND GRASS: A Book of Rhymes (verse; illustrated by Rowland Emett) (Faber, 1941) £25
THE OLD LION and Other Stories (illustrated by Irene Hawkins) (Faber, 1942)..£25
MR BUMPS AND HIS MONKEY (originally published in 'The Lord Fish' under the title 'The Old Lion';
 illustrated by Dorothy P. Lathrop) (J.C. Winston, US, [1942])...£25
THE MAGIC JACKET and Other Stories (illustrated by Irene Hawkins) (Faber, 1943)...£30
COLLECTED RHYMES AND VERSES (verse; illustrated by Berthold Wolpe) (Faber, 1944) £20
THE SCARECROW and Other Stories (illustrated by Irene Hawkins) (Faber, 1945) £25
THE THREE ROYAL MONKEYS (illustrated by Mildred Eldridge) (Faber, 1946)..£10
THE DUTCH CHEESE and Other Stories (illustrated by Irene Hawkins) (Faber, 1946)..£15
COLLECTED STORIES FOR CHILDREN (illustrated by Irene Hawkins) (Faber, 1947)...£15
COLLECTED STORIES FOR CHILDREN (illustrated by Robin Jacques) (Faber, 1957)..£15
RHYMES AND VERSES: Collected Poems for Children (verse; illustrated by Elinore Blaisdell) (Holt, US, [1947]).................£20
JACK AND THE BEANSTALK (adapted from 'Told Again') (Hulton Press, 1951) £10
DICK WHITTINGTON (adapted from 'Told Again'; illustrated by Ionicus) (Hulton Press, 1951)...............................£10
SNOW-WHITE (adapted from 'Told Again'; illustrated by David Walsh) (Hulton Press, 1952) £10
CINDERELLA (adapted from 'Told Again'; illustrated by Ionicus) (Hulton Press, 1952)..£10

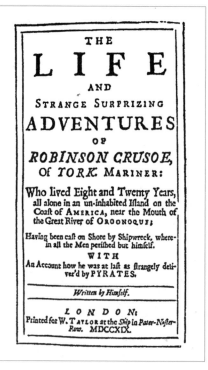

This is the true first edition of the children's classic
The Life and Strange Surprising Adventures of
Robinson Crusoe *by Daniel Defoe.*

SELECTED STORIES AND VERSE (paperback) (Puffin, 1952) £3
THE STORY OF JOSEPH (illustrated by Edward Ardizzone) (Faber, 1958) £30
THE STORY OF MOSES (illustrated by Edward Ardizzone) (Faber, 1959) £30
THE STORY OF SAMUEL AND SAUL (illustrated by Edward Ardizzone) (Faber, 1960) £30
A PENNY A DAY (illustrated by Paul Kennedy) (Knopf, US, 1960) £15
POEMS. Edited by Eleanor Graham (verse; paperback) (Puffin, 1962) £4

DEARMER, Mabel

British illustrator. Born: Mabel White in 1872. Studied art at the Herkomer School, Bushey, subsequently illustrating a number of children's books, many of them written by herself. Died: 1915.

Prices are for books in Very Good condition.

Books Written and Illustrated by Mabel Dearmer

ROUND-ABOUT-RHYMES by Mrs Percy Dearmer (Blackie, [1898]) £225
THE BOOK OF PENNY TOYS (Macmillan, 1899) £200
THE NOAH'S ARK GEOGRAPHY (Macmillan, 1900) £200
THE COCKYOLLY BIRD (Hodder & Stoughton, 1914) £200
BRER RABBIT AND MR FOX (Joseph Williams, [1914]) £200

Books Written by Mabel Dearmer

A CHILD'S LIFE OF CHRIST (illustrated by Eleanor Fortescue-Brickdale) (Methuen, 1906) £50
THE PLAYMATE: A Christmas Mystery Play (illustrated by Helen Stratton) (Mowbray, 1910)....£65

Books Illustrated by Mabel Dearmer

WYMPS and Other Fairy Tales by Evelyn Sharp (John Lane, 1897) £100
ALL THE WAY FAIRYLAND by Evelyn Sharp (John Lane, 1898) £100
THE STORY OF THE SEVEN YOUNG GOSLINGS by Laurence Housman (Blackie, [1899]) £150

DEFOE, Daniel

British author. Born: Daniel Foe in London in 1660/61, the son of Noncomformist parents. Following a disastrous attempt to establish himself as a merchant, he became a prolific writer of political tracts and 'novels', publishing his best-known work, *Robinson Crusoe*, in 1719. Although not intended for young readers, it has long been established as a children's classic. Died: 1731.

Prices are for books in Good condition, rebound (pre-1850) or in original cloth.

ROBINSON CRUSOE (as 'The Life and Strange Surprizing Adventures of Robinson Crusoe'; anonymous;
   first edition, first issue) (W. Taylor, 1719) £15,000
ROBINSON CRUSOE (as 'The Life and Strange Surprizing Adventures of Robinson Crusoe';
   anonymous; later impressions) (W. Taylor, 1719) £2,000
ROBINSON CRUSOE (illustrated by E. McKnight Kauffer; limited to 525 copies) (Etchells & MacDonald, 1929) £600
ROBINSON CRUSOE (illustrated by Edward Ardizzone) (Nonesuch Press, 1968) £50
ROBINSON CRUSOE (illustrated by Edward Gordon Craig; limited to 500 copies; morocco-backed cloth binding; in slipcase)
   (Basilisk Press, 1979) £600
THE FARTHER ADVENTURES OF ROBINSON CRUSOE (anonymous) (W. Taylor, 1719) £2,000
SERIOUS REFLECTIONS DURING THE LIFE AND SURPRISING ADVENTURES OF ROBINSON CRUSOE
   (anonymous) (W. Taylor, 1720) £2,000
ROBINSON CRUSOE (first joint edition of the first two novels; made up of the [abridged] seventh edition of
   'The Life and Strange Adventures of Robinson Crusoe' and the fifth edition of
   'The Farther Adventures of Robinson Crusoe'; two volumes) (W. Mears/T. Woodward, 1726)............... the set £800
ROBINSON CRUSOE (as 'The Life and Strange Surprising Adventures of Robinson Crusoe';
   illustrated by Thomas Stothard; introduction by George Chalmers; two volumes) (John Stockdale, 1790)............. the set £800
ROBINSON CRUSOE (first joint edition of all three novels; as 'The Life and Adventures of Robinson Crusoe';
   includes 'The True-Born Englishman, a Satire' and 'The Original Power of the People of England Examined and
   Asserted'; three volumes) (Printed at the Logographic Press; sold by J. Walter, 1790)....................... the set £800
ROBINSON CRUSOE (illustrated by George Cruikshank and Thomas Stothard;
   introductory verses by Bernard Barton; two volumes) (John Major, 1831)....................... the set £800
ROBINSON CRUSOE (illustrated by J. Ayton Symington) (Dent, 1903)....................................£40
ROBINSON CRUSOE (as 'The Life and Strange Surprising Adventures of Robinson Crusoe'; illustrated by
   Thomas Stothard; introduction by Charles Whibley; limited to 775 copies; three volumes) (Constable, 1925)........ the set £800

'DENNIS THE MENACE' ANNUALS

Popular spin-offs from the *Beano* comics and annuals. Published biennially by D.C. Thomson.

Prices are for annuals in Very Good condition (with cover description in brackets).

DENNIS THE MENACE 1956 (Dennis holding a tin of paint) £120
DENNIS THE MENACE 1958 (Dennis on go-cart speeding down a hill,
   knocking down a policeman, sweep and painter) £60
DENNIS THE MENACE 1960 (Dennis underwater using pincers on swimmer's foot) £35
DENNIS THE MENACE 1962 (Dennis holding a large caricature head of himself over his own head)....................£30
DENNIS THE MENACE 1964 (Dennis's head bursting through a black and white paper sheet)....................£25
DENNIS THE MENACE 1968 ....£20

DENNIS THE MENACE 1970 & 1972 .... each **£15**
DENNIS THE MENACE 1974 & 1976 .... each **£12**
DENNIS THE MENACE 1978 .... **£10**
DENNIS THE MENACE 1980 .... **£6**
DENNIS THE MENACE 1982 .... **£5**
DENNIS THE MENACE 1984-Present .... each **£4**

'DESPERATE DAN' ANNUALS

Popular spin-offs from the *Dandy* comics and annuals, published by D.C. Thomson.

Prices are for annuals in Very Good condition.

DESPERATE DAN 1954 .... **£140**
THE DESPERATE DAN BOOK 1979 .... **£8**

DETMOLD, Maurice and Edward

British illustrators. Born: Charles Frederick and Edward Barton Detmold on 21st November 1883, subsequently changing their middle names to 'Maurice' and 'Julius' respectively. Both brothers excelled at representing animals, having studied them at London's Zoological Gardens. Collaborated on an edition of *The Jungle Book*, before Charles committed suicide in 1908. Edward continued to illustrate books until the late 1920s. Died: 1957.

Prices are for books in Very Good condition.

Books Illustrated by Maurice and Edward Detmold

PICTURES FROM BIRDLAND (Dent, 1899).. **£350**
SIXTEEN ILLUSTRATION OF SUBJECTS FROM KIPLING'S 'JUNGLE BOOK'
  (in portfolio) (Macmillan, 1903)... **£1,500**
THE JUNGLE BOOK (Macmillan, 1908)... **£150**

Books Illustrated by Edward Detmold

THE FABLES OF AESOP (Hodder & Stoughton, 1909) **£125**
THE FABLES OF AESOP (limited to 750 copies, signed by the artist) (Hodder & Stoughton, 1909)............ **£500**
BIRDS AND BEASTS by Camille Lemonnier (George Allen, 1911)... **£60**
THE BOOK OF BABY BEASTS by Florence E. Dugdale (Henry Frowde/Hodder & Stoughton, [1911])............ **£75**
THE LIFE OF THE BEE by Maurice Maeterlinck (George Allen, 1911).. **£150**
HOURS OF GLADNESS by Maurice Maeterlinck (George Allen, 1912)... **£125**
THE BOOK OF BABY BIRDS by Florence E. Dugdale (Henry Frowde/Hodder & Stoughton, [1912])............ **£100**
THE BOOK OF BABY PETS by Florence E. Dugdale (Henry Frowde/Hodder & Stoughton, [1915]) **£100**
THE BOOK OF BABY DOGS by Charles J. Kaberry (Henry Frowde/Hodder & Stoughton, [1915])............ **£100**
TWENTY-FOUR NATURE PICTURES (in portfolio) (Dent, [1919])... **£500**
BIRDS IN TOWN AND VILLAGE by W.H. Hudson (Dent, 1919).. **£50**
OUR LITTLE NEIGHBOURS by Charles J. Kaberry (Henry Frowde/Hodder & Stoughton, [1921])............ **£100**
FABRE'S BOOK OF INSECTS by J.H.C. Fabre (Hodder & Stoughton, [1921]) **£175**
RAINBOW HOUSES FOR BOYS AND GIRLS by Arthur Vine Hall (Cape, 1923) **£70**
THE ARABIAN NIGHTS – TALES FROM THE THOUSAND AND ONE NIGHTS
  (Hodder & Stoughton, [1924]) **£350**
THE ARABIAN NIGHTS – TALES FROM THE THOUSAND AND ONE NIGHTS
  (limited to 100 copies, signed by the artist) (Hodder & Stoughton, [1924]) **£1,000**
THE FANTASTIC CREATURES OF EDWARD JULIUS DETMOLD (paperback) (Pan, 1976)....................... **£20**

'DICK BARTON'

'Dick Barton – Special Agent' was a popular radio program on the BBC Light Programme from 1946 to 1951. It spawned a number of collectable items listed below.

Prices are for books in Very Good condition.

Books

DICK BARTON – SPECIAL AGENT by Edward J. Mason & Geoffrey Webb (no dustjacket) (Contact Publications, 1950) **£5**
THE INSIDE STORY OF DICK BARTON by Geoffrey Webb (Convoy, 1950)....................................... **£12**
THE RETURN OF DICK BARTON (paperback) (Atlas Publications, 1952)... **£15**
THE BLACK PANTHER (paperback) (Paladin Press, 1952) **£15**
JAIL BREAK (paperback) (Paladin Press, 1952)... **£15**
DICK BARTON, SPECIAL AGENT by Elwyn Jones (in dustjacket) (Arthur Barker, 1977) **£15**
THE GREAT TOBACCO CONSPIRACY by Mike Dorrell (paperback) (Star, 1978)............................... **£5**
THE MYSTERY OF THE MISSING FORMULA by Mike Dorrell (paperback) (Star, 1978).................... **£5**
THE CASE OF THE VANISHING HOUSE by Alan Radnor (paperback) (Star, 1978)........................... **£5**
THE GOLD BULLION SWINDLE by Larry Pryce (paperback) (Star, 1978)....................................... **£5**
DICK BARTON, SPECIAL AGENT ANNUAL (Brown Watson, 1978) **£7**

Magazines/comics

STRAND MAGAZINE 'How Dick Barton Reads' (October 1949) **£7**

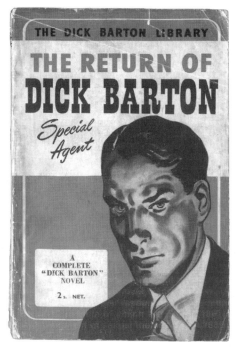

The Detmold brothers collaborated on only two books, including an edition of **The Jungle Book** *before Maurice's tragic death.*

Dick Barton! Special Agent! A very rare spin-off from the radio adventure series which ran from 1946 to 1951.

COMET (Amalgamated Press) 'Dick Barton and the Flying Saucer Mystery' (11 April-13 June 1953)...................................each £3
COMET (Amalgamated Press) 'Dick Barton in Peril on the Moon' (20 June-1 August 1953)...each £3
COMET (Amalgamated Press) 'Dick Barton and the Grey Ghost' (8 August-10 October 1953)..each £3
SUPER DETECTIVE LIBRARY (Amalgamated Press) No. 12 'Dick Barton Finds the City Under the Sea' (1953)....................£22

DICKENS, Charles

British author. Born: Portsmouth, 1812. The great novelist wrote few works specifically for young readers, but his 'Christmas Books' — notably *A Christmas Carol* (1843) — are of equal appeal to both children and adults. Died: 1870.

Prices are for books in Very Good condition with dustjackets where applicable.

A CHRISTMAS CAROL: Being a Ghost Story of Christmas (trial issue [proof stage];
  illustrated by John Leech) (Chapman & Hall, 1844 [1843]) £20,000
A CHRISTMAS CAROL (first edition, first issue; first chapter headed 'Stave 1'; illustrated by John Leech)
  (Chapman & Hall, 1843)..£10,000
A CHRISTMAS CAROL (first edition, second issue; first chapter headed 'Stave One'; illustrated by John Leech)
  (Chapman & Hall, 1843)..£3,000
A CHRISTMAS CAROL (second edition; illustrated by John Leech) (Chapman & Hall, 1844 [1843])....................................£1,250
A CHRISTMAS CAROL (illustrated by Charles E. Brock) (Dent, 1905) £30
A CHRISTMAS CAROL (illustrated by Arthur Rackham; issued with dustjacket) (Heinemann, 1915)...................................£350
A CHRISTMAS CAROL (illustrated by Arthur Rackham; limited to 530 copies, signed by the artist) (Heinemann, 1915).......£1,500
A CHRISTMAS CAROL (illustrated by Honor C. Appleton) (Simpkin, Marshall, Hamilton, Kent, 1920) £45
A CHRISTMAS CAROL (illustrated by John Leech; issued without dustjacket) (King Penguin, 1946)......................................£10
A CHRISTMAS CAROL (with stills from the film 'Scrooge'; issued with dustjacket) (Ward Lock, 1951) £25
A CHRISTMAS CAROL (illustrated by Ronald Searle; issued with dustjacket) (Perpetua, 1961) £25
THE CHIMES: A Goblin Story of Some Bells that Rang an Old Year Out and a New Year In (first edition, first issue;
  illustrated by Daniel Maclise, Richard Doyle, John Leech and William C. Stanfield) (Chapman & Hall, 1845 [1844]) £300
THE CHIMES (first edition, second issue; illustrated by Daniel Maclise, Richard Doyle,
  John Leech and William C. Stanfield) (Chapman & Hall, 1845 [1844]) £175
THE CHIMES (illustrated by Hugh Thomson) (Hodder & Stoughton, [1913])..£35
THE CRICKET ON THE HEARTH: A Fairy Tale of Home (first edition, with 'Daily News' advert pink slip inserted; illustrated
  by Daniel Maclise, Richard Doyle, William C. Stanfield, John Leech and Edwin Landseer) (Bradbury & Evans, 1846 [1845])....£600
THE CRICKET ON THE HEARTH: A Fairy Tale of Home (first edition, without pink slip inserted; illustrated by
  Daniel Maclise, Richard Doyle, William C. Stanfield, John Leech and Edwin Landseer) (Bradbury & Evans, 1846 [1845]) £150

THE CRICKET ON THE HEARTH: A Fairy Tale of Home (illustrated by Hugh Thomson) (Golden Cockerel Press, 1933) £60
THE BATTLE OF LIFE: A Love Story (first edition, first issue; illustrated by Daniel Maclise, Richard Doyle,
William C. Stanfield and John Leech) (Bradbury & Evans, 1846) £2,250
THE BATTLE OF LIFE: A Love Story (first edition, second issue; illustrated by Daniel Maclise, Richard Doyle,
William C. Stanfield and John Leech) (Bradbury & Evans, 1846) £300
THE BATTLE OF LIFE: A Love Story (first edition, third issue; illustrated by Daniel Maclise, Richard Doyle,
William C. Stanfield and John Leech) (Bradbury & Evans, 1846) £1,200
THE BATTLE OF LIFE: A Love Story (first edition, fourth issue; illustrated by Daniel Maclise, Richard Doyle,
William C. Stanfield and John Leech) (Bradbury & Evans, 1846) £200
THE HAUNTED MAN AND THE GHOST'S BARGAIN: A Fancy for Christmas Time (illustrated by John Tenniel,
William C. Stanfield, Frank Stone and John Leech) (Bradbury & Evans, 1848)... £200
CHRISTMAS BOOKS (Chapman & Hall, 1852)... £60
CHRISTMAS BOOKS (illustrated by H. M. Brock) (Harrap, 1932) £25
A CHILD'S HISTORY OF ENGLAND (frontispiece by F.W. Topham; three volumes) (Bradbury & Evans, 1852-54) £300
THE MAGIC FISHBONE (illustrated by S.B. Pearse) (Saint Catherine Press/Nisbet, [1912]) £30
THE HOLLY TREE and Other Christmas Stories (illustrated by E.H. Shepard) (Partridge, [1926])......................... £50
A LIFE OF OUR LORD: Written for his Children (Associated Newspapers, 1934)... £10

DICKINSON, Peter

British author. Born: Zambia, 1927. Awarded Carnegie Medal in 1980. His first three highly successful 'Changes' books were followed by others with distant and exotic settings.

Prices are for books in Very Good condition with dustjackets where applicable.

THE WEATHERMONGER (Gollancz, 1968).. £35
HEARTSEASE (illustrated by Robert Hales) (Gollancz, 1969) £25
THE DEVIL'S CHILDREN (illustrated by Robert Hales) (Gollancz, 1970) £25
EMMA TUPPER'S DIARY (Gollancz, 1971).. £20
THE DANCING BEAR (illustrated by David Smee) (Gollancz, 1972)... £20
THE IRON LION (illustrated by Marc Brown) (Allen & Unwin, 1973) £20
THE GIFT (illustrated by Gareth Floyd) (Gollancz, 1973).. £20
PRESTO! (Hutchinson, 1975) £20

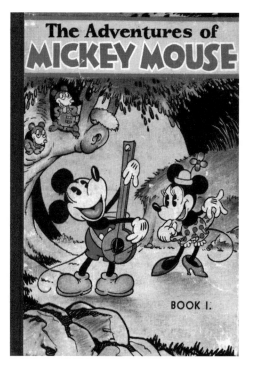

Items relating to Walt Disney and Mickey Mouse remain most desirable, although prices have stalled in recent years.

THE CHANGES (Gollancz, 1975)...£45
THE BLUE HAWK (illustrated by David Smee) (Gollancz, 1976) £20
KING AND JOKER (Hodder & Stoughton, 1976)..£20
ANNERTON PIT (Gollancz, 1977)..£20
WALKING DEAD (Hodder & Stoughton, 1977)...£20
HEPZIBAH (illustrated by Sue Porter) (Eel Pie, 1978)..£20
TULKA (Gollancz, 1979)...£20
THE FLIGHT OF DRAGONS (illustrated by Wayne Anderson) (Gollancz,1979).........................£20
CITY OF GOLD (illustrated by Michael Foreman) (Gollancz, 1980) £20
THE SEVENTH RAVEN (Gollancz, 1981) £20
A SUMMER IN THE TWENTIES (Hodder & Stoughton, 1981)..£20
HEALER (Gollancz, 1983) £10
HINDSIGHT (The Bodley Head, 1983) £10
GIANT COLD (illustrated by Alan Cober) (Gollancz, 1984)...£10
A BOX OF NOTHING (illustrated by Ian Newsham) (Gollancz, 1985)..£10
DEATH OF A UNICORN (paperback) (Hamlyn, 1985)..£10
MOLE HOLE (illustrated by Jean Claverie) (Blackie, 1987)..£10
EVA (Gollancz, 1988)...£10
MERLIN DREAMS (illustrated by Alan Lee) (Gollancz, 1988) £15
SKELETON-IN-WAITING (The Bodley Head, 1989) £10
AK (Gollancz, 1990)...£10
PLAY DEAD (The Bodley Head, 1991) £10
THE YELLOW ROOM CONSPIRACY (London : Little Brown, 1994)..£10

DISNEY, Walt

The American film-maker, Walt Disney (1901-66), adapted many classic children's stories for the screen, notably *Snow White and the Seven Dwarfs* (1937), *Alice in Wonderland* (1951), *Peter Pan* (1953), *The Sword in the Stone* (1963) and *The Jungle Book* (1967). These, and original works featuring Mickey Mouse, Donald Duck and the studio's other characters, prompted a number of spin-off publications.

Prices are for books in Very Good condition.

MICKEY MOUSE BOOK by B. Bobette (Bibo & Lang, 1930) £1,000
MICKEY CHERCHEUR D'OR (Hachette, France, 1931) £300
MICKEY MOUSE MOVIE STORIES (Dean, 1931)..£400
MICKEY MOUSE STORY BOOK (David McKay, 1931)..£600
THE ADVENTURES OF MICKEY MOUSE: Book 1 (David McKay, 1931)...................................£625
MORE ADVENTURES OF MICKEY MOUSE (Dean, 1932)..£350
MICKEY MOUSE (Dean: 'Great Big Midget Books' series, [1933])...£250
MICKY MAUS IM ZIRKUS (German version of 'Mickey Mouse at the Circus'; three pop-up pictures)
    (Verlag Bollmann, [c.1933])..£700
MINNI MAUS UND DAS ENTLEIN (German version of 'Minnie Mouse and the Little Duck'; three pop-up pictures)
    (Verlag Bollmann, [c.1933])..£700
THE POP-UP MICKEY MOUSE (three pop-up pictures) (Whitman, 1933).................................£700
THE POP-UP MINNIE MOUSE (Whitman, US, 1933)..£700
THE POP-UP SILLY SYMPHONIES: Babes in the Woods and King Neptune (Whitman, US, 1933)....£600
THREE LITTLE PIGS (Whitman, US, 1933) £150
WHO'S AFRAID OF THE BIG BAD WOLF: The Three Little Pigs (David McKay, 1933).............£100
MICKEY IN KING ARTHUR'S COURT (four pop-up pictures) (Dean, [1934]) £700
MICKEY MOUSE AND HIS HORSE TANGLEFOOT (Whitman, US, 1934).................................£100
MICKEY MOUSE IN GIANT LAND (Collins, 1934)...£200
MICKEY MOUSE WINS THE RACE (Whitman, US, 1934) £125
SANTA'S WORKSHOP: From 'Silly Symphony' (Collins, [c.1934])..£125
THE PIED PIPER (John Lane: The Bodley Head, 1934) £200
DONALD DUCK (Whitman, US, 1935)...£125
MICKEY MOUSE AND THE MAGIC CARPET (Whitman, US, [1935])..£150
MICKEY MOUSE CRUSOE (Collins, [1935]) £175
MICKEY MOUSE MOVIE STORIES BOOK 2 (Dean, [1935])..£450
THE THREE ORPHAN KITTENS (Whitman, US, 1935)...£125
THE TORTOISE AND THE HARE (Dean, 1935) £100
THE WALT DISNEY SILLY SYMPHONY OMNIBUS (John Lane: The Bodley Head, 1935)..........£175
PRINCESS ELIZABETH GIFT BOOK (includes two Mickey Mouse colour plates and Disney endpapers)
    (Hodder & Stoughton, [1935]) £40
MICKEY MOUSE AT THE CARNIVAL (Collins: 'Wee Little Books' series, 1936) £150
THE THREE ORPHAN KITTENS (Dean, 1936)...£100
MICKEY MOUSE'S MISFORTUNE (Collins: 'Wee Little Books' series, 1936) £150
DONALD DUCK AND HIS MISADVENTURES (Whitman: 'The Better Little Books' series, US, 1937)....£100
SNOW WHITE AND THE SEVEN DWARFS. Adapted from Grimm's Fairy Tales (Whitman, US, 1937)....£140
FERDINAND THE BULL (Whitman, US, 1938)..£40
MICKEY MOUSE IN THE RACE FOR RICHES (Whitman: 'The Better Little Books' series, US, 1938)....£100
PLUTO'S PLAYTIME (Juvenile Productions, [1938]) £120

SNOW WHITE ANNUAL (Dean, [1938]) £120
THE STORY OF CLARABELLE COW (Whitman, US, 1938)...£60
WALT DISNEY'S SNOW WHITE SKETCH BOOK (Collins, [1938])...£500
SCHOOL DAYS IN DISNEYVILLE (Heath, 1939)..£30
SNOW WHITE AND THE MAGIC MIRROR (3-D plates; with special spectacles) (Dean, [1939])...............£100
SNOW WHITE AND THE SEVEN DWARFS (Collins, c1939)...£120
WALT DISNEY'S 'PINOCCHIO' (film scenario with illustrations; adapted from 'Adventures of Pinocchio';
    limited to 100 numbered copies; comb-bound) (Collins, [1939])...£200
WALT DISNEY TELLS THE STORY OF 'PINOCCHIO' (paperback) (Whitman, US, 1939)........................£900
WALT DISNEY'S VERSION OF 'PINOCCHIO' (pictorial boards) (Collins, 1940)......................................£60
BAMBI (Collins, [c1940])..£100
DONALD DUCK GETS FED UP (Whitman: 'The Better Little Books' series, US, 1940)............................£100
DUMBO PAINTING BOOK (Collins, [c1940])..£30
FATHER NOAH'S ARK. From the film 'Silly Symphony' (small format; without colour plates)
    (Birn, [c1940])..£70
FATHER NOAH'S ARK (quarto; with colour plates) (Birn, [c1940])..£175
THE PINOCCHIO STORY BOOK (Collins, 1940) £70
THE DISNEYLAND OMNIBUS (Dean, 1940)...£70
WALT DISNEY WONDER BOOK (Sunshine Press, [c1940])...£70
WALT DISNEY'S 'FANTASIA' by Deems Taylor (Simon & Schuster, US, 1940).....................................£500
MICKEY MOUSE AND THE DUDE RANCH BANDIT (Whitman, US, 1943) £250
THE NUTCRACKER SUITE (Collins, 1943) £100
BAMBI (Heath, 1944)...£30
DONALD DUCK AND HIS FRIENDS: As Told by Jean Ayer (Heath, 1944) £50
MICKEY SEES THE USA (Heath, 1944)...£30
MICKEY'S VOYAGE (Hachette, France 1948)...£50
POOR PLUTO (Whitman, US, 1948)..£40
THE CINDERELLA MAGIC WAND BOOK (3-D; with special spectacles) (Dean 1950)...........................£100
WALT DISNEY'S TREASURE ISLAND (Collins, 1950) £25
WALT DISNEY'S THUMPER ANNUAL (Odhams, 1952)...£30
PETER PAN CHILDREN'S ALBUM (Walt Disney, 1952)...£50
PETER PAN (Walt Disney, 1953)..£50
PLUTO'S PAINTING BOOK (Adprint, 1953) £30
MICKEY MOUSE ALPINISTE (Hachette, France, 1954) £150
LADY AND THE TRAMP AT THE ZOO (Adprint, 1955) £20
WALT DISNEY'S LADY AND THE TRAMP. Based on the Story by Ward Greene
    (Dean, [1955])..£45

*A rare **Mickey Mouse Annual** from 1933 plus the tie-in colour annual for the **Three Little Pigs**, issued in 1933 and worth £150 today.*

WALT DISNEY'S CROSSWORD PUZZLE BOOK (Birn, 1960) £15
DONALD DUCK'S POP-UP CIRCUS (Purnell, 1970) £40
THE DISNEY POSTER BOOK (introduction by Maurice Sendak; 22 large colour plates; card covers)
   (Academy Editions, [1977]) £30
PINOCCHIO (pop-up book) (Walt Disney, 1981) £25
WALT DISNEY'S TREASURY OF CARTOON CLASSICS (Abrams, 1981) £12
WALT DISNEY'S MOVIE POSTER BOOK (Walt Disney, 1989) £15
SNOW WHITE TEACHES THE SEVEN DWARFS TO KNIT (Walt Disney, no date) £100
THE ROBBER KITTEN (Whitman, US, no date) £125
THE STORY OF CASEY JNR THE LITTLE ENGINE WHO SAVED A CIRCUS AND ALL THE ANIMALS
   (Collins, no date) £50

'Mickey Mouse' Annuals
MICKEY MOUSE ANNUAL 1931 (Dean, 1930) £500
MICKEY MOUSE ANNUAL 1932-40 (Dean) .... each £250
MICKEY MOUSE ANNUAL 1941-45 (Dean) .... each £125
MICKEY MOUSE ANNUAL 1946-49 (Dean) .... each £60
MICKEY MOUSE ANNUAL 1950-59 (Dean) .... each £40
MICKEY MOUSE ANNUAL 1960-65 (Dean) .... each £20

'Donald Duck' Annuals
DONALD DUCK'S ANNUAL 1939 (Collins) £400
DONALD DUCK'S ANNUAL 1940 (Collins) £250
DONALD DUCK'S ANNUAL 1941 (Collins) £175
DONALD DUCK'S ANNUAL 1942 (Collins) £150

DIXON, Franklin W.
House name, under which the 'Hardy Boys' novels, featuring Frank and Joe Hardy, were written.

Prices are for U.K. editions in Very Good condition with dustjackets where applicable.

'Hardy Boys' Books
HUNTING FOR HIDDEN GOLD (Harold Hill, 1951) £25
THE MARK ON THE DOOR (Harold Hill, 1957) £12
THE MYSTERY OF THE DISAPPEARING FLOOR (Sampson Low Marston, 1961) £20
THE MYSTERY OF THE FLYING EXPRESS (Sampson Low Marston, 1961) £20
THE MYSTERY OF THE DESERT GIANT (Sampson Low Marston, 1963) £20
THE MYSTERY AT DEVIL'S PAW (Sampson Low Marston, 1963) £20
THE FLICKERING TORCH MYSTERY (Sampson Low Marston, 1963) £20
THE MYSTERY OF THE CHINESE JUNK (Sampson Low Marston, 1963) £20
THE CLUE OF THE BROKEN BLADE (Sampson Low Marston, 1963) £20
THE GHOST AT SKELETON ROCK (Sampson Low Marston, 1964) £20
THE VIKING SYMBOL MYSTERY (Sampson Low Marston, 1964) £20
THE CLUE IN THE EMBERS (Sampson Low Marston, 1965) £20
THE HOODED HAWK MYSTERY (Sampson Low Marston, 1965) £20
THE YELLOW FEATHER MYSTERY (Sampson Low Marston, 1965) £20
THE SECRET OF PIRATE'S HILL (Sampson Low Marston, 1965) £20
THE CRISSCROSS SHADOW (Sampson Low Marston, 1965) £20
THE HAUNTED FORT (Sampson Low Marston, 1966) £20
THE WAILING SIREN MYSTERY (Sampson Low Marston, 1966) £20
SECRET OF THE WILD CAT SWAMP (Sampson Low Marston, 1966) £20
THE MYSTERY OF THE MELTED COINS (Sampson Low Marston, 1967) £15
THE MYSTERY OF THE SPIRAL BRIDGE (Sampson Low Marston, 1967) £15
THE TWISTED CLAW (Macdonald, 1968) £15
THE SINISTER SIGNPOST (Macdonald, 1969) £15
THE SECRET AGENT ON FLIGHT 101 (Macdonald, 1969) £15
THE CLUE OF THE SCREECHING OWL (Macdonald, 1969) £15
THE MYSTERY OF THE AZTEC WARRIOR (Collins, 1971) £15
THE SECRET OF THE OLD MILL (Collins, 1972) £15
THE SHORE ROAD MYSTERY (Collins, 1972) £15
THE GREAT AIRPORT MYSTERY (Collins, 1972) £12
THE MYSTERY OF THE WHALE TATTOO (paperback) (Armada, 1973) £5
MISSING CHUMS (Collins, 1974) £12
SIGN OF THE CROOKED ARROW (paperback) (Armada, 1975) £5
THE SECRET OF SKULL MOUNTAIN (Collins, [1977]) £12
DANGER ON VAMPIRE TRAIL (Collins, [1977]) £12
THE MYSTERIOUS CARAVAN (1977) £12
THE SECRET OF THE CAVES (paperback) (Armada, 1977) £5
WHILE THE CLOCK TICKED (paperback) (Armada, 1979) £5
THE SHORT-WAVE MYSTERY (Collins, 1980) £12
THE SECRET PANEL (Collins, 1980) £12

DIXON, Franklin W.

THE SECRET WARNING (Collins, 1980)..£12
A FIGURE IN HIDING (Collins, 1980)...£10
THE SECRET OF THE LOST TUNNEL (Collins, 1980)...£10
THE WITCHMASTER'S KEY (Collins, 1980)...£10
THE STING OF THE SCORPION (Collins, 1980)...£10
THE MYSTERY OF THE SAMURAI SWORD (illustrated by Leslie Morrill)
 (Angus & Robertson, 1980)..£10
NIGHT OF THE WEREWOLF (illustrated by Leslie Morrill) (Angus & Robertson, 1980) £10
THE APEMAN'S SECRET (illustrated by Leslie Morrill) (Angus & Robertson, 1980) £10
THE PENTAGON SPY (illustrated by Leslie Morrill) (Angus & Robertson, 1980)........£10
THE MUMMY CASE (Angus & Robertson, 1981)..£10
THE STONE IDOL (illustrated by Leslie Morrill) (Angus & Robertson, 1982)............£10
THE VANISHING THIEVES (illustrated by Leslie Morrill) (Angus & Robertson, 1982)....£10
THE OUTLAW'S SILVER (illustrated by Leslie Morrill) (Angus & Robertson, 1982)....£10
THE SUBMARINE CAPER (illustrated by Leslie Morrill) (Angus & Robertson, 1982)....£10
THE MYSTERY OF SMUGGLER'S COVE (Angus & Robertson, 1982)....................£5
THE TOWER TREASURE (Angus & Robertson, 1982)..£5
TRACK OF THE ZOMBIE (Angus & Robertson, 1983)..£5
THE BILLION DOLLAR RANSOM (illustrated by Leslie Morrill)
 (Angus & Robertson, 1983)..£10
THE VOODOO PLOT (Angus & Robertson, 1983) £10
THE TIC-TAC TERROR (Angus & Robertson, 1983)...£10
'SUPER SLEUTHS' SERIES (by Carolyn Keene and Franklin W. Dixon; seven books)
 (Angus & Robertson, 1983)..each £6
CAVE-IN (Angus & Robertson, 1984)...£10
THE CRIMSON FLAME (Angus & Robertson, 1984)...£10
TRAPPED AT SEA (Angus & Roberston, 1984) £10
GAME PLAN FOR DISASTER (Angus & Robertson, 1984)...................................£10
THE BLACKWING PUZZLE (Angus & Robertson, 1985).......................................£7
THE DEMON'S DEN (Angus & Robertson, 1985)...£7
THE SKYFIRE PUZZLE (Angus & Robertson, 1986)...£7
THE SWAMP MONSTER (Angus & Robertson, 1986)...£8
REVENGE OF THE DESERT PHANTOM (Angus & Robertson, 1986)...................£8

'DOCTOR WHO' BOOKS AND ANNUALS

The BBC's hugely popular children's science fiction drama series was launched in 1963 and inspired a number of spin-off books and annuals.

Prices are for books and annuals in Very Good condition.

'Doctor Who' Annuals

1966 (William Hartnell as 'Doctor Who') (World Distributors) £35
1967 (William Hartnell as 'Doctor Who') (World Distributors) £60
1968 (Patrick Troughton as 'Doctor Who') (World Distributors) £70
1969 (Patrick Troughton as 'Doctor Who') (World Distributors) £60
1970 (Patrick Troughton as 'Doctor Who') (World Distributors) £30
1971 (Jon Pertwee as 'Doctor Who') (World Distributors) £70
1973 (Jon Pertwee as 'Doctor Who') (World Distributors) £15
1974 (Jon Pertwee as 'Doctor Who') (World Distributors) £15
1975 (Jon Pertwee as 'Doctor Who') (World Distributors) £15
1976 (Tom Baker as 'Doctor Who') (World Distributors) £8
1977 (Tom Baker as 'Doctor Who') (World Distributors) £8
1978 (Tom Baker as 'Doctor Who') (World Distributors) £8
1979 (Tom Baker as 'Doctor Who') (World Distributors) £8
1980 (Tom Baker as 'Doctor Who') (World Distributors) £8
1981 (Tom Baker as 'Doctor Who') (World Distributors) £8
1982 (Tom Baker and Peter Davison as 'Doctor Who'; with cover date) (World Distributors) £8
1983 (Peter Davison as 'Doctor Who'; without cover date) (World Distributors) £8
1984 (Peter Davison as 'Doctor Who') (World Distributors)...................................£8
1985 (Colin Baker as 'Doctor Who') (World Distributors)......................................£8
1986 (Colin Baker as 'Doctor Who') (World Distributors)......................................£8

'Dalek' Books

THE DALEK BOOK 1964 (Souvenir/Panther)..£75
THE DALEK WORLD 1965 (Souvenir/Panther)..£65
THE DALEK OUTER SPACE BOOK 1966 (Souvenir/Panther)..............................£75
TERRY NATION'S DALEK 1976 (World Distributors)..£15
TERRY NATION'S DALEK 1977 (World Distributors)..£15
TERRY NATION'S DALEK 1978 (World Distributors)..£10
TERRY NATION'S DALEK 1979 (World Distributors)..£10

Two rare Dr Who publications from his earliest incarnations. For collectors after more detail, Peter Haining's **Doctor Who: A Celebration** *(1983) remains one of the most comprehensive books ever written about the Doctor.*

Other Annuals

DOCTOR WHO AND THE INVASION FROM SPACE (World Distributors, 1966)................................**£50**
THE AMAZING WORLD OF DOCTOR WHO (World Distributors, 1976)...**£10**
DOCTOR WHO — ADVENTURES IN TIME AND SPACE (compilation from previous annuals) (World Distributors, 1981)..........**£8**
K9 ANNUAL (World Distributors, 1983)...**£5**

Target Novels

DOCTOR WHO NOVELS (Wingate/W.H. Allen, 1974-1988).. each **£8**
DOCTOR WHO NOVELS (with black logo; paperback) (Target, 1973-1975) .... each **£5**
DOCTOR WHO NOVELS (with diamond crescent logo; paperback) (Target, 1975-1981) .... each **£2**
DOCTOR WHO NOVELS (with neon logo; paperback) (Target, 1981-1988)........................... each **£2**
DOCTOR WHO NOVELS (with asteroid logo; paperback) (Target, 1987-Present) .... each **£2**
JUNIOR DOCTOR WHO AND THE GIANT ROBOT by Terrance Dicks (W.H. Allen, 1979)................**£8**
JUNIOR DOCTOR WHO AND THE GIANT ROBOT by Terrance Dicks (paperback) (Target, 1980) **£3**
JUNIOR TARGET AND THE BRAIN OF MORBUS by Terrance Dicks (W.H. Allen, 1980) **£8**
JUNIOR TARGET AND THE BRAIN OF MORBUS by Terrance Dicks (paperback) (Target, 1980)............**£3**
THE FIVE DOCTORS by Terrance Dicks (paperback) (Target, 1983)..**£3**
THE TWO DOCTORS by Robert Holmes (paperback) (Target, 1985)......................................**£4**
THE COMPANIONS OF DOCTOR WHO (paperback) (Target, 1986-1987).......................... each **£2**

Other Novels

DOCTOR WHO IN AN EXCITING ADVENTURE WITH THE DALEKS by David Whitaker (Muller, 1964)................**£20**
DOCTOR WHO IN AN EXCITING ADVENTURE WITH THE DALEKS by David Whitaker (paperback) (Armada, 1965) **£6**
DOCTOR WHO IN AN EXCITING ADVENTURE WITH THE DALEKS by David Whitaker (paperback) (Avon, US 1967)........**£10**
DOCTOR WHO AND THE CRUSADERS by David Whitaker (Muller, 1965) **£10**
DOCTOR WHO AND THE CRUSADERS by David Whitaker (paperback) (Dragon, 1967)..................**£6**
DOCTOR WHO AND THE ZARBI by Bill Strutton (Muller, 1965) **£10**
K9 AND THE TIME TRAP by Dave Martin (paperback) (Sparrow, 1980)..................................**£3**
K9 AND THE BEAST OF VEGA by Dave Martin (paperback) (Sparrow, 1980) **£3**
K9 AND THE ZETA RESCUE by Dave Martin (paperback) (Sparrow, 1980) **£3**
K9 AND THE MISSING PLANET by Dave Martin (paperback) (Sparrow, 1980) **£3**
SEARCH FOR THE DOCTOR by David Martin (Severn House, 1986).....................................**£10**
CRISIS IN SPACE by Michael Holt (Severn House, 1986)..**£10**
THE GARDEN OF EVIL by David Martin (Severn House, 1986)..**£10**
RACE AGAINST TIME by Pip and Jane Baker (Severn House, 1986) **£10**
MISSION TO VENUS by William Emms (Severn House, 1986) **£10**
INVASION OF THE ORMAZOIDS by Philip Martin (Severn House, 1986)................................**£10**

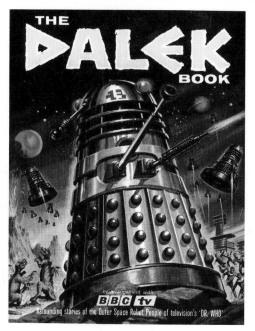

The first 1964 **Dalek Book** *is worth £75 in today's market.*

Non-Fiction Titles

THE DALEK POCKET BOOK AND SPACE TRAVELLER'S GUIDE by Terry Nation (paperback) (Panther, 1965)......................£20
THE DOCTOR WHO MONSTER BOOK by Terrance Dicks (paperback) (Target, 1975) £6
THE SECOND DOCTOR WHO MONSTER BOOK by Terrance Dicks (paperback) (Target, 1976)................................£6
THE ADVENTURES OF K9 AND OTHER MECHANICAL CREATURES by Terrance Dicks (paperback) (Target, 1975) £3
TERRY NATION'S DALEK SPECIAL (paperback) (Target, 1979) £3
THE DOCTOR WHO QUIZ BOOK by Nigel Robinson (paperback) (Target, 1981)..£2
THE DOCTOR WHO CROSSWORD BOOK by Nigel Robinson (paperback) (Target, 1982) £2
DOCTOR WHO QUIZ BOOKS by Michael Holt (paperback) (Magnet, 1982-83) .... each £1
THE SECOND DOCTOR WHO QUIZ BOOK by Nigel Robinson (paperback) (Target, 1983) £2
DOCTOR WHO: BRAIN-TEASERS AND MIND BENDERS by Adrian Heath (paperback) (Target, 1984)...................£2
THE DOCTOR WHO PUZZLE BOOK by Michael Holt (paperback) (Magnet, 1985)...£1
THE THIRD DOCTOR WHO QUIZ BOOK by Nigel Robinson (paperback) (Target, 1985)......................................£2

'Doctor Who' Reference Books: Large-Format

DOCTOR WHO: THE MAKING OF A TELEVISION SERIES by Alan Road (Deutsch, 1982) £10
DOCTOR WHO: THE MAKING OF A TELEVISION SERIES by Alan Road (paperback) (Puffin, 1983)........................£4
THE DOCTOR WHO TECHNICAL MANUAL by Mark Harris (Severn House, 1983) £10
THE DOCTOR WHO TECHNICAL MANUAL by Mark Harris (paperback) (Sphere, 1983) £2
DOCTOR WHO: A CELEBRATION by Peter Haining (W.H. Allen, 1983) £10
DOCTOR WHO: A CELEBRATION by Peter Haining (limited to 500 copies; leather binding) (W.H. Allen, 1983) £35
DOCTOR WHO: THE KEY TO TIME by Peter Haining (W.H. Allen, 1984)...£10
DOCTOR WHO: THE KEY TO TIME by Peter Haining (limited to 500 copies; leather binding) (W.H. Allen, 1984)....................£35
DOCTOR WHO: THE KEY TO TIME by Peter Haining (paperback) (Comet, 1987)..£4
THE DOCTOR WHO PATTERN BOOK by Joy Gammon (W.H. Allen, 1986)...£3
THE DOCTOR WHO PATTERN BOOK by Joy Gammon (paperback) (W.H. Allen, 1986) £2
DOCTOR WHO: THE TARDIS INSIDE OUT by John Nathan-Turner (Piccadilly, 1985) £5
DOCTOR WHO: THE TARDIS INSIDE OUT by John Nathan-Turner (paperback) (Piccadilly, 1985) £3
THE DOCTOR WHO COOKBOOK by Gary Downie (W.H. Allen, 1985)...£4
THE DOCTOR WHO COOKBOOK by Gary Downie (paperback) (Star, 1986)..£2
THE DOCTOR WHO ILLUSTRATED A-Z by Lesley Standring (W.H. Allen, 1985)...£10
THE DOCTOR WHO ILLUSTRATED A-Z by Lesley Standring (paperback) (Star, 1987)..£4
TIMEVIEW: THE COMPLETE DOCTOR WHO ILLUSTRATIONS OF FRANK BELLAMY
    Text by David Bellamy (Who Dares Publishing, 1985)..£8
TIMEVIEW: THE COMPLETE DOCTOR WHO ILLUSTRATIONS OF FRANK BELLAMY
    Text by David Bellamy (paperback) (Who Dares Publishing, 1985) £5
DOCTOR WHO: THE EARLY YEARS by Jeremy Bentham (W.H. Allen, 1986)...£20

DOCTOR WHO: THE EARLY YEARS by Jeremy Bentham (limited to 500 copies; leather binding) (W.H. Allen, 1986) **£60**
DOCTOR WHO: THE EARLY YEARS by Jeremy Bentham (paperback) (Comet, 1988) **£6**
THE DOCTOR WHO FILE by Peter Haining (W.H. Allen, 1986)..**£10**
THE DOCTOR WHO FILE by Peter Haining (paperback) (W.H. Allen, 1992) **£3**
DOCTOR WHO: THE COMPANIONS by John Nathan-Turner (Piccadilly, 1986) **£5**
DOCTOR WHO: THE COMPANIONS by John Nathan-Turner (paperback) (Piccadilly, 1986) **£3**
DOCTOR WHO: SPECIAL EFFECTS by Mat Irvine (Hutchinson, 1986) **£6**
DOCTOR WHO: SPECIAL EFFECTS by Mat Irvine (paperback) (Beaver, 1986)..**£3**
DOCTOR WHO: THE TIME-TRAVELLERS' GUIDE by Peter Haining (W.H. Allen, 1987) **£10**
DOCTOR WHO: THE TIME-TRAVELLERS' GUIDE by Peter Haining (paperback) (Comet, 1989) **£3**
DOCTOR WHO: 25 GLORIOUS YEARS by Peter Haining (W.H. Allen/Planet, 1988)..**£10**
DOCTOR WHO: 25 GLORIOUS YEARS by Peter Haining (paperback) (Virgin, 1990) **£5**
DOCTOR WHO: CYBERMEN by David Banks (Who Dares Publishing, 1988)..**£20**
DOCTOR WHO: THE CYBERMEN by David Banks (silver leather binding) (Who Dares Publishing, 1988)............**£90**
DOCTOR WHO: THE CYBERMEN by David Banks (paperback) (Virgin, 1990)..**£5**
DOCTOR WHO YEARBOOK (boards; issued without dustjacket) (Marvel, 1991) **£3**
DOCTOR WHO: THE GALLIFREY CHRONICLES by John Peel (Doctor Who, 1991) **£12**
DOCTOR WHO YEARBOOK 1993 (boards; issued without dustjacket) (Marvel, 1992)..................................**£3**
DOCTOR WHO: THE MONSTERS by Adrian Rigleford and Andrew Skilleter (Doctor Who, 1992)....................**£12**
DOCTOR WHO: THE SIXTIES by David J. Howe, Mark Stammers and Stephen James Walker (Doctor Who, 1992)..............**£12**
DOCTOR WHO: THE SIXTIES by David J. Howe, Mark Stammers and Stephen James Walker (Doctor Who, 1993)..............**£10**
DOCTOR WHO YEARBOOK 1994 (boards; issued without dustjacket) (Marvel, 1993)..................................**£4**
DOCTOR WHO — TIMEFRAME: THE ILLUSTRATED HISTORY by David J. Howe (Doctor Who, 1993)................**£12**

'Doctor Who' Reference Books: Small-Format

THE MAKING OF DOCTOR WHO by Malcolm Hulke and Terrance Dicks (paperback) (Piccolo, 1972)..............**£10**
THE MAKING OF DOCTOR WHO by Malcolm Hulke and Terrance Dicks (revised edition; paperback)
  (Target/Wyndham, 1976) **£5**
A DAY WITH A TV PRODUCER by Graham Rickard (Wayland, 1980)..**£6**
THE DOCTOR WHO PROGRAMME GUIDE — VOLUME ONE by Jean-Marc Lofficier (W. H. Allen, 1981)............**£10**
THE DOCTOR WHO PROGRAMME GUIDE — VOLUME ONE by Jean-Marc Lofficier (paperback) (Target, 1981) **£3**
THE DOCTOR WHO PROGRAMME GUIDE — VOLUME TWO by Jean-Marc Lofficier (W.H. Allen, 1981) **£10**
THE DOCTOR WHO PROGRAMME GUIDE — VOLUME TWO by Jean-Marc Lofficier (paperback) (Target, 1981)............**£3**
DOCTOR WHO: THE UNFOLDING TEXT by John Tulloch and Manuel Alvarado (Macmillan, 1983)................**£10**
DOCTOR WHO: THE UNFOLDING TEXT by John Tulloch and Manuel Alvarado (paperback) (Macmillan, 1983) **£3**
DOCTOR WHO: TRAVEL WITHOUT THE TARDIS by Jean Airey and Laurie Haldeman (paperback) (Target, 1986)..................**£2**
ENCYCLOPEDIA OF THE WORLDS OF DOCTOR WHO: A-D by David Saunders (Piccadilly, 1987) **£6**
ENCYCLOPEDIA OF THE WORLDS OF DOCTOR WHO: A-D by David Saunders (paperback) (Knight, 1988)........**£2**
THE OFFICIAL DOCTOR WHO AND THE DALEKS BOOK by John Peel and Terry Nation (paperback)
  (St Martins Press, US, 1989)..**£3**
ENCYCLOPEDIA OF THE WORLDS OF DOCTOR WHO: E-K by David Saunders (Piccadilly, 1989) **£6**
ENCYCLOPEDIA OF THE WORLDS OF DOCTOR WHO: E-K by David Saunders (paperback) (Knight, 1989)........**£2**
DOCTOR WHO: THE PROGRAMME GUIDE by Jean-Marc Lofficier (paperback) (Target, 1989) **£2**
ENCYCLOPEDIA OF THE WORLDS OF DOCTOR WHO: L-R by David Saunders (Piccadilly, 1990)....................**£6**
DOCTOR WHO: THE TERRESTRIAL INDEX by Jean-Marc Lofficier (paperback) (Target, 1991)....................**£2**
DOCTOR WHO: THE UNIVERSAL DATA BANK by Jean-Marc Lofficier (paperback) (Doctor Who, 1992) **£3**
DOCTOR WHO: THE HANDBOOK — THE FOURTH DOCTOR by David J. Howe, Mark Stammers and
  Stephen James Walker (paperback) (Doctor Who, 1992) **£2**
DOCTOR WHO: THE HANDBOOK — THE SIXTH DOCTOR by David J. Howe, Mark Stammers and
  Stephen James Walker (paperback) (Doctor Who, 1993) **£3**

Magazines and Pamphlets

RADIO TIMES — DOCTOR WHO: 10th ANNIVERSARY SPECIAL (November, 1973) **£50**
DOCTOR WHO: THE DEVELOPING ART by Jeremy Bentham (pamphlet) (British Film Institute, October 1983)........................**£5**
RADIO TIMES — DOCTOR WHO: 20th ANNIVERSARY SPECIAL (November 1983)..**£25**
DOCTOR WHO: 30th ANNIVERSARY SPECIAL (based on the '10th Anniversary Special') (Marvel, 1993) **£6**

DOYLE, Richard

Irish illustrator. Born in 1824, he was one of the main contributors to _Punch_ during the 1840s, illustrating a number of children's works following his departure from the title in 1850. Died: 1883.

Prices are for books in Very Good condition.

THE FAIRY RING: A New Collection of Popular Tales by J. and W. Grimm. Translated by J.E. Taylor (John Murray, 1846).......**£1,200**
FAIRY TALES FROM ALL NATIONS by Anthony R. Montalba (Chapman & Hall, 1849) **£200**
BOOK OF BALLADS by Sir Theodore Martin (written under the pseudonym 'Bon Gaultier';
  illustrated by Richard Doyle and others) (Orr, [1849])..**£150**
THE ENCHANTED DOLL: A Fairy Tale for Little People by Mark Lemon (Bradbury & Evans, 1849) **£100**
REBECCA AND ROWENA: A Romance upon Romance by W.M. Thackeray (Chapman & Hall, 1850) **£325**
THE KING OF THE GOLDEN RIVER: A Legend of Stiria by John Ruskin (Smith Elder, 1851) **£600**
JUVENILE CALENDAR AND ZODIAC FLOWERS by E.L. Hervey (Sampson Low, [1855])................................**£120**
MERRY PICTURES. By the Comic Hands of H.K. Browne, Richard Doyle and Others (Kent, 1857)....................**£80**

DOYLE, Richard

THE SCOURING OF THE WHITE HORSE by Thomas Hughes (Macmillan, 1859 [1858])......................................**£180**
AN OLD FAIRY TALE TOLD ANEW by J.R. Planché (Routledge, [1865])..**£60**
FAIRY TALES by Mark Lemon (illustrated by Richard Doyle and C.H. Bennett) (Bradbury Evans, 1868)..................**£175**
CHRISTMAS BOOKS by Charles Dickens (illustrated by Richard Doyle and others) (Chapman & Hall, 1869)...........**£125**
PUCK ON PEGASUS by H.C. Pennell (Routledge, 1869, [1868])..**£180**
IN FAIRYLAND: A Series of Pictures from the Elf World (with a poem by William Allingham) (Longmans, 1870 [1869]).......**£750**
SNOW-WHITE AND ROSY RED and Other Famous Fairy Tales (Dean, [1871])..**£270**
THE ENCHANTED CROW and Other Famous Fairy Tales (Dean, [1871]) **£200**
FEAST OF THE DWARFS and Other Famous Fairy Tales (Dean, [1871])...**£200**
FORTUNE'S FAVOURITE and Other Famous Fairy Tales (Dean, [1871])...**£90**
HOMER FOR THE HOLIDAYS by a Boy of Twelve (with extracts from Poe's translation; fifteen plates)
(Pall Mall Gazette Extras, [1883]) **£75**
THE PRINCESS NOBODY: A Tale of Fairy Land by Andrew Lang (illustrations after drawings by Richard Doyle;
printed in colour by Edmund Evans) (Longmans, [1884])..**£500**
JACK THE GIANT KILLER (Eyre & Spottiswoode, 1888)..**£300**
THE DOYLE FAIRY BOOK by A.R. Montalba (Dean, 1890)..**£200**
THE SAD STORY OF A PIG AND LITTLE GIRL by Madeline Wyndham (London, [1901]) **£120**
THE ENCHANTED DOLL by Mark Lemon (illustrated by Richard Doyle and C.H. Bennett) (Bradbury Evans, 1903)..............**£140**

DOYLE, Roddy
Irish author, dramatist and screenwriter. Born: 1958. The author of such novels as *The Commitments* and *The Snapper*, has also penned a handful of children's titles.
Prices are for books in Very Good condition with dustjackets.
NOT JUST FOR CHRISTMAS (paperback) (New Island Books, Dublin, 1999) **£5**
THE GIGGLER TREATMENT (Scholastic Press, 2000) **£15**
ROVER SAVES CHRISTMAS (Scholastic Press, 2001) **£15**
THE MEANWHILE ADVENTURES (Scholastic Press, 2004) **£5**

DULAC, Edmund
French illustrator. Born: Toulouse, 1882. Came to London in his early twenties, where he quickly established himself as a rival to Arthur Rackham, illustrating a number of expensive 'gift book' editions of classic children's works, including the *Arabian Nights* (1907). He also worked as a stage designer. Died: 1953.
Prices are for books in Very Good condition without dustjackets.

Books Written and Illustrated by Edmund Dulac
LYRICS PATHETIC AND HUMOROUS FROM A TO Z (24 colour plates by Edmund Dulac) (Warne, 1908)................**£350**
LYRICS PATHETIC AND HUMOROUS FROM A TO Z (portfolio of plates; in cloth-covered box;
limited to 160 copies) (Warne, 1909) **£2,500**
A FAIRY GARLAND: Being Fairy Tales from the Old French (twelve colour plates by Edmund Dulac) (Cassell, 1928) **£250**
A FAIRY GARLAND: Being Fairy Tales from the Old French (twelve colour plates by Edmund Dulac;
De Luxe edition: limited to 1,000 copies, signed by the artist) (Cassell, 1928) **£450**

Books Illustrated by Edmund Dulac
NOVELS OF THE SISTERS BRONTË (ten volumes; six colour plates by Edmund Dulac in each volume)
(Dent, 1905).. each **£50**
FAIRIES I HAVE MET by Mrs R. Stawell (eight colour plates by Edmund Dulac) (John Lane, [1907]) **£100**
FAIRIES I HAVE MET (eight colour plates by Edmund Dulac) (Hodder & Stoughton, [1910])..............................**£100**
MY DAYS WITH THE FAIRIES by Mrs. R. Stawell (new enlarged edition of above;
eight colour plates by Edmund Dulac) (Hodder & Stoughton, [1913])..**£175**
STORIES FROM THE ARABIAN NIGHTS Retold by Laurence Housman (fifty colour plates by Edmund Dulac)
(Hodder & Stoughton, 1907) **£350**
STORIES FROM THE ARABIAN NIGHTS(fifty colour plates by Edmund Dulac; De Luxe edition: limited to
350 copies, signed by the artist) (Hodder & Stoughton, 1907)..**£1,750**
THE TEMPEST by William Shakespeare (forty colour plates by Edmund Dulac) (Hodder & Stoughton, [1908])......**£250**
THE TEMPEST (forty colour plates by Edmund Dulac; De Luxe edition:
limited to 500 copies, signed by the artist) (Hodder & Stoughton, [1908]) **£1,500**
THE RUBAIYAT OF OMAR KHAYYAM (twenty plates by Edmund Dulac) (Hodder & Stoughton, [1909])..............**£350**
THE RUBAIYAT OF OMAR KHAYYAM (twenty plates by Edmund Dulac; De Luxe edition: limited to 750 copies,
signed by the artist) (Hodder & Stoughton, [1909])...**£1,750**
THE SLEEPING BEAUTY and Other Fairy Tales by A.T. Quiller Couch (thirty colour plates by Edmund Dulac)
(Hodder & Stoughton, [1910]) **£500**
THE SLEEPING BEAUTY (thirty colour plates by Edmund Dulac; De Luxe edition:
limited to 1,000 copies, signed by the artist) (Hodder & Stoughton, [1910]) **£1,000**
STORIES FROM HANS ANDERSEN (28 colour plates by Edmund Dulac) (Hodder & Stoughton, [1911])..............**£300**
STORIES FROM HANS ANDERSEN (28 colour plates by Edmund Dulac; De Luxe edition: limited to 750 copies,
signed by the artist) (Hodder & Stoughton, [1911])...**£1,500**
THE BELLS and Other Poems by Edgar Allan Poe (28 colour plates by Edmund Dulac) (Hodder & Stoughton, [1912]) **£250**
THE BELLS (28 colour plates by Edmund Dulac; De Luxe edition: limited to 750 copies, signed by the artist)
(Hodder & Stoughton, [1912]) **£750**

*One of Richard Doyle's illustrations from his first work, **The Fairy Ring** (1846).*

PRINCESS BADOURA: A Tale from The Arabian Nights Retold by Laurence Housman
(ten colour plates by Edmund Dulac) (Hodder & Stoughton, 1913) **£400**

PRINCESS BADOURA (ten colour plates by Edmund Dulac; De Luxe edition: limited to 750 copies, signed by the artist)
(Hodder & Stoughton, 1913) **£1,700**

SINBAD THE SAILOR and Other Stories from The Arabian Nights (23 colour plates by Edmund Dulac)
(Hodder & Stoughton, 1914) **£600**

SINBAD THE SAILOR (23 colour plates by Edmund Dulac;
De Luxe edition: limited to 500 copies, signed by the artist) (Hodder & Stoughton, 1914)......................**£2,500**

EDMUND DULAC'S PICTURE-BOOK FOR THE FRENCH RED CROSS (twenty colour plates by Edmund Dulac)
(Hodder & Stoughton, [1915]) **£80**

THE DREAMER OF DREAMS by Queen Marie of Roumania (six colour plates by Edmund Dulac)
Hodder & Stoughton, [1915])...**£50**

THE STEALERS OF LIGHT by Queen Marie of Roumania (two colour plates by Edmund Dulac)
(Hodder & Stoughton, 1916)..**£45**

EDMUND DULAC'S FAIRY BOOK (fifteen colour plates by Edmund Dulac) (Hodder & Stoughton, 1916) **£170**

EDMUND DULAC'S FAIRY BOOK (fifteen colour plates by Edmund Dulac; De Luxe edition: limited to 350 copies,
signed by the artist) (Hodder & Stoughton, 1916)...**£1,200**

TANGLEWOOD TALES by Nathaniel Hawthorne (fourteen colour plates by Edmund Dulac)
(Hodder & Stoughton, [1918]) **£150**

TANGLEWOOD TALES (fourteen colour plates; De Luxe edition:
limited to 500 copies, signed by the artist) (Hodder & Stoughton, [1918]) **£750**

THE KINGDOM OF THE PEARL by Leonard Rosenthal (ten colour plates by Edmund Dulac; limited to 675 copies)
(Nisbet, [1920])...**£400**

THE KINGDOM OF THE PEARL (ten colour plates by Edmund Dulac; De Luxe edition:
limited to 100 copies, signed by the author) (Nisbet, [1920]) **£2,000**

FOUR PLAYS FOR DANCERS by W.B. Yeats (seven illustrations from Dulac's designs) (Macmillan, 1921)............**£200**

THE GREEN LACQUER PAVILION by Helen De V. Beauclerk (nine black-and-white illustrations by
Edmund Dulac and a portrait of author) (Collins, 1926) **£35**

TREASURE ISLAND by Robert Louis Stevenson (twelve colour plates by Edmund Dulac) (Benn, 1927)...............**£350**

TREASURE ISLAND (twelve colour plates by Edmund Dulac; De Luxe edition:
limited to fifty copies, signed by the artist) (Benn, 1927)...**£4,000**

GODS AND MORTALS IN LOVE by Hugh Ross Williamson (nine colour plates by Edmund Dulac)
(Country Life, [1935])..**£175**

THE DAUGHTERS OF THE STARS by Mary C. Crary (two colour plates by Edmund Dulac) (Hatchard, 1939)........**£40**

THE DAUGHTERS OF THE STARS by Mary C. Crary (two colour plates by Edmund Dulac; De Luxe edition:
limited to 500 copies, signed by the artist) (Hatchard, 1939)...**£170**

THE GOLDEN COCKEREL. Adapted from Alexander Pushkin (limited to 1,500 numbered copies,
signed by the artist) (Limited Editions Club, US, 1950) **£300**

DEATH HIMSELF LISTENED AND SAID, "GO ON LITTLE NIGHTINGALE. GO ON"

A typically creepy plate by Edmund Dulac, one of 28 to be found in his edition of **Stories from Hans Andersen** *(1911).*

DUMAS, Alexandre

French author. Born: Villers-Cotterets, 1802. Like Dickens, the great French novelist wrote few works specifically for children, but his best-known adult titles — notably *The Count of Monte-Cristo* and *The Three Musketeers* (both 1846) — have been adapted for young readers. Died: 1870.

Prices are for books in Very Good condition.

GOOD LADY BERTHA'S HONEY BROTH (illustrated by Bertall) (Chapman & Hall: 'Picture Story Books' series, 1846).........**£150**
GOOD LADY BERTHA'S HONEY BROTH (as 'The Honey-Stew of Countess Bertha') (Bohn, 1846)..................................**£125**
GOOD LADY BERTHA'S HONEY BROTH (as 'The Honey-Stew of Lady Bertha') (Jeremiah How, 1846)...........................**£125**
THE STORY OF A NUTCRACKER (illustrated by Bertall) (Chapman & Hall: 'Picture Story Books' series, 1846)......................**£150**
THE STORY OF A NUTCRACKER (as 'Princess Pirlipatine and the Nutcracker'; illustrated by Violet Dale)
(Philip Allan, 1918)..**£30**
CAPTAIN PAMPHILE: Episodes (Longmans, 1892)..**£30**
CAPTAIN PAMPHILE (as 'Adventures of Captain Pamphile'; paperback) (Methuen, [1904])......................................**£15**
CAPTAIN PAMPHILE (as 'Adventures of Captain Pamphile'; illustrated by Frank Adams; hardback) (Methuen, [1905])............**£25**
LYDERIC: Count of Flanders (paperback) (Gowans & Gray, 1903)..**£15**
LA JEUNESSE DE PIERROT (Blackie, 1906)...**£20**
THE DUMAS FAIRY TALE BOOK (illustrated by Harry Rountree) (Warne, 1924)..**£40**
THE PHANTOM WHITE HARE and Other Stories (issued with dustjacket) (Canongate, 1989)..................................**£15**

'DUMPY' BOOKS

A popular series of numbered, small-format books, selected by E.V. Lucas and published by Grant Richards and later by Chatto & Windus. Helen Bannerman's *Little Black Sambo* was the fourth title in the series.

Prices are for books in Very Good condition.

NO. 1: THE FLAMP, THE AMELIORATOR AND THE SCHOOLBOY'S APPRENTICE by E.V. Lucas (Grant Richards, 1897)........**£100**
NO. 2: MRS TURNER'S CAUTIONARY STORIES (Grant Richards, 1897)...**£80**
NO. 3: THE BAD FAMILY AND OTHER STORIES by Mrs Fenwick (Grant Richards, 1899) **£80**
NO. 4: THE STORY OF LITTLE BLACK SAMBO by Helen Bannerman (illustrated by the author)
(Grant Richards, 1899)..**£6,000**
NO. 5: THE BOUNTIFUL LADY by Thomas Cobb (Grant Richards, 1900) **£80**
NO. 6: A CAT BOOK by E.V. Lucas (illustrated by H. Officer Smith) (Grant Richards, 1901)...................................**£70**
NO. 7: A FLOWER BOOK by Eden Coybee (illustrated by Nellie Benson) (Grant Richards, 1901).............................**£70**
NO. 8: THE PINK KNIGHT by J. R. Monsell (illustrated by the author) (Grant Richards, 1901)................................**£70**
NO. 9: THE LITTLE CLOWN by Thomas Cobb (Grant Richards, 1901)..**£70**
NO. 10: A HORSE BOOK by Mary Tourtel (Grant Richards, 1901)...**£175**
NO. 11: LITTLE PEOPLE: An Alphabet by T.W.H. Crosland (Grant Richards, 1901)..**£100**
NO. 12: A DOG BOOK by Ethel Bicknell (illustrated by C. Moore Park) (Grant Richards, 1902).............................**£80**
NO. 13: THE ADVENTURES OF SAMUEL AND SELINA by Jean C. Archer (Grant Richards, 1902)..........................**£70**
NO. 14: THE LITTLE LOST GIRL by Eleanor Raper (Grant Richards, 1902)...**£70**
NO. 15: DOLLIES by Richard Hunter (illustrated by Ruth Cobb) (Grant Richards, 1902)......................................**£100**
NO. 16: THE BAD MRS GINGER by Honor C. Appleton (illustrated by the author) (Grant Richards, 1902)..............**£90**
NO. 17: PETER PIPER'S PRACTICAL PRINCIPLES (Grant Richards, 1902)..**£70**
NO. 18: LITTLE WHITE BARBARA (Grant Richards, 1902)...**£75**
NO. 19: JAPANESE DUMPY (Grant Richards, 1903)..**£85**
NO. 20: TOWLOCKS AND HIS WOODEN HORSE by Alice Appleton (illustrated by Honor C. Appleton)
(Grant Richards, 1903)...**£100**
NO. 21: THE THREE LITTLE FOXES by Mary Tourtel (Grant Richards, 1903)...**£175**
NO. 22: THE OLD MAN'S BAG by T.W.H. Crosland (illustrated by J.R. Monsell) (Grant Richards, 1903) **£80**
NO. 23: THE THREE GOBLINS by M.G. Taggart (Grant Richards, 1903)...**£75**
NO. 24: DUMPY PROVERBS by Honor C. Appleton (illustrated by the author) (Grant Richards, 1903)...................**£100**
NO. 25: MORE DOLLIES by Richard Hunter (illustrated by Ruth Cobb) (Grant Richards, 1903)............................**£100**
NO. 26: LITTLE YELLOW WANG-LO by M.C. Bell (Grant Richards, 1903)...**£90**
NO. 27: PLAIN JANE (Grant Richards, 1903) **£80**
NO. 28: THE SOOTY MAN (Grant Richards, 1903)..**£80**
NO. 29: FISHY WINKLE by Jean Archer (illustrated by the author) (Grant Richards, 1903) **£80**
NO. 30: ROSALIND (Grant Richards, 1904)...**£80**
NO. 31: SAMMY AND THE SNARLIWINK (Grant Richards, 1904) **£80**
NO. 32: THE MOTOR CAR DUMPY BOOK by T.W.H. Crosland (illustrated by J.R. Monsell)
(Grant Richards, 1904)...**£150**
NO. 33: IRENE'S CHRISTMAS PARTY by Richard Hunter (illustrated by Ruth Cobb) (Grant Richards, 1904) **£70**
NO. 34: THE LITTLE SOLDIER BOOK by Jessie Pope (illustrated by Henry Mayor) (Chatto & Windus, 1905).......**£70**
NO. 35: A DUTCH DOLL'S DITTIES (Chatto & Windus, 1905)..**£80**
NO. 36: TEN LITTLE NIGGER BOYS (Chatto & Windus, 1905)..**£100**
NO. 37: HUMPTY DUMPTY'S LITTLE SON (Chatto & Windus, 1907) **£80**
NO. 38: SIMPLE SIMON (Chatto & Windus, 1907)..**£80**
NO. 39: THE LITTLE FRENCHMAN (Chatto & Windus, 1908) **£80**
NO. 40: THE POTATO BOOK, or The Story of an Irish Potato by Lily Schofield (Chatto & Windus, 1908)...............**£80**

E

'EAGLE'

Popular British comic of the 1950s and '60s. The comic itself was launched on 14th April 1950, the first annual appearing the following year. Among the title's many popular characters were 'Harris Tweed, Extra Special Agent' and 'Dan Dare'.

Prices are for comics/annuals/books in Very Good condition with dustjackets where applicable. See also 'Dan Dare'.

'Eagle' Comic

EAGLE ISSUE 1 (Hulton/LongacreOdhams/IPC, 14th April 1950) £170

'Eagle' Annuals

NO. 1 (Hulton Press, September 1951)..£30
NO. 2 (Hulton Press, September 1952)..£20
NO. 3 (Hulton Press, September 1953)..£15
NO. 4 (Hulton Press, September 1954)..£15
NO. 5 (Hulton Press, September 1955)..£15
NO. 6 (Hulton Press, September 1956)..£15
NO. 7 (Hulton Press, 1957)..£15
NO. 8 (Hulton Press, 1958)..£15
NO. 9 (Hulton Press, 1959)..£15
NO. 10 (Hulton Press, 1960)..£15
NO. 11 (Longacre Press, 1961)..£15
NO. 12 (issued without dustjacket) (Longacre Press, 1962) £12
NO. 13 (issued without dustjacket) (Longacre Press, 1963) £12
NO. 14 (issued without dustjacket) (Longacre Press, 1964) £12
NO. 15 (issued without dustjacket) (Longacre Press, 1965) £12
NO. 16 (issued without dustjacket) (Longacre Press, 1966) £12
NO. 17 (issued without dustjacket) (Longacre Press, 1967) £12
NO. 18 (issued without dustjacket) (Longacre Press, 1968) £12
Later Issues (issued without dustjackets)..each £12

Others

RIDERS OF THE RANGE ANNUAL (Juvenille Productions, 1951-1956) ....each £10
RIDERS OF THE RANGE ANNUAL (Hulton Press, 1957-60) ....each £10
RIDERS OF THE RANGE ANNUAL (Hulton Press, 1961-62) ....each £20
JEFF ARNOLD ON THE BOZEMAN TRAIL (issued without dustjacket) (Juvenille Productions, [c1962]) £25
EAGLE BOOK OF MAGIC (press-out) (1950s) £150
THE EAGLE BOOK OF ADVENTURE STORIES (includes W.E. Johns' story 'Strange Freight') (1950)....................£25
EAGLE BOOK OF RECORDS AND CHAMPIONS (1951)..£15
P.C.49 EAGLE STRIP CARTOON BOOK (Preview Publications, 1953)..£20
P.C.49 EAGLE STRIP CARTOON BOOK NO. 2 (Preview Publications, 1954) £20
EAGLE SPECIAL INVESTIGATOR by Max Hastings (Joseph, 1953)..£12
EAGLE BOOK OF TRAINS (1953) £10
EAGLE BOOK OF AIRCRAFT (1953) £10
EAGLE SPORTS ANNUAL NO. 1 (1953)...£12
ADVENTURE CALLING by Max Hastings (novel) (1953)...£10
EAGLE SPORTS ANNUAL NO. 2 (1954)...£12
EAGLE SPORTS ANNUAL NO. 3-Onwards ....each £12
SERGEANT LUCK'S SECRET MISSION (novel) (1956) £15
THE BADEN POWELL STORY (1957) £65
I WANT TO BE...: An Eagle Book of Careers (Hulton Press, 1957)..£15
EAGLE BOOK OF TRAINS (Hulton Press, 1957) £10
THE HAPPY WARRIOR (1958)..£35
LUCK OF THE LEGION'S FOREIGN ADVENTURE (novel) (1958) £20
EAGLE BOOK OF HOBBIES (Hulton Press, 1958) £15
JACK O'LANTERN AND THE FIGHTING COCK (novel) (1958)..£10
EAGLE BOOK OF CARS AND MOTOR SPORTS (Hulton Press, 1958) £15
EAGLE BOOK OF SHIPS AND BOATS (Hulton Press, 1959)..£15
EAGLE BOOK OF RECORDS AND CHAMPIONS (Hulton Press, 1959)..£25
EAGLE BOOK OF MODEL AIRCRAFT by Ray Malmstrom (Hulton Press, 1959) £20
BEST OF EAGLE ANNUAL 1951-59 ....£10
EAGLE BOOK OF MODEL BOATS by Ray Malmstrom (Longacre Press, 1960) £20
EAGLE BOOK OF TRAINS (Longacre Press, 1960)..£15
EAGLE BOOK OF SPACECRAFT MODELS by Ray Malmstrom (Longacre Press, 1960)................................£20
EAGLE BOOK OF POLICE AND DETECTION by R.M. Harrison (Longacre Press, 1960)................................£20
EAGLE BOOK OF MODEL CARS by Ray Malmstrom (Longacre Press, 1961)..£20

*The rare first **Riders of the Range** Eagle annual, inspired by the popular radio serial of the same name.*

Black Hunting Whip (1950) is one of eleven titles in Monica Edwards' popular 'Punchbowl Farm' series, worth £40 today.

EAGLE BOOK OF THE WEST by Charles Chilton (Longacre Press, 1961)..£10
EAGLE BOOK OF HOW IT WORKS (Longacre Press, 1962)..£10
EAGLE BOOK OF FIGHTING SERVICES (Longacre Press, 1962)..£15
EAGLE FOOTBALL ANNUAL 1962 ....£5
EAGLE FOOTBALL ANNUAL 1963 ....£5
EAGLE BOOK OF AMAZING STORIES (1974)...£5
EAGLE: THE UNIVERSE (Eagle/Girl Book)..£18
EAGLE EXPLORING THE ARTS (Eagle/Girl Book) £13
EAGLE NEW BOOK OF TRAINS £8
EAGLE BOOK OF MODERN WONDERS £5
EAGLE BOOK OF BALSA MODELS £15
EAGLE BOOK OF ROCKS AND SPACE TRAVEL £20
EAGLE BOOK OF NEW AIRCRAFT £10
EAGLE CLASSIC — ADVENTURES OF PC 49 (paperback) (Hawk)...£8
EAGLE CLASSIC — HARRIS TWEED (paperback) (Hawk)...£8
EAGLE CLASSIC — FRASER OF AFRICA (paperback) (Hawk) £8
EAGLE CLASSIC — RIDERS OF THE RANGE (paperback) (Hawk)...£8
EAGLE CORGI CLASSICS (limited edition) £25

EDWARDS, Monica

British author. Born: Belper, Derbyshire, in 1912. Well-known for her 'Romney Marsh' and 'Punchbowl Farm' series based on real people and places. Died: 1998

Prices are for books in Very Good condition with dustjackets.

'Punchbowl Farm' Books

NO MISTAKING CORKER (Collins, 1947)..£50
BLACK HUNTING WHIP (Collins, 1950)...£40
PUNCHBOWL MIDNIGHT (Collins, 1951)..£40
SPIRIT OF PUNCHBOWL FARM (Collins, 1952) £45
THE WANDERER (Collins, 1953)..£40
PUNCHBOWL HARVEST (Collins, 1954) £45
FRENCHMAN'S SECRET (Collins, 1956)...£40

THE COWNAPPERS (Collins, 1958)..£40
THE OUTSIDER (Collins, 1961) £35
FIRE IN THE PUNCHBOWL (Collins, 1965) £36
THE WILD ONE (Collins, 1967)...£45

'Romney Marsh' Books
WISH FOR A PONY (Collins, 1947) £35
THE SUMMER OF THE GREAT SECRET (Collins, 1948) £35
THE MIDNIGHT HORSE (Collins, 1949) £45
THE WHITE RIDERS (Collins, 1950)..£45
CARGO OF HORSES (Collins, 1951) £35
HIDDEN IN A DREAM (Collins, 1952) £35
STORM AHEAD (Collins, 1953) £45
NO ENTRY (Collins, 1954)..£40
THE NIGHTBIRD (Collins, 1955)..£45
OPERATION SEABIRD (Collins, 1957)..£40
STRANGERS TO THE MARSH (Collins, 1957) £35
NO GOING BACK (Collins, 1960) £35
THE HOODWINKER (Collins, 1962) £35
DOLPHIN SUMMER (Collins, 1963)..£35
A WIND IS BLOWING (Collins, 1969)...£45

Others
JOAN GOES FARMING ('Career books for girls') (The Bodley Head, 1954)..£25
RENNIE GOES RIDING ('Career books for girls') (The Bodley Head, 1956) £25
KILLER DOG (Collins, 1959)...£25
UNDER THE ROSE (Collins, 1968)...£25

ELIOT, T.S.
American poet. Born: Thomas Stearns Eliot in Missouri, U.S., in 1888. Eliot's only children's work, *Old Possum's Book of Practical Cats*, takes its title from the nickname given to him by Ezra Pound. A sequence of light verses, it was initially issued in a dustjacket designed by the poet himself, although a new edition with illustrations by Nicolas Bentley followed soon after. The poems provided the inspiration for Andrew Lloyd Webber's hit musical, *Cats* (1981). Died: 1965.

Prices are for books in Very Good condition with dustjackets.

OLD POSSUM'S BOOK OF PRACTICAL CATS (Faber, 1939)..£750
OLD POSSUM'S BOOK OF PRACTICAL CATS (illustrated by Nicolas Bentley) (Faber, 1940).....................£200
GROWLTIGER'S LAST STAND and Other Poems (illustrated by Errol Le Cain) (Faber, 1986).....................£35
MR MISTOFFELEES (illustrated by Errol Le Cain) (Faber, 1990) £35

EMETT, Rowland
British illustrator. Born: London, 1906. Studied at the Birmingham School of Arts and Crafts, subsequently working as a commercial artist before submitting his first illustration to *Punch* in 1939. Best known for his drawings of old-fashioned railway locomotives and other fantastic machines, but has also illustrated two books by Walter de la Mare. Awarded an OBE in 1978. Died: 1990.

Prices are for books in Very Good condition with dustjackets.

PEACOCK PIE by Walter De La Mare (Faber, 1941) £30
BELLS & GRASS: A Book of Rhymes by Walter De La Mare (Faber, 1941)..£30
ANTHONY & ANTIMACASSAR by Mary Emett (Faber, [1943])..£40
THE EMETT FESTIVAL RAILWAY (paperback) (Puffin: 'Cut-Out Book' No. 7, 1951) £40
NELLIE COME HOME (Faber, 1952)..£35

ESTES, Eleanor
American author. Born: Connecticut, 1906. Still popular for her 'Moffat' books. Awarded the Newbery Medal for *Ginger Pye* in 1952. Died: 1988.

Prices are for books in Very Good condition with dustjackets where applicable.

THE MOFFATS (illustrated by Louis Slobodkin) (Harcourt Brace, US, 1941)...£50
THE MOFFATS (illustrated by Louis Slobodkin) (The Bodley Head, 1959) £30
THE MIDDLE MOFFAT (illustrated by Louis Slobodkin) (Harcourt Brace, US, 1942) £50
THE MIDDLE MOFFAT (illustrated by Louis Slobodkin) (The Bodley Head, 1960).....................................£25
RUFUS M (illustrated by Louis Slobodkin) (Harcourt Brace, US, 1943)..£30
RUFUS M (illustrated by Louis Slobodkin) (The Bodley Head, 1960) £20
THE SUN AND THE WIND AND MR TODD (illustrated by Louis Slobodkin) (Harcourt Brace, US, 1943).........£25
THE SLEEPING GIANT AND OTHER STORIES (illustrated by Eleanor Estes) (Harcourt Brace, US, 1948)............£20
GINGER PYE (illustrated by the author) (Harcourt Brace, US, 1951)...£20
GINGER PYE (illustrated by the author) (The Bodley Head, 1961) £20

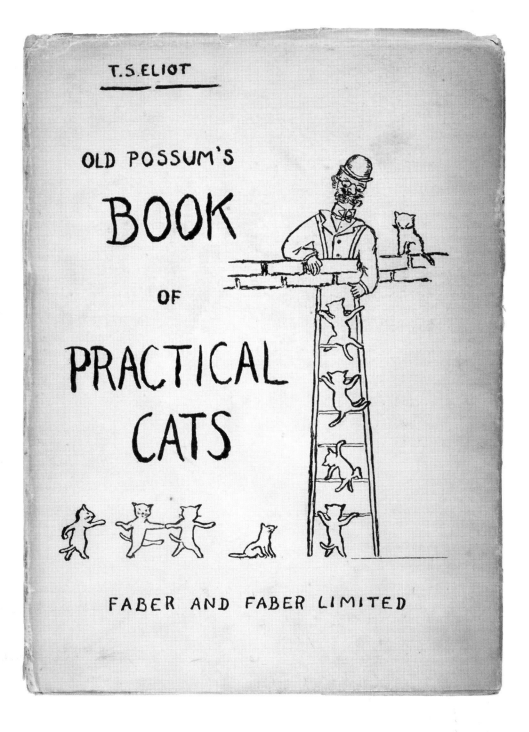

The original dustjacket from T.S. Eliot's only children's book, issued by Faber & Faber in 1939.

A LITTLE OVEN (illustrated by the author) (Harcourt Brace, US, 1955) £20
PINKY PYE (illustrated by Edward Ardizzone) (Harcourt Brace, US, 1958) £30
PINKY PYE (illustrated by Edward Ardizzone) (Constable, 1959) £30
THE WITCH FAMILY (illustrated by Edward Ardizzone) (Harcourt Brace, US, 1960) £35
THE WITCH FAMILY (illustrated by Edward Ardizzone) (Constable, 1962)...£35
THE ALLEY (illustrated by Edward Ardizzone) (Harcourt Brace, US, 1964)...£25
MIRANDA THE GREAT (illustrated by Edward Ardizzone) (Harcourt Brace, US, 1967)...£20
THE TUNNEL OF HUGSY GOODE (illustrated by Edward Ardizzone) (Harcourt Brace, US, 1972) £15
THE COAT-HANGER CHRISTMAS TREE (illustrated by Susanne Suba) (Atheneum, US, 1973)..................................£20
THE COAT-HANGER CHRISTMAS TREE (illustrated by Susanne Suba) (OUP, 1976)...£20
THE LOST UMBRELLA OF KIM CHU (illustrated by Jacqueline Ayer) (Atheneum, US, 1978) £15
THE MOFFAT MUSEUM (Harcourt Brace, US, 1983)..£10
THE CURIOUS ADVENTURES OF JIMMY MCGEE (illustrated by John O'Brien) (Harcourt Brace, US, 1987) £10

Play
THE LOLLIPOP PRINCESS: A PLAY FOR PAPER DOLLS (illustrated by the author) (Harcourt Brace,US, 1969)...........£15

EWING, Juliana Horatia
British author. Born: Juliana Horatia Gatty in Yorkshire in 1841. Her mother, Margaret Gatty, was a writer of children's stories and, in 1866, founded *Aunt Judy's Magazine*, to which her daughter became a frequent contributor. Her first collection of children's stories had appeared in 1862, and was followed by many more books, notably *The Brownies and Other Tales* (1870) — which gave its name to the junior Girl Guides — *Jan of the Windmill* (1876) and *Jackanapes* (1884). Among the artists who illustrated her works were George Cruikshank and Randolph Caldecott. Kipling and E. Nesbit both admired her writing. Died: 1885.

Prices are for books in Very Good condition.

MELCHIOR'S DREAM and Other Tales by J.H.Gatty (Bell & Daldy, 1862) £40
MRS OVERTHEWAY'S REMEMBRANCES (illustrated by J.A. Pasquier and Joseph Wolf) (Bell & Daldy, 1869)...........£40
THE BROWNIES and Other Tales (illustrated by George Cruikshank) (Bell & Daldy, 1870) £45
THE BROWNIES and Other Stories (illustrated by E.H. Shepard) (Dent: 'Illustrated Children's Classics' series, 1954)...........£50
A FLAT IRON FOR A FARTHING, or Some Passages in the Life of an Only Son (Bell & Daldy, 1873)..........................£30
LOB LIE-BY-THE-FIRE, or The Luck of Lingborough and Other Tales (illustrated by George Cruikshank) (Bell, 1874) £35
LOB LIE-BY-THE-FIRE (illustrated by Randolph Caldecott) (SPCK, [1885])..£20
SIX TO SIXTEEN: A Story For Girls (illustrated by Mrs W. Allingham) (Bell, 1876 [1875]) £25
JAN OF THE WINDMILL: A Story of the Plains (Bell, 1876)...£25
A GREAT EMERGENCY and Other Tales (Bell, 1877)...£25
WE AND THE WORLD: A Book for Boys (Bell, 1881 [1880])...£25
BROTHERS OF PITY and Other Tales of Beasts and Men (SPCK, [1882]) £25
OLD-FASHIONED FAIRY TALES (SPCK, [1882]) £50
BLUE AND RED, or The Discontented Lobster (verse; illustrated by R. André) (SPCK, [1883])...................................£50
MASTER FRITZ (illustrated by R. André) (SPCK, [1883])...£40
OUR GARDEN (verse; illustrated by R. André) (SPCK, [1883])..£40
A SOLDIER'S CHILDREN (illustrated by R. André) (SPCK, 1883) £40
A SWEET LITTLE DEAR (illustrated by R. André) (SPCK, [1883]) £30
THREE LITTLE NEST-BIRDS (illustrated by R. André) (SPCK, [1883])...£30
A WEEK SPENT IN A GLASS POND BY THE GREAT WATER BEETLE (illustrated by R. André and others)
    (Wells Gardner, [1883]) £30
THE DOLLS' WASH (verse; illustrated by R. André) (SPCK, [1883]) £30
A SOLDIER'S CHILDREN and Five Other Tales in Verse (omnibus; illustrated by R. André) (SPCK, [1883]) £40
DOLLS' HOUSEKEEPING (illustrated by R. André) (SPCK, [1884])...£30
DADDY DARWIN'S DOVECOT: A Country Tale (illustrated by Randolph Caldecott) (SPCK, [1884])...........................£20
JACKANAPES (illustrated by Randolph Caldecott) (SPCK, 1884 [1883])..£20
JACKANAPES (contains 'Daddy Darwin's Dovecot' and 'Lob Lie-By-The-Fire'; illustrated by Randolph Caldecott)
    (SPCK, [1892]) £25
JACKANAPES (illustrated by Tasha Tudor) (OUP, U.S., 1948)...£50
THE BLUE BELLS ON THE LEA (illustrated by R. André) (SPCK, [1884])..£50
LITTLE BOYS AND WOODEN HORSES (illustrated by R. André) (SPCK, [1884])...£30
PAPA POODLE AND OTHER PETS (verse; illustrated by R. André) (SPCK, [1884])...£25
TONGUES IN TREES (illustrated by R. André) (SPCK, [1884])..£25
'TOUCH HIM IF YOU DARE': A Tale of the Hedge (illustrated by R. André) (SPCK, [1884])......................................£25
THE STORY OF A SHORT LIFE (SPCK, [1885])..£10
POEMS OF CHILD LIFE AND COUNTRY LIFE (six books; illustrated by R. André; wraps) (SPCK, 1885).....................the set £60
MARY'S MEADOW, and LETTERS FROM A LITTLE GARDEN. Edited by H.K.F. Gatty (SPCK, [1886]).......................£15
DANDELION CLOCKS and Other Tales (illustrated by Gordon Browne and others) (SPCK, [1887]).............................£15
THE PEACE-EGG and A CHRISTMAS MUMMING PLAY (illustrated by Gordon Browne) (SPCK, [1887]) £15
SNAP-DRAGONS. Edited by H.K.F. Gatty (contains 'A Tale of Christmas Eve', 'And Old Father Christmas' and
    'An Old Fashioned Tale of the Young Days of a Grumpy Old God-Father'; illustrated by Gordon Browne)
    (SPCK, [1888]) £20
MOTHER'S BIRTHDAY REVIEW and Seven Other Tales in Verse (omnibus; illustrated by R. André; boards)
    (SPCK, 1888) £40

F

FALKNER, John Meade
British author. Born: 1858. A bibliophile and scholar, Falkner wrote two mystery stories — *The Lost Stradivarius* (1895) and *The Nebuly Coat* (1903) — as well as the classic children's novel, *Moonfleet* (1898). Died: 1932.
Price is for books in Very Good condition.
MOONFLEET (Arnold, 1898)..£250

FARJEON, Eleanor
British author. Born: 1881. Daughter of the novelist, B.L. Farjeon. Received virtually no formal education, but was encouraged to write from an early age. Produced several volumes of verse for children, notably *Nursery Rhymes of London Town* (1916), as well as fairy tales (*Martin Pippin in the Apple Orchard*, 1921), stories and plays. Her volume of stories, *The Little Bookroom*, won her the Carnegie Medal and the Hans Christian Andersen International Medal. She was a friend of Edward Thomas and Walter de la Mare. Died: 1965.
Prices are for books in Very Good condition (with dustjackets after 1931).
PAN-WORSHIP and Other Poems (Elkin Mathews, 1908)...£20
DREAM-SONGS FOR THE BELOVED (Orpheus Press, 1911) £20
TREES (Fellowship Books, 1913)..£20
NURSERY RHYMES OF LONDON TOWN (illustrated by Macdonald Gill) (Duckworth, 1916) £90
MORE NURSERY RHYMES OF LONDON TOWN (illustrated by Macdonald Gill) (Duckworth, 1917)...£90
ALL THE WAY TO ALFRISTON (verse; illustrated by Robin Guthrie) (Morland Press, 1918)...........£80
SONNETS AND POEMS (Blackwell, 1918)..£20
SINGING GAMES FOR CHILDREN (illustrated by J. Littlejohns) (Dent, [1919]) £70
A FIRST CHAPBOOK OF ROUNDS (verse; illustrated by John Garside; issued without dustjacket)
    (Dent, 1919)...£45
A SECOND CHAPBOOK OF ROUNDS (verse; illustrated by John Garside; issued without dustjacket)
    (Dent, 1919)...£35
GYPSY AND GINGER (Dent, 1920)...£25
MARTIN PIPPIN IN THE APPLE-ORCHARD (Collins, 1921)..£35
MARTIN PIPPIN IN THE APPLE-ORCHARD (illustrated by C.E. Brock) (Collins, 1925) £50
TUNES OF A PENNY PIPER (illustrated by John Aveten) (Selwyn & Blount, 1922).......................£25
SONGS FOR MUSIC AND LYRICAL POEMS (illustrated by John Aveten) (Selwyn & Blount, 1922) ...£25
THE SOUL OF KOL NIKON (Collins, [1923])..£30
ALL THE YEAR ROUND (verse) (Collins, [1923]) £25
THE COUNTRY CHILD'S ALPHABET (verse; illustrated by William Michael Rothenstein)
    (Poetry Bookshop, 1924)...£130
THE TOWN CHILD'S ALPHABET (illustrated by David Jones) (Poetry Bookshop, 1924) £130
MIGHTY MEN: Achilles to Julius Caesar (non-fiction) (Blackwell, 1924)......................................£20
MIGHTY MEN: Beowulf to Harold (non-fiction) (Blackwell, 1925)..£20
MIGHTY MEN (omnibus; contains both volumes) (Blackwell, 1928)..£25
SONGS FROM 'PUNCH' FOR CHILDREN (verse; card covers) (Saville, 1925) £35
YOUNG FOLK AND OLD (High House Press, 1925) £25
TOM COBBLE (Blackwell, [1925])..£35
FAITHFUL JENNY DOVE and Other Tales (Collins, [1925])..£25
NUTS AND MAY: A Medley for Children (illustrated by Rosalind Thorneycroft) (Collins, [1926]) ...£90
JOAN'S DOOR (illustrated by Will Townsend) (Collins, [1926])...£30
SINGING GAMES FROM ARCADY (verse) (Blackwell, 1926)..£25
THE WONDERFUL KNIGHT (illustrated by Doris Pailthorpe) (Blackwell, [1927])............................£25
THE KING'S BARN, or Joan's Tale (Collins, [1927])..£25
THE MILL OF DREAMS, or Jennifer's Tale (Collins, [1927])...£25
YOUNG GERARD, or Joyce's Tale (Collins, [1927]) £25
COME CHRISTMAS (illustrated by Molly McArthur) (Collins, 1927)..£25
A BAD DAY FOR MARTHA (illustrated by Eugine Richards) (Blackwell, [1928]) £25
KALEIDOSCOPE (Collins, [1928]) £20
KALEIDOSCOPE (illustrated by Edward Ardizzone) (OUP, 1963)..£45
AN ALPHABET OF MAGIC (illustrated by Margaret W. Tarrant) (Medici Society, 1928) £80
OPEN WINKINS, or Jessica's Tale (Collins, 1928)..£35
A COLLECTION OF POEMS (Collins, [1929]) £35
THE PERFECT ZOO (Harrap, 1929)..£25
THE KING'S DAUGHTER CRIES FOR THE MOON (illustrated by May Smith)
    (Blackwell, [1929])..£30
THE TALE OF TOM TIDDLER (illustrated by Norman Tealby) (Collins, 1929)..................................£50
WESTWOODS (illustrated by May Smith) (Blackwell, 1930)..£25
TALES FROM CHAUCER: The Canterbury Tales Done into Prose by Eleanor Farjeon
    (illustrated by W. Russell Flint) (Medici Society, 1930) £120

FARJEON, Eleanor

THE OLD NURSE'S STOCKING BASKET (illustrated by E. Herbert Whydale)
(University of London, [1931]) £30
THE OLD NURSE'S STOCKING BASKET (illustrated by Edward Ardizzone) (OUP, 1965).................. £35
LADYBROOK (Collins, 1931).. £35
PERKIN THE PEDLAR (illustrated by Clare Leighton) (Faber, 1932).. £75
KATY KRUSE AT THE SEASIDE, or The Deserted Islanders (Harrap, 1932) £35
KINGS AND QUEENS. With Herbert Farjeon (illustrated by Rosalind Thorneycroft) (Gollancz, 1932).... £80
THE FAIR OF ST. JAMES: A Fantasia (Faber, 1932) £40
AMELIARANNE'S PRIZE PACKET (illustrated by S.B. Pearse) (Harrap, 1933) £80
PANNYCHIS (illustrated by Clare Leighton; limited to 200 copies) (High House Press, 1933) £90
HEROES AND HEROINES (with Herbert Farjeon; illustrated by Rosalind Thorneycroft)
(Gollancz, 1933) £45
OVER THE GARDEN WALL (illustrated by Gwen Raverat) (Faber, 1933) £75
AMELIARANNE'S WASHING DAY (illustrated by S.B. Pearse) (Harrap, 1934) £75
ITALIAN PEEPSHOW and Other Stories (illustrated by Rosalind Thorneycroft) (Blackwell, 1934) £25
ITALIAN PEEPSHOW and Other Stories (illustrated by Edward Ardizzone) (OUP, 1960) £35
JIM AT THE CORNER and Other Stories (illustrated by Irene Mountfort) (Blackwell, 1934)................. £25
JIM AT THE CORNER and Other Stories (illustrated by Edward Ardizzone) (OUP, 1958).................... £45
THE OLD SAILOR'S YARN BOX (illustrated by Irene Mountfort) (Stokes, 1934).................................. £20
THE CLUMBER PUP (illustrated by Irene Mountfort) (Blackwell, [1934])... £40
AND I DANCE MINE OWN CHILD (illustrated by Irene Mountfort) (Blackwell, [1935]).......................... £25
A NURSERY IN THE NINETIES (Gollancz, 1935) £25
JIM AND THE PIRATES (illustrated by Richard Naish) (Blackwell, [1936]).. £25
TEN SAINTS (non-fiction; illustrated by Helen Sewell) (OUP, 1936)... £25
LECTOR READINGS (illustrated by Ruth Westcott) (Nelson, 1936) £12
HUMMING BIRD (Joseph, 1936)... £20
MARTIN PIPPIN IN THE DAISY-FIELD (illustrated by Isobel and John Morton-Sale)
(Joseph, 1937) £40
THE WONDERS OF HERODOTUS (illustrated by Edmund Nelson) (Nelson, 1937)............................. £12
PALADINS IN SPAIN (illustrated by Katharine Tozer) (Nelson, 1937)... £20
SING FOR YOUR SUPPER (illustrated by Isobel and John Morton-Sale) (Joseph, 1938) £25
SONGS OF KINGS AND QUEENS (with Herbert Farjeon) (Arnold, 1938)... £20
ONE FOOT IN FAIRYLAND: Sixteen Tales (illustrated by Robert Lawson) (Joseph, 1938).................. £35
GRANNIE GRAY: Children's Plays and Games with Music and Without (illustrated by J. Jefferson Farjeon)
(Dent, 1939)... £25
GRANNIE GRAY: Children's Plays and Games with Music and Without (illustrated by Peggy Fortnum)
(OUP, 1956).. £25
A SUSSEX ALPHABET (illustrated by Sheila M Thompson) (Pear Tree Press, 1939)......................... £200
THE NEW BOOK OF DAYS (illustrated by Philip Gough and M.W. Hawes) (OUP, 1941) £35
BRAVE OLD WOMAN (Joseph, 1941).. £35
MAGIC CASEMENTS (Allen & Unwin, 1941).. £25
CHERRYSTONES (illustrated by Isobel and John Morton-Sale) (Joseph, 1942) £30
GOLDEN CONEY (Joseph, [1943])... £25
THE FAIR VENETIAN (Joseph, 1943).. £25
AMELIARANNE GIVES A CONCERT (illustrated by S.B. Pearse) (Harrap, 1944)................................ £70
THE MULBERRY BUSH (illustrated by Isobel and John Morton-Sale) (Joseph, 1945) £25
A PRAYER FOR LITTLE THINGS (Houghton Mifflin, U.S., 1945).. £30
DARK WORLD OF ANIMALS (illustrated by T. Stoney) (Sylvan Press, 1945) £25
ARIADNE AND THE BULL (Joseph, 1945).. £25
THE GLASS SLIPPER (with Herbert Farjeon; play; illustrated by Hugh Stevens) (Wingate 1946) £20
THE GLASS SLIPPER (illustrated by E.H. Shepard) (OUP, 1955).. £35
FIRST AND SECOND LOVE (verse) (Joseph, 1947) £20
LOVE AFFAIR (Joseph, 1947).. £20
THE STARRY FLOOR (illustrated by Isobel and John Morton-Sale) (Joseph, 1949) £30
MRS MALONE (illustrated by David Knight) (Joseph, 1950) £30
MRS MALONE (illustrated by Edward Ardizzone) (OUP, 1962).. £45
SILVER SAND AND SNOW (Joseph, 1951) £30
THE SILVER CURLEW: A Fairy Tale (play; wraps) (Samuel French, [1953]) £20
THE SILVER CURLEW: A Fairy Tale (illustrated by E.H. Shepard) (OUP, 1953)................................... £40
THE LITTLE BOOKROOM (illustrated by Edward Ardizzone) (OUP, 1955).. £50
THE CHILDREN'S BELLS: A Selection of Poems (illustrated by Peggy Fortnum) (OUP, 1957)........... £30
A PUFFIN QUARTET OF POETS: Eleanor Farjeon, James Reeves, E.V. Rieu and Ian Seraillier
(selected with introductory notes by Eleanor Graham; illustrated by Diana Bloomfield; paperback)
(Puffin, 1958) £7
ELEANOR FARJEON'S BOOK: Stories, Verses, Plays (illustrated by Edward Ardizzone; paperback)
(Puffin, 1960) £20
MORNING HAS BROKEN (verse; illustrated by Gordon Stowell) (Mowbray, 1981) £12
INVITATION TO A MOUSE and Other Poems. Chosen by Annabel Farjeon (illustrated by Antony Maitland)
(Pelham, 1981) £12
THE LITTLE DRESSMAKER (illustrated by Charles Front) (Julia MacRae, 1984)................................ £12

FARRAR, F.W.

British author. Born: Frederick William Farrar in India in 1831. Educated at Kings William's College and London and Cambridge Universities, subsequently becoming a Fellow of Trinity College. Taught at Harrow and was appointed headmaster of Marlborough College, before becoming a Canon of Westminster and finally Dean of Canterbury. Wrote a handful of boys' stories, of which the best known is *Eric, or Little by Little* (1858). Also produced a large number of works on theology, education and other subjects. Died: 1903.

Prices are for books in Very Good condition.

ERIC, or Little By Little: A Tale of Roslyn School (A. & C. Black, 1858)...£400
ERIC, or Little By Little: A Tale of Roslyn School (illustrated by Gordon Browne) (A. & C. Black, 1894) £30
ST WINIFRED'S (anonymous) (A. & C. Black, 1862) £200
ST WINIFRED'S, or The World of School (illustrated by Gordon Browne)
      (A. & C. Black, 1905)...£30

FARROW, G.E.

British author. Born: George Edward Farrow in 1862. Wrote a number of nonsense books in the style of Edward Lear, of which the best known is *The Wallypug of Why* (1895). Died: 1920.

Prices are for books in Very Good condition.

THE WALLYPUG OF WHY (illustrated by Harry Furniss; vignettes by Dorothy Furniss)
      (Hutchinson, [1895])...£140
THE KING'S GARDENS: An Allegory (illustrated by A.L. Bowley) (Hutchinson, 1896)...............................£50
THE MISSING PRINCE (illustrated by Harry Furniss; vignettes by Dorothy Furniss) (Hutchinson, 1896) £60
THE WALLYPUG IN LONDON (illustrated by Alan Wright) (Methuen, 1898 [1897]).................................£90
ADVENTURES IN WALLYPUG-LAND (illustrated by Alan Wright) (Methuen, 1898)................................£90
THE LITTLE PANJANDRUM'S DODO (illustrated by Alan Wright) (Skeffington, 1899) £80
THE MANDARIN'S KITE, or Little Tsu-Foo and Another Boy (illustrated by Alan Wright)
      (Skeffington,1900)..£40
BAKER MINOR AND THE DRAGON (illustrated by Alan Wright) (Pearson, 1902 [1901]).........................£70
THE NEW PANJANDRUM (illustrated by Alan Wright) (Pearson, 1902 [1901]).................................£60
AN A.B.C. OF EVERY-DAY PEOPLE (illustrated by John Hassall) (Dean, [1902]).............................£175
IN SEARCH OF THE WALLYPUG (illustrated by Alan Wright) (Pearson, 1903 [1902]).........................£80
ABSURD DITTIES (illustrated by John Hassall) (Routledge, 1903)...£70
PROFESSOR PHILANDERPAN (Pearson, 1904 [1903]) £60
ALL ABOUT THE WALLY-PUG (Raphael Tuck [printed in Germany], [1904]).................................£70
THE CINEMATOGRAPH TRAIN and Other Stories (illustrated by Alan Wright) (Johnson, 1904)..................£80
PIXIE PICKLES: The Adventures of Pixene and Pixette in their Woodland Haunts (illustrated by H.B. Neilson)
      (Skeffington, [1904])..£80
WALLYPUG TALES (illustrated) (Raphael Tuck [printed in Germany], [1904])...............................£120
ROUND THE WORLD A.B.C. (verse; illustrated by John Hassall) (Nister [printed in Germany], [1904])...........£120
THE WALLYPUG BIRTHDAY BOOK (illustrated by Alan Wright) (Routledge, 1904).............................£60
THE WALLYPUG IN FOGLAND (illustrated by Alan Wright) (Pearson, 1904) £80
LOVELY MAN (Being the Views of Mistress A. Grosspatch) (cover illustration by John Hassall)
      (Skeffington, 1904)..£90
RUFF AND READY: The Fairy Guide by May Byron and G.E. Farrow (illustrated by John Hassall)
      (Cooke, [1905])...£100
THE MYSTERIOUS 'MR PUNCH': A School Story (Christian Knowledge Society, [1905]) £50
THE WALLYPUG BOOK (illustrated by Harry Furniss) (Treherne, [1905])...................................£60
THE WALLYPUG IN THE MOON, or His Badjesty (illustrated by Alan Wright) (Pearson, 1905) £60
THE ADVENTURES OF JI (illustrated by G.C. Tresidder) (Partridge, [1906]).............................£50
ESSAYS IN BACON: An Autograph Book (Treherne, [1906])...£50
THE ESCAPE OF THE MULLINGONG: A Zoological Nightmare (illustrated by Gordon Browne)
      (Blackie, 1907 [1906])..£50
THE ADVENTURES OF A DODO (illustrated by Willy Pogány) (Unwin, [1907])................................£75
THE DWINDLEBERRY ZOO (illustrated by Gordon Browne) (Blackie, 1909 [1908])...........................£75
A MYSTERIOUS VOYAGE, or The Adventures of a Dodo (illustrated by K.M. Roberts) (Partridge, [1910])...........£75
THE MYSTERIOUS SHIN SHIRA (Hodder & Stoughton, [1915])...£40
ZOO BABIES (illustrated by Cecil Aldin) (Frowde/Hodder & Stoughton, 1913)..............................£150
DON'T TELL (illustrated by John Hassall) (Cooke, no date)...£50
TEN LITTLE JAPPY CHAPS (illustrated by John Hassall) (Treherne: 'Stump Books' series, no date)...........£50

'FATHER TUCK'S' ANNUALS

Popular series of annuals published by Raphael Tuck between 1898 (dated 1899) and 1935. Those from the 1930s include 'Come to Life Pictures', full-colour panoramas which stand up when the books are opened. The annuals were great favourites of the Royal Family.

Prices are for annuals in Very Good condition.

FATHER TUCK'S ANNUAL (Raphael Tuck, [1899-1931]).. each £35
TUCK'S ANNUAL (Raphael Tuck, [1932-1935]).. each £30
FATHER TUCK'S ANNUAL (with 'pop-up' panoramics; several issued during 1930s) .... each £60

This first edition of G.E. Farrow's excellent Carroll-inspired children's fantasy, **The Wallypug of Why** *(1895).*

'FELIX' ANNUALS

Felix the Cat was the creation of the Pat Sullivan Studio, and was the first animated film character to win a worldwide audience. Launched in America in 1919, he was particularly popular in Britain, appearing in strip form in the *Pearson's Weekly* and the *Illustrated Sunday Herald* and inspiring a series of annuals and other spin-offs.

Prices are for annuals in Very Good condition.

FELIX ANNUAL 1923	£120
FELIX ANNUAL 1924-30	each £100
THE FELIX ANNUAL: Picture Stories of the Famous Film Cat (London, [1926])	£80
FELIX THE CAT ANNUAL 1956 (World Distributors)	£60
FELIX THE CAT ANNUAL (London, [1961])	£40
FELIX THE CAT ANNUAL (Purnell, 1962)	£40

FENN, George Manville

British author. Born in London in 1831. In addition to over sixty adult novels, his even greater number of boys' adventure stories were enormously popular. He was a good friend and biographer of G.A. Henty. Died: 1909.

Prices are for books in Very Good condition in the original binding.

Boys' fiction

HOLLOWDELL GRANGE (Routledge, 1866)	£250
FEATHERLAND; or, How the Birds Lived at Greenlawn (Griffith & Farran, 1866)	£250
OFF TO THE WILDS (Sampson Low, 1881)	£100
IN THE KING'S NAME (Blackie, [1882])	£100
NAT THE NATURALIST (Blackie, 1883 [1882])	£100
DUTCH THE DIVER (Cassell, [1883])	£60
MIDDY AND ENSIGN (Griffith & Farran, 1883)	£100
THE GOLDEN MAGNET (Blackie, 1884 [1883])	£100
THE SILVER CANON (Sampson Low, 1884)	£100
BUNYIP LAND (Blackie, 1885 [1884])	£100
MENHARDOC (Blackie, 1885 [1884])	£100
A TERRIBLE COWARD, AND SON PHILIP (Blackie, [1885])	£60
BROWNSMITH'S BOY (Blackie, 1886 [1885])	£100
PATIENCE WINS (Blackie, 1886 [1885])	£100
DEVON BOYS (Blackie, 1887 [1886])	£100
YUSSUF THE GUIDE (Blackie, 1887 [1886])	£100
IN MARINE ARMOUR (paperback) (S.P.C.K.: 'Penny Library of Fiction' series, [1887])	£25
LORD JOHN (paperback) (S.P.C.K.: 'Penny Library of Fiction' series, [1887])	£25
DICK O' THE FENS (Blackie, 1888 [1887])	£75
MOTHER CAREY'S CHICKEN (Blackie, 1888 [1887])	£75
QUICKSILVER (Blackie, 1889 [1888])	£50
CROWN AND SCEPTRE (S.P.C.K., [1889])	£75
STAUNCH (paperback) (S.P.C.K.: 'Penny Library of Fiction' series, [1889])	£35
THREE BOYS (Griffith & Farran, [1889])	£60
CUTLASS AND CUDGEL (Griffith & Farran, [1890])	£60
THE CRYSTAL HUNTERS (Partridge, [1890])	£75
MASS' GEORGE (S.P.C.K., [1890])	£100
MUTINY OF THE 'HELEN GRAY' (paperback) (S.P.C.K.: 'Penny Library of Fiction' series, [1890])	£35
NOLENS VOLENS (Partridge, [1890])	£60
SYD BELTON (Methuen, 1891)	£60
BURR JUNIOR: HIS STRUGGLES AND STUDIES AT OLD BROWNE'S SCHOOL (Griffith & Farran, [1891])	£100
THE RAJAH OF DAH (Chambers, 1891)	£60
TO THE WEST (S.P.C.K., 1891)	£60
THE DINGO BOYS (Chambers, 1892)	£60
THE WEATHERCOCK (Griffith & Farran, 1892)	£60
GIL THE GUNNER (S.P.C.K., [1892])	£60
THE GRAND CHACO (Partridge, [1892])	£40
BEGUMBAGH (Chambers, 1893)	£40
THE BLACK BAR (Sampson Low, 1893)	£60
BLUE JACKETS (Griffith & Farran, [1893])	£60
SAIL-HO! (S.P.C.K., [1893])	£60
STEVE YOUNG (Partridge, [1893])	£60
REAL GOLD (Chambers, 1894 [1893])	£60
DIAMOND DYKE (Chambers, 1894)	£60
FIRE ISLAND (Sampson Low, 1894)	£60
FIRST IN THE FIELD (Partridge, [1894])	£60
THE VAST ABYSS (S.P.C.K., [1894])	£60
CORMORANT CRAG (Partridge, [1895])	£60
PLANTER JACK (S.P.C.K., [1895])	£60
THE QUEEN'S SCARLET (Cassell, 1895)	£175

ROY ROYLAND (Chambers, 1896 [1895])..£60
JACK AT SEA (S.P.C.K., [1896])...£60
THE BLACK TOR (Chambers, 1896)...£60
IN HONOUR'S CAUSE (Partridge, [1896])..£40
SMITH'S WEAKNESS (S.P.C.K., [1896])..£40
FRANK AND SAXON (S.P.C.K., [1897])...£60
THE LITTLE SKIPPER (Nister, [1897]) £40
VINCE THE REBEL (Chambers, 1897)...£60
DRAW SWORDS! (Chambers, 1898)..£40
NIC REVEL (Chambers, 1898) £60
OUR SOLDIER BOY (Nister, [1898])..£40
THE SILVER SALVORS (S.P.C.K., [1898])..£60
JUNGLE AND STREAM (Partridge, 1898)..£60
FIX BAY'NETS! (Chambers, 1899)..£40
KING O'THE BEACH (Nister, [1899])..£40
YOUNG ROBIN HOOD (Nister, [1899])..£30
NED LEGER (S.P.C.K., [1899])...£40
IN THE MAHDI'S GRASP (Partridge, [1899])..£40
KING ROBERT'S PAGE (Nister, [1900])..£40
OLD GOLD (Nister, [1900])..£60
UNCLE BART (S.P.C.K., [1900])...£40
CHARGE! (Chambers, 1900)...£40
A DASH FROM DIAMOND CITY (Nister, [1901])...£60
CHING, THE CHINAMAN (S.P.C.K., [1901])..£40
THE KING'S SONS (Nister, [1901])..£30
THE KOPJE GARRISON (Chambers, 1901) £40
RUNNING AMOK (Chatto & Windus, 1901)...£60
PULABAD (Chapman & Hall: 'Young People's Library' Vol 4, 1901).......................................£40
SOMETHING LIKE A SNAKE (Warwick Brothers, Canada, [1901])..£75
THE PERIL FINDERS (S.P.C.K., [1902])..£40
STAN LYNN (Chambers, 1902) £60
THE ROUGH STONES and A BAD DAY'S FISHING (Nister, [1902])....................................£30
THE LOST MIDDY (Nister, [1902]) £40
COASTGUARD JACK (Nister, [1902]) £40
A YOUNG HERO (Nister, [1903])..£40
FITZ THE FILIBUSTER (S.P.C.K., [1903])...£40
THE KING'S ESQUIRES (Grant Richards, 1903) £60
WALSH, THE WONDER-WORKER (Chambers, 1903) £40
WILL OF THE MILL (Collins, [1903])...£40
THE POWDER MONKEY (Nister, [1904])...£40
GLYN SEVERN'S SCHOOL-DAYS (Chambers, 1904) £40
MARCUS: YOUNG CENTURION (Nister, [1904])..£40
THE OCEAN CAT'S-PAW (S.P.C.K., [1904])..£40
TO WIN OR TO DIE (Partridge, [1904])..£40
NEPHEW JACK (S.P.C.K., [1905])..£40
SHOULDER ARMS! (Chambers, 1905) £40
TRAPPER DAN (Partridge, [1905])...£40
DEAD MAN'S LAND (Partridge, [1906])..£40
HUNTING THE SKIPPER (S.P.C.K., [1906])..£40
'TENTION! (Chambers, 1906) £40
TRAPPED BY MALAYS (Chambers, 1907) £60
JACK THE RASCAL (Everett, [1909])...£75

Christmas Annuals & Numbers

'ONCE A WEEK' CHRISTMAS NUMBERS:
'SHIP AHOY!' (wrappers) (1873)..£40
SIXTY PER CENT (wrappers) (1874) £40
JACK IN THE BOX (wrappers) (1875)...£40
'LAND AHEAD!' (wrappers) (1876)...£40
GOBLIN ROCK (wrappers) (1877) £40
'G.M. FENN'S CHRISTMAS ANNUAL':
EVE AT THE WHEEL (Ward & Downey, 1885) £75

Others

'CABBY' (On Cabbies in General) (Virtue, 1864)...£300
THE WORLD OF WIT AND HUMOUR Edited by G.M. Fenn (Cassell, 1871)...........................£60
A BOOK OF FAIR WOMEN Edited by G.M. Fenn (Cassell, 1873)...£60
ADVENTURES OF WORKING MEN (Cassell, [1881]) £60
FRIENDS I HAVE MADE (Cassell, [1881]) £60
Ditto (as 'COBWEB'S FATHER') (Cassell, [1883])...£60
POVERTY CORNER (Cassell, [1882]) £80
MY PATIENTS (Cassell, [1883]) £60
CAPTAIN JACK (with others) (Nister, [1896]) £40

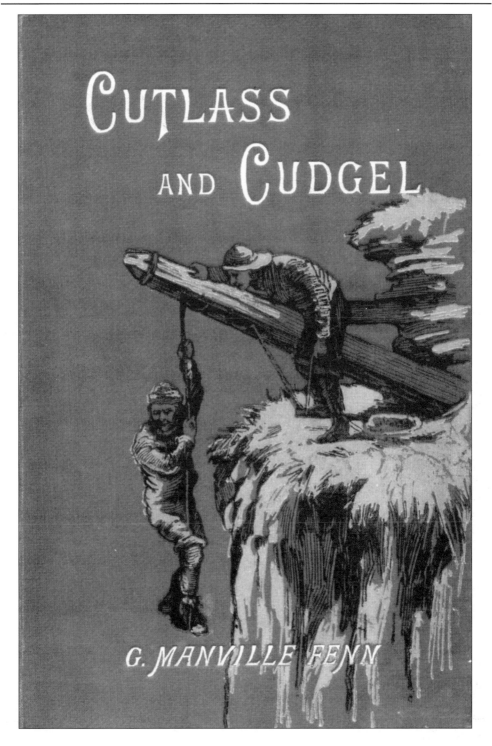

The dynamic, action-packed pictorial boards of all G. Manville Fenn's adventure stories are popular with collectors.

IN BATTLE AND BREEZE (with G.A. Henty & W. Clark Russell) (Blackie, 1896 [1895]) £80
MEMOIR OF B.F. STEVENS (Privately printed, 1903)...£60
THE KHEDIVE'S COUNTRY: The Nile Valley and Its Products (travel) (Cassell, 1904) £80
GEORGE ALFRED HENTY (Blackie, 1907)..£200

FINNEMORE, John

British children's author. Born: 1863. Finnemore was headmaster at Tanygarreg School on Mynydd Bach, Cardiganshire. He penned a large number of boys' stories and other books for children, although he is best remembered for the 'Teddy Lester' series, all set in Slapton School, which first appeared in the *Boys' Realm* story paper, before being published in book form. They were also reprinted in the 1950s. Died: 1928.

Prices are for books in Very Good condition.

THREE SCHOOL CHUMS (W. & R. Chambers, 1907)...£15
HIS FIRST TERM (W. & R. Chambers, 1909)...£15
TEDDY LESTER'S CHUMS (W. & R. Chambers, 1910) £15
TEDDY LESTER'S SCHOOLDAYS (W. & R. Chambers, 1914)..£15
TEDDY LESTER, CAPTAIN OF CRICKET (W. & R. Chambers, 1916) £15
TEDDY LESTER IN THE FIFTH (W. & R. Chambers, 1921) £15

'FILM FUN'

British comic, published by Amalgamated Press and containing stories featuring movie stars such as Harold Lloyd, Buster Keaton and Laurel and Hardy. The comic itself was launched on 17th January 1920, but the first annual didn't appear until 1938. The last edition was dated 1961.

Prices are for comics/annuals in Very Good condition.

FILM FUN ISSUE 1 (17th January 1920) £90
FILM FUN ANNUAL 1938 ....£200
FILM FUN ANNUAL 1939 ....£150
FILM FUN ANNUAL 1940 ....£100
FILM FUN ANNUAL 1941 ....£75
FILM FUN ANNUAL 1942 ....£75
FILM FUN ANNUAL 1943 ....£75
FILM FUN ANNUAL 1944 ....£75
FILM FUN ANNUAL 1945 ....£45
FILM FUN ANNUAL 1946 ....£45
FILM FUN ANNUAL 1947 ....£45
FILM FUN ANNUAL 1948 ....£45
FILM FUN ANNUAL 1949 ....£45
FILM FUN ANNUAL 1950 ....£45
FILM FUN ANNUAL 1951 ....£25
FILM FUN ANNUAL 1952-60 ....each £15
FILM FUN ANNUAL 1961 ....£20

FIRMIN, Peter

British illustrator. Born: Harwich, Essex, 1928. Studied at Colchester School of Art and Central School of Art in London. Worked as a freelance and commercial illustrator before beginning a successful collaboration with the writer, Oliver Postgate, in 1958. Together they have created the children's television programmes, *The Clangers*, *Noggin the Nog*, *Bagpuss* and *Ivor the Engine*, all of which inspired spin-off books. Firmin also made the puppet, Basil Brush, for BBC TV. Two of his daughters, Charlotte and Hannah Firmin, have become successful illustrators.

Prices are for books in Very Good condition with dustjackets where applicable.

IVOR THE ENGINE (with Oliver Postgate) (Abelard-Schuman, [1962]) £40
NOGGIN AND THE WHALE (with Oliver Postgate) (Ward, 1965)...£20
NOGGIN THE KING (with Oliver Postgate) (Ward, 1965)..£20
NOGBAD AND THE ELEPHANTS (with Oliver Postgate) (Kaye & Ward, 1967)............................£20
NOGGIN AND THE MOON MOUSE (with Oliver Postgate) (Kaye & Ward, 1967)..........................£20
TOG SEES THE WORLD: A Pogles' Wood Story (with Oliver Postgate) (Hamlyn, 1967).................£12
THE SAGA OF NOGGIN THE NOG (with Oliver Postgate) (Kaye & Ward, 1968)...........................£15

FISCHEL, Ana

British author. Creator of the 'Zartarbia Tales' series of children's books.

Prices are for books in Fine condition with dustjackets where applicable.

ISABELLA ZOPHIE AND LE CIRQUE DE MAGIQUE (paperback) (Pen Press, 2004) £10
ISABELLA ZOPHIE AND LE CIRQUE DE MAGIQUE (paperback; Limited Signed Review Copy) (Pen Press, 2004) £30
ISABELLA ZOPHIE AND LE CIRQUE DE MAGIQUE (Limited Signed Hardback) (Pen Press, 2004) £15
ISABELLA ZOPHIE AND THE HOTEL GASTRONOMIC (paperback; Pen Press, 2005) £10
ISABELLA ZOPHIE AND THE HOTEL GASTRONOMIC (paperback; Review Copy; 300 copies) (Pen Press, 2005)...............£12

*Laurel and Hardy were regular cover stars for the **Film Fun Annual**, including the first published in 1938 (top left), today worth £200.*

FLEMING, Ian

British author. Born: Ian Lancaster Fleming in 1908. Fleming is best known for the 'James Bond' novels, but also enjoyed great success with his three children's books featuring the wonder car, Chitty-Chitty-Bang-Bang. Roald Dahl wrote the script for the successful 1967 film version. Died: 1964.

Prices are for books in Very Good condition.

CHITTY-CHITTY-BANG-BANG, THE MAGICAL CAR: ADVENTURE NUMBER 1 (illustrated by John Burningham) (Cape, 1964).....**£200**
CHITTY-CHITTY-BANG-BANG, THE MAGICAL CAR: ADVENTURE NUMBER 2 (illustrated by John Burningham) (Cape, 1964).....**£200**
CHITTY-CHITTY-BANG-BANG, THE MAGICAL CAR: ADVENTURE NUMBER 3 (illustrated by John Burningham) (Cape, 1965).....**£200**
THE COMPLETE ADVENTURES OF THE MAGICAL CAR (omnibus edition; illustrated by John Burningham) (Cape, 1971)....**£80**

FOLKARD, Charles

British illustrator. Born: Charles James Folkard in Lewisham in 1878. Studied at the St. John's Wood School of Art and Goldsmith's College School of Art, subsequently illustrating many classic children's works as well as creating the strip cartoon, Teddy Tail, which ran in the *Daily Mail* from 1915 to 1960. He also wrote a number of children's plays. Died: 1963.

Prices are for books in Very Good condition (with dustjackets after 1940).

'Teddy Tail' Books (all written and illustrated by Charles Folkard; boards; issued without dustjackets)

THE ADVENTURES OF TEDDY TAIL OF THE DAILY MAIL (A. & C. Black, 1915).....**£35**
TEDDY TAIL IN NURSERY RHYME LAND (A. & C. Black, 1915).....**£35**
TEDDY TAIL IN FAIRYLAND (A. & C. Black, 1916).....**£30**
TEDDY TAIL IN HISTORYLAND (A. & C. Black, 1917).....**£25**
TEDDY TAIL'S FAIRY TALE (A. & C. Black, 1919).....**£25**
TEDDY TAIL IN BABYLAND (A. & C. Black, 1919).....**£25**
TEDDY TAIL AT THE SEASIDE (A. & C. Black, 1920).....**£25**
TEDDY TAIL'S ALPHABET (A. & C. Black, 1921).....**£25**
TEDDY TAIL IN TOYLAND (A. & C. Black, 1922).....**£25**
TEDDY TAIL'S ADVENTURES IN THE A B SEA (A. & C. Black, 1926).....**£25**

Other Books Illustrated by Charles Folkard

SWISS FAMILY ROBINSON by J.R. Wyss (Dent, 1910).....**£30**
THE FLINT HEART by Eden Phillpotts (sixteen black-and-white illustrations by Charles Folkard) (Smith Elder, 1910).....**£35**
PINOCCHIO by Carlo Collodi (Dent, 1911).....**£100**
THE CHILDREN'S SHAKESPEARE. Edited by Alice S. Hoffman (Dent, 1911).....**£70**
GRIMMS' FAIRY TALES (A. & C. Black, 1911).....**£50**
AESOP'S FABLES (A. & C. Black, 1912).....**£35**
JOLLY CALLE and Other Swedish Fairy Tales by Helena Nyblom (Dent, [1913]).....**£45**
THE JACKDAW OF RHEIMS by Richard Barham (Gay & Hancock, 1913).....**£125**
THE ARABIAN NIGHTS (A. & C. Black, 1913).....**£50**
BELGIAN PLAYMATES by Nellie Pollock (Gay & Hancock, 1914).....**£30**
OTTOMAN WONDER TALES by Lucy Garnett (A. & C. Black, 1915).....**£30**
MOTHER GOOSE'S NURSERY RHYMES. Edited by L.E. Walter (A. & C. Black, [1919]).....**£70**
MOTHER GOOSE'S NURSERY TALES. Edited by L.E. Walter (second edition) (A. & C. Black, 1923).....**£50**
BRITISH FAIRY AND FOLK TALES. Edited by William J. Glover (A. & C. Black, 1920).....**£40**
WITCH'S HOLLOW by Arthur Brook (eight colour plates and other illustrations by Charles Folkard) (A. & C. Black, 1920).....**£45**
SONGS FROM ALICE IN WONDERLAND AND THROUGH THE LOOKING-GLASS by Lewis Carroll (A. & C. Black, 1921).....**£100**
THE MAGIC EGG by Dorothy Black (A. & C. Black, 1922).....**£50**
GRANNY'S WONDERFUL CHAIR by Frances Browne (A. & C. Black, 1925).....**£20**
TALES FROM SHAKESPEARE by Charles and Mary Lamb (Dent, [1926]).....**£100**
THE TROUBLES OF A GNOME by Zofja Kossak-Szczucka (A. & C. Black, 1928).....**£40**
ALICE'S ADVENTURES IN WONDERLAND by Lewis Carroll (A. & C. Black, 1929).....**£50**
THE LAND OF NURSERY RHYME by Alice Daglish and Ernest Rhys (Dent, 1932).....**£30**
TALES OF THE TAUNUS MOUNTAINS by Olive Dehn (Blackwell, 1937).....**£30**
GRIMMS' FAIRY TALES (Dent, 1949).....**£30**
THE PRINCESS AND CURDIE by George MacDonald (Dent, 1949).....**£40**
THE PRINCESS AND THE GOBLIN by George MacDonald (Dent, 1949).....**£50**
PINOCCHIO (the original translation by M.A. Murray, revised by G. Tassinari) (Dent, 1951).....**£40**
THE BOOK OF NONSENSE Edited by Roger Lancelyn Green (Dent, 1956).....**£35**

FOREMAN, Michael

British illustrator. Born: Pakefield, Suffolk, in 1938. Studied at Lowestoft School of Art and at the Royal College of Art, subsequently lecturing at the latter as well as other art schools. Has won several awards for his children's illustrations, notably the Kurt Maschler Award in 1982. He has also written a number of children's books.

Prices are for books in Very Good condition with dustjackets where applicable.

POEMS FOR CHILDREN 1950-1961. Chosen by Michael Baldwin (Routledge, 1962).....**£50**
THE PERFECT PRESENT (Hamish Hamilton, 1967).....**£65**

THE TWO GIANTS (Brockhampton Press, 1967)..£45
THE GREAT SLEIGH ROBBERY (Hamish Hamilton, 1968)...£35
HORATIO (Hamish Hamilton, 1970)..£30
MOOSE (Hamish Hamilton, 1971)..£25
DINOSAURS AND ALL THAT RUBBISH (Hamish Hamilton, 1972)..£25
MR NOAH AND THE SECOND FLOOD by Sheila Burnford (Gollancz, 1973)..................................£20
WAR AND PEAS (Hamish Hamilton, 1974)..£20
RAINBOW RIDER by Jane Yolen (Collins, 1975)..£20
ALL THE KING'S HORSES (Hamish Hamilton, 1976)..£20
HANS ANDERSEN — HIS CLASSIC FAIRYTALES (translated by Eric Haugaard) (Gollancz, 1976)........£25
MONKEY AND THE THREE WIZARDS (Collins, 1976)...£25
THE STONE BOOK by Alan Garner (Collins, 1976)...£35
TOM FOBBLE'S DAY by Alan Garner (Collins, 1977)...£45
GRANNY REARDUN by Alan Garner (Collins, 1977)...£45
PANDA'S PUZZLE, AND HIS VOYAGE OF DISCOVERY (Hamish Hamilton, 1977).......................£20
TEENY-TINY AND THE WITCH WOMAN by Barbara Walker (Andersen Press, 1977)....................£20
THE AIMER GATE by Alan Garner (Collins, 1978)...£40
BROTHERS GRIMM: POPULAR FOLK TALES (Gollancz, 1978)...£25
MICKEY'S KITCHEN CONTEST (Andersen Press, 1978)..£25
THE SELFISH GIANT by Oscar Wilde (Kaye & Ward, 1978)..£25
WINTER'S TALES (illustrated by Freire White and Michael Foreman) (Benn, 1979)........................£20
CITY OF GOLD and Other Stories from the Old Testament by Peter Dickinson (Gollancz, 1980)........£25
THE PIG PLANTAGENET by Allen Andrews (Hutchinson, 1980)...£20
THE TIGER WHO LOST HIS STRIPES (Andersen Press, 1980)...£20
THE FAITHFULL BULL by Ernest Hemingway (Hamish Hamilton, 1980)..£35
FAIRY TALES (Pavilion, 1981)..£25
TRICK A TRACKER (Gollancz, 1981)...£20
PANDA AND THE ODD LION (Hamish Hamilton, 1981)...£20
SLEEPING BEAUTY AND OTHER FAVOURITE TALES (Gollancz, 1982)..£30
THE MAGIC MOUSE AND THE MILLIONAIRE (Hamish Hamilton, 1982)...£20
LAND OF DREAMS (Andersen Press, 1982)..£20
A CHRISTMAS CAROL (Gollancz, 1983)...£25
THE SAGA OF ERIK THE VIKING (Pavilion, 1983)..£25
CAT AND CANARY (Andersen Press, 1984)..£45
A CAT AND MOUSE LOVE STORY by Nanette Newman (Heinemann, 1984)...................................£20
PANDA AND THE BUNYIPS (Hamish Hamilton, 1984)...£20
LAND OF DREAMS (Andersen Press, 1984)..£20
SHAKESPEARE STORIES by Leon Garfield (Gollancz, 1985)..£25
SHAKESPEARE STORIES BOOK NUMBER 2 (Gollancz, 1994)..£15
BRONTOSAURUS SUPERSTAR (Hamish Hamilton, 1985)...£25
NICOBOBINUS by Terry Jones (Joseph, 1985)..£25
SEASONS OF SPLENDOUR by Madhur Jaffrey (Pavilion, 1985)..£25
A CHILD'S GARDEN OF VERSES by R.L. Stevenson (Gollancz, 1985)...£30
I'LL TAKE YOU TO MRS COLE (Andersen Press, 1985)...£20
EARLY IN THE MORNING by Charles Causley (Viking/Kestrel, 1986)..£20
TALES FOR THE TELLING: Irish Folk and Fairy Stories (Pavilion, 1986)..£25
THE MAGIC OINTMENT and Other Cornish Legends by Eric Quayle (Andersen Press, 1986)........£25
PANDA AND THE BUSHFIRE (Hamish Hamilton, 1986)...£20
BEN'S BOX (Methuen, 1986)..£20
BEN'S BOX (pop-up book) (Hodder & Stoughton, [1986])..£30
JUST SO STORIES (Kestrel, 1987)...£25
BEN'S BABY (Andersen Press, 1987)..£10
EDMOND WENT FAR AWAY by Martin Bax (Walker, 1988)..£12
PETER PAN AND WENDY (Pavilion, 1988)...£40
WAR BOY: A Country Childhood (Pavilion, 1989)..£25
MICHAEL FOREMAN'S WORLD OF FAIRY TALES (Pavilion, 1990)..£35
THE BOY WHO SAILED WITH COLUMBUS (Pavilion, 1991)..£25
DAD I CAN'T SLEEP (Anderson Press, 1994)...£30
SHAKESPEARE STORIES BOOK NUMBER 2 (Gollancz, 1994)..£15
JOAN OF ARC (Pavilion, 1998)..£25

FOREST, Antonia

British author. Born Patricia Rubenstein, London, 1915. Well-known for her 'Marlowe family' series set in upper-middle-class background with strong characterisation and insight into relationships. Died: 2004.

Prices are for books in Very Good condition with dustjackets.

AUTUMN TERM (illustrated by Marjorie Owens) (Faber, 1948)...£35
THE MARLOWS AND THE TRAITOR (illustrated by Doritie Kettlewell) (Faber, 1953)....................£35
FALCONER'S LURE: The Story of a Summer Holiday (illustrated by Tasha Kallin) (Faber, 1957)........£90
END OF TERM (Faber, 1959)...£50

PETER'S ROOM (Faber, 1961)	£75
THE THURSDAY KIDNAPPING (Faber, 1963)	£40
THE THUGGERY AFFAIR (Faber, 1965)	£30
THE READY-MADE FAMILY (Faber, 1967)	£45
THE PLAYER'S BOY (Faber, 1970)	£45
THE PLAYERS AND THE REBELS (Faber, 1971)	£45
THE CRICKET TERM (Faber, 1974)	£30
THE ATTIC TERM (Faber, 1976)	£30
RUN AWAY HOME (Faber, 1982)	£70

FORESTER, C.S.

British author. Born: Cecil Louis Troughton Smith in 1899. Forester is best known for the 'Hornblower' series of navel adventure novels, but also enjoyed great success with his two children's books. Died: 1966.

Prices are for books in Very Good condition with dustjackets.

POO-POO AND THE DRAGON (Michael Joseph, 1942)	£60
POO-POO AND THE DRAGON (Little Brown, US, 1942)	£50
THE BARBARY PIRATES (Random House, US, 1953)	£50
THE BARBARY PIRATES (first UK edition) Macdonald, 1956)	£25

FUNKE, Cornelia

German children's author. Born: 1958. Cornelia Funke's debut, The Thief Lord, was published in her homeland of Germany in 2000, winning rave reviews, before being issued in this country two years later. Below is a selected bibliography.

Prices are for books in Fine condition with dustjackets.

THE THIEF LORD (first print run of 1,000 copies) (The Chicken House, 2002)	£35
INKHEART (paperback) (The Chicken House, 2004)	£15
DRAGON RIDER (500 copies, signed & numbered, slipcase, red endpapers) (The Chicken House, 2004)	£40
DRAGON RIDER (500 copies, signed, red endpapers) (The Chicken House, 2004)	£30
INKSPELL (The Chicken House, 2005)	£15

Two children's books by authors better known for their adult series –
Ian Fleming's 'James Bond' books and C.S. Forester's 'Hornblower' novels.

G

GARDAM, Jane

British author. Born: Yorkshire, 1928. Has written several excellent novels of adolescence. After her first five books, she produced a series of readers for younger children, notably *Bridget and William*.

Prices are for books in Very Good condition with dustjacket where applicable.

A FEW FAIR DAYS (illustrated by Peggy Fortnum) (Hamish Hamilton, 1971) £25
A LONG WAY FROM VERONA (Hamish Hamilton, 1971) £25
THE SUMMER AFTER THE FUNERAL (Hamish Hamilton, 1973)..£25
BLACK FACES WHITE FACES (Hamish Hamilton, 1975)..£15
BILGEWATER (Hamish Hamilton, 1976)..£20
THE HOLLOW LAND (illustrated by Janet Rawlins) (Macrae, 1981) £15
BRIDGET AND WILLIAM (illustrated by Janet Rawlins) (Macrae,1981)................................£15
HORSE (illustrated by Janet Rawlins) (MacRae, 1982) £15
CRUSOE'S DAUGHTER (Hamish Hamilton, 1985) £20
KIT (illustrated by William Geldart) (MacRae, 1986) £15
KIT IN BOOTS (illustrated by William Geldart) (MacRae, 1986)..£15
THROUGH THE DOLL'S HOUSE DOOR (MacRae, 1987) £15
GOING INTO A DARK HOUSE (short stories) (Sinclair-Stevenson, 1994) £10
FAITH FOX (Sinclair-Stevenson, 1996)..£10

GARFIELD, Leon

British author. Born: Brighton, 1921. Served in the Medical Corps during the war, subsequently working as a hospital lab technician before becoming a full-time writer in 1966. His first novel, *Jack Holborn* (1964), was intended for adults but, on his editor's advice, was rewritten for younger readers. This was followed by many more children's novels, often set in the past, the most notable of which are *Smith* (1967) and *The Drummer Boy* (1970). His books are noted for their frank treatment of sexual themes. Died: 1996.

Prices are for books in Very Good condition with dustjackets.

'Apprentices' Books

THE LAMPLIGHTER'S FUNERAL (illustrated by Antony Maitland) (Heinemann, 1976)....................£20
MIRROR, MIRROR (illustrated by Antony Maitland) (Heinemann, 1976)..£15
MOSS AND BLISTER (illustrated by Faith Jaques) (Heinemann, 1976)..£15
THE CLOAK (illustrated by Faith Jaques) (Heinemann, 1976)..£15
THE VALENTINE (illustrated by Faith Jaques) (Heinemann, 1977)..£15
LABOUR IN VAIN (illustrated by Faith Jaques) (Heinemann, 1977) £15
THE FOOL (illustrated by Faith Jaques) (Heinemann, 1977) £15
ROSY STARLING (illustrated by Faith Jaques) (Heinemann, 1977) £15
THE DUMB CAKE (illustrated by Faith Jaques) (Heinemann, 1977)..£10
TOM TITMARSH'S DEVIL (illustrated by Faith Jaques) (Heinemann, 1977) £10
THE FILTHY BEAST (illustrated by Faith Jaques) (Heinemann, 1978)..£10
THE ENEMY (illustrated by Faith Jaques) (Heinemann, 1978)..£10

Others

JACK HOLBORN (illustrated by Antony Maitland) (Constable, 1964) £50
DEVIL-IN-THE-FOG (illustrated by Antony Maitland) (Constable, 1966) £30
SMITH (illustrated by Antony Maitland) (Constable, 1967)..£25
BLACK JACK (illustrated by Antony Maitland) (Longman, 1968)..£25
MISTER CORBETT'S GHOST and Other Stories (illustrated by Antony Maitland) (Longman, 1969)...£20
THE RESTLESS GHOST: Three Stories (illustrated by Saul Lambert) (Pantheon, U.S., 1969)....................£15
THE BOY AND THE MONKEY (illustrated by Trevor Ridley) (Heinemann, 1969) £15
THE DRUMMER BOY (illustrated by Antony Maitland) (Longman, 1970)..£20
THE GOD BENEATH THE SEA (with Edward Blishen; non-fiction; illustrated by Charles Keeping) (Longman, 1970) £15
THE STRANGE AFFAIR OF ADELAIDE HARRIS (illustrated by Fritz Wegner) (Longman, 1971)..............£15
THE CAPTAIN'S WATCH (illustrated by Trevor Ridley) (Heinemann, 1972)....................................£15
THE GHOST DOWNSTAIRS (illustrated by Antony Maitland) (Longman, 1972)................................£15
CHILD O'WAR: The True Story of a Boy Sailor in Nelson's Navy. Recreated by Leon Garfield in consultation with
    David Proctor (non-fiction; illustrated by Antony Maitland) (Collins, 1972) £20
THE GOLDEN SHADOW (with Edward Blishen; non-fiction; illustrated by Charles Keeping) (Longman, 1973)...........£15
LUCIFER WILKINS (illustrated by Trevor Ridley) (Heinemann, 1973) £20
THE SOUND OF COACHES (illustrated by John Lawrence) (Kestrel, 1974)....................................£25
THE PRISONERS OF SEPTEMBER (paperback) (Puffin, 1975) £15
THE PLEASURE GARDEN (illustrated by Fritz Wegner) (Kestrel, 1976)..£20
THE HOUSE OF HANOVER: England in the Eighteenth Century (non-fiction) (Deutsch, 1976)....................£15
AN ADELAIDE GHOST (Ward Lock, 1977) £10
THE CONFIDENCE MAN (Kestrel, 1978) £10

BOSTOCK AND HARRIS, or The Night of the Comet (illustrated by Martin Cottam)
(Kestrel, 1979) **£10**
JOHN DIAMOND (illustrated by Antony Maitland) (Kestrel, 1980) **£15**
FAIR'S FAIR (illustrated by Margaret Chamberlain) (Macdonald, 1981) **£10**
KING NIMROD'S TOWER (illustrated by Michael Bragg) (Methuen, 1982) **£15**
THE WRITING ON THE WALL (illustrated by Michael Bragg) (Methuen, 1983) **£10**
THE KING IN THE GARDEN (illustrated by Michael Bragg) (Methuen, 1984) **£10**
GUILT AND GINGERBREAD (illustrated by Fritz Wegner) (Viking Kestrel, 1984) **£10**
THE WEDDING GHOST (illustrated by Charles Keeping) (OUP, 1985) **£10**
SHAKESPEARE STORIES (illustrated by Michael Foreman) (Gollancz, 1985) **£20**
THE DECEMBER ROSE (Viking Kestrel, 1986) **£10**
BLEWCOAT BOY (Gollancz/National Trust, 1988) **£10**

GARNER, Alan

British author. Born: Congleton, Cheshire, in 1934. Following a long period of illness, he studied at
Manchester Grammar School and Magdalen College, Oxford, where he read Classics. Inspired by William
Golding's *Lord of the Flies*, he wrote the fantasy novel, *The Weirdstone of Brisingamen* (1960), at the
age of 22, and has followed it up with a small number of highly accomplished and sophisticated books for
children. He still lives in Cheshire.

Prices are for books in Very Good condition with dustjackets.

THE WEIRDSTONE OF BRISINGAMEN: A Tale of Alderley (Collins, 1960) **£500**
THE MOON OF GOMRATH (Collins, 1963) **£300**
ELIDOR (illustrated by Charles Keeping) (Collins, 1965) **£200**
HOLLY FROM THE BONGS: A Nativity Play (music by William Mayne) (Collins, 1966) **£50**
THE OLD MAN OF MOW (photographs by Roger Hill) (Collins, 1966 [1967]) **£50**
THE OWL SERVICE (Collins, 1967) **£70**
RED SHIFT (Collins, 1973) **£45**
POTTER THOMPSON (play; music by Gordon Crosse) (OUP, 1975) **£30**
THE GUIZER: A Book of Fools (Hamish Hamilton, 1975) **£40**
THE BREADHORSE (verse; illustrated by Albin Trowski) (Collins, 1975) **£40**
THE STONE BOOK (illustrated by Michael Foreman) (Collins: 'Craftsmanship' series No. 1, 1976) **£35**
TOM FOBBLE'S DAY (illustrated by Michael Foreman) (Collins: 'Craftsmanship' series No. 2, 1977) **£45**
GRANNY REARDUN (illustrated by Michael Foreman) (Collins: 'Craftsmanship' series No. 3, 1977) **£45**
THE AIMER GATE (illustrated by Michael Foreman) (Collins: 'Craftsmanship' series No. 4, 1978) **£40**
FAIRY TALES OF GOLD (four books: 'The Girl of the Golden Gate', 'The Golden Brothers',
'The Princess and the Golden Mane' and 'The Three Golden Heads of the Well') (Collins, 1979) .... each **£15**
THE LAD OF THE GAD (Collins, 1980) **£20**
BOOK OF BRITISH FAIRY TALES (Collins, 1984) **£15**
A BAG OF MOONSHINE (illustrated by Patrick Lynch) (Collins, 1986) **£12**
ONCE UPON A TIME... (Dorling Kindersley, 1993) **£12**
SANDLOPER (Harvill Press, 1996) **£15**
LITTLE RED HEN (illustrated by Norman Messenger; paper boards)
(Dorling Kindersley: 'Nursery Tales' series, 1997) **£5**
THE VOICE THAT THUNDERS (Harvill Press, 1998) **£8**
THE WELL OF THE WIND by Alan Garner and Herve Blondon
(Dorling Kindersley, 1998) **£12**

GARNETT, Eve

British author-illustrator. Born: Worcestershire, 1900. Awarded Carnegie Medal, 1938. Best known for her
'Ruggles family', the first successful true-life depiction of a working class family. Died: 1991.

Prices are for books in Very Good condition with dustjackets where applicable.

Books Written and illustrated by Eve Garnett

THE FAMILY FROM ONE END STREET AND SOME OF THEIR ADVENTURES (Muller, 1937) **£100**
IS IT WELL WITH THE CHILD? (Muller, 1938) **£30**
IN AND OUT AND ROUNDABOUT: STORIES OF A LITTLE TOWN (Muller 1948) **£50**
A BOOK OF SEASONS (anthology) (OUP, 1952) **£30**
FURTHER ADVENTURES OF THE FAMILY FROM ONE END STREET (Heinemann,1956) **£60**
HOLIDAY AT THE DEW DROP INN: A ONE END STREET STORY (Heinemann, 1962) **£50**
TO GREENLANDS ICY MOUNTAINS (Heinemann, 1968) **£20**
FIRST AFFECTIONS (Muller, 1982) **£20**

Books Illustrated by Eve Garnett

THE LONDON CHILD by Evelyn Sharp (John Lane, 1927) **£60**
THE BARONS OF CRASHBANIA by Norman Hunter (Blackwell, 1932) **£50**
A CHILD'S GARDEN OF VERSES by Robert Louis Stevenson (paperback)
(Penguin: 'Puffin Story Books', 1948) **£10**
A GOLDEN LAND Edited by James Reeves (illustrated by Eve Garnett and others)
(Constable, 1958) **£20**

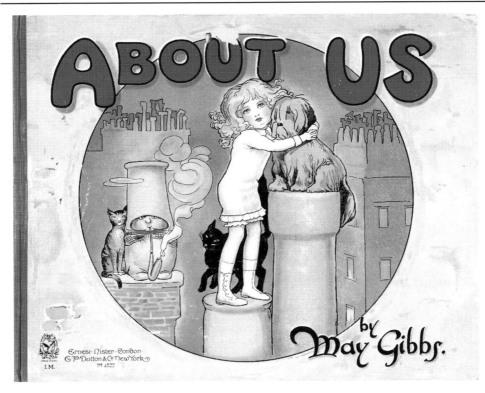

'Gumnut Babies' author May Gibbs' first book was issued in 1912 by Nister and is currently worth £750.

GIBBONS, Stella

British author. Born: London, 1902. Best known for her classic comic novel, *Cold Comfort Farm* (1932), but published a solitary children's work in 1935. Died: 1989.

Price is for book in Very Good condition with dustjacket.

THE UNTIDY GNOME (Longmans, 1935)..£150

GIBBS, May

Australian author-illustrator. Born: Cecilia May Gibbs in Surrey in 1877. Emigrated to Australia with her family in 1881. Studied at Church of England Girls' School, Perth, Chelsea Polytechnic and Henry Blackburn School of Black and White Art in London. Drew on the flora and fauna of Western Australia for her highly successful series of books featuring the 'gumnut babies', beginning in 1918 with *Snugglepot and Cuddlepie: Their Adventures Wonderful*. She also drew a long-running newspaper strip featuring two similar characters, Bib and Bub. Her works always attract keen bidding at auction. In 2001 we valued *About Us* at £100, but a copy sold for £966 at Dominic Winter Book Auctions in December 2003. Died: 1969.

Prices are for books in Very Good condition.

Books Written and Illustrated by May Gibbs

ABOUT US (Nister, 1912)...£750
GUM BLOSSOM BABIES (pamphlet) (Angus & Robertson, Sydney, 1916)...£250
GUMNUT BABIES (pamphlet) (Angus & Robertson, Sydney, 1916)...£250
BORONIA BABIES (pamphlet) (Angus & Robertson, Sydney, 1917)..£150
FLANNEL FLOWERS and Other Bush Babies (pamphlet) (Angus & Robertson, Sydney, 1917) £125
WATTLE BABIES (pamphlet) (Angus & Robertson, Sydney, 1918)...£125
SNUGGLEPOT AND CUDDLEPIE: Their Adventures Wonderful (Angus & Robertson, Sydney, 1918) £350
LITTE RAGGED BLOSSOM and More about Snugglepot and Cuddlepie
  (Angus & Robertson, Sydney, 1920)..£300
LITTLE OBELIA and Further Adventures of Ragged Blossom, Snugglepot and Cuddlepie
  (Angus & Robertson, Sydney, 1921)..£300
NUTTYBUB AND NITTERSING (Osboldstone, Melbourne, 1923) £140
CHUCKLEBUD AND WUNKYDOO (Osboldstone, Melbourne, 1924)...£120

A classic example of a May Gibbs illustration and the omnibus edition of **Snugglepot and Cuddlepie** *(right).*

CHUCKLEBUD AND WUNKYDOO (as 'Two Little Gumnuts') (Cornstalk, Sydney, 1929)..**£100**
BIB AND BUB: THEIR ADVENTURES (verse; two volumes) (Cornstalk, Sydney, 1925)...........................the set **£350**
THE FURTHER ADVENTURES OF BIB AND BUB (verse) (Cornstalk, Sydney, 1927) **£200**
MORE FUNNY STORIES ABOUT OLD FRIENDS, BIB AND BUB (verse) (Cornstalk, Sydney, 1928) **£175**
BIB AND BUB IN GUMNUT TOWN (Halstead, Waterloo, 1929)..**£225**
BIB AND BUB PAINTING BOOK: New Stories (Penfold, Sydney, [c.1930s])...**£225**
GUMNUTS (Angus & Robertson, Sydney, 1940)..**£70**
SCOTTY IN GUMNUT LAND (Angus & Robertson, Sydney, 1941) **£70**
SCOTTY IN GUMNUT LAND (Angus & Robertson, 1956) **£40**
MR AND MRS BEAR AND FRIENDS (Angus & Robertson, Sydney, 1943) **£55**
MR AND MRS BEAR AND FRIENDS (Angus & Robertson, 1957) **£35**
THE COMPLETE ADVENTURES OF SNUGGLEPOT AND CUDDLEPIE (contains 'Snugglepot and Cuddlepie',
  'Little Ragged Blossom' and 'Little Obelia') (Angus & Robertson, 1946)..**£125**
PRINCE DANDE LION: A Garden Whim-Wham (Ure Smith, Sydney, 1953)..**£45**
PRINCE DANDE LION: A Garden Whim-Wham (Angus & Robertson, 1954) **£20**
ALPHABET FRIEZE (Angus & Robertson, Sydney, 1984)..**£15**
THE MAY GIBBS COLLECTION: GUMNUT CLASSICS. Edited by Maureen Walsh (two volumes)
  (Angus & Robertson, Sydney, 1985)..the set **£250**

Book Illustrated by May Gibbs
BARONS AND KINGS (1215-1485) by Estelle Ross (illustrated by May Gibbs and Stephen Reid) (Harrap, 1912)....................**£40**

GIRAUD, S.L.
British editor and book designer. Born: Stephen Louis Gerard. Began his career working in the promotions
department of the *Daily Express*. Creator, with Theodore Brown, of the modern 'pop-up' annual, with the
Daily Express Children's Annual and, subsequently, the 'Bookano' series. His ideas were copied by Harold
Lentz in America. Died: 1951.
Prices are for books in Very Good condition with all pop-ups in working order.
THE STORY OF JESUS (Strand Publications, 1934) **£40**
HANS ANDERSEN'S FAIRY STORIES (Strand Publications, 1936)..**£75**
ADVENTURE AND BUILDING BOOK (Strand Publications, 1936)..**£50**
BOOKANO STORIES: With Pictures that Spring Up in Model Form. Edited by S.L. Giraud
  (Strand Publications: 'Bookano Living Pictures' series, [1936-])..**£80**
BOOKANO ZOO: Animals in Fact, Fancy and Fun. Edited and produced by S.L. Giraud
  (Strand Publications, [1939])..**£70**
BOOKANO NO. 1: Goblins in a Carpenter's Shop, with Sound Effects of Sawing Wood!
  (Strand Publications, 1934) **£100**
BOOKANO NO. 2: Cottage, with Semi-Transparent Fairy (Strand Publications, 1935) **£90**

BOOKANO NO. 3 (Strand Publications, 1936) £80
BOOKANO NO. 4 (Strand Publications, 1937) £80
BOOKANO NO. 5 (Strand Publications, 1938) £70
BOOKANO NO. 6 (Strand Publications, 1939) £70
BOOKANO NO. 7 (Strand Publications, 1940) £70
BOOKANO NO. 8 (Strand Publications, 1941) £70
BOOKANO NO. 9 (Strand Publications, 1942) £70
BOOKANO NO. 10 (Strand Publications, 1943) £60
BOOKANO NO. 11 (Strand Publications, 1944) £60
BOOKANO NO. 12 (Strand Publications, 1945) £60
BOOKANO NO. 13 (Strand Publications, 1946) £60
BOOKANO NO. 14 (Strand Publications, 1947) £60
BOOKANO NO. 15 (Strand Publications, 1948) £60
BOOKANO NO. 16: **Tower Bridge** (Strand Publications, 1949) £85
BOOKANO STORIES NO. 17 (Strand Publications, 1950) £100

'GIRL'

British comic published between 1953 and 1965. The title was launched by Hulton as a sister paper to *Eagle*, and was the first post-war British comic aimed specifically at girls.

Prices are for comics/annuals in Very Good condition.

GIRL ISSUE 1 (Hulton Press, 2nd November 1951) £55
GIRL ANNUAL (Hulton Press, 1953) £20
GIRL ANNUAL (Hulton Press, 1954-57) .... each £10
GIRL ANNUAL (Hulton Press, 1958) £8
GIRL ANNUAL (Hulton Press, 1959-60) .... each £7
GIRL ANNUAL (Longacre Press, 1961-62) .... each £7
GIRL ANNUAL (Longacre Press, 1963) £5
GIRL ANNUAL (Longacre Press, 1964-65) .... each £5

'GIRL'S OWN'

British story paper/annual published by the Religious Tract Society between 1880 and 1941. The paper itself was launched in January 1880 as a companion to the bestselling *Boy's Own Paper*, and continued, under various titles, until 1965, by which time it was known as *Heiress*. The *Girl's Own Annual* was the first ever annual for girls. Vols. 1-29 edited by Charles Peters, Vols. 30-53 by Flora Klickman.

Prices are for volumes/story papers in Very Good condition.

VOLUMES 1-29 (3rd January 1880-26th September 1908) (weekly issues of 'Girl's Own Paper' bound as annual, in 'Girl's Own Annual'; picture boards, or other bindings, with Index. Summer or Christmas Supplements for the current or preceding year are sometimes included in these bound volumes) .... each £30

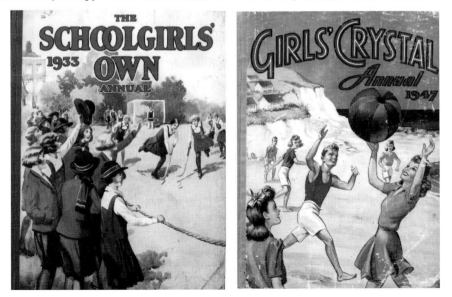

*The jolly pictorial boards of the **Schoolgirls' Own** and **Girls' Crystal** annuals from 1933 and 1947 respectively.*

VOLUMES 30-49 (October 1908-September 1928) (monthly issues of 'Girl's Own Paper & Woman's Magazine'
bound in 'Girl's Own Annual' boards or other bindings) .... each £30
GIRLS OWN PAPER (January 1918 issue contains 'Thomas' by Richmal Crompton) **£25**
GIRLS OWN PAPER (April 1918 contains 'Mrs. Tempest' by Richmal Crompton)... **£25**
VOLUMES 50-51 (October 1928-September 1930) (monthly issue of 'Woman's Magazine & Girl's Own Paper'
bound in 'Girl's Own Annual' picture boards or other bindings) .... each £35
VOLUMES 52-53 (October 1930-September 1932) (monthly issues of 'Girl's Own Paper' bound in
'Girl's Own Annual' picture boards) .... each £35
VOLUMES 54-56 (October 1932-September 1941) (monthly issues of 'Girl's Own Paper' bound in
'Girl's Own Annual' plain boards) .... each £35
GIRLS OWN PAPER (Volume 57 [1935/6] contains 'Peggy and the Brotherhood'
by Elsie H. Oxenham and 'The Robins Make Good' by Elinor Brent-Dyer) .... each **£15** volume **£45**
VOLUMES 57-61 (October 1935-September 1940) (monthly issues of 'Girl's Own Paper' bound in
'Girl's Own Annual' plain boards; containing runs of Elsie J. Oxenham stories)....................................... each **£50**
GIRLS OWN PAPER (Volume 60 [1938/9] contains
'Patch and a Pawn' by Elsie H. Oxenham) .... each **£15** volume **£45**
VOLUME 62 (October 1940-September 1941) (monthly issues of 'Girl's Own Paper' bound in 'Girl's Own Annual'
plain boards; contains first ever publication of 'Worrals of the WAAF' by W.E. Johns and
'The Ravensdale Mystery' by W.E. Johns writing as William Earle)............................... each **£15** volume **£65**

'GIRL'S REALM'

British story paper/annual of the early 1900s, published by Hutchinson. Originally intended to be more
progressive than established rivals like the *Girl's Own Paper*, but was resolutely conformist by the time
it ceased publication in 1915.
Prices are for annuals in Very Good condition in original cloth.

THE GIRL'S REALM: Volumes 1-17 plus late extra volume [November 1915] (November 1908-November 1915)........ each **£20**

'GIRLS' CRYSTAL'

British story paper published by Amalgamated Press between 1940 and 1976. The paper itself,
originally entitled *The Crystal*, was launched on 26th October 1935, becoming *The Girls' Crystal Weekly*
from No. 10 onwards. After 908 issues, the title became a comic, and strip stories were introduced into
the annuals.
Prices are for annuals in Very Good condition.

GIRLS' CRYSTAL (No. 1, 1935)...**£20**
GIRLS' CRYSTAL (1935-1963) .... each **£4**
GIRLS' CRYSTAL ANNUAL 1940 [1939] **£25**
GIRLS' CRYSTAL ANNUAL 1941-43 .... each **£18**
GIRLS' CRYSTAL ANNUAL 1944-49 .... each **£15**
GIRLS' CRYSTAL ANNUAL 1950-53 .... each **£10**
GIRLS' CRYSTAL ANNUAL 1954-58 .... each **£7**
GIRLS' CRYSTAL ANNUAL 1959-68 .... each **£5**
GIRLS' CRYSTAL ANNUAL 1969-76 .... each **£3**

Other Amalgamated Press schoolgirl story papers/annuals

THE SCHOOL FRIEND (No 1, 1919)..**£35**
THE SCHOOL FRIEND 1919-1925 (original series)... each **£5**
THE SCHOOL FRIEND 1925-1929 (new series) .... each **£4**
THE SCHOOLGIRL (No. 1, 1929)...**£20**
THE SCHOOLGIRL 1929-1940 .... each **£4**
THE SCHOOLGIRLS OWN (No. 1, 1921)...**£35**
THE SCHOOLGIRLS OWN 1921-1936.. each **£5**
THE SCHOOLGIRLS OWN LIBRARY 1922-1940 (Pre-war series; 'Morcove' & 'Cliff House' issues) .... each **£10**
THE SCHOOLGIRLS OWN LIBRARY 1922-1940 (Pre-war series; other issues) .... each **£7**
THE SCHOOLGIRLS OWN LIBRARY 1946-1963 (Second series) .... each **£4**
SCHOOL FRIEND (No. 1, 1950) **£35**
SCHOOL FRIEND 1950-1965 .... each **£4**
SCHOOLGIRLS PICTURE LIBRARY 1957-1965 ('Silent Three' issues) .... each **£8**
SCHOOLGIRLS PICTURE LIBRARY 1957-1965 (Other issues) .... each **£5**
THE SCHOOLGIRLS OWN ANNUAL (1923-1943)
(Copies retaining the clear tissue jacket overprinted with the title date etc, add 50% premium)
THE SCHOOLGIRLS OWN ANNUAL 1923-1929 (Alfred Bestall cover artwork)... each **£20**
THE SCHOOLGIRLS OWN ANNUAL 1930-1937... each **£12**
THE SCHOOLGIRLS OWN ANNUAL 1938-1943... each **£20**
THE SCHOOL FRIEND ANNUAL (1927-1981)
(Copies retaining the clear tissue jacket overprinted with the title date etc, add 50% premium)
THE SCHOOL FRIEND ANNUAL 1927-1937 .... each **£12**
THE SCHOOL FRIEND ANNUAL 1938-1943 .... each **£25**
THE SCHOOL FRIEND ANNUAL 1944-1960 .... each **£15**
THE SCHOOL FRIEND ANNUAL 1961-1968 .... each **£12**
THE SCHOOL FRIEND ANNUAL 1969-1981 .... each **£4**

*This Goble plate from **The Water Babies** shows why he is one of the more collectable artists from the Golden Age of illustration.*

GOBLE, Warwick

British illustrator. Born: London, 1862. Studied at the City of London School and Westminster School of Art, subsequently joining the staff of the *Pall Mall Gazette* and *Westminster Gazette* as an artist. Illustrated many colour plate books for A. & C. Black and Macmillan, his style showing the strong influence of Japanese and Chinese art. Travelled extensively, visiting the battlefields of France in 1919. Died: 1943.

Prices are for books in Very Good condition without dustjackets.

THE GRIM HOUSE by Mrs Molesworth (Nisbet, 1899)..£40
THE WATER BABIES by Charles Kingsley (32 colour plates by Warwick Goble)
(Macmillan, 1909)...£350
THE WATER BABIES by Charles Kingsley (32 colour plates by Warwick Goble; limited to 260 copies)
(Macmillan, 1909)..£1,500
THE WATER BABIES by Charles Kingsley (sixteen colour plates by Warwick Goble)
(Macmillan, 1910)...£100
THE WATER BABIES by Charles Kingsley (reissue; sixteen colour plates by Warwick Goble)
(Macmillan, 1922)..£80
GREEN WILLOW and Other Japanese Fairy Tales by Grace James (forty colour plates by Warwick Goble)
(Macmillan, 1910)...£600
GREEN WILLOW and Other Japanese Fairy Tales by Grace James (forty colour plates by Warwick Goble;
De Luxe edition: limited to 500 copies) (Macmillan, 1910) £2,000
GREEN WILLOW and Other Japanese Fairy Tales by Grace James (sixteen colour plates by Warwick Goble)
(Macmillan, 1912)...£100
GREEN WILLOW and Other Japanese Fairy Tales by Grace James
(reissue; sixteen colour plates by Warwick Goble) (Macmillan, 1923).......................................£70
FOLK TALES OF BENGAL by De Lala Vihari (Macmillan, 1912)...£200
FOLK TALES OF BENGAL by De Lala Vihari (limited to 150 copies) (Macmillan, 1912)..........£1,000
PEEPS AT MANY LANDS — TURKEY by Julius Van Millingen (twelve colour plates by Warwick Goble)
(A. & C. Black, 1911)...£30
STORIES FROM THE PENTAMERONE by Giovanni Battista Basile (Macmillan, 1911)...............£175
STORIES FROM THE PENTAMERONE by Giovanni Battista Basile (De Luxe edition: limited to 150 copies)
(Macmillan, 1911)..£1,000
THE FAIRY BOOK by D.M. Craik (32 colour plates by Warwick Goble) (Macmillan, 1913)........£250
THE BOOK OF FAIRY POETRY. Edited by Dora Owen (sixteen colour plates by Warwick Goble)
(Longmans, 1920)..£350

GODDEN, Rumer

British author. Born: Sussex, 1907. Spent most of her life in India, the setting for much of her work. Writer of well-made, traditional children's stories, notably her 'Doll' books. Died: 1998.

Prices are for books in Very Good condition with dustjackets where applicable.

THE DOLL'S HOUSE (illustrated by Dana Saintsbury) (Joseph, 1947)...£50
IN NOAH'S ARK (verse) (Joseph, 1949)...£25
THE MOUSEWIFE (illustrated by Dana Saintsbury) (Macmillan, 1951)...£30
IMPUNITY JANE: The Story of a Pocket Doll (illustrated by Adrienne Adams) (Macmillan, 1955) £30
THE FAIRY DOLL (illustrated by Adrienne Adams) (Macmillan, 1956)...£30
MOUSE HOUSE (illustrated by Adrienne Adams) (Macmillan, 1958) £30
THE GREENGAGE SUMMER (Macmillan, 1958)..£25
THE STORY OF HOLLY AND IVY (illustrated by Adrienne Adams) (Macmillan, 1958) £25
CANDY FLOSS (illustrated by Adrienne Adams) (Macmillan, 1960)...£25
ST JEROME AND THE LION (verse) (illustrated by Jean Primrose) (Macmillan, 1961)................£25
MISS HAPPINESS AND MISS FLOWER (illustrated by Jean Primrose) (Macmillan, 1961) £25
LITTLE PLUM (illustrated by Jean Primrose) (Macmillan, 1963)...£25
HOME IS THE SAILOR (illustrated by Jean Primrose) (Macmillan, 1964)....................................£25
THE KITCHEN MADONNA (illustrated by Carol Barker) (Macmillan, 1967)..................................£20
SWANS AND TURTLES (Macmillan, 1968) £25
OPERATION SIPPACIK (illustrated by Carol Barker) (Macmillan, 1969).......................................£20
THE TALE OF THE TALES: THE BEATRIX POTTER BALLET (Frederick Warne, 1971)...............£15
THE OLD WOMAN WHO LIVED IN A VINEGAR BOTTLE (illustrated by Mairi Hedderwick)
(Macmillan, 1972)...£20
THE DIDDAKOI (illustrated by Creina Glegg) (Macmillan, 1972) £20
MR MCFADDEN'S HALLOWE'EN (illustrated by Ann Strugnell) (Macmillan, 1975).....................£20
THE ROCKING HORSE SECRET (illustrated by Juliet Stanwell Smith) (Macmillan, 1977)............£20
A KINDLE OF KITTENS (illustrated by Lynne Byrnes) (Macmillan, 1978) £20
THE DRAGON OF OG (illustrated by Pauline Baynes) (Macmillan, 1981).....................................£20
THE VALIANT CHATTI-MAKER (illustrated by Jeroo Roy) (Macmillan, 1983) £25
FOUR DOLLS (illustrated by Pauline Baynes) (Macmillan, 1983) £25
THURSDAY'S CHILDREN (Macmillan, 1984)..£10
FU-DOG (illustrated by Valerie Littlewood) (Julia McRae Books, 1989)..£10
GREAT GRANDFATHER'S HOUSE (Macmillan, 1993)..£10
LISTEN TO THE NIGHTINGALE (Macmillan, 1993)..£10
PREMLATA AND THE FESTIVAL OF LIGHTS (Macmillan, 1993)...£10

GOODALL, John S.

British illustrator. Born: John Strickland Goodall in Heacham, Norfolk, in 1908. He studied at the Royal Academy Schools (1925-29) and began to contribute *to* the *Radio Times* and other magazines. After service in the Second World War and a period of commissioned portrait paintings, he turned to book illustration, often employing Victorian themes and settings. Died: 1996.

Prices are for books in Very Good condition with dustjackets where applicable.

Books Written and Illustrated by John S Goodall

DR OWL'S PARTY: A Tale for Children (Blackie, 1954)	£20
FIELD MOUSE HOUSE (Blackie, 1954)	£20
SHREWBETTINA'S BIRTHDAY (Macmillan, 1970)	£20
THE MIDNIGHT ADVENTURES OF KELLY, DOT, AND ESMERALDA (Macmillan, 1972)	£20
CREEPY CASTLE (Macmillan, 1975)	£20
NAUGHTY NANCY THE BAD BRIDESMAID (Macmillan, 1975)	£20
PADDY PORK'S HOLIDAY (Macmillan, 1976)	£20
PADDY'S EVENING OUT (Macmillan, 1978)	£20
LITTLE RED RIDING HOOD (Deutsch 1980)	£20
PADDY'S NEW HAT (Macmillan, 1980)	£20
THE ADVENTURES OF PADDY PORK (Macmillan, 1980)	£20
THE BALLOONING ADVENTURES OF PADDY PORK (Macmillan, 1980)	£20
SHREWBETTINA GOES TO WORK (pop-up book) (Macmillan, 1981)	£25
PADDY FINDS A JOB (pop-up book) (Macmillan, 1981)	£25
LAVINIA'S COTTAGE (pop-up book) (Macmillan, 1982)	£25
PADDY GOES TRAVELLING (Macmillan, 1982)	£20
PADDY UNDER WATER (Macmillan, 1984)	£20
PADDY PORK TO THE RESCUE (Deutsch, 1985)	£20
PUSS IN BOOTS (Deutsch, 1990)	£20

Books Illustrated by John S Goodall

FIVE CHILDREN AND IT by E Nesbit (Random House, 1948)	£30
THE PHOENIX AND THE CARPET by E Nesbit (Random House, 1948)	£30
THE STORY OF THE AMULET by E Nesbit (Random House, 1949)	£30
FIGHT FOR FREEDOM by Ian Serraillier (Heinemann, 1965)	£30

GOREY, Edward

American author/illustrator. Born: Chicago, 1925. Best known for 1957's *The Doubtful Guest* and the macabre *Gashlycrumb Tinies*. Most of his books are gothic, macabre pastiches of Victorian and Edwardian instructional books for children. The author wrote under various names, usually anagrams of Edward Gorey, and The Fantod Press was Gorey's own publishing imprint. Unless otherwise noted, titles without jackets are either pictorial hardbacks or books issued in stiff card pictorial wrappers. We have only included Gorey's original works – he also illustrated many books by other authors. Our prices also reflect the fact that his works tend to sell for far more in the US. Died: 2000.

Prices are for first editions in Very Good condition with dustjackets where applicable.

THE UNSTRUNG HARP; OR, MR. EARBRASS WRITES A NOVEL (Duell, Sloan and Pearce/Little Brown, US, 1953)	£70
THE LISTING ATTIC (Sloan and Pearce/Little, Brown and Company, US, 1954)	£70
THE LISTING ATTIC (as THE LISTING ATTIC [and] THE UNSTRUNG HARP) (No d/j) (Abelard, UK, 1974)	£15
THE DOUBTFUL GUEST (Doubleday, US, 1957)	£35
THE DOUBTFUL GUEST (Putnam, UK, 1958)	£25
THE OBJECT-LESSON (Doubleday, US, 1958)	£35
THE OBJECT-LESSON (Anthony Blond, UK, 1958)	£25
THE BUG BOOK (No d/j, 600 copies) (Looking Glass Library, US, 1959)	£70
THE BUG BOOK (trade edition) (Epstein & Carroll, US, 1960)	£30
THE FATAL LOZENGE: AN ALPHABET (No d/j. First edition has '$1.25' stamped on the front) (Ivan Obolensky, US, 1960)	£25
THE FATAL LOZENGE: AN ALPHABET (as THE GOREY ALPHABET; No d/j) (Constable, UK, 1961)	£15
THE HAPLESS CHILD (No d/j) (Ivan Obolensky, US, 1961)	£25
THE HAPLESS CHILD (No d/j) (Anthony Blond, UK, 1961)	£10
THE HAPLESS CHILD (First hardback edition) (Dodd, Mead & Company, US, 1980)	£25
THE CURIOUS SOFA (by 'Ogdred Weary', no d/j, a notice on the copyright page stating 'this is copy no. 83 of an edition limited to 212 copies' appears in every copy) (Ivan Obolensky, US, 1961)	£25
THE CURIOUS SOFA (First hardcover edition) (Mead and Company, US, 1980)	£25
THE WILLOWDALE HANDCAR; OR THE RETURN OF THE BLACK DOLL (No d/j) (Bobbs-Merrill, US, 1962)	£15
THE WILLOWDALE HANDCAR; OR THE RETURN OF THE BLACK DOLL (First hardcover edition) (Dodd, Mead, US, 1979)	£25
THE BEASTLY BABY (by 'Ogdred Weary', limited to 500 copies) (The Fantod Press, US, 1962)	£50
THE BEASTLY BABY (No d/j) (Blue Eyed Dog, UK, [1995])	£25
THE VINEGAR WORKS / THREE VOLUMES OF MORAL INSTRUCTION (no d/js) (Three-volume slipcased set enclosing THE GASHLYCRUMB TINIES: OR, AFTER THE OUTING, THE INSECT GOD and THE WEST WING) (Simon and Schuster, US, 1963)	£125

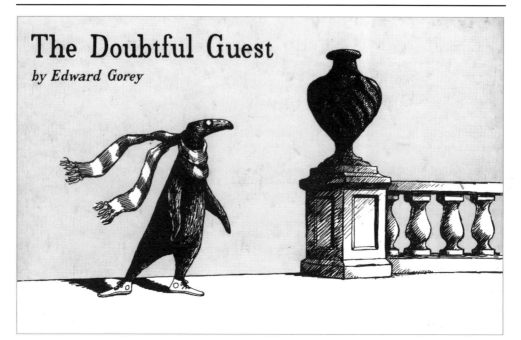

The Doubtful Guest
by Edward Gorey

The Doubtful Guest was first published in America in 1957 and remains Gorey's most popular children's book.

THE WUGGLY UMP (J.B. Lippincott, US, 1963) **£35**
[THE NURSERY FRIEZE] (No d/j. Limited to 500 copies. '15' is stamped on the front wrapper, 'TWO' is stamped
  on the rear. This was Gorey's 15th book and the second by The Fantod Press) (The Fantod Press, US, 1964) **£50**
THE SINKING SPELL (No d/j) (Ivan Obolensky, US, 1964) **£25**
THE REMEMBERED VISIT; A STORY TAKEN FROM LIFE (Simon and Schuster, US, 1965) **£35**
THREE BOOKS FROM THE FANTOD PRESS (No d/j. Limited to 500 copies. Three volumes in envelope including
  THE EVIL GARDEN, THE PIOUS INFANT and THE INANIMATE TRAGEDY) (The Fantod Press, US, 1966) **£125**
THE GILDED BAT (Simon and Schuster, US, 1966) **£35**
THE GILDED BAT (Jonathan Cape, UK, 1967) **£25**
THE UTTER ZOO (Meredith Press, US, 1967) **£50**
FLETCHER AND ZENOBIA (by Victoria Chess and Edward Gorey) (Meredith Press, US, 1967) **£50**
THE OTHER STATUE; THE SECRETS: VOLUME ONE (Simon and Schuster, US, 1968) **£35**
THE BLUE ASPIC (Meredith Press, US, 1968) **£50**
THE IRON TONIC: OR, A WINTER AFTERNOON IN LONELY VALLEY
  (No d/j. 200 numbered and 26 lettered copies signed) (Albondocani Press, US, 1969) ....**£125 / £250**
THE EPILEPTIC BICYCLE (First edition has '$3' on d/j) (Dodd, Mead & Company, US, 1969) **£35**
WHY WE HAVE DAY AND NIGHT (by Peter F. Neumeyer & Edward Gorey) (Young Scott Books, US, 1970) **£50**
THREE BOOKS FROM THE FANTOD PRESS [II] (No d/j. Limited to 500 copies. Three volumes in envelope including
  THE CHINESE OBELISKS, FOURTH ALPHABET, DONALD HAS A DIFFICULTY and THE OSBICK BIRD)
  (The Fantod Press, US, 1970) **£125**
THE SOPPING THURSDAY (Limited to 500 numbered copies signed by Edward Gorey. No d/j)
  (Gotham Book Mart & Gallery, US, 1970) **£125**
THE SOPPING THURSDAY (de luxe edition. Limited to 26 lettered copies signed by Edward Gorey,
  each with an original drawing by Edward Gorey laid in. No D/J) (Gotham Book Mart & Gallery, US, 1970) **£300**
THE SOPPING THURSDAY (Trade edition. No d/j) (Capricorn Press, US, 1971) **£25**
THREE BOOKS FROM THE FANTOD PRESS [III] (Limited to 500 copies. Three volumes in envelope including THE
  DERANGED COUSINS: OR, WHATEVER, THE ELEVENTH EPISODE and [THE UNTITLED BOOK])
  (The Fantod Press, US, 1971) **£125**
THREE BOOKS FROM THE FANTOD PRESS [III]
  (Limited to 26 lettered copies signed by Edward Gorey) (The Fantod Press, US, 1971) **£250**
STORY FOR SARA: WHAT HAPPENED TO A LITTLE GIRL (No d/j. 500 numbered and 26 lettered copies
  signed by Edward Gorey) (Albondocani Press, US, 1971) ....**£125 / £250**
THE SALT HERRING (by 'Charles Cros', no d/j, limited to 300 numbered
  and 26 lettered copies signed by Edward Gorey) (Gotham Book Mart & Gallery, US, 1971) ....**£125 / £250**
FLETCHER AND ZENOBIA SAVE THE CIRCUS (Illustrated by Victoria Chess, text by Edward Gorey)
  (Dodd, Mead & Company, US, 1971) **£35**
LEAVES FROM A MISLAID ALBUM (17 cards, laid into an olive-green folder, enclosed in envelope.
  Limited to 500 numbered copies) (Gotham Book Mart, US, 1972) **£80**

LEAVES FROM A MISLAID ALBUM (18 cards, laid into a folding box, tied with a black ribbon.
Limited to 50 roman-numeraled copies and 26 lettered copies signed by Edward Gorey)
(Gotham Book Mart & Gallery, US, 1972) ....£150 / £250

THE AWDREY-GORE LEGACY (Dodd, Mead, US, 1972)..£35

AMPHIGOREY (G.P. Putnam's, US, 1972)..£50

AMPHIGOREY (Enclosed in a black slipcase. 50 numbered signed copies, each with an original watercolor
and ink drawing) (G.P. Putnam's, US, 1972)...£700

THE LAVENDER LEOTARD: OR, GOING A LOT TO THE NEW YORK CITY BALLET
(Gotham Book Mart, US, 1973) (Limited to 1,000 copies. No d/j)...£50

THE LAVENDER LEOTARD (Limited to 100 numbered and 26 lettered copies signed by Edward Gorey. No d/j)
(Gotham Book Mart, 1973) ....£125 / £250

THE BLACK DOLL, A SILENT FILM (Gotham Book Mart, US, 1973) £50

THE BLACK DOLL, A SILENT FILM (No d/j, in slipcase. Limited to 100 numbered and 26 lettered copies
signed by Edward Gorey)(Gotham Book Mart, 1973)...£125 / £250

THE ABANDONED SOCK / THE DISRESPECTFUL SUMMONS / THE LOST LIONS
(Issued as three-volume set FANTOD IV, THREE BOOKS FROM THE FANTOD PRESS in a white envelope.
No d/j. Limited to 500 copies) (The Fantod Press, US, 1972)..£125

THE ABANDONED SOCK / THE DISRESPECTFUL SUMMONS / THE LOST LIONS
(26 lettered copies, each signed by Edward Gorey. No d/j, slipcase) (The Fantod Press, US, 1972) £250

A LIMERICK (No d/j. Issued in both brown and orange wrappers) (Salt-Works Press, US, 1973)..................£50

CATEGOREY: FIFTY DRAWINGS (No d/j) (Gotham Book Mart, US, 1973) £50

CATEGOREY: FIFTY DRAWINGS (No d/j. 100 numbered copies and 26 lettered copies signed by Edward Gorey)
(Gotham Books Mart, US, 1973)..£125 / £250

THE GLORIOUS NOSEBLEED, FIFTH ALPHABET (Dodd, Mead, US, 1974) £35

THE GLORIOUS NOSEBLEED, FIFTH ALPHABET
(Dodd, Mead, US, 1974) (250 numbered copies and 26 lettered copies signed by Edward Gorey) .....£125 / £250

L'HEURE BLEUE (No d/j. 500 numbered copies signed by Edward Gorey) (The Fantod Press, US, 1975)............£125

L'HEURE BLEUE (No d/j. Limited to 26 lettered copies signed by Edward Gorey. There were also 58 numbered copies
signed by Edward Gorey printed in an alternate blue stamping) (The Fantod Press, US, 1975) ....£250 / £175

AMPHIGOREY, TOO (G.P. Putnam's, US, 1975)..£50

LES PASSEMENTERIES HORRIBLES (No d/j. 300 numbered and 26 lettered copies signed by Edward Gorey)
(Albondocani Press, US, 1976) ....£125 / £250

THE BROKEN SPOKE (Dodd, Mead, US, 1976) £35

THE BROKEN SPOKE (250 numbered and 26 lettered copies signed by Edward Gorey) (Dodd, Mead, US, 1976)......£125 / £250

THE BROKEN SPOKE (Ernest Benn, 1979)...£25

THE LOATHSOME COUPLE (Dodd, Mead, US, 1977) £35

THE LOATHSOME COUPLE (Limited to 250 numbered and 26 lettered copies
signed by Edward Gorey) (Dodd, Mead, US, 1977) ....£125 / £250

DOGEAR WRYDE POSTCARDS: ALMS FOR OBLIVION SERIES (16 postcards enclosed in white envelope)
(Fantod Press, US, 1978)...£70

THE GREEN BEADS (No d/j. 400 numbered and 26 lettered copies signed by Edward Gorey)
(Albondocani Press, US, 1978)..£125 / £250

DRACULA, A TOY THEATRE (No d/j. Spiral bound) (Charles Scribner's, US, 1979) £50

GOREY POSTERS (No d/j) (Harry N. Abrams, US, 1979)...£50

DOGEAR WRYDE POSTCARDS: INTERPRETIVE SERIES (13 post cards enclosed in white envelope)
(Fantod Press, US, 1979) £70

DOGEAR WRYDE POSTCARDS: INTERPRETIVE SERIES
(50 numbered and 26 lettered sets of postcards, all hand-painted in watercolors by Edward Gorey)..................£500

DOGEAR WRYDE POSTCARDS: NEGLECTED MURDERESSES SERIES (12 post cards enclosed in
white envelope. 250 sets, numbered and signed by Edward Gorey) (Fantod Press, US, 1980)..........................£150

DANCING CATS AND NEGLECTED MURDERESSES (No d/j) (Workman Publishing, US, 1980) £35

DANCING CATS AND NEGLECTED MURDERESSES (No d/j. A limited run of 500 numbered and
26 lettered signed copies with a tipped-in colophon leaf and alternate wrapper design)....................£125 / £250

DANCING CATS AND NEGLECTED MURDERESSES (No d/j) (J.M. Dent, UK, 1980)................................£15

LES URNES UTILES (No d/j. 400 numbered and 26 lettered copies signed by Edward Gorey)
(Halty-Ferguson, US, 1980) ....£125 / £250

F. M. R. A. (33 unbound leaves of various sizes enclosed in linen clamshell box.
400 numbered copies, signed by Edward Gorey) (Andrew Alpern, US, 1980)..£125

LE MELANGE FUNESTE (No d/j. 500 numbered and 26 lettered copies signed by Edward Gorey)
(Gotham Book Mart, US, 1981)...£125 / £250

THE DWINDLING PARTY (No d/j) (Random House, US, 1982) £15

THE DWINDLING PARTY (No d/j) (Heinemann, UK, 1982) £10

THE WATER FLOWERS (Congdon & Weed, US, 1982) £35

THE PRUNE PEOPLE (Limited to 400 numbered and 26 lettered copies signed by Edward Gorey)
(Albondocani Press, US, 1983)..£125 / £250

THE ECLECTIC ABECEDARIUM (No d/j. 300 copies [numbered 101 to 400] signed by Edward Gorey)
(Anne & David Bromer, US, 1983) £125

THE ECLECTIC ABECEDARIUM (No d/j in slipcase. 100 copies [numbered 1 to 100] each drawing hand-painted
in multi-colored watercolours by Edward Gorey) (Anne & David Bromer, US, 1983).......................................£700

AMPHIGOREY ALSO (Congdon & Weed, US, 1983)..£50

AMPHIGOREY ALSO (250 numbered and 26 lettered copies signed by Edward Gorey)
(Congdon & Weed, US, 1983)...£125 / £250

E.D. WARD: A MERCURIAL BEAR (No d/j) (Gotham Book Mart, US, 1983)...£35

THE TUNNEL CALAMITY (No d/j. Clear plastic eye-piece fitted into cover board) (G.P. Putnam's, US, 1984)..........................£25
LES ECHANGES MALANDREUX (No d/j. 500 numbered and 26 lettered copies signed by Edward Gorey)
(Metacom Press, US, 1985)...£125 / £250
THE PRUNE PEOPLE II (No d/j. 300 numbered and 26 lettered copies signed by Edward Gorey)
(Albondocani Press, US, 1985)..£125 / £250
THE IMPROVABLE LANDSCAPE (No d/j. 300 numbered and 26 lettered copies signed by Edward Gorey)
(A Piermont Book/Albondocani Press, US, 1986)...£125 / £250
THE RAGING TIDE: OR, THE BLACK DOLL'S IMBROGLIO
(Beaufort Books Publishers /A Peter Weed Book, US, 1987)...£50
Q.R.V. (400 copies, 290 of which are numbered and signed by Edward Gorey,
including 110 deluxe limited signed copies issued in a slipcase) (Anne and David Bromer, US, 1989)..........£70 / £125 / £175
Q.R.V (as THE UNIVERSAL SOLVENT; No d/j) (The Fantod Press, US, 1990)..£35
THE DRIPPING FAUCET; FOURTEEN HUNDRED & FIFTY EIGHT TINY, TEDIOUS, & TERRIBLE TALES
(No d/j. 500 numbered and 26 hand-colored lettered signed copies) (Metacom Press, US, 1989)................£125 / £500
DOGEAR WRYDE POSTCARDS: TRAGEDIES TOPIARES SERIES
(12 postcards in white envelope. 250 numbered and signed sets) (Privately Printed, US, 1989)............................£150
DOGEAR WRYDE POSTCARDS: MENACED OBJECTS SERIES (16 postcards in white envelope.
250 numbered and signed sets) (No publisher, US, 1989)...£150
THE HELPLESS DOORKNOB: A SHUFFLED STORY (20 laminated cards in plastic box.
Limited to 500 numbered and signed sets) (No publisher, US, 1989)...£125
DOGEAR WRYDE POSTCARDS: WHATEVER NEXT? SERIES (12 postcards in white envelope.
250 sets, numbered and signed by Edward Gorey) (No publisher, US, 1990)..£150
THE TUNING FORK (No d/j, 500 numbered and signed copies.
First separate edition, originally published in AMPHIGOREY ALSO) (The Fantod Press, US, 1990)..........................£70
THE STUPID JOKE (No d/j, 500 numbered and signed copies) (The Fantod Press, US, 1990).................................£70
THE FRAUGHT SETTEE (No d/j, 500 numbered and signed copies) (The Fantod Press, US, 1990).........................£70
LA BALLADE TROUBLANTE (No d/j) (The Fantod Press, US, 1991)..£15
THE GRAND PASSION: A NOVEL (No d/j, issued in white envelope. 500 numbered and signed copies)
(The Fantod Press, US, 1991)...£70
THE DOLEFUL DOMESTICITY; ANOTHER NOVEL (No d/j, issued in white envelope.
500 numbered and signed copies) (The Fantod Press, US, 1991)...£70
THE BETRAYED CONFIDENCE: SEVEN SERIES OF DOGEAR WRYDE POSTCARDS
(Bound volume of seven previously issued 'Dogear Wryde' postcard series) (Parnasuss Imprints, US, 1992) £50
THE BETRAYED CONFIDENCE (deluxe edition. Issued in black slipcase. 250 boxed copies with additional loose plate)
(Parnasuss Imprints, US, 1992)..£125
THE POINTLESS BOOK: OR, NATURE & ART (by 'Garrod Weedy', no d/j) (The Fantod Press, US, 1993) £25
THE FLOATING ELEPHANT [PLUS] THE DANCING ROCK (Printed back to back.
100 copies numbered and signed by Edward Gorey) (The Fantod Press, US, 1993)..£125
FIGBASH ACROBATE ('by Aedwyrd Gore, 500 numbered and 26 lettered copies signed by Edward Gorey. No d/j)
(The Fantod Press, US, 1994)..£70 / £125
THE RETRIEVED LOCKET (500 numbered and 26 lettered copies signed by Edward Gorey. No d/j)
(The Fantod Press, US, 1994)..£70 / £125
THE UNKNOWN VEGETABLE (500 numbered copies signed by Edward Gorey. No d/j) (The Fantod Press, US, 1995)..........£70
THE FANTOD PACK; INTERPRETED BY MADAME GROEDA WEYRD (20 laminated printed cards and booklet issued in
grey box. Limited to 750 numbered and 26 lettered copies signed by Edward Gorey) (Gotham Book Mart, US, 1995) ....£50 / £125
THE FANTOD PACK; INTERPRETED BY MADAME GROEDA WEYRD
(20 cards wrapped in a yellow sheet. Produced without Gorey's permission) (Owl Press, US, [1996]) £25
Q.R.V. HIKUPTAH: A DOZEN DOGEAR WRYDE POSTCARDS (12 postcards in white envelope with pictorial stamping.
Limited to 500 sets, numbered and signed by Edward Gorey) (The Fantod Press, US, 1996) £70
THE JUST DESSERT: THOUGHTFUL ALPHABET XI
(750 numbered and 26 lettered copies signed by Edward Gorey. No d/j) (The Fantod Press, US, 1997) ....£50 / £125
THE DEADLY BLOTTER: THOUGHTFUL ALPHABET XVII (750 numbered and 26 lettered copies
signed by Edward Gorey. No d/j) (The Fantod Press, US, 1997)...£50 / £125
THE HAUNTED TEA-COSY: A DISPIRITED AND DISTASTEFUL DIVERSION FOR CHRISTMAS (Harcourt Brace, US, 1997)......£12
THE HAUNTED TEA-COSY: A DISPIRITED AND DISTASTEFUL DIVERSION FOR CHRISTMAS
(Issued in a navy blue slipcase, with d/j. Limited to 500 numbered and 26 lettered copies signed by Edward Gorey)
(Harcourt Brace, US, 1997)..£50 / £125
THE HEADLESS BUST: A MELANCHOLY MEDITATION ON THE FALSE MILLENNIUM
(A sequel to THE HAUNTED TEA-COSY) (Harcourt Brace, US, 1999)...£12
THE HEADLESS BUST: A MELANCHOLY MEDITATION ON THE FALSE MILLENNIUM
(Issued in a green cloth slipcase. Limited to 750 numbered and 26 lettered copies signed by Edward Gorey.
Accompanied by a 15" Bahhumbug beanbag cloth doll.) (Harcourt Brace, US, 1999) ....£50 / £175

GOSCINNY, René and UDERZO, Albert

French writer/artist team. Born in 1926 and 1927 respectively, the two men have — together or separately — worked on many comic strips, but are best-known for their series of books featuring the 'indomitable Gaul', Asterix. He made his first appearance in the French magazine, *Pilote*, in 1959, and has since featured in well over two dozen books. Goscinny also created the characters Lucky Luke, Ompa-pa, Iznogoud and Nicholas, although in collaboration with other artists. He died in 1977.
Prices are for books in Very Good condition.

'Asterix' Books
ASTERIX THE GAUL (Brockhampton Press, 1969) £60
ASTERIX AND CLEOPATRA (Brockhampton Press, 1969) £50

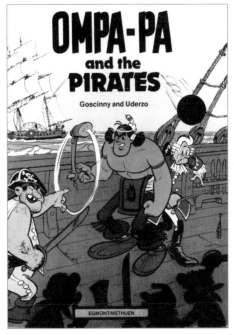

Two of the most popular 'Asterix' adventures were reprinted in this unusual compendium volume in 1977.

The third volume in the less well-known 'Ompa-Pa' series, also first published in hardback pictorial boards in 1977.

ASTERIX THE GLADIATOR (Brockhampton Press, 1969) **£50**
ASTERIX IN BRITAIN (Brockhampton Press, 1970).. **£40**
ASTERIX THE LEGIONARY (Brockhampton Press, 1970) **£40**
ASTERIX IN SPAIN (Brockhampton Press, 1971) **£30**
ASTERIX AND THE BIG FIGHT (Brockhampton Press, 1971) **£30**
ASTERIX AND THE ROMAN AGENT (Brockhampton Press, 1972)... **£30**
ASTERIX AT THE OLYMPIC GAMES (Brockhampton Press, 1972).. **£30**
ASTERIX IN SWITZERLAND (Brockhampton Press, 1973)... **£30**
THE MANSIONS OF THE GODS (Brockhampton Press, 1973).. **£30**
ASTERIX AND THE LAUREL WREATH (Brockhampton Press, 1974)... **£30**
ASTERIX AND THE GOTHS (Brockhampton Press, 1974).. **£30**
ASTERIX AND THE SOOTHSAYER (Brockhampton Press, 1975)... **£30**
ASTERIX AND THE GOLDEN SICKLE (Hodder & Stoughton, 1975)... **£20**
ASTERIX AND THE GREAT CROSSING (Hodder & Stoughton, 1976)... **£20**
ASTERIX AND THE CAULDRON (Hodder & Stoughton, 1976)... **£20**
ASTERIX AND THE CIRCUS OF ROME (push-out book) (GeminiScan Publishing, 1976)................................. **£40**
ASTERIX AND THE CHIEFTAN'S SHIELD (Hodder & Stoughton, 1977)... **£20**
ASTERIX AND CAESAR'S GIFT (Hodder & Stoughton, 1977).. **£20**
ASTERIX AND THE NORMANS (Hodder & Stoughton, 1978) **£20**
ASTERIX AND THE TWELVE TASKS (push-out book) (GeminiScan Publishing, 1978).................................... **£40**
ASTRERIX AND THE PIRATES (push-out book) (GeminiScan Publishing, 1978).. **£40**
OBELIX AND CO. (Hodder & Stoughton, 1979) **£20**
ASTERIX AND THE BANQUET (Hodder & Stoughton, 1979)... **£20**
ASTERIX IN CORSICA (Hodder & Stoughton, 1979 [1980]) **£20**
THREE ADVENTURES OF ASTERIX (contains 'Asterix in Britain', 'Asterix in Switzerland' and 'Asterix the Gaul')
   (Hodder & Stoughton, [1979]) **£15**
ASTERIX IN BELGIUM (Hodder & Stoughton, 1980).. **£15**
ASTERIX AND THE GREAT DIVIDE (Hodder & Stoughton, 1981)... **£15**
ASTERIX AND THE BLACK GOLD (Hodder & Stoughton, 1982) **£15**
ADVENTURES OF ASTERIX (contains 'Asterix the Gaul', 'Asterix and the Soothsayer', 'Asterix and the Goths' and
   'Asterix and Caesar's Gift') (Hodder & Stoughton, 1982) **£15**
ASTERIX AND SON (Hodder & Stoughton, 1983)... **£15**
ASTERIX AND THE MAGIC CARPET (Hodder & Stoughton, 1988) **£10**
HOW OBELIX FELL INTO THE MAGIC POTION WHEN HE WAS A LITTLE BOY (Hodder & Stoughton, 1989)....... **£10**
ASTERIX AND THE SECRET WEAPON (Hodder & Stoughton, 1991) **£10**

'Asterix' Film Books

THE TWELVE TASKS OF ASTERIX (contains 'The Race', 'The Javelin', 'The Judo Match', 'The Isle of Pleasure', 'The Magician', 'The Chef', 'The Cave of the Beast', 'The Place that Sends You Mad', 'The Crocodiles', 'The Old Man of the Mountains', 'The Ghostly Legionnaires' and 'The Circus') (Hodder & Stoughton, 1978) £10
ASTERIX VERSUS CAESAR (Hodder & Stoughton, 1986) £5
OPERATION GETAFIX (Hodder & Stoughton, 1990) £5
ASTERIX TASK PACK (contains 'The Race', 'The Javelin', 'The Judo Match', 'The Isle of Pleasure', 'The Magician', 'The Chef', 'The Cave of the Beast', 'The Place that Sends You Mad', 'The Crocodiles', 'The Old Man of the Mountains', 'The Legionnaires' and 'The Circus') (Hodder & Stoughton, 1976) ..... each £5

'Ompa-Pa' Books

OMPA-PA AND BROTHER TWO SCALP (Methuen, 1977) £20
OMPA-PA SAVES THE DAY (Methuen, 1977) £20
OMPA-PA AND THE PIRATES (Methuen, 1977) £20
OMPA-PA AND THE SECRET MISSION (Methuen, 1978) £15
OMPA-PA AND THE PRUSSIANS (Methuen, 1978) £15

'Lucky Luke' Books (Goscinny and Morris)

JESSE JAMES (Brockhampton Press, 1972) £20
THE STAGE COACH (Brockhampton Press, 1972) £15
DALTON CITY (Brockhampton Press, 1973) £15
THE TENDERFOOT (Brockhampton Press, 1974) £15
WESTERN CIRCUS (Hodder & Stoughton, 1974) £15
APACHE CANYON (Hodder & Stoughton, 1974) £12
MA DALTON (Hodder & Stoughton, 1980) £12
THE DASHING WHITE COWBOY (Hodder & Stoughton, 1982) £12
CURING THE DALTONS (Hodder & Stoughton, 1982) £12

'Iznogoud' Books (Goscinny and Tabary)

IZNOGOUD ON HOLIDAY (Methuen, 1977) £12
IZNOGOUD THE INFAMOUS (Methuen, 1977) £12
THE WICKED WILES OF IZNOGOUD (Methuen, 1978) £10
IZNOGOUD AND THE MAGIC COMPUTER (Methuen, 1978) £10
A CARROT FOR IZNOGOUD (Egmont, 1979) £10
IZNOGOUD AND THE DAY OF MISRULE (Egmont, 1979) £10
IZNOGOUD ROCKETS TO STARDOM (Egmont, 1980) £12
IZNOGOUD AND THE MAGIC CARPET (Egmont, 1980) £12

'Nicholas' Books (Goscinny and Sempé)

YOUNG NICHOLAS (issued with dustjacket) (Hutchinson, 1961) £55
NICHOLAS AND THE GANG AT SCHOOL (Abelard-Schuman, 1976) £15
NICHOLAS AND THE GANG (Abelard-Schuman, 1977) £15
NICHOLAS AND THE GANG AGAIN (Abelard-Schuman, 1977) £12
NICHOLAS ON HOLIDAY (Abelard-Schuman, 1978) £12
NICHOLAS AT LARGE (Abelard-Schuman, 1979) £12

GOUDGE, Elizabeth

British author. Born: Wells, Somerset, in 1900. Awarded the Carnegie Medal in 1947. Her books are old-fashioned, with an openly religious element. Notable for *The Little White Horse*. Died: 1984.
Prices are for books in Very Good condition with dustjackets where applicable.

THE FAIRIES' BABY and Other Stories (Foyles, 1919) £80
SISTER OF THE ANGELS: A Christmas Story (illustrated by C. Walter Hodges) (Duckworth, 1939) £20
SMOKY-HOUSE (illustrated by C. Walter Hodges) (Duckworth, 1940) £35
HENRIETTA'S HOUSE (illustrated by Lorna R. Steele) (University of London Press/Hodder & Stoughton, 1942) £35
THE LITTLE WHITE HORSE (illustrated by C. Walter Hodges) (University of London Press, 1946) £70
MAKE-BELIEVE (illustrated by C. Walter Hodges) (Duckworth, 1949) £40
THE VALLEY OF SONG (illustrated by Steven Spurrier) (University of London Press, 1951) £40
LINNETS AND VALERIANS (illustrated by Ian Ribbons) (Brockhampton Press, 1964) £40
I SAW THREE SHIPS (illustrated by Richard Kennedy) (Brockhampton Press, 1969) £40
THE LOST ANGEL (illustrated by Shirley Hughes) (Hodder & Stoughton, 1971) £25

GRAHAME, Kenneth

British author. Born: Edinburgh, 1859. Educated at St. Edward's School, Oxford, he was unable to attend university for financial reasons, instead obtaining a clerkship at the Bank of England, where he remained until 1908. Enjoyed modest success as an essayist before establishing his reputation with the story collections, *The Golden Age* (1895) and *Dream Days* (1898), and finally the classic children's novel, *The Wind in the Willows* (1908). The last was brilliantly illustrated by E.H. Shepard in 1931. Grahame's only son, Alastair, committed suicide while a student at Oxford in 1920. Died: 1932.
Prices are for books in Very Good condition with dustjackets where applicable.

PAGAN PAPERS (frontispiece by Aubrey Beardsley) (John Lane/Elkin Matthews, 1894 [1893]) £150

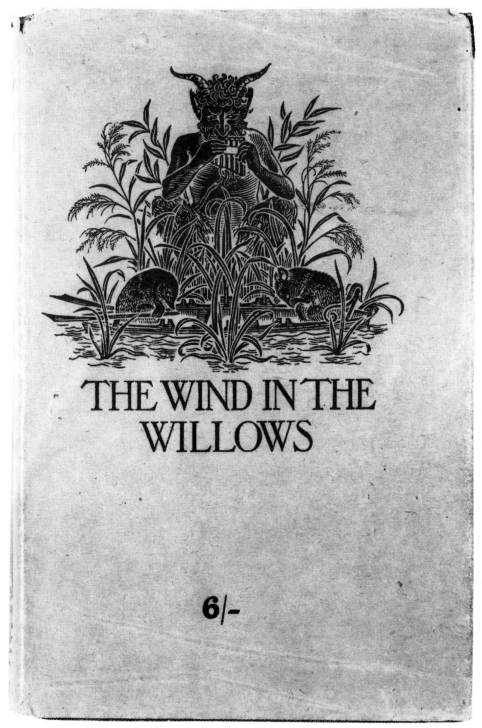

The incredibly rare buff dustjacket designed by Graham Robertson for the
*first edition of **The Wind in the Willows** (1908), today worth around £45,000.*

The first edition of **The Wind in the Willows** *in its more common state – without a dustjacket. For most people, E.H. Shepard's illustrations, first issued in this edition by Methuen in 1931 (right), remain unsurpassed.*

THE GOLDEN AGE (John Lane, 1895)..**£200**
THE GOLDEN AGE (illustrated by Maxfield Parrish) (John Lane, 1900)..**£100**
THE GOLDEN AGE (illustrated by R.J. Enraght-Moony) (John Lane: The Bodley Head, 1915 [1914]) **£40**
THE GOLDEN AGE (illustrated by Lois Lenski) (The Bodley Head, 1922) **£50**
THE GOLDEN AGE (illustrated by E.H. Shepard; in dustjacket) (The Bodley Head, 1928)......................**£150**
THE GOLDEN AGE (illustrated by E.H. Shepard; limited to 275 copies, signed by the author and artist; in slipcase)
(The Bodley Head, 1928)..**£600**
DREAM DAYS (John Lane, 1898)..**£300**
DREAM DAYS (illustrated by Lois Lenski) (The Bodley Head, 1922)..**£60**
DREAM DAYS (illustrated by E.H. Shepard; in dustjacket) (The Bodley Head, 1930)..............................**£150**
DREAM DAYS (illustrated by E.H. Shepard; limited to 275 copies, signed by the author and artist)
(The Bodley Head, 1930)..**£600**
THE GOLDEN AGE and DREAM DAYS (omnibus; illustrated by Charles Keeping; in dustjacket)
(The Bodley Head, 1962) **£80**
THE WIND IN THE WILLOWS (frontispiece by Graham Robertson; with dustjacket) (Methuen, 1908)...........**£45,000**
THE WIND IN THE WILLOWS (frontispiece by Graham Robertson; without dustjacket) (Methuen, 1908)............**£5,000**
THE WIND IN THE WILLOWS (illustrated by E.H. Shepard; with dustjacket) (Methuen, 1931)....................**£600**
THE WIND IN THE WILLOWS (illustrated by E.H. Shepard; limited to 200 copies, signed by the author and artist;
issued with dustjacket) (Methuen, 1931)..**£4,000**
THE WIND IN THE WILLOWS (illustrated by Arthur Rackham; limited to 2,020 numbered copies,
signed by the designer, Bruce Rogers; in slipcase) (Limited Editions Club, U.S., 1940) **£1,000**
THE WIND IN THE WILLOWS (illustrated by Arthur Rackham; in dustjacket) (Heritage, U.S., 1940)..............**£100**
FIRST WHISPER OF 'THE WIND IN THE WILLOWS' Edited by Elspeth Grahame (in dustjacket) (Methuen, 1944) **£35**
THE WIND IN THE WILLOWS (illustrated by Arthur Rackham; omits several of the colour plates from
the original American edition; in dustjacket) (Methuen, 1950) **£150**
THE WIND IN THE WILLOWS (illustrated by Arthur Rackham; limited to 500 copies; in box) (Methuen, 1951)...............**£1,500**
THE WIND IN THE WILLOWS (illustrated by E.H. Shepard; colour plates; in dustjacket) (Methuen, 1959)......**£125**
THE WIND IN THE WILLOWS (illustrated by E.H. Shepard; first full-colour edition; in dustjacket) (Methuen, 1971) **£60**
THE WIND IN THE WILLOWS (illustrated by Arthur Rackham; twelve colour plates and fifteen line drawings)
(Methuen Children's Books, 1975; in dustjacket) **£50**
THE WIND IN THE WILLOWS (illustrated by Michael Hague; in dustjacket) (Holt, U.S., 1980)....................**£50**
THE WIND IN THE WILLOWS (illustrated by Michael Hague; in dustjacket) (Methuen, 1980) **£40**
THE WIND IN THE WILLOWS (illustrated by John Burningham; in slipcase; in dustjacket)
(Viking, 1983) **£80**
THE CAMBRIDGE BOOK OF POETRY FOR CHILDREN Edited by Kenneth Grahame (CUP, 1916) **£40**

THE KENNETH GRAHAME BOOK
(contains 'The Golden Age', 'Dream Days' and 'The Wind in the Willows') (Methuen, 1932)....................................£35
SWEET HOME (adapted from 'The Wind in the Willows'; in dustjacket) (Methuen, 1946)...£30
TOAD GOES CARAVANNING (adapted from 'The Wind in the Willows'; in dustjacket) (Methuen, 1947) £30
BERTIE'S ESCAPADE (reprinted from 'First Whisper of "The Wind in the Willows"') (Methuen, 1949)...................£60
THE RELUCTANT DRAGON (illustrated by Michael Hague; in dustjacket) (Holt, US, 1983)....................................£25
MY DEAREST MOUSE: The 'Wind in the Willows' Letters (in dustjacket) (Methuen, 1988)...................................£25

GRAVES, Robert

British author. Born: Robert von Ranke Graves in 1895. Best known for his poetry and adult novels, notably *I, Claudius* (1934), but also wrote a number of verse and prose works for children. Died: 1985.

Prices are for books in Very Good condition with dustjackets where applicable.

THE PENNY FIDDLE: Poems for Children (illustrated by Edward Ardizzone) (Cassell, 1960)............................£100
THE BIG GREEN BOOK (illustrated by Maurice Sendak) (Crowell-Crozier, U.S., 1962)..£60
THE BIG GREEN BOOK (illustrated by Maurice Sendak; paperback) (Puffin, 1978) £20
ANN AT HIGHWOOD HALL: Poems for Children (illustrated by Edward Ardizzone) (Cassell, 1964)................£90
TWO WISE CHILDREN (illustrated by Ralph Pinto) (Quist, U.S., 1967) £35
THE POOR BOY WHO FOLLOWED HIS STAR (Cassell, 1968) £25
AN ANCIENT CASTLE (Peter Owen, 1980) £15

GREENAWAY, Kate

British author-illustrator. Born: London, 1846, but spent the formative years of her childhood in Rolleston, a village in Nottinghamshire. Studied at the Female School of Art in South Kensington and the Slade School, subsequently working as a freelance painter/illustrator before Edmund Evans published her first solo 'picture book', the hugely successful *Under the Window*, in 1879. Many more followed, as well as several almanacks. Enjoyed a long friendship with John Ruskin, who was a great admirer of her work. Died: 1901.

Prices are for books in Very Good condition.

Books

AUNT LOUISA'S NURSERY FAVOURITE (Warne, 1870)..£350
DIAMONDS AND TOADS (Warne, 1871) £900
PUCK AND BLOSSOM by Rosa Mulholland (Marcus Ward, 1875) £250
FAIRY GIFTS; or A Wallet of Wonders by Kathleen Knox (Griffith & Farran, 1875).....................................£225
SEVEN BIRTHDAYS by Kathleen Knox (Griffith & Farran, 1876)...£225
THE QUIVER OF LOVE: A Collection of Valentines Ancient and Modern (Marcus Ward, 1876) £120
TOPO: A Tale About English Children in Italy by G.E. Brunefile (Marcus Ward, 1878)................................£100
UNDER THE WINDOW by Kate Greenaway (verse) (Routledge, 1879) £250
THE 'LITTLE FOLKS' PAINTING BOOK (Cassell, Petter & Galpin, 1879)..£300
KATE GREENAWAY'S BIRTHDAY BOOK FOR CHILDREN (Routledge, 1880)...£150
MOTHER GOOSE, or The Old Nursery Rhymes (Routledge, 1881)...£175
A DAY IN A CHILD'S LIFE (music by Myles Birket Foster) (Routledge, 1881) £250
LITTLE ANN and Other Poems by J. & A. Taylor (Routledge, 1883) £140
LANGUAGE OF FLOWERS (Routledge, 1884)..£125
A PAINTING BOOK (wrappers) (Routledge, 1884)..£225
SONGS FOR THE NURSERY (Routledge, 1884)...£125
MARIGOLD GARDEN (Routledge, 1885)...£250
KATE GREENAWAY'S ALBUM (limited to eight copies) (Routledge, 1885)...£7,000
KATE GREENAWAY'S ALPHABET (miniature book; card covers) (Routledge, 1885)..................................£120
ENGLISH SPELLING BOOK (Routledge, 1885)..£120
DAME WIGGINS OF LEE AND HER SEVEN WONDERFUL CATS (George Allen, 1885) £40
AN APPLE PIE (Routledge, 1886) £300
RHYMES FOR THE YOUNG FOLK (Cassell, 1886)..£100
QUEEN VICTORIA'S JUBILEE GARLAND (Routledge, 1887)..£200
BABY'S BIRTHDAY BOOK (Marcus Ward, 1887)...£125
THE PIED PIPER OF HAMELIN by Robert Browning (Routledge, 1888) £150
THE ROYAL PROGRESS OF KING PEPITO by Beatrice Cresswell (SPCK, 1889)..£150
KATE GREENAWAY'S BOOK OF GAMES (Routledge, 1889) £300
THE APRIL BABY'S BOOK OF TUNES by the author of 'Elizabeth and Her German Garden' (Macmillan, 1900)........£150
LITTLEDOM CASTLE and Other Tales by Mabel H. Spielmann (illustrated by Kate Greenaway and others)
(Routledge, 1903)..£100

Almanacks (prices are for Almancks without their original envelope. If these are present, prices should be tripled)

1883 (pictorial boards) (Routledge, [1882])..£200
1884 (pictorial wrappers) (Routledge, [1883])...£200
1885 (pictorial boards) (Routledge, [1884])...£175
1886 (pictorial boards) (Routledge, [1885])...£150
1887 (pictorial boards) (Routledge, [1886])...£100
1888 (pictorial boards) (Routledge, [1887])...£100

1889 (pictorial boards) (Routledge, [1888])......	**£150**
1890 (pictorial boards) (Routledge, [1889])......	**£100**
1891 (pictorial boards) (Routledge, [1890])......	**£100**
1892 (pictorial boards) (Routledge, [1891])......	**£100**
1893 (pictorial boards) (Routledge, [1892])......	**£100**
1894 (pictorial boards) (Routledge, [1893])......	**£100**
1895 (pictorial boards) (Routledge, [1894])......	**£100**

The 1896 was never published

1897 (leather binding) (Routledge, [1896])	**£600**
1924 (pictorial boards) (Routledge, [1923])......	**£50**
1925 (pictorial boards) (Routledge, [1924])......	**£50**
1926 (pictorial boards) (Routledge, [1925])......	**£50**
1927 (pictorial boards) (Routledge, [1926])......	**£50**
1928 (pictorial boards) (Routledge, [1927])......	**£50**
1929 (leather binding) (Routledge, [1928])	**£100**

Calendars

CALENDAR OF THE SEASONS (Marcus Ward, 1876/1877/1881/1882)	each **£75**
A CALENDAR OF THE MONTHS (Marcus Ward, 1884)......	**£50**
KATE GREENAWAY'S CALENDAR (Routledge, 1884/1897/1899)	each **£100**

A charming illustration by Kate Greenaway, produced for Routledge in the 1880s. Her early almanacks were issued in flimsy envelopes, and you can expect to pay three times as much for copies with these intact.

GREENE, Graham

British author. Born: 1904. The great novelist wrote four 'picture books', the first for Eyre & Spottiswoode while he working as a director of the firm. Originally illustrated by Dorothy Craigie, they were later reissued with pictures by Edward Ardizzone. Died: 1993.

Prices are for books in Very Good condition with dustjackets.

THE LITTLE TRAIN (anonymous; illustrated by Dorothy Craigie) (Eyre & Spottiswoode, [1946])..**£600**
THE LITTLE TRAIN(illustrated by Edward Ardizzone) (The Bodley Head, 1973) **£100**
THE LITTLE FIRE ENGINE (illustrated by Dorothy Craigie) (Parrish, [1950])...**£400**
THE LITTLE FIRE ENGINE (illustrated by Edward Ardizzone) (The Bodley Head, 1973) **£100**
THE LITTLE HORSE BUS (illustrated by Dorothy Craigie) (Parrish, [1952])...**£350**
THE LITTLE HORSE BUS (illustrated by Edward Ardizzone) (The Bodley Head, 1974)...**£100**
THE LITTLE STEAM ROLLER (illustrated by Dorothy Craigie) (Parrish, [1953]) **£350**
THE LITTLE STEAM ROLLER (illustrated by Edward Ardizzone) (The Bodley Head, 1974)..**£100**

'GREYFRIARS HOLIDAY' ANNUALS

British annual almost entirely devoted to the work of 'Frank Richards' (Charles Hamilton), containing stories and features about his most popular schools, Rookwood, St. Jim's and Greyfriars. Published by Amalgamated Press, it was launched in 1919 under the title *The Holiday Annual for Boys and Girls*, but was renamed *The Greyfriars Holiday Annual for Boys and Girls* for the next issue. The title was killed off by the war, the final edition appearing in 1941.

Prices are for books in Very Good condition.

THE HOLIDAY ANNUAL ANNUAL FOR BOYS AND GIRLS 1920 [1919] **£50**
THE GREYFRIARS HOLIDAY ANNUAL FOR BOYS AND GIRLS 1921 [1920] **£35**
THE GREYFRIARS HOLIDAY ANNUAL FOR BOYS AND GIRLS 1922 [1921]-1937 [1936] ....each **£35**
THE GREYFRIARS HOLIDAY ANNUAL FOR BOYS AND GIRLS 1938 [1937]-1939 [1938] ....each **£35**
THE GREYFRIARS HOLIDAY ANNUAL FOR BOYS AND GIRLS 1940 [1939]-1941 [1940] ....each **£30**

The third of Graham Greene's four collaborations with Dorothy Craigie, worth £350.

187

GRIMM, Jacob and Wilhelm

German philologists and collectors of fairy tales. Jacob Ludwig Carl Grimm and Wilhelm Carl Grimm were born in Hanau, near Frankfurt, in 1785 and 1786 respectively. They both studied at Marburg University, where they developed their interest in German folk literature. Their first volume of *Kinder-und Hausmärchen* ('Nursery and Household Tales') was published in 1812, the second appearing two years later. Amongst the tales included in these volumes were versions of 'Little Red Riding-Hood', 'The Sleeping Beauty' and 'Hansel and Gretel'. They were first translated into English by a London lawyer, Edgar Taylor, appearing in two volumes along with illustrations by George Cruikshank. The first comprehensive edition was that of Margaret Hunt (1884), which featured an introduction by Andrew Lang. The brothers died in 1863 and 1859 respectively.

Prices are for books in Very Good condition (with dustjackets after 1971).

GERMAN POPULAR STORIES (first English edition; illustrated by George Cruikshank; translated by Edgar Taylor; two volumes) (C. Baldwin, 1824-26) .... the set **£750**

THE FAIRY RING: A New Collection of Popular Tales (illustrated by R. Doyle; translated by Edgar Taylor) (John Murray, 1846) **£1,200**

HOUSEHOLD STORIES (illustrated by E.H. Wehnert; new translation; two volumes) (Addey, 1853) **£175**

GRIMM'S GOBLINS (illustrated by 'Phiz') ('Fairy Books for Boys and Girls', [1861]) **£175**

HOUSEHOLD STORIES (illustrated by Walter Crane; translated by L. Crane) (Macmillan, 1882) **£90**

FAIRY TALES OF THE BROTHERS GRIMM (illustrated by Arthur Rackham; translated by Mrs Edgar Lucas) (Freemantle, 1900) **£300**

GRIMM'S FAIRY TALES (illustrated by John Hassall) (Sands, 1902) **£80**

GRIMM'S FAIRY TALES. Selected and edited for little folk (illustrated by Helen Stratton) (Blackie, [1903]) **£20**

GRIMM'S FAIRY TALES. Edited by J.R. Monsell (illustrated by J.R. Monsell) (Cassell, 1908) **£30**

GRIMM'S FAIRY TALES. Selected and retold by Githa Sowerby (illustrated by Millicent Sowerby) (Grant Richards, 1909) **£100**

FAIRY TALES OF THE BROTHERS GRIMM (illustrated by Arthur Rackham; translated by Mrs Edgar Lucas) (Constable, 1909) **£750**

FAIRY TALES OF THE BROTHERS GRIMM (illustrated by Arthur Rackham; limited to 750 copies, signed by the artist) (Constable, 1909) **£3,000**

FAIRY TALES OF THE BROTHERS GRIMM (illustrated by Arthur Rackham) (Constable, 1920) **£300**

FAIRY TALES OF THE BROTHERS GRIMM (illustrated by Arthur Rackham) (Heinemann, [1925]) **£150**

GRIMM'S FAIRY TALES (illustrated by Mabel Lucie Attwell) (Cassell, [1910]) **£120**

GRIMM'S FAIRY TALES (illustrated by Charles Robinson; translated by L.L. Weedon) (Children's Classics, [1910]) **£50**

GRIMM'S FAIRY TALES (illustrated by Charles Folkard; introduction by John Ruskin) (A. & C. Black, 1911) **£40**

GRIMM'S FAIRY STORIES (illustrated by Mabel Lucie Attwell) (Raphael Tuck, 1912) **£150**

GRIMM'S FAIRY TALES (illustrated by Monro S. Orr) (Harrap, 1914) **£25**

LITTLE BROTHER AND LITTLE SISTER (illustrated by Arthur Rackham) (Constable, 1917) **£300**

LITTLE BROTHER AND LITTLE SISTER (illustrated by Arthur Rackham; with extra plate; limited to 525 copies, signed by the artist) (Constable, 1917) .... **£2,000** (without extra plate: **£1,250**)

SNOWDROP and Other Tales (illustrated by Arthur Rackham; reprint from 'Fairy Tales of the Brothers Grimm' [1909]) (Constable, 1920) **£400**

GRIMM'S FAIRY TALES (illustrated by Anne Anderson) (Collins, [1922]) **£75**

GRIMM'S FAIRY TALES (illustrated by Louis Rhead) (Harper, [1923]) **£25**

HANSEL AND GRETEL and Other Stories (illustrated by Kay Nielsen) (Hodder & Stoughton, [1925]) **£800**

HANSEL AND GRETEL and Other Stories (illustrated by Kay Nielsen; limited to 600 copies, signed by the artist; cream buckram binding) (Hodder & Stoughton, [1925]) **£2,000**

GRIMM'S FAIRY TALES (illustrated by Ruth Moorwood and Harry Rountree) (Nelson, [1932]) **£30**

TALES FROM GRIMM (illustrated and translated by Wanda Gág; issued with dustjacket) (Faber, 1937) **£50**

FAIRY TALES: Thirteen Tales (illustrated by R.A. Brandt) (Peter Lunn, 1944) **£10**

HOUSEHOLD TALES (illustrated by Mervyn Peake; issued with dustjacket) (Eyre & Spottiswoode, 1946) **£60**

GRIMMS' FAIRY TALES (illustrated by Charles Folkard) (Dent, 1949) **£30**

GRIMM'S OTHER TALES: A New Selection by Wilhelm Hansen. Translated and edited by Ruth Michaelis-Jena and Arthur Ratcliff (illustrated by Gwenda Morgan) (Golden Cockerel Press, 1956) **£30**

GRIMM'S FOLK TALES (illustrated by George Cruikshank; translated by Eleanor Quarrie; issued without dustjacket) (Folio Society, 1965) **£20**

SIX FAIRY TALES FROM THE BROTHERS GRIMM (illustrated by David Hockney; translated by Heiner Bastian; issued without dustjacket) (Petersburg Press/OUP, [1970]) **£40**

SIX FAIRY TALES FROM THE BROTHERS GRIMM (illustrated by David Hockney; translated by Heiner Bastian; limited to 575 numbered copies, signed by the artist; issued without dustjacket) (Petersburg Press/Kasmin Gallery, [1970]) **£2,750**

THE JUNIPER TREE and Other Tales from Grimm (illustrated by Maurice Sendak; selected by Lore Segal and Maurice Sendak; translated by Lore Segal and Randall Jarrell; two volumes; issued with dustjackets; in slipcase) (Farrar, Strauss & Giroux, U.S., 1973) .... the set **£85**

THE JUNIPER TREE and Other Tales from Grimm (illustrated by Maurice Sendak; selected by Lore Segal and Maurice Sendak; translated by Lore Segal and Randall Jarrell; two volumes; issued with dustjackets; in slipcase) (The Bodley Head, 1974) .... the set **£75**

KING GRISLY-BEARD (illustrated by Maurice Sendak) (The Bodley Head, 1974) **£30**

BROTHERS GRIMM: POPULAR FOLK TALES (illustrated by Michael Foreman) (Gollancz, 1978) **£25**

DEAR MILI (illustrated by Maurice Sendak) (Michael di Capua/Farrar, Strauss & Giroux, U.S., 1988) **£35**

DEAR MILI (illustrated by Maurice Sendak) (Viking Kestrel, 1988) **£30**

An Arthur Rackham plate from 1900's **Fairy Tales of the Brothers Grimm***, translated by Mrs Edgar Lucas.*

HADDON, Mark

British author, illustrator and screenwriter. Born: 1962. Wrote several books for children before *The Curious Incident of the Dog in the Night-Time* won the Whitbread Book of the Year in 2003. Also writes the popular 'Agent Z' series, worth around £4 each.

Prices are for books in Fine condition with dustjackets where applicable.

GILBERT'S GOBSTOPPER (issued without dustjacket) (Dutton Children's Books, 1988)..£15
TONI AND THE TOMATO SOUP (issued without dustjacket) (Hamish Hamilton, 1989)..£10
A NARROW ESCAPE FOR PRINCESS SHARON (issued without dustjacket) (Hamish Hamilton, 1989)...............£10
GRIDZBI SPUDVETCH! (paperback) (Walker Books, 1993)...£10
TITCH JOHNSON (issued without dustjacket) (Walker Books, 1993)..£10
REAL PORKY PHILIPS (issued without dustjacket) (A & C Black, 1994) £10
THE SEA OF TRANQUILITY (issued without dustjacket) (Collins, 1996)...£10
OCEAN STAR EXPRESS (Collins, 2001) £10
THE CURIOUS INCIDENT OF THE DOG IN THE NIGHT-TIME (first edition) (Cape, 2003)...................................£35
THE CURIOUS INCIDENT OF THE DOG IN THE NIGHT-TIME (first adult edition) (Cape, 2003)...........................£30
THE CURIOUS INCIDENT OF THE DOG IN THE NIGHT-TIME (limited edition of 1,000 copies,
  signed, numbered, no dustjacket and plain slipcase with sticker; book itself is 'adult' edition,
  although slipcase sticker depicts original children's cover; Waterstone's exclusive) (Cape, 2004)......................£30
A SPOT OF BOTHER (Cape, 2006)..£10

HAGUE, Michael

American artist. Born in Los Angeles in 1948, Hague has established an international reputation as an illustrator of children's classics, notably *The Wind in the Willows* (1980).

Prices are for books in Very Good condition with dustjackets where applicable.

EAST OF THE SUN AND WEST OF THE MOON (Harcourt Brace, US, 1980)..£40
THE WIND IN THE WILLOWS by Kenneth Grahame (Holt, US, 1980)..£50
THE WIND IN THE WILLOWS by Kenneth Grahame (Methuen, 1980)...£40
MICHAEL HAGUE'S FAVOURITE HANS CHRISTIAN ANDERSEN FAIRY TALES (Holt, US, 1981)......................£30
THE MAN WHO KEPT HOUSE (Harcourt Brace, US, 1981)...£35
THE NIGHT BEFORE CHRISTMAS by Clement C. Moore (Holt, US, 1981)..£30
THE WIZARD OF OZ by L. Frank Baum (Holt, US, 1982)...£40
THE DRAGON KITE (Harcourt Brace, US, 1982)...£25
THE RELUCTANT DRAGON by Kenneth Grahame (Holt, US, 1983)...£25
THE LION, THE WITCH AND THE WARDROBE by C.S. Lewis (Macmillan, US, 1983)...£60
THE HOBBIT by J.R.R. Tolkien (Houghton Mifflin, US, 1984) £60
THE HOBBIT by J.R.R. Tolkien (as 'The Illustrated Hobbit') (Allen & Unwin, 1984)...£60
MOTHER GOOSE: A Collection of Nursery Rhymes Edited by Michael Hague (Holt, US, 1984)........................£25
ALPHABEARS (Holt, US, 1984) £25
AESOP'S FABLES Edited by Michael Hague (Holt, US, 1985)..£30
A CHILD'S BOOK OF PRAYERS (Holt, US, 1985) £20
ALICE'S ADVENTURES IN WONDERLAND by Lewis Carroll (Holt, US, 1985) £30
ALICE'S ADVENTURES IN WONDERLAND by Lewis Carroll (Methuen, 1985)..£25
THE LEGEND OF THE VEERY BIRD (Harcourt, US, 1985) £25
OUT OF THE NURSERY, INTO THE NIGHT (Holt, US, 1986)..£25
NUMBEARS: A Counting Book (Holt, US, 1986)..£25
MICHAEL HAGUE'S WORLD OF UNICORNS (Holt, US, 1986)...£20
THE SECRET GARDEN by F.H. Burnett (Holt, US, 1987)..£30
PETER PAN by J.M. Barrie (Holt, US, 1987)..£35
THE LAND OF NOD and Other Poems for Children by R.L. Stevenson. Edited by Michael Hague (Holt, US, 1988) £25
THE UNICORN ALPHABET by Marianna Mayer (Mayer, US, 1989) £20
CINDERELLA and Other Tales from Perrault (Holt, US, 1989)..£20
BEAR HUGS (Holt, US, 1989)...£12
A UNICORN JOURNAL (Arcade, US, 1990)..£18
MY SECRET GARDEN DIARY (Arcade, US, 1990)...£12
OUR BABY: A BOOK OF RECORDS AND MEMORIES (Arcade, US, 1990) £15
MAGIC MOMENTS: A BOOK OF DAYS (Arcade, US, 1990)..£15
WE WISH YOU A MERRY CHRISTMAS (Holt, US, 1990) £10
BOX OF CHRISTMAS CAROLS (includes 'Jingle Bells', 'Deck the Halls' and 'O Christmas Tree') (Holt, US, 1990-)......the set £35
THE BORROWERS by Mary Norton (Harcourt Brace, US, 1991)..£30
THE FAIRY TALES OF OSCAR WILDE (Holt, US, 1993)..£15
TEDDY BEAR TEDDY BEAR (Morrow, US, 1993)..£10
THE RAINBOW FAIRY BOOK by Andrew Lang (Books of Wonder, US, 1993)..£10
THE LITTLE MERMAID by Hans Christian Andersen (Holt, US, 1994)...£10
THE CHILDREN'S BOOK OF VIRTUES by William J. Bennett (Simon &Schuster, US, 1995)...............................£10

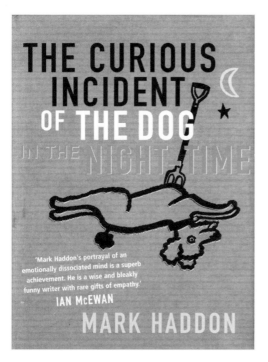

The less-common adult edition of Mark Haddon's 2003 bestseller (see opposite page).

THE OWL AND THE PUSSY-CAT and Other Nonsense Poems by Edward Lear (North-South, US, 1995) **£10**
THE PERFECT PRESENT (illustrated by the author) (Morrow, US, 1996)... **£10**
THE CHILDREN'S BOOK OF HEROES by William J. Bennett (Simon &Schuster, US, 1997)...................................... **£10**
CALANDARBEARS: A Book of Months by Kathleen Hague (Holt, US, 1997) **£15**

HALE, Kathleen
British author-illustrator. Born: Scotland, 1898. Studied at Manchester and Central Schools of Art. Worked as secretary to the painter, Augustus John, and as a freelance artist before publishing the first of her 'Orlando' books, *Orlando the Marmalade Cat: A Camping Holiday*, in 1938. Her autobiography, *A Slender Reputation*, appeared in 1994. Died: 2000.

Prices are for books in Very Good condition with dustjackets where applicable.

'Orlando' Books (all Written and Illustrated by Kathleen Hale)
ORLANDO THE MARMALADE CAT: A CAMPING HOLIDAY (in dustjacket) (Country Life, [1938]) **£450**
ORLANDO THE MARMALADE CAT: A TRIP ABROAD (in dustjacket) (Country Life, [1938]) **£400**
ORLANDO'S EVENING OUT (paperback) (Puffin: 'Picture Books' series No. PP14, [1941])... **£40**
ORLANDO'S EVENING OUT (boards) (Puffin: 'Picture Books' series No. PP14, [1941]).. **£75**
ORLANDO'S HOME LIFE (paperback) (Puffin: 'Picture Books' series No. PP26, [1942])... **£40**
ORLANDO'S HOME LIFE (boards) (Puffin: 'Picture Books' series No. PP26, [1942]).. **£75**
ORLANDO THE MARMALADE CAT BUYS A FARM (card covers) (Country Life, 1942) **£300**
ORLANDO THE MARMALADE CAT: HIS SILVER WEDDING (card covers) (Country Life, 1944).. **£300**
ORLANDO THE MARMALADE CAT BECOMES A DOCTOR (card covers) (Country Life, 1944) **£200**
ORLANDO'S INVISIBLE PYJAMAS (paperback) (Transatlantic Arts, 1947).. **£125**
ORLANDO THE MARMALADE CAT KEEPS A DOG (in dustjacket) (Country Life, 1949) **£350**
ORLANDO THE JUDGE (paperback) (John Murray, 1950)... **£80**
ORLANDO THE MARMALADE CAT: A SEASIDE HOLIDAY (in dustjacket) (Country Life, 1952) **£250**
ORLANDO'S ZOO (paperback) (John Murray, 1954) **£50**
ORLANDO THE MARMALADE CAT: THE FRISKY HOUSEWIFE (boards, no dustjacket) (Country Life, 1956)....................... **£75**
ORLANDO'S MAGIC CARPET (in dustjacket) (John Murray, 1958)... **£100**
ORLANDO THE MARMALADE CAT BUYS A COTTAGE (boards, no dustjacket) (Country Life, 1963) **£75**
ORLANDO AND THE THREE GRACES (in dustjacket) (John Murray, 1965) **£100**
ORLANDO THE MARMALADE CAT GOES TO THE MOON (in dustjacket) (John Murray, 1968).. **£75**
ORLANDO THE MARMALADE CAT AND THE WATER CATS (boards, no dustjacket) (Cape, 1972) **£60**

'Peep-Show' Books (all Written and Illustrated by Kathleen Hale)
ORLANDO'S COUNTRY LIFE (Chatto & Windus, 1950)... **£150**
PUSS-IN-BOOTS (Chatto & Windus, 1951) **£150**

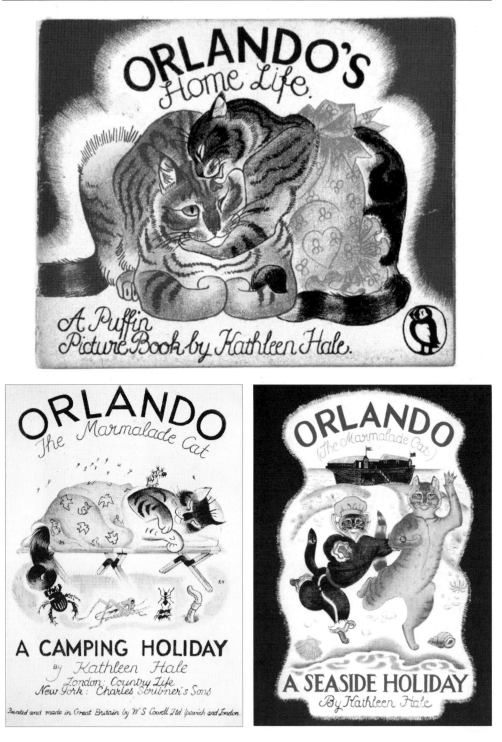

A trio of very collectable 'Orlando the Marmalade Cat' books by Kathleen Hale, including the rare 'Puffin Picture Book' edition.

Other Books Written and Illustrated by Kathleen Hale

'HENRIETTA' THE FAITHFUL HEN (boards, no dustjacket) (Transatlantic Arts, 1943).......................................£100
MANDA THE JERSEY CALF (boards, no dustjacket) (John Murray, 1952)..£60
HENRIETTA'S MAGIC EGG (boards, no dustjacket) (Allen & Unwin, 1973)..£60

Books Illustrated by Kathleen Hale

I DON'T MIX MUCH WITH FAIRIES by Molly Harrower (Eyre & Spottiswoode, 1928)................................£90
PLAIN JANE by Molly Harrower (Eyre & Spottiswoode, 1929)..£75
BASIL SEAL RIDES AGAIN by Evelyn Waugh (in dustjacket) (limited to 750 numbered copies, signed by the author)
    (Chapman & Hall, 1963)..£400

HARGREAVES, Roger

British author-illustrator. Born: 1925. Was working as the director of a London advertising agency when, in the early 1970s, he achieved enormous fame with the 'Mr Men' series of picture books. These were followed by the 'Timbuctoo' and 'Little Miss' series. Died: 1988.

Prices are for books in Fine condition.

'Mr Men' Books

MR BUMP (Thurman, 1971) £15
MR GREED (Thurman, 1971)...............................£15
MR HAPPY (Thurman, 1971) £15
MR DAYDREAM (Thurman, 1972) £15
MR SILLY (Thurman, 1972) £15
MR SMALL (Thurman, 1972)...............................£15
MR UPPITY (Thurman, 1972)..............................£15
MR BOUNCE (Thurman, 1976)............................£15
MR CHATTERBOX (Thurman, 1976) £15
MR DIZZY (Thurman, 1976) £15
MR FORGETFUL (Thurman, 1976).........................£15
MR FUNNY (Thurman, 1976) £15
MR IMPOSSIBLE (Thurman, 1976)........................£15
MR JELLY (Thurman, 1976) £15
MR MEAN (Thurman, 1976) £15
MR MEN'S CHRISTMAS (Thurman, 1976)................£15
MR MEN ON HOLIDAY (Thurman, 1976) £15
MR MUDDLE (Thurman, 1976)............................£15
MR NOISY (Thurman, 1976)...............................£15
MR STRONG (Thurman, 1976) £15
MR MEN'S SPORTS DAY (Thurman, 1977) £10
MR SMALL'S COLOURING BOOK (Thurman, 1977) £10
MR BUSY (Thurman, 1978)................................£10
MR CLUMSY (Thurman, 1978)............................£10
MR CLEVER (Thurman, 1978) £10
MR MISCHIEF (Thurman, 1978)...........................£10
MR NONSENSE (Thurman, 1978).........................£10
MR QUIET (Thurman, 1978)...............................£10
MR RUSH (Thurman, 1978)................................£10
MR SKINNY (Thurman, 1978) £10

MR SNEEZE (Thurman, 1971) £15
MR SLOW (Thurman, 1971)...............................£15
MR NOSEY (Thurman, 1971)..............................£15
MR WORRY (Thurman, 1978)..............................£10
MR TALL (Thurman, 1978)................................£10
MY OWN MR MEN STORYBOOK (Mirror Books, 1978)....£10
THE MR MEN ABC (Thurman, 1978) £10
THE MR MEN NO. 1 (Mirror Books, 1978)................£10
THE MR MEN [NO. 2] (Mirror Books, 1978) £10
MR GRUMPY (Thurman, 1979)............................£10
MR TRUMPET (Thurman, 1979) £10
MR TRUMPET'S FRUIT (Thurman, 1979)..................£10
MR GREEDY GOES SHOPPING (Thurman, [1979])........£10
MR HAPPY AT THE SEASIDE (Thurman, [1979])..........£10
MR SILLY ON THE FARM (Thurman, [1979])...............£10
MR TICKLE IN THE PARK (Thurman, [1979])..............£10
THE SECOND MR MEN STORYBOOK
    (Mirror Books, 1979).................................£10
MY VERY OWN MR MEN STORYBOOK
    (Thurman, 1979).....................................£6
MR FUNNY AT THE CIRCUS (Thurman, 1980)..............£6
MR MUDDLE GOES TO SCHOOL (Thurman, 1980)........£6
MR NOSEY FOLLOWS HIS NOSE (Thurman, 1980)..........£6
MR STRONG TO THE RESCUE (Thurman, 1980).............£6
THE MR MEN RAINY DAY BOOK (Thurman, 1980).........£6
THE THIRD MR MEN STORYBOOK (Mirror Books, 1980)..£6
MR CHRISTMAS (Thurman, 1984) £6
MR MEN NUMBER FUN (Thurman, 1984) £6
MY VERY OWN MR MEN BIRTHDAY BOOK
    (Thurman, 1984).....................................£6

'Little Miss' Books

LITTLE MISS BOSSY (Thurman, 1981)....................£6
LITTLE MISS HELPFUL (Thurman, 1981)..................£6
LITTLE MISS LATE (Thurman, 1981)......................£6
LITTLE MISS NAUGHTY (Thurman, 1981)................£6
LITTLE MISS NEAT (Thurman, 1981) £6
LITTLE MISS PLUMP (Thurman, 1981)...................£6
LITTLE MISS SCATTERBRAIN (Thurman, 1981) £6
LITTLE MISS SHY (Thurman, 1981)......................£6
LITTLE MISS SPLENDID (Thurman, 1981) £6
LITTLE MISS SUNSHINE (Thurman, 1981)...............£6
LITTLE MISS TINY (Thurman, 1981) £6

LITTLE MISS TROUBLE (Thurman, 1981)..................£6
LITTLE MISS MAGIC (Thurman, 1982) £6
LITTLE MISS CHATTERBOX (Thurman, 1984)..............£6
LITTLE MISS CONTRARY (Thurman, 1984).................£6
LITTLE MISS COOK BOOK (Thurman, 1984) £6
LITTLE MISS DOTTY (Thurman, 1984)....................£6
LITTLE MISS FICKLE (Thurman, 1984) £6
LITTLE MISS LUCKY (Thurman, 1984) £6
LITTLE MISS STAR (Thurman, 1984).....................£6
LITTLE MISS TWINS (Thurman, 1984) £6

'Hippo, Potto & Mouse' Books

HIPPO, POTTO & MOUSE (Hodder & Stoughton, 1976)......£6
HIPPO LEAVES HOME (Hodder & Stoughton, 1976)..........£6

MOUSE GETS CAUGHT (Hodder & Stoughton, 1976) £6
POTTO FINDS A JOB (Hodder & Stoughton, 1976)............£6

'Roar' Books

ROAR (Hodder & Stoughton, 1979)..£6
ROAR'S DAY OF MISTAKES (Hodder & Stoughton, 1981) £6

HARGREAVES, Roger

Two of Roger Hargeaves' very successful 'Mr Men' books. Even in Fine condition, these are only worth from £5 to £10.

*Ever versatile, Hargreaves turned his attention to ordinary household objects in his witty 1981 picture book, **Things**.*

'Timbuctoo' Books

WOOF: A SORT OF DOG FROM TIMBUCTOO! (Hodder & Stoughton, 1978) £6
BUZZ: A SORT OF BEE FROM TIMBUCTOO! (Hodder & Stoughton, 1978) £6
CHIRP: A SORT OF BIRD FROM TIMBUCTOO! (Hodder & Stoughton, 1978) £6
HISS: A SORT OF SNAKE FROM TIMBUCTOO! (Hodder & Stoughton, 1978) £6
MEOW: A SORT OF CAT FROM TIMBUCTOO! (Hodder & Stoughton, 1978)..£6
MOO: A SORT OF COW FROM TIMBUCTOO! (Hodder & Stoughton, 1978)..£6
NEIGH: A SORT OF HORSE FROM TIMBUCTOO! (Hodder & Stoughton, 1978) £6
OINK: A SORT OF PIG FROM TIMBUCTOO! (Hodder & Stoughton, 1978) £6
SQUEAK: A SORT OF MOUSE FROM TIMBUCTOO! (Hodder & Stoughton, 1978)..£6
TRUMPET: A SORT OF ELEPHANT FROM TIMBUCTOO! (Hodder & Stoughton, 1978) £6
SNAP!: A SORT OF CROCODILE FROM TIMBUCTOO! (Hodder & Stoughton, 1978)..£6
ROAR: A SORT OF LION FROM TIMBUCTOO! (Hodder & Stoughton, 1978) £6
BAA: A SORT OF SHEEP FROM TIMBUCTOO! (Hodder & Stoughton, 1979)..£6
BLEAT: A SORT OF GOAT FROM TIMBUCTOO! (Hodder & Stoughton, 1979)..£6
CHATTER : A SORT OF MONKEY FROM TIMBUCTOO! (Hodder & Stoughton, 1979)..£6
CLUCK: A SORT OF HEN FROM TIMBUCTOO! (Hodder & Stoughton, 1979) £6
CROAK: A SORT OF FROG FROM TIMBUCTOO! (Hodder & Stoughton, 1979) £6
GRIZZLE: A SORT OF BEAR FROM TIMBUCTOO! (Hodder & Stoughton, 1979)..£6
GROWL: A SORT OF TIGER FROM TIMBUCTOO! (Hodder & Stoughton, 1979)..£6
HONK: A SORT OF SEAL FROM TIMBUCTOO! (Hodder & Stoughton, 1979) £6
HOOT: A SORT OF OWL FROM TIMBUCTOO! (Hodder & Stoughton, 1979) £6
PUFF: A SORT OF PANDA FROM TIMBUCTOO! (Hodder & Stoughton, 1979)..£6
QUACK: A SORT OF DUCK FROM TIMBUCTOO! (Hodder & Stoughton, 1979)..£6
SNIFF: A SORT OF RABBIT FROM TIMBUCTOO! (Hodder & Stoughton, 1979) £6
SQUAWK: A SORT OF PARROT FROM TIMBUCTOO! (Hodder & Stoughton, 1979) £6
TRUMPET (Purnell, 1979)..£6
AN APPLE FOR OINK (Hamlyn, 1981)..£6
HISS AND THE STORM (Hamlyn, 1981) £6
MOO'S FANCY HATS (Hamlyn, 1981)..£6
NEIGH MOVES HOUSE (Hamlyn, 1981)..£6

Others

COUNT WORM (Hodder & Stoughton, 1976) £6
GRANDFATHER CLOCK (Hodder & Stoughton, 1977)..£6

ALBERT THE ALPHABETICAL ELEPHANT (Hodder & Stoughton, 1977)..£6
THINGS (Hodder & Stoughton, 1981)..£6
ONCE UPON A WORM (Hodder & Stoughton, 1982)...£6
I AM A BOOK (Hodder & Stoughton, 1984) £6

HARRIS, Joel Chandler

American author. Born: Georgia, 1848. Worked as a printer's devil and then journalist before writing the 'Uncle Remus' stories, which were based on the folksongs and stories of the blacks of the American South. Originally published in the *Atlanta Constitution*, these were first issued in book form in 1880 under the title *Uncle Remus: His Songs and His Sayings*, and were followed by several sequels. Died: 1908.

Prices are for books in Very Good condition.

UNCLE REMUS: His Songs and his Sayings, The Folk-Lore of the Old Plantation
(illustrated by Frederick Church and James Moser) (Appleton, US, 1881 [1880]) £4,000
UNCLE REMUS and His Legends of the Old Plantation (animal tales only) (Bogue, 1881)..................£350
UNCLE REMUS, or Mr Fox, Mr Rabbit and Mr Terrapin (enlarged edition, including 'His Songs and His Sayings' as well as the animal tales) (Routledge, 1881)..£350
UNCLE REMUS: His Songs and his Sayings, The Folk-Lore of the Old Plantation (Ward Lock, [1883])...........................£350
NIGHTS WITH UNCLE REMUS: Myths and Legends of the Old Plantation (Tribner, US, [1883])................£350
DADDY JAKE THE RUNAWAY (Appleton, US, 1889)...£2,000
UNCLE REMUS AND HIS FRIENDS: Old Plantation Stories, Songs, Ballads, etc. (Osgood McIlvaine, 1892) £225
UNCLE REMUS: His Songs and his Sayings (reprint of the 1881 Routledge edition) (Routledge, 1895)............................£200
MR RABBIT AT HOME (sequel to 'Little Mr Thimblefinger and his Queer Country'; illustrated by O. Herford) (Osgood McIlvaine, 1895) £175
THE TAR-BABY and Other Rhymes of Uncle Remus (verse) (Appleton, US, 1904)..........................£2,000
UNCLE REMUS (illustrated by Harry Rountree and René Bull) (Nelson, [1906])....................................£125
LITTLE MR THIMBLEFINGER AND HIS QUEER COUNTRY (illustrated by O. Herford) (Osgood McIlvaine, 1894) £130
WALLY WANDEROON AND HIS STORY-TELLING MACHINE (Grant Richards, UK/US, 1904)......................£80
A LITTLE UNION SCOUT (Duckworth [printed in the US], 1904)..£80
UNCLE REMUS AND BRER RABBIT (Appleton, US, 1907) £250
THE BISHOP AND THE BOOGERMAN (illustrated by Charlotte Harding) (John Murray, 1909).................£70

HASSALL, John

British illustrator. Born: Walmer, Devon, in 1868. Educated at Newton Abbot College and Neuenheim College, Heidelberg, later studying in Antwerp and Paris. From 1895 onwards, he worked as a cartoonist and advertising artist, before turning his attention to children's books. He was one of the first members of the London Sketch Club, becoming President in 1903. Founded the New Art School with Charles van Havermaet. His daughter was the wood engraver, Joan Hassall. Died: 1948.

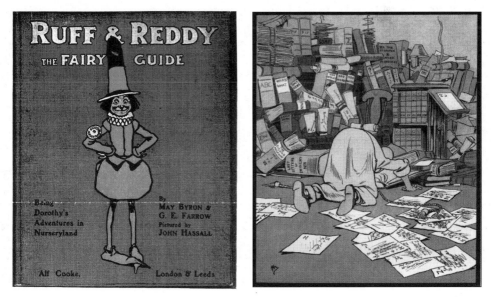

*The decorated cloth boards of the **Ruff & Reddy: The Fairy Guide** and an illustration from **An ABC Book of Everyday People** by John Hassall. Today Hassall's is best remembered for designing the 'Skegness is SO Bracing' rail poster.*

HASSALL, John

Prices are for books in Very Good condition.

TWO WELL-WORN SHOE STORIES (illustrated by John Hassall and Cecil Aldin) (Sands, 1899)................................**£250**

THE WOULDBEGOODS by E. Nesbit (illustrated by John Hassall and Arthur Buckland) (Unwin, 1901)................................**£300**

AN A.B.C. OF EVERY-DAY PEOPLE by G.E. Farrow (Dean, [1902])...**£175**

GRIMM'S FAIRY TALES (twelve illustrations by John Hassall) (Sands, 1902) **£100**

THE PANTOMIME A.B.C. by R. Carse (Sands, [1902])...**£125**

SIX AND TWENTY BOYS AND GIRLS by G.C. Bingham (verse) (Blackie, [1902]) **£50**

ABSURD DITTIES by G.E. Farrow (Routledge, 1903)..**£75**

ROUND THE WORLD A.B.C. by G.E. Farrow (Nister [printed in Germany], [1904]) **£120**

THE TWINS by Edward Shirley (verse) (Nelson, [1904]) **£70**

THE OLD NURSERY STORIES AND RHYMES (Blackie, [1904])...**£175**

ALL THE BEST NURSERY STORIES AND RHYMES (Blackie, [1905])...**£175**

RUFF AND REDDY: The Fairy Guide by May Byron and G.E. Farrow (Cooke, [1905]).................................**£100**

PUG PETER: KING OF MOUSELAND by E. Nesbit (illustrated by John Hassall and Harry Rountree) (Cooke, [1905])...........**£120**

THE MAGIC SHOP by May Byron (Cooke, [1905])...**£50**

SPORT AND PLAY: A Picture Book by Edward Shirley (Nelson, [1907])..**£50**

THE HAPPY ANNUAL by Cecil Aldin and John Hassall (Heinemann, 1907)..**£70**

GOOD QUEEN BESS 1533-1603: A Book for Children by B. Girvin (David Nutt, [1907])..............................**£50**

MOTHER GOOSE'S NURSERY RHYMES. Edited by Walter C. Jerrold (Blackie, 1909 [1908])......................**£65**

GULLIVER'S TRAVELS by Jonathan Swift (Nelson, [1908])...**£50**

THE PRINCESS AND THE DRAGON by S.H. Hamer (illustrated by John Hassall and T. Butler-Stoney) (Duckworth, [1908])....**£40**

MISS MANNERS by Aileen Orr (Andrew Melrose, 1909)..**£90**

TALES AND TALKS FOR NURSERY LAND (illustrated by John Hassall and others) (Blackie, [1909]).........**£45**

THE DOLL'S DIARY by Rose H. Thomas (24 illustrations by John Hassall) (Grant Richards, 1909)..............**£55**

FRIDAY AND SATURDAY: The Adventures of Two Little Pickles by May Byron (verse) (Frowde/Hodder & Stoughton, [1910])......**£45**

THE SLEEPING BEAUTY and Other Tales from Perrault by C. Perrault (Blackie, [1912])..............................**£55**

CHILDREN'S PAINTING BOOK. In Aid of the Belgium Relief Fund by Thomas R. Arkell
(illustrated by John Hassall, R.I. Jingles and Reginald Arkell) (Odhams Press, 1914) **£40**

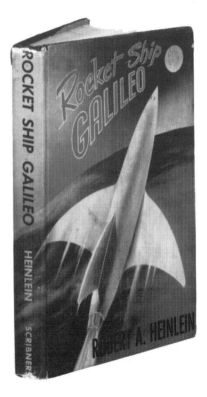

The very rare first edition, first issue of the author's first book which was published in green pictorial cloth with vignette title and illustrations by Frederick Church and James Moser. The second issue was bound in red cloth.

*American SF author Robert A. Heinlein's first and most collectable novel for children **Rocket Ship Galileo**.*

THE HASSALL PAINTING BOOK (Lawrence & Jellicoe, [1915])..£50
THE PETER PAN PAINTING BOOK (Hodder & Stoughton, [1915])...£50
WITH LOVE FROM DADDY: Letters to a Child by R.H. Lindo (Stanley Paul, [1918])...............................£40
THE HASSALL A.B.C.: A Children's Picture Book (Collins, [1918])..£70
BLACKIE'S POPULAR FAIRY TALES (Blackie, [1921])..£30
OUR DIARY, or Teddy and Me (Nelson, [1928])..£50
ROBINSON CRUSOE, THE SWISS FAMILY ROBINSON AND GULLIVER'S TRAVELS (Blackie, 1930)............£30
BLACKIE'S POPULAR NURSERY STORIES (Blackie, [1931])...£20
DON'T TELL (Cooke, no date)...£50
TEN LITTLE JAPPY CHAPS (Treherne: 'Stump Books' series, no date)...£50

HAWTHORNE, Nathaniel

American author. Born: Massachusetts 1804. One of the great American novelists and short story writers of the mid-nineteenth century. His two most celebrated works for adults, *The Scarlet Letter* (1850) and *The House of the Seven Gables* (1851), were both deeply rooted in the extreme Puritanism of New England and his own family history – his notorious ancestor, John Hathorne, was one of the Salem judges who persecuted local 'witches' in 1692. Many famous artists illustrated Nathaniel's works and he is credited as being the first major American author to focus literary attention on the child and to write specifically for younger readers, with two celebrated books retelling Greek myths for children. Died: 1864.

Prices are for books in Good condition (up to 1900); very good condition (after 1900) in original bindings.

PETER PARLEY'S UNIVERSAL HISTORY On the Basis of Geography For the Use of Families
  (Anonymous) (American Stationers Co., John B. Russell, US, 1837; 2 volumes) £1,500
GRANDFATHER'S CHAIR: A History for Youth (E.P. Peabody; Wiley & Putnam, US, 1841) £600
FAMOUS OLD PEOPLE: Being the second Epoch of Grandfather's Chair (E.P. Peabody, US, 1841) £600
LIBERTY TREE: With the Last Words of Grandfather's Chair (E.P. Peabody, US, 1841) £600
BIOGRAPHICAL STORIES FOR CHILDREN (Taffan & Dennet, US, 1842) £400
HAWTHORNE'S HISTORICAL TALES FOR YOUTH (Taffan & Dennet, US, 1842; containing above four titles in two vols)............£600
HAWTHORNE'S HISTORICAL TALES FOR YOUTH as 'TRUE STORIES FROM HISTORY AND BIOGRAPHY'
  (Ticknor, Reed and Fields, US, 1851)..£400
A WONDER-BOOK FOR GIRLS AND BOYS (Ticknor, Reed and Fields, 1852 [November 1851]) £1,000
A WONDER-BOOK (H. Bohn, 1851)..£400
A WONDER-BOOK (G. Routledge, 1851)..£400
A WONDER-BOOK (Illustrated by Walter Crane) (Osgood McIlvaine, 1892)...£200
A WONDER-BOOK (Illustrated by Arthur Rackham; red cloth; with dustjacket) (Hodder & Stoughton, [1922]) £350
A WONDER-BOOK (Limited to 600 copies, signed by Rackham; cream buckram; with dustjacket)
  (Hodder & Stoughton, [1922])...£1,250
TANGLEWOOD TALES FOR GIRLS AND BOYS (Chapman & Hall, 1853)..£800
TANGLEWOOD TALES (Ticknor, Reed and Fields, 1853) £800
TANGLEWOOD TALES (Illustrated by Willy Pogany) (T. Fisher Unwin, 1909) £60
TANGLEWOOD TALES (Illustrated by Edmond Dulac) (Hodder & Stoughton, 1918)..............................£150
TANGLEWOOD TALES (Hodder & Stoughton, 1918; limited to 500 copies, signed by Dulac) £750

HEINLEIN, Robert A.

SF author. Born: 1907. Frank Robertson described Heinlein as "the one author who raised SF from the gutter of pulp space opera to the altitude of original and breathtaking concepts". The great American writer of many influential titles for adults, also penned these very collectable books aimed at the juvenile market. Died: 1988.

Prices are for books in Very Good condition with dustjackets.

ROCKET SHIP GALILEO (1st state dustjacket priced $2.00) (Scribner's, US, 1947) £550
ROCKET SHIP GALILEO (paperback) (New English Library, UK, 1971) £25
SPACE CADET (1st state dustjacket priced $2.50) (Scribner's, US, 1948) £350
SPACE CADET (Gollancz, UK, 1966) £125
RED PLANET (Scribner's, US, 1949)...£325
RED PLANET (Gollancz, UK, 1963)..£130
FARMER IN THE SKY (Scribner's, US, 1950) £150
FARMER IN THE SKY (Gollancz, UK, 1962) £100
BETWEEN PLANETS (Scribner's, US, 1951)...£200
BETWEEN PLANETS (Gollancz, UK, 1968)..£100
THE ROLLING STONES (Scribner's, US, 1952)...£225
THE ROLLING STONES (as 'SPACE FAMILY STONE') (Gollancz, UK, 1969)..£100
STARMAN JONES (Scribners, US, 1953)..£150
STARMAN JONES (Sidgwick & Jackson, UK, 1954)..£60
THE STAR BEAST (Scribner's, US, 1954)...£100
THE STAR BEAST (New English Library, UK, 1971)..£50
TUNNEL IN THE SKY (Scribner's, US, 1955)...£100
TUNNEL IN THE SKY (Gollancz, UK, 1965)...£50
TIME FOR THE STARS (Scribner's, US, 1956) £200

HEINLEIN, Robert A.

TIME FOR THE STARS (Gollancz, UK, 1963) **£100**
CITIZEN OF THE GALAXY (Scribner's, US, 1957) **£160**
CITIZEN OF THE GALAXY (Gollancz, UK, 1969) **£70**
HAVE SPACE SUIT - WILL TRAVEL (Scribner's, US, 1958) **£250**
HAVE SPACE SUIT - WILL TRAVEL (Gollancz, UK, 1970) **£50**
STARSHIP TROOPERS (Putnam, US, 1959) **£1000**
STARSHIP TROOPERS(New English Library, UK, 1961) **£100**
PODKAYNE OF MARS (Putnam, US, 1963) **£450**
PODKAYNE OF MARS (paperback) (New English Library, UK, 1969) **£8**
PODKAYNE OF MARS (New English Library, UK, 1977) **£35**

HENTY, G.A.

British author. Born: George Alfred Henty at Trumpington, Cambridgeshire, in 1832. After a sickly childhood, he went to Westminster School and Cambridge, where he read Classics. Joined the army on the outbreak of the Crimean War, leaving five years later to become a roving war correspondent. His hugely successful career as a novelist began in 1867 with the publication of *A Search for a Secret*, his first book for young readers, *Out on the Pampas, or The Young Settlers* (1871), appearing four years later. Despite his success as a novelist, he continued to report on foreign conflicts until 1876. He edited the story papers, *Union Jack* and *Boys' Own Magazine*, and collaborated on an annual, *Camps and Quarters*. Died: 1902.

Prices are for books in Very Good condition.

THE MARCH TO MAGDALA (Tinsley Brothers, 1868) **£2,000**
ALL BUT LOST (three volumes; blue boards) (Tinsley Brothers, 1869) .... the set **£2,500**
OUT ON THE PAMPAS, or The Young Settlers (illustrated by J.B. Zwecker; blue or brown boards)
  (Griffith & Farran, 1871 [1870]) **£900**
THE YOUNG FRANC-TIREURS (blue, red or green boards) (Griffith & Farran, 1872 [1871]) **£700**
THE MARCH TO COOMASSIE (second edition; blue boards) (Tinsley Brothers, 1874) **£450**
SEASIDE MAIDENS (orange boards) (Tinsley Brothers, 1880) **£600**
THE YOUNG BUGLERS (illustrated by J. Proctor; red or green boards; with adverts dated October 1879)
  (Griffith & Farran, 1880 [1879]) **£500**
THE CORNET OF HORSE (red boards; with adverts dated January 1881) (Sampson Low & Marston, 1881) **£500**
IN TIMES OF PERIL (red or blue boards; with adverts dated October 1881) (Griffith & Farran, 1881) **£700**
FACING DEATH (blue or brown boards) (Blackie, [1882 — though some first edition copies are apparently dated 1883]) **£500**
WINING HIS SPURS (published in the US as 'Fighting the Saracens' and 'The Boy Knights'; red boards)
  (Sampson Low & Marston, 1882) **£550**
FRIENDS THOUGH DIVIDED (red, blue brown or green boards; adverts dated September 1883) (Griffith & Farran, 1883) **£400**
JACK ARCHER (published in the US as 'The Fall of Sebastopol'; red boards) (Sampson Low & Marston, 1883) **£400**
UNDER DRAKE'S FLAG (green or brown boards) (Blackie, 1883 [1882]) **£200**
BY SHEER PLUCK (red boards; with adverts headed 'New Series for 1885') (Blackie, 1884 [1883]) **£300**
WITH CLIVE IN INDIA (red, brown or blue boards) (Blackie, 1884 [1883]) **£200**
THE YOUNG COLONISTS (blue and gold boards) (Routledge, 1885 [1884]) **£200**
TRUE TO THE OLD FLAG (blue, grey, red or green boards) (Blackie, 1885 [1884]) **£200**
IN FREEDOM'S CAUSE (blue, brown or red boards) (Blackie, 1885 [1884]) **£100**
ST. GEORGE FOR ENGLAND (brown, blue or green boards) (Blackie, 1885 [1884]) **£100**
THE LION OF THE NORTH (brown or green boards) (Blackie, 1886 [1885]) **£140**
THE DRAGON AND THE RAVEN (brown or green boards) (Blackie, 1886 [1885]) **£200**
FOR NAME AND FAME (brown or grey boards) (Blackie, 1886 [1885]) **£300**
THROUGH THE FRAY (brown or red boards) (Blackie, 1886 [1885]) **£150**
YARNS ON THE BEACH (brown or red boards) (Blackie, 1886 [1885]) **£300**
THE YOUNG CARTHAGINIAN (blue or green boards) (Blackie, 1887 [1886]) **£200**
THE BRAVEST OF THE BRAVE (red or blue boards) (Blackie, 1887 [1886]) **£150**
A FINAL RECKONING (illustrated by W.B. Wollen; blue or green boards) (Blackie, 1887 [1886]) **£100**
WITH WOLFE IN CANADA (illustrated by Gordon Browne; green, blue or red boards) (Blackie 1887 [1886]) **£200**
THE SOVEREIGN READER: Scenes from the Life and Reign of Queen Victoria (red or purple boards) (Blackie, [1887]) ... **£150**
IN THE REIGN OF TERROR (red, blue, grey or green boards) (Blackie, 1888) **£150**
STURDY AND STRONG (red, blue or orange boards) (Blackie, 1888 [1887]) **£150**
ORANGE AND GREEN (red, blue or orange boards) (Blackie 1888 [1887]) **£100**
BONNIE PRINCE CHARLIE (brown or red boards) (Blackie, 1888 [1887]) **£100**
FOR THE TEMPLE (brown, red or blue boards) (Blackie, 1888 [1887]) **£200**
GABRIEL ALLEN MP (red boards) (Spencer & Blackett, [1888]) **£250**
CAPTAIN BAYLEY'S HEIR (red, brown or blue boards) (Blackie, 1889) **£100**
THE CAT OF BUBASTES (blue, brown, grey or green boards) (Blackie, 1889 [1888]) **£200**
THE LION OF ST MARK (red, blue or grey boards) (Blackie, 1889 [1888]) **£80**
THE CURSE OF CARNE'S HOLD (two volumes; blue boards) (Spencer & Blackett, 1889) ...... the set **£500**
THE PLAGUE SHIP (wraps) (SPCK: 'Penny Library of Fiction' series, 1889) **£600**
BY PIKE AND DYKE (brown or green boards) (Blackie, 1890 [1889]) **£120**
ONE OF THE 28TH (red, brown, green or blue boards) (Blackie, 1890 [1889]) **£200**
TALES OF DARING AND DANGER (blue or green boards) (Blackie, 1889 [1890]) **£300**
WITH LEE IN VIRGINIA (brown or blue boards) (Blackie, 1890 [1889]) **£150**

Most collectors of G.A. Henty's boys' adventure stories are happy to amass copies in their original decorated pictorial boards. Survivors still in the plain buff jackets (bottom right) are very rare indeed. All our prices relate to books without jackets.

THOSE OTHER ANIMALS (illustrated by H. Weir; green boards) (Henry & Co, [1891]) **£250**
BY ENGLAND'S AID (blue or brown boards) (Blackie, 1891 [1890]) **£150**
BY RIGHT OF CONQUEST (green or brown boards) (Blackie, 1891 [1890]) **£100**
MAORI AND SETTLER (brown, blue, red or green boards) (Blackie, 1891) **£100**
A CHAPTER OF ADVENTURES (published in the US as 'The Young Midshipman'; blue or grey boards)
    (Blackie, 1891 [1890]) **£1,000**
A HIDDEN FOE (two volumes; grey boards) (Sampson Low & Marston, [1891]) **£2,000**
THE DASH FOR KHARTOUM (brown, red, grey or green boards) (Blackie, 1892 [1891]) **£100**

HELD FAST FOR ENGLAND (red, grey or brown boards) (Blackie, 1892 [1891]) **£100**
REDSKIN AND COWBOY (red, green or brown boards) (Blackie, 1892 [1891]) **£100**
THE RANCH IN THE VALLEY (wraps) (SPCK: 'Penny Library of Fiction' series, 1892) **£500**
BERIC THE BRITON (blue or brown boards) (Blackie, 1893 [1892]) **£150**
CONDEMNED AS A NIHILIST (brown or blue boards) (Blackie, 1893 [1892])..**£150**
IN GREEK WATERS (grey, brown or green boards) (Blackie, 1893 [1892])..**£100**
TALES FROM THE WORKS OF G.A. HENTY (red boards) (Blackie, 1893) **£100**
RUJUB THE JUGGLER (published in the US as 'In the Days of the Mutiny'; three volumes, blue boards)
    (Chatto & Windus, 1893) ....the set **£750**
A JACOBITE EXILE (brown, green, grey or blue boards) (Blackie, 1894 [1893])..**£200**
THROUGH THE SIKH WAR (green boards) (Blackie, 1894 [1893])..**£100**
ST BARTHOLOMEW'S EVE (green, blue or red boards) (Blackie, 1894 [1893]) **£100**
DOROTHY'S DOUBLE (three volumes) (Chatto & Windus, 1894)..**£750**
WHEN LONDON BURNED (blue boards) (Blackie, 1895 [1894])..**£200**
CUTHBERT HARTINGTON and A WOMAN OF THE COMMUNE (F.V. White, 1895)..**£200**
WULF THE SAXON (green boards) (Blackie, 1895 [1894])..**£75**
IN THE HEART OR THE ROCKIES (grey boards) (Blackie, 1895 [1894])..**£100**
A KNIGHT OF THE WHITE CROSS (green boards) (Blackie, 1896 [1895]) **£150**
BEARS AND DACOITS (Blackie, [1896])..**£300**
SURLY JOE (wraps) (Blackie, [1896])..**£200**
WHITE-FACED DICK (limp cloth cover) (Blackie, [1896])..**£200**
THROUGH RUSSIAN SNOWS (grey boards) (Blackie, 1896 [1895]) **£100**
THE TIGER OF MYSORE (blue boards) (Blackie, 1896 [1895])..**£100**
ON THE IRRAWADDY (blue boards) (Blackie, 1897 [1896])..**£150**
AT AGINCOURT (grey boards; with adverts containing no reviews of this title) (Blackie, 1897)............................**£150**
WITH COCHRANE THE DAUNTLESS (blue boards) (Blackie, 1897) **£100**
THE QUEEN'S CUP (three volumes; green or blue boards) (Chatto & Windus, 1897)..**£600**
WITH MOORE AT CORUNNA (green or blue boards) (Blackie, 1898 [1897])..**£100**
COLONEL THORNDYKE'S SECRET (published in the US in an abridged form as
    'The Brahmin's Treasure'; pink boards) (Chatto & Windus, 1898)..**£150**
WITH FREDERICK THE GREAT (red boards; with adverts either headed 'Books for Young People'
    or 'Illustrated Story Books') (Blackie, 1898 [1897])..**£100**
UNDER WELLINGTON'S COMMAND (blue boards) (Blackie, 1899 [1898]) **£100**
AT ABOUKIR AND ACRE (red boards) (Blackie, 1899 [1898]) **£100**
BOTH SIDES THE BORDER (blue boards) (Blackie, 1899 [1898])..**£75**
THE LOST HEIR (green boards; with adverts) (James Bowden, 1899) **£150**
ON THE SPANISH MAIN (red wraps) (Chambers, [1899])..**£100**
AT DUTY'S CALL (Chambers, [1899])..**£75**
A ROVING COMMISSION (illustrated by W. Rainey; red boards) (Blackie, 1900 [1899])....................................**£100**
WON BY THE SWORD (illustrated by C.M. Sheldon; blue boards) (Blackie, 1900 [1899]) **£75**
NO SURRENDER! (red boards) (Blackie, 1900 [1899])..**£100**
DO YOUR DUTY (blue or green boards) (Blackie, [1900])..**£150**
THE SOUL SURVIVORS (red wraps) (Chambers, [1901]) **£100**
IN THE IRISH BRIGADE (green boards; with 32 pages of adverts) (Blackie, 1901 [1900])................................**£100**
OUT WITH GARIBALDI (blue boards) (Blackie, 1901 [1900])..**£75**
JOHN HAWKE'S FORTUNE (paper cover) (Chapman & Hall: 'Young People's Library' series, 1901)..................**£65**
WITH BULLER IN NATAL (blue boards) (Blackie, 1901)..**£65**
QUEEN VICTORIA (purple boards) (Blackie, 1901)..**£50**
TO HERAT AND CABUL (blue boards) (Blackie, 1902 [1901])..**£70**
WITH ROBERTS TO PRETORIA (red boards) (Blackie, 1902 [1901])..**£160**
AT THE POINT OF THE BAYONET (green boards) (Blackie, 1902 [1901])..**£150**
IN THE HANDS OF THE CAVE DWELLERS (Blackie, 1903 [1902])..**£150**
THE TREASURE OF THE INCAS (green boards) (Blackie, 1903 [1902])..**£75**
WITH THE BRITISH LEGION (blue or green boards) (Blackie, 1903 [1902])..**£75**
WITH KITCHENER IN THE SOUDAN (red boards) (Blackie, 1903 [1902]) **£65**
THROUGH THREE CAMPAIGNS (red boards) (Blackie, 1904 [1903])..**£65**
WITH THE ALLIES TO PEKIN (green boards) (Blackie, 1904 [1903])..**£65**
BY CONDUCT AND COURAGE (red boards; with either 381 or 384 numbered pages) (Blackie, 1905 [1904])........................**£100**
GALLANT DEEDS (white or grey boards) (Chambers, 1905)..**£65**
IN THE HANDS OF THE MALAYS (red boards) (Blackie, 1905) **£65**
AMONG THE BUSHRANGERS (adapted from 'A Final Reckoning') (Blackie, 1906) **£40**
THE YOUNG CAPTAIN (adapted from 'With Clive in India') (Blackie, 1906) **£40**
THE TWO PRISONERS (adapted from 'A Soldier's Daughter') (Blackie, 1906 [1905])......................................**£40**
CAST ASHORE (adapted from 'Under Drake's Flag') (Blackie, 1906)..**£35**
CHARLIE MARRYAT (adapted from 'With Clive in India') (Blackie, 1906) **£35**
CORNET WALTER (adapted from 'Orange and Green') (Blackie, 1906) **£35**
A HIGHLAND CHIEF (adapted from 'In Freedom's Cause') (Blackie, 1906)..**£35**
AN INDIAN RAID (adapted from 'Redskin and Cowboy') (Blackie, 1906)..**£35**
A SOLDIER'S DAUGHTER (red, blue or green boards) (Blackie, 1906 [1905]) **£65**

HERGÉ

Belgium author-illustrator. Born: George Rémi in Brussels in 1907. In 1925, he joined the Catholic newspaper, *Le XX Siècle*, for which he created the boy reporter-cum-detective, Tintin. The character first appeared in the children's supplement, *Le Petit Vingtième*, in 1929, in a story entitled 'Tintin au Pays de Soviets'. This was published in book form in 1930, and was followed by another 22 adventures up to 1976. The first of the books to appear in English were *The Crab with the Golden Claws* and *King Ottokar's Sceptre*, which were published simultaneously in 1958. Died: 1983.

Prices are for books in Very Good condition.

'Tintin' Story Books

THE CRAB WITH THE GOLDEN CLAWS (Methuen, 1958) £50
KING OTTOKAR'S SCEPTRE (Methuen, 1958)...£50
THE SECRET OF THE UNICORN (Methuen, 1959)..£40
RED RACKHAM'S TREASURE (Methuen, 1959) £40
DESTINATION MOON (Methuen, 1959)...£50
EXPLORERS ON THE MOON (Methuen, 1959)...£50
THE CALCULUS AFFAIR (Methuen, 1960) £40
THE RED SEA SHARKS (Methuen, 1960) £40
THE SHOOTING STAR (Methuen, 1961)..£30
TINTIN IN TIBET (Methuen, 1962) £40
THE SEVEN CRYSTAL BALLS (Methuen, 1962) £30
PRISONERS OF THE SUN (Methuen, 1962)..£30
THE CASTAFIORE EMERALD (Methuen, 1963)..£30
THE BLACK ISLAND (Methuen, 1966)..£30
FLIGHT 714 (Methuen, 1968)...£25
CIGARS OF THE PHARAOH (Methuen, 1971) £25
THE LAND OF BLACK GOLD (Methuen, 1972) £25
THE BROKEN EAR (Methuen, 1975) £25
TINTIN AND THE PICAROS (Methuen, 1976)..£20
TINTIN IN AMERICA (Methuen, 1978)..£20
THE BLUE LOTUS (Methuen, 1983)..£20
TINTIN IN THE LAND OF THE SOVIETS (Sundancer, 1989) £20
TINTIN AND ALPH-ART (Sundancer, 1990) £20
TINTIN IN THE CONGO (Sundancer, 1991) £20

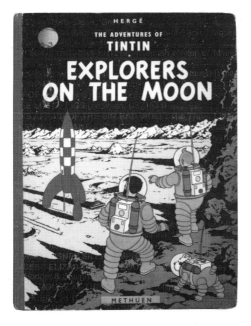

*For 1959's **Explorers on the Moon** Hergé had a scale model of a moon rocket especially made to facilitate accurate drawing.*

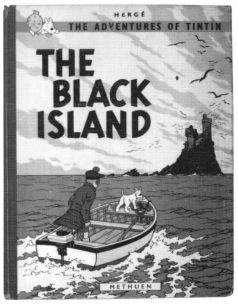

*The first British edition of the revised and redrawn version of **The Black Island** (1966) is worth at least £30 today.*

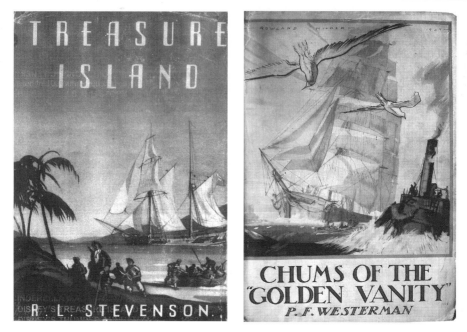

Two seabound children's books illustrated by Rowland Hilder, an artist primarily known for his depiction of the countryside.

'Tintin' Film Books
TINTIN AND THE GOLDEN FLEECE (Methuen, 1965) £25
TINTIN AND THE BLUE ORANGES (Methuen, 1967) £20
TINTIN AND THE LAKE OF SHARKS (Methuen, 1973) £15

Other 'Tintin' Books
THE MAKING OF TINTIN (Methuen, 1983) £20
THE MAKING OF TINTIN: IN THE WORLD OF THE INCA (Methuen, 1985) £20
THE MAKING OF TINTIN: MISSION TO THE MOON (Methuen, 1989) £20
THE MAKING OF TINTIN: CIGARS OF THE PHARAOH/THE BLUE LOTUS (Methuen, 1995) £20

'Jo, Zette & Jocko' Books
THE VALLEY OF THE COBRAS (Methuen, 1986) £15
THE STRATOSHIP H22. PART ONE: MR PUMP'S LEGACY (Methuen, 1987) £15
THE STRATOSHIP H22. PART TWO: DESTINATION NEW YORK (Methuen, 1987) £15

'Quick & Flupke' Books
DOUBLE TROUBLE (Mammoth, 1992) £10
TWO OF A KIND (Mammoth, 1992) £10

Others
POPOL OUT WEST (Methuen, 1969) £25

HERRIOT, James
British author. Born: James Alfred Wight in Sunderland in 1916. Studied at Glasgow Veterinary College, subsequently joining a practice in the Yorkshire Dales in 1937. Best known for his enormously successful books of 'rural reminiscences', including *If Only They Could Talk* (1970) and *The Lord God Made Them All* (1981), but also wrote a handful of children's works. Died: 1995.

Prices are for books in Very Good condition with dustjackets where applicable.

IF ONLY THEY COULD TALK (Joseph, 1970) £40
IT SHOULDN'T HAPPEN TO A VET (Joseph, 1972) £20
LET SLEEPING VETS LIE (Joseph, 1973) £15
VET IN HARNESS (Joseph, 1974) £10
ALL CREATURES GREAT AND SMALL (omnibus) (Joseph, 1975) £15
VETS MIGHT FLY (Joseph, 1976) £10
ALL THINGS BRIGHT AND BEAUTIFUL (omnibus) (Joseph, 1976) £10
VET IN A SPIN (Joseph, 1977) £10

ALL THINGS WISE AND WONDERFUL (omnibus) (Joseph, 1978)..£10
JAMES HERRIOT'S YORKSHIRE (Joseph, 1979)..£10
THE LORD GOD MADE THEM ALL (Joseph, 1981)...£10
THE BEST OF JAMES HERRIOT (Joseph, 1982)..£10
MOSES THE KITTEN (illustrated by Peter Barrett) (Joseph, 1984)..£15
ONLY ONE WOOF (illustrated by Peter Barrett) (Joseph, 1985)...£15
JAMES HERRIOT'S DOG STORIES (Joseph, 1986)...£10
THE CHRISTMAS DAY KITTEN (illustrated by Ruth Brown) (Joseph, 1986) £20
BONNY'S BIG DAY (Joseph, 1987)...£15
THE MARKET SQUARE DOG (Joseph, 1989)..£15
OSCAR, CAT-ABOUT-TOWN (illustrated by Ruth Brown) (Joseph, 1990)..£20
SMUDGE'S DAY OUT (illustrated by Ruth Brown) (Joseph, 1991) £15
BLOSSOM COMES HOME (illustrated by Ruth Brown) (Joseph, 1991)..£15
EVERY LIVING THING (Joseph, 1992)...£10
JAMES HERRIOT'S FAVOURITE DOG STORIES (Joseph, 1992)..£10
JAMES HERRIOT'S CAT STORIES (Joseph, 1994)..£10

HIGSON, Charlie
British author. Born: 1958. Former *First Show* star who penned four adult thrillers before being given permission by the Ian Fleming estate to write the 'Teen Bond' series.
Prices are for books in Very Good condition.

SILVERFIN (paperback) (first print, incorrectly states next novel arriving 'October 2005) (Puffin, 2005)...............£10
SILVERFIN (uncorrected proof copy; paperback) (Puffin, 2005)..£20
SILVERFIN ('Limited Collectors' Edition'; 999 signed, numbered limited hardbacks; slipcase) (Puffin, 2006) £25
BLOODFEVER (paperback) (Puffin, 2006)..£7
BLOODFEVER (uncorrected proof copy; paperback) (Puffin, 2006) £20

HILDER, Rowland
Artist & illustrator. Born: Long Island, New York, 1905, to British parents. Artist primarily known for his depiction of the English countryside – indeed the terms 'Rowland Hilder Landscape' and the adjective 'Hilderesque' have found their way into the English language. He illustrated several classic works, penned his own books, and drew for many boys' story books. Died: 1993.
Prices are for books in Very Good condition with dustjackets.

By Percy F. Westerman
EAST IN THE "GOLDEN GRAIN" (Blackie, [1925]) £30
THE LUCK OF THE "GOLDEN DAWN" (Blackie, [1926]) £30
THE RIDDLE OF THE AIR (Blackie, [1926]) £30
CHUMS OF THE "GOLDEN VANITY" (Blackie, [1927]) £30
THE JUNIOR CADET (Blackie, [1928]) £30
PAT STOBART IN THE "GOLDEN DAWN" (Blackie, [1929]) £30
THE SENIOR CADET (Blackie, [1931])...£30
ALL HANDS TO THE BOATS! (Blackie, [1932]) £30
THE BLACK HAWK (Blackie, 1934) £30
THE RED PIRATE (Blackie, [1935]) £30

By John Lesterman
THE ADVENTURES OF A TRAFALGAR LAD (Jonathan Cape, 1926) £40
A SAILOR OF NAPOLEON (Jonathan Cape, 1927) (illustrated with Richard Southern) £40
A PAIR OF ROVERS (Jonathan Cape, 1928) £40
THE SECOND MATE OF THE MYRADALE (Jonathan Cape, 1929) £40

Others
TRUE TALES OF THE SEA by C. Fox-Smith (Oxford University Press, 1932) £30
THE MIDNIGHT FOLK by John Masefield (Heinemann, 1931)..£120
NO SURRENDER by Harold Avery (Nelson, 1933) £20
FIRE DOWN BELOW by W.M.W. Watt (Frederick Muller, 1935) £20
THEY WENT TO THE ISLAND by L.A.G. Strong (Dent, 1940) £20

HILL, Eric
British author. Born: London, 1927. Creator of the popular 'Spot' series.
Prices are for books in Very Good condition with dustjackets where applicable.

'Spot' Books
WHERE'S SPOT ? (Heinemann, 1980)...£6
SPOT'S FIRST WALK (Heinemann, 1981) £6
SPOT'S BIRTHDAY PARTY (Heinemann, 1982)...£6
SPOT'S FIRST CHRISTMAS (Heinemann, 1983) £6

HILL, Eric

SPOT'S BUSY YEAR (colouring book) (Putnam, 1983) £6
SPOT TELLS THE TIME (colouring book) (Putnam, 1983) £6
SPOT'S ALPHABET (colouring book) (Putnam, 1983)..£6
SPOT LEARNS TO COUNT(colouring book) (Putnam, 1983)..£6
HERE'S SPOT (Heinemann, 1984) £6
SPOT GOES TO SCHOOL (Heinemann, 1984)..£6
PLAY WITH SPOT (Heinemann, 1985) £6
SPOT GOES TO THE BEACH (Heinemann, 1985)..£6
SPOT AT THE FAIR (Heinemann, 1985)...£6
SPOT AT THE FARM (Heinemann, 1985)...£6
SPOT GOES ON HOLIDAY (Heinemann, 1985)...£6
SPOT GOES TO THE CIRCUS (Heinemann, 1986)...£5
SPOT LOOKS AT COLOURS (Heinemann, 1986)...£5
SPOT LOOKS AT SHAPES (Heinemann, 1986) £5
SPOT'S FIRST WORDS (Heinemann, 1986)..£5
SPOT GOES TO THE FARM (Heinemann, 1987)...£5
SPOT'S FIRST PICNIC (Heinemann, 1987)...£5
SPOT'S HOSPITAL VISIT (Heinemann, 1987) £5
SPOT'S FIRST EASTER (Heinemann, 1988)...£5
SPOT COUNTS FROM ONE TO TEN (Heinemann, 1989)..£5
SPOT LOOKS AT OPPOSITES (Heinemann, 1989)...£5
SPOT LOOKS AT THE WEATHER (Heinemann, 1989)...£5
SPOT'S BABY SISTER (Heinemann, 1989)...£5
SPOT SLEEPS OVER (Heinemann, 1990) £4
SPOT GOES TO THE PARK (Heinemann, 1991)...£4
SPOT IN THE GARDEN (Heinemann, 1991)..£4
SPOT'S TOY BOX (Heinemann, 1991)..£4
SPOT AT HOME (Heinemann, 1991) £4

'Peek-A-Book' Series for Children; Self-Illustrated

NURSEY RHYMES (Heinemann, 1982) £5
OPPOSITES (Heinemann, 1982)...£5
ANIMALS (Heinemann, 1982) £5
WHO DOES WHAT ? (Heinemann, 1982)..£5
BABY ANIMALS (Heinemann, 1984)..£5
MORE OPPOSITES (Heinemann, 1984)..£5

'Baby Bear Story-Book' Series For Children; Self-Illustrated

AT HOME, (Heinemann, 1983) £5
MY PETS (Heinemann, 1983)..£5
THE PARK (Heinemann,1983) £5
UP THERE (Heinemann, 1983) £5
BABY BEAR'S BEDTIME (Heinemann, 1984) £5
GOOD MORNING, BABY BEAR (Heinemann, 1984)...£5

HILL, Lorna

British author. Born: Durham, 1902. *A Dream of Sadler's Wells* (1950) was the first of a long series of interlocking ballet novels based on her daughter's training at the Sadler Wells Ballet School (now Royal Ballet School). Her realistic picture of family life, *The Vicarage Children*, appeared in 1961. Died: 1991.

Prices are for books in Very Good condition with dustjackets where applicable.

'Marjorie' Books

MARJORIE AND CO (Art and Educational, 1948)..£30
MARJORIE AND CO (Nelson, 1958) £15
STOLEN HOLIDAY (Art and Educational, 1948)..£30
STOLEN HOLIDAY (Nelson, 1956) £15
BORDER PEEL (Art and Educational, 1950) £30
BORDER PEEL (Nelson, 1956)...£20
CASTLE IN NORTHUMBRIA (Burke, 1953) £25
NO MEDALS FOR GUY (Nelson, 1962) £15
NORTHERN LIGHTS (paperback) (Privately published, 1999)..£20

'Patience' Books

THEY CALLED HER PATIENCE (Burke, 1951)..£25
THEY CALLED HER PATIENCE (Burke, 1958)...£15
IT WAS ALL THROUGH PATIENCE (Burke, 1952)..£25
IT WAS ALL THROUGH PATIENCE (Burke, 1961)...£15
SO GUY CAME TOO (Burke, 1954)...£20
SO GUY CAME TOO (Burke, 1959)...£15

THE FIVE SHILLING HOLIDAY (Burke, 1955) £20
THE FIVE SHILLING HOLIDAY (Burke, 1960) £15

'Sadler's Wells' Books
A DREAM OF SADLER'S WELLS (Evans, 1950) £20
VERONICA AT THE WELLS (Evans, 1951).. £20
MASQUERADE AT THE WELLS (Evans, 1952) £20
NO CASTANETS AT THE WELLS (Evans, 1953) £20
JANE LEAVES THE WELLS (Evans, 1953) £20
ELLA AT THE WELLS (Evans, 1954) £20
RETURN TO THE WELLS (Evans, 1955)... £20
ROSANNA JOINS THE WELLS (Evans, 1956) £20
PRINCIPAL ROLE (Evans, 1957)... £20
SWAN FEATHER (Evans, 1958) £20
DRESS-REHEARSAL (Evans, 1959) £20
BACK-STAGE (Evans, 1960) £20
VICKI IN VENICE (Evans, 1962) £25
THE SECRET (Evans, 1964) £30

'Dancing Peel' Books
DANCING PEEL (Nelson, 1954).. £20
DANCER'S PEEL (Nelson, 1955) £20
THE LITTLE DANCER (Nelson, 1956)... £20
DANCER IN THE WINGS (Nelson, 1958).. £25
DANCER IN DANGER (Nelson, 1960) £25
DANCER ON HOLIDAY (Nelson, 1962) £25

'Vicarage Children' Books
THE VICARAGE CHILDREN (Evans, 1961)... £25
MORE ABOUT MANDY (Evans, 1963).. £25
THE VICARAGE CHILDREN IN SKYE (Evans, 1966) £25

HILL, Stuart
British author. Born: 1958. Children's fantasy novel *The Cry of the Icemark* won the Ottakar's Children's Book Prize. Selected bibliography.

Prices are for books in Very Good condition with dustjackets where applicable.

THE CRY OF THE ICEMARK (The Chicken House, 2005) £10
THE CRY OF THE ICEMARK (1,000 copies signed and numbered, with dustjacket and illustrated slipcase; green endpapers)
(The Chicken House, 2005) £35
BLADE OF FIRE (part II of the 'Chronicles of Icemark') (The Chicken House, 2006).. £7

HOBAN, Russell
American author, resident in Britain since 1969. Born: Russell Conwell Hoban in Lansdale, Pennsylvania, in 1925. Studied at the Philadelphia Museum School of Industrial Art, subsequently working as an illustrator and advertising copywriter. As well as his many children's books — several of them illustrated by his first wife, Lillian — he has written a number of adult novels, notably *The Lion of Boaz-Jachin and Jachin-Boaz* (1973) and *Riddley Walker* (1980).

Prices are for books in Very Good condition with dustjackets where applicable.

WHAT DOES IT DO AND HOW DOES IT WORK? Power Shovel, Dump Truck and Other Heavy Machines (non-fiction)
(Harper, US, 1959) £60
THE ATOMIC SUBMARINE: A Practice Combat Patrol Under the Sea (non-fiction) (Harper, US, [1960]) £20
BEDTIME FOR FRANCES (illustrated by Garth Williams) (Harper, US, [1960]) £45
HERMAN THE LOSER (illustrated by Lillian Hoban) (Harper, US, 1961)... £25
THE SONG IN MY DRUM (illustrated by Lillian Hoban) (Harper, US, 1962) £25
LONDON MEN AND ENGLISH MEN (illustrated by Lillian Hoban) (Harper, US, 1962)... £25
SOME SNOW SAID HELLO (illustrated by Lillian Hoban) (Harper, US, [1963]) £25
THE SORELY TRYING DAY (illustrated by Lillian Hoban) (Harper, US, 1964).. £25
A BABY SISTER FOR FRANCES (illustrated by Lillian Hoban) (Harper, US, 1964) £30
BREAD AND JAM FOR FRANCES (illustrated by Lillian Hoban) (Harper, US, 1964).. £30
NOTHING TO DO (illustrated by Lillian Hoban) (Harper, US, 1964)... £20
TOM AND THE TWO HANDLES (illustrated by Lillian Hoban) (Harper, US, 1965) £20
WHAT HAPPENED WHEN JACK AND DAISY TRIED TO FOOL THE TOOTH FAIRIES (Four Winds Press, US, 1965)........... £30
GOODNIGHT (verse; illustrated by Lillian Hoban) (Norton, US, 1966)... £20
HENRY AND THE MONSTROUS DIN (illustrated by Lillian Hoban) (Harper, US, 1966) £20
THE LITTLE BRUTE FAMILY (illustrated by Lillian Hoban) (Macmillan, US, 1966)... £35
SAVE MY PLACE (illustrated by Lillian Hoban) (Norton, US, 1967) £15
CHARLIE THE TRAMP (illustrated by Lillian Hoban) (Four Winds Press, US, 1967) £25
THE MOUSE AND HIS CHILD (illustrated by Lillian Hoban) (Harper, US, 1967)... £45

THE PEDALLING MAN and Other Poems (illustrated by Lillian Hoban) (Norton, US, 1968)..£20
A BIRTHDAY FOR FRANCES (illustrated by Lillian Hoban) (Harper, US, 1968) £30
THE STONE DOLL OF SISTER BRUTE (illustrated by Lillian Hoban) (Macmillan, US, 1968)..................................£30
HARVEY'S HIDEOUT (illustrated by Lillian Hoban) (Parents' Magazine Press, US, 1969) £20
BEST FRIENDS FOR FRANCES (illustrated by Lillian Hoban) (Harper, US, 1969)...£25
THE MOLE FAMILY'S CHRISTMAS (illustrated by Lillian Hoban) (Parents' Magazine Press, US, 1969) £20
UGLY BIRD (illustrated by Lillian Hoban) (Macmillan, US, 1969) £20
A BARGAIN FOR FRANCES (illustrated by Lillian Hoban) (Harper, US, 1970)..£30
EMMET OTTER'S JUG-BAND CHRISTMAS (Parents' Magazine Press, US, 1971) £20
EGG THOUGHTS and Other Frances Songs (Harper, US, 1972)...£25
THE SEA-THING CHILD (illustrated by Brom Hoban) (Gollancz, 1972)..£20
LETITIA RABBIT'S STRING SONG (illustrated by Mary Chalmers) (Coward McCann, US, 1973).........................£20
HOW TOM BEAT CAPTAIN NAJORK AND HIS HIRED SPORTSMEN (illustrated by Quentin Blake) (Cape, 1974)..................£25
TEN WHAT? A Mystery Counting Book (illustrated by Sylvie Selig) (Cape, 1974)..£20
DINNER AT ALBERTA'S (illustrated by James Marshall) (Crowell, US, 1975) £20
CROCODILE AND PIERROT (illustrated by Sylvie Selig) (Cape, 1975) £20
A NEAR THING FOR CAPTAIN NAJORK (illustrated by Quentin Blake) (Cape, 1975)..£25
ARTHUR'S NEW POWER (illustrated by Byron Barton) (Crowell, US, 1978) £15
THE TWENTY ELEPHANT RESTAURANT (illustrated by Emily Arnold McCully) (Atheneum, US, 1978)................£20
THE DANCING TIGERS (illustrated by David Gentleman) (Cape, 1979)..£20
LA CORONA AND THE TIN FROG (illustrated by Nicola Bayley) (Cape, 1979) £25
FLAT CAT (illustrated by Clive Scruton) (Methuen, 1980) £10
ACE DRAGON LTD. (illustrated by Quentin Blake) (Cape, 1980)...£15
THE SERPENT TOWER (illustrated by David Scott) (Methuen, 1981)..£10
THE GREAT FRUIT GUM ROBBERY (illustrated by Colin McNaughton) (Methuen, 1981)....................................£15
THEY CAME FROM AARGH! (illustrated by Colin McNaughton) (Methuen, 1981)..£15
THE BATTLE OF ZORMLA (illustrated by Colin McNaughton) (Methuen, 1982)...£12
THE FLIGHT OF BEMBEL RUDZUK (Methuen, 1982)...£12
BIG JOHN TURKLE (illustrated by Martin Baynton) (Walker, 1983)..£10
JIM FROG (illustrated by Martin Baynton) (Walker, 1983) £10
CHARLIE MEADOWS (illustrated by Martin Baynton) (Walker, 1984)...£12
LAVINIA BAT (illustrated by Martin Baynton) (Walker, 1985)...£15
THE RAIN DOOR (illustrated by Quentin Blake) (Gollancz, 1986)...£20
THE MARZIPAN PIG (illustrated by Quentin Blake) (Cape, 1986) £20
JIM HEDGEHOG'S SUPERNATURAL CHRISTMAS (Clarion Books, US, 1992)..£10
M.O.L.E. (Much Overworked Little Earthmover) (illustrated by Jan Pienkowski) (Cape, 1993)...............................£15
A BARGAIN FOR FRANCES (illustrated by Lilian Hoban) (HarperCollins, US, 1998) £5

HOCKNEY, David

British artist. Born: Bradford, 1937. Studied Bradford Grammar School and the Royal College of Art. Best-known as a painter, he has also produced illustrations to a number of works, both adult and juvenile, often in limited as well as trade editions.

Price is for books in Very Good condition.

SIX FAIRY TALES FROM THE BROTHERS GRIMM (translated by Heiner Bastian) (Petersburg Press/OUP, [1970])...............£50
SIX FAIRY TALES FROM THE BROTHERS GRIMM (translated by Heiner Bastian; limited to 575 numbered copies,
signed by the artist) (Petersburg Press/Kasmin Gallery, [1970]) £3,000

HODGETTS, Sheila

British author, best known for the 'Toby Twirl' series of books published by Sampson Low Marston in the 1940s and '50s and illustrated by Edward Jeffrey.

Prices are for books in Very Good condition with dustjackets where applicable.

TOBY TWIRL ANNUALS (Sampson Low, 1946-1958) ....each £30
ONE MAGIC NIGHT (illustrated by Edward Jeffrey) (Sampson Low, [1947])..£30
THE SLEEPING CITY (illustrated by Edward Jeffrey) (Sampson Low, [1947])..£30
TOBY TWIRL RESCUES PRINCE APRICOT (illustrated by Edward Jeffrey) (Sampson Low, [1947])....................£40
THE TOBY TWIRL STORY BOOK (illustrated by Edward Jeffrey) (Sampson Low, [1947])....................................£30
TOBY TWIRL AND THE MERMAID PRINCESS (Sampson Low, [1948]) £30
TOBY TWIRL LIBRARY (eight books; illustrated by Edward Jeffrey) (Sampson Low, [1949-1954]) ....each £20
SLEEPY TIME TALES (Sampson Low, [1951-])...£20
THE TOBY TWIRL COLOUR STRIP ADVENTURE BOOK (illustrated by Edward Jeffrey) (Sampson Low, [1952]) £30
THE NEW TOBY TWIRL COLOUR STRIP ADVENTURE BOOK (illustrated by Edward Jeffrey) (Sampson Low, [1953])..........£30
THE ADVENTURE TWINS COLOUR STRIP BOOK (illustrated by R. MacGillivray) (Sampson Low, [1953])..............£20
THRILLS WITH THE ADVENTURE TWINS (illustrated by R. MacGillivray) (Sampson Low, [1954]) £20
TOBY TWIRL ON DAPPLE HEATH (strip book; illustrated by Edward Jeffrey; card covers) (Sampson Low, [1954])......£30
TOBY TWIRL AND THE TALKING POODLE (illustrated by Edward Jeffrey) (Sampson Low, [1954]).....................£30
THE ADVENTURE TWINS COLOUR STRIP BOOK (illustrated by R. MacGillivray) (Sampson Low, [1955])..............£20
THE NEW TOBY TWIRL COLOUR STRIP ADVENTURE BOOK (illustrated by Edward Jeffrey)
(Sampson Low, [1955]) £20

Heinrich Hoffman is best known for his famous collection of child's fables which he wrote for the young patients at a lunatic asylum.

HOFFMANN, Heinrich

German author-illustrator. Born: Frankfurt, 1809. Studied medicine, and began writing stories for the young patients at a lunatic asylum in which he worked. *Struwwelpeter* ('Shock-headed Peter'), his famous collection of child's fables, was first published under the title *Lustige Gesichten und drollige Bilder* ('Merry Stories and Funny Pictures') in 1845, an English translation published in Leipzig appearing three years later. The book was a huge success, going through 100 editions in its first thirty years. Hoffmann wrote other picture books, but none enjoyed the same popularity. Died: 1894.

Prices are for books in Very Good condition.

THE ENGLISH STRUWWELPETER, or Pretty Stories and Funny Pictures for Little Children Translated from the German
(first English edition) (Leipzig, 1848) **£5,000**
DEAN'S SIXPENNY 'ENGLISH STRUWWELPETERS' (thirteen books: Nos. 1-9, 11-14) (Dean, [1859]) .... each **£150**
THE ENGLISH STRUWWELPETER, or Pretty Stories and Funny Pictures for Little Children
(twelfth edition; printed on one side of the leaf only) (Friedrich Volckmar, Leipzig, [1860]) **£275**
DER STRUWWELPETER: Oder Lustige Geschichten und Drollige Bilder Für Kinder von 3-6 Jahren
(100th German edition; printed on one side of the leaf only; with an additional leaf 'zur hundersten Auflage')
(Frankfurt, [1876]) **£140**
STRUWWELPETER, or Merry Stories and Funny Pictures (printed on one side of the leaf only)
(Blackie, 1903) **£100**
THE ENGLISH STRUWWELPETER, or Pretty Stories and Funny Pictures (Routledge, [1909]) **£100**
STRUWWELPETER (printed on one side of the leaf only) (Blackie, [1928]) **£80**
THE LATIN STRUWWELPETER (translated by W.H.D. Rouse) (Blackie, 1934) **£100**
SLOVENLY PETER (translated by Mark Twain; limited to 1,500 copies) (Limited Editions Club, US, 1935) **£450**

DER STRUWWELPETER (Wiesbaden, [1950]) £80
STRUWWELPETER (illustrated by J. and A.G. Johnstone) (Gifford, 1950) £60
STRUWWELPETER (Blackie, [1960]) £50
PETRUS ERICIUS — STRUWWELPETER: Lepidse Historiolse ab Hugone Henrico Paoli Latinis Versibus Enarratae
(Florentiae, [1960]) £50
KING NUT-CRACKER, or The Dream of Poor Reinhold: A Fairy Tale (translated by J.R. Planché)
(London [printed in Leipzig], [1853])...£900
KING NUT-CRACKER AND THE POOR BOY, REINHOLD: A Christmas Story with Pictures
(translated by A.H.) (London, 1854) £800
KING NUT-CRACKER (translated by J.R. Planché) ([1927])...£80
KINDERGARTEN TOYS and How to Use Them: A Practical Explanation of the First Six Gifts of Froebel's Kindergarten
(London, [1874]) £175
KINDERGARTEN TOYS and How to Use Them: A Practical Explanation of the First Six Gifts of Froebel's Kindergarten
(second edition) (London, [1877]) £100

'Struwwelpeter' Pastiches

THE EGYPTIAN STRUWWELPETER: Being the Struwwelpeter Papyrus, with full text and original vignettes from
the Vienna Papyri (H. Grevel, [1899]) £275
SWOLLEN-HEADED WILLIAM: A Satire upon the Emperor William II, founded upon H. Hoffmann's 'Struwwelpeter'.
Adapted by E.V. Lucas (illustrations adapted by G. Morrow) (Methuen, 1914) £80
THE MODERN STRUWWELPETER by Jan Struther (illustrated by E.H. Shepard) (Methuen, 1936)......................£225

'HOOD'S COMIC' ANNUALS

Popular British annual, edited by Tom Hood (1835-74), son of the poet, Thomas Hood (1799-1845). Tom Hood also wrote and illustrated many children's books, including *Fairy Realm* (1865), a selection of Perrault's fairy tales retold in verse.

Prices are for annuals in Very Good condition.

THE COMIC ANNUAL by Thomas Hood 1830-1842 ([1829-41]).. each £50
THE COMIC ANNUAL by Thomas Hood 1843-1867 ([1842-66]).. each £40
TOM HOOD'S COMIC ANNUAL 1868-1876 ([1867-1875] — no issue for 1869) .... each £35
HOOD'S COMIC ANNUAL 1877-1895 ([1876-94]) .... each £30
HOOD'S ANNUAL ([1895-1897]).. each £25

HOROWITZ, Anthony

British author. Born in North London in 1955. Creator of the bestselling novels starring Teen Spy sensation Alex Rider. He has also written the less collectable 'Diamond Brothers' and 'Groosham Grange' series of children's books, alongside many horror stories for adults.

Prices are for books in Very Good condition.

STORMBREAKER (paperback) (Walker Books, 2000)..£10
STORMBREAKER ('Special Limited Edition'; 750 signed, numbered hardback copies; slipcase) (Walker Books, 2005)............£20
POINT BLANC (paperback) (Walker Books, 2001)...£5
SKELETON KEY(paperback) (Walker Books, 2002) £5
EAGLE STRIKE (paperback) (Walker Books, 2003) £5
SCORPIA (paperback) (Walker Books, 2004) £5
ARK ANGEL (paperback) (Walker Books, 2005) £5

HORWOOD, William

British author. Born: 1944. Began as an English teacher, then worked as a freelance journalist for the *Financial Times*, *Guardian* and *Reader's Digest*. Notable for his 'Duncton Wood' series and for his sequels to *The Wind in the Willows*.

Prices are for books in Very Good condition with dustjackets where applicable.

THE WILLOWS IN WINTER (illustrated by Patrick Benson) (HarperCollins, 1993) £30
TOAD TRIUMPHANT (illustrated by Patrick Benson) (HarperCollins, 1995)..£18
THE WILLOWS AND BEYOND (HarperCollins, 1998) £18
WILLOWS AT CHRISTMAS (HarperCollins, 1999)...£12

HUGHES, Richard

British author. Born: Richard Arthur Warren Hughes in Caterham, Surrey, in 1900. Best known for his adult novels, including *A High Wind in Jamaica* (1929) and *The Fox in the Attic* (1961), but also produced a handful of children's works. Died: 1976.

Prices are for books in Very Good condition with dustjackets where applicable.

BURIAL, AND THE DARK CHILD (limited to sixty copies) (Privately printed, 1930)..£700
THE SPIDER'S PALACE and Other Stories (illustrated by George Charlton) (Chatto & Windus, 1931)..............£60
DON'T BLAME ME! and Other Stories (illustrated by Fritz Eichenberg) (Chatto & Windus, 1940) £30
GERTRUDE'S CHILD (illustrated by Rick Schreiter) (Quist, US, 1967) £18
THE WONDER DOG (illustrated by Antony Maitland)
(Chatto & Windus: 'Collected Children's Stories' series, 1977) £12

HUGHES, Shirley

British author-illustrator. Born: West Kirby, the Wirral, in 1927. She trained at Liverpool Art School and the Ruskin School of Art, Oxford. Awarded Kate Greenaway Medal in 1977 and the Eleanor Farjeon Award in 1984. Has illustrated numerous young children's books as well as her own, where the emphasis is on the richness and detail of the pictures. Awarded the OBE in 1999.

Prices are for books in Very Good condition with dustjackets where applicable.

Books Written and Illustrated by Shirley Hughes

'Lucy and Tom' Books

LUCY AND TOM'S DAY (boards) (Gollancz, 1960) £45
LUCY AND TOM GO TO SCHOOL (boards) (Gollancz, 1973)...£40
LUCY AND TOM AT THE SEASIDE (boards) (Gollancz, 1976) £40
LUCY AND TOM'S CHRISTMAS (boards) (Gollancz, 1981)..£30
LUCY AND TOM'S ABC (boards) (Gollancz 1984)...£20
LUCY AND TOM'S 1,2,3 (boards) (Gollancz, 1987) £20
LUCY AND TOM'S WORLD (boards) (Gollancz, 1993)..£20

'Alfie' Books

ALFIE GETS IN FIRST (boards) (The Bodley Head, 1981)..£30
ALFIE'S FEET (boards) (The Bodley Head,1982) £20
ALFIE GIVES A HAND (boards) (The Bodley Head, 1983 ....£20
AN EVENING AT ALFIE'S (boards) (The Bodley Head, 1984)..£20
THE BIG ALFIE AND ANNIE ROSE STORYBOOK (The Bodley Head, 1988)........................£15
ALFIE'S ALPHABET (boards) (The Bodley Head, 1988)..£15
THE BIG ALFIE OUT OF DOORS STORYBOOK (Walker, 1989)..£15
THE ALFIE COLLECTION (The Bodley Head, 1992)..£15
THE ALFIE TREASURY (The Bodley Head, 1994)..£15
ALFIE AND THE BIRTHDAY SURPRISE (The Bodley Head, 1997).......................................£10

'Charlie Moon' Books

HERE COMES CHARLIE MOON (The Bodley Head, 1980) £10
CHARLIE MOON AND THE BIG BONANZA BUST UP (The Bodley Head, 1985) £10

'Chips' Books

CHIPS AND JESSIE (The Bodley Head, 1985) £10
ANOTHER HELPING OF CHIPS (The Bodley Head, 1986)..£10

Others

THE TROUBLE WITH JACK (The Bodley Head, 1970)...£15
SALLY'S SECRET (The Bodley Head, 1973) £15
HELPERS (The Bodley Head, 1975)..£15
BEING TOGETHER (boards) (Walker, 1977) £10
DOGGER (boards) (The Bodley Head, 1977) £25
IT'S TOO FRIGHTENING FOR ME ! (Hodder and Stoughton, 1977)......................................£10
MOVING MOLLY (boards) (The Bodley Head, 1978) £15
UP AND UP (The Bodley Head, 1979)...£15
OVER THE MOON: A BOOK OF SAYINGS (Faber, 1980) £15
NOISY (boards) (Walker, 1985) £5
WHEN WE WENT TO THE PARK (boards) (Walker, 1985)..£5
BATHWATER'S HOT (boards) (Walker, 1985)...£5
TWO SHOES, NEW SHOES (boards) (Walker, 1986) £5
COLOURS (boards) (Walker, 1986)...£5
ALL SHAPES AND SIZES (boards) (Walker, 1986) £5
OUT AND ABOUT (boards) (Walker, 1988) £5
THE BIG CONCRETE LORRY (boards) (Walker, 1989)...£5
ANGEL MAE (boards) (Walker, 1989)...£5
MOTYN (boards) (CLC, 1990) £5
THE SNOW LADY (boards) (Walker, 1990)...£5
WHEELS (boards) (Walker, 1991)...£5
LLYR MAWR STRAEON ALFIE YN YR AWYR AGORED (boards) (CLC,1992) £5
BOUNCING (boards) (Walker, 1993)..£5
GIVING (boards) (Walker, 1993)..£5
STORIES BY FIRELIGHT (Lothrop, 1993)...£5
STRAEON YNG NGOLAU'R TAN (boards) (CLC, 1993) £5
CHATTING (boards) (Walker,1994) £5
HIDING (boards) (Walker, 1994)..£5
RHYMES FOR ANNIE ROSE (The Bodley Head, 1995) £10
ENCHANTMENT IN THE GARDEN (The Bodley Head, 1996) £10
TALES OF TROTTER STREET (Walker, 1996)...£10
THE NURSERY COLLECTION (Walker, 1997)...£10

PLAYING (Walker, 1997) £5
THE LION AND THE UNICORN (Cape, 1998) £10
ABEL'S MOON (The Bodley Head, 1999)...£10

Books Illustrated by Shirley Hughes

THE HILL WAR by Olivia Fitzroy (Collins, 1950)...£25
FOURWINDS ISLAND by Vega Stewart (Collins, 1951)......................................£25
GREAT-UNCLE TOBY by John R. Hale (Faber, 1951)..£25
WORLD'S END WAS HOME by Nan Chauncy (OUP, 1952)...............................£25
FOLLOW THE FOOTPRINTS by William Mayne (OUP, 1953)............................£30
A WEEK OF STORIES by Doris Rust (Faber, 1953)..£20
THE JOURNEY OF JOHNNY REW by Anne Barrett (Collins, 1954)..................£20
ALL THROUGH THE NIGHT by Rachel Field (Collins, 1954).............................£20
THE WORLD UPSIDE DOWN by William Mayne (OUP, 1954)............................£30
A STORY A DAY by Doris Rust (Faber, 1954) £15
THE BELL FAMILY by Noel Streatfeild (Collins, 1954)......................................£20
THE BOYS' COUNTRY BOOK by John Moore (Collins, 1955).........................£10
ALL SORTS OF DAYS by Doris Rust (Faber, 1955)...£10
LOST LORRENDEN by Mabel Esther Allan (Blackie, 1956)............................£10
MR PUNCH'S CAP by Kathleen Fidler (Lutterworth, 1956)..............................£10
THE MAN OF THE HOUSE by Allan Campbell Maclean (Collins, 1956).........£10
WILLIAM AND THE LORRY by Diana Ross (Faber, 1956)................................£15
THE ANIMALS AT NUMBER ELEVEN by Doris Rust (Faber, 1956)...............£10
GUNS IN THE WILD by Ian Serraillier (Heinemann, 1956)..............................£20
MYSTERY ON RAINBOW ISLAND by Dorothy Clewes (Collins, 1957)..........£20
COME TO THE FAIR. Edited by Barbara Ireson (Faber 1957).........................£10
THE ANIMALS AT ROSE COTTAGE by Doris Rust (Faber, 1957)................£10
KATY AT HOME by Ian Serraillier (Heinemann, 1957) £20
THE MYSTERY OF THE JADE-GREEN CADILLAC by Dorothy Clewes (Collins, 1958).......£10
THE BOY AND THE DONKEY by Diana Pullein-Thomson (Collins, 1958)......£10
MIXED-MUDDLY ISLAND by Doris Rust (Faber, 1958)...................................£10
KATY AT SCHOOL by Ian Serraillier, based on a story by Susan Coolidge (Heinemann, 1959) £20
NOEL STREATFEILD'S BALLET ANNUAL by Noel Streatfeild (Collins, 1959).......£10
THE LOST TOWER TREASURE by Dorothy Clewes (Collins, 1960) £10
ROLLING ON by Mary Cockett (Methuen, 1960)..£10
FELL FARM CAMPERS by Marjorie Lloyd (paperback) (Penguin, 1960) £5
NEW TOWN: A Story About the Bell Family by Noel Streatfeild (Collins, 1960)......£15
FLOWERING SPRING by Elfrida Vipont (OUP, 1960) £10
THE SINGING STRINGS by Dorothy Clewes (Collins, 1961)..........................£10
MARY ANN GOES TO HOSPITAL by Mary Crockett (Methuen, 1961)..........£10
FAIRY TALES by Hans Andersen (translated by Caroline Peachey) (Blackie, 1961)......£30
THE BRONZE CHRYSANTHEMUM by Sheena Porter (OUP, 1961).............£10
PLAIN JANE by Barbara Softly (Macmillan, 1961)...£10
THE PAINTED GARDEN by Noel Streatfeild (paperback) (Puffin, 1961).......£5
COTTAGE BY THE LOCK by Mary Crockett (Methuen, 1962) £10
MY NAUGHTY LITTLE SISTER by Dorothy Edwards (Methuen, 1962).......£30
MY NAUGHTY LITTLE SISTER'S FRIENDS by Dorothy Edwards (Methuen, 1962) £25
PLACE MILL by Barbara Softly (Macmillan, 1962)..£10
THE SIGN OF THE UNICORN by Mabel Esther Allan (Dent, 1963)..............£10
THE SHINTY BOYS by Margaret Macpherson (Collins, 1963).......................£10
TALES OF TIGGS FARM by Helen Morgan (Faber, 1963)............................£10
MEET MARY KATE by Helen Morgan (Faber, 1963)......................................£10
WILLY IS MY BROTHER by Peggy Parish (Gollancz, 1963).........................£10
THE MERRY-GO-ROUND by Diana Ross (Lutterworth, 1963).......................£15
FIONA ON THE FOURTEENTH FLOOR by Mabel Esther Allan (Dent, 1964).......£10
OPERATION SMUGGLE by Dorothy Clewes (Collins, 1964)........................£10
THE CAT AND MRS CARY by Doris Gates (Methuen, 1964)........................£10
STORIES FROM GRIMM by Roger Lancelyn Green (Blackie, 1964).............£20
ROLLER SKATES by Ruth Sawyer (The Bodley Head, 1964) £10
A STONE IN A POOL by Barbara Softly (Macmillan, 1964)...........................£10
JACKO AND OTHER STORIES by Jean Sutcliffe (The Bodley Head 1964) £10
TIM RABBIT'S DOZEN by Alison Uttley (Faber, 1964).................................£25
TALES THE MUSES TOLD by Roger Lancelyn Green (The Bodley Head, 1965).......£10
A DREAM OF DRAGONS by Helen Morgan (Faber, 1965)..........................£10
LUCINDA'S YEAR OF JUBILEE by Ruth Sawyer (The Bodley Head, 1965).......£10
KATE AND THE FAMILY TREE by Margaret Storey (The Bodley Head, 1965).......£10
THE TWELVE DANCING PRINCESSES by Margaret Storey (Nelson, 1965).......£10
THE WITCH'S DAUGHTER by Nina Bawden (Gollancz,1966)......................£25
LITTLE BEAR'S PONY by Donald Bisset (Benn, 1966) £10
WAYLAND'S KEEP by Angela Bull (Collins, 1966).......................................£10

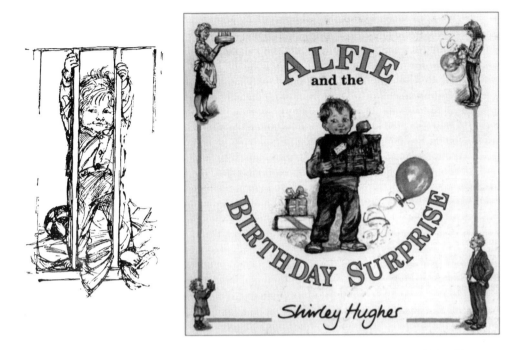

Alfie and the Birthday Surprise (1997) is one of many Shirley Hughes books to feature her mischievous little toddler.

FABER BOOK OF NURSERY STORIES by Barbara Ireson (Faber, 1966) £15
SATCHKIN PATCHKIN by Helen Morgan (Faber, 1966)..£10
SOMETHING TO DO by Septima (paperback) (Penguin, 1966) £5
THE SMALLEST DOLL by Margaret Storey (Faber, 1966) £10
THE SMALLEST BRIDESMAID by Margaret Storey (Faber, 1966) £10
WISH ON A PIG by Barbara Ward (Collins, 1966) £10
PORTERHOUSE MAJOR by Margaret J. Baker (Methuen, 1967)..£10
STORIES FOR SIX YEAR OLDS by Sara and Stephen Corrin (Faber, 1967) £10
A DAY ON BIG O by Helen Cresswell (Benn, 1967)..£10
MARY KATE AND THE JUMBLE BEAR by Helen Morgan (Faber, 1967)..£10
THE WOOD STREET SECRET by Mabel Esther Allan (Methuen, 1968)..£10
FLUTES AND CYMBALS. Edited by Leonard Clark (The Bodley Head, 1968) £10
WHEN MY NAUGHTY LITTLE SISTER WAS GOOD by Dorothy Edwards (Methuen, 1968) £15
THE NEW TENANTS by Margaret Macpherson (Collins, 1968)..£10
ROBIN'S REAL ENGINE and Other Stories by William Mayne (Hamish Hamilton, 1968)................£10
THE TOFFEE JOIN by William Mayne (Hamish Hamilton: 'Gazelle' series, 1968)..............................£20
MRS PINNY AND THE BLOWING DAY by Helen Morgan (Faber, 1968)..£10
HOME AND AWAY by Ann Thwaite (Brockhampton Press, 1968)...£10
A CROWN FOR A QUEEN by Ursula Moray Williams (Hamish Hamilton, 1968)................................£10
THE TOYMAKER'S DAUGHTER by Ursula Moray Williams (Hamish Hamilton,1968)..........................£10
THE BICYCLE WHEEL by Ruth Ainsworth (Hamish Hamilton, 1969)..£10
GOLDIE by Irma Chilton (Hamish Hamilton, 1969)..£10
ALL ABOUT MY NAUGHTY LITTLE SISTER by Dorothy Edwards (Methuen, 1969)...........................£15
MOSHIE CAT: TRUE ADVENTURES OF A MALLORQUIN KITTEN by Helen Griffiths
    (Hutchinson,1969)...£15
MRS PINNY AND THE SUDDEN SNOW by Helen Morgan (Faber, 1969) £10
CINDERELLA, OR THE LITTLE GLASS SLIPPER by Charles Perrault (Methuen, 1969)....................£20
THE RUTH AINSWORTH BOOK by Ruth Ainsworth (Heinemann, 1970)..£20
THE WOOD STREET GROUP by Mabel Esther Allan (Methuen, 1970)..£10
THE JADE- GREEN CADILLAC by Dorothy Clewes (Howard Baker, 1970) £10
ADVENTURE ON RAINBOW ISLAND by Dorothy Clewes (Howard Baker, 1970)...............................£10
RAINBOW PAVEMENT by Helen Cresswell (Benn, 1970) £10
MORE NAUGHTY LITTLE SISTER STORIES by Dorothy Edwards (Methuen,1970) £10

HUGHES, Shirley

EIGHT DAYS TO CHRISTMAS by Geraldine Kaye (Macmillan, 1970)......................................£10
MARY KATE AND THE SCHOOL BUS by Helen Morgan (Faber, 1970)..............................£10
MORE FAIRY TALES by Caroline Peachey (Blackie, 1970)......................................£10
THE THREE TOYMAKERS by Ursula Moray Williams (Hamish Hamilton,1970) £10
MALKIN'S MOUNTAIN by Ursula Moray Williams (Hamish Hamilton, 1970)................£10
THE WOOD STREET RIVALS by Mabel Esther Allan (Methuen, 1971)...........................£15
SQUIB by Nina Bawden (Gollancz, 1971)......................................£15
STORIES FOR EIGHT YEAR OLDS by Sara and Stephen Corrin (Faber, 1971)............£10
THE LITTLE CAT THAT COULD NOT SLEEP by Frances Margaret Fox (Faber, 1971) £10
THE LOST ANGEL by Elizabeth Goudge (Hodder & Stoughton,1971)..........................£10
FREDERICO by Helen Griffiths (Hutchinson, 1971)......................................£10
MOTHER FARTHING'S LUCK by Helen Morgan (Faber, 1971) £10
ROBBIE'S MOB by Jo Rice (World's Work, 1971)......................................£10
THE SMELL OF PRIVET by Barbara Sleigh (Hutchinson, 1971) £10
THE LITTLE BROOMSTICK by Mary Stewart (Brockhampton Press, 1971)..................£10
DANCING DAY by Robina Beccles Willson (Benn, 1971)......................................£10
HOSPITAL DAY by Leila Berg (Macmillan, 1972)......................................£10
L'ARC EN CIEL by Helen Cresswell (Benn, 1972) £10
LES JEUNES CORSAIRS by Helen Cresswell (Benn, 1972).....................................£10
MOTHER'S HELP by Sara Dickinson (Collins, 1972) £10
GINGER by Geraldine Kaye (Macmillan, 1972)......................................£10
THE FIRST MARGARET MAHY STORYBOOK by Margaret Mahy (Dent, 1972)..............£10
MRS PINNY AND THE SALTY SEA DAY by Helen Morgan (Faber, 1972).....................£10
THE THIRTEEN DAYS OF CHRISTMAS by Jenny Overton (Faber, 1972)......................£10
THE HOUSE IN THE SQUARE by Joan G. Robinson (Collins, 1972)...........................£10
ANOTHER LUCKY DIP by Ruth Ainsworth (paperback) (Puffin, 1973)..........................£5
THE WOOD STREET HELPERS by Mabel Esther Allan (Methuen, 1973) £10
STORIES FOR FIVE YEAR OLDS by Sara and Stephen Corrin (Faber, 1973)..............£10
THE HOLLYWELL FAMILY by Margaret Kornitzer (The Bodley Head, 1973)................£10
THE SECOND MARGARET MAHY STORYBOOK by Margaret Mahy (Dent, 1973)..........£10
THE PHANTOM FISHERBOY: TALES OF MYSTERY AND MAGIC by Ruth Ainsworth (Deutsch, 1974) £10
STORIES FOR UNDER FIVES by Sara and Stephen Corrin (Faber, 1974)...................£10
MISS HENDY'S HOUSE by Joan Drake (Brockhampton, Press, 1974) £10
MY NAUGHTY LITTLE SISTER AND BAD HARRY by Dorothy Edwards (Methuen, 1974) £10
THE GAUNTLET FAIR by Alison Farthing (Chatto & Windus, 1974)............................£10
AWAY FROM WOOD STREET by Mabel Esther Allan (Methuen, 1975).......................£10
HAZY MOUNTAIN by Donald Bisset (boards) (Kestrel, 1975)......................................£5
THE THIRD MARGARET MAHY STORYBOOK by Magaret Mahy (Dent, 1975) £10
PETER PAN AND WENDY by J.M. Barrie (Hodder & Stoughton, 1976)........................£15
MY NAUGHTY LITTLE SISTER GOES FISHING by Dorothy Edwards (Methuen, 1976) £15
TATTERCOATS AND OTHER FOLK TALES by Winifred Finlay (Kaye & Ward, 1976).........£10
THE SNAKE CROOK by Ruth Tomalin (Faber, 1976) £10
THE NOEL STREATFEILD BIRTHDAY STORY BOOK by Noel Streatfeild, John Pudney and others
    (illustrated by Shirley Hughes and others) (Dent, 1976)......................................£15
MAKE HAY WHILE THE SUN SHINES by Alison M. Abel (Faber, 1977)......................£15
THE PHANTOM ROUNDABOUT by Ruth Ainsworth (Deutsch,1977) £10
DONKEY DAYS by Helen Cresswell (Benn, 1977) £10
MY NAUGHTY LITTLE SISTER AND BAD HARRY'S RABBIT by Dorothy Edwards (Methuen, 1977)......£15
A THRONE FOR SESAME by Helen Young (Deutsch, 1977) £10
MORE STORIES FOR SEVEN YEAR OLDS by Sara and Stephen Corrin (Faber, 1978).........£10
POTTLE PIG by Nancy Northcote (Kaye & Ward, 1978) £10
THE TROUBLE WITH DRAGONS by Olive Selfridge (Addison-Wesley, 1978) £10
THE SNAILMAN by Barbara Sivers (Little Brown, 1978)......................................£10
FROM SPRING TO SPRING: STORIES OF THE FOUR SEASONS by Alison Uttley (Faber, 1978)........£20
STORIES FOR NINE YEAR OLDS by Sara and Stephen Corrins (Faber, 1979)..............£10
MY NAUGHTY LITTLE SISTER AT THE FAIR by Dorothy Edwards (Methuen, 1979)..........£15
BOGWOPPIT by Ursula Moray Williams (Hamish Hamilton, 1979)...........................£10
THE PIRATE SHIP and Other Stories by Ruth Ainsworth (Heinemann, 1980) £10
WITCHDUST by Mary Welfare (Murray, 1980)......................................£10
A CAT'S TALE by Rikki Cate (Methuen, 1982) £10
COUSIN PONS by Honore de Balzac (translated and with an introduction by Herbert J Hunt; in slipcase)
    (The Folio Society, 1984)......................................£15
FIVE TO EIGHT by Dorothy Butler (The Bodley Head, 1985)......................................£10
MAHY MAGIC by Margaret Mahy (Dent, 1986) £10
THE HORRIBLE STORY AND OTHERS by Margaret Mahy (Dent, 1987)........................£25
THE SECRET GARDEN by Frances Hodgson Burnett (Gollancz, 1988)......................£15
THE BOY WHO BOUNCED AND OTHER MAGIC TALES by Magaret Mahy (paperback)
    (Puffin, 1988)......................................£5
CHOCOLATE PORRIDGE and Other Stories by Magaret Mahy (paperback) (Puffin, 1989)........£10

MY NAUGHTY LITTLE SISTER STORYBOOK by Dorothy Edwards (Methuen, 1991)......£10
RAINBOW TALES by Alison Uttley (Young Piper, 1991).......£10
THE GIRL WITH THE GREEN EAR by Magaret Mahy (Dent, 1991) £10
LITTLE WOMEN by Louisa May Alcott (paperback) (Puffin, 1994).......£10
THE RAILWAY CHILDREN by Edith Nesbit (Macmillan, 1994) £15
BABIES NEED BOOKS by Dorothy Butler (paperback) (Penguin,1995) £5
THE COMPLETE MY NAUGHTY LITTLE SISTER STORYBOOK by Dorothy Edwards (Methuen, 1997) £10

HUGHES, Ted

British poet. Born: Edward James Hughes in Mytholmroyd, Yorkshire, in 1930. Studied at Pembroke College, Cambridge. Married the poet, Sylvia Plath, in 1963. Appointed Poet Laureate in 1984. Although best known for his adult poetry, collected in volumes such as *The Hawk in the Rain* (1957) and *Lupercal* (1960), he has also written a number of books of children's verse, notably *Meet My Folks!* (1961) and *The Earth-Owl and Other Moon-People* (1963), as well as plays and stories for young readers. Perhaps his best-known children's work is the novel, *The Iron Man* (1968). Died: 1998.

Prices are for books in Very Good condition with dustjackets.

MEET MY FOLKS! (illustrated by George Adamson) (Faber, 1961).......£100
HOW THE WHALE BECAME (illustrated by George Adamson) (Faber, 1963).......£75
THE EARTH-OWL AND OTHER MOON-PEOPLE (verse; illustrated by R.A. Brandt) (Faber, 1963) £50
NESSIE THE MANNERLESS MONSTER (verse; illustrated by Gerald Rose) (Faber, 1964).......£60
POETRY IN THE MAKING: An Anthology of Poems and Programmes from 'Listening and Writing'
(Faber, 1967).......£60
THE IRON MAN: A Story in Five Nights (illustrated by George Adamson) (Faber, 1968) £60
FIVE AUTUMN SONGS FOR CHILDREN'S VOICES (illustrated by Nina Carroll; limited to 500 copies: copies 3-11
— verses in manuscript; with one illustration in watercolour) (Gilberton, 1968 [1970]).......£270
FIVE AUTUMN SONGS FOR CHILDREN'S VOICES (illustrated by Nina Carroll; limited to 500 copies: copies 12-37
— verses in manuscript) (Gilberton, 1968 [1970]) £220
FIVE AUTUMN SONGS FOR CHILDREN'S VOICES (illustrated by Nina Carroll; limited to 500 copies: copies 38-188
— signed by the author) (Gilberton, 1968 [1970]).......£100
FIVE AUTUMN SONGS FOR CHILDREN'S VOICES (illustrated by Nina Carroll; limited to 500 copies: copies 189-500
— numbered) (Gilberton, 1968 [1970]).......£50
SPRING, SUMMER, AUTUMN, WINTER (limited to 140 numbered copies, signed by the author)
(Rainbow Press, 1974).......£200
SPRING, SUMMER, AUTUMN, WINTER (as 'Seasons Songs') (Faber, 1976).......£30
EARTH MOON (limited to 200 numbered copies, signed by the author) (Rainbow Press,1976).......£175
MOON BELLS AND OTHER POEMS (Chatto Windus, 1978).......£20
UNDER THE NORTH STAR (verse; illustrated by Leonard Baskin) (Faber, 1981) £30
WHAT IS THE TRUTH? A Farmyard Fable for the Young (illustrated by R.J. Lloyd)
(Faber, 1984).......£25
FFANGS THE VAMPIRE BAT AND THE KISS OF TRUTH (illustrated by Chris Riddell)
(Faber, 1986).......£20
THE CAT AND THE CUCKOO (Sunstone Press, [1987]).......£25
THE MERMAID'S PURSE (Faber, 1991) £20
THE IRON WOMAN (Faber, 1993).......£15
COLLECTED ANIMAL POEMS (four volumes) (Faber, 1994).......the set £40
DREAM FIGHTER AND OTHER CREATION TALES (Faber, 1995).......£15
SHAGGY AND SPOTTY (Faber, 1997).......£15

HUGHES, Thomas

British author. Born: Uffington, Berkshire, in 1822. Studied at Rugby School and Oriel College, Oxford. His experiences at Rugby provided the inspiration for his best-known work, *Tom Brown's Schooldays* (1857). A Christian Socialist, Hughes co-founded the Working Men's College in London and was elected to Parliament in 1865. Became a County Court judge in 1882. Died: 1896.

Prices are for books in Very Good condition.

TOM BROWN'S SCHOOLDAYS: By an Old Boy (blue cloth) (Macmillan, 1857).......£700
TOM BROWN'S SCHOOLDAYS (early reprints) (Macmillan, 1857-60).......£125
TOM BROWN'S SCHOOLDAYS (paperback) (Tauchnitz, Germany, 1858) £75
TOM BROWN'S SCHOOLDAYS (first illustrated edition; illustrated by Arthur Hughes and Sidney Prior Hall)
(Macmillan, 1869 [1868]).......£90
TOM BROWN'S SCHOOLDAYS (illustrated by Edmund J. Sullivan) (Macmillan, 1896) £50
TOM BROWN'S SCHOOLDAYS (illustrated by E.H. Shepard) (Methuen, [1904]).......£125
TOM BROWN'S SCHOOLDAYS (illustrated by Hugh Thomson) (Ginn, US, [1918]).......£40
THE SCOURING OF THE WHITE HORSE (illustrated by Richard Doyle) (Macmillan, 1859) £180
TOM BROWN AT OXFORD (three volumes) (Macmillan, 1861).......the set £325
NOTES FOR BOYS — AND THEIR FATHERS — ON MORALS, MIND AND MANNERS
(non-fiction) (Elliot Stock, 1885) £30
VACATION RAMBLES. Edited by his Daughter (non-fiction) (Macmillan, 1895).......£35
EARLY MEMORIES FOR THE CHILDREN (non-fiction) (Thomas Burleigh, 1899) £170

HUNTER, Norman

British author. Born: Sydenham, Kent, in 1899. Studied at Beckenham School, subsequently becoming an advertising copywriter. Submitted stories to various publications, including *The Merry-Go-Round* and the *Boy's Own Paper*, as well as the BBC's *Children's Hour*, before launching the 'Professor Branestawm' series in 1933 with *The Incredible Adventures of Professor Branestawm*. Also wrote a number of books on conjuring. Died: 1995.

Prices are for books in Very Good condition with dustjackets where applicable.

'Professor Branestawm' Books

THE INCREDIBLE ADVENTURES OF PROFESSOR BRANESTAWM (illustrated by W. Heath Robinson)
(John Lane: The Bodley Head, 1933) £150
PROFESSOR BRANESTAWM'S TREASURE HUNT and Other Incredible Adventures (illustrated by James Arnold)
(John Lane: The Bodley Head, 1937) £100
STORIES OF PROFESSOR BRANESTAWM (illustrated by W. Heath Robinson; card wraps) (Arnold, [1939]) £40
THE PECULIAR TRIUMPH OF PROFESSOR BRANESTAWM (illustrated by George Adamson)
(The Bodley Head, 1970) £35
PROFESSOR BRANESTAWM UP THE POLE (illustrated by George Adamson) (The Bodley Head, 1972)................£25
PROFESSOR BRANESTAWM'S DICTIONARY (illustrated by Derek Cousins) (The Bodley Head, 1973).................£20
PROFESSOR BRANESTAWM'S GREAT REVOLUTION (The Bodley Head, 1974)...£20
PROFESSOR BRANESTAWM'S COMPENDIUM OF CONUNDRUMS, RIDDLES, PUZZLES,
BRAIN-TWISTERS AND DOTTY DESCRIPTIONS (The Bodley Head, 1975)...£15
PROFESSOR BRANESTAWM'S DO-IT-YOURSELF HANDBOOK (The Bodley Head, 1976).................................£15
PROFESSOR BRANESTAWM 'ROUND THE BEND (The Bodley Head, 1977) £25
PROFESSOR BRANESTAWM'S PERILOUS PUDDING (The Bodley Head, 1979)...£25
THE BEST OF BRANESTAWM (The Bodley Head, 1980)..£15
PROFESSOR BRANESTAWM'S POCKET MOTOR CAR (The Bodley Head, 1981) £12
PROFESSOR BRANESTAWM AND THE WILD LETTERS (The Bodley Head, 1981) £12
PROFESSOR BRANESTAWM'S MOUSE WAR (The Bodley Head, 1982)..£12
PROFESSOR BRANESTAWM'S BUILDING BUST-UP (The Bodley Head, 1982)...£12
PROFESSOR BRANESTAWM'S POCKET MOTOR CAR (contains 'Professor Branestawm's Pocket Motor Car' and
'Professor Branestawm and the Wild Letters'; paperback) (Puffin, 1982) £5
PROFESSOR BRANESTAWM'S CRUNCHY CROCKERY (The Bodley Head, 1983) £10
PROFESSOR BRANESTAWM'S HAIR-RAISING IDEA (The Bodley Head, 1983) £10
PROFESSOR BRANESTAWM'S MOUSE WAR (contains 'Professor Branestawm's Mouse War' and
'Professor Branestawm's Building Bust-Up'; paperback) (Puffin, 1984) £5
PROFESSOR BRANESTAWM'S CRUNCHY CROCKERY (contains 'Professor Branestawm's Crunchy Crockery' and
'Professor Branestawm's Hair-Raising Idea'; paperback) (Puffin, 1993) £5

Others

THE BAD BARONS OF CRASHBANIA (illustrated by Eve Garnett) (Blackwell, [1932]).....................................£50
LARKY LEGENDS (illustrated by James Arnold) (John Lane: The Bodley Head, 1938) £125
LARKY LEGENDS (as 'The Dribblesome Teapots and Other Incredible Stories') (The Bodley Head, 1969)...............£40
JINGLE TALES (illustrated by Gordon Robinson) (Warne, [1930])..£70
JINGLE TALES (illustrated by Gordon Robinson; paperback) (Warne, [1941])..£30
PUFFIN BOOK OF MAGIC (paperback) (Puffin, 1968) £7
THE HOME-MADE DRAGON and Other Incredible Stories (The Bodley Head, 1971) £20
THE FRANTIC PHANTOM and Other Incredible Stories (illustrated by Geraldine Spence)
(The Bodley Head, 1973)...£20
WIZARDS ARE A NUISANCE (paperback) (BBC, 1973)..£20
NORMAN HUNTER'S BOOK OF MAGIC (The Bodley Head, 1974) £12
LONG LIVE THEIR MAJESTIES! (paperback) (Blackie, 1975)..£5
DUST-UP AT THE ROYAL DISCO and Other Incredible Stories (The Bodley Head, 1975) £20
COUNT BAKWERDZ ON THE CARPET and Other Incredible Stories (The Bodley Head, 1979)......................£20
SNEEZE AND BE SLAIN and Other Incredible Stories (The Bodley Head, 1980) £20

HUXLEY, Aldous

British author. Born: Godalming, 1894. The author of *Brave New World* only wrote one children's novel which was issued posthumously. Died: 1963.

Prices are for books in Very Good condition with dustjackets.

THE CROWS OF PEARBLOSSOM (illustrated by Barbara Cooney) (Chatto & Windus, 1967)......................£40

IRVING, Washington

American author. Born in New York City in 1783. Left school at sixteen and worked in a law office. Travelled in Europe during 1804-6. Enjoyed huge success with *The Sketch Book of Geoffrey Crayon, Gent*, which included the story of 'Rip Van Winkle' and 'The Legend of Sleepy Hollow', and his account of an 'Old Christmas' in England. *Bracebridge Hall, or The Humorists* further showed his affinity with English life. Between 1829 and 1832, Irving was secretary to the American legation in London, and received a gold medal from the Royal Society of Literature and an honorary degree from Oxford University. Died: 1859.

Prices are for books in Very Good condition.

THE SKETCH BOOK OF GEOFFREY CRAYON, GENT (seven numbers: first and second state wrappers)
(C.S. Van Winkle, US, May 1819 to September 1820) .... £3,000 / £2,000
THE SKETCHBOOK OF GEOFFREY CRAYON, GENT (two volumes) (John Miller, 1820) .... the set £3,000
THE SKETCHBOOK OF GEOFFREY CRAYON, GENT (with 120 engravings on wood) (Bell & Daldy, 1865) £700
BRACEBRIDGE HALL, or THE HUMORISTS: A Medley. By Geoffrey Crayon. Gent (two volumes)
(C.S. Van Winkle, US, 1822) £2,000
BRACEBRIDGE HALL, or THE HUMORISTS: A Medley. By Geoffrey Crayon. Gent (two volumes)
(John Murray, 1822) £1,500
BRACEBRIDGE HALL (illustrated by Randolph Caldecott) (Macmillan, 1877 [1876]) £35
OLD CHRISTMAS (illustrated by Randolph Caldecott) (Macmillan, 1876) £35
OLD CHRISTMAS (illustrated by Cecil Aldin) (Hodder & Stoughton, 1908) £130
OLD CHRISTMAS (illustrated by Frank Dadd) (G.P. Putnam's, U.K./US, 1916) £40
RIP VAN WINKLE (illustrated by Gordon Browne) (Blackie, 1887 [1886]) £40
RIP VAN WINKLE and THE LEGEND OF SLEEPY HOLLOW (illustrated by G.H. Broughton) (Macmillan, 1893) £40
RIP VAN WINKLE (illustrated by Arthur Rackham) (Heinemann, 1905) £800
RIP VAN WINKLE (illustrated by Arthur Rackham; limited to 250 copies, signed by the artist; vellum binding)
(Heinemann, 1905) £3,500
RIP VAN WINKLE (illustrated by Charles Robinson) (T.C. & E.C. Jack, 1913) £40
RIP VAN WINKLE (illustrated by N.C. Wyeth) (David McKay, US, 1921) £40
THE LEGEND OF SLEEPY (illustrated by Arthur Keller) (Grant Richards, 1909) £30
THE LEGEND OF SLEEPY HOLLOW (illustrated by Arthur Rackham) (Harrap, 1928) £150
THE LEGEND OF SLEEPY HOLLOW (illustrated by Arthur Rackham; limted to 375 copies,
signed by the artist; vellum binding) (Harrap, 1928) £750

One of Arthur Rackham's illustrations for Washington Irving's **Rip Van Winkle**. *He also illustrated* **The Legend of Sleepy Hollow**.

JACOBS, Joseph

Anglo-Australian folklorist. Born: Sydney, Australia, in 1854. Educated at London University and King's College, Cambridge. Edited the British journal, *Folk-Lore*, as well as the *Jewish Encyclopedia*. His two collections, *English Fairy Tales* (1890) and *More English Fairy Tales* (1894), were enormously influential, and were followed by volumes devoted to Celtic and Indian folk tales. Died: 1916.

Prices are for books in Very Good condition.

ENGLISH FAIRY TALES (illustrated by J.D. Batten) (David Nutt, 1890) £50
CELTIC FAIRY TALES (illustrated by J.D. Batten) (David Nutt, 1892 [1891]) £50
INDIAN FAIRY TALES (illustrated by J.D. Batten) (David Nutt, 1892)..£50
INDIAN FAIRY TALES (illustrated by J.D. Batten; limited to 160 copies; printed on Japanese vellum) (David Nutt, 1892).......£120
MORE ENGLISH FAIRY TALES (illustrated by J.D. Batten) (David Nutt, 1894 [1893])..£50
MORE ENGLISH FAIRY TALES (limited to 160 copies; printed on Japanese vellum) (David Nutt, 1894 [1893]).....................£120
MORE CELTIC FAIRY TALES (illustrated by J.D. Batten) (David Nutt, 1894) £50
AESOP'S FABLES (illustrated by Richard Heighway) (Macmillan, 1894) £20
THE BOOK OF WONDER VOYAGES (illustrated by J.D. Batten) (David Nutt, 1896)..£60
THE BOOK OF WONDER VOYAGES (illustrated by J.D. Batten; ltd to 100 copies; printed on Japanese vellum) (David Nutt, 1896) £120
ENGLISH FAIRY TALES (revised third edition; illustrated by J.D. Batten) (David Nutt, 1898)......................................£40

JACQUES, Brian

British author. Born: Liverpool, 1939. A playwright and radio presenter for Radio Merseyside, he is best known for the popular 'Redwall' series.

Prices are for books in Very Good condition with dustjackets where applicable.

REDWALL (Hutchinson, 1986) £30
MOSSFLOWER (Hutchinson, 1988)..£30
MATTIMEO (Hutchinson, 1989) £30
MARIEL OF REDWALL (Hutchinson, 1991) £30
SALAMANDASTRON (Hutchinson, 1992) £30
MARTIN THE WARRIOR : A Tale of Redwall (Hutchinson, 1993) £20
THE BELLMAKER (Hutchinson, 1994)..£30
OUTCAST OF REDWALL (Hutchinson, 1995)..£25
THE PEARLS OF LUTRA (Hutchinson, 1996)..£20
THE LONG PATROL: A Tale of Redwall (Hutchinson, 1997)..£20
REDWALL MAP AND THE REDWALL RIDER (Hutchinson, 1997)..£20
RED FOX (Hutchinson, 1997)..£30
MARLFOX (Hutchinson, 1998) £30
REDWALL ABBEY (Hutchinson, 1998)..£20
LORD BROCKTREE (Hutchinson, 1999)..£10
LEGEND OF LUKE (Hutchinson, 1999)..£10
REDWALL FAMILY TREE (Hutchinson, 1999)..£10

JAMES, Grace

British author. Born: Tokyo, Japan, in 1885. Her father worked with the Naval Mission in Japan where the family lived until she was twelve years old. Her best-known books feature John and Mary, who are based on her nephew and niece. Died: 1965.

Prices are for books in Very Good condition with dustjackets where applicable.

'John and Mary' Books

JOHN AND MARY (illustrated by Mary Gardiner) (Muller, 1935) £30
MORE ABOUT JOHN AND MARY (illustrated by Mary Gardiner) (Muller, 1936) £30
JOHN AND MARY ABROAD (illustrated by Mary Gardiner) (Muller, 1937) £30
JOHN AND MARY, DETECTIVES (illustrated by Mary Gardiner) (Muller, 1938) £30
JOHN AND MARY'S SECRET SOCIETY (illustrated by Mary Gardiner) (Muller, 1939)..£30
JOHN AND MARY'S VISITORS (illustrated by Mary Gardiner) (Muller, 1940)..£30
NEW FRIENDS FOR JOHN AND MARY (illustrated by Mary Gardiner) (Muller, 1941)..£30
JOHN AND MARY AND MISS ROSE BROWN (illustrated by Mary Gardiner) (Muller, 1942) £30
JOHN AND MARY AT SCHOOL (illustrated by Mary Gardiner) (Muller, 1943) £25
JOHN AND MARY'S YOUTH CLUB (illustrated by Mary Gardiner) (Muller, 1945)..£25
JOHN AND MARY AT RIVERTON (illustrated by Mary Gardiner) (Muller, 1946)..£25
THE ADVENTURES OF JOHN AND MARY (illustrated by Mary Gardiner) (Muller, 1947)..£25
JOHN AND MARY'S AUNT (illustrated by Mary Gardiner) (Muller, 1950)..£25
JOHN AND MARY IN ROME (illustrated by Mary Gardiner) (Muller, 1954) £25
JOHN AND MARY'S FAIRY TALES (illustrated by Mary Gardiner) (Muller, 1955) £25
JOHN AND MARY BY LAND AND SEA (illustrated by Mary Gardiner) (Muller, 1956)..£25

The first edition of Tove Jansson's **Comet in Moominland** *(1951) and an illustration from* **Moominsummer Madness** *(1955), showing a behatted Moominpappa.*

JOHN AND MARY'S JAPANESE FAIRY TALES (illustrated by Mary Gardiner) (Muller, 1957) **£25**
JOHN AND MARY AND LISETTA (illustrated by Mary Gardiner) (Muller, 1958) **£25**
JOHN AND MARY'S TREASURES (illustrated by Mary Gardiner) (Muller, 1960) **£20**
JOHN AND MARY REVISIT ROME (illustrated by Mary Gardiner) (Muller, 1963) **£20**

Others
GREEN WILLOW AND OTHER JAPANESE FAIRY TALES (forty colour plates by Warwick Goble) (Macmillan, 1910) **£600**
GREEN WILLOW AND OTHER JAPANESE FAIRY TALES (forty colour plates by Warwick Goble;
    De Luxe edition: limited to 500 copies) (Macmillan, 1910) **£2,000**
GREEN WILLOW AND OTHER JAPANESE FAIRY TALES (sixteen colour plates by Warwick Goble) (Macmillan, 1912) **£100**
GREEN WILLOW AND OTHER JAPANESE FAIRY TALES (reissue; sixteen colour plates by Warwick Goble) (Macmillan, 1923)...... **£70**
THE BLAKES AND THE BLACKETTS (illustrated by Mary Gardiner) (Muller, 1939) **£30**
NIBS (illustrated by Mary Gardiner) (Muller, 1951)... **£30**
NIBS AND THE NEW WORLD (illustrated by Mary Gardiner) (Muller, 1953) **£30**

Plays
THE DANCING SHOES (wrappers) (French's Plays for Juvenile Performers, 1921).. **£15**
THE PORK PIE HAT A Victorian Play in Two Acts (wrappers) (French's Plays for Schoolgirls, No.2, 1922)............................. **£15**
THE CUCUMBER RING: A Chinese Play (verse; wrappers) (French's Plays for Juvenile Performers, No.1, 1924) **£15**
THE JELLYFISH (wrappers) (French's Plays for Juvenile Performers, No.14, 1931) **£15**
ROBERT AND LOUISA (wrappers) (French's Plays for Boys, 1931)... **£15**
THE THREE DWARF TREES. From an Old Japanese Play (wrappers) (French's Plays for Juvenile performers, No.33, 1936)....... **£15**

JAMES, M.R.
British author. Born: Montague Rhodes James in 1862. Educated at Eton and King's College, Cambridge, becoming Provost of Eton in 1918. Best known for his *Ghost Stories of an Antiquary* (1904), he wrote a single children's work and also translated a volume of Hans Christian Andersen's stories. Awarded the Order of Merit in 1930. Died: 1936.
Prices are for books in Very Good condition with dustjackets.
THE FIVE JARS (illustrated by Gilbert James) (Arnold, 1922) **£300**
HANS ANDERSEN, FORTY STORIES (illustrated by Christine Jackson; translated by M.R. James) (Faber, 1930)................... **£40**
HANS ANDERSEN, FORTY-TWO STORIES (illustrated by Robin Jacques; translated by M.R. James) (Faber, 1953).............. **£30**

JANSSON, Tove
Finnish author-illustrator. Born: 1914. Began her famous 'Moomin' series with *Comet in Moominland*, first published in Britain in 1951. Like its sequels, this book was written in Swedish and illustrated by its author. The London *Evening News* ran a 'Moomin' comic strip between 1954 and 1968. Died: 2001.
Prices are for books in Very Good condition with dustjackets where applicable.
FINN FAMILY MOOMINTROLL (illustrated by the author) (Benn, 1950).. **£200**
COMET IN MOOMINLAND (illustrated by the author) (Benn, 1951) **£100**
THE EXPLOITS OF MOOMINPAPPA: Described by Himself (illustrated by the author) (Benn, 1952)......................... **£85**
THE BOOK ABOUT MOOMIN, MYMBLE AND LITTLE MY (illustrated by the author) (Benn, 1953)...................................... **£225**
MOOMINSUMMER MADNESS (illustrated by the author) (Benn, 1955)... **£100**
MOOMIN (picture book; quarto; illustrated by the author) (Wingate, 1957) **£120**

MOOMINLAND MIDWINTER (illustrated by the author) (Benn, 1958) £100
WHO WILL COMFORT TOFFLE? (illustrated by the author) (Benn, 1960) £130
TALES FROM MOOMINVALLEY (illustrated by the author) (Benn, 1963)...£50
MOMMINPAPPA AT SEA (illustrated by the author) (Benn, 1966) £50
MOOMINVALLEY IN NOVEMBER (illustrated by the author) (Benn, 1971)...£50
DANGEROUS JOURNEY (illustrated by the author) (Benn, 1978)...£100

JARVIS, Robin

British author-illustrator. Born in Liverpool. Worked as model-maker for film and TV. Notable for the 'Deptford Trilogy'.

Prices are for books in Very Good condition with dustjackets where applicable.

'Deptford Mice' Books

THE DARK PORTAL (Macdonald, 1989)..£40
THE CRYSTAL PRISON (Macdonald, 1989)...£20
THE FINAL RECKONING (Simon & Schuster, 1990) £20

'Deptford Histories' Books

THE ALCHYMIST'S CAT (Simon & Schuster, 1991) £15
THE OAKEN THRONE (Simon & Schuster, 1993)...£15

'Whitby' Books

THE WHITBY WITCHES (boards/paperback) (Simon & Schuster, 1991)...£12 / £5
A WARLOCK IN WHITBY (boards/paperback) (Simon & Schuster, 1992)..£12 / £5
THE WHITBY CHILD (boards/paperback) (Simon & Schuster, 1994) ....£12 / £5

'Tales From the Wyrd Museum' Books

THE WOVEN PATH (Collins, 1995)..£12
THE RAVEN'S KNOT (Collins, 1996)..£12
THE FATAL STRAND (Collins, 1998)...£12

'Hagwood' Books

THORN OGRES OF HAGWOOD (Puffin Books, 1999)...£8

JEFFERIES, Richard

British author. Born: Coate, Wiltshire, in 1848. Worked on the *North Wilts Herald* before moving to London in 1877. Jefferies wrote several volumes of essays — mainly on country matters — and adult novels (including the Wellsian romance, *After London, or Wild England*, 1895), but also published two enduring works for children, *Wood Magic* (1881) and its sequel, *Bevis: The Story of a Boy* (1882). Died: 1887.

Prices are for books in Very Good condition.

WOOD MAGIC (two volumes) (Cassell, Peter & Galpin, 1881) ....the set £250
BEVIS: THE STORY OF A BOY (three volumes) (Sampson Low, 1882) ....the set £1,000

JOHNS, Captain W.E.

British author. Born: William Earle Johns in Hertford in 1893. Worked as a surveyor after school, serving in the army and, from 1916 onwards, the newly-formed Royal Flying Corps during the First World War. Remained in the Air Force until 1930, when he became a newspaper air correspondent and founded the magazine, *Popular Flying*, in the pages of which his famous character, Biggles (Major James Bigglesworth, DSO, MC), first appeared. A versatile author, Johns also wrote science fiction novels for young readers, and even a book on gardening. The publicity surrounding his centenary in 1993 showed that interest in his work is as great as ever. Died: 1968.

Prices are for books in Very Good condition with dustjackets in similar condition. Hamilton/OUP editions are extremely rare in this state and Fine copies would fetch a premium

'Biggles' Books

THE CAMELS ARE COMING (written under the pseudonym 'William Earle') (John Hamilton, [1932])...................£2,500
THE CAMELS ARE COMING (paperback) ('Boys' Friend Library' No. 614, 1938) £250
THE CRUISE OF THE CONDOR (John Hamilton, [1933]) £1,800
THE CRUISE OF THE CONDOR (paperback) ('Boys' Friend Library' No. 617, 1938) £250
"BIGGLES" OF THE CAMEL SQUADRON (John Hamilton, [1934])...£1,800
BIGGLES FLIES AGAIN (John Hamilton, [1934])..£1,800
BIGGLES FLIES AGAIN (paperback) ('Boys' Friend Library' No. 630, 1938) £250
BIGGLES LEARNS TO FLY (paperback) ('Boys' Friend Library' No. 469, 1935).....................................£1,000
BIGGLES LEARNS TO FLY (first hardback edition) (Brockhampton Press, 1955)..................................£75
BIGGLES IN FRANCE (paperback) ('Boys' Friend Library' No. 501, 1935) £1,100
THE BLACK PERIL: A 'Biggles' Story (John Hamilton, [1935]) £2,500
BIGGLES FLIES EAST (OUP, 1935) £1,500
BIGGLES FLIES EAST (paperback) ('Boys' Friend Library' No. 621, 1938) £250
BIGGLES HITS THE TRAIL (OUP, 1935) £1,500

BIGGLES & CO (OUP, 1936) £1,500
BIGGLES IN AFRICA (OUP, 1936) £1,500
BIGGLES — AIR COMMODORE (OUP, 1937) £1,500
BIGGLES FLIES WEST (OUP, 1937) £1,500
BIGGLES FLIES SOUTH (OUP, 1938) £1,500
BIGGLES GOES TO WAR (OUP, 1938) £1,500
BIGGLES GOES TO WAR (paperback) ('Boys' Friend Library' No. 610, 1938) £250
THE BIGGLES OMNIBUS (contains 'Biggles Flies East', 'Biggles Hits the Trail' and 'Biggles and Co.') (OUP, 1938)............£1,500
THE RESCUE FLIGHT: A Biggles Story (OUP, 1939)...£1,500
BIGGLES IN SPAIN (OUP, 1939)...£1,250
BIGGLES FLIES NORTH (OUP, 1939)..£1,250
BIGGLES — SECRET AGENT (OUP, 1940) £1,250
BIGGLES IN THE BALTIC: A Tale of the Second Great War (OUP, 1940) £1,200
BIGGLES IN THE SOUTH SEAS (OUP, 1940)...£1,200
THE BIGGLES FLYING OMNIBUS (contains 'Biggles Flies North', 'Biggles Flies South' and 'Biggles Flies West') (OUP, 1940).......£1,500
BIGGLES DEFIES THE SWASTIKA (OUP, 1941)..£1,200
SPITFIRE PARADE: Stories of Biggles in War-Time (OUP, 1941)....................................£1,200
BIGGLES SEES IT THROUGH (OUP, 1941) £1,200
BIGGLES FLIES AGAIN (paperback) (Penguin No. 348, 1941)..£200
THE THIRD BIGGLES OMNIBUS (contains 'Biggles in Spain', 'Biggles Goes to War' and 'Biggles in the Baltic') (OUP, 1941) £1,200
BIGGLES IN THE JUNGLE (OUP, 1942)...£1,000
BIGGLES SWEEPS THE DESERT (Hodder & Stoughton, 1942) £85
BIGGLES — CHARTER PILOT (OUP, 1943) £900
BIGGLES IN BORNEO (OUP, 1943)..£800
BIGGLES 'FAILS TO RETURN' (Hodder & Stoughton, 1943)...£85
BIGGLES IN THE ORIENT (Hodder & Stoughton, 1945) £85
BIGGLES DELIVERS THE GOODS (Hodder & Stoughton, 1946)..£85
SERGEANT BIGGLESWORTH C.I.D. (Hodder & Stoughton, 1947)......................................£85
BIGGLES' SECOND CASE (Hodder & Stoughton, 1948)..£85
BIGGLES HUNTS BIG GAME (Hodder & Stoughton, 1948)...£60
BIGGLES TAKES A HOLIDAY (Hodder & Stoughton, 1949)..£55
BIGGLES BREAKS THE SILENCE (Hodder & Stoughton, 1949)...£40
BIGGLES GETS HIS MEN (Hodder & Stoughton, 1950)..£40
BIGGLES — AIR DETECTIVE (issued without a dustjacket) (Marks & Spencer, 1950) £15
ANOTHER JOB FOR BIGGLES (Hodder & Stoughton, 1951)..£20
BIGGLES GOES TO SCHOOL (Hodder & Stoughton, 1951)..£35
BIGGLES WORKS IT OUT (Hodder & Stoughton, 1951)..£40
BIGGLES TAKES THE CASE (Hodder & Stoughton, 1952)..£35
BIGGLES FOLLOWS ON (Hodder & Stoughton, 1952) £35
BIGGLES AND THE BLACK RAIDER (Hodder & Stoughton, 1953) £35
BIGGLES IN THE BLUE (Brockhampton Press, 1953) £40
BIGGLES IN THE GOBI (Hodder & Stoughton, 1953)..£45
BIGGLES OF THE SPECIAL AIR POLICE (Thames, [1953])..£20
THE FIRST BIGGLES OMNIBUS (contains 'Biggles Sweeps the Desert', 'Biggles in the Orient',
'Biggles Delivers the Goods' and 'Biggles "Fails to Return"') (Hodder & Stoughton, 1953) ..£35
BIGGLES CUTS IT FINE (Hodder & Stoughton, 1954)..£45
BIGGLES AND THE PIRATE TREASURE and Other Biggles Adventures (Brockhampton Press, 1954) £45
BIGGLES, FOREIGN LEGIONNAIRE (Hodder & Stoughton, 1954) £45
BIGGLES, PIONEER AIRFIGHTER (Thames, [1954]) £20
BIGGLES IN AUSTRALIA (Hodder & Stoughton, 1955)...£45
BIGGLES' CHINESE PUZZLE and Other Biggles Adventures (Brockhampton Press, 1955) £45
BIGGLES OF 266 (Thames, [1956])...£20
NO REST FOR BIGGLES (Hodder & Stoughton, 1956)..£45
BIGGLES TAKES CHARGE (Brockhampton Press, 1956)..£45
THE BIGGLES AIR DETECTIVE OMNIBUS (contains 'Sergeant Bigglesworth C.I.D.', 'Biggles' Second Case',
'Another Job for Biggles' and 'Biggles Works it Out') (Hodder & Stoughton, 1956) £45
BIGGLES MAKES ENDS MEET (Hodder & Stoughton, 1957)..£45
BIGGLES OF THE INTERPOL (Brockhampton Press, 1957)..£60
BIGGLES ON THE HOME FRONT (Hodder & Stoughton, 1957)..£60
BIGGLES PRESSES ON (Brockhampton Press, 1958)..£45
BIGGLES ON MYSTERY ISLAND (Hodder & Stoughton, 1958)...£45
BIGGLES BURIES A HATCHET (Brockhampton Press, 1958) £50
BIGGLES IN MEXICO (Brockhampton Press, 1959) £45
BIGGLES' COMBINED OPERATION (Hodder & Stoughton, 1959)......................................£45
BIGGLES AT WORLD'S END (Brockhampton Press, 1959)..£45
BIGGLES AND THE LEOPARDS OF ZINN (Brockhampton Press, 1960).............................£50
BIGGLES GOES HOME (Hodder & Stoughton, 1960)..£50
BIGGLES AND THE POOR RICH BOY (Brockhampton Press, 1961)...................................£35
BIGGLES FORMS A SYNDICATE (Hodder & Stoughton, 1961)..£50

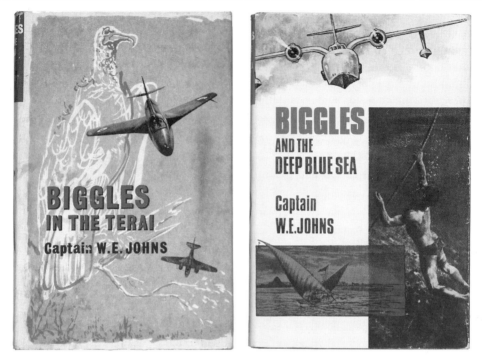

During the 1960s, the popularity of the 'Biggles' stories by Captain W.E. Johns gradually began to wane . . .

BIGGLES AND THE MISSING MILLIONAIRE (Brockhampton Press, 1961) £35
BIGGLES GOES ALONE (Hodder & Stoughton, 1962) £80
ORCHIDS FOR BIGGLES (Brockhampton Press, 1962) £50
BIGGLES SETS A TRAP (Hodder & Stoughton, 1962) £100
BIGGLES TAKES IT ROUGH (Brockhampton Press, 1963) £100
BIGGLES FLIES TO WORK (Dean, 1963) £15
BIGGLES TAKES A HAND (Hodder & Stoughton, 1963) £100
BIGGLES' SPECIAL CASE (Brockhampton Press, 1963) £80
BIGGLES AND THE PLANE THAT DISAPPEARED: A Story of the Air Police (Hodder & Stoughton, 1963) £180
BIGGLES AND THE LOST SOVEREIGNS (Brockhampton Press, 1964) £120
BIGGLES AND THE BLACK MASK (Hodder & Stoughton, 1964) £180
BIGGLES INVESTIGATES and Other Stories of the Air Police (Brockhampton Press, 1964) £150
BIGGLES LOOKS BACK: A Story of Biggles and the Air Police (Hodder & Stoughton, 1965) £100
BIGGLES AND THE PLOT THAT FAILED (Brockhampton Press, 1965) £180
BIGGLES AND THE BLUE MOON (Brockhampton Press, 1965) £200
BIGGLES SCORES A BULL (Hodder & Stoughton, 1965) £180
THE BIGGLES ADVENTURE OMNIBUS (contains 'Biggles Gets his Men', 'No Rest for Biggles',
'Another Job for Biggles' and 'Biggles Takes a Holiday') (Hodder & Stoughton, 1965) £45
BIGGLES IN THE TERAI (Brockhampton Press, 1966) £250
BIGGLES AND THE GUN RUNNERS (Brockhampton Press, 1966) £250
BIGGLES SORTS IT OUT (Brockhampton Press, 1967) £225
BIGGLES AND THE DARK INTRUDER (paperback) (Knight, 1967) £25
BIGGLES AND THE PENITENT THIEF (Brockhampton Press, 1967) £200
BIGGLES AND THE DEEP BLUE SEA (Brockhampton Press, 1968) £450
THE BOY BIGGLES (Dean, 1968) £15
BIGGLES IN THE UNDERWORLD (Brockhampton Press, 1968) £225
BIGGLES AND THE LITTLE GREEN GOD (Brockhampton Press, 1969) £300
BIGGLES AND THE NOBLE LORD (Brockhampton Press, 1969) £300
BIGGLES SEES TOO MUCH (Brockhampton Press, 1970) £300
BIGGLES OF THE ROYAL FLYING CORPS (Purnell, 1978) £20
THE BUMPER BIGGLES BOOK (Chancellor, 1983) £15
THE BEST OF BIGGLES (Chancellor, 1985) £15
BIGGLES DOES SOME HOMEWORK (card wraps; limited to 300 numbered copies) (Wright & Schofield, 1997) £750
BIGGLES AIR ACE: THE UNCOLLECTED STORIES (card wraps; limited to 300 numbered copies) (Norman Wright, 1999) £200

. . . the upshot for collectors is that later adventures are almost as rare as the early Oxford University Press titles.

'Worrals' Books

WORRALS OF THE W.A.A.F. (Lutterworth Press, 1941) £200
WORRALS CARRIES ON (Lutterworth Press, 1942) £100
WORRALS FLIES AGAIN (Hodder & Stoughton, 1942) £70
WORRALS ON THE WAR-PATH (Hodder & Stoughton, 1943) £40
WORRALS GOES EAST (Hodder & Stoughton, 1944) £40
WORRALS OF THE ISLANDS: A Story of the War in the Pacific (Hodder & Stoughton, 1945) £40
WORRALS IN THE WILDS (Hodder & Stoughton, 1947) £35
WORRALS DOWN UNDER (Lutterworth Press, 1948) £35
WORRALS GOES AFOOT (Lutterworth Press, 1949) £35
WORRALS IN THE WASTELANDS (Lutterworth Press, 1949) £30
WORRALS INVESTIGATES (Lutterworth Press, 1950) £30
THE CHILDREN'S GIFT BOOK (contains a 'Worrals' short story) (Odhams Press, 1946) £20

'Gimlet' Books

KING OF THE COMMANDOS (University of London Press, 1943) £45
GIMLET GOES AGAIN (University of London Press, 1944) £30
GIMLET COMES HOME (University of London Press, 1946) £25
GIMLET MOPS UP (Brockhampton Press, 1947) £25
GIMLET'S ORIENTAL QUEST (Brockhampton Press, 1948) £25
GIMLET LENDS A HAND (Brockhampton Press, 1949) £25
GIMLET BORES IN (Brockhampton Press, 1950) £25
GIMLET OFF THE MAP (Brockhampton Press, 1951) £20
GIMLET GETS THE ANSWER (Brockhampton Press, 1952) £20
GIMLET TAKES A JOB (Brockhampton Press, 1954) £20

Science Fiction Books

KINGS OF SPACE: A Story of Interplanetary Explorations (Hodder & Stoughton, 1954) £30
RETURN TO MARS (Hodder & Stoughton, 1955) £30
NOW TO THE STARS (Hodder & Stoughton, 1956) £35
TO OUTER SPACE (Hodder & Stoughton, 1957) £40
THE EDGE OF BEYOND (Hodder & Stoughton, 1958) £40
THE DEATH RAYS OF ARDILLA (Hodder & Stoughton, 1959) £50
TO WORLDS UNKNOWN: A Story of Interplanetary Explorations (Hodder & Stoughton, 1960) £50

JOHNS, Captain W.E.

THE QUEST FOR THE PERFECT PLANET (Hodder & Stoughton, 1961)...£20
WORLDS OF WONDER: More Adventures in Space (Hodder & Stoughton, 1962)......................£25
THE MAN WHO VANISHED INTO SPACE (Hodder & Stoughton, 1963) £25

Others Books Written or Edited by W.E. Johns

MOSSYFACE (written under the pseudonym 'William Earle') ('The Weekly Telegraph Novel' No. 121, 1922)........................£3,500
MOSSYFACE (paper covers) (Mellifont, [1932])...£2,500
MOSSYFACE (Buckram bound, no jacket; limited to 300 numbered copies) (Trendler/Wright, 1994)....................£80
WINGS: A Book of Flying Adventures. Edited by W.E. Johns (Hamilton, [1931]) £300
MODERN BOYS BOOK OF AIRCRAFT (Amalgamated Press, 1931).......................................£100
THE PICTORIAL FLYING COURSE by H.M. Schofield and F/O W.E. Johns (John Hamilton, [1932])....................£305
FIGHTING PLANES AND ACES (plates, including portraits) (John Hamilton, [1932])..................£300
THE SPY FLYERS (illustrated by Howard Leigh) (John Hamilton, 1933) £500
THE SPY FLYERS (paperback) ('Boys' Friend Library' No. 625, 1938)....................................£250
THE SPY FLYERS (card wrappers; limited to 300 numbered copies) (Norman Wright, 2002) £50
THE RAID (John Hamilton, [1935])...£400
THE AIR VC's (John Hamilton, [1935])..£350
SOME MILESTONES IN AVIATION (John Hamilton, [1935]) £200
THRILLING FLIGHTS. Edited by W.E. Johns (John Hamilton, [1935])...................................£300
BLUE BLOOD RUNS RED (written under the pseudonym 'Jon Early') (Newnes, [1936]).................£1,000
BLUE BLOOD RUNS RED (card wrappers, limited to 300 numbered copies)
    (Norman Wright, 1988)...£75
MODERN BOY'S BOOK OF ADVENTURE STORIES (Amalgamated Press, 1936)...................£75
ACE HIGH (Ace, 1936)...£100
AIR ADVENTURES (Ace, 1936)...£100
SKY HIGH: A 'Steeley' Adventure (Newnes, [1936])..£550
SKY HIGH (Latimer House, 1951)..£50
STEELEY FLIES AGAIN (Newnes, [1936])...£650
STEELEY FLIES AGAIN (Latimer House, 1951) £50
FLYING STORIES (John Hamilton, 1937)...£100
MURDER BY AIR: A 'Steeley' Adventure (Newnes, [1937])..£650
MURDER BY AIR(Latimer House, 1951)..£50
THE PASSING SHOW (My Garden/Newnes, 1937)..£100
DESERT NIGHT: A Romance (John Hamilton, [1938]) £250
THE MURDER AT CASTLE DEEPING: A 'Steeley' Adventure (John Hamilton, [1938])..............£1,250
THE MURDER AT CASTLE DEEPING(Latimer House 1951) £50
CHAMPION OF THE MAIN (OUP, 1938) £400
WINGS OF ROMANCE: A 'Steeley' Adventure (Newnes, 1939) £650
WINGS OF ROMANCE(Latimer House 1951)...£50
MODERN BOY'S BOOK OF PIRATES (Amalgamated Press, [1939])....................................£250
THE UNKNOWN QUANTITY
    (please note, our prices is for the geuine first with crest on spine) (John Hamilton, [1940])....................£500
THE UNKNOWN QUANTITY (John Hamilton reprints)..£350
THE UNKNOWN QUANTITY (card wrappers, limited to 300 numbered copies) (Norman Wright, 2003)....................£50
SINISTER SERVICE: A Tale (OUP, 1942)...£125
COMRADES IN ARMS (contains a 'Biggles', 'Worrals' and 'Gimlet' short story) (Hodder & Stoughton, 1947) £40
THE RUSTLERS OF RATTLESNAKE VALLEY (Nelson, 1948) £30
DR VANE ANSWERS THE CALL (Latimer House, 1950)..£175
DR VANE ANSWERS THE CALL (card wrappers, limited to 300 numbered copies) (Norman Wright, 2003) £20
SHORT SORTIES (Latimer House, 1950)..£175
SKY FEVER and Other Stories (Latimer House, 1953)..£175
ADVENTURE BOUND (illustrated by Douglas Relf) (Nelson, 1955) £15
ADVENTURE UNLIMITED (illustrated by Douglas Relf) (Nelson, 1957)..................................£15
NO MOTIVE FOR MURDER (Hodder & Stoughton, 1958) £180
NO MOTIVE FOR MURDER (card wrappers, limited to 300 numbered copies, each signed by Margaret Collins,
    niece of W.E. Johns) (Norman Wright, 2005)..£20
THE MAN WHO LOST HIS WAY (Macdonald, 1959) £180
THE MAN WHO LOST HIS WAY (card wrappers, limited to 300 numbered copies) (Norman Wright, 2004)............£20
THE BIGGLES BOOK OF HEROES (Parrish, 1959)...£75
ADVENTURES OF THE JUNIOR DETECTION CLUB (Parrish, 1960)....................................£75
WHERE THE GOLDEN EAGLE SOARS (Hodder & Stoughton, 1960).................................£50
THE BIGGLES BOOK OF TREASURE HUNTING (Parrish, 1962)..£50
THE COCKPIT (contains the W.E. Johns story 'Ace of Spades') (John Hamilton, [1943]).................£75
OUT OF THE BLUE (John Hamilton, no date)...£75
AIR STORIES BY FLIGHT LIEUTENANT (no date)...£75
STEELEY AND THE MISSING PAGE & Other Stories (card wrappers, limited to 300 numbered copies)
    (Norman Wright, 2000)...£70
DESERT ADVENTURES (omnibus comprising 'Desert Night' and 'The Raid') (card wrappers, limited to 300 numbered copies)
    (Norman Wright, 2001)...£60
WINGED JUSTICE & Other Uncollected Stories (card wrappers, limited to 300 numbered copies)
    (Norman Wright, 2001)...£100

Books Illustrated by W.E. Johns
DESERT WINGS by Covington Clarke (John Hamilton, [1931]) £80
ACES UP by Covington Clarke (John Hamilton, [1931]).. £35
FOR VALOUR by Covington Clarke (John Hamilton, [1931]) £35

JONES, Diana Wynne
British author. Born: 1934. A writer of unconventional fantasy stories with modern settings but featuring witches and mythological figures.

Prices are for books in Very Good condition with dustjackets where applicable.

WILKINS' TOOTH (illustrated by Julia Rodber) (Macmillan, 1973)..£40
WILKINS' TOOTH (as 'Witch's Business') (illustrated by Julia Rodber) (Dutton, U.S., 1974) £20
THE OGRE DOWNSTAIRS (Macmillan, 1974) £25
EIGHT DAYS OF LUKE (Macmillan, 1975)...£25
CART AND CWIDDER (Macmillan, 1975)..£25
DOGSBODY (Macmillan, 1975)..£25
POWER OF THREE (Macmillan, 1976)..£20
CHARMED LIFE (Macmillan, 1977) £15
DROWNED AMNET (Macmillan, 1977)..£15
WHO GOT RID OF ANGUS FLINT (illustrated by John Sewell) (Evans, 1978) £15
THE SPELLCOATS (Macmillan, 1979)...£15
THE MAGICIANS OF CAPRONA (Macmillan, 1980) £15
THE FOUR GRANNIES (illustrated by Thelma Lambert) (Hamish Hamilton, 1980)...£15
THE HOMEWARD BOUNDERS (Macmillan, 1981)...£10
THE TIME OF THE GHOST (Macmillan, 1981)..£10
WITCH WEEK (Macmillan, 1982)..£10
WARLOCK AT THE WHEEL (Macmillan, 1984) £10
ARCHER'S GOON (Methuen, 1984) £10
FIRE AND HEMLOCK (Methuen, 1985)...£10
A TALE OF THE CITY (Methuen, 1987)...£10
THE LIVES OF CHRISTOPHER CHANT (Macmillan, 1988)..£10
CHAIR PERSON (Macmillan, 1988)...£10
CASTLE IN THE AIR (Macmillan, 1990) £8
BLACK MARIA (Macmillan, 1991) £8
YES, DEAR (Macmillan, 1992) £8
A SUDDEN WILD MAGIC (Macmillan, 1992)..£8
STOPPING FOR A SPELL (Macmillan, 1993) £5

*The wraparound dustjacket for Diana Wynne Jones' 1982 novel, **Witch Week**, was illustrated by Ionicus.*

A TOUGH GUIDE TO FANTASY LAND (Macmillan, 1996) £5
DEEP SECRET (Macmillan, 1997) £5
LORD OF DERKHOLM (Macmillan, 1998)...£5

'JOURNEY INTO SPACE'

The BBC's very popular science fiction radio serial was written by Charles Chilton and ran for over 60 episodes during the 1950s. The following collectable items were issued in the wake of its phenomenal success.

Prices are for books and comics in Very Good condition with dustjackets where applicable.

Books by Charles Chilton

JOURNEY INTO SPACE (Herbert Jenkins, 1954) £55
THE RED PLANET (Herbert Jenkins, 1956) £55
THE WORLD IN PERIL (Herbert Jenkins, 1960) £55
JOURNEY INTO SPACE (paperback) (Pan, 1956)...£6
JOURNEY INTO SPACE (paperback) (Digit, 1963) £4
THE RED PLANET (paperback) (Pan, 1960)..£5
THE RED PLANET (paperback) (Digit, 1963) £4
THE WORLD IN PERIL (paperback) (Pan, 1962)..£5

Comics

EXPRESS WEEKLY (Beaverbrook, 1956-1957) .... each £3

'JOY STREET' ANNUALS

British annual, published by Blackwell during the 1920s and '30s. Among the contributors were Walter de la Mare, Hilaire Belloc, G.K. Chesterton and A.A. Milne. The monthly magazine, *The Merry-Go-Round*, grew out of the title.

Prices are for annuals in Very Good condition with dustjackets.

NUMBER ONE JOY STREET: A Medley of Prose and Verse for Boys and Girls ([1923])........................£40
NUMBER TWO JOY STREET ([1924]) £40
NUMBER THREE JOY STREET ([1925]) £40
NUMBER FOUR JOY STREET ([1926]) £30
NUMBER FIVE JOY STREET ([1927])...£30
NUMBER SIX JOY STREET ([1928])...£30
NUMBER SEVEN JOY STREET ([1929]) £30
NUMBER EIGHT JOY STREET ([1930])..£30
NUMBER NINE JOY STREET ([1931])...£30
NUMBER TEN JOY STREET ([1932]) £30
NUMBER ELEVEN JOY STREET ([1933]) £30
NUMBER TWELVE JOY STREET ([1934]) £30
NUMBER TWELVE 'A' JOY STREET ([1935])...£30
NUMBER FOURTEEN JOY STREET ([1936])..£30

Three rare spin-off books penned by Charles Chilton, the creator of the popular science fiction BBC radio serial **Journey into Space.**

KÄSTNER, Erich

German author. Born: Dresden, 1899. Educated at König Georg Gymnasium and, after service in the First World War, Leipzig University. Moved to Berlin in 1927, where he worked as a freelance journalist. As well as *Emil and the Detectives* (1931) and his other children's books, he also wrote a handful of adult works, notably the novel, *Fabian* (1932), and a volume of verse, *Let's Face It* (1963). Died: 1974.

Prices are for books in Very Good condition with dustjackets.

EMIL AND THE DETECTIVES (illustrated by Walter Trier) (Cape, 1931)...£200
ANNALUISE AND ANTON (illustrated by Walter Trier) (Cape, 1932) £125
THE 35TH OF MAY (illustrated by Walter Trier) (Cape, 1933)..£55
THE FLYING CLASSROOM (illustrated by Walter Trier) (Cape, 1934) £70
EMIL AND THE THREE TWINS (illustrated by Walter Trier) (Cape, 1935) £70
EMIL (contains 'Emil and the Detectives', 'Emil and the Three Twins' and 'The 35th of May') (Cape, 1949) £25
LOTTIE AND LISA (illustrated by Walter Trier) (Cape, 1950)..£70
THE ANIMALS CONFERENCE (Collins, 1955) £80
WHEN I WAS A LITTLE BOY (autobiography) (Cape, 1959)..£25
LET'S FACE IT (verse) (Cape, 1963)..£30
THE LITTLE MAN (illustrated by Horst Lemke) (Cape, 1966)..£35
TILL EULENSPIEGEL THE CLOWN (illustrated by Walter Trier) (Cape, 1967)...£85
PUSS IN BOOTS (illustrated by Walter Trier) (Cape, 1967) £45
THE LITTLE MAN AND THE LITTLE MISS (illustrated by Horst Lemke) (Cape, 1969)..................................£25

KEENE, Carolyn

House name, under which – amongst others – the popular 'Nancy Drew' novels were written. Many of the books were the work of the American author, Harriet S. Adams. Born: 1894. Died: 1982.

Prices are for U.K. editions in Very Good condition with dustjackets where applicable.

'Nancy Drew' Books

THE SECRET OF THE OLD CLOCK (Harold Hill, 1954) £15
THE HIDDEN STAIRCASE (Harold Hill, 1954)...£15
THE BUNGALOW MYSTERY (Harold Hill, 1954)...£15

Emil meets his 'detectives' in an illustration from the original edition of Kästner's story.

THE MYSTERY OF LILAC INN (Harold Hill, 1954)..£15
THE SECRET AT SHADOW RANCH (Harold Hill, 1954)..£15
THE SECRET AT RED GATE FARM (Harold Hill, 1954)..£15
THE CLUE IN THE DIARY (Harold Hill, 1960)..£12
NANCY'S MYSTERIOUS LETTER (Harold Hill, 1960)..£12
THE SIGN OF THE TWISTED CANDLES (Harold Hill, 1960)..£12
THE PASSWORD TO LARKSPUR LANE (Harold Hill, 1960)..£12
THE CLUE OF THE BROKEN LOCKET (Harold Hill, 1963)..£12
THE MESSAGE IN THE HOLLOW OAK (Harold Hill, 1963)..£12
THE MYSTERY OF THE FIRE DRAGON (Harold Hill, 1963)..£12
THE CLUE OF THE DANCING PUPPET (Harold Hill, 1963)..£12
THE SECRET OF THE GOLDEN PAVILION (Harold Hill, 1963)..£12
THE HIDDEN WINDOW MYSTERY (Harold Hill, 1964)..£12
THE HAUNTED SHOWBOAT (Harold Hill, 1964)..£12
THE MOONSTONE CASTLE MYSTERY (Harold Hill, 1964)..£12
THE CLUE OF THE WHISTLING BAGPIPES (Harold Hill, 1964)..£12
THE CLUE OF THE VELVET MASK (Harold Hill, 1965)..£12
THE WITCHTREE SYMBOL (Harold Hill, 1965)..£12
THE RINGMASTER'S SECRET (Harold Hill, 1965)..£12
THE SCARLET SLIPPER MYSTERY (Harold Hill, 1965)..£12
THE CLUE OF THE BLACK EYE (Harold Hill, 1966)..£12
THE PHANTOM OF PINE HILL (Harold Hill, 1966)..£12
THE SECRET OF THE WOODEN LADY (Harold Hill, 1966)..£12
THE CLUE OF THE LEANING CHIMNEY (Harold Hill, 1966)..£12
MYSTERY OF THE 99 STEPS (Harold Hill, 1967)..£12
THE CLUE IN THE OLD ALBUM (Harold Hill, 1967)..£12
THE GHOST OF BLACKWOOD HALL (Harold Hill, 1967)..£12
THE CLUE IN THE CROSSWORD CIPHER (Harold Hill, 1968)..£12
TWIN DILEMMA (Harold Hill, 1968)..£12
SWAMI'S RING (Harold Hill, 1968)..£12
QUEST OF THE MISSING MAP (Collins, 1971)..£10
THE INVISIBLE INTRUDER (Collins, 1972)..£10
THE WHISPERING STATUE (Collins, 1972)..£10
THE MYSTERY OF THE MOSS-COVERED MANSION (Collins, 1973)..£10
THE CLUE IN THE CRUMBLING WALL (paperback) (Armada, 1978)..£5
THE FLYING SAUCER MYSTERY (Angus & Robertson, 1980)..£10
THE CROOKED BANNISTER (Collins, 1980)..£10
THE SKY PHANTOM (Collins, 1980)..£10
THE THIRTEENTH PEARL (Collins, 1980)..£10
THE MYSTERIOUS MANNEQUIN (Collins, 1980)..£10
THE TRIPLE HOAX (Angus & Robertson, 1980)..£10
THE SECRET IN THE OLD ATTIC (paperback) (Armada, 1980)..£5
THE SECRET IN THE OLD LACE (Harold Hill, 1981)..£10
THE KACHINA DOLL MYSTERY (Harold Hill, 1982)..£10
THE GREEK SYMBOL MYSTERY (Angus & Robertson, 1982)..£10
THE SECRET OF THE SWISS CHALET (Sparrow, 1982)..£10
RACE AGAINST TIME (Harold Hill, 1983)..£10
THE MYSTERY OF THE IVORY CHARM (paperback) (Armada, 1983)..£5
MYSTERY OF THE WINGED LION (Harold Hill, 1983)..£10
THE EMERALD-EYED CAT MYSTERY (Harold Hill, 1985)..£10
THE CLUE IN THE OLD STAGE-COACH (paperback) (Armada, 1985)..£5
THE BLUEBEARD ROOM (Harold Hill, 1986)..£5
THE ESKIMO'S SECRET (Harold Hill, 1986)..£5
THE MYSTERIOUS IMAGE (Harold Hill, 1986)..£5
THE PHANTOM OF VENICE (Harold Hill, 1986)..£7
THE SECRET OF THE FORGOTTEN CITY (paperback) (Armada, 1987)..£5
THE DOUBLE JINX MYSTERY (paperback) (Armada, 1987)..£5
THE STRANGE MESSAGE IN THE PARCHMENT (paperback) (Armada, 1988)..£5
THE SPIDER SAPPHIRE MYSTERY (paperback) (Armada, 1992)..£5

'Dana Girls' Books

THE MYSTERY OF THE STONE TIGER (Severn House, 1972)..£5
THE RIDDLE OF THE FROZEN FOUNTAIN (Sparrow, 1981)..£5
THE SECRET OF THE SILVER DOLPHIN (Severn House, 1983)..£5

Others

'SUPER SLEUTHS' SERIES (with Franklin Dixon; seven books) (paperback) (Armada, 1983) .... each £5
DANGER ON ICE (with Franklin Dixon; illustrated by Paul Frame; paperback) (Armada: 'Be a Detective' series, 1985)...............£5
THE SECRET OF THE KNIGHT'S SWORD (with Franklin Dixon; illustrated by Paul Frame; paperback)
    (Armada: 'Be a Detective' series, 1985)..£5

KEEPING, Charles

British author-illustrator. Born: London, 1924. Died: 1988.

Prices are for books in Very Good condition with dustjackets where applicable.

Books Written and Illustrated by Charles Keeping

BLACK DOLLY (Brockhampton Press, 1966)..£35
SHAUN AND THE CART-HORSE (OUP, 1966)...£35
CHARLEY, CHARLOTTE AND THE GOLDEN CANARY (OUP, 1967)...............................£35
ALFIE AND THE FERRY BOAT (OUP, 1968)..£25
JOSEPH'S YARD (OUP, 1969)..£25
THROUGH THE WINDOW (OUP, 1970)...£25
THE GARDEN SHED (OUP, 1971)...£25
THE SPIDER'S WEB (OUP, 1972)...£25
THE NANNY GOAT AND THE FIERCE DOG (Abelard-Schuman, 1973).........................£25
RICHARD (OUP, 1973)...£25
THE RAILWAY PASSAGE (OUP, 1974)...£20
WASTEGROUND CIRCUS (OUP,1975)..£15
INTER-CITY (OUP, 1977)...£15
MISS EMILY AND THE BIRD OF MAKE-BELIEVE (Hutchinson, 1978)..........................£15
WILLIE'S FIRE-ENGINE (OUP, 1980)..£15
SAMMY STREETSINGER (OUP, 1984)...£15

Books Illustrated by Charles Keeping

THE SILVER BRANCH by Rosemary Sutcliff (OUP, 1957)..£25
WARRIOR SCARLET by Rosemary Sutcliff (OUP, 1958)..£25
THE LANTERN BEARERS by Rosemary Sutcliff (OUP, 1959) £25
KNIGHT'S FEE by Rosemary Sutcliff (OUP, 1960)...£25
DAWN WIND by Rosemary Sutcliff (OUP, 1961)..£25
BEOWULF. Retold by Rosemary Sutcliff (The Bodley Head, 1961) £25
THE GOLDEN AGE and DREAM DAYS (omnibus) by Kenneth Grahame (The Bodley Head, 1962) £80
THE HORNED HELMET by Henry Treece (Brockhampton Press, 1963)............................£20
THE LAST OF THE VIKINGS by Henry Treece (Brockhampton Press, 1964).....................£25
THE MARK OF THE HORSE LORD by Rosemary Sutcliff (OUP, 1965).............................£25
HEROES AND HISTORY by Rosemary Sutcliff (Batsford, 1965) £25
ELIDOR by Alan Garner (Collins, 1965) £200
BENT IS THE BOW by Geoffrey Trease (Nelson, 1965) £20
RED TOWERS OF GRANADA by Geoffrey Trease (Macmillan, 1966)..............................£20
THE COLD FLAME. Based on a Tale from the Collection of the Brothers Grimm (Hamish Hamilton, 1967) £20
THE GOD BENEATH THE SEA by Leon Garfield and Edward Blishen (non-fiction) (Longman, 1970) £15
THE GOLDEN SHADOW by Leon Garfield and Edward Blishen (Longman, 1973)..............£15
THE CAPRICORN BRACELET by Rosemary Sutcliff (OUP, 1973)....................................£15
ABOUT THE SLEEPING BEAUTY by P.L. Travers (Collins, 1977).....................................£35
BLOOD FEUD by Rosemary Sutcliff (OUP, 1977)...£15
THE ROBBERS by Nina Bawden (Gollancz, 1979)...£15
THE WEDDING GHOST by Leon Garfield (OUP, 1985) £10
CHARLES KEEPING'S BOOK OF CLASSIC GHOST STORIES (Blackie, 1986)...............£15
CHARLES KEEPING'S TALES OF THE MACABRE (Blackie, 1987)..................................£15

KING, Clive

British author. Born: 1924. Best known for *Stig of the Dump* (1963), he has written a handful of other children's books, many of them reflecting his work overseas with the British Council.

Prices are for books in Very Good condition with dustjackets where applicable.

HAMID OF ALEPPO (illustrated by Luigi Percie Giovanetti) (Macmillan, US, 1958)..........£50
THE TOWN THAT WENT SOUTH (illustrated by Maurice Bartlett) (Macmillan, US, 1959) £50
STIG OF THE DUMP (illustrated by Edward Ardizzone; paperback) (Puffin Original, 1963)....£30
STIG OF THE DUMP (illustrated by Edward Ardizzone) (Hamilton, 1965) £25
THE TWENTY-TWO LETTERS (illustrated by Richard Kennedy) (Hamilton, 1966)..............£25
THE TWENTY-TWO LETTERS (simultaneous paperback edition; illustrated by Richard Kennedy) (Puffin, 1966)......£5
THE NIGHT THE WATER CAME (illustrated by Mark Peppé) (Longman, 1973)..................£20
SNAKES AND SNAKES (illustrated by Richard Kennedy) (Kestrel, 1975) £20
ME AND MY MILLION (Kestrel, 1976) £20
HIGH JACKS, LOW JACKS (illustrated by Jacqueline Atkinson; laminated boards) (Benn, 1976)........£12
FIRST DAY OUT (illustrated by Jacqueline Atkinson; laminated boards) (Benn, 1976)........£12
ACCIDENT (illustrated by Jacqueline Atkinson; laminated boards) (Benn, 1976) £12
THE SECRET (illustrated by Jacqueline Atkinson; laminated boards) (Benn, 1976) £12
THE DEVIL'S CUT (illustrated by Val Biro) (Hodder & Stoughton, 1978) £20
THE BIRDS FROM AFRICA (illustrated by Diana Groves; laminated boards) (Macdonald, 1980)........£12
NINNY'S BOAT (illustrated by Ian Newsham) (Kestrel, 1980) £15

THE SOUND OF PROPELLERS (illustrated by David Perkins; d/j illustration by Fred Gambino) (Viking Kestrel, 1986) £15
THE SEASHORE PEOPLE (Viking Kestrel, 1987)...£15
ADVENTURE STORIES (as editor; anthology; laminated boards) (Kingfisher, 1988) £5
A TOUCH OF CLASS (laminated boards) (The Bodley Head, 1995) £5

KING, Jessie M.

Scottish illustrator. Born: Jessie Marion King in 1875. Studied at the Glasgow School of Art, where she was influenced by the work of Charles Rennie Mackintosh. Subsequently worked as a muralist and costume and jewellery designer, as well as providing illustrations for various books and magazines (notably *The Studio*). Settled in Scotland in 1913 after spending two years in Paris. Died: 1949.

Prices are for books in Very Good condition.

THE HEROES by Charles Kingsley (Routledge, 1907)...£200
A HOUSE OF POMEGRANATES by Oscar Wilde (sixteen illustrations by Jessie M. King) (Methuen, 1915)...........£500
THE LITTLE WHITE TOWN OF NEVER-WEARY (Harrap, [1917])...£275
A CAROL: GOOD KING WENCESLAS (adapted by J.M. Neale) (The Studio, [1919])..£220
GOOD KING WENCESLAS (Harold Hill, [1920]) £125
HOW CINDERELLA WAS ABLE TO GO TO THE BALL by Jessie M. King (brochure; printed on batik)
  (Foulis, [1924])...£525
THE ENCHANTED CAPITAL OF SCOTLAND: A Tale of Mystery and Adventure by Isobel K.C. Steele
  (limited to 500 copies) (1945)...£550
MUMMY'S BEDTIME STORY BOOK by 'Marion' (Harrap, [1917])..£275

Mummy's Bedtime Story Book by 'Marion' is a fine example of Jessie M. King's illustrative style.

KING-SMITH, Dick

British author. Born: Gloucestershire, 1922. His novels are distinguished by their pace and humour. *The Sheep-Pig* was filmed as *Babe* in 1995. He has penned another 30 books in the last decade which we have not included in the list, all worth around the £5 mark.

Prices are for books in Fine condition with dustjackets where applicable.

Fiction/Verse

THE FOX BUSTERS (illustrated by Jon Miller) (Gollancz, 1978)	£45
DAGGIE DOGFOOT (illustrated by Mary Rayner) (Gollancz, 1980)	£40
THE MOUSE BUTCHER (illustrated by Wendy Smith) (Gollancz, 1981)	£30
MAGNUS POWDERMOUSE (illustrated by Mary Rayner) (Gollancz, 1982)	£25
THE QUEEN'S NOSE (illustrated by Jill Bennett) (Gollancz, 1983)	£25
THE SHEEP-PIG (illustrated by Mary Rayner) (Gollancz, 1983)	£30
HARRY'S MAD (illustrated by Jill Bennett) (Gollancz, 1984)	£25
SADDLEBOTTOM (illustrated by Alice Englander) (Gollancz, 1985)	£20
LIGHTNING FRED (illustrated by Michael Bragg) (Heinemann: 'Banana Books', 1985)	£15
YOB (illustrated by Abigail Pizer) (Heinemann: 'Banana Books', 1986)	£15
H. PRINCE (illustrated by Martin Honeysett) (Walker, 1986)	£15
FARMER BUNGLE FORGETS (illustrated by Martin Honeysett) (Walker, 1986)	£15
E.S.P.: ERIC STANLEY PIGEON (Illustrated by Peter Wingham) (André Deutsch, 1986)	£15
NOAH'S BROTHER (illustrated by Ian Newsham) (Gollancz, 1986)	£15
DUMPLING (illustrated by Jo Davies) (Hamish Hamilton, 1986)	£15
THE HODGEHEG (illustrated by Linda Birch) (Hamish Hamilton, 1987)	£15
FRIENDS AND BROTHERS (illustrated by Susan Hellard) (Heinemann: 'Banana Books', 1987)	£15
CUCKOOBUSH FARM (illustrated by Kazuko) (Orchard, 1987)	£10
GEORGE SPEAKS (illustrated by Judy Brown) (Viking Kestrel, 1988)	£12
MARTIN'S MICE (illustrated by Jez Alborough) (Gollancz, 1988)	£12
THE JENIUS (illustrated by Peter Firmin) (Gollancz, 1988)	£12
EMILY'S LEGS (illustrated by Katinka Kew) (Macdonald, 1988)	£12
DODO COMES TO TUMBLEDOWN FARM (illustrated by John Sharp) (Heinemann, 1988)	£12
SOPHIE'S SNAIL (illustrated by David Perkins) (Walker, 1988)	£12
THE TOBY MAN (illustrated by Ian Newsham) (Gollancz, 1989)	£12
ALICE AND FLOWER AND FOXIANNA (paperback) (Heinemann, 1989)	£5
BEWARE OF THE BULL! (paperback) (Heinemann, 1989)	£5
HENRY POND THE POET (illustrated by Larry Wilkes) (Hodder & Stoughton: 'Roosters' series, 1989)	£5
THE TROUBLE WITH EDWARD (Hodder & Stoughton: 'Roosters' series, 1989)	£5
DODOS ARE FOREVER (illustrated by David Perkins) (Viking Kestrel, 1989)	£10
BLESSU (illustrated by Adrienne Kennaway) (Hamish Hamilton, 1990)	£5
ACE: THE VERY IMPORTANT PIG (illustrated by Liz Graham-Yooll) (Gollancz, 1990)	£10
THE JOLLY WITCH (illustrated by F. Rodgers) (Simon & Schuster, 1990)	£10
PADDY'S POT OF GOLD (illustrated by David Parkins) (Viking, 1990)	£10
THE WATERHORSE (illustrated by David Parkins) (Viking, 1990)	£10
ALPHABEASTS (illustrated by Quentin Blake) (Gollancz, 1990)	£15
THE WHISTLING PIGLET (illustrated by N. Johnson) (Walker, 1990)	£6
JUNGLE JINGLES and Other Stories (illustrated by Jonathan Allen) (Doubleday, 1990)	£10
THE CUCKOO CHILD (illustrated by David Perkins) (Viking, 1991)	£10
SOPHIE'S TOM (illustrated by David Parking) (Walker, 1991) (paperback)	£5
THE GUARD DOG (illustrated by Joceyln Wild) (Doubleday, 1991)	£10
LIGHTNING STRIKES TWICE (illustrated by A. Pizer; paperback) (Mammoth, 1991)	£5
CARUSO'S COOL CATS (paperback) (BBC/Longman, 1991)	£5
SOPHIE HITS SIX (illustrated by David Parkins) (Walker, 1991)	£5
HORACE AND MAURICE (illustrated by Semi Sweeten) (Doubleday, 1991)	£10
FIND THE WHITE HORSE (Viking, 1991)	£10
TRIFFIC PIG BOOK (Gollancz, 1991)	£20
BLESSU and DUMPLING (paperback) (Puffin, 1992)	£5
FARM TALES (illustrated by Liz Graham-Yooll; paperback) (Little Mammoth, 1992)	£5
LADY DAISY (illustrated by N. Harris) (Viking, 1992)	£10
PRETTY POLLY (illustrated by David Parkins) (Viking, 1992)	£10
THE GHOST AT CODLIN CASTLE and Other Stories (illustrated by Amanda Harvey) (Viking, 1992)	£10
THE FINGER EATER (illustrated by Arthur Robins) (Walker, 1992)	£5
SUPER TRIFFIC PIGS (paperback) (Gollancz, 1992)	£3
TOPSY-TURVY STORYBOOK (illustrated by John Eastwood) (Gollancz, 1992)	£10
UNCLE BUMPO (illustrated by Toni Goffe) (André Deutsch, 1993)	£10
THE SWOOSE (illustrated by Judy Brown) (Viking: 'Kite Books', 1993)	£5
THE INVISIBLE DOG (Viking: 'Kite Books', 1993)	£5
HORSE PIE (illustrated by Valerie Littlewood) (Doubleday, 1993)	£10
DRAGON BOY (illustrated by Jocelyn Wild) (Viking, 1993)	£10
A NARROW SQUEAK and Other Animal Stories (illustrated by Amanda Harvey) (Viking, 1993)	£10
THE MERRYTHOUGHT (illustrated by Mike Reid) (Viking, 1993)	£10

SOPHIE IN THE SADDLE (illustrated by David Parkins) (Walker, 1993) £5
YOUR FAVOURITE FARM STORIES (illustrated by J. Sharp) (Dean, 1993) £5
THE SCHOOLMOUSE (illustrated by Phil Garner) (Viking, 1994) £10
CONNIE AND ROLLO (illustrated by Judy Brown) (Doubleday, 1994) £10
HARRIET'S HARE (illustrated by Valerie Littlewood) (Doubleday, 1994) £10
MR POTTER'S PET (illustrated by Hilda Owen) (Viking, 1994) £5
THE EXCITEMENT OF BEING ERNEST (illustrated by Nigel McMullen) (Simon & Schuster, 1994) £10
SOPHIE IS SEVEN (illustrated by David Parkins) (Walker, 1994) £5
ANIMAL PARADE: A Collection of Stories and Poems (illustrated by Jocelyn Wild; paperback) (Mammoth, 1994) £5
BOBBY THE BAD (illustrated by Julie Anderson; paperback) (Hippo Scholastic Books, 1994) £3
WARLOCK WATSON (illustrated by Julie Anderson; paperback) (Hippo/Scholastic Books, 1995) £5
KING MAX THE LAST (Hamish Hamilton, 1995) £5
SOPHIE'S LUCKY (illustrated by David Perkins) (Walker, 1995) £5
ALL BECAUSE OF JACKSON (illustrated by John Eastwood) (Doubleday, 1995) £10
THE TERRIBLE TRINS (Viking, 1995) £10
PHILIBERT THE FIRST (Viking, 1995) £10
OMNIBOMBULATOR (Doubleday, 1995) £10
HAPPY MOUSEDAY (Doubleday, 1995) £10
CLEVER DUCK (illustrated by M. Terry) (Viking: 'Kite Books', 1996) £6
DIRTY GERTIE MACKINTOSH (illustrated by Ros Asquith; verse; boards) (Doubleday, 1996) £10

Non-fiction

PETS FOR KEEPS (illustrated by Alan Saunders; paperback) (Puffin, 1986) £5
COUNTRY WATCH (illustrated by Catherine Bradbury; paperback) (Puffin, 1987) £5
TOWN WATCH (illustrated by Catherine Bradbury; paperback) (Puffln, 1987) £5
WATER WATCH (illustrated by Catherine Bradbury; paperback) (Puffin, 1988) £5
ALL PIGS ARE BEAUTIFUL (illustrated by Anita Jeram) (Walker, 1993) £5
I LOVE GUINEA PIGS (illustrated by Anita Jeram) (Walker, 1994) £5

KINGSLEY, Charles

British author. Born: Devon, 1819. Educated at Helston Grammar School and Cambridge University. Ordained shortly before his marriage in 1844, subsequently launching the periodical, *Politics for the People*, with his fellow Christian Socialist, Thomas Hughes. Appointed Regius Professor of Modern History at Cambridge in 1860, and was later Governor of Trinidad. As well as his well-known children book, *Ditto* (1863), he wrote a number of works for older readers, including the historical romances, *Westward Ho!* (1855) and *Hereward the Wake* (1866), and the political novels, *Yeast* (1848) and *Alton Locke* (1850). Died: 1875.

Prices are for books in Very Good condition.

GLAUCUS, or The Wonders of the Shore (Macmillan, 1855) £400
WESTWARD HO! (three volumes) (Macmillan, 1855) .... the set £600
THE HEROES, or Greek Fairy Tales for My Children (illustrated by the author) (Macmillan, 1856 [1855]) £300
THE HEROES (illustrated by Jessie M. King) (Routledge, 1907) £200
THE HEROES (illustrated by W. Russell Flint; limited to 500 numbered copies) (P. Lee Warner / Riccardi Press, 1912) £500
THE HEROES (illustrated by W. Russell Flint; limited to 12 copies, printed on vellum) (P. Lee Warner / Riccardi Press, 1912) . £1,200
THE WATER BABIES: A Fairy Tale for a Land-Baby
(illustrated by J. Noel Paton; 200 copies containing the verse, 'L'Envoi') (Macmillan, 1863) £1,000
THE WATER BABIES (illustrated by J. Noel Paton; later issues) (Macmillan, 1863) £400
THE WATER BABIES (illustrated by Linley Sambourne) (Macmillan, 1865) £100
THE WATER BABIES (illustrated by J. Noel Paton and Percival Skelton) (Macmillan, 1869) £50
THE WATER BABIES (illustrated by Katherine Cameron) (T.C. & E.C. Jack, [1905]) £50
THE WATER BABIES (illustrated by Margaret Tarrant) (Dent, 1908) £100
THE WATER BABIES (illustrated by Arthur Dixon) (Nister, [1908]) £35
THE WATER BABIES (illustrated by Alice B. Woodward) (Blackie, 1909) £60
THE WATER BABIES (illustrated by Warwick Goble) (Macmillan, 1909) £350
THE WATER BABIES (illustrated by Warwick Goble; limited to 260 numbered copies; in slipcase) (Macmillan, 1909) £1,500
THE WATER BABIES (illustrated by Warwick Goble; reissues) (Macmillan, 1910 & 1922) .... £80/£60
THE WATER BABIES (illustrated by W. Heath Robinson) (Constable, 1915) £175
THE WATER BABIES (illustrated by Mabel Lucie Attwell; abridged version) (Raphael Tuck, [1915]) £160
THE WATER BABIES (illustrated by Jessie Willcox Smith) (Dodd Mead, US, 1916) £200
THE WATER BABIES (illustrated by Jessie Willcox Smith) (Hodder & Stoughton, [1916]) £200
THE WATER BABIES (illustrated by Jessie Willcox Smith) (Hodder & Stoughton/Boots the Chemist, [c.1930]) £75
THE WATER BABIES (illustrated by Jessie Willcox Smith; facsimile of the original 1916 edition;
limited to 500 numbered copies; in slipcase) (Hodder & Stoughton, 1981) £100
THE WATER BABIES (illustrated by Gordon Robinson) (J.A. Sharp, 1919) £20
THE WATER BABIES (illustrated by Harry G. Theaker) (Ward Lock, [1922]) £40
THE WATER BABIES (illustrated by Anne Anderson) (T.C. & E.C. Jack, [1924]) £130
THE WATER BABIES (illustrated by Rosalie K. Fry) (Dent, 1957) £25
HEREWARD THE WAKE (two volumes) (Macmillan, 1866) .... the set £400
MADAM HOW AND LADY WHY, or First Lessons in Earth Lore for Children (London, 1870) £150

KINGSTON, W.H.G.

British author. Born: 1814. William Henry Giles Kignston spent much of his youth in Oporto where his father was a merchant. Prolific writer of adventure stories for boys, notably *Peter the Whaler* (1851) and *The Three Midshipmen* (1873) and its sequels. He also edited a number of annuals and periodicals for boys, including the first *Union Jack*. He was voted second only to Dickens in a boys' poll of 1884, mainly because of the exuberance of his young heroes and graphic naval descriptions. The following list is only a small selection from his complete bibliography of 165 titles. Died: 1880.

Prices are for books in Good condition.

PETER THE WHALER: His Life and Adventures in the Arctic Regions (Grant, 1851)......£100
MANCO, THE PERUVIAN CHIEF, or An Englishman's Adventures in the Country of the Incas
  (Grant, 1853 [1852]).......£60
SALT WATER (Griffith & Farran, 1857 [1856]).......£40
THE EARLY LIFE OF OLD JACK: A Tale for Boys (Nelson, 1858).......£40
OLD JACK: A Tale for Boys (Nelson, 1859).......£40
ROUND THE WORLD: A Tale for Boys (Nelson, 1859).......£40
WILL WEATHERHELM: Yarns of an Old Sailor (Griffith & Farran, 1859).......£30
MY FIRST VOYAGE TO SOUTHERN SEAS (Nelson, 1860).......£30
DIGBY HEATHCOTE, or The Early Days of a Country Gentleman's Son and Heir
  (Routledge, Warne & Routledge, 1860).......£30
ERNEST BRACEBRIDGE, or School-Boy Days (Sampson Low, 1860 [1859]).......£30
TRUE BLUE (Griffith & Farran, 1862 [1861]).......£30
MARMADUKE MERRY THE MIDSHIPMAN (Routledge, 1862).......£30
PAUL GERRARD, THE CABIN BOY (Routledge, 1866).......£30
THE ROYAL MERCHANT, or Events in the Days of Sir Thomas Gresham (Partridge, 1870).......£20
IN THE WILDS OF AFRICA: A Tale for Boys (Nelson, 1871 [1870]).......£40
ON THE BANKS OF THE AMAZON (Nelson, 1872).......£75
THE TRAPPER'S SON (London/Edinburgh, 1873).......£30
THE THREE MIDSHIPMEN (Griffith & Farran, 1873 [1872]).......£30
HURRICANE HURRY (illustrated by R. Huttula) (Griffith & Farran, 1874).......£30
ELDOL THE DRUID (Partridge, 1874).......£30
THE TWO SHIPMATES (SPCK, 1874).......£30
STORIES OF ANIMAL SAGACITY (illustrated by Harrison Weir) (Nelson, 1874).......£30
THE HEROIC WIFE, or The Wanderers on the Amazon (illustrated by H.W. Petherick) (Griffith & Farran, 1874).......£30
THE SOUTH SEA WHALER (Nelson, 1875).......£25
THE THREE LIEUTENANTS, or Naval Life in the Nineteenth Century (illustrated by D.H. Friston) (Griffith & Farran, 1875).......£30
SAVED FROM THE SEA (Nelson, 1876 [1875]).......£25
THE THREE COMMANDERS (Griffith & Farran, 1876 [1875]).......£40
SNOW-SHOES AND CANOES (Sampson Low, 1876).......£20
THE YOUNG RAJAH: A Story of Indian Life and Adventure (Nelson, 1876).......£25
THE WANDERERS: Adventures in Trinidad (Nelson, 1876).......£20
TWICE LOST: A Story of Shipwreck and Adventure (Nelson, 1876).......£20
THE YOUNG LLANERO (Nelson, 1877).......£20
IN THE ROCKY MOUNTAINS (Nelson, 1878 [1877]).......£20
WITH AXE AND RIFLE, or The Western Pioneers (Sampson Low, 1878).......£20
IN NEW GRANADA, or Heroes and Patriots: A Tale for Boys (Nelson, 1879).......£20
IN THE WILDS OF FLORIDA: A Tale of Warfare and Hunting (Nelson, 1880).......£60
THE GOLDEN GRASSHOPPER: A Story of the Days of Sir Thomas Gresham (Religious Tract Society, 1880).......£15
AMONG THE RED-SKINS, or Over the Rocky Mountains (Cassell, 1880).......£30
THE HEIR OF KILFINNAN (Sampson Low, 1881 [1880]).......£20
ROGER WILLOUGHBY: A Story of the Times of Benbow (Nisbet, 1881 [1880]).......£20
PADDY FINN: Adventures Afloat and Ashore (Griffith & Farran, 1883).......£25
FROM POWDER MONKEY TO ADMIRAL (Hodder, 1883).......£20

KIPLING, Rudyard

British author. Born: Bombay, 1865. Brought to England in 1871, later studying at the United Services College, Westward Ho! Returned to India in 1882, spending the next seven years working as a journalist and short story-writer. Lived in the United States from 1892 to 1896, subsequently settling permanently in England. Kipling is a rare example of an author who is equally celebrated for his children's works as his adult ones. Among the former are the two *Jungle Books* (1894/95), *Stalky & Co* (1899), *Just So Stories* (1902) and *Puck of Pook's Hill* (1906). Some of these books contain illustrations either by him or his father, John Lockwood Kipling. Despite the unfashionability of many of Kipling's views, his children's works have remained enduring classics of the genre. Died: 1936.

Prices are for books in Very Good condition.

THE JUNGLE BOOK (illustrated by J. Lockwood Kipling, W.H. Drake and P. Frenzeny) (Macmillan, 1894).......£1,500
THE SECOND JUNGLE BOOK (illustrated by J. Lockwood Kipling) (Macmillan, 1895).......£400
SIXTEEN ILLUSTRATIONS OF SUBJECTS FROM KIPLING'S 'JUNGLE BOOK' (illustrated by M. and E. Detmold)
  (Macmillan, 1903).......£1,500

*Kipling's best-loved children's books including the two **Jungle Book** volumes and the pictorial boards of his **Just So Stories**.*

THE JUNGLE BOOK (illustrated by M. and E. Detmold) (Macmillan, 1908)..£150
THE TWO JUNGLE BOOKS (Macmillan, 1924)..£35
ALL THE MOWGLI STORIES (illustrated by Stuart Tresilian; issued with dustjacket) (Macmillan, 1933)............£35
ALL THE MOWGLI STORIES (illustrated by Stuart Tresilian; leather binding; issued with dustjacket) (Macmillan, 1933)..........£45
CAPTAINS COURAGEOUS: A Story of the Grand Banks (illustrated by I.W. Taber) (Macmillan, 1897)....................£70
STALKY & CO (Macmillan, 1899)...£100
KIM (illustrated by J. Lockwood Kipling) (Macmillan, 1901)...£80
JUST SO STORIES FOR LITTLE CHILDREN (illustrated by the author) (Macmillan, 1902) £500
PUCK OF POOK'S HILL (illustrated by H.R. Millar) (Macmillan, 1906) £70
PUCK OF POOK'S HILL (illustrated by Arthur Rackham) (Doubleday, US, 1906)...............................£250
A SONG OF THE ENGLISH (verse; illustrated by W. Heath Robinson) (Hodder & Stoughton, 1909) £350
REWARDS AND FAIRIES (illustrated by Frank Craig) (Macmillan, 1910)......................................£75
THE COLLECTED VERSE OF RUDYARD KIPLING (illustrated by W. Heath Robinson) (Doubleday Page, US, 1910)...........£250
A HISTORY OF ENGLAND (with C.R.L. Fletcher; quarto) (OUP/Hodder & Stoughton, 1911)....................£40
A HISTORY OF ENGLAND (octavo edition for use in schools) (OUP/Hodder & Stoughton, 1911)...............£20
LAND AND SEA TALES FOR SCOUTS AND GUIDES (Macmillan, 1923)...£35
TOOMAI OF THE ELEPHANTS (tie-in with the film 'Elephant Boy'; issued with dustjacket) (Macmillan, 1937)........................£10

KNATCHBULL-HUGESSEN, E.H.

British author. Born: Edward Hugessen Knatchbull-Hugessen in 1829. Between 1869 and 1886, he published several volumes of original fairy stories, of which the first was *Stories for my Children* (1869). Modelled on tales of Hans Andersen, these were an important influence on J.R.R. Tolkien. Knatchbull-Hugessen was a great-nephew of Jane Austen, and briefly served as a junior minister in Gladstone's government. Towards the end of his life, Knatchbull-Hugessen received a baronetcy, becoming the first Baron Brabourne. Died: 1893.

Prices are for books in Good condition.

STORIES FOR MY CHILDREN (Macmillan, 1869)..£35
CRACKERS FOR CHRISTMAS: More Stories by E.K.H. (Macmillan, 1870).....................................£35
CRACKERS FOR CHRISTMAS: More Stories by E.K.H. (new edition) (Routledge, 1883 [1882])...............£25
MOONSHINE: Fairy Stories (illustrated by W. Brunton) (Macmillan, 1871).....................................£35
TALES AT TEA-TIME: Fairy Stories (illustrated by W. Brunton) (Macmillan, 1872)..............................£40
QUEER FOLK: Seven Stories (illustrated by S.E. Waller) (Macmillan, 1873)...................................£40
QUEER FOLK: Seven Stories (new edition) (Routledge, 1883 [1882])..£25
WHISPERS FROM FAIRYLAND (Longmans Green, 1875 [1874]) £30
HIGGLEDY-PIGGLEDY, or Stories for Everybody and Everybody's Children
    (Longmans Green, 1875)...£60
UNCLE JOE'S STORIES (illustrated by E. Griset) (Routledge, 1879 [1878]) £40
OTHER STORIES (illustrated by E. Griset) (Routledge, 1880 [1879])...£40
THE MOUNTAIN-SPRITE'S KINGDOM and Other Stories (illustrated by E. Griset) (Routledge, 1881 [1880]) £40
FERDINAND'S ADVENTURE and Other Stories (illustrated by E. Griset) (Routledge, 1883 [1882])...............£40
FRIENDS AND FOES FROM FAIRY LAND (illustrated by L. Sambourne) (Longmans, 1886 [1885])...............£40
ELLA'S FAULT: Jack Frost's Little Prisoners (with Stella Austin and S. Baring Gould) (Skeffington, 1887)....................£30
THE MAGIC OAK TREE AND PRINCE FILDERKIN (Unwin, 1894)..£30
SOME WHISPERS FROM FAIRYLAND (contains 'The Lost Prince' and 'The Silver Fairies' from 'Whispers from Fairy-Land')
    (Blackie, [1933])..£10

L

LADYBIRD BOOKS

Highly successful children's imprint derived from the activities of Loughborough bookseller, Henry Wills (later Wills & Hepworth), who launched the 'Ladybird' logo in 1915. The first book to appear under the imprint was *Little Stories for Little People*, an annual-sized volume published in 1916. An unknown number of similar sized books continued to appear for many years, although only a handful are listed here as so few have survived, and the publishing records have been lost. As is noted below, the majority of these early titles are worth around £50. The distinctive pocket-sized 'Ladybird' was a result of Second World War paper shortages. The first of these was *Bunnikin's Picnic Party* (1940), issued in boards and a dustjacket. Later editions/issues have no jackets.

Prices are for books in Very Good condition with dustjackets where applicable.

Pre-1940 books

LITTLE STORIES FOR LITTLE PEOPLE (issued in decorative boards) (1916) £100
ABC PICTURE BOOK (issued in decorative boards) (1916) £70

> *The remaining large format pre-1940 books are worth around £50+ each. They have no
> Ladybird logo, normally carrying the word 'The Ladybird Series' somewhere on the cover.
> Known titles include THE LADYBIRD DOLLY'S PICTURE BOOK; ABC OF TRAINS AND MOTORS;
> MRS TABBY; OUR ROVER and THE FAIRY ENGINE*

Rhyming Stories – Series 401

BUNNIKIN'S PICNIC PARTY (1940), Augusine J. MacGregor £80
THE FIRST DAY OF THE HOLIDAYS (1940), Augusine J. MacGregor £70
GINGER'S ADVENTURES (1940), Augusine J. MacGregor £70
SMOKE AND FLUFF (1941), E. M. Coghlin £60
JEREMY'S DAY IN THE COUNTRY (1941), E. M. Coghlin £70
BOB BUSHTAIL'S ADVENTURE (1941), E. M. Coghlin £60
DOWNY DUCKLING (1946), Walter Perring £60
PIGGLY PLAYS TRUANT (1946), Walter Perring £60
LOST AT THE FAIR (1948), Walter Perring £50
THE RUNAWAY (1948), Walter Perring £70
MR. BADGER TO THE RESCUE (1949), Walter Perring £70
BUNNY'S FIRST BIRTHDAY (1950), Walter Perring £70
THE BUNNY-FLUFF'S MOVING DAY (1950), Walter Perring £70
THE GREEN UMBRELLA (1950), Walter Perring £70
PIPPETY'S UNLUCKY DAY (1952), Walter Perring £80
JONATHAN'S SHOPPING DAY (1952), Walter Perring £80
FIVE LITTLE KITTENS (1955), Walter Perring £80
HIGH TIDE (1956), Walter Perring £175

Fairy Stories and Rhymes – Series 413

BABY'S FIRST BOOK (1954), B. Lewis £70

The Adventures of Wonk – Series 417

GOING TO SEA (1941), Muriel Levy £125
STRAWBERRIES AND CREAM (1941), Muriel Levy £125
FIREWORKS (1941), Muriel Levy £125
THE SECRET (1945), Muriel Levy £200
THE CIRCUS (1948), Muriel Levy £125
THE SNOWMAN (1948), Muriel Levy £125

Uncle Mac – Series 455

IN THE TRAIN WITH UNCLE MAC (1945) £40
IN THE COUNTRY WITH UNCLE MAC (1946) £20
BESIDE THE SEA WITH UNCLE MAC (1959) £20

Tasseltip Tales – Series 474

A LITTLE SILK APRON (1947), Dorothy Richards £60
MR. MOLE'S HOUSEWARMING PARTY (1947), Dorothy Richards £60
THE FLICKERDICK (1947), Dorothy Richards £60
CLATTER! CLATTER! BANG!!! (1948), Dorothy Richards £60
THE FIRST DAY OF SPRING (1950), Dorothy Richards £70
THE FLOWER SHOW (1953), Dorothy Richards £70

TInker's Wig – Series 478

THE TINKER'S WIG (1947), John Saunders £60

Series 497

TIPTOES, THE MISCHIEVOUS KITTEN (1949) £10
THE WISE ROBIN (1950) £10

An unknown quantity of these rare pre-war large-format Ladybird books were produced, and all are worth around the £50 mark in Very Good condition. The familiar pocket Ladybirds began when wartime paper shortages forced the publishers to reduce sizes.

Series 522
THE CHILD OF THE TEMPLE (1953)..£10
THE SHEPHERD BOY OF BETHLEHEM (1954) £10
THE LITTLE LORD JESUS (1954) £10
THE STORY OF JESUS (1955)..£10
JESUS BY THE SEA OF GALILEE (1958) £10
JESUS CALLS HIS DISCIPLES (1959)..£10

Series 536
A BOOK OF BRITISH BIRDS AND THEIR NESTS (1953)..£10
A SECOND BOOK OF BRITISH BIRDS AND THEIRS NESTS (1954) £10
A THIRD BOOK OF BRITISH BIRDS AND THEIR NESTS (1954)...£8
BRITISH WILD FLOWERS (1957) £8
BRITISH WILD FLOWERS (1958) £10
WHAT TO LOOK FOR IN WINTER (1959) £8
WHAT TO LOOK FOR IN SUMMER (1960)..£8
WHAT TO LOOK FOR IN AUTUMN (1960) £5
WHAT TO LOOK FOR IN SPRING (1961)..£5
THE WEATHER (1962)...£4
BOOK OF TREES (1963)...£4
POND LIFE (1966)...£4
YOUR BODY (1967)..£4
GARDEN BIRDS (1967)..£4
SEA AND ESTUARY BIRDS (1967)..£4

Series 538
THE IMPATIENT HORSE (1953), George Murray..£400

Series 561
KING ALFRED THE GREAT (1956)..£10
WILLIAM THE CONQUEROR (1956)..£10
SIR WALTER RALEIGH (1957)..£10
THE STORY OF NELSON (1957) £10
THE FIRST QUEEN ELIZABETH (1958) £10
FLORENCE NIGHTINGALE (1959) £8
JULIUS CAESAR AND ROMAN BRITAIN (1959) £8
THE STORY OF CHARLES II (1960)..£8
DAVID LIVINGSTONE (1960)...£8
STONE AGE MAN IN BRITAIN (1961)...£8

Three examples from the 'Adventures of Wonk' Ladybird series, written by Muriel Levy. All were originally issued in dustjackets.

THE STORY OF HENRY V (1962)..£8
OLIVER CROMWELL (1963)...£5
ALEXANDER THE GREAT (1963)...£5
RICHARD THE LIONHEART (1965)..£5
CLEOPATRA AND ANCIENT EGYPT (1966)...£5
THE KINGS AND QUEENS OF ENGLAND (Book 1; 1968)...£5
THE KINGS AND QUEENS OF ENGLAND (Book 2; 1968)...£5
NAPOLEON (1968)...£5

Series 563
PUPPIES AND KITTENS (1956)..£10
THE FARM (1958)..£10
GOING TO SCHOOL (1959)..£10
THE ZOO (1960)..£8

Transport – Series 584
BRITISH RAILWAY LOCOMOTIVES (1964), D. L. Joiner £30

Series 587
FLIGHT ONE: AUSTRALIA (1958)...£10
FLIGHT TWO: CANADA (1959)..£8
FLIGHT THREE: USA (1959)..£8

Series 601
THE STORY OF FLIGHT (1960)..£10
GREAT INVENTIONS (1961)..£5
THE STORY OF RAILWAYS (1961)..£5
THE STORY OF SHIPS (1961)..£5
THE STORY OF THE MOTOR CAR (1962)...£5
THE STORY OF HOUSES AND HOMES (1963)..£5
THE STORY OF CLOTHES AND COSTUMES (1964)..£5
CHURCHES AND CATHEDRALS (1964)...£5
THE STORY OF OIL (1968) £5
THE STORY OF NEWSPAPERS (1969)..£5
THE STORY OF PRINTING (1970)...£5

Series 606A
JESUS THE HELPER (1960) £5
JESUS THE FRIEND (1961) £5
BABY JESUS (1961)...£5
CHILDREN OF THE BIBLE (1962)...£5
A FIRST BOOK OF SAINTS (1963)..£5

Series 606B
THE FIREMAN (1960) £8
THE POLICEMAN (1961)..£5
THE NURSE (1963) £5
THE FISHERMAN (1963) £5

THE BUILDER (1965)...£5
THE POSTMAN (1965)..£5
THE MINER (1965) :...£5
THE SOLDIER (1966)..£5
THE AIRMAN IN THE ROYAL AIR FORCE (1967) £5

Series 606C
THE STORY OF CRICKET (1964) £5
THE STORY OF FOOTBALL (1964)...£5

Well Loved Tales – Series 606D
CINDERELLA (1964), Vera Southgate..£80
THE ELVES AND THE SHOEMAKER (1965)..£5
THREE LITTLE PIGS (1965)..£5
SLEEPING BEAUTY (1965)..£5
DICK WHITTINGTON AND HIS CAT (1966)...£5
THE PRINCESS AND THE PEA (1967)..£5
THE MAGIC PORRIDGE POT (1971)...£5
THE BIG PANCAKE (1972)...£5
THE OLD WOMAN AND HER PIG (1973)...£5
THE MUSICIANS OF BREMEN (1974)...£5

Series 606E
ELECTRICITY (1966) £5
GAS (1967) £5
WATER SUPPLY (1969) £5

Series 612
THE LORD'S PRAYER (1961) £8
BOOK OF PRAYERS (1964)..£10

Early Learning – Series 622
THE LADYBIRD ABC (1962) £30

Series 633
THINGS TO MAKE (1963)...£8
TOYS AND GAMES TO MAKE (1966)..£5
STAMP COLLECTING (1969) £5
HOW TO SWIM AND DIVE (1971) £5
LEARNING TO SEW (1972)..£5

Series 649
ANIMALS, BIRDS AND PLANTS OF THE BIBLE (1963)..£5
WHAT TO LOOK FOR INSIDE A CHURCH (1972) £5
WHAT TO LOOK FOR OUTSIDE A CHURCH (1972)..£5

Series 651
ANIMALS AND HOW THEY LIVE (1965) £5
BIRDS AND HOW THEY LIVE (1966) £5

Series 654
HOW IT WORKS – THE MOTOR CAR (1965) £8
HOW IT WORKS – THE COMPUTER (1969) £5
HOW IT WORKS – PRINTING PROCESSES (1971) £5

Series 662
THE STORY OF MUSIC (1968)...£5
BALLET (1969)..£5
THE LIVES OF GREAT COMPOSERS (Book 1; 1969)..£5
THE LIVES OF GREAT COMPOSERS (Book 2; 1969)..£5

Series 706
CUB SCOUTS (1970)...£5
SCOUTS (1971)..£5
BROWNIE GUIDE (1978)...£5
GIRL GUIDE (1980)...£5

Series 707
THE STORY OF THE INDIANS (1973)..£5
THE BATTLE OF THE LITTLE BIG HORN (1976)...£5

Series 727
WILD LIFE IN BRITAIN (1972)...£5
DISAPPEARING MAMMALS (1973)...£5
WHAT ON EARTH ARE WE DOING (1976) £5

BUTTERFLIES AND MOTHS (1978) £5
HEDGES (1979)...£5
UNDERSTANDING THE SEA (1979) £5

Series 737
WATER (1973) £4
MAN IN THE AIR (1973)...£4
MAN AND HIS CAR (1974) £4
UNDER THE GROUND (1975)...£5
THE STREAM (1975)...£5

Royalty Series
THE QUEEN (1983) £5
PRINCE CHARLES (1981)...£5
THE QUEEN MOTHER (1982) £10
THE PRINCESS OF WALES (1982) £10
WILLIAM AND HENRY (1982) £10
THE ROYAL WEDDING: PRINCE CHARLES (1981)..£10
THE ROYAL WEDDING: PRINCE ANDREW (1986) £5

Miscellaneous
OUR FRIEND (series 6a; 1964)..£5
SUNNY DAYS (series 8a; 1964) £5
FUN AT THE FARM (series 4b; 1965) £5
THE BIG HOUSE (series 8b; 1966)...£8
JUMP FROM THE SKY (series 9b; 1966)...£5
ADVENTURE ON THE ISLAND (series 10a; 1966) £5
MYSTERY ON THE ISLAND (series 11a; 1966) £5
THE HOLIDAY CAMP MYSTERY (series 12a; 1966)..£8
THE CARNIVAL (series 1b; 1967)...£5
ADVENTURE AT THE CASTLE (series 10b; 1967)...£5
BOOKS ARE EXCITING (series 11c; 1967) £5
MOUNTAIN ADVENTURE (series 12b; 1967) £5
YOU MUST BE JOKING (Save the Children Fund; 1986)..£5
THE LADYBIRD 50th ANNIVERSARY COMPETITION BOOK (1990)..£8
INDEX OF UK FIRST EDITIONS (Published in Dustjackets 1940-65) 6th Edition, 2001, A4 Booklet, Steve Rudge......... in print £11

LA FONTAINE, Jean de
French author. Born: Champagne, France, in 1621. Wrote several volumes of adult poetry, but is best known today for his *Fables* – either original, or drawn from Aesop or other classical sources – first published under the title *Fables Choisies Mises en Vers* in 1668. These were first translated into English in 1734, and have been reprinted many times since. Died: 1695.

Prices are for books in Very Good condition with dustjackets where applicable.

FABLES (twelve volumes) (France, 1668-94) ....the set **£15,000**
FABLES (first English edition) (London, 1734)..**£2,000**
LA FONTAINE'S FABLES (translated by R. Thomson) (France, 1806) **£500**
FABLES (illustrated by J.J. Grandville; two volumes) (France, 1838)..............................the set **£2,000**
FABLES (illustrated by Gustave Doré; two volumes) (Hachette, Paris, 1867)...................the set **£400**
THE FABLES OF LA FONTAINE (illustrated by Gustave Doré; translated into English verse by Walter Thornbury)
(Cassell, 1868) **£250**
THE FABLES OF LA FONTAINE (illustrated by Stephen Gooden; translated into English verse by Edward Marsh;
two volumes; issued with dustjackets) (Heinemann, 1931) ....the set **£125**
LA FONTAINE'S FABLES (translated into English verse by Sir Edward Marsh; issued with dustjacket)
(Dent: 'Everyman's Library' series, 1953)..**£12**
THE LION AND THE RAT (illustrated and retold by Brian Wildsmith; issued with dustjacket) (OUP, 1963)...............**£30**
THE NORTH WIND AND THE SUN (illustrated and retold by Brian Wildsmith; issued with dustjacket) (OUP, 1964)..................**£30**
THE RICH MAN AND THE SHOE-MAKER (illustrated and retold by Brian Wildsmith; issued with dustjacket)(OUP, 1965)........**£30**
THE HARE AND THE TORTOISE (illustrated and retold by Brian Wildsmith; issued with dustjacket) (OUP, 1966) **£30**
THE FABLES OF LA FONTAINE, including his 'Life of Aesop' (illustrated by J.B. Oudry; translated by Kitty Muggeridge)
(Collins, 1973) **£25**

LAMB, Charles and Mary
British authors. Born: London, in 1775 and 1764 respectively. Charles was educated at Christ's Hospital, subsequently obtaining a clerkship at East India House, where he remained for thirty years. Mary stabbed her mother to death in 1796 and was committed to a lunatic asylum. Following her release in 1799, she lived with her brother until his death in 1834. The two of them collaborated on a number of children's books, most notably their *Tales from Shakespear* of 1807. Charles also achieved great fame with his adult *Essays of Elia* (1823/33). Mary died in 1847.

Prices are for books in Very Good condition.

*A complete set of Andrew Lang's famous coloured 'Fairy Book' series. The first **Blue Fairy Book** remains the most collectable, currently valued at £750.*

THE KING AND QUEEN OF HEARTS (verse; wraps) (Godwin: 'Juvenile Library' series, 1805) **£800**
THE KING AND QUEEN OF HEARTS (facsimile of the first edition; introduction by E.V. Lucas) (Methuen, 1902)...................**£100**
TALES FROM SHAKESPEAR (two volumes) (Hodgkins, 1807)...the set **£2,000**
TALES FROM SHAKESPEARE (illustrated by Arthur Rackham) (Dent: 'Temple Classics' series, 1899) **£100**
TALES FROM SHAKESPEARE (Nister, [c.1900]) **£75**
TALES FROM SHAKESPEARE (illustrated by Arthur Rackham) (Dent, 1909)..**£200**
TALES FROM SHAKESPEARE (illustrated by Arthur Rackham; limited to 750 numbered copies, signed by the artist)
(Dent, 1909)..**£1,000**
TALES FROM SHAKESPEARE (illustrated by Charles Folkard) (Dent, [1926]) **£100**
THE ADVENTURES OF ULYSSES (adapted from Chapman's translation of the 'Odyssey';
illustrated by C. Heath after H. Corbould; boards) (Godwin: 'Juvenile Library' series, 1808)....................................**£600**
MRS LEICESTER'S SCHOOL (anonymous) (Godwin: 'Juvenile Library' series, 1809)...**£900**
POETRY FOR CHILDREN (anonymous; wrappers) (Godwin: 'Juvenile Library' series, 1809) **£700**
A BOOK EXPLAINING THE RANKS AND DIGNITIES OF BRITISH SOCIETY (boards)
(Tabart: 'Juvenile and School Library' series, 1809)...**£700**
PRINCE DORUS: A Poetical Version of an Ancient Tale (wraps) (Godwin: 'Juvenile Library' series, 1811)...........................**£700**
BEAUTY AND THE BEAST (wraps) (Godwin: 'Juvenile Library' series, [1811]) **£700**
BEAUTY AND THE BEAST (introduction by Andrew Lang; boards) (Field & Tuer/Leadenhall Press, [1887])...........................**£100**
MR H, or Beware a Bad Name (play) (Carey, US, 1813)...**£225**
A MASQUE OF DAYS (illustrated by Walter Crane) (Cassell, 1901)..**£225**
STORIES FOR CHILDREN (illustrated by Charles Robinson and W. Green) (Dent, 1902) **£80**

LANG, Andrew

Scottish folklorist. Born: Selkirk, Scotland, in 1844. Educated at Edinburgh Academy, St. Andrew's University and Balliol College, Oxford. Subsequently became a Fellow of Merton College, but moved to London in the early 1870s where he worked as a freelance journalist, writing leaders for the *Daily News* and collaborating on translations of the *Odyssey* and the *Iliad*. Wrote/compiled a large number of children's works, but is best known for his 'Fairy Book' series, beginning with *The Blue Fairy Book* in 1889 and ending with *The Lilac Fairy Book* in 1910. Also collaborated with H. Rider Haggard on a novel, *The World's Desire* (1890). As a reviewer/publisher's reader, he forwarded the careers of Haggard, Rudyard Kipling, Arthur Conan Doyle, Walter de la Mare, F. Anstey and E. Nesbit. Died: 1912.

Prices are for books in Very Good condition.

'Fairy' Books

THE **BLUE FAIRY BOOK** (illustrated by Henry J. Ford and G.P. Jacomb Hood) (Longmans, 1889) **£750**
THE **RED FAIRY BOOK** (illustrated by Henry J. Ford and L. Speed) (Longmans, 1890) **£350**
THE **GREEN FAIRY BOOK** (illustrated by Henry J. Ford) (Longmans, 1892) **£350**
THE **YELLOW FAIRY BOOK** (illustrated by Henry J. Ford) (Longmans, 1894) **£350**
THE **PINK FAIRY BOOK** (illustrated by Henry J. Ford) (Longmans, 1897) **£300**
THE **GREY FAIRY BOOK** (illustrated by Henry J. Ford) (Longmans, 1900) **£275**
THE **VIOLET FAIRY BOOK** (illustrated by Henry J. Ford) (Longmans, 1901) **£275**
THE **CRIMSON FAIRY BOOK** (illustrated by Henry J. Ford) (Longmans, 1903) **£275**
THE **BROWN FAIRY BOOK** (illustrated by Henry J. Ford) (Longmans, 1904) **£275**
THE **ORANGE FAIRY BOOK** (illustrated by Henry J. Ford) (Longmans, 1906) **£225**
THE **OLIVE FAIRY BOOK** (illustrated by Henry J. Ford) (Longmans, 1907) **£225**
THE **LILAC FAIRY BOOK** (illustrated by Henry J. Ford) (Longmans, 1910) **£225**

Others

THE **PRINCESS NOBODY: A Tale of Fairy Land** (illustrated by Richard Doyle)
(Longmans, [1884]) **£750**
JOHNNY NUT AND THE GOLDEN GOOSE (Longmans, 1888) **£120**
THE **GOLD OF FAIRNILEE** (illustrated by T. Scott and E.A. Lemann) (Arrowsmith, [1888]) **£140**
PRINCE PRIGIO (illustrated by Gordon Browne) (Arrowsmith, 1889) **£120**
THE **WORLD'S DESIRE** (with H. Rider Haggard) (Longmans, 1890) **£80**
THE **BLUE POETRY BOOK** (illustrated by Henry J. Ford and Lancelot Speed)
(Longmans, 1891) **£120**
THE **TRUE STORY BOOK** (illustrated by L. Bogle, Lucien Davis, Henry J Ford, C.H.M. Kerr and Lancelot Speed)
(Longmans, 1893) **£100**
PRINCE RICARDO OF PANTOUFLIA: Being the Adventures of Prince Prigio's Son
(illustrated by Gordon Browne) (Arrowsmith, [1893]) **£100**
THE **RED TRUE STORY BOOK** (illustrated by Henry J. Ford) (Longmans, 1895) **£90**
THE **ANIMAL STORY BOOK** (illustrated by Henry J. Ford) (Longmans, 1896) **£90**
THE **ARABIAN NIGHTS ENTERTAINMENTS.** Edited by Andrew Lang (illustrated by Henry J. Ford)
(Longmans, 1898) **£225**
THE **RED BOOK OF ANIMAL STORIES** (illustrated by Henry J. Ford) (Longmans, 1899) **£90**
THE **BOOK OF ROMANCE** (illustrated by Henry J. Ford) (Longmans, 1902) **£120**
THE **RED ROMANCE BOOK** (illustrated by Henry J. Ford) (Longmans, 1905) **£140**
TALES OF A FAIRY COURT (contains 'Prince Prigio' and 'Prince Ricardo of Pantouflia'; illustrated by A.A. Dixon)
(Arrowsmith, [1907]) **£120**
TALES OF TROY AND GREECE (illustrated by Henry J. Ford) (Longmans, 1907) **£100**
THE **BOOK OF PRINCES AND PRINCESSES** (illustrated by Henry J. Ford) (Longmans, 1908) **£120**
THE **RED BOOK OF HEROES** (illustrated by Henry J. Ford) (Longmans, 1909) **£120**
THE **ALL SORTS OF STORIES BOOK** (illustrated by Henry J. Ford) (Longmans, 1911) **£90**
THE **BOOK OF SAINTS AND HEROES** (illustrated by Henry J. Ford) (Longmans, 1912) **£90**
THE **STRANGE STORY BOOK** (illustrated by Henry J. Ford) (Longmans, 1913) **£100**
THE **ROSE FAIRY BOOK** (illustrated by Vera Bock) (Longmans, [1948]) **£120**

*Illustrator Errol Le Cain is becoming increasingly collectable. His edition of **The Pied Piper of Hamelin** is now valued at £20.*

*The first UK hardback edition of **A Wizard of Earthsea**. The book was originally published as a Puffin paperback in 1971.*

LAWSON, Robert

American author-illustrator. Born: 1892. The creator of 'Uncle Analdas', an irascible old rabbit, who appeared in several stories. Won the Newbery Medal for *Rabbit Hill* (1944). Died: 1957.

Prices are for books in Very Good condition with dustjackets.

Books Written and Illustrated by Robert Lawson

BEN AND ME (Little Brown, US, 1939)..£150
THEY WERE STRONG AND GOOD (Little Brown, US, 1940)..£75
I DISCOVER COLUMBUS (Little Brown, US, 1941)..£100
COUNTRY COLIC (Little Brown, US, 1944)..£75
RABBIT HILL (Viking, US, 1944)...£75
AT THAT TIME (Viking, US, 1947)..£45
THE FABULOUS FLIGHT (Little Brown, US, 1949)...£45
ROBBUT, A TALE OF TAILS (Heinemann, 1949)...£40
MR REVERE AND I (Little Brown, US, 1953)..£55
THE TOUGH OF WINTER (Little Brown US, 1954)..£40
CAPT KIDD'S CAT (Muller, 1956)...£55
THE GREAT WHEEL (Viking, US, 1964)..£70

Books Illustrated by Robert Lawson

THE WEE MEN OF BALLYWOODEN by Arthur Mason (Heinemann, 1931)..£70
THE STORY OF FERDINAND by Munro Leaf (Hamish Hamilton, 1937)..£60
ONE FOOT IN FAIRYLAND: Sixteen Tales by Eleanor Farjeon (Joseph, 1938).....................................£35
WEE GILLIS by Munro Leaf (Viking, US, 1938)..£60
MR POPPER'S PENGUINS by Richard and Florence Atwater (Harrap, 1939)..£40
POO-POO AND THE DRAGONS by C.S. Forester (Joseph, 1942)..£200
ADAM OF THE ROAD by Janet Gray (A. & C. Black, 1943)..£35
SIMPSON AND SAMPSON by Munro Leaf (Warne, 1944)..£35

LE CAIN, Errol

British author-illustrator. Born: Singapore, 1941. Worked in advertising and animation for TV and films. He wrote and illustrated several books for children, but most of his work was for other writers. He won the Kate Greenaway Medal *with Hiawatha's Childhood* in 1985. Died: 1989.

Prices are for books in Very Good condition with dustjackets where applicable.

Books Illustrated by Errol Le Cain

SIR ORFEO by Anthea Davis (Faber, 1970)..£20
THE CHILD IN THE BAMBOO GROVE by Rosemary Harris (Faber, 1971)..£15
THE BEACHCOMBERS by Helen Cresswell (Faber, 1972)...£15
THE KING'S WHITE ELEPHANT by Rosemary Harris (Faber, 1973)..£15
THE LOTUS AND THE GRAIL by Rosemary Harris (Faber, 1974)...£15
THE FLYING SHIP by Rosemary Harris (Faber, 1975)..£15
THORN ROSE. Taken from the Brothers Grimm by Errol Le Cain (Faber, 1975)................................£35
THE LITTLE DOG OF FO by Rosemary Harris (Faber, 1976)...£15
THE SLY CORMORANT AND THE FISHES by Brian Patten (verse) (Kestrel, 1977)...............................£25
THE TWELVE DANCING PRINCESSES Taken from the Brothers Grimm by Erroll Le Cain (Faber, 1978).........£25
BEAUTY AND THE BEAST by Rosemary Harris (Faber, 1979)...£15
THE SNOW QUEEN New Adapted Version from Hans Christian Andersen by Naomi Lewis (Kestrel, 1979).....£25
MRS FOX'S WEDDING by Sara and Stephen Corrin (Faber, 1980)..£20
THE THREE MAGIC GIFTS by Riordan James (Kaye & Ward, 1980)..£20
ALADDIN AND THE WONDERFUL LAMP Retold by Andrew Lang (pictorial boards) (Faber, 1981)...............£25
MOLLY WHUPPIE Retold by Walter de la Mare (pictorial boards) (Faber, 1983).................................£20
HIAWATHA'S CHILDHOOD by Henry Wadsworth Longfellow (Faber, 1984)..£30
GROWLTIGER'S LAST STAND and Other Poems by T.S. Eliot (Faber, 1986)......................................£35
THE ENCHANTER'S DAUGHTER by Antonia Barber (Cape, 1987)...£20
CHRISTMAS 1993 or SANTA'S LAST RIDE by Leslie Bricasse (Faber, 1987).....................................£20
THE PIED PIPER OF HAMELIN Retold by Sara and Stephen Corrin (Faber, 1988)................................£20
TAIL FEATHERS FROM MOTHER GOOSE by Iona Opie (illustrated by Nicola Bayley, Babette Cole and Erroll Le Cain) (Walker, 1988) £25
THE CHRISTMAS STOCKINGS by Mathew Price (Angus and Robertson, 1989).................................£20
MR MISTOFFELEES by T.S. Eliot (Faber, 1990) £35

LE GUIN, Ursula

American author. Born: Ursula Kroeber in Berkeley, California, in 1929. Educated at Radcliffe College, Massachusetts, and Columbia University. Married the historian, Charles A. Le Guin, in 1953. Best known for her 'Earthsea' trilogy of children's novels, she has also written a number of science fiction/fantasy works for adults.

Prices are for books in Very Good condition with dustjackets.

A WIZARD OF EARTHSEA (first issue, vertical line on title page, dustjacket priced $3.95) (Parnassus Press, US, 1968)..£1,000
A WIZARD OF EARTHSEA (second issue, dustjacket unpriced) (Parnassus Press, US, 1968)................£100
A WIZARD OF EARTHSEA (illustrated by Ruth Robbins; paperback) (Puffin, 1971) £10
A WIZARD OF EARTHSEA (Gollancz, 1971)..£150
THE TOMBS OF ATUAN (Atheneum, US, 1971)..£200
THE TOMBS OF ATUAN (Gollancz, 1972)...£120
THE FARTHEST SHORE (Atheneum, US, 1972) £175
THE FARTHEST SHORE (Gollancz, 1973)..£100
A VERY LONG WAY FROM ANYWHERE ELSE (Gollancz, 1976) £40
A VERY LONG WAY FROM ANYWHERE ELSE (as 'Very Far Away from Anywhere Else') (Atheneum, US, 1976).................£45
EARTHSEA (omnibus) (Gollancz, 1977)..£45
LEESE WEBSTER (Atheneum, US, 1979)..£40
THE BEGINNING PLACE (Harper, US, 1980)..£40
THRESHOLD, or The Beginning Place (Gollancz, 1980) £40
LEESE WEBSTER (Gollancz, 1981)...£40
VISIT FROM DR KATZ (picture book; boards) (Collins, 1988)..£15
VISIT FROM DR KATZ (picture book) (Atheneum, US, 1988)..£15
CATWINGS (Orchard, US, 1988)...£15
CATWINGS RETURN (Orchard, US, 1989)...£15
FIRE AND STONE (Atheneum, US, 1989)...£15
TEHANU (Gollancz, 1990)...£20
TEHANU (Atheneum, US, 1990) £20

LE MAIR, H. Willebeek

Dutch illustrator. Born: Henriette Willebeek Le Mair in Rotterdam in 1889. Her first book, *Premières Rondes Enfantines*, was published when she was only fifteen, but she is best known in Britain for her later nursery rhyme illustrations. She ran a primary school for several years. Died: 1966.

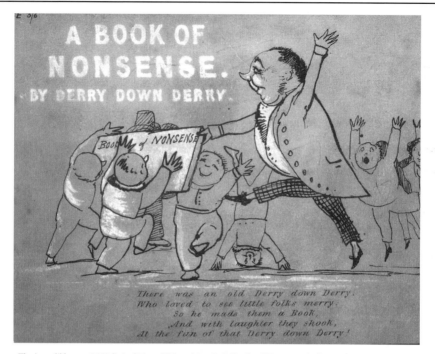

The incredibly rare 1846 first edition of Edward Lear's **A Book of Nonsense** *by 'Derry Down Derry'.*

Prices are for books in Very Good condition.

OUR OLD NURSERY RHYMES (Augener, 1911) **£250**
OUR OLD NURSERY RHYMES (De Luxe edition; signed by the artist; vellum binding) (Augener, 1911) **£2,250**
LITTLE SONGS OF LONG AGO (Augener, 1912) **£250**
LITTLE SONGS OF LONG AGO (De Luxe edition; signed by the artist; vellum binding) (Augener, 1912) **£2,250**
AUNTIE'S LITTLE RHYME BOOK (Augener, 1913) **£140**
NURSIE'S LITTLE RHYME BOOK (Augener, 1913) **£140**
GRANNY'S LITTLE RHYME BOOK (Augener, 1913) **£140**
SCHUMANN'S PIANO ALBUM OF CHILDREN'S PIECES (Augener, [1913]) **£175**
MOTHER'S LITTLE RHYME BOOK (Augener, [1913]) **£140**
THE CHILDREN'S CORNER by Rosie Helen Elkin (Augener, [1914]) **£250**
THE CHILDREN'S CORNER by Rosie Helen Elkin (De Luxe edition; signed by the artist; vellum binding)
    (Augener, 1914) **£2,250**
OLD NURSERY RHYMES (Augener, [1914]) **£250**
LITTLE PEOPLE by Rosie Helen Elkin (Augener, [1915]) **£250**
OLD DUTCH NURSERY RHYMES (Augener, 1917) **£250**
DADDY'S LITTLE RHYME BOOK (Augener, [c.1920]) **£140**
BABY'S LITTLE RHYME BOOK (Augener, [c.1920]) **£140**
A GALLERY OF CHILDREN by A.A. Milne (Stanley Paul, 1925) **£500**
A GALLERY OF CHILDREN by A.A. Milne (limited to 500 numbered copies, signed by the author) (Stanley Paul, 1925) **£1,000**
A CHILD'S GARDEN OF VERSE by R.L. Stevenson (Harrap, 1931) **£225**
TWENTY JAKATA TALES. Retold by Noor Inayat Khan (Harrap, 1939) **£120**
CHRISTMAS CAROLS FOR YOUNG PEOPLE by Dawn and Peter Cope (Fine Books, 1976) **£50**

LEAR, Edward

British author-illustrator. Born: London, 1812. An accomplished artist, Lear published a book of *Illustrations of the Family of Psittacidae, or Parrots* **when he was only twenty. Inspired by the limerick collection,** *Anecdotes and Adventures of Fifteen Gentlemen,* **he began to write humorous verses, the best of which were included in his** *Book of Nonsense* **(1846). Lear spent long periods in Italy and the Greek Islands during the 1840s and 1850s, recording his experiences in a number of books. Died: 1888.**

Prices are for books in Very Good condition with dustjackets where applicable.

A BOOK OF NONSENSE (written under the pseudonym 'Derry Down Derry';
    illustrated by the author; two volumes; wraps) (Thomas Maclean, 1846) .... the set **£70,000**
A BOOK OF NONSENSE by Edward Lear (enlarged edition; illustrated by the author) (Routledge, [1861]) **£700**

There was an Old Man with a beard, who said, "It is just as I feared!—
Two Owls and a Hen, four Larks and a Wren,
Have all built their nests in my beard!"

A classic pose from one of Edward Lear's illustrations in the first edition of **A Book of Nonsese.**

NONSENSE SONGS, STORIES, BOTANY AND ALPHABETS (illustrated by the author)
(Robert John Bush, 1871) **£900**
MORE NONSENSE, PICTURES, RHYMES, BOTANY, ETC. (illustrated by the author)
(Robert John Bush, 1872 [1874]) **£700**
LAUGHABLE LYRICS: A Fourth Book of Nonsense Poems, Songs, Botany, Music, etc.
(illustrated by the author) (Robert John Bush, 1877 [1876]) **£600**
THE JUMBLIES and Other Nonsense Poems, Songs, Botany, Music (illustrated by the author)
(Warne, 1877 [1876]) **£300**
NONSENSE DROLLERIES (contains 'The Owl and the Pussy Cat' and 'The Duck and the Kangaroo';
illustrated by W. Foster) (Warne, 1889) **£175**
A NONSENSE BIRTHDAY BOOK (illustrated by the author) (Warne, [1894]) **£200**
NONSENSE SONGS AND STORIES (introduction by Edward Strachey) (Warne, 1895) **£125**
NONSENSE SONGS AND STORIES (illustrated by L. Leslie Brooke) (Warne, 1900) **£80**
THE PELICAN CHORUS and Other Nonsense Verses (illustrated by L. Leslie Brooke) (Warne, 1900) ..**£125**
QUEERY LEARY NONSENSE. Edited by Lady Strachey (illustrated by the author; introduction by the Earl of Cromer)
(Mills & Boon, 1911) **£85**
THE LEAR COLOURED BIRD BOOK FOR CHILDREN (illustrated by the author; foreword by J. St. Loe Strachey)
(Mills & Boon, [1912]) **£80**
CALICO PIE (illustrated by the author) (Warne, [1924]) **£100**
THE OWL AND THE PUSSY CAT (illustrated by the author) (Warne, [1924]) **£100**
A BOOK OF NONSENSE. Edited by Ernest Rhys (contains works by Edward Lear and various other authors;
illustrated by the authors; issued with dustjacket) (Dent: 'Everyman's Library' series, [1917]) **£60**
THE POBBLE (illustrated by the author; limited to fifty copies) (Hugh Sharp, 1934) **£400**
THE QUANGLE WANGLE'S HAT (illustrated by the author; limited to fifty copies) (Hugh Sharp, 1933)..........**£400**
NONSENSE SONGS AND LAUGHABLE LYRICS (illustrated by the author; limited to 950 copies)
(Peter Pauper Press, US, 1935) **£100**
EDWARD LEAR'S NONSENSE SONGS (illustrated by the author; issued with dustjacket) (Chatto & Windus, 1938)................**£75**
A BOOK OF LEAR. Edited by R.L. Megroz (illustrated by the author; paperback; issued with dustjacket) (Penguin, 1939)........**£20**
EDWARD LEAR'S NONSENSE OMNIBUS (illustrated by the author; issued with dustjacket) (Warne, 1943) **£30**
THE COMPLETE NONSENSE OF EDWARD LEAR. Edited and with an introduction by Holbrook Jackson
(illustrated by the author; issued with dustjacket) (Faber, 1947) **£30**
THE COMPLETE NONSENSE SONGS OF EDWARD LEAR (illustrated by the author;
introduction by Leonard Russell; issued with dustjacket) (Grey Walls Press, 1947) **£20**
EDWARD LEAR'S NONSENSE ALPHABET (illustrated by G.S. Sherwood; issued with dustjacket)
(Collins, [1949]) **£75**
A NONSENSE ALPHABET (illustrated by the author; issued with dustjacket) (HMSO, 1952) **£40**
TEAPOTS AND QUAILS and Other Nonsense. Edited and introduced by Angus Davidson and Philip Hofer
(illustrated by the author; issued with dustjacket) (John Murray, 1953) **£50**
ABC (illustrated by the author; issued with dustjacket) (Constable: 'Young Books' series, 1965)................**£30**

LEWIS, C. Day

**Anglo-Irish author. Born: Cecil Day Lewis in Ireland in 1904. Best known for his adult poetry — he
was appointed Poet Laureate in 1968 — his children's story, *The Otterbury Incident,* has been a firm favourite
since it was first published in 1948. He has also written a number of detective novels under the
pseudonym, 'Nicholas Blake'. Died: 1972.**

Prices are for books in Very Good condition with dustjackets.

DICK WILLOUGHBY (Blackwell, [1933]) **£40**
POETRY FOR YOU: A Book for Boys and Girls on the Enjoyment of Poetry (Blackwell, 1944) **£30**
THE OTTERBURY INCIDENT: A Tale (illustrated by Edward Ardizzone) (Putnam, 1948) **£40**

LEWIS, C.S.

British author. Born: Clive Staples Lewis in Belfast in 1898. Educated at Malvern College and University College, Oxford. In 1925, he was made a Fellow of Magdalen College, remaining there until 1954, when he received a Cambridge professorship. At Oxford, he was a member of the informal group known as the 'Inklings', along with Charles Williams and J.R.R. Tolkien. His Christian faith is evident in his bestselling 'Narnia' series of children's books (1950-56), as well as several non-fiction works for adults (notably *The Screwtape Letters*, 1942). He also wrote a handful of accomplished science fiction novels. His short-lived marriage to the American, Joy Davidman, was the subject of the 1994 film, *Shadowlands*. Died: 1963.

Prices are for books in Very Good condition with dustjackets,

THE LION, THE WITCH AND THE WARDROBE (illustrated by Pauline Baynes) (Bles, 1950) **£6,000**
THE LION, THE WITCH AND THE WARDROBE (illustrated by Michael Hague) (Macmillan, US, 1983).................................. **£60**
PRINCE CASPIAN: THE RETURN TO NARNIA (illustrated by Pauline Baynes) (Bles, 1951) **£1,500**
THE VOYAGE OF THE DAWN TREADER (illustrated by Pauline Baynes) (Bles, 1952)... **£1,500**
THE SILVER CHAIR (illustrated by Pauline Baynes) (Bles, 1953) **£2,000**
THE HORSE AND HIS BOY (illustrated by Pauline Baynes) (Bles, 1954).. **£1,500**
THE MAGICIAN'S NEPHEW (illustrated by Pauline Baynes) (The Bodley Head, 1955) **£800**
THE LAST BATTLE (illustrated by Pauline Baynes) (The Bodley Head, 1956) **£800**

LINDGREN, Astrid

Swedish author. Born: Vimmerby, Sweden, in 1907. Has written over fifty children's books, including adventure and detective stories, but is best known for *Pippi Longstocking* (1954) and its many sequels. In the mid-Forties, she became a children's books editor with the Stockholm publishers, Raban & Sjøren. Died: 2002.

Prices are for books in Very Good condition with dustjackets where applicable.

PIPPI LONGSTOCKING (illustrated by Richard Kennedy; translated by Edna Harup) (OUP, 1954) **£125**
PIPPI GOES ABROAD (illustrated by Richard Kennedy; translated by Marianne Turner) (OUP, 1956) **£100**
PIPPI IN THE SOUTH SEAS (illustrated by Richard Kennedy; translated by Marianne Turner) (OUP, 1957)............................... **£85**

Five of the seven first editions which make up C.S. Lewis's 'Narnia' books.

NORIKO-SAN GIRL OF JAPAN (illustrated by Anna Riwkin-Brick; translated by Leila Bery) (Methuen, 1958).............£60
ERIC AND KARLSSON-ON-THE-ROOF (illustrated by Richard Kennedy; translated by Marianne Turner)
    (OUP, 1958).............£55
SIA LIVES ON KILIMANJARO (photographs by Anna Riwkin-Brick) (Methuen, 1959) £55
CIRCUS CHILD (photographs by Anna Riwkin-Brick) (Methuen, 1960) £40
MY SWEDISH COUSINS (photographs by Anna Riwkin-Brick) (Macmillan, [1960]) £40
MY SWEDISH COUSINS (photographs by Anna Riwkin-Brick) (Methuen: 'Children Everywhere' series, 1961).............£40
RASMUS AND THE TRAMP (illustrated by Eric Palmquist; translated by Gerry Bothmer) (Methuen, 1961).............£40
RASMUS AND THE VAGABOND, RASMUS AND THE TRAMP (Methuen, 1961).............£40
THE TOMTEN (adapted by Astrid Lindgren from a poem by Victor Rydberg; illustrated by Harald Wiberg)
    (Constable, 1962).............£40
KATI IN ITALY (illustrated by Daniel Dupuy) (Brockhampton Press, 1962) £40
DIRK LIVES IN HOLLAND (with Anna Riwken-Brick) (Methuen: 'Children Everywhere' series, 1963).............£20
MARKO LIVES IN YUGOSLAVIA (with Anna Riwken-Brick) (Methuen: 'Children Everywhere' series, 1963).............£20
MADICKEN (illustrated by Ilon Wikland; translated by Marianne Turner) (OUP, 1963).............£25
THE SIX BULLERBY CHILDREN (illustrated by Ilon Wikland; translated by Evelyn Ramsden) (Methuen, 1963).............£20
CHRISTMAS IN THE STABLE (illustrated by Harald Wiberg; translated by Anthea Bell) (Brockhampton Press, 1963).............£20
CHERRY TIME AT BULLERBY (illustrated by Ilon Wikland; translated by Florence Lamborn) (Methuen, 1964).............£20
HAPPY DAYS AT BULLERBY (Methuen, 1964).............£20
CHRISTMAS AT BULLERBY (illustrated by Ilon Wikland) (Methuen, 1964).............£20
KATI IN AMERICA (illustrated by Daniel Dupuy; translated by Marianne Turner) (Brockhampton Press, 1964).............£15
SIMON SMALL MOVES IN (illustrated by Ilon Wikland; translated by Marianne Turner)
    (Burke: 'Read for Fun' series, 1965).............£15
GERDA LIVES IN NORWAY (with Anna Riwken-Brick) (Methuen, 1965).............£15
THE FOX AND THE TOMTEN (after a poem by Karl-Erik Forsslund; illustrated by Harald Wiberg) (Constable, [1966]).............£25
KATI IN PARIS (illustrated by Daniel Dupuy) (Brockhampton Press, 1966) £12
BRENDA HELPS GRANDMOTHER (illustrated by Ilon Wikland; translated by Marianne Helweg)
    (Burke: 'Read for Fun' series, 1966).............£30
A DAY AT BULLERBY (Methuen, 1967).............£20
NOY LIVES IN THAILAND (photographs by Anna Riwkin-Brick) (Methuen: 'Children Everywhere' series, 1967).............£15
SEACROW ISLAND (Oliver & Boyd, 1968).............£15
SCRAP AND THE PIRATES (Oliver & Boyd, 1968).............£15
THE MISCHIEVOUS MARTENS (Methuen, 1968).............£15
MATTI LIVES IN FINLAND (photographs by Anna Riwkin-Brick) (Methuen: 'Children Everywhere' series, 1969).............£15
LOTTA LEAVES HOME (Methuen, 1969).............£15
LOTTA'S BIKE (Methuen, 1973) £15
EMIL'S PRANKS (Brockhampton Press, 1973) £15
EMIL AND HIS CLEVER PIG (Brockhampton Press, 1974) £15
MY VERY OWN SISTER (Methuen, 1974).............£15
THE BROTHERS LIONHEART (illustrated by Ilon Wikland; translated by John Tate) (Brockhampton Press, 1975).............£15
KARLSSON FLIES AGAIN (Methuen, 1977).............£15
EMIL AND LINA'S BAD TOOTH (Brockhampton Press, 1977).............£15
LOTTA'S CHRISTMAS SURPRISE (Methuen, 1978) £15
MARDIE (Methuen, 1979).............£15
I WANT TO GO TO SCHOOL TOO (Methuen, 1980) £15
THE WORLD'S BEST KARLSON (Methuen, 1980).............£15
THAT'S MY BABY (Methuen, 1980) £15
SPRINGTIME AT BULLERBY (Methuen, 1981) £15
MARDIE TO THE RESCUE (Methuen, 1981).............£15
THE RUNAWAY SLEIGH RIDE (illustrated by Ilon Wikland; laminated boards) (Methuen, 1984) £10
THE ROBBER'S DAUGHTER (illustrated by Ilon Wikland; translated by Patricia Crampton) (Methuen, 1984).............£15
MY NIGHTINGALE IS SINGING (Methuen, 1985).............£15
EMIL'S LITTLE SISTER (Hodder & Stoughton, 1985).............£15
EMIL'S STICKY PROBLEM (Hodder & Stoughton, 1986).............£15
THE DRAGON WITH RED EYES (Methuen, 1986).............£15
THE GHOST OF SKINNY JACK (Methuen, 1988).............£15
LOTTA'S EASTER SURPRISE (illustrated by Ilon Wikland; translated by Patricia Crampton; laminated boards)
    (Raben Strogren, 1991).............£10

LINDSAY, Norman

Australian author-illustrator. Born: 1879. Worked as chief cartoonist of the Sydney *Bulletin*, and wrote
and illustrated several novels, including the works of Dickens and Balzac. He wrote his classic children's
novel, *The Magic Pudding* (1918), as a distraction from the horrors of the First World War, later dismissing
it as a "little bundle of piffle". A follow-up, *The Flyaway Highway* (1936), was less successful. Died: 1969.

Prices are for books in Very Good condition with dustjackets.

THE MAGIC PUDDING: The Adventures of Bunyip Bluegum (illustrated by the author) (Sydney, 1918) £2,000
THE MAGIC PUDDING (Angus & Robertson, Sydney, 1930).............£150
THE MAGIC PUDDING (Hamish Hamilton, 1936) £75
THE FLYAWAY HIGHWAY (Angus & Robertson, Sydney, 1936).............£75

LINGARD, Joan

Scottish author. Born: Edinburgh, in 1932. She spent her formative years in Belfast, which provided the background for her first book *The Twelfth of July* (1970). Awarded the West German Buxtehuder Bulle in 1986 for *Across the Barricades*, and the Scottish Arts Council Children's Book Award 1999 for *Tom and the Tree House.* She was awarded the MBE in 1998.

Prices are for books in Very Good condition with dustjackets where applicable.

THE TWELFTH DAY OF CHRISTMAS (Hamish Hamilton, 1970)...£40
FRYING AS USUAL (illustrated by Pricilla Clive) (Hamish Hamilton, 1971)..£35
ACROSS THE BARRICADES (Hamish Hamilton, 1972)..£30
INTO EXILE (Hamish Hamilton, 1973)...£30
THE CLEARANCE (Hamish Hamilton, 1974)..£25
THE RESETTLING (Hamish Hamilton, 1975)...£25
A PROPER PLACE (Hamish Hamilton, 1975)...£25
THE PILGRIMAGE (Hamish Hamilton, 1976)...£20
HOSTAGES TO FORTUNE (Hamish Hamilton, 1976)...£20
THE REUNION (Hamish Hamilton, 1977)...£20
SNAKE AMONG THE SUNFLOWERS (Hamish Hamilton, 1977)..£20
THE GOOSEBERRY (Hamish Hamilton, 1978)...£20
THE FILE ON FRAULIEN BERG (Macrae, 1980)..£20
STRANGERS IN THE HOUSE (Hamish Hamilton, 1981)...£20
THE WINTER VISITOR (Hamish Hamilton, 1983)..£15
THE FREEDOM MACHINE (Hamish Hamilton, 1986)..£15
THE GUILTY PARTY (Hamish Hamilton, 1987)...£15
RAGS AND RICHES (Hamish Hamilton, 1988)...£10
THE WOMEN'S HOUSE (Hamish Hamilton, 1989)..£10
TUG OF WAR (Hamish Hamilton, 1989)..£10
GLAD RAGS (Hamish Hamilton, 1990)...£10
SECRETS AND SURPRISES (illustrated by Jacqui Thomas) (Macmillan, 1991).....................................£10
BETWEEN TWO WORLDS (Hamish Hamilton, 1991)..£10
HANDS OFF OUR SCHOOL (Hamish Hamilton, 1992)..£10
NIGHT FIRES (Hamish Hamilton, 1993)..£10
CLEVER CLIVE AND LOOPY LUCY (illustrated by Jacqui Thomas) (Macmillan, 1993)...........................£10
SLOW FLO AND BOOMERANG BILL (illustrated by Jacqui Thomas) (Macmillan, 1994).........................£10
LIZZIE'S LEAVING (Hamish Hamilton, 1995)..£10
SULKY SUZY, JITTERY JACK (Hamish Hamilton)...£10
A SECRET PLACE (Hodder, 1998)...£10
DARK SHADOWS (Hamish Hamilton, 1998)...£10
TOM AND THE TREE HOUSE (illustrated by Paul Howard) (Hodder, 1998)...£10
THE EGG THIEVES (illustrated by Paul Howard) (Hodder, 1999)..£10
NATASHA'S WILL (Hamish Hamilton, 2000) £10
RIVER EYES (Hodder, 2000)..£10

Picture Books

CAN YOU FIND SAMMY THE HAMSTER? (illustrated by Jan Lewis)
  (Walker Books, 1990)   £5
MORAG AND THE LAMB (illustrated by Patricia Casey) (Walker, 1991)...£5

'LITTLE FOLKS' MAGAZINE

British illustrated magazine published by Cassell. Harry Rountree was among the artists who contributed to the series. Bound into half-yearly volumes.

Prices are for bound copies in Very Good condition. Volumes bound in publisher's special pictorial boards sell for more than double these prices.

LITTLE FOLKS 1875-1895 (Vols. 1-42) .... each £40
LITTLE FOLKS 1896-1897 (Vols. 43-46) .... each £50
LITTLE FOLKS 1898 (Vol. 47) £35
LITTLE FOLKS 1898-1903 (Vols. 48-58) .... each £60
LITTLE FOLKS 1904 (Vol. 59) £35
LITTLE FOLKS 1904-1906 (Vols. 60-63) .... each £60
LITTLE FOLKS 1906-1907 (Vols. 64-65) .... each £35
LITTLE FOLKS 1907 (Vol. 66) £50
LITTLE FOLKS 1908 (Vols. 67-68) .... each £35
LITTLE FOLKS 1909 (Vol. 69) £50
LITTLE FOLKS 1909-1915 (Vols. 70-82) .... each £50
LITTLE FOLKS 1916-1933 (Vols. 83-118) .... each £30

LIVELY, Penelope

British author. Born: Penelope Margaret Lively in Cairo in 1933. Educated at St. Anne's College, Oxford. Although best known as an adult novelist — she won the Booker Prize for *Moon Tiger* in 1986 — Penelope Lively began her career writing for children. Her most famous work for young readers is probably *The Ghost of Thomas Kempe* (1973), for which she was awarded the Carnegie Medal.

Prices are for books in Very Good condition with dustjackets.

ASTERCOTE (illustrated by Antony Maitland) (Heinemann, 1970)..£40
THE WHISPERING KNIGHTS (illustrated by Gareth Floyd) (Heinemann, 1971)...............................£35
THE WILD HUNT OF HAGWORTHY (illustrated by Juliet Mozley) (Heinemann, 1971)....................£35
THE DRIFTWAY (Heinemann, 1972)..£35
THE GHOST OF THOMAS KEMPE (illustrated by Anthony Maitland) (Heinemann, 1973).............£30
THE HOUSE IN NORHAM GARDENS (Heinemann, 1974)..£30
GOING BACK (Heinemann, 1975)...£25
BOY WITHOUT A NAME (Heinemann, 1975)...£25
A STITCH IN TIME (Heinemann, 1976)..£25
THE STAINED GLASS WINDOW (illustrated by Michael Pollard) (Abelard-Schuman, 1976)..........£20
FANNY'S SISTER (illustrated by John Lawrence) (Heinemann, 1976)..£20
THE VOYAGE OF QV 66 (illustrated by Harold Jones) (Heinemann, 1978)..................................£20
FANNY AND THE MONSTERS (illustrated by John Lawrence) (Heinemann, 1979).......................£20
FANNY AND THE BATTLE OF POTTER'S PIECE (illustrated by John Lawrence) (Heinemann, 1981)...£20
THE REVENGE OF SAMUEL STOKES (Heinemann, 1981)...£15
UNINVITED GHOSTS and Other Stories (illustrated by John Lawrence) (Heinemann, 1984).........£15
A HOUSE INSIDE OUT (illustrated by David Parkins) (Deutsch, 1987).......................................£12

LOFTING, Hugh

British author-illustrator. Born: Hugh John Lofting in Maidenhead, Berkshire, in 1889. Educated at Massachusetts Institute of Technology and London Polytechnic. Moved to the United States in 1912, where he supported himself by writing for humorous magazines. Joined the Irish Guards in 1916, being invalided out in 1917. His humour and deep compassion — particularly for animals — are evident in *The Story of Doctor Dolittle* (1920) and its many sequels. Died: 1947.

Prices are for books in Very Good condition with dustjackets.

THE STORY OF DOCTOR DOLITTLE (Stokes, US, 1920)..£1,500
THE STORY OF DOCTOR DOLITTLE (illustrated by the author) (Cape, 1922) £350
THE VOYAGES OF DOCTOR DOLITTLE (illustrated by the author) (Stokes, US, 1922) £600
THE VOYAGES OF DOCTOR DOLITTLE (illustrated by the author) (Cape, 1923)..........................£300
DOCTOR DOLITTLE'S POST OFFICE (illustrated by the author) (Stokes, US, [1923])..................£400
DOCTOR DOLITTLE'S POST OFFICE (illustrated by the author) (Cape, 1924) £200
THE STORY OF MRS TUBBS (illustrated by the author) (Stokes, US, 1923)...............................£225
THE STORY OF MRS TUBBS (illustrated by the author) (Cape, 1924) £175
PORRIDGE POETRY (illustrated by the author) (Cape, 1925) £125
DOCTOR DOLITTLE'S CIRCUS (illustrated by the author) (Cape, 1925).....................................£150
DOCTOR DOLITTLE'S ZOO (illustrated by the author) (Cape, 1926)..£125
DOCTOR DOLITTLE'S CARAVAN (illustrated by the author) (Stokes, US, 1926) £150
DOCTOR DOLITTLE'S CARAVAN (illustrated by the author) (Cape, 1927)...................................£125
DOCTOR DOLITTLE'S GARDEN (illustrated by the author) (Cape, 1928)....................................£110
DOCTOR DOLITTLE IN THE MOON (illustrated by the author) (Cape, 1929)................................£125
NOISY NORA (illustrated by the author) (Cape, 1929) £70
THE TWILIGHT OF MAGIC (illustrated by Lois Lenski) (Cape, 1930) £70
DOCTOR DOLITTLE'S RETURN (illustrated by the author) (Stokes, US, 1930).............................£125
GUB GUB'S BOOK (illustrated by the author) (Cape, 1932)...£70
DOCTOR DOLITTLE'S RETURN (illustrated by the author) (Cape, 1933) £100
DOCTOR DOLITTLE'S BIRTHDAY BOOK (Stokes, US, 1935)...£100
TOMMY, TILLY AND MRS TUBBS (illustrated by the author) (Cape, 1937).................................£40
VICTORY FOR THE SLAIN (Cape, 1942)..£40
DOCTOR DOLITTLE AND THE SECRET LAKE (illustrated by the author) (Cape, 1949)..................£125
DOCTOR DOLITTLE AND THE GREEN CANARY (illustrated by the author) (Cape, 1951)................£110
DOCTOR DOLITTLE'S PUDDLEBY ADVENTURES (illustrated by the author) (Cape, 1953)...............£100
DOCTOR DOLITTLE: A TREASURY. Compiled by Olga Fricker (illustrated by the author) (Cape, 1968)...............£40
DOCTOR DOLITTLE AND HIS FRIENDS (illustrated by Leon Jason) (Collins, 1968).......................£12

LONDON, Jack

American author. Born: John Griffith Chaney in San Francisco in 1876. Educated at various schools in Oakland, subsequently entering Berkeley University as a Special Student. Travelled to the Yukon in 1897, his experiences there providing the basis for a number of bestselling stories and novels, two of which — *The Call of the Wild* (1903) and *White Fang* (1905) — have become established children's classics. Died: 1916.

Prices are for books in Very Good condition.

THE CALL OF THE WILD (illustrated by Philip R. Goodwin and Charles Livingston Bull) (Macmillan, US, 1903)..**£1,000**

THE CALL OF THE WILD (illustrated by Philip R. Goodwin and Charles Livingston Bull) (Heinemann, 1903)...**£300**

TALES OF THE FISH PATROL (Macmillan, US, 1905)...**£100**

TALES OF THE FISH PATROL (Heinemann, 1906)...**£75**

WHITE FANG (Macmillan, US, 1905)...**£150**

WHITE FANG (Methuen, 1907)...**£100**

LONE RANGER, The

A selection of rare and collectable books about the Western adventurer, all written by 'Fran Striker'.

Prices are for books in Very Good condition with dustjackets where applicable.

THE LONE RANGER (by Gaylord DuBois; later revised and credited to Fran Striker) (Grosset & Dunlap, US, 1936)..............**£150**

THE LONE RANGER AND THE MYSTERY RANCH (Grosset & Dunlap, US, 1938) **£35**

THE LONE RANGER AND THE GOLD ROBBERY (Grosset & Dunlap, 1939) **£40**

THE LONE RANGER AND THE OUTLAW STRONGHOLD (Grosset and Dunlap, US, 1939) **£150**

THE LONE RANGER AND TONTO (Grosset & Dunlap, US, 1940) **£150**

THE LONE RANGER AT THE HAUNTED GULCH (Grosset & Dunlap, US, 1941)........................**£50**

THE LONE RANGER TRAPS THE SMUGGLERS (Grosset & Dunlap, US, 1942) **£50**

THE LONE RANGER RIDES AGAIN (Grosset & Dunlap, US, 1943) **£25**

THE LONE RANGER RIDES NORTH (Grosset & Dunlap, US, 1946)..**£25**

THE LONE RANGER AND THE SILVER BULLET (Grosset & Dunlap, US, 1947)........................**£40**

THE LONE RANGER ON THE POWDERHORN TRAIL (Grosset & Dunlap, US, 1949)................**£20**

THE LONE RANGER IN WILD HORSE CANYON (Grosset & Dunlap, US, 1950)........................**£25**

THE LONE RANGER WEST OF MAVERICK PASS (Grosset & Dunlap, US, 1951)......................**£25**

THE LONE RANGER'S NEW DEPUTY (Simon & Schuster, US, 1951) **£25**

THE LONE RANGER AT GUNSIGHT MESA (Grosset & Dunlap, US, 1953) **£40**

THE LONE RANGER AND THE BITTER SPRING FEUD (Grosset & Dunlap, US, 1954) **£40**

THE LONE RANGER AND TROUBLE ON THE SANTA FE (Grosset & Dunlap, US, 1955) **£40**

THE LONE RANGER ON THE RED BUTTE TRAIL (Grosset & Dunlap, US, 1956) **£25**

THE LONE RANGER AND THE CODE OF THE WEST (Grosset & Dunlap, US, 1957) **£60**

THE LEGEND OF THE LONE RANGER
(movie novelisation by Gary McCarthy) (paperback; Ballantine Books, US, 1981).........................**£6**

'Big Little Books' *(All issued in laminated pictorial boards)*

THE LONE RANGER AND HIS HORSE SILVER (Whitman, US, 1935)..**£100**

THE LONE RANGER AND THE VANISHING HERD (Whitman, US, 1936) **£100**

THE LONE RANGER AND THE MENACE OF MURDER VALLEY (Whitman, US, 1938)..............**£120**

THE LONE RANGER AND DEAD MEN'S MINE (Whitman, US, 1939) **£120**

THE LONE RANGER AND THE BLACK SHIRT HIGHWAYMAN (Whitman, US, 1939)................**£120**

THE LONE RANGER FOLLOWS THROUGH (Whitman, US, 1941) **£100**

THE LONE RANGER ON THE BARBARY COAST (Whitman, US, 1944) **£100**

THE LONE RANGER AND THE SILVER BULLET (Whitman, US, 1946) **£75**

THE LONE RANGER AND THE SECRET OF SOMBER CANYON (Whitman, US, 1950) **£75**

'Fast Action Story Book' *(All issued in laminated pictorial boards)*

THE LONE RANGER AND THE LOST VALLEY (Whitman, US, 1938) **£50**

'Better Little Books' *(All issued in laminated pictorial boards)*

THE LONE RANGER AND THE RED RENEGADES (Whitman, US, 1939)....................................**£100**

THE LONE RANGER AND THE SECRET WEAPON (Whitman, US, 1943)....................................**£35**

'Little Golden Books' *(All issued in laminated pictorial boards)*

THE LONE RANGER AND TONTO (Whitman, US, 1957) **£20**

THE LONE RANGER AND THE TALKING PONY (Whitman, US, 1958) **£20**

LUCAS, E.V.

British author. Born: Edward Verrall Lucas in Eltham, Kent, in 1868. He acquired much of his education working in a Brighton bookshop. Thereafter he wrote prolifically on a great variety of subjects, including art, literature and travel. He edited the works of Charles and Mary Lamb (1903-35) and a number of books for children, including *Old Fashion Tales* (1905). Died: 1938.

Prices are for books in Very Good condition.

THE SCHOOLBOY'S APPRENTICE (Methuen, 1897)...**£30**

A BOOK OF VERSES FOR CHILDREN. Edited by E.V. Lucas (Grant Richards, 1897)......................**£30**

THE FLAMP, THE AMELIORATOR AND THE SCHOOLBOY'S APPRENTICE (Grant Richards: 'Dumpy Book' No.1, 1897)...**£100**

A CAT BOOK (illustrated by H Officer Smith) (Grant Richards: 'Dumpy Book' No.6, 1897)................**£65**

THE BOOK OF SHOPS (illustrated by F.D. Bedford) (Grant Richards, 1899)...................................**£350**

FOUR AND TWENTY TOILERS (illustrated by F.D. Bedford) (Grant Richards, 1900).......................**£200**

THREE HUNDRED GAMES AND PASTIMES (Grant Richards, 1903)..**£45**

OLD FASHIONED TALES (Wells Gardner, 1905)...**£30**

FORGOTTEN TALES OF LONG AGO (Wells Gardner, 1906) **£30**

RUNAWAYS AND CASTAWAYS (illustrated by F.D. Bedford) (Wells Gardner, 1908)..£50
THE SLOWCOACH: A Story of Roadside Adventure (illustrated by M.V. Wheelhouse) (Wells Gardner, 1910) £75
SWOLLEN-HEADED WILLIAM. Adapted by E.V. Lucas (illustrated by G. Morrow) (Methuen, 1914)....................£60
PLAYTIME & COMPANY: A Book for Children (illustrated by E.H. Shepard) (Methuen, 1925) £100

LYNCH, Patricia

Irish author. Born: Cork, 1898. Her work amalgamates the traditional folktale with the present-day children's story. One of her best-known books is *The Turf-Cutter's Donkey* (1934). Died: 1972.

Prices are for books in Very Good condition with dustjackets where applicable.

THE GREEN DRAGON (illustrated by Dorothy Hardy) (Harrap, 1925)..£55
THE COBBLER'S APPRENTICE (illustrated by Mildred R. Lamb) (Shaylor, 1930).................................£50
KING OF THE TINKERS (illustrated by Katherine C. Lloyd) (Dent, 1938) £40
THE GREY GOOSE OF KILNEVEN (illustrated by John Keating) (Dent, 1939) £40
FIDDLER'S QUEST (illustrated by Isobel Morton-Sale) (Dent, 1941)..£35
LISHEEN AT THE VALLEY FARM and Other Stories (illustrated by Beatrice Salkeld)
    (Gayfield Press, Dublin, 1945)..£30
KNIGHTS OF GOD: Stories of the Irish Saints (illustrated by Alfred E. Kerr) (Hollis & Carter, 1945).............£35
THE MAD O'HARA'S (illustrated by Elizabeth Rivers) (Dent, 1948) £30
STRANGERS AT THE FAIR and Other Stories (illustrated by Eileen Coghlan; paperback) (Penguin, 1949) £12
THE SEVENTH PIG and Other Irish Fairy Tales (illustrated by Jerome Sullivan) (Dent, 1950).....................£30
THE DARK SAILOR OF YOUGHAL (illustrated by Jerome Sullivan) (Dent, 1951)...................................£30
THE BOY AT THE SWINGING LANTERN (illustrated by Joan Kiddell-Monroe) (Dent, 1952)..........................£30
TALES OF IRISH ENCHANTMENT (legends; illustrated by Fergus O'Ryan) (Burn Oates, 1952)........................£30
TALES OF IRISH ENCHANTMENT (legends; illustrated by Fergus O'Ryan) (Clonmore & Reynolds, Dublin, 1952)........£25
DELIA DALY OF GALLOPING GREEN (illustrated by Joan Kiddell-Monroe) (Dent, 1953)............................£30
ORLA OF BURREN (illustrated by Joan Kiddell-Monroe) (Dent, 1954)..£30
TINKER BOY (illustrated by Harry Kernoff) (Dent, 1955)..£30
THE BOOKSHOP ON THE QUAY (illustrated by Peggy Fortnum) (Dent, 1956)......................................£30
FIONA LEAPS THE BONFIRE (illustrated by Peggy Fortnum) (Dent, 1957) £30
COBBLER'S LUCK (illustrated by Christopher Brooker) (Burke, 1957)..£30
THE OLD BLACK SEA CHEST : A Story of Bantry Bay (illustrated by Peggy Fortnum) (Dent, 1958)................£30
THE STONE HOUSE AT KILGOBBIN (illustrated by Christopher Brooker) (Burke, 1959)...........................£30
THE RUNAWAYS (Blackwell, 1959) £25
JINNY THE CHANGELING (illustrated by Peggy Fortnum) (Dent, 1959)..£30
THE BLACK GOAT OF SLIEVEMORE and Other Irish Tales (revised edition of 'The Seventh Pig and
    Other Irish Fairy Tales') (Dent, 1959)..£25
SALLY FROM CORK (illustrated by Elizabeth Grant) (Dent, 1960)...£20
THE LOST FISHERMAN OF CARRIGMOR (illustrated by Christopher Brooker) (Burke, 1960) £20
RYAN'S FORT (illustrated by Elizabeth Grant) (Dent, 1961)...£20
THE LONGEST WAY ROUND (illustrated by D.G. Valentine) (Burke, 1961).......................................£20
THE GOLDEN CADDY (illustrated by Juliette Palmer) (Dent, 1962)..£20
THE HOUSE BY LOUGH NEAGH (illustrated by Nina Ross) (Dent, 1963) £20
HOLIDAY AT ROSQUIN (illustrated by Mary Shillabeer) (Dent, 1964)..£20
THE TWISTED KEY and Other Stories (illustrated by Joan Kiddell-Monroe) (Harrap, 1964).....................£20
MONA OF THE ISLE (illustrated by Mary Shillabeer) (Dent, 1965)..£20
BACK OF BEYOND (illustrated by Susannah Holden) (Dent, 1966)..£20
THE KERRY CARAVAN (illustrated by James Hunt) (Dent, 1967)..£20

'Turf-Cutter's Donkey' Books

THE TURF-CUTTER'S DONKEY: An Irish Story of Mystery and Adventure (illustrated by Jack B. Yeats)
    (Dent, 1934)...£150
THE TURF-CUTTER'S DONKEY GOES VISITING: The Story of an Island Holiday
    (illustrated by George Altendorf) (Dent, 1935) £50
LONG EARS: The Story of a Little Grey Donkey (illustrated by Joan Kiddell-Monroe) (Dent, 1943)..............£30
THE TURF-CUTTER'S DONKEY KICKS UP HIS HEELS (illustrated by Eileen Coghlan) (Dutton, US, 1939)..............£45
THE TURF-CUTTER'S DONKEY KICKS UP HIS HEELS (illustrated by Eileen Coghlan)
    (Browne & Nolan, Dublin, 1946)...£40

'Brogeen' Books

BROGEEN OF THE STEPPING STONES (illustrated by Alfred Kerr) (Kerr-Cross Publishing, 1947)..................£40
BROGEEN FOLLOWS THE MAGIC TUNE (illustrated by Peggy Fortnum) (Burke, 1952) £30
BROGEEN AND THE GREEN SHOES (illustrated by Peggy Fortnum) (Burke, 1953)..................................£30
BROGEEN AND THE BRONZE LIZARD (illustrated by Grace Golden) (Burke, 1954) £30
BROGEEN AND THE PRINCESS OF SHEEN (illustrated by Christopher Brooker) (Burke, 1955)......................£30
BROGEEN AND THE LOST CASTLE (illustrated by Christopher Brooker) (Burke, 1956)............................£30
BROGEEN AND THE BLACK ENCHANTER (illustrated by Christopher Brooker) (Burke, 1958)........................£30
BROGEEN AND THE LITTLE WIND (illustrated by Beryl Sanders) (Burke, 1962)..................................£30
BROGEEN AND THE RED FEZ (illustrated by Beryl Sanders) (Burke, 1963)......................................£30
GUESTS AT THE BEECH TREE: A Brogeen Story (illustrated by Beryl Sanders) (Burke, 1964) £30

M

MACDONALD, George

Scottish author. Born: Huntly, Aberdeenshire, in 1824. Won a bursary to King's College, Aberdeen. Moved to London in 1845, subsequently serving as a Congregationalist minister before becoming Professor of English Literature at Bedford College. Began his literary career with the dramatic poem, *Within and Without* (1855), and the adult fairy tale, *Phantastes* (1858), his earliest children's stories being collected as *Dealings with the Fairies* in 1867. His best-known works, *At the Back of the North Wind* (1871) and *The Princess and the Goblin* (1872), were both initially serialised in Alexander Strahan's *Good Words for the Young*. These were followed by many more children's works, notably *The Princess and Curdie* (1883). Mark Twain, John Ruskin, Lewis Carroll and William Morris (who bought Kelmscott House in Hammersmith from MacDonald) were amongst his friends. Died: 1905.

Prices are for books in Very Good condition with dustjackets where applicable.

DEALINGS WITH THE FAIRIES (illustrated by Arthur Hughes) (Strahan, 1867) £2,000
AT THE BACK OF THE NORTH WIND (illustrated by Arthur Hughes) (Strahan, 1871) £2,000
AT THE BACK OF THE NORTH WIND (illustrated by Jessie Willcox Smith) (David McKay, US, 1920)................. £250
AT THE BACK OF THE NORTH WIND (illustrated by E.H. Shepard; issued with dustjacket) (Dent, 1956)........... £60
AT THE BACK OF THE NORTH WIND (illustrated by Charles Mozley; issued with dustjacket) (Nonesuch Press, 1963).......... £45
RANALD BANNERMAN'S BOYHOOD (illustrated by Arthur Hughes) (Strahan, 1871) £700
RANALD BANNERMAN'S BOYHOOD (illustrated by Arthur Hughes) (Blackie, [1890]) £50
RANALD BANNERMAN'S BOYHOOD (illustrated by M.V. Wheelhouse) (Blackie, [1912]) £40
THE PRINCESS AND THE GOBLIN (illustrated by Arthur Hughes) (Strahan, 1872) £1,500
THE PRINCESS AND THE GOBLIN (illustrated by Arthur Hughes and Helen Stratton) (Blackie, 1911) £60
THE PRINCESS AND THE GOBLIN (illustrated by Jessie Willcox Smith) (David McKay, US, 1921).................. £200
THE PRINCESS AND THE GOBLIN (illustrated by Charles Folkard; issued with dustjacket) (Dent, 1949)........ £50
GUTTA PERCHA WILLIE: THE WORKING GENIUS (illustrated by Arthur Hughes) (Henry S. King, 1873).......... £500
GUTTA PERCHA WILLIE: THE WORKING GENIUS (as 'The History of Gutta Percha Willie') (Blackie, 1887)........ £50
THE WISE WOMAN: A PARABLE (Strahan, 1875) £200
THE WISE WOMAN (as 'The Lost Princess, or The Wise Woman'; illustrated by A.G. Walker) (Wells Gardner, 1895) £100
THE LOST PRINCESS (as 'The Lost Princess'; illustrated by 'BB'; issued with dustjacket) (Dent, 1967)............ £50
THE PRINCESS AND CURDIE (illustrated by James Allen) (Chatto & Windus, 1883 [1882])................................ £400
THE PRINCESS AND CURDIE (illustrated by Helen Stratton) (Blackie, 1911) £35
THE PRINCESS AND CURDIE (illustrated by Charles Folkard; issued with dustjacket) (Dent, 1949) £40
THE PRINCESS AND CURDIE (illustrated by Peter Warne; issued with dustjacket) (Ark Publishing, 1979) £25
CROSS PURPOSE and THE SHADOWS (illustrated by H.M. Brock) (Blackie, [1886]) £30
THE LIGHT PRINCESS and Other Fairy Stories (illustrated by L. Leslie Brooke) (Blackie, [1890])................... £125
THE LIGHT PRINCESS (illustated by F.D. Bedford) (Blackie, [c.1926]) £40
THE LIGHT PRINCESS and Other Tales of Fantasy (contains all eight of George MacDonald's short fairy stories; introduction by Roger Lancelyn Green; illustrated by Arthur Hughes; issued with dustjacket) (Gollancz, 1961)................... £40
THE LIGHT PRINCESS (illustrated by Maurice Sendak; issued with dustjacket) (The Bodley Head, 1969) £50
THE GOLDEN KEY (illustrated by Maurice Sendak; afterword by W.H. Auden; issued with dustjacket) (The Bodley Head, 1972) £40

MARCHANT, Bessie

British author. Born: Elizabeth Marchant in Petham, Kent, in 1862. Educated at Petham County Primary School. Moved to London while in her early twenties, where she taught at a Baptist school. Hugely prolific author of stories for both girls and boys, many of them set overseas, despite the fact that Marchant herself never left Britain. Died: 1941.

Prices are for books in Very Good condition.

BROKEN BARRIERS (Toulson, 1889) £45
UNDER CLEARER SKIES (James Knapp, 1892)... £45
THE OLD HOUSE BY THE WATER (Religious Tract Society, [1894]) £25
IN THE CRADLE OF THE NORTH WIND: A Tale (W.P. Nimmo, 1896).. £30
WEASEL TIM: A Tale (Robert Culley, [1896]).. £40
YUPPIE: The Land Beyond the Flood (Robert Culley, [1898]) £25
THE BONDED THREE: A Tale (illustrated by William Rainey) (Blackie, [1898])... £30
AMONG THE TORCHES OF THE ANDES: A Tale (W.P. Nimmo, 1898)... £20
THE HUMBLING OF MARK LESTER (Simpkin Marshall, [1899]) £35
THE RAJAH'S DAUGHTER, or The Half-Moon Girl (Partridge, 1899).. £25
TELL-TALE-TIT (Robert Culley, [1899]) £35
WINNING HIS WAY: A Story for Boys (Gall & Inglis, [1899]) £20
CECILY FROME, THE CAPTAIN'S DAUGHTER (W.P. Nimmo, [1900]) £15
THE GHOST OF ROCK GRANGE (SPCK, [1900]) £40
THE GIRL CAPTIVES: A Story of the Indian Frontier (illustrated by William Rainey) (Blackie, 1900 [1899]) £15
IN THE TOILS OF THE TRIBESMEN: A Story of the Indian Frontier (Gall & Inglis, [1900]).............................. £25

*Two Charles Folkard plates from the 1949 edition of **The Princess and the Goblin** by George MacDonald. The book is worth £50 today.*

Canada provided the setting for A Daughter of the Ranges, a typically stirring 'outback' tale of girlish pluck and clean living!

With one or two exceptions, later Bessie Marchant titles like this one are worth between £10 and £25 in Very Good condition.

THE DEBT OF THE DAMERALS (Clarke, 1905)..£15
HOPE'S TRYST: A Story of the Siberian Frontier (Blackie, 1905) £20
THE MYSTERIOUS CITY (illustrated by W.S. Stacey) (SPCK, [1905])...£30
QUEEN OF SHINDY FLAT (illustrated by Charles Sheldon) (Wells Gardner, 1905).......................................£30
ATHABASCA BILLI: A Tale of the Far West (illustrated by H. Piffard) (SPCK, [1906])..................................£20
A DAUGHTER OF THE RANGES: A Story of Western Canada (illustrated by A.A. Dixon) (Blackie, 1906 [1905])....................£20
KENEALY'S RIDE: A Tale of the Pampas (Gall & Inglis, [1906])..£20
MAISIE'S DISCOVERY (illustrated by R. Tod) (Collins, [1906])..£30
UNCLE GREG'S MANHUNT: A Story of Texan Horse Thieves (Robert Culley, [1906]) £30
DARLING OF SANDY POINT (illustrated by Harold Piffard) (SPCK, [1907])..£15
A GIRL OF THE FORTUNATE ISLES (illustrated by Paul Hardy) (Blackie, 1907 [1906]) £15
JULIETTE, THE MAIL CARRIER (illustrated by R. Tod) (Collins, [1907]) £25
THE MYSTERY OF THE SILVER RUN (Wells Gardner, 1907)..£15
NO ORDINARY GIRL: A Story of Central America (illustrated by Frances Ewan) (Blackie, 1908 [1907])......£15
THE APPLE LADY (illustrated by G. Soper) (Collins, [1908])...£25
ROLF THE REBEL (illustrated by W.S. Stacey) (SPCK, [1908]) £15
SISTERS OF SILVER CREEK: A Story of Western Canada (illustrated by Robert Hope) (Blackie, 1908 [1907])....................£15
A COURAGEOUS GIRL: A Story of Uruguay (illustrated by William Rainey) (Blackie, 1909 [1908])..............£30
DAUGHTERS OF THE DOMINION: A Story of the Canadian Frontier (Blackie, 1909 [1908]).......................£15
AN ISLAND HEROINE (illustrated by W.H. Margetson) (Collins, [1909])..£15
JENNY'S ADVENTURE, or On the Trial for Klondyke (Butcher, [1909])...£15
THE ADVENTURES OF PHYLLIS: A Story of the Argentine (illustrated by F. Whiting) (Cassell, [1910]) £15
A COUNTESS FROM CANADA (illustrated by Cyrus Cuneo) (Blackie, 1910) £20
THE BLACK COCKATOO: A Story of Western Australia (illustrated by Lancelot Speed) (Religious Tract Society, [1910]) £35
THE DEPUTY BOSS: A Tale of British Honduras (illustrated by Oscar Wilson) (SPCK, [1910])....................£20
MOLLY OF ONE TREE BEND: A Story of a Girl's Heroism on the Veldt (Butcher, [1910]).............................£25
THREE GIRLS IN MEXICO: A Tale of Life in the Interior (illustrated by William Rainey) (Blackie, 1910) £25
A COUNTESS FROM CANADA: A Story of Life in the Back-woods (illustrated by Cyrus Cuneo) (Blackie, 1911)..................£15
GRETA'S DOMAIN: A Tale of Chiloé (illustrated by William Rainey) (Blackie, 1911) £15
REDWOOD RANCH (illustrated by Harold Piffard) (SPCK, 1911) £15
THE FERRY HOUSE GIRLS: An Australian Story (illustrated by W.R.S. Scott) (Blackie, 1912)....................£35

Like so many of Marchant's novels, **A Girl of Distinction** *was set overseas, even though the author never left Britain!*

A GIRL OF DISTINCTION: A Tale of the Karroo (illustrated by William Rainey) (Blackie, 1912)..£25
HIS GREAT SURRENDER (illustrated by Gordon Browne) (SPCK, [1912])...£15
A PRINCESS OF SERVIA: A Story of To-Day (illustrated by William Rainey) (Blackie, [1912])...............................£40
SIBYL OF ST PIERRE: A Tale of Martinique (illustrated by William Rainey) (Wells Gardner, 1912).........................£25
THE WESTERN SCOUT (illustrated by W.S. Stacey) (SPCK, 1912)...£20
A GIRL OF THE NORTHLAND (illustrated by N. Tenison) (Hodder & Stoughton, 1913)...£15

MARCHANT, Bessie

THE YOUNGEST SISTER: A Tale of Manitoba (illustrated by William Rainey) (Blackie, 1913 [1912]))..................................£20
THE ADVENTUROUS SEVEN: Their Hazardous Undertaking (illustrated by W.R.S. Scott) (Blackie, [1914]))..................£15
A MYSTERIOUS INHERITANCE: A Story of Adventure in British Columbia (Blackie, [1914]).....................................£15
HELEN OF THE BLACK MOUNTAIN: A Story of Montenegro (Blackie, [1914])..£15
THE HEROINE OF THE RANCH: A Story of Tierra Del Fuego (illustrated by Cyrus Cuneo) (Blackie, 1914) £15
THE LOYALTY OF HESTER HOPE: A Story of British Columbia (illustrated by William Rainey)
    (Blackie, [1914])..£25
DENVER WILSON'S DOUBLE: A Story of New Mexico (illustrated by W. Douglas Almond) (Blackie, [1915]) £15
A GIRL AND A CARAVAN: The Story of Irma's Quest in Persia (Blackie, [1915])..£25
MOLLY ANGEL'S ADVENTURES: A Story of Belgium under German Occupation (Blackie, [1915]).........................£30
A GIRL MUNITION WORKER (Blackie, [1916])...£25
JOYCE HARRINGTON'S TRUST: An Argentine Mystery (Blackie, 1916 [1915])...£20
THE UNKNOWN ISLAND: A Tale of Adventure in the Seychelles (Blackie, [1916]).......................................£15
A CANADIAN FARM MYSTERY, or Pam the Pioneer (Blackie, 1917 [1916])...£15
A V.A.D. IN SALONICA: A Tale of a Girl's Work in The Great War (Blackie, [1917])...................................£30
CYNTHIA WINS: A Tale of the Rocky Mountains (illustrated by John E. Sutcliffe) (Blackie, [1918]) £20
A DANGEROUS MISSION: A Tale of Russia in Revolution (illustrated by Wal Paget) (Blackie, [1918]).................£20
THE GOLD-MARKED CHARM: The Story of a Mystery in the Blue Nile Country
    (Blackie, 1918)...£15
LOIS IN CHARGE, or A Girl of Grit: The Story of a Plantation in Brazil
    (illustrated by Cyrus Cuneo) (Blackie, [1918])..£20
NORAH TO THE RESCUE: A Story of the Philippines (Blackie, [1919])...£15
A TRANSPORT GIRL IN FRANCE (Blackie, [1919])...£15
SALLY MAKES GOOD: A Story of Tasmania (illustrated by Leo Bates) (Blackie, [1920])...............................£25
THE GIRL OF THE PAMPAS (Blackie, [1921])...£15
ISLAND BORN: A Tale of Hawaii (illustrated by Leo Bates) (Blackie, [1921]).......................................£30
THE MISTRESS OF PURITY GAP (Cassell, [1921])..£15
HARRIET GOES A-ROAMING (Blackie, [1922])...£10
THE FORTUNES OF PRUE (Ward Lock, 1923) £10
RACHEL OUT WEST (illustrated by Henry Coller) (Blackie, [1923])...£10
A BID FOR SAFETY (Ward Lock, 1924)...£10
DIANA CARRIES ON (Nelson, [1924])..£10
THE MOST POPULAR GIRL IN THE SCHOOL (Partridge, [1924])..£10
SYLVIA'S SECRET (illustrated by W.E. Wightman) (Blackie, [1924])..£10
HER OWN KIN (Blackie, [1925])..£10
TO SAVE HER SCHOOL (illustrated by H.L. Bacon) (Partridge, 1925)...£15
BY HONOUR BOUND (Nelson, [1925])..£15
DELMAYNE'S ADVENTURES (Collins, 1925) £15
COUSIN PETER'S MONEY (Sheldon, 1926) £15
DI THE DAUNTLESS (illustrated by W.E. Wightman) (Blackie, [1926])..£10
MILLICENT GWENT, SCHOOLGIRL (Warne, [1926])..£15
MOLLY IN THE WEST (illustrated by F.E. Hiley) (Blackie, [1927]) £10
THE TWO NEW GIRLS (Warne, [1927])..£12
GLENALLAN'S DAUGHTERS (Nelson, [1928])..£15
LUCIE'S LUCK (illustrated by F.E. Hiley) (Blackie, [1928])...£10
THE BANNISTER TWINS (illustrated by E. Brier) (Nelson, [1929])...£10
HILDA HOLDS ON (illustrated by F.E. Hiley) (Blackie, [1929])...£12
HOW NELL SCORED (Nelson, [1929])..£10
LAUREL THE LEADER (Blackie, [1930])..£12
CUCKOO OF THE LOG RAFT (Newnes, [1931])...£10
TWO ON THEIR OWN (illustrated by F.E. Hiley) (Blackie, [1931])..£10
THE HOMESTEADER GIRL (illustrated by V. Cooley) (Nelson, [1932])...£15
JANE FILLS THE BREACH (illustrated by F.E. Hiley) (Blackie, [1932])..£10
SILLA THE SEVENTH (Newnes, 1932) £10
DEBORAH'S FIND (illustrated by Henry Coller) (Blackie, [1933])..£10
THE COURAGE OF KATRINE (Warne, 1934)...£10
HOSEA'S GIRL (Hutchinson, 1934) £15
LESBIA'S LITTLE BLUNDER (Warne, [1934])...£10
ERICA'S RANCH (Blackie, [1934])..£10
ANNA OF THE TENTERFORD (illustrated by F.E. Hiley) (Blackie, [1935])...£10
FELICITY'S FORTUNE (Blackie, [1936])..£10
NANCY AFLOAT (Nelson, [1936])..£12
A DAUGHTER OF THE DESERT (Blackie, 1937) £10
TOMMY'S TREK (with 'Peter's Sparrow' by Mary Burns) (Blackie, [1937])...£10
MISS WILMER'S GANG (illustrated by J.A. May) (Blackie, 1938)...£10
WAIFS OF WOLLAMOO: A Story for Girls (Warne, [1938])...£25
A GIRL UNDAUNTED, or The Honey Queen (illustrated by J.A. May) (Blackie, 1939).................................£10
MARTA THE MAINSTAY (Blackie, [1940])..£12
TWO OF A KIND (Blackie, 1941)..£10
THE TRIUMPHS OF THREE (Blackie, [1942])...£10

MARRYAT, Captain

British author. Born: Frederick Marryat in London in 1792. Entered the Royal Navy in 1806, seeing action on board Lord Cochrane's frigate, 'H.M.S. Impérieuse', and subsequently serving in the American war of 1812 and on St. Helena, where he made a death-bed sketch of Napoleon. His first book, a *Code of Signals* for merchant ships, was published in 1817, and was followed by a *Suggestion for the Abolition of Impressment* (1822) and many adventure novels. These included several for children, notably *Masterman Ready* (1841-42) and *The Children of the New Forest* (1847). Settled in Langham, Norfolk, where he pursued a number of disastrous and expensive experiments in agriculture. Died: 1848.

Prices are for books in Good condition.

THE NAVAL OFFICER, or Scenes and Adventures in the Life of Frank Mildmay
(anonymous; three volumes) (Colburn, 1829)..the set **£350**
THE KING'S OWN (anonymous; three volumes) (Colburn & Bentley, 1830).................................the set **£225**
NEWTON FORSTER, or The Merchant Service (anonymous; three volumes) (James Cochrane, 1832) ....the set **£200**
PETER SIMPLE (anonymous; three volumes) (Saunders & Otley, 1834) ....the set **£400**
PETER SIMPLE (second edition; three volumes; reset text) (Saunders & Otley, 1834)......................the set **£275**
JACOB FAITHFUL (anonymous; three volumes) (Saunders & Otley, 1834)..................................the set **£400**
JACOB FAITHFUL (illustrated by R.W. Buss; three volumes) (Saunders & Otley, 1837)......................the set **£400**
JACOB FAITHFUL (illustrated by R.W. Buss; introduction by George Saintsbury; limited to 750 copies; two volumes)
(Constable, 1928)..the set **£175**
THE PACHA OF MANY TALES (short stories; anonymous; three volumes) (Saunders & Otley, 1835) ....the set **£185**
THE PIRATE and THE THREE CUTTERS (novellas; one volume) (Longmans Green, 1836)......................**£150**
JAPHET IN SEARCH OF A FATHER (anonymous; three volumes) (Saunders & Otley, 1836)....................the set **£225**
MR MIDSHIPMAN EASY (anonymous; three volumes) (Saunders & Otley, 1836) ....the set **£350**
SNARLEYYOW, or The Dog Fiend (anonymous; three volumes) (Colburn, 1837)...............................the set **£225**
THE PHANTOM SHIP (three volumes) (Colburn, 1839)..the set **£475**
POOR JACK (twelve monthly parts; octavo) (Longmans Green, January-December 1840)......................the set **£350**
POOR JACK (first edition in book form; illustrated by Clarkson Stanfield) (Longmans Green, 1840)....................**£225**
MASTERMAN READY, or The Wreck of the Pacific. Written for Young People (illustrated by the author; three volumes)
(Longmans Green, 1841-1842)..the set **£350**
JOSEPH RUSHBROOK, or The Poacher (anonymous; three volumes) (Longmans Green, 1841) ....the set **£175**
PERCIVAL KEENE (three volumes) (Colburn, 1842)...the set **£175**
NARRATIVE OF THE TRAVELS AND ADVENTURES OF MONSIEUR VIOLET IN CALIFORNIA, SONORA,
AND WESTERN TEXAS (three volumes) (Longmans Green, 1843)..the set **£700**
NARRATIVE OF THE TRAVELS AND ADVENTURES OF MONSIEUR VIOLET... (as 'The Travels and Romantic Adventures
of Monsieur Violet, among the Snake Indians and Wild Tribes of the Great Western Prairies') (Longmans Green, 1843)..**£350**
THE SETTLERS IN CANADA. Written for Young People (two volumes) (Longmans Green, 1844)..................the set **£175**
THE MISSION, or Scenes in Africa. Written for Young People (two volumes) (Longmans Green, 1845)..................the set **£200**
THE PRIVATEERSMAN, or One Hundred Years Ago (two volumes) (Longmans Green, 1846) ....the set **£175**
THE CHILDREN OF THE NEW FOREST (illustrated by Frank Marryat; two volumes) (Hurst, [1847]) ....the set **£900**
THE LITTLE SAVAGE (two volumes) (Hurst, 1848-49) ....the set **£200**

MARTIN, J.P.

British author. Born: Scarborough, Yorkshire, 1880. Became a Methodist minister in 1902. His stories belong to the distinctive English tradition of high-spirited fantasy, his six 'Uncle' books developing a struggle for supremacy between virtue and villainy. Died: 1966.

Prices are for books in Very Good condition with dustjackets.

UNCLE (illustrated by Quentin Blake) (Cape, 1964) **£50**
UNCLE CLEANS UP (illustrated by Quentin Blake) (Cape, 1965) **£50**
UNCLE AND HIS DETECTIVE (illustrated by Quentin Blake) (Cape, 1966) **£45**
UNCLE AND HIS TREACLE TROUBLE (illustrated by Quentin Blake) (Cape, 1967) **£45**
UNCLE AND CLAUDIUS THE CAMEL (illustrated by Quentin Blake) (Cape, 1969)............................**£45**
UNCLE AND THE BATTLE FOR BADGERTOWN (illustrated by Quentin Blake) (Cape, 1973)....................**£45**

MASEFIELD, John

British author. Born: 1878. Poet Laureate from 1930 to 1967, and — like his three successors (C. Day Lewis, John Betjeman and Ted Hughes) — a very popular writer for children. His most collectable fantasies are *The Midnight Folk* (1927) and *The Box of Delights* (1935), both of which have been dramatised on radio and TV. Died: 1967.

Prices are for books in Very Good condition (with dustjackets after 1920).

LOST ENDEAVOUR (Wells Gardner, 1910)...**£60**
MARTIN HYDE (Wells Gardner, 1910)...**£60**
A BOOK OF DISCOVERIES (Wells Gardner, 1910)...**£45**
JIM DAVIS (Wells Gardner, 1911)..**£100**
THE MIDNIGHT FOLK (Heinemann, 1927)..**£60**
THE MIDNIGHT FOLK (illustrated by Rowland Hilder) (Heinemann, 1931) **£120**
THE BIRD OF DAWNING (Heinemann, 1933)...**£50**
THE BOX OF DELIGHTS (Heinemann, 1935)...**£150**
DEAD NED (Heinemann, 1938)...**£50**
LIVE AND KICKING NED (Heinemann, 1939)..**£50**

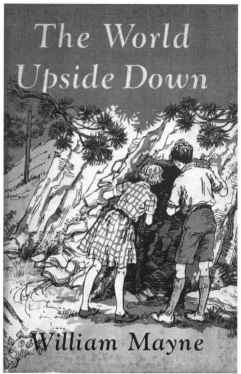

The first of J.P. Martin's six 'Uncle' books is now worth £50 in Very Good condition with the Quentin Blake dustjacket.

*The same amount should secure a Very Good first of William Mayne's second book, **The World Turned Upside Down**.*

MAYNE, William

British author. Born: William Cyril Mayne in Hull in 1928. Educated at Canterbury Cathedral Choir School, subsequently working for the BBC and as a teacher. His first novel was published in 1953, since when he has written over 100 more. Lectured at Deakin University, Geelong, in 1976/77, and in 1979 was granted a one-year Fellowship in Creative Writing at Rolle College in Exmouth. He lives in Yorkshire.

Prices are for books in Very Good condition with dustjackets where applicable.

FOLLOW THE FOOTPRINTS (illustrated by Shirley Hughes) (OUP, 1953)...£30
THE WORLD UPSIDE DOWN (illustrated by Shirley Hughes) (OUP, 1954) £50
A SWARM IN MAY (illustrated by C. Walter Hodges) (OUP, 1955) £45
THE MEMBER FOR THE MARSH (illustrated by Lynton Lamb) (OUP, 1956) £45
CHORISTERS' CAKE (illustrated by C. Walter Hodges) (OUP, 1956)...£45
THE BLUE BOAT (illustrated by Geraldine Spence) (OUP, 1957)...£35
A GRASS ROPE (illustrated by Lynton Lamb) (OUP, 1957) £40
THE LONG NIGHT (illustrated by 'BB') (Blackwell, 1957 [1958])..£125
UNDERGROUND ALLEY (illustrated by Marcia Lane Foster) (OUP, 1958)..£30
THE GOBBLING BILLY (written under the pseudonym 'Dynely James'; with Dick Caesar) (Gollancz, 1959) £45
THE GOBBLING BILLY (Brockhampton Press, 1969)...£15
THIRTEEN O'CLOCK (illustrated by 'BB') (Blackwell, 1959)...£50
THE THUMBSTICK (illustrated by Tessa Theobald) (OUP, 1959) £25
THE ROLLING SEASON (illustrated by Christopher Brooker) (OUP, 1960)..£25
CATHEDRAL WEDNESDAY (illustrated by C. Walter Hodges) (OUP, 1960)...£25
THE FISHING PARTY (illustrated by Christopher Brooker) (Hamish Hamilton, 1960) £25
SUMMER VISITORS (illustrated by William Stobbs) (OUP, 1961)..£25
THE CHANGELING (illustrated by Victor G. Ambrus) (OUP, 1961)...£25
THE GLASS BALL (illustrated by Janet Duchesne) (Hamish Hamilton, 1961)...£25
THE LAST BUS (illustrated by Margery Gill) (Hamish Hamilton, 1962)..£25
THE TWELVE DANCERS (illustrated by Lynton Lamb) (Hamish Hamilton, 1962)..£25
THE MAN FROM THE NORTH POLE (illustrated by Prudence Seward) (Hamish Hamilton, 1963)...........................£25
ON THE STEPPING STONES (illustrated by Prudence Seward) (Hamish Hamilton, 1963) £25

WORDS AND MUSIC (illustrated by Lynton Lamb) (Hamish Hamilton, 1963)...**£25**
PLOT NIGHT (illustrated by Janet Duchesne) (Hamish Hamilton, 1963)..**£25**
A PARCEL OF TREES (illustrated by Margery Gill; paperback) (Puffin, 1963) **£10**
WATER BOATMAN (illustrated by Anne Linton) (Hamish Hamilton, 1964)...**£20**
WHISTLING RUFUS (illustrated by Raymond Briggs) (Hamish Hamilton, 1964) **£25**
SAND (illustrated by Margery Gill) (Hamish Hamilton, 1964)...**£20**
A DAY WITHOUT WIND (illustrated by Margery Gill) (Hamish Hamilton, 1964)................................**£20**
THE BIG WHEEL AND THE LITTLE WHEEL (illustrated by Janet Duchesne) (Hamish Hamilton, 1965) **£20**
PIG IN THE MIDDLE (illustrated by Mary Russon) (Hamish Hamilton, 1965)..................................**£20**
NO MORE SCHOOL (illustrated by Peter Warner) (Hamish Hamilton, 1965) **£20**
DORMOUSE TALES (five books: 'The Lost Thimble', 'The Steam Roller', 'The Picnic', 'The Football' and
   'The Tea Party'; written under the pseudonym 'Charles Molin'; illustrated by Leslie Wood)
   (Hamish Hamilton, 1966)... each **£10**
EARTHFASTS (Hamish Hamilton, 1966) **£20**
ROOFTOPS (illustrated by Mary Russon) (Hamish Hamilton, 1966) **£20**
THE OLD ZION (illustrated by Margery Gill) (Hamish Hamilton, 1966) **£20**
THE BATTLEFIELD (illustrated by Mary Russon) (Hamish Hamilton, 1967)....................................**£20**
THE BIG EGG (illustrated by Margery Gill) (Hamish Hamilton, 1967) **£20**
THE TOFFEE JOIN (illustrated by Shirley Hughes) (Hamish Hamilton, 1968) **£20**
OVER THE HILLS AND FAR AWAY (Hamish Hamilton, 1968) **£20**
THE YELLOW AEROPLANE (illustrated by Trevor Stubley) (Hamish Hamilton, 1968).....................**£20**
THE HOUSE ON FAIRMOUNT (illustrated by Fritz Wegner) (Hamish Hamilton, 1968)....................**£20**
THE HILL ROAD (Dutton, 1969) **£10**
RAVENSGILL (Hamish Hamilton, 1970)...**£20**
ROYAL HARRY (Hamish Hamilton, 1971) **£20**
A GAME OF DARK (Hamish Hamilton, 1971) **£20**
THE INCLINE (illustrated by Trevor Stubley) (Hamish Hamilton, 1972)...**£20**
THE SWALLOWS (written under the pseudonym 'Martin Cobalt') (Heinemann, 1972).....................**£20**
ROBIN'S REAL ENGINE (illustrated by Mary Dinsdale) (Hamish Hamilton, 1972)..........................**£20**
SKIFFY (illustrated by Nicholas Fisk) (Hamish Hamilton, 1972) **£20**
THE JERSEY SHORE (Hamish Hamilton, 1973) **£20**
A YEAR AND A DAY (illustrated by Krystyna Turska) (Hamish Hamilton, 1976)..............................**£15**
PARTY PANTS (illustrated by Joanna Stubs) (Knight, 1977)...**£10**
MAX'S DREAM (illustrated by Laszio Acs) (Hamish Hamilton, 1977)...**£15**
IT (Hamish Hamilton, 1977)...**£15**
WHILE THE BELLS RING (illustrated by Janet Rawlins) (Hamish Hamilton, 1979).........................**£20**
SALT RIVER TIMES (illustrated by Elizabeth Honey) (Hamish Hamilton, 1980)..............................**£15**
THE MOUSE AND THE EGG (illustrated by Krystyna Turska) (Julia MacRae, 1980)........................**£20**
THE PATCHWORK CAT (illustrated by Nicola Bayley) (Cape, 1981)..**£30**
ALL THE KING'S MEN (Cape, 1982)..**£15**
WINTER QUARTERS (Cape, 1982)..**£15**
SKIFFY AND THE TWIN PLANETS (Hamish Hamilton, 1982) **£15**
A SMALL PUDDING FOR WEE GOWRIE and Other Stories of Underground Creatures
   (Macmillan, 1983)...**£15**
THE MOULDY (illustrated by Nicola Bayley) (Cape, 1983)..**£25**
THE RED BOOK OF HOB STORIES (illustrated by Patrick Benson) (Walker, 1984).......................**£15**
THE GREEN BOOK OF HOB STORIES (illustrated by Patrick Benson) (Walker, 1984)...................**£15**
THE YELLOW BOOK OF HOB STORIES (illustrated by Patrick Benson) (Walker, 1984) **£15**
THE BLUE BOOK OF HOB STORIES (illustrated by Patrick Benson) (Walker, 1984)......................**£15**
DRIFT (Cape, 1985)..**£10**
BARNABAS WALKS (illustrated by B. Firth) (Walker: 'Animal Library' series, 1986) **£10**
COME, COME TO MY CORNER (illustrated by Kenneth Lilly) (Walker: 'Animal Library' series, 1986) **£10**
TIBBER (illustrated by Jonathan Heale) (Walker: 'Animal Library' series, 1986)...........................**£10**
CORBIE (illustrated by Peter Visscher) (Walker: 'Animal Library' series, 1986) **£10**
GIDEON AHOY! (Viking Kestrel, 1987) **£12**
KELPIE (Cape, 1987)..**£12**
THE BLEMYAH STORIES (illustrated by Juan Wijguard) (Walker, 1987) **£12**
ANTAR AND THE EAGLES (Walker, 1989)...**£12**
HOUSE IN TOWN (Walker, 1989)..**£12**
NETTA NEXT (Hamish Hamilton, 1990) **£10**
THURSDAY CREATURE (Heinemann, 1990)..**£10**
COMPLETE BOOK OF HOB STORIES (Walker, 1991) **£20**
TIGER'S RAILWAY (Walker, 1991)...**£8**
LOW TIDE (Cape, 1992)...**£8**
AND NETTA AGAIN (Hamish Hamilton, 1992) **£8**
EGG TIMER (Heinemann, 1993)...**£8**
OH GRANDMA (Hamish Hamilton, 1993) **£8**
CUDDY (Cape, 1994)...**£8**
BELLS ON HER TOES (Hamish Hamilton, 1994)...**£8**
MIDNIGHT FAIR (Hodder Children's Books, 1997)...**£4**

MEADE, L.T.

Irish author. Born: Elizabeth Thomasina Meade in Brandon, County Cork, in 1844. Prolific writer for the middle-class child, especially school stories for girls in which she stressed adolescent passion. Her most famous story is *Beyond the Blue Mountains* (1893). Died: 1914.

Prices are for books in Good condition.

LOTTIE'S LAST HOME (Shaw, 1875)..£30
KNIGHT OF TODAY (Shaw, 1877)..£20
SCAMP AND I (Shaw, 1877)..£25
BEL AND MARJORY (Shaw, 1878)..£25
THE CHILDREN'S KINGDOM (Shaw, 1878)..£20
YOUR BROTHER AND MINE (Shaw, 1878)..£20
WATER LILLIES and Other Tales (Shaw, 1878)..£20
DOT AND HER TREASURES (Shaw, 1879)..£20
WATER GIPSIES (Shaw, 1879)..£20
A DWELLER IN TENTS (Isbister, 1880)..£20
MOU-SETSE by L.T. Meade with THE ORPHAN'S PILGRIMAGE by T. Von Gumbert (Isbister, 1880) £20
THE FLOATING LIGHT OF RING-FINNAN, AND THE GUARDIAN ANGELS (MacNiven, 1880)......................£20
MOTHER HERRING'S CHICKEN (Isbister, 1881)..£15
A LONDON BABY (Nisbet, 1882)..£15
THE CHILDREN'S PILGRIMAGE (Nisbet, 1883)..£15
HERMIE'S ROSE-BUDS and Other Stories (Hodder & Stoughton, 1883)..£15
THE AUTOCRAT OF THE NURSERY (Hodder & Stoughton, 1884) £15
A BAND OF THREE (Isbister, 1884)..£15
SCARLET ANEMONES (Hodder & Stoughton, 1884)..£15
THE TWO SISTERS (Hodder & Stoughton, 1884)..£15
THE ANGEL OF LOVE (Hodder & Stoughton, 1885)..£15
A LITTLE SILVER TRUMPET (Hodder & Stoughton, 1885) £15
A WORLD OF GIRLS (Cassell, 1886)..£15
DADDY'S BOY (Hatchards, 1887)..£15
THE O'DONNELLS OF INCHFAWN (Hatchards, 1887)..£15
THE PALACE BEAUTIFUL (Cassell, 1887)..£15
SWEET NANCY (Partridge, 1887)..£15
DEB AND THE DUCHESS (Hatchard, 1888)..£15
NOBODY'S NEIGHBOURS (Isbister, 1888)..£15
A FARTHINGFUL (Chambers, 1889) £15
THE GOLDEN LADY (Chambers, 1889)..£15
THE LADY OF THE FOREST (Partridge, 1889)..£15
THE LITTLE PRINCESS OF TOWER HILL (Partridge, 1889)..£15
POOR MISS CAROLINA (Chambers, 1889)..£15
A NEW-FASHIONED GIRL (Cassell, 1889) £15
THE BERESFORD PRIZE (Longman, 1890) £15
DICKORY DOCK (Chambers, 1890)..£15
ENGAGED TO BE MARRIED (Simpkin Marshall, 1890) £15
HEART OF GOLD (Warne, 1890) £15
JUST A LOVE STORY (Blackett, 1890) £15
MARIGOLD (Partridge, 1890)..£15
HEPSY GIPSY (Methuen, 1891)..£15
THE CHILDREN OF WILTON CHASE (Chambers, 1891)..£20
A SWEET GIRL-GRADUATE (Cassell, 1891)..£20
LITTLE MARY and Other Stories (Chambers, 1891) £15
BASHFUL FIFTEEN (Cassell, 1892)..£20
FOUR ON AN ISLAND (Chambers, 1892)..£20
OUT OF THE FASHION (Methuen, 1892)..£15
A RING OF RUBIES (Cassell, 1892)..£15
BEYOND THE BLUE MOUNTAINS (Cassell, 1893)..£100
A YOUNG MUTINEER (Wells Gardner, 1893)..£15
BETTY (Chambers, 1894)..£15
IN AN IRON GRIP (two volumes) (Chatto & Windus, 1894)... the set £25
RED ROSE AND TIGER LILY (Cassell, 1894)..£12
GIRLS, NEW AND OLD (Chambers, 1895)..£20
THE LEAST OF THESE and Other Stories (Chambers, 1895)..£12
CATALINA, ART STUDENT (Chambers, 1896)..£20
A GIRL IN TEN THOUSAND (Oliphant, 1896)..£12
GOOD LUCK (Nisbet, 1896)..£12
A LITTLE MOTHER TO THE OTHERS (White, 1896)..£12
MERRY GIRLS OF ENGLAND (Cassell, 1896) £12
PLAYMATES (Chambers, 1896)..£12
THE WHITE TZAR (Russell, 1896)..£12

THE HOUSE OF SURPRISES (Longman, 1896)..£12
BAD LITTLE HANNAH (White, 1897)...£12
A HANDFUL OF SILVER (Oliphant, 1897)..£12
WILD KITTY (Chambers, 1897)...£12
CAVE PERILOUS (RTS, 1898)...£12
A BUNCH OF CHERRIES (Isbister, 1898)...£12
THE CLEVEREST WOMAN IN ENGLAND (Nisbet, 1898)..£12
MARY GIFFORD, MB (Wells Gardner, 1898)..£12
THE GIRLS OF ST WODE'S (Chambers 1898)...£20
THE REBELLION OF LIL CARRINGTON (Cassell, 1898) £20
THE SIREN (White, 1898)...£12
ADVENTURESS (Chatto & Windus, 1899)...£12
ALL SORTS (Nisbet, 1899) £12
LIGHT O' THE MORNING (Chambers, 1899)..£12
THE ODDS AND EVENS (Chambers,1899)..£12
WAGES (Nisbet, 1900) £12
A PLUCKY GIRL (Chambers, 1900) £12
THE BEAUFORTS (Griffith & Farran, 1900)..£12
A BRAVE POOR THING (Isbister, 1900)..£12
DADDY'S GIRL (Newnes, 1900) £12
MISS NONENTITY (Chambers, 1900)..£20
SEVEN MAIDS (Chambers, 1900) £12
A SISTER OF THE RED CROSS (Nelson, 1900) £12
IN TIME OF ROSES (Nelson, 1900)...£12
IN TIME OF ROSES (Nister, 1900)..£35
WHEELS OF IRON (Nisbet, 1901)...£12
THE BLUE DIAMOND (Chatto & Windus, 1901) £12
COSEY CORNER (Chambers, 1901) £12
GIRLS OF THE TRUE BLUE (Chambers, 1901)..£20
THE NEW MRS LASCELLES (Clarke, 1901) £12
A STUMBLE BY THE WAY (Chatto & Windus, 1901)..£12
A VERY NAUGHTY GIRL (Chambers, 1901)..£20
DRIFT (Methuen, 1902) £12
MARGARET (White, 1902)..£12
THE PURSUIT OF PENELOPE (Digby Long, 1902)...£12
THE PRINCESS WHO GAVE ALL AWAY AND THE NAUGHTY ONE OF THE FAMILY
   (Nister, 1902)...£12
GIRLS OF THE FOREST (Chambers, 1902) £20
QUEEN ROSE (Chambers, 1902) £12
THE REBEL OF THE SCHOOL (Chambers, 1902) £20
THE SQUIRE'S LITTLE GIRL (Chambers, 1902)...£12
THROUGH PERIL FOR A WIFE (Digby Long, 1902)...£12
RESURGAM (Methuen, 1903)...£12
ROSEBURY (Chatto & Windus, 1903)..£12
PETER THE PILGRIM (Chambers, 1903)...£12
THE WITCH MAID (Nisbet, 1903) £12
THE BURDEN OF HER YOUTH (Long, 1903)...£12
BY MUTUAL CONSENT (Long, 1903)..£12
A GAY CHARMER (Chambers, 1903)...£12
THE MANOR SCHOOL (Chambers,1903)..£20
THAT BRILLIANT PEGGY (Hodder & Stoughton, 1903)...£20
A MAID OF MYSTERY (White, 1904)...£20
THE ADVENTURES OF MIRANDA (John Long, 1904)..£20
AT THE BACK OF THE WORLD (Hurst & Blackett, 1904)..£15
THE LADY CAKE-MAKER (Hodder & Stoughton, 1904)...£12
CASTLE POVERTY (Nisbet, 1904)..£10
LOVE TRIUMPHANT (T. Fisher Unwin, 1904) £12
A MADCAP (Cassell, 1904)...£15
NURSE CHARLOTTE (John Long, 1904) £12
THE GIRLS OF MRS PRITCHARD'S SCHOOL (Chambers, 1904)...................................£15
A MODERN TOMBOY (Chambers, 1904)...£15
PETRONELLA AND THE COMING OF POLLY (Chambers, 1904) £12
WILFUL COUSIN KATE (Chambers, 1905) £12
BESS OF DELANEY'S (Digby Long, 1905) £12
HIS MASCOT (John Long, 1905) £12
LITTLE WIFE HESTER (John Long, 1905) £12
LOVEDAY (Hodder & Stoughton, 1905) £12
OLD READMONEY'S DAUGHTER (Partridge, 1905) £12
VIRGINIA (Digby Long, 1905)..£12

Title	Price
DUMPS (Chambers, 1905)	£12
A BEVY OF GIRLS (Chambers, 1905)	£15
THE COLONEL AND THE BOY (Hodder & Stoughton, 1906)	£12
THE FACE OF JULIET (John Long, 1906)	£12
THE GIRL AND HER FORTUNE (Hodder & Stoughton, 1906)	£12
THE HEART OF HELEN (John Long, 1906)	£12
THE HOME OF SWEET CONTENT (White, 1906)	£12
IN THE FLOWER OF HER YOUTH (Nisbet, 1906)	£12
THE MAID WITH THE GOGGLES (Digby Long, 1906)	£12
SUE (Chambers, 1906)	£12
VICTORY (Methuen, 1906)	£12
THE HILL-TOP GIRL (Chambers, 1906)	£15
TURQUOISE AND RUBY (illustrated by Mabel Lucie Attwell) (Chambers, 1906)	£50
THE COLONEL'S CONQUEST (Jacobs, US, 1907)	£12
THE CURSE OF THE FEVERALS (John Long, 1907)	£12
A GIRL FROM AMERICA (Chambers, 1907)	£12
THE HOME OF SILENCE (Sisley, 1907)	£12
KINDRED SPIRITS (John Long, 1907)	£12
THE LADY OF DELIGHT (Hodder & Stoughton, 1907)	£12
LITTLE JOSEPHINE (John Long, 1907)	£12
THE LITTLE SCHOOL-MOTHERS (Cassell, 1907)	£15
THE LOVE OF SUSAN CARDIGAN (Digby Long, 1907)	£12
THE RED CAP OF LIBERTY (Nisbet, 1907)	£12
THE RED RUTH (Laurie, 1907)	£12
THE SCAMP FAMILY (Chambers, 1907)	£15
THREE GIRLS FROM SCHOOL (Chambers, 1907)	£15
THE SCHOOL FAVOURITE (Chambers, 1908)	£15
THE AIM OF HER LIFE (John Long, 1908)	£12
A LOVELY FRIEND and Other Stories (Digby Long, 1908)	£10
THE COURT-HARMAN GIRLS (Chambers, 1908)	£15
THE COURTSHIP OF SYBIL (John Long, 1908)	£10
HETTY BERESFORD (Hodder & Stoughton, 1908)	£10
SARAH'S MOTHER (Hodder & Stoughton, 1908)	£10
THE SCHOOL FAVOURITE (Chambers, 1908	£15
THE SCHOOL QUEENS (Chambers, 1908)	£15
AYLWYN'S FRIENDS (Chambers, 1909)	£10
BETTY VIVIAN (Chambers, 1909)	£10
BLUE OF THE SEA (Nisbet, 1909	£10
BROTHER OR HUSBAND (White, 1909)	£10
THE FOUNTAIN OF BEAUTY (John Lane, 1909)	£10
I WILL SING A NEW SONG (Hodder & Stoughton, 1909)	£10
THE PRINCESS OF THE REVELS (Chambers, 1909)	£10
THE STORMY PETREL (Hurst & Blackett, 1909)	£10
THE ABC GIRL (White, 1910)	£15
BELINDA TREHERNE (John Long, 1910)	£10
A GIRL OF TODAY (John Long, 1910)	£10
LADY ANNE (Nisbet, 1910)	£10
MISS GWENDOLINE (John Long, 1910)	£10
NANCE KENNEDY (Partridge, 1910)	£10
PRETTY GIRL AND THE OTHERS (Chambers,1910)	£10
ROSE REGINA (Chambers, 1910)	£10
A BUNCH OF COUSINS AND THE BARN "BOYS" (Chambers, 1911)	£10
DESBOROUGH'S WIFE (Digby Long, 1911)	£10
THE DOCTOR'S CHILDREN (Chambers, 1911)	£10
FOR DEAR DAD (Chambers, 1911)	£10
THE GIRL FROM SPAIN (Digby Long, 1911)	£10
MOTHER AND SON (Ward Lock, 1911)	£10
RUFFLES (Stanley Paul, 1911)	£10
THE SOUL OF MARGARET RAND (Ward Lock, 1911)	£10
DADDY'S GIRL, AND CONSUELO'S QUEST OF HAPPINESS (New York Book Co, US, 1911)	£10
THE GIRLS OF MERTON COLLEGE (Hurst, US, 1911)	£10
CORPORAL VIOLET (Hodder & Stoughton, 1912)	£10
A GIRL OF THE PEOPLE (Everett, 1912)	£10
KITTY O'DONOVAN (Chambers, 1912)	£10
LORD AND LADY KITTY (White, 1912)	£10
LOVE'S CROSS ROADS (Stanley Paul, 1912)	£10
PEGGY FROM KERRY (Chambers, 1912)	£10
THE CHESTERTON GIRL GRADUATES (Chambers, 1913)	£10
THE GIRLS OF ABINGER CLOSE (Chambers, 1913)	£10

THE GIRLS OF KING'S ROYAL (Chambers, 1913)..£10
THE PASSION OF KATHLEEN DUVEEN (Stanley Paul, 1913)..£10
A BAND OF MIRTH (illustrated by Mabel Lucie Attwell) (Chambers, 1914)................................£50
COL TRACEY'S WIFE (Aldine, 1914)..£10
ELIZABETH'S PRISON (Stanley Paul, 1914)..£10
A GIRL OF HIGH ADVENTURE (Chambers, 1914)..£10
HER HAPPY FACE (Ward Lock, 1914)..£10
THE QUEEN OF JOY (Chambers, 1914)...£10
THE WOOING OF MONICA (John Long, 1914)..£10
THE DARLING OF THE SCHOOL (Chambers, 1915)..£10
GREATER THAN GOLD (Ward Lock, 1915)...£10
JILL THE IRRESISTIBLE (Chambers, 1915)...£10
HOLLYHOCK (Chambers, 1916)..£10
MADGE MOSTYN'S NIECES (Chambers, 1916)..£10
THE MAID INDOMITABLE (Ward Lock, 1916)..£10
MOTHER MARY (Chambers, 1916)..£10
DAUGHTERS OF TODAY (Hodder & Stoughton, 1916)..£10
BETTER THAN RICHES (Chambers, 1917)...£10
THE FAIRY GODMOTHER (Chambers, 1917)..£10
MISS PATRICIA (John Long, 1925)..£15
ROSES AND THORNS (John Long, 1928)..£15

MEGGENDORFER, Lothar

German illustrator and creator of movable picture books. Born: 1847. Worked for many years on the German equivalent of *Punch*. Created movable books for a variety of publishers, including Braun & Schneider of Munich and the British firm, Dean & Son. Best known for books like *Always Jolly!* and *Travels of Little Lord Thumb and his Man Damien* (both 1891), in which puppet figures are made to move by pulling on a tab. Died: 1925.

Prices are for books in Very Good condition and in full working order. Note that prices vary considerably according to condition. Many titles have been reissued over the last twenty years, and these reprints are worth between £20 and £40.

Two fine examples of the 'funny movable toybooks' perfected by the brilliant German illustrator, Lothar Meggendorfer (1847-1925).

MEGGENDORFER, Lothar

NEU LEBENDE BILDER (Braun & Schneider, Munich, [c1880])...£1,250
AUS DER KINDRERSTUBE (Esslingen, [c1885])..£1,250
BEWEGLICHE SCHATTENBILDER (H. Vorstellung, Munich, [1886])...£1,250
NAH UND FERN. Ein Tierbilderbuch zum Ziehen (Munich, [1887])..£1,250
INTERNATIONALER ZIRKUS (H. Grevel, 1887)..£1,250
ARTISTIC PUSSY AND HER STUDIO: Moving Pictures and Other Tales (L.W. Walter, US, [c1890])........£1,250
THE CITY PARK: A Panoramic Stand-Up Book (H. Grevel, [c1890])..£1,250
MILITARITCHES ZIEBITDERBUCH (Munich, [c1890])..£1,250
AFFENTHEATER (Munich, [c1890])...£1,250
FROM FAR AND NEAR (H. Grevel, [c1890])...£1,250
HUTOMATEN THEATER (Stuttgart, [c1890])...£1,250
LEBENDE TIERBILDER (Braun & Schneider, Munich, [c1890]) £1,250
TRANSFORMATION SCENES (H. Grevel, [c1890])..£1,250
ZWOLF SCHONE GESCHICHTEN (Munich, [c1890])...£1,250
COMIC ACTORS: A New Movable Toybook (H. Grevel, [1891])...£1,250
ALWAYS JOLLY! A Movable Toybook (H. Grevel, [1891]) £1,250
CURIOUS CREATURES: A New Movable Toybook of All Kinds of Animals (H. Grevel, [1891])................£1,250
MERRY COMPANY: A Funny Movable Toybook (H. Grevel, [1891])..£1,250
TRAVELS OF LITTLE LORD THUMB AND HIS MAN DAMIEN: A Movable Toybook
    (H. Grevel, [1891])...£1,250
ALL ALIVE (H. Grevel, [c1892]) £1,250
HUMOROUS PICTURE BOOK (H. Grevel, [1894]) £1,250
LOOK AT ME! A New Movable Toybook (H. Grevel, [1894])..£1,250
COMICS FACE: A Movable Toybook (H. Grevel, [1895])...£1,250
SCENES OF ANIMAL LIFE: A Movable Toybook (H. Grevel, [1895])..£1,250
WHAT'S O'CLOCK? A Toy Book to Teach Children the Time (H. Grevel, [1897])....................................£1,250
NUR FUR BRAVE KINDER (J.F. Schreiber, 1899) £1,250
CLOWN PUTTY FACE: The Quick Change Artist (H. Grevel, [1900])..£1,250
THE DOLL'S HOUSE: A Present for Good Little Children (H. Grevel, [c1900])..£1,250
OUR AUNTS: A Humorous Album of 400 Transformations (H. Grevel, [1900] £1,250
THE TRICKS OF NAUGHTY BOYS: A Series of Amusing Transformation Scenes (H. Grevel, [1900]) £1,250
COMIC ZOOLOGY (H. Grevel, 1902)..£1,250

MILLIGAN, Spike

British comedian. Born: India, 1918. The former Goon's off-beat, witty and anarchic humour in stories and verse had great appeal to children. Died 2002.

Prices are for books in Very Good condition with dustjackets where applicable.

SILLY VERSE FOR KIDS (Dobson, 1959)..£175
A BOOK OF MILLIGANIMALS (Dobson, 1968) £25
THE BALD TWIT LION (Dobson, 1968)...£25
MILLIGAN'S ARK (illustrated by Giles, Ronald Searle, Ralph Steadman and Terry Gilliam) (Hobbs, 1971).........£15
BAD JELLY THE WITCH: A Fairy Story (Hobbs/Joseph, 1973) £25
BAD JELLY THE WITCH: A Fairy Story (with extra illustrations) (Virgin, 2000) £10
DIP THE PUPPY: A Fairy Story; with The Terrible Monster Jelly (Hobbs/Joseph, 1974).........................£25
GOBLINS (illustrated by W Heath Robinson) (Hutchinson, 1978) £12
UNSPUN SOCKS FROM A CHICKEN'S LAUNDRY (Hobbs/Joseph, 1981) £15
SIR NOBONK AND THE TERRIBLE, AWFUL, DREADFUL, NAUGHTY, NASTY DRAGON
    (Hobbs/Joseph, 1982) £20
FLEAS, KNEES & HIDDEN ELEPHANTS (Boxtree, 1994)...£6
HUTCHINSON'S TREASURY OF CHILDREN'S LITERATURE (anthology) (Hutchinson, 1995)......................£10
A CHILDREN'S TREASURY OF MILLIGAN (anthology) (Virgin, 1999)...£12

MILLS, Annette

British author. Born: 1894. Mills was best known for her series of stories featuring Muffin the Mule. She was the sister of the actor, John Mills. Died: 1955.

Prices are for books in Very Good condition with dustjackets where applicable.

MUFFIN THE MULE (illustrated by Molly Blake) (University of London Press, 1949)......................................£45
MORE ABOUT MUFFIN (illustrated by Molly Blake) (University of London Press, 1950)...............................£40
MUFFIN AND THE MAGIC HAT (illustrated by Molly Blake) (University of London Press, [1951]) £35
HERE COMES MUFFIN (illustrated by Molly Blake) (University of London Press, [1952])..............................£35
JENNIFER AND THE FLOWER FAIRIES (illustrated by Molly Blake) (News of the World, [1952])..................£25
PRUDENCE KITTEN (illustrated by Molly Blake) (University of London Press, [1952]).................................£25
MUFFIN AT THE SEASIDE (illustrated by Molly Blake) (University of London Press, [1953]).......................£35
COLONEL CROCK (illustrated by Edward Andrewes) (Harrap, 1953) £15
MUFFIN'S SPLENDID ADVENTURE (illustrated by Molly Blake) (University of London Press, [1954]).........£35
MERRY MUFFIN BOOKS (three books; illustrated by Neville Main) (Brockhampton Press, 1954).......... each £20
PRUDENCE KITTEN AND PUFFER OF CHILDREN'S TELEVISION (illustrated by George Fry)
    (Publicity Productions, [1955])..£12

MILNE, A.A.

British author. Born: Alan Alexander Milne in London in 1882. Educated at Westminster School and Trinity College, Cambridge, where he read mathematics. Became assistant editor of *Punch* at the age of 24, remaining with the magazine until the outbreak of the First World War, when he joined the army. He had his first literary success as a playwright, but was encouraged to write children's verse by Rose Fyleman, who published his poem, 'The Dormouse and the Doctor', in *The Merry-Go-Round*. His first collection, *When We Were Very Young* (1924), sold half a million copies in its first ten years, and was followed by another volume of verse, *Now We Are Six* (1927), and the story-books, *Winnie-the-Pooh* (1926) and *The House at Pooh Corner* (1928). Thereafter, he concentrated on the theatre, producing only two more children's works, notably *Toad of Toad Hall* (1929), a stage version of Kenneth Grahame's *The Wind in the Willows*. Died: 1956.

Prices are for books in Very Good condition with dustjackets where applicable.

ONCE ON A TIME: A Fairy Story (illustrated by H.M. Brock) (Hodder & Stoughton, 1917)..£150
ONCE ON A TIME (illustrated by Charles Robinson) (Hodder & Stoughton, [1925]) £120
WHEN WE WERE VERY YOUNG (verse; illustrated by E.H. Shepard) (Methuen, 1924)......................................£5,000
WHEN WE WERE VERY YOUNG (verse; illustrated by E.H. Shepard; limited to 100 numbered copies,
    signed by the author and artist) (Methuen, 1924)..£6,000
WHEN WE WERE VERY YOUNG (verse; illustrated by E.H. Shepard; limited to 300 numbered copies,
    signed by Christopher Milne) (Methuen, 1974) £500
VESPERS: A Poem (illustrated by E.H. Shepard; music by H. Fraser-Simson) (Methuen, [1924])......................£150
MAKE-BELIEVE: A Children's Play in a Prologue and Three Acts (lyrics by C.E. Burton) (Methuen, 1925) £100
A GALLERY OF CHILDREN (illustrated by H. Willebeek le Mair under the pseudonym 'Saida') (Stanley Paul, 1925)............£500
A GALLERY OF CHILDREN (illustrated by H. Willebeek le Mair under the pseudonym 'Saida';
    limited to 500 numbered copies, signed by the author) (Stanley Paul, 1925)..........................£1,000
THE KING'S BREAKFAST (illustrated by E.H. Shepard; music by H. Fraser-Simson) (Methuen, 1925)................£200
WINNIE-THE-POOH (stories; illustrated by E.H. Shepard) (Methuen, 1926) £2,500
WINNIE-THE-POOH (stories; illustrated by E.H. Shepard; De Luxe edition: red, green or blue leather binding; in slipcase)
    (Methuen, 1926) £3,000
WINNIE-THE-POOH (stories; illustrated by E.H. Shepard; limited to 350 copies, signed by the author and artist)
    (Methuen, 1926)..£5,000
WINNIE-THE-POOH (stories; illustrated in colour by E.H. Shepard) (Methuen, 1973)...............................£80
WINNIE-THE-POOH (stories; illustrated by E.H. Shepard; limited to 300 numbered copies,
    signed by the artist) (Methuen, 1973) £600

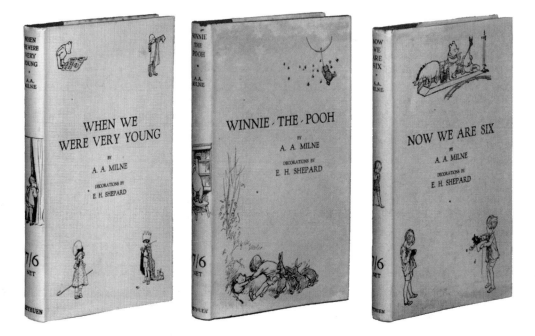

Three of A.A. Milne's best-known works in their rare dustjackets. All these books were also issued in signed, limited editions.

One of E.H. Shepard's famous illustrations of Winnie-the-Pooh and Christopher Robin from the first edition of **The House at Pooh Corner** *(1928).*

WINNIE-THE-POOH AND EEYORE'S TAIL: A Pop-Up Picture Book (adapted by A. Schenk from the original illustrations by E.H. Shepard) (Methuen, [1953]) £100

WINNIE-THE-POOH AND THE BEES: A Pop-Up Picture Book (adapted by A. Schenk from the original illustrations by E.H. Shepard) (Methuen, [1953]) £100

TEDDY BEAR and Other Songs From 'When We Were Very Young' (illustrated by A.A. Milne; music by H. Fraser-Simson) (Methuen, 1926)...£220

NOW WE ARE SIX (verse; illustrated by E.H. Shepard) (Methuen, 1927).................................£850

NOW WE ARE SIX (verse; illustrated by E.H. Shepard; De Luxe edition: red, blue or green leather binding; in slipcase) (Methuen, 1927)...£1,750

NOW WE ARE SIX (verse; illustrated by E.H. Shepard; limited to 200 numbered copies, signed by the author and artist) (Methuen, 1927)...£2,000

NOW WE ARE SIX (verse; illustrated by E.H. Shepard; limited to 300 numbered copies, signed by Christopher Milne) (Methuen, 1976)...£500

SONGS FROM 'NOW WE ARE SIX' (music by H. Fraser-Simson) (Methuen, 1927)...................£250

MORE VERY YOUNG SONGS (Methuen, 1928)...£200

THE HOUSE AT POOH CORNER (stories; illustrated by E.H. Shepard) (Methuen, 1928)..........£1,250

THE HOUSE AT POOH CORNER (stories; illustrated by E.H. Shepard; De Luxe edition: red, green or blue leather binding; in slipcase) (Methuen, 1928)..£2,500

THE HOUSE AT POOH CORNER (stories; illustrated by E.H. Shepard; limited to 350 numbered copies, signed by the author and artist) (Methuen, 1928)..£4,000

THE HOUSE AT POOH CORNER (illustrated in colour by E.H. Shepard) (Methuen, 1974)............£60

THE CHRISTOPHER ROBIN CALENDAR (verse; illustrated by E.H. Shepard) (Methuen: 'Ephemerides' series, [1928])..£75

THE CHRISTOPHER ROBIN STORY BOOK (selections from 'When We Were Very Young', 'Now We Are Six', 'Winnie-the-Pooh' and 'The House at Pooh Corner'; new preface by the author) (Methuen, 1929).........£400

THE HUMS OF POOH (illustrated by E.H. Shepard; music by H. Fraser-Simson) (Methuen, 1929).........£200

TOAD OF TOAD HALL: A Play Taken from Kenneth Grahame's 'The Wind in the Willows' (Methuen, 1929).....................£100

TOAD OF TOAD HALL (limited to 200 numbered copies, signed by Kenneth Grahame and A.A. Milne) (Methuen, 1929)...£1,250

TALES OF POOH (selections from 'Winnie-the-Pooh' and 'The House at Pooh Corner'; illustrated by E.H. Shepard) (Methuen: 'Modern Classics' series, [1930])..............................£200

THE CHRISTOPHER ROBIN BIRTHDAY BOOK (selections from 'When We Were Very Young', 'Now We Are Six', 'Winnie-the-Pooh' and 'The House at Pooh Corner'; illustrated by E.H. Shepard) (Methuen, 1930).........£150

THE CHRISTOPHER ROBIN VERSES (contains 'When We Were Very Young' and 'Now We Are Six'; illustrated by E.H. Shepard) (Methuen, 1932)..£250

INTRODUCING WINNIE-THE-POOH (Methuen, 1947) £75

THE WORLD OF POOH (eight new colour plates by E.H. Shepard) (Methuen, 1958)...................£100

THE WORLD OF CHRISTOPHER ROBIN (eight new colour plates by E.H. Shepard) (Methuen, 1959)........£100

PRINCE RABBIT and THE PRINCESS WHO COULD NOT LAUGH (illustrated by Mary Shepard) (Ward Lock, 1966)...........£30

THE POOH STORY BOOK (new illustrations and colour plates by E.H. Shepard) (Methuen, 1967)..........£60

THE CHRISTOPHER ROBIN VERSE BOOK (illustrated in colour by E.H. Shepard) (Methuen, 1969)........£60

MOLESWORTH, Mrs

British author. Born: Mary Louisa Stewart in Manchester in 1839. An enormously prolific author, she began by writing adult novels, but turned to children's fiction on the advice of the illustrator, Sir Noel Paton. Amongst her best-known titles are *The Cuckoo Clock* (1877), *The Tapestry Room* (1879) and *The Carved Lions* (1895). Although rather dated now, her books have been admired by Swinburne, Gillian Avery and Roger Lancelyn Green. The 35 Macmillan books are the most attractive titles for collectors. Died: 1921.
Prices are for books in Very Good condition.

Macmillan series (1875-1911)

TELL ME A STORY (written under the pseudonym 'Ennis Graham'; illustrated by Walter Crane) (Macmillan, 1875).................£80
CARROTS: Just a Little Boy (written under the pseudonym 'Ennis Graham'; illustrated by Walter Crane) (Macmillan, 1876)...........£80
THE CUCKOO CLOCK (written under the pseudonym 'Ennis Graham'; illustrated by Walter Crane) (Macmillan, 1877)...........£80
THE CUCKOO CLOCK (illustrated by Charles E. Brock) (Chambers, 1931) £30
THE CUCKOO CLOCK (illustrated by E.H. Shepard) (Dent, 'Children's Illustrated Classics' series, 1954) £30
GRANDMOTHER DEAR (illustrated by Walter Crane) (Macmillan, 1878)...£60
THE TAPESTRY ROOM (illustrated by Walter Crane) (Macmillan, 1879) £60
A CHRISTMAS CHILD (illustrated by Walter Crane) (Macmillan, 1880)..£60
THE ADVENTURES OF HERR BABY (illustrated by Walter Crane) (Macmillan, 1881).....................................£40
ROSY (illustrated by Walter Crane) (Macmillan, 1882)..£40
TWO LITTLE WAIFS (illustrated by Walter Crane) (Macmillan, 1883) £40
CHRISTMAS-TREE LAND (illustrated by Walter Crane) (Macmillan, 1884) £40
US: An Old-Fashioned Story (illustrated by Walter Crane) (Macmillan, 1885).......................................£40
FOUR WIND'S FARM (illustrated by Walter Crane) (Macmillan, 1887)...£40
LITTLE MISS PEGGY (illustrated by Walter Crane) (Macmillan, 1887)...£40
A CHRISTMAS POSY (illustrated by Walter Crane) (Macmillan, 1888)..£40
THE RECTORY CHILDREN (illustrated by Walter Crane) (Macmillan, 1889) £40
THE CHILDREN OF THE CASTLE (illustrated by Walter Crane) (Macmillan, 1890)......................................£40
NURSE HEATHERDALE'S STORY (illustrated by L. Leslie Brooke) (Macmillan, 1891)...................................£40
THE GIRLS AND I: A Veracious History (illustrated by L. Leslie Brooke) (Macmillan, 1892) £40
MARY: A Nursery Story for Very Little Children (illustrated by L. Leslie Brooke) (Macmillan, 1893)..............£40
MY NEW HOME (illustrated by L. Leslie Brooke) (Macmillan, 1894) £40
THE CARVED LIONS (illustrated by L. Leslie Brooke) (Macmillan, 1895) £30
SHEILA'S MYSTERY (illustrated by L. Leslie Brooke) (Macmillan, 1895)..£30
THE ORIEL WINDOW (illustrated by L. Leslie Brooke) (Macmillan, 1896)..£30
MISS MOUSE AND HER BOYS (illustrated by L. Leslie Brooke) (Macmillan, 1897).....................................£30
THE MAGIC NUTS (illustrated by Rosie Pitman) (Macmillan, 1898)..£25
THIS AND THAT: A Tale of Two Tinies (illustrated by Hugh Thomson) (Macmillan, 1899).............................£35
THE HOUSE THAT GREW (illustrated by Alice B. Woodward) (Macmillan, 1900)..£30
THE WOOD-PIGEONS AND MARY (illustrated by H.R. Millar) (Macmillan, 1901)..£30
PETERKIN (illustrated by H.R. Millar) (Macmillan, 1902)...£30
THE RUBY RING (illustrated by Rosie Pitman) (Macmillan, 1904)...£20
JASPER: A Story for Children (illustrated by Gertrude D. Holland) (Macmillan, 1906).............................£20
THE LITTLE GUEST: A Story for Children (illustrated by Gertrude D. Holland) (Macmillan, 1907)...................£20
FAIRIES — OF SORTS (illustrated by Gertrude D. Holland) (Macmillan, 1908).......................................£20
THE STORY OF A YEAR (illustrated by Gertrude D. Holland) (Macmillan, 1910)......................................£20
FAIRIES AFIELD (illustrated by Gertrude D. Holland) (Macmillan, 1911)...£20

Other children's books

HERMY: The Story of a Little Girl (illustrated by Mary Ellen Edwards) (Routledge, 1881 [1880]).................£40
HERMY (illustrated by Lewis Baumer) (Chambers, 1898)..£20
HOODIE (illustrated by Mary Ellen Edwards) (Routledge, 1882) £40
HOODIE (illustrated by Lewis Baumer) (Chambers, 1897)...£20
THE BOYS AND I (illustrated by Mary Ellen Edwards) (Routledge, 1883)..£30
SUMMER STORIES FOR BOYS AND GIRLS (illustrated by Mary Ellen Edwards) (Macmillan, 1882)........................£40
THE LITTLE OLD PORTRAIT (illustrated by W. Gunston) (SPCK, [1884])...£30
THE LITTLE OLD PORTRAIT (as 'EDMEE: A Tale fo the French Revolution'; illustrated by Gertrude Demain Holland) (Macmillan, 1916)..£20
SILVERTHORNS (illustrated by J. Noel Paton) (Hatchards, [1887])..£40
THE PALACE IN THE GARDEN (illustrated by Harriet M. Bennett) (Hatchards, 1887)..................................£25
THE ABBEY BY THE SEA and FELIX, AN OUTCAST (illustrated by Frank Dadd) (SPCK, [1887]) £25
FIVE MINUTES' STORIES (illustrated by Gordon Browne and others) (SPCK, [1888]).................................£30
A HOUSE TO LET (illustrated by W.J. Morgan) (SPCK, [1889])..£25
THE OLD PINCUSHION, or Aunt Clotilda's Guests (illustrated by Mrs A. Hope) (Griffith & Farran, [1889]) £25
THE OLD PINCUSHION (illustrated by Mabel Lucie Attwell) (Chambers, 1910)..£60
NESTA, or Fragments of a Little Life (Chambers, 1889) £25
GREAT UNCLE HOOT-TOOT (illustrated by Gordon Browne and others) (SPCK, [1889]) £25
TWELVE TINY TALES (illustrated by W.J. Morgan) (SPCK, [1889]) £30
FAMILY TROUBLES (MR NOBODY) (illustrated by W.J. Morgan) (SPCK, [1890]) £30
LITTLE MOTHER BUNCH (illustrated by Mary Ellen Edwards) (Cassell, 1890)...£30
THE STORY OF A SPRING MORNING and Other Tales (illustrated by Mary Ellen Edwards) (Longman, 1890) £30

THE GREEN CASKET and Other Stories (illustrated by R. Barnes and W.J. Morgan) (Chambers, 1890)..£30
THE LUCKY DUCKS and Other Stories (illustrated by W.J. Morgan) (SPCK, [1891])............£30
SWEET CONTENT (illustrated by William Rainey) (Griffith & Farran, 1891)............................£40
AN ENCHANTED GARDEN — FAIRY STORIES (illustrated by W.J. Hennessy) (Unwin, 1892) £60
STORIES OF THE SAINTS FOR CHILDREN (Longmans, 1892) £30
FARTHINGS: The Story of a Stray and a Waif (illustrated by G.M. Broadley) (Wells Gardner, 1892)....£30
ROBIN REDBREAST: A Story for Girls (illustrated by Robert Barnes) (Chambers, 1892) £30
THE NEXT-DOOR HOUSE (illustrated by W. Hatherell) (Cassell, 1892)....................................£30
THE MAN WITH THE PAN-PIPES and Other Stories (illustrated by W.J. Morgan) (SPCK, [1892])....£30
STUDIES AND STORIES (short stories, illustrated by Walter Crane) (A.D. Innes, 1893) £40
THE THIRTEEN LITTLE BLACK PIGS and Other Stories (illustrated by W.J. Morgan) (SPCK, [1893]) £30
OPPOSITE NEIGHBOURS and Other Stories (illustrated by W.J. Morgan) (SPCK, [1895])..........£20
FRIENDLY JOEY and Other Stories (illustrated by W.J. Morgan) (SPCK, [1896]) £20
STORIES FOR CHILDREN IN ILLUSTRATION OF THE LORD'S PRAYER
(illustrated by Gordon Browne and others)
(Gardner & Darton, 1897)..£25
GREYLING TOWERS: A Story for the Young (illustrated by Percy Tarrant) (Chambers, 1898) £25
THE CHILDREN'S HOUR (Nelson, [1899]) £30
THE THREE WITCHES (illustrated by Lewis Baumer) (Chambers, [1900]) £30
'MY PRETTY' AND HER LITTLE BROTHER 'TOO' and Other Stories (illustrated by Lewis Baumer)
(Chambers, [1901])..£30
THE BLUE BABY and Other Stories (illustrated by Maud C. Foster) (Unwin, [1901]) £30
THE BLUE BABY (illustrated by Lewis Baumer) (Chambers, 1904) £20
THE MYSTERY OF THE PINEWOOD AND HOLLOW TREE HOUSE (illustrated by A.A. Dixon) (Nister, 1903) £30
THE BOLTED DOOR and Other Stories (illustrated by L. Baumer) (Chambers, [1906])..........£30
THE FEBRUARY BOYS (illustrated by Mabel Lucie Attwell) (Chambers, 1909) £60
FAIRY STORIES Edited by Roger Lancelyn Green (issued with dustjacket) (Harvill, 1957) £10

Teenage novels & stories

LETTICE (illustrated by Frank Dadd) (SPCK, [1884]) £30
A CHARGE FULFILLED (illustrated by R. Caton Woodville) (SPCK, [1886])............................£30
THE THIRD MISS St QUENTIN (Hatchards, 1888) £25
NEIGHBOURS (illustrated by Mary Ellen Edwards) (Hatchards, 1889)....................................£25
THE BEWITCHED LAMP (illustrated by Robert Barnes) (Chambers, 1891) £30
THE RED GRANGE (illustrated by Gordon Browne) (Methuen, 1891)......................................£30
IMOGEN, or Only Eighteen (illustrated by H.A. Bone) (Chambers, 1892) £30
LEONA (Cassell, 1892)..£30
BLANCHE: A Story for Girls (illustrated by Robert Barnes) (Chambers, 1894 [1893]) £30
OLIVIA: A Story for Girls (illustrated by Robert Barnes) (Chambers, 1895 [1894])................£30
WHITE TURRETS (illustrated by William Rainey) (Chambers, 1896 [1895])............................£20
PHILIPPA (illustrated by J. Finnemore) (Chambers, 1897 [1896])..£20
MEG LANGHOLME, or The Day After Tomorrow (illustrated by William Rainey) (Chambers, 1897) £20
THE LAUREL WALK (Isbister, 1898)..£20
THE GRIM HOUSE (illustrated by Warwick Goble) (Nisbet, 1899)..£30

MONTGOMERY, L.M.

Canadian author. Born: Lucy Maud Montgomery in Clifton, Prince Edward Island, in 1874. Studied to be a teacher, but joined the *Halifax Chronicle* in 1901, having already contributed poems and stories to various papers. Her bestselling novel, *Anne of Green Gables* (1908), was followed by a number of sequels. Died: 1942.

Prices are for books in Very Good condition with dustjackets.

'Anne Shirley' Books

ANNE OF GREEN GABLES (illustrated by M.A. and W.A. Claus) (Page, US, 1908)....................£3,000
ANNE OF GREEN GABLES (illustrated by M.A. and W.A. Claus) (Pitman, 1908)......................£1,000
ANNE OF AVONLEA (Pitman, 1909) £175
CHRONICLES OF AVONLEA (Sampson Low, 1912)..£120
ANNE OF THE ISLAND (Pitman, 1915)..£140
ANNE'S HOUSE OF DREAMS (Constable, 1917) £90
RAINBOW VALLEY (Constable, 1920)..£120
RILLA OF INGLESIDE (Hodder & Stoughton, [1921]) £85
FURTHER CHRONICLES OF AVONLEA (Harrap, 1925) £120
ANNE OF WINDY WILLOWS (Harrap, 1936) £40
ANNE OF INGLESIDE (Harrap, 1939) £40

'Emily Starr' Books

EMILY OF NEW MOON (Hodder & Stoughton, [1923])..£150
EMILY CLIMBS (Hodder & Stoughton, [1925])..£120
EMILY'S QUEST (Hodder & Stoughton, [1927])..£75

'Pat Gardiner' Books

PAT OF SILVER BUSH (Hodder & Stoughton, [1933]) £50
MISTRESS PAT (Harrap, 1935)..£55

Others

KILMENY OF THE ORCHARD (illustrated by George Gibbs) (Pitman, 1910) £200
THE STORY GIRL (Pitman, 1911)...£220
THE GOLDEN ROAD (Cassell, 1914)..£220
THE WATCHMAN and Other Poems (Constable, 1920) £55
THE BLUE CASTLE (Hodder & Stoughton, [1926])..£60
MAGIC FOR MARIGOLD (Hodder & Stoughton, [1929])...£60
AUNT BECKY BEGAN IT (Hodder & Stoughton, [1931])..£60
JANE OF LANTERN HILL (Harrap, 1937)..£40
THE ROAD TO YESTERDAY (Angus & Robertson, 1975)..£20
THE DOCTOR'S SWEETHEART and Other Stories (Harrap, 1979)..£20

'MOTHER GOOSE'

The figure of 'Mother Goose' as a teller of folk tales and rhymes has its roots in both German and French folklore. Its English origins can be traced back to the first translation of Charles Perrault's *Histories, or Tales of Past Times* (1729; *Histories, ou Contes du temps passé*), where the expression 'Contes de Ma Mère L'Oye' was translated as 'Mother Goose's Tales'. Subsequent edition of the stories were published under the title, *Mother Goose's Tales,* and the phrase became commonplace to describe any book of 'traditional' rhymes or fables, especially in America.

Prices are for books in Very Good condition.

THE ENTERTAINING TALES OF MOTHER GOOSE (Lumsden, [c1815])..£1,750
MOTHER GOOSE'S MELODY Containing the Most Celebrated Songs of the Old British Nurses (Marshall, 1817)........£1,000
MOTHER GOOSE, or Harlequin and the Golden Egg: An Original Shadow Pantomime (London, 1864) £600
MOTHER GOOSE'S MELODIES (illustrated by J. Ralson Chase) (Philadelphia, US, [1870])....................................£500
MOTHER GOOSE'S MELODIES FOR CHILDREN, or Songs for the Nursery Edited by G.A.R.
  (illustrated by H.L. Stephens and G. Fay) (London, 1872 [1871]) £500

*A plate from Arthur Rackham's 1913 edition of **Mother Goose**, issued by Heinemann in both trade and limited editions.*

MOTHER GOOSE'S NURSERY RHYMES (illustrated by Sir John Gilbert, John Tenniel and others) (Routledge, 1877 [1876]).......£120
MOTHER GOOSE'S JINGLES (illustrated by H. Weir, Walter Crane and others) (London, 1878 [1877]).................................£100
MOTHER GOOSE'S NURSERY RHYMES AND FAIRY TALES (two volumes) (Routledge, 1878 [1877]).....................the set £55
MOTHER GOOSE, or The Old Nursery Rhymes (illustrated by Kate Greenaway) (Routledge, [1881]).................................£170
OLD MOTHER GOOSE and Other Rhymes (illustrated by H. Weir) (Routledge, [1886])...£60
MOTHER GOOSE'S NURSERY RHYMES, TALES AND JINGLES (Warne, [1890])...£50
OLD MOTHER GOOSE'S RHYMES AND TALES (illustrated by Constance Haslewood) (Warne, 1890)..............................£50
LITTLE MOTHER GOOSE (illustrated by Jessie Watkins) (Ward, [1892]) £125
MOTHER GOOSE IN PROSE: Nursery Rhymes with Stories Founded on Them by L. Frank Baum
   (illustrated by M. Parrish) (Chicago, US, [1897])..£3,000
DENSLOW'S MOTHER GOOSE: Being the Old Familiar Rhymes and Jingles of Mother Goose
   Edited by W.W. Denslow (illustrated by W.W. Denslow) (New York, US, 1901)...£1,200
MOTHER GOOSE'S NURSERY RHYMES (illustrated by Mabel Chadburn) (Dent, 1903)..£50
MOTHER GOOSE'S NURSERY RHYMES Edited by Walter C. Jerrold (illustrated by John Hassall) (Blackie, 1909 [1908]).......£55
MOTHER GOOSE'S BOOK OF NURSERY RHYMES AND SONGS Edited by Ernest and Grace Rhys (Dent, [1910]).............£30
MOTHER GOOSE (illustrated by Mabel Lucie Attwell) (Raphael Tuck, 1910)..£150
MOTHER GOOSE JINGLES (Nister, [c.1910])..£75
MOTHER GOOSE: The Old Nursery Rhymes (illustrated by Arthur Rackham) (Heinemann, [1913])..............................£300
MOTHER GOOSE: The Old Nursery Rhymes (illustrated by Arthur Rackham; limited to 1,130 copies,
   signed by the artist) (Heinemann, [1913])..£1,000
THE LITTLE MOTHER GOOSE (illustrated by Jessie Willcox Smith; selected and adapted by Samuel McChord Crothers)
   (Dodd Mead, US, [1915])..£70
MOTHER GOOSE'S NURSERY RHYMES. Edited by L.E. Walter (illustrated by Charles Folkard)
   (A. & C. Black, [1919])..£70
MOTHER GOOSE'S NURSERY RHYMES. Edited by L.E. Walter (illustrated by Charles Folkard; second edition)
   (A. & C. Black, 1923)..£50
THE BOYD SMITH MOTHER GOOSE (illustrated by E. Boyd Smith; text collated by Lawrence Elmendorf)
   (Putnam, 1920)...£50
THE OLD MOTHER GOOSE NURSERY RHYME BOOK (illustrated by Anne Anderson) (Nelson, [1926]).......................£85
MOTHER GOOSE NURSERY RHYMES (illustrated by Charles Robinson) (Collins, [1928])....................................£75
MOTHER GOOSE: Nursery Rhymes (illustrated by Margaret W. Tarrant) (Ward Lock, [1929]).............................£60
WILLY POGÁNY'S MOTHER GOOSE (illustrated by Willy Pogány) (Nelson, U.K./US, [1929])...............................£150
MOTHER GOOSE (illustrated by Sybil Tawse) (Harrap, 1932)..£40
THE POP-UP MOTHER GOOSE (New York, US, [1933])..£400
MOTHER GOOSE RHYMES (illustrated by S.B. Pearse and Winifred M. Ackroyd) (Coker, [1935])........................£50
MOTHER GOOSE: The Old Nursery Rhymes (illustrated by Arthur Rackham; two volumes) (Heinemann, [1952]).....the set £150
THE MOTHER GOOSE TREASURY (illustrated by Raymond Briggs) (Hamish Hamilton, 1966)................................£60
MOTHER GOOSE: A Collection of Nursery Rhymes. Edited by Michael Hague (Holt, US, 1984)...........................£25
TAIL FEATHERS FROM MOTHER GOOSE: The Opie Rhyme Book by Iona and Peter Opie (Pavilion, 1988) £25

MURPHY, Jill

British author-illustrator. Born: London, 1949. Author of the 'Worst Witch' series.

Prices are for books in Very Good condition with dustjackets where applicable.

THE WORST WITCH (Allison & Busby, 1974) £30
THE WORST WITCH STRIKES AGAIN (Allison & Busby, 1980) £25
A BAD SPELL FOR THE WORST WITCH (Kestrel, 1982) £15
WHATEVER NEXT? (Walker, 1983)...£12
GEOFFREY STRANGEWAYS (Walker, 1990)..£12
WORLDS APART (Walker, 1991)..£10
THE WORST WITCH ALL AT SEA (Viking, 1993)...£10

Picture Books 1-5

ON THE WAY HOME (Walker, 1982)...£10
ALL IN ONE PIECE (Walker, 1987)..£10
PEACE AT LAST (Walker, 1988)...£10
A PIECE OF CAKE (Walker, 1994)...£10
FIVE MINUTES PEACE (Walker, 1995) £10
THE LAST NOO-NOO (Walker, 1995)..£10

MURRAY, Peter

British author. Born 1951. Award-winning creator of the 'Mokee Joe' series of shorter children's novels.

Prices are for books in Fine condition.

MOKEE JOE IS COMING! (paperback) (Pen Press, 2003) £15
MOKEE JOE IS COMING! (Review Copy, 100 copies) (Pen Press, 2003)..£40
MOKEE JOE IS COMING! (paperback) (Hodder, 2004)..£10
MOKEE JOE RECHARGED (paperback) (Hodder, 2004) £5
MOKEE JOE – THE DOOMSDAY TRAIL (paperback) (Hodder, 2005) £5
BONEBREAKER (book 1 in a series) (paperback) (Hodder, 2005) £5

N

NASH, Ogden

Born: 1902. America's humorous laureate, probably the most quoted of all twentieth-century US poets. He was a droll critic of human frailty and absurdity, with an ingenious play on words. 15 of his 40 books were specifically written for children. Three were illustrated by his daughter Linell. Died: 1971.

Prices are for books in Very Good condition with dustjackets.

THE CRICKET OF CARADOR (with Joseph Alger) (Doubleday Page, US, 1925) £100
PARENTS KEEP OUT: Elderly Poems for Youngerly Readers (illustrated by Marton Wells)
(Little Brown, US, 1951) £20
PARENTS KEEP OUT (Dent, 1962) £15
THE CHRISTMAS THAT ALMOST WASN'T (illustrated by Linell Nash)
(Little Brown, US, 1957) £20
THE CHRISTMAS THAT ALMOST WASN'T (Dent, 1958) £15
CUSTARD THE DRAGON (illustrated by Linell Nash) (Little Brown, US, 1959) £20
CUSTARD THE DRAGON (Dent, 1960) £15
A BOY IS A BOY: The Fun of Being a Boy (illustrated by Arthur Shilstone)
(Franklin Watts, US, [1960]) £20
A BOY IS A BOY (Dent, 1961) £15
CUSTARD THE DRAGON AND THE WICKED KNIGHT
(illustrated by Linell Nash) (Little Brown, US, 1961) £20
THE NEW NUTCRACKER SUITE and Other Innocent Verses
(designed and illustrated by Ivan Chermakoyeff) (Little Brown, US, 1962) £30
GIRLS ARE SILLY (illustrated by Lawrence Beall Smith) (Franklin Watts, US [1962]) £20
GIRLS ARE SILLY (illustrated by Joan Kiddell-Monroe) (Dent, 1964) £15
THE ADVENTURES OF ISABEL (illustrated by Walter Lorraine) (Little Brown, US, 1963) £20
A BOY AND HIS ROOM (illustrated by Lawrence Beall Smith) (Franklin Watts, US, [1963]) £20
A BOY AND HIS ROOM and THE ADVENTURES OF ISABEL (illustrated by Ionicus) (Dent, 1964) £20
THE UNTOLD ADVENTURES OF SANTA CLAUS (Little Brown, US, 1964) £20
THE UNTOLD ADVENTURES OF SANTA CLAUS (illustrated by Ionicus) (Dent, 1964) £20
THE ANIMAL GARDEN (illustrated by Hilary Knight) (M. Evans, US, 1965) £20
THE CRUISE OF THE AARDVARK (illustrated by Wendy Watson) (M. Evans, US, 1967) £20
THE MYSTERIOUS OUPHE (illustrated by Frank Darling) (Spadea Press, US, 1967) £30
AN OGDEN NASH OMNIBOOK (contains THE CHRISTMAS THAT ALMOST WASN'T; A BOY AND HIS ROOM;
and GIRLS ARE SILLY) (Dent, 1967) £20
THE SCROOBIOUS PIP by Edward Lear. Completed by Ogden Nash (illustrated by Nancy Ekholm Burkett)
(Harper & Row, US, 1968) £20
CUSTARD AND COMPANY Selected and Illustrated by Quentin Blake
(Kestrel Books, 1974) £15

NEEDHAM, Violet

British author. Born: 1876. She was 63 when her first novel, *The Black Riders* (1939), was published, although she had submitted it unsuccessfully to several firms twenty years earlier. This was followed by seventeen more children's books, most of them illustrated by her friend and neighbour, Joyce Bruce. Eight of her novels are set in a series of imaginary Central European countries, reflecting her childhood travels on the Continent. Died: 1967.

Prices are for books in Very Good condition with dustjackets.

THE BLACK RIDERS (illustrated by Anne Bullen) (Collins, 1939) £150
THE EMERALD CROWN (illustrated by Anne Bullen) (Collins, 1940) £100
THE STORMY PETREL (illustrated by Joyce Bruce) (Collins, 1942) £100
THE HORN OF MERLYNS (illustrated by Joyce Bruce) (Collins, 1943) £75
THE WOODS OF WINDRI (illustrated by Joyce Bruce) (Collins, 1944) £40
THE HOUSE OF THE PALADIN (illustrated by Joyce Bruce) (Collins, 1945) £40
THE CHANGELING OF MONTE LUCIO (illustrated by Joyce Bruce) (Collins, 1946) £40
THE BELL OF THE FOUR EVANGELISTS (illustrated by Joyce Bruce) (Collins, 1947) £75
THE BOY IN RED (illustrated by Joyce Bruce) (Collins, 1948) £50
THE BETRAYER (illustrated by Joyce Bruce) (Collins, 1950) £50
PANDORA OF PARRHAM ROYAL (illustrated by Joyce Bruce) (Collins, 1951) £120
THE AVENUE (illustrated by Joyce Bruce) (Collins, 1952) £60
HOW MANY MILES TO BABYLON? (illustrated by Joyce Bruce) (Collins, 1953) £120
ADVENTURES AT HAMPTON COURT (illustrated by Will Nickless) (Lutterworth Press, 1954) £120
RICHARD AND THE GOLDEN HORSE SHOE (illustrated by Joyce Bruce) (Collins, 1954) £150
THE GREAT HOUSE OF ESTRAVILLE (illustrated by Joyce Bruce) (Collins, 1955) £150
THE SECRET OF THE WHITE PEACOCK (illustrated by Joyce Bruce) (Collins, 1956) £120
ADVENTURES AT WINDSOR CASTLE (illustrated by David Walsh) (Lutterworth Press, 1957) £120
THE RED ROSE OF RUVINA (illustrated by Richard Kennedy) (Collins, 1957) £100

NESBIT, E.

British author. Born: Edith Nesbit in Kennington, London, in 1858. Following the death of her father when she was four, she spent the next nine years travelling with her family in France and Germany, during which time she had little formal schooling. She had her first poem accepted for publication when she was fifteen, and continued to write for various magazines after her marriage to Hubert Bland, one of the founder members of the Fabian Society, in 1880. She thought of herself primarily as a poet, but following the success of *The Story of the Treasure Seekers* (1899), parts of which had originally appeared in *Pall Mall* and *Windsor* magazines, she concentrated on writing for children. Among her best-known works in the field are *Five Children and It* (1902), *The Phoenix and the Carpet* (1904) and *The Railway Children* (1906). Died: 1924.

Prices are for books in Very Good condition (with dustjackets after 1940).

THE STORY OF THE TREASURE SEEKERS: Being the Adventures of the Bastable Children in Search of a Fortune
(illustrated by Gordon Browne & Lewis Baumer) (T. Fisher Unwin, 1899) £400
THE BOOK OF DRAGONS (illustrated by H.R. Millar and H. Granville Fell) (Harper, 1901 [1900]) £400
9 UNLIKELY TALES FOR CHILDREN (illustrated by H.R. Millar & Claude Shepperson) (T. Fisher Unwin, 1901)....................£300
THE WOULDBEGOODS: Being the Further Adventures of the Treasure Seekers
(illustrated by Arthur Buckland and John Hassall) (T. Fisher Unwin, 1901)...£300
FIVE CHILDREN AND IT (illustrated by H.R. Millar) (T. Fisher Unwin, 1902) £300
THE PHOENIX AND THE CARPET (illustrated by H.R. Millar) (Newnes [1904])...£300
THE NEW TREASURE SEEKERS (illustrated by Gordon Browne and Lewis Baumer) (T. Fisher Unwin, 1904)....................£300
OSWALD BASTABLE AND OTHERS (illustrated by C.E. Brock and H.R. Millar) (Wells Gardner, 1905)............£300
THE RAILWAY CHILDREN (illustrated by C.E.Brock) (Wells Gardner, 1906)...£1,200
THE STORY OF THE AMULET (illustrated by H.R.Millar) (T. Fisher Unwin, 1906) £250
THE ENCHANTED CASTLE (illustrated by H.R. Millar) (T. Fisher Unwin, 1907)..£250
THE HOUSE OF ARDEN (illustrated by H.R. Millar) (T. Fisher Unwin, 1908) £300
HARDING'S LUCK (illustrated by H.R. Millar) (Hodder & Stoughton, 1909) £300
THE MAGIC CITY (illustrated by H.R. Millar) (Macmillan, 1910) £300
THE WONDERFUL GARDEN, or The Three Cs (illustrated by H.R. Millar) (Macmillan, 1911) £200
THE MAGIC WORLD (illustrated by H.R. Millar and Spencer Pryse) (Macmillan, 1912)...£200
WET MAGIC (illustrated by H.R. Millar) (T. Werner Laurie [l913])..£200
FIVE OF US - AND MADELINE (edited by Mrs C. Sharp) (illustrated by Nora Unwin) (T. Fisher Unwin, 1925) £100
COMPLETE HISTORY OF THE BASTABLE FAMILY (illustrated by H.R. Millar and others) (Ernest Benn, 1928) £100

Other children's books (for younger readers)
DOGGY TALES (illustrated by Lucy Kemp-Welch) (Marcus Ward [1895]) £80
PUSSY TALES (illustrated by Lucy Kemp-Welch) (Marcus Ward [1895])..£80
TALES OF THE CLOCK (illustrated by Helen Jackson) (Raphael Tuck, 1895) £60
TALES TOLD IN THE TWILIGHT (Nister, 1897) £100
THE CHILDREN'S SHAKESPEARE (illustrated by Frances Brundage) (Raphael Tuck, 1897) £60
ROYAL CHILDREN OF ENGLISH HISTORY (illustrated by Frances Brundage) (Raphael Tuck, 1897) £60
A BOOK OF DOGS (illustrated by Winifred Austin) (Dent, 1898)..£60
PUSSY AND DOGGY TALES (illustrated by Lucy Kemp-Welch) (Dent, 1899)...£80
THE REVOLT OF THE TOYS and WHAT COMES OF QUARRELLING (illustrated by Ambrose Dudley) (Nister [1902]) £150
THE RAINBOW QUEEN and Other Stories (Raphael Tuck [l903]) £60
PLAYTIME STORIES (Raphael Tuck, 1903) £60
THE STORY OF FIVE REBELLIOUS DOLLS (Nister, 1904) £150
CAT TALES (with Rosamund Bland) (illustrated by Isabel Watkin) (Nister, 1904) £100
PUG PETER: KING OF MOUSELAND (illustrated by Harry Rountree and John Hassall) (Alf Cooke [1905]) £150
THE OLD NURSERY STORIES (illustrated by W.H. Margetson) (Hodder & Stoughton/H.Frowde, 1908) £60
THESE LITTLE ONES (illustrated by Spencer Pryse) (George Allen, 1909)...£60
CHILDREN'S STORIES FROM ENGLISH HISTORY (with Doris Ashley) (illustrated by John H. Bacon and Howard Davie)
(Raphael Tuck, 1914)..£40
FAIRY STORIES (Edited by Naomi Lewis, issued with dustjacket, illustrated by Brian Robb) (Ernest Benn, 1977) £15

Verse
LAYS AND LEGENDS Two volumes (Longman, 1886 & 1892) ....the set £80
THE LILY AND THE CROSS (Griffith Farran, 1887)...£60
THE STAR OF BETHLEHEM (Nister, 1887) £150
LEAVES OF LIFE (Longman, 1888)..£60
THE MESSAGE OF THE DOVE: An Easter Poem (H.J. Drane, 1888) £60
EASTER-TIDE: POEMS (H.J. Drane, 1888) £60
LANDSCAPE AND SONG (H.J. Drane, 1888)...£60
BY LAND AND SEA (H.J. Drane, 1888) £60
THE LILIES ROUND THE CROSS: AN EASTER MEMORIAL (with Helen J.Wood) (Nister [1889])............................£150
CORALS: SEA SONGS (Nister [1889])..£300
SONGS OF TWO SEASONS (illustrated by J. MacIntyre) (Raphael Tuck [1890])...£250
SWEET LAVENDER (Nister [1892])...£150
THE VOYAGE OF COLUMBUS, 1492: THE DISCOVERY OF AMERICA (illustrated by Will and Frances Brundage)
(Raphael Tuck, 1892)..£200
OUR FRIENDS AND ALL ABOUT THEM (Raphael Tuck [1893]) £150

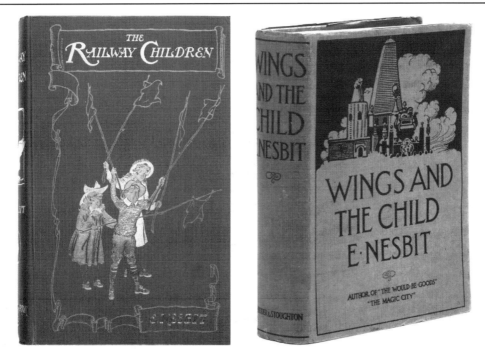

*Edith Nesbit wrote many stories that have become children's classics, including her most famous work, **The Railway Children** (1906), plus **The Story of the Treasure Seekers** (1899), its sequel **The Wouldbegoods** (1901), and **Five Children and It** (1902).*

FLOWERS I BRING AND SONGS I SING (as 'E. Bland') (Raphael Tuck [1893]) **£100**
THE GIRL'S OWN BIRTHDAY BOOK (H.J. Drane [l894]).. **£30**
HOLLY AND MISTLETOE: A Book of Christmas Verse (with Norman Gale and Richard Le Gallienne)
    (Marcus Ward [1895]).. **£60**
A POMANDER OF VERSE (John Lane, 1895)... **£80**
ROSE LEAVES (Nister [1895]).. **£150**
AS HAPPY AS A KING (illustrated by S. Rosamund Praeger) (Marcus Ward [1896]).......................... **£80**
DINNA FORGET (with G.C. Bingham) (Nister, 1897).. **£100**
SONGS OF LOVE AND EMPIRE (Constable, 1898).. **£60**
TO WISH YOU EVERY JOY (Raphael Tuck, 1901) **£60**
THE RAINBOW AND THE ROSE (Longman, 1905).. **£40**
JESUS IN LONDON: A Poem (Fifield, 1908)... **£40**

Play
CINDERELLA (Sidgwick & Jackson, 1909) **£40**

Miscellaneous
WINGS AND THE CHILD: OR, THE BUILDING OF MAGIC CITIES (Hodder & Stoughton, 1913)
    (illustrated by George Barraud) **£150**
LONG AGO WHEN I WAS YOUNG (illustrated by Edward Ardizzone. With dustjacket) (Whiting & Wheaton, 1966)................. **£30**

Anthologies of children's stories
LISTEN LONG AND LISTEN WELL (Raphael Tuck, 1893) **£100**
SUNNY TALES FOR SNOWY DAYS (Raphael Tuck, 1893) **£100**
TOLD BY SUNBEAMS & ME (Raphael Tuck, 1893) **£100**
FUR AND FEATHERS: Tales for All Weathers (Raphael Tuck, 1894) **£100**
LADS AND LASSIES (Raphael Tuck, 1894) **£100**
TALES THAT ARE TRUE, FOR BROWN EYES AND BLUE (illustrated by M.Goodman) (Raphael Tuck, 1894) **£100**
TALES TO DELIGHT, FROM MORNING TILL NIGHT (illustrated by M.Goodman) (Raphael Tuck, 1894) **£100**
HOURS IN MANY LANDS: Stories and Poems (illustrated by Frances Brundage) (Raphael Tuck, 1894) **£100**
TREASURES FROM STORYLAND (Raphael Tuck 1895)... **£100**
DULCIE'S LANTERN & other stories (with Theo Gift and Mrs Worthington) (Griffith Farran, 1895) **£80**
DOG TALES (with A. Guest and Emily R. Watson) (illustrated by R.K.Mounsey) (Raphael Tuck, 1898) **£100**
HIDE AND SEEK TALES (Nister [l909])... **£100**
MY SEASIDE STORY BOOK (with George Manville Fenn) (Nister, 1911) **£80**
OUR NEW STORY BOOK (illustrated by Elsie Wood and Louis Wain) (Nister, 1913)............................. **£100**

NICHOLS, Beverley

British author. Born: 1898. He wrote four children's books about a magic wood, beginning with *The Tree That Sat Down* (1945). Died: 1983.

Prices are for books in Very Good condition in dustjackets.

THE TREE THAT SAT DOWN (illustrated by Isobel and John Morton-Sale) (Cape, 1945) £25
THE STREAM THAT STOOD STILL (illustrated by Richard Kennedy) (Cape, 1948)................................£25
THE MOUNTAIN OF MAGIC (illustrated by Peggy Fortnum) (Cape, 1950) £25
THE WICKEDEST WITCH IN THE WORLD (W.H. Allen, 1971)..£25

NIELSEN, Kay

Danish illustrator. Born in Copenhagen in 1886. Studied art at Colarossi's and the Academie Julien in Paris. Moved to London in 1911, where he was commissioned to illustrate Sir Arthur Quiller-Couch's *In Powder and Crinoline* (1913) by Hodder & Stoughton. This was followed by handsome 'Gift Book' editions of the fairy tales of Hans Andersen (1924) and the Brothers Grimm (*Hansel and Gretel*, 1925). Moved to California in 1938 hoping to find work as a set designer in Hollywood, but met with little success. Died: 1957.

Prices are for books in Very Good condition.

IN POWDER AND CRINOLINE Old Fairy Tales retold by Sir Arthur Quiller-Couch
   (24 colour plates by Kay Nielsen; cloth binding) (Hodder & Stoughton, [1913])................................£800
IN POWDER AND CRINOLINE (26 colour plates by Kay Nielsen; Large Paper edition) (Hodder & Stoughton, [1913]) £1,200
IN POWDER AND CRINOLINE (26 colour plates by Kay Nielsen; De Luxe edition: limited to 500 copies,
   signed by the artist; green vellum binding) (Hodder & Stoughton, [1913]) £2,500
EAST OF THE SUN AND WEST OF THE MOON: Old Tales from the North retold by Peter C. Asbjörnsen and
   Jorgen Moe (25 colour plates by Kay Nielsen; blue cloth binding) (Hodder & Stoughton, [1914]) £1,750
EAST OF THE SUN AND WEST OF THE MOON (25 colour plates by Kay Nielsen; De Luxe edition:
   limited to 500 copies signed by Artist; 25 colour plates; white vellum binding) (Hodder & Stoughton, [1914])................£8,000
HANS ANDERSEN'S FAIRY TALES (twelve colour plates by Kay Nielsen; blue cloth binding) (Hodder & Stoughton, [1924])........£700

One of Kay Nielsen's plates from In **Powder and Crinoline**, *the book that launched his career as a book illustrator.*

HANS ANDERSEN'S FAIRY TALES (twelve colour plates by Kay Nielsen; De Luxe edition: limited to 500 copies, signed by the artist; blue cloth binding, issued with dustjacket / or white vellum binding) (Hodder & Stoughton, [1924])...**£2,000 / £3,000**
HANSEL AND GRETEL and Other Stories (twelve colour plates by Kay Nielsen) (Hodder & Stoughton, [1925])...................**£800**
HANSEL AND GRETEL and Other Stories (twelve colour plates by Kay Nielsen; limited to 600 copies, signed by the artist; cream buckram binding) (Hodder & Stoughton, [1925])................................**£2,500**
RED MAGIC A Collection of the World's Best Fairy Tales from all Countries Edited and arranged by Romer Wilson (red cloth binding) (Cape, 1930)...**£400**

NISTER, Ernest

German publisher of movable picture books. Although based in Nuremburg, Nister set up a London office in 1888 which, under the direction of the writer Robert Ellice Mack, provided many of the designs for the firm's books. These contained a variety of novelties, including 'pop-up' panoramas, revolving pictures, and 'slat' mechanisms that replace one picture with another at the pull of a tab.

Prices are for books in Very Good condition.

Pop-Up Books

LITTLE PETS, PANORAMA PICTURES ON VIEW WITHIN (Nister, [c1893]) **£500**
PEEPS INTO FAIRYLAND by F.E. Weatherly (Nister, [c1895]) **£500**
THE MODEL MENAGERIE by L.L. Weedon and Evelyn Fletcher (Nister, [c1895]) **£550**
THE LAND OF LONG AGO (illustrated by E. Stuart Hardy) (Nister, [c1898]) **£700**

Movables and Panorama Books

LITTLE FOLK'S SURPRISES by Hope Myrtoun (verse; illustrations by Percy Hickling) (Nister, [c1890])...............................**£500**
WONDERLAND PICTURES (Nister, [c1890]) **£500**
MAGIC MOMENTS (Nister, [c1892]) **£500**

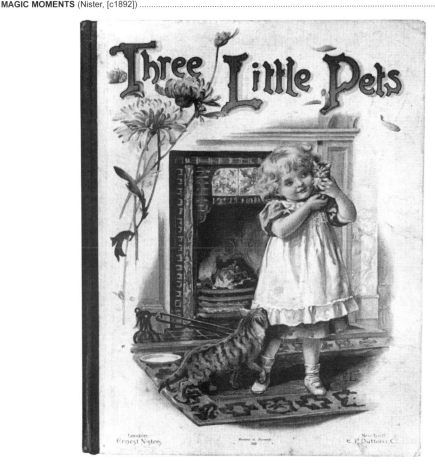

A fine example of a Nister picture book from the late 1890s. Like all the others, it was printed in Bavaria.

NISTER, Ernest

TWINKLING PICTURES by L.L. Weedon (verse) (Nister, [c1892])..£500
PLEASANT PASTIME PICTURES (Nister, [c1895]) £500
MORE PLEASANT SURPRISES by F.E. Weatherly (movable book) (Nister, [1895])...............................£500
CHANGING PETS (Nister, [c1905])...£250
COME AND GO!: A Novel Book for Children by Clifton Bingham (verse) (Nister, [c1905]) £1,200

'Nister's Holiday' Annuals

NISTER'S HOLIDAY ANNUAL: Pictures and Stories for Little Folk Edited by R.E. Mack (Nister, [1888-1916]) .... each £200

Others

WINTER SONGS AND SKETCHES Edited by E. Nesbit and R. Ellice Mack (Nister/Griffith Farran, [c1880])...........................£50
SCENES FROM THE BIBLE (picture puzzle book; contains four jigsaws; in box) (Nister, [c1880]).............£100
WHEN ALL IS YOUNG by Robert E. Mack (verse; illustrated by Harriet M. Bennet) (Nister/Dutton, US, 1888) £200
DICK AND HIS DOG (shaped picture book) (Nister, [c1890])..£100
PLAY HOUR STORY BOOK (Nister, [c1890])..£75
GULLIVER'S TRAVELS (illustrated by A. Jackson) (Nister, [c1890])..£75
AS THY DAYS, SO SHALL THY STRENGTH BE (Nister, [c1890])...£75
HOLLOW TREE HOUSE by E. Nesbit, Mrs Molesworth and others (Nister, [1892]).................................£90
PICTURE HOUSE (Nister, 1893) £300
PICTURES AND PLUMS FOR FINGERS AND THUMBS (Nister, [c1893])...£300
SHORT AND SWEET STORIES (Nister, [c1893])..£60
NISTER'S NONSENSE (verse and prose by various authors) (Nister, [1894])...£75
MORE NISTER'S NONSENSE (verse and prose by various authors) (Nister, [1894]).................................£75
PICTURE BOOK GARDEN AND STORY LAND (short stories and verse) (Nister, 1894) £300
MORE JINGLES, JOKES AND FUNNY FOLKS by Louis Wain and Clifton Bingham (Nister, 1898) £250
PATHWAY OF FLOWERS — A CALENDAR FOR 1898 (with silk ties) (Nister, [c1898])............................£75
THREE LITTLE PETS (Nister, [c1898])...£100
PICTURE COMPANIONS (Nister, [c1899])..£300
WHEN MOTHER WAS A LITTLE GIRL by Blanchard (verse) (Nister, [c1900])..£400
PIG TALES by Lilian Gask (Nister, [c1900])...£75
AS WITH GLADNESS (pamphlet) (Nister, [c1900]) £50
MY LITTLE CIRCUS BOOK by Lavine Helmer (Nister, [c1900]) £40
THE GAMES BOOK FOR BOYS AND GIRLS (Nister, [c1900])...£80
KING ROBERT'S PAGE (Nister, 1900) £50
LET'S PRETEND (Nister, [c1900])..£200
MERRY CHILDREN'S NURSERY RHYMES (Nister, [c1900])...£80
LAMBS' TALES FROM SHAKESPEARE (Nister, [c1900])..£60
NURSERY TALES (illustrated by E. Stuart Hardy) (Nister, [c1900]) £40
MY DOLLY'S TOY BOOK (untearable book) (Nister, [c1900])..£150
COSY CORNER STORIES (Nister, [c1900]) £60
GRANDMA'S MEMORIES by Mary D. Brine (illustrated by Ambrose Dudley) (Nister/Dutton, US, [c1900])............£50
WARRIORS BRAVE: A Story of Little Lead Soldiers (illustrated by M.M. Jamieson)
   (Nister: 'Little Mother' series, [c1900])...£175
A BOOK OF GNOMES by E. Weatherly (Nister, [c1900])..£300
THE DANDY LION by Louis Wain and Clifton Bingham (Nister, [c1900])...£300
FUN ALL THE WAY (Nister, 1900) £100
FUN AND FROLIC by Louis Wain and Clifton Bingham (Nister, [1902])...£650
FUN FOR EVERYONE (Nister, 1902)...£100
THE REVOLT OF THE TOYS AND WHAT BECAME OF QUARRELLING: Two Stories by E. Nesbit (Nister, 1902)............£150
THE DOINGS OF A DEAR LITTLE COUPLE BY MARY BRINE (Nister, [c1902]) £50
MARCUS THE YOUNG CENTURION by George Manville Fenn (Nister, 1904) £60
SHAKESPEARE'S HEROINES by Anna Jameson (Nister, [c1904])..£50
THE STORY OF THE FIVE REBELLIOUS DOLLS (Nister, 1904)...£200
FUNNY FAVOURITES by Clifton Bingham (Nister, 1904) £300
PAUL CRESWICK IN ALFRED'S DAY (Nister, [c1905])..£30
DICK OF TEMPLE BAR by M.C. Roswell (illustrated by I. Thackeray) (Nister/Dutton, US, [c1905])............£35
OH! SUCH FUN (Nister, [c1905])..£60
STORIES AND RHYMES FOR HOLIDAY TIMES (Nister, [c1907]) £60
FAIRY TALES (illustrated by Arthur A. Dixon) (Nister, 1908)..£60
FULL OF FUN by Clifton Bingham (Nister, [c1908])...£300
HIDE AND SEEK STORIES (Nister, [c1909])...£75
PLAYTIME STORIES (Nister, [c1909]) £50
THE POET AND OTHER ANIMALS (illustrated by H.G.H. Thompson) (Nister, [1909])............................£175
FAVOURITE FAIRY TALES (Nister, [c1910]) £60
HAPPY HEARTS AND MERRY EYES (Nister, [c1910])...£60
MOTHER GOOSE JINGLES (Nister, [c1910])...£80
MY SEASIDE STORY BOOK by E. Nesbit and George Manville Fenn (Nister, 1911) £60
OUR NEW STORY BOOK by E. Nesbit and others (Nister/Dutton, US, 1913) £75
ROSY CHEEKS FUNNY BOOK (Nister, [c1917]) £100
WILD ANIMAL TALES (Nister, [c1917]) £50

NIX, Garth

Australian author. Born: 1963. Writer of many children's books, the best-known of which is the 'Old Kingdom' series (listed below), once dubbed 'fantasy that reads like realism' by Philip Pullman. Selected bibliography.

Prices are for books in Fine condition in dustjackets.

SABRIEL (Eos, 1996)..£35
SABRIEL (Collins, 2002) £10
LIRAEL: DAUGHTER OF THE CLAYR (HarperCollins, 2001).................................£8
ABHORSEN (HarperCollins, 2003) £5
THE CREATURE OF THE CASE (HarperCollins, 2005)..£5

NORTON, Mary

British author. Born: Mary Pearson in London in 1903. Educated at St. Margaret's Convent, East Grinstead, and Lilian Baylis's Old Vic Theatre School, subsequently working as an actress. Her first children's work, *The Magic Bed-Knob* (1945), was the inspiration for the Disney film, *Bedknobs and Broomsticks* (1971), but she is best known for her 'Borrowers' books, featuring the diminutive Clock family. She moved to Ireland in 1972. Died: 1992.

Prices are for books in Very Good condition with dustjackets.

'Bedknobs' Books

THE MAGIC BED-KNOB (illustrated by Joan Kiddell-Monroe)
(Dent, 1945)...£100
BONFIRES AND BROOMSTICKS (illustrated by Mary Adshead)
(Dent, 1947)...£80
BEDKNOB AND BROOMSTICK (adapted from 'The Magic Bed-Knob' and 'Bonfires and Broomsticks';
illustrated by Erik Blegvad) (Dent, 1957)..£30

'Borrowers' Books

THE BORROWERS (illustrated by Diana Stanley) (Dent, 1952) £125
THE BORROWERS (illustrated by Michael Hague) (Harcourt Brace, US, 1991).....£30
THE BORROWERS AFIELD (illustrated by Diana Stanley) (Dent, 1955) £100
THE BORROWERS AFLOAT (illustrated by Diana Stanley) (Dent, 1959) £80
THE BORROWERS ALOFT (illustrated by Diana Stanley) (Dent, 1961) £45
THE BORROWERS OMNIBUS (contains 'The Borrowers', 'The Borrowers Afield',
'The Borrowers Afloat' and 'The Borrowers Aloft'; illustrated by Diana Stanley) (Dent, 1966) ...£35
POOR STAINLESS (Dent, 1971)..£15
THE BORROWERS AVENGED (illustrated by Pauline Baynes)
(Kestrel, 1982)...£15

Others

ARE ALL THE GIANTS DEAD? (illustrated by Brian Froud)
(Dent, 1975)...£25

*The four first edition volumes in Mary Norton's 'Borrowers' series published between in 1952 and 1961. She also wrote **The Magic Bed-Knob** in 1945, which was the inspiration for the 1971 Disney film **Bedknobs and Broomsticks**.*

O'BRIAN, Patrick

British historical novelist and translator. Born: Richard Patrick Russ, 1914. Best known for the popular 'Jack Aubrey' series of nautical adventures, O'Brian also penned a handful of juvenile and children's titles. Died: 2000.

Prices are for books in Very Good condition with dustjackets.

As Patrick O'Brian
THE ROAD TO SAMARCAND (Hart-Davis, 1954) £250
THE GOLDEN OCEAN (Hart-Davis, 1956) £175
THE GOLDEN OCEAN (J. Day, US, 1957)..£125
THE GOLDEN OCEAN (Revised Edition) (Macmillan, 1970) £20
THE GOLDEN OCEAN (Revised Edition) (Norton, US, 1994)..£20
THE UNKNOWN SHORE (Hart Davis, 1959)...£100
THE UNKNOWN SHORE (Norton, US, 1995)..£20
MEN OF WAR (Collins, 1974)..£25

As 'R.P. Russ'
CAESAR: THE LIFE STORY OF A PANDA LEOPARD (illustrated by Harry Rountree) (Putnam, 1930)..............£1,000
CAESAR: THE LIFE STORY OF A PANDA LEOPARD ('by Patrick O'Brian') (The British Library, 1999) £12
BEASTS ROYAL (illustrated by Harry Rountree) (Putnam, 1934)...£1,000
HUSSEIN: AN ENTERTAINMENT (Oxford University Press, 1938)...£1,000
HUSSEIN: AN ENTERTAINMENT ('by Patrick O'Brian') (The British Library, 1999).......................................£12

ODGERS, Chris

British author and illustrator. Born: 1977. Burst onto the scene with *Fall* in 2003, which won immediate praise for the quality of writing and illustrations.

Prices are for books in Fine condition with dustjackets.

FALL (Atlantic, 2003) £15
FALL (signed, dated, illustrated) (Atlantic, 2003)..£40
FALL (100 signed, dated, numbered; slipcase) (Atlantic, 2003) £75
FALL (limited edition of 13 signed, dated, numbered, slipcased 'Black Cat' copies) (Atlantic, 2003)............£250
MULE (no dustjacket; pictorial boards) (Sawhorse Books, 2005) £15
MULE (no dustjacket; pictorial boards; 100 signed, dated, numbered) (Sawhorse Books, 2005)....................£20
MULE (no dustjacket; pictorial boards; 20 signed, dated, numbered 'Black Cat' copies) (Sawhorse Books, 2005) £35

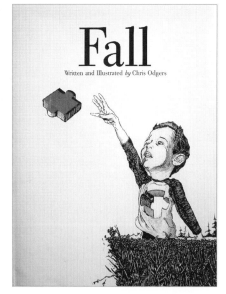

Chris Odgers' debut was only published in 2003 but has already become a well established modern collectable.

OOR WULLIE, YOUR WULLIE, A'BODY'S WULLIE!

*The 1949 **Oor Wullie** book, now worth £800 in Very Good condition. This was previously mistaken for the 1951 edition.*

'OOR WULLIE' ANNUALS

Spin-offs from Dudley Watkins' popular strip, 'The Broons', published biennially by D.C. Thomson The annuals were undated before 1967, and there were no editions for 1945 and 1947 due to paper shortages.

Prices are for annuals in Very Good condition (with cover description for undated annuals).

OOR WULLIE 1941 (Oor Wullie sitting on bucket)..£2,000
OOR WULLIE 1943 (Oor Wullie standing next to a bucket with frog)..£1,000
OOR WULLIE 1949 (sixteen caption portraits of Oor Wullie)..£700
OOR WULLIE 1951 (large head-and-shoulders portrait of Oor Wullie) £500
OOR WULLIE 1953 (Oor Wullie's year month-by-month)..£300
OOR WULLIE 1955 (Oor Wullie reading a copy of 'Oor Wullie') £175
OOR WULLIE 1957 (Oor Wullie snowman sitting on a bucket, with a cabin in the background)..........£125
OOR WULLIE 1959 (Oor Wullie looking over fence with his body painted on the front)......................£80
OOR WULLIE 1961 (Oor Wullie sitting at table holding a knife and fork)..£60
OOR WULLIE 1963 (Oor Wullie walking beside a brick wall, his shadow in the shape of a policeman) ...£45
OOR WULLIE 1965 (Oor Wullie polishing a bucket)..£40
OOR WULLIE 1967 ....£20
OOR WULLIE 1969 ....£20
OOR WULLIE 1971 ....£15
OOR WULLIE 1973 ....£15
OOR WULLIE 1974 ....£10
OOR WULLIE 1975-79 ....each £6
OOR WULLIE 1981-Present ....each £5

OPIE, Iona and Peter

British folklorists. Born: Peter Mason Opie and Iona Margaret Balfour Archibald in 1918 and 1923 respectively. Educated at Eton, Peter published an autobiography, *I Want to Be a Success*, at the age of only 21. Following wartime service with the Royal Sussex Regiment, he joined the BBC and wrote two more volumes of reminiscences. He married Iona in 1943 and, following the birth of their first child in 1944, the two of them set about studying the folklore of childhood, subsequently co-compiling several volumes of nursery rhymes and children's verses. Both of them were awarded honorary Masterships of Arts from Oxford University in 1962. Peter died in 1982.

Prices are for books in Very Good condition with dustjackets.

I SAW ESAU: Traditional Rhymes of Youth (Williams & Norgate, 1947)..£80
I SAW ESAU: Traditional Rhymes of Youth (illustrated by Maurice Sendak) (Walker, 1992)..................£25
THE OXFORD DICTIONARY OF NURSERY RHYMES (Clarendon Press, 1951)....................................£70
THE OXFORD NURSERY RHYME BOOK (illustrated by Joan Hassall)
    (Clarendon Press, 1955) £60
CHRISTMAS PARTY GAMES (OUP, US, 1957)...£60
THE LORE AND LANGUAGE OF SCHOOLCHILDREN (Clarendon Press, 1959)..............................£60
THE PUFFIN BOOK OF NURSERY RHYMES (illustrated by Pauline Baynes; paperback)
    (Puffin, 1963)..£10
A FAMILY BOOK OF NURSERY RHYMES (Clarendon Press, 1964)..£40
CHILDREN'S GAMES IN STREET AND PLAYGROUND (Clarendon Press, 1969)..............................£40
THE OXFORD BOOK OF CHILDREN'S VERSE (Clarendon Press, 1973)..£25
THREE CENTURIES OF NURSERY RHYMES AND POETRY FOR CHILDREN
    (exhibition catalogue) (National Book League, [1973])...£40
THREE CENTURIES OF NURSERY RHYMES AND POETRY FOR CHILDREN
    (exhibition catalogue; enlarged edition) (National Book League, 1977) £40
THE CLASSIC FAIRY TALES (1974)..£30
A NURSERY COMPANION (Clarendon Press, 1980)..£30
THE SINGING GAME (Pavilion, 1985)..£30
BABIES: AN UNSENTIMENTAL ANTHOLOGY (illustrated by Bob Graham)
    (John Murray, 1990) £15
CHILDREN'S GAMES WITH THINGS (OUP, 1997) £15

Books by Iona Opie

DITTIES FOR THE NURSERY (illustrated by Monica Walker) (OUP, 1954) £50
TAIL FEATHERS FROM MOTHER GOOSE: THE OPIE RHYME BOOK (Walker, 1988) £25
THE TREASURES OF CHILDHOOD: BOOKS, TOYS AND GAMES FROM THE OPIE COLLECTION
    (with Robert Opie and Brian Alderson) (Pavilion, 1989) £30
THE PEOPLE IN THE PLAYGROUND (OUP, 1993) £15
'MY VERY FIRST MOTHER GOOSE' SERIES
    (illustrated by Rosemary Wells; board books; no dustjackets) (Walker, 1996) ....each: £5

Books by Peter Opie

I WANT TO BE A SUCCESS (Michael Joseph, 1939) £30
HAVING HELD THE NETTLE (tales) (Torchstream Books, 1945) £20
THE CASE OF BEING A YOUNG MAN (Wells & Gardner, 1946) £20

A Nursery Companion (1980) is one of several volumes about children's literature compiled by folklorists, Iona and Peter Opie. This edition of I Saw Esau was illustrated by Maurice Sendak and published in 1992.

OUTCAULT, Richard Felton

American illustrator, best known for the 'Buster Brown' books. Born: 1863. Died: 1928.

Prices are for books in Very Good condition.

BUSTER BROWN BUSY BODY (Chambers, 1903) £120
BUSTER BROWN (Chambers, [1904]) £110
BUSTER BROWN (Stokes, US, 1904) £100
BUSTER BROWN ABROAD (illustrated by the author) (Chambers, [1905]) £95
TIGE — HIS STORY (illustrated by the author) (Stokes, US, [1905]) £150
MY RESOLUTIONS: BUSTER BROWN (Stokes, US, 1906) £95
BUSTER BROWN (Dean, [1906]) £70
BUSTER BROWN'S MAXIMS FOR MEN (Chambers, [1907]) £55
BUSTER BROWN NUGGETS (Dean, [1908]) £45
BUSTER BROWN'S AUTOBIOGRAPHY (Chambers, [1909]) £45
BUSTER AND TIGE HERE AGAIN (Stokes, US, 1914) £45

OUTHWAITE, Ida Rentoul

Australian author-illustrator. Born: Ida Rentoul in 1888. Illustrated a number of picture books in the first four decades of this century, including several written by her sister, Annie R. Rentoul. Died: 1960.

Prices are for books in Very Good condition.

ELVES AND FAIRIES (Lothian, Melbourne/Sydney, 1916) £750
ELVES AND FAIRIES (limited to 1500 copies, signed by the artist)
   (Lothian, Melbourne/Sydney, 1916) £2,000
THE ENCHANTED FOREST (with Grenbry Outhwaite; sixteen colour plates and fifteen black-and-white plates
   by Ida Rentoul Outhwaite) (A. & C. Black, 1921) £750
THE ENCHANTED FOREST (with Grenbry Outhwaite; sixteen colour plates and fifteen black-and-white plates
   by Ida Rentoul Outhwaite; limited to 500 copies, signed by the artist) (A. & C. Black, 1921) ...£2,000
THE LITTLE GREEN ROAD TO FAIRYLAND (with Annie R. Rentoul; eight colour plates and eight black-and-white plates
   by Ida Rentoul Outhwaite; limited to 300 copies, signed by the artist) (A. & C. Black, 1922) ...£2,000
THE LITTLE GREEN ROAD TO FAIRYLAND (A. & C. Black, 1922) £750
THE LITTLE GREEN ROAD TO FAIRYLAND (second edition) (A. & C. Black, 1925) £450
THE LITTLE FAIRY SISTER (A. & C. Black, 1923) £400
THE LITTLE FAIRY SISTER (second edition) (A. & C. Black, 1929) £300
FAIRYLAND OF IDA RENTOUL OUTHWAITE by Annie R. Rentoul, Grenbry Outhwaite and Ida Rentoul Outhwaite
   (verse and stories; limited to 1,000 copies, signed by the artist) (Ramsay, Melbourne, 1926) ...£2,000
FAIRYLAND OF IDA RENTOUL OUTHWAITE (Stokes, US, 1929) £1,000
FAIRYLAND OF IDA RENTOUL OUTHWAITE (A. & C. Black, 1931) £750
BLOSSOM: A Fairy Story (A. & C. Black, 1928) £300
BUNNY AND BROWNIE: The Adventures of George and Wiggle by Ida Rentoul Outhwaite (A. & C. Black, 1930) £500
A BUNCH OF WILD FLOWERS by Ida Rentoul Outhwaite (Angus & Robertson, Sydney, 1933) £300
THE OTHER SIDE OF NOWHERE by Tarella Quin (Lothian, Melbourne/Sydney, 1934) £300
CHIMNEY TOWN by Tarell Quin Daskein (stories) (A. & C. Black, 1934) £150
SIXPENCE TO SPEND (Australia, 1935) £300

OXENBURY, Helen

British author-illustrator. Born: Suffolk, 1938. Married John Burningham in 1964. Awarded Kate Greenaway Medal in 1969. A very successful series of board books for Walker in the 1980s established her as a household name. These were followed later by fourteen 'Tom and Pippo' books.

Prices are for books in Very Good condition with dustjackets where applicable.

Books Written and Illustrated by Helen Oxenbury

HELEN OXENBURY'S ABC OF THINGS (Heinemann, 1971) £15
PIG TALE (Heinemann, 1973) £15
THE QUEEN AND ROSIE RANDALL (Heinemann, 1978) £15
729 ANIMAL ALLSORTS (Methuen, 1980) £10
BILL AND STANLEY (Benn, 1981) £10
BEDTIME (Walker, 1982) £10
MOTHER'S HELPER (Walker, 1982) £10
SHOPPING TRIP (Walker, 1982) £10
GOOD NIGHT, GOOD MORNING (Walker, 1982) £10
BEACH DAY (Walker, 1982) £10
NUMBERS OF THINGS (London, Delacorte, 1983) £15
THE BIRTHDAY PARTY (Walker, 1983) £10
THE DRIVE (Walker, 1983) £10
THE FIRST CHECK-UP (Walker,1983) £10
THE DANCING CLASS (Walker, 1983) £10
EATING OUT (Walker, 1983) £10
PLAYSCHOOL (Walker, 1983) £10
GRAN AND GRANPA (Walker, 1984) £10
THE VISITOR (Walker, 1984) £10
OUR DOG (Walker, 1984) £10
THE HELEN OXENBURY NURSERY STORY BOOK
    (Walker, 1985) £15
I CAN (Walker, 1986) £10
I HEAR (Walker, 1986) £10
I SEE (Walker, 1986) £10
I TOUCH (Walker, 1986) £10
BABY'S FIRST BOOK AND DOLL (Walker, 1986) £10
ALL FALL DOWN (Walker, 1987) £10
SAY GOODNIGHT (Walker, 1987) £10
TICKLE TICKLE (Walker, 1987) £10
CLAP HANDS (Walker, 1987) £10
MONKEY SEE, MONKEY DO (Walker, 1991) £10
THE HELEN OXENBURY NURSERY TREASURY (Heinemann, 1992) £15
THE THREE LITTLE WOLVES AND THE BIG, BAD PIG
    (Heinemann, 1993) £10

'Tom and Pippo' Books

TOM AND PIPPO GO FOR A WALK (Walker, 1988) £15
TOM AND PIPPO MAKE A MESS (Walker, 1988) £15
TOM AND PIPPO READ A STORY (Walker, 1988) £15
TOM AND PIPPO AND THE WASHING MACHINE (Walker, 1988) £15
TOM AND PIPPO'S DAY (Walker, 1988) £15
TOM AND PIPPO GO SHOPPING (Walker, 1989) £15
TOM AND PIPPO SEE THE MOON (Walker, 1989) £15
TOM AND PIPPO IN THE GARDEN (Walker, 1989) £15
TOM AND PIPPO IN THE SNOW (Walker, 1989) £15
TOM AND PIPPO MAKE A FRIEND (Walker, 1989) £15
PIPPO GETS LOST (Walker, 1989) £15

Others

GREAT BIG ENORMOUS TURNIP by Alexei Tolstoy
    (Watts, 1968) £10
THE HUNTING OF THE SNARK by Lewis Carroll
    (Heinemann, 1970) £15
CAKES AND CUSTARD by Brian Alderson (Heinemann, 1974) £30
A CHILD'S BOOK OF MANNERS by Fay Maschler
    (Cape, 1978) £15
ALL FALL DOWN (Walker, 1987) £10
FARMER DUCK (Walker, 1991) £10
SO MUCH by Trish Cooke (Walker, 1994) £10
IT'S MY BIRTHDAY (Walker, 1994) £5
ALICE'S ADVENTURES IN WONDERLAND by Lewis Carroll
    (Walker,1999) £20

OXENHAM, Elsie J.

British author. Born: Elsie Jeanette Dunkerley in Southport in 1880. She took her pseudonym from that of her father, the novelist John Oxenham ('J.O.'). Under this name, she wrote many school novels, the best-known set in the imaginary Abbey School, Wycombe, based on Cleeve Abbey in Somerset. She was an enthusiastic supporter of the English Folk Dance Society and the American Camp Fire Movement. Died: 1960.

Prices are for books in Very Good condition (with dustjackets after 1937 — after 1931 for 'Abbey' books).

'Abbey' Books

GIRLS OF THE HAMLET CLUB (illustrated by H.C. Earnshaw) (Chambers, 1914)......................£750
THE ABBEY GIRLS (illustrated by Arthur A. Dixon) (Collins, [1920])......................£275
THE GIRLS OF THE ABBEY SCHOOL (illustrated by Elsie Anna Wood) (Collins, [1921])......................£175
THE ABBEY GIRLS GO BACK TO SCHOOL (illustrated by Elsie Anna Wood) (Collins, [1922])......................£175
THE NEW ABBEY GIRLS (illustrated by Elsie Anna Wood) (Collins, [1923])......................£175
THE ABBEY GIRLS AGAIN (illustrated by Elsie Anna Wood) (Collins, [1924])......................£175
THE ABBEY GIRLS IN TOWN (illustrated by Rosa C. Petherick) (Collins, [1925])......................£175
QUEEN OF THE ABBEY GIRLS (illustrated by E.J. Kealey) (Collins, [1926])......................£175
JEN OF THE ABBEY SCHOOL (Collins, [1927])......................£175
THE ABBEY GIRLS WIN THROUGH (Collins, [1928])......................£175
THE ABBEY SCHOOL (omnibus; illustrated by Elsie Anna Wood) (Collins, [1928])......................£175
THE ABBEY GIRLS AT HOME (illustrated by Inder Burns) (Collins, [1929])......................£70
THE GIRLS OF ROCKLANDS SCHOOL (adapted from 'Jen of the Abbey School') (Collins, 1929)......................£40
THE SECOND TERM AT ROCKLANDS (adapted from 'Jen of the Abbey School') (Collins, [1930])......................£40
THE ABBEY GIRLS PLAY UP (Collins, [1930])......................£140
THE THIRD TERM AT ROCKLANDS (adapted from 'Jen of the Abbey School') (Collins, [1931])......................£50
THE ABBEY GIRLS ON TRIAL (Collins, [1931])......................£140
THE GIRLS OF SQUIRREL HOUSE (adapted from 'Rosamund's Victory') (Collins, [1932])......................£40
BIDDY'S SECRET: A Romance of the Abbey Girls (Chambers, 1932)......................£850
THE E.J. OXENHAM OMNIBUS (contains 'The Abbey Girls Win Through', 'The Abbey Girls at Home' and
    'The Abbey Girls Play Up'; issued without dustjacket) (Collins, [1932])......................£100
ROSAMUND'S VICTORY: A Romance of the Abbey Girls (Harrap, 1933)......................£275
MAIDLIN TO THE RESCUE: A Story of the Abbey Girls (illustrated by Rene Cloke) (Chambers, 1934)......................£800
THE CALL OF THE ABBEY SCHOOL (adapted from 'Queen of the Abbey Girls') (Collins, [1934])......................£25
JOY'S NEW ADVENTURE: A Romance of the Abbey Girls (illustrated by Rene Cloke) (Chambers, 1935)......................£800
MAIDLIN BEARS THE TORCH: An Abbey Story (Religious Tract Societ/Girl's Own Paper, [1937])......................£800
ROSAMUND'S TUCK-SHOP: A School Story (Religious Tract Society/Girl's Own Paper, [1937])......................£250
ROSAMUND'S CASTLE (Religious Tract Society/Girl's Own Paper, [1938])......................£800
SCHOOLDAYS AT THE ABBEY (Collins, 1938)......................£65
SECRETS OF THE ABBEY (illustrated by Heade) (Collins, 1939)......................£65
STOWAWAYS IN THE ABBEY (illustrated by Heade) (Collins, 1940)......................£65
JANDY MAC COMES BACK (illustrated by Heade) (Collins, 1941)......................£55
MAID OF THE ABBEY (illustrated by Heade) (Collins, 1943)......................£35
TWO JOANS AT THE ABBEY (illustrated by Margaret Horder) (Collins, 1945)......................£50
AN ABBEY CHAMPION (illustrated by Margaret Horder) (Muller, 1946)......................£150
ROBINS IN THE ABBEY (illustrated by Margaret Horder) (Collins, 1947)......................£35
A FIDDLER FOR THE ABBEY (illustrated by Margaret Horder) (Muller, 1948)......................£150
GUARDIANS OF THE ABBEY (illustrated by Margaret Horder) (Muller, 1950)......................£150
SCHOOLGIRL JEN AT THE ABBEY (Collins, [1950])......................£35
STRANGERS AT THE ABBEY (Collins, 1951)......................£35
RACHEL IN THE ABBEY (illustrated by M.D. Neilson) (Muller, 1951)......................£150
SELMA AT THE ABBEY (Collins, 1952)......................£25
A DANCER FROM THE ABBEY (Collins, 1953)......................£25
THE SONG OF THE ABBEY (Collins, 1954)......................£25
TOMBOYS AT THE ABBEY (illustrated by Frank Varty) (Collins, 1957)......................£25
TWO QUEENS AT THE ABBEY (Collins, 1959)......................£30

Others

GOBLIN ISLAND (illustrated by Thomas Heath Robinson) (Collins, [1907])......................£150
A PRINCESS IN TATTERS (illustrated by Frank Adams) (Collins, [1908])......................£120
THE CONQUEST OF CHRISTINA (illustrated by G.B. Foyster) (Collins, [1909])......................£140
THE GIRL WHO WOULDN'T MAKE FRIENDS (illustrated by P.B. Hickling) (Nelson, [1909])......................£75
MISTRESS NANCIEBEL (illustrated by James Durden) (Hodder & Stoughton, 1910 [1909])......................£110
A HOLIDAY QUEEN (illustrated by E.A. Overnell) (Collins, [1910])......................£120
ROSALY'S NEW SCHOOL (illustrated by T.J. Overnell) (Chambers, 1913)......................£110
SCHOOLGIRLS AND SCOUTS (illustrated by Arthur A. Dixon) (Collins, [1914])......................£100
AT SCHOOL WITH THE ROUNDHEADS (illustrated by H.C. Earnshaw) (Chambers, 1915)......................£140
FINDING HER FAMILY (illustrated by W.S. Stacey) (SPCK, [1916])......................£150
THE TUCK-SHOP GIRL: A School Story of Girl Guides (illustrated by H.C. Earnshaw) (Chambers, 1916)......................£180
A SCHOOL CAMP FIRE (illustrated by Percy Tarrant) (Chambers, 1917)......................£150

THE SCHOOL OF UPS AND DOWNS: The Story of a Summer Camp (illustrated by H.C. Earnshaw) (Chambers, 1918).....**£225**
EXPELLED FROM SCHOOL (illustrated by Victor Prout) (Collins, [1919]) **£60**
A GO-AHEAD SCHOOLGIRL (illustrated by H.C. Earnshaw) (Chambers, 1919)................................**£175**
THE SCHOOL TORMENT (illustrated by H.C. Earnshaw) (Chambers, 1920)....................................**£175**
THE TWINS OF CASTLE CHARMING (Swarthmore Press, [1920])..**£300**
THE TWO FORM CAPTAINS (illustrated by Percy Tarrant) (Chambers, 1921) **£185**
THE CAPTAIN OF THE FIFTH (illustrated by Percy Tarrant) (Chambers, 1922) **£150**
PATIENCE JOAN, OUTSIDER (Cassell, [1922])..**£130**
THE JUNIOR CAPTAIN (illustrated by Percy Tarrant) (Chambers, [1923]) **£150**
THE SCHOOL WITHOUT A NAME (illustrated by Nina K. Brisley) (Chambers, [1924])................**£300**
THE GIRLS OF GWYNFA (Warne, 1924) **£100**
'TICKLES', or The School that was Different (Partridge, [1924]) **£70**
THE TESTING OF THE TORMENT (illustrated by P.B. Hickling) (Cassell, 1925) **£120**
VEN AT GREGORY'S (illustrated by Nina K. Brisley) (Chambers, [1925])....................................**£225**
THE CAMP FIRE TORMENT (illustrated by Enid W. Browne) (Chambers, 1926)............................**£155**
THE TROUBLES OF TAZY (illustrated by Percy Tarrant) (Chambers, [1926])................................**£200**
PATIENCE AND HER PROBLEMS (illustrated by Molly Benatar) (Chambers, [1927])....................**£150**
PEGGY MAKES GOOD (Partridge, [1927]) **£50**
THE CRISIS IN CAMP KEEMA (illustrated by Percy Tarrant) (Chambers, [1928]) **£175**
DEB AT SCHOOL (illustrated by Nina K. Brisley) (Chambers, 1929) **£175**
DOROTHY'S DILEMMA (illustrated by Nina K. Brisley) (Chambers, 1930) **£175**
DEB OF SEA HOUSE (Chambers, 1931) **£175**
THE CAMP MYSTERY (Collins, [1932])..**£60**
THE REFORMATION OF JINTY (Chambers, 1933) **£175**
JINTY'S PATROL (Newnes, [1934])..**£80**
PEGGY AND THE BROTHERHOOD (Religious Tract Society/Girl's Own Paper, [1936])................**£135**
DAMARIS AT DOROTHY'S (Sheldon Press, [1937])..**£130**
SYLVIA OF SARN (Warne, 1937) **£60**
DAMARIS DANCES (illustrated by Margaret Horder) (OUP, 1940) **£40**
PATCH AND A PAWN (Warne, 1940)..**£55**
ADVENTURE FOR TWO (illustrated by Margaret Horder) (OUP, 1941)..**£45**
PERNEL WINS (illustrated by Margaret Horder) (Muller, 1942) **£100**
ELSA PUTS THINGS RIGHT (Muller, 1944) **£100**
DARING DORANNE (Muller, 1945) **£100**
THE SECRETS OF VAIRY (illustrated by Margaret Horder) (Muller, 1947)..................................**£100**
MARGERY MEETS THE ROSES (Lutterworth Press, 1947)..**£110**
NEW GIRLS AT WOOD END (Blackie, 1957)..**£130**

Maidlin to the Rescue (1934), one of Elsie J. Oxenham's famous 'Abbey' books, is worth £800 in Very Good condition.

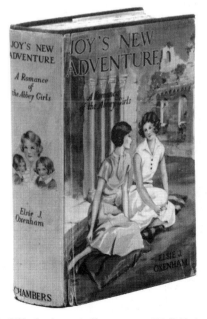

The 'Abbey' series eventually ran to some 44 individual titles. Joy's New Adventure was published by Collins in 1941.

PAOLINI, Christopher

American author. Born: 1983. The 500-page *Eragon* was written when home-educated Paolini was 15 and then edited and self-published by his parents. This story of a farm boy who finds a dragon's egg, was then discovered by US publishers Knopf, who paid nearly £250,000 for the rights. The movie version was released in Christmas 2006.

Prices are for books in Fine condition in dustjackets where applicable.

ERAGON Inheritance Book One (paperback) Paolini International, US, 2002)...£500
ERAGON (first hardback edition) (Knopf, US, 2003)..£50
ERAGON (Doubleday, 2004) £20
ERAGON (paperback) (Corgi, 2005) £20
ELDEST (Knopf, US, 2005) £20
ELDEST (Doubleday, 2005)..£20
ELDEST (paperback) (Corgi, UK, 2006)...£20

PARDOE, Margot

British author. Born: Margot Mary Pardoe in London in 1902. Studied at Abbotts Hill School, Hertfordshire, and trained to be an opera singer. Made her debut as a children's writer with *The Far Island* (1936), but is best known for the 'Bunkle' series, which began with *Four Plus Bunkle* (1939). She has also written romance-thrillers and 'time-travel' historical novels for young readers. Died: 1996.

Prices are for books in Very Good condition in dustjackets.

THE FAR ISLAND: A Story for Girls and Boys (illustrated by R.M. Turvey) (Routledge, 1936)............£60
FOUR PLUS BUNKLE (illustrated by J.D. Evans) (Routledge, 1939) £120
BUNKLE BEGAN IT (illustrated by Julie Neild) (Routledge, 1942)...£70
BUNKLE BUTTS IN (illustrated by Julie Neild) (Routledge, 1943) £70
BUNKLE BOUGHT IT (illustrated by Julie Neild) (Routledge, 1945)...£60

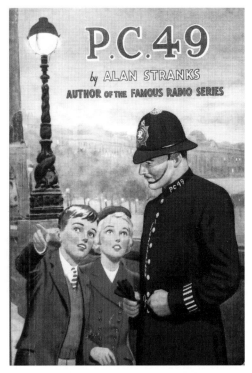

*A tie-in annual from the popular radio serial **P.C.49**, following the adventures of the ordinary bobby on the beat.*

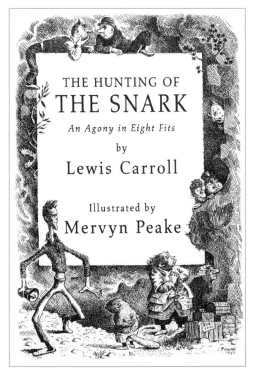

*The Mervyn Peake-illustrated edition of Lewis Carroll's nonsense epic, **The Hunting of the Snark,** was first published in 1941.*

BUNKLE BREAKS AWAY (illustrated by Julie Neild) (Routledge, 1947) £60
BUNKLE AND BELINDA (illustrated by Julie Neild) (Routledge, 1947) £50
BUNKLE BAFFLES THEM (illustrated by Julie Neild) (Routledge, 1949)..£50
BUNKLE WENT FOR SIX (illustrated by Julie Neild) (Routledge, 1950)..£50
BUNKLE GETS BUSY (illustrated by Julie Neild) (Routledge, 1951)..£60
THE GHOST BOAT (with Howard Biggs; illustrated by Webster Murray) (Hodder & Stoughton, 1951) £35
BUNKLE'S BRAINWAVE (illustrated by Mary Smith) (Routledge, 1952)...£60
BUNKLE SCENTS A CLUE (illustrated by Pamela Kemp) (Routledge, 1953)..£60
THE BOAT SEEKERS (illustrated by B. Kay) (Hodder & Stoughton, 1953)..£30
CHARLES ARRIVING (illustrated by Leslie Atkinson) (Routledge, 1954)...£30
THE DUTCH BOAT (illustrated by Leslie Atkinson) (Hodder & Stoughton, 1955) £30
MAY MADRIGAL (illustrated by Leslie Atkinson) (Routledge, 1955) £25
ARGLE'S MIST (illustrated by Leslie Atkinson) (Routledge, 1956)..£25
THE NAMELESS BOAT (illustrated by Leslie Atkinson) (Hodder & Stoughton, 1957)...£30
ARGLE'S CAUSEWAY (illustrated by Leslie Atkinson) (Routledge, 1958)...£25
ARGLE'S ORACLE (illustrated by Audrey Fawley) (Routledge, 1959)...£25
THE GREEK BOAT MYSTERY (Hodder & Stoughton, [1960])..£25
BUNKLE BRINGS IT OFF (illustrated by Audrey Fawley) (Routledge, 1961) £50

'P.C.49'

Created specifically for radio by Alan Stranks, P.C.49 (Police Constable Archibald Berkeley-Willoughby) was an ordinary bobby on the beat, solving crime in the late 1940s and early '50s. The popular fictional policeman also spawned a number of collectable items.

Prices are for annuals, magazines and comics in Very Good condition.

Annuals

P.C.49 (Juvenile Productions, 1951)...£12
ON DUTY WITH P.C.49 (Juvenile Productions, 1952) £10
ON THE BEAT WITH P.C.49 (Preview Productions, 1953)...£12
P.C.49 EAGLE STRIP CARTOON BOOK (Preview Productions, 1953) £20
P.C.49 EAGLE STRIP CARTOON BOOK NUMBER 2 (Andrew Dakers, 1954) £20
P.C.49 ANNUAL (Andrew Dakers, 1955)..£20
THE ADVENTURES OF P.C.49 (Eagle Classics: Hawk Books, 1990) £8

Magazines/Comics

RADIO TIMES 'The Case of the Christmas Copper' (by Alan Stranks) (1949, Christmas edition).................................£12
EAGLE (Hulton Press 14th April 1950-March 1957) Vol. 1 No. 1 ....£175
EAGLE Vol. 1 No.2 ....£45
EAGLE Vol. 1 Nos. 3-20 ....each £8
EAGLE All other issues ....each £3

PEAKE, Mervyn

British author-illustrator. Born: Mervyn Laurence Peake in China in 1911. Studied painting at the Royal Academy Schools in London. Wrote a number of children's books, of which the best known are the three 'Gormenghast' novels, and also illustrated several children's classics, including *Treasure Island* (1949) and the two 'Alice' books (1954). Never recovered from a breakdown brought on by his war service. Died: 1968.

Prices are for books in Very Good condition with dustjackets.

Books Written and Illustrated by Mervyn Peake

CAPTAIN SLAUGHTERBOARD DROPS ANCHOR (Country Life, 1939) £3,000
CAPTAIN SLAUGHTERBOARD DROPS ANCHOR (Eyre & Spottiswoode, 1945) £200
TITUS GROAN (Eyre & Spottiswode, 1946) £250
LETTERS FROM A LOST UNCLE from Polar Regions (Eyre & Spottiswoode, 1948)..£150
GORMENGHAST (Eyre & Spottiswoode, 1950)..£150
TITUS ALONE (Eyre & Spottiswoode, 1959) £100
A BOOK OF NONSENSE (Peter Owen, 1972) £30

Books Illustrated by Mervyn Peake

RIDE A COCK-HORSE and Other Nursery Rhymes (Chatto & Windus, 1940)...£250
THE HUNTING OF THE SNARK by Lewis Carroll (Chatto & Windus, 1941)..£100
THE HUNTING OF THE SNARK by Lewis Carroll (Chatto & Windus: 'Zodiac Books' series, 1941)....................................£50
RIME OF THE ANCIENT MARINER by Samuel Coleridge (Chatto & Windus, 1943)...£50
HOUSEHOLD TALES by the Brothers Grimm (Eyre & Spottiswoode, 1946)..£100
ALICE'S ADVENTURES IN WONDERLAND and THROUGH THE LOOKING GLASS by Lewis Carroll
  (Zephyr Books, Sweden, 1946)..£200
ALICE'S ADVENTURES IN WONDERLAND and THROUGH THE LOOKING GLASS (Wingate, 1954)...£120
TREASURE ISLAND by Robert Louis Stevenson (Eyre & Spottiswoode, 1949) £50
THE SWISS FAMILY ROBINSON by J. Wyss (Heirloom Library, [1950])..£30
THE BOOK OF LYONNE by Burgess Drake (The Falcon Press, 1952)...£40
THE YOUNG BLACKBIRD by E. Clepham Palmer (Wingate, 1954) £40

THE WONDERFUL LIFE & ADVENTURES OF TOM THUMB by Paul Britten Austin
(two volumes; card covers; issued without dustjackets)
(Radiotjänst, Sweden, 1954 & 1955) ....the set **£150**
A POT OF GOLD and Two Other Tales by Aaron Judah (Faber, 1959)......................................**£30**
SKETCHES FROM BLEAK HOUSE (Methuen, 1983) **£20**

PEARCE, Philippa

British author. Born: Ann Philippa Pearce in Great Shelford, Cambridgeshire, in 1920. Studied at Girton College, Cambridge, subsequently working as a civil servant, a BBC radio producer and a children's book editor. Won the Carnegie Medal for her second book, *Tom's Midnight Garden* (1958), subsequently producing a steady stream of novels, story collections and picture books.
Prices are for books in Very Good condition with dustjackets where applicable.

MINNOW ON THE SAY (illustrated by Edward Ardizzone) (OUP, 1955) **£60**
TOM'S MIDNIGHT GARDEN (illustrated by Susan Einzig) (OUP, 1958).....................................**£75**
STILL JIM AND SILENT JIM (Blackwell, 1959 [1960])...**£25**
MRS COCKLE'S CAT (illustrated by Antony Maitland) (Constable, 1961) **£25**
A DOG SO SMALL (illustrated by Antony Maitland) (Constable, 1962).....................................**£25**
THE STRANGE SUNFLOWER (illustrated by Kathleen Williams; issued without dustjacket)
(Nelson, 1966)...**£10**
THE CHILDREN OF THE HOUSE. Written with Brian Fairfax-Lucy (illustrated by John Sergeant)
(Longman, 1968)...**£20**
THE ELM STREET LOT (illustrated by Maina Martinez; paperback) (BBC, 1969).......................**£6**
THE SQUIRREL WIFE (illustrated by Derek Collard) (Longman, 1971) **£15**
WHAT THE NEIGHBOURS DID and Other Stories (illustrated by Faith Jaques) (Longman, 1972) **£15**
THE SHADOW-CAGE and Other Tales of the Supernatural (illustrated by Janet Archer) (Kestrel, 1977)...**£15**
THE BATTLE OF BUBBLE AND SQUEAK (illustrated by Alan Barker) (Deutsch, 1978) **£15**
WINGS OF COURAGE (illustrated by Hilary Abrahams) (Kestrel, 1982).................................**£15**
THE WAY TO SATTIN SHORE (illustrated by Charlotte Voake) (Kestrel, 1983) **£15**
LION AT SCHOOL and Other Stories (illustrated by Caroline Sharpe) (Viking, 1985) **£15**
WHO'S AFRAID? and Other Strange Stories (illustrated by Peter Melnyczuk)
(Viking Kestrel, 1986)...**£15**
EMILY'S OWN ELEPHANT (illustrated by John Lawrence) (MacRae, 1987)...........................**£15**
THE TOOTHBALL (illustrated by Helen Ganly) (Deutsch, 1987)...**£15**
FREDDY (illustrated by David Armitage) (Deutsch, 1988)..**£15**
OLD BELLE'S SUMMER HOLIDAY (illustrated by William Geldart) (Deutsch, 1989) **£15**
HERE COMES TOD (illustrated by Adriano Gon) (Walker, 1992) **£10**
THE LITTLE WHITE MEN (illustrated by Gillian McClure) (Deutsch, 1996)..............................**£10**
THE ROPE, AND OTHER STORIES (paperback) (Puffin, 2000)...**£5**

PEARSE, S.B.

British illustrator. Born: Susan Beatrice Pearse in Fair Oak, Hampshire, in 1878. Studied at the Royal College of Art. Best-known for her 'Ameliaranne' books, but also contributed illustrations to *Little Folks* and *Playbox Annual*. Designed the 'two-children' poster for Start-Rite shoes. Died: 1980.
Prices are for books in Very Good condition with dustjackets where applicable.

THE PENDLETON TWINS by E.M. Jameson (Hodder & Stoughton, 1908)...............................**£100**
THE MAGIC FISHBONE by Charles Dickens (Saint Catherine Press/Nisbet, [1912]) **£40**
AMELIARANNE AND THE GREEN UMBRELLA by Constance Heward (Harrap, 1920) **£175**
THE TWINS AND TABIFFA by Constance Heward (Harrap, 1923)..**£125**
AMELIARANNE CINEMA STAR by Constance Heward (Harrap, 1924)...................................**£125**
AMELIARANNE IN TOWN by Natalie Joan (Harrap, 1930)...**£110**
THE PARTY BOOK by Madeline Barnes (Blackie, [c1930]) **£75**
AMELIARANNE AT THE CIRCUS by Margaret Gilmour (Harrap, 1931)..................................**£110**
AMELIARANNE AND THE BIG TREASURE by Natalie Joan (Harrap, 1932).........................**£100**
AMELIARANNE'S PRIZE PACKET by Eleanor Farjeon (Harrap, 1933)..................................**£100**
AMELIARANNE'S WASHING DAY by Eleanor Farjeon (Harrap, 1934)....................................**£95**
AMELIARANNE AT THE SEASIDE by Margaret Gilmour (Harrap, 1935).................................**£70**
MOTHER GOOSE RHYMES (illustrated by S.B. Pearse and Winifred M. Ackroyd) (Coker, [1935])...**£55**
AMELIARANNE AT THE ZOO by K.L. Thompson (Harrap, 1936) **£70**
AMELIARANNE AT THE FARM by Constance Heward (Harrap, 1937).....................................**£70**
AMELIARANNE GIVES A CHRISTMAS PARTY by Constance Heward (Harrap, 1938)...............**£70**
AMELIARANNE KEEPS SCHOOL by Constance Heward (Harrap, 1940)...............................**£65**
AMELIARANNE GOES TOURING by Constance Heward (Harrap, 1941)................................**£65**
AMELIARANNE AND THE JUMBLE SALE by Eileen M. Osborne (Harrap, 1943).....................**£65**
AMELIARANNE GIVES A CONCERT by Eleanor Farjeon (Harrap, 1944).................................**£65**
AMELIARANNE BRIDESMAID by Ethelberta Morris (Harrap, 1946).......................................**£65**
AMELIARANNE GOES DIGGING by Lorna Wood (Harrap, 1948)...**£65**
NURSERY VERSERY by Patience Strong (Muller, 1948) **£25**
ADVENTURES OF CHRISTABEL, JANE AND CHIRPY by Constance Heward (Harrap, 1955) **£15**

PENGUIN BOOKS

British publishing house. Born 1935. Following Penguin's successful launch, owner Allen Lane decided to start an imprint of paperbacks specifically aimed at children. The most famous was Puffin, but lesser-known names include Ptarmigan, Porpoise and Peacock. Below is a selected bibliography (with catalogue numbers) of the most collectable.

Prices are for books in Very Good condition.

Penguin
P348 BIGGLES FLIES AGAIN by W.E. Johns (1941) £100

Puffin (b1940)
<u>PUFFIN PICTURE BOOKS</u>
PP1 WAR ON LAND by James Holland (1940) £20
PP2 WAR AT SEA by James Holland (1940) £20
PP3 WAR IN THE AIR by James Gardner (1940) £20

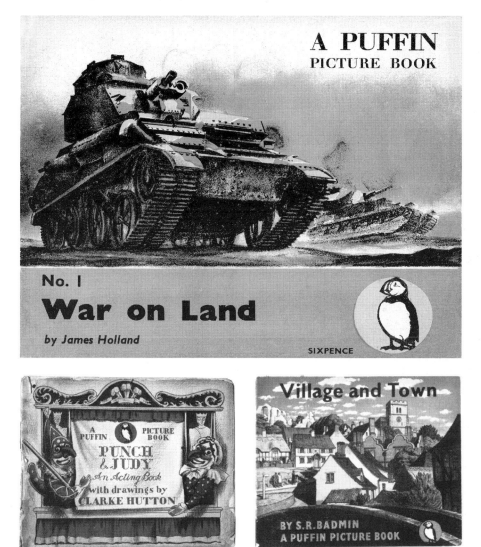

The familiar landscape format of the collectable (but very fragile) Puffin Picture Books.

PP4 **ON THE FARM** by James Gardner (1940) £8
PP5 **A BOOK OF INSECTS** by James Holland & Richard James (1941) £5
PP6 **FLOWERS OF THE FIELD** by Marion Rivers-Moore (1941) £5
PP7 **ANIMALS OF THE COUNTRYSIDE** by Arnrid Johnston (1941) £5
PP8 **GREAT DEEDS OF THE WAR** by Roland Davies (1941)..£20
PP9 **POND AND RIVER LIFE** by Brynhild Parker & Alwyn Richards (1941)...£5
PP10 **A BOOK OF TRAINS** by W.J. Bassett Lowke & F. Courtney (1941)..£5
PP11 **A BOOK OF SHIPS** by A.C. Hardy, Laurence Dunn & M.J. Hardy (1942) £5
PP12 **A BOOK OF RIGMAROLES** by Enid Marx (1945)...£15
PP13 **HAMISH** by Joanna Cannan & Anne Bullen (1944) £10
PP14 **ORLANDO'S EVENING OUT** by Kathleen Hale (1941)..£40
PP15 **LO CHENG** by Chiang Yee (1942) £8
PP26 **ORLANDO'S HOME LIFE** by Kathleen Hale (1942)...£40
PP27 **PUNCH AND JUDY** by Clarke Hutton (1942)..£20
PP31 **TREES IN BRITAIN** by S.R. Badmin (1943)..£4
PP38 **ABOUT A MOTOR CAR** by Phyllis Ladyman (1946) £4
PP43 **OUR HORSES** by Lionel Edwards (1945)..£5
PP56 **DOGS** by Maurice Wilson (1946)..£4
PP68 **THE STORY OF OIL** by J.D.H. Goldsworthy & W.C. Ives (1951) £4
PP75 **THE THEATRE AT WORK** by James Cleaver (1947)...£5
PP85 **MITLA AND LUPE** by Jose Sancha (1948)..£10
PP90 **BIRDS OF THE ESTUARY** by C.F. Tunnicliffe (1952)..£20
PP100 **EVEREST IS CLIMBED** by Wilfred Noyce & Richard Taylor (1954) £6
PP108 **CHURCHES AND CATHEDRALS** by Helen & Richard Leacroft (c1956)..£4
PP111 **DISCOVERY OF THE POLES** by Quintin Riley & Richard Taylor (1957)..£6
PUFFIN STORY BOOKS
PS1 **WORZEL GUMMIDGE** by Barbara Euphan Todd (1941) £8
PS2 **CORNISH ADVENTURE** by Derek McCulloch (1941)..£5
PS3 **THE CUCKOO CLOCK** by Mrs Molesworth (1941) £5
PS4 **GARRAM THE HUNTER, A BOY OF THE HILL TRIBES** by Herbert Best (1941) £5
PS5 **SMOKY, THE STORY OF A HORSE** by Will James (1941)..£5
PS6 **THE INSECT MAN** by Eleanor Doorly (1942) £5
PS7 **THE FAMILY FROM ONE END STREET** by Eve Garnett (1942)..£5
PS11 **CARCAJOU** by R.G. Montgomery (1943) £5
PS12 **MARZOUK, THE STORY OF A LYNX** by Vitaly Bianchi (1944)..£5
PS15 **GAY-NECK** by Dhan Gopal Mukerji (1944) £5
PS16 **MY FRIEND MR. LEAKY** by J.B.S. Haldane (1944) £5
PS19 **COCONUT ISLAND** by Robert Gibbings (1946) £5
PS21 **WE'LL MEET IN ENGLAND** by Kitty Barnes (1946)..£5
PS22 **A CHILD'S GARDEN OF VERSES** by R.L. Stevenson (1948) £5
PS25 **DAVID GOES TO ZULULAND** by K. Marshall (1946)..£5
PS27 **STORMALONG** by Alan Villiers (1946) £5
PS29 **NO OTHER WHITE MEN** by Julia Davis (1946)...£5
PS35 **ALICE'S ADVENTURES IN WONDERLAND** by Lewis Carroll (1946) £5
PS36 **TREASURE ISLAND** by R.L. Stevenson (1946)...£5
PS39 **COLUMBUS SAILS** by C. Walter Hodges (1947)..£5
PS42 **THE SECRET OF DEAD MAN'S COVE** by R.J. McGregor (1948)...£5
PS50 **CHILDREN OF THE NEW FOREST** by Captain Marryat (1948)..£5
PS60 **TARKA THE OTTER** by Henry Williamson (1949)..£5
PS73 **KING ARTHUR AND HIS KNIGHTS OF THE ROUND TABLE** by Roger Lancelyn Green (Puffin original) (1953) £4
PS86 **GOING TO THE BALLET** by Arnold Haskell (1954) £4
PS135 **THE STORY OF JESUS** by Eleanor Graham (1959) £4
PS149 **LUCKY DIP** by Ruth Ainsworth (1961) £7
PS153 **THE WOOL PACK** by Cynthia Harnett (1961) £4
PS159 **TELL ME A STORY** by Ed. E. Colwell (1962)..£6
PS161 **THE HOBBIT** by J.R.R. Tolkien (1961)..£25
PS196 **STIG OF THE DUMP** by Clive King (Puffin original) (1963) £30
PS239 **GOBBOLINO THE WITCH'S CAT** by Ursula Moray Williams (1965) £4
BABY PUFFIN
BP1 **ABC** by Dorothy Chapman (1943)...£60
PUFFIN CUT-OUT BOOKS
PC1-3 **A COTSWOLD VILLAGE** by L.A. Dovey (1947)..£35
PC4 **A THEATRE YOU CAN MAKE** by Jane Cummings (1948) £35
PC5 **THE HIGH TOBY** by J.B. Priestley & Doris Zinkeisen (1948)..£35
PC6 *NEVER ISSUED*
PC7 **THE EMETT FESTIVAL RAILWAY** by Rowland Emett & Victor Keeling (1951).......................................£40
PC7a-9 **A HALF-TIMBERED VILLAGE** by L.A. Dovey (1951) £35
PC10 *NEVER ISSUED*
PC11 **TREASURE ISLAND** by L.A. Dovey (1953) £35

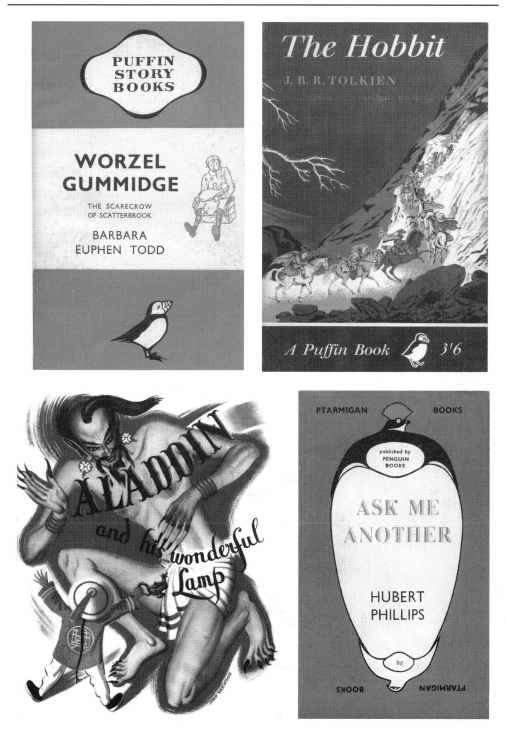

Four rarities from the penguin stable. Clockwise from top left: The first Puffin Story Book, **Worzel Gummidge**, *the Puffin issue of J.R.R. Tolkien's* **The Hobbit**, *and rare examples from the short-lived 'Porpoise' and 'Ptarmigan' imprints.*

Ptarmigan (b1945) *A series of game, puzzle and quiz books aimed at children.*
PT1 ASK ME ANOTHER by Hubert Phillips (1945) £12

Porpoise (b1948) *A short-lived stab at the hardback children's market.*
J1 ALADDIN AND HIS WONDERFUL LAMP (with d/j; illustrated by John Harwood) (1948).........................£35
J2 PAUL THE HERO OF THE FIRE (with d/j; written and illustrated by Edward Ardizzone) (1948)................£35
J3 THE UGLY DUCKLING (with d/j; by Hans Andersen, illustrated by Will Nickless) (1949)........................£40
J4 THE FLYING POSTMAN (with d/j; written and illustrated by V.H. Drummond) (1949)...............................£40

Peacock (b1962) *A series aimed at the gap between children's and adult reading.*
PK1 NATIONAL VELVET by Enid Bagnold (1962) £12

PEPPER, Frank S.

British comics writer. Born: 1910. Creator of many famous children's characters including 'Roy of the Rovers', 'Rockfist Rogan', 'Danny of the Dazzlers' and 'Captain Condor'. From the early 1930s until the late 1970s, Pepper contributed to scores of boys' papers, comics, annuals and books. Died: 1988.

Prices are for comics and books in Very Good condition with dustjackets where applicable. Comic values assume an average comic from the year. 'No. 1' issues would be worth well above the price given.

Story papers written as 'John Marshall' (published by the Amalgamated Press)
TRIUMPH 'Ware That Crazy Skybird!' (1937).. each £5
CHAMPION 'The 'Down-But-Not-Out' Rangers' (1937).. each £5
CHAMPION 'Chippy Always Set the Pace' (1937) .... each £5
CHAMPION 'Sky-High With Cloudy Kaye' (1937) .... each £5
CHAMPION 'Sergeant Dunn's Fighting Sportsmen' (1937-1938) .... each £5
CHAMPION 'The Hide-and-Seek Speed Star' (1938) .... each £5
CHAMPION 'Secret Enemy of the Skating Lumberjacks' (1938) .... each £5
CHAMPION 'Q.9 the Boxing Spy' (1939)... each £5
CHAMPION 'Boxing Boss of the Convict Castaways' (1939)... each £5
CHAMPION 'Skipper of the Stony Broke Cricketers' (1941) .... each £4
CHAMPION 'The Ice Ace from Nowhere' (1949)... each £3
CHAMPION 'Danny of the Dazzlers' (1949-1952) .... each £3
CHAMPION 'The Secret Service Six-Hitter' (1952) .... each £3
CHAMPION 'The Fastest Winger in Football' (1952-1953) .... each £3
CHAMPION 'Salty Blake - the Sea-Dog Centre-Forward' (1953).. each £3
CHAMPION 'The Lad With the Test Match Touch' (1953) .... each £3
CHAMPION 'The Mystery Goalie from Jamaica' (1953) .... each £3
CHAMPION 'Crusaders for the Cup' (1953-1954) .... each £3
CHAMPION 'The Come-Back Centre-Forward' (1954) .... each £3

Story papers written as 'Hal Wilton' (published by the Amalgamated Press)
TRIUMPH 'Snapshot Sammy' (1932).. each £5
TRIUMPH 'Typhoon of the South Seas' (1932) .... each £5
TRIUMPH 'Shanghai Soo' (1933) .... each £5
TRIUMPH 'Rory's Racing Midget' (1935)... each £5
TRIUMPH 'In Africa with Rory's Racing Midget' (1935-1936)... each £5
TRIUMPH 'Doomed to the Big House' (1936) .... each £5
TRIUMPH 'Fighters of the Ming-Fu Menace' (1936).. each £5
TRIUMPH 'The Big-Shot from Nowhere' (1936-1937).. each £5
TRIUMPH 'Detective Peter Farrell' (1937-1940)... each £8
CHAMPION 'Steam-Hammer Hogan – the Fighting Docker' (1936).. each £5
CHAMPION 'The Wrestling Hercules' (1936) .... each £5
CHAMPION 'Tearaway the Stunting Racehorse' (1936) .... each £5
CHAMPION 'Buck Gordon's Speed-Track Avengers' (1937)... each £5
CHAMPION 'The Boxing Legionnaire' (1937).. each £5
CHAMPION 'Zoom the Racing Speed-Cop' (1937) .... each £5
CHAMPION 'The Boxing G-Man' (1937-1938) .... each £5
CHAMPION 'The Wild West Heavyweight' (1938)... each £5
CHAMPION 'The Boxing Convict' (1938) .... each £5
CHAMPION 'Rockfist Rogan' many series from (1938-1955) .... each £4

Comics written as 'John Morion' (published by the Amalgamated Press/Fleetway/IPC)
KNOCKOUT 'In Old London Town' (illustrated by Eric Parker, Robert Macgillivray) (1949)................ each £3
KNOCKOUT 'When Blackbeard Sailed the Seas' (illustrated by Derek Eyles) (1949) .... each £3
KNOCKOUT 'Beau Brummell' (illustrated by Eric Parker) (1950-1951) .... each £3
COMET 'Roy of the Rangers' (illustrated by Robert Macgillivray) (1949)... each £4
SUN 'The New Adventures of Monte Cristo' (three series, illustrated by Eric Parker) (1949)............. each £4

Comics written as 'Frank S. Pepper' (published by the Amalgamated Press/Fleetway/IPC)
LION 'Captain Condor' (1952-1964) .... each £3
LION 'Bruce Kent invites you to Spot the Clues' (1957-1964).. each £2

LION "Sky High' Tales' (1961)... each £2
LION 'The Day the World Drowned' (1968-1969).. each £2
LION 'Torville's Touchstone'/'Spellbinder' (1970-1974)... each £2
LION 'The Jigsaw Journey' (1971)... each £2
LION 'The Steel Commando' (1971-1974) .... each £2
LION 'Noah's Ark' (1972-1973) 'The Flying Fortress' (1973).. each £2
LION 'The Team Terry Kept in a Box' (1973-1974).. each £2
LION 'Sark the Sleeper' (1973-1974)... each £2
TORNADO 'Victor Drago and the China-Town Terror' (1979) .... each £3

Comics written as 'Hal Wilton' (published by the Amalgamated Press/Fleetway/IPC)
LION 'Sgt. Ron Noble in The Great Invasion Mystery' 1955 .... each £3
LION 'Secret Mission to Norway' 1955-1956 .... each £3
LION 'Gunsmoke Smith' 1956-1957 .... each £3
LION 'Rockfist Rogan' 1966 .... each £2
LION 'Sergeant Samson of the Mounties' 1956-1957 .... each £2

Comics written as 'John Marshall' (published by the Amalgamated Press/Fleetway/IPC)
LION 'The Toughest Team in the League' 1958-1959 .... each £2
TIGER 'Tales of Whitestoke School' 1954-1955 .... each £2
TIGER 'Daring Escape Stories' (feature) 1954-1955 .... each £2
TIGER 'King of the Skating Aces' 1955 .... each £2
TIGER 'Rockfist Rogan' 1955-1956 .... each £2

Comics written as 'Stewart Colwyn' (published by the Amalgamated Press/Fleetway/IPC)
TIGER 'Roy of the Rovers' 1954
TIGER 'Biff Bailey - Fighting Fury' 1956 -1959 .... each £2

Annuals (published by the Amalgamated Press/Fleetway)
CHAMPION ANNUAL (as 'Hal Wilton' & 'John Marshall') 1939-1942 .... each £15
CHAMPION ANNUAL (as 'Hal Wilton' & 'John Marshall') 1947-1956 .... each £12
LION ANNUAL (as Frank S. Pepper, 'Hal Wilton' & 'Harry Clements') 1954-1961.. each £12

Books (published by Stewart Pepper & Son)
ROCKFIST ROGAN by 'Hal Wilton' (with dustjacket) (1950)... £30
ROCKFIST AT THE NORTH POLE by 'Hal Wilton' (with dustjacket) (1951)... £30
ROCKFIST IN THE KINGDOM OF THE KHAN by 'Hal Wilton' (with dustjacket) (1952)............................. £30

PERRAULT, Charles

French author-folklorist. Born: Paris, 1628. Studied law, subsequently working in Louis XIV's civil service. His first collection of traditional fairy stories, *Histoires ou contes du temps passé* (1697), contained versions of 'Little Red Riding Hood', 'Bluebeard', 'Cinderella', 'Hop o' my Thumb' and 'Puss in Boots'. Elected to the Académie Française in 1671. Died: 1703.

Prices are for books in Very Good condition.

HISTOIRES, OU CONTES DU TEMPS PASSE, AVEC DES MORALITEZ (Paris, 1697)..................................£12,000
LES CONTES DE PERRAULT (illustrated by Gustav Doré) (Paris, 1862)..£350
PERRAULT'S POPULAR TALES. Edited by Andrew Lang (Clarendon Press, 1888)..£50
TALES OF PASSED TIMES (illustrated by Charles Robinson)
   (Dent: 'Temple Classics for Young People' series, [1899]))..£60
CONTES DE PERRAULT. Adapted by Kathleen Fitzgerald (illustrated by Margaret Tarrant) (Siegle & Hill, 1910)......................£75
PERRAULT'S FAIRY TALES (illustrated by Honor C. Appleton; translated by S.R. Littlewood) (Herbert Daniel, [1911]) £75
THE SLEEPING BEAUTY and Other Tales (illustrated by John Hassall) (Blackie, [1912])................................£60
FAIRY TALES (illustrated by Charles Robinson) (Dent, [1913])...£60
CINDERELLA Adapted by E.L. Elias (illustrated by Willy Pogány) (Harrap, [1915]) £50
CINDERELLA Adapted by Githa Sowerby (illustrated by Millicent Sowerby) (Hodder & Stoughton, [1915])..............£80
CINDERELLA Adapted by Charles S. Evans (illustrated by Arthur Rackham) (Heinemann, 1919) £100
CINDERELLA Adapted by Charles S. Evans (illustrated by Arthur Rackham; De Luxe edition: limited to 525 copies,
   signed by the artist; on handmade paper) (Heinemann, 1919) £600
CINDERELLA Adapted by Charles S. Evans (illustrated by Arthur Rackham; De Luxe vellum edition:
   limited to 325 copies, signed by the artist; on Japanese vellum) (Heinemann, 1919) £1,000
THE SLEEPING BEAUTY Adapted by Charles S. Evans (illustrated by Arthur Rackham) (Heinemann, 1920)......................£100
THE SLEEPING BEAUTY Adapted by Charles S. Evans (illustrated by Arthur Rackham; with extra plate;
   limited to 625 copies, signed by the artist) (Heinemann, 1920)...£600
OLD TIME STORIES (illustrated by W. Heath Robinson; translated by A.E. Johnson) (Constable, 1921) £350
THE FAIRY TALES OF CHARLES PERRAULT (illustrated by Harry Clarke; cloth or buckram binding)
   (Harrap, [1922]) £250
THE FAIRY TALES OF CHARLES PERRAULT (illustrated by Harry Clarke; De Luxe edition:
   Persian Levant leather binding) (Harrap, [1922]) £500
TALES OF PAST TIMES (illustrated by John Austen) (Selwyn & Blount, 1922)...£75
TALES OF PAST TIMES (illustrated by John Austen; limited to 200 copies, signed by the artist)
   (Selwyn & Blount, 1922)...£200
CINDERELLA and Other Tales from Perrault (illustrated by Michael Hague) (Holt, US, 1989) £20

PETO, Gladys

British illustrator. Born: Gladys Emma Peto in Maidenhead, Berkshire, in 1890. Studied at the Maidenhead School of Art, subsequently working as a fabric and pottery designer as well as illustrator. Contributed an illustrated diary to the *Sketch* between 1915 annd 1926, subsequently publishing a number of lighthearted travel books. Produced a series of children's annuals in the 1930s. Died: 1977.

Prices are for books in Very Good condition.

GLADYS PETO'S CHILDREN ANNUAL 1923 (Sampson Low, 1923) £100
GLADYS PETO'S CHILDREN ANNUAL 1924 (Sampson Low, 1924) £95
DAPHNE AND THE FAIRY and Other Stories (Sampson Low, 1924)...£120
JOAN'S VISIT TO TOYLAND and Other Tales (Sampson Low, 1924)...£120
SNOWMAN and Other Tales (Sampson Low, 1924)..£110
GLADYS PETO'S CHILDREN'S BOOK (Sampson Low, 1925)...£90
THE CHINA COW and Other Stories by Sewell Stokes and others
   (Sampson Low, [1929]) £90
GLADYS PETO'S BEDTIME STORIES (Shaw, [1931])...£90
TWILIGHT STORIES (Shaw, [1932])..£65
GLADYS PETO'S GIRLS' OWN STORIES (Shaw, [1933]) £65
SUNSHINE TALES (Shaw, [1935])..£55
THE FOUR-LEAVED CLOVER and Other Stories (Juvenile Productions, [1937]).................................£50

PEYTON, K.M.

British author. Born: Kathleen Wendy Herald in Birmingham in 1929. Studied at Wimbledon High School and Manchester Art School. Published her first book, *Sabre: The Horse from the Sea* (1948), when she was only nineteen, and has since written many more, notably the 'Flambards' series. She won the Carnegie Medal for the second book in the sequence, *The Edge of the Cloud* (1969). Collaborated with her husband, Michael Peyton, on several early stories, subsequently retaining his initial on her books.

Prices are for books in Very Good condition with dustjackets.

SABRE: The Horse from the Sea (written under the name 'Kathleen Herald'; illustrated by Lionel Edwards)
   (A. & C. Black, 1948) £30
THE MANDRAKE: A Pony (written under the name 'Kathleen Herald'; illustrated by Lionel Edwards)
   (A. & C. Black, 1949)..£30
CRAB THE ROAN (written under the name 'Kathleen Herald'; illustrated by Peter Biegel)
   (A. & C. Black, 1953)...£20
NORTH TO ADVENTURE (Collins, 1958)..£15
STORMCOCK MEETS TROUBLE (Collins, 1961)...£10
THE HARD WAY HOME (illustrated by R.A. Branton) (Collins, 1962)..£10
WINDFALL (illustrated by Victor G. Ambrus) (OUP, 1962)...£15
BROWNSEA SILVER (illustrated by Victor G. Ambrus) (Collins, 1964)..£10
THE MAPLIN BIRD (illustrated by Victor G. Ambrus) (OUP, 1964) £10
THE PLAN FOR BIRDSMARSH (illustrated by Victor G. Ambrus) (OUP, 1965)..................................£20
THUNDER IN THE SKY (illustrated by Victor G. Ambrus) (OUP, 1966) £10
FLAMBARDS (illustrated by Victor G. Ambrus) (OUP, 1967)...£25
FLY-BY-NIGHT (illustrated by the author) (OUP, 1968)...£15
THE EDGE OF THE CLOUD (illustrated by Victor G. Ambrus) (OUP, 1969).....................................£20
FLAMBARDS IN THE SUMMER (OUP, 1969)..£20
PENNINGTON'S SEVENTEENTH SUMMER (illustrated by the author)
   (OUP, 1970)..£10
THE BEETHOVEN MEDAL (illustrated by the author) (OUP, 1971)..£10
A PATTERN OF ROSES (illustrated by the author) (OUP, 1972)..£10
PENNINGTON'S HEIR (illustrated by the author) (OUP, 1973) £10
THE TEAM (illustrated by the author) (OUP, 1975)..£20
THE RIGHT-HAND MAN (illustrated by Victor G. Ambrus)
   (OUP, 1977)..£15
PROVE YOURSELF A HERO (OUP, 1977) £10
A MIDSUMMER NIGHT'S DEATH (OUP, 1978)..£10
MARION'S ANGELS (OUP, 1979)..£10
MARION'S ANGELS (as 'Falling Angel') (Methuen, 1983) £10
FLAMBARDS DIVIDED (OUP, 1981)...£15
DEAR FRED (illustrated by the author) (The Bodley Head, 1981)..£10
GOING HOME (illustrated by the author) (OUP, 1982)...£10
WHO, SIR? ME, SIR? (OUP, 1983)..£10
THE LAST DITCH (OUP, 1984)...£10
FROGGETT'S REVENGE (OUP, 1985)..£10
PLAIN JACK (illustrated by the author) (OUP, 1988)..£10
DOWNHILL ALL THE WAY (OUP, 1988) £10
SKYLARK (OUP, 1989) £10
DARKLING (paperback) (Corgi, 1989)...£3

PIENKOWSKI, Jan

Polish illustrator. Born: Jan Michel Pienkowski in Warsaw in 1936. Studied in London and at King's College, Cambridge. Began his artistic career by designing posters and greetings cards, but later turned to children's book illustration, winning the Kate Greenaway Medal for his drawings for Joan Aiken's *The Kingdom Under the Sea* (1971). Perhaps his finest works are the pop-up books, *Haunted House* (1979) and *Robot* (1981), the first of which has sold over one million copies.

Prices are for books in Very Good condition with dustjackets where applicable.

'Pop-Up' Books

HAUNTED HOUSE (Heinemann, 1979)	£50
DINNERTIME (Minipop; with Anne Carter) (Gallery Five, 1981)	£10
ROBOT (Heinemann, 1981)	£35
LITTLE MONSTERS (Minipop) (Orchard, 1986)	£20
SMALL TALK (Minipop) (Orchard, 1987)	£10
FANCY THAT (Minipop) (Orchard, 1991)	£10
DOORBELL (Orchard, 1992)	£8
ABC DINOSAUR (Heinemann, 1993)	£20

Other Books Written and Illustrated by Jan Pienkowski

NUMBERS (Heinemann, 1973)	£10
COLOURS (Heinemann, 1973)	£10
SHAPES (Heinemann, 1973)	£10
SIZES (Heinemann, 1973)	£10
HOMES (Heinemann, 1979)	£10
WEATHER (Heinemann, 1979)	£10
ABC (Heinemann, 1980)	£10
TIME (Heinemann, 1980)	£10
QUEST FOR THE GLOOP (with Helen Nicoll) (Heinemann, 1980)	£12
GOSSIP (Heinemann/Gallery Five, 1983)	£10
ABC COLOURING BOOK (paperback) (Puffin, 1984)	£8
123 COLOURING BOOK (paperback) (Puffin, 1984)	£8
CHRISTMAS: The King James Version (Heinemann, 1984)	£20
FARM: Colouring Book (paperback) (Puffin, 1985)	£8
FARM: Nursery Book (Heinemann, 1985)	£10
ZOO: Colouring Book (paperback) (Puffin, 1985)	£8
ZOO: Nursery Book (Heinemann, 1985)	£10
I'M CAT (Walker, 1985)	£10
I'M FROG (Walker, 1985)	£10
I'M MOUSE (Walker, 1985)	£10
I'M PANDA (Walker, 1985)	£10
FOOD (Heinemann, 1986)	£10
FACES (Heinemann, 1986)	£10
EASTER: The King James Version (Heinemann, 1989)	£20
OH MY! A FLY! (Orchard, 1989)	£10
EGGS FOR TEA (Orchard, 1989)	£10
PET FOOD (Orchard, 1989)	£10

'Meg and Mog' Books, all written by Helen Nicoll, illustrated by Jan Pienkowski

MEG AND MOG (Heinemann, 1972)	£20
MEG'S CAR (Heinemann, 1975)	£20
MEG'S CASTLE (Heinemann, 1975)	£20
MEG'S VEG (Heinemann, 1976)	£15
MOG'S MUMPS (Heinemann, 1976)	£15
MEG AND MOG BIRTHDAY BOOK (Heinemann, 1979)	£15
MOG AT THE ZOO (Heinemann, 1982)	£15
MOG IN THE FOG (Heinemann, 1984)	£15
OWL AT SCHOOL (Heinemann, 1984)	£10

Other Books Illustrated by Jan Pienkowski

ANNIE, BRIDGET AND CHARLIE: An ABC for Children of Rhymes by Jessie Gertrude Townsend (1967)	£25
A NECKLACE OF RAINDROPS and Other Stories by Joan Aiken (Cape, 1968)	£30
THE KINGDOM UNDER THE SEA and Other Stories by Joan Aiken (Cape, 1971)	£25
GHOSTS AND BOGLES by Dinah Starkey (Hutchinson, 1976)	£25
THE AMBER MOUNTAIN and Other Folk Stories by Agnes Szudek (Hutchinson, 1976)	£20
JACK AND THE BEANSTALK by Jacob and Wilhelm Grimm (translated by Joseph Jacobs; issued without dustjacket) (Heinemann/Gallery Five: 'Jan Pienkowski's Fairy Tale Library' series, 1977)	£15
SNOW WHITE by Jacob and Wilhelm Grimm (issued without dustjacket) (Heinemann/Gallery Five: 'Jan Pienkowski's Fairy Tale Library' series, 1977)	£15
SLEEPING BEAUTY by Jacob and Wilhelm Grimm (translated by David Walser; issued without dustjacket) (Heinemann/Gallery Five: 'Jan Pienkowski's Fairy Tale Library' series, 1977)	£15

HANSEL AND GRETEL by Jacob and Wilhelm Grimm (issued without dustjacket) (Heinemann/Gallery Five: 'Jan Pienkowski's Fairy Tale Library' series, 1977)..**£15**
PUSS IN BOOTS by Charles Perrault (translated by David Walser; issued without dustjacket) (Heinemann/Gallery Five: 'Jan Pienkowski Fairy Tale Library' series, 1977)..**£15**
CINDERELLA by Charles Perrault (translated by David Walser; issued without dustjacket) (Heinemann/Gallery Five: 'Jan Pienkowski's Fairy Tale Library' series, 1977)..**£15**
JAN PIENKOWSKI'S FAIRY TALE LIBRARY (six books: 'Jack and the Beanstalk', 'Snow White', 'Sleeping Beauty', 'Hansel and Gretel', 'Puss in Boots' and 'Cinderella'; in box; issued without dustjackets) (Heinemann/Gallery Five, 1977) ....the set **£100**
TALE OF A ONE-WAY STREET and Other Stories by Joan Aiken (Cape, 1978) **£25**
PAST EIGHT O'CLOCK by Joan Aiken (Cape, 1986)...**£15**
A FOOT IN THE GRAVE by Joan Aiken (Cape, 1989) **£20**
HOME SWEET HOME (Orchard, 1989) **£10**
M.O.L.E. (Much Overworked Little Earthmover) by Russell Hoban (Cape, 1993).......................................**£15**
GOODNIGHT MOO (Orion, 1994) **£5**
BRONTO'S BRUNCH (Orion, 1994)...**£5**

'PIP & SQUEAK (& WILFRED)' ANNUALS

British comic annuals featuring — respectively — a dog, a penguin and a baby rabbit. The original strip ran in the *Daily Mirror* from 1919 to 1953.

Prices are for annuals in Very Good condition.

'Pip & Squeak' Annuals
PIP & SQUEAK ANNUAL (Daily Mirror, 1923 [1922]-35) .... each **£25**
PIP & SQUEAK ANNUAL (Daily Mirror, 1936-40) .... each **£20**

'Wilfred's' Annuals
WILFRED'S ANNUAL (Daily Mirror, 1924-35) .... each **£25**
WILFRED'S ANNUAL (Daily Mirror, 1936-39) .... each **£20**

'Pip, Squeak & Wilfred' Annuals
PIP, SQUEAK & WILFRED ANNUAL (Daily Mirror, [1953-55]) .... each **£12**

'PLAYBOX' ANNUALS

Highly influential British comic annuals, published by Amalgamated Press between 1909 and 1956. Its best-known character was Tiger Tim, who first appeared in the *Daily Mirror* in 1904, subsequently featuring in the magazine supplements, *The Playbox* and *The Playhour*, before being chosen for the *Playbox Annual*. Also included were several of W. Heath Robinson's eccentric 'inventions' from the *Strand*.

Prices are for annuals in Very Good condition.

PLAYBOX ANNUAL 1909 ....**£60**
PLAYBOX ANNUAL 1910 ....**£40**
PLAYBOX ANNUAL 1911 ....**£35**
PLAYBOX ANNUAL 1912-15 .... each **£30**
PLAYBOX ANNUAL 1916-20 .... each **£25**
PLAYBOX ANNUAL 1921-42 .... each **£20**
PLAYBOX ANNUAL 1943-46 .... each **£18**
PLAYBOX ANNUAL 1947-48 .... each **£15**
PLAYBOX ANNUAL 1949 ....**£12**
PLAYBOX ANNUAL 1950-51 .... each **£10**
PLAYBOX ANNUAL 1952 ....**£8**
PLAYBOX ANNUAL 1953-56 .... each **£7**

POGÁNY, Willy

Hungarian illustrator. Born: Vilmos Andreas Pogány in Szeged, Hungary, in 1882. Studied at the Technical University of Budapest and the Budapest Art School. Lived in London between 1906 and 1914, during which time he illustrated a number of children's books for Harrap and other publishers, notably *A Treasury of Verse for Little Children* (1908), *Folk Tales from Many Lands* (1910) and *The Hungarian Fairy Book* (1913). The quality of his work declined following his move to America in 1914, although he continued to be a prolific illustrator and also worked as a set designer on several classic films, notably Boris Karloff's *The Mummy*. Died: 1955.

Prices are for books in Very Good condition.

THE WELSH FAIRY BOOK by W. Jenkyn Thomas (100 illustrations by Willy Pogány) (Unwin, [1907]) **£125**
THE ADVENTURES OF A DODO by G.E. Farrow (seventy illustrations by Willy Pogány) (Unwin, [1907]) **£75**
MILLY AND OLLY by Mrs Humphey Ward (48 illustrations by Willy Pogány) (Unwin, 1907)..**£40**
A TREASURY OF VERSE FOR LITTLE CHILDREN by Madalen G. Edgar (Harrap, [1908]) **£100**
THE RUBAIYAT OF OMAR KHAYYAM (24 colour illustrations by Willy Pogány) (Harrap, 1909) **£100**
THE RUBAIYAT OF OMAR KHAYYAM (24 colour illustrations by Willy Pogány; De Luxe edition: limited to 500 copies, signed by the artist) (Harrap, 1909) **£600**

TANGLEWOOD TALES by Nathaniel Hawthorne (Unwin, [1909]) £60
NORSE WONDER TALES by Sir George Dasent (Collins, [1909]) £20
GISLI THE OUTLAW by Sir George Dasent (Harrap, [1909]).. £20
THE RIME OF THE ANCIENT MARINER by S.T. Coleridge (twenty colour illustrations by Willy Pogány)
(Harrap, 1910) £400
THE RIME OF THE ANCIENT MARINER by S.T. Coleridge (twenty colour illustrations by Willy Pogány;
limited to 525 copies, signed by the artist) (Harrap, 1910) £1,500
THE BLUE LAGOON by H. de Vere Stacpoole (Unwin, 1910).. £125
FOLK TALES FROM MANY LANDS by Lilian Gask (Harrap, 1910).. £100
THE WITCH'S KITCHEN, or The India Rubber Doctor by Gerald Young (Harrap, [1910]) £60
TANNHAUSER by Richard Wagner (eight colour plates by Willy Pogány) (Harrap, 1911)............................ £150
TANNHAUSER by Richard Wagner (eight colour plates by Willy Pogány; limited to 525 copies,
signed by the artist) (Harrap, 1911)... £500
PARSIFAL by Richard Wagner (eight colour plates by Willy Pogány) (Harrap, 1912)................................. £150
PARSIFAL by Richard Wagner (eight colour plates by Willy Pogány; limited to 525 copies, signed by the artist)
(Harrap, 1912).. £500
THE FAIRIES AND THE CHRISTMAS CHILD by Lilian Gask (Harrap, [1912]).. £40
THE TALE OF LOHENGRIN by Richard Wagner (eight colour plates by Willy Pogány) (Harrap, 1913)...... £150
THE TALE OF LOHENGRIN by Richard Wagner (eight colour plates by Willy Pogány;
limited to 525 copies, signed by the artist) (Harrap, 1913) £500
ATTA TROLL by Heinrich Heine (Sidgwick & Jackson, 1913) £60
THE HUNGARIAN FAIRY BOOK by Nandor Pogány (Unwin, 1913) £120
FORTY-FOUR TURKISH FAIRY TALES by Ignacz Kunos (Harrap, [1913]) £50
FORTY-FOUR TURKISH FAIRY TALES by Ignacz Kunos (De Luxe edition: leather binding) (Harrap, [1913])........... £70
WILLY POGÁNY CHILDREN (five books: 'Children at the Pole', 'Hiawatha', 'Red Riding Hood',
'Robinson Crusoe' and 'The Three Bears') (Harrap, [1914]).. each £50
THE CHILDREN IN JAPAN by Grace Bartruse (Harrap, [1915]).. £40
CINDERELLA Adapted by E.L. Elias (Harrap, [1915]) £40
THE GINGERBREAD MAN by Lionel Fable (Harrap, [1915]).. £60
MORE TALES FROM THE ARABIAN NIGHTS by Frances J. Olcott (Holt, US, 1915) £45
HOME BOOK OF VERSE FOR YOUNG CHILDREN Edited by B.E. Stevenson (Holt, US, 1915) £20
STORIES TO TELL THE LITTLEST ONES by Sara Cone Bryant (Houghton Mifflin, US, 1916)................... £20

*This is frequently quoted as being one the most
beautiful books ever published.* **The Rime of the
Ancient Mariner** *as 'presented' by Willy Pogány,
was first printed in 1910.*

STORIES TO TELL THE LITTLEST ONES by Sara Cone Bryant (Harrap, 1918)...£20
THE KING OF IRELAND'S SON by Padraic Colum (Macmillan, US, 1916) £40
THE KING OF IRELAND'S SON by Padraic Colum (Harrap, 1920) £50
BIBLE STORIES TO READ AND TELL by Frances J. Olcott (Houghton Mifflin, US, 1916)..................................£15
TALES OF THE PERSIAN GENII by Frances J. Olcott (Houghton Mifflin, US, 1917) £30
TALES OF THE PERSIAN GENII by Frances J. Olcott (Harrap, 1919)..£30
GULLIVER'S TRAVELS by Jonathan Swift. Adapted by Padraic Colum (Macmillan, US, 1917)......................£50
GULLIVER'S TRAVELS by Jonathan Swift. Adapted by Padraic Colum (Harrap, 1919)................................£50
LITTLE TAILOR OF THE WINDING WAY by Gertrude Crownfield (Macmillan, US, 1917) £20
POLLY'S GARDEN by Helen Ward Banks (Macmillan, US, 1918)..£30
THE ADVENTURES OF ODYSSEUS AND THE TALE OF TROY by Padraic Colum (Macmillan, US, 1918) £50
THE ADVENTURES OF ODYSSEUS AND THE TALE OF TROY by Padraic Colum (Harrap, [1920])................£50
CHILDREN'S PLAYS by Eleanor and Ada Skinner (Appleton, US, 1919)...£20
UNCLE DAVIE'S CHILDREN by Agnes McClelland Daulton (Macmillan, US, 1920)...£20
THE CHILDREN OF ODIN A Book of Northern Myths by Padraic Colum (Macmillan, US, 1920)...................£30
THE CHILDREN OF ODIN A Book of Northern Myths by Padraic Colum (Harrap, 1922) £30
THE GOLDEN FLEECE and the Heroes Who Lived Before Achilles by Padraic Colum
(Macmillan, US, 1921)...£30
THE ADVENTURES OF HAROUN EL RASCHID by Frances J. Olcott (Holt, US, 1923)....................................£30
FAIRY FLOWERS: Nature Legends of Fact and Fantasy by Isidora Newman (Holt, US, 1926)....................£200
FAIRY FLOWERS: Nature Legends of Fact and Fantasy by Isidora Newman (Humphrey Milford, [1926])...........£200
GEORGE WASHINGTON GOES AROUND THE WORLD by Margaret L. Thomas (Nelson, 1927) £20
LOOKING OUT FOR JIMMIE by Helen H. Flanders (Dent [printed in the US], [1928]) £25
TISZA TALES by Rosika Schwimmer (Doubleday Doran, US, [1928])..£40
ALICE'S ADVENTURES IN WONDERLAND by Lewis Carroll (Dutton, US, 1929) £50
ALICE'S ADVENTURES IN WONDERLAND by Lewis Carroll (signed, limited edition, 200 copies) (Dutton, US, 1929) £400
WILLY POGÁNY'S MOTHER GOOSE (Nelson, UK/US, [1929])..£150
MAGYAR FAIRY TALES by Nandor Pogány (Dutton, US, 1930) £60
THE WIMP AND THE WOODLE by Helen von Kolnitz Hyer (Suttonhouse, US, 1935) £30
THE CHILDREN'S GULLIVER (adapted by F.H. Lee) (Harrap, 1935) £30
THE GOOSE GIRL OF NURNBERG by H.S. Hawley (Suttonhouse, US, 1936)..£30
COPPA HAMBA by Blanche Ambrose (Suttonhouse, US, 1936) £30
HOW SANTA FOUND THE COBBLER'S SHOP by Margaretta Harmon (Suttonhouse, US, 1936)...............£30
THE GOLDEN COCKEREL by Alexander Pushkin (adapted by Elaine Pogány) (Nelson, US, 1938)..............£90
PETERKIN by Elaine and Willy Pogány (McKay, US, 1940)...£80
THE FRENZIED PRINCE: Being Heroic Stories of Ancient Ireland by Padraic Colum (McKay, US, 1943)...........£45
RUNNING AWAY WITH NEBBY by Philis Garrard (McKay, US, 1944) £60

PORTER, Eleanor H.

American author. Born: Eleanor Hodgman Porter in 1868. Wrote a number of popular children's novels, but is best known for *Pollyanna* (1913), about a good-natured girl whose sunny temperament overcomes all adversity. Sequels were written by a number of other authors. Died: 1920.

Prices are for books in Very Good condition in dustjackets where applicable.

CROSS CURRENTS (illustrated by William Stecher) (Wilde, 1907)...£75
CROSS CURRENTS (illustrated by William Stecher) (Harrap, 1928)..£25
THE TURN OF THE TIDE (illustrated by Frank Merrill) (Wilde, 1908)..£60
THE TURN OF THE TIDE (illustrated by Frank Merrill) (Harrap, 1928)...£25
THE SUNBRIDGE GIRLS AT SIX STAR RANCH (written under the pseudonym 'Eleanor Stuart'; illustrated by Frank Murch)
(Page, US, 1913)..£80
THE SUNBRIDGE GIRLS AT SIX STAR RANCH (as 'Six Star Ranch') (Stanley Paul, 1916) £50
POLLYANNA (illustrated by Stockton Mulford) (Page, US, 1913)...£325
POLLYANNA (illustrated by Stockton Mulford) (Pitman, 1913)..£175
POLLYANNA GROWS UP (illustrated by H. Weston Taylor) (Page, US, 1915)..£125
POLLYANNA GROWS UP (illustrated by H. Weston Taylor) (Pitman, 1915) £100
MISS BILLY (Stanley Paul, 1914)...£35
MISS BILLY — MARRIED (Page, US, 1914)...£35
MISS BILLY — MARRIED (Stanley Paul, 1915)..£35
MISS BILLY'S DECISION (Stanley Paul, [1915])..£35
JUST DAVID (Constable, 1916)...£35
THE ROAD TO UNDERSTANDING (Constable, [1917]) £25
OH, MONEY! MONEY! (Constable, 1918) £30
KEITH'S DARK TOWER (Constable, 1919)...£30
MARY MARIE (Constable, UK/US, [1920])...£20
THE STORY OF MARCO (Stanley Paul, [1920]) £20
SISTER SUE (Constable, UK/US, [1921]) £20
MONEY, LOVE AND KATE, together with 'The Story of a Nickel' (Hodder & Stoughton, [1924]) £25
LITTLE PARDNER and Other Stories (Hodder & Stoughton, 1926)...£20
THE 'MISS BILLY' STORIES (contains 'Miss Billy', 'Miss Billy's Decision' and 'Miss Billy Married') (Harrap, 1927)...................£20

PORTER, Gene Stratton

American author. Born: Geneva Grace Stratton Porter in Wabash County, Indiana, in 1863. As well as her children's books, she wrote extensively on natural history. Died: 1924.

Prices are for books in Very Good condition.

FRECKLES (illustrated by E. Stetson Crawford) (Doubleday, US, 1904) £100
FRECKLES (illustrated by E. Stetson Crawford) (John Murray, 1905) £50
A GIRL OF THE LIMBERLOST (illustrated by Wladyslaw T. Benda) (Doubleday, US, 1909) £150
A GIRL OF THE LIMBERLOST (illustrated by Wladyslaw T. Benda) (Hodder & Stoughton, 1911).......................£100
MORNING FACE (illustrated by the author) (Doubleday, US, 1916)..£10
MORNING FACE (illustrated by the author) (John Murray, 1916)..£60
THE MAGIC GARDEN (illustrated by Lee Thayer) (Doubleday, US, 1917)...£40
THE MAGIC GARDEN (illustrated by Lee Thayer) (Hutchinson, [1927])..£25
THE WHITE FLAG (John Murray, 1923) £75

POTTER, Beatrix

British author-illustrator. Born: Helen Beatrix Potter in London in 1866. Educated at home by governesses, and showed an early love of art and of nature. In 1893, she sketched out her 'Tale of Peter Rabbit' in a letter to the son of one of her governesses, and eight years later she had the work privately printed in an edition of 250 copies. A trade edition was later issued by Frederick Warne, who published all her subsequent picture books. Died: 1943.

Prices are for books in Very Good condition.

A HAPPY PAIR by Frederick E. Weatherly (the exceptionally rare first book illustrated by Beatrix Potter –
    under 10 copies are thought to have survived; 6 chromolithographed illustrations each signed 'H.B.P.'
    together with wrapper design by Beatrix Potter; pictorial wrappers) (Hildesheimer & Faulkner, [1890]).......................£15,000+
THE TALE OF PETER RABBIT (limited to 250 copies; flat spine) (Privately printed, [1901])..£50,000+
THE TALE OF PETER RABBIT (limited to 200 copies; round spine) (Privately printed, 1902)..£25,000
THE TALE OF PETER RABBIT (trade edition in cloth) (Warne, [1902])...£15,000
THE TALE OF PETER RABBIT (trade edition in boards) (Warne, [1902])..£6,000
THE TALE OF PETER RABBIT (De Luxe edition) (Warne, 1902) £12,500
THE TAILOR OF GLOUCESTER (limited to 500 copies) (Privately printed, 1902)..£10,000+
THE TAILOR OF GLOUCESTER (first trade edition) (Warne, 1903)..£3,500

Left: The first self-published edition of Beatrix Potter's famous debut, identified by the tell-tale flat spine. Above: Her debut published work as an illustrator is a very scarce item in any condition and dates from 1890.

The second 'Glad' book by Eleanor H. Porter, still in its very scarce dustjacket and worth at least £100 today.

*The splendid cover artwork for the second **Wham! Annual** issued in 1967 by Power Comics.*

THE TAILOR OF GLOUCESTER (De Luxe edition) (Warne, 1903) £6,500
THE TALE OF SQUIRREL NUTKIN (trade edition) (Warne, 1903) £2,500
THE TALE OF SQUIRREL NUTKIN (De Luxe edition) (Warne, 1903) £8,000
THE TALE OF BENJAMIN BUNNY (Warne, 1904) £1,000
THE TALE OF BENJAMIN BUNNY (decorated cloth binding) (Warne, 1904) £2,500
THE TALE OF TWO BAD MICE (Warne, 1904) £600
THE TALE OF TWO BAD MICE (decorated cloth binding) (Warne, 1904) £2,000
THE TALE OF MRS TIGGY-WINKLE (Warne, 1905) £500
THE TALE OF MRS TIGGY-WINKLE (decorated cloth binding) (Warne, 1905) £2,000
THE PIE AND THE PATTY-PAN (large format) (Warne, 1905) £400
THE TALE OF MR JEREMY FISHER (Warne, 1906) £400
THE STORY OF A FIERCE BAD RABBIT (panorama) (Warne, 1906) £600
THE STORY OF MISS MOPPET (panorama) (Warne, 1906) £600
THE TALE OF TOM KITTEN (Warne, 1907) £400
THE TALE OF JEMIMA PUDDLE-DUCK (Warne, 1908) £600
THE ROLY-POLY PUDDING (large format) (Warne, 1908) £300
THE ROLY-POLY PUDDING (as 'The Tale of Samuel Whiskers') (Warne, [1926]) £600
THE TALE OF THE FLOPSY BUNNIES (Warne, 1909) £600
THE TALE OF THE FLOPSY BUNNIES (decorated cloth binding) (Warne, 1909) £2,000
GINGER & PICKLES (large format) (Warne, 1909) £500
THE TALE OF MRS TITTLEMOUSE (Warne, 1910) £400
PETER RABBIT'S PAINTING BOOK (Warne, [1911]) £600
THE TALE OF TIMMY TIPTOES (Warne, 1911) £500
THE TALE OF MR TOD (Warne, 1912) £500
THE TALE OF PIGLING BLAND (Warne, 1913) £500
APPLEY DAPPLY'S NURSERY RHYMES (Warne, 1917) £600
TOM KITTEN'S PAINTING BOOK (Warne, 1917) £500
THE TALE OF JOHNNY TOWN-MOUSE (Warne, [1918]) £400
CECILY PARSLEY'S NURSERY RHYMES (small format) (Warne, 1922) £1,000
JEMIMA PUDDLE-DUCK'S PAINTING BOOK (Warne, [1925]) £500
PETER RABBIT'S ALMANAC FOR 1929 (Warne, [1928]) £500
THE FAIRY CARAVAN (McKay, US, 1929) £200
THE FAIRY CARAVAN (issued with dustjacket) (Warne, 1952) £80

THE TALE OF LITTLE PIG ROBINSON (large format) (Warne, [1930]) £300
SISTER ANNE (McKay, US, 1932) £300
WAG-BY-WALL (limited to 100 copies) (Warne, [1944]) £600
JEMIMA PUDDLE-DUCK'S PAINTING BOOK From the Original Designs by B. Potter (Warne, [1954]) £80
JEREMY FISHER'S PAINTING BOOK From the Original Designs by B. Potter (Warne, [1954]) £80
PETER RABBIT'S PAINTING BOOK From the Original Designs by B. Potter (Warne, [1954]) £80
TOM KITTEN'S PAINTING BOOK From the Original Designs by B. Potter (Warne, [1954]) £80
THE TALE OF THE FAITHFUL DOVE (illustrated by Marie Angel; limited to 100 copies)
    (Warne, [1955]) £400
THE TAILOR OF GLOUCESTER (facsimile; limited to 1,500 numbered copies; in box) (Warne, 1968) £100
THE TAILOR OF GLOUCESTER (facsimile of the original manuscript) (Warne, 1969) £60
THE SLY OLD CAT (issued with dustjacket) (Warne, 1971) £50
THE TALE OF TUPENNY (illustrated by Marie Angel; issued with dustjacket) (Warne, 1973) £40
THE TALE OF PETER RABBIT (boxed set; contains facsimiles of the 1901 first edition,
    the first Warne cloth-bound edition of 1902, and the original 'Peter Rabbit' letter from Beatrix Potter;
    limited to 750 numbered sets) (Warne, 1993) .... the set £200

POWER COMICS
British comics publishers popular in the 1960s and '70s.
Prices are for comics/annuals in Very Good condition. Published by Odhams Press unless otherwise indicated.

WHAM! 1 (20th June 1964) £55
WHAM! 1 (With free gift – Fun Gun) £90
WHAM! ANNUAL (1966) £8
WHAM! ANNUAL (1967-1969) .... each £6
WHAM! ANNUAL (1970-1971) .... each £4
WHAM! ANNUAL (IPC, 1972) £3
WHAM! AND POW! ANNUAL (IPC, 1973-1974) .... each £3
SMASH! 1 (5 February 1966) £80
SMASH! 1 (With free gift – Big Bang Gun) £110
SMASH! ANNUAL (1967) £7
SMASH! POW! IT'S FANTASTIC SUMMER SPECIAL (1968) £30
SMASH! HOLIDAY SPECIAL (IPC, 1969-1970) .... each £15
SMASH! ANNUAL (1968-1970) .... each £5
SMASH! ANNUAL (IPC, 1971-1976) .... each £3
SMASH! FUN BOOK (IPC, 1971) £8
POW! 1 (21st January 1967) £30
POW! 1 (With free gift – Spidermatic Gun and ammo) £70
POW! ANNUAL (1968) £5
POW! ANNUAL (1969-1971) .... each £3
FANTASTIC 1 (18th February 1967) £10
FANTASTIC 1 (With free gift – Pennant/Wallet) £20
FANTASTIC ANNUAL (1968) £5
FANTASTIC ANNUAL (1969-1970) .... each £3
TERRIFIC 1 (15th April 1967) £7
TERRIFIC 1 (With free gift – Iron Man Transfer) £12

PRATCHETT, Terry
British author. Born: Beaconsfield, 1948. Best known for his hugely successful series of humorous
science fantasy novels set in the imaginary 'Discworld', but began his career with a children's novel,
The Carpet People (1971), subsequently producing the 'Bromeliad' trilogy (*Truckers*, *Diggers* and *Wings*),
a series featuring the youngster, Johnny Maxwell, and further children's titles set in 'Discworld'.
Prices are for books in Very Good condition with dustjackets.

THE CARPET PEOPLE (illustrated by the author) (Colin Smythe, 1971) £700
THE CARPET PEOPLE (revised edition; unillustrated) (Gollancz, 1992) £30

Bromeliad Trilogy
TRUCKERS (Doubleday, 1989) £40
DIGGERS (Doubleday, 1990) £30
WINGS (Doubleday, 1990) £30

Johnny Maxwell Series
ONLY YOU CAN SAVE MANKIND (Doubleday, 1992) £25
JOHNNY AND THE DEAD (Doubleday, 1993) £20
JOHNNY AND THE BOMB (Doubleday, 1996) £20

Discworld Children's Books
THE AMAZING MAURICE AND HIS EDUCATED RODENTS (Doubleday, 2001) £15
THE WEE FREE MEN (Doubleday, 2003) £15
A HAT FULL OF SKY (Doubleday, 2004) £12

*Long before he found huge success with the 'Discworld' series, Terry Pratchett made his debut with **The Carpet People**, published by Colin Smythe in 1971, and encased in this dustjacket designed by the author. It is worth at least £700 today.*

PRESTON, Chloe

British author-illustrator. Born: 1887. She illustrated stories by May Byron and Tom Preston, notably those featuring the 'Peek-a-Boos' and the little wooden 'Chunkies'. She also designed numerous postcards for Valentines and Raphael Tuck, soft toys for Farnells and nursery designs for Paragon China Co. Died: 1969.

Prices are for books in Good condition.

'Peek-a-Boo' Books

THE PEEK-A-BOOS (Henry Frowde/Hodder & Stoughton, 1911)	£100
THE PEEK-A-BOOS IN WINTER (verses and illustrations) (Henry Frowde/Hodder & Stoughton, 1911)	£100
THE PEEK-A-BOO BUNNIES by Z.H. [G.H. Vyse] (Henry Frowde/Hodder & Stoughton, 1912)	£100
THE PEEK-A-BOOS AMONG THE BUNNIES by Z.H. [G.H. Vyse] (Henry Frowde/Hodder & Stoughton, 1912)	£100
THE PEEK-A-BOOS JAPS by Tom Preston (Henry Frowde/Hodder & Stoughton, 1912)	£100
THE PEEK-A-BOOS' HOLIDAY by Tom Preston (Henry Frowde/Hodder & Stoughton, 1912)	£100
THE PEEK-A-BOO TWINS by Tom Preston (Henry Frowde/Hodder & Stoughton, 1913)	£100
THE PEEK-A-BOOS IN TOWN by May Byron (Henry Frowde/Hodder & Stoughton, 1913)	£100
THE PEEK-A-BOOS' DESERT ISLAND by Max Byron (Henry Frowde/Hodder & Stoughton, 1914)	£150
THE PEEK-A-BOOS AT THE ZOO by May Bryon (Henry Frowde/Hodder & Stoughton, 1914)	£100
THE PEEK-A-BOOS AT SCHOOL by May Byron (Henry Frowde/Hodder & Stoughton, 1915)	£100
THE PEEK-A-BOOS IN CAMP by May Byron (Henry Frowde/Hodder & Stoughton, 1915)	£100
THE PEEK-A-BOOS IN WAR TIME by May Byron (Henry Frowde/Hodder & Stoughton, 1916)	£100
THE PEEK-A-BOO FARMERS by May Byron (Henry Frowde/Hodder & Stoughton, 1917)	£100
THE PEEK-A-BOO CIRCUS by May Byron (Humphrey Milford, 1919)	£100
THE PEEK-A-BOO CHRISTMAS by May Byron (Humphrey Milford, 1920)	£100
THE PEEK-A-BOO GARDENERS (Humphrey Milford, 1921)	£100
THE PEEK-A-BOO BOOKLETS by May Byron (Humphrey Milford, 1916-)	each £20
THE PEEK-A-BOOS GO SHOPPING (Humphrey Milford, 1922)	£100
THE PEEK-A-BOO GIPSIES by May Byron (OUP, 1923)	£100
THE PEEK-A-BOO PLAY BOOKS (Humphrey Milford, 1927-)	each £20

'Chunkies' Books

THE CHUNKIES by May Byron (Humphrey Milford, 1916)	£75
FIVE BAD CHUNKIES by May Byron (Humphrey Milford, 1921)	£75

THE CHUNKIES' ADVENTURES (Humphrey Milford, 1921)..£75
THE CHUNKY BOOKLETS (Humphrey Milford, 1921-)..each £20
THE CHUNKIES' PLAY BOOK (OUP, 1930)..£75

Others

ZH (illustrated by Chloe Preston and George Howard-Vyse) (Hodder & Stoughton, [c1913]).................£50
WILLIAM AND WOGGS by May Byron (Hodder & Stoughton, 1915) £50
BOB THE BOLD by Ella Maclennan (Hodder & Stoughton, [c1920])...£50
LITTLE TOMMY TUCKER and Other Stories (Samuel Lowe Kenosha, 1940)...£50
NURSERY RHYMES FOR CHILDREN (Samuel Lowe Kenosha, 1942) £50

PRICE, Evadne

British author. Born: Helen Zenna Smith in 1896. Best known for her children's novels featuring 'Jane' Turpin, a female William Brown. Also wrote adult novels under her own name. Died: 1985.

Prices are for books in Very Good condition with dustjackets.

JUST JANE (John Hamilton, [1928])...£150
JUST JANE (illustrated by Frank R. Grey) (Robert Hale, 1937)...£50
MEET JANE (Marriott, 1930)...£100
MEET JANE (illustrated by Frank R. Grey) (Robert Hale, 1937)..£50
ENTER — JANE (Newnes, [1932])..£100
ENTER — JANE (illustrated by Frank R. Grey) (Robert Hale, 1937)..£50
JANE THE FOURTH (illustrated by Frank R. Grey) (Robert Hale, 1937)...£70
JANE THE SLEUTH (illustrated by Frank R. Grey) (Robert Hale, 1939)..£60
JANE THE UNLUCKY (illustrated by Frank R. Grey) (Robert Hale, 1939)...£45
JANE THE POPULAR (illustrated by Frank R. Grey) (Robert Hale, 1939)...£45
JANE THE PATIENT (illustrated by Frank R. Grey) (Robert Hale, 1940)...£40
JANE GETS BUSY (illustrated by Frank R. Grey) (Robert Hale, 1940)...£40
JANE AT WAR (illustrated by Frank R. Grey) (Robert Hale, 1947) £40
JANE AND CO (selections from various books; illustrated by Frank R. Grey)
(Macmillan, 1985)...£15

PRICE, Willard

American author. Born: Peterborough, Ontario, Canada, in 1887. Best known for the highly improbable adventures of Hal and Roger Hunt in realistic settings. Died: 1983.

Prices are for books in Very Good condition with dustjackets

AMAZON ADVENTURE (illustrated by George Hartmann) (Cape, 1951) £25
SOUTH SEA ADVENTURE (Cape, 1952)..£25
UNDERWATER ADVENTURE (Cape, 1955)...£20
VOLCANO ADVENTURE (Cape, 1956)..£20
WHALE ADVENTURE (Cape, 1960)...£20
AFRICAN ADVENTURE (Cape, 1963)...£20
ELEPHANT ADVENTURE (Cape, 1964)..£20
SAFARI ADVENTURE (Cape, 1966)...£20
LION ADVENTURE (Cape, 1967) £15
GORILLA ADVENTURE (Cape, 1969)...£15
DIVING ADVENTURE (Cape, 1970)...£15
CANNIBAL ADVENTURE (illustrated by Pat Marriott) (Cape, 1972)...£15
TIGER ADVENTURE (illustrated by Pat Marriott) (Cape, 1979)..£15
ARCTIC ADVENTURE (illustrated by Pat Marriott) (Cape, 1980)..£15

'PRIZE' ANNUALS

Early British annuals published by Dean. Edited by J.E. Clarke up to 1875.

Prices are for annuals in Very Good condition.

THE CHILDREN'S PRIZE 1863-75 ....each £40
THE PRIZE FOR GIRLS AND BOYS 1876-23 ....each £30

PRØYSEN, Alf

Norwegian author. Born: 1914. Creator of 'Mrs Pepperpot' series, all illustrated by Björn Berg. Died: 1970.

Prices are for books in Very Good condition with dustjackets where applicable.

LITTLE OLD MRS PEPPERPOT and Other Stories (illustrated by Björn Berg) (Hutchinson, 1959) £40
MRS PEPPERPOT AGAIN and Other Stories (illustrated by Björn Berg) (Hutchinson, 1960).....................£30
MRS PEPPERPOT TO THE RESCUE and Other Stories (illustrated by Björn Berg) (Hutchinson, 1963)....£25
MRS PEPPERPOT IN THE MAGIC WOOD and Other Stories (illustrated by Björn Berg)
(Hutchinson, 1968)...£20
MRS PEPPERPOT'S BUSY DAY (illustrated by Björn Berg) (Hutchinson, 1970)....................................£20
MRS PEPPERPOT'S OUTING (illustrated by Björn Berg) (Hutchinson, 1971) £20
MRS PEPPERPOT'S CHRISTMAS (illustrated by Björn Berg) (Hutchinson, 1972)..................................£20
MRS PEPPERPOT'S YEAR (illustrated by Björn Berg) (Hutchinson, 1973) £20

PUDNEY, John
British author. Born: Langley, Buckinghamshire, in 1909. Notable for the 'Fred and I' adventure stories and the 'Hartwarp' series for the younger age group. Died: 1977.
Prices are for books in Very Good condition with dustjackets where applicable.

SATURDAY ADVENTURE (Evans, 1950) £15
SUNDAY ADVENTURE (Evans, 1951) £15
MONDAY ADVENTURE (Evans, 1952) £15
TUESDAY ADVENTURE: The Affray in the Sardanger Fjord (Evans, 1953) £15
WEDNESDAY ADVENTURE (Evans, 1954) £15
THURSDAY ADVENTURE: The Stolen Airliner (Evans, 1955) £15
FRIDAY ADVENTURE (Evans, 1956) £15
SPRING ADVENTURE (illustrated by Douglas Relf) (Evans, 1961) £15
SUMMER ADVENTURE (illustrated by Douglas Relf) (Evans, 1962) £15
AUTUMN ADVENTURE (illustrated by Douglas Relf) (Evans, 1963) £15
WINTER ADVENTURE (illustrated by Douglas Relf) (Evans, 1964) £15
THE GRANDFATHER CLOCK (illustrated by Peggy Beetles) (Hamish Hamilton, 1957) £10
CROSSING THE ROAD (illustrated by Janet and Anne Grahame Johnstone) (Hamish Hamilton, 1958) £10
THE HARTWARP LIGHT RAILWAY (illustrated by Ferelith Eccles Williams) (Hamish Hamilton, 1962) £10
THE HARTWARP DUMP (illustrated by Ferelith Eccles Williams) (Hamish Hamilton, 1962) £10
THE HARTWARP BALLOON (illustrated by Ferelith Eccles Williams) (Hamish Hamilton, 1962) £10
THE HARTWARP CIRCUS (illustrated by Ferelith Eccles Williams) (Hamish Hamilton, 1963) £10
THE HARTWARP BAKEHOUSE (illustrated by Ferelith Eccles Williams) (Hamish Hamilton, 1964) £10
THE HARTWARP EXPLOSION (illustrated by Ferelith Eccles Williams) (Hanish Hamilton, 1965) £10
THE HARTWARP JETS (illustrated by Ferelith Eccles Williams) (Hamish Hamilton, 1967) £10
TUNNEL TO THE SKY (illustrated by Christine Marsh) (Hamish Hamilton, 1965) £10
THE NOEL STREATFEILD BIRTHDAY STORY BOOK by Noel Streatfeild, John Pudney and others
(illustrated by Shirley Hughes and others) (Dent, 1976) £15

PULLMAN, Philip
Prize-winning British author. Born: 1946. History was made in 2002 when Pullman's compelling finale to the 'His Dark Materials' trilogy *The Amber Spyglass* won the Whitbread Book of the Year prize. It was the first time the coveted prize had been won by a children's book – the judges agreed that Pullman's 'superlative achievement' transcended all age barriers. His bestselling trilogy also remain his most avidly sought rarities, although prices have cooled since peaking around 2004.
Prices are for books in Fine condition with dustjackets where applicable.

'His Dark Materials' trilogy
NORTHERN LIGHTS (Scholastic, 1995) £3,000
THE SUBTLE KNIFE (Scholastic, 1997) £1,000
THE AMBER SPYGLASS (Scholastic, 2001) £75
HIS DARK MATERIALS (omnibus edition) (Scholastic, 2001) £25
Ditto (Boxed Set. Three volumes; paperback; in box) (Scholastic/Point, 2001) £20
LYRA'S OXFORD (with John Lawrence. Postcards, a map of Oxford,
and a short story set in the 'His Dark Materials' universe) (no dustjacket) (Fickling, 2003) £12

'Sally Lockhart' books
THE RUBY IN THE SMOKE (OUP, 1985) £1,000
THE SHADOW IN THE PLATE (OUP, 1986) £500
THE TIGER IN THE WELL (Viking, 1991) £250
THE TIN PRINCESS (paperback) (Puffin/OUP, 1994) £30

Others
THE HAUNTED STORM (New English Library, 1971) £2,000
GALATEA (Gollancz, 1979) £300
COUNT KARLSTEIN or The Ride of the Demon Huntsman (Chatto & Windus, 1982) £700
HOW TO BE COOL (paperback) (Heinemann, 1987) £30
SPRING-HEELED JACK: A Story of Bravery and Evil (boards, no dustjacket) (Doubleday, 1989) £400
THE BROKEN BRIDGE (paperback) (Macmillan, 1990) £100
THE WHITE MERCEDES (Pan Macmillan, 1992) £350
THE WONDERFUL STORY OF ALADDIN AND THE ENCHANTED LAMP (Andre Deutsch, 1993) £100
SHERLOCK HOLMES AND THE ADVENTURE OF THE LIMEHOUSE HORROR (paperback)
(Nelson, 1993) £150
THE NEW CUT GANG: THUNDERBOLT'S WAXWORK (boards, no dustjacket) (Viking, 1994) £200
THE NEW CUT GANG: THE GAS-FITTER'S BALL (boards, no dustjacket) (Viking, 1995) £200
THE FIREWORK-MAKER'S DAUGHTER (boards, no dustjacket) (Doubleday, 1995) £200
CLOCKWORK or All Wound Up (illustrated by Peter Bailey; boards, no dustjacket) (Doubleday, 1996) £300
MOSSYCOAT (illustrated by Peter Bailey; paperback) (Scholastic Hippo, 1998) £20
I WAS A RAT! (illustrated by Peter Bailey; boards, no dustjacket) (Doubleday, 1999) £200
PUSS IN BOATS; or, The Ogre, The Ghouls and the Windmill (Doubleday, 2000) £10
THE SCARECROW AND HIS SERVANT (Doubleday, 2004) £10

PYLE, Howard

American author-illustrator. Born: Wilmington, Delaware, in 1853. Began contributing illustrated fables to *St. Nicholas* magazine at the age of 21, subsequently achieving fame with *The Merry Adventures of Robin Hood* (1883), which he both wrote and illustrated. This was followed by several historical and adventure novels, three collections of fairy tales and a four-volume retelling of the legends of King Arthur. N.C. Wyeth, Maxfield Parrish and Jessie Willcox Smith were amongst his pupils. Died: 1911.

Prices are for books in Very Good condition.

THE MERRY ADVENTURES OF ROBIN HOOD of Great Renown in Nottinghamshire (Scribner, US, 1883)......................£300
THE MERRY ADVENTURES OF ROBIN HOOD of Great Renown in Nottinghamshire (Sampson Low, 1883)......................£50
PEPPER AND SALT, or Seasoning for Young Folk (stories) (Sampson Low, US, 1886) £200
PEPPER AND SALT, or Seasoning for Young Folk (stories) (Sampson Low, 1888)..£100
THE WONDER CLOCK, or Four and Twenty Marvellous Tales (stories; with Katherine Pyle)
   (Harper, US, 1888) £250
OTTO OF THE SILVER HAND (novel) (Sampson Low, 1888) £200
THE ROSE OF PARADISE (Harper, US, 1888)...£200
MEN OF IRON (novel) (Osgood McIlvaine, 1892 [1891])..£200
TWILIGHT LAND (Osgood McIlvaine, 1895 [1894]) £200
THE STORY OF JACK BALLISTER'S FORTUNES (novel) (Century, US, 1895) £200
THE STORY OF JACK BALLISTER'S FORTUNES (novel) (Osgood McIlvaine, 1897 [1896])..£200
THE GARDEN BEHIND THE MOON: A Real Story of the Moon Angel (novel) (Lawrence & Bullen, 1896)..................£200
THE STORY OF KING ARTHUR AND HIS KNIGHTS (Newnes, 1903)...£200
THE STORY OF KING ARTHUR AND HIS KNIGHTS by Howard Pyle (Scribner's, US, 1903) £200
THE STORY OF THE CHAMPIONS OF THE ROUND TABLE (Newnes, 1905)..£200
THE STORY OF THE CHAMPIONS OF THE ROUND TABLE by Howard Pyle (Scribner's, US, 1905)...................£200
THE STORY OF LAUNCELOT AND HIS COMPANIONS (Chapman & Hall, 1907) £200
THE STORY OF SIR LAUNCELOT AND HIS COMPANIONS by Howard Pyle (Scribner's, US, 1907).....................£200
THE STORY OF THE GRAIL AND THE PASSING OF ARTHUR by Howard Pyle (Scribner's, US, 1911)..................£200
THE RUBY OF KISHMOOR (Harper, US, 1908)..£200
HOWARD PYLE'S BOOK OF PIRATES. Compiled by Merle Johnson (Harper, US, 1921) £100

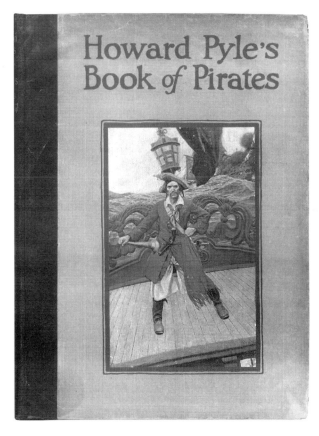

*The splendid cover of **Howard Pyle's Book of Pirates** (1921).*

R

RACKHAM, Arthur

British illustrator. Born: London, 1867. Studied at the City of London School and the Lambeth School of Art. Began by contributing illustrations to the *Westminster Budget, Little Folks* and other magazines, launching his career as a highly successful illustrator of children's books with editions of the *Ingoldsby Legends* (1898), Lambs *Tales from Shakespeare* (1899) and the Grimms' *Fairy Tales* (1900). Most of his pre-First World War 'Gift Books' were issued in sumptuous limited editions as well as standard trade editions. Married the Irish portrait painter, Edyth Starkie, in 1903. Died: 1939.

Prices are for books in Very Good condition.

THE ZANKIWANK AND THE BLETHERWITCH by S.J.A. Fitzgerald (seventeen full-page drawings and
    24 smaller drawings by Arthur Rackham) (Dent, 1896) £1,500
TWO OLD LADIES by Maggie Browne (four colour plates and nineteen black-and-white illustrations by
    Arthur Rackham) (Cassell, 1897)..£500
TWO OLD LADIES by Maggie Browne (as 'The Surprising Adventures of Tuppy and Tue')
    (Cassell, 1904) £250
THE INGOLDSBY LEGENDS by Richard H. Barham (Dent, 1898) £150
THE INGOLDSBY LEGENDS by Richard H. Barham (Dent, 1907) £300
THE INGOLDSBY LEGENDS by Richard H. Barham (limited to 560 copies, signed by the artist)
    (Dent, 1907)..£1,000
TALES FROM SHAKESPEARE by Charles and Mary Lamb (twelve illustrations by Arthur Rackham)
    (Dent: 'Temple Classics' series, 1899) £100
TALES FROM SHAKESPEARE by Charles and Mary Lamb (Dent, 1909)..£200
TALES FROM SHAKESPEARE by Charles and Mary Lamb (limited to 750 copies, signed by the artist)
    (Dent, 1909)..£1,000
GULLIVER'S TRAVELS by Jonathan Swift (Dent: 'Temple Classics' series, 1900)...£75
GULLIVER'S TRAVELS by Jonathan Swift (Dent, 1909) £200
GULLIVER'S TRAVELS by Jonathan Swift (with extra plate; limited to 750 copies, signed by the artist)
    (Dent, 1909)..£1,000
GULLIVER'S TRAVELS by Jonathan Swift (adapted by F.C. Tilney)
    (Dent: 'Tales for Children from Many Lands' series, [1913])...£50
GULLIVER'S TRAVELS by Jonathan Swift (Dent: 'Children's Illustrated Classics' series, 1952).............................£20
FAIRY TALES OF THE BROTHERS GRIMM (Freemantle, 1900)...£300
FAIRY TALES OF THE BROTHERS GRIMM (translated by Mrs Edgar Lucas)
    (Constable, 1909) £750

*The origibnal dustjacket for the first trade edition
of **Fairy Tales by Hans Andersen**. The book was
issued both trade and De Luxe editions.*

One of twelve plates by Arthur Rackham for **The Peter Pan Portfolio** *(1912).*

Rackham illustrated many gift-book editions of works by Hans Christian Andersen and the brothers Grimm.

FAIRY TALES OF THE BROTHERS GRIMM (limited to 750 copies, signed by the artist) (Constable, 1909) **£3,000**
FAIRY TALES OF THE BROTHERS GRIMM (Constable, 1920)...**£300**
FAIRY TALES OF THE BROTHERS GRIMM (Heinemann, [1925]) **£150**
THE GREEK HEROES (four colour plates and eight black-and-white illustrations by Arthur Rackham) (Cassell, 1903) **£80**
THE GREEK HEROES (reissue of 1903 edition; four colour plates and eight black-and-white illustrations by Arthur Rackham)
(Cassell, 1910) **£60**
KINGDOMS CURIOUS by Myra Hamilton (illustrated by Arthur Rackham, H.R. Millar and others) (Heinemann, 1905)...........**£100**
RIP VAN WINKLE by Washington Irving (Heinemann, 1905) **£800**
RIP VAN WINKLE by Washington Irving (limited to 250 copies, signed by the artist) (Heinemann, 1905)...................**£3,500**
PUCK OF POOK'S HILL by Rudyard Kipling (four colour plates by Arthur Rackham) (Doubleday Page, US, 1906)................**£200**
PETER PAN IN KENSINGTON GARDENS by J.M. Barrie (Hodder & Stoughton, [1906]) **£1,000**
PETER PAN IN KENSINGTON GARDENS by J.M. Barrie (limited to 500 copies, signed by the artist)
(Hodder & Stoughton, [1906]) **£4,000**
PETER PAN IN KENSINGTON GARDENS by J.M. Barrie (new edition) (Hodder & Stoughton, 1912)...................**£1,500**
PETER PAN IN KENSINGTON GARDENS by J.M. Barrie (new edition)
(De-Luxe edition in vellum) (Hodder & Stoughton, [1912]) **£1,500**
PETER PAN IN KENSINGTON GARDENS by J.M. Barrie (new edition) (trade edition in green cloth)
(Hodder & Stoughton, [1912]) **£600**
PETER PAN IN KENSINGTON GARDENS (facsimile of the 1912 edition; limited to 500 numbered copies)
(Hodder & Stoughton, 1983) **£150**
J.M. BARRIE'S PETER PAN IN KENSINGTON GARDENS by M.C. Byron (Hodder & Stoughton, [1929]) **£50**
THE PETER PAN PORTFOLIO (limited to 500 copies, numbered 101-600) (Hodder & Stoughton, [1912])...................**£3,000**
THE PETER PAN PORTFOLIO (limited to twenty copies, each plate signed by the artist) (Hodder & Stoughton, 1912)......**£10,000**
ALICE'S ADVENTURES IN WONDERLAND by Lewis Carroll (with poem by Austin Dobson; green cloth binding)
(Heinemann, [1907])..**£300**
ALICE'S ADVENTURES IN WONDERLAND by Lewis Carroll (with poem by Austin Dobson;
De Luxe edition: limited to 1,130 copies [unsigned]; white vellum binding) (Heinemann, [1907])................**£1,750**
THE LAND OF ENCHANTMENT (Cassell, 1907)..**£200**
A MIDSUMMER NIGHT'S DREAM by William Shakespeare (Heinemann, 1908) **£450**
A MIDSUMMER NIGHT'S DREAM by William Shakespeare (limited to 1,000 copies, signed by the artist)
(Heinemann, 1908)..**£1,500**
UNDINE by Friedrich de la Motte Fouqué (translated by W.L. Courtney) (Heinemann, 1909) **£200**
UNDINE by Friedrich de la Motte Fouqué (translated by W.L. Courtney; limited to 1,000 copies, signed by the artist)
(Heinemann, 1909)...**£1,000**
THE RAINBOW BOOK by Mabel H. Spielmann (illustrated by Arthur Rackham and others) (Chatto & Windus, 1909) **£100**
THE BOOK OF BETTY BARBER by Maggie Browne (Duckworth, [1910])..**£500**
STORIES OF KING ARTHUR by A.L. Haydon (four colour plates and other illustrations by Arthur Rackham)
(Cassell, 1910) **£75**
AESOP'S FABLES (translated by V.S. Vernon Jones) (Heinemann, 1912) **£200**
AESOP'S FABLES (translated by V.S. Vernon Jones; limited to 1,450 copies, signed by the artist) (Heinemann, 1912) **£1,000**
MOTHER GOOSE: The Old Nursery Rhymes (Heinemann, [1913]) **£300**
MOTHER GOOSE: The Old Nursery Rhymes (limited to 1,130 copies, signed by the artist) (Heinemann, [1913])...............**£1,000**
MOTHER GOOSE: The Old Nursery Rhymes (two volumes) (Heinemann, [1952]) ....the set **£150**
ARTHUR RACKHAM'S BOOK OF PICTURES (introduction by Sir Arthur Quiller-Couch) (Heinemann, 1913)........................**£300**
ARTHUR RACKHAM'S BOOK OF PICTURES (introduction by Sir Arthur Quiller-Couch;
limited to 1,030 copies, signed by the artist) (Heinemann, 1913)...**£1,000**
A CHRISTMAS CAROL by Charles Dickens (Heinemann, 1915) **£400**
A CHRISTMAS CAROL by Charles Dickens (limited to 530 copies, signed by the artist) (Heinemann, 1915) **£1,500**
THE ALLIES' FAIRY BOOK (Heinemann, [1916]) **£100**
THE ALLIES' FAIRY BOOK (limited to 525 copies, signed by the artist) (Heinemann, [1916])..............................**£750**
LITTLE BROTHER AND LITTLE SISTER by the Brothers Grimm (Constable, 1917)......................................**£300**
LITTLE BROTHER AND LITTLE SISTER by the Brothers Grimm (with extra plate;
limited to 525 copies, signed by the artist) (Constable, 1917).........................**£2,000** (without extra plate: **£1,250**)
THE ROMANCE OF KING ARTHUR by Thomas Malory (Macmillan, 1917)..**£300**
THE ROMANCE OF KING ARTHUR by Thomas Malory (limited to 500 copies, signed by the artist) (Macmillan, 1917) **£1,000**
ENGLISH FAIRY TALES RETOLD by Flora A. Steel (Macmillan, 1918)..**£200**
ENGLISH FAIRY TALES RETOLD by Flora A. Steel (limited to 500 copies, signed by the artist) (Macmillan, 1918).............**£1,000**
THE SPRINGTIDE OF LIFE by A.C. Swinburne (Heinemann, 1918) **£100**
THE SPRINGTIDE OF LIFE by A.C. Swinburne (with extra plate; limited to 765 copies, signed by the artist)
(Heinemann, 1918)...**£500**
SOME BRITISH BALLADS (Constable, [1919]) **£150**
SOME BRITISH BALLADS (limited to 575 copies, signed by the artist) (Constable, [1919]) **£1,000**
SOME BRITISH BALLADS (Heinemann, [1924])...**£60**
CINDERELLA Adapted by Charles S. Evans (Heinemann, 1919)...**£100**
CINDERELLA Adapted by Charles S. Evans (De Luxe edition: limited to 525 copies,
signed by the artist; on handmade paper) (Heinemann, 1919) **£600**
CINDERELLA Adapted by Charles S. Evans (De Luxe vellum edition: limited to 325 copies,
signed by the artist; on Japanese vellum) (Heinemann, 1919)...**£1,000**
SNOWDROP and Other Tales by the Brothers Grimm (reprint from 'Fairy Tales of the Brothers Grimm' [1909])
(Constable, 1920)..**£200**
HANSEL AND GRETEL and Other Tales by the Brothers Grimm (reprint from 'Fairy Tales of the Brothers Grimm' [1909])
(Constable, 1920)..**£200**

'They quaffed liquor in profound silence.' Rackham's illustration from the 1905 edition of Washington Irving's **Rip Van Winkle**.

THE SLEEPING BEAUTY Adapted by Charles S. Evans (Heinemann, 1920)..£100
THE SLEEPING BEAUTY Adapted by Charles S. Evans (with extra plate; limited to 625 copies,
  signed by the artist) (Heinemann, 1920)..£600
IRISH FAIRY TALES by James Stephens (Macmillan, 1920)..£200
IRISH FAIRY TALES by James Stephens (limited to 520 copies, signed by the artist) (Macmillan, 1920)......£1,000
A DISH OF APPLES by Eden Phillpotts (Hodder & Stoughton, [1921])...................................£100
A DISH OF APPLES by Eden Phillpotts (limited to 500 copies, signed by the artist) (Hodder & Stoughton, [1921])......£600
A WONDER BOOK by Nathaniel Hawthorne (Hodder & Stoughton, 1922)...................................£200
A WONDER BOOK by Nathaniel Hawthorne (limited to 600 copies, signed by the artist)
  (Hodder & Stoughton, [1922])..£800
WHERE THE BLUE BEGINS by Christopher Morley (Heinemann, [1925])...................................£150
WHERE THE BLUE BEGINS by Christopher Morley (limited to 175 copies, signed by the artist)
  (Heinemann, [1925])..£600
POOR CECCO by Margery Williams Bianco (Chatto & Windus, 1925).....................................£150
POOR CECCO by Margery Williams Bianco (limited to 105 copies, signed by the author) (Doran, US, [1925])......£5,000
THE LEGEND OF SLEEPY HOLLOW by Washington Irving (Harrap, 1928)...................................£150
THE LEGEND OF SLEEPY HOLLOW by Washington Irving (limited to 375 copies,
  signed by the artist; vellum binding) (Harrap, 1928)....................................£750
THE NIGHT BEFORE CHRISTMAS: A Visit from St. Nicholas by Clement C. Moore (wrappers) (Harrap, 1931)......£75
THE NIGHT BEFORE CHRISTMAS: A Visit from St. Nicholas by Clement C. Moore (limited to 550 copies,
  signed by the artist) (Harrap, 1931)..£1,000
THE CHIMES by Charles Dickens (limited to 1,500 copies, signed by the artist; in slipcase)
  (Limited Editions Club, US, 1931)...£400
THE KING OF THE GOLDEN RIVER by John Ruskin (wrappers) (Harrap, 1932)............................£75
THE KING OF THE GOLDEN RIVER by John Ruskin (limited to 570 copies, signed by the artist) (Harrap, 1932)......£500
FAIRY TALES by Hans C. Andersen (selected and illustrated by Arthur Rackham) (Harrap, 1932)......£200
FAIRY TALES by Hans C. Andersen (selected and illustrated by Arthur Rackham; limited to 525 copies,
  signed by the artist) (Harrap, 1932)..£1,500
GOBLIN MARKET by Christina G. Rossetti (wrappers) (Harrap, 1933).................................£75
GOBLIN MARKET by Christina G. Rossetti (limited to 410 copies, signed by the artist) (Harrap, 1933)......£600
THE ARTHUR RACKHAM FAIRY BOOK (Harrap, 1933)..£150
THE ARTHUR RACKHAM FAIRY BOOK (limited to 460 copies, signed by the artist) (Harrap, 1933)......£800
THE PIED PIPER OF HAMELIN by Robert Browning (Harrap 1934)......................................£75
THE PIED PIPER OF HAMELIN by Robert Browning (limited to 410 copies, signed by the artist) (Harrap, 1934)......£600
THE WIND IN THE WILLOWS by Kenneth Grahame (limited to 2,020 numbered copies, signed by the designer,
  Bruce Rogers; in slipcase) (Limited Editions Club, US, 1940)............................£1,000
THE WIND IN THE WILLOWS by Kenneth Grahame (Heritage, US, 1940).................................£100
THE WIND IN THE WILLOWS by Kenneth Grahame (omits several of the colour plates from the original American edition)
  (Methuen, 1950)...£150
THE WIND IN THE WILLOWS by Kenneth Grahame (limited to 500 copies; in box) (Methuen, 1951)......£1,500
THE WIND IN THE WILLOWS by Kenneth Grahame (twelve colour plates and fifteen line drawings by Arthur Rackham)
  (Methuen, 1975)...£75

'RADIO FUN' ANNUALS

British comic annual published by Amalgamated Press and featuring the stars of British radio, notably Arthur Askey, Tommy Trinder and Duggie Wakefield.

Prices are for annuals in Very Good condition.

RADIO FUN ANNUAL 1940 ....£120
RADIO FUN ANNUAL 1941 ....£100
RADIO FUN ANNUAL 1942 ....£75
RADIO FUN ANNUAL 1943 ....£65
RADIO FUN ANNUAL 1944 ....£60
RADIO FUN ANNUAL 1945 ....£55
RADIO FUN ANNUAL 1946 ....£50
RADIO FUN ANNUAL 1947-48 ....each £45
RADIO FUN ANNUAL 1949 ....£40
RADIO FUN ANNUAL 1950-55 ....each £35
RADIO FUN ANNUAL 1956-58 ....each £20
RADIO FUN ANNUAL 1959-60 ....each £15

RAE, Gwynedd

British author. Born: 1892. The creator of 'Mary Plain', the bear from Berne, Switzerland, who featured in a series of droll and endearing stories with a discreet touch of fantasy. Died: 1977.

Prices are for books in Very Good condition with dustjackets where applicable.

MOSTLY MARY (Routledge, 1930) £75
ALL MARY (Routledge, 1931) £45
MARY PLAIN ON HOLIDAY (illustrated by Irene Williamson) (Routledge, 1937) £40
MARY PLAIN IN TROUBLE (Routledge, 1940) £40

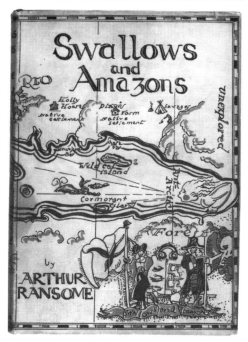

*'Big-Hearted' Arthur Askey was a regular cover star of the long-running British comic **Radio Fun**.*

Swallows and Amazons was the first book in Ransome's much-loved series following the adventures of the Walker family.

MARY PLAIN IN WAR-TIME (Routledge, 1942) £40
MARY PLAIN'S BIG ADVENTURE (Routledge, 1944) £40
MARY PLAIN IN TOWN (Routledge, 1947)...£40
MARY PLAIN TO THE RESCUE (Routledge, 1950)...£40
MARY PLAIN AND THE TWINS (illustrated by Irene Williamson) (Routledge, 1952) £40
MARY PLAIN GOES BOB-A-JOBBING (illustrated by Irene Williamson) (Routledge, 1954) £40
MARY PLAIN GOES TO AMERICA (illustrated by Irene Williamson) (Routledge, 1957) £40
MARY PLAIN VIP (illustrated by Irene Williamson) (Routledge, 1961)...£40
MARY PLAIN'S "WHODUNIT" (Routledge, 1965) £40

RANSOME, Arthur
British author. Born: Arthur Michell Ransome in Leeds in 1884. Studied at Rugby School and Leeds University, leaving the latter at the age of seventeen to become an office boy at the publishers, Grant Richards. Gave up his job in 1903 to become a freelance writer, contributing essays and articles to a variety of publications and subsequently becoming overseas correspondent for the *Manchester Guardian*. Left the paper in 1929 to write *Swallows and Amazons* (1930), the first in a series of books describing the Walker family's adventures in the Lake District. Amongst his many other books were critical studies of Edgar Allan Poe (1910) and Oscar Wilde (1912). Died: 1967.
Prices are for books in Very Good condition (with dustjackets after 1920).

'Swallows and Amazons' Books
SWALLOWS AND AMAZONS (vignette and endpaper & frontispiece maps illustrated by Stephen [Steven] Spurrier)
    (Cape, 1930)...£1,500
SWALLOWS AND AMAZONS (illustrated by Clifford Webb) (Cape, 1931)..£250
SWALLOWS AND AMAZONS (illustrated by Arthur Ransome) (Cape, 1938) £150
THE SWALLOWS & AMAZONS (original draft of 'Swallows and Amazons'; issued in pictorial boards with dustjacket
    (50 copies) or pictorial wrappers [500 copies]) (Amazon Publications/The Arthur Ransome Society, 1997)...............£50 / £20
SWALLOWDALE (illustrated by Clifford Webb) (Cape, 1931) £750
SWALLOWDALE (illustrated by Arthur Ransome) (Cape, 1936)..£75
PETER DUCK (illustrated by the author) (Cape, 1932)..£250
WINTER HOLIDAY (illustrated by the author) (Cape, 1933)..£300
COOT CLUB (illustrated by the author and Helene Carter) (Cape, 1934) £300
PIGEON POST (illustrated by the author) (Cape, 1936) £200
WE DIDN'T MEAN TO GO TO SEA (illustrated by the author) (Cape, 1937) £150

SECRET WATER (illustrated by the author) (Cape, 1939)..£120
THE BIG SIX (illustrated by the author) (Cape, 1940)..£120
MISSEE LEE (illustrated by the author) (Cape, 1941)..£100
THE PICTS AND THE MARTYRS, or Not Welcome At All (illustrated by the author) (Cape, 1943) £100
GREAT NORTHERN? (Cape, 1947) £100
COOTS IN THE NORTH and Other Stories (Cape, 1988) £12

Others

THE CHILD'S BOOK OF THE SEASONS (non-fiction) (Treherne, 1906)...£75
POND AND STREAM (non-fiction) (Treherne, 1906)..£75
THE THINGS IN OUR GARDEN (ncn-fiction) (Treherne, 1906)...£75
HIGHWAYS AND BYWAYS IN FAIRYLAND (Alston Rivers: 'Pinafore Library' series, [1906]).............................£100
THE IMP AND THE ELF AND THE OGRE (contains 'The Child's Book of the Seasons', 'Pond and Stream' and
'The Things in Our Garden') (Nisbet, 1910)..£100
OLD PETER'S RUSSIAN TALES (illustrated by Dmitri Mitrokhin) (T.C. & E.C. Jack, 1916) £150
ALADDIN AND HIS WONDERFUL LAMP (illustrated by Mackenzie) (Nisbet, [1919])..£150
ALADDIN AND HIS WONDERFUL LAMP (limited to 250 numbered copies, signed by the artist; illustrated by Mackenzie)
(Nisbet, [1919])...£1,500
THE SOLDIER AND DEATH: A Russian Folk Tale (Privately printed, 1920) £50
THE WAR OF THE BIRDS AND THE BEASTS AND OTHER RUSSIAN TALES (Cape, 1984)...........................£12
THE BLUE TREACLE: The Story of an Escape (issued in paper boards [25 copies] or wrappers [375 copies])
(The Arthur Ransome Society, 1993) ....£40 / £20
ALADDIN AND HIS LAMP in Five Scenes of Ten Minutes Each (wrappers [80 copies])
(The Arthur Ransome Society, 1997) £10

REEVES, James

British author. Born: London, 1909. Prolific wrtiter of prose and verse for both children and adults,
and edited many other books. His *Complete Poems for Children*, illustrated by Edward Ardizzone,
was published in 1973. Died: 1978.

Prices are for books in Very Good condition with dustjackets where applicable.

THE WANDERING MOON (illustrated by Evadne Rowan) (Heinemann, 1950)..£25
MULCASTER MARKET Three Plays for Young People (illustrated by Dudley Cutler) (Heinemann, 1951) £25
THE BLACKBIRD IN THE LILAC (verse; illustrated by Edward Ardizzone) (OUP, 1952) £50
THE KING WHO TOOK SUNSHINE (Heinemann, 1954) £20
ENGLISH FABLES AND FAIRY STORIES, RETOLD (illustrated by Joan Kiddell-Monroe) (Blackie, 1954) £20
PIGEONS AND PRINCESSES (illustrated by Edward Ardizzone) (Heinemann, 1956) £45
A HEALTH TO JOHN PATCH A Ballad Operetta (Boosey, 1957) £20
PREFABULOUS ANIMILES (illustrated by Edward Ardizzone) (Heinemann, 1957) £40
WANDERING MOON (illustrated by Edward Ardizzone) (Heinemann, 1957)...£40
A GOLDEN LAND Edited by James Reeves (illustrated by Gillian Conway, Eve Garnett and others) (Constable 1958) £25
MULBRIDGE MANOR (illustrated by Geraldine Spence) (Heinemann, 1958) £20
TITUS IN TROUBLE (illustrated by Edward Ardizzone) (The Bodley Head, 1959) £45
EXPLOITS OF DON QUIXOTE, RETOLD (illustrated by Edward Ardizzone) (Blackie, 1959) £45
RAGGED ROBIN (illustrated by Jane Paton) (Heinemann, 1961)..£20
FABLES FROM AESOP, RETOLD (illustrated by Maurice Wilson) (Blackie, 1961)...£20
HURDY-GURDY: Selected Poems for Children (illustrated by Edward Ardizzone) (Heinemann, 1961) £45
SAILOR RUMBELOW AND BRITTANIA (illustrated by Edward Ardizzone) (Dutton, 1962) £45
THE STRANGE LIGHT (illustrated by Lynton Lamb) (Heinemann, 1964)..£30
THREE TALL TALES: Chosen from Traditional Sources (illustrated by Edward Ardizzone) (Abelard-Schuman, 1964) £35
THE STORY OF JACKIE THIMBLE (illustrated by Edward Ardizzone) (Chatto & Windus, 1965)........................£35
THE ROAD TO A KINGDOM: Stories from the Old and New Testaments (illustrated by Richard Kennedy)
(Heinemann, 1965)..£20
THE PILLAR-BOX THIEVES (illustrated by Dick Hart) (Nelson, 1965) £25
THE SECRET SHOEMAKERS and Other Stories (illustrated by Edward Ardizzone) (Abelard-Schuman, 1966).......£45
THE COLD FLAME: Based on a Tale from the Collection of the Brothers Grimm (illustrated by Charles Keeping)
(Hamish Hamilton, 1967)..£25
RHYMING WILL (illustrated by Edward Ardizzone) (Hamish Hamilton, 1967)..£30
THE CHRISTMAS BOOKS (illustrated by Raymond Briggs) (Heinemann, 1968)..£35
MR HORROX AND THE GRATCH (illustrated by Quentin Blake) (Abelard-Schuman, 1969)............................£30
HEROES AND MONSTERS: Legends of Ancient Greece Retold – Gods and Voyagers
(illustrated by Sarah Nechamkin) (Blackie, 1969)..£20
THE ANGEL AND THE DONKEY (illustrated by Edward Ardizzone) (Hamish Hamilton, 1969) £25
MAILDON THE VOYAGER (illustrated by John Lawrence) (Hamish Hamilton, 1971) £20
HOW THE MOON BEGAN (illustrated by Edward Ardizzone) (Abelard-Schuman, 1971).................................£25
THE PATH OF GOLD (illustrated by Krystyna Turska) (Hamish Hamilton, 1972) £25
COMPLETE POEMS FOR CHILDREN (illustrated by Edward Ardizzone) (Heinemann, 1973) £30
THE FORBIDDEN FOREST and Other Stories (illustrated by Raymond Briggs) (Heinemann, 1973) £30
THE VOYAGE OF ODYSSEUS: Homer's Odyssey Retold (Blackie, 1973)..£20
TWO GREEDY BEARS (illustrated by Gareth Floyd) (Hamish Hamilton, 1974) £20

THE LION THAT FLEW (illustrated by Edward Ardizzone) (Chatto & Windus, 1974) £30
MORE PREFABULOUS ANIMILES (illustrated by Edward Ardizzone) (Heinemann, 1975) £30
THE CLEVER MOUSE (illustrated by Barbara Swiderska) (Chatto & Windus, 1976) £20
QUEST AND CONQUEST: Pilgrim's Progress Retold (illustrated by Joanna Troughton) (Blackie, 1976)..................£12
ARCADIAN BALLADS (illustrated by Edward Ardizzone) (Heinemann, 1977)..£25
EGGTIME STORIES (illustrated by Colin McNaughton) (Blackie, 1978) £12
THE JAMES REEVES STORYBOOK (illustrated by Edward Ardizzone) (Heinemann, 1978)..................................£30
A PRINCE IN DANGER (illustrated by Gareth Floyd) (Kaye & Ward, 1979) £12
SNOW-WHITE AND ROSE-RED (illustrated by Jenny Rodwell) (Andersen Press, 1979)....................................£12

RICHARDS, Frank

British author. Born: Charles Harold St. John Hamilton in Ealing, London, in 1876. Studied at various day schools in West London, including Thorne House, but never attended a boarding school. Began to write in his teens, contributing boys' stories to, amongst other titles, Pearson's *Big Budget* and, from 1895 onwards, the Harmsworth magazines *Pluck*, *Gem* and *Magnet*. His first 'Greyfriars' story, featuring the immortal Billy Bunter, appeared in the opening issue of *Magnet* under the pseudonym, 'Frank Richards', derived from a character in Scott's *Rob Roy* and his brother, Richard Hamilton. After *Gem* and *Magnet* folded during the war, Richards wrote a series of successful 'Greyfriars' novels for Skilton and, later, Cassell. Died: 1961.

Prices are for books in Very Good condition with dustjackets.

'Billy Bunter' Books

BILLY BUNTER OF GREYFRIARS SCHOOL (illustrated by R.J. Macdonald) (Charles Skilton, 1947) £75
BILLY BUNTER'S BANKNOTE (Charles Skilton, 1948)..£50
BILLY BUNTER'S BARRING-OUT (illustrated by R.J. Macdonald) (Charles Skilton, 1948) £50
BILLY BUNTER IN BRAZIL (Charles Skilton, 1949)..£50
BILLY BUNTER'S CHRISTMAS PARTY (illustrated by R.J. Macdonald) (Charles Skilton, 1949)........................£50
BILLY BUNTER'S BENEFIT (illustrated by R.J. Macdonald) (Charles Skilton, 1950)..£45
BILLY BUNTER AMONG THE CANNIBALS (illustrated by R.J. Macdonald) (Charles Skilton, 1950) £45
BILLY BUNTER'S POSTAL ORDER (illustrated by R.J. Macdonald) (Charles Skilton, 1951)..............................£45
BILLY BUNTER BUTTS IN (illustrated by R.J. Macdonald) (Charles Skilton, 1951)..£45
BILLY BUNTER AND THE BLUE MAURITIUS (illustrated by R.J. Macdonald) (Charles Skilton, 1952) £55
BILLY BUNTER'S BEANFEAST (illustrated by R.J. Macdonald) (Cassell, 1952) £45
BILLY BUNTER'S BRAIN-WAVE (illustrated by R.J. Macdonald) (Cassell, 1953)...£40
BILLY BUNTER'S FIRST CASE (illustrated by R.J. Macdonald) (Cassell, 1953) £40
BILLY BUNTER'S OWN (annual; some were issued with jackets, add 50%) (Mandeville/Oxenhoath Press, [1953-61]) .... each £12
BILLY BUNTER THE BOLD (illustrated by R.J. Macdonald) (Cassell, 1954) £30
BUNTER DOES HIS BEST (illustrated by R.J. Macdonald) (Cassell, 1954)...£30
BILLY BUNTER'S DOUBLE (illustrated by R.J. Macdonald) (Cassell, 1955) £30
BACKING UP BILLY BUNTER (illustrated by C.H. Chapman) (Cassell, 1955) £30
LORD BILLY BUNTER (illustrated by C.H. Chapman) (Cassell, 1956)..£30
THE BANISHING OF BILLY BUNTER (illustrated by C.H. Chapman) (Cassell, 1956)......................................£30
BILLY BUNTER'S BOLT (illustrated by C.H. Chapman) (Cassell, 1957)..£30
BILLY BUNTER AFLOAT (illustrated by C.H. Chapman) (Cassell, 1957)...£30
BILLY BUNTER'S BARGAIN (illustrated by C.H. Chapman) (Cassell, 1958)...£30
BILLY BUNTER THE HIKER (illustrated by C.H. Chapman) (Cassell, 1958)...£30
BUNTER OUT OF BOUNDS (illustrated by C.H. Chapman) (Cassell, 1959)...£30
BUNTER COMES FOR CHRISTMAS (illustrated by C.H. Chapman) (Cassell, 1959) £30
BUNTER THE BAD LAD (illustrated by C.H. Chapman) (Cassell, 1960)..£30
BUNTER KEEPS IT DARK (illustrated by C.H. Chapman) (Cassell, 1960) £30
BILLY BUNTER'S TREASURE-HUNT (illustrated by C.H. Chapman) (Cassell, 1961)..£25
BILLY BUNTER AT BUTLINS (illustrated by C.H. Chapman) (Cassell, 1961) £22
BILLY BUNTER AT BUTLINS (Butlin's 'Beaver Club' edition; issued with TV tie-in dustjacket) (Cassell, 1961)........................£12
BUNTER THE VENTRILOQUIST (illustrated by C.H. Chapman) (Cassell, 1961)...£30
BUNTER THE CARAVANNER (illustrated by C.H. Chapman) (Cassell, 1962)...£22
BILLY BUNTER'S BODYGUARD (illustrated by C.H. Chapman) (Cassell, 1962) £22
BIG CHIEF BUNTER (illustrated by C.H. Chapman) (Cassell, 1963)...£22
JUST LIKE BUNTER (illustrated by C.H. Chapman) (Cassell, 1963)...£22
BUNTER THE STOWAWAY (illustrated by C.H. Chapman) (Cassell, 1964) £22
THANKS TO BUNTER (illustrated by C.H. Chapman) (Cassell, 1964) £22
BUNTER THE SPORTSMAN (illustrated by C.H. Chapman) (Cassell, 1965) £22
BUNTER'S LAST FLING (illustrated by C.H. Chapman) (Cassell, 1965)..£22
BUNTER THE TOUGH GUY OF GREYFRIARS (Armada paperbacks, 1965)...£4
BUNTER AND THE PHANTOM OF THE TOWERS (Armada paperbacks, 1965)..£4
BUNTER'S HOLIDAY CRUISE (Armada paperbacks, 1965)..£4
BUNTER THE RACKETEER (Armada paperbacks, 1965)...£4
BILLY BUNTERS HOLIDAY ANNUAL (Odhams, 1966)..£10
BEST OF MAGNET AND GEM (large format card wraps) (Fleetway, 1967) £8

Billy Bunter's Brain-Wave (1953) was one of the last 'Bunter' books to be illustrated by Richards' old colleague R.J. Macdonald.

By 1965's Bunter's Last Fling his place had been taken by the late great C.H. Chapman.

BILLY BUNTER'S BIG TOP (Merlin paperback, 1967)..£4
BILLY BUNTER AND THE MAN FROM SOUTH AMERICA (Merlin paperback, 1967)...............£4
BILLY BUNTER AND THE SCHOOL REBELLION (Merlin paperback, 1967).............................£4
BILLY BUNTER AND THE SECRET ENEMY (Merlin paperback, 1967)....................................£4
BILLY BUNTER AND THE CROOKED CAPTAIN (Merlin paperback, 1968)...............................£4
BILLY BUNTER'S CONVICT (Merlin paperback, 1968) £4
BILLY BUNTER – SPORTSMAN (Merlin paperback, 1968)...£4
BILLY BUNTER AND THE BANK ROBBER (Merlin paperback, 1968)......................................£4
BILLY BUNTER'S BAD LUCK (Armada paperbacks, 1971) £4
BILLY BUNTER'S BARGAIN (Armada paperbacks, 1971) £4

'Jack' Books
JACK OF ALL TRADES (Mandeville, 1950)..£25
JACK'S THE LAD (Spring Books, 1957) £15
JACK OF THE CIRCUS (Spring Books, 1957) £15

Books written as 'Martin Clifford'
THE SECRET OF THE STUDY (Mandeville, 1949)...£15
TALBOT'S SECRET (Mandeville, 1949)..£15
TOM MERRY AND CO OF ST JIM'S (Mandeville, 1949) £12
TOM MERRY'S ANNUAL (Mandeville, 1949) £12
RALLYING ROUND GUSSY (Mandeville, 1950)..£18
TOM MERRY'S OWN (Mandeville, 1950)..£12
THE SCAPEGRACE OF ST JIM'S (Mandeville, 1951)..£15
THE NEW TOM MERRY'S OWN (Mandeville, 1951)...£12
THE RIVALS OF ROOKWOOD (written under the pseudonym 'Owen Conquest') (Mandeville, 1951).............£15
TOM MERRY'S SECRET (paperback) (Hamilton, 1952)..£6
TOM MERRY'S RIVAL (paperback) (Hamilton, 1952)..£6
THE MAN FROM THE PAST (paperback) (Hamilton, 1952)...£4
WHO RAGGED RAILTON? (paperback) (Hamilton, 1952) £4
SKIMPOLE'S SNAPSHOT (paperback) (Hamilton, 1952) £4
TROUBLE FOR TRIMBLE (paperback) (Hamilton, 1952) £4

*Frank Richards wrote countless 'Bunter' stories for **The Magnet** and contributed to many other British story papers.*

D'ARCY IN DANGER (paperback) (Hamilton, 1952) £4
D'ARCY ON THE WARPATH (paperback) (Hamilton, 1952) £4
D'ARCY'S DISAPPEARANCE (paperback) (Hamilton, 1952) £4
D'ARCY THE REFORMER (paperback) (Hamilton, 1952) £4
D'ARCY'S DAY OFF (paperback) (Hamilton, 1952) £4
TROUBLE FOR TOM MERRY (Spring Books, 1953) £10
DOWN AND OUT (Spring Books, 1953) £10
CARDEW'S CATCH (Spring Books, 1954) £10
THE DISAPPEARANCE OF TOM MERRY (Spring Books, 1954) £10
TOM MERRY'S OWN (Mandeville, 1954) £12
THROUGH THICK AND THIN (Spring Books, 1955) £10
TOM MERRY'S TRIUMPH (Spring Books, 1956) £10
TOM MERRY & CO, CARAVANNERS (Spring Books, 1956) £8

Books Written as 'Hilda Richards'
BESSIE BUNTER OF CLIFF HOUSE SCHOOL (illustrated by R.J. Macdonald)
   (Charles Skilton, 1949) £70

Others
THE SECRET OF THE SCHOOL (booklet) (Merrett, 1946) £10
THE BLACK SHEEP OF SPARSHOTT (booklet) (Merrett, 1946) £10
FIRST MAN IN (booklet) (Merrett, 1946) £10
LOOKING AFTER LAMB (booklet) (Merrett, 1946) £10
THE HERO OF SPARSHOTT (booklet) (Merrett, 1946) £10
PLUCK WILL TELL (booklet) (Merrett, 1946) £10
TOP STUDY AT TOPHAM (booklet) (Matthew, 1947) £10
BUNNY BINKS ON THE WARPATH (booklet) (Matthew, 1947) £10
THE DANDY OF TOPHAM (booklet) (Matthew, 1947) £10
SENT TO COVENTRY (booklet) (Matthew, 1947) £10
THE LONE TEXAN (Atlantic, 1954) £30
THE LONE TEXAN (paperback) (Atlantic, 1954) £12

Richards rarities
'HALFPENNY GEM'
No. 3 (first 'Tom Merry' Story) £35
Numbers 5, 7,9,11-48 ....each £15
'THE GEM': NEW SERIES
Number 1 ....£25
Issues published between 1908 and 1914 (excluding double numbers) ....each £7
Double numbers published between 1908 and 1914 ....each £25
Issues published between 1915 and 1925 ....each £7
Issues published between 1925 and 1931 ....each £5
Issues published between 1931 and 1939 (other than issues with W.E. Johns serial instalments) ....each £5

'THE MAGNET'

Number 1	**£250**
Number 1 (facsimile)	**£5**
Number 2	**£50**
Number 3	**£35**
Issues published between 1908 and 1915 (red covers; excluding double numbers)	each **£7**
Double numbers published between 1908 and 1915	each **£15**
Issues published between 1915 and 1922 (in blue and white covers)	each **£7**
Issues published between 1922 and 1926 (in blue and orange covers)	each **£7**
Issues published between 1927 and 1933 (in blue and orange covers)	each **£10**
Issues published between 1934 and 1937 (in blue and orange covers)	each **£7**
Issues published between 1937 and 1940 (in salmon-coloured covers)	each **£5**
Final number (1,683)	**£10**

'BOYS' FRIEND LIBRARY': FIRST SERIES

Number 30: 'Tom Merry and Co'	**£25**
Number 38: 'Tom Merry's Conquest'	**£25**
Number 237: 'King Cricket'	**£35**
Number 276: 'Through Thick and Thin'	**£15**
Number 288: 'The Boy Without a Name'	**£25**
Number 328: 'Rivals and Chums'	**£25**
Number 367: 'Cousin Ethel's Schooldays'	**£15**
Number 383: 'After Lights Out'	**£15**
Number 417: 'Frank Richards' Schooldays'	**£12**

'BOYS' FRIEND LIBRARY': NEW SERIES

'Rio Kid' issues (all under the 'Ralph Redway' byline)	each **£10**
'Ken King' issues (all under the 'Charles Hamilton' byline)	each **£10**

THE GREYFRIARS HOLIDAY ANNUAL *Issues retaining their tissue wrappers sell for 25%-35% more*

1920 issue (published September 1919)	**£35**
1921-1928 issues	each **£35**
1929-1940 issues	each **£25**
1941 (final issue)	**£35**

BOYS' FRIEND WEEKLY *Issues with 'Rookwood' stories by Owen Conquest*

Number 715 (first 'Rookwood' issue)	**£15**
Numbers 716-1,298	each **£5**

GREYFRIARS HERALD: FIRST SERIES *1915*

Number 1	**£35**
Numbers 2-18	each **£5**

SCHOOL FRIEND: FIRST SERIES *1919 issues written by Charles Hamilton as 'Hilda Richards'*

Number 1	**£70**
Numbers 2-6	each **£12**

SCHOOLBOYS' OWN LIBRARY

Number 1: 'The Greyfriars Players'	**£35**
Numbers 2-166 (64-page issues featuring Greyfriars, St Jim's and Rookwood)	each **£10**
Numbers 167-411 (96-page issues featuring Rookwood and Cedar Creek)	each **£10**
Numbers 167-411 (96-page issues featuring Greyfriars and St Jim's)	each **£5**
'DETECTIVE' SERIES Numbers 1-4 (booklet format) Merrett 1945/6	each **£12**
'ROMANCE' SERIES Numbers 1-4 (booklet format under the name 'Winston Cardew') Merrett 1945/6	each **£12**
'HEADLAND HOUSE' SERIES Numbers 1-3 (Merrett, 1946)	each **£10**
'MASCOT SCHOOLBOYS' SERIES Numbers 1-4 (Matthews, 1949)	each **£10**
'MASCOT SCHOOLGIRLS' SERIES Numbers 1-4 (Matthews, 1949)	each **£10**

Miscellaneous

CHUMS OF LYNWOOD (Shields, [1940s])	**£12**
FOURTH FORM AT LYNWOOD (J.B. Publications, [1940s])	**£12**
BILLY BUNTER'S MYSTERY CHRISTMAS (play adapted by Maurice McLouchlin) (Samuel French, 1959)	**£25**

'RIDERS OF THE RANGE'

Below is a list of collectable items produced in the wake of the BBC's popular Western radio serial 'Riders of the Range', which kicked off in January 1949, becoming a popular show among younger listeners.

Prices are for annuals and books in Very Good condition.

RIDERS OF THE RANGE ANNUAL (Juvenile Productions, 1951-1956)	each **£10**
RIDERS OF THE RANGE ANNUAL (Hulton Press, 1957-1960)	each **£10**
RIDERS OF THE RANGE ANNUAL (Hulton Press, 1961-1962)	each **£20**
JEFF ARNOLD ON THE BOZEMAN TRAIL (Juvenile Productions, 1954)	**£25**
RIDERS OF THE RANGE (Eagle Classics: Hawk Books, 1990)	**£8**

'ROBIN HOOD' BOOKS AND ANNUALS

Legendary English outlaw who, despite continuing controversy over his origins and/or identity, has inspired countless books and ephemera from the early seventeenth century onwards.

Prices are for books in Very Good condition with dustjackets where applicable.

'Robin Hood' Books

LIFE AND BALLADS OF ROBIN HOOD (Milner & Sowerby, 1865) £500
THE MERRY ADVENTURES OF ROBIN HOOD of Great Renown in Nottinghamshire by Howard Pyle
   (Scribner, US, 1883)..£350
THE MERRY ADVENTURES OF ROBIN HOOD of Great Renown in Nottinghamshire by Howard Pyle
   (Sampson Low, 1883)..£75
STORIES OF ROBIN HOOD by H.E. Marshall (illustrated by A.S. Forrest)
   ('Told to the Children' series, [1905])..£15
ROBIN HOOD by H. Gilbert (illustrated by Walter Crane) (T.C. & E.C. Jack, 1912)..£50
ROBIN HOOD, HIS DEEDS AND ADVENTURES AS RECOUNTED IN OLD ENGLISH BALLADS
   (selected and illustrated by Lucy Fitch Perkins) (T.C. & E.C. Jack, [1913])...£125
GILBERT THE OUTLAW by D.H. Parry (Cassell, 1917) £20
STORIES OF ROBIN HOOD (Aldine, 1925) £20
THE MERRY MEN (Aldine, 1927)..£20
ROBIN HOOD AND HIS MERRY MEN by E. Charles Vivian (illustrated by Harry G. Theaker)
   (Ward Lock, [1927])..£30
ROBIN OF SHERWOOD (Aldine, 1928)..£20
TALES OF ROBIN HOOD by Enid Blyton (Newnes: 'John O'London's Children's Library' series, [1930])...........£30
MORE ADVENTURES WITH ROBIN HOOD (Aldine, 1930) £20
BOWS AGAINST THE BARONS by Geoffrey Trease (Martin Lawrence, 1934)...£40
THE CHILDREN'S ROBIN HOOD. Retold by Frank H. Lee (Harrap, 1934)...£15
THE ADVENTURES OF ROBIN HOOD (tie-in with the film 'The Adventures of Robin Hood', starring Errol Flynn;
   eight colour plates) (Ward Lock, [1939])...£75
THE ADVENTURES OF ROBIN HOOD (reissue of the 1939 tie-in edition; eight colour plates) (Ward Lock, [1954])....£50
PICTURE SHOW OF ROBIN HOOD (card wrappers) (Juvenile Publications, circa 1940) £15
THE CHRONICLES OF ROBIN HOOD by Rosemary Sutcliff (illustrated by C. Walter Hodges) (OUP, 1950) £30
ROBIN HOOD by Antonia Fraser (illustrated by Victor Ambrus) (Weidenfeld & Nicolson: 'Heirloom Library' series, 1955) £15
THE ADVENTURES OF ROBIN HOOD. Collected and retold by Roger Lancelyn Green (paperback)
   (Penguin, 1956)..£10
ROBIN AND HIS MERRY MEN by Ian Serraillier (illustrated by Victor Ambrus) (OUP, 1969).........................£20
ROBIN OF SHERWOOD by Richard Carpenter (paperback) (Puffin, 1985)..£5

'Robin Hood' Comics and Annuals

ROBIN HOOD by Pierce Egan Junior ('Penny Part-Works', bound) (circa 1840s)...............................£120-£180
ROBIN HOOD AND THE OUTLAWS OF SHERWOOD FOREST by George Emmett
   ('Penny Part-Works', bound) (1868-69) ....n/a
ROBIN HOOD LIBRARY Nos. 1-88 (First Series) (Aldine, 1901-06) .... each £10
THRILLER COMICS/THRILLER PICTURE LIBRARY
   (issues containing comic strip 'Robin Hood Told in Pictures'; 56 in all) (Fleetway, 1951-63) .... each £8
THE ADVENTURES OF ROBIN HOOD NO 1 (Adprint/Rand McNally, 1956)...£15
THE ADVENTURES OF ROBIN HOOD NO 2 (Adprint/Rand McNally, 1957)...£12
THE ADVENTURES OF ROBIN HOOD NO 3 (with dustjacket) Adprint, 1958) £20
THE ADVENTURES OF ROBIN HOOD NO 4 (Adprint, 1959) £12
ROBIN HOOD ANNUAL 1957 (Amalgamated Press, 1956)..£15
ROBIN HOOD ANNUAL 1958 (Amalgamated Press, 1957)..£15
ROBIN HOOD ANNUAL 1959 (Amalgamated Press, 1958)..£15
ROBIN HOOD ANNUAL 1960 (Fleetway, 1959)..£15
ROBIN OF SHERWOOD ANNUAL 1986 (World International, 1985) £5

ROBINSON, Charles

British illustrator. Born: London, 1870, son of the wood engraver, Thomas Robinson, and the elder brother of the illustrator, W. Heath Robinson. Studied at Islington High School and Highbury School of Art. Established his reputation with his 1896 edition of Stevenson's *A Child's Garden of Verses*, and went on to illustrate more than 100 further titles. Died: 1937.

Prices are for books in Very Good condition.

Books Written and Illustrated by Charles Robinson

CHRISTMAS DREAMS (written under the pseudonym 'Awfly Weirdly')
   (Marcus Ward, 1896)..£150
THE TEN LITTLE BABIES (SPCK, [1905])..£150
FANCIFUL FOWLS (Dent, 1906)..£100
PECULIAR PIGGIES (Dent, 1906)..£100
BLACK BUNNIES (Blackie, [1907]) £100
BLACK DOGGIES (Blackie, [1907])..£100
BLACK SAMBOS (Blackie, [1907])...£150

'Picture Books for Children' by Walter Copeland
Illustrated by Charles Robinson

THE BOOK OF THE ZOO (Dent, 1902)..£100
THE BLACK CAT BOOK (Blackie, [1905])...£125
THE BOOK OF DUCKS AND DUTCHIES (Blackie, 1905)..£100
THE BOOK OF THE DUTCH DOLLS (Blackie, 1905)...£125
THE BOOK OF THE FAN (Blackie, 1905)...£125
THE BOOK OF THE LITTLE JDs (Blackie, 1905)..£100
THE BOOK OF THE MANDARINFANTS (Blackie, 1905)..£125
THE BOOK OF THE LITTLE DUTCH DOTS (Blackie, 1905)...£125
THE SILLY SUBMARINE (Blackie, 1906)...£100
THE BOOK OF DOLLY'S DOINGS (Blackie, 1906)..£125
BOUNCING BABIES (Blackie, 1906)...£100
THE BOOK OF DOLLY'S HOUSE (Blackie, 1906)...£125
THE BOOK OF DOLLY-LAND (Blackie, 1906)..£125
AWFUL AIRSHIP (Blackie, 1906)...£150
MAD MOTOR (Blackie, 1906)...£125
THE SWEET SHOP (Blackie, 1907)..£100
THE TOY SHOP (Blackie, 1907)..£100
THE CAKE SHOP (Blackie, 1907)..£100
BABES AND BLOSSOMS (Blackie, [1908])..£150
THE BOOK OF OTHER PEOPLE (Blackie, 1908)...£100
THE BOOK OF SAILORS (Blackie, 1908)..£100
THE BOOK OF SOLDIERS (Blackie, 1908)...£125

Other Books Illustrated by Charles Robinson

AESOP'S FABLES (Dent: 'Banbury Cross' series, 1895)...£100
THE INFANT READER (Macmillan, 1895)..£50
THE FIRST PRIMER (Macmillan, 1895)...£50
THE SECOND PRIMER (Macmillan, 1895)..£50
A CHILD'S GARDEN OF VERSES by R.L. Stevenson (John Lane: The Bodley Head, 1896 [1895])..............£350
A CHILD'S GARDEN OF VERSES by R.L. Stevenson (reissue) (John Lane: The Bodley Head, 1921)...........£150
ANIMALS IN THE WRONG PLACES by E. Carrington (Bell, 1896)...£50
MINSTREL DICK by C.R. Coleridge (Gardner Darton, 1896)...£50
MAKE BELIEVE by H.D. Lowry (John Lane, 1896)...£50
THE CHILD WORLD by G. Setoun (John Lane, 1896)..£50
DOBBIES' LITTLE MASTER by Mrs A. Bell (Bell, 1897)..£50
LULLABY LAND: Songs of Childhood by E. Field (selected by K. Grahame) (John Lane, 1898 [1897])......£100
KING LONGBEARD by B. MacGregor (John Lane, 1898 [1897])...£50
LILLIPUT LYRICS by W.B. Rands. Edited R. Brimley Johnson (John Lane, 1899 [1898])..........£50
THE NEW NOAH'S ARK by J.J. Bell (verse) (John Lane, 1899 [1898])....................................£50
TALES OF PASSED TIMES by Charles Perrault (Dent: 'Temple Classic for Young People' series, [1899])....£50
THE MASTER MOSAIC-WORKERS by George Sand (twelve illustrations by Charles Robinson; translated by C.C. Johnson) (Dent: 'Temple Classics for Young People' series, 1899).......................................£50
FAIRY TALES FROM HANS CHRISTIAN ANDERSEN (illustrated by Charles, Thomas and William Heath Robinson; translated by Mrs E. Lucas) (Dent, 1899)..£125
CHILD VOICES by William Edward Cule (Andrew Melrose, [1899])..£50
JACK OF ALL TRADES by John Joy Bell (verse) (John Lane, 1900 [1899])..............................£50
THE SUITORS OF APRILLE by N. Garstin (John Lane, 1900 [1899])...£50
PIERRETTE by H. de Vere Stacpoole (John Lane, 1900 [1899])..£60
THE LITTLE LIVES OF THE SAINTS by Rev Percy Dearmer (Wells Gardner, 1900)...............£50
SINTRAM AND HIS COMPANIONS by F.H.C. de la Motte Fouque (Dent, 1900).......................£50
THE TRUE ANNALS OF FAIRYLAND: The Reign of King Herla. Edited by W. Canton (Dent, 1900)..........£50
THE ADVENTURES OF ODYSSEUS by Homer. Retold by F.S. Marvin, R.J.G. Mayor and F.M. Stawell (Dent, [1900])..£50
THE TRUE ANNALS OF FAIRYLAND: The Reign of Old King Cole. Edited by J.M. Gibbon (three volumes) (Dent, 1901)...the set £100
THE BOOK OF DAYS FOR LITTLE ONES by Clare Bridgman (Dent, 1901).............................£200
THE FARM BOOK FOR LITTLE ONES by Walter Copeland (Dent, [1901])..............................£175
THE TRUE ANNALS OF FAIRY-LAND: The Reign of King Oberon. Edited by Walter Jerrold (three volumes) (Dent, 1902)..the set £100
STORIES FOR CHILDREN by Charles and Mary Lamb (illustrated by Charles Robinson and W. Green) (Dent, 1902)..£60
THE BAIRNS CORONATION BOOK by Clare Bridgman (Dent, [1902])....................................£85
NONSENSE! NONSENSE! by Walter Jerrold (Blackie, 1902)...£65
THE SHOPPING DAY by C. Bridgman (Dent, 1902)..£55
THE MOTHERS' BOOK OF SONG. Compiled by John Henry Burn (Wells Gardner, [1902]).....£30
THE BIG BOOK OF NURSERY RHYMES. Edited by J. Jerrold (Blackie, [1903])....................£150
FIRESIDE SAINTS by Douglas W. Jerrold (Blackie, 1903)..£20
THE CLOUD KINGDOM by I.H. Wallis (John Lane, [1905])...£35

ROBINSON, Charles

A BOOKFUL OF FUN (Sealey Clark, [1905])..£45
ROAD, RAIL AND SEA by Clare Jerrold (Blackie, [1906]) £100
BABY TOWN BALLADS by 'Netta' (Sealey Clark, 1906)..£50
THE CHILD'S CHRISTMAS by E. Sharp (Blackie, [1906])..£50
THE STORY OF THE WEATHERCOCK by E. Sharp (Blackie, [1907])....................................£75
PRINCE BABILLON by 'Netta' (Sealey Clark, 1907)..£50
ALICE'S ADVENTURES IN WONDERLAND by Lewis Carroll (eight colour plates and 112 other illustrations by
    Charles Robinson) (Cassell, 1907)..£150
SONGS OF LOVE AND PRAISE by A. Matheson (Dent, 1907)..£40
THE FAIRIES' FOUNTAIN by Countess E. Martinengo-Cesaresco (Fairbairns, 1908) £70
SONGS OF HAPPY CHILDHOOD by I. Maunder (Sealey Clark, 1908)....................................£55
IN THE BEGINNING by S.B. Macy (Sealey Clark, 1910)..£50
THE VANISHING PRINCES by N. Syrett (David Nutt, [1910])..£50
BROWNIKINS AND OTHER FANCIES by Ruth Arkwright (music by J.W. Wilson) (Wells Gardner, [1910]).....£50
GRIMM'S FAIRY TALES (translated by L.L. Weedon) (Nister: 'Children's Classics' series, [1910])................£50
BABES AND BIRDS by Jessie Pope (Blackie, [1910])..£50
THE SECRET GARDEN by F. Hodgson Burnett (Heinemann, 1911) £350
THE BIG BOOK OF FAIRY TALES Edited by Walter Jerrold (Blackie, 1911)........................£200
THE SENSITIVE PLANT by Percy Bysshe Shelley (Heinemann, [1911]).............................£350
THE BABY SCOUTS by Jessie Pope (Blackie, [1911])..£65
BABES AND BEASTS by Jessie Pope (Blackie, [1912])..£65
THE FOUR GARDENS by 'Handasyde' (Heinemann, 1912) £60
THE BIG BOOK OF FABLES Edited by Walter Jerrold (Blackie, 1912)................................£175
BEE, THE PRINCESS OF THE DWARFS by Anatole France (translated by Peter Wright) (Dent, 1912) £50
FAIRY TALES by Charles Perrault (Dent: 'Tales for Children from Many Lands' series, [1913])...............£50
MARGARET'S BOOK by H. Fielding-Hall (Hutchinson, [1913])..£150
TOPSY TURVY by W.J. Minnion (The Connoisseur, 1913)..£50
THE HAPPY PRINCE and Other Tales by Oscar Wilde (Duckworth, 1913)..........................£250
THE HAPPY PRINCE and Other Tales by Oscar Wilde (limited to 250 copies, signed by the artist; vellum binding)
    (Duckworth, 1913) £1,000
THE OPEN WINDOW by E. Temple Thurston (Chambers, 1913)..£35
A CHILD'S BOOK OF EMPIRE by A.T. Morris (Blackie, [1914]) £35
OUR SENTIMENTAL GARDEN by A. and E. Castle (Heinemann, 1914) £75
FROM THE ARABIAN NIGHTS ENTERTAINMENTS: The Story of Prince Ahmed and the Fairy Perie Banou
    (Gay & Hancock, [1915])..£50
SONGS AND SONNETS OF SHAKESPEARE (Duckworth, 1915) £125
WHAT HAPPENED AT CHRISTMAS by Evelyn Sharp (Blackie, [1915])..............................£55
THE LITTLE HUNCHBACK ZIA by F. Hodgson Burnett (Heinemann, 1916)..........................£60
BRIDGET'S FAIRIES by Mrs M. Stevenson (Religious Tract Society, [1919])........................£50
SONGS OF HAPPY CHILDHOOD by I. Maunder (Sealey Clark, 1920)..................................£50
TEDDY'S YEAR WITH THE FAIRIES by M. Elsie Gullick (Religious Tract Society, [1920]) £60
THE CHILDREN'S GARLAND OF VERSES by G. Rhys (Dent, 1921)....................................£60
FATHER TIME STORIES by John G. Stevenson (Religious Tract Society, [1921])..................£25
DORIS AND DAVID ALL ALONE by Elizabeth Marc (Hutchinson, [1922])............................£35
ONCE ON A TIME by A.A. Milne (Hodder & Stoughton, [1925])..£120
FATHER TIME STORIES by John G. Stevenson (Religious Tract Society, [1925])..................£50
THE SAINT'S GARDEN by W. Radcliffe (Religious Tract Society, 1927)................................£15
MOTHER GOOSE NURSERY RHYMES (Collins, [1928]) £75
THE RUBAIYAT OF OMAR KHAYYAM (introduction by Laurence Housman; translated by Edward Fitzgerald)
    (Collins, [1928])..£100
GRANNY'S BOOK OF FAIRY STORIES (Blackie, 1930)..£50
YOUNG HOPEFUL by Jennie Dunbar (Herbert Jenkins, 1932)..£50

ROBINSON, W. Heath

British author-illustrator. Born: William Heath Robinson in London in 1872, the son of the wood engraver, Thomas Robinson, and the younger brother of the illustrator, Charles Robinson. Studied at the Islington School of Art and the Royal Academy Schools. His first important works were editions of *Don Quixote* and Hans Andersen's *Fairy Tales* (both 1897), but his distinctive style was first evident in the illustrations for his own comic tale, *The Adventures of Uncle Lubin* (1902). Wrote and illustrated several more children's books, but is perhaps best known for the weird and wonderful 'inventions' he drew for the *Strand* magazine. Died: 1944.

Prices are for books in Very Good condition.

DANISH FAIRY TALES AND LEGENDS by H.C. Andersen (sixteen illustrations by W. Heath Robinson)
    (Sands, 1897)..£100
THE LIFE AND EXPLOITS OF DON QUIXOTE by Cervantes (sixteen illustrations by W. Heath Robinson)
    (Sands, 1897)..£100
THE PILGRIM'S PROGRESS by John Bunyan (24 illustrations by W. Heath Robinson) (Sands, 1897).........£75
THE GIANT CRAB and Other Tales from Old India by W.H.D. Rouse (David Nutt, 1897) £350

ROBINSON, W. Heath

THE QUEEN'S STORY BOOK Edited by L. Gomme (Constable, 1898)..£60
THE ARABIAN NIGHTS ENTERTAINMENTS (Newnes/Constable, 1899)..................................£100
FAIRY TALES FROM HANS CHRISTIAN ANDERSEN (illustrated by W. Heath Robinson,
  Charles Robinson and Thomas Heath Robinson) (Dent, 1899)..£100
THE TALKING THRUSH by William Crooke (Dent, 1899)..£300
TALES FOR TOBY by A.R. Hope (Dent, 1900)..£50
THE ADVENTURES OF DON QUIXOTE OF LA MANCHA by Cervantes (Dent, 1902)..............£80
MEDIAEVAL STORIES by J.H.E. Schuck (Sands, 1902)..£70
THE ADVENTURES OF UNCLE LUBIN (Grant Richards, 1902)......................................£1,000
THE ADVENTURES OF UNCLE LUBIN (new edition) (Grant Richards, 1925)........................£100
THE SURPRISING TRAVELS AND ADVENTURES OF BARON MUNCHAUSEN by R.E. Raspe
  (Grant Richards, 1902)..£100
RAMA AND THE MONKEYS. Edited by G. Hodgson (Dent, 1903)..£70
THE CHILD'S ARABIAN NIGHTS (Grant Richards, 1903)..£250
STORIES FROM THE ILIAD. Edited by Jeanie Lang (T.C. & E.C. Jack, [1906])........................£40
STORIES FROM THE ODYSSEY. Edited by Jeanie Lang (T.C. & E.C. Jack, [1906])....................£40
THE MONARCHS OF MERRY ENGLAND by Roland Carse (Cooke, [1908])............................£175
MORE MONARCHS OF MERRY ENGLAND by Roland Carse (Cooke, [1908])..........................£175
THE MONARCHS OF MERRY ENGLAND and MORE MONARCHS OF MERRY ENGLAND by Roland Carse
  (four parts; ten plates by W. Heath Robinson in each) (Unwin, [1908]).....................the set £225
A SONG OF THE ENGLISH by Rudyard Kipling (thirty colour plates by W. Heath Robinson)
  (Hodder & Stoughton, 1909)..£200
THE COLLECTED VERSE OF RUDYARD KIPLING (Doubleday Page, US, 1910)......................£250
BILL THE MINDER (Constable, 1912)..£500
BILL THE MINDER (De Luxe edition: limited to 380 copies, signed by the author; vellum binding)
  (Constable, 1912)..£1,500
HANS ANDERSEN'S FAIRY TALES (Constable, 1913)..£600
HANS ANDERSEN'S FAIRY TALES (De Luxe edition: limited to 100 copies signed by artist; vellum binding)
  (Constable, 1913)..£3,000
THE WATER BABIES by Charles Kingsley (Constable, 1915)..£175
PEACOCK PIE by Walter de la Mare (Constable, [1916])..£75
GET ON WITH IT (cartoons) (Robinson & Birch, [1920])..£130
OLD TIME STORIES by Charles Perrault (Constable, 1921)..£300
FLY PAPERS (cartoons) (Duckworth, [1921])..£80
THE HOME-MADE CAR (Duckworth, [1921])..£125
PETER QUIP IN SEARCH OF A FRIEND (Partridge, [1922])..£750
HANS ANDERSEN'S FAIRY TALES (new edition) (Hodder & Stoughton, [1923])......................£100
TOPSY TURVY TALES by E.S. Munro (John Lane: The Bodley Head, 1923)............................£100
BILL THE MINDER (Hodder & Stoughton, [1924])..£10
HANS ANDERSEN'S FAIRY TALES (Boots edition; reissue of 1923 edition) (Hodder & Stoughton, [1927])...£80

*The undated 1922 first edition of Robinson's **Peter Quip in Search of a Friend**, today worth £750.*

*The rare dustjacket from the hugely successful **Bill the Minder** (1912), written and illustrated by William Heath Robinson.*

THE INCREDIBLE ADVENTURES OF PROFESSOR BRANESTAWM by Norman Hunter
(24 illustrations by W. Heath Robinson) (John Lane: The Bodley Head, 1933) £150
HEATH ROBINSON'S BOOK OF GOBLINS (contains stories from F.T. Vernaleken's 'In the Land of Marvels')
(Hutchinson, [1934]) £150
MY LINE OF LIFE (autobiography) (Blackie, 1938) £150
LET'S LAUGH: A Book of Humorous Inventions (Hutchinson, [1939]) £40
STORIES OF PROFESSOR BRANESTAWM by Norman Hunter (card wraps) (Arnold, [1939])............................£40
ONCE UPON A TIME by L.M.C. Clopet (Muller, 1944) £175

'ROSEBUD' ANNUALS

Early British annual published by James Clark. It was the first annual to contain the work of the celebrated cat artist, Louis Wain.

Prices are for annuals in Very Good condition. Annuals containing illustrations by Louis Wain sell for up to four times this price.

THE ROSEBUD ANNUAL 1889 [1890] – Onwards [c.1915] .... each £40

ROSS, Diana

British author. Born: Malta, 1910. Well known for her 'Little Red Engine' series, illustrated by herself and signed 'Gri'. Died: 2000.

Prices are for books in Very Good condition with dustjackets where applicable.

'Little Red Engine' Books

THE LITTLE RED ENGINE GETS A NAME (illustrated by George Lewitt-Him) (Faber, 1942)....................................£35
THE STORY OF THE LITTLE RED ENGINE (illustrated by Leslie Wood) (Faber, 1945) £35
THE LITTLE RED ENGINE GOES TO MARKET (illustrated by Leslie Wood) (Faber, 1946)..................................£25
THE LITTLE RED ENGINE GOES TO TOWN (illustrated by Leslie Wood) (Faber, 1952) £25
THE LITTLE RED ENGINE GOES TRAVELLING (illustrated by Leslie Wood) (Faber, 1955)................................£25
THE LITTLE RED ENGINE AND THE ROCKET (illustrated by Leslie Wood) (Faber, 1956)..................................£25
THE LITTLE RED ENGINE GOES HOME (illustrated by Leslie Wood) (Faber, 1958)..£25
THE LITTLE RED ENGINE GOES TO BE MENDED (illustrated by Leslie Wood) (Faber, 1966)...........................£25
THE LITTLE RED ENGINE AND THE TADDLECOMBE OUTING (illustrated by Leslie Wood) (Faber, 1968)........£25
THE LITTLE RED ENGINE GOES CAROLLING (illustrated by Leslie Wood) (Faber, 1971)...................................£25

Others

THE WORLD AT WORK: Getting You Things (Country Life, 1939) £40
THE WORLD AT WORK: Making You Things (Country Life, 1939) £40
THE STORY OF THE BEETLE WHO LIVED ALONE (illustrated by Margaret Kaye) (Faber, 1941)........................£30
UNCLE ANTY'S ALBUM (illustrated by Antony Denny) (Faber, 1941) £30
THE GOLDEN HEN and Other Stories (illustrated by Gri) (Faber, 1942) £30
THE WILD CHERRY (illustrated by Gri) (Faber, 1943) £30
NURSERY TALES (illustrated by Nancy Innes) (Faber, 1944)..£30
THE STORY OF LOUISA (illustrated by Margaret Kaye) (Penguin, 1945)..£30
WHOO, WHOO, THE WIND BLEW (illustrated by Leslie Wood) (Faber, 1946)..£20
THE TOOTER and Other Nursery Tales (illustrated by Irene Hawkins) (Faber, 1951)...£20
THE ENORMOUS APPLE PIE AND OTHER MISS PUSSY TALES (illustrated by Peggy Fortnum) (Lutterworth Press, 1951) £30
EBENEZER THE BIG BALLOON (illustrated by Leslie Wood) (Faber, 1952)..£20
THE BRIDAL GOWN and Other Stories (illustrated by Gri) (Faber, 1952) £20
THE BRAN TUB (illustrated by Gri) (Lutterworth Press, 1954)...£15
WILLIAM AND THE LORRY (illustrated by Shiley Hughes) (Faber, 1956)..£15
CHILD OF AIR (illustrated by Gri) (Lutterworth Press, 1957)..£15
THE DREADFUL BOY (illustrated by Prudence Seward) (Hamish Hamilton, 1959) £15
THE MERRY-GO-ROUND (illustrated by Shirley Hughes) (Lutterworth Press, 1963)..£15
OLD PERISHER (illustrated by Edward Ardizzone) (Faber, 1965)..£35
NOTHING TO DO (illustrated by Constance Marshall) (Hamish Hamilton, 1966)...£15
I LOVE MY LIFE WITH AN A: WHERE IS HE? (illustrated by Leslie Wood) (Faber, 1972) £15

ROSSETTI, Christina

British poet. Born: Christina Georgina Rossetti in London in 1830, the younger sister of the poet and painter, D.G. Rossetti. She contributed some verses to the Pre-Raphaelite journal, *The Germ*, and published her first collection, *Goblin Market and Other Poems*, in 1862. The title-poem has become something of a children's classic, and has been illustrated by Arthur Rackham (1933) amongst others. She also wrote the well-known hymn, 'In the bleak mid winter'. Died: 1894.

Prices are for books in Very Good condition.

GOBLIN MARKET and Other Poems (illustrated by D.G. Rossetti) (Macmillan, 1862)......................................£1,250
THE PRINCE'S PROGRESS and Other Poems (illustrated by D.G. Rossetti) (Macmillan, 1866) £600
SING-SONG: A Nursery Rhyme Book (illustrated by Arthur Hughes) (Macmillan, 1872).....................................£400
SPEAKING LIKENESSES (illustrated by Arthur Hughes) (Macmillan, 1874)..£100
MAUDE: A Story for Girls (introduction by W.M. Rossetti) (Bowden, 1897) £45

ROUNTREE, Harry

Illustrator. Born: New Zealand, 1878. Rountree began his career as a lithographer at a commercial studio in Auckland, before moving to London where he was discovered by *Little Folks* editor S.H. Hamer. He was known for drawing animals with a humorous flair, with dense detail and rich colour. Died: 1950.

Prices are for books in Very Good condition (in dustjackets after 1925).

ALICE'S ADVENTURES IN WONDERLAND by Lewis Carroll (Nelson, 1908)..**£100**
THROUGH THE LOOKING GLASS by Lewis Carroll (Nelson, 1928) **£50**
THE LOST WORLD by Arthur Conan Doyle (Hodder & Stoughton, [1912]) **£500**
THE LOST WORLD by Arthur Conan Doyle (Large Paper edition, limited to 1,000 copies,
    but only 190 copies of this first issue sold) (Hodder & Stoughton, [1912])......................................**£1,250**
THE LOST WORLD by Arthur Conan Doyle (Large Paper edition, comprising the second issue of 810 copies)
    (Henry Frowde/Hodder & Stoughton, [1912])...**£700**
THE POISON BELT by Arthur Conan Doyle (Hodder & Stoughton, 1913) **£100**
CAESAR: THE LIFE STORY OF A PANDA LEOPARD by R.P. Russ (later known as 'Patrick O'Brian') (Putnam, 1930) **£1,000**
THE CHILDREN OF CHERRY-TREE FARM by Enid Blyton (illustrated by Harry Rountree) (Country Life, 1940) **£40**
THE CHILDREN OF WILLOW FARM: A Tale of Life on a Farm by Enid Blyton
    (illustrated by Harry Rountree) (Country Life, 1942) **£35**

A fine example of work by the great New Zealand illustrator Harry Rountree.

ROWLING, J.K.

British author. Born: Chepstow, Kent, in 1965. After attending Exeter University she worked for Amnesty International and later taught English in Portugal. She now lives in Edinburgh. Her numerous British and foreign awards for each of her 'Harry Potter' books include the British Book Awards' Children's Book of the Year, 1997, 1998 and 1999, and the Nestle Smarties Book Prize 9-11 years, 1997, 1998 and 1999. She was the bestselling author of 1999, 2000, 2001, 2002, and 2004 and in the UK and awarded the OBE in 2000. Pleased note that signed editions are relatively rare and any genuine signatures would add a premium to the prices below. However, collectors beware as J.K. Rowling has gone on record saying that she has seen many forged signatures on the market.

Prices are for books in Fine condition with dustjackets where applicable.

HARRY POTTER AND THE PHILOSOPHER'S STONE (print-run of 500 copies; laminated boards; issued without dustjacket; Wendy Cooling endorsement quote on front cover; cascading number line of 10 to 1 on copyright page) (Bloomsbury, 1997)................................**£10,000**

HARRY POTTER AND THE PHILOSOPHER'S STONE (second issue; laminated boards with dustjacket; cascading number line of 10 to 2 on copyright page) (Bloomsbury, 1997).................................**£2,500**

HARRY POTTER AND THE PHILOSOPHER'S STONE (first paperback edition: standard cover) (Bloomsbury, 1997) **£100**

HARRY POTTER AND THE PHILOSOPHER'S STONE (paperback: 'adult' cover) (Bloomsbury, 1998) **£75**

HARRY POTTER AND THE PHILOSOPHER'S STONE (collectors' edition: limited to 4,000 copies; red cloth) (Bloomsbury, 1999) **£300**

HARRY POTTER AND THE PHILOSOPHER'S STONE (uncorrected proof: 200 copies; issued without dustjacket; plain white and yellow cover; paperback) (Bloomsbury, 1997) **£2,000**

HARRY POTTER AND THE PHILOSOPHER'S STONE (first children's large print edition; paperback) (Bloomsbury, 2001) **£25**

HARRY POTTER AND THE CHAMBER OF SECRETS (print-run of 10,150 copies; laminated boards and dustjacket; cascading number line of 10 to 1 on copyright page; first state jacket has a circular promotional flash on the front which reads 'J.K. Rowling 1997 Smarties Award Winner shortlisted for the 1997 Carnegie Medal' and a black endorsement at the bottom that reads '"Inventive and action-packed" *The Bookseller*". The words 'Harry Potter and the Philosopher's Stone' are also printed without italics on the front inner flap) (Bloomsbury, 1998).....................**£1,250**

HARRY POTTER AND THE CHAMBER OF SECRETS (first paperback edition: standard cover) (Bloomsbury, 1998) **£20**

HARRY POTTER AND THE CHAMBER OF SECRETS (paperback: 'adult' cover) (Bloomsbury, 1999)...................................**£20**

HARRY POTTER AND THE CHAMBER OF SECRETS (collectors' edition: limited to 4,000 copies; pale blue cloth) (Bloomsbury, 1999) **£100**

HARRY POTTER AND THE CHAMBER OF SECRETS (uncorrected proof: 300 copies; issued without dustjacket; paperback) (Bloomsbury, 1998) **£1,200**

HARRY POTTER AND THE CHAMBER OF SECRETS (first children's large print edition; paperback) (Bloomsbury, 2002).......**£25**

HARRY POTTER AND THE PRISONER OF AZKABAN (1,000 copies, first state: which has 'Joanne Rowling' on verso of title-page, text misalignment p7; cascading number line of 10 to 1 on copyright page) (Bloomsbury, 1999)..........**£1,200**

HARRY POTTER AND THE PRISONER OF AZKABAN (9,000 copies, first printing, second state: 'J.K. Rowling' on verso of title-page with 'Clay . . . St Ives'; also with cascading number line of 10 to 1 on copyright page) (Bloomsbury, 1999) **£350**

The signed deluxe collectors' editions of the first four J.K. Rowling novels are together worth over £3,000.

HARRY POTTER AND THE PRISONER OF AZKABAN (trade hardback: first printing, third state: 'J.K. Rowling' on verso of title-page, 'Clay . . . St Ives' omitted, two pages of adverts at rear cascading number line of 10 to 1 on copyright page) (Bloomsbury, 1999)...**£100**

HARRY POTTER AND THE PRISONER OF AZKABAN (first paperback edition: standard cover) (Bloomsbury, 2000) **£10**

HARRY POTTER AND THE PRISONER OF AZKABAN (paperback: 'adult' cover) (Bloomsbury, 2000)....................**£8**

HARRY POTTER AND THE PRISONER OF AZKABAN (collectors' edition: limited to 1,000 copies; green cloth; 'Joanne Rowling' on copyright page – although this also appears on same later issues – and complete cascading number line of 10 to 1 on copyright page) (Bloomsbury, 1999)...**£1,000**

HARRY POTTER AND THE PRISONER OF AZKABAN (uncorrected proof: first state, limited to approximately 50 copies; issued without dustjacket; purple and white paperback) (Bloomsbury, 1999)....................**£1,250**

HARRY POTTER AND THE PRISONER OF AZKABAN (uncorrected proof: second state, limited to approximately 250 copies) (Bloomsbury, 1999)...**£800**

HARRY POTTER AND THE PRISONER OF AZKABAN (first children's large print edition; paperback) (Bloomsbury, 2002) **£25**

HARRY POTTER AND THE GOBLET OF FIRE (unknown print-run; laminated boards and dustjacket; first edition on copyright page; first issue has print error on page 503 'Dumbledore, come!' spoken by Crouch rather than Fudge) (Bloomsbury, 2000)..**£45**

HARRY POTTER AND THE GOBLET OF FIRE (collectors' edition: blue cloth; 'Joanne Rowling' on copyright page and complete cascading number line of 10 to 1 on copyright page) (Bloomsbury, 2000)........................**£55**

HARRY POTTER AND THE GOBLET OF FIRE (first paperback edition) (Bloomsbury, 2001) **£10**

HARRY POTTER AND THE GOBLET OF FIRE (first adult edition: paperback) (Bloomsbury, 2001)....................**£12**

HARRY POTTER AND THE GOBLET OF FIRE (first children's large print edition; paperback) (Bloomsbury, 2002).................**£20**

HARRY POTTER AND THE ORDER OF THE PHOENIX (unknown print-run; laminated boards and dustjacket; first edition on copyright page; cascading number line of 10 to 1 on copyright page) (Bloomsbury, 2003)...........................**£25**

HARRY POTTER AND THE ORDER OF THE PHOENIX (first adult edition: hardback) (Bloomsbury, 2003) **£15**

HARRY POTTER AND THE ORDER OF THE PHOENIX (first children's large print edition; paperback) (Bloomsbury, 2003) **£20**

HARRY POTTER AND THE ORDER OF THE PHOENIX (collectors' edition; hardback) (Bloomsbury, 2003) **£30**

HARRY POTTER AND THE HALF-BLOOD PRINCE (unknown print-run; laminated boards and dustjacket; first edition on copyright page; cascading number line of 10 to 1 on copyright page) (Bloomsbury, 2005) **£12**

HARRY POTTER AND THE HALF-BLOOD PRINCE (first paperback edition) (Bloomsbury, 2005) **£5**

HARRY POTTER AND THE HALF-BLOOD PRINCE (first adult edition: hardback) (Bloomsbury, 2005) **£5**

HARRY POTTER AND THE HALF-BLOOD PRINCE (first children's large print edition; paperback) (Bloomsbury, 2005) **£20**

HARRY POTTER AND THE HALF-BLOOD PRINCE (collectors' edition; hardback) (Bloomsbury, 2005) **£25**

'Harry Potter' Box Sets

HARRY POTTER GIRT SET (hardback of 'Philosopher's Stone and 'Chamber of Secrets') (Bloomsbury, 1998).......................**£80**

HARRY POTTER AND THE GOBLET OF FIRE (first edition and deluxe edition together in slipcase with signed watercolour from artist Jason Cockcroft as frontis and/or signed bookplate from Rowling) (Bloomsbury, 2001)..............**£1,000**

HARRY POTTER AND THE ORDER OF THE PHOENIX (hardback first edition multiple issue with poster in presentation box) (Bloomsbury, 2003) **£70**

HARRY POTTER DELUXE EDITION BOX SET (Bloomsbury, 2004)...**£150**

Other 'Harry Potter' books

QUIDDITCH THROUGH THE AGES (cascading number line 10 to 1; paperback) (Bloomsbury, 2001)........................**£5**

FANTASTIC BEASTS AND WHERE TO FIND THEM (cascading number line 10 to 1; paperback) (Bloomsbury, 2001) **£5**

HARRY POTTER'S SCHOOL BOOKS (by 'Kennilworthy Whisp'; satchel set of above two books with 'Hogwarts library' book plate; prices assumes bag is still sealed) (Bloomsbury, 2001)..**£20**

'RUPERT' ANNUALS

Popular series of annuals published by the *Daily Express* and featuring the adventures of Rupert Bear. The character was the creation of Mary Tourtel and first appeared in the paper on 8th November 1920. The 'Rupert' annuals were launched in 1936, one year after the strip had been taken over by Alfred Bestall (1892-1986). From 1976 it was drawn by John Harrold.

Prices are for books and annuals in Very Good condition.

'Rupert' Annuals

1936 (with dustjacket) (Daily Express)............**£3,000**	**1960-66** ('Magic Painting' pages coloured in)	
1936 (without dustjacket) (Daily Express).........**£500**	(Daily Express)....................................each **£45**	
1937 & 1938 (Daily Express)..................each **£500**	**1967-68** ('Magic Painting' pages coloured in)	
1939-41 (Daily Express).........................each **£600**	(Daily Express)....................................each **£40**	
1942 (wraps) (Daily Express)..........................**£700**	**1960-66** ('Magic Painting' pages not coloured in)	
1943 (wraps) (Daily Express)..........................**£500**	(Daily Express)..................................each **£130**	
1944 (wraps) (Daily Express)..........................**£300**	**1967-68** ('Magic Painting' pages not coloured in)	
1945 (wraps) (Daily Express)..........................**£250**	(Daily Express)..................................each **£120**	
1946 & 1947 (wraps) (Daily Express).......each **£250**	**1969** (Daily Express)......................................**£25**	
1948 & 1949 (wraps) (Daily Express).......each **£300**	**1970-89** (Daily Express).............................each **£10**	
1950-54 (boards) (Daily Express)............each **£150**	**1990-98** (Daily Express).............................each **£10**	
1955-59 (boards) (Daily Express) ....each **£100**	**1999- to date** (Daily Express)....................each **£5**	

Facsimiles (prices are for annuals in Mint condition with dustjackets/slipcases where applicable)

1936 (issued with dustjacket) (Daily Express, 1985).........**£140**
1937 (Daily Express, 1986)...**£80**
1938 (Daily Express, 1989)...**£100**
1939 (Daily Express, 1991)..**£30**
1940 & 1941 (Pedigree, 1992 & 1993).....................each **£30**

1942 (in slipcase) (Pedigree, 1994) **£100**
1943 (in slipcase) (Pedigree, 1995) **£50**
1944 (in slipcase) (Pedigree, 1996) **£40**
1945 (in slipcase) (Pedigree, 1997) **£45**
1948-50 (in slipcase)(Pedigree, 1998-2000) ....each **£25**

'Monster Rupert' Books (with cover description)

1931 (Rupert watching wolf leap from bed) (Sampson Low, no date)..**£900**
1932 (Rupert sitting on a log) (Sampson Low, no date) **£800**
1933 (Rupert being hidden by female bird) (Sampson Low, no date)...**£800**
1934 (Rupert and small boy in storeroom) (Sampson Low, no date)..**£800**

'The Monster Rupert' Books (with cover description)

1948 (Rupert sitting on a log; with dustjacket) (Sampson Low, no date) **£80**
1949 (Rupert watching fox leap from bed; with dustjacket) (Sampson Low, no date)..**£125**
1950 (Rupert helping small boy out of hole; issued with dustjacket) (Sampson Low, no date) **£70**

'Adventure' Series

NO. 1 (Daily Express) **£50**
NOS. 2-9 (Daily Express).....................................each **£30**
NO. 10 (Daily Express) **£35**
NOS. 11-20 (Daily Express)................................each **£30**
NOS. 21-30 (Daily Express).................................each **£35**
NOS. 31-35 (Daily Express)..................................each **£35**

NOS. 36-40 (Daily Express) ....each **£40**
NOS. 41-46 (Daily Express) ....each **£60**
NOS. 47-48 (Daily Express) ....each **£80**
NO. 49 (Daily Express)..**£100**
NO. 50 (Daily Express)..**£125**

RUSKIN, John

British author. Born: Surrey, 1819. Studied at Christ Church, Oxford. The celebrated critic and philosopher wrote only two children's books, the first, *The King of the Golden River* (1851), was one of the earliest English fantasies for children. He was a friend of, and influence on, the children's artist, Kate Greenaway. Died: 1900.

Prices are for books in Very Good condition.

THE KING OF THE GOLDEN RIVER, or The Black Brothers: A Legend of Stiria (illustrated by Richard Doyle)
(Smith Elder, 1851)...**£650**
THE KING OF THE GOLDEN RIVER (illustrated by Arthur Rackham; wrappers) (Harrap, 1932)...............................**£75**
THE KING OF THE GOLDEN RIVER (illustrated by Arthur Rackham; limited to 750 copies, signed by the artist)
(Harrap, 1932) **£500**
THE ETHICS OF THE DUST (Smith Elder, 1866)...**£600**
DAME WIGGINS OF LEE AND HER SEVEN WONDERFUL CATS Edited from the original 1823 version by John Ruskin
(illustrated by Kate Greenaway and others; with original verses by John Ruskin) (George Allen, 1885) **£175**

RYAN, John

British author. Born: Edinburgh, 1921. Began as art master at Harrow and later became a cartoonist for the *Catholic Herald*. Created the popular children's animated TV series, *Captain Pugwash*.

Prices are for books in Very Good condition with dustjackets where applicable.

Books Written and Illustrated by John Ryan

CAPTAIN PUGWASH (The Bodley Head, 1957)..**£70**
PUGWASH ALOFT (The Bodley Head, 1958) **£50**
PUGWASH AND THE GHOST SHIP (The Bodley Head, 1962)..**£40**
PUGWASH IN THE PACIFIC (The Bodley Head, 1973) **£30**
CAPTAIN PUGWASH ANNUAL 1976 (World Distributors, 1975)..**£20**
DODO'S DELIGHT or Doodle and the State Secret (Deutsch, 1977)..**£10**
DOODLE'S HOMEWORK (Deutsch, 1978)..**£5**
CROCKLE AND THE KITE (Hamlyn, 1980)...**£10**
ALL ABOARD (Hamlyn, 1980)...**£10**
PUGWASH AND THE FANCY-DRESS PARTY (The Bodley Head, 1982)..**£20**
CAPTAIN PUGWASH: THE QUEST OF THE GOLDEN HANDSHAKE (The Bodley Head, 1983)................................**£20**
CAPTAIN PUGWASH: THE BATTLE OF BUNKUM BAY (pictorial boards; illustrated by the author)
(The Bodley Head, 1984) **£15**
PUGWASH AND THE MIDNIGHT FEAST and PUGWASH AND THE WRECKERS (paperback)
(Puffin, 1986) **£10**
EAGLE CLASSICS – HARRIS TWEED, EXTRA SPECIAL AGENT (Hawk Books, 1990)..**£6**
CAPTAIN PUGWASH AND THE HUGE REWARD (Gungarden Books, 1991)..**£10**
THE CAPTAIN PUGWASH COLLECTION (Ted Smart, 1992) **£10**
FATSO THE FATHEAD (The Bodley Head, 1993)..**£10**
MUDGE THE SMUGGLER (Macmillan, 1995) **£10**
GIANT-KILLER: The Story of David and Goliath and the Man who Carried the Shield (Lion Picture Story, 1995) **£5**

S

SAINT-EXUPÉRY, Antoine de

French author. Born: Lyons, France, in 1900. Was a commercial pilot during the 1930s and '40s, drawing on his experiences for several adult novels about aviation. His only children's book, *The Little Prince* (1943), was first published in America, in both French and English. Saint-Exupéry died whilst on a reconnaissance flight in 1944.

Prices are for books in Very Good condition with dustjackets.

THE LITTLE PRINCE (illustrated by the author; translated by Katherine Woods) (Reynel & Hitchcock, US, 1943) **£500**
THE LITTLE PRINCE (illustrated by the author; translated by Katherine Woods; limited to 500 copies)
(Reynel & Hitchcock, US, 1943)...**£2,500**
THE LITTLE PRINCE (illustrated by the author; translated by Katherine Woods) (Heinemann, 1945)......................................**£500**

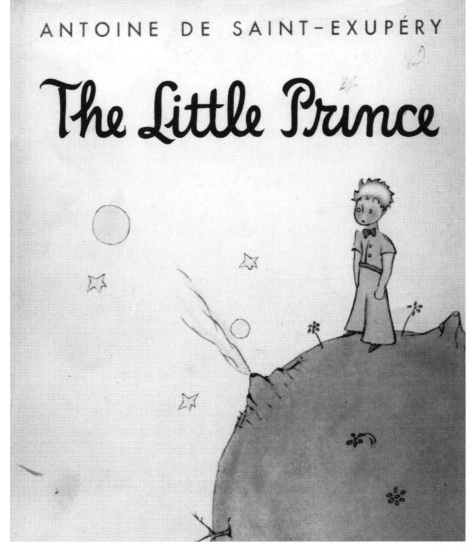

The iconic dustjacket that encased the original English issue of the French author's first and only children's book.

The Gay Dolphin Adventure (1945) was the third novel in Malcolm Saville's enduringly popular 'Lone Pine' series.

The first edition of **The Neglected Mountain** *(1953) features this atmospheric dustjacket designed by Bertram Prance.*

SAVILLE, Malcolm

British author. Born: Leonard Malcolm Saville in Hastings, Sussex, in 1901. Educated privately, subsequently working for Amalgamated Press and the publishers, Cassell and George Newnes. Wrote a large number of children's books, but is best-known for the series featuring a group of children known as the 'Lone Piners' who were introduced in his first novel, *Mystery at Witchend* (1943). Died: 1982.

Prices are for books in Very Good condition with dustjackets.

'Lone Pine' Books

MYSTERY AT WITCHEND (illustrated by G.E. Breary) (Newnes, 1943)..£225
SEVEN WHITE GATES (illustrated by Bertram Prance) (Newnes, 1944)..£175
THE GAY DOLPHIN ADVENTURE (illustrated by Bertram Prance) (Newnes, 1945) £100
THE SECRET OF GREY WALLS (illustrated by Bertram Prance) (Newnes, 1947)...£100
LONE PINE FIVE (illustrated by Bertram Prance) (Newnes, 1949) £100
'The Flower-Show Hat' (in THE GUIDE GIFT BOOK, 1950) £25
THE ELUSIVE GRASSHOPPER (illustrated by Bertram Prance) (Newnes, 1951)..£75
THE NEGLECTED MOUNTAIN (illustrated by Bertram Prance) (Newnes, 1953) £75
SAUCERS OVER THE MOOR (illustrated by Bertram Prance) (Newnes, 1955) £75
WINGS OVER WITCHEND (Newnes, 1956)..£75
LONE PINE LONDON (Newnes, 1957)..£55
THE SECRET OF THE GORGE (Newnes, 1958) £55
MYSTERY MINE (Newnes, 1959)..£55
SEA WITCH COMES HOME (Newnes, 1960)..£55
NOT SCARLET BUT GOLD (illustrated by A.R. Whitear) (Newnes, 1962)...£55
TREASURE AT AMORYS (illustrated by T.R. Freeman) (Newnes, 1964) £60
MAN WITH THREE FINGERS (illustrated by Michael Whittlesea) (Newnes, 1966)..£100
RYE ROYAL (Collins, 1969)..£75
STRANGERS AT WITCHEND (Collins, 1970)..£60
WHERE'S MY GIRL (Collins, 1972) £80
HOME TO WITCHEND (paperback) (Armada, 1978)...£25
HOME TO WITCHEND (Severn House, 1979)...£80

'Jilly Family' Books

REDSHANK'S WARNING (illustrated by Lunt Roberts) (Lutterworth Press, 1948)..£50

TWO FAIR PLAITS (illustrated by Lunt Roberts) (Lutterworth Press, 1948) £40
STRANGERS AT SNOWFELL (illustrated by Wynne) (Lutterworth Press, 1949) £40
THE SIGN OF THE ALPINE ROSE (illustrated by Wynne) (Lutterworth Press, 1950)..£30
THE LUCK OF SALLOWBY (illustrated by Tidden Reeves) (Lutterworth Press, 1952)..£30
THE AMBERMERE TREASURE (illustrated by Marcia Lane Foster) (Lutterworth Press, 1953)......................................£35

'Buckingham Family' Books
THE MASTER OF MARYKNOLL (illustrated by Alice Bush) (Evans, 1950)..£50
THE BUCKINGHAMS AT RAVENSWYKE (illustrated by Alice Bush) (Evans, 1952) £50
THE LONG PASSAGE (illustrated by Alice Bush) (Evans, [1954])..£40
A PALACE FOR THE BUCKINGHAMS (illustrated by Alice Bush) (Evans, 1963)...£50
THE SECRET OF VILLA ROSA (Collins, 1971) £35
DIAMONDS IN THE SKY (Collins, 1974) £40

'Marston Baines' Books
THREE TOWERS IN TUSCANY (Heinemann, 1963) £35
THE PURPLE VALLEY (Heinemann, 1964)...£30
DARK DANGER (Heinemann, 1965) £30
WHITE FIRE (Heinemann, 1966)..£50
POWER OF THREE (Heinemann, 1968)..£35
THE DAGGER AND THE FLAME (Heinemann, 1970)...£35
MARSTON MASTER SPY (Heinemann, 1978)...£60

'Mike and Mary' Books
TROUBLE AT TOWNSEND (illustrated by Lunt Roberts) (Transatlantic Arts, 1945)...£30
THE RIDDLE OF THE PAINTED BOX (illustrated by Lunt Roberts) (Carrington, 1947)...£30
THE FLYING FISH ADVENTURE (illustrated by Lunt Roberts) (John Murray, 1950)..£30
WHERE THE BUS STOPPED (Blackwell, 1955 [1956])..£40
YOUNG JOHNNY BIMBO (illustrated by Lunt Roberts) (John Murray, 1956) £30
THE FOURTH KEY (illustrated by Lunt Roberts) (John Murray, 1957)..£30

'Susan and Bill' Books
SUSAN, BILL AND THE WOLF-DOG (illustrated by E.H. Shepard) (Nelson, 1954) £40
SUSAN, BILL AND THE IVY-CLAD OAK (illustrated by E.H. Shepard) (Nelson, 1954) £40
SUSAN, BILL AND THE VANISHING BOY (illustrated by E.H. Shepard) (Nelson, 1955)...£35
SUSAN, BILL AND THE GOLDEN CLOCK (illustrated by E.H. Shepard) (Nelson, 1955) £35
SUSAN, BILL AND THE DARK STRANGER (illustrated by E.H. Shepard) (Nelson, 1956)..£35
SUSAN, BILL AND THE 'SAUCY KATE' (illustrated by E.H. Shepard) (Nelson, [1956]) £35
SUSAN, BILL AND THE BRIGHT STAR CIRCUS (illustrated by T.R. Freeman) (Nelson, [1960])....................................£35
SUSAN, BILL AND THE PIRATES BOLD (illustrated by T.R. Freeman) (Nelson, [1961])...£35

'Nettleford' Books
ALL SUMMER THROUGH (illustrated by Joan Kiddell-Monroe) (Hodder & Stoughton, 1951)......................................£30
CHRISTMAS AT NETTLEFORD (illustrated by Joan Kiddell-Monroe) (Hodder & Stoughton, 1953)...............................£30
SPRING COMES TO NETTLEFORD (illustrated by Joan Kiddell-Monroe) (Hodder & Stoughton, 1954)..........................£30
THE SECRET OF BUZZARD SCAR (illustrated by Joan Kiddell-Monroe) (Hodder & Stoughton, 1955) £30

'Lucy and Humf' Books
FOUR-AND-TWENTY BLACKBIRDS (illustrated by Lilian Buchanan) (Newnes, 1959)...£45
THE SECRET GALLEYBIRD PIT (adapted from 'Four-and-Twenty Blackbirds'; paperback) (Armada, 1968) £8
GOOD DOG DANDY (paperback) (Armada, 1971) £8
GOOD DOG DANDY (hardback) (White Lion, 1977) £20
THE ROMAN TREASURE MYSTERY (paperback) (Armada, 1973)...£15

Others
COUNTRY SCRAPBOOK FOR BOYS AND GIRLS (non-fiction) (National Magazine Co, [1944]) £20
COUNTRY SCRAPBOOK FOR BOYS AND GIRLS (non-fiction; revised and enlarged edition)
   (Gramol, 1945) £20
OPEN AIR SCRAPBOOK FOR BOYS AND GIRLS (non-fiction) (Gramol, [1945]) £20
SEASIDE SCRAPBOOK FOR BOYS AND GIRLS (non-fiction) (Gramol, 1946) £20
JANE'S COUNTRY YEAR (non-fiction; illustrated by Bernard Bowerman) (Newnes, 1946) £35
THE ADVENTURE OF THE LIFEBOAT SERVICE (non-fiction) (Macdonald, 1950)..£30
CORONATION GIFT BOOK FOR BOYS AND GIRLS (non-fiction) (Daily Graphic/Pitkin, 1952)......................................£25
THE SECRET OF THE HIDDEN POOL (illustrated by Lunt Roberts) (John Murray, 1953) £30
YOUNG JOHNNIE BIMBO (illustrated by Lunt Roberts) (John Murray, 1956)..£30
READ ALOUD TALES FOR SUNNY STORIES. Edited by Malcom Saville (Newnes, 1956)..£10
TREASURE AT THE MILL (illustrated by Harry Pettit) (Newnes, 1957)..£50
KING OF KINGS (non-fiction) (Nelson, [1958]) £25
KING OF KINGS (non-fiction; revised edition) (Lion, 1975) £20
SMALL CREATURES (non-fiction; illustrated by John T. Kenney) (Edmund Ward, 1959) £40
MALCOLM SAVILLE'S COUNTRY BOOK (non-fiction) (Cassell, 1961) £20
MALCOLM SAVILLE'S SEASIDE BOOK (non-fiction) (Cassell, 1962) £20

*Dartmoor provides the setting for **Saucers Over the Moor**, which is now worth £75 in Very Good condition with the jacket.*

Saville has also produced a number of non-fiction works, including this sensitively-written life of Christ from 1958.

THE THIN GREY MAN (illustrated by Desmond Knight) (Macmillan, 1966)..£40
STRANGE STORY (Mowbray, 1967)...£25
COME TO LONDON: A Personal Introduction to the World's Greatest City (non-fiction) (Heinemann 1967) £25
COME TO DEVON (non-fiction) (Benn 1969)...£25
COME TO CORNWALL (non-fiction) (Benn, 1969)..£25
COME TO SOMERSET (non-fiction) (Benn, 1970) £25
SEE HOW IT GROWS (non-fiction; illustrated by Robert Micklewright) (OUP, 1971)...£20
EAT WHAT YOU GROW (non-fiction; illustrated by Robert Micklewright; paperback) (Carousel, 1975) £12
PORTRAIT OF RYE (non-fiction; illustrated by Michael Renton; paperback) (Goulden, 1976).................................£25
PORTRAIT OF RYE (revised edition; updated by Mark O'Hanlon; paperback) (O'Hanlon, 1999) £5
DISCOVERING THE WOODLAND (non-fiction; illustrated by Elsie Wrigley; paperback) (Carousel, 1978)...............£10
THE COUNTRYSIDE QUIZ (non-fiction; illustrated by Robert Micklewright; paperback) (Carousel, 1978) £8
THE WONDER WHY BOOK OF EXPLORING A WOOD (non-fiction; paperback) (Transworld, 1979)..........................£8
THE WONDER WHY BOOK OF EXPLORING THE SEASIDE (non-fiction; paperback) (Transworld, 1979).................£8
WORD OF ALL SEASONS (non-fiction; illustrated by E. and P. Wrigley) (Lutterworth Press, 1979) £25
THE WONDER WHY BOOK OF WILD FLOWERS THROUGH THE YEAR (non-fiction; paperback) (Transworld, 1980) £8
THE STORY OF WINCHELSEA CHURCH (non-fiction) (Winchelsea Church, [c1980]) £6
THE SEASHORE QUIZ (non-fiction; paperback) (Carousel, 1981) £4
THE SILDENT HILLS OF SHROPSHIRE (with Mark O'Hanlon; paperback; non-fiction) (O'Hanlon, 1998)...................£5

SCARRY, Richard

American author-illustrator. Born: Richard McClure Scarry in Boston, Massachusetts, in 1919. Has produced many large format 'picture books', distinguished by their vast range of animal characters and well-filled pages. Died: 1994.

Prices are for books in Very Good to Fine condition with dustjackets where applicable.

THE ANIMALS' MERRY CHRISTMAS by Kathryn Jackson (Simon & Schuster, US, 1950)......................................£40
THE ANIMALS' MERRY CHRISTMAS by Kathryn Jackson (Collins, 1977)..£5
THE GREAT BIG CAR AND TRUCK BOOK (Simon & Schuster, US, 1951)..£25
RABBIT AND HIS FRIENDS (Simon & Schuster, US, 1953)..£30
RABBIT AND HIS FRIENDS (Muller, 1954) £25
NURSERY TALES (Simon & Schuster, US, 1958) £18
NAUGHTY BUNNY (Golden Press, US, 1959) £22

NAUGHTY BUNNY (Muller, 1959)..£18
TINKER AND TANKER (Doubleday, US, 1960)...£18
TINKER AND TANKER (Hamlyn, 1969)..£12
TINKER AND TANKER OUT WEST (Doubleday, US, 1961)...£18
TINKER AND TANKER OUT WEST (Hamlyn, 1969)..£12
TINKER AND TANKER AND THE PIRATES (Doubleday, US, 1961)..£18
TINKER AND TANKER AND THEIR SPACE SHIP (Doubleday, US, 1961)..£18
MANNERS (Golden Press, US, 1962)..£18
TINKER AND TANKER, KNIGHTS OF THE ROUND TABLE (Doubleday, US, 1963)........................£18
TINKER AND TANKER, KNIGHTS OF THE ROUND TABLE (Hamlyn, 1969)....................................£12
TINKER AND TANKER IN AFRICA (Doubleday, US, 1963)...£18
TINKER AND TANKER IN AFRICA (Hamlyn, 1969)..£12
A TINKER AND TANKER COLOURING BOOK (Doubleday, US, 1963)..£12
BEST WORD BOOK EVER (Golden Press, US, 1963)...£18
BEST WORD BOOK EVER (Hamlyn, 1964)...£12
WHAT ANIMALS DO (Golden Press, US, 1963)...£18
THE ROOSTER STRUTS (Golden Press, US, 1963)...£18
THE ROOSTER STRUTS (as 'The Golden Happy Book of Animals') (Golden Press, US, 1964).......£12
THE ROOSTER STRUTS (as 'Animals') (Hamlyn, 1964)...£10
POLITE ELEPHANT (Golden Press, US, 1964)...£18
IS THIS THE HOUSE OF MISTRESS MOUSE? (Golden Press, US, 1964)....................................£18
ANIMAL MOTHER GOOSE (Golden Press, US, 1964)...£18
ANIMAL MOTHER GOOSE (Hamlyn, 1965)...£12
BEST NURSERY RHYMES EVER (Golden Press, US, 1964)...£18
BEST NURSERY RHYMES EVER (Hamlyn, 1971)..£12
TEENY TINY TALES (Golden Press, US, 1965)...£18
TEENY TINY TALES (Hamlyn, 1970)...£12
THE SANTA CLAUS BOOK (Golden Press, US, 1965)...£18
THE BUNNY BOOK (Golden Press, US, 1965)...£18
THE BUNNY BOOK (Hamlyn, 1966)..£12
BUSY BUSY WORLD (Golden Press, US, 1965)...£18
BUSY BUSY WORLD (Hamlyn, 1966)..£12
STORYBOOK DICTIONARY (Random House, US, 1966)...£12
THE EGG IN THE HOLE BOOK (Golden Press, US, 1967)..£18
PLANES (Golden Press, US, 1967)..£12
TRAINS (Golden Press, US, 1967)...£12
BOATS (Golden Press, US, 1967)..£12
CARS (Golden Press, US, 1967)...£12
THE EARLY BIRD (Random House, US, 1968)...£12
THE EARLY BIRD (Collins, 1970)..£6
WHAT DO PEOPLE DO ALL DAY? (Random House, US, 1968)..£12
WHAT DO PEOPLE DO ALL DAY? (Collins, 1969)..£6
THE GREAT PIE ROBBERY (Random House, US, 1969)..£12
THE GREAT PIE ROBBERY (Collins, 1969)...£6
THE SUPERMARKET MYSTERY (Random House, US, 1969)..£12
THE SUPERMARKET MYSTERY (Collins, 1969)..£6
GREAT BIG SCHOOLHOUSE (Random House, US, 1969)...£12
GREAT BIG SCHOOLHOUSE (Collins, 1969)..£6
THINGS TO KNOW (Random House, US, 1970)...£6
THINGS TO KNOW (Collins, 1976)...£6
GREAT BIG AIR BOOK (Random House, US, 1971)..£12
GREAT BIG AIR BOOK (Collins, 1971)...£6
ABC WORD BOOK (Random House, US, 1971)..£12
ABC WORD BOOK (Collins, 1972)...£6
LOOK AND LEARN LIBRARY (four books: 'Best Stories Ever', 'Fun with Words', 'Going Places' and
   'Things to Know') (Golden Press, US, 1971)...each £6
FUNNIEST STORYBOOK EVER (Random House, US, 1972)...£12
FUNNIEST STORYBOOK EVER (Collins, 1972)...£6
NICKY GOES TO THE DOCTOR (Golden Press, US, 1972)...£12
NICKY GOES TO THE DOCTOR (Hamlyn, 1972)...£6
HOP ABOARD, HERE WE GO! (Random House, US, 1972)...£12
HOP ABOARD, HERE WE GO! (Hamlyn, 1972)..£6
GREAT BIG MYSTERY BOOK (Collins, 1973)..£6
SILLY STORIES (Golden Press, US, 1973)..£12
SILLY STORIES (Hamlyn, 1974)..£6
BABYKINS AND HIS FAMILY (Golden Press, US, 1973)..£12
BABYKINS AND HIS FAMILY (Hamlyn, 1974)...£6
FIND YOUR ABCs (Random House, US, 1973)..£10
PLEASE AND THANK YOU BOOK (Random House, US, 1973)...£10

SCARRY, Richard

CARS AND TRUCKS AND THINGS THAT GO (Golden Press, US, 1974) £6
CARS AND TRUCKS AND THINGS THAT GO (Collins, 1974).. £6
EUROPEAN WORD BOOK (Hamlyn, 1974)... £10
BEST RAINY DAY BOOK EVER (Random House, US, 1974)... £10
BEST RAINY DAY BOOK EVER (Hamlyn, 1975)... £6
GREAT STEAMBOAT MYSTERY (Random House, US, 1975) £10
GREAT STEAMBOAT MYSTERY (Collins, 1976).. £6
ALL DAY LONG by J.D. Bevington (Hamlyn, 1975)... £6
WITH THE ANIMALS by J.D. Bevington (Hamlyn, 1975) £6
WORK AND PLAY BOOK (Collins, 1975).. £6
ANIMAL NURSERY TALES (Golden Press, US, 1975).. £10
ANIMAL NURSERY TALES (Collins, 1975)... £6
FAVOURITE STORYBOOK (Random House, US, 1976) £10
FAVOURITE STORYBOOK (Collins, 1976)... £6
BUSY TOWN, BUSY PEOPLE (Random House, US, 1976)... £10
BUSY TOWN, BUSY PEOPLE (Collins, 1976).. £6
STORYTIME (Collins, 1976).. £6
ALL DAY LONG (Golden Press: 'Look-Look' series, US, 1976) £6
ALL DAY LONG (Hamlyn: 'Look-Look' series, 1977).. £6
ALL YEAR LONG (Golden Press: 'Look-Look' series, US, 1976) £6
ALL YEAR LONG (Hamlyn: 'Look-Look' series, 1977) £6
IN MY TOWN (Golden Press: 'Look-Look' series, US, 1976)... £6
IN MY TOWN (Hamlyn: 'Look-Look' series, 1977).. £6
LEARN TO COUNT (Golden Press: 'Look-Look' series, US, 1976)... £6
LEARN TO COUNT (Hamlyn: 'Look-Look' series, 1977) £6
ABOUT ANIMALS (Golden Press: 'Look-Look' series, US, 1976)... £6
ABOUT ANIMALS (Hamlyn: 'Look-Look' series, 1977)... £6
AT WORK (Golden Press: 'Look-Look' series, US, 1976).. £6
AT WORK (Hamlyn: 'Look-Look' series, 1977).. £6
MY HOUSE (Golden Press: 'Look-Look' series, US, 1976)... £6
MY HOUSE (Hamlyn: 'Look-Look' series, 1977) £6
ON THE FARM (Golden Press: 'Look-Look' series, US, 1976).. £6
ON THE FARM (Hamlyn: 'Look-Look' series, 1977).. £6
ON VACATION (Golden Press: 'Look-Look' series, US, 1976).. £6
ON VACATION (Hamlyn: 'Look-Look' series, 1977).. £6
SHORT AND TALL (Golden Press: 'Look-Look' series, US, 1976) £6
SHORT AND TALL (Hamlyn: 'Look-Look' series, 1977) £6
TEENY TINY ABC (Golden Press, US, 1976) £6
TEENY TINY ABC (Hamlyn, 1975)... £6
EARLY WORDS (Random House, US, 1976) £6
EARLY WORDS (Collins, 1977) £6
COLOUR BOOK (Random House, US, 1976)... £6
COLOUR BOOK (Collins, 1977).. £6
LAUGH AND LEARN LIBRARY (Collins, 1976) £6
PICTURE DICTIONARY (Collins, 1976).. £6
LITTLE ABC (Random House, US, 1976) £6
LITTLE ABC (Collins, 1976) £6
BUSIEST PEOPLE EVER (Random House, US, 1976)... £6
BUSIEST PEOPLE EVER (Collins, 1977)... £6
BEST COUNTING BOOK EVER (Random House, US, 1976) £6
BEST COUNTING BOOK EVER (Collins, 1977)... £6
LOWLY WORM STORY BOOK (contains 'The Talking Bread', 'Please Move to the Back of the Bus'
    'Lowly Worm's Birthday' and 'Rudolf's Aeroplane') (Random House, US, 1977) £6
LOWLY WORM STORY BOOK (Collins, 1979).. £6
BUSY, BUSY WORD BOOK (Collins, 1977) £6
MR FIXIT and Other Stories (Collins, 1977) £6
LITTLE BEDTIME BOOK (Collins, 1977).. £6
BEST MAKE-IT BOOK EVER (Random House, US, 1977) £6
BEST MAKE-IT BOOK EVER (Collins, 1978)... £6
LITTLE COUNTING BOOK (Random House, US, 1978)... £6
LITTLE COUNTING BOOK (as 'Busy-Busy Counting Book') (Collins, 1977).. £6
LOWLY WORM SNIFFY BOOK (Random House, US, 1978)... £6
POSTMAN PIG AND HIS BUSY NEIGHBOURS (Random House, US, 1978)... £6
POSTMAN PIG AND HIS BUSY NEIGHBOURS (Collins, 1978) £6
TOY BOOK (Random House, US, 1978).. £6
TOY BOOK (Collins, 1979).. £6
STORIES TO COLOUR (Random House, US, 1978) £6
STORIES TO COLOUR (Collins, 1979)... £6
HOLIDAY BOOK (Collins, 1979) £6

FIRST RICHARD SCARRY OMNIBUS (contains 'Cars and Trucks and Things That Go', 'Busiest People Ever' and 'Best Counting Book Ever') (Collins, [1979])..£10
MIX OR MATCH STORYBOOK (Random House, US, 1979)...£6
MIX OR MATCH BOOK (Collins, 1980)..£6
BEST FIRST BOOK EVER (Random House, US, 1979)...£6
BEST FIRST BOOK EVER (Collins, 1980)..£6
HUCKLE'S BOOK (Random House, US, 1979) £6
HUCKLE'S BOOK (Collins, 1979) £6
BUSYTOWN POP-UP BOOK (Random House, US, 1979)..£6
BUSYTOWN POP-UP BOOK (Collins, 1980) £6
CAN YOU COUNT? (Collins, 1979) £6
LOWLY WORM THINGS ON WHEELS (Random House, US, 1980)...£6
LOWLY WORM THINGS ON WHEELS (Collins, 1979) £6
LOWLY WORM WHERE DOES IT COME FROM BOOK (Random House, US, 1980) £6
LOWLY WORM WHERE DOES IT COME FROM BOOK (Collins, 1979)..£6
LOWLY WORM TELL-TIME BOOK (Random House, US, 1980) £6
LOWLY WORM TELL-TIME BOOK (Collins, 1979)...£6
PEASANT PIG AND THE TERRIBLE DRAGON (Random House, US, 1980)...£6
PEASANT PIG AND THE TERRIBLE DRAGON (Collins, 1981) £6
THE THREE LITTLE PIGS (Collins, 1981)..£6
LOWLY WORM WORD BOOK (Random House, US, 1981)...£6
LOWLY WORM WORD BOOK (Collins, 1982)..£6
CHRISTMAS MICE (Golden Press, US, 1981) £6
BEST CHRISTMAS BOOK EVER (Random House, US, 1981)...£6
BEST CHRISTMAS BOOK EVER (Collins, 1981)..£6
THE WOLF AND THE SEVEN KIDS (Collins, 1981)..£6
LITTLE RED RIDING HOOD (Collins, 1981)...£6
GOLDILOCKS AND THE THREE BEARS (Collins, 1981)...£6
BUSY HOUSES (Random House, US, 1981)...£6
BUSY HOUSES (Collins, 1982)..£6
FOUR BUSY WORD BOOKS (Random House, US, 1982)...£6
BUSYTOWN SHAPE BOOKS (Collins, 1982) £6
STICKER BOOKS (three books: 'On Holiday', 'At School' and 'I Can Count to Eleven') (Collins, 1982)...........each £6
BOARD BOOKS (four books: 'Colours', 'Words', 'My House' and 'Things I Do') (Collins, 1982)...........each £6
OLD MOTHER HUBBARD AND OTHER RHYMES (Hamlyn, 1983) £6
THIS LITTLE PIG WENT TO MARKET AND OTHER RHYMES (Hamlyn, 1983).....................................£6
ONE, TWO, BUCKLE MY SHOE AND OTHER RHYMES (Hamlyn, 1983)...£6
LITTLE MISS MUFFET AND OTHER RHYMES (Hamlyn, 1983)..£6
MEET THE ANIMALS text by J.D. Bevington (Hamlyn, 1984)...£6
PIG WILL AND PIG WON'T: A Book of Manners (Collins, 1984)...£6
BEST BUMPER BOOK EVER (contains 'What Do People Do All Day', 'ABC Work Book' and 'Funniest Storybook Ever') (Collins, 1984) £6
THE BEST MISTAKES EVER! and Other Stories (Random House, US, 1984).......................................£6
THE BEST MISTAKES EVER! and Other Stories (Collins, 1985) £6
THE BIGGEST WORD BOOK EVER (Hamlyn, 1986)..£6
BIG AND LITTLE (Western, US, 1987) £6
THE BUSY FUN AND LEARN BOOK (Hamlyn, 1987)..£6
THE BEST EVER MUSIC BOOK (Random House, US, 1987) £6
THE BEST EVER MUSIC BOOK (Hamlyn, 1987)..£6
BOARD BOOKS (four books: 'Going Places on the Water', 'Going Places in the Air', 'Going Places in the Car' and 'Going Places with Goldbug') (Collins, 1987)...........each £5
SPLISH SPLASH SOUNDS (Western, US 1987) £4
BUSY WORKERS (Western, US, 1988)...£4
COUNTING COLOUR (Western, US, 1992)...£4
COPY COLOUR (Western, US, 1992) £4
MAGIC PAINTING (World International, 1992)..£4
BIGGEST POP-UP EVER (World International, 1992)...£12
ABC's (Western: 'Golden Little-Look Books' series, US, 1992)..£4
MR FUMBLE'S STICKER FUN (World International, 1992) £4
BEST FRIEND EVER (Western: 'Golden Little-Look Books' series, 1992)..£4
NURSERY RHYMES (Western, US, 1993)...£4
STORY BOOK (Dean, 1993) £4
GETTING READY FOR SCHOOL (Dean, 1993)..£4
TINKER AND TANKER STORYBOOK (Dean, 1993) £4
HUCKLE CAT'S BUSIEST DAY EVER (World International, 1993)...£4
MR FIXIT (pop-up book) (World International, 1993)..£6
MR FUMBLE (pop-up book) (World International, 1993) £7
BANANAS GORILLA (pop-up book) (World International, 1993)..£7
BEST LITTLE WORD BOOK EVER (Western, US, 1993) £4
BEST BUSY YEAR EVER (Western, US, 1993)..£4

SCARRY, Richard

BEST FAIRYTALES EVER (World International, 1993) £4
SLEEPING CAR ADVENTURE (Western, US, 1994) £4
SNOWSTORM SURPRISE (Western, US, 1994) £4
WORDS AND COUNTING 4-5 YEARS (Dean, 1994) £4
BIGGEST CATCH EVER (Western, US, 1994) £4
BUSIEST FIREFIGHTERS EVER (Western, US, 1994) £4
DINGO, THE WORST DRIVER EVER (Western, US, 1994) £4
FLOATING BANANAS (Western, US, 1994) £4
LETTERS AND NUMBERS 3-4 YEARS (Dean, 1994) £4
MR FUMBLE'S COFFEE SHOP DISASTER (Western, US, 1994) £4
READING AND SUMS 5-6 YEARS (Dean, 1994) £4

SEARLE, Ronald

British illustrator. Born: St Andrews, Cambridge, in 1920. Studied at Cambridge School of Art. Drew his first 'St. Trinian's' cartoon in 1941 whilst stationed in Scotland with the army, enjoying huge success with the subsequent series of books and with his illustrations for Geoffrey Willans' four 'Molesworth' titles. Moved to France in 1961 following a breakdown. Provided the animated sequences for the films *Those Magnificent Men in their Flying Machines* (1965) and *Monte Carlo or Bust* (1969).

Prices are for books in Very Good condition with dustjackets where applicable.

'Molesworth' Books (all Written by Geoffrey Willans and illustrated by Ronald Searle)
DOWN WITH SKOOL (Parrish, 1953) £20
HOW TO BE TOPP (Parrish, 1954) £15
WHIZZ FOR ATOMS (Parrish, 1956) £15
THE COMPLEET MOLESWORTH (contains 'Down with Skool', 'How to Be Topp' and 'Whizz for Atoms') (Parrish, 1958) £15
BACK IN THE JUG AGANE (Parrish, 1959) £15

'St Trinian's' Books
HURRAH FOR ST. TRINIAN'S! (foreword by D.B. Wyndham Lewis) (Macdonald, 1948) £35

*The innocent joys of school life, as depicted by the incomparable Ronald Searle in **Hurrah for St. Trinian's!** (1948).*

THE FEMALE APPROACH (includes some 'St Trinian's' cartoons; preface by Sir Max Beerbohm) (Macdonald, 1949).............£15
BACK TO THE SLAUGHTERHOUSE (includes some 'St Trinian's' cartoons) (Macdonald, 1951) £20
THE TERROR OF ST. TRINIAN'S (with D.B. Wyndham Lewis) (Parrish, 1952)...£20
SOULS IN TORMENT (includes some 'St Trinian's' cartoons) (Perpetua, 1953)..£20
THE ST. TRINIAN'S STORY (with Kaye Webb) (Perpetua, 1959)..£20

Others

JOHN GILPIN by William Cowper (Chiswick Press, 1952) £30
JOHN GILPIN by William Cowper (King Penguin, 1953)..£15
A CHRISTMAS CAROL by Charles Dickens (Perpetua, 1961) £25
OLIVER TWIST by Charles Dickens (Joseph, 1962)...£25
GREAT EXPECTATIONS by Charles Dickens (Joseph, 1962)...£25
THE HUNCHBACK OF NOTRE-DAME by Victor Hugo (Readers Digest, 1966)...£25
THE ADVENTURES OF BARON MUNCHAUSEN by R.E. Raspe (Pantheon, US, 1969) £25

SENDAK, Maurice

American illustrator. Born: Maurice Bernard Sendak in New York in 1928. Studied at Lafayette High School, subsequently working as a window-dresser and enjoying his first major success as an illustrator with Ruth Krauss's *A Hole is to Dig* (1952). Best known for his 1963 picture book, *Where the Wild Things Are*.

Prices are for books in Very Good condition with dustjackets where applicable.

WONDERFUL FARM by Marcel Aymé (Harper, US, 1951)..£175
MAGGIE ROSE – HER BIRTHDAY CHRISTMAS by R. Sawyer (Harper, US, 1952)..£140
A HOLE IS TO DIG: A First Book of First Definitions by Ruth Krauss (Harper, US, 1952)...............................£120
A HOLE IS TO DIG: A First Book of First Definitions by Ruth Krauss (Hamish Hamilton, 1963) £70
SHADRACH by Meindart de Jong (Harper, US, 1953) £75
A VERY SPECIAL HOUSE by Ruth Krauss (Harper, US, 1953)..£100
I'LL BE YOU AND YOU BE ME by Ruth Krauss (Harper, US, 1954)..£200
MAGIC PICTURES by Marcel Aymé (Harper, US, 1954)..£85
THE WHEEL ON THE SCHOOL by Meindart de Jong (Harper, US, 1954)..£70
THE WHEEL ON THE SCHOOL by Meindart de Jong (Lutterworth Press, 1956)...£50
I WANT TO PAINT MY BATHROOM BLUE by Ruth Krauss (Harper, US, 1954)..£70
TIN FIDDLE by E. Tripp (OUP, 1954) £70
THE LITTLE COW AND THE TURTLE by Meindart de Jong (Harper, US, 1955) £60
THE LITTLE COW AND THE TURTLE by Meindart de Jong (Lutterworth Press, 1961)...£50
WHAT CAN YOU DO WITH A SHOE? by B.S. de Regniers (Harper, US, 1955)...£70
CHARLOTTE AND THE WHITE HORSE by Ruth Krauss (Harper, US, 1955)..£90
CHARLOTTE AND THE WHITE HORSE by Ruth Krauss (The Bodley Head, 1977) £50
KENNY'S WINDOW: A Tale for Children (Harper, US, [1956])...£130
THE HOUSE OF SIXTY FATHERS by Meindart de Jong (Harper, US, 1956)..£50
HAPPY RAIN by Maurice Sendak (Harper, US, 1956)...£70
VERY FAR AWAY: A Tale by Maurice Sendak (Harper, US, 1957) £250
VERY FAR AWAY by Maurice Sendak (World's Work, 1960) £85
LITTLE BEAR by Else Holmelund Minarik (Harper, US, 1957)...£85
LITTLE BEAR by Else Holmelund Minarik (World's Work, 1958)...£50

Sendak's most famous and sought-after work, published in the US in 1964, is now worth £2,000 in Very Good condition.

WHAT DO YOU SAY DEAR by Sesyle Joslin (Faber, 1958) **£65**
NO FIGHTING, NO BITING! by Else Holmelund Minarik (Harper, US, 1958) **£185**
NO FIGHTING, NO BITING! by Else Holmelund Minarik (Tadworth, 1969) **£50**
THE ACROBAT (Privately printed, 1959) **£135**
FATHER BEAR COMES HOME by Else Holmelund Minarik (Harper, US, 1959) **£70**
FATHER BEAR COMES HOME by Else Holmelund Minarik (World's Work, 1960) **£50**
THE MOON JUMPERS by Janice May Udry (Harper, US, 1959) **£65**
THE MOON JUMPERS by Janice May Udry (The Bodley Head, 1979) **£45**
LITTLE BEAR'S FRIEND by Else Holmelund Minarik (Harper, US, 1960) **£70**
LITTLE BEAR'S FRIEND by Else Holmelund Minarik (World's Work, 1961) **£50**
THE SIGN ON ROSIE'S DOOR by Maurice Sendak (Harper US, 1960) **£300**
THE SIGN ON ROSIE'S DOOR (Hamish Hamilton, 1969) **£40**
DWARF LONG-NOSE by Wilhelm Hauff (translated by Doris Orgel) (Random House, US, 1960) **£60**
DWARF LONG-NOSE by Wilhelm Hauff (translated by Doris Orgel) (The Bodley Head, 1979) **£35**
LITTLE BEAR'S VISIT by Else Holmelund Minarik (Harper, US, 1961) **£70**
LITTLE BEAR'S VISIT by Else Holmelund Minarik (World's Work, 1962) **£50**
THE NUTSHELL LIBRARY by Maurice Sendak (verse; four books: 'Alligators All Around',
  'Chicken Soup with Rice', 'One Was Johnny' and 'Pierre'; in slipcase) (Harper, US, 1962) .... the set **£135**
THE NUTSHELL LIBRARY by Maurice Sendak (verse; four books: 'Alligators All Around',
  'Chicken Soup with Rice', 'One Was Johnny' and 'Pierre'; in slipcase) (Collins, 1964) .... the set **£100**
THE BIG GREEN BOOK by Robert Graves (Crowell-Crozier, US, 1962) **£50**
THE BIG GREEN BOOK by Robert Graves (paperback) (Puffin, 1978) **£10**
WHERE THE WILD THINGS ARE by Maurice Sendak (Harper, US, 1963) **£2,000**
WHERE THE WILD THINGS ARE by Maurice Sendak (The Bodley Head, 1967) **£400**
THE GRIFFIN AND THE MINOR CANON by Frank R. Stockton (Holt, US, 1963) **£100**
THE GRIFFIN AND THE MINOR CANON by Frank R. Stockton (Collins, 1968) **£75**
THE BAT-POET by Randall Jarrell (McMillan, US, 1964) **£50**
THE BAT-POET by Randall Jarrell (Kestrel, 1977) **£35**
THE BEE-MAN OF ORN by Frank R. Stockton (Holt, US, 1964) **£60**
THE BEE-MAN OF ORN by Frank R. Stockton (Collins, 1967) **£45**
PLEASANT FIELDMOUSE by Jan Wahl (Harper, US, 1964) **£40**
PLEASANT FIELDMOUSE by Jan Wahl (Tadworth, 1969) **£25**
HECTOR PROTECTOR and AS I WENT OVER THE WATER (verse) (Harper, US, 1965) **£70**
HECTOR PROTECTOR and AS I WENT OVER THE WATER (verse) (The Bodley Head, 1967) **£55**
ANIMAL PEOPLE by Randall Jarrell (Random House, US, 1965) **£50**
THE ANIMAL FAMILY by Randall Jarrell (Pantheon, US, 1965) **£85**
THE ANIMAL FAMILY by Randall Jarrell (Hart-Davis, 1967) **£50**
HIGGLETY PIGGLETY POP! or There Must be More to Life by Maurice Sendak (Harper, US, 1967) **£50**
HIGGLETY PIGGLETY POP! or There Must be More to Life by Maurice Sendak (The Bodley Head, 1969) **£40**
A KISS FOR LITTLE BEAR by Else Holmelund Minarik (Harper, US, 1968) **£50**
A KISS FOR LITTLE BEAR by Else Holmelund Minarik (World's Work, 1969) **£40**
MR RABBIT AND THE LOVELY PRESENT by Charlotte Zolotow (The Bodley Head, 1968) **£40**
LULLABIES AND NIGHT SONGS (The Bodley Head, 1969) **£55**
THE LIGHT PRINCESS by George MacDonald (The Bodley Head, 1969) **£50**
IN THE NIGHT KITCHEN (Harper, US, 1970) **£125**
IN THE NIGHT KITCHEN (The Bodley Head, 1971) **£60**
ZLATEH THE GOAT and Other Stories by Isaac Bashevis Singer (Longmans, 1970) **£25**
THE MAGICIAN: A Counting Book (Rosenbach, US, 1971) **£45**
PICTURES (Harper, US, 1971) **£55**
PICTURES (The Bodley Head, 1972) **£35**
IN SARAH'S ROOM (The Bodley Head, 1972) **£30**
FANTASY SKETCHES (Rosenbach, US, 1972) **£25**
THE GOLDEN KEY by George MacDonald (afterword by W.H. Auden; issued with dustjacket)
  (The Bodley Head, 1972) **£40**
THE JUNIPER TREE and Other Tales from Grimm (selected by Lore Segal and Maurice Sendak;
  translated by Lore Segal and Randall Jarrell; two volumes; issued with dustjackets; in slipcase)
  (Farrar, Straus & Giroux, US, 1973) .... the set **£85**
THE JUNIPER TREE and Other Tales from Grimm (selected by Lore Segal and Maurice Sendak; translated by
  Lore Segal and Randall Jarrell; two volumes; issued with dustjackets; in slipcase) (The Bodley Head, 1974) .... the set **£75**
KING GRISLY-BEARD by Wilhelm and Jacob Grimm (The Bodley Head, 1974) **£30**
REALLY ROSIE (play; adapted from 'The Sign on Rosie's Door' and 'The Nutshell Library') (Harper, 1975) **£35**
SEVEN LITTLE MONSTERS by Maurice Sendak (Harper, US, 1976) **£45**
SEVEN LITTLE MONSTERS by Maurice Sendak (The Bodley Head, 1977) **£35**
FLY BY NIGHT by Randall Jarrell (Farrar, Straus & Giroux, US, 1976) **£45**
FLY BY NIGHT by Randall Jarrell (The Bodley Head, 1977) **£35**
SOME SWELL PUP, or Are You Sure You Want a Dog? by Maurice Sendak and Matthew Margolis
  (Farrar, Straus & Giroux, 1976) **£50**
SOME SWELL PUP, or Are You Sure You Want a Dog? by Maurice Sendak and Matthew Margolis
  (The Bodley Head, 1976) **£30**

CINDERELLA (Heinemann/Gallery Five, 1977) £20
THE ART OF MAURICE SENDAK by G. Selma Lanes (The Bodley Head, 1980) £90
OUTSIDE OVER THERE by Maurice Sendak (Harper, US, 1981) £30
OUTSIDE OVER THERE by Maurice Sendak (The Bodley Head, 1981) £25
THE NUTCRACKER by E.T.A. Hoffmann (translated by Ralph Manheim) (Harper, US, 1984) £70
THE NUTCRACKER by E.T.A. Hoffman (The Bodley Head, 1984) £65
LOVE FOR THREE ORANGES (Farrar, Strauss & Giroux, US, 1984) £60
LOVE FOR THREE ORANGES (The Bodley Head, 1984) £45
THE CUNNING LITTLE VIXEN by Rudolf Tesnohlidek (Farrar, Straus & Giroux, US, 1985) £75
IN GRANDPA'S HOUSE by P. Sendak (The Bodley Head, 1986) £30
THE POSTERS (Harmony, 1987) £60
THE POSTERS (The Bodley Head, 1987) £30
DEAR MILI by Wilhelm Grimm (Michael di Capua/Farrar, Straus & Giroux, US, 1988) £35
DEAR MILI by Wilhelm Grimm (Viking Kestrel, 1988) £30
I SAW ESAU by Iona Opie (Walker, 1992) £25

SEREDY, Kate

American (originally Hungarian) author-illustrator. Born: Budapest, 1899. She drew upon her Hungarian background for several stories, notably *The Good Master* (1935). Won the Newbery Medal for *The White Stag* (1937). Died: 1975.

Prices are for books in Very Good condition with dustjackets where applicable.

Books Written and Illustrated by Kate Seredy

THE GOOD MASTER (Viking Press, US, 1935) £50
THE GOOD MASTER (Harrap, 1937) £45
LISTENING (Viking Press, US 1936) £40
THE WHITE STAG (Viking Press, US, 1937) £30
THE WHITE STAG (Harrap, 1938) £25
THE SINGING TREE (Viking Press, US, 1939) £30
THE SINGING TREE (Harrap, 1940) £30
A TREE FOR PETER (Viking Press, US, 1941) £30
THE OPEN GATE (Viking Press, US, 1943) £30

They Raced for Treasure was Ian Serraillier's second children's book. It was published by Jonathan Cape in 1946.

His 1956 book, The Silver Sword, is now valued at £50 in Very Good condition with the C. Walter Hodges dustjacket.

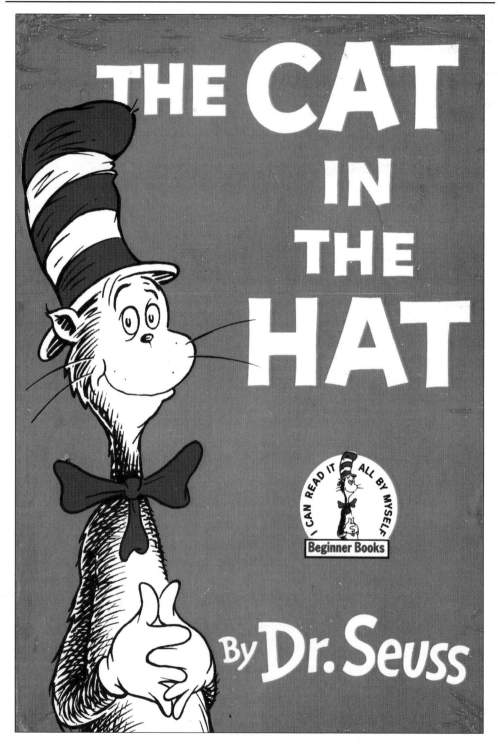

Dr. Seuss's fourteenth book **The Cat in the Hat** *(1957), remains his most famous and avidly-sought.*

THE OPEN GATE (Harrap, 1947)..£25
THE CHESTRY OAK (Viking Press, US, 1948) £45
THE CHESTRY OAK (Harrap, 1957)..£30
GYPSY (Viking Press, US, 1951) £20
GYPSY (Harrap, 1952)..£15
PHILOMENA (Viking Press, US, 1955) £30
PHILOMENA (Harrap, 1957) £20
THE TENEMENT TREE (Viking Press, US, 1959)..£20
THE TENEMENT TREE (Harrap, 1960) £15
A BRAND-NEW UNCLE (Viking Press, US, 1961) £15
LAZY TINKS (Viking Press, US, 1962)..£10
LAZY TINKS (Harrap, 1964)..£10

SERRAILLIER, Ian

British author. Born: 1912. Best known for *The Silver Sword* (1956), also several adventure stories and a verse retelling of *Beowulf* in *The Windmill Book of Ballads* (1962). Died: 1994.

Prices are for books in Very Good condition with dustjackets where applicable.

THE WEAVER BIRDS (verse; illustrated) (Macmillan, 1944)..£35
THEY RACED FOR TREASURE (illustrated by C. Walter Hodges) (Cape, 1946)................£30
FLIGHT TO ADVENTURE (illustrated by C. Walter Hodges) (Cape, 1946)........................£30
CAPTAIN BOUNDSABOARD AND THE PIRATE (illustrated by Michael Bartlett and Arline Braybrooke) (Cape, 1949)............£30
THERE'S NO ESCAPE (illustrated by C. Walter Hodges) (Cape, 1950)............................£30
JUNGLE ADVENTURE Based on a Story by R.M. Ballantyne (illustrated by Vera Jarman) (Heinemann, 1953).......................£20
THE ADVENTURES OF DICK VARLEY. Based on a Story by R.M. Ballantyne (illustrated by Vera Jarman) (Heinemann, 1955).......£20
BEOWULF THE WARRIOR (verse; illustrated by Mark Severidon) (OUP, 1954)................£20
MAKING GOOD (illustrated by Vera Jarman) (Heinemann, 1955) £25
THE SILVER SWORD (illustrated by C. Walter Hodges) (Cape, 1956).................................£50
GUNS IN THE WILD Based on a Story by R.M. Ballantyne (illustrated by Shirley Hughes) (Heinemann, 1956)..........£20
KATY AT HOME. Based on a Story by Susan Coolidge (illustrated by Shirley Hughes) (Heinemann, 1957)...........£20
KATY AT SCHOOL Based on a Story by Susan Coolidge (illustrated by Shirley Hughes) (Heinemann, 1959)...........£20
THE IVORY HORN Retold from the Song of Roland (illustrated by William Stobbs) (Oxford University Press, 1960) £15
THE GORGON'S HEAD: The Song of Perseus (illustrated by William Stobbs) (Oxford University Press, 1961) £15
THE WINDMILL BOOK OF BALLADS (illustrated by Mark Severin and Leonard Rosoman) (Heinemann, 1962)...........£20
THE WAY OF DANGER: The Story of Theseus (illustrated by William Stobbs) (Oxford University Press, 1962).......................£15
THE CLASHING ROCKS: The Story of Jason (illustrated by William Stobbs) (Oxford University Press, 1962)....................£15
THE ENCHANTED ISLAND: Stories from Shakespeare (illustrated by Peter Farmer) (Oxford University Press, 1964) £15
THE CAVE OF DEATH (illustrated by Stuart Tresilian) (Heinemann, 1965)........................£20
FIGHT FOR FREEDOM (illustrated by John S. Goodall) (Heinemann, 1965) £20
A FALL FROM THE SKY: The Story of Daedalus (illustrated by William Stobbs) (Nelson, 1966)................£15
CHAUCER AND HIS WORLD (Lutterworth Press, 1967)...£15
HAVELOK THE WARRIOR (illustrated by Elaine Raphael) (Hamish Hamilton, 1968).........£15
ROBIN HOOD AND HIS MERRY MEN (illustrated by Victor Ambrus) (OUP, 1969)............£20
THE TALE OF THREE LANDLUBBERS (illustrated by Raymond Briggs) (Hamish Hamilton, 1970)..................£20
HERACLES THE STRONG (illustrated by Rocco Negri) (Hamish Hamilton, 1971)..............£15

SEUSS, Dr

American author-illustrator. Born: Theodor Seuss Geisel in Springfield, Massachusetts, in 1904. Studied at Dartmouth College and Lincoln College, Oxford, subsequently working as a freelance cartoonist and film animator. Produced many popular picture books, of which the best known is *The Cat in the Hat* (1957). Received a doctorate from Dartmouth College in 1955. Died: 1991.

Prices are for books in Very Good condition with dustjackets.

AND TO THINK THAT I SAW IT ON MULBERRY STREET (Vanguard Press, US, 1937)........................£100
AND TO THINK THAT I SAW IT ON MULBERRY STREET (Country Life, 1939) £100
THE 500 HATS OF BARTHOLOMEW CUBBINS (Vanguard Press, US, 1938) £150
THE 500 HATS OF BARTHOLOMEW CUBBINS (OUP, [1940])...£100
THE SEVEN LADY GODIVAS (Random House, US, 1939)..£250
THE KING'S STILTS (Random House, US, 1939)..£200
THE KING'S STILTS (Hamish Hamilton, 1942)...£100
HORTON HATCHES THE EGG (Random House, US, 1940)...£200
HORTON HATCHES THE EGG (Hamish Hamilton, 1942) £100
HORTON HATCHES THE EGG (reissue) (Collins, 1962)...£60
McELLIGOT'S POOL (Random House, US, 1947) £150
McELLIGOT'S POOL (Collins, 1975)..£40
THIDWICK THE BIG-HEARTED MOOSE (Random House, US, 1948).............................£150
THIDWICK THE BIG-HEARTED MOOSE (Collins, 1968) £40
BARTHOLOMEW AND THE OOBLECK (Random House, US, 1949) £150
IF I RAN THE ZOO (Random House, US, 1950) £150

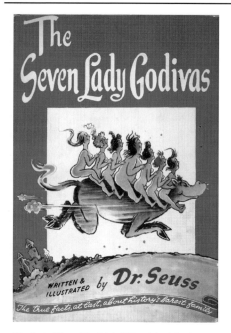

The first edition of the third children's book by the 'Grinch' creator was only ever published in America.

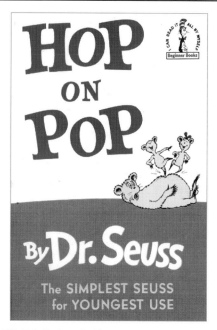

This 1963 'Beginner Book' Hop on Pop features his typically bold cover artowrk. Today it is worth around £100.

SCRAMBLED EGGS SUPER! (Random House, US, 1953)	£150
HORTON HEARS A WHO! (Random House, US, 1954)	£150
HORTON HEARS A WHO! (Collins, 1976)	£30
ON BEYOND ZEBRA (Random House, US, 1955)	£150
IF I RAN THE CIRCUS (Random House, US, 1956)	£150
IF I RAN THE CIRCUS (Collins, 1969)	£60
THE CAT IN THE HAT (Random House, US, 1957)	£1,000
THE CAT IN THE HAT (Hutchinson, 1958)	£200
THE CAT IN THE HAT (Collins, 1961)	£100
HOW THE GRINCH STOLE CHRISTMAS (Random House, US, 1957)	£300
HOW THE GRINCH STOLE CHRISTMAS (Collins, 1973)	£75
THE CAT IN THE HAT COMES BACK (Random House, US, 1958)	£300
THE CAT IN THE HAT COMES BACK (Collins, 1961)	£75
YERTLE THE TURTLE (Random House, US, 1958)	£150
YERTLE THE TURTLE (Collins, 1963)	£50
HAPPY BIRTHDAY TO YOU! (Random House, US, 1959)	£150
ONE FISH, TWO FISH, RED FISH, BLUE FISH (Random House, US, 1960)	£150
ONE FISH, TWO FISH, RED FISH, BLUE FISH (Collins, 1960)	£75
GREEN EGGS AND HAM (Random House, US, 1960)	£150
GREEN EGGS AND HAM (Collins, 1962)	£60
THE SNEETCHES and WHAT WAS I SCARED OF? (Random House, US, 1961)	£150
THE SNEETCHES and WHAT WAS I SCARED OF? (Collins, 1965)	£40
SLEEP BOOK (Random House, US, 1962)	£100
SLEEP BOOK (Collins, 1964)	£40
HOP ON POP (Random House, US, 1963)	£100
HOP ON POP (Collins, 1964)	£40
DR SEUSS ABC (Random House, US, 1963)	£100
DR SEUSS ABC (Collins, 1964)	£40
THE CAT IN THE HAT DICTIONARY, BY THE CAT HIMSELF (with Philip D. Eastman) (Random House, US, 1964)	£100
FOX IN SOCKS (Random House, US, 1965)	£100
FOX IN SOCKS (Collins, 1966)	£50
I HAD TROUBLE IN GETTING TO SOLLA SOLLEW (Random House, US, 1965)	£150
I HAD TROUBLE IN GETTING TO SOLLA SOLLEW (Collins, 1967)	£100
THE CAT IN THE HAT SONGBOOK (Random House, US, 1967)	£100
THE CAT IN THE HAT STORYBOOK (Collins, 1968)	£60

THE FOOT BOOK (Random House, US, 1968)..**£75**
THE FOOT BOOK (Collins, 1969)..**£50**
MY BOOK ABOUT ME (with Roy McKie) (Random House, US, 1969).................................**£60**
MY BOOK ABOUT ME (with Roy McKie) (Collins, 1973)...**£30**
I CAN LICK 30 TIGERS TODAY (Random House, US, 1969)..**£75**
I CAN LICK 30 TIGERS TODAY (Collins, 1970)..**£50**
I CAN DRAW IT MYSELF (Random House, US, 1970)...**£75**
MR BROWN CAN MOO, CAN YOU? (Random House, US, 1970)......................................**£60**
MR BROWN CAN MOO, CAN YOU? (Collins, 1971)..**£40**
THE LORAX (Random House, US, 1971)..**£75**
THE LORAX (Collins, 1972)...**£40**
MARVIN K. MOONEY WILL YOU PLEASE GO NOW? (Random House, US, 1972).........**£30**
MARVIN K. MOONEY WILL YOU PLEASE GO NOW? (Collins, 1973).............................**£20**
DID I EVER TELL YOU HOW LUCKY YOU ARE? (Random House, US, 1973)................**£40**
DID I EVER TELL YOU HOW LUCKY YOU ARE? (Collins, 1974)...................................**£30**
THE SHAPE OF ME AND OTHER STUFF (Random House, US, 1973).............................**£25**
THE SHAPE OF ME AND OTHER STUFF (Collins, 1974)...**£15**
THERE'S A WOCKET IN MY POCKET! (Random House, US, 1974)................................**£30**
THERE'S A WOCKET IN MY POCKET! (Collins, 1975)..**£20**
DR SEUSS STORYTIME (four volumes) (Random House, US, 1974).................the set **£60**
DR SEUSS STORYTIME (four volumes) (Collins, 1979)...................................the set **£30**
A GREAT DAY FOR UP! (illustrated by Quentin Blake) (Random House, US, 1974)........**£25**
A GREAT DAY FOR UP! (illustrated by Quentin Blake) (Collins, 1975)............................**£15**
OH, THE THINKS YOU CAN THINK (Random House, US, 1975)......................................**£30**
OH, THE THINKS YOU CAN THINK (Collins, 1976)..**£25**
THE CAT'S QUIZZER (Random House, US, 1976)..**£40**
THE CAT'S QUIZZER (Collins, 1977)..**£40**
I CAN READ WITH MY EYES SHUT! (Random House, US, 1978)...................................**£30**
I CAN READ WITH MY EYES SHUT! (Collins, 1979)...**£30**
OH SAY CAN YOU SAY? (Random House, US, 1979)..**£30**
OH SAY CAN YOU SAY? (Collins, 1980)..**£20**
HUNCHES IN BUNCHES (Random House, US, 1982)...**£40**
HUNCHES IN BUNCHES (Collins, 1982)..**£40**
THE BUTTER BATTLE BOOK (Random House, US, 1984)...**£60**
THE BUTTER BATTLE BOOK (Collins, 1984)...**£40**
BEGINNER BOOK DICTIONARY (Random House, US, 1986)..**£30**
BEGINNER BOOK DICTIONARY (Collins, 1987)..**£20**
I'M NOT GOING TO GET UP TODAY (Random House, US, 1987).....................................**£30**
I'M NOT GOING TO GET UP TODAY (Collins, 1988)...**£20**
OH, THE PLACES YOU'LL GO (Random House, US, 1990)..**£30**
OH, THE PLACES YOU'LL GO (Collins, 1990)..**£20**
DAISY-HEAD MAYZIE (Random House, US, 1995)..**£20**
DAISY-HEAD MAYZIE (Collins, 1999)..**£15**

Books Written as 'Theo Le Sieg'

TEN APPLES UP ON TOP (illustrated by Roy McKie) (Random House, US, 1961)............**£25**
TEN APPLES UP ON TOP (illustrated by Roy McKie) (Collins, 1963)..............................**£15**
I WISH THAT I HAD DUCK FEET (illustrated by B. Tobey) (Random House, US, 1965)....**£25**
I WISH THAT I HAD DUCK FEET (illustrated by B. Tobey) (Collins, 1967)......................**£15**
COME OVER TO MY HOUSE (illustrated by Richard Erdoes) (Random House, US, 1966)...**£25**
COME OVER TO MY HOUSE (illustrated by Richard Erdoes) (Collins, 1967)..................**£15**
THE EYE BOOK (illustrated by Roy McKie) (Random House, US, 1968)...........................**£25**
THE EYE BOOK (illustrated by Roy McKie) (Collins, 1969)..**£15**
IN A PEOPLE HOUSE (illustrated by Roy McKie) (Random House, US, 1972)..................**£20**
IN A PEOPLE HOUSE (illustrated by Roy McKie) (Collins, 1973)....................................**£10**
THE MANY MICE OF MR BRICE (illustrated by Roy McKie) (Random House, US, 1973)..**£20**
THE MANY MICE OF MR BRICE (illustrated by Roy McKie) (Collins, 1974).....................**£10**
WACKY WEDNESDAY (illustrated by George Booth) (Random House, US, 1974)............**£15**
WACKY WEDNESDAY (illustrated by George Booth) (Collins, 1975)..............................**£10**
WOULD YOU RATHER BE A BULLFROG? (illustrated by Roy McKie) (Random House, US, 1975)....**£15**
WOULD YOU RATHER BE A BULLFROG? (illustrated by Roy McKie) (Collins, 1976).......**£10**
HOOPER HUMPERDINK — ? NOT HIM! (illustrated by Charles E. Martin) (Random House, US 1976)....**£15**
HOOPER HUMPERDINK — ? NOT HIM! (illustrated by Charles E. Martin) (Collins, 1977)....**£10**
PLEASE TRY TO REMEMBER THE FIRST OF OCTEMBER (illustrated by Art Cunnings) (Random House, US, 1977)....**£20**
PLEASE TRY TO REMEMBER THE FIRST OF OCTEMBER (illustrated by Art Cunnings) (Collins, 1978)....**£10**
MAYBE YOU SHOULD FLY A JET! MAYBE YOU SHOULD BE A VET! (illustrated by Michael J. Smollin)
    (Random House, US, 1980)..**£20**
MAYBE YOU SHOULD BE A VET! (Collins, 1981)...**£10**
THE TOOTH BOOK (illustrated by Roy McKie) (Random House, US, 1981)......................**£20**
THE TOOTH BOOK (illustrated by Roy McKie) (Collins, 1982)..**£10**

The pictorial gilt cloth covers of the first British edition of Anna Sewell's influential children's novel.

*This later edition of **Black Beauty** features colour plates and a dustjacket designed by Cecil Aldin (1912).*

SEWELL, Anna

British author. Born: Great Yarmouth, Norfolk, in 1820, the daughter of the writer, Mary Sewell. Studied at a Quaker school until the age of fifteen, when she became a semi-invalid following a fall. Her only novel, *Black Beauty* (1877), was written to encourage the better treatment of horses and was published only five months before her death in 1878.

Prices are for books in Very Good condition.

BLACK BEAUTY: His Grooms and Companions. The Autobiography of a Horse.
Translated from the original equine by Anna Sewell (Jarrold, 1877) £12,000
BLACK BEAUTY (illustrated by John Beer) (Jarrold, 1894)..£100
BLACK BEAUTY (illustrated by Maude Scrivener and others) (Jarrold, [1909])..£60
BLACK BEAUTY (illustrated by Cecil Aldin) (Jarrold, [1912])..£125
BLACK BEAUTY (illustrated by Lucy Kemp-Welch) (Dent, 1915)..£100
BLACK BEAUTY (illustrated by Lucy Kemp-Welch; limited to 600 copies, signed by the artist) (Dent, 1915).........................£550
BLACK BEAUTY (illustrated by Alice B. Woodward) (Bell, 1931) £60
BLACK BEAUTY (illustrated by Rowland Wheelwright) (Harrap, 1932)..£50
BLACK BEAUTY (illustrated by Lionel Edwards) (Lunn, 1946)..£50

SHAW, Jane

Scottish author. Born: Jean Bell Shaw Patrick in Glasgow in 1910. Studied at Park School, Glasgow, Glasgow University and the Maria Grey Training College, London. Worked for the Times Book Club and the publishers, Collins, before publishing her first two children's works, *My Own Book of Baby Beasts* and *My Own Book of Other Lands*, in 1938 under the name 'Jean Patrick'. *Breton Holiday*, her first book to appear under the pseudonym 'Jane Shaw', followed a year later. Her best-known works are the eleven novels featuring the schoolgirl, Susan Lyle, beginning with *Susan Pulls the Strings* (1952). She also contributed short stories to several Collins annuals during the 1940s. Lived in South Africa for many years, working in the Children's Bookshop in Johannesburg.

Prices are for books in Very Good condition with dustjackets.

MY OWN BOOK OF BABY BEASTS (written under the name 'Jean Patrick') (Collins, 1938)..£8
MY OWN BOOK OF OTHER LANDS (written under the name 'Jean Patrick') (Collins, 1938)..£8
BRETON HOLIDAY (reissued as 'Breton Adventure') (Collins, 1939) £15
BERMESE HOLIDAY (reissued as 'Bermese Adventure') (Collins, 1940)..£15

HIGHLAND HOLIDAY (Collins, 1942) £15
MAGIC SHIPS (Collins, 1943) £15
THE HOUSE OF THE GLIMMERING LIGHT (Collins, 1943) £15
THE CREW OF THE BELINDA (Collins, 1945) £15
THE MOOCHERS (Lutterworth Press, 1950) £15
THE MOOCHERS ABROAD (Lutterworth Press, 1951) £15
MOOCHERS AND PREFECTS (Lutterworth Press, 1951) £15
SUSAN PULLS THE STRINGS (Collins, 1952) £10
FARM FRIENDS (Collins, 1953) £8
PUPPY TALES (Collins, 1953) £8
PENNY FOOLISH (Nelson, 1953) £10
TWOPENCE COLOURED (Nelson, 1954) £10
SUSAN'S HELPING HAND (Collins, 1955) £10
THREEPENNY BIT (Nelson, 1955) £10
FOURPENNY FAIR (Nelson, 1956) £12
SUSAN RUSHES IN (Collins, 1956) £10
LOOKING AFTER THOMAS (Nelson, 1957) £5
SUSAN INTERFERES (Collins, 1957) £10
FIVEPENNY MYSTERY (Nelson, 1958) £12
CROOKED SIXPENCE (Nelson, 1958) £12
SUSAN AT SCHOOL (Collins, 1958) £10
WILLOW GREEN MYSTERY (Nelson, 1958) £6
UNCLE REMUS STORIES (Retold) (Collins, 1960) £10
SUSAN MUDDLES THROUGH (Collins, 1960) £12
THE TALL MAN (Nelson, 1960) £6
VENTURE TO SOUTH AFRICA (Nelson, 1960) £15
HEIDI GROWS UP (Retold) (Collins, 1961) £10
NEW HOUSE AT NORTHMEAD (Nelson, 1961) £15
SUSAN'S TRYING TERM (Collins, 1961) £12
NO TROUBLE FOR SUSAN (Collins, 1962) £15
LEFT-HANDED TUMFY (Lutterworth Press, 1962) £7
CROOKS TOUR (Collins, 1962) £7
NORTHMEAD NUISANCE (Nelson, 1963) £15
ANYTHING CAN HAPPEN (Nelson, 1964) £15
NOTHING HAPPENED AFTER ALL (Nelson, 1965) £15
SUSAN'S KIND HEART (Collins, 1965) £15
PADDY TURNS DETECTIVE (written under the pseudonym 'Jean Bell'; paperback) (Collins: 'Spitfire' series, 1967) £3
THE PENHALLOW MYSTERY (written under the pseudonym 'Jean Bell'; paperback) (Collins: 'Spitfire' series, 1967) £3
WHERE IS SUSAN? (Collins, 1968) £15
A JOB FOR SUSAN (Collins, 1969) £15
BRER RABBIT AND BRER FOX (Collins, 1969) £10

SHEPARD, E.H.

British illustrator. Born: Ernest Howard Shepard in London in 1879. Studied at St. Paul's School, Heatherley's and the Royal Academy Schools. By 1914, he was a regular contributor to *Punch*, which led to a commission to illustrate A.A. Milne's *When We Were Very Young* (1924), and later his 'Winnie-the-Pooh' books. Subsequently illustrated such children's classics as *Bevis* (1932) and Hans Andersen's fairy tales (1961), but his masterpiece is undoubtedly his edition of Kenneth Grahame's *The Wind in the Willows* (1931). Died: 1976.

Prices are for books in Very Good condition with dustjackets where applicable.

Books by A.A. Milne Illustrated by E.H. Shepard

WHEN WE WERE VERY YOUNG (verse) (Methuen, 1924) £5,000
WHEN WE WERE VERY YOUNG (limited to 100 numbered copies, signed by the author and artist)
  (Methuen, 1924) £6,000
WHEN WE WERE VERY YOUNG (limited to 300 numbered copies, signed by Christopher Milne)
  (Methuen, 1974) £500
VESPERS: A Poem (verse; music by H. Fraser-Simson) (Methuen, [1924]) £150
THE KING'S BREAKFAST (music by H. Fraser-Simson) (Methuen, 1925) £200
WINNIE-THE-POOH (stories) (Methuen, 1926) £2,500
WINNIE-THE-POOH (limited to 350 copies, signed by the author and artist) (Methuen, 1926) £5,000
WINNIE-THE-POOH (De Luxe edition: red, green or blue leather binding; in slipcase) (Methuen, 1926) £3,000
WINNIE-THE-POOH (illustrated in colour by E.H. Shepard) (Methuen, 1973) £80
WINNIE-THE-POOH (limited to 300 numbered copies, signed by Christopher Milne) (Methuen, 1976) £600
NOW WE ARE SIX (verse) (Methuen, 1927) £850
NOW WE ARE SIX (limited to 200 numbered copies, signed by the author and artist) (Methuen, 1927) £2,000
NOW WE ARE SIX (De Luxe edition: red, blue or green leather binding; in slipcase) (Methuen, 1927) £1,750
NOW WE ARE SIX (limited to 300 numbered copies, signed by Christopher Milne) (Methuen, 1976) £500
THE HOUSE AT POOH CORNER (stories) (Methuen, 1928) £1,250

This E.H. Shepard illustration was used on both the jacket and front board of the 1928 edition of Kenneth Grahame's **The Golden Age***.*

THE HOUSE AT POOH CORNER (limited to 350 numbered copies, signed by the author and artist)
(Methuen, 1928) **£4,000**
THE HOUSE AT POOH CORNER (De Luxe edition: red, green or blue leather binding; in slipcase)
(Methuen, 1928) **£2,500**
THE HOUSE AT POOH CORNER (illustrated in colour by E.H. Shepard) (Methuen, 1974) **£60**
THE CHRISTOPHER ROBIN CALENDAR (verses) (Methuen, [1928]) **£75**
THE CHRISTOPHER ROBIN STORY BOOK (selections from 'When We Were Very Young',
'Now We Are Six', 'Winnie-the-Pooh' and 'The House at Pooh Corner'; new preface by the author)
(Methuen, 1929) **£400**
THE HUMS OF POOH (music by H. Fraser-Simson) (Methuen, 1929) **£200**
TALES OF POOH (selections from 'Winnie-the-Pooh' and 'The House at Pooh Corner'; 87 illustrations by E.H. Shepard)
(Methuen, [1930]) **£200**
THE CHRISTOPHER ROBIN BIRTHDAY BOOK (selections from 'When We Were Very Young',
'Now We Are Six', 'Winnie-the-Pooh' and 'The House at Pooh Corner') (Methuen, 1930) **£150**
THE CHRISTOPHER ROBIN VERSES (contains 'When We Were Very Young' and 'Now We Are Six';
twelve plates and text decorations by E.H. Shepard) (Methuen, 1932) **£250**
WINNIE-THE-POOH AND EEYORE'S TAIL: A Pop-Up Picture Book (adapted by A. Schenk from the
original illustrations by E.H. Shepard) (Methuen, [1953]) **£75**
WINNIE-THE-POOH AND THE BEES: A Pop-Up Picture Book (adapted by A. Schenk from the
original illustrations by E.H. Shepard) (Methuen, [1953]) **£75**
THE WORLD OF POOH (contains 'Winnie-the-Pooh' and 'The House at Pooh Corner';
eight new colour plates by E.H. Shepard) (Methuen, 1958) **£100**
THE WORLD OF CHRISTOPHER ROBIN (contains 'When We Were Very Young' and 'Now We Are Six';
eight new colour plates by E.H. Shepard) (Methuen, 1959) **£100**
THE POOH STORY BOOK (new illustrations and colour plates by E.H. Shepard) (Methuen, 1967) **£60**
THE CHRISTOPHER ROBIN VERSE BOOK (illustrated in colour by E.H. Shepard) (Methuen, 1969) **£60**
THE POOH COOK BOOK by Katie Stewart (Methuen, 1971) **£25**
THE HUMS OF POOH: Lyrics by Pooh, Additional Lyrics by Eeyore (Methuen, [1972]) **£40**
THE POOH SKETCH BOOK (Methuen, 1982) **£20**

Books by Kenneth Grahame Illustrated by E.H. Shepard

THE GOLDEN AGE (The Bodley Head, 1928) **£150**
THE GOLDEN AGE (limited to 275 copies, signed by the author and artist; in slipcase) (The Bodley Head, 1928) **£600**

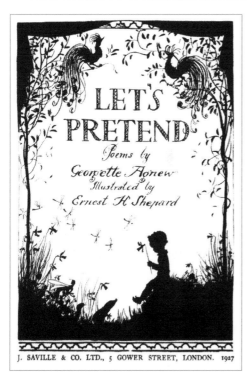

*Ernest H. Shepard's jacket design for an edition of
poems by Georgette Agnew, issued by Saville in 1927.*

*The beautiful title illustration from the 1930 Kenneth
Grahame-E.H. Shepard collaboration **Dream Days**.*

THE GOLDEN AGE (The Bodley Head, 1973) £25
DREAM DAYS (The Bodley Head, 1930)..£150
DREAM DAYS (The Bodley Head, 1973)..£25
DREAM DAYS (limited to 275 copies, signed by the author and artist; in slipcase) (The Bodley Head, 1930) £600
THE WIND IN THE WILLOWS (first Shepard edition [38th edition]) (Methuen, 1931).......................................£600
THE WIND IN THE WILLOWS (illustrated by E.H. Shepard; limited to 200 copies, signed by the author and artist)
(Methuen, 1931)..£4,000
THE WIND IN THE WILLOWS (colour plates by E.H. Shepard) (Methuen, 1959)...£125
THE WIND IN THE WILLOWS (first full-colour Shepard edition [105th]) (Methuen, 1971)...............................£60
BERTIE'S ESCAPADE (reprinted from 'First Whisper of "The Wind in the Willows"') (Methuen, 1949)................£60

Books by Malcolm Saville Illustrated by E.H. Shepard
SUSAN, BILL AND THE WOLF-DOG (Nelson, 1954) £40
SUSAN, BILL AND THE IVY-CLAD OAK (Nelson, 1954) £40
SUSAN, BILL AND THE VANISHING BOY (Nelson, 1955) £35
SUSAN, BILL AND THE GOLDEN CLOCK (Nelson, 1955) £35
SUSAN, BILL AND THE DARK STRANGER (Nelson, 1956) £35
SUSAN, BILL AND THE 'SAUCY KATE' (Nelson, [1956]) £35

Other Books Illustrated by E.H. Shepard
TOM BROWN'S SCHOOLDAYS by Thomas Hughes (Methuen, [1904])...£100
PLAYTIME AND COMPANY by E.V. Lucas (Methuen, 1925)...£100
THE HOLLY TREE and Other Christmas Stories by Charles Dickens (Partridge, [1926])..............................£50
LET'S PRETEND by Georgette Agnew (Saville, 1927)..£50
THE LITTLE ONE'S LOG by Eva Violet Isaacs, Marchioness of Reading (Partridge, 1927).............................£40
CHRISTMAS POEMS by John Drinkwater (Sidgwick & Jackson, 1931) £25
BEVIS by Richard Jefferies (Cape, 1932)..£60
THE SEVENTH DAUGHTER by Barbara Euphan Todd (Burns Oates, 1935)...£50
THE MODERN STRUWWELPETER by Jan Struther (Methuen, 1936)...£200
THE ISLANDERS by Roland Pertwee (Methuen, 1950)..£40
THE SILVER CURLEW: A Fairy Tale by Eleanor Farjeon (OUP, 1953)...£35
THE BROWNIES and Other Stories by J.H. Ewing (Dent: 'Children's Illustrated Classics' series, 1954)...............£50
THE CUCKOO CLOCK by Mrs Molesworth (Dent: 'Children's Illustrated Classics' series, 1954) £30
THE GLASS SLIPPER by Eleanor Farjeon (OUP, 1955)...£30
FROGMORTON by Susan Colling (Collins, 1955)..£30
MODERN FAIRY STORIES. Chosen and Introduced by Roger Lancelyn Green
(Dent: 'Children's Illustrated Classics' series, 1955)..£25
AT THE BACK OF THE NORTH WIND by George MacDonald (Dent: 'Children's Illustrated Classics' series, 1956) £60
THE SECRET GARDEN by Frances Hodgson Burnett (1956) £40
THE PANCAKE Edited by J.H. Fassett (Ginn, 1957)...£30
BRIAR ROSE Edited by J.H. Fassett (Ginn, 1958) £30
OLD GREEK FAIRY TALES by Roger Lancelyn Green (Bell, [1958])...£25
HANS ANDERSEN'S FAIRY TALES by Hans Christian Andersen (translated by L.W. Kingland) (OUP, 1961) £30
A NOBLE COMPANY Edited by J. Compton (1961)...£25
THE FLATTERED FLYING FISH and Other Poems by E.V. Rieu (Methuen, 1962) £25

Books Written & Illustrated by E.H. Shepard
FUN AND FANTASY: A Book of Drawings (Methuen, 1927)...£65
DRAWN FROM MEMORY: On the Author's Childhood (Methuen, 1957) £65
DRAWN FROM LIFE: On the Author's Childhood (sequel to the above) (Methuen, 1961)...............................£45
BEN AND BROCK (Methuen, 1965)..£30
BETSY AND JOE (Methuen, 1966) £25

SIMMONDS, Posy

British author & illustrator. Born: Berkshire, 1945. Rosemary Elizabeth 'Posy' Simmonds is a British newspaper cartoonist, writer and illustrator of children's books. She is best known for her long association with The Guardian, for which she draws the cartoon titled 'Tamara Drewe'.

Prices are for books in Fine condition, issued in laminated pictorial boards and without dustjackets unless otherwise stated.

Written & illustrated by Posy Simmonds
FRED (Jonathan Cape, 1987)..£15
LULU AND THE FLYING BABIES (Jonathan Cape, 1988) £10
LULU AND THE CHOCOLATE WEDDING (paperback) (Jonathan Cape, 1990) £7
BOUNCING BUFFALO (Jonathan Cape, 1994)..£12
F-FREEZING ABC (Jonathan Cape, 1995) £8
LAVENDER (Jonathan Cape, 2003)..£12
BAKER CAT (Jonathan Cape, 2004) £15

Illustrated by Posy Simmonds
RABBITING ON AND OTHER POEMS by Kit Wright (paperback) (Fontana, 1978)...£12
THE CAPTAIN HOOK AFFAIR by Humphrey Carpenter (issued with dust jacket) (Allen & Unwin, 1979)...................£10

HOT DOG AND OTHER POEMS by Kit Wright (paperback) (Kestrel, 1981) £8
THE YOUNG VISITERS by Daisy Ashford (issued with dust jacket) (Chatto & Windus, 1984)........................£10
CAT AMONG THE PIGEONS by Kit Wright (Viking, 1987)...£6
MATILDA WHO TOLD LIES, AND WAS BURNED TO DEATH by Hilaire Belloc (issued with dust jacket)
(Jonathan Cape, 1991) £15
GREAT SNAKES by Kit Wright (Viking, 1994) £12
CAUTIONARY TALES AND OTHER VERSES by Hilaire Belloc (Folio Society, 1997).................................£10
ONE DOG AND HIS MAN by Trevor Grove (paperback) (Atlantic Books, 2003) £5

SMITH, Dodie

British author. Born: Dorothy Gladys Smith in Lancashire in 1896. Best known for her 1956 children's classic, *The One Hundred and One Dalmatians*, brilliantly filmed by Disney in 1960. She also wrote a number of adult plays and the novel, *I Capture the Castle* (1952). Died: 1990.

Prices are for books in Very Good condition with dustjackets.

I CAPTURE THE CASTLE (Heinemann, 1949) £60
THE ONE HUNDRED AND ONE DALMATIANS (Heinemann, 1956)...£85
THE STARLIGHT BARKING: More About the Hundred and One Dalmatians
(illustrated by Janet and Anne Grahame-Johnstone) (Heinemann, 1967)...£45
THE MIDNIGHT KITTENS (W.H. Allen, 1978)..£30

SMITH, Jessie Willcox

American illustrator. Born: Philadelphia, 1863. Studied with Howard Pyle at the Philadelphia Fine Art Institute, subsequently specialising in children's books. Died: 1935.

Prices are for books in Very Good condition.

Written & illustrated by Jessie Willcox Smith

BOTH SIDES (Nisbet, 1887)..£100
STEPHEN GILMORE'S DREAM, or Coals of Fire (Nisbet, 1887) £75
DICKENS' CHILDREN: A Calendar of 1912 (Scribners, US, [1911]) £100

Illustrated by Jessie Willcox Smith

EVANGELINE by H.W. Longfellow (illustrated by Jessie Willcox Smith and V. Oakley)
(Houghton Mifflin, US, 1897) £100
AN OLD FASHIONED GIRL by Louisa May Alcott (Little Brown, US, 1902)..£40
THE BOOK OF THE CHILD by Mabel Humphrey (Stokes, US, 1903)...£400
RHYMES OF REAL CHILDREN by Elizabeth Sage Goodwin (Duffield, US, 1903)...............................£150
IN THE CLOSED ROOM by Frances Hodgson Burnett (McClure Philips, US, 1904) £100
A CHILD'S GARDEN OF VERSES by R.L. Stevenson (Scribners, US, 1905) £150
DREAM BLOCKS by Aileen C. Higgins (Duffield, US, 1908)..£85
THE SEVEN AGES OF CHILDHOOD by Carolyn Wells (Moffat Yard, US, 1909)................................£100
A CHILD'S BOOK OF OLD VERSES (Duffield, US, 1910) £150
A CHILD'S BOOK OF STORIES. Complied by Penrhyn Wingfield Coussens (Duffield, US, 1911) £100
THE NOW-A-DAYS FAIRY BOOK by Anna A. Chapin (Dodd Mead, US, 1911) £75
'TWAS THE NIGHT BEFORE CHRISTMAS by Clement Moore (Houghton Mifflin, US, 1912)..................£100
LITTLE WOMEN by Louisa M. Alcott (Little Brown, US, 1915)..£50
A CHILD'S STAMP BOOK OF OLD VERSES (Duffield, US, 1915)..£100
WHEN CHRISTMAS COMES AROUND by Priscilla Underwood (Duffield, US, 1915) £100
THE EVERYDAY FAIRY BOOK by Anna A. Chapin (Dodd Mead, US, 1915) £75
THE LITTLE MOTHER GOOSE (selected and adapted by Samuel McChord Crothers)
(Dodd Mead, US, [1915]) £70
THE WATER BABIES by Charles Kingsley (Dodd Mead, US, 1916) £150
THE WATER BABIES by Charles Kingsley (Hodder & Stoughton, [1916]) £150
THE WATER BABIES by Charles Kingsley (Hodder & Stoughton/Boots the Chemist, [c.1930])................£75
THE WATER BABIES by Charles Kingsley (facsimile of the original 1916 edition;
limited to 500 numbered copies; in slipcase) (Hodder & Stoughton, 1981).....................................£95
THE WAY TO WONDERLAND by Mary Stewart Sheldon (Dodd Mead, US, 1917)...............................£100
AT THE BACK OF THE NORTH WIND by George MacDonald (David McKay, US, 1920) £250
A CHILD'S BOOK OF MODERN STORIES Edited by Ada and Eleanor Skinner (anthology)
(Duffield, US, 1920)...£60
THE PRINCESS AND THE GOBLIN by George MacDonald (David McKay, US, 1921)..........................£200
A LITTLE CHILD'S BOOK OF STORIES. Edited by Ada and Eleanor Skinner (anthology)
(Duffield, US, 1922)...£55
HEIDI by Johanna Spyri (David McKay, US, 1922) £250
A VERY LITTLE CHILD'S BOOK OF STORIES. Edited by Ada and Eleanor Skinner (anthology)
(Duffield, US, 1923)...£55
A CHILD'S PRAYER by Cora Cassard Toogood (David McKay, US, 1925).......................................£55
THE CHILDREN OF DICKENS. Compiled by S. McChord Crothers (Scribners, US, 1925).....................£55
A CHILD'S BOOK OF COUNTRY STORIES. Edited by Ada and Eleanor Skinner (anthology)
(Duffield, US, 1925)...£55

SNICKET, Lemony

Pseudonym of American author Daniel Handler. Born: 1970. His phenomenally successful thirteen-volume 'A Series of Unfortunate Events' books have all been bestsellers and inspired one big budget Hollywood adaptation to date. Figures from Nielsen BookScan revealed that Handler was responsible for no fewer than six of the twenty bestselling children's hardbacks in 2006.

Prices are for books in Near Mint condition.

A Series of Unfortunate Events (with illustrated) *All illustrated by Brett Helquist*

THE BAD BEGINNING (Harper Collins, US, 1999) (wraparound)..£300
THE BAD BEGINNING (Advance reading copy. Bound with THE REPTILE ROOM. Paperback) (HarperCollins, US, 1999) £300
THE BAD BEGINNING (Egmont, UK, 2001) (wraparound) £75
THE BAD BEGINNING (Egmont, UK, 2003) 'Collector's Edition'. Larger size hardback £15
THE BAD BEGINNING ('Limited Edition'. Deluxe, leather bound, slip-cased, individually signed. 2,000 copies)
(Egmont, UK, 2003) £100
THE BAD BEGINNING ('Special edition'. Includes printed picture of the 'Marvellous Marriage' in paper frame. Slipcase)
(HarperCollins, US, 2003) £40
THE REPTILE ROOM (Harper Collins, US, 1999) £100
THE REPTILE ROOM (Egmont, UK, 2001)..£30
THE WIDE WINDOW (Harper Collins, US, 2000) £75
THE WIDE WINDOW (Egmont, UK, 2001)..£20
THE MISERABLE MILL (Harper Collins, US, 2000)..£60
THE MISERABLE MILL (Egmont, UK, 2002) £15
THE AUSTERE ACADEMY (Harper Collins, US, 2000) (wraparound)..£30
THE AUSTERE ACADEMY (Advance Reading Copy, paperback) (Harper Collins, US, 2000) £30
THE AUSTERE ACADEMY (wraparound) (Egmont, UK, 2002) £25
THE ERSATZ ELEVATOR (first state price: $8.95) (Harper Collins, US, 2001) £25
THE ERSATZ ELEVATOR (wraparound) (Egmont, UK, 2002) £15
THE VILE VILLAGE (first state price: $9.95) (Harper Collins, US, 2001)..£15
THE VILE VILLAGE (wraparound) (Egmont, UK, 2002)..£10
THE HOSTILE HOSPITAL (first state price: $9.95) (Harper Collins, US, 2001)..£10
THE HOSTILE HOSPITAL (wraparound) (Egmont, UK, 2001)...£10
THE HOSTILE HOSPITAL (Exclusive Waterstones edition. Reversable dustjacket: on reverse spoof book:
'The Luckiest Kids in the World, Book 1 – The Pony Party') (Egmont, UK, 2001) £20
THE CARNIVOROUS CARNIVAL (first state price: $10.90) (Harper Collins, US, 2002) £10
THE CARNIVOROUS CARNIVAL (Egmont, UK, 2003) £6

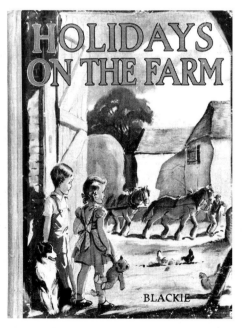

This 1944 Blackie volume is illustrated by Eileen Soper, best known for her illustrations for the 'Famous Five' series.

*Soper's 1947 edition of **Alice in Wonderland** is now valued at £40 in Very Good condition with the dustjacket.*

THE SLIPPERY SLOPE (Harper Collins, US, 2003) £10
THE SLIPPERY SLOPE (Egmont, UK, 2004) £6
THE GRIM GROTTO (Harper Collins, US, 2004) £10
THE GRIM GROTTO (Egmont, UK, 2004) £10
THE PENULTIMATE PERIL (Harper Collins, US, 2005) ....new £6.99
THE PENULTIMATE PERIL (Egmont, UK, 2005) ....new £6.99
THE END (Harper Collins, US, 2006) ....new £6.99
THE END (Egmont, UK, 2006) ....new £6.99

Omnibus/boxed editions

A BOX OF UNFORTUNATE EVENTS (omnibus, includes books 1 to 4)
(Harper Collins, US, 2001) £30
A BOX OF UNFORTUNATE EVENTS (Egmont, UK, 2002) £30
A SERIES OF UNFORTUNATE EVENTS
(W.H. Smith Omnibus edition, including books 1-3) (Egmont, UK, 2001) (wraparound) £20
A SERIES OF UNFORTUNATE EVENTS (W.H. Smith Omnibus edition, including books 4-6, plus chapter from
'The Vile Village' (Egmont, UK, 2001) (wraparound)...£20
A SERIES OF UNFORTUNATE EVENTS (Egmont, UK, 2004)
(Film tie-in omnibus edition, includes books 1-3 bound together £10
A SERIES OF UNFORTUNATE EVENTS: THE TROUBLE BEGINS (Harper Collins, US, 2004)
(Boxed film tie-in edition of the first three books) £15

Non-series

THE BABY IN THE MANGER (32-page hardback, illustrated by Lisa Brown, limited to 65 numbered copies,
signed/embossed/dated by author and signed by illustrator) (Monotreme Press, US, 2002) £500
LEMONY SNICKET: THE UNAUTHORIZED AUTOBIOGRAPHY (Hardback with reversible spoof dustjacket)
(Harper Collins, US, 2002) £20
BEHIND THE SCENES WITH COUNT OLAF (film tie-in paperback) (Egmont, UK, 2004) £5
THE BLANK BOOK (Harper Collins, US, 2004) £5
THE BLANK BOOK (Egmont, UK, 2004) £5
BEATRICE LETTERS (correspondence, in an accordion-style folder) (Egmont, UK, 2006) .... new £12.99

SOPER, Eileen

British illustrator. Born: 1905. She was encouraged by her father, the artist George Soper (1870-1942) and was elected to The Print Makers Society of California in 1921 after her first exhibition of etchings. She illustrated the entire series of Enid Blyton's 'Famous Five' adventures and a vast range of other books. She was a founder member of the Society of Wildlife Artists (1964) and a member of the Royal Society of Miniature Painters (1972). Died:1990.

Prices are for books in Very Good condition with dustjackets.

Books Written and Illustrated by Eileen Soper

HAPPY RABBIT (Macmillan, 1947)..£60
DORMOUSE AWAKE (Macmillan, 1948) £60
SAIL AWAY SHREW (Macmillan, 1949)..£60

'Famous Five' Books Illustrated by Eileen Soper

FIVE ON A TREASURE ISLAND: An Adventure Story (Hodder & Stoughton, 1942)....................................£1,200
FIVE GO ADVENTURING AGAIN (Hodder & Stoughton, 1943)...£500
FIVE RUN AWAY TOGETHER (Hodder & Stoughton, 1944)...£500
FIVE GO TO SMUGGLERS' TOP (Hodder & Stoughton, 1945)..£500
FIVE GO OFF IN A CARAVAN (Hodder & Stoughton, 1946)..£500
FIVE ON KIRRIN ISLAND AGAIN (Hodder & Stoughton, 1947)...£500
FIVE GO OFF TO CAMP (Hodder & Stoughton, 1948) £120
FIVE GET INTO TROUBLE (Hodder & Stoughton, 1949)...£100
FIVE FALL INTO ADVENTURE (Hodder & Stoughton, 1950)..£75
FIVE ON A HIKE TOGETHER (Hodder & Stoughton, 1951)...£55
FIVE HAVE A WONDERFUL TIME (Hodder & Stoughton, 1952)..£55
FIVE GO DOWN TO THE SEA (Hodder & Stoughton, 1953) £45
FIVE GO TO MYSTERY MOOR (Hodder & Stoughton, 1954)...£45
FIVE HAVE PLENTY OF FUN (Hodder & Stoughton, 1955)...£40
FIVE ON A SECRET TRAIL (Hodder & Stoughton, 1956)...£40
FIVE GO TO BILLYCOCK HILL (Hodder & Stoughton, 1957)..£40
FIVE GET INTO A FIX (Hodder & Stoughton, 1958)..£35
FIVE ON FINNISTON FARM (Hodder & Stoughton, 1960)..£35
FIVE GO TO DEMON'S ROCK (Hodder & Stoughton, 1961)...£35
FIVE HAVE A MYSTERY TO SOLVE (Hodder & Stoughton, 1962)...£35
FIVE ARE TOGETHER AGAIN (Hodder & Stoughton, 1963)...£35
THE FAMOUS FIVE SPECIAL (contains 'Five go off to Camp', 'Five go off in a Caravan' and
'Five Have a Wonderful Time') (Hodder & Stoughton, 1959)...£35
THE FAMOUS FIVE BIG BOOK (contains 'Five on a Treasure Island', 'Five Go Adventuring Again' and
'Five Run Away Together') (Hodder & Stoughton, 1964)..£35

Other Enid Blyton Books Illustrated by Eileen Soper

I'LL TELL YOU A STORY (Macmillan, 1942)..£15
ENID BLYTON'S MERRY STORY BOOK (Hodder & Stoughton, 1943)..£30
THE TOYS COME TO LIFE (Brockhampton Press, [1944])...£30
COME TO THE CIRCUS (Brockhampton Press, [1944]) £30
ENID BLYTON'S JOLLY STORY BOOK (Hodder & Stoughton, 1944) £30
POLLY PIGLET (Brockhampton Press, [1944])..£30
TALES FROM THE BIBLE (Methuen, 1944)...£30
THE BLUE STORY BOOK (Methuen, 1945)...£30
THE CONJURING WIZARD and Other Stories (Macmillan, 1945)...£30
THE RUNAWAY KITTEN (Brockhampton Press, [1945])..£30
THE TWINS GO TO NURSERY-RHYME LAND (Brockhampton Press, [1945])......................................£30
THE TEDDY BEAR'S PARTY (Brockhampton Press, [1945]) £30
THE BAD LITTLE MONKEY (Brockhampton Press, [1946])...£30
ENID BLYTON'S GAY STORY BOOK (Hodder & Stoughton, 1946)..£35
THE LITTLE WHITE DUCK and Other Stories (Macmillan, 1946)..£30
THE SURPRISING CARAVAN (Brockhampton Press, 1946)...£30
THE TRAIN THAT LOST ITS WAY (Brockhampton Press, [1946]) £30
AT SEASIDE COTTAGE (Brockhampton Press, [1947])..£25
THE GREEN STORY BOOK (Methuen, 1947)..£25
ENID BLYTON'S LUCKY STORY BOOK (Hodder & Stoughton, 1947)...£30
SECRET OF THE OLD MILL (Brockhampton Press, [1948]) £30
TALES OF THE TWINS (Brockhampton Press, [1948])..£20
THE ASTONISHING LADDER and Other Stories (Macmillan, 1950)...£30
THE THREE NAUGHTY CHILDREN and Other Stories (Macmillan, 1950) £30
TRICKY THE GOBLIN and Other Stories (Macmillan, 1950)...£25
ENID BLYTON'S BOOK OF THE YEAR (music by Alec Rowley) (Evans, 1950)...................................£25
ENID BLYTON'S BRIGHT STORY BOOK (Brockhampton Press, 1952)...£25
MY FIRST NATURE BOOK (Macmillan, 1952)..£10
ENID BLYTON'S FRIENDLY STORY BOOK (Brockhampton Press, 1954)...£25

Other Books Illustrated by Eileen Soper

A CASTLE FOR JOHN-PETER by Ursula Moray Williams (Harrap, 1941)..£15
MALTA: A KITTEN by Mary Moore (Macmillan, 1943)...£15
RABBIT TALES by Mary Moore (Macmillan 1944) £15
COUNTRY DAYS by E. Gould (Blackie, 1944) £15
HOLIDAYS ON THE FARM by E. Gould (Blackie, 1944) £15
HAPPY DAYS ON THE FARM by E. Gould (Blackie, 1944) £15
ALICE IN WONDERLAND by Lewis Carroll (Harrap, 1947)...£40
THE SONG OF LAMBERT by Mazo de la Roch (Macmillan, 1955)...£25
HOW TO OBSERVE WILD ANIMALS by Maxwell Knight (Routledge, 1957).......................................£15
BULLY AND THE BADGER by Charles Malins (Robert Yeatman, 1974)..£15
NO BADGERS IN MY WOOD by Phil Drabble (Michael Joseph, 1979)...£15

SOWERBY, Millicent

British illustrator. Born: Amy Millicent Sowerby in 1878, the daughter of the illustrator, J.G. Sowerby. Largely self-taught, she collaborated with her sister, Githa Sowerby, on a series of children's books, as well as illustrating such classics as *Alice in Wonderland* (1907) and Stevenson's *A Child's Garden of Verses* (1908). Died: 1967.

Prices are for books in Very Good condition.

THE WISE BOOK by Githa Sowerby (Dent, 1906) £80
ALICE'S ADVENTURES IN WONDERLAND by Lewis Carroll (Chatto & Windus, 1907).....................£120
THE BUMBLETOES by Githa Sowerby (verse) (Chatto & Windus, 1907) £80
CHILDHOOD by Githa Sowerby (verse) (Chatto & Windus, 1907)..£90
YESTERDAY'S CHILDREN by Githa Sowerby (verse) (Chatto & Windus, 1908).................................£55
A CHILD'S GARDEN OF VERSES by R.L. Stevenson (Chatto & Windus, 1908).................................£100
GRIMM'S FAIRY TALES. Selected and retold by Githa Sowerby (twelve colour illustrations by Millicent Sowerby)
    (Grant Richards, 1909)..£100
THE HAPPY BOOK by Githa Sowerby (Hodder & Stoughton, [1909])..£60
LITTLE PLAYS FOR LITTLE PEOPLE by Githa Sowerby (Hodder & Stoughton, [1910])....................£60
THE MERRY BOOK by Githa Sowerby (Hodder & Stoughton, [1911])..£60
MY BIRTHDAY by Githa Sowerby (Hodder & Stoughton, [1911])..£55
POEMS OF CHILDHOOD by Githa Sowerby (Hodder & Stoughton, [1912]) £55
THE PRETTY BOOK by Githa Sowerby (verse) (Frowde, [1915])..£60
CINDERELLA. Adapted by Githa Sowerby (Hodder & Stoughton, [1915])..£70
THE DAINTY BOOK by Githa Sowerby (verse) (Hodder & Stoughton, [1915])...................................£60
THE GAY BOOK by Githa Sowerby (verse) (Hodder & Stoughton, [1915])..£60
THE BRIGHT BOOK by Githa Sowerby (verse) (Hodder & Stoughton, [1916]) £60
THE BONNIE BOOK by Githa Sowerby (verse) (Humphrey Milford, [1918]) £60
THE WISE BOOK by Githa Sowerby (verse) (Milford & Warner, [1921])..£60

*Three early editions of the most famous children's book by Joanna Spyri following the adventures of Swiss orphan girl **Heidi**.*

SPYRI, Johanna

Swiss author. Born: Johanna Heusser in Zurich in 1827. Wrote a number of children's books, but is best known for *Heidi*, about a Swiss orphan girl. Died: 1901.

Prices are for books in Very Good condition (with dustjackets after 1930).

HEIDI'S EARLY EXPERIENCES: A Story for Children (Sampson Low, 1884) £1,500
HEIDI'S FURTHER EXPERIENCES: A Story for Children (Sampson Low, 1884)...£1,500
HEIDI: Her Years of Wandering and Learning (translated by Louise Brooks) (Boston, US, 1885 [1884])............£1,000
HEIDI (illustrated by Lizzie Lawson) (Dent, [1909])..£100
HEIDI (cloth and leather bindings) (Dent: 'Everyman's Library' series, 1910)..£15
HEIDI (illustrated by Maria L. Kirk; translated by Elisabeth P. Stork) (Lippincott, US, [1919]) £60
HEIDI (illustrated by Jessie Willcox Smith; issued with dustjacket) (David McKay, US, 1922)..........................£250
HEIDI (illustrated by Anne Anderson) (David McKay, US, 1923)...£50
HEIDI (illustrated by Anne Anderson; translated by Helene S. White) (Harrap, 1924).................................£75
SHIRLEY TEMPLE IN 'HEIDI' (tie-in with the film 'Heidi', starring Shirley Temple, with dustjacket) (Saalfield, US, 1937) £50
HEIDI (illustrated by Pelagie Doane; translated by M. Rosenbaum; issued with dustjacket) (Collins, 1938) £15
HEIDI (illustrated by Maginel Wright Enright) (Rand McNally, US: 'Windermere' series, 1939)........................£15
HEIDI (illustrated by Janet & Anne Grahame Johnstone; issued with dustjacket) (Heirloom Library, 1949) £15
HEIDI (illustrated by Vincent O. Cohen; issued with dustjacket) (Dent, 1950).......................................£10
HEIDI (illustrated by Raymond Sheppard; translated by Marian Edwardes; issued with dustjacket) (Blackie, 1955) £10
HEIDI (illustrated by Cecil Leslie; translated by Eileen Hall; paperback) (Puffin, 1956)................................£3
GRITLI'S CHILDREN (Cupples & Hurd, US/UK, 1887) £600
SWISS STORIES FOR CHILDREN (translated by L. Wheelock) (Blackie, 1889 [1888]) £250
IN SAFE KEEPING (translated by L. Wheelock) (Blackie, [1896])...£100
HEIMATLOS: Two Stories for Children, and Those Who Love Children
   (illustrated by Frederick Richardson; translated by Emma Stelter Hopkins) (Ginn, US, 1912) £75
MONI THE GOAT-BOY (Lippincott, US/UK, 1916)..£30
CORNELLI (illustrated by Maria L. Kirk; translated by Elisabeth P. Stork) (Lippincott, US/UK, 1920) £50
MÄZLI: A Story of the Swiss Valleys (translated by Elisabeth P. Stork) (Lippincott, US/UK, 1921) £50
FRANCESCA AT HINTERWALD (Lippincott, US/UK, [1923]) £50
VINZI: A Story of the Swiss Alps (translated by Elisabeth P. Stork) (Lippincott, US/UK, 1923).....................£30
DORA (translated by Elisabeth P. Stork) (Lippincott, US/UK, [1924]) £30
THE NEW YEAR'S CAROL (translated by Grace Edwards) (Houghton Mifflin, US, 1924)...........................£30
CHILDREN OF THE ALPS (translated by Elisabeth P. Stork) (Lippincott, US/UK, [1925]) £30
EVELI, THE LITTLE SINGER (translated by Elisabeth P. Stork) (Lippincott, US/UK, [1926])........................£30
THE FAIRY OF INTRA (illustrated by M.J. Marshall) (Lippincott, US/UK, [1926]) £30
PEPPINO (translated by Elisabeth P. Stork) (Lippincott, US/UK, [1926])..£30
JÖRLI, or The Stauffer Mill (illustrated by B. Greer; translated by Elisabeth P. Stork) (Lippincott, US/UK, 1928).....£30
SWISS STORIES FROM MADAME JOHANNA SPYRI and Two Stories from Madame Kabalinsky
   (Gresham, [1930]) £15
ALL ALONE IN THE WORLD: 'The Story of Rico' and 'Wiseli's Way' (illustrated by Michael Ross;
   translated by M.E. Calthrop; issued with dustjacket) (Dent, 1958)..£15

'Heidi' books by other authors

HEIDI GROWS UP by Charles Tritten (illustrated by Pelagi Doane) (Collins, 1939) £15
HEIDI'S CHILDREN by Charles Tritten (illustrated by Pelagi Doane) (Collins, 1939) £15
HEIDI ANNUAL (laminated boards) (Grandreams, 1982 & 1983) £4

STEADMAN, Ralph

British illustrator. Born: Liverpool, 1936. Studied at Abergele Grammar School and the London College of Printing. Best known for his grotesque illustrations for magazines such as *Private Eye* and the *New Statesman*, but has illustrated a handful of children's books, winning the Francis Williams Award for his edition of *Alice in Wonderland* (1967).

Prices are for books in Very Good condition with dustjackets.

FLY AWAY PETER by Frank Dickens (Dobson, 1964)..£40
THE BIG SQUIRREL AND THE LITTLE RHINOCEROS by Mischa Damjan (Dobson, 1965) £35
ALICE IN WONDERLAND by Lewis Carroll (Dobson, 1967)..£70
RALPH STEADMAN'S JELLY BOOK (Dobson, 1967) £50
THE LITTLE RED COMPUTER (McGraw, US, 1969)...£40
TWO CATS IN AMERICA by Mischa Damjan (Longman, 1970)..£35
THROUGH THE LOOKING GLASS AND WHAT ALICE FOUND THERE by Lewis Carroll (MacGibbon & Kee, 1972) £60
RALPH STEADMAN'S BUMPER TO BUMPER BOOK FOR CHILDREN (Pan, 1973)..................................£30
THE BRIDGE (Collins, 1974)...£25
THE HUNTING OF THE SNARK (Dempsey, 1975) £50
CHERRYWOOD CANNON. Based on a story by Dimitri Sidjanski (Paddington Press, 1978)......................£30
EMERGENCY MOUSE by Bernard Stone (Anderson Press, 1978) £25
INSPECTOR MOUSE by Bernard Stone (Anderson Press, 1980)...£25
QUASIMODO MOUSE by Bernard Stone (Anderson Press, 1984) £25
TREASURE ISLAND (Harrap, 1985)..£35
THE COMPLETE ALICE AND THE HUNTING OF THE SNARK (Cape, 1986) £40

STEVENSON, Robert Louis

Scottish author. Born: Robert Lewis Balfour Stevenson in Edinburgh in 1850. Studied at Edinburgh Academy and Edinburgh University. Enjoyed his first success with *Travels with a Donkey* (1879), but is now best known for his adventure stories, *Treasure Island* (1883) and *Kidnapped* (1886), and the macabre tale, *The Strange Case of Dr Jekyll and Mr Hyde* (1886). Other children's works include *The Black Arrow* (1888) and *A Child's Garden of Verses* (1885). Settled in the Pacific island of Samoa in 1891. Died: 1894.

Prices are for books in Very Good condition.

TREASURE ISLAND (Cassell, 1883)...£5,000
TREASURE ISLAND (illustrated by Mervyn Peake, with dustjacket) (Eyre & Spottiswoode, 1949)..............£50
TREASURE ISLAND (illustrated by Ralph Steadman; with dustjacket) (Harrap, 1985)................................£35
A CHILD'S GARDEN OF VERSES (Longmans Green, 1885)..£3,000
A CHILD'S GARDEN OF VERSES (illustrated by Charles Robinson) (John Lane: The Bodley Head, 1896 [1895])..........£350
A CHILD'S GARDEN OF VERSES (illustrated by Charles Robinson; reissue) (John Lane: The Bodley Head, 1921) £150
A CHILD'S GARDEN OF VERSES (illustrated by Jessie Willcox Smith) (Scribners, US, 1905) £150
A CHILD'S GARDEN OF VERSES (illustrated by Millicent Sowerby) (Chatto & Windus, 1908) £100
A CHILD'S GARDEN OF VERSES (illustrated by H. Willebeek Le Mair) (Harrap, 1931) £200
SONGS WITH MUSIC FROM 'A CHILD'S GARDEN OF VERSES' (illustrated by Margaret Tarrant) (T.C. & E.C. Jack, [1918])..........£50
KIDNAPPED (Cassell, 1886)...£2,500
THE MERRY MEN and Other Tales (Chatto & Windus, 1887) £100
THE BLACK ARROW (Cassell, 1888) £80
THE MASTER OF BALLANTRAE (Cassell, 1889)...£350
THE LAND OF NOD and Other Poems for Children. Edited by Michael Hague (Holt, US, 1988).................£25

STOKER, Bram

Irish author. Born: Abraham Stoker in Dublin in 1847. The author of *Dracula* wrote a single children's work, a collection of weird, allegorical fables for young readers. Died: 1912.

Prices are for books in Very Good condition.

UNDER THE SUNSET (illustrated by W. Fitzgerald and W.V. Cockburn; full parchment vellum binding)
   (Sampson Low, 1882 [1881]) £300
UNDER THE SUNSET (second edition; green cloth binding) (Sampson Low, 1882)...................................£150

STRANG, Herbert

Pseudonym of George Herbert Ely (1866-1958) and C. James l'Estrange (1867-1947). Unique collaboration between two men as 'Herbert Strang' produced a huge number of patriotic adventure stories in addition to editing Herbert Strang annuals.

Prices are for books in Good condition.

'Herbert Strang's Historical Series'

WITH MARLBOROUGH TO MALPLAQUET (with Richard Stead) (Hodder & Stoughton, 1908).................£10
WITH THE BLACK PRINCE (with Richard Stead) (Hodder & Stoughton, 1908) £10
A MARINER OF ENGLAND (with Richard Stead) (Hodder & Stoughton, 1908)..£10
ONE OF RUPERT'S HORSE (with Richard Stead) (Hodder & Stoughton, 1908) £10

LION-HEART (with Richard Stead) (Hodder & Stoughton, 1908)..£10
CLAUD THE ARCHER (with John Aston) (Hodder & Stoughton, 1908)..£10
IN THE FOREST (with John Aston) (Hodder & Stoughton, 1908)...£10
ROGER THE SCOUT (with George Lawrence) (Hodder & Stoughton, 1908)..£10
FOR THE WHITE ROSE (with George Lawrence) (Hodder & Stoughton, 1908)...£10

'Strang's Penny Books'

THREE BOYS AT THE FAIR (Humphrey Milford, 1926-27)...£10
KITTY'S KITTEN (Humphrey Milford, 1926-27) £10
THE CINEMA DOG (Humphrey Milford, 1926-27)...£10
BILL SAWYER'S VC (Humphrey Milford, 1926-27) £10
THE GAME OF BROWNIES (Humphrey Milford, 1926-27)..£10
JENNY'S ARK (Humphrey Milford, 1926-27) £10
BAA-BAA AND THE WIDE WORLD (Humphrey Milford, 1926-27) £10
TOM LEAVES SCHOOL (Humphrey Milford, 1926-27)...£10
THE MISCHIEF-MAKING MAGPIE (Humphrey Milford, 1926-27)..£10
A RIDE WITH ROBIN HOOD (Humphrey Milford, 1926-27)..£10
PETE'S ELEPHANT (Humphrey Milford, 1926-27) £10
TEN POUNDS REWARD (Humphrey Milford, 1926-27)..£10
ADOLF'S DOG (Humphrey Milford, 1926-27)..£10
THE ADVENTURES OF A PENNY STAMP (Humphrey Milford, 1926-27)...£10
DON'T BE TOO SURE (Humphrey Milford, 1926-27) £10
JACK AND JOCKO (Humphrey Milford, 1926-27)..£10
THE PRINCESS AND THE ROBBERS (Humphrey Milford, 1926-27) £10
THE CHRISTMAS FAIRY (Humphrey Milford, 1926-27)...£10
THE SEVEN SONS (Humphrey Milford, 1926-27) £10
THE RED CANDLE (Humphrey Milford, 1926-27)..£10
THE MILLER'S DAUGHTER (Humphrey Milford, 1926-27)...£10
THE GREY GOOSE FEATHERS (Humphrey Milford, 1926-27) £10
THE BIRTHDAY PRESENT (Humphrey Milford, 1926-27)..£10
THERE WAS A LITTLE PIG (Humphrey Milford, 1926-27)...£10
THE MAGIC SMOKE (Humphrey Milford, 1926-27)...£10
THE CHILDREN OF THE FERRY (Humphrey Milford, 1926-27)...£10
SUGAR CANDY TOWN (Humphrey Milford, 1926-27)...£10
LITTLE MR PIXIE (Humphrey Milford, 1926-27)..£10
THE LITTLE SEA HORSE (Humphrey Milford, 1926-27)...£10
THE LITTLE BLUE-GREY HARE (Humphrey Milford, 1926-27) £10

Others

TOM BURNABY (Blackie, 1904) £60
BOYS OF THE LIGHT BRIGADE (Blackie, 1904)..£50
KOBO (illustrated by William Rainey) (Blackie, 1904)...£40
BROWN OF MOUKDEN (Blackie, 1905)...£40
BROWN OF MOUKDEN (reissued as 'Jack Brown in China') (OUP, 1923)...£20
THE ADVENTURES OF HARRY ROCHESTER (illustrated by William Rainey) (Blackie, 1905).....................£25
JACK HARDY (illustrated by William Rainey) (Hodder & Stoughton, 1905)...£25
ONE OF CLIVE'S HEROES (illustrated by William Rainey) (Hodder & Stoughton, 1906)..............................£25
SAMBA (illustrated by William Rainey) (Hodder & Stoughton, 1906)..£25
ROB THE RANGER (illustrated by W.H. Margetson) (Hodder & Stoughton, 1907)..£25
WITH DRAKE ON THE SPANISH MAIN (illustrated by Archibald Webb) (Hodder & Stoughton, 1907)...........£25
KING OF THE AIR (illustrated by W.E. Webster) (Hodder & Stoughton, 1907)...£25
HUMPHREY BOLD (Hodder & Stoughton, 1908) £25
BARCLAY OF THE GUIDES (illustrated by H.W. Koekkoek) (Hodder & Stoughton, 1908)............................£25
LORD OF THE SEAS (illustrated by C. Fleming Williams) (Hodder & Stoughton, 1908)...............................£25
PALM TREE ISLAND (illustrated by Archibald Webb and Alan Wright) (Hodder & Stoughton, 1909) £25
SETTLERS AND SCOUTS (illustrated by T.C. Dugdale) (Hodder & Stoughton, 1909)..................................£25
SWIFT AND SURE (Hodder & Stoughton, 1909)...£25
THE CRUISE OF THE GYRO-CAR (illustrated by A.C. Michael) (Hodder & Stoughton, 1910).......................£25
THE ADVENTURES OF DICK TREVANION (illustrated by William Rainey) (Hodder & Stoughton, 1910).......£25
ROUND THE WORLD IN SEVEN DAYS (illustrated by A.C. Michael) (Hodder & Stoughton, 1910)...............£25
THE FLYING BOAT (illustrated by T.C. Dugdale) (Hodder & Stoughton, 1911) £25
THE AIR SCOUT (illustrated by W.R.S. Stott) (Hodder & Stoughton, 1911)..£25
THE MOTOR SCOUT (illustrated by Cyril Cuneo) (Hodder & Stoughton, 1912)..£25
THE AIR PATROL (illustrated by Cyril Cuneo) (Hodder & Stoughton, 1912)..£25
CERDIC THE SAXON (illustrated by L.L. Weedon) (Hodder & Stoughton, 1913)...£25
A LITTLE NORMAN MAID (Hodder & Stoughton, 1913)...£25
SULTAN JIM, EMPIRE-BUILDER (Hodder & Stoughton, 1913)..£25
A GENTLEMAN-AT-ARMS (Hodder & Stoughton, 1914) £25
A HERO OF LIEGE (Hodder & Stoughton, 1914) £25
FIGHTING WITH FRENCH (Hodder & Stoughton, 1915)...£25
THE BOY WHO WOULD NOT LEARN (OUP, 1915)..£25

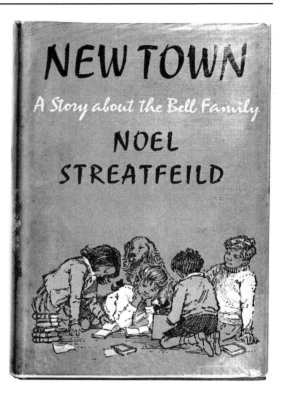

Above: One of Ruth Gervis's illustrations from Streatfeild's most famous work, **Ballet Shoues** *(1936), now valued at £50. Right: Noel Streatfeild's* **New Town** *(1960) is valued at £20 in Very Good condition with the Shirley Hughes-designed dustjacket.*

THE SILVER SHOT (OUP, 1915)	**£25**
IN TRAFALGAR'S BAY (OUP, 1915)	**£25**
BURTON OF THE FLYING CORPS (Hodder & Stoughton, 1916)	**£25**
FRANK FORESTER (Hodder & Stoughton, 1916)	**£25**
THE OLD MAN OF THE MOUNTAIN (illustrated by Rene Bull) (Hodder & Stoughton, 1916)	**£25**
THROUGH THE ENEMY'S LINES (illustrated by H.E. Elcock) (Hodder & Stoughton, 1916)	**£25**
CARRY ON! (illustrated by H.E. Elcock and H. Evison) (Hodder & Stoughton, 1917)	**£25**
WITH HAIG ON THE SOMME (OUP, 1917)	**£25**
STEADY, BOYS, STEADY (Hodder & Stoughton, 1917)	**£25**
THE LONG TRAIL (OUP, 1918)	**£25**
TOM WILLOUGHBY'S SCOUTS (OUP, 1919)	**£25**
THE BLUE RAIDER (OUP, 1919)	**£25**
BRIGHT IDEAS (illustrated by C.E. Brock) (OUP, 1920)	**£25**
NO MAN'S ISLAND (illustrated by C.E. Brock) (OUP, 1921)	**£25**
THE CAVE IN THE HILLS (OUP, 1922)	**£25**
BASTABLE COVE (OUP, 1922)	**£25**
WINNING HIS NAME (illustrated by C.E. Brock) (OUP, 1922)	**£25**
HONOUR FIRST (illustrated by W.E. Wightman) (OUP, 1923)	**£25**
TRUE AS STEEL (illustrated by C.E. Brock) (OUP, 1923)	**£25**
A THOUSAND MILES AN HOUR (OUP, 1924)	**£25**
THE HEIR OF A HUNDRED KINGS (OUP, 1924)	**£25**
YOUNG JACK (OUP, 1924)	**£25**
MARTIN OF OLD LONDON (OUP, 1925)	**£25**
OLWYN'S SECRET (OUP, 1925)	**£25**
DAN BOLTON'S DISCOVERY (OUP, 1926)	**£25**
LOST IN LONDON (OUP, 1927)	**£15**
THE RIVER PIRATES (OUP, 1927)	**£15**
THE RIDERS (OUP, 1928)	**£10**
ON LONDON RIVER (OUP, 1929)	**£10**
SHIPS AND THEIR STORY: Scouting stories (OUP, 1931)	**£10**
DICKON OF THE CHASE (OUP, 1931)	**£10**
A SERVANT OF JOHN COMPANY (OUP, 1932)	**£10**

STREATFEILD, Noel

British author. Born: Sussex, 1895. Studied at the Academy of Dramatic Art, London, subsequently working as an actress until she turned to writing in 1929. Produced a handful of adult novels until the success of *Ballet Shoes* (1936) launched her as a children's author. Awarded the Carnegie Medal for *The Circus is Coming* (1938), and an OBE in 1983. Died: 1986.

Prices are for books in Very Good condition with dustjackets where applicable.

THE WHICHARTS (Heinemann, 1931) £50
TOP AND BOTTOMS (Heinemann, 1933) £45
SHEPHERDESS OF SHEEP (Heinemann, 1934) £45
THE CHILDREN'S MATINEE (plays) (Heinemann, 1934) £30
BALLET SHOES: A Story of Three Children on the Stage (illustrated by Ruth Gervis) (Dent, 1936)......... £200
IT PAYS TO BE GOOD (Heinemann, 1936)... £25
WISDOM TEETH (play) (Samuel French: 'Acting Edition', [1936]) £15
TENNIS SHOES (illustrated by D.L. Mays) (Dent, 1937) £250
CAROLINE ENGLAND (Heinemann, 1937).. £25
THE CIRCUS IS COMING (illustrated by Steven Spurrier) (Dent, 1938).. £40
DENNIS THE DRAGON (verse; illustrated by Ruth Gervis) (Dent, 1939) £20
LUKE (Heinemann, 1939)... £20
THE HOUSE IN CORNWALL (illustrated by D.L. Mays) (Dent, 1940) £20
THE WINTER IS PAST (Collins, [1940])... £20
THE CHILDREN OF PRIMROSE LANE (illustrated by Marcia Lane Foster) (Dent, 1941) £20
HARLEQUINADE (illustrated by Clarke Hutton) (Chatto & Windus, 1943)... £20
CURTAIN UP (illustrated by D.L. Mays) (Dent, 1944) £20
MYRA CARROL (Collins, 1944)... £20
SAPLINGS (Collins, 1945).. £25
PARTY FROCK (illustrated by Anna Zinkeisen) (Collins, 1946).. £30
THE PAINTED GARDEN (illustrated by Ley Kenyon) (Collins, 1949).. £20
OSBERT (Rand McNally, US, 1950)... £15
MOTHERING SUNDAY (Collins, 1950).. £20
THE YEARS OF GRACE. Edited by Noel Streatfeild (essays by various authors) (Evans, 1950)............ £15
THE THEATER CAT (illustrated by Susanne Shuba) (Rand McNally, US, 1951)...................................... £15
WHITE BOOTS (illustrated by Milein Cosman) (Collins, 1951).. £20
THE PICTURE STORY OF BRITAIN (non-fiction) (Watts, US, 1951)... £10
AUNT CLARA (Collins, 1952)... £20
THE FEARLESS TREASURE: A Story of England from Then to Now (illustrated by Dorothea Braby)
    (Joseph, 1953)... £15
THE FIRST BOOK OF BALLET (non-fiction) (Watts, US, 1953).. £15
BY SPECIAL REQUEST. Edited by Noel Streatfeild (stories by various authors) (Collins, 1953)............ £15
THE BELL FAMILY (illustrated by Shirley Hughes) (Collins, 1954) £20
GROWING UP GRACEFULLY: Etiquette. Edited by Noel Streatfeild (illustrated by John Dugan) (Arthur Barker, 1955) £7
THE DAY BEFORE YESTERDAY: Firsthand Stories of Fifty Years Ago.
    Edited by Noel Streatfeild (stories by various authors; illustrated by Dick Hart) (Collins, 1956)......... £10
THE GREY FAMILY (illustrated by Pat Marriott) (Hamish Hamilton, 1956) £15
JUDITH (Collins, 1956) £15
THE FIRST BOOK OF BALLET (non-fiction) (Bailey & Swinfen, 1956).. £15
WINTLE'S WONDERS (illustrated by Richard Kennedy) (Collins, 1957) £15
THE FIRST BOOK OF ENGLAND (non-fiction; illustrated by Gioia Fiammenghi) (Watts, US, [1958]) £10
THE FIRST BOOK OF ENGLAND (non-fiction; illustrated by Gioia Fiammenghi) (Bailey & Swinfen, 1958) £10
QUEEN VICTORIA (non-fiction; illustrated by Robert Frankenburg) (Random House, US, 1958)............ £10
QUEEN VICTORIA (non-fiction; illustrated by Robert Frankenburg) (W.H. Allen, 1961) £10
THE ROYAL BALLET SCHOOL (non-fiction; photographs by Gabor Denes) (Collins, 1959) £15
NOEL STREATFEILD'S BALLET ANNUAL (non-fiction) (Collins, 1959)... £12
BABY BOOK SERIES (twelve parts) (Arthur Barker, 1959)... each £10
BERTRAM (illustrated by Margery Gill) (Hamish Hamilton, 1959).. £10
CHRISTMAS WITH THE CHRYSTALS (Blackwell, 1959 [1960]).. £12
LOOK AT THE CIRCUS (non-fiction) (Hamish Hamilton, 1960) £8
NEW TOWN: A Story about the Bell Family (illustrated by Shirley Hughes) (Collins, 1960)..................... £15
THE PAINTED GARDEN: A Story of a Holiday in Hollywood (illustrated by Shirley Hughes; paperback) (Puffin, 1961)........... £5
THE SILENT SPEAKER (Collins, 1961)... £8
APPLE BOUGH (illustrated by Margery Gill) (Collins, 1962) £15
LISA GOES TO RUSSIA (illustrated by Geraldine Spence) (Collins, 1963)... £8
A VICARAGE FAMILY (illustrated by Charles Mozley) (Collins, 1963)... £12
CONFIRMATION AND AFTER. Edited by Noel Streatfeild (Heinemann, 1963) £5
PRISKA by Merja Otava. Edited by Noel Streatfeild (Benn, 1964) £6
THE CHILDREN ON THE TOP FLOOR (illustrated by Jillian Willet) (Collins, 1964)................................ £12
THE THAMES: LONDON'S RIVER (non-fiction; illustrated by Kurt Wiese) (Champaign Garrard, US, 1964)
THE THAMES: LONDON'S RIVER (non-fiction; illustrated by Kurt Wiese) (Muller, 1966) £6
LET'S GO COACHING (illustrated by Peter Warner) (Hamish Hamilton, 1965).. £8

AWAY FROM THE VICARAGE (Collins, 1965)..£20
THE GROWING SUMMER (illustrated by Edward Ardizzone) (Collins, 1966)..........................£35
OLD CHAIRS TO MEND (illustrated by Barry Wilkinson) (Hamish Hamilton, 1966) £15
ENJOYING OPERA (non-fiction; illustrated by Hilary Abrahams) (Dobson, 1966)..................£5
BEFORE CONFIRMATION (non-fiction) (Heinemann, 1967)...£5
THE FIRST BOOK OF SHOES (non-fiction) (Watts, US, 1967) £5
THE FIRST BOOKS OF SHOES (non-fiction) (Watts, 1971) £5
CALDICOTT PLACE (illustrated by Betty Maxey) (Collins, 1967) £20
THE BARROW LANE GANG (BBC, 1968)..£5
GEMMA (illustrated by Betty Maxey) (May Fair, 1968) £4
GEMMA AND SISTERS (illustrated by Betty Maxey) (May Fair, 1968) £4
NICHOLAS by Marlie Brande. Edited by Noel Streatfeild (Benn, 1968)...............................£6
GEMMA ALONE (May Fair, 1969)..£4
GOODBYE GEMMA (May Fair, 1969)..£4
THURSDAY'S CHILD (illustrated by Peggy Fortnum) (Collins, 1970) £20
RED RIDING HOOD (non-fiction) (Benn, 1970) £8
SLEEPY NICHOLAS by Marle Brande. Edited by Noel Streatfeild (Benn, 1970)....................£8
BEYOND THE VICARAGE (Collins, 1971) £15
BALLET SHOES FOR ANNA (illustrated by Mary Dinsdale) (Collins, 1972) £15
THE BOY PHAROAH, TUTANKHAMEN (non-fiction) (Joseph, 1972).....................................£10
THE NOEL STREATFEILD SUMMER HOLIDAY BOOK (illustrated by Sara Silcock) (Dent, 1973)......£7
THE NOEL STREATFEILD CHRISTMAS HOLIDAY BOOK (illustrated by Sara Silcock) (Dent, 1973)....£7
THE NOEL STREATFEILD EASTER HOLIDAY BOOK (illustrated by Sara Silcock) (Dent, 1974).......£7
WHEN THE SIREN WAILED (illustrated by Margery Gill) (Collins, 1974) £10
GRAN-NANNIE (Joseph, 1975)...£15
A YOUNG PERSON'S GUIDE TO BALLET (non-fiction) (Warne, 1975) £6
FAR TO GO (Illustrated by Charles Mozley) (Collins, 1976) £15
THE NOEL STREATFEILD BIRTHDAY STORY BOOK (Dent, 1976) £7
THE NOEL STREATFEILD WEEKEND STORY BOOK (Dent, 1977)..£7
MEET THE MAITLANDS (illustrated by Antony Maitland) (W.H. Allen, 1978).........................£12
THE MAITLANDS: ALL CHANGE AT CUCKLY PLACE (illustrated by Antony Maitland) (W.H. Allen, 1979)............£10

STUDDY, G.E.

British artist. Born: 1878. Best known as the creator of Bonzo the dog. Died: 1948.

Prices are for books and annuals in Very Good condition.

'Bonzo' Annuals

BONZO LAUGHTER ANNUAL [1935] £140
BONZO'S ANNUAL (Bonzo sitting on throne) [1936] £125
BONZO'S ANNUAL (Bonzo dressed as clown with balloon) [1937]..£120
BONZO'S ANNUAL (Bonzo skipping) [1938]..£120
BONZO'S ANNUAL (Bonzo and jack-in-the-box) [1947] £50
BONZO'S ANNUAL (Bonzo with a donkey and cart) [1948]...£50
BONZO'S ANNUAL (Bonzo wearing a fez and firing a peashooter) [1949] £50
BONZO'S ANNUAL (Bonzo with parrot) [1950]...£50
BONZO'S ANNUAL (Bonzo as a cowboy) [1951] £45
BONZO'S ANNUAL (Bonzo on a moon rocket) [1952]...£40
THE BONZO PORTFOLIO (1-10) ....each £250

'Bonzo' Books

BONZO'S HAPPY DAY (Dunlop Press, no date)...£150
BONZO'S LEAP YEAR (Dunlop Press, no date)..£150
BONZO'S HAPPY FAMILY (Dunlop Press, no date)..£150
BONZO'S LITTLE HOLIDAY (Dunlop Press, no date) £150
BACHELOR BONZO (Dunlop Press, no date)...£150
BONZO'S BRAN PIE (Dunlop Press, no date) £150
BONZO PAINTING BOOK (Swain, [1924]) £150
MR BONZO COMES TO TOWN (Swain, [1925])..£150
BAD BOY BONZO (Swain, [1925]) £150
BONZO'S SEASIDE HOLIDAY (Swain, [1925])..£150
BONZO'S COUNTRY HOLIDAY (Swain, [1925])...£150
THE GOOD DEEDS OF BONZO (Swain, [1925]) £150
THE ADVENTURES OF BONZO (Swain, [1925]) £150
THE BONZO BOOK (Partridge, [1925]) £200
THE NEW BONZO BOOK (Partridge, [1927])...£200
THE BONZOOLOO BOOK (Partridge, [1929])...£200
BONZO AND US (Partridge, 1931) £160
BONZO: The Great Big Holiday Book (cover shows Bonzo on rocking horse) (Dean, 1934) ...£75
BONZO: The Great Big Holiday Book (cover shows Bonzo's head) (Dean, 1934).................£75
BONZO COLOURING BOOK (Dean, [1934]) £70

Others
A BOX OF TRICKS (Swain, no date) £100
A LUCKY DIP (Swain, [c1920s]) £100
PUPPY TAILS (Swain, [c1920s]) £100
THE STUDDY DOGS PORTFOLIOS (six portfolios; colour plates) (The Sketch, [1922-1925]) .... each £250
UNCLE'S ANIMAL BOOK by G.E. Studdy (verse) (Warne, [1923]) £200
JEEK by G.E. Studdy (Hamish Hamilton, 1940) £175

STYLES, Showell
British author: Born: Sutton Coldfield, 1908. One of the most prolific and versatile writers of modern times, Showell Styles' vast bibliography includes crime novels, historical novels, thrillers, guidebooks, mountaineering books and a number of children's books. His first was *The Lost Glacier* (1955), a story aimed at older children involving a hunt for the Abominable Snowman or Yeti, in the Himalayas.

Prices are for books in Very Good condition with dustjackets where applicable.

'Quinn' series
MIDSHIPMAN QUINN (Faber, 1956) £15
MIDSHIPMAN QUINN (Vanguard Press, US, 1956) £12
MIDSHIPMAN QUINN (Longmans: 'Heritage of Literature' series, 1961) £12
MIDSHIPMAN QUINN (paperback) (Atlantic Publishing, 1968) £2
MIDSHIPMAN QUINN (paperback) (Hamlyn: 'Beaver Books' series, 1976) £2
QUINN OF THE FURY (Faber, 1958) £12
QUINN OF THE FURY (Vanguard Press, US, 1958) £12
QUINN OF THE FURY (paperback) (Atlantic Publishing, 1968) £2
MIDSHIPMAN QUINN WINS THROUGH (Faber, 1961) £12
MIDSHIPMAN QUINN WINS THROUGH (as 'MIDSHIPMAN QUINN AND DENISE THE SPY') (Vanguard Press, US, 1961) £15
QUINN AT TRAFALGAR (Faber, 1965) £10
QUINN AT TRAFALGAR (Vanguard Press, US, 1965) £10
THE MIDSHIPMAN QUINN COLLECTION (paperback) (Bethlehem Books, US, 1999) £12

'Tiger Patrol' series
TIGER PATROL (Collins, 1957) £8
TIGER PATROL (Collins: 'Seagull Library' series, 1966) £8
TIGER PATROL (pictorial boards) (The Children's Press, 1970) £3
THE TIGER PATROL WINS THROUGH (Collins, 1958) £8
THE TIGER PATROL AT SEA (Collins, 1958) £8
THE TIGER PATROL PRESSES ON (Collins, 1961) £8

'Peter Byrd' series
THE FLYING ENSIGN (Faber, 1960) £10
THE FLYING ENSIGN (as 'GREENCOATS AGAINST NAPOLEON') (Vanguard Press, US, 1960) £15
BYRD OF THE 95th (Faber, 1962) £10
BYRD OF THE 95th (as 'THUNDER OVER SPAIN') (Vanguard Press, US, 1962) £15

'Hughes Family' series
THE SHOP IN THE MOUNTAIN (Gollancz, 1961) £12
THE SHOP IN THE MOUNTAIN (Vanguard Press, US, 1961) £12
THE SHOP IN THE MOUNTAIN (paperback) (Atlantic Publishing, 1968) £3
THE LADDER OF SNOW (Gollancz, 1962) £12
THE LADDER OF SNOW (Vanguard Press, US, 1962) £12
THE LADDER OF SNOW (paperback) (Atlantic Publishing, 1968) £2
A NECKLACE OF GLACIERS (Gollancz, 1963) £12
A NECKLACE OF GLACIERS (paperback) (Atlantic Publishing, 1968) £2
THE PASS OF MORNING (Gollancz, 1966) £12
THE PASS OF MORNING (Ives Washburn, US, 1966) £12
THE PASS OF MORNING (paperback) (Atlantic Publishing, 1968) £2

'Mr Fiddle' series
MR FIDDLE (Hamish Hamilton: 'Antelope Books' series, 1965) £10
MR FIDDLE'S PIG (Hamish Hamilton: 'Antelope Books' series, 1966) £10
MR FIDDLE'S BAND (Hamish Hamilton: 'Antelope Books' series, 1967) £10
A CASE FOR MR FIDDLE (Hamish Hamilton: 'Antelope Books' series, 1969) £10
A CASE FOR MR FIDDLE (Later Editions) (Hamish Hamilton: 'Antelope Books' series, 1970 & 1973) .... each £8

'Wolf Cub' series
RED FOR ADVENTURE (Brockhampton Press, 1965) £8
RED FOR ADVENTURE (White Lion, 1976) £8
WOLF CUB ISLAND (Brockhampton Press, 1966) £8
THE SEA CUB (Brockhampton Press, 1967) £8
CUBS OF THE CASTLE (Brockhampton Press, 1969) £8
CUBS ON THE JOB (Brockhampton Press, 1972) £8

'Able Seaman Jones' series

INDESTRUCTIBLE JONES (Faber, 1967) £10
INDESTRUCTIBLE JONES (Ives Washburn, US, 1968) £12
JONES'S PRIVATE NAVY (Faber, 1969) £10

'John & Ann Davies' series

JOURNEY WITH A SECRET (Gollancz, 1968) £12
JOURNEY WITH A SECRET (Meredith Press, US, 1969).. £12
JOURNEY WITH A SECRET (as 'MYSTERY OF THE FLEEING GIRL'; paperback) (Scholastic Book Services, US, 1970) £8
A TENT ON TOP (Gollancz, 1971)... £12

Others

THE LOST GLACIER (Hart-Davis, 1955)... £15
THE LOST GLACIER (Vanguard Press, US, 1956)... £15
KAMI THE SHERPA (Brockhampton Press: 'Brock Real Life Adventures' series, 1957) £15
KAMI THE SHERPA (Second Impression) (Brockhampton Press, 1959)... £8
KAMI THE SHERPA (as 'SHERPA ADVENTURE') (Vanguard Press, US, 1960)....................................... £15
HOW MOUNTAINS ARE CLIMBED (Routledge & Kegan Paul, 1958).. £8
HOW UNDERGROUND BRITAIN IS EXPLORED (Routledge & Kegan Paul, 1959)..................................... £8
THE BATTLE OF COTTON (Constable, 1960) £15
THE LOST POTHOLE (Brockhampton Press: 'Brock Real Life Adventures' series, 1961).......................... £15
THE LOST POTHOLE (Children's Book Club, 1961) £5
THE LOST POTHOLE (White Lion, 1974) £6
THE BATTLE OF STEAM (Constable, 1961).. £20
LOOK AT MOUNTAINS (Hamish Hamilton, 1962).. £10
THE CAMP IN THE HILLS (Ernest Benn, 1964).. £15
THE CAMP IN THE HILLS (included in 'BANDIT ONE') (Ernest Bonn,1964).. £15
GREENHORN'S CRUISE (Brockhampton Press: 'Brock Real Life Adventures' series, 1964)...................... £15
GREENHORN'S CRUISE (Van Nostrand, US, 1964).. £15
GREENHORN'S CRUISE (White Lion, 1976) £5
FIRST UP EVEREST (Coward-McCann, US, 1969).. £15
THE SNOWDON RANGERS (Faber, 1970) £10
THE FORBIDDEN FRONTIERS (Hamish Hamilton Children's Books, 1970)... £15
MARTY'S MOUNTAIN (Heinemann: 'Red Apple Books' series, 1973).. £5

SUTCLIFF, Rosemary

British author. Born: Surrey, 1920. Regarded as one of the leading writers of historical novels, enjoyed by adults and children. Particularly notable are *The Eagle of the Ninth* (1954) and *Warrior Scarlet* (1958). Died: 1992.

Prices are for books in Very Good condition with dustjackets where applicable.

THE CHRONICLES OF ROBIN HOOD (illustrated by C. Walter Hodges) (OUP, 1950) £30
THE QUEEN ELIZABETH STORY (illustrated by C. Walter Hodges) (OUP, 1950)....................................... £30
THE ARMOURER'S HOUSE (illustrated by C. Walter Hodges) (OUP, 1951)... £30
BROTHER DUSTY-FEET (illustrated by C. Walter Hodges) (OUP, 1952)... £30
SIMON (illustrated by Richard Kennedy) (OUP, 1953) £30
THE EAGLE OF THE NINTH (illustrated by C. Walter Hodges) (OUP, 1954)... £35
OUTCAST (illustrated by Richard Kennedy) (OUP, 1955)... £25
THE SHIELD RING (illustrated by C. Walter Hodges) (OUP, 1956).. £25
THE SILVER BRANCH (illustrated by Charles Keeping) (OUP, 1957) £25
WARRIOR SCARLET (illustrated by Charles Keeping) (OUP, 1958)... £25
THE LANTERN BEARERS (illustrated by Charles Keeping) (OUP, 1959).. £25
THE RIDER ON THE WHITE HORSE (Hodder & Stoughton, 1959) £35
THE BRIDGE BUILDERS (Blackwell, 1959) £20
KNIGHT'S FEE (illustrated by Charles Keeping) (OUP, 1960).. £25
HOUSES AND HISTORY (illustrated by William Stobbs) (Batsford, 1960).. £20
DAWN WIND (illustrated by Charles Keeping) (OUP, 1961) £25
BEOWULF (illustrated by Charles Keeping) (The Bodley Head, 1961) £25
THE HOUND OF ULSTER (illustrated by Victor Ambrus) (The Bodley Head, 1963)..................................... £20
SWORD AT SUNSET (Hodder & Stoughton, 1963) £20
THE MARK OF THE HORSE LORD (illustrated by Charles Keeping) (OUP, 1965)....................................... £25
A SAXON SETTLER (illustrated by John Lawrence) (OUP, 1965) £20
HEROES AND HISTORY (illustrated by Charles Keeping) (Batsford, 1965).. £25
THE CHIEF'S DAUGHTER (illustrated by Victor Ambrus) (Hamish Hamilton, 1967) £20
THE HIGH DEEDS OF FINN MACCOOL (illustrated by Michael Charlton) (The Bodley Head, 1967)............ £15
A CIRCLET OF OAK LEAVES (illustrated by Victor Ambrus) (Hamish Hamilton, 1968)............................... £15
THE FLOWERS OF ADONIS (Hodder & Stoughton, 1969).. £30
THE WITCH'S BRAT (illustrated by Robert Micklewright) (OUP,1970).. £15
THE TRUCE OF THE GAMES (illustrated by Victor Ambrus) (Hamish Hamilton, 1971)............................... £15
TRISTAN AND ISEULT (illustrated by Victor Ambrus) (TheBodley Head, 1971)... £15

HEATHER, OAK, AND OLIVE: Three Stories (illustrated by Victor Ambrus) (Dutton, 1972)..£15
THE CAPRICORN BRACELET (illustrated by Charles Keeping) (OUP,1973) £15
THE CHANGELING (illustrated by Victor Ambrus) (Hamish Hamilton, 1974)..£15
WE LIVED IN DRUMFYVIE (illustrated by Margaret Lyford-Pike) (Blackie, 1975) £15
BLOOD FEUD (illustrated by Charles Keeping) (OUP, 1977) £15
SHIFTING SANDS (illustrated by Laszlo Acs) (Hamish Hamilton, 1977)..£15
SUN HORSE, MOON HORSE (illustrated by Shirley Felts) (The Bodley Head, 1977) £15
SONG FOR A DARK QUEEN (Pelham, 1978)..£20
THE LIGHT BEYOND THE FOREST: The Quest for the Holy Grail (illustrated by Shirley Felts) (The Bodley Head, 1979) £15
FRONTIER WOLF (OUP, 1980)...£15
THE SWORD AND THE CIRCLE: King Arthur and the Knights of the Round Table (illustrated by Shirley Felts)
(The Bodley Head, 1981)...£12
EAGLE'S EGG (illustrated by Victor Ambrus) (Hamish Hamilton, 1981) £15
THE ROAD TO CAMLANN: The Death of King Arthur (illustrated by Shirley Felts) (The Bodley Head, 1981).............£12
BONNY DUNDEE (The Bodley Head, 1982)..£15
THE ROUNDABOUT HORSE (illustrated by Alan Marks) (Hamish Hamilton, 1986) £10
FLAME-COLOURED TAFFETA (OUP, 1986) £10
A LITTLE DOG LIKE YOU (illustrated by Jane Johnson) (Orchard, 1987) £10

SWIFT, Jonathan

Anglo-Irish author. Born: Dublin, 1667. Studied at Kilkenny Grammar School and Trinity College, Dublin.
His novel, *Gulliver's Travels*, has become a children's classic, although invariably in a revised form. Any
copies of the first edition at auction are invariably rebound in leather (or calf), never in the very rare
original bindings/boards. Died: 1745.

Prices are for books in Very Good condition (with dustjackets after 1940).

TRAVELS INTO SEVERAL REMOTE NATIONS OF THE WORLD by Lemuel Gulliver
(two volumes; rebound in leather) (London, 1726)...the set £20,000
GULLIVER'S TRAVELS (illustrated by H.K. Browne) (Warne, [1879]) £60
GULLIVER'S TRAVELS (illustrated by Gordon Browne) (Routledge, [1880])...£60
GULLIVER'S TRAVELS (illustrated by A.E. Jackson) (Nister, [c1890])..£60
GULLIVER'S TRAVELS (illustrated by C.E. Brock; preface by H. Craik) (London, 1894) £40
GULLIVER'S TRAVELS (illustrated by Arthur Rackham) (Dent, 1900) £75
GULLIVER'S TRAVELS (illustrated by Arthur Rackham) (Dent, 1909) £200
GULLIVER'S TRAVELS (illustrated by Arthur Rackham; with extra plate; limited to 750 copies, signed by the artist)
(Dent, 1909)..£1,000
GULLIVER'S TRAVELS (illustrated by Arthur Rackham; adapted by F.C. Tilney)
(Dent: 'Tales for Children from Many Lands' series, [1913])..£50
GULLIVER'S TRAVELS (illustrated by John Hassall) (Nelson, [1908])..£50
GULLIVER'S TRAVELS. Adapted by Padraic Colum (illustrated by Willy Pogány) (Macmillan, US, 1917) £50
GULLIVER'S TRAVELS. Adapted by Padraic Colum (illustrated by Willy Pogány) (Harrap, 1919)............................£50
GULLIVER'S TRAVELS (illustrated by Jean de Bosschere) (Heinemann, 1920) £75
GULLIVER'S TRAVELS (illustrated by Louis Rhead) (Harper, US, [1923])...£40
TRAVELS INTO REMOTE NATIONS OF THE WORLD by Lemuel Gulliver (illustrated by David Jones;
limited to 480 copies; two volumes) (Golden Cockerel Press, 1925) ....the set £2,000
GULLIVER'S TRAVELS (illustrated by Rex Whistler; De Luxe edition: twelve hand-coloured engraved plates;
limited to 195 copies; two volumes; in slipcase) (Cresset Press, 1930)..the set £3,000
THE CHILDREN'S GULLIVER. Adapted by F.H. Lee (illustrated by Willy Pogány) (Harrap, 1935).............................£30
GULLIVER'S TRAVELS (illustrated by Jack Matthews) (Routledge, 1947)...£20
GULLIVER'S TRAVELS (illustrated by Edward Bawden) (Folio Society, 1948) £35

*Arguabbly the finest illustrated edition
of Jonathan Swift's Gulliver's Travels,
with plates by Athur Rackham was
issued in 1909.*

TARRANT, Margaret W.

British illustrator. Born in 1888, the daughter of the artist, Percy Tarrant. Studied at Clapham School of Art and Heatherley's. Began her career designing cards and calendars for the Medici Society, subsequently illustrating a number of children's classics. She was a close friend of Cicely Mary Barker. Died: 1959.

Prices are for books in Very Good condition (with dustjackets after 1920).

Books Written and Illustrated by Margaret W. Tarrant

OUR DAY: A Book of Nursery Times and Playtime Rhymes (48 colour plates by Margaret W. Tarrant) (Ward Lock, [1923]).........£70
THE MARGARET TARRANT BIRTHDAY BOOK. Compiled by Frank S. Cole (Medici Society, [1932]).................£70
JOAN IN FLOWERLAND by Margaret W. Tarrant and Lewis Dutton (Warne, [1935]) £70
THE MARGARET TARRANT NURSERY RHYME BOOK (Collins, [1944]) £70

Books Illustrated by Margaret W. Tarrant

THE WATER-BABIES by Charles Kingsley (Dent, 1908) £120
CONTES DE PERRAULT Adapted by Kathleen Fitzgerald (Siegle & Hill, 1910) £85
THE BOOK OF SPRING (George Allen, 1910).................£100
THE BOOK OF SUMMER (George Allen, 1910).................£100
THE BOOK OF AUTUMN (George Allen, 1910) £100
THE BOOK OF WINTER (George Allen, 1910).................£100
THE BOOK OF THE SEASONS (verse; selected by George A.B. Dewar) (George Allen, 1910).................£220
THE PIED PIPER OF HAMELIN by Robert Browning (Dent, 1912) £85
GOBLIN MARKET by Christina Rossetti (Routledge/Dutton, US, [1912]).................£80
MERRY ANIMAL TALES by Madge A. Bigham (Harrap, 1913).................£75
NURSERY RHYMES (48 colour plates by Margaret W. Tarrant) (Ward Lock: 'Rainbow' series, 1914).................£60
THE LITTLEST ONE by Marion St. John Webb (verse) (Harrap, 1914).................£60
GAMES FOR PLAYTIME AND PARTIES: With and Without Music, for Children of All Ages by S.V. Wilman
(T.C. & E.C. Jack, [1914]).................£120
A PICTURE BIRTHDAY-BOOK FOR BOYS AND GIRLS by Frank Cole (Harrap, [1915]).................£100
FAIRY TALES. Edited by Harry Golding (48 colour plates by Margaret W. Tarrant) (Ward Lock, 1915) £70
THE GIRLHOOD OF FAMOUS WOMEN by F.J. Snell (Harrap, 1915).................£30
ALICE'S ADVENTURES IN WONDERLAND by Lewis Carroll (48 colour plates by Margaret W. Tarrant)
(Ward Lock, 1916).................£130
FAIRY STORIES FROM HANS CHRISTIAN ANDERSEN (48 colour plates by Margaret W. Tarrant)
(Ward Lock, 1917).................£80

'Hare's Foot Clover', one of the plates from Margaret Tarrant's
Joan in Flowerland, *which she co-wrote with Lewis Dutton.*

The Goblin Market from Christina Rossetti's classic poem, as depicted by Margaret Tarrant in her 1912 edition of the work.

KNOCK THREE TIMES: A Tale for Children by Marion St.John Webb (Harrap, 1917) £90
SONGS WITH MUSIC FROM 'A CHILD'S GARDEN OF VERSES' by R.L. Stevenson (T.C. & E.C. Jack, [1918]) £70
VERSES FOR CHILDREN Edited by H. Golding (48 colour plates by Margaret W. Tarrant) (Ward Lock, 1918) £80
IN WHEELABOUT AND COCKALONE by Grace Rhys (illustrated by Margaret W. Tarrant and Megan Rhys)
  (G.G. Harrap & Co, 1918) £30
THE TOOKEY AND ALICE MARY TALES by Robert de M. Rudolf (Harrap, 1919) £45
ELIZ'BETH, PHIL AND ME by Marion St. John Webb (Harrap, 1919) £70
ZOO DAYS by Harry Golding (48 colour plates by Margaret W. Tarrant) (Ward Lock, 1919) £70
THE ANIMAL ABC by Harry Golding (Ward Lock, 1920) £175
THE LITTLEST ONE AGAIN by Marion St. John Webb (Harrap, 1923) £60
THE FOREST FAIRIES by Marion St. John Webb (verse) (Modern Art Society, [1925]) £120
THE HOUSE FAIRIES by Marion St. John Webb (verse) (Modern Art Society, [1925]) £120
THE HEATH FAIRIES by Marion St. John Webb (verse) (Modern Art Society, [1925]) £120
THE SEED FAIRIES by Marion St. John Webb (verse) (Modern Art Society, [1925]) £120
THE INSECT FAIRIES by Marion St. John Webb (verse) (Modern Art Society, [1925]) £120
THE POND FAIRIES by Marion St. John Webb (verse) (Modern Art Society, 1925) £120
THE SEA-SHORE FAIRIES by Marion St. John Webb (verse) (Modern Art Society, [1925]) £120
THE WILD-FRUIT FAIRIES by Marion St. John Webb (verse) (Modern Art Society, [1925]) £120
RHYMES OF OLD TIMES (Medici Society, 1925) £60
THE TALES THE LETTERS TELL (five books; illustrated by M.W. Tarrant and others) (Grant Educational, 1925) .... each £40
THE MAGIC LAMPLIGHTER by Marion St John Webb (verse) (Medici Society, 1926) £60
THE WEATHER FAIRIES by Marion St John Webb (Modern Art Society, [1927]) £120
THE TWILIGHT FAIRIES by Marion St John Webb (Modern Art Society, [1928]) £120
AN ALPHABET OF MAGIC by Eleanor Farjeon (Medici Society, 1928) £100
THE ORCHARD FAIRIES by Marion St John Webb (verse) (Modern Art Society, [1928]) £125
MOTHER GOOSE: Nursery Rhymes (24 colour plates by Margaret W. Tarrant) (Ward Lock, [1929]) £80
OUR ANIMAL FRIENDS by Harry Golding (Ward Lock: 'Sunshine' series, [1930]) £60
SIMPLE COMPOSITION STEPS by Rose Meeres (written under the pseudonym 'S.N.D.') (Grant Educational, [1930]) £40
THE SONGS THE LETTERS SING by Rose Meeres (written under the pseudonym 'S.N.D.') (Grant Educational, [1930]) .... each £40
THE HIDDEN YEARS by John Oxenham (fourteen illustrations by Margaret W. Tarrant) (Longmans, 1931) £40
MAGIC HOUSES by Barbara Todd (verse) (Medici Society, [1932]) £150
MAGIC FLOWERS by Barbara Todd (verse) (Medici Society, [1933]) £150
DREAMLAND FAIRIES by Mary Gann (Duckworth, 1936) £175
FLOWERS OF THE COUNTRYSIDE (illustrated by Margaret W. Tarrant, M. Forestier and Eileen & Eva Soper)
  (Medici Society, 1943) £70
JOHANN THE WOOD CARVER by Gilmore Wood (Warne, 1949) £40
THE STORY OF CHRISTMAS (Medici Society, 1952) £15

'TARZAN' Rivals

The character 'Tarzan' was created by Edgar Rice Burroughs for adult readers, making his first appearance in American pulp title *All-Story* in October 1912. The success of the series inspired a host of copycat characters, mainly aimed at children or young adults. Below is a list of some of the most collectable.

Prices are for books in Very Good condition with dustjackets where applicable.

'Bomba the Jungle Boy' by Roy Rockwood

BOMBA THE JUNGLE BOY (Cupples & Leon, US, 1926) £25
BOMBA THE JUNGLE BOY AT THE MOVING MOUNTAIN (Cupples & Leon, US, 1926) £25
BOMBA THE JUNGLE BOY AT THE GIANT CATARACT (Cupples & Leon, US, 1926) £25
BOMBA THE JUNGLE BOY ON JAGUAR ISLAND (Cupples & Leon, US, 1927) £25
BOMBA THE JUNGLE BOY IN THE ABANDONED CITY (Cupples & Leon, US, 1927) £25
BOMBA THE JUNGLE BOY ON THE TERROR TRAIL (Cupples & Leon, US, 1928) £25
BOMBA THE JUNGLE BOY IN THE SWAMP OF DEATH (Cupples & Leon, US, 1929) £25
BOMBA THE JUNGLE BOY AMONG THE SLAVES (Cupples & Leon, US, 1929) £25
BOMBA THE JUNGLE BOY ON THE UNDERGROUND RIVER (Cupples & Leon, US, 1930) £25
BOMBA THE JUNGLE BOY AND THE LOST EXPLORERS (Cupples & Leon, US, 1930) £25
BOMBA THE JUNGLE BOY IN A STRANGE LAND (Cupples & Leon, US, 1931) £25
BOMBA THE JUNGLE BOY AMONG THE PYGMIES (Cupples & Leon, US, 1931) £25
BOMBA THE JUNGLE BOY AND THE CANNIBALS (Cupples & Leon, US, 1931) £25
BOMBA THE JUNGLE BOY AND THE PAINTED HUNTERS (Cupples & Leon, US, 1932) £25
BOMBA THE JUNGLE BOY AND THE RIVER DEMONS (Cupples & Leon, US, 1933) £25
BOMBA THE JUNGLE BOY AND THE HOSTILE CHIEFTAIN (Cupples & Leon, US, 1934) £25
BOMBA THE JUNGLE BOY TRAPPED BY THE CYCLONE (Cupples & Leon, US, 1935) £25
BOMBA THE JUNGLE BOY IN THE LAND OF BURNING LAVA (Cupples & Leon, US, 1936) £25
BOMBA THE JUNGLE BOY IN THE PERILOUS KINGDOM (Cupples & Leon, US, 1937) £25
BOMBA THE JUNGLE BOY IN THE STEAMING GROTTO (Cupples & Leon, US, 1938) £25

'Kaspa the Lion Man' by C.T. Stoneham

THE LION'S WAY: A STORY OF MEN AND LIONS (Hutchinson, 1931) £100
THE LION'S WAY: A STORY OF MEN AND LIONS (as 'KING OF THE JUNGLE') (Grossett & Dunlap, US, 1931) £100
KASPA THE LION MAN (Methuen, 1933) £100

'Tahara' by Harold M. Sherman

TAHARA, BOY MYSTIC OF INDIA (Goldsmith, US, 1933) £15
TAHARA AMONG THE AFRICAN TRIBES (Goldsmith, US, 1933) £15
TAHARA, BOY KING OF THE DESERT (Goldsmith, US, 1933)..£15
TAHARA IN THE LAND OF YUCATAN (Goldsmith, US, 1933)...£15

'Sorak' by Harvey D. Richards

SORAK OF THE MALAY JUNGLE (Cupples & Leon, US, 1934) £15
SORAK AND THE CLOUDED TIGER (Cupples & Leon, US, 1934)..£15
SORAK AND THE SULTAN'S ANKUS (Cupples & Leon, US, 1934)..£15
SORAK AND THE TREE MEN (Cupples & Leon, US, 1936) £15

'Kioga' by William L. Chester

HAWK OF THE WILDERNESS (Harper, US, 1936)...£25
HAWK OF THE WILDERNESS (paperback) (Ace, US, 1966)..£6
KIOGA OF THE WILDERNESS (paperback) (Daw, US, 1976) £4
ONE AGAINST A WILDERNESS (paperback)(Daw, US, 1977)...£4
KIOGA OF THE UNKNOWN LAND (paperback)(Daw, US, 1978)..£4

'Jan of the Jungle' by Otis Adelbert Kline

CALL OF THE SAVAGE (Clode, US, 1937)...£25
CALL OF THE SAVAGE (as 'JAN OF THE JUNGLE'; paperback)
    (Ace, US, 1966)..£8
JAN IN INDIA (Fictioneer, US, 1974)...£15

'Bantan' by Maurice B. Gardner

BANTAN, GOD-LIKE ISLANDER (Meador, US, 1937)..£25
BANTAN AND THE ISLAND GODDESS (Meador, US, 1942) £25
BANTAN DEFIANT (Greenwich Books, US, 1955)..£20
BANTAN VALIANT (Meador, US, 1957) £20
BANTAN'S ISLAND PERIL (Meador, US, 1959) £20
BANTAN INCREDIBLE (Forum, US, 1960) £20
BANTAN PRIMEVAL (Forum, US, 1961) £15
BANTAN FEARLESS (Forum, US, 1963) £15
ISLAND PARADISE AND OTHERS (Forum, US, 1964)..£15
BANTAN AND THE MERMAIDS (Gaus, US, 1970)...£15
BANTAN'S QUEST (Gaus, US, 1974) £15
THE ANCESTORS OF BANTAN (Gaus, US, 1976) £15
THE NEW ADVENTURES OF BANTAN (Gaus, US, 1977)..£15

'Tana' by Alan Connell

LORDS OF THE SERPENT LAND (paperback) (Curranong Publications, Australia, 1945) £30
PRISONERS IN SERPENT LAND (paperback) (Curranong Publications, Australia, 1945) £30
WARRIORS OF SERPENT LAND (paperback) (Curranong Publications, Australia, 1945) £30

'Azan the Apeman' by Marco Garron

THE LOST CITY (paperback) (Curtis Warren, 1950) £60
THE MISSING SAFARI (paperback) (Curtis Warren, 1950)...£60
TRIBAL WAR (paperback) (Curtis Warren, 1951)...£60
WHITE FANGS (paperback) (Curtis Warren, 1951) £60
KING HUNTERS (paperback) (Curtis Warren, 1951) £60
JUNGLE FEVER (paperback) (Curtis Warren, 1951)...£60

'Rex Brandon, White Hunter' by Marco Garon

JUNGLE ALLIES (paperback) (Curtis Warren, 1951) £30
DEATH WARRIORS (paperback) (Curtis Warren, 1951) £30
BLACK FURY (paperback) (Curtis Warren, 1951)...£30
WHITE GOLD (paperback) (Curtis Warren, 1951) £30
BLACK SPORT (paperback) (Curtis Warren, 1951) £30
BUSH CLAWS (paperback) (Curtis Warren, 1951) £30
SILENT RIVER (paperback) (Curtis Warren, 1951) £30
VELDT WARRIORS (paperback) (Curtis Warren, 1951)...£30
LEOPARD GOD (paperback) (Curtis Warren, 1951) £30
SNAKE VALLEY (paperback) (Curtis Warren, 1952) £30
FIRE TRIBES (paperback) (Curtis Warren, 1952) £30
MOUNTAIN GOLD (paperback) (Curtis Warren, 1952)...£30

'Anjani, White God of the Jungle' by Earl Titan

THE GOLD OF AKADA (paperback) (Scion, 1951) £35
THE GOLD OF AKADA (paperback) (Gryphon Books, US, 1997) £10
ANJANI THE MIGHTY (paperback) (Scion, 1951) £35
ANJANI THE MIGHTY (paperback) (Gryphon Books, US, 1997)..£10

'Shuna' by John King
SHUNA, WHITE QUEEN OF THE JUNGLE (paperback) (Harborough, 1951) £30
SHUNA AND THE LOST TRIBE (paperback) (Harborough, 1951) £30

'Jacare' by Victor Norwood
THE UNTAMED (paperback) (Scion, 1951) £30
THE CAVES OF DEATH (paperback) (Scion, 1951) £30
THE TEMPLE OF THE DEAD (paperback) (Scion, 1951) £30
THE SKULL OF KANAIMA (paperback) (Scion, 1951) £30
THE ISLAND OF CREEPING DEATH (paperback) (Scion, 1952) £30
CRY OF THE BEAST (paperback) (Scion, 1953) £30
DRUMS ALONG THE AMAZON (paperback) (Scion, 1953) £30

'Polaris Janess' by Charles B. Stilson
POLARIS OF THE SNOWS (Avalon, US, 1965) £25
MINOS OF SARDANES (Avalon, US, 1966) £25
POLARIS AND THE IMMORTALS (Avalon, US, 1968) £25

'Lord Grandith' by Philip José Farmer
A FEAST UNKNOWN (Essex House, US, 1969) £25
LORD OF THE TREES (paperback) (Ace, US, 1970) £6
THE MAD GOBLIN (paperback) (Ace, US, 1970) £6

'Jongor' by Robert Moore Williams
JONGOR OF LOST LAND (paperback) (Popular Library, US, 1970) £4
THE RETURN OF JONGOR (paperback) (Popular Library, US, 1970) £4
JONGOR FIGHTS BACK (paperback) (Popular Library, US, 1970) £4

'Balzan of the Cat People' by Wallace Moore
THE BLOOD STONES (paperback) (Pyramid, US, 1975) £3
THE CAVERNS OF MADNESS (paperback) (Pyramid, US, 1976) £3
THE LIGHTS OF ZETAR (paperback) (Pyramid, US, 1976) £3

'Bunduki' by J.T. Edson
BUNDUKI (paperback) (Corgi, 1975) £3
BUNDUKI AND DAWN (paperback) (Corgi, 1976) £3
SACRIFICE FOR THE QUAGGA GOD (paperback) (Corgi, 1976) £3
FEARLESS MASTER OF THE JUNGLE (paperback) (Corgi, 1980) £3

Others
OZAR THE AZTEC by Valentine Wood (Gramol, 1935) £30
SOJAR OF TITAN by Manly Wade Wellman (Crestwood, US, 1949) £15
ZAMBA OF THE JUNGLE by John Raymond (paperback) (John Spencer, 1951) £30
LORD TYGER by Philip José Farmer (Doubleday, US, 1970) £15
MARVEL COMICS 1 (features 'Ka-Zar') (Timely/Atlas, US, October/November 1939) £10,000
JUNGLE COMICS 1 (features 'Käanga') (Fiction House, US, 1940) £30

TAYLOR, G.P.
British children's author. Born: 1961. Following numerous rejection letters from major publishers Reverend G.P. Taylor sold his motorbike to fund a private publication of 2,500 paperback copies of his first novel, *Shadowmancer*, issued by Mount Publishing in October 2002. After being scooped by Faber this title changed hands for silly amounts, before prices began to plateau.
Prices are for books in Fine condition with dustjackets where applicable.

SHADOWMANCER (paperback; 2,500 copies) (Mount Publishing, 2002) £500
SHADOWMANCER (paperback) (Faber & Faber, 2003) £5
SHADOWMANCER (Special Edition, hardcover) (Faber & Faber, 2003) £15
SHADOWMANCER (adult edition, paperback) (Faber & Faber, 2004) £5
SHADOWMANCER (hardcover) (Charisma House, 2004) £8
WORMWOOD (paperback, true first edition) (Faber & Faber, 2004) £5
WORMWOOD (first hardback edition) (Faber & Faber, 2004) £10
TERSIAS (Faber & Faber, 2005) £8
TERSIAS (paperback) (Faber & Faber, 2006) £5

THACKERAY, W.M.
British author. Born: William Makepeace Thackeray in Calcutta in 1811. Studied at Charterhouse and Trinity College, Cambridge. The author of *Vanity Fair* (1847) wrote a series of 'Christmas Books' between 1846 and 1855, of which the last, *The Rose and the Ring*, has been the most enduring. Died: 1863.
Prices are for books in Very Good condition.

'Christmas' Books
MRS PERKINS' BALL (illustrated by the author) (Chapman & Hall, [1847]) £500

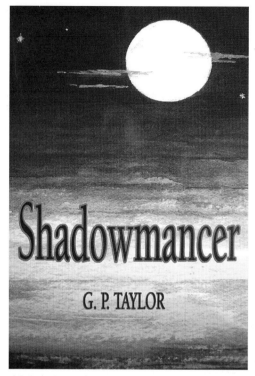

Hugh Thomson remains very popular with collectors and this illustrated fairy book is worth £225 today.

G.P. Taylor is part of a new wave of collectable children's authors and his self-published debut has become a regular at auction.

OUR STREET (illustrated by the author) (Chapman & Hall, 1848) **£500**
DR BIRCH AND HIS YOUNG FRIENDS (illustrated by the author) (Chapman & Hall, 1849) **£500**
REBECCA AND ROWENA: A Romance upon Romance (illustrated by Richard Doyle) (Chapman & Hall, 1850) **£500**
THE KICKLEBURYS ON THE RHINE (Smith Elder, 1850) **£500**
THE ROSE AND THE RING, or The History of Prince Giglio and Prince Bulbo:
    A Far-Side Pantomime for Great and Small Children (illustrated by the author) (Smith Elder, 1855) **£800**

THOMPSON, Kay

American author. Born: 1912. Best known for her 'Eloise' books. She was also a well-known star of stage and film musicals, notably *Funny Face* with Fred Astaire. Died: 1998.

Prices are for books in Very Good condition with dustjackets.

ELOISE: A Book for Precocious Grown-ups (illustrated by Hilary Knight) (Simon & Schuster, US, 1955) **£150**
ELOISE: A Book for Precocious Grown-ups (Max Reinhardt UK, 1957) **£150**
ELOISE: A Book for Precocious Grown-ups
    (Simon & Schuster, US, 1995; limited to 250 copies, signed by Thompson and Knight) (In slipcase; no dustjacket) **£150**
ELOISE IN PARIS (illustrated by Hilary Knight) (Simon & Schuster, US, 1957) **£150**
ELOISE IN PARIS (Max Reinhardt, UK, 1958) **£150**
ELOISE IN PARIS (Simon & Schuster, US, 1999; limited to 250 copies, signed by Knight) (In slipcase; no dustjacket) **£150**
ELOISE AT CHRISTMASTIME (illustrated by Hilary Knight) (Random House, US, 1958) **£200**
ELOISE AT CHRISTMASTIME (Max Reinhardt, UK, 1959) **£250**
ELOISE AT CHRISTMASTIME (Simon & Schuster, US, 1999; limited to 250 copies, signed by Knight) (In slipcase; no dustjacket) **£150**
ELOISE IN MOSCOW (illustrated by Hilary Knight) (Simon & Schuster, US, 1959).. **£150**
ELOISE IN MOSCOW (Max Reinhardt, UK, 1960) **£150**
ELOISE IN MOSCOW (Simon & Schuster, us, 2000; limited to 250 copies, signed by Knight) (In slipcase; no dustjacket) **£120**
ELOISE TAKES A BAWTH (illustrated by Hilary Knight, with additional Plumbing by Matt Crowley)
    (Simon & Schuster, US, 2002) **£15**

Other 'Eloise' titles

THE ABSOLUTELY ESSENTIAL ELOISE (illustrated by Hilary Knight, with Scrapbook written by Marie Brenner)
    (Simon & Schuster, US, 1999) **£15**
ELOISE: THE ULTIMATE EDITION (contains ELOISE; ELOISE IN PARIS; ELOISE AT CHRISTMASTIME;
    and ELOISE IN MOSCOW) (illustrated by Hilary Knight) (Simon & Schuster, US, 2000)....................................... **£15**

ELOISE'S GUIDE TO LIFE, or how to eat, dress, travel, behave, and stay six forever
(illustrated by Hilary Knight) (Simon & Schuster, US, 2000)..£10

Others

KAY THOMPSON'S MISS POOKY PECKINPAUGH, and her secret private boyfriends
complete with telephone numbers (illustrated by Joe Eula) (Harper & Row, US, 1970) £75

THOMSON, Hugh

British artist-illustrator. Born: Coleraine, Co. Londonderry, in 1860. Had little formal training, serving his apprenticeship at the card manufacturers, Marcus Ward. Made his first contributions to the *English Illustrated Magazine*, subsequently illustrating a number of classic works, specialising in those written or set in the eighteenth century. An important influence on C.E. and H.M. Brock. Died: 1920.

Prices are for books in Very Good condition.

THE PIPER OF HAMELIN by R.W. Buchanan (Heinemann, 1893)..£50
JACK THE GIANT KILLER (Macmillan, 1898) £225
THIS AND THAT: A Tale of Two Tinies by Mrs Molesworth (Macmillan, 1899)........................£35
THE CHIMES by Charles Dickens (Hodder & Stoughton, [1913])...£35
TOM BROWN'S SCHOOLDAYS by Thomas Hughes. Edited by H.C. Bradby (Ginn, US, [1918])........£35
THE CRICKET ON THE HEARTH by Charles Dickens (introduction by Walter de la Mare) (Golden Cockerel Press, 1933).......£60

THURBER, James

American author-illustrator. Born: James Grover Thurber in 1894. Best known for his humorous contributions to the *New Yorker* magazine, Thurber also wrote a handful of children's books, of which *The 13 Clocks* (1950) and *The Wonderful O* (1955) are the best known. Died: 1961.

Prices are for books in Very Good condition with dustjackets.

MANY MOONS (illustrated by Louis Slobodkin) (Harcourt Brace, US, 1943)...............................£100
MANY MOONS (illustrated by Louis Slobodkin) (Hamish Hamilton, 1944)..................................£70
THE GREAT QUILLOW (illustrated by Doris Lee) (Harcourt Brace, US, 1944).............................£70
THE WHITE DEER (illustrated by James Thurber and Don Freeman) (Harcourt Brace, US, 1945)............£60
THE WHITE DEER (illustrated by James Thurber and Don Freeman) (Hamish Hamilton, 1946)............£50
THE 13 CLOCKS (illustrated by Mark [Marc] Simont) (Simon & Schuster, US, 1950) £60
THE 13 CLOCKS (illustrated by Marc Simont) (Hamish Hamilton, 1951)....................................£50
THE WONDERFUL O (illustrated by Marc Simont) (Simon & Schuster, US, 1957) £50
THE WONDERFUL O (illustrated by Marc Simont) (Hamish Hamilton, 1958)..............................£40

TIMLIN, William M.

British author-illustrator. Born: William Mitcheson Timlin in Ashington, Northumberland, in 1892. Studied at Morpeth Grammar School and the Armstrong School of Art in Newcastle. Moved to South Africa in 1912. His solitary children's book, *The Ship that Sailed to Mars* (1923), is one of the classic works of fantasy. Died: 1943.

Price is for books in Very Good condition with dustjackets.

THE SHIP THAT SAILED TO MARS: A Fantasy (illustrated by the author) (Harrap, [1923]) £2,000

TODD, Barbara Euphan

British author. Born: Yorkshire, 1897. Prolific children's author, best known for her series of novels featuring the walking, talking scarecrow, Worzel Gummidge. Under the pseudonym 'Euphan', Todd contributed a number of humorous verses to *Punch* in the 1920s. Died: 1976.

Prices are for books in Very Good condition with dustjackets where applicable.

THE 'NORMOUS SATURDAY FAIRY BOOK (with Marjory Royce and Moira Meighn) (Stanley Paul, 1924) £60
THE 'NORMOUS SUNDAY STORY BOOK (with Marjory Royce and Moira Meighn) (Stanley Paul, 1925) £50
THE VERY GOOD WALKERS (with Marjory Royce; illustrated by H.R. Millar) (Methuen, 1925)......£50
MR BLOSSOM'S SHOP (Nelson, [1929]) £60
HAPPY COTTAGE (with Marjory Royce) (Collins, [1930]) £60
MAGIC HOUSES (verse) (Medici Society, [1932])..£150
MAGIC FLOWERS (verse) (Medici Society, [1933])...£150
SOUTH COUNTRY SECRETS: A Description of Southern England Written in the Form of a Tale
(written with John Graham Bower under the pseudonyms 'Euphan' and 'Klaxon') (Burns Oates, 1935) £60
THE SEVENTH DAUGHTER (illustrated by E.H. Shepard) (Burns Oates, 1935) £60
THE TOUCHSTONE: Tales (with 'Klaxon' [John Graham Bower]) (Burns Oates, 1936) £60
WORZEL GUMMIDGE, or The Scarecrow of Scatterbrook (illustrated by Elizabeth Alldridge) (Burns Oates, 1936)............£180
WORZEL GUMMIDGE AGAIN (illustrated by Elizabeth Alldridge) (Burns Oates, 1937)............£150
THE MYSTERY TRAIN (University of London, 1937) £60
THE SPLENDID PICNIC (University of London, 1937) £60
MORE ABOUT WORZEL GUMMIDGE (Burns Oates, 1938) £100
MR DOCK'S GARDEN (illustrated by Ruth Westcott) (Arnold, [1939]).....................................£60
GERTRUDE THE GREEDY GOOSE (illustrated by Benjamin Rabier) (Muller, [1939]).................£60

THOMPSON, Kay

THE HOUSE THAT RAN BEHIND (with Esther Boumphrey) (Muller, 1943) £50
MISS RANSKILL COMES HOME (Chapman & Hall, 1946) £40
WORZEL GUMMIDGE AND SAUCY NANCY (illustrated by Will Nickless) (Hollis & Carter, 1947) £60
WORZEL GUMMIDGE TAKES A HOLIDAY (illustrated by Will Nickless) (Hollis & Carter, 1949) £60
ALOYSIUS LET LOOSE by John Graham Bower (written under the pseudonym 'Klaxon',
     with Barbara Euphan Todd; illustrated by A.E. Batchelor) (Collins, 1950) £50
EARTHY MANGOLD AND WORZEL GUMMIDGE (illustrated by J.J. Crockford) (Hollis & Carter, 1954) £60
WORZEL GUMMIDGE AND THE RAILWAY SCARECROWS (illustrated by Jill Crockford) (Evans, 1955)........ £60
WORZEL GUMMIDGE AT THE CIRCUS (illustrated by Jill Crockford) (Evans, 1956)................................. £60
THE BOY WITH THE GREEN THUMB (illustrated by Charlotte Hough) (Hamish Hamilton, 1956)............... £20
THE WIZARD AND THE UNICORN (illustrated by Prudence Seward) (Hamish Hamilton, 1957) £20
WORZEL GUMMIDGE AND THE TREASURE SHIP (illustrated by Jill Crockford) (Evans, 1958)................. £40
THE SHOP AROUND THE CORNER (illustrated by Olive Coughlan) (Hamish Hamilton, 1959)................... £20
DETECTIVE WORZEL GUMMIDGE (illustrated by Jill Crockford) (Evans, 1963)...................................... £60
THE SHOP BY THE SEA (illustrated by Sarah Garland) (Hamish Hamilton, 1966)................................... £20
THE CLOCK SHOP (illustrated by Jill Crockford) (World's Work, 1967) £20
THE SHOP ON WHEELS (illustrated by Jill Crockford) (World's Work, 1968) £20
THE BOX IN THE ATTIC (illustrated by Lynette Hemmant) (World's Work, 1970) £12
THE WAND FROM FRANCE (illustrated by Lynette Hemmant) (World's Work, [1972]) £12

TOLKIEN, J.R.R.

British author. Born: John Ronald Reuel Tolkien in Bloemfontein, South Africa, in 1892. Studied at King Edward's School, Birmingham, and Exeter College, Oxford. Appointed Professor of Anglo-Saxon at Oxford in 1925. Published a number of scholarly works on philology and English literature, but is best-known for his three books about the mythical land of 'Middle Earth', *The Hobbit* (1937), *The Lord of the Rings* (1954-55) and *The Silmarillion* (1977), the last begun while he was a soldier in the First World War. Drew tremendous strength and inspiration from his friendship with C.S. Lewis, the two of them forming an informal literary society known as 'The Inklings'. Died: 1973.

Prices are for books in Very Good condition with dustjackets where applicable.
The US edition is listed only where it precedes the UK edition.

'The Hobbit, or There and Back Again'
FIRST EDITION (illustrated by the author) (Allen & Unwin, 1937) £25,000
SECOND IMPRESSION (four new colour plates by the author) (Allen & Unwin, 1938)............................ £4,000
SECOND EDITION (contains revised version of 'Riddle in the Dark') (Allen & Unwin, 1951) £50
FIRST PAPERBACK EDITION (Puffin, 1961) £8
THIRD (REVISED) EDITION (Allen & Unwin, 1966) £20
SCHOOLS EDITION (introduction by R.S. Fowler; paperback) (Allen & Unwin, 1972)............................. £5
DE LUXE EDITION (some of Tolkien's original illustrations coloured by H.E. Riddett; in slipcase)
     (Allen & Unwin, 1976).. £150
FIRST FOLIO SOCIETY EDITION (Society's own binding of Allen & Unwin's 1976 De Luxe edition; in slipcase)
     (Folio Society, 1976).. £100
SECOND FOLIO SOCIETY EDITION (illustrated by Eric Fraser; in slipcase) (Folio Society, 1979)............... £15
MICHAEL HAGUE EDITION (Houghton Mifflin, US, 1984)... £15
MICHAEL HAGUE EDITION (as 'The Illustrated Hobbit') (Allen & Unwin, 1984)...................................... £15
FIFTIETH ANNIVERSARY EDITION (new introduction by Christopher Tolkien) (Allen & Unwin, 1987) £20
DE LUXE FIFTIETH ANNIVERSARY EDITION (limited to 500 copies; leather binding) (Allen & Unwin, 1987).......£200
THE ANNOTATED HOBBIT (annotated by Douglas A. Anderson) (Unwin Hyman, 1988)........................... £15
CENTENARY EDITION (Harper Collins, 1991) £25
THE HOBBIT: THE GRAPHIC NOVEL (illustrated by David Wenzel; adapted by Charles Dixon with Sean Demming)
     (Grafton, 1991)... £8

'The Lord of the Rings'
'The Fellowship of the Ring, being the First Part of "The Lord of the Rings"'
FIRST EDITION (Allen & Unwin, 1954) £4,000
REVISED EDITION (new foreword and prologue by author) (Allen & Unwin, 1966) £150
CENTENARY EDITION (Harper Collins, 1991) £15

'The Two Towers, being the Second Part of "The Lord of the Rings"'
FIRST EDITION (Allen & Unwin, 1954) £3,500
REVISED EDITION (Allen & Unwin, 1966)... £150
CENTENARY EDITION (Harper Collins, 1991) £15

'The Return of the King, being the Third Part of "The Lord of the Rings"'
FIRST EDITION (Allen & Unwin, 1955) £3,000
REVISED EDITION (Allen & Unwin, 1966)... £150
CENTENARY EDITION (Harper Collins, 1991) £15

'The Lord of the Rings'
COMPLETE SET OF FIRST EDITIONS (three volumes) (Allen & Unwin, 1954-55) .... the set **£10,000**
FIRST COMBINED EDITION (three volumes; in grey box) (Allen & Unwin, 1962) .... the set **£200**

*Tolkien greatly admired the work of artist Pauline Baynes and she illustrated both **Smith of Wootton Major** and **The Adventures of Tom Bombadil**. Also pictured is a complete first edition set of **The Lord of the Rings** trilogy, and **Mr Bliss**, a lighthearted picture book that wasn't published until 1982, nine years after the author's death. Very Good copies are now worth £15.*

DE LUXE COMBINED EDITION (three volumes; black buckram bindings; gilt edges;
in box decorated by Pauline Baynes) (Allen & Unwin, 1964) .... the set **£300**
FIRST PAPERBACK EDITION (one volume) (Allen & Unwin, 1968) **£20**
DE-LUXE INDIA PAPER EDITION (one volume; in slipcase; India paper) (Allen & Unwin, 1969) **£750**
THREE-VOLUME PAPERBACK EDITION (Allen & Unwin, 1974) .... the set **£25**
FOLIO SOCIETY EDITION (illustrated by Ingahild Grathmer; illustrations drawn by Eric Fraser;
three volumes; in box) (Folio Society, 1977) .... the set **£60**
25TH ANNIVERSARY EDITION (three volumes plus sixteen-page booklet; paperbacks; in box) (Unwin, [1980]) .... the set **£30**
THREE-VOLUME BOXED EDITION (Unwin Hyman, 1985) .... the set **£50**
CENTENARY EDITION (three volumes; in box) (Harper Collins, 1991) .... the set **£50**
ILLUSTRATED CENTENARY EDITION (illustrated by Alan Lee) (Harper Collins, 1991) **£30**
DE LUXE ILLUSTRATED CENTENARY EDITION (limited to 250 numbered copies, signed by the artist;
quarter leather binding; in slipcase) (Harper Collins, 1991) **£300**
ONE-VOLUME CENTENARY EDITION (Harper Collins, 1992) **£20**

'The Silmarillion'

FIRST EDITION: Billing & Sons issue (printed by Billing & Sons; cloth binding) (Allen & Unwin, 1977) **£50**
FIRST EDITION: Clowes issue (printed by William Clowes; cloth or paper binding) (Allen & Unwin, 1977) **£20**
DE LUXE EDITION (limited to 900 numbered [101-1,000] copies; leather binding; printed by William Clowes)
(Allen & Unwin, 1982) **£400**
SIGNED DE LUXE EDITION (limited to 100 numbered [1-100] copies, signed by Christopher Tolkien;
leather binding; printed by William Clowes) (Allen & Unwin, 1982) **£200**
CENTENARY EDITION (Harper Collins, 1992) **£15**

'The History of Middle-Earth' (all books edited by Christopher Tolkien)

THE BOOK OF LOST TALES Part 1 (Volume I of 'The History of Middle-Earth') (Allen & Unwin, 1983) .... **£300+**
THE BOOK OF LOST TALES Part 2 (Volume II of 'The History of Middle-Earth') (Allen & Unwin, 1984) **£300**
THE LAYS OF BELERIAND (Volume III of 'The History of Middle-Earth') (Allen & Unwin, 1985) **£100**
THE SHAPING OF MIDDLE-EARTH (Volume IV of 'The History of Middle-Earth') (Allen & Unwin, 1986) **£250**
THE LOST ROAD (Volume V of 'The History of Middle-Earth') (Unwin Hyman, 1987) **£250**
THE RETURN OF THE SHADOW: The History of 'The Lord of the Rings' Part 1
(Volume VI of 'The History of Middle-Earth') (Unwin Hyman, 1988) **£150**
THE TREASON OF ISENGARD: The History of 'The Lord of the Rings' Part 2
(Volume VII of 'The History of Middle-Earth') (Unwin Hyman, 1989) **£75**

THE WAR OF THE RING: The History of 'The Lord of the Rings' Part 3
(Volume VIII of 'The History of Middle-Earth') (Unwin Hyman, 1990) **£150**
SAURON DEFEATED: The History of 'The Lord of the Rings' Part 4
(Volume IX of 'The History of Middle-Earth') (HarperCollins, 1992) **£200**
MORGOTH'S RING (HarperCollins, 1993) **£200**
THE WAR OF THE JEWELS (HarperCollins, 1994) **£300**
THE PEOPLES OF MIDDLE-EARTH (paperback) (HarperCollins, 1996) **£20**

Other 'Middle-Earth' Books

THE ADVENTURES OF TOM BOMBADIL and Other Verses from 'The Red Book'
(illustrated by Pauline Baynes) (Allen & Unwin, 1962)...................................**£200**
THE ADVENTURES OF TOM BOMBADIL and Other Verses from 'The Red Book'
(with 'Farmer Giles of Ham') (Unwin, 1975)...................................**£10**
THE ADVENTURES OF TOM BOMBADIL and Other Verses from 'The Red Book'
(illustrated by Roger Garland) (Unwin Hyman, 1990) **£10**
THE ROAD GOES EVER ON: A Song Cycle (music by Donald Swann) (Houghton Mifflin, US, 1967) **£45**
THE ROAD GOES EVER ON: A Song Cycle (music by Donald Swann) (Allen & Unwin, 1968).......**£35**
BILBO'S LAST SONG (illustrated by Pauline Baynes; poster) (Allen & Unwin, 1974) **£30**
BILBO'S LAST SONG (illustrated by Pauline Baynes; hardback) (Unwin Hyman, 1990)...................................**£15**
BILBO'S LAST SONG (illustrated by Pauline Baynes; paperback) (Arrow, 1992) **£3**
THE FILM BOOK OF J.R.R. TOLKIEN'S 'THE LORD OF THE RINGS' (130 stills from the film; paperback)
(Methuen, Toronto, 1978)...................................**£5**
THE FILM BOOK OF J.R.R. TOLKIEN'S 'THE LORD OF THE RINGS' (130 stills from the film; paperback)
(Fantasy Film Books, 1979) **£5**
UNFINISHED TALES OF NUMENOR AND MIDDLE-EARTH. Edited by Christopher Tolkien (Allen & Unwin, 1980)...................................**£40**
STORIES FROM THE THIRD AGE (contains 'The Hobbit', 'The Lord of the Rings' and 'The Silmarillion';
four volumes; paperbacks; in box) (Unwin, [1980])...................................the set **£10**
THE MIDDLE-EARTH COLLECTION (contains 'The Hobbit', 'The Lord of the Rings' and 'The Silmarillion';
five volumes; paperbacks; in box) (Unwin, [1980]) ....the set **£10**

Books About 'Middle-Earth'

A GUIDE TO MIDDLE-EARTH by Robert Foster (Mirage Press, US, 1971)...................................**£20**
A GUIDE TO MIDDLE-EARTH by Robert Foster (revised edition; as 'The Complete Guide to Middle-Earth,
from "The Hobbit" to "The Silmarillion"') (Allen & Unwin, 1978)...................................**£10**
A TOLKIEN COMPASS. Edited by Jared Lobdell (includes Tolkien's 'Guide to the Names in "The Lord of the Rings"')
(Open Court, US, 1975) **£20**
THE TOLKIEN COMPANION by J.E.A. Tyler (illustrated by Kevin Reilly) (Macmillan, 1976) **£20**
THE TOLKIEN COMPANION by J.E.A. Tyler (revised edition; as 'The New Tolkien Companion') (Macmillan, 1979) **£20**
J.R.R. TOLKIEN: THE COMPLETE GUIDE (includes Foster's 'The Complete Guide to Middle-Earth' and
Humphrey Carpenter's 'J.R.R. Tolkien: A Biography'; paperback; in slipcase) (Unwin, 1978)...................................**£10**
AN INTRODUCTION TO ELVISH: and to Other Tongues and Proper Names . . . of Middle-Earth. Edited by Jim Allan
(Bran's Head, 1978) **£20**
A MIDDLE-EARTH ALBUM by Joan Wyatt (Thames & Hudson, 1979) **£20**
A TOLKIEN BESTIARY by David Day (illustrated by Ian Miller) (Mitchell Beazley, 1979) **£20**
THE TOLKIEN QUIZ-BOOK by Bart Andrews and Bernice Zuber (paperback) (Sphere, 1979)...................................**£2**
THE MIDDLE-EARTH QUIZ BOOK by Suzanne Buchholz (paperback) (Thames & Hudson, 1980) **£3**
A READER'S GUIDE TO 'THE SILMARILLION' by Paul H. Kocker (Thames & Hudson, 1980) **£20**
JOURNEYS OF FRODO by Barbara Strachey (paperback) (Allen & Unwin, 1981) **£5**
AN ATLAS OF MIDDLE-EARTH by Karen Fenstad (Houghton Mifflin, US, 1981)...................................**£20**
THE TOLKIEN QUIZ BOOK by Nigel Robinson and Linda Wilson (paperback) (Star, 1981) **£2**
THE ROAD TO MIDDLE-EARTH by Tom Shippey (Allen & Unwin, 1982) **£20**
A DICTIONARY OF QUENYA AND OF PROTO-ELDARIN Compiled by J.C. Bradfield ([J.C. Bradfield], 1982) **£20**
THE SONG OF MIDDLE-EARTH: J.R.R. Tolkien's Themes, Symbols and Myths by David Harvey (Allen & Unwin, 1985).....**£20**
A TOLKIEN THESAURUS by Richard A. Blackwelder (Garland, US, 1990) **£50**
TOLKIEN: THE ILLUSTRATED ENCYCLOPEDIA by David Day (Mitchell Beazley, 1991)...................................**£20**

Others

OXFORD POETRY 1915 Edited by G.D.H. Cole and T.W. Earp (includes Tolkien's poem 'Goblin Feet') (Blackwell, 1915).......**£400**
OXFORD POETRY 1914-1916 (includes Tolkien's poem 'Goblin Feet') (Blackwell, 1917)...................................**£150**
THE BOOK OF FAIRY POETRY Edited by Dora Owen (includes Tolkien's poem 'Goblin Feet') (Longmans, 1920) **£100**
FIFTY NEW POEMS FOR CHILDREN (includes Tolkien's poem 'Goblin Feet') (Blackwell, 1922)...................................**£30**
FARMER GILES OF HAM (illustrated by Pauline Baynes) (Allen & Unwin, 1949)...................................**£250**
FARMER GILES OF HAM (illustrated by Roger Garland) (Unwin Hyman, 1990)...................................**£15**
TREE AND LEAF (includes Tolkien's essay 'On Fairy-Stories' and his story 'Leaf by Niggle') (Allen & Unwin, 1964)...............**£100**
TREE AND LEAF (paperback; simultaneous with the above) (Allen & Unwin, 1964) **£15**
TREE AND LEAF (revised edition; contains first printing of the full version of the poem 'Mythopoeia') (Unwin Hyman, 1988) **£20**
WINTER'S TALES FOR CHILDREN 1 Edited by Caroline Hillier (includes Tolkien's poems 'Once Upon a Time' and
'The Dragon's Visit') (Macmillan, 1965)...................................**£20**
THE TOLKIEN READER (contains 'The Homecoming of Beorhtnoth', 'On Fairy-Stories', 'Leaf by Niggle',
'Farmer Giles of Ham' and 'The Adventures of Tom Bombadil') (Ballantine, US, 1966)...................................**£30**
SMITH OF WOOTTON MAJOR (boards; issued without dustjacket) (Allen & Unwin, 1967) **£40**
SMITH OF WOOTTON MAJOR (illustrated by Roger Garland) (Unwin Hyman, 1990)...................................**£10**
SMITH OF WOOTTON MAJOR and FARMER GILES OF HAM (paperback) (Ballantine, US, [1969]) **£5**

THE HAMISH HAMILTON BOOK OF DRAGONS Edited by Roger Lancelyn Green (includes Tolkien's poem 'The Hoard')
(Hamish Hamilton, 1970)..£15
THE HOMECOMING OF BEORHTNOTH (Allen & Unwin, 1975)..£20
TREE AND LEAF, SMITH OF WOOTTON MAJOR and THE HOMECOMING OF BEORHTNOTH (paperback) (Unwin, 1975)...£3
FARMER GILES OF HAM and THE ADVENTURES OF TOM BOMBADIL (paperback) (Unwin, 1975).................£3
THE FATHER CHRISTMAS LETTERS Edited by Baillie Tolkien (Allen & Unwin, 1976)............................£30
DRAWINGS BY TOLKIEN (exhibition catalogue; introduction by Baillie Tolkien and Humphrey Carpenter)
(Ashmolean Museum, Oxford/National Book League, 1976)..£15
PICTURES BY J.R.R. TOLKIEN (in slipcase) (Allen & Unwin, 1979)...£150
POEMS AND STORIES (contains 'The Adventures of Tom Bombadil', 'The Homecoming of Beorhtnoth Beorhtelm's Son',
'On Fairy-Stories', 'Leaf by Niggle', 'Farmer Giles of Ham' and 'Smith of Wootton Major';
illustrated by Pauline Baynes; in box) (Allen & Unwin, 1980)..£150
THE LETTERS OF J.R.R. TOLKIEN Edited by Humphrey Carpenter and Christopher Tolkien (Allen & Unwin, 1981)...............£20
MR BLISS (Allen & Unwin, 1982)..£15
SMITH OF WOOTTON MAJOR and LEAF BY NIGGLE (illustrated by Pauline Baynes; paperback) (Unwin, 1983)..................£3
THE HOMECOMING OF BEORHTNOTH (pamphlet; limited to 300 copies) (Anglo Saxon Books, 1991) £30

'TOPPER'

Popular British comic, published by D.C. Thomson. The comic itself was launched on 7th February 1953, the first *Topper Book* appearing later that year. All the annuals published up until 1959 were oblong in format. All were issued in boards except the first, which had card covers.

Prices are for comics/annuals in Very Good condition.

TOPPER (7th February 1953)..£135
THE TOPPER PICTURE BOOK...£100
THE TOPPER BOOK 1955..£50
THE TOPPER BOOK 1956-57 ....each £30
THE TOPPER BOOK 1958-59 ....each £25
THE TOPPER BOOK 1960..£20
THE TOPPER BOOK 1961..£15
THE TOPPER BOOK 1962-65 ....each £15
THE TOPPER BOOK 1966-69 ....each £10
THE TOPPER BOOK 1970..£8
THE TOPPER BOOK 1971-72 ....each £6
THE TOPPER BOOK 1973-79 ....each £4
THE TOPPER BOOK 1980-Present ....each £3

TOURTEL, Mary

British author-illustrator. Born: Mary Caldwell in Canterbury, Kent, in 1873. Contributed two titles to Grant Richards' famous 'Dumpy Books' series, but is best-known as the creator of Rupert Bear, launched in the *Daily Express* in November 1920 as a rival to the *Daily Mail*'s 'Teddy Tail'. She was forced to abandon the strip in 1935 due to failing eyesight. See also the 'Rupert Annuals' entry. Died: 1948.

Prices are for books in Very Good condition.

Early 'Rupert' Books

THE ADVENTURES OF RUPERT THE LITTLE LOST BEAR Reprinted from the 'Daily Express'
(Nelson, [1921])..£950
THE LITTLE BEAR AND THE FAIRY CHILD Reprinted from the 'Daily Express' (Nelson, [1922])................£1,050
MARGOT THE MIDGET AND LITTLE BEAR'S CHRISTMAS. Reprinted from the 'Daily Express'
(Nelson, [1922])..£950
THE LITTLE BEAR AND THE OGRES (Nelson, 1922)..£1,050
'RUPERT LITTLE BEAR'S ADVENTURES' (three books) (Sampson Low, 1924-25) .... each: £850
'RUPERT – LITTLE BEAR SERIES' (six books) (Sampson Low, 1925-27)... each: £400

'Little Bear Library' Books

NO. 1: RUPERT AND THE ENCHANTED PRINCESS (Sampson Low, [1928]) £70
NO. 2: RUPERT AND THE BLACK DWARF (Sa\mpson Low, [1928])...£60
NO. 3: RUPERT AND HIS PET MONKEY (Sampson Low, [1928])...£55
NO. 4: RUPERT AND HIS FRIEND MARGOT and RUPERT, MARGOT AND THE FAIRIES
(Sampson Low, [1928]) £55
NO. 5: RUPERT IN THE WOOD OF MYSTERY (Sampson Low, [1929]) £55
NO. 6: FURTHER ADVENTURES OF RUPERT AND HIS PET MONKEY and RUPERT AND THE STOLEN APPLES
(Sampson Low, [1929]) £55
NO. 7: RUPERT AND THE THREE ROBBERS (Sampson Low, [1929])..£55
NO. 8: RUPERT, THE KNIGHT AND THE LADY and RUPERT AND THE WISE GOAT'S BIRTHDAY CAKE
(Sampson Low, [1929]) £55
NO. 9: RUPERT AND THE CIRCUS CLOWN (Sampson Low, [1929])...£50
NO. 10: RUPERT AND THE MAGIC HAT (Sampson Low, [1929])...£50
NO. 11: RUPERT AND THE LITTLE PRINCE (Sampson Low, [1930])...£50
NO. 12 : RUPERT AND KING PIPPIN (Sampson Low, [1930])..£50

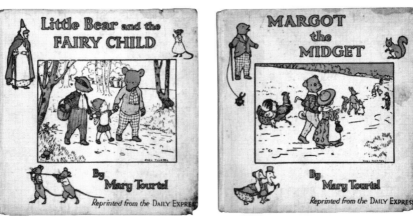

The Adventures of Rupert the Little Lost Bear (*Thomas Nelson, [1921]*) *represents the first appearance of 'Rupert' in book form.*

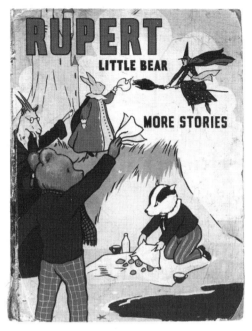

*One of the rare **Monster Rupert** volumes published by Sampson Low during the 1930s.*

*This edition of **Rupert Little Bear, More Stories** was issued in 1939 and is currently worth around £500.*

NO. 33: RUPERT AND THE MAGIC TOYMAN (Sampson Low, [1933]) **£50**
NO. 34: RUPERT AND BILL KEEP SHOP and RUPERT'S CHRISTMAS THRILLS
(Sampson Low, [1933]) **£50**
NO. 35: RUPERT AND ALGERNON and RUPERT AND THE WHITE DOVE
(Sampson Low, [1934]) **£50**
NO. 36: RUPERT AND BEPPO AGAIN (Sampson Low, [1934]).. **£50**
NO. 37 : RUPERT AND DAPPLE (Sampson Low, [1934]) **£50**
NO. 38: RUPERT AND BILL'S AEROPLANE ADVENTURE (Sampson Low, [1934]).................................... **£50**
NO. 39: RUPERT AND THE MAGICIAN'S UMBRELLA (Sampson Low, [1934]).. **£50**
NO. 40: RUPERT AND BILL AND THE PIRATES (Sampson Low, [1935]) **£50**
NO. 41: RUPERT AT THE SEASIDE and RUPERT AND BINGO (Sampson Low, [1935])............................ **£50**
NO. 42 : RUPERT GETS CAPTURED and RUPERT AND THE SNOW BABE'S CHRISTMAS ADVENTURES
(Sampson Low, [1935]) **£50**
NO. 43: RUPERT, THE MANIKIN AND THE BLACK KNIGHT (Sampson Low, [1935])................................ **£50**
NO. 44: RUPERT AND THE GREEDY PRINCESS (Sampson Low, [1935]).. **£50**
NO. 45 : RUPERT AND BILL'S SEASIDE HOLIDAY and RUPERT AND THE TWINS' BIRTHDAY CAKE
(Sampson Low, [1936]) **£50**
NO. 46: RUPERT AND EDWARD AND THE CIRCUS and RUPERT AND THE SNOWMAN
(Sampson Low, [1936]) **£50**

Other 'Rupert' Books

DAILY EXPRESS CHILDREN'S ANNUAL 1930-31 (Lane, 1930-31).. each **£150**
DAILY EXPRESS CHILDREN'S ANNUAL 1932-34 (Lane, 1932-34).. each **£100**
MONSTER RUPERT (four volumes) (Sampson Low, 1931-34).. each **£900**
MONSTER RUPERT (three volumes) (Sampson Low, 1948-50)... each **£50**
MONSTER RUPERT (with all cut-outs intact [200 in total]) (Sampson Low, 1950) **£55**
MONSTER RUPERT (with all cut-outs intact [120 in total]) (Sampson Low, 1953) **£50**
THE RUPERT STORY BOOK (Sampson Low, [1938]).. **£500**
RUPERT LITTLE BEAR, MORE STORIES (Sampson Low, [1939]) **£500**
RUPERT AGAIN (Sampson Low, [1940])... **£500**

Others

A HORSE BOOK by Mary Tourtel (Grant Richards: 'Dumpy Books for Children' series No. 10, 1901) **£175**
THE HUMPTY DUMPTY BOOK: Nursery Rhymes Told in Pictures
(Treherne, [1902])... **£175**
THE THREE LITTLE FOXES by Mary Tourtel
(Grant Richards: 'Dumpy Books for Children's series No. 21, 1903).. **£175**

TOWNSEND, John Rowe

British author. Born: Yorkshire, 1922. He has a considerable reputation, especially for *The Intruder* (1969) and his history of children's literature, *Written for Children* (1965; revised: 1974 & 1983).

Prices are for books in Very Good condition with dustjackets where applicable.

GUMBLE'S YARD (illustrated by Dick Hart) (Hutchinson, 1961) £70
HELL'S EDGE (Hutchinson, 1963) £55
WIDDERSHINS CRESCENT (Hutchinson, 1965) £55
WIDDERSHINS CRESCENT (as 'Goodbye to Gumble's Yard'; paperback) (Puffin, 1981) £15
THE HALLERSAGE SOUND (Hutchinson, 1966) £35
PIRATE'S ISLAND (illustrated by Douglas Hall) (OUP, 1968) £35
THE INTRUDER (illustrated by Graham Humphrey) (OUP, 1969) £35
GOODNIGHT, PROF, LOVE (illustrated by Peter Farmer) (OUP, 1970) £30
THE SUMMER PEOPLE (illustrated by Robert Micklewright) (OUP, 1972) £30
A WISH FOR WINGS (illustrated by Philip Gough) (Heinemann, 1972) £30
FOREST OF THE NIGHT (OUP, 1974) £30
NOAH'S CASTLE (OUP, 1975) £30
TOP OF THE WORLD (illustrated by Nikki Jones) (OUP, 1976) £25
THE XANADU MANUSCRIPT (illustrated by Paul Ritchie) (OUP, 1977) £25
KING CREATURE, COME (OUP, 1980) £20
THE ISLANDERS (OUP, 1981) £20
CLEVER DICK (OUP, 1982) £20
A FOREIGN AFFAIR (Kestrel, 1982) £15
DAN ALONE (Kestrel, 1983) £15
CLOUDY-BRIGHT (Kestrel, 1984) £15
TOM TIDDLER'S GROUND (illustrated by Marke Peppe) (Viking Kestrel, 1986) £15
THE PERSUADING STICK (Viking Kestrel, 1986) £15
ROB'S PLACE (Viking Kestrel, 1987) £15

TOZER, Katharine

British author-illustrator. Born: 1905. Best known for her series of books featuring the toy elephant, Mumfie. Died: 1943.

Prices are for books in Very Good condition with dustjackets.

Books Written and Illustrated by Katharine Tozer

THE WANDERINGS OF MUMFIE (John Murray, 1935) £80
HERE COMES MUMFIE (John Murray, 1936) £65
MUMFIE THE ADMIRAL (John Murray, 1937) £60
MUMFIE'S PICTURE BOOK (selected by Eiluned Lewis) (John Murray, 1937) £60
MUMFIE'S MAGIC BOX (John Murray, 1938) £60
MUMFIE'S UNCLE SAMUEL (John Murray, 1939) £60
NOAH: The Story of Another Ark (John Murray, 1940) £20
THE ADVENTURES OF ALFIE (John Murray, 1941) £20
MUMFIE MARCHES ON (John Murray, 1942) £40

Books Illustrated by Katharine Tozer

PALADINS IN SPAIN by Eleanor Farjeon (Nelson, 1937) £15
THE CHINESE CHILDREN NEXT DOOR by Pearl S. Buck (Methuen, 1943) £15

TRANTER, Nigel

Scottish author. Born: 1909. Celebrated Scots author, particularly admired for his historical novels, and writer of several Western novels under the pen-name 'Nye Tredgold'. He began writing children's books in the late 1950s, producing twelve in all, each with black-and-white illustrations. Died: 2000.

Prices are for books in Very Good condition with dustjackets.

SPANIARD'S ISLE (Brockhampton Press, 1958) £45
BORDER RIDING (Brockhampton Press, 1959) £35
NESTOR THE MONSTER (Brockhampton Press, 1960) £70
BIRDS OF A FEATHER (Brockhampton Press, 1961) £40
THE DEER POACHERS (Blackie, 1961) £30
SOMETHING VERY FISHY (Collins, 1963) £15
GIVE A DOG A BAD NAME (Collins, 1963) £20
GIVE A DOG A BAD NAME (as 'SMOKE ACROSS THE HIGHLANDS') (Platt & Monk, US, 1964) £15
SILVER ISLAND (Nelson, 1964) £35
PURSUIT (Collins, 1965) £35
TINKER TESS (Dobson Books, 1967) £50
FIRE AND HIGH WATER (Collins, 1967) £35
TO THE RESCUE (Dobson Books, 1968) £35

One of Mary Shepard's illustrations from the 1934 first edition of **Mary Poppins**. *This book is worth £500 today.*

TRAVERS, P.L.

Australian author. Born: Pamela Lyndon Goff in Queensland, Australia, in 1899. Moved to Britain in 1923, working as an actress and dancer until 1936. She wrote a number of children's books, but is best known for her 'Mary Poppins' stories, which inspired Walt Disney's memorable 1964 film starring Julie Andrews. Died: 1996.

Prices are for books in Very Good condition with dustjackets.

MARY POPPINS (illustrated by Mary Shepard) (Howe, 1934)...£500
MARY POPPINS COMES BACK (illustrated by Mary Shepard) (Dickson & Thompson, 1935)...............................£150
HAPPY EVER AFTER (illustrated by Mary Shepard) (Privately printed, 1940) £200
I GO BY SEA, I GO BY LAND (illustrated by Gertrude Hermes) (Davies, 1941)...£75
MARY POPPINS OPENS THE DOOR (illustrated by Mary Shepard and Agnes Sims) (Davies, 1944)...................£100
MARY POPPINS IN THE PARK (illustrated by Mary Shepard) (Davies, 1952)..£80
THE FOX AT THE MANGER (illustrated by Thomas Bewick) (Collins, 1963) £50
MARY POPPINS FROM A TO Z (illustrated by Mary Shepard) (Collins, 1963)...£50
FRIEND MONKEY (Collins, 1972)...£20
ABOUT THE SLEEPING BEAUTY (illustrated by Charles Keeping) (Collins, 1977) £35
MARY POPPINS IN THE KITCHEN (with Maurice Moore-Betty; illustrated by Mary Shepard) (Collins, 1977)...........£15
MARY POPPINS IN CHERRY TREE LANE (illustrated by Mary Shepard) (Collins, 1982)................................£15

TREASE, Geoffrey

British author. Born: Robert Geoffrey Trease in Nottingham in 1909. Studied at Nottingham High School and Queen's College, Oxford. Worked as a teacher and journalist before publishing his first novel, *Bows against the Barons*, in 1934. Like many of his works, this book reflects the author's strong left-wing convictions. Has also written a study of children's writing, *Tales Out of School* (1948). Died: 1998.

Prices are for books in Very Good condition with dustjackets.

BOWS AGAINST THE BARONS (illustrated by Michael Boland) (Martin Lawrence, 1934) £40
COMRADES FOR THE CHARTER (illustrated by Michael Boland) (Martin Lawrence, 1934).............................£40
UNSLEEPING SWORD (Martin Lawrence, 1934)..£35
THE CALL TO ARMS (Martin Lawrence, 1935)..£35
MISSING FROM HOME (illustrated by Scott) (Lawrence & Wishart, [1936])...£30
RED COMET: A Tale of Travel in the USSR (illustrated by Fred Ellis) (Lawrence & Wishart, 1937).................£30
THE CHRISTMAS HOLIDAY MYSTERY (illustrated by Alfred Sindall) (A. & C. Black, 1937) £30
MYSTERY ON THE MOORS (illustrated by Alfred Sindall) (A. & C. Black, 1937)..£30
DETECTIVES OF THE DALES (illustrated by J.C.B. Knight) (A. & C. Black, 1938) £30
IN THE LAND OF THE MOGUL: A Story of the East India Company's First Adventure in India
    (illustrated by J.C.B. Knight) (Blackwell, 1938)..£30
THE DRAGON WHO WAS DIFFERENT and Other Plays for Children (Muller, 1938) £30
NORTH SEA SPY (Fore, [1939])...£30
CLEM VOROSHILVO: The Red Marshal (Pilot Press, [1940]) £25

TREASE, Geoffrey

CUE FOR TREASON (illustrated by Beatrice Goldsmith) (Blackwell, 1940)..£25
THE RUNNING OF THE DEER (illustrated by W. Lindsay Cable) (Harrap, [1941]) £20
THE GREY ADVENTURER (illustrated by Beatrice Goldsmith) (Blackwell, 1942) £25
BLACK NIGHT, RED MORNING (illustrated by Donia Nachsen) (Shakespeare Head Press, 1944) £25
ARMY WITHOUT BANNERS (Fore, 1945) £25
TRUMPETS IN THE WEST (illustrated by Alan Blyth) (Blackwell, 1947)......................................£25
SILVER GUARD (illustrated by Alan Blyth) (Blackwell, 1948)..£25
THE HILLS OF VARNA (illustrated by Treyer Evans) (Macmillan, 1948) £25
TALES OUT OF SCHOOL (Heinemann, 1948)..£15
THE MYSTERY OF MOORSIDE FARM (illustrated by Alan Blyth) (Blackwell, 1949) £25
NO BOATS ON BANNERMERE (illustrated by Richard Kennedy) (Heinemann, 1949)................£30
THE SECRET FIORD (illustrated by H.M. Brock) (Macmillan, 1949)...£25
FORTUNE, MY FOE: The Story of Sir Walter Raleigh (Methuen 1949) £25
THE YOUNG TRAVELLER IN INDIA AND PAKISTAN (Phoenix House, 1949) £15
UNDER BLACK BANNER (illustrated by Richard Kennedy) (Heinemann, 1951).........................£25
ENJOYING BOOKS (Phoenix House: 'Excursions Series for Young People', 1951) £10
THE CROWN OF VIOLET (illustrated by C. Walter Hodges) (Macmillan, 1952)..........................£25
THE BARONS' HOSTAGE: A Story of Simon de Montfort (illustrated by Alan Jessett) (Phoenix House, 1952) £25
BLACK BANNER PLAYERS (illustrated by Richard Kennedy) (Heinemann, 1952).....................£25
THE PAGEANT BOOKS. Edited by Geoffrey Trease (Phoenix House, 1952) £10
THE NEW HOUSE AT HARDALE (Lutterworth Press, 1953)..£15
THE SILKEN SECRET (illustrated by Alan Jessett) (Blackwell, 1953) £25
THE SEVEN QUEENS OF ENGLAND (Heinemann, 1953)...£15
THE SHADOW OF SPAIN and Other Plays (Blackwell, [1953])..£10
THE YOUNG TRAVELLER IN ENGLAND AND WALES (Phoenix House, 1953) £10
BLACK BANNER ABROAD (Heinemann, 1954)..£25
THE YOUNG TRAVELLER IN GREECE (Phoenix House, 1955 [1956]) £10
THE FAIR FLOWER OF DANGER (Blackwell, 1955 [1956])..£20
WORD TO CAESAR (illustrated by Geoffrey Whittam) (Macmillan, 1955 [1956]).......................£20
SIX OF THE BEST by Kitty Barne and others. Edited by G. Trease (stories) (Blackwell, 1955)....£15
THE SEVEN KINGS OF ENGLAND (illustrated by Leslie Atkinson) (Heinemann, 1955)............£12
IN THE BLOOD (Blackwell, [1956])..£20
THE GATES OF BANNERDALE (Heinemann, 1956)...£20
SECRET OF SHAM (Blackwell, [1956])...£20
SNARED NIGHTINGALE (Macmillan, 1957)...£20
MIST OVER ATHELNEY (illustrated by R.S. Sherriffs and J.L. Stokle) (Macmillan, 1958) £20
EDWARD ELGAR: MAKER OF MUSIC (adapted from the play 'Elgar of England') (Macmillan, 1959).........£15
SO WILD THE HEART (Macmillan, 1959) £20
THE MAYTHORN STORY (illustrated by Robert Hodgson) (Heinemann, 1960) £20
THUNDER OF VALMY (illustrated by John S. Goodall) (Macmillan, 1960)................................£15
THE YOUNG WRITER (illustrated by Carl Hollander) (Nelson, [1961]) £10
WOLFGANG MOZART: The Young Composer (Macmillan 1961)..£10
CHANGE AT MAYTHORN (illustrated by Robert Hodgson) (Heinemann, 1962).........................£15
FOLLOW MY BLACK PLUME (illustrated by Brian Wildsmith) (Macmillan, 1963) £30
THE ITALIAN STORY: From the Earliest Times to 1946 (Macmillan, 1963)...........................£10
A THOUSAND FOR SICILY (illustrated by Brian Wildsmith) (Macmillan, 1964).........................£30
SEVEN STAGES (Heinemann, 1964)...£15
THE DUTCH ARE COMING (illustrated by Lynette Hemmant) (Hamish Hamilton, 1965)............£15
BENT IS THE BOW (illustrated by Charles Keeping) (Nelson, 1965)...£20
THE RED TOWERS OF GRANADA (illustrated by Charles Keeping) (Macmillan, 1966).............£20
COMPANIONS OF FORTUNE by René Guiullot (translated by G. Trease) (Childrens Library, 1967)........£10
THE WHITE NIGHTS OF ST. PETERSBURG (illustrated by William Stobbs) (Macmillan, 1967).......£15
THE RUNAWAY SERF (illustrated by Mary Russon) (Hamilton, 1968).......................................£15
SEVEN SOVEREIGN QUEENS (Heinemann, [1968])...£10
BYRON: A Poet Dangerous to Know (Macmillan, 1969) £15
A MASQUE FOR THE QUEEN (illustrated by Krystyna Turska) (Hamish Hamilton, 1970) £15
THE CONDOTIERRI: Soldiers of Fortune (Thames & Hudson, [1970]).................................£15
A WHIFF OF BURNT BOATS (Macmillan, 1971)...£15
HORSEMEN ON THE HILLS (Macmillan, 1971)...£15
A SHIP TO ROME (illustrated by Leslie Atkinson) (Heinemann, 1972)......................................£15
SAMUEL PEPYS AND HIS WORLD (Thames & Hudson, [1972])..£10
A VOICE IN THE NIGHT (illustrated by Sara Silcock) (Heinemann, 1973) £15
POPINJAY STAIRS (Macmillan, 1973)..£15
D.H. LAWRENCE: The Phoenix and the Flame (Macmillan, 1973)..£20
DAYS TO REMEMBER: A Garland of Historic Anniversaries (illustrated by Joanna Troughton) (Heinemann, 1973)..............£15
THE CHOCOLATE BOY (illustrated by David Walker) (Heinemann, 1975)................................£15
THE IRON TSAR (Macmillan, 1975)..£15
WHEN THE DRUMS BEAT (illustrated by Janet Marsh) (Heinemann, 1976)..............................£15
VIOLET FOR BONAPARTE (Macmillan, 1976) £15

THE SEAS OF MORNING (illustrated by David Smee; paperback) (Puffin, 1976)...£5
THE SPY CATCHERS (illustrated by Geoffrey Bargery) (Hamish Hamilton, 1976)...£15
THE FIELD OF THE FORTY FOOTSTEPS (Macmillan, 1977)...£15
THE CLAWS OF THE EAGLE (illustrated by Ionicus) (Heinemann, 1977)..£15
MANDEVILLE (Macmillan, 1980)..£10
A WOOD BY MOONLIGHT and Other Stories (Chatto & Windus, 1981)..£10
SARABAND FOR SHADOWS (Macmillan, 1982)..£10
THE CORMORANT VENTURE (Macmillan, 1984)...£10
TOMORROW IS A STRANGER (Heinemann, 1987)...£10

TREECE, Henry

British author. Born: Wednesbury, Staffordshire, in 1911. Studied at Wednesbury High School and Birmingham University. Taught English at Barton-on-Humber Grammar School in Lincolnshire between 1946 and 1959. Began his literary career as a poet and was co-founder of the New Apocalypse movement, but turned to novel writing in the early 1950s, producing a series of historical novels for adults and children. Died: 1966.

Prices are for books in Very Good condition with dustjackets.

LEGIONS OF THE EAGLE (illustrated by Christine Price) (The Bodley Head, 1954) £40
THE EAGLES HAVE FLOWN (illustrated by Christine Price) (The Bodley Head, 1954) £35
DESPERATE JOURNEY: A Tale (illustrated by Richard Kennedy) (Faber, 1954)..£30
ASK FOR KING BILLY (illustrated by Richard Kennedy) (Faber, 1955)..£30
VIKING'S DAWN (illustrated by Christine Price) (The Bodley Head, 1955)..£30
HOUNDS OF THE KING (illustrated by Christine Price) (The Bodley Head, 1955) £30
MEN OF THE HILLS (illustrated by Christine Price) (The Bodley Head, 1957)..£30
THE ROAD TO MIKLAGARD (illustrated by Christine Price) (The Bodley Head, 1957)....................................£20
HUNTER HUNTED (illustrated by Richard Kennedy) (Faber, 1957)..£20
DON'T EXPECT ANY MERCY! (Faber, 1958) £20
THE CHILDREN'S CRUSADE (illustrated by Christine Price) (The Bodley Head, 1958) £20
THE RETURN OF ROBINSON CRUSOE (illustrated by Will Nickless) (Hulton Press, [1958])..........................£30
THE BOMBARD (illustrated by Christine Price) (The Bodley Head, 1959) £20
WICKHAM AND THE ARMADA (illustrated by Hookway Cowles) (Hulton Press, 1959)....................................£20
CASTLES AND KINGS (non-fiction; illustrated by C. Walter Hodges) (Batsford, 1959) £20
VIKING'S SUNSET (illustrated by Christine Price) (The Bodley Head, 1960)..£20
RED SETTLEMENT (The Bodley Head, 1960) £20
THE TRUE BOOK ABOUT CASTLES (non-fiction; illustrated by G.H. Channing) (Muller, 1960) £10
THE JET BEADS (illustrated by W.A. Sillince) (Brockhampton Press, 1961)...£20
THE GOLDEN ONE (illustrated by William Stobbs) (The Bodley Head, 1961)...£20
MAN WITH A SWORD (illustrated by William Stobbs) (The Bodley Head, 1962) £20
WAR DOG (illustrated by Roger Payne) (Brockhampton Press, 1962)..£20
HORNED HELMET (illustrated by Charles Keeping) (Brockhampton Press, 1963) £20
KNOW ABOUT THE CRUSADES (non-fiction) (Blackie, [1963]) £15
FIGHTING MEN: How Men have Fought Through the Ages (with Ronald Ewart Oakeshott)
   (Brockhampton Press, 1963)..£15
THE BURNING OF NJAL (illustrated by Bernard Blatch) (The Bodley Head, 1963) £15
THE LAST OF THE VIKINGS (illustrated by Charles Keeping) (Brockhampton Press, 1964).............................£25
HOUNDS OF THE KING, with Two Radio Plays (contains 'Hounds of the King', 'Harold Godwinson' and 'William,
   Duke of Normandy'; illustrated by Stuart Tresilian) (Longman, 1965) £15
THE BRONZE SWORD (illustrated by Mary Russon)
   (Hamish Hamilton: 'Antelope Books' series, 1965)..£10
SPLINTERED SWORD (illustrated by Charles Keeping)
   (Brockhampton Press, 1965)...£25
KILLER IN DARK GLASSES (Faber, 1965) £20
BANG, YOU'RE DEAD! (Faber, 1966)...£20
THE QUEEN'S BROOCH (Hamish Hamilton, 1966)..£15
SWORDS FROM THE NORTH (illustrated by Charles Keeping) (Faber, 1967)..£15
THE WINDSWEPT CITY (illustrated by Faith Jaques) (Hamish Hamilton, 1967)...£10
VINLAND THE GOOD (illustrated by William Stobbs) (The Bodley Head, 1967)...£15
THE DREAM-TIME (illustrated by Charles Keeping) (Brockhampton Press, 1967)..£30
THE INVADERS (illustrated by Charles Keeping) (Brockhampton Press, 1972) £20
LEGIONS OF THE EAGLE (The Bodley Head, 1972)...£15

TREVOR, Elleston

British author. Born: 1920. Also wrote as Mansell Black, Roger Fitzalan, Adam Hall, Simon Rattray, Warwick Scott, Caesar Smith, Lesley Stone. Writer of adult mystery and crime, and lively action and animal stories for children. Died: 1995.

Prices are for books in Very Good condition with dustjackets.

DEEP WOOD (illustrated by David Williams) (Gerald G. Swan, 1945) £50

WUMPUS (illustrated by J. McCail) (Gerald G. Swan, 1945)...£55
WUMPUS AGAIN (illustrated by J. McCail) (Gerald G. Swan, 1946) £50
HEATHER HILL (Gerald G. Swan, 1946)..£30
MORE ABOUT WUMPUS (illustrated by J. McCail) (Gerald G. Swan, 1947)......................£45
THE WIZARD OF THE WOOD (illustrated by Leslie Atkinson) (Falcon Press, 1948)..............£45
THE SECRET TRAVELLERS (illustrated by David Williams) (Gerald G. Swan, 1948)..............£30
BADGER'S MOON (illustrated by Leslie Atkinson) (Falcon Press, 1949)..............................£30
ANT'S CASTLE (illustrated by David Williams) (Falcon Press, 1949)...................................£25
MOLE'S CASTLE (illustrated by Leslie Atkinson) (Falcon Press, 1950)................................£25
SWEETHALLOW VALLEY (illustrated by Leslie Atkinson) (Falcon Press, 1950) £20

TUDOR, Tasha

American author-illustrator. Born Starling Burgess in 1915. Wrote poetry, fairy tales and a series of 'Becky' books. Best known for her first book, *Pumpkin Moonshine* (1938).

Prices are for books in Very Good condition with dustjackets where applicable.

Books Written and Illustrated by Tasha Tudor

PUMPKIN MOONSHINE (OUP, 1938)..£1,500
ALEXANDER THE GREAT (OUP, 1939) £500
THE COUNTRY FAIR (OUP, 1940) £400
SNOW BEFORE CHRISTMAS (OUP, 1941)...£400
A TALE FOR EASTER (OUP, 1941)..£150
DORCAS PORCAS (OUP, 1942)...£300
THE WHITE GOOSE (OUP, 1943)..£200
LINSEY WOOLSEY (OUP, 1946)...£200
THISTLY B (OUP, 1949) £250
AMANDA AND THE BEAR (OUP, 1951) £200
EDGAR ALLAN CROW (OUP, 1953)...£100
A IS FOR ANNABELLE (verse) (OUP, 1954) £200
1 IS ONE (verse) (Rand McNally, US, [1956])..£60
AROUND THE YEAR (OUP, 1957)..£150
AND SO IT WAS (Westminster Press, 1958) £60
AND SO IT WAS (paperback) (Westminster Press, 1988)...£15
BECKY'S BIRTHDAY (Viking, US, 1960)..£60
THE TASHA TUDOR BOOK OF FAIRY TALES (Platt & Munk, US, 1961).........................£75
BECKY'S CHRISTMAS (Viking, US, 1961)...£60
WINGS FROM THE WIND (Lippincott, US, 1964)..£75
TASHA TUDOR'S FAVOURITE STORIES (Lippincott, US, 1965).....................................£75
TAKE JOY! THE TASHA TUDOR CHRISTMAS BOOK (World, US, 1966).........................£50
FIRST DELIGHTS: A Book About the Five Senses (Platt & Munk, US, 1966).....................£50
FIRST POEMS OF CHILDHOOD (Platt & Munk, US, 1967)..£25
CORGIVILLE FAIR (Crowell, US, 1971)..£150
TASHA TUDOR'S FIVE SENSES (Platt & Munk, US, 1978)..£60
THE SPRINGS OF JOY (Rand McNally, US, 1979)..£60
TASHA TUDOR'S SEASON'S OF DELIGHT: A Year on an Old-Fashioned Farm
(a three-dimensional pop-up book) (Philomel, US, 1986)..£60
THE PRIVATE WORLD OF TASHA TUDOR (Little Brown, US, 1992)...............................£40
THE TASHA TUDOR COOKBOOK RECIPES AND REMINISCENCES
(Little Brown, US, 1993) £40
THE DOLL'S CHRISTMAS (Simon & Schuster, US, 1999) £30
ALL FOR LOVE (Simon & Schuster, US, 2000)...£30

Books Illustrated by Tasha Tudor

THE DOLL'S HOUSE by Rumer Godden (Viking, US, 1947) £50
THE DOLL'S HOUSE by Rumer Godden (Macmillan, 1963)...£50
JACKANAPES by Juliana H. Ewing (OUP, US, 1948)...£125
FIRST PRAYERS (OUP, US, 1952)..£125
FIRST GRACES (Henry Z. Walck, US, 1955) £100
FIRST GRACES (Lutterworth Press, 1964)...£10
THE TWENTY THIRD PSALM-MINIATURE (St Onge Press, 1965) £65
REAL DIARY OF A REAL BOY by Henry Shute (The Noone House, US, 1967) £45
MORE PRAYERS (Lutterworth Press, 1968)..£10
THE LORD IS MY SHEPHERD (Philomel, US, 1980)..£30
A CHILD'S GARDEN OF VERSES by R.L. Stevenson (Rand McNally, US, 1981) £35
THE NEW ENGLAND BUTT'RY SHELF ALMANAC by Mary Mason Campbell
(Stephen Greene, US, 1982)...£35
A BASKET OF HERBS : A Book of American Sentiments Edited by Mary Campbell
(Stephen Greene, US, 1983)...£200
GIVE US THIS DAY THE LORD'S PRAYER (paperback)
(Paper Star, US, 1987)..£10

TV ANNUALS

The following is a selection of collectable television tie-in annuals, arranged in alphabetical order in three seperate decades.

Prices are for annuals in Very Good condition.

1950s

THE ADVENTURES OF ROBIN HOOD (Adprint, 1956)..£20
THE ADVENTURES OF ROBIN HOOD (Adprint, 1957-59).. each £10
THE ADVENTURES OF ROBIN HOOD (Adprint, 1960 onwards) .... each £8
ATV SHOW BOOK/ATV TELEVISION SHOW/STAR BOOK (LTA Robinson/Purnell, 1950s) .... each £12
ATV SHOW BOOK/ATV TELEVISION SHOW/STAR BOOK (LTA Robinson/Purnell, 1960s) .... each £10
BRONCO LAYNE (World Distributors, 1959) £12
BRONCO LAYNE (World Distributors, 1960-64) .... each £8
CHAMPION THE WONDER HORSE/CHAMPION THE WONDER HORSE COMIC ANNUAL
   (Daily Mirror/World Distributors/Purnell, [1953])...£15
CHAMPION THE WONDER HORSE/CHAMPION THE WONDER HORSE COMIC ANNUAL
   (Daily Mirror/World Distributors/Purnell, 1954-56).. each £10
CHAMPION THE WONDER HORSE/CHAMPION THE WONDER HORSE COMIC ANNUAL
   (Daily Mirror/World Distributors/Purnell, 1961 & 1962) .... each £8
CIRCUS BOY' (Daily Mirror, 1958-60).. each £12
GIRL FILM AND TELEVISION ANNUAL (Hulton/Odhams, 1957)..£20
GIRL FILM AND TELEVISION ANNUAL (Hulton/Odhams, 1958 & 1959) .... each £15
GIRL FILM AND TELEVISION ANNUAL (Hulton/Odhams, 1960 onwards) .... each £8
HAWKEYE AND THE LAST OF THE MOHICANS (Adprint, 1958)..£12
HAWKEYE AND THE LAST OF THE MOHICANS (Adprint, 1959)...£8
THE LONE RANGER/LONE RANGER ADVENTURE STORIES (Adprint/World Distributors/Brown Watson, 1957-60) .... each £12
THE LONE RANGER/LONE RANGER ADVENTURE STORIES (Adprint/World Distributors/Brown Watson, 1964-69)............. each £8
THE LONE RANGER/LONE RANGER ADVENTURE STORIES (Adprint/World Distributors/Brown Watson, 1970s) .... each £3
ROY ROGERS' BUMPER BOOK (Adprint, 1950s)... each £15
ROY ROGERS COWBOY ANNUAL (World Distributors, 1952-59)... each £15
ROY ROGERS COWBOY ANNUAL (World Distributors, 1960 onwards) .... each £8
ROY ROGERS' STORIES (Adprint, 1956) £20
ROY ROGERS' STORIES (Adprint, 1957-59) .... each £12
ROY ROGERS' STORIES (Adprint, 1960 onwards).. each £8
TELEVISION ANNUAL (Omnibus Press, 1954-59).. each £15
TELEVISION FAVOURITES COMIC ANNUAL (World, 1958) £20
TENDERFOOT (World, 1959)...£15
TV ANNUAL (Amalgamated Press, 1950s) .... each £15
TV COMIC/NEW MIGHTY TV COMIC ANNUAL (News of the World/Beaverbrook/TV/Polystyle, 1954)............£30
TV COMIC/NEW MIGHTY TV COMIC ANNUAL (News of the World/Beaverbrook/TV/Polystyle, 1955)............£20
TV COMIC/NEW MIGHTY TV COMIC ANNUAL (News of the World/Beaverbrook/TV/Polystyle, 1956-59) .... each £15
TV COMIC/NEW MIGHTY TV COMIC ANNUAL (News of the World/Beaverbrook/TV/Polystyle, 1960-69)......... each £12
TV COMIC/NEW MIGHTY TV COMIC ANNUAL (News of the World/Beaverbrook/TV/Polystyle, 1970-73) .... each £8
TV COMIC/NEW MIGHTY TV COMIC ANNUAL (News of the World/Beaverbrook/TV/Polystyle, 1973-84)......... each £6
'TV MIRROR ANNUAL (Amalgamated Press, 1950s) .... each £12
WAGON TRAIN/BIG TV BUMPER BOOK (World Distributors/Daily Mirror/Peveril, 1959)....................£15
WAGON TRAIN/BIG TV BUMPER BOOK (World Distributors/Daily Mirror/Peveril, 1960-62)............ each £12
WAGON TRAIN/BIG TV BUMPER BOOK (World Distributors/Daily Mirror/Peveril, 1962 onwards) .... each £8
WESTERN ROUND-UP ANNUAL (World, 1955-58) .... each £12
WESTERN TV AND FILM ANNUAL (Macdonald/Purnell, 1959) £12
WESTERN TV AND FILM ANNUAL (Macdonald/Purnell, 1964) £8

1960s

ADAM ADAMANT (Unknown, 1968)..£8
ANDY PANDY (Purnell, 1967) £8
THE ANGELS (City, 1967)...£15
ATOM ANT (Atlas, 1968) £25
AVENGERS (Diana Rigg) (Souvenir/Atlas, 1967) £15
AVENGERS (Linda Thorson) (Souvenir/Atlas, 1968) £12
AVENGERS (Linda Thorson) (Souvenir/Atlas, 1969) £15
BATMAN (Atlas/Top Sellers, 1960/61)...£80
BATMAN (Atlas/Top Sellers, 1961/62)...£55
BATMAN (Atlas/Top Sellers, 1962/63)...£35
BATMAN (Atlas/Top Sellers, 1963/64)...£25
BATMAN (Atlas/Top Sellers, 1964-67)... each £25
BATMAN (Adam West photo cover) (Atlas/Top Sellers, 1968)...£25
BATMAN (Atlas/Top Sellers, 1969-72).. each £15
BATMAN (Atlas/Top Sellers, 1973-79)... each £8
BATMAN (Atlas/Top Sellers, 1980-95)... each £6

THE BEAVER (Fairhaven Books, 1960s) .... each £15
THE BEVERLY HILLBILLIES (World, 1960s) £15
BEWITCHED (World, 1966) £25
BEWITCHED (World, 1967) £15
THE BOOK OF BLUE PETER/THE BLUE PETER ANNUAL(BBC, 1964) £80
THE BOOK OF BLUE PETER/THE BLUE PETER ANNUAL(BBC, 1965) £30
THE BOOK OF BLUE PETER/THE BLUE PETER ANNUAL(BBC, 1966) £15
THE BOOK OF BLUE PETER/THE BLUE PETER ANNUAL(BBC, 1967-75) .... each £8
THE BOOK OF BLUE PETER/THE BLUE PETER ANNUAL(BBC, 1976-85) .... each £6
THE BOOK OF BLUE PETER/THE BLUE PETER ANNUAL(BBC, 1986-92/1998) .... each £3
THE BOOK OF BLUE PETER/THE BLUE PETER ANNUAL(withdrawn) (BBC, 1999) £8
BONANZA (World Distributors/Purnell, 1962 & 1963) .... each £12
BONANZA (World Distributors/Purnell, 1964-69) .... each £10
BUGS BUNNY (World, 1960s) .... each £12
BUGS BUNNY (World, 1970s) .... each £8
BUGS BUNNY (World, 1980s) .... each £6
BURKE'S LAW (World, 1965) £12
CAPTAIN SCARLET (City Magazines, 1968) £20
CAPTAIN SCARLET (City Magazines, 1969) £12
CAPTAIN SCARLET & THUNDERBIRDS (City Magazines, 1970) £20
CHEYENNE (World, 1960) £15
CHEYENNE (World, 1961-65) .... each £8
CHEYENNE, A TELEVISION STORYBOOK (New Town Printers, 1961 & 1962) .... each £12
DAKTARI (World, 1967) £12
DAKTARI (World, 1968-70) .... each £8
THE DALEK BOOK (Souvenir/Panther, 1964) £70
THE DALEK WORLD (Souvenir/Panther, 1965) £60
THE DALEK OUTER SPACE BOOK (Souvenir/Panther, 1966) £70
DANGER MAN (Atlas/World, 1964) £15
DANGER MAN (Atlas/World, 1965-67) .... each £12
DANGER MAN TELEVISION STORYBOOK (PBS, 1965) £15
DANGER MAN "TOP TV SERIES" (Young World, 1965) £12
DR KILDARE (World, 1964-66) .... each £12
DOCTOR WHO (World/Marvel, 1966) £35
DOCTOR WHO (World/Marvel, 1967) £60
DOCTOR WHO (World/Marvel, 1968) £70
DOCTOR WHO (World/Marvel, 1969) £60
DOCTOR WHO (World/Marvel, 1970) £30
DOCTOR WHO (World/Marvel, 1971) £70
DOCTOR WHO (World/Marvel, 1973-75) .... each £15
DOCTOR WHO (World/Marvel, 1976-86) .... each £8
DOCTOR WHO AND THE INVASION FROM SPACE (World, 1965) £55
EMERGENCY WARD 10 GIRL'S ANNUAL (Purnell, 1963) £15
EMERGENCY WARD 10 GIRL'S ANNUAL (Purnell, 1964) £12
FIREBALL XL5 (Century 21, 1964) £35
FIREBALL XL5 (Century 21, 1965) £25
FIREBALL XL5 (Century 21, 1966 & 1967) .... each £15
FOUR FEATHER FALLS (Collins, 1961 & 1962) .... each £35
THE GIRL FROM U.N.C.L.E. (World, 1968 & 1969) .... each £15
THE GIRL FROM U.N.C.L.E. (World, 1970) £10
THE HIGH CHAPARRAL (World, 1970-73) .... each £10
THE IMPOSSIBLES (Atlas, 1969) £15
JOE 90 (City, 1969 & 1970) .... each £15
JOE 90: TOP SECRET COMIC (City, 1970) £12
JOE 90 STORY BOOK (City, 1969) £10
JONNY QUEST (World, 1966 & 1967) .... each £20
LANCER (World, 1970) £10
LAND OF THE GIANTS (World, 1970 & 1971) .... each £10
LAND OF THE GIANTS TELEVISION STORY BOOK (PBS, 1969) £10
LARAMIE (World/Purnell/Dean & Son, 1960-65) .... each £15
LAREDO (World, 1966) £12
THE LEGEND OF CUSTER (Atlas, 1968) £12
THE MAN FROM U.N.C.L.E. (World, 1966-69) .... each £15
THE OUTER LIMITS (World, 1966 & 1967) .... each £12
PINKY & PERKY (Purnell, 1960s) .... each £10
PINKY & PERKY (Purnell, 1970s) .... each £6
PIPPIN (Polystyle, 1960s) .... each £8
PIPPIN (Polystyle, 1970s) .... each £8
PIPPIN (Polystyle, 1980s) .... each £3

*There's a thriving market for TV tie-in books, annuals and comics, and this **Bewitched Annual** from 1966 is currently worth £25.*

PIXIE AND DIXIE WITH MR JINKS (World, 1960s)..each **£12**
PIXIE AND DIXIE WITH MR JINKS (World, 1970s)..each **£8**
POPEYE (Adprint/Purnell/Brown Watson/Pemberton/World/Grandreams, 1960) **£12**
POPEYE (Adprint/Purnell/Brown Watson/Pemberton/World/Grandreams, 1961-65)..each **£8**
POPEYE (Adprint/Purnell/Brown Watson/Pemberton/World/Grandreams, 1966-69)..each **£6**
POPEYE (Adprint/Purnell/Brown Watson/Pemberton/World/Grandreams, 1970 onwards)..each **£3**

TV ANNUALS

PROJECT SWORD (City, 1968)..£15
RAWHIDE (Dean & Sons, 1960)..£15
RAWHIDE (Dean & Sons, 1961-65)... each £12
RAWHIDE (Dean & Sons, 1966 onwards).. each £8
RAWHIDE TELEVISION STORYBOOK (New Town Printers, 1961).......................£12
ROGER MOORE ADVENTURE BOOK (Panther/Souvenir, 1966)..........................£8
THE SAINT (World/PBS, 1968-70)... each £10
THE SAINT (World/PBS, 1973).. £8
THE SAINT TELEVISION STORYBOOK (PBS, 1971)...£8
SGT BILKO (World, 1960-62).. each £15
SKIPPY THE BUSH KANGAROO (World, 1970-73).. each £8
SOOTY (Daily Mirror/Purnell/World, 1960s)... each £12
SOOTY (Daily Mirror/Purnell/World, 1970s)... each £8
SOOTY (Daily Mirror/Purnell/World, 1980s)... each £3
SOOTY (Daily Mirror/Purnell/World, 1990s)... each £2
STAR TREK (World/Stafford Pemberton/Grandreams, 1968)............................£15
STAR TREK (World/Stafford Pemberton/Grandreams, 1969 & 1970)........... each £12
STAR TREK (World/Stafford Pemberton/Grandreams, 1971-75)................... each £8
STAR TREK (World/Stafford Pemberton/Grandreams, 1976-79)................... each £6
STAR TV & FILM ANNUAL (Odhams, 1960s)... each £8
STAR & TV FUN (Odhams, 1968)..£8
STINGRAY (City, 1966)..£20
STINGRAY (City, 1967)..£12
SUPERCAR/MIKE MERCURY IN SUPERCAR (Collins, 1962)...........................£25
SUPERCAR/MIKE MERCURY IN SUPERCAR (Collins, 1963 & 1964)......... each £25
TALES OF WELLS FARGO (World/Purnell/Peveril/Swan, 1961).......................£12
TALES OF WELLS FARGO ('Big TV Bumper Book') (World/Purnell/Peveril/Swan, 1962) ...£8
TALES OF WELLS FARGO ('TV Storybook') (World/Purnell/Peveril/Swan, 1964) £8
TARZAN (World/Brown Watson, 1965 & 1966)... each £8
TARZAN (World/Brown Watson, 1967-71)... each £8
TARZAN (World/Brown Watson, 1973-80)... each £6
TEMPLE HOUSTON (World, 1965)...£8
TERRYTOON PLAYHOUSE (Purnell, 1964)..£12
THUNDERBIRDS (City/Century 21/Purnell, 1966)..£25
THUNDERBIRDS (City/Century 21/Purnell, 1967)..£15
THUNDERBIRDS (City/Century 21/Purnell, 1968)..£10
THUNDERBIRDS (City/Century 21/Purnell, 1971)..£8
THUNDERBIRDS (City/Century 21/Purnell, 1972)..£10
TOP CAT (World, 1960s) .... each £20
TOP CAT (World, 1970s)... each £8
TRUMPTON (Purnell, 1968-72) .... each £8
TV CENTURY 21/TV 21 (City/Fleetway, 1966)..£20
TV CENTURY 21/TV 21 (City/Fleetway, 1967 & 1968)................................ each £12
TV CENTURY 21/TV 21 (City/Fleetway, 1969 & 1970) .... each £10
TV CENTURY 21/TV 21 (City/Fleetway, 1971-73).. each £8
TV CRIMEBUSTERS (TV, 1962)..£20
TV TORNADO (World, 1968)..£15
TV TORNADO (World, 1969-1971)... each £12
TWILIGHT ZONE (World, 1964)..£15
VOYAGE TO THE BOTTOM OF THE SEA (World, 1966)................................£20
VOYAGE TO THE BOTTOM OF THE SEA (World, 1967)................................£15
VOYAGE TO THE BOTTOM OF THE SEA (World, 1968)................................£12
WOODY WOODPECKER (1960s)... each £8
WOODY WOODPECKER (1970s-80s).. each £6
YOGI BEAR (World, 1960s)... each £15
Z CARS (World, 1964) £10
Z CARS (World, 1965-67) .... each £8
Z CARS (World, 1970s) .... each £8

1970s

ALIAS SMITH AND JONES (World, 1976) £8
ALIAS SMITH AND JONES (World, 1977) £6
ANGELS (World, 1970s).. each £6
BABAR (BBC/Odhams, 1971)...£6
BARBAPAPA (World, 1976 & 1977)... each £6
BARETTA (Brown Watson, 1977)...£8
BATTLESTAR GALACTICA (Grandreams, 1979) £8
HANNA BARBERA'S BIG SHOW (Brown Watson, 1973)..................................£12
BIONIC WOMAN (Grandreams, 1978 & 1979) .... each £8
BLACK BEAUTY (Opal Quill/World, 1975-80) .... each £6

BLACK BEAUTY (Opal Quill/World, 1985) £3
BLAKE'S SEVEN (World, 1979 & 1980) .... each £8
BLAKE'S SEVEN (World, 1981) £10
CHARLIE'S ANGELS (Stafford Pemberton, 1978-81) .... each £12
CLUE CLUB (World, 1979) £10
COUNTDOWN (Polystyle, 1972) £12
COUNTDOWN (Polystyle, 1973) £8
DAD'S ARMY (World, 1973-78) .... each £8
TERRY NATION'S DALEK (World, 1976 & 1977) .... each £12
TERRY NATION'S DALEK (World, 1978 & 1979) .... each £8
DAVID CASSIDY (World, 1974 & 1975) .... each £10
DEPUTY DAWG (World, 1970-74) .... each £8
DOUGAL ANNUAL (BBC/Odhams, 1971-73) .... each £8
DYNOMUTT & MUMBLY (World, 1979) £6
EMERGENCY! (World, 1979) £8
FOLLYFOOT (World, 1975 & 1976) .... each £6
FUNKY PHANTOM (Brown Watson, 1974) £8
GEMINI MAN (Brown Watson, 1977) £12
HAPPY DAYS (Stafford Pemberton, 1979) £10
HAPPY DAYS (Stafford Pemberton, 1980-82) .... each £6
HAZELL (Stafford Pemberton, 1979 & 1980) .... each £6
HARLEM GLOBETROTTERS (Brown Watson, 1973 & 1974) .... each £8
HONG KONG PHOOEY (1975) £8
INCREDIBLE HULK (Marvel/Grandreams, 1977-85) .... each £8
JUST WILLIAM (World, 1978 & 1979) .... each £3
KOJAK (Stafford Pemberton, 1977-79) .... each £8
KUNG FU (Brown Watson, 1975-77) .... each £8
LANCER (World, 1970) £8
LAMB CHOP (World, 1972) £6
LARRY HARMON'S LAUREL AND HARDY (Brown Watson, 1970) £12
LARRY HARMON'S LAUREL AND HARDY (Brown Watson, 1971-75) .... each £8
LOGAN'S RUN (Brown Watson, 1979) £6
LOOK-IN TELEVISION ANNUAL (Independent Television Publications, 1972) £12
LOOK-IN TELEVISION ANNUAL (Independent Television Publications, 1973-79) ..... each £8
LOOK-IN TELEVISION ANNUAL (Independent Television Publications, 1980-91) ..... each £6
LOOK-IN TV COMEDY ANNUAL (ITP, 1975 & 1976) .... each £6
THE MAGICIAN (Brown Watson, 1976) £8
MUPPET SHOW (Brown Watson, 1978-80) .... each £6
NEW AVENGERS (Brown Watson, 1978 & 1979) .... each £10
OREGON TRAIL (Stafford Pemberton, 1979) £6
PARTRIDGE FAMILY (World, 1973-75) .... each £12
PINK PANTHER (Brown Watson, 1970s) .... each £6
PLANET OF THE APES (World, 1976 & 1977) .... each £8
THE QUEST (Brown Watson, 1977) £8
RETURN OF THE SAINT (Stafford Pemberton, 1979 & 1980) .... each £6
SCOOBY DOO (Brown Watson/World/Marvel, 1970s) .... each £12
SCOOBY DOO (Brown Watson/World/Marvel, 1980s) £8
SCOOBY DOO (Brown Watson/World/Marvel, 1981-90) .... each £6
SIX MILLION DOLLAR MAN (World/Stafford Pemberton, 1976) £8
SIX MILLION DOLLAR MAN (World/Stafford Pemberton, 1977-79) .... each £6
SPACE 1999 (World/Whitham, 1976) £8
SPACE 1999 (World/Whitham, 1977-79) .... each £6
SPACE 1999 (World/Whitham, 1980) £10
STAR MAIDENS (Stafford Pemberton, 1978) £6
STARSKY & HUTCH (Stafford Pemberton, 1978-80) .... each £8
HANNA BARBERA'S SUPER TV HEROES (Brown Watson, 1976 & 1977) .... each £12
THE SWEENEY (Brown Watson, 1977-79) .... each £6
TOM & JERRY/WORLD OF TOM & JERRY (World/PBS, 1970s) .... each £6
TOM & JERRY/WORLD OF TOM & JERRY (World/PBS, 1977) £8
TOM & JERRY/WORLD OF TOM & JERRY (World/PBS, 1980s-90s) .... each £3
TOP OF THE POPS (World, 1974-79) .... each £6
TOP OF THE POPS (World, 1980-83) .... each £3
TV ACTION (Polystyle, 1973 & 1974) .... each £8
TWO RONNIES (Brown Watson, 1979) £6
UFO (Polystyle, 1970) £8
WACKY RACES (Brown Watson, 1974) £12
THE WOMBLES (World, 1970s) .... each £6
THE WOMBLES (World, 1980s-99) .... each £3
WONDERFUL WORLD OF DISNEY (Fleetway, 1977-79) .... each £6

TWAIN, Mark

American author. Born: Samuel Langhorne Clemens in Missouri in 1835. Left school at twelve, subsequently working as a printer and river-boatman. Became a reporter during the Civil War, adopting the pseudonym, Mark Twain (a boatmen's call meaning 'two fathoms deep'). As well as such classic children's works as *The Adventures of Tom Sawyer* (1876), *Huckleberry Finn* (1884) and *The Prince and the Pauper* (1881), he wrote a number of satirical novels and volumes of reminiscences. Died: 1910.

Prices are for books in Very Good condition (in dustjackets after 1940).

THE CELEBRATED JUMPING FROG OF CALAVERAS COUNTY AND OTHER SKETCHES (wrappers) (Routledge, 1867).....£2,500
THE INNOCENTS ABROAD or THE NEW PILGRIM'S PROGRESS (two volumes) Hotten, [1870]) £800
ROUGHING IT (Routledge, 1872) £500
THE INNOCENTS AT HOME (Routledge, 1872)..£500
A CURIOUS DREAM AND OTHER SKETCHES (Routledge, [1872])..£350
MARK TWAIN'S SKETCHES (Routledge, 1872)..£250
THE CHOICE HUMOROUS WORKS (Hotten, [1873])..£250
THE GILDED AGE (with C.D. Warner; three volumes) (Routledge, 1874) ....the set £700
INFORMATION WANTED AND OTHER SKETCHES (Routledge, [1876])...£350
THE ADVENTURES OF TOM SAWYER (Chatto & Windus, 1876)..£5,000
THE ADVENTURES OF TOM SAWYER (illustrated by Keith Vaughan; Introduction by Graham Hu)
    (Paul Elek: 'Camden Classics' series, 1947)...£20
THE ADVENTURES OF TOM SAWYER (illustrated by Edward Ardizzone) (Heinemann, 1961)............£25
A TRAMP ABROAD (two volumes) (Chatto & Windus, 1880) ....the set £175
THE PRINCE AND THE PAUPER: A Tale for Young People of All Ages (Chatto & Windus, 1881)........£500
THE STOLEN WHITE ELEPHANT (Chatto & Windus, 1882)...£175
LIFF ON THE MISSISSIPPI (Chatto & Windus, 1883)..£500
THE ADVENTURES OF HUCKLEBERRY FINN, Tom Sawyer's Comrade (illustrated by E.W. Kemble)
    (Chatto & Windus, 1884) £1,800
THE ADVENTURES OF HUCKLEBERRY FINN, Tom Sawyer's Comrade (illustrated by Edward Burra)
    (Paul Elec: 'Camden Classics' series, 1947)..£20
THE ADVENTURES OF HUCKLEBERRY FINN, Tom Sawyer's Comrade (illustrated by Edward Ardizzone)
    (Heinemann, 1961)...£25
MARK TWAIN'S LIBRARY OF HUMOUR (illustrated by E.W. Kemble) (Chatto & Windus, 1888)..........£250
A YANKEE AT THE COURT OF KING ARTHUR (illustrated by Dan Beard) Chatto & Windus, 1889).......£175
THE AMERICAN CLAIMANT (Chatto & Windus, 1892) £80
THE $1,000,000 BANK NOTE (Chatto & Windus, 1893)..£80
TOM SAWYER ABROAD (illustrated by Dan Beard) (Chatto & Windus, 1894) £250
PUDD'NHEAD WILSON (Chatto & Windus, 1894)..£350
TOM SAWYER, DETECTIVE: As Told by Huck Finn, and Other Tales (Chatto & Windus, 1897 [1896]) £250
MORE TRAMPS ABROAD (Chatto & Windus, 1897)...£100
THE MAN THAT CORRUPTED HADLEYBURG (Chatto & Windus, 1900) £150
A DOUBLE BARRELLED DETECTIVE STORY (Chatto & Windus, 1902) £100
EXTRACTS FROM ADAM'S DIARY (Harper, UK/US, 1904)...£100
A DOG'S TALE (Harper, UK/US, 1904)...£100
EVE'S DIARY (Harper, UK/US, 1906) £100
THE $30,000 BEQUEST (Harper, UK/US, 1906) £80
A HORSE'S TALE (Harper, UK/US, 1907)..£60

*Samuel Langhore Clemens' first children's book, **The Celebrated Jumping Frog of Calaveras County and other Sketches,** is worth around £2,500, while his tale, **The Prince and the Pauper,** we currently value at £500 in Very Good condition.*

UPTON, Florence K.

Anglo-American illustrator. Born: Florence Kate Upton in New York in 1873, but moved permanently to England in 1893. Created the 'Golliwogg' in a series of picture books which were written by her mother, Bertha Upton (1849-1912), beginning with *The Adventures of Two Dutch Dolls and a 'Golliwogg'* (1895). The books started a 'Golliwogg' craze and spawned a whole range of ephemera and novelty items. Died: 1922.

Prices are for books in Very Good condition.

THE ADVENTURES OF TWO DUTCH DOLLS AND A GOLLIWOGG by Bertha Upton (verse) (Longmans, [1895]) **£400**
THE GOLLIWOGG'S BICYCLE CLUB by Bertha Upton (verse) (Longmans, [1896]) **£350**
LITTLE HEARTS by Bertha Upton (Routledge, 1897) **£350**
THE VEGE-MEN'S REVENGE by Bertha Upton (verse) (Longmans, [1897]) **£350**
THE GOLLIWOGG AT THE SEA-SIDE by Bertha Upton (verse) (Longmans, 1898) **£350**
THE GOLLIWOGG IN WAR! by Bertha Upton (verse) (Longmans, 1899) **£350**
THE GOLLIWOGG'S POLAR ADVENTURES by Bertha Upton (verse) (Longmans, [1900]) **£350**
THE GOLLIWOGG'S "AUTO-GO-CART" by Bertha Upton (verse) (Longmans, [1901]) **£350**
THE GOLLIWOGG'S AIR-SHIP by Bertha Upton (verse) (Longmans, [1902]) **£350**
THE GOLLIWOGG'S CIRCUS by Bertha Upton (verse) (Longmans, [1903]) **£350**
THE GOLLIWOGG IN HOLLAND by Bertha Upton (verse) (Longmans, [1904]) **£350**
THE GOLLIWOGG'S FOX-HUNT by Bertha Upton (verse) (Longmans, [1905]) **£350**
THE GOLLIWOGG'S DESERT ISLAND by Bertha Upton (verse) (Longmans, [1906]) **£350**
THE GOLLIWOGG'S CHRISTMAS by Bertha Upton (verse) (Longmans, 1907) **£450**
THE ADVENTURES OF BORBEE AND THE WISP: The Story of a Sophisticated Little Girl and
    an Unsophisticated Little Boy by Florence K. Upton (Longmans, 1908) **£350**
GOLLIWOGG IN THE AFRICAN JUNGLE by Bertha Upton (verse) (Longmans, 1909) **£400**

The 'Golliwogg' picture books, written by Bertha Upton and illustrated by her daughter, Florence. All fetch three-figure sums in Very Good condition, and these four are together worth £1,400.

UTTLEY, Alison

British author. Born: Cromford, Derbyshire, in 1884. Studied at Manchester and Cambridge Universities, subsequently working as a schoolteacher. Wrote a number of children's books, but is best known for her 'Little Grey Rabbit' series, and for those featuring Sam Pig. Also wrote a play about the life and works of Hans Andersen. Died: 1976.

Prices are for books in Very Good condition with dustjackets.

'Grey Rabbit' Books

THE SQUIRREL, THE HARE AND THE LITTLE GREY RABBIT (illustrated by Margaret Tempest) (Heinemann, 1929).........£150
HOW LITTLE GREY RABBIT GOT BACK HER TAIL (illustrated by Margaret Tempest) (Heinemann, 1930)...........£130
THE GREAT ADVENTURE OF HARE (illustrated by Margaret Tempest) (Heinemann, 1931) £130
THE STORY OF FUZZYPEG THE HEDGEHOG (illustrated by Margaret Tempest) (Heinemann, 1932) £130
SQUIRREL GOES SKATING (illustrated by Margaret Tempest) (Collins, 1934) £130
WISE OWL'S STORY (illustrated by Margaret Tempest) (Collins, 1935)....................£130
LITTLE GREY RABBIT'S PARTY (illustrated by Margaret Tempest) (Collins, 1936)....................£130
THE KNOT SQUIRREL TIED (illustrated by Margaret Tempest) (Collins, 1937)....................£130
FUZZYPEG GOES TO SCHOOL (illustrated by Margaret Tempest) (Collins, 1938) £130
LITTLE GREY RABBIT'S CHRISTMAS (illustrated by Margaret Tempest) (Collins, 1939) £130
MY LITTLE GREY RABBIT PAINTING BOOK (illustrated by Margaret Tempest) (Collins, 1940)....................£130
MOLDY WARP THE MOLE (illustrated by Margaret Tempest) (Collins, 1940)....................£100
HARE JOINS THE HOME GUARD (illustrated by Margaret Tempest) (Collins, 1942)....................£125
LITTLE GREY RABBIT'S WASHING DAY (illustrated by Margaret Tempest) (Collins, 1942)....................£75
WATER RAT'S PICNIC (illustrated by Margaret Tempest) (Collins, 1943)....................£75
LITTLE GREY RABBIT'S BIRTHDAY (illustrated by Margaret Tempest) (Collins, 1944) £75
THE SPECKLEDY HEN (illustrated by Margaret Tempest) (Collins, 1945) £70
LITTLE GREY RABBIT TO THE RESCUE (play; illustrated by Margaret Tempest) (Collins, 1945)....................£50
LITTLE GREY RABBIT AND THE WEASELS (illustrated by Margaret Tempest) (Collins, 1947) £50
GREY RABBIT AND THE WANDERING HEDGEHOG (illustrated by Margaret Tempest) (Collins, 1948)....................£50
LITTLE GREY RABBIT MAKES LACE (illustrated by Margaret Tempest) (Collins, 1950) £50
HARE AND THE EASTER EGGS (illustrated by Margaret Tempest) (Collins, 1952)....................£50
LITTLE GREY RABBIT'S VALENTINE (illustrated by Margaret Tempest) (Collins, 1953) £50
LITTLE GREY RABBIT GOES TO THE SEA (illustrated by Margaret Tempest) (Collins, 1954)....................£50
HARE AND GUY FAWKES (illustrated by Margaret Tempest) (Collins, 1956)....................£50
LITTLE GREY RABBIT'S PAINT-BOX (illustrated by Margaret Tempest) (Collins, [1958]) £50

The second of Alison Uttley's 'Grey Rabbit' books, now worth £130 in Very Good condition with the Margaret Tempest jacket.

All the books were issued in dustjackets, but even without them they have a great deal of charm, as this example shows.

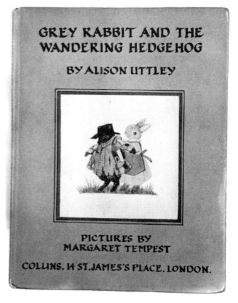

*The front board of **Little Grey Rabbit's Christmas** (1939) features a very appropriate 'snowflake' background design.*

*Post-war titles like **Grey Rabbit and the Wandering Hedgehog** are worth £40-£50 in their original dustjackets.*

GREY RABBIT FINDS A SHOE (illustrated by Margaret Tempest) (Collins, 1960)..£50
GREY RABBIT AND THE CIRCUS (illustrated by Margaret Tempest) (Collins, 1961) £50
THREE LITTLE GREY RABBIT PLAYS (contains 'The Grey Rabbit's Hospital', 'The Robber' and 'A Christmas Story')
    (Heinemann, 1961)...£40
GREY RABBIT'S MAY DAY (illustrated by Margaret Tempest) (Collins, 1963) £40
HARE GOES SHOPPING (illustrated by Margaret Tempest) (Collins, 1965) £40
LITTLE GREY RABBIT'S PANCAKE DAY (illustrated by Margaret Tempest) (Collins, 1967).............................£40
LITTLE GREY RABBIT GOES TO THE NORTH POLE (illustrated by Katherine Wigglesworth) (Collins, 1970) £40
FUZZYPEG'S BROTHER (illustrated by Katherine Wigglesworth) (Heinemann, 1971)..£40
LITTLE GREY RABBIT'S SPRING CLEANING PARTY (illustrated by Katherine Wigglesworth) (Collins, 1972).......£40
LITTLE GREY RABBIT AND THE SNOW-BABY (illustrated by Katherine Wigglesworth) (Collins, 1973) £40
HARE AND THE RAINBOW (illustrated by Katherine Wigglesworth) (Collins, 1975)...£40

'Sam Pig' Books
TALES OF THE FOUR PIGS AND BROCK THE BADGER (illustrated by Alec Buckels) (Faber, 1939) £100
THE ADVENTURES OF SAM PIG (illustrated by Francis Gower) (Faber, 1940)..£70
SAM PIG GOES TO MARKET (illustrated by A.E. Kennedy) (Faber, 1941)...£55
SIX TALES OF BROCK THE BADGER (illustrated by Alec Buckels and Francis Gower) (Faber, 1941)...............£50
SIX TALES OF SAM PIG (illustrated by Francis Gower) (Faber, 1941) £50
SIX TALES OF THE FOUR PIGS (illustrated by Alec Buckels) (Faber, 1941)...£45
SAM PIG AND SALLY (illustrated by A.E. Kennedy) (Faber, 1942) £45
SAM PIG AT THE CIRCUS (illustrated by A.E. Kennedy) (Faber, 1943)...£45
SAM PIG IN TROUBLE (illustrated by A.E. Kennedy) (Faber, 1948) £45
YOURS EVER, SAM PIG (illustrated by A.E. Kennedy) (Faber, 1951)..£40
SAM PIG AND THE SINGING GATE (illustrated by A.E. Kennedy) (Faber, 1955) £40
SAM PIG GOES TO THE SEASIDE (illustrated by A.E. Kennedy) (Faber, 1960)..£40
THE SAM PIG STORYBOOK (illustrated by Cecil Leslie) (Faber, 1965)..£30

'Tim Rabbit' Books
THE ADVENTURES OF NO ORDINARY RABBIT (illustrated by Alec Buckels) (Faber, [1937]).............................£100
TEN TALES OF TIM RABBIT (illustrated by Alec Buckels) (Faber, 1941)..£50
ADVENTURES OF TIM RABBIT (illustrated by A.E. Kennedy) (Faber, 1945)..£50
TIM RABBIT AND COMPANY (illustrated by A.E. Kennedy) (Faber, 1959) £40
TIM RABBIT'S DOZEN (illustrated by Shirley Hughes) (Faber, 1964) £30

'Little Brown Mouse' Books
SNUG AND SERENA MEET A QUEEN (illustrated by Katherine Wigglesworth) (Heinemann, 1950)....................£60
SNUG AND SERENA PICK COWSLIPS (illustrated by Katherine Wigglesworth) (Heinemann, 1950) £55

GOING TO THE FAIR (illustrated by Katherine Wigglesworth) (Heinemann, 1951)..£40
TOAD'S CASTLE (illustrated by Katherine Wigglesworth) (Heinemann, 1951)...£40
MRS MOUSE SPRING-CLEANS (illustrated by Katherine Wigglesworth) (Heinemann, 1952) £40
CHRISTMAS AT THE ROSE AND CROWN (illustrated by Katherine Wigglesworth) (Heinemann, 1952) £40
THE GYPSY HEDGEHOGS (illustrated by Katherine Wigglesworth) (Heinemann, 1953) £40
SNUG AND THE CHIMNEY-SWEEPER (illustrated by Katherine Wigglesworth) (Heinemann, 1953) £40
THE MOUSE TELEGRAMS (illustrated by Katherine Wigglesworth) (Heinemann, 1955) £40
THE FLOWER SHOW (illustrated by Katherine Wigglesworth) (Heinemann, 1955) £40
SNUG AND THE SILVER SPOON (illustrated by Katherine Wigglesworth) (Heinemann, 1957) £35
MR STOAT WALKS IN (illustrated by Katherine Wigglesworth) (Heinemann, 1957)...£35
SNUG AND SERENA COUNT TWELVE (illustrated by Katherine Wigglesworth) (Heinemann, 1959)..................£30
SNUG AND SERENA GO TO TOWN (illustrated by Katherine Wigglesworth) (Heinemann, 1961).......................£30
THE BROWN MOUSE BOOK: Magical Tales of Two Little Mice (illustrated by Katherine Wigglesworth) (Heinemann, 1971) £35

'Little Red Fox' Books
LITTLE RED FOX AND THE WICKED UNCLE (illustrated by Katherine Wigglesworth) (Heinemann, 1954)...........................£125
LITTLE RED FOX AND CINDERELLA (illustrated by Katherine Wigglesworth) (Heinemann, 1956) £100
LITTLE RED FOX AND THE MAGIC MOON (illustrated by Katherine Wigglesworth) (Heinemann, 1958)............£100
LITTLE RED FOX AND THE UNICORN (illustrated by Katherine Wigglesworth) (Heinemann, 1962) £70
THE LITTLE RED FOX AND THE BIG TREE (illustrated by Jennie Corbett) (Heinemann, 1968)..........................£60

Others
THE COUNTRY CHILD (illustrated by C.F. Tunnicliffe) (Faber, 1931) £125
MOONSHINE AND MAGIC (illustrated by William Townsend) (Faber, 1932)...£100
THE ADVENTURES OF PETER AND JUDY IN BUNNYLAND (illustrated by L. Young) (Collins, 1935)................£80
CANDLELIGHT TALES (illustrated by Elinor Bellingham-Smith) (Faber, 1936)...£70
AMBUSH OF YOUNG DAYS (Faber, 1937)..£60
MUSTARD, PEPPER AND SALT (illustrated by Gwen Raverat) (Faber, 1938) £90
HIGH MEADOWS (Faber, 1938) £60
A TRAVELLER IN TIME (illustrated by Phyllis Bray) (Faber, 1939)...£40
THE FARM ON THE HILL (Faber, 1941) £35
NINE STARLIGHT TALES (illustrated by Irene Hawkins) (Faber, 1942) £35
TEN CANDLELIGHT TALES (selections from 'Candlelight Tales') (Faber, 1942) £35
CUCKOO CHERRY-TREE (illustrated by Irene Hawkins) (Faber, 1943) £35
COUNTRY HOARD (illustrated by C.F. Tunnicliffe) (Faber, 1943) £40
THE SPICE WOMAN'S BASKET and Other Tales (illustrated by Irene Hawkins) (Faber, 1944).........................£40
MRS NIMBLE AND MR BUMBLE (illustrated by Horace Knowles) (James, 1944) £50
SOME MOONSHINE TALES (illustrated by Sarah Nechamkin) (Faber, 1945)...£30
THE WEATHER COCK and Other Stories (illustrated by Nancy Innes) (Faber, 1945) £35
WHEN ALL IS DONE (Faber, 1945)...£35
COUNTRY THINGS (illustrated by C.F. Tunnicliffe) (Faber, 1946)..£45
THE WASHERWOMAN'S CHILD: A Play on the Life and Stories of Hans Christian Andersen
(illustrated by Irene Hawkins) (Faber, 1946) £40
JOHN BARLEYCORN: Twelve Tales of Fairy and Magic (illustrated by Philip Hepworth) (Faber, 1948)................£45

A selection that show how the series expanded and introduced new characters: Hare, Squirrel and Moldy Warp the Mole.

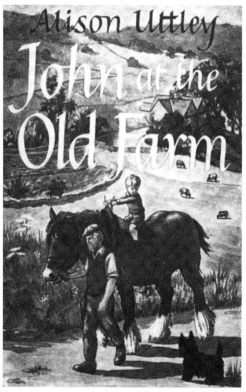

After the 'Grey Rabbit' books, Uttley's best-known works are those featuring Sam Pig. This is the tenth title in the series.

Uttley also wrote a number of 'miscellaneous' titles, like this story about a young boy's holiday on his grandfather's farm.

CARTS AND CANDLESTICKS (essays; illustrated by C.F. Tunnicliffe) (Faber, 1948) **£45**
IN PRAISE OF COUNTRY LIFE: An Anthology. Edited by Alison Uttley (Muller, 1949) **£40**
THE COBBLER'S SHOP and Other Tales (illustrated by Irene Hawkins) (Faber, 1950) **£40**
MACDUFF (illustrated by A.E. Kennedy) (Faber, 1950) **£30**
AMBUSH OF YOUNG DAYS (illustrated by C.F. Tunnicliffe) (Faber, 1951 [1952]) **£45**
PLOWMEN'S CLOCKS (essays; illustrated by C.F. Tunnicliffe) (Faber, 1952) **£45**
THE STUFF OF DREAMS (Faber, 1953) **£30**
MAGIC IN MY POCKET: A Selection of Tales (illustrated by Judith Brook; paperback) (Puffin, 1957) **£15**
THE SWANS FLY OVER (illustrated by C.F. Tunnicliffe) (Faber, 1959) **£45**
SOMETHING FOR NOTHING (illustrated by C.F. Tunnicliffe) (Faber, 1960) **£45**
JOHN AT THE OLD FARM (illustrated by Jennifer Miles) (Heinemann, 1960) **£50**
THE LITTLE KNIFE WHO DID ALL THE WORK: Twelve Tales of Magic (illustrated by Pauline Baynes) (Faber, 1962) **£30**
WILD HONEY (illustrated by C.F. Tunnicliffe) (Faber, 1962) **£45**
CUCKOO IN JUNE (illustrated by C.F. Tunnicliffe) (Faber, 1964) **£45**
THE MOUSE, THE RABBIT AND THE LITTLE WHITE HEN (illustrated by Jennie Corbett; boards)
     (Heinemann: 'Cowslip' series, 1966) **£25**
ENCHANTMENT (illustrated by Jennie Corbett; boards) (Heinemann: 'Cowslip' series, 1966) **£25**
A PECK OF GOLD (illustrated by C.F. Tunnicliffe) (Faber, 1966) **£45**
THE BUTTON-BOX and Other Essays (illustrated by C.F. Tunnicliffe) (Faber, 1968) **£45**
LAVENDER SHOES: Eight Tales of Enchantment (illustrated by Janina Ede) (Faber, 1970) **£25**
A TEN O'CLOCK SCHOLAR and Other Essays (illustrated by C.F. Tunnicliffe) (Faber, 1970) **£45**
SECRET PLACES and Other Essays (illustrated by C.F. Tunnicliffe) (Faber, 1972) **£60**
FAIRY TALES. Edited by Kathleen Lines (illustrated by Ann Strugwell) (Faber, 1975) **£25**
FROM SPRING TO SPRING: Stories of the Four Seasons. Edited by Kathleen Lines
     (anthology; illustrated by Shirley Hughes) (Faber, 1978) **£20**
STORIES FOR CHRISTMAS. Chosen by Kathleen Lines (illustrated by Gavin Rowe) (Faber, 1977) **£20**

V

VERNE, Jules

French author. Born: Nantes, 1828. Famous for his escapist adventure novels and short stories. Died: 1905.

Prices are for books in Very Good condition (with dustjackets after 1950).

FIVE WEEKS IN A BALLOON (Chapman & Hall, 1870) £4,000
A JOURNEY TO THE CENTRE OF THE EARTH (Griffith & Farran, 1872 [1871]) £5,000
TWENTY THOUSAND LEAGUES UNDER THE SEA (Sampson Low, 1873 [1872]) £8,000
FROM THE EARTH TO THE MOON DIRECT IN 97 HOURS, 20 MINUTES, AND A TRIP ROUND IT (Sampson Low, 1873)....£3,000
MERIDIANA: The Adventures of Three Englishmen and Three Russians in South Africa (Sampson Low, 1873) £1,500
THE FUR COUNTRY (Sampson Low, 1874 [1873])...£1,500
AROUND THE WORLD IN EIGHTY DAYS (Sampson Low, 1874 [1873]) £6,000
A FLOATING CITY, AND THE BLOCKADE RUNNERS (Sampson Low, 1874) £1,500
DR OX'S EXPERIMENT and Other Stories (Sampson Low, 1875) £600
THE MYSTERIOUS ISLAND (three volumes : 'Dropped from the Clouds', 'Abandoned' and
'The Secret of the Island') (Sampson Low, 1875)...the set £3,000
THE ENGLISH AT THE NORTH POLE – I: THE ADVENTURES OF CAPTAIN HATTERAS (Routledge, 1875 [1874])............£600
THE ENGLISH AT THE NORTH POLE – II: THE FIELD OF ICE (Routledge, 1876) £600
THE SURVIVORS OF THE 'CHANCELLOR' (Sampson Low, 1875) £600
MARTIN PAZ (Sampson Low, 1876) £600
A WINTER AMID THE ICE and Other Stories (Sampson Low, 1876) £600
A VOYAGE ROUND THE WORLD (three volumes: 'South America', 'Australia' & 'New Zealand') (Routledge, 1876-77) ...... the set £2,000
MICHAEL STROGOFF (Sampson Low, 1877 [1876])..£1,000
THE CHILD OF THE CAVERN (Sampson Low, 1877)..£1,000
HECTOR SERVADAC (Sampson Low, 1878) £1,000
DICK SANDS, THE BOY CAPTAIN (Sampson Low, 1879 [1878])...£1,000
THE BEGUM'S FORTUNE (Sampson Low, 1880 [1879])...£1,000
THE TRIBULATIONS OF A CHINAMAN (Sampson Low, 1880) £800
THE STEAM HOUSE (two volumes: 'Demon of Cawnpore' and 'Tigers and Traitors') (Sampson Low, 1881) .... the set £2,000
THE GIANT RAFT (two volumes: 'Down the Amazon' and 'The Cryptogram') (Sampson Low, 1881)......................... the set £1,500
GODFREY MORGAN, A CALIFORNIAN MYSTERY (Sampson Low, 1883) £1,000
THE GREEN RAY (Sampson Low, 1883)..£1,000
KERABAN THE INFLEXIBLE (two vols: 'The Captain of the Guidara' & 'Scarpante the Spy') (Sampson Low, 1884-85) ...... the set £2,000
THE VANISHED DIAMOND (Sampson Low, 1885)..£1,000
THE ARCHIPELAGO ON FIRE (Sampson Low, 1886) £1,000
MATHIAS SANDORF (Sampson Low, 1886) £1,000
THE CLIPPER OF THE CLOUDS (Sampson Low, 1887)..£1,000
THE LOTTERY TICKET (Sampson Low, 1887) £1,000
THE FLIGHT TO FRANCE (Sampson Low, 1888) £1,000
NORTH AGAINST SOUTH (Sampson Low, 1888)..£1,000
ADRIFT IN THE PACIFIC (Sampson Low, 1889)...£1,000
A FAMILY WITHOUT A NAME (Sampson Low, 1891 [1890])..£1,000
THE PURCHASE OF THE NORTH POLE (Sampson Low, 1891 [1890]) £1,000
CAESAR CASCABEL (Sampson Low, 1891)...£1,000
MISTRESS BRANICAN (Sampson Low, 1892)...£1,000
THE CASTLE OF THE CARPATHIANS (Sampson Low, 1893) £1,000
CLAUDIUS BOMBARNAC (Sampson Low, 1894)...£1,000
FOUNDLING MICK (Sampson Low, 1895)...£1,000
CAPTAIN ANTIFER (Sampson Low, 1895) £1,000
THE FLOATING ISLAND (Sampson Low, 1896) £1,000
CLOVIS DARDENTOR (Sampson Low, 1897)...£1,000
FOR THE FLAG (Sampson Low, 1897) £1,000
AN ANTARCTIC MYSTERY (Sampson Low, 1898)..£1,500
THE WILL OF AN ECCENTRIC (Sampson Low, 1900)...£1,500
THE CHASE OF THE GOLDEN METEOR (Grant Richards, 1909) £400
MASTER OF THE WORLD (Sampson Low, [1914])..£400
THE LIGHTHOUSE AT THE END OF THE WORLD (Sampson Low, [1923])..£300
THEIR ISLAND HOME (Sampson Low, [1923]) £300
THE CASTAWAYS OF THE FLAG (Sampson Low, [1923]) £300
INTO THE NIGER BEND (Arco, 1960) £50
THE CITY IN THE SAHARA (Arco, 1960)...£50
THE SURVIVORS OF THE JONATHAN: The Masterless Man (Arco, 1962) £50
THE UNWILLING DICTATOR (Arco, 1962)...£50
THE GOLDEN VOLCANO: The Claim on Forty Mile Creek (Arco, 1962) £50
FLOOD AND FAME (Arco, 1962)..£50
THE SECRET OF THE WILLHELM STORITZ (Arco, 1964)...£50

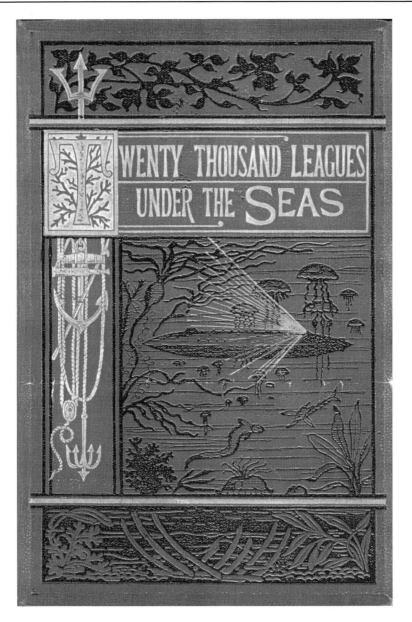

*Jules Verne's novels are full of wonderful inventions like the Nautilus submarine from **Twenty Thousand Leagues Under the Seas**.*

WAIN, Louis

British illustrator. Born: London, 1860. Studied at the West London School of Art, joining the *Illustrated Sporting and Dramatic News* as a journalist/illustrator in 1882. Began his highly successful career as a cat illustrator in 1886 with *Madame Tabby's Establishment*, producing his first annual in 1901. Worked in America between 1908 and 1910. Committed to a mental hospital in 1924 following an attack on his sister. With such a prolific output, it is very hard to be sure about many of the first editions, and it is also impossible to prove which ones were written by him as well. Died: 1939.

Prices are for books in Very Good condition. 'Et al' indicates that he was not the sole illustrator. Authors are listed where known.

MADAME TABBY'S ESTABLISHMENT (by 'Kari') (Macmillan, 1886) £700
OUR FARM: THE TROUBLE AND SUCCESSES THEREOF (by F.W. Pattenden) (James Clarke, 1888) £150
AUNT LOUISA'S JUMBLE BOOK (Frederick Warne, c1890)..£150
DREAMS BY FRENCH FIRESIDES: STORIES (by Richard Leander, pseudonym, translated by
　　J. Raleigh from the German) (A & C Black, 1890)..£300
LAUGH AND GROW WISE (New York: McLoughlin, c1890)...£200
A BOOK OF DRAWINGS (et al) (Privately printed for Mr And Mrs F T Davies, 1891)....................................N/A
BIRD PICTURES (et al; by Laura Jewry Valentine) (Warne, 1892) £80
DOG PICTURES (et al; by Laura Jewry Valentine) (Warne, 1892)...£80
CAT PICTURES (et al; by Laura Jewry Valentine) (Warne, 1892)...£80
PETER, A CAT O'ONE TAIL: HIS LIFE AND ADVENTURES (by Charles Morley) (Pall Mall Gazette, 1892)........£500
OLD RABBIT, THE VOODOO AND OTHER SORCERERS (et al; by Mary Alicia Owen) (T. Fisher Unwin, 1893)....£200
NOVEL NOTES (et al; by Jerome K. Jerome) (The Leadenhall Press, 1893)..£40
LAMENT OF BILLY VILLY (by Emily Rowley Watson) (Raphael Tuck, 1894) £300
MERRY MADCAPS (et al) (S.W. Partridge, c1895) £150
PUPPY DOGS' TALES (by 'Puppy Dogs', pseudonym) (Thomas Nelson, 1896)..£300
MISS LOVEMOUSE'S LETTERS (by 'Miss Lovemouse', pseudonym) (Thomas Nelson, 1896)............................£300
THE CHILDREN'S TABLEAUX: The Three Little Kittens (by Many authors) (Ernest Nister, 1896)....................£300
COMICAL CUSTOMERS AT THE NEW STORES OF COMICAL RHYMES AND STORIES (et al) (Ernest Nister, 1896).........£200
DOCTOR QUACK & HIS COMICAL CURES (et al) (Ernest Nister, 1896) (sold with HAPPY SCHOOLDAYS)............the pair £300
THE CHILDREN'S PEEPSHOW (et al; by Clifton Bingham) (Ernest Nister, c1896) £200
STORIES FROM LOWLY LIFE (by C.M. Duppa) (Macmillan, 1898)..£200
JINGLES, JOKES, AND FUNNY FOLKS (et al; by Clifton Bingham) (Ernest Nister, 1898) £200
Ditto (a pirate edition) (McLoughlin, US, 1898)..£200
PUSSY'S MIXTURE OF VERSE AND PICTURE (et al; by Clifton Bingham) (Ernest Nister, 1898) £200
THE MONKEY THAT WOULD NOT KILL (by Henry Drummond) (Hodder & Stoughton, 1898) £100
MORE JINGLES, JOKES, AND FUNNY FOLKS (by Clifton Bingham) (Ernest Nister, 1898) £200
IN DOORS AND OUT (et al) (Blackie, 1899)..£100
PUSSIES AND PUPPIES (S.W. Partridge, 1899)...£400
THE DANDY LION (by Clifton Bingham) (Ernest Nister, 1900)...£400
FUN ALL THE WAY (Nister, 1900) £200
PUSSIES AT WORK (Raphael Tuck, c1900) £400
COMICAL DOINGS (et al; many authors) (Ernest Nister, c1900)..£150
CATLAND (by 'Father Tuck' pseud) (Raphael Tuck, 1901)..£600
THE LIVING ANIMALS OF THE WORLD (by C.J. Cornish) ([1901])...£200
LOUIS WAIN'S ANNUAL (Ed: Stanhope Sprigg) (Anthony Treherne, 1901) £400
CATS (by 'Grimalkin' pseud) (Sands, 1901) £1,000
FAITHFUL FRIENDS: PICTURES AND STORIES FOR LITTLE FOLK (et al) (Blackie, 1901)................................£150
PA CATS, MA CATS, AND THEIR KITTENS (by 'Father Tuck' pseud) (Raphael Tuck, [1902]) £1,000
A PUSSIE'S DIARY (by Edith Warry. 'Diploma' series) (Dean, 1902)...£300
FUN AND FROLIC (by Clifton Bingham) (Ernest Nister, 1902)...£700
ALL SORTS OF CATS (by Clifton Bingham) (Ernest Nister / NY E.P. Dutton, No 747, 1902)...........................£600
LOUIS WAIN'S ANNUAL FOR 1902 (Ed: Stanhope Sprigg) (Anthony Treherne, 1902)..................................£400
PING-PONG CALENDER FOR 1903 (by Clifton Bingham) (Raphael Tuck, [1902]) £300
PING-PONG AS SEEN BY LOUIS WAIN (by Clifton Bingham) (Raphael Tuck, 1902).....................................£600
THE LOUIS WAIN NURSERY BOOK (James Clarke, 1902) £300
LOUIS WAIN'S CATS AND DOGS (Raphael Tuck, 1902)..£400
FUN FOR EVERYONE (Ernest Nister, c1902) £200
EVER SO FUN (Ernest Nister, c1902)...£100
LOUIS WAIN'S ANNUAL 1903 (Ed: T.F.G. Coates) (Hutchinson, 1903)...£400
LOUIS WAIN'S SUMMER BOOK (Hutchinson, 1903)...£200
LOUIS WAIN'S BABY PICTURE BOOK (James Clarke, 1903)..£400
LOUIS WAIN'S DOG PAINTING BOOK ('Little Artist' series) (Raphael Tuck, 1903) £400
LOUIS WAIN'S CAT PAINTING BOOK ('Little Artist' series) (Raphael Tuck, 1903)......................................£400
FATHER TUCK'S POSTCARD PAINTING BOOK (Raphael Tuck, 1903)...£300
CATLAND ABC (Raphael Tuck, [1903]) £800

Cat books are always popular with collectors, and none more so than those by Louis Wain. He was a prolific illustrator and new discoveries are being made all the time. Indeed our Wain bibliography lists several new titles unknown at the time of our previous edition.

WAIN, Louis

BIG DOGS, LITTLE DOGS, CATS AND KITTENS (Raphael Tuck, 1903)..£1,000
CAT LIFE (Raphael Tuck, 1903)...£600
CATLAND 'PANORAMA' (Raphael Tuck, c1903) (multi-hinged folding board book) £600
COMIC ANIMALS ABC: VERSES AND PICTURES (Collins, [1903])...£400
WITH FATHER TUCK TO ANIMAL LAND (Ed. Edric Vredenburg) (Raphael Tuck, 1903) £600
FAIRY TALES (by Grace C Floyd) (Raphael Tuck, c1903) £300
WITH LOUIS WAIN TO FAIRYLAND (by Nora Chesson) (Raphael Tuck, 1903)....................................£1,200
KITTENLAND (by Clifton Bingham) (Collins, 1903) £1,200
THE LOUIS WAIN KITTEN BOOK (Anthony Treherne, [1903]) £1,000
PUPPYLAND: PICTURES AND PLAY (by Clifton Bingham) (Collins, 1903) £300
PUSS IN BOOTS (Anthony Treherne, 1904)...£600
CLAWS AND PAWS: STORIES AND PICTURES FROM KITTENLAND AND PUPPYLAND
     (et al; by Clifton Bingham) (Nister, [1904])..£800
FUNNY ANIMALS AND STORIES ABOUT THEM (et al) (James Clarke, 1904)..£300
KITS AND CATS ('Little Pets' series) (Raphael Tuck, 1904)...£600
IN ANIMAL LAND WITH LOUIS WAIN (S.W. Partridge, 1904)...£600
FUNNY FAVOURITES (by Clifton Bingham) (Ernest Nister, 1904)..£600
STORIES FROM PUSSYLAND (The Piccanninies Picture Pocket Book series, one of five books
issued in red cloth case. et al; by S. Sutton Smith) (Sands, 1904)...£300
LOUIS WAIN'S ANNUAL 1905 (Ed: R.S. Pengally) (P.S. King, 1905) £300
LOUIS WAIN'S ANIMAL SHOW with Stories in Prose & Verse (James Clarke, 1905) £400
CAT TALES (by W.L. Alden) (Digby, Long, 1905) £400
ANIMAL ANTICS: FUNNY PICTURES: MERRY RHYMES (et al) (S.W. Partridge, 1905) £200
FROLICS IN FAIRYLAND (by Grace C. Floyd) (Raphael Tuck, c1905)..£300
MY BOOK OF FUNNY FOLK (Charles H. Kelly, 1905)...£150
MY CAT AND DOG BOOK (Charles H. Kelly, 1905)...£150
MY CAT BOOK (Charles H. Kelly, 1905)...£200
NURSERY RHYMES PICTURED BY LOUIS WAIN (Raphael Tuck, c1905)...£400
FUN AT ZOO (by Clifton Bingham) (Collins, 1906) £300
ANIMAL FUN (et al) (James Clarke, 1906)..£150
AT THE PANTOMIME WITH LOUIS WAIN (by Grace C. Floyd) (Raphael Tuck, No. 6788, c1906)............£300
MIXED PICKLES BOTTLED BY LOUIS WAIN (Ed: Edric Vredenburg. 'Welcome Gift' series) (Raphael Tuck, c1906) £300
NURSERY CATS (Board Book. 'Indestructible' series) (Raphael Tuck, c1906) £300
PANTOMIME PUSSIES (by Grace C. Floyd) (Raphael Tuck, c1906)...£300
LOUIS WAIN'S SUMMER BOOK FOR 1906 (P.S. King, 1906)...£400
PRANKS AND PURRS IN PUSSYLAND (title page reads Pussies Purrs and Pranks. et al) (Charles H. Kelly, 1906) £200
PLAYTIME IN PUSSYLAND (by Clifton Bingham) (Alfe Cooke, c1906)...£400
IN CAT AND DOG LAND WITH LOUIS WAIN (Raphael Tuck, c1906)...£400
LOUIS WAIN'S ANNUAL FOR 1906 (John F. Shaw, 1906)...£300

Although Wain's cats were usually depicted in human poses, they invariably retained their distinctly feline grace and charm.

LOUIS WAIN'S ANNUAL 1907 (Bemrose, 1907) £300
ANIMAL GAMBOLS (et al) (James Clarke, 1907) £150
THE ADVENTURES OF FRISKERS AND HIS FRIENDS (by Marian Isabel Hurrell) (Robert Culley, 1907) £400
A CAT'S DIARY (Edith Warry) (Dean's Pinafore Series, No. 62, 1907) (Called 'A Pussie's Diary' on title page) £300
'MEPHISTOPHELES' THE AUTOBIOGRAPHY OF A TABBY CAT (by Keiro - Charles Yates Stephenson) (Jarrold, 1907).....£400
THE MARVELLOUS STORY OF PUSS IN BOOTS (possibly a pirate edition) (Chicago: M.A. Donohue, 1908).................£200
ANIMAL PLAYTIME (et al) (James Clarke, 1908)...£300
FULL OF FUN (by Clifton Bingham) (Ernest Nister, 1908)...£400
ANIMAL PRANKS, ABC (et al) (James Clarke, 1908) £200
CAT'S CRADLE: A PICTURE-BOOK FOR LITTLE FOLK (by May Byron) (Blackie, [1908])......................................£400
THE KINGS AND THE CATS, Munster Fairy Tales for Young and Old (by John Hannon) (Burns and Oates, 1908) £400
KITTENLAND HOLIDAYS (et al) (Collins, c1908)..£200
A LITTLE BOOK OF PUSSY CATS (Little Folks Library, 1908) £300
LOUIS WAIN'S ANNUAL 1908 (Bemrose, 1908) £300
LOUIS WAIN'S ANNUAL 1909–10 (George Allen, 1909)..£300
HOLIDAY STORIES AND RHYMES (et al; by Clifton Bingham) (Ernest Nister, c1909).....................................£150
HOLIDAYS IN ANIMAL LAND (et al; by A.W. Ridler) (James Clarke, 1909) £400
TWO CATS AT LARGE: A BOOK OF SURPRISES (by S.C. Woodhouse) (George Routledge, 1910)....................£600
WHO SAID CATS? ('Favourite' series) (New York: The International Art Publishing Company, c1910) £150
THE MERRY ANIMAL PICTURE BOOK (by A.W. Ridler) (James Clarke, 1910)..£400
MRS GAMP'S STORY BOOK (et al) (Unknown publisher, c1910)...£200
FUNNY FOLK IN ANIMAL LAND (et al; by 'Uncle Frank', pseudonym) (S.W. Partridge, 1910)..........................£150
THE HAPPY FAMILY (by Edric Vredenburg et al) (Raphael Tuck, 1910)..£1,000
SUCH FUN WITH LOUIS WAIN (by Norman Gale et al) (Raphael Tuck, c1910) £300
SOMEBODY'S PUSSIES (Raphael Tuck, c1910)..£300
LOUIS WAIN'S ANNUAL 1910–11 (George Allen, 1910)..£300
LOUIS WAIN'S ANNUAL 1911 (John F. Shaw, 1911)...£300
LOUIS WAIN'S ANNUAL 1911–12 (John F. Shaw, 1911)...£300
LOUIS WAIN'S ANNUAL STREET (P.S. King & Sons, 1911) £300
ANIMALS IN FUN-LAND (et al; A W Ridler) (James Clarke, 1911)..£400
CATS AT SCHOOL (by S.C. Woodhouse) (George Routledge, 1911)...£600
THE CAT SCOUTS: A PICTURE BOOK FOR LITTLE FOLK (by Jessie Pope) (Blackie, 1912) £400
DAYS IN CATLAND WITH LOUIS WAIN 'PANORAMA' (by Arthur Barnaby) (Raphael Tuck, [1912])...................£1,500+
WITH LOUIS WAIN IN PUSSYLAND (Shape Book. "Hurrah" series. by Norman Gale) (Raphael Tuck, c1912) £300
CATS OF MANY LANDS (by Norman Gale) (Raphael Tuck, No. 9972, 'Wonderland' Series, c1912) £300
LOUIS WAIN'S PAINTING BOOK (John F. Shaw, c1912)...£300
LIFE IN CATLAND (by Norman Gale) (Raphael Tuck, c 1912) £300
IN STORY LAND WITH LOUIS WAIN (Raphael Tuck, 1912)...£600
LOUIS WAIN'S ANNUAL 1912 (John F. Shaw, 1912) £300
PUSSYLAND PICTURES BY LOUIS WAIN ('Playtime' series) (Raphael Tuck, c1912) £300
LOUIS WAIN'S FATHER CHRISTMAS (John F. Shaw, 1912)...£300
LOUIS WAIN'S HAPPY LAND (by A.W. Ridler) (John F. Shaw, 1912)..£300
PLEASURES IN PUSSYTOWN (by Norman Gale. 'Nursery' series) (Raphael Tuck, c1912) £300
MERRY TIMES IN ANIMAL-LAND (et al; by A.W. Ridler) (James Clarke, 1912)...£200
PICTURELAND FUN (et al) (Ernest Nister, 1913)...£200
PAGES OF FUN (Ernest Nister, 1913) £300
LOUIS WAIN'S ANNUAL 1913 (John F. Shaw, 1913) £300
ANIMAL HAPPYLAND (et al; by A W Ridler) (James Clarke, 1913)..£300
HAPPY HOURS WITH LOUIS WAIN (John F. Shaw, 1913) £400
IN LOUIS WAIN LAND (John F. Shaw, c1913) £400
A CAT ALPHABET, AND PICTURE BOOK FOR LITTLE FOLK (Blackie, [1914])...£600
ANIMAL PICTURE-LAND (et al; by A W Ridler) (James Clarke, 1914) £300
TINKER, TAILOR (by Edric Vredenburg) (Raphael Tuck, 1914)...£600
A DOG'S DAY (et al) (Collins, c1914) £70
IN CATLAND (Father Tuck's Panorama Series) (John F. Shaw, c1914)...£300
LOUIS WAIN'S ANNUAL 1914 (John F. Shaw, 1914) £200
LOUIS WAIN'S ANNUAL 1915 (John F. Shaw, 1915) £200
ANIMAL FANCY-LAND (et al, by A.W. Ridler) (James Clarke, 1915) £300
DADDY CAT (by May Byron) (Blackie, [1915])..£600
HOLIDAY FRIENDS (et al, by Clifton Bingham) (Raphael Tuck, c1915) £120
CAT STORIES: TALES FOR LITTLE PEOPLE (et al, by Ann Stephenson) (Aldine, 1915)................................£70
AMONG OUR FRIENDS (et al) (Raphael Tuck, c1915)..£100
A TRIP TO CATLAND (Raphael Tuck, c1915) (Father Tuck's 'Holiday' series)...£300
FROLICSOME FRIENDS (by Jessie Pope) (Blackie, 1915) £200
PRINTER'S PIE (et al) (Sphere & Tatler, 1915) £60
TO NURSERY LAND WITH LOUIS WAIN (Ed: Edric Vredenburg, 'Golden Gift' series) (Raphael Tuck, c1915).......£300
OUR DARLINGS (et al) (Shaw, c1915)..£50
LITTLE SOLDIERS (by May Crommelin) (Hutchinson, [1915]) £300
PAGES TO PLEASE YOU ('Golden Gift' series) (Raphael Tuck, c1916) £200

MERRY TIMES WITH LOUIS WAIN (by Dorothy Black et al. 'Golden Gift' series) (Raphael Tuck, 1916)..................£400
PUSSY CATS ABC (S.W. Partridge, 1916) £300
CATS OF ALL SORTS (Geographia, c1916) £300
I'LL TELL YOU A STORY (Ed: Edric Vredenburg, 'Furry Mascot' series) (Raphael Tuck, c1916).................£100
TERRIER, VC, A BLACK AND TAN HERO (by Julia Lowndes Tracey) (Aldine, 1916) £300
LITTLE RED RIDING HOOD AND OTHER TALES (Gale & Polden, [1917]) £300
HAPPY SCHOOLDAYS (by 'Freckles') (Gale and Polden, [1917])..£300
CATS AT PLAY (Blackie, 1917)...£400
ROSY CHEEKS FUNNY BOOK (Ernest Nister [c1917]) £150
CINDERELLA AND OTHER FAIRY TALES (Gale and Polden, 1917) £300
BILLIECAT FAMILY FROLICS (Gale and Polden, c1918) £300
ANIMAL JOLLITIES (et al) (James Clarke, c1919) £150
THE ANIMAL JOY-BOOK (et al; by E H Jeffs) (James Clarke, c1919) £150
IN WAIN LAND (John F. Shaw, 1919) £300
JOCK THE BOW WOW (Shape Book) (Valentine Book Toys, 1919) £200
ANIMAL FROLICS (et al; by A.W. Ridler) (James Clarke, 1919)..£150
THE FARMYARD PUSSIES, TALES FOR LITTLE PEOPLE (Aldine, c 1919)..£200
TATTERS, THE PUPPY (Shape Book) (Valentine, 1919) £200
FLOSSY AND FLUFFY (Valentine, 1919) £200
LOUIS WAIN'S 'DOGGIE' PAINTING BOOK (Shape Book) (Valentine, 1919)...£200
LOUIS WAIN'S 'KITTENS' PAINTING BOOK (Shape Book) (Valentine, 1919)...£200
LOUIS WAIN'S 'CATS' PAINTING BOOK (Shape Book) (Valentine, 1919)..£200
I'LL TELL YOU A TALE (Ed: Edric Vredenburg, 'Furry Mascot' series, black furry cat with movable tail on cover)
     (Raphael Tuck, c1920)...£200
THE STORY OF TABBYKIN TOWN IN SCHOOL AND AT PLAY (by 'Kittycat', pseudonym) (C.N. Faulkner, 1920) £300
VERY FUNNY (Scott and Sleeman, 1920) £200
SWING HIGH – SWING LOW (et al) (Springfield MBY McLoughlin Bros, c1920)...£150
THE TALE OF LITTLE PRISCILLA PURR (by Cecily M. Rutley) (Valentine, 1920)..£600
THE TALE OF NAUGHTY KITTY CAT (by Cecily M. Rutley) (Valentine, 1920)..£300
THE TALE OF PETER PUSSKIN (by Cecily M. Rutley) (Valentine, 1920)...£300
THE TALE OF THE TABBY TWINS (by Cecily M. Rutley) (Valentine, 1920) £300
LOUIS WAIN'S CAT MASCOT POSTCARD PAINTING BOOK ('Little Artist' series) (Raphael Tuck, c1920)...........£150
LOUIS WAIN'S DOG MASCOT POSTCARD PAINTING BOOK ('Little Artist' series) (Raphael Tuck, c1920)...........£150
LOUIS WAIN'S MERRY MASCOT POSTCARD PAINTING BOOK ('Little Artist' series) (Raphael Tuck, c1920).......£150
'LITTLE PEOPLE' (Transfer Pictures, Series 211, Louis Wain's Mascots. 36 cat and dog mounted transfers
     contained in original printed wrappers. Unusual item in VG condition) (Raphael Tuck, c1920)................£100
EVERY CHILD'S OWN PICTURE BOOK (by Grace C. Floyd. 'Wonder' series,
     with 24 perforated coloured picture labels for child to paste in) (Raphael Tuck, [c1920])........................£300
CATS AT PLAY (Blackie, c1920) £300
PUSSY LAND (Shape Book) (Geographia, 1920)...£400
SOMEBODY'S PUSSIES (Board Book) (Raphael Tuck, c1920) £200
ADVENTURES OF PETER PUSS (Raphael Tuck, c1920) £300
BUSY PUSSIES (Blackie, c1920s)...£300
THE JOY BOOK 1922, A Picture and Story Annual for Little Folk
     (Many authors, one long story: 'The Adventures of Patrick Persian') (Hulton, 1921)...............................£200
THE PUSSY ROCKER: POLLY PUSS (by Cecily M Rutley. Shape Book with rolling eyes) (Valentine Rocker Book, 1921) £300
THE PUPPY ROCKER: PETER PUP (Shape Book with rolling eyes. by Cecily M. Rutley) (Valentine Rocker Book, 1921)......£300
THE TEDDY ROCKER: THE: NAUGHTY TEDDY BEAR (Shape Book with rolling eyes. by Cecily M. Rutley) (Valentine, 1921) £300
THE BIG ABC BOOK (et al) (Blackie, 1921) £150
LOUIS WAIN'S ANNUAL 1921 (Hutchinson, 1921) £200
CHARLIE'S ADVENTURES (Valentine, 1922) £400
THE KITTEN'S HOUSE (Valentine, 1922) £400
LOUIS WAIN'S CHILDREN'S BOOK (Hutchinson, 1923) £300
SOUVENIR OF LOUIS WAIN'S WORK (Louis Wain Fund, 1925) £200
ANIMALS 'XTRA' AND LOUIS WAIN'S ANNUAL (Louis Wain Fund, 1925)..£200
LOUIS WAIN'S ANIMAL BOOK (Collins, 1928) £200
BLACKIE'S EASY STORY BOOK (et al) (Blackie, c1930) £60
KITS AND CATS (With 'Louis Wain in Pussyland' on the title page. 'Hurrah' series Shape Book)
     (by Anon. [Norman Gale]) (Raphael Tuck, 1930s) £200
LOST, STOLEN OR STRAYED (by Marion Ashmore) (Eyre & Spottiswode, 1934) £150
LOUIS WAIN'S GREAT BIG MIDGET BOOK (et al) (Dean, 1934) £200
THE PICTURE BOOK OF KITTENS (et al; by Jessie Pope) (Ward, Lock, 1935) £150
LITTLE FROLIC (et al) (Juvenile Productions, c1936) £60
MY OWN PICTURE BOOK (et al) (Ward, Lock & Co, 1938) £60

Books of unknown date

CATS AND DOGS (et al) (Children's Press); CATS AND KITTENS: STORIES AND PICTURES (Ed: Mabel Mackintosh) (John Shaw); THE CHILDREN'S NATURAL HISTORY (Unknown); FAVOURITE FAIRY TALES PAINTING BOOK: POST CARDS TO PAINT (Valentine); FUN AND FROLIC (Collins); IN DOORS AND OUT (et al) (Blackie); KIT-CATS (London?, imprint 'W'); LES DISTRACTIONS DE MINET (Paris: Raphael Tuck); MY DOGGIE BOOK (John F. Shaw); NURSERY RHYMES PAINTING BOOK: POST CARDS TO PAINT (Valentine); OUR DARLINGS (et al) (John F. Shaw); THE PET

PUSSY (et al. 'Tiny Tots' series) (Raphael Tuck); **ROUND THE FARMYARD PAINTING BOOK: POST CARDS TO PAINT** (Valentine); **SOME CATS FOR PAINTING: POSTCARD PAINTING BOOK** ('Little Artist' series) (Raphael Tuck); **TO NURSERY LAND WITH LOUIS WAIN** (Ed: Edric Vredenberg. 'Golden Gift' series) (Raphael Tuck); **TOMMY'S FRIGHT, THE STORY OF A PERSIAN KITTEN** (one of six in envelope) (Home Chat Bedtime Booklets)

Periodicals in which Wain drawings may be found

Boy's Own Paper, Captain, Cassells' Magazine, Childrens' Friend, Crampton's Magazine, English Illustrated Magazine, Father Tuck's Annual, Graphic, Harmsworth London Magazine, Idler, Illustrated London News, Illustrated Sporting & Dramatic News, Infants' Magazine, Jabberwock, Lady's Magazine, Leisure Hour, Little Dots, Little Folks, MAP, Nister's Holiday Annual, Our Own Magazine, Pearson's Weekly, Playmates, Playbox Annual, Playbox Annual, Rosebud Annual, School Girl's Annual, Sketch, Smith's Weekly, Strand Magazine, Windsor Magazine

WALSH, Jill Paton

British author. Born: London, 1937. Her books are aimed at adolescents but are enjoyed by older and younger readers. Notable for *Goldengrove* (1972) and its sequel, *Unleaving* (1976). Won the Whitbread Award for *The Emperor's Winding-Sheet* in 1974.

Prices are for books in Very Good condition with dustjackets where applicable.

HENGEST'S TALE (illustrated by Janet Margrie) (Macmillan, 1966)..£40
THE DOLPHIN CROSSING (Macmillan, 1967)..£30
WORDHOARD: Anglo-Saxon Stories (with Kevin Crossley-Holland) (Macmillan, 1969)........................£20
FIREWEED (Macmillan, 1969)..£20
GOLDENGROVE (Macmillan, 1972) £20
TOOLMAKER (illustrated by Jeroo Roy) (Macmillan, 1973)..£20
THE DAWNSTONE (illustrated by Mary Dinsdale) (Hamish Hamilton, 1973)....................................£20
THE EMPEROR'S WINDING SHEET (Macmillan, 1974)..£20
THE BUTTY BOY (illustrated by Juliette Palmer) (Macmillan, 1975) £20
THE BUTTY BOY (as 'The Huffler'; illustrated by Juliette Palmer) (Farrar Straus, US, 1975)................£20
THE ISLAND SUNRISE: Prehistoric Britain (Deutsch, 1975) £20
UNLEAVING (Macmillan, 1976)..£20
CROSSING THE SALAMIS (illustrated by David Smee) (Heinemann, 1977) £10
THE WALLS OF ATHENS (illustrated by David Smee) (Heinemann, 1977) £10
PERSIAN GOLD (illustrated by David Smee) (Heinemann, 1978) £10
CHILDREN OF THE FOX (contains 'Crossing to Salamis', 'The Walls of Athens' and 'Persian Gold')
   (Farrar Straus, US, 1978)..£10
A CHANCE CHILD (Macmillan, 1978)..£10
THE GREEN BOOK (illustrated by Joanna Stubbs) (Macmillan, 1981)...£10
BABYLON (illustrated by Jenny Northway) (Deutsch, 1982) £10
A PARCEL OF PATTERNS (Kestrel, 1983)..£10
LOST AND FOUND (illustrated by Mary Rayner) (Deutsch, 1984)...£10
GAFFER SAMSON'S LUCK (illustrated by Brock Cole) (Farrar Straus, US, 1984)............................£10
GAFFER SAMSON'S LUCK (illustrated by Brock Cole) (Viking Kestrel, 1985).................................£10
PEPI AND THE SECRET NAMES (Frances Lincoln, 1994) £10

WARNER, Rex

British author. Born: Birmingham, 1905. One of the most highly-regarded writers of the period spanning the Second World War. His thoughtful allegorical novels led to him being acclaimed 'the English Kafka'. However, his first published book was boy's adventure story, *The Kite*. Died: 1986.

Prices are for books in Very Good condition with dustjackets.

THE KITE (Basil Blackwell: 'Tales of Action' series No 8, 1936) £85
THE KITE (Basil Blackwell, 1943)..£15
THE KITE (Revised Edition; illustrated by Edward Pagram) (Hamish Hamilton: 'Big Reindeer Books' series, 1963)...................£10
THE KITE (Revised Edition; illustrated by Edward Pagram) (Hamish Hamilton: 'Heron' series, 1963).......................................£10

WEBB, Marion St John

British author. Born: Hampstead, London in the 1890s. Her first book, *The Littlest One*, which appeared in 1914, was enormously successful, as were the 'Mr Papingay' books. Died: 1930.

Prices are for books in Good condition (with dustjackets after 1920).

'Littlest' Books

THE LITTLEST ONE (illustrated by Margaret W. Tarrant) (Harrap, 1914) £50
THE LITTLEST ONE (Harrap, 1918)..£35
THE LITTLEST ONE – HIS BOOK (illustrated by Margaret W. Tarrant and Kathleen I. Nixon; music by Ralph Dunstan)
   (Harrap, 1923) £40
THE LITTLEST ONE AGAIN (illustrated by Margaret W. Tarrant and Kathleen I. Nixon) (Harrap, 1923)...............£35
THE LITTLEST ONE – HIS BOOK and THE LITTLEST ONE AGAIN (with additional poems)
   (illustrated by A.H. Watson) (Harrap, 1927) £40
THE LITTLEST ONE'S THIRD BOOK (Harrap, 1928)..£35
THE LITTLEST ONE IN BETWEEN (Harrap, 1929) £35

'Fairies' Books

THE FLOWER FAIRIES (Modern Art Society, [1923])......£100
THE SEED FAIRIES (Modern Art Society, [1923])......£100
THE INSECT FAIRIES (illustrated by Margaret W. Tarrant) (Modern Art Society, [1925])......£100
THE FOREST FAIRIES (illustrated by Margaret W. Tarrant) (Modern Art Society, [1925])......£100
THE ORCHARD FAIRIES (illustrated by Margaret W. Tarrant) (Modern Art Society, [1925])......£100
THE HOUSE FAIRIES (illustrated by Margaret W. Tarrant) (Modern Art Society, [1925])......£100
THE POND FAIRIES (illustrated by Margaret W. Tarrant) (Modern Art Society, [1925])......£100
THE SEA-SHORE FAIRIES (illustrated by Margaret W. Tarrant) (Modern Art Society, [1925])......£100
THE HEATH FAIRIES (Modern Art Society, [1927])......£100
THE WEATHER FAIRIES (illustrated by Margaret W. Tarrant) (Modern Art Society, [1927])......£100
THE TWILIGHT FAIRIES (illustrations by Margaret W. Tarrant) (Modern Art Society, [1928])......£100
THE WILD FRUIT FAIRIES (illustrated by Margaret W. Tarrant) (Modern Art Society, [1932])......£100

'Mr Papingay' Books

THE LITTLE ROUND HOUSE (Stanley Paul, 1924)......£30
THE LITTLE ROUND HOUSE (as 'Mr Papingay and the Little Round House') (Newnes, 1936)......£25
MR PAPINGAY'S CARAVAN (illustrated by Frank Rogers) (Collins, [1929])......£25
MR PAPINGAY'S FLYING SHOP (Collins, [1931])......£25
MR PAPINGAY'S SHIP (Stanley Paul, 1925)......£25
MR PAPINGAY'S SHIP (Newnes, [1936])......£25
MR PAPINGAY'S SHIP (illustrated by Jean Walmsley Heap) (Collins, 1957)......£25

Others

KNOCK THREE TIMES (illustrated by Margaret W. Tarrant) (Harrap, 1917)......£70
THE GIRLS OF CHEQUERTREES (Harrap, 1918)......£30
ELIZ'BETH PHIL AND ME (illustrated by Margaret W. Tarrant) (Harrap, 1919)......£50
THE HOUSE WITH A TWISTING PASSAGE (illustrated by Doris M. Palmer) (Harrap, 1922)......£50
THE MAGIC LAMPLIGHTER (illustrated by Margaret W. Tarrant) (Medici Society, 1926)......£45
JOHN AND ME & THE DICKERY DOG (illustrated by A.H. Watson) (Harrap, 1930)......£30
TWICE TEN (University of London Press, 1931)......£20

WEBSTER, Jean

American author. Born: Alice Jane Chandler Webster in 1876, the daughter of Mark Twain's business partner, Charles L. Webster. Best known for her 1912 novel, *Daddy Long-Legs*, which was later filmed with Mary Pickford in the lead role. Died: 1916.

Prices are for books in Very Good condition.

WHEN PATTY WENT TO COLLEGE (Century, US, 1903)......£100
THE WHEAT PRINCESS (Century, US, 1905)......£75
JERRY JUNIOR (illustrated by Orson Lowell) (Century, US, 1907)......£60
MUCH ADO ABOUT PETER (illustrated by Charlotte Harding and Harry Linnell) (Doubleday Page, US, 1909)......£60
MUCH ADO ABOUT PETER (Hodder & Stoughton, [1917])......£30
JUST PATTY (illustrated by C.M. Relyea) (Century, US, 1911)......£50
DADDY LONG-LEGS (illustrated by the author) (Century, US, 1912)......£150
DADDY LONG-LEGS (illustrated by the author) (Hodder & Stoughton, 1913)......£50
DADDY LONG-LEGS: A Comedy in Four Acts (play) (Samuel French: 'Standard Library' edition, UK/US, [1922])......£15
DADDY LONG-LEGS (illustrated by Edward Ardizzone) (Brockhampton Press, 1966)......£45
JUST PATTY (Hodder & Stoughton, 1915)......£35
PATTY AND PRISCILLA (Hodder & Stoughton, [1915])......£50
DEAR ENEMY (illustrated by the author) (Century, US, 1915)......£35
DEAR ENEMY (Hodder & Stoughton, [1915])......£20
THE FOUR-POOLS MYSTERY (Hodder & Stoughton, 1916)......£40
THE WHEAT PRINCESS (Hodder & Stoughton, 1916)......£35
JERRY (Hodder & Stoughton, [1916])......£30

WELCH, Ronald

British author. Born: Glamorganshire, 1909. Ronald Welch was the pseudonym of Ronald Felton, who wrote authentic, exciting historical novels. Awarded the Carnegie Medal for *Knight Crusader* in 1955. Died: 1982.

Prices are for books in Very Good condition with dustjackets where applicable.

THE BLACK CAR MYSTERY (Pitman, 1950)......£30
THE CLOCK STOOD STILL (Pitman, 1951)......£30
THE GAUNTLET (illustrated by T.R. Freeman) (OUP, 1951)......£30
KNIGHT CRUSADER (illustrated by William Stobbs) (OUP, 1954)......£25
SKER HOUSE (written under the pseudonym 'Ronald Felton') (Hutchinson, 1954)......£25
CAPTAIN OF DRAGOONS (illustrated by William Stobbs) (OUP, 1956)......£25
THE LONG BOW (Blackwell, 1957)......£20
MOHAWK VALLEY (illustrated by William Stobbs) (OUP, 1958)......£20

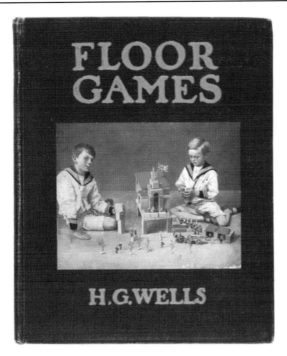

H.G. Wells produced three children's books, the first of which was written for his sons who also appear on the cover illustration. This book is currently worth £350 in Very Good condition.

CAPTAIN OF FOOT (illustrated by William Stobbs) (OUP, 1959)......£20
ESCAPE FROM FRANCE (illustrated by William Stobbs) (OUP, 1960) £20
FOR THE KING (illustrated by William Stobbs) (OUP, 1961)......£20
NICHOLAS CAREY (illustrated by William Stobbs) (OUP, 1963) £20
BOWMAN OF CRECY (illustrated by Ian Ribbons) (OUP, 1966)......£20
THE HAWK (illustrated by Gareth Floyd) (OUP, 1967)......£20
SUN OF YORK (illustrated by Doreen Roberts) (OUP, 1970) £20
THE GALLEON (illustrated by Victor Ambrus) (OUP, 1971) £20
TANK COMMANDER (illustrated by Victor Ambrus) (OUP, 1972) £20
ZULU WARRIOR (illustrated by David Harris) (David & Charles, 1974)......£20
ENSIGN CAREY (illustrated by Victor Ambrus) (OUP, 1976)......£20

WELLS, H.G.
British author. Born: Herbert George Wells in 1866. The great science fiction novelist wrote three works for children, the best-known of which, *The Adventures of Tommy*, was written in 1898 for the daughter of a friend, but not published until 1929. Died: 1946.

Prices are for books in Very Good condition with dustjackets.

FLOOR GAMES (Palmer, 1911) £250
LITTLE WARS: A Game for Boys (Palmer, 1913) £150
THE ADVENTURES OF TOMMY (illustrated by the author) (Harrap, 1929) £100

WESTALL, Robert
British author. Born in Newcastle in 1929. Studied at Durham University and the Slade School, subsequently working as an art master at schools in Birmingham and Chester. Won the Carnegie Medal with his first children's book, *The Machine Gunners* (1975), and later with *The Scarecrows* (1981). Died: 1993.

Prices are for books in Very Good condition with dustjackets where applicable.

THE MACHINE GUNNERS (Macmillan, 1975)......£30
THE WIND EYE (Macmillan, 1976)......£20
THE WATCH HOUSE (Macmillan, 1977)......£20
THE DEVIL ON THE ROAD (Macmillan, 1978) £20
FATHOM FIVE (Macmillan, 1979)......£20
THE SCARECROWS (Chatto & Windus, 1981)......£15
BREAK OF DARK (Chatto & Windus, 1982) £15
FUTURETRACK 5 (Kestrel, 1983) £15

THE HAUNTING OF CHAS McGILL (Macmillan, 1983)...£15
THE CATS OF SEROSTER (Macmillan, 1984)..£10
THE CHILDREN OF THE BLITZ: Memoirs of Wartime Childhood. Edited by Robert Westall (Viking, 1985)...........£10
RACHEL AND THE ANGEL (Macmillan, 1986)..£10
URN BURIAL (Viking Kestrel, 1987)...£10
ROSALIE (Macmillan, 1987)...£10
GHOSTS AND JOURNEYS (Macmillan, 1988)...£10
GHOST ABBEY (Macmillan, 1988)..£10
THE CREATURE IN THE DARK (Blackie, 1988)..£10
BLITZCAT (Macmillan, 1989)..£10
A WALK ON THE WILD SIDE (Methuen, 1989)..£10
OLD MAN ON A HORSE (Blackie, 1989)...£10
ECHOES OF WAR (Viking Kestrel, 1989)..£10
CAT! (Viking Kestrel, 1989)...£10
THE CALL (Viking Kestrel, 1989)..£10
IF CATS COULD FLY (Methuen, 1990)...£10
STORMSEARCH (Blackie, 1990)..£10
THE PROMISE (Macmillan, 1990)..£10
KINGDOM BY THE SEA (Methuen 1990)...£10
YAXLEY'S CAT (Macmillan, 1991)...£10
THE CHRISTMAS CAT (Methuen, 1991)...£10
THE CHRISTMAS GHOST (Methuen, 1992)...£10
GULF (Methuen, 1992)...£10
FEARFUL LOVERS (Macmillan, 1992)..£10
THE STONES OF MUNCASTER CATHEDRAL (Viking, 1993)..£10
A PLACE FOR ME (Macmillan, 1993)..£10
THE WHEATSTONE POND (Viking, 1993)..£10
FALLING INTO GLORY (Methuen, 1993)..£10
A TIME OF FIRE (Macmilan, 1994)...£10
NIGHTMARE (Methuen, 1995)..£10
CHILDREN OF THE BLITZ (Macmillan, 1995)...£10

The Young Cavalier was one of the first of many stirring boys' adventures to come from the prolific pen of Percy F. Westerman.

Westerman flew the flag during the First World War with morale-boosting novels like A Lively Bit of The Front (1918).

WESTERMAN, Percy F.

British author. Born: Percy Francis Westerman in 1876. Served with the RAF during the WWI. Wrote well over 100 novels, but is probably best known for those featuring the pilot, Colin Standish. Voted the most popular boys' author in Britain in the late 1930s. All values after 1920 assume the presence of a dustjacket; all prices for books before that date are without jackets. Publishing records cannot confirm whether titles from this period were issued with jackets, and we prefer not to price what may not exist. Died: 1959.

Prices are for books in Very Good condition with dustjackets (after 1920).

Historical tales
A LAD OF GRIT (illustrated by E.S. Hodgson) (Blackie, 1908) £75
THE WINNING OF THE GOLDEN SPURS (Nisbet, 1911) £60
THE YOUNG CAVALIER (illustrated by Gordon Browne) (Pearson, 1911) £60
THE QUEST OF THE "GOLDEN HOPE" (illustrated by Frank Wiles) (Blackie, 1912)........................£60
UNDER KING HENRY'S BANNERS (illustrated by John Campbell) (Pilgrim Press, 1914)................£30
'GAINST THE MIGHT OF SPAIN (illustrated by Savile Lumley) (Pilgrim Press, 1914)....................£30
THE LAST OF THE BUCCANEERS (illustrated by John de Walton) (Blackie, 1937)..........................£25
BOB STRICKLAND'S LOG (illustrated by Jack Matthew) (Blackie, 1953)...£15
DAVENTRY'S QUEST (illustrated by P.A. Jobson) (Blackie, 1955)..£15
JACK CRADDOCK'S COMMISSION (illustrated by Edward Osmond) (Blackie, 1958)........................£15

Science fiction
THE FLYING SUBMARINE (illustrated by John de Walton) (Nisbet, 1912)..£30
THE SEA MONARCH (illustrated by E.S. Hodgson) (Black, 1912) £30
THE RIVAL SUBMARINES (illustrated by C. Fleming Williams) (Partridge, 1913) £30
THE DREADNOUGHT OF THE AIR (illustrated by C. Fleming Williams) (Partridge, 1914)................£20
THE SECRET BATTLEPLANE (illustrated by Ernest Prater) (Blackie, 1916)......................................£20
THE WAR OF THE WIRELESS WAVES (illustrated by W.E. Wightman) (Oxford University Press, 1923) £25
ON THE WINGS OF THE WIND (illustrated by W.E. Wigfull) (Blackie, 1928)......................................£25
THE SECRET OF THE PLATEAU (illustrated by W.E. Wigfull) (Blackie, 1931)....................................£25

Stories of WWI
THE DISPATCH-RIDERS (illustrated by Frank Gillett) (Blackie, 1915)...£20
THE FIGHT FOR CONSTANTINOPLE (illustrated by W.E. Wigfull) (Blackie, 1915)..............................£20
A SUB OF THE RNR (illustrated by W.E. Wigfull) (Partridge, 1915)..£20
ROUNDING UP THE RAIDER (illustrated by E.S. Hodgson) (Blackie, 1916) £20
A WATCH OF THE NORTH SEA (illustrated by C.M. Padday) (Partridge, 1917) £20
DEEDS OF PLUCK AND DARING IN THE GREAT WAR (Blackie, 1917) £20
TO THE FORE WITH THE TANKS! (illustrated by Dudley Tennant) (Partridge, 1918) £20
UNDER THE WHITE ENSIGN (illustrated by E.S. Hodgson) (Blackie, 1918) £20
THE FRITZSTRAFERS (illustrated by Stanley L. Wood) (Partridge, 1918)...£20
BILLY BARCROFT R.N.A.S. (Partridge, 1918)...£20
A LIVELY BIT OF THE FRONT (illustrated by Wal Paget) (Blackie, 1918) £20
THE SECRET CHANNEL AND OTHER STORIES (Black, 1918) £20
THE SUBMARINE HUNTERS (illustrated by E.S. Hodgson) (Blackie, 1918)......................................£20
WITH BEATTY OFF JUTLAND (illustrated by Frank Gillett) (Blackie, 1918) £20
WILMSHURST OF THE FRONTIER FORCE (illustrated by Ernest Prater) (Partridge, 1918) £20
A SUB AND A SUBMARINE (illustrated by E.S. Hodgson) (Blackie, 1919)..£20
WINNING HIS WINGS (illustrated by E.S. Hodgson) (Blackie, 1919) £20
THE THICK OF THE FRAY AT ZEEBRUGGE, APRIL 1918 (illustrated by W.E. Wigfull) (Blackie, 1919)....£20
THE MYSTERY SHIP (illustrated by A. Morrow) (Partridge, 1920) £25
KEEPERS OF THE NARROW SEAS (reprint of The Fritzstrafers) (illustrated by Stanley L. Wood) (Partridge, 1931)................£25

Stories with scouting interest
THE SCOUTS OF SEAL ISLAND (illustrated by Ernest Prater) (Black, 1913) £30
THE SEA SCOUTS OF THE "PETREL" (illustrated by Ernest Prater) (Black, 1914) £30
SEA SCOUTS ALL (illustrated by Charles Pears) (Blackie, 1920) £15
SEA SCOUTS ABROAD (illustrated by Charles Pears) (Blackie, 1921) £25
SEA SCOUTS UP-CHANNEL (illustrated by C.M. Padday) (Blackie, 1922) £25
THE BOYS OF THE "PUFFIN" (illustrated by G.W. Goss) (Partridge, 1925) £25
THE SEA SCOUTS OF THE "KESTREL" (Seeley, 1925)...£25
THE MYSTERY OF THE BROADS (illustrated by E.A. Cox) (Blackie, 1930)..£25
HAUNTED HARBOUR (illustrated by John de Walton) (Blackie, 1937) £25
SEA SCOUTS AT DUNKIRK (illustrated by J.C.B. Knight) (Blackie, 1941)..£25
"SEA SCOUTS, ALERT!" (illustrated by G. Graham) (Blackie, 1955) £15

'The Golden Line' stories
A CADET OF THE MERCANTILE MARINE (illustrated by W.E. Wigfull) (Blackie, 1923)......................£30
THE GOOD SHIP "GOLDEN EFFORT" (illustrated by W.E. Wigfull) (Blackie, 1923) £30
EAST IN THE "GOLDEN GRAIN" (illustrated by Rowland Hilder) (Blackie, [1925])...............................£30
THE LUCK OF THE "GOLDEN DAWN" (illustrated by Rowland Hilder) (Blackie, [1926]).......................£30

A selection of rare dustjacketed books by Westerman, who became Blackie's most successful author after G.A. Henty. His works are not particularly valuable, but are avidly sought by collectors of boys' adventure stories.

CHUMS OF THE "GOLDEN VANITY" (illustrated by Rowland Hilder) (Blackie, [1927]) £30
THE JUNIOR CADET (illustrated by Rowland Hilder) (Blackie, [1928]).. £30
PAT STOBART IN THE "GOLDEN DAWN" (illustrated by Rowland Hilder) (Blackie, [1929])................. £30
LESLIE DEXTER, CADET (illustrated by Norman Hepple) (Blackie, 1930) £30
THE SENIOR CADET (illustrated by Rowland Hilder) (Blackie, [1931]) £30
ALL HANDS TO THE BOATS! (illustrated by Rowland Hilder) (Blackie, [1932]) £30
ON BOARD THE "GOLDEN EFFORT" (Blackie, 1935)... £30
THE "GOLDEN GLEANER" (illustrated by M. MacKinlay) (Blackie, 1948).. £15
WORKING THEIR PASSAGE (illustrated by Ellis Silas) (Blackie, 1951).. £15
ROUND THE WORLD IN THE "GOLDEN GLEANER" (illustrated by Jack Matthew)(Blackie, 1952) £15
ROLLING DOWN TO RIO (illustrated by R.G. Campbell) (Blackie, 1953)... £15

'Alan Carr'
HIS FIRST SHIP (illustrated by D.L. Mays) (Blackie, 1936) £20
HIS UNFINISHED VOYAGE (illustrated by D.L. Mays) (Blackie, 1937).. £25
CADET ALAN CARR (illustrated by D.L. Mays) (Blackie, 1938) £25
IN EASTERN SEAS (illustrated by D.L. Mays) (Blackie, 1939) £25
THE WAR AND ALAN CARR (illustrated by E. Boye Uden) (Blackie, 1940).. £25
WAR CARGO (illustrated by E. Boye Uden) (Blackie, 1941).. £25
ALAN CARR IN THE NEAR EAST (illustrated by E. Boye Uden) (Blackie, 1942).................................. £25
ALAN CARR IN THE ARCTIC (illustrated by E. Boye Uden) (Blackie, 1943).. £25
SECRET CONVOY (illustrated by Terence Cuneo) (Blackie, 1944).. £25
ALAN CARR IN COMMAND (illustrated by Terence Cuneo) (Blackie, 1945).. £25
BY LUCK AND BY PLUCK (illustrated by Terence Cuneo) (Blackie, 1946).. £25

'Standish'
THE AMIR'S RUBY (illustrated by W.E. Wigfull) (Blackie, 1932) £25
THE WESTOW TALISMAN (illustrated by W.E. Wigfull) (Blackie, 1934).. £25
STANDISH OF THE AIR POLICE (illustrated by W.E. Wigfull) (Blackie, 1935) £20
RINGED BY FIRE (illustrated by W.E. Wigfull) (Blackie, 1936).. £25
STANDISH GETS HIS MAN (illustrated by W.E. Wigfull) (Blackie, 1938).. £25
STANDISH LOSES HIS MAN (illustrated by W.E. Wigfull) (Blackie, 1939)... £25
STANDISH PULLS IT OFF (illustrated by W.E. Wigfull) (Blackie, 1940)... £25
STANDISH HOLDS ON (illustrated by W.E. Wigfull) (Blackie, 1941)... £25
BEYOND THE BURMA ROAD (illustrated by Victor Bertoglio) (Blackie, 1949)..................................... £15
Standish then made brief appearances in
SABARINDA ISLAND (illustrated by A. Barclay) (Blackie, 1950) £15
THE MYSTERY OF NIX HALL (illustrated by D.C. Eyles) (Blackie, 1950)... £15
THE MISSING DIPLOMAT (illustrated by R.G. Campbell) (Blackie, 1953).. £15

'John Cloche' stories
AT GRIPS WITH THE SWASTIKA (illustrated by Leo Bates) (Blackie, 1940) £25
FIGHTING FOR FREEDOM (illustrated by Terence Cuneo) (Blackie, 1941)... £25
SUB-LIEUTENANT JOHN CLOCHE (illustrated by H. Pym) (Blackie, 1943)... £25
ENGAGE THE ENEMY CLOSELY (illustrated by Terence Cuneo) (Blackie, 1944)............................... £25
OPERATIONS SUCCESSFULLY EXECUTED (illustrated by S. Drigin) (Blackie, 1945)........................ £25
RETURN TO BASE (illustrated by Leslie Wilcox) (Blackie, 1946) £25
THE MYSTERY OF THE KEY (illustrated by Ellis Silas) (Blackie, 1948)... £15

Stories of WWII
WHEN THE ALLIES SWEPT THE SEAS (illustrated by J.C.B. Knight) (Blackie, 1940) £25
DESTROYER'S LUCK (illustrated by R.W. Jobson) (Blackie, 1942).. £25
ON GUARD FOR ENGLAND (illustrated by J.C.B. Knight) (Blackie, 1942)... £25
WITH THE COMMANDOS (illustrated by S. Van Abbe) (Blackie, 1943).. £25
COMBINED OPERATIONS (illustrated by S. Van Abbe) (Blackie, 1944) £25
ONE OF THE MANY (illustrated by Ellis Silas) (Blackie, 1945) £25
SQUADRON LEADER (illustrated by Terence Cuneo) (Blackie, 1946).. £25

Adventure stories
CAPTURED AT TRIPOLI (illustrated by Charles Seldon) (Blackie, 1912) £30
THE STOLEN CRUISER (illustrated by D.L. Walton) (Jarrolds, 1913) £25
WHEN EAST MEETS WEST (illustrated by C.M. Padday) (Blackie, 1913).. £30
THE SEA-GIRT FORTRESS (illustrated by W.E. Wigfull) (Blackie, 1914).. £30
BUILDING THE EMPIRE (Jarrolds, 1914)... £20
THE NAMELESS ISLAND (illustrated by E.S. Hodgson) (Partridge, 1915) £20
THE TREASURE OF THE "SAN PHILIPO" (R.T.S., 1916).. £20
'MIDST ARCTIC PERILS (illustrated by W.E. Wigfull) (Pearson, 1919).. £15
THE AIRSHIP "GOLDEN HIND" (illustrated by C. Fleming Williams) (Partridge, 1920).......................... £25
THE SALVING OF THE "FUSI YAMA" (illustrated by E.S. Hodgson) (Blackie, 1920)............................. £25
THE THIRD OFFICER (illustrated by E.S. Hodgson) (Blackie, 1921).. £25
THE WIRELESS OFFICER (illustrated by W.E. Wigfull) (Blackie, 1922).. £25
THE PIRATE SUBMARINE (illustrated by Galli) (Nisbet, 1923).. £25
CLIPPED WINGS (illustrated by E.S. Hodgson) (Blackie, 1923)... £25

SINCLAIR'S LUCK (Partridge, 1924)..£25
CAPTAIN CAIN (illustrated by John de Walton) (Nisbet, 1924)..£25
THE TREASURE OF THE SACRED LAKE (Pearson, 1924)..£25
UNCONQUERED WINGS (illustrated by E.S. Hodgson) (Blackie, 1924)..£25
CLINTON'S QUEST (illustrated by R.B. Ogle) (Pearson, 1925)..£25
THE BUCCANEERS OF BOYA (illustrated by William Rainey) (Blackie, 1925)............................£25
ANNESLEY'S DOUBLE (illustrated by J.H. Hartley) (Black, 1926)..£25
KING OF KILBA (illustrated by W.E. Wigfull) (Ward Lock, 1926)..£25
THE RIDDLE OF THE AIR (illustrated by Rowland Hilder) (Blackie, 1926)..................................£30
THE TERROR OF THE SEAS (illustrated by W.E. Wigfull) (Ward Lock, 1927)..............................£25
MYSTERY ISLAND (illustrated by Savile Lumley)(Oxford University Press, 1927)......................£25
CAPTAIN BLUNDELL'S TREASURE (illustrated by J. Cameron) (Blackie, 1927)..........................£25
IN THE CLUTCHES OF THE DYAKS (illustrated by F. Marston)(Partridge, 1927)........................£25
A SHANGHAI ADVENTURE (illustrated by Leo Bates) (Blackie, 1928)..£25
RIVALS OF THE REEF (illustrated by Kenneth Inns) (Blackie, 1929)..£25
CAPTAIN STARLIGHT (illustrated by W.E. Wigfull) (Blackie, 1929)..£25
CAPTAIN SANG (illustrated by M. MacKinlay) (Blackie, 1930)..£25
IN DEFIANCE OF THE BAN (illustrated by E.S. Hodgson) (Blackie, 1931)..................................£25
CAPTAIN FOSDYKE'S GOLD (illustrated by E.S. Hodgson) (Blackie, 1932)................................£25
KING FOR A MONTH (illustrated by Comerford Watson) (Blackie, 1933)....................................£25
ROCKS AHEAD! (illustrated by D.L. Mays) (Blackie, 1933)..£25
THE WHITE ARAB (illustrated by Henry Coller) (Blackie, 1933)..£25
THE DISAPPEARING DHOW (illustrated by D.L. Mays) (Blackie, 1933)......................................£25
CHASING THE "PLEIAD" (Blackie, 1933)..£25
TALES OF THE SEA (by P.F.W. and others) (illustrated by Terence Cuneo) (Tuck, 1934)............£25
ANDY-ALL-ALONE (illustrated by D.L. Mays) (Blackie, 1934)..£25
THE BLACK HAWK (illustrated by Rowland Hilder) (Blackie, 1934)..£30
THE RED PIRATE (illustrated by Rowland Hilder) (Blackie, [1935])..£30
SLEUTHS OF THE AIR (illustrated by Comerford Watson) (Blackie, 1935)..................................£25
THE CALL OF THE SEA (illustrated by D.L. Mays) (Blackie, 1935)..£25
CAPTAIN FLICK (illustrated by E.S. Hodgson) (Blackie, 1936)..£25
TIRELESS WINGS (illustrated by Comerford Watson) (Blackie, 1936)..£25
MIDSHIPMAN RAXWORTHY (illustrated by E.S. Hodgson) (Blackie, 1936)................................£25
WINGED MIGHT (illustrated by E.R. Grover) (Blackie, 1937)..£25
UNDER FIRE IN SPAIN (illustrated by Ernest Prater) (Blackie, 1937)..£25
MIDSHIPMAN WEBB'S TREASURE (illustrated by D.L. Mays) (Blackie, 1937)..........................£25
THE BULLDOG BREED (illustrated by E. Boyce Uden) (Blackie, 1939)......................................£25
THE EAGLE'S TALONS (illustrated by M MacKinlay) (Blackie, 1940)..£25
IN DANGEROUS WATERS (Blackie, 1940)..£25
SECRET FLIGHT (illustrated by Gordon Hogg) (Blackie, 1942)..£25
UNFETTERED MIGHT (illustrated by S. Jezzard) (Blackie, 1947)..£15
TRAPPED IN THE JUNGLE (illustrated by A.S. Forrest) (Blackie, 1947)......................................£15
THE PHANTOM SUBMARINE (illustrated by J.C.B. Knight) (Blackie, 1947)................................£15
FIRST OVER (illustrated by Ellis Silas) (Blackie, 1948)..£15
MISSING BELIEVED LOST (illustrated by Will Nickless) (Blackie, 1949)....................................£15
CONTRABAND (illustrated by A. Barclay) (Blackie, 1949)..£15
BY SEA AND AIR (Blackie, 1950)..£15
DESOLATION ISLAND (illustrated by W. Gale) (Blackie, 1950)..£15
HELD TO RANSOM (illustrated by Ellis Silas) (Blackie, 1951)..£15
THE ISLE OF MYSTERY (illustrated by Philip) (Blackie, 1951)..£15
SABOTAGE (illustrated by Ellis Silas) (Blackie, 1952)..£15
DANGEROUS CARGO (illustrated by W. Gale) (Blackie, 1952)..£15
WRESTED FROM THE DEEP (illustrated by Robert Johnston) (Blackie, 1954)............................£15
A MIDSHIPMAN OF THE FLEET (illustrated by P.A. Jobson) (Blackie, 1954)............................£15
THE JU-JU HAND (Blackie, 1954)..£15
THE DARK SECRET (illustrated by Victor Bertoglio) (Blackie, 1954)..£15
THE LURE OF THE LAGOON (illustrated by E. Kearon) (Blackie, 1955)....................................£15
HELD IN THE FROZEN NORTH (illustrated by Edward Osmond) (Blackie, 1956)......................£15
THE MYSTERY OF THE "SEMPIONE" (illustrated by P.B. Batchelor) (Blackie, 1957)................£15
MISTAKEN IDENTITY (illustrated by Robert Johnston) (Blackie, 1959)......................................£15

Omnibuses

THE PERCY F. WESTERMAN OMNIBUS BOOK (contains 'Sea scouts All' [1920], 'Sea Scouts Abroad' [1921], 'Sea Scouts Up-Channel' [1922]) (Blackie, 1935)..£35
THE NEW PERCY F. WESTERMAN OMNIBUS BOOK (contains 'The Junior Cadet' [1928], 'The Salving of the Fusi Yama' [1920], 'Under the White Ensign' [1918]) (Blackie, 1939)..................£35
THE PERCY WESTERMAN OMNIBUS (contains 'The Pirate Submarine' [1923], 'Captain Cain' [1924], 'The Flying Submarine' [1912]) (Nisbet, 1930)..£35

Others

THE LOG OF A SNOB (social satire, illustrated by W.E. Wigfull) (Chapman & Hall, 1914)........£35
THE MYSTERY OF STOCKMERE SCHOOL (his only school story, illustrated by A. Pearse) (Partridge, 1924).........£30

WHISTLER, Rex

British artist and illustrator. Born: Dorset, 1905. Reginald John 'Rex' Whistler was the essence of the 'Bright Young Things' generation of the 1920s, who designed West End theatre sets, the Café at the Tate Gallery, Wedgwood china and books. He illustrated works by Evelyn Waugh and Walter de la Mare as well as titles for children (of which a selected list is printed below). He was killed on 18th July 1944 while serving in the 2nd (Armoured) Battalion in Normandy.

Prices are for books in Very Good condition with dustjackets.

GULLIVER'S TRAVELS by Jonathan Swift (2 vols; super-royal quarto, limited to 195 sets printed on hand-made paper, bound in half green niger morocco) (Cresset Press, 1930) **£3,500**
DESERT ISLANDS and ROBINSON CRUSOE by Walter de la Mare
(Faber & Faber/Fountain Press, February 1930; limited to 650 copies, signed by author)...............................**£250**
DESERT ISLANDS and ROBINSON CRUSOE (Trade edition) (Faber & Faber, April 1930) **£50**
FAIRY TALES AND LEGENDS by Hans C. Andersen (Cobden-Sanderson, 1935; limited to 200 copies, signed by Whistler) **£350**
FAIRY TALES AND LEGENDS Trade edition (Cobden-Sanderson, 1935) **£50**
¡OHO! (John Lane the Bodley Head, 1946) **£50**

WHITE, E.B.

American author. Born: Elwyn Brooks White in 1899. A regular contributor to *New Yorker*, he also wrote a handful of children's books, of which *Stuart Little* (1945) is the best-known and there have been two film versions. Died: 1985.

Prices are for books in Very Good condition with dustjackets.

STUART LITTLE (illustrated by Garth Williams) (Harper, US, 1945)...**£500**
STUART LITTLE (illustrated by Garth Williams) (Hamish Hamilton, 1946) **£200**
CHARLOTTE'S WEB (illustrated by Garth Williams) (Harper, US, 1952)...**£350**
CHARLOTTE'S WEB (illustrated by Garth Williams) (Hamish Hamilton, 1952) **£80**
THE SECOND TREE FROM THE CORNER (Harper, US, 1954) **£25**
THE SECOND TREE FROM THE CORNER (Hamish Hamilton, 1954) **£15**
TRUMPET OF THE SWAN (Harper, US, 1970) **£40**
TRUMPET OF THE SWAN (illustrated by Edward Frascino) (Hamish Hamilton, 1970)..**£30**

*E.B. White wrote a handful of children's book, and two have become modern classics. **Stuart Little** was first issued in 1945, with **Charlotte's Web** appearing seven years later. Pictured are the original American first editions, both illustrated by Garth Williams.*

WHITE, T.H.

British author. Born: Terence Hanbury White in Bombay in 1906. Studied at Cheltenham College and Cambridge University, subsequently teaching English as Stowe School. Best-known for the Arthurian tetralogy, *The Once and Future King* (1958). Died: 1964.

Prices are for books in Very Good condition with dustjackets.

Arthurian Saga

THE SWORD IN THE STONE (illustrated by the author) (Collins, 1938) £600
THE WITCH IN THE WOOD (illustrated by the author) (Collins, 1940) £600
THE ILL-MADE KNIGHT (illustrated by the author) (Collins, 1941)...£400
THE ONCE AND FUTURE KING (omnibus edition; contains (1) *The Sword in the Stone*, revised with two new chapters; (2) *The Witch in the Wood*, rewritten and retitled *The Queen of Air and Darkness*; *The Ill-Made Knight*, largely unaltered; and *The Candle in the Wind*, published here for the first time) (Collins, 1958)..£150
THE BOOK OF MERLYN: Unpublished Conclustion to The Once and Future King (University of Texas Press, US, 1977)......£30
THE BOOK OF MERLYN (Collins, 1978)..£30

Other works

MISTRESS MASHAM'S REPOSE (Cape, 1947) £60
THE ELEPHANT AND THE KANGAROO (Cape, 1948) £60
THE GOSHAWK (Cape, 1951) £60
THE MASTER: An Adventure Story (Cape, 1957)...£40
THE GODSTONE AND THE BLACKYMOR (illustrated by Edward Ardizzone) (Cape, 1959).........................£40

WIGGIN, Kate Douglas

American author. Born: Kate Douglas Smith in Philadelphia in 1856. Trained as a kindergarten teacher, and wrote her first children's book, *The Story of Patsy* (1883), to raise money for the movement. Her 1903 novel, *Rebecca of Sunnybrook Farm*, provided Mary Pickford with one of her most famous roles in 1918. Died: 1923.

Prices are for books in Very Good condition.

THE STORY OF PATSY (Privately printed, US, 1883)..£2,000
THE STORY OF PATSY (Gay & Bird, 1889) £250
THE BIRDS' CHRISTMAS CAROL (Murdock, US, 1887) £1,250
THE BIRDS' CHRISTMAS CAROL (Gay & Bird, 1891)..£280
A SUMMER IN A CAÑON: A Californian Story (Houghton Mifflin, US, 1890) £800
A SUMMER IN A CAÑON: A Californian Story (Gay & Bird, 1896)..£200
TIMOTHY'S QUEST: A Story (Houghton Mifflin, US, 1892) £500
TIMOTHY'S QUEST (Gay & Bird, 1893 [1892])...£200
A CATHEDRAL COURTSHIP AND PENELOPE'S ENGLISH EXPERIENCES (Gay & Bird, 1893)................£350
POLLY OLIVER'S PROBLEM: A Story for Girls (Houghton Mifflin, US, 1893) £200
POLLY OLIVER'S PROBLEM: A Story for Girls (Gay & Bird, 1894)..£100
THE VILLAGE WATCH TOWER and Other Tales (Gay & Bird, 1895)..£150
MARM LISA (Chapters I-X) (Gay & Bird, [1896])..£120
PENELOPE'S PROGRESS (Watt, 1897)..£250
PENELOPE'S EXPERIENCES IN SCOTLAND (Gay & Bird, 1898)..£200
PENELOPE'S EXPERIENCES IN ENGLAND (illustrated by C.E. Brock) (Houghton Mifflin, US, 1900) £150
PENELOPE'S ENGLISH EXPERIENCES (illustrated by C.E. Brock) (Houghton Mifflin, US, 1900)............£150
PENELOPE'S IRISH EXPERIENCES (Gay & Bird, 1901)...£150
THE DIARY OF A GOOSE GIRL (illustrated by C.A. Shepperson) (Gay & Bird, 1902) £150
HALF-A-DOZEN HOUSEKEEPERS: A Story for Girls (Kelly, [1903])...£80
HALF-A-DOZEN HOUSEKEEPERS: A Story for Girls (illustrated by Mills Thompson) (Gay & Bird, [1903])............£70
REBECCA OF SUNNYBROOK FARM (Houghton Mifflin, US, 1903)..£250
ROSE O' THE RIVER (illustrated by George Wright) (Constable, US, 1905).......................................£80
THE OLD PEABODY PEW: A Christmas Romance of a Country Church (illustrated by Alice Barber Stephens) (Constable, [1907])..£70
NEW CHRONICLES OF REBECCA (Houghton Mifflin, US, 1907)...£150
SUSANNA AND SUE (Houghton Mifflin, US, 1909)..£60
ROBINETTA (with Mary Findlater, Jane Findlater and Allan McAulay) (Gay & Hancock, 1911) £40
MOTHER CAREY (Hodder & Stoughton, [1911])..£60
NEW CHRONICLES OF REBECCA OF SUNNYBROOK FARM (Hodder & Stoughton, [1912]) £70
A CHILD'S JOURNEY WITH DICKENS (Houghton Mifflin, US, 1912)..£50
THE STORY OF WAITSTILL BAXTER (illustrated by H.M. Brett) (Hodder & Stoughton, [1913]) £50
BLUEBEARD: A Musical Fantasy (Harper, UK/US, 1914)..£60
PENELOPE'S POSTSCRIPTS (Hodder & Stoughton, 1915)...£70
THE ROMANCE OF A CHRISTMAS CARD (Hodder & Stoughton, [1916])..£60
LADIES-IN-WAITING (Hodder & Stoughton, [1919])...£50
CREEPING JENNY and Other New England Stories (Houghton Mifflin, US, 1924)...............................£45
TWILIGHT STORIES: More Tales for the Story Hour (Houghton Mifflin, US, 1925) £45
MOTHER CAREY'S CHICKENS (play; with Nora Archibald Smith) (Samuel French: 'Standard Library' edition, UK/US, [1925]) £10
REBECCA OF SUNNYBROOK FARM (play) (Samuel French: 'Acting' edition, [1932]).........................£15

WILDE, Oscar

Irish author. Born: Oscar Fingal O'Flahertie Wills Wilde in 1854. The great playwright wrote a handful of Hans Andersen-style fairy stories for children, collected under the title *The Happy Prince and Other Tales* in 1888. A later collection, *A House of Pomegranates*, is not a children's book, but is aimed at an adult readership. Died: 1900.

Prices are for books in Very Good condition (with dustjackets after 1950).

THE HAPPY PRINCE and Other Tales (illustrated by Walter Crane and G. Jacomb-Hood) (David Nutt, 1888)........................£750
THE HAPPY PRINCE and Other Tales (edition limited to 75 copies signed by the author and publisher)
(David Nutt, 1888) £3,000
THE HAPPY PRINCE and Other Tales (illustrated by Charles Robinson) (Duckworth, 1913)......................£250
THE HAPPY PRINCE and Other Tales (illustrated by Charles Robinson; De Luxe edition: limited to 250 copies
signed by the artist; vellum binding) (Duckworth, 1913)...£1,000
A HOUSE OF POMEGRANATES (illustrated by Charles Ricketts and C.H. Shannon) (Osgood & McIlvaine, 1891) £750
A HOUSE OF POMEGRANATES (illustrated by Jessie M. King) (Methuen, 1915)...............................£500
THE HAPPY PRINCE and A HOUSE OF POMEGRANATES: The Complete Fairy Stories of Oscar Wilde
(illustrated by Philippe Jullian) (Duckworth, 1952) £30
THE SELFISH GIANT (illustrated by Michael Foreman) (Kaye & Ward, 1978)..£20

WILDER, Laura Ingalls

American author. Born: Laura Ingalls in 1867. Best known for the semi-autobiographical 'Little House' books, which were based on her childhood experiences. The first novel in the series, *Little House in the Big Woods*, was published in 1932, when Wilder was 65 years old. The books have become well-known in Britain thanks to the television series, *Little House on the Prairie*. Died: 1957.

Prices are for books in Very Good condition with dustjackets where applicable.

LITTLE HOUSE IN THE BIG WOODS (illustrated by Helen Sewell) (Harper, US, 1932) £500
LITTLE HOUSE IN THE BIG WOODS (illustrated by Garth Williams) (Methuen, 1956)........................£200
FARMER BOY (illustrated by Helen Sewell) (Harper, US, 1933)..£300
FARMER BOY (illustrated by Garth Williams) (Lutterworth Press, 1965)......................................£60
LITTLE HOUSE ON THE PRAIRIE (illustrated by Helen Sewell) (Harper, US, 1935) £325
LITTLE HOUSE ON THE PRAIRIE (illustrated by Garth Williams) (Methuen, 1957)........................£175
ON THE BANKS OF PLUM CREEK (illustrated by Helen Sewell and Mildred Boyle) (Harper, US, 1937) £300
ON THE BANKS OF PLUM CREEK (illustrated by Garth Williams) (Methuen, 1958)........................£80
BY THE SHORES OF SILVER LAKE (illustrated by Helen Sewell and Mildred Boyle) (Harper, US, 1939)...............£275
BY THE SHORES OF SILVER LAKE (illustrated by Garth Williams) (Lutterworth Press, 1961)........................£50
THE LONG WINTER (illustrated by Helen Sewell and Mildred Boyle) (Harper, US, 1940)........................£275
THE LONG WINTER (illustrated by Garth Williams) (Lutterworth Press, 1961) £50
LITTLE TOWN ON THE PRAIRIE (illustrated by Helen Sewell and Mildred Boyle) (Harper, US, [1941]) £275
LITTLE TOWN ON THE PRAIRIE (illustrated by Garth Williams) (Lutterworth Press, 1963)........................£50
THESE HAPPY GOLDEN YEARS (illustrated by Helen Sewell and Mildred Boyle) (Harper, US, 1943)...............£275
THESE HAPPY GOLDEN YEARS (illustrated by Garth Williams) (Lutterworth Press, 1964)........................£50
THE FIRST FOUR YEARS (illustrated by Garth Williams; epilogue by Rose Wilder) (Harper, US, 1971)........................£60
THE FIRST FOUR YEARS (illustrated by Garth Williams; epilogue by Rose Wilder) (Lutterworth Press, 1973) £40
THE FIRST FOUR YEARS (illustrated by Garth Williams; epilogue by Rose Wilder; paperback) (Puffin, 1978)........................£20
WEST FROM HOME (Harper & Row, US, 1974) £40

WILDSMITH, Brian

British illustrator. Born: Penistone, Yorkshire, in 1930. He illustrated *The Oxford Book of Poetry for Children* (1960) and the 1981 edition of *Arabian Nights*. He won the Kate Greenaway Medal for *Brian Wildsmith's ABC* (1962) and produced a series of picture books based on fables by La Fontaine (1963 onwards).

Prices are for books in Very Good condition with dustjackets where applicable.

Books Written and Illustrated by Brian Wildsmith

TALES FROM THE ARABIAN NIGHTS (OUP, 1961)..£25
BRIAN WILDSMITH'S ABC (OUP, 1962)...£30
BRIAN WILDSMITH'S BIRDS (OUP, 1963)..£30
THE LION AND THE RAT by Jean de La Fontaine (OUP, 1963) £25
THE NORTH WIND AND THE SUN by Jean de La Fontaine (OUP, 1964)..£25
1 2 3 (OUP, 1964) £20
THE RICH MAN AND THE SHOE-MAKER by Jean de La Fontaine (OUP, 1965) £25
THE HARE AND THE TORTOISE by Jean de La Fontaine (OUP, 1966)..£25
BRIAN WILDSMITH'S WILD ANIMALS (OUP, 1968)...£20
BRIAN WILDSMITH'S FISHES (OUP, 1969)...£20
BRIAN WILDSMITH'S PUZZLES (OUP, 1970)...£20
BRIAN WILDSMITH'S CIRCUS (OUP, 1970)...£20
LITTLE WOOD DUCK (OUP, 1972) £20
THE TWELVE DAYS OF CHRISTMAS by Jean de La Fontaine (illustrated by Brian Wildsmith) (OUP, 1972)........................£25
WHAT THE MOON SAW (OUP, 1978)..£10

WILDSMITH, Brian

HUNTER AND HIS DOG (OUP, 1979) £10
ANIMAL GAMES (OUP, 1980) £10
ANIMAL HOMES (OUP, 1980) £10
ANIMAL SHAPES (OUP, 1980) £10
ANIMAL TRICKS (OUP, 1980) £10
PROFESSOR NOAH'S SPACESHIP (OUP, 1980) £10
SEASONS (OUP, 1980) £20
DAISY (OUP, 1984) £20
THE TUNNEL (OUP, 1993) £30

Books Illustrated by Brian Wildsmith

THE OXFORD BOOK OF POETRY FOR CHILDREN (OUP, 1963) £35
FOLLOW MY BLACK PLUME by Geoffrey Trease (Macmillan, 1963) £30
THE KNIGHTS OF KING MIDAS by Paul Berna (paperback) (Penguin, 1964) £5
A THOUSAND FOR SICILY by Geoffrey Trease (Macmillan, 1964) £30
CHILD'S GARDEN OF VERSES by R.L. Stevenson (OUP, 1966) £20
BLUE BIRD by Maurice Maeterlinck (OUP, 1976) £20

WILLARD, Barbara

British author. Born: Sussex, 1909. Has written many adult works as well as more than fifty children's books, of which the 'Mantlemass' novels are the best known. Died: 1994.

Prices are for books in Very Good condition with dustjackets.

SNAIL AND THE PENNITHORNES (illustrated by Geoffrey Fletcher) (Epworth Press, 1957) £25
SNAIL AND THE PENNITHORNES NEXT TIME (illustrated by Geoffrey Fletcher)
(Epworth Press, 1958) £20
THE HOUSE WITH ROOTS (illustrated by Robert Hodgson) (Constable, [1959]) £15
SON OF CHARLEMAGNE (illustrated by Emil Weiss) (Heinemann, 1960) £15
SNAIL AND THE PENNITHORNES AND THE PRINCESS (illustrated by Geoffrey Fletcher)
(Epworth Press, 1960) £20
THE DIPPERS AND JO (illustrated by Jean Harper) (Hamish Hamilton, 1960) £15
EIGHT FOR A SECRET (illustrated by Lewis Hart) (Constable, [1960]) £15
THE PENNY PONY (illustrated by Juliette Palmer) (Hamish Hamilton, 1961) £15
IF ALL THE SWORDS IN ENGLAND (illustrated by Robert M. Sax) (Burns & Oates, 1961) ... £15
STOP THE TRAIN! (illustrated by Jean Harper) (Hamish Hamilton, 1961) £12
THE SUMMER WITH SPIKE (illustrated by Anne Linton) (Constable, [1961]) £12
DUCK ON A POND (illustrated by Mary Rose Hardy) (Constable, [1962]) £12
HETTY (illustrated by Pamela Mara) (Constable, [1962]) £12
THE BATTLE OF WEDNESDAY WEEK (illustrated by Douglas Hall) (Constable: 'Young Books' series, [1963]) £12
THE DIPPERS AND THE HIGH-FLYING KITE (illustrated by Maureen Eckersley) (Hamish Hamilton, 1963) £12
THE SUDDENLY GANG (illustrated by Lynne Hemmant) (Hamish Hamilton, 1963) £12
THE PRAM RACE (illustrated by Constance Marshall) (Hamish Hamilton, 1964) £12
A DOG AND A HALF (illustrated by Jane Paton) (Hamish Hamilton, 1964) £12

The Velverteen Rabbit was first issued by Heinemann in 1922 with four full-page and three double-page colour lithographs by William Nicholson. The dustjacket is extremely scarce and in 2005 this copy sold at Dominic Winter Book Auctions for £8,600.

THREE AND ONE TO CARRY (illustrated by Douglas Hall) (Constable: 'Young Books' series, [1964]) **£12**
AUGUSTINE CAME TO KENT (illustrated by Hans Guggenheim) (World's Work, 1964)... **£12**
THE WILD IDEA (illustrated by Douglas Bissett) (Hamish Hamilton, 1965) **£12**
CHARITY AT HOME (illustrated by Douglas Hall) (Constable: 'Young Books' series, [1965])... **£12**
SURPRISE ISLAND (illustrated by Jane Paton) (Hamish Hamilton, 1966) **£12**
THE RICHLEIGHS OF TANTAMOUNT (illustrated by C. Walter Hodges) (Constable, 1966).. **£12**
THE GROVE OF GREEN HOLLY (illustrated by Gareth Floyd) (Constable, 1967)... **£15**
THE PET CLUB (illustrated by Lynne Hemmant) (Hamish Hamilton, 1967)... **£12**
TO LONDON! TO LONDON! (illustrated by Antony Maitland) (Longman, 1968).. **£20**
HURRAH FOR ROSIE! (illustrated by Gareth Floyd) (Hutchinson, 1968) **£12**
ROYAL ROSIE (illustrated by Gareth Floyd) (Hutchinson, 1968) **£12**
THE FAMILY TOWER (Constable: 'Young Books' series, [1968]).. **£12**
THE TOPPLING TOWERS (Longman, 1969) **£12**
THE POCKET MOUSE (illustrated by Mary Russon) (Hamish Hamilton, 1969)... **£12**
JUNIOR MOTORIST: The Driver's Apprentice (with Frances Howell; non-fiction; illustrated by Ionicus)
(Collins, 1969) **£12**
CHICHESTER AND LEWES (non-fiction; illustrated by Graham Humphreys) (Longman, 1970)... **£12**
THE LARK AND THE LAUREL (illustrated by Gareth Floyd) (Longman, 1970)... **£30**
PRISCILLA PENTECOST (illustrated by Doreen Roberts) (Hamish Hamilton, 1970) **£12**
THE REINDEER SLIPPERS (illustrated by Tessa Jordan) (Hamish Hamilton, 1970) **£12**
THE SPRIG OF BROOM (illustrated by Paul Shardlow) (Longman, 1971) **£20**
A COLD WIND BLOWING (Longman, 1972)... **£20**
THE DRAGON BOX (illustrated by Tessa Jordan) (Hamish Hamilton, 1972)... **£12**
JUBILEE! (illustrated by Hilary Abrahams) (Heinemann, 1973).. **£12**
THE IRON LILY (Longman, 1973)... **£20**
HARROW AND HARVEST (Kestrel, 1974)... **£20**
HAPPY FAMILIES Edited by Barbara Willard (anthology) (Hamilton, 1974) **£12**
THE GIANT'S FEAST by Max Bollinger (illustrated by Monika Laimgruber; translated by Barbara Willard)
(Hamish Hamilton, 1975)... **£15**
FIELD AND FOREST Edited by Barbara Willard (illustrated by Faith Jaques) (Kestrel, 1975) **£15**
CONVENT CAT (illustrated by Bunchu Iguchi; translated by Barbara Willard) (Hamish Hamilton 1975)................................. **£15**
THE MILLER'S BOY (illustrated by Gareth Floyd) (Kestrel, 1976)... **£12**
BRIDESMAID (illustrated by Jane Paton) (Hamish Hamilton, 1976) **£12**
THE ELDEST SON (Kestrel, 1977) **£12**
THE COUNTRY MAID (Hamish Hamilton, 1978) **£12**
THE GARDENER'S GRANDCHILDREN (illustrated by Gordon King) (Kestrel, 1978) **£10**
SPELL ME A WITCH (illustrated by Phillida Gili) (Hamish Hamilton, 1979) **£10**
A FLIGHT OF SWANS (Kestrel, 1980).. **£15**
THE KEYS OF MANTLEMASS (Kestrel, 1981) **£25**
SUMMER SEASON (Julia MacRae, 1981)... **£10**
FAMOUS ROWENA LAMONT (Hardy, 1983)... **£10**
THE QUEEN OF THE PHARISEES' CHILDREN (Julia MacRae, 1983) **£10**
SMILEY TIGER (illustrated by Laszelo Acs) (Julia MacRae, 1984) **£10**
NED ONLY (Julia MacRae, 1985).. **£10**

WILLIAMS, Kit

British illustrator, best known for his unique visual puzzle-book, *Masquerade* (1979). The book – which was the idea of the publisher, Tom Maschler – contained clues to a hidden treasure, which was eventually found in 1982.

Prices are for books in Very Good condition.

MASQUERADE (boards; issued without dustjacket) (Cape, 1979)... **£20**
UNTITLED (title can be found by solving clues concealed within the text and illustrations; boards;
issued without dustjacket) (Cape, 1984).. **£15**
OUT OF ONE EYE: The Art of Kit Williams (issued with dustjacket) (Cape, 1986)... **£15**

WILLIAMS, Margery

British author. Born: London, 1881. Her first novel for adults was published when she was only 17 years old and she continued to author books for adults until the 1920s. The classic *Velveteen Rabbit; or how toys became real* was her first attempt at writing for children. A copy still in its very rare dustjacket sold at Dominic Winter Book Auctions in December 2005 for £8,600. These are her two most famous collectables. Died: 1944.

Prices are for books in Very Good condition with dustjackets where applicable.

THE VELVETEEN RABBIT (in very rare dustjacket; four full page and three double-page colour
lithographs by William Nicholson; pictorial boards) (Heinemann, 1922)... **£7,000**
POOR CECCO (Trade edition, 7 colour plates & 24 black-and-white illustrations by Arthur Rackham;
yellow cloth; with dustjacket) (Chatto & Windus, 1925 [May 1926]) **£250**
POOR CECCO (Limited edition of 105, signed, with 7 plates by A. Rackham, in parchment-backed boards & slipcase)
(George H. Doran, US, 1925) **£5,000**
POOR CECCO (US trade edition; as above; blue cloth) (George H. Doran, US, 1925)... **£350**

WILLIAMSON, Henry

British author. Born: London, 1895. Studied at Colfe's Grammar School, Lewisham, and served with the Bedfordshire Regiment during the First World War, subsequently settling in North Devon. Completed two major series of novels, the 'Flax of Dreams' and 'Chronicle of Ancient Sunlight' sequences, but is best-known for his animals books, notably *Tarka the Otter* (1927) and *Salar the Salmon* (1935). Died: 1977.

Prices are for books in Very Good condition with dustjackets where applicable.

THE PEREGRINE'S SAGA (illustrated by Warwick Reynolds) (Collins,1923; limited to 600 copies) £600
THE PEREGRINE'S SAGA (enlarged and revised edition) (illustrated by C.F. Tunnicliffe) (Putnam, 1934) £60
THE OLD STAG (Putnam, 1926) £80
THE OLD STAG and Other Hunting Stories (enlarged and revised edition)
   (illustrated by C.F. Tunnicliffe) (Putnam, 1933) £80
STUMBERLEAF (story from THE OLD STAG) (wrappers; designed by Lionel Edwards)(Putnam, 1928) £80
TARKA THE OTTER (private printing for subscribers only; limited to 100 copies,
   signed by the author, with additional owl sketch; full vellum binding) (Putnam, August 1927)..................£800
TARKA THE OTTER (First trade edition; limited to 1,000 copies) (Putnam, October 1927) £200
TARKA THE OTTER (First unlimited edition) (Putnam, October 1927) £80
TARKA THE OTTER (Fourth edition, "slightly revised, following suggestions of T.E.L.") (Putnam, 1928) £40
TARKA THE OTTER (First illustrated edition, with wood engravings by C.F. Tunnicliffe) (Putnam, 1932) £80
TARKA THE OTTER (illustrated by Barry Driscoll) (Nonesuch Press, 1964) £30
THE LONE SWALLOWS and Other Essays of Boyhood and Youth (illustrated by C.FTunnicliffe) (Putnam, 1933)................£60
THE STAR-BORN (illustrated by C.F. Tunnicliffe) (Faber & Faber, 1933)...£60
THE STAR-BORN (ditto; limited, signed edition) (Faber & Faber, 1933)..£150
THE STAR-BORN (revised edition) (Faber & Faber, 1948) £15
SALAR THE SALMON (Faber & Faber, 1935) £80
SALAR THE SALMON (illustrated in colour by CF.Tunnicliffe) (Putnam, 1936)..£300
COLLECTED NATURE STORIES (five volumes: TARKA THE OTTER, SALAR THE SALMON,
   THE OLD STAG, THE PEREGRINE'S SAGA and THE LONE SWALLOWS)
   (illustrated by C.F. Tunnicliffe) (Putnam, 1946; limited to 500 sets) .... the set £150
SCRIBBLING LARK (Faber & Faber, 1949) £30
COLLECTED NATURE STORIES (omnibus, containing stories from THE PEREGRINE'S SAGA, THE OLD STAG
   and TALES OF MOORLAND AND ESTUARY; with a new introduction by the author)
   (illustrated by C.F. Tunnicliffe and Broom Lynne) (Macdonald, 1970) £30
THE SCANDAROON (illustrated by Ken Lilly) (Macdonald, 1972) £20
THE SCANDAROON (illustrated by Ken Lilly) (Macdonald, 1972; limited to 250 copies,
   signed by the author; imitation leather, in slipcase) £60
THE HENRY WILLIAMSON ANIMAL SAGA (anthology) (Macdonald/Jane's, 1974)..£15

WILSON, Jacqueline

Award-winning British author and children's laureate, best known for the 'Tracy Beaker' books. Born: 1945. Her early Macmillan thrillers and OUP titles were normally issued in jackets. Very few of her more recent titles appeared with jackets.

Prices are for books in Fine condition in dustjackets where applicable.

HIDE AND SEEK (Macmillan, 1972) £65
RICKY'S BIRTHDAY (Macmillan, 1973) £35
TRUTH OR DARE (Macmillan, 1973) £55
SNAP (Macmillan, 1974) £55
LET'S PRETEND (Macmillan, 1976) £55
MAKING HATE (Macmillan, 1977) £50
NOBODY'S PERFECT (Oxford University Press, 1983) £60
WAITING FOR THE SKY TO FALL (Oxford University Press, 1983) £45
THE KILLER TADPOLE (Hamish Hamilton, 1984) £25
THE OTHER SIDE (Oxford University Press, 1984) £45
THE SCHOOL TRIP (Hamish Hamilton, 1984) £15
HOW TO SURVIVE SUMMER CAMP (illustrated by Sue Heap) (Oxford University Press, 1985) £45
AMBER (Oxford University Press, 1986) £30
THE MONSTER IN THE CUPBOARD (Blackie, 1986) £10
GLUBBSLYME (illustrated by Jane Cope) (Oxford University Press, 1987) £45
LONELY HEARTS (paperback) (Armada, 1987) £8
SUPERSLEUTH (paperback) (Armada, 1987) £8
THE POWER OF THE SHADE (Oxford University Press, 1987) £30
RAT RACE (paperback) (Armada, 1988) £8
THIS GIRL (Oxford University Press, 1988) £20
VAMPIRE (paperback) (Armada, 1988) £5
FALLING APART (Oxford University Press, 1989) £15
IS THERE ANYBODY THERE? VOLUME 1 – SPIRIT RAISING (paperback) (Armada, 1989) £3
THE LEFT-OUTS (Blackie, 1989) £15
THE PARTY IN THE LIFT (Blackie, 1989) £15
IS THERE ANYBODY THERE? VOLUME 2 – CRYSTAL GAZING (paperback) (Armada, 1990) £3

TAKE A GOOD LOOK (illustrated by Michael Salter) (Blackie, 1990) **£15**
THE DREAM PALACE (Oxford University Press, 1991) **£15**
THE STORY OF TRACY BEAKER (illustrated by Nick Sharratt) (Doubleday, 1991) **£60**
THE STORY OF TRACY BEAKER (Collectors' Edition) (Doubleday, 2001) **£5**
THE WEREPUPPY (illustrated by Janet Robertson) (Blackie, 1991) **£10**
MARK SPARK (illustrated by Janet Robertson and Bethan Matthews) (Hamish Hamilton, 1991) **£10**
THE SUITCASE KID (illustrated by Nick Sharratt) (Doubleday, 1992) **£60**
THE SUITCASE KID (Collectors' Edition) (Doubleday, 2001) **£5**
VIDEO ROSE (illustrated by Janet Robertson) (Blackie, 1992) **£30**
DEEP BLUE (Oxford University Press, 1993) **£15**
MARK SPARK IN THE DARK (illustrated by Janet Robertson and Bethan Matthews) (Hamish Hamilton, 1993) **£10**
THE MUM-MINDER (illustrated by Nick Sharratt) (Doubleday, 1993) **£45**
COME BACK, TEDDY! (Longman, 1994) **£5**
FREDDY'S TEDDY (Longman, 1994) **£5**
TEDDY AT THE FAIR (Longman, 1994) **£5**
TEDDY GOES SWIMMING (Longman, 1994) **£5**
THE BED AND BREAKFAST STAR (illustrated by Nick Sharratt) (Doubleday, 1994) **£25**
THE WEREPUPPY ON HOLIDAY (illustrated by Janet Robertson) (Blackie, 1994) **£15**
TWIN TROUBLE (Methuen, 1994) **£15**
CLIFFHANGER (illustrated by Nick Sharratt) (paperback) (Corgi Yearling, 1995) **£8**
DOUBLE ACT (illustrated by Nick Sharratt and Sue Heap) (Doubleday, 1995) **£12**
DOUBLE ACT (Collectors' Edition) (Doubleday, 2001) **£5**
JIMMY JELLY (illustrated by Lucy Keijser) (Piccadilly Press, 1995) **£8**
LOVE FROM KATIE (Ginn, 1995) **£5**
MY BROTHER BERNADETTE (Heinemann, 1995) **£8**
SOPHIE'S SECRET DIARY (Ginn, 1995) **£5**
THE DINOSAUR'S PACKED LUNCH (illustrated by Nick Sharratt) (Doubleday, 1995)............................ **£15**
BAD GIRLS (illustrated by Nick Sharratt) (Doubleday, 1996) **£15**
BEAUTY AND THE BEAST (A & C Black, 1996)... **£8**
CONNIE AND THE WATER BABIES (Methuen, 1996) **£8**
MR COOL (Kingfisher, 1996) **£5**
GIRLS IN LOVE (illustrated by Nick Sharratt) (Doubleday, 1997).. **£10**
THE LOTTIE PROJECT (illustrated by Nick Sharratt) (Doubleday, 1997) **£10**
THE MONSTER STORY-TELLER (illustrated by Nick Sharratt) (Doubleday, 1997).................................. **£10**
BURIED ALIVE! (illustrated by Nick Sharratt) (Doubleday, 1998) **£5**
GIRLS UNDER PRESSURE (illustrated by Nick Sharratt) (Doubleday, 1998) **£5**
RAPUNZEL (Scholastic, 1998) **£5**
GIRLS OUT LATE (illustrated by Nick Sharratt) (Doubleday, 1999) **£5**
MONSTER EYEBALLS (illustrated by Stephen Lewis) (Heinemann, 1999) **£8**
THE ILLUSTRATED MUM (illustrated by Nick Sharratt) (Doubleday, 1999) **£8**
LIZZIE ZIPMOUTH (paperback) (illustrated by Nick Sharratt) (Corgi, 2000) **£5**
THE DARE GAME (illustrated by Nick Sharratt) (Doubleday, 2000) **£5**
VICKY ANGEL (illustrated by Nick Sharratt) (Doubleday, 2000) **£5**
DUSTBIN BABY (illustrated by Nick Sharratt) (Doubleday, 2001) **£5**
SLEEP-OVERS (illustrated by Nick Sharratt) (Doubleday, 2001) **£5**
THE CAT MUMMY (illustrated by Nick Sharratt) (Doubleday, 2001) **£5**
GIRLS IN TEARS (illustrated by Nick Sharratt) Doubleday, 2002) **£5**
SECRETS (illustrated by Nick Sharratt) (Doubleday, 2002) **£5**
THE WORRY WEBSITE (illustrated by Nick Sharratt) (Doubleday, 2002) **£10**
LOLA ROSE (illustrated by Nick Sharratt) (Doubleday, 2003) **£8**
MIDNIGHT (illustrated by Nick Sharratt) (DOUBLEDAY, 2003) **£8**
BEST FRIENDS (illustrated by Nick Sharratt) (Doubleday, 2004) **£5**
THE DIAMOND GIRLS (illustrated by Nick Sharratt) (Doubleday, 2004) **£5**
CLEAN BREAK (illustrated by Nick Sharratt) (Doubleday, 2005) **£5**
LOVE LESSONS (illustrated by Nick Sharratt) (Doubleday, 2005) **£5**

WODEHOUSE, P.G.

British author. Born: Pelham Grenville Wodehouse in Guildford in 1881. Studied at Dulwich College, subsequently working in a Hong Kong bank before becoming a freelance writer. Began his career contributing school stories to *Captain* magazine, later producing a handful of novels in the genre. The last of these, *Mike* (1909), includes the first appearance of the character, Psmith, who later featured in a number of adult novels. Died: 1975.

Prices are for books in Very Good condition (with dustjackets after 1930).

THE POTHUNTERS (silver chalice on front cover) (A. & C. Black, 1902)..**£2,000**
THE POTHUNTERS (pictorial cover) (A. & C. Black, 1902)...**£800**
A PREFECT'S UNCLE (illustrated by R. Noel Pocock) (A. & C. Black, 1903) ....no adverts **£1,500** / adverts **£1,000**
TALES OF ST AUSTIN'S (illustrated by R. Noel Pocock) (A. & C. Black, 1903) **£1,000**
THE GOLD BAT (illustrated by T.M.R. Whitwell) (A. & C. Black, 1904)..**£800**

*The celebrated humorist P.G. Wodehouse began his career writing stories for **Captain** magazine, going on to pen a number of novels for younger readers. This 1902 first edition of **The Pothunters** (identified by the silver chalice on the front) is worth £2,000 today.*

WILLIAM TELL TOLD AGAIN (1st issue; top edge gilt; 2 pages of advertisements)
(with J.W. Houghton; illustrated by P. Dadd) (A. & C. Black, 1904)..£800
THE HEAD OF KAY'S (illustrated by T.M.R. Whitwell; without advertising supplement)
(A. & C. Black, 1905)..£1,250
THE HEAD OF KAY'S (illustrated by T.M.R. Whitwell; with advertising supplement)
(A. & C. Black, 1905)..£1,000
THE WHITE FEATHER (illustrated by W. Townend) (A. & C. Black, 1907)..£800
MIKE: A Public School Story (illustrated by T.M.R. Whitwell; without advertising supplement)
(A. & C. Black, 1909)..£2,000
MIKE: A Public School Story (illustrated by T.M.R. Whitwell; with advertising supplement)
(A. & C. Black, 1910)..£1,500
ENTER PSMITH (revised version of second half of 'Mike'; issued with dustjacket)
(A. & C. Black, 1935)..£400
MIKE AND PSMITH (issued with dustjacket) (Herbert Jenkins, 1953) £125
MIKE AT WRYKYN (revised version of first half of 'Mike'; issued with dustjacket)
(Herbert Jenkins, 1953)..£125

WOOD, Lawson
British illustrator. Born: Highgate, London, in 1878, the grandson of the landscape painter, L.J. Wood. Studied at the Slade School and Heatherley's, serving in the Royal Flying Corps during the Great War. Wood was Pearson's chief artist for six years, and also contributed to the *Graphic* and *Illustrated London News*. Died: 1957.

Prices are for books in Very Good condition.

THE BOW-WOW BOOK by John C. Kernahan (illustrated by L. Wood and L. Raven-Hill)
(Nisbet, 1912)..£250
A BASKET OF PLUMS by R. Waylett (Gale & Polden, [1916])..£100
A BOX OF CRACKERS by R. Waylett (Gale & Polden, [1916])..£100
THE 'MR' BOOKS (Warne, [1916]) ....each £50

*A series of comic creations by British illustrator Lawson Wood, featuring his most famous and collectable character 'Gran'Pop'. These were originally published in titles such as **Mischief Makers** and **Popular Gran'Pop** (both 1946).*

'SPLINTERS' (Duckworth, [1916])...£85
THE MR AND MRS BOOKS (Warne, [1918]) ....each £40
THE 'MRS' BOOKS (Warne, [1920])...each £40
RUMMY TALES: A Series of Illustrated Children's Books (Warne, [1920]) ....each £40
THE 'RUMMY TALES' PAINTING BOOK (Warne, [1921]) £50
RUMMY TALES: A Series of Illustrated Booklets for Children (Warne, [1922]) ....each £30
THE NOO-ZOO TALES: A Series of illustrated Children's Books (Warne, [1922]) ....each £30
'BOOK TOYS' SERIES by Lawson Wood (Valentine, [1925])...each £45
THE 'LAWSON WOOD' COLOUR BOOK SERIES (Partridge, [1925] ....each £30
JOLLY RHYMES by Lawson Wood (Nelson, [1926])...£40
THE SCOT 'SCOTCHED' by Lawson Wood (Newnes, [1927])...£60
THE LAWSON WOOD NURSERY RHYME BOOK (board book) (Nelson, [c1930]).......................£100
LAWSON WOOD'S FUN FAIR by Lawson Wood (Arundel, [1931])...£200
THE OLD NURSERY RHYMES (Nelson, [1933])..£300
GRAN'POP'S ANNUAL ([Dean], [1935])..each £75
A BEDTIME PICTURE BOOK (Birn, [1943])...£50
GRAN'POP'S BOOK OF FUN (Birn, [1943]) £65
MERRY MONKEYS (Birn, [1946]) £35
MISCHIEF MAKERS (Birn, 1946)...£25
POPULAR GRAN'POP (Birn, 1946)...£50
LAWSON WOOD'S ANNUAL ([Dean], [1951-52])..each £40

WRIGHT, Sean

British author and illustrator. Born: 1959. Creator of the very popular 'Jesse Jameson' books and a children's fantasy series which began with *The Twisted Root of Jaarfindor* in 2004.

Prices are for books in Very Good condition with dustjackets where applicable.

'Jesse Jameson' series
JESSE JAMESON AND THE GOLDEN GLOW (paperback) (Crowswing, 2003)................................£15
JESSE JAMESON AND THE BOGIE BEAST (Crowswing, 2003)...£10
JESSE JAMESON AND THE CURSE OF CALDAZAR (Crowswing, 2004)..£8
JESSE JAMESON AND THE VAMPIRE VAULT (Crowswing, 2004)..£8
JESSE JAMESON AND THE STONEHENGE OF SPELFINDIAL (Crowswing, 2006)........................£8

'Elriad Myth & Legend' series
THE TWISTED ROOT OF JAARFINDOR (signed/dated) (Crowswing, 2004) £30
JAARFINDOR REMADE (Crowswing, 2006)...£15

Others
DARK TALES OF TIME AND SPACE (500 hardbacks; signed) (Crowswing, 2005)........................£20
DARK TALES OF TIME AND SPACE (30 limited edition signed hardbacks; slipcase) (Crowswing, 2005) £20
DARK TALES OF TIME AND SPACE (paperback) (Crowswing, 2005) £5
WICKED OR WHAT? (hardcover) (Crowswing, 2005)...£20

WYSS, J.D.

Swiss author. Born: Johann David Wyss in Switzerland in 1743. Served as a chaplain in the Swiss army, writing his famous story, *The Swiss Family Robinson*, for the entertainment of his four sons. One of them, Johann Rudolf Wyss, was responsible for the story's publication in 1813, an English version – translated by William Godwin and published by his wife, Mary – appearing the following year. Died: 1818.

Prices are for books in Very Good condition.

THE FAMILY ROBINSON CRUSOE (translated by William Godwin; two volumes) (M.J. Godwin, 1814) ....the set £5,000
THE SWISS FAMILY ROBINSON (second edition; two volumes) (M.J. Godwin, 1818)..............................the set £2,500
SWISS FAMILY ROBINSON (translated by J. Lovell) (London, [1869]).......................................£300
THE SWISS FAMILY ROBINSON (translated by W.H. Davenport Adams; introduction by C. Nodier) (London, 1870 [1869])..£150
THE SWISS FAMILY ROBINSON (translated by Mrs H.B. Paull) (London, [1877]) £125
THE SWISS FAMILY ROBINSON (Routledge, [1885])...£100
THE SWISS FAMILY ROBINSON. Edited with Notes by A. Gardiner (J. Heywood, 1886).............£60
THE SWISS FAMILY ROBINSON (translated by Mrs H.B. Paull) (Warne: 'Chandos Classics' series, [1890])...........£60
THE SWISS FAMILY ROBINSON (illustrated by J. Finnemore; translated by E.A. Brayley Hodgetts) (Newnes, 1897 [1896])...£60
THE SWISS FAMILY ROBINSON (Blackie, 1905)..£30
THE SWISS FAMILY ROBINSON (illustrated by Charles Folkard) (Dent, 1910)............................£45
THE SWISS FAMILY ROBINSON. Edited by W.H.G. Kingston (illustrated by Ernest Prater; introduction by Walter Jerrold) (Nister/Dutton, US: 'Children's Classics' series, [1910])...................£45
THE SWISS FAMILY ROBINSON (illustrated by Gordon Browne) (Cassell, [1910]).....................£35
THE CHILDREN'S SWISS FAMILY ROBINSON Adapted by F.H. Lee (illustrated by Honor C. Appleton) (Harrap, 1938)..£25
THE SWISS FAMILY ROBINSON (illustrated by Mervyn Peake) (Heirloom Library, 1950) £30

Y

YONGE, Charlotte M.

British author. Born: Otterbourne, near Winchester, in 1823. The author of over 150 works, she is best known for her 'Langley' books and *The Heir of Redclyffe* (1853). Died: 1901.

Prices are for books in Good condition.

'Aunt Charlotte's Stories'

AUNT CHARLOTTE'S STORIES OF ENGLISH HISTORY FOR THE LITTLE ONES
(Marcus Ward, 1873)..£40
AUNT CHARLOTTE'S STORIES OF BIBLE HISTORY (Marcus Ward, 1875) £40
AUNT CHARLOTTE'S STORIES OF GREEK HISTORY (Marcus Ward, 1876) £40
AUNT CHARLOTTE'S STORIES OF ROMAN HISTORY (Marcus Ward, 1877) £40
AUNT CHARLOTTE'S STORIES OF GERMAN HISTORY (Marcus Ward, 1878).................................£40
AUNT CHARLOTTE'S STORIES OF AMERICAN HISTORY (Marcus Ward, 1883)...............................£40
AUNT CHARLOTTE'S STORIES OF FRENCH HISTORY (Marcus Ward, 1884) £40
AUNT CHARLOTTE'S STORIES OF BIBLE HISTORY FOR YOUNG DISCIPLES
(John C. Winston, 1909)..£60

Others

LANGLEY SCHOOL (Macmillan, 1850) £150
THE HEIR OF REDCLYFFE (Macmillan, 1853) £300
THE LITTLE DUKE (Parker, 1854)..£250
HEARTSEASE, or The Brother's Wife (Parker, 1854) £75
THE LANCES OF LYNWOOD (Parker, 1855)..£75
THE HISTORY OF SIR THOMAS THUMB (Constable, 1855)...£75
THE DAISY CHAIN, or Aspirations (Parker, 1856)..£100
DYNEVOR TERRACE, or The Clue of Life (Parker, 1857) £100
PIGEON PIE: A Tale of Roundhead Times (Mozley, 1860) £100
THE TRIAL: More Links of the Daisy Chain (Macmillan, 1864)...£200
THE DOVE IN THE EAGLE'S NEST (two volumes) (Macmillan, 1866) ....the set £200
THE CHAPLET OF PEARLS (two volumes) (Macmillan, 1868)..............................the set £150
A BOOK OF WORTHIES (Macmillan, 1869)..£75
THE CAGED LION (Macmillan, 1870)...£75
LADY HESTOR, or Ursula's Narrative (Macmillan, 1870) £75
THE PILLARS OF THE HOUSE, or Under Wode, Under Road
(four volumes) (Macmillan, 1873)...the set £150
WOMANKIND (Mozley & Smith, 1876)..£100
A MAN OF OTHER DAYS (two volumes) (Hurst & Blackett, 1877) ....the set £50
THE STORY OF THE CHRISTIANS AND MOORS IN SPAIN (Macmillan, 1878)............................£60
MAGNUM BONUM, or Mother Carey's Brood (three volumes) (Macmillan, 1879)...........the set £180
BYWORDS: Tales Old and New (Macmillan, 1880)..£45
UNKNOWN TO HISTORY: A Story of the Captivity of Mary of Scotland
(two volumes) (Macmillan, 1882)...the set £100
STRAY PEARLS, Memoirs of Margaret de Ribaumont Viscontess of Bellaise
(illustrated by W.J. Hennessy)
(two volumes) (Macmillan, 1883)...the set £100
THE ARMOURER'S PRENTICES (two volumes) (Macmillan, 1884)..........................the set £150
THE TWO SIDES OF THE SHIELD (two volumes) (Macmillan, 1885)........................the set £250
CHANTRY HOUSE (two volumes) (Macmillan, 1886)...the set £120
THE PRINCE AND THE PAGE: A Story of the Last Crusade (illustrated by Marguerite de Angeli)
(Macmillan, 1886) £50
UNDER THE STORM, or Steadfast's Change (National Society Depository, 1887)......................£40
BEACHCROFT AT ROCKSTONE (two volumes) (Macmillan, 1888) ....the set £200
MORE BYWORDS (Macmillan, 1890)...£35
THE CONSTABLE'S TOWER (National Society Depository, 1891)...£35
GRISLY GRISELL, or the Laidly Lady of Whitburn (two volumes) (Macmillan, 1893)........the set £140
A TALE OF THE CHEDDAR CAVES ONE HUNDRED YEARS AGO (Wells Clare Son & Co, 1891)........£35
THE RELEASE OF CAROLINE'S FRENCH KINDRED (Macmillan, 1896) £35
AN OLD WOMAN'S OUTLOOK IN A HAMPSHIRE VILLAGE (Macmillan, 1897) £30
FOUNDED ON PAPER, or Up Hill and Down Hill Between the Two Jubilees
(National Society Depository, 1898)..£40
MODERN BROODS, or Developments Unlooked For (Macmillan, 1900)....................................£35
A BOOK OF GOLDEN DEEDS (illustrated by W. Rainey) (S.W. Partridge, 1914)........................£15
LITTLE LUCY'S WONDERFUL GLOBE (illustrated by Anne Merriman Peck) (Harper, 1927)............£25

Index

411

Grading your book

Below are the Standard Conditions for grading secondhand books and their dustjackets. The five basic conditions accepted by collectors all over the world are listed here, together with a description of what each one means.

Mint

This means that the book is in perfect condition. It is complete with its dustjacket and is impossible to distinguish from a new copy.
DUSTJACKET: as new.

Fine

The book appears to be in excellent condition. Closer examination, however, will show evidence of ownership and storage. There may also be a small inscription to or by the previous owner, but generally the book is in near perfect condition.
DUSTJACKET: as new, but with very slight rubbing on corners.

Very Good

Slightly less than Fine condition. Apart from slight foxing or fading, the book has no faults.
DUSTJACKET: clean with excellent colouring, but with slight rubbing to most edges and corners.

Good

It is obvious that the book is secondhand. However, apart from minor faults, it must always be assumed that books in Good condition are complete in all respects, unless described otherwise.
DUSTJACKET: fairly clean with almost perfect colouring, but suffering from marks, slight creasing and other signs of wear. Most of the edges are rubbed or have very small tears in them.

Poor

A book in this category is in really bad condition. It may be warped, the preliminary pages may be missing, and the spine irreparably damaged. The text is complete but the book is really only suitable to read.
DUSTJACKET: tatty and grubby, and may well be marked, creased or torn.

Ready Reckoner of Prices

This Ready Reckoner will help you work out the value of a book in any condition. For example, if you have a book which we value at £10 in Fine condition, but which is only in Good condition, you can read across the appropriate line and find the correct value of your book – in this case, £5. Please note that Poor condition books worth less than £10 in Fine condition are virtually worthless to collectors. However, Poor condition books may be worth many times more if they contain intact, well-preserved illustrations.

Mint	Fine	Very Good	Good	Poor
10,000	8,000	6,000	3,000	500
5,000	4,000	3,000	1,500	250
2,000	1,500	1,000	500	60
1,000	800	600	300	40
750	600	450	200	30
500	400	300	150	20
200	180	150	80	10
150	135	125	70	8
100	90	75	40	5
75	65	55	30	4
50	45	40	20	3
40	35	30	18	2.50
30	27	22	13	2
25	22	18	10	1.50
20	17	15	8	1
15	13	11	7	1
12	10	8	5	-
10	8	6.50	4	-
9	7	5.75	3.50	-
8	6	4.50	2.50	-
7	5	3.75	2	-
6	4.50	3.50	1.50	-
5	4	3	1	-
4	3.50	2.50	50p	-
3	2.50	2	50p	-
2	1.75	1.30	-	-

Subscribe to **BOOK** AND MAGAZINE **COLLECTOR**

Make sure you get your copy of *BMC* every month by subscribing now!

- Up to £20 off the cover price
- FREE £60 book listing advert in every issue!
- FREE postage and packaging
- Money back guarantee
- Back issues available at half price!
- Get your copy before it goes on sale in the shops

3 EASY WAYS TO SUBSCRIBE

1 ☎ **Phone SUBS HOTLINE 0208 752 8193**

2 **E-mail** janice.mayne@metropolis.co.uk

3 ✉ **Post** BMC Subs, Unit 101, 140 Wales Farm Road, London, W3 6UG